BOOKS by

His Divine Grace

A.C. Bhaktivedanta Swami Prabhupāda

published by Krishna Books Inc.

Bhagavad-gītā As It Is

Śrīmad Bhāgavatam, First Canto

Kṛṣṇa, the Supreme Personality of Godhead

Teachings of Lord Chaitanya

Śrī Īśopaniṣad

The Nectar of Devotion

The Nectar of Instruction

The Science of Self-Realization

Rāja-vidyā: The King of Knowledge

Easy Journey to Other Planets

Kṛṣṇa, the Reservoir of Pleasure

The Perfection of Yoga

Beyond Birth and Death

On Chanting Hare Krishna

KṚṢṆA

The Supreme Personality of Godhead

KṚṢṆA

The Supreme Personality of Godhead

A Summary Study of Śrīla Vyāsadeva's *Śrīmad-Bhāgavatam*, Tenth Canto.

His Divine Grace
A.C. Bhaktivedanta Swami Prabhupāda

Founder-Ācārya of the International Society for Krishna Consciousness

KṚṢṆA

The Supreme Personality of Godhead

contains the original text and art published by
the Bhaktivedanta Book Trust in 1972.

Krishna Books Inc is licensed by the Bhaktivedanta Book Trust
to print and publish the pre-1978 literary works of
His Divine Grace A.C. Bhaktivedanta Swami Prabhupāda.

To obtain further information contact Krishna Books Inc
on the Internet at http://www.krishnabooks.org
by email: info@krishnabooks.org

Krishna Books Inc

578 Washington Blvd. Suite 808
Marina del Rey, CA 90292 USA

Library of Congress Catalog Card Number: 74-118081
2010 English Edition ISBN: 978-1-60293-007-0

Printed and bound by Thomson Press (India) Ltd.

To My Father, Gour Mohon De (1849-1930)

a pure devotee of Kṛṣṇa, who raised me as a Kṛṣṇa conscious child from the beginning of my life. In my boyhood ages he instructed me how to play the *mṛdaṅga*. He gave me Rādhā-Kṛṣṇa Vigraha to worship, and he gave me Jagannātha-Ratha to duly observe the festival as my childhood play. He was kind to me, and I imbibed from him the ideas later on solidified by my spiritual master, the eternal father.

Contents

From Apple

Everybody is looking for KṚṢṆA.

Some don't realize that they are, but they are.

KṚṢṆA is GOD, the Source of all that exists, the Cause of all that is, was, or ever will be.

As GOD is unlimited, HE has many Names.

Allah-Buddha-Jehova-Rama: All are KṚṢṆA, all are ONE.

God is not abstract; He has both the impersonal and the personal aspects to His personality which is SUPREME, ETERNAL, BLISSFUL, and full of KNOWLEDGE. As a single drop of water has the same qualities as an ocean of water, so has our consciousness the qualities of GOD'S consciousness . . . but through our identification and attachment with material energy (physical body, sense pleasures, material possessions, ego, etc.) our true TRANSCENDENTAL CONSCIOUSNESS has been polluted, and like a dirty mirror it is unable to reflect a pure image.

With many lives our association with the TEMPORARY has grown. This impermanent body, a bag of bones and flesh, is mistaken for our true self, and we have accepted this temporary condition to be final.

Through all ages, great SAINTS have remained as living proof that this non-temporary, permanent state of GOD CONSCIOUSNESS can be revived in all living Souls. Each soul is potentially divine.

Kṛṣṇa says in *Bhagavad Gita:* "Steady in the Self, being freed from all material contamination, the yogi achieves the highest perfectional stage of happiness in touch with the Supreme Consciousness." (VI, 28)

YOGA (a scientific method for GOD (SELF) realization) is the process by which we purify our consciousness, stop further pollution, and arrive at the state of Perfection, full KNOWLEDGE, full BLISS.

If there's a God, I want to see Him. It's pointless to believe in something without proof, and Kṛṣṇa Consciousness and meditation are methods where you can actually obtain GOD perception. You can actually see God, and hear Him, play with Him. It might sound crazy, but He is actually there, actually with you.

There are many yogic Paths—Raja, Jnana, Hatha, Kriya, Karma, Bhakti—which are *all* acclaimed by the MASTERS of each method.

SWAMI BHAKTIVEDANTA is as his title says, a BHAKTI Yogi following the path of DEVOTION. By serving GOD through each thought, word, and DEED, and by chanting of HIS Holy Names, the devotee quickly develops God-consciousness. By chanting

Hare Kṛṣṇa, Hare Kṛṣṇa
Kṛṣṇa Kṛṣṇa, Hare Hare
Hare Rāma, Hare Rāma
Rāma Rāma, Hare Hare

one inevitably arrives at KṚṢṆA Consciousness. (The proof of the pudding is in the eating!)

I request that you take advantage of this book *KṚṢṆA,* and enter into its understanding. I also request that you make an appointment to meet your God now, through the self liberating process of YOGA (UNION) and GIVE PEACE A CHANCE.

ALL YOU NEED IS LOVE (KRISHNA) HARI BOL

George Harrison 31/3/70

Apple Corps Ltd 3 Savile Row London W1 Gerrard 2772/3993 Telex Apcore London

Preface

nivṛtta-tarṣair upagīyamānād
bhavauṣadhāc chrotramano'bhirāmāt
ka uttama-śloka-guṇānuvādāt
pumān virajyeta vinā paśughnāt
(Śrīmad-Bhāgavatam 10.1.4)

In these Western countries, when someone sees the cover of a book like *Kṛṣṇa,* he immediately asks, "Who is Kṛṣṇa? Who is the girl with Kṛṣṇa?" etc.

The immediate answer is that Kṛṣṇa is the Supreme Personality of Godhead. How is that? Because He conforms in exact detail to descriptions of the Supreme Being, the Godhead. In other words, Kṛṣṇa is the Godhead because He is all-attractive. Outside the principle of all-attraction, there is no meaning to the word Godhead. How is it one can be all-attractive? First of all, if one is very wealthy, if he has great riches, he becomes attractive to the people in general. Similarly, if someone is very powerful, he also becomes attractive, and if someone is very famous, he also becomes attractive, and if someone is very beautiful or wise or unattached to all kinds of possessions, he also becomes attractive. So from practical experience we can observe that one is attractive due to 1) wealth, 2) power, 3) fame, 4) beauty, 5) wisdom, and 6) renunciation. One who is in possession of all six of these opulences at the same time, who possesses them to an unlimited degree, is understood to be the Supreme Personality of Godhead. These opulences of the Godhead are delineated by Parāśara Muni, a great Vedic authority.

We have seen many rich persons, many powerful persons, many famous persons, many beautiful persons, many learned and scholarly persons, and persons in the renounced order of life unattached to material possessions.

But we have never seen any one person who is unlimitedly and simultaneously wealthy, powerful, famous, beautiful, wise and unattached, like Kṛṣṇa, in the history of humanity. Kṛṣṇa, the Supreme Personality of Godhead, is an historical person who appeared on this earth 5,000 years ago. He stayed on this earth for 125 years and played exactly like a human being, but His activities were unparalleled. From the very moment of His appearance to the moment of His disappearance, every one of His activities is unparalleled in the history of the world, and therefore anyone who knows what we mean by Godhead will accept Kṛṣṇa as the Supreme Personality of Godhead. No one is equal to the Godhead, and no one is greater than Him. That is the import of the familiar saying, "God is great."

There are various classes of men in the world who speak of God in different ways, but according to Vedic literatures and according to the great *ācāryas,* the authorized persons versed in the knowledge of God, in all ages, like *ācāryas* Śaṅkara, Rāmānuja, Madhva, Viṣṇusvāmī, Lord Caitanya and all their followers by disciplic succession, all unanimously agree that Kṛṣṇa is the Supreme Personality of Godhead. As far as we, the followers of Vedic civilization, are concerned, we accept the Vedic history of the whole universe, which consists of different planetary systems called Svargalokas, or the higher planetary system, Martyalokas, or the intermediary planetary system, and Pātālalokas, or the lower planetary system. The modern historians of this earth cannot supply historical evidences of events that occurred before 5,000 years ago, and the anthropologists say that 40,000 years ago Homo sapiens had not appeared on this planet because evolution had not reached that point. But the Vedic histories, the *Purāṇas* and *Mahābhārata,* relate human histories which extend millions and billions of years into the past.

For example, from these literatures we are given the histories of Kṛṣṇa's appearances and disappearances millions and billions of years ago. In the Fourth Chapter of the *Bhagavad-gītā* Kṛṣṇa tells Arjuna that both He and Arjuna had had many births before and that He (Kṛṣṇa) could remember all of them and that Arjuna could not. This illustrates the difference between the knowledge of Kṛṣṇa and that of Arjuna. Arjuna might have been a very great warrior, a well-cultured member of the Kuru dynasty, but after all, he was an ordinary human being, whereas Kṛṣṇa, the Supreme Personality of Godhead, is the possessor of unlimited knowledge. Because He possesses unlimited knowledge, Kṛṣṇa has a memory that is boundless.

Kṛṣṇa's knowledge is so perfect that He remembers all the incidences of His appearances some millions and billions of years in the past, but Arjuna's memory and knowledge are limited by time and space, for he is an ordinary human being. In the Fourth Chapter Kṛṣṇa states that He can remember instructing the lessons of the *Bhagavad-gītā* some millions of years ago to the sun-god, Vivasvān.

Nowadays it is the fashion of the atheistic class of men to try to become God by following some mystic process. Generally the atheists claim to be God by dint of their imagination or their meditational prowess. Kṛṣṇa is not that kind of God. He does not become God by manufacturing some mystic process of meditation, nor does He become God by undergoing the severe austerities of the mystic yogic exercises. Properly speaking, He never *becomes* God because He is the Godhead in all circumstances.

Within the prison of His maternal uncle Kaṁsa, where His father and mother were confined, Kṛṣṇa appeared outside His mother's body as the four-handed Viṣṇu-Nārāyaṇa. Then He turned Himself into a baby and told His father to carry Him to the house of Nanda Mahārāja and his wife Yaśodā. When Kṛṣṇa was just a small baby the gigantic demoness Pūtanā attempted to kill Him, but when He sucked her breast He pulled out her life. That is the difference between the real Godhead and a God manufactured in the mystic factory. Kṛṣṇa had no chance to practice the mystic *yoga* process, yet He manifested Himself as the Supreme Personality of Godhead at every step, from infancy to childhood, from childhood to boyhood, and from boyhood to young manhood. In this book *Kṛṣṇa,* all of His activities as a human being are described. Although Kṛṣṇa plays like a human being, He always maintains His identity as the Supreme Personality of Godhead.

Since Kṛṣṇa is all-attractive, one should know that all his desires should be focused on Kṛṣṇa. In the *Bhagavad-gītā* it is said that the individual person is the proprietor or master of the body, but Kṛṣṇa, who is the Supersoul present in everyone's heart, is the supreme proprietor and supreme master of each and every individual body. As such, if we concentrate our loving propensities upon Kṛṣṇa only, then immediately universal love, unity and tranquility will be automatically realized. When one waters the root of a tree, he automatically waters the branches, twigs, leaves and flowers; when one supplies food to the stomach through the mouth, he satisfies all the various parts of the body.

The art of focusing one's attention on the Supreme and giving one's love to Him is called Kṛṣṇa consciousness. We have inaugerated the Kṛṣṇa consciousness movement so that everyone can satisfy his propensity for loving others simply by directing his love towards Kṛṣṇa. The whole world is very much anxious to satisfy the dormant propensity of love for others, but the inventions of various methods like socialism, communism, altruism, humanitarianism, nationalism, and whatever else may be manufactured for the peace and prosperity of the world, are all useless and frustrating because of our gross ignorance of the art of loving Kṛṣṇa. Generally people think that by advancing the cause of moral principles and religious rites, they will be happy. Others may think that happiness can be achieved by economic development, and yet others think that simply by sense gratification they will be happy. But the real fact is that people can only be happy by loving Kṛṣṇa.

Kṛṣṇa can perfectly reciprocate one's loving propensities in different relationships called mellows or *rasas*. Basically there are twelve loving relationships. One can love Kṛṣṇa as the supreme unknown, as the supreme master, the supreme friend, the supreme child, the supreme lover. These are the five basic love *rasas*. One can also love Kṛṣṇa indirectly in seven different relationships, which are apparently different from the five primary relationships. All in all, however, if one simply reposes his dormant loving propensity in Kṛṣṇa, then his life becomes successful. This is not a fiction but is a fact that can be realized by practical application. One can directly perceive the effects that love for Kṛṣṇa has on his life.

In the Ninth Chapter of the *Bhagavad-gītā* this science of Kṛṣṇa consciousness is called the king of all knowledge, the king of all confidential things, and the supreme science of transcendental realization. Yet we can directly experience the results of this science of Kṛṣṇa consciousness because it is very easy to practice and is very pleasurable. Whatever percentage of Kṛṣṇa consciousness we can perform will become an eternal asset to our life, for it is imperishable in all circumstances. It has now been actually proved that today's confused and frustrated younger generation in the Western countries can directly perceive the results of chanelling the loving propensity toward Kṛṣṇa alone.

It is said that although one executes severe austerities, penances and sacrifices in his life, if he fails to awaken his dormant love for Kṛṣṇa, then all his penances are to be considered useless. On the other hand, if one has awakened his dormant love for Kṛṣṇa, then what is the use in executing austerities and penances unnecessarily?

The Kṛṣṇa consciousness movement is the unique gift of Lord Caitanya to the fallen souls of this age. It is a very simple method which has actually been carried out during the last four years in the Western countries, and there is no doubt that this movement can satisfy the dormant loving propensities of humanity. This book *Kṛṣṇa* is another presentation to help the Kṛṣṇa consciousness movement in the Western world. This transcendental literature is published in two parts with profuse illustrations.

People love to read various kinds of fiction to spend their time and energy. Now this tendency can be directed to Kṛṣṇa. The result will be the imperishable satisfaction of the soul, both individually and collectively.

It is said in the *Bhagavad-gītā* that even a little effort expended on the path of Kṛṣṇa consciousness can save one from the greatest danger. Hundreds of thousands of examples can be cited of people who have escaped the greatest dangers of life due to a slight advancement in Kṛṣṇa consciousness. We therefore request everyone to take advantage of this great transcendental literature. One will find that by reading one page after another, an immense treasure of knowledge in art, science, literature, philosophy and religion will be revealed, and ultimately, by reading this one book, *Kṛṣṇa*, love of Godhead will fructify.

My grateful acknowledgement is due to Śrīmān George Harrison, now chanting Hare Kṛṣṇa, for his liberal contribution of $19,000 to meet the entire cost of printing this volume. May Kṛṣṇa bestow upon this nice boy further advancement in Kṛṣṇa consciousness.

And at last my ever-willing blessings are bestowed upon Śrīmān Śyāmasundaradāsa Adhikārī, Śrīmān Brahmānandadāsa Brahmacārī, Śrīmān Hayagrīvadāsa Adhikārī, Śrīman Satsvarūpadāsa Adhikārī, Śrīmatī Devahūti Devī, Śrīmatī Jaduräṇī Dāsī, Śrīmān Muralīdharadāsa Brahmacārī, Śrīmān Bhāradvājadāsa Adhikārī, and Śrīmān Pradyumnadāsa Adhikārī, etc., for their hard labor in different ways to make this publication a great success.

Hare Kṛṣṇa.

Advent Day of Śrīla
Bhaktisiddhānta Sarasvatī

February 26th, 1970
ISKCON Headquarters
3764 Watseka Avenue
Los Angeles, California

Introduction

Kṛṣṇa! Kṛṣṇa! Kṛṣṇa! Kṛṣṇa! Kṛṣṇa! Kṛṣṇa! Kṛṣṇa! he!
Kṛṣṇa! Kṛṣṇa! Kṛṣṇa! Kṛṣṇa! Kṛṣṇa! Kṛṣṇa! Kṛṣṇa! he!
Kṛṣṇa! Kṛṣṇa! Kṛṣṇa! Kṛṣṇa! Kṛṣṇa! Kṛṣṇa! rakṣa mām!
Kṛṣṇa! Kṛṣṇa! Kṛṣṇa! Kṛṣṇa! Kṛṣṇa! Kṛṣṇa! pāhi mām!
Rāma! Rāghava! Rāma! Rāghava! Rāma! Rāghava! rakṣa mām!
Kṛṣṇa! Keśava! Kṛṣṇa! Keśava! Kṛṣṇa! Keśava! pāhi mām!

Caitanya-caritāmṛta (Madhya 7.96)

While attempting to write this book, *Kṛṣṇa,* let me first offer my respectful obeisances unto my spiritual master, Om Viṣṇupāda 108 Śrī Śrīmad Bhaktisiddhānta Sarasvatī Gosvāmī Mahārāja Prabhupāda. Then let me offer my respectful obeisances to the ocean of mercy, Lord Śrī Kṛṣṇa Caitanya Mahāprabhu. He is the Supreme Personality of Godhead, Kṛṣṇa Himself, appearing in the role of a devotee just to distribute the highest principles of devotional service. Lord Caitanya began His preaching from the country known as Gauḍadeśa (West Bengal). And as I belong to the Mādhva-Gauḍīya-sampradāya, I must therefore offer my respectful obeisances to our disciplic succession. This Mādhva-Gauḍīya-sampradāya is also known as Brahma-sampradāya because the disciplic succession originally began from Brahmā. Brahmā instructed the sage Nārada, Nārada instructed Vyāsadeva, and Vyāsadeva instructed Madhva Muni or Madhvācārya. Mādhavendra Purī, the originator of Mādhva-Gauḍīya-sampradāya, belonged to the Madhvācārya disciplic succession; he had many renowned disciples both in the *sannyāsa* (renounced) and household orders of life, disciples such as Nityānanda Prabhu, Advaita Prabhu and Īśvara Purī. Īśvara Purī happened to be the spiritual master of Lord Caitanya Mahāprabhu. So let us offer our respectful obeisances to Īśvara Purī, Nityānanda Prabhu, Śrī Advaita Ācārya Prabhu, Śrīvāsa Paṇḍit and Śrī Gadādhara Paṇḍit. Next, let us offer our respectful obeisances to Svarūpa-Dāmodara, who acted as the private secretary to Lord Caitanya Mahāprabhu; and let us offer our respectful obeisances to Śrī Vāsudeva Datta and the constant attendant of Lord Caitanya, Śrī Govinda, and the constant friend of Lord Caitanya, Mukunda, and also to Murāri Gupta. And let us offer our respectful obeisances to the six Gosvāmīs of Vṛndāvana, Śrī Rūpa Gosvāmī, Śrī Sanātana Gosvāmī, Śrī Raghunātha Bhaṭṭa Gosvāmī, Śrī Gopāla Bhaṭṭa Gosvāmī, Śrī Jīva Gosvāmī and Śrī Raghunātha Dāsa Gosvāmī.

Kṛṣṇa Himself has explained in the *Bhagavad-gītā* that He is the Supreme Personality of Godhead. Whenever there are discrepancies in the regulative principles of man's religious life and a prominence of irreligious activities, He appears on this earthly planet. In other words, when Lord Śrī Kṛṣṇa appeared, there was a necessity of minimizing the load of sinful activities accumulated on this planet, or in this universe. For affairs of the material creation, Lord Mahā-Viṣṇu, the plenary portion of Kṛṣṇa, is in charge.

When the Lord descends, the incarnation emanates from Viṣṇu. Mahā-Viṣṇu is the original cause of material creation, and from Him Garbhodakaśāyi-Viṣṇu expands, and then Kṣīrodakaśāyi-Viṣṇu. Generally, all the incarnations appearing within this material universe are plenary expansions from Kṣīrodakaśāyi-Viṣṇu. Therefore, the business of minimizing the overload of sinful activities on this earth does not belong to the Supreme Personality of Godhead, Kṛṣṇa Himself. But when Kṛṣṇa appears, all the Viṣṇu expansions also join with Him. Kṛṣṇa's different expansions, namely Nārāyaṇa, the quadrupal expansion of Vāsudeva, Saṅkarṣaṇa, Pradyumna and Aniruddha, as well as the partial plenary expansion of Matsya or the incarnation of fish, and other *yuga-avatāras* (incarnations for the millennium), and the *manvantara-avatāras,* the incarnations of Manus—all combine together and appear with the body of Kṛṣṇa, the Supreme Personality of Godhead. Kṛṣṇa is the complete whole, and all plenary expansions and incarnations always live with Him.

When Kṛṣṇa appeared, Lord Viṣṇu was also with Him. Kṛṣṇa actually appears to demonstrate His Vṛndāvana pastimes and to attract the fortunate conditioned souls and invite them back home, back to Godhead. The killing of the demons was simultaneous to His Vṛndāvana activities and was carried out only by the Viṣṇu portion of Kṛṣṇa.

In the *Bhagavad-gītā,* Eighth Chapter, 20th verse, it is stated that there is another eternal nature, the spiritual sky, which is transcendental to this manifested and nonmanifested matter. The manifested world can be seen in the form of many stars and planetary systems, such as the sun, moon, etc., but beyond this there is a nonmanifested portion which is not approachable to anyone in this body. And beyond that nonmanifested matter there is the spiritual kingdom. That kingdom is described in the *Bhagavad-gītā* as supreme and eternal. It is never annihilated. This material nature is subjected to repeated creation and annihilation. But that part, the spiritual nature, remains as it is, eternally.

The supreme abode of the Personality of Godhead, Kṛṣṇa, is also described in the *Brahma-saṁhitā* as the abode of *cintāmaṇi.* That abode of Lord Kṛṣṇa known as Goloka Vṛndāvana is full of palaces made of touchstone. There the trees are called desire trees, and the cows are called *surabhi.* The Lord is served there by hundreds and thousands of goddesses of fortune. His name is Govinda, the Primeval Lord, and He is the cause of all causes. There the Lord plays His flute, His eyes are like lotus petals, and the color of His body is like that of a beautiful cloud. On His head is a peacock feather. He is so attractive that He excels thousands of cupids. Lord Kṛṣṇa gives only a little hint in the *Gītā* of His personal abode which is the supermost planet in the spiritual kingdom. But in the *Śrīmad-Bhāgavatam,* Kṛṣṇa actually appears with all His paraphernalia and demonstrates His activities in Vṛndāvana, then at Mathurā, and then at Dvārakā. The subject matter of this book will gradually reveal all these activities.

The family in which Kṛṣṇa appeared is called the Yadu dynasty. This Yadu dynasty belongs to the family descending from Soma, the god in the moon planet. There are two different *kṣatriya* families of the royal order, one descending from the king of the moon planet and the other descending from the king of the sun planet. Whenever the Supreme Personality of Godhead appears, He generally appears in a *kṣatriya* family because He has to establish religious principles or the life of righteousness. The *kṣatriya* family is the protector of the human race, according to the Vedic system. When the Supreme Personality of Godhead appeared as Lord Rāmacandra, He appeared in the family descending from the sun-god, known as Raghu-vaṁśa; and when He appeared as Lord Kṛṣṇa, He did so in the family of Yadu-vaṁśa. There is a long list of the kings of the Yadu-vaṁśa in the Ninth Canto, 24th chapter of *Śrīmad-Bhāgavatam.* All of them were great powerful kings. Kṛṣṇa's father's name was Vasudeva, son of Śūrasena, descending from the Yadu dynasty. Actually, the Supreme Personality of Godhead does not belong to any dynasty of this material world, but the family in which the Supreme Personality of Godhead appears becomes famous, by His grace. For example, sandalwood is produced in the states of Malaya. Sandalwood has its own qualifications apart from Malaya, but because, accidently, this wood is mainly produced in the states of Malaya, it is known as Malayan sandalwood. Similarly, Kṛṣṇa the Supreme Personality of Godhead belongs to everyone, but just as the sun rises from the east, although there are other directions from which it could rise, so, by His own choice, the Lord appears in a particular family, and that family becomes famous.

When Kṛṣṇa appears, all His plenary expansions also appear with Him. Kṛṣṇa appeared along with Balarāma (Baladeva), who is known as His elder brother. Balarāma is the origin of Saṅkarṣaṇa, of the quadrupal expansion. Balarāma is also the plenary expansion of Kṛṣṇa. In this book, the attempt will be made to show how Kṛṣṇa appeared in the family of the Yadu dynasty and how He displayed His transcendental characteristics. This is very vividly described in the *Śrīmad-Bhāgavatam*—specifically, the Tenth Canto—and the basis of this book will be *Śrīmad-Bhāgavatam.*

The pastimes of the Lord are generally heard and relished by liberated souls. Those who are conditioned souls are interested in reading fictional stories of the material activities of some common man. Narrations describing the transcendental activities of the Lord are found in *Śrīmad-Bhāgavatam* and other *Purāṇas.* But, the conditioned souls still prefer to study ordinary narrations. They are not so interested in studying the narrations of the pastimes of the Lord, Kṛṣṇa. And yet, the descriptions of the pastimes of Lord Kṛṣṇa are so attractive that they are relishable for all classes of men. There are three classes of men in this world. One class consists of liberated souls, another consists of those who are trying to be liberated, and the third consists of materialistic men. Whether one is liberated or is trying to be liberated, or is even grossly materialistic, the pastimes of Lord Kṛṣṇa are worth studying.

Liberated souls have no interest in materialistic activities. The impersonalist theory that after liberation one becomes inactive and needs hear nothing does not prove that a liberated person is actually inactive. A living soul cannot be inactive. He is either active in the conditioned state or in the liberated state. A diseased person, for example, is also active, but his activities are all painful. The same person, when freed from the diseased condition, is still active, but in the healthy condition the activities are full of pleasure. Similarly, the impersonalists manage to get freed from the diseased conditional activities, but they have no information of activities in the healthy condition. Those who are actually liberated and in full knowledge take to hearing the activities of Kṛṣṇa; such engagement is pure spiritual activity.

It is essential for persons who are actually liberated to hear about the pastimes of Kṛṣṇa. That is the supreme relishable subject matter for one in the liberated state. Also, if persons who are trying to be liberated hear such narrations as *Bhagavad-gītā* and *Śrīmad-Bhāgavatam,* then their path of liberation becomes very clear. *Bhagavad-gītā* is the preliminary study of *Śrīmad-Bhāgavatam.* By studying the *Gītā,* one becomes fully conscious of the position of Lord Kṛṣṇa; and when he is situated at the lotus feet of Kṛṣṇa, he understands the narrations of Kṛṣṇa as described in the *Śrīmad-Bhāgavatam.* Lord Caitanya has therefore advised His followers that their business is to propagate *Kṛṣṇa-kathā.*

Kṛṣṇa-kathā means narrations about Kṛṣṇa. There are two *Kṛṣṇa-kathās:* narrations *spoken by Kṛṣṇa* and narrations *spoken about Kṛṣṇa. Bhagavad-gītā* is the narration or the philosophy or the science of God, spoken by Kṛṣṇa Himself. *Śrīmad-Bhāgavatam* is the narration about the activities and transcendental pastimes of Kṛṣṇa. Both are *Kṛṣṇa-kathā.* It is the order of Lord Caitanya that *Kṛṣṇa-kathā* should be spread all over the world, because if the conditioned souls, suffering under the pangs of material existence, take to *Kṛṣṇa-kathā,* then their path of liberation will be open and clear. The purpose of presenting this book is primarily to induce people to understand Kṛṣṇa or *Kṛṣṇa-kathā,* because thereby they can become freed from material bondage.

This *Kṛṣṇa-kathā* will also be very much appealing to the most materialistic persons because Kṛṣṇa's pastimes with the *gopīs* (cowherd girls) are exactly like the loving affairs between young girls and boys within this material world. Actually, the sex feeling found in human society is not unnatural because this same sex feeling is there in the original Personality of Godhead. The pleasure potency is called Śrīmatī Rādhārāṇī. The attraction of loving affairs on the basis of sex feeling is the original feature of the Supreme Personality of Godhead, and we, the conditioned souls, being part and parcel of the Supreme, have such feelings also, but they are experienced within a perverted, minute condition. Therefore, when those who are after sex life in this material world hear about Kṛṣṇa's pastimes with the *gopīs,* they will relish transcendental pleasure, although it appears to be materialistic. The advantage will be that they will gradually be elevated to the spiritual platform. In the *Bhāgavatam* it is stated that if one hears the pastimes of Lord Kṛṣṇa with the gopīs *from authorities with submission,* then he will be promoted to the platform of transcendental loving service to the Lord, and the material disease of lust within his heart will be completely vanquished. In other words, it will counteract the material sex life.

Kṛṣṇa will be appealing to the liberated souls and to persons who are trying to be liberated, as well as to the gross, conditioned materialist.

According to the statement of Mahārāja Parīkṣit, who heard about Kṛṣṇa from Śukadeva Gosvāmī, *Kṛṣṇa-kathā* is equally applicable to every human being, in whatever condition of life he is in. Everyone will appreciate it to the highest magnitude. But Mahārāja Parīkṣit also warned that persons who are simply engaged in killing animals and in killing themselves may not be very much attracted to *Kṛṣṇa-kathā*. In other words, ordinary persons who are following the regulative moral principles of scriptures, no matter in what condition they are found, will certainly be attracted, but not persons who are killing themselves. The exact word used in the *Śrīmad-Bhāgavatam* is *paśughna*, which means killing animals or killing oneself. Persons who are not self-realized and who are not interested in spiritual realization are killing themselves; they are committing suicide. Because this human form of life is especially meant for self-realization, by neglecting this important part of his activities, one simply wastes his time like the animals. So he is *paśughna*. The other meaning of the word refers to those who are actually killing animals. This means persons who are animal eaters (even dog eaters), and they are all engaged in killing animals in so many ways, such as hunting, opening slaughterhouses, etc. Such persons cannot be interested in *Kṛṣṇa-kathā*.

King Parīkṣit was especially interested in hearing *Kṛṣṇa-kathā* because he knew that his forefathers and particularly his grandfather, Arjuna, were victorious in the great battle of Kurukṣetra only because of Kṛṣṇa. We may also take this material world as a battlefield of Kurukṣetra. Everyone is struggling hard for existence in this battlefield, and at every step there is danger. According to Mahārāja Parīkṣit, the battlefield of Kurukṣetra was just like a vast ocean full of dangerous animals. His grandfather Arjuna had to fight with such great heroes as Bhīṣma, Droṇa, Karṇa, and many others who were not ordinary fighters. Such warriors have been compared to the *timiṅgila* fish in the ocean. The *timiṅgila* fish can very easily swallow up big whales. The great fighters on the battlefield of Kurukṣetra could swallow many, many Arjunas very easily, but simply due to Kṛṣṇa's mercy, Arjuna was able to kill all of them. Just as one can cross with no exertion over the little pit of water contained in the hoofprint of a calf, so Arjuna, by the grace of Kṛṣṇa, was able to very easily jump over the ocean of the battle of Kurukṣetra.

Mahārāja Parīkṣit very much appreciated Kṛṣṇa's activities for many other reasons. Not only was his grandfather saved by Kṛṣṇa, but he himself also was saved by Kṛṣṇa. At the end of the battle of Kurukṣetra, all the members of the Kuru dynasty, both the sons and grandsons on the side of Dhṛtarāṣṭra, as well as those on the side of the Pāṇḍavas, died in the fighting. Except the five Pāṇḍava brothers, everyone died on the battlefield of Kurukṣetra. Mahārāja Parīkṣit was at that time within the embryo of his mother. His father, Abhimanyu, the son of Arjuna, also died on the battlefield of Kurukṣetra, and so Mahārāja Parīkṣit was a posthumous child. When he was in the womb of his mother, a *brahmāstra* weapon was released by Aśvatthāmā to kill the child. When Parīkṣit Mahārāja's mother, Uttarā, approached Kṛṣṇa, Kṛṣṇa, seeing the danger of abortion, entered her womb as the Supersoul and saved Mahārāja Parīkṣit. Mahārāja Parīkṣit's other name is Viṣṇurāta because he was saved by Lord Viṣṇu Himself while still within the womb.

Thus everyone, in any condition of life, should be interested in hearing about Kṛṣṇa and His activities because He is the Supreme Absolute Truth, the Personality of Godhead. He is all-pervading; He is living within everyone's heart, and He is living as His universal form. And yet, as described in the *Bhagavad-gītā,* He appears as He is in the human society just to invite everyone to His transcendental abode, back to home, back to Godhead. Everyone should be interested in knowing about Kṛṣṇa, and this book is presented with this purpose: that people may know about Kṛṣṇa and be perfectly benefitted in this human form of life.

In the Ninth Canto of *Śrīmad-Bhāgavatam,* Śrī Baladeva is described as the son of Rohiṇī, a wife of Vasudeva. Vasudeva, the father of Kṛṣṇa, had sixteen wives, and one of them was Rohiṇī, the mother of Balarāma. But Balarāma is also described as the son of Devakī, so how could He be the son of both Devakī and Rohiṇī? This was one of the questions put by Mahārāja Parīkṣit to Śukadeva Gosvāmī, and it will be answered in due course. Mahārāja Parīkṣit also asked Śukadeva Gosvāmī why Śrī Kṛṣṇa, just after His appearance as the son of Vasudeva, was immediately carried to the house of Nanda Mahārāja in Vṛndāvana, Gokula. He also wanted to know what the activities of Lord Kṛṣṇa were while He was in Vṛndāvana and while He was in Mathurā. Besides that, he was especially inquisitive to know why Kṛṣṇa killed His maternal uncle, Kaṁsa. Kaṁsa, being the brother of His mother, was a very intimate superior to Kṛṣṇa, so how was it that He killed Kaṁsa? Also, he asked how many years Lord Kṛṣṇa remained in human society, how many years He reigned over the kingdom of Dvārakā, and how many wives He accepted there. A *kṣatriya* king is generally accustomed to accept more than one wife; therefore Mahārāja Parīkṣit also inquired about His number of wives. The subject matter of this book is Śukadeva Gosvāmī's answering of these and other questions asked by Mahārāja Parīkṣit.

The position of Mahārāja Parīkṣit and Śukadeva Gosvāmī is unique.

Mahārāja Parīkṣit is the right person to hear about the transcendental pastimes of Kṛṣṇa, and Śukadeva Gosvāmī is the right person to describe them. If such a fortunate combination is made possible, then *Kṛṣṇa-kathā* immediately becomes revealed, and people may benefit to the highest possible degree from such a conversation.

This narration was presented by Śukadeva Gosvāmī when Mahārāja Parīkṣit was prepared to give up his body, fasting on the bank of the Ganges. In order to assure Śukadeva Gosvāmī that by hearing *Kṛṣṇa-kathā* he would not feel tired, Mahārāja Parīkṣit expressed himself very frankly: "Hunger and thirst may give trouble to ordinary persons or to me, but the topics of Kṛṣṇa are so nice that one can continue to hear about them without feeling tired because such hearing situates one in the transcendental position." It is understood that one must be very fortunate to hear about *Kṛṣṇa-kathā* seriously, like Mahārāja Parīkṣit. He was especially intent on the subject matter because he was expecting death at any moment. Every one of us should be conscious of death at every moment. This life is not at all assured; at any time one can die. It does not matter whether one is a young man or an old man. So before death takes place, we must be *fully* Kṛṣṇa conscious.

At the point of his death, King Parīkṣit was hearing *Śrīmad-Bhāgavatam* from Śukadeva Gosvāmī. When King Parīkṣit expressed his untiring desire to hear about Kṛṣṇa, Śukadeva Gosvāmī was very pleased. Śukadeva was the greatest of all *Bhāgavata* reciters, and thus he began to speak about Kṛṣṇa's pastimes, which destroy all inauspiciousness in this age of Kali. Śukadeva Gosvāmī thanked the King for his eagerness to hear about Kṛṣṇa, and he encouraged him by saying, "My dear King, your intelligence is very keen because you are so eager to hear about the pastimes of Kṛṣṇa." He informed Mahārāja Parīkṣit that hearing and chanting of the pastimes of Kṛṣṇa are so auspicious that the process purifies the three varieties of men involved: he who recites the transcendental topics of Kṛṣṇa, he who hears such topics, and he who inquires about Him. These pastimes are just like the Ganges water which flows from the toe of Lord Viṣṇu: they purify the three worlds, the upper, middle and lower planetary systems.

1 / Advent of Lord Kṛṣṇa

Once the world was overburdened by the unnecessary defense force of different kings, who were actually demons, but were posing themselves as the royal order. At that time, the whole world became perturbed, and the predominating deity of this earth, known as Bhūmi, went to see Lord Brahmā to tell of her calamaties due to the demoniac kings. Bhūmi assumed the shape of a cow and presented herself before Lord Brahmā with tears in her eyes. She was bereaved and was weeping just to invoke the Lord's compassion. She related the calamitous position of the earth, and after hearing this, Lord Brahmā became much aggrieved, and he at once started for the ocean of milk, where Lord Viṣṇu resides. Lord Brahmā was accompanied by all the demigods headed by Lord Śiva, and Bhūmi also followed. Arriving on the shore of the milk ocean, Lord Brahmā began to pacify the Lord Viṣṇu who formerly saved the earthly planet by assuming the transcendental form of a boar.

In the Vedic *mantras*, there is a particular type of prayer called *Puruṣa-sūkta.* Generally, the demigods offer their obeisances unto Viṣṇu, the Supreme Personality of Godhead, by chanting the *Puruṣa-sūkta.* It is understood herein that the predominating deity of every planet can see the supreme lord of this universe, Brahmā, whenever there is some disturbance in his planet. And Brahmā can approach the Supreme Lord Viṣṇu, not by seeing Him directly, but by standing on the shore of the ocean of milk. There is a planet within this universe called *Śvetadvīpa,* and on that planet there is an ocean of milk. It is understood from various Vedic literatures that just as there is the ocean of salt water within this planet, there are various kinds of oceans in other planets. Somewhere there is an ocean of milk, somewhere there is an ocean of oil, and somewhere there is an ocean of liquor and many other types of oceans. *Puruṣa-sūkta* is the standard prayer which the demigods recite to appease the Supreme Personality of Godhead, Kṣīrodakaśāyī-Viṣṇu. Because He is lying on the ocean of milk, He is called Kṣīrodakaśāyī-Viṣṇu. He is the Supreme Personality of Godhead, through whom all the incarnations within this universe appear.

After all the demigods offered the *Puruṣa-sūkta* prayer to the Supreme Personality of Godhead, they apparently heard no response. Then Lord Brahmā personally sat in meditation, and there was a message-transmission from Lord Viṣṇu to Brahmā. Brahmā then broadcast the message to the demigods. That is the system of receiving Vedic knowledge. The Vedic knowledge is received first by Brahmā from the Supreme Personality of Godhead, through the medium of the heart. As stated in the beginning of *Śrīmad-Bhāgavatam, tene brahma hṛdā:* the transcendental knowledge of the *Vedas* was transmitted to Lord Brahmā through the heart. Here also, in the same way, only Brahmā could understand the message transmitted by Lord Viṣṇu, and he broadcast it to the demigods for their immediate action. The message was: the Supreme Personality of Godhead will appear on the earth very soon along with His supreme powerful potencies, and as long as He remains on the earth planet to execute His mission of annihilating the demons and establishing the devotees, the demigods should also remain there to assist Him. They should all immediately take birth in the family of the Yadu dynasty, wherein the Lord will also appear in due course of time.

The Supreme Personality of Godhead Himself, Kṛṣṇa, personally appeared as the son of Vasudeva. Before He appeared, all the demigods, along with their wives, appeared in different pious families in the world just to assist the Lord in executing His mission. The exact word used here is *tatpriyārtham,* which means the demigods should appear on the earth in order to please the Lord. In other words, any living entity who lives only to satisfy the Lord is a demigod. The demigods were further informed that the plenary portion of Lord Kṛṣṇa, Ananta, who is maintaining the universal planets by extending his millions of hoods, would also appear on earth before Lord Kṛṣṇa's appearance. They were also informed that the external potency of Viṣṇu *(māyā),* with whom all the conditioned souls are enamoured, would also appear just to execute the purpose of the Supreme Lord.

After instructing and pacifying all the demigods, as well as Bhūmi, with sweet words, Lord Brahmā, the father of all *prajāpatis,* or progenitors of universal population, departed for his own abode, the highest material planet, called Brahmaloka.

The leader of the Yadu dynasty, King Śūrasena, was ruling over the country known as Mathurā (the district of Mathurā) as well as the district known as Śūrasena. On account of the rule of King Śūrasena, Mathurā became the capital city of all the kings of the Yadus. Mathurā was also made the capital of the kings of the Yadu dynasty because the Yadus were a very pious family and knew that Mathurā is the place where Lord Śrī Kṛṣṇa lives eternally, just as He also lives in Dvārakā.

Once upon a time, Vasudeva, the son of Śūrasena, just after marrying Devakī, was going home on his chariot with his newly wedded wife. The father of Devakī, known as Devaka, had contributed a sufficient dowery because he was very affectionate toward his daughter. He had contributed hundreds of chariots completely decorated with gold equipment. At that time, Kaṁsa, the son of Ugrasena, in order to please his sister, Devakī, had voluntarily taken the reins of the horses of Vasudeva's chariot and was driving. According to the custom of the Vedic civilization, when a girl is married, the brother takes the sister and brother-in-law to their home. Because the newly married girl may feel too much separation from her father's family, the brother goes with her until she reaches her father-in-law's house. The full dowery contributed by Devaka was as follows: 400 elephants fully decorated with golden garlands, 15,000 decorated horses, and 1800 chariots. He also arranged for two hundred beautiful girls to follow his daughter. The *kṣatriya* system of marriage, still current in India, dictates that when a *kṣatriya* is married, a few dozen of the bride's young girl friends (in addition to the bride) go to the house of the king. The followers of the queen are called maidservants, but actually they act as friends of the queen. This practice is prevalent from time immemorial, traceable at least to the time before the advent of Lord Kṛṣṇa 5,000 years ago. So Vasudeva brought home another two hundred beautiful girls along with his wife.

While the bride and bridegroom were passing along on the chariot, there were different kinds of musical instruments playing to indicate the auspicious moment. There were conchshells, bugles, drums and kettledrums; combined together, they were vibrating a nice concert. The procession was passing very pleasingly, and Kaṁsa was driving the chariot, when suddenly there was a miraculous sound vibrated from the sky which especially announced to Kaṁsa: "Kaṁsa: you are such a fool. You are driving the chariot of your sister and your brother-in-law, but you do not know that the eighth child of this sister will kill you."

Kaṁsa was the son of Ugrasena, of the Bhoja dynasty. It is said that Kaṁsa was the most demonic of all the Bhoja dynasty kings. Immediately after hearing the prophecy from the sky, he caught hold of Devakī's hair and was just about to kill her with his sword. Vasudeva was astonished at Kaṁsa's behavior, and in order to pacify the cruel, shameless brother-in-law, he began to speak as follows, with great reason and evidence. He said, "My dear brother-in-law Kaṁsa, you are the most famous king of the Bhoja dynasty, and people know that you are the greatest warrior and a valiant king. How is it that you are so infuriated that you are prepared to kill a woman who is your own sister at this auspicious time of her marriage? Why should you be so much afraid of death? Death is already born along with your birth. From the very day you took your birth, you began to die. Suppose you are twenty-five years old; that means you have already died twenty-five years. Every moment, every second, you are dying. Why then should you be so much afraid of death? Final death is inevitable. You may die either today or in a hundred years; you cannot avoid death. Why should you be so much afraid? Actually, death means annihilation of the present body. As soon as the present body stops functioning and mixes with the five elements of material nature, the living entity within the body accepts another body, according to his present action and reaction. It is just as when a man walks on the street; he puts forward his foot, and when he is confident that his foot is situated on sound ground, he lifts the other foot. In this way, one after another, the body changes and the soul transmigrates. See how the plantworms change from one twig to another so carefully! Similarly, the living entity changes his body as soon as the higher authorities decide on his next body. As long as a living entity is conditioned within this material world, he must take material bodies one after another. His next particular body is offered by the laws of nature, according to the actions and reactions of this life.

"This body is exactly like one of the bodies which we always see in dreams. During our dream of sleep, we create so many bodies according to mental creation. We have seen gold and we have also seen a mountain, so in a dream we can see a golden mountain by combining the two ideas. Sometimes in dreams, we see that we have a body which is flying in the sky, and at that time we completely forget our present body. Similarly, these bodies are changing. When you have one body, you forget the past body. During a dream, we may make contact with so many new kinds of bodies, but when we are awake we forget them all. And actually these material bodies are the creations of our mental activities. But at the present moment we do not recollect our past bodies.

"The nature of the mind is flickering. Sometimes it accepts something, and immediately it rejects the same thing. Accepting and rejecting is the process of the mind in contact with the five objects of sense gratification:

form, taste, smell, sound, and touch. In its speculative way, the mind comes in touch with the objects of sense gratification, and when the living entity desires a particular type of body, he gets it. Therefore, the body is an offering by the laws of material nature. The living entity accepts a body and comes out again into the material world to enjoy or suffer according to the construction of the body. Unless we have a particular type of body, we cannot enjoy or suffer according to our mental proclivities inherited from the previous life. The particular type of body is actually offered to us according to our mental condition at the time of death.

"The luminous planets like the sun, moon or the stars reflect themselves in different types of reservoirs, like water, oil or ghee. The reflection moves according to the movement of the reservoir. The reflection of the moon is on the water, and the moving water makes the moon also appear to be moving, but actually the moon is not moving. Similarly, by mental concoction, the living entity attains different kinds of bodies, although actually he has no connection with such bodies. But on account of illusion, being enchanted by the influence of *māyā,* the living entity thinks that he belongs to a particular type of body. That is the way of conditioned life. Suppose a living entity is now in a human form of body. He thinks that he belongs to the human community, or a particular country or particular place. He identifies himself in that way and unnecessarily prepares for another body which is not required by him. Such desires and mental concoctions are the cause of different types of body. The covering influence of material nature is so strong that the living entity is satisfied in whatever body he gets, and he identifies with that body with great pleasure. Therefore, I beg to request you not to be overwhelmed by the dictation of your mind and body."

Vasudeva thus requested Kaṁsa not to be envious of his newly married sister. One should not be envious of anyone because envy is the cause of fear both in this world and in the next when one is before Yamarāja (the lord of punishment after death). Vasudeva appealed to Kaṁsa on behalf of Devakī, stating that she was his younger sister. He also appealed at an auspicious moment, at the time of marriage. A younger sister or brother are supposed to be protected as one's children. "The position is overall so delicate," Vasudeva reasoned, "that if you kill her, it will go against your high reputation."

Vasudeva tried to pacify Kaṁsa by good instruction as well as by philosophical discrimination, but Kaṁsa was not to be pacified because his association was demoniac. Because of his demoniac associations, he was always a demon, although born in a very high royal family. A demon never cares for any good instruction. He is just like a determined thief: one can give him moral instruction, but it will not be effective. Similarly, those who are demoniac or atheistic by nature can hardly assimilate any good instruction, however authorized it may be. That is the difference between demigod and demon. Those who can accept good instruction and try to live their lives in that way are called demigods, and those who are unable to take such good instruction are called demons. Failing in his attempt to pacify Kaṁsa, Vasudeva wondered how he would protect his wife Devakī. When there is imminent danger, an intelligent person should try to avoid the dangerous position as far as possible. But if, in spite of endeavoring by all intelligence, one fails to avoid the dangerous position, there is no fault on his part. One should try his best to execute his duties, but if the attempt fails, he is not at fault.

Vasudeva thought of his wife as follows: "For the present let me save the life of Devakī, then later on, if there are children, I shall see how to save them." He further thought, "If in the future I get a child who can kill Kaṁsa–just as Kaṁsa is thinking–then both Devakī and the child will be saved because the law of Providence is inconceivable. But now, some way or other, let me save the life of Devakī."

There is no certainty how a living entity contacts a certain type of body, just as there is no certainty how the blazing fire comes in contact with a certain type of wood in the forest. When there is a forest fire, it is experienced that the blazing fire sometimes leaps over one tree and catches another by the influence of the wind. Similarly, a living entity may be very careful and fearful in the matter of executing his duties, but it is still very difficult for him to know what type of body he is going to get in the next life. Mahārāja Bharata was very faithfully executing the duties of self-realization, but by chance he contacted temporary affection for a deer, and he had to accept his next life in the body of a deer.

Vasudeva, after deliberating on how to save his wife, began to speak to Kaṁsa with great respect, although Kaṁsa was the most sinful man. Sometimes it happens that a most virtuous person like Vasudeva has to flatter a person like Kaṁsa, a most vicious person. That is the way of all diplomatic transactions. Although Vasudeva was deeply aggrieved, he presented himself outwardly as cheerful. He addressed the shameless Kaṁsa in that way because he was so atrocious. Vasudeva said to Kaṁsa, "My dear brother-in-law, please consider that you have no danger from your sister. You are awaiting some danger because you have heard a prophetic voice in the sky. But the danger is to come from the sons of your sister, who are not present now. And who knows? There may or may not be sons in the future.

Considering all this, you are safe for the present. Nor is there cause of fear from your sister. If there are any sons born of her, I promise that I shall present all of them to you for necessary action."

Kaṁsa knew the value of Vasudeva's word of honor, and he was convinced by his argument. For the time being, he desisted from the heinous killing of his sister. Thus Vasudeva was pleased and praised the decision of Kaṁsa. In this way, he returned to his home.

After due course of time, Vasudeva and Devakī gave birth to eight male children, as well as one daughter. When the first son was born, Vasudeva kept his word of honor and immediately brought the child before Kaṁsa. It is said that Vasudeva was very much elevated and famous for his word of honor, and he wanted to maintain this fame. Although it was very painful for Vasudeva to hand over the newly born child, Kaṁsa was very glad to receive him. But he became a little compassionate with the behavior of Vasudeva. This event is very exemplary. For a great soul like Vasudeva, there is nothing considered to be painful in the course of discharging one's duty. A learned person like Vasudeva carries out his duties without hesitation. On the other hand, a demon like Kaṁsa never hesitates in committing any abominable action. It is said, therefore, that a saintly person can tolerate all kinds of miserable conditions of life, a learned man can discharge his duties without awaiting favorable circumstances, a heinous person like Kaṁsa can act in any sinful way, and a devotee can sacrifice everything to satisfy the Supreme Personality of Godhead.

Kaṁsa became satisfied by the action of Vasudeva. He was surprised to see Vasudeva keeping his promise, and being compassionate upon him and pleased, he began to speak as follows: "My dear Vasudeva, you need not present this child to me. I am not in danger from this child. I have heard that the eighth child born of you and Devakī will kill me. Why should I accept this child unnecessarily? You can take him back."

When Vasudeva was returning home with his first-born child, although he was pleased by the behavior of Kaṁsa, he could not believe in him because he knew that Kaṁsa was uncontrolled. An atheistic person cannot be firm in his word of honor. One who cannot control the senses cannot be steady in his determination. The great politician, Cāṇakya Paṇḍit, said, "Never put your trust in a diplomat or in a woman." Those who are addicted to unrestricted sense gratification can never be truthful, nor can they be trusted with any faith.

At that time the great sage Nārada came to Kaṁsa. He was informed of Kaṁsa's becoming compassionate to Vasudeva and returning his first-born child. Nārada was very anxious to accelerate the descent of Lord Kṛṣṇa as soon as possible. He therefore informed Kaṁsa that personalities like Nanda Mahārāja and all the cowherd men and girls and the wives of the cowherd men in Vṛndāvana, and, on the other side, Vasudeva, his father Śūrasena and all his relatives born in the family of Vṛṣṇi of the Yadu Dynasty, were preparing for the appearance of the Lord. Nārada warned Kaṁsa to be careful of the friends and well-wishers and all the demigods taking birth in those families. Kaṁsa and his friends and advisors were all demons. Demons are always afraid of demigods. After being thus informed by Nārada about the appearance of the demigods in different families, Kaṁsa at once became alert. He understood that since the demigods had already appeared, Lord Viṣṇu must be coming soon. He at once arrested both his brother-in-law Vasudeva and Devakī and put them behind prison bars.

Within the prison, shackled in iron chains, Vasudeva and Devakī gave birth to a male child year after year, and Kaṁsa, thinking each of the babies to be the incarnation of Viṣṇu, killed them one after another. He was particularly afraid of the eighth child, but after the visit of Nārada, he came to the conclusion that any child might be Kṛṣṇa. Therefore it was better to kill all the babies who took birth of Devakī and Vasudeva.

This action of Kaṁsa is not very difficult to understand. There are many instances in the history of the world of persons in the royal order who have killed father, brother, or a whole family and friends for the satisfaction of their ambitions. There is nothing astonishing about this, for the demoniac can kill anyone for their nefarious ambitions.

Kaṁsa was made aware of his previous birth by the grace of Nārada. He learned that in his previous birth he was a demon of the name Kālanemi and that he was killed by Viṣṇu. Having taken his birth in the Bhoja family, he decided to become the deadly enemy of the Yadu dynasty; Kṛṣṇa was going to take birth in that family, and Kaṁsa was very much afraid that he would be killed by Kṛṣṇa, just as he was killed in his last birth.

He first of all imprisoned his father Ugrasena because he was the chief king among the Yadu, Bhoja, and Andhaka dynasties, and he also occupied the kingdom of Śūrasena, Vasudeva's father. He declared himself the king of all such places.

Thus ends the Bhaktivedanta purport of the First Chapter of Kṛṣṇa, *"Advent of Lord Kṛṣṇa."*

His Divine Grace A.C. Bhaktivedanta Swami Prabhupāda
Founder- Āchārya of the International Society for Krishna Consciousness

“Dear mother Devakī, within your womb is the Supreme Personality of Godhead…” (p. 22)

“Therefore I request You to conceal this four-armed form of Your Lordship which holds the four symbols of Viṣṇu…” (p. 29)

Having spoken thus in the presence of His father and mother, the Lord turned Himself into an ordinary child and remained silent. (p. 30)

Lord Kṛṣṇa played on the lap of Devakī just like an ordinary child. (p. 30)

The night was very dark, but Vasudeva could see everything just as in the sunlight. (p. 30)

Vasudeva silently entered the house and exchanged his son for the girl. (p. 31)

The joyous vibrations at Kṛṣṇa's birth ceremony could be heard in all the pasturing grounds and houses. (p. 38)

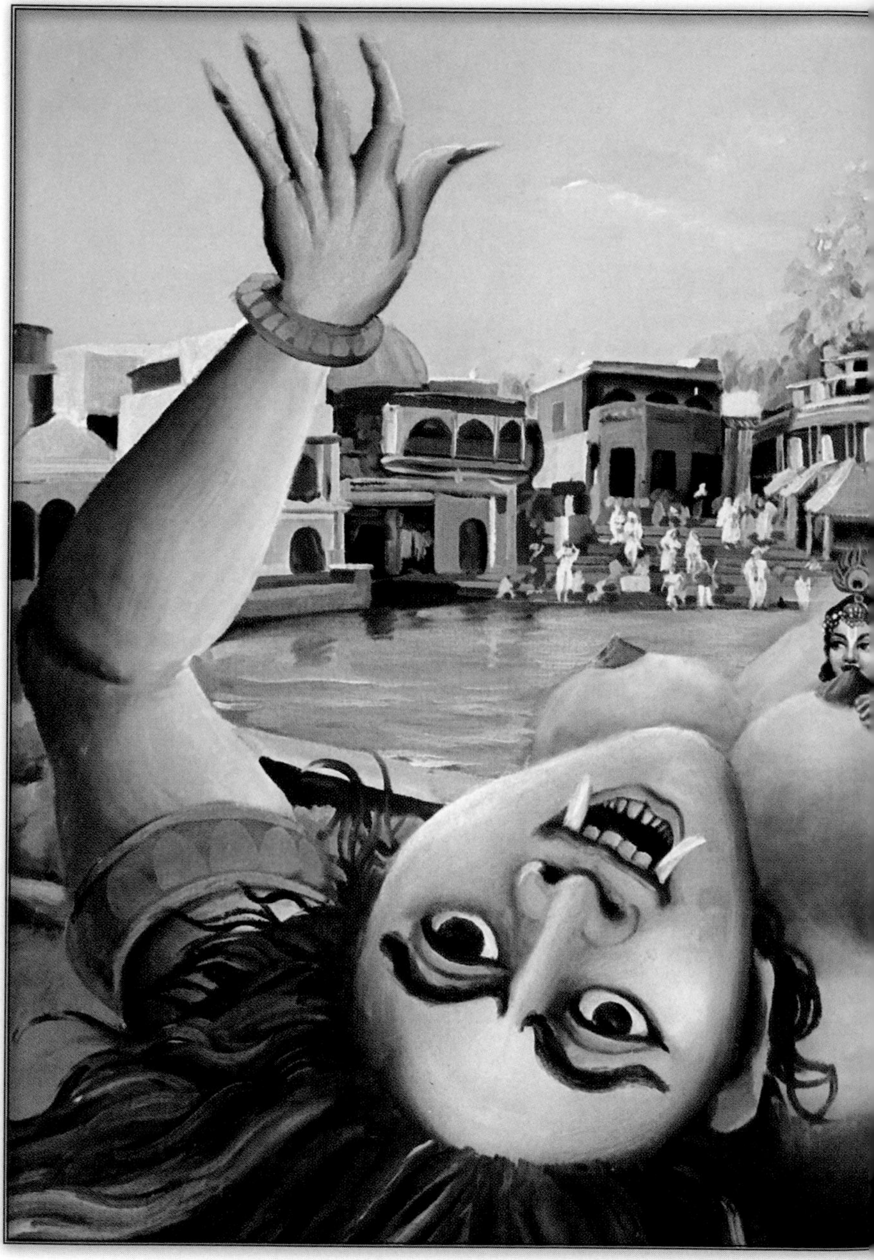

“Oh child, leave me, leave me!” (p. 46)

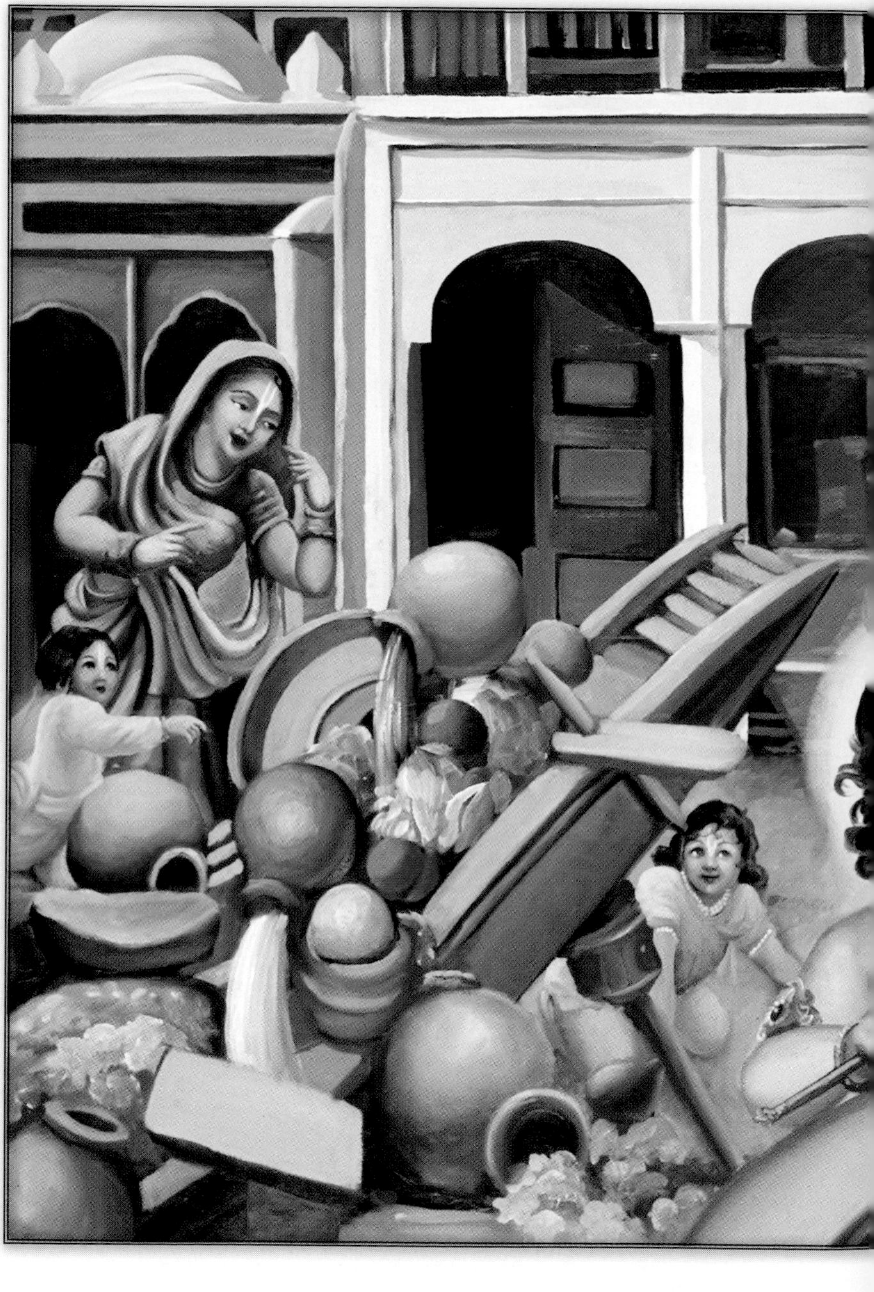

No one could ascertain the cause of the cart's falling. (p. 52)

Tṛṇāvarta felt the baby to be as heavy as a mountain. (p. 53)

"All day They simply make arrangements to steal our butter and yogurt." (p. 61)

2 / Prayers by the Demigods for Lord Kṛṣṇa in the Womb

King Kaṁsa not only occupied the kingdoms of the Yadu, Bhoja, and Andhaka dynasties and the kingdom of Śūrasena, but he also made alliances with all the other demoniac kings, as follows: the demon Pralamba, demon Baka, demon Cāṇūra, demon Tṛṇāvarta, demon Aghāsura, demon Muṣṭika, demon Ariṣṭa, demon Dvivida, demon Pūtanā, demon Keśī and demon Dhenuka. At that time, Jarāsandha was the king of Magadha province (known at present as Behar state). Thus by his diplomatic policy, Kaṁsa consolidated the most powerful kingdom of his time, under the protection of Jarāsandha. He made further alliances with such kings as Bāṇāsura and Bhaumāsura, until he was the strongest. Then he began to behave most inimically towards the Yadu dynasty into which Kṛṣṇa was to take His birth.

Being harassed by Kaṁsa, the kings of the Yadu, Bhoja and Andhaka dynasties began to take shelter in different states such as the state of the Kurus, the state of the Pañcālas and the states known as Kekaya, Śālva, Vidarbha, Niṣadha, Videha and Kośala. Kaṁsa broke the solidarity of the Yadu Kingdom, as well as the Bhoja and Andhaka. He made his position the most solid within the vast tract of land known at that time as Bhāratavarṣa.

When Kaṁsa killed the six babies of Devakī and Vasudeva one after another, many friends and relatives of Kaṁsa approached him and requested him to discontinue these heinous activities. But all of them became worshipers of Kaṁsa.

When Devakī became pregnant for the seventh time, a plenary expansion of Kṛṣṇa known as Ananta appeared within her womb. Devakī was overwhelmed both with jubilation and lamentation. She was joyful, for she could understand that Lord Viṣṇu had taken shelter within her womb, but at the same time she was sorry that as soon as her child would come out,

Kaṁsa would kill Him. At that time, the Supreme Personality of Godhead, Kṛṣṇa, being compassionate upon the fearful condition of the Yadus, due to atrocities committed by Kaṁsa, ordered the appearance of His *Yogamāyā,* or His internal potency. Kṛṣṇa is the Lord of the universe, but He is especially the Lord of the Yadu dynasty.

This *Yogamāyā* is the principal potency of the Personality of Godhead. In the *Vedas* it is stated that the Lord, the Supreme Personality of Godhead, has multipotencies. *Parāsya śaktir vividhaiva śrūyate.* All the different potencies are acting externally and internally, and *Yogamāyā* is the chief of all potencies. He ordered the appearance of *Yogamāyā* in the land of Vrajabhūmi, in Vṛndāvana, which is always decorated and full with beautiful cows. In Vṛndāvana, Rohiṇī, one of the wives of Vasudeva, was residing at the house of King Nanda and Queen Yaśodā. Not only Rohiṇī, but many others in the Yadu dynasty were scattered all over the country due to their fear of the atrocities of Kaṁsa. Some of them were even living in the caves of the mountains.

The Lord thus informed *Yogamāyā:* "Under the imprisonment of Kaṁsa are Devakī and Vasudeva, and at the present moment, My plenary expansion, Śeṣa, is within the womb of Devakī. You can arrange the transfer of Śeṣa from the womb of Devakī to the womb of Rohiṇī. After this arrangement, I am personally going to appear in the womb of Devakī with My full potencies. Then I shall appear as the son of Devakī and Vasudeva. And you shall appear as the daughter of Nanda and Yaśodā in Vṛndāvana.

"Since you will appear as My contemporary sister, people within the world will worship you with all kinds of valuable presentations: incense, candles, flowers and offerings of sacrifice. You shall quickly satisfy their desires for sense gratification. People who are after materialistic affection will worship you under the different forms of your expansions, which will be named Durgā, Bhadrakālī, Vijayā, Vaiṣṇavī, Kumudā, Caṇḍikā, Kṛṣṇā, Mādhavī, Kanyakā, Māyā, Nārāyaṇī, Īśānī, Śāradā and Ambikā."

Kṛṣṇa and *Yogamāyā* appeared as brother and sister—the Supreme Powerful and the supreme power. Although there is no clear distinction between the Powerful and the power, power is always subordinate to the Powerful. Those who are materialistic are worshippers of the power, but those who are transcendentalists are worshippers of the Powerful. Kṛṣṇa is the Supreme Powerful, and Durgā is the supreme power within the material world. Actually people in the Vedic culture worship both the Powerful and the power. There are many hundreds of thousands of temples of Viṣṇu and Devī, and sometimes they are worshipped simultaneously. The worshipper of the power, Durgā, or the external energy of Kṛṣṇa, may achieve all kinds of material success very easily, but anyone who wants to be elevated transcendentally must engage in worshipping the Powerful in Kṛṣṇa consciousness.

The Lord also declared to *Yogamāyā* that His plenary expansion, Ananta Śeṣa, was within the womb of Devakī. On account of being forcibly attracted to the womb of Rohiṇī, He would be known as Saṅkarṣaṇa and would be the source of all spiritual power or *bala,* by which one could be able to attain the highest bliss of life which is called *ramaṇa.* Therefore the plenary portion Ananta would be known after His appearance either as Saṅkarṣaṇa or Balarāma.

In the *Upaniṣads* it is stated, *Nāyam ātma bala hinena labhya.* The purport is that one cannot attain the Supreme or any form of self-realization without being sufficiently favored by Balarāma. *Bala* does not mean physical strength. No one can attain spiritual perfection by physical strength. One must have the spiritual strength which is infused by Balarāma or Saṅkarṣaṇa. *Ananta* or *Śeṣa* is the power which sustains all the planets in their different positions. Materially this sustaining power is known as the law of gravitation, but actually it is the display of the potency of Saṅkarṣaṇa. Balarāma or Saṅkarṣaṇa is spiritual power, or the original spiritual master. Therefore Lord Nityānanda Prabhu, who is also the incarnation of Balarāma, is the original spiritual master. And the spiritual master is the representative of Balarāma, the Supreme Personality of Godhead, who supplies spiritual strength. In the *Caitanya-caritāmṛta* it is confirmed that the spiritual master is the manifestation of the mercy of Kṛṣṇa.

When *Yogamāyā* was thus ordered by the Supreme Personality of Godhead, she circumambulated the Lord and then appeared within this material world according to His order. When the Supreme Powerful Personality of Godhead transferred Lord Śeṣa from the womb of Devakī to the womb of Rohiṇī, both of them were under the spell of *Yogamāyā,* which is also called *yoga-nidrā.* When this was done, people understood that Devakī's seventh pregnancy was a miscarriage. Thus although Balarāma appeared as the son of Devakī, He was transferred to the womb of Rohiṇī to appear as her son. After this arrangement, the Supreme Personality of Godhead, Kṛṣṇa, who is always ready to place His full potencies in His unalloyed devotees, entered as the Lord of the whole creation within the mind of Vasudeva. It is understood in this connection that Lord Kṛṣṇa first of all situated Himself in the unalloyed heart of Devakī. He was not put into the womb of Devakī by seminal discharge. The Supreme Personality of Godhead, by His inconceivable potency, can appear in any way. It is not necessary for Him to appear in the ordinary way by seminal injection within the womb of a woman.

When Vasudeva was sustaining the form of the Supreme Personality of Godhead within his heart, he appeared just like the glowing sun whose shining rays are always unbearable and scorching to the common man. The form of the Lord situated in the pure unalloyed heart of Vasudeva is not different from the original form of Kṛṣṇa. The appearance of the form of Kṛṣṇa anywhere, and specifically within the heart, is called *dhāma. Dhāma* does not only refer to Kṛṣṇa's form, but His name, His form, His quality and His paraphernalia. Everything becomes manifest simultaneously.

Thus the eternal form of the Supreme Personality of Godhead with full potencies was transferred from the mind of Vasudeva to the mind of Devakī, exactly as the setting sun's rays are transferred to the full moon rising in the east.

Kṛṣṇa, the Supreme Personality of Godhead, entered the body of Devakī from the body of Vasudeva. He was beyond the conditions of the ordinary living entity. When Kṛṣṇa is there, it is to be understood that all His plenary expansions, such as Nārāyaṇa, and incarnations like Lord Nṛsiṁha, Varāha, etc., are with Him, and they are not subject to the conditions of material existence. In this way, Devakī became the residence of the Supreme Personality of Godhead who is one without a second and the cause of all creation. Devakī became the residence of the Absolute Truth, but because she was within the house of Kaṁsa, she looked just like a supressed fire, or like misused education. When fire is covered by the walls of a pot or is kept in a jug, the illuminating rays of the fire cannot be very much appreciated. Similarly, misused knowledge, which does not benefit the people in general, is not very much appreciated. So Devakī was kept within the prison walls of Kaṁsa's palace, and no one could see her transcendental beauty which resulted from her conceiving the Supreme Personality of Godhead.

Kaṁsa, however, saw the transcendental beauty of his sister Devakī, and he at once concluded that the Supreme Personality of Godhead had taken shelter in her womb. She had never before looked so wonderfully beautiful. He could distinctly understand that there was something wonderful within the womb of Devakī. In this way, Kaṁsa became perturbed. He was sure that the Supreme Personality of Godhead would kill him in the future and that He had now come. Kaṁsa began to think: "What is to be done with Devakī? Surely she has Viṣṇu or Kṛṣṇa within her womb, so it is certain that Kṛṣṇa has come to execute the mission of the demigods. And even if I immediately kill Devakī, His mission cannot be frustrated." Kaṁsa knew very well that no one can frustrate the purpose of Viṣṇu. Any intelligent man can understand that the laws of God cannot be violated. His purpose will be served in spite of all impediments offered by the demons. Kaṁsa thought: "If I kill Devakī at the present moment, Viṣṇu will enforce His supreme will more vehemently. To kill Devakī just now would be a most abominable act. No one desires to kill his reputation, even in an awkward situation; if I kill Devakī now, my reputation will be spoiled. Devakī is a woman, and she is under my shelter; she is pregnant, and if I kill her, immediately all my reputation, the result of pious activities and duration of life, will be finished."

He also further deliberated: "A person who is too cruel, even in this lifetime is as good as dead. No one likes a cruel person during his lifetime, and after his death, people curse him. On account of his self-identification with the body, he must be degraded and pushed into the darkest region of hell." Kaṁsa thus meditated on all the pros and cons of killing Devakī at that time.

Kaṁsa finally decided not to kill Devakī right away but to wait for the inevitable future. But his mind became absorbed in animosity against the Personality of Godhead. He patiently waited for the deliverance of the child, expecting to kill Him, as he had done previously with the other babies of Devakī. Thus being merged in the ocean of animosity against the Personality of Godhead, he began to think of Kṛṣṇa and Viṣṇu while sitting, while sleeping, while walking, while eating, while working—in all the situations of his life. His mind became so much absorbed with the thought of the Supreme Personality of Godhead that indirectly he could see only Kṛṣṇa or Viṣṇu around him. Unfortunately, although his mind was so absorbed in the thought of Viṣṇu, he is not recognized as a devotee because he was thinking of Kṛṣṇa as an enemy. The state of mind of a great devotee is also to be always absorbed in Kṛṣṇa, but a devotee thinks of Him favorably, not unfavorably. To think of Kṛṣṇa favorably is Kṛṣṇa consciousness, but to think of Kṛṣṇa unfavorably is not Kṛṣṇa consciousness.

At this time Lord Brahmā and Lord Śiva, accompanied by great sages like Nārada and followed by many other demigods, invisibly appeared in the house of Kaṁsa. They began to pray for the Supreme Personality of Godhead in select prayers which are very pleasing to the devotees and which award fulfillment of their desires. The first words they spoke acclaimed that the Lord is true to His vow. As stated in the *Bhagavad-gītā*,

Kṛṣṇa descends in this material world just to protect the pious and destroy the impious. That is His vow. The demigods could understand that the Lord had taken His residence within the womb of Devakī in order to fulfill this vow. The demigods were very glad that the Lord was appearing to fulfill His mission, and they addressed Him as *satyam param,* or the Supreme Absolute Truth.

Everyone is searching after the truth. That is the philosophical way of life. The demigods give information that the Supreme Absolute Truth is Kṛṣṇa. One who becomes fully Kṛṣṇa conscious can attain the Absolute Truth. Kṛṣṇa is the Absolute Truth. Relative truth is not truth in all the three phases of eternal time. Time is divided into past, present and future. Kṛṣṇa is Truth always, past, present and future. In the material world everything is being controlled by supreme time, in the course of past, present and future. But before the creation, Kṛṣṇa was existing, and when there is creation, everything is resting in Kṛṣṇa, and when this creation is finished, Kṛṣṇa will remain. Therefore, He is Absolute Truth in all circumstances. If there is any truth within this material world, it emanates from the Supreme Truth, Kṛṣṇa. If there is any opulence within this material world, the cause of the opulence is Kṛṣṇa. If there is any reputation within this material world, the cause of the reputation is Kṛṣṇa. If there is any strength within this material world, the cause of such strength is Kṛṣṇa. If there is any wisdom and education within this material world, the cause of such wisdom and education is Kṛṣṇa. Therefore Kṛṣṇa is the source of all relative truths.

This material world is composed of five principal elements: earth, water, fire, air and ether, and all such elements are emanations from Kṛṣṇa. The material scientists accept these primary five elements as the cause of material manifestation, but the elements in their gross and subtle states are produced by Kṛṣṇa. The living entities who are working within this material world are also products of His marginal potency. In the Seventh Chapter of the *Bhagavad-gītā,* it is clearly stated that the whole manifestation is a combination of two kinds of energies of Kṛṣṇa, the superior energy and the inferior energy. The living entities are the superior energy, and the dead material elements are His inferior energy. In its dormant stage, everything remains in Kṛṣṇa.

The demigods continued to offer their respectful prayers unto the supreme form of the Personality of Godhead, Kṛṣṇa, by analytical study of the material manifestation. What is this material manifestation? It is just like a tree. A tree stands on the ground. Similarly, the tree of the material manifestation is standing on the ground of material nature. This material manifestation is compared with a tree because a tree is ultimately cut off in due course of time. A tree is called *vṛkṣa. Vṛkṣa* means that thing which will be ultimately cut off. Therefore, this tree of the material manifestation cannot be accepted as the Ultimate Truth. The influence of time is on the material manifestation, but Kṛṣṇa's body is eternal. He existed before the material manifestation, He is existing while the material manifestation is continuing, and when it will be dissolved, He will continue to exist.

The *Kaṭha Upaniṣad* also cites this example of the tree of material manifestation standing on the ground of material nature. This tree has two kinds of fruits, distress and happiness. Those who are living on the tree of the body are just like two birds. One bird is the localized aspect of Kṛṣṇa known as the Paramātmā, and the other bird is the living entity. The living entity is eating the fruits of this material manifestation. Sometimes he eats the fruit of happiness, and sometimes he eats the fruit of distress. But the other bird is not interested in eating the fruit of distress or happiness because he is self-satisfied. The *Kaṭha Upaniṣad* states that one bird on the tree of the body is eating the fruits, and the other bird is simply witnessing. The roots of this tree extend in three directions. That means the root of the tree is the three modes of material nature: goodness, passion and ignorance. Just as the tree's root expands, so, by association of the modes of material nature (goodness, passion and ignorance), one expands his duration of material existence. The taste of the fruits are of four kinds: religiosity, economic development, sense gratification and ultimately, liberation. According to the different associations in the three modes of material nature, the living entities are tasting different kinds of religiosity, different kinds of economic development, different kinds of sense gratification and different kinds of liberation. Practically all material work is performed in ignorance, but because there are three qualities, sometimes the quality of ignorance is covered with goodness or passion. The taste of these material fruits is accepted through five senses. The five sense organs through which knowledge is acquired are subjected to six kinds of whips: lamentation, illusion, infirmity, death, hunger and thirst. This material body, or the material manifestation, is covered by seven layers: skin, muscle, flesh, marrow, bone, fat and semina. The branches of the tree are eight: earth, water, fire, air, ether, mind, intelligence and ego. There are nine gates in this body: the two eyes, two nostrils, two ears, one mouth, one genital, one rectum. And there are ten kinds of internal air passing within the body: *prāṇa, apāna, udāna, vyāna, samāna,* etc. The two birds seated in this tree, as explained above, are the living entity and the localized Supreme Personality of Godhead.

The root cause of the material manifestation described here is the Supreme Personality of Godhead. The Supreme Personality of Godhead expands Himself and takes charge of the three qualities of the material world. Viṣṇu takes charge of the modes of goodness, Brahmā takes charge of the modes of passion, and Lord Śiva takes charge of the modes of ignorance. Brahmā, by the modes of passion, creates this manifestation, Lord Viṣṇu maintains this manifestation by the modes of goodness, and Lord Śiva annihilates it by the modes of ignorance. The whole creation ultimately rests in the Supreme Lord. He is the cause of creation, maintenance and dissolution. And when the whole manifestation is dissolved, in its subtle form as the energy of the Lord, it rests within the body of the Supreme Lord.

"At the present," the demigods prayed, "the Supreme Lord Kṛṣṇa is appearing just for the maintenance of this manifestation." Actually the Supreme Cause is one, but, being deluded by the three modes of material nature, less intelligent persons see that the material world is manifested through different causes. Those who are intelligent can see that the cause is one, Kṛṣṇa. As it is stated in the *Brahma-saṁhitā: sarva-kāraṇa-kāraṇam.* Kṛṣṇa, the Supreme Personality of Godhead, is the cause of all causes. Brahmā is the deputed agent for creation, Viṣṇu is the expansion of Kṛṣṇa for maintenance, and Lord Śiva is the expansion of Kṛṣṇa for dissolution.

"Our dear Lord," the demigods prayed, "it is very difficult to understand Your eternal form of personality. People in general are unable to understand Your actual form; therefore You are personally descending to exhibit Your original eternal form. Somehow people can understand the different incarnations of Your Lordship, but they are puzzled to understand the eternal form of Kṛṣṇa with two hands, moving among human beings exactly like one of them. This eternal form of Your Lordship is ever increasing in transcendental pleasure for the devotees. But for the nondevotees, this form is very dangerous." As stated in the *Bhagavad-gītā*, Kṛṣṇa is very pleasing to the *sādhu.* It is said, *paritrāṇāya sādhūnām.* But this form is very dangerous for the demons because Kṛṣṇa also descends to kill the demons. He is, therefore, simultaneously pleasing to the devotees and dangerous to the demons.

"Our dear lotus-eyed Lord, You are the source of pure goodness. There are many great sages who simply by *samādhi,* or transcendentally meditating upon Your lotus feet and thus being absorbed in Your thought, have easily transformed the great ocean of nescience created by the material nature to no more than water in a calf's hoofprint." The purpose of meditation is to focus the mind upon the Personality of Godhead, beginning from

His lotus feet. Simply by meditation on the lotus feet of the Lord, great sages cross over this vast ocean of material existence without difficulty.

"O self-illuminated one, the great saintly persons who have crossed over the ocean of nescience, by the help of the transcendental boat of Your lotus feet, have not taken away that boat. It is still lying on this side." The demigods are using a nice simile. If one takes a boat to cross over a river, the boat also goes with one to the other side of the river. And so when one reaches the destination, how can the same boat be available to those who are still on the other side? To answer this difficulty, the demigods say in their prayer that the boat is not taken away. The devotees still remaining on the other side are able to pass over the ocean of material nature because the pure devotees do not take the boat with them when they cross over. When one simply approaches the boat, the whole ocean of material nescience is reduced to the size of water in a calf's hoofprint. Therefore, the devotees do not need to take a boat to the other side; they simply cross the ocean immediately. Because the great saintly persons are compassionate toward all conditioned souls, the boat is still lying at the lotus feet of the Lord. One can meditate upon His feet at any time, and by so doing, one can cross over the great ocean of material existence.

Meditation means concentration upon the lotus feet of the Lord. Lotus feet indicate the Supreme Personality of Godhead. Those who are impersonalists do not recognize the lotus feet of the Lord, and therefore their object of meditation is something impersonal. The demigods express their mature verdict that persons who are interested in meditating on something void or impersonal cannot cross over the ocean of nescience. Such persons are simply imagining that they have become liberated. "O lotus-eyed Lord! Their intelligence is contaminated because they fail to meditate upon the lotus feet of Your Lordship." As a result of this neglectful activity, the impersonalists fall down again into the material way of conditioned life, although they may temporarily rise up to the point of impersonal realization. Impersonalists, after undergoing severe austerities and penances, merge themselves into the Brahman effulgence or impersonal Brahman existence. But their minds are not free from material contamination; they have simply tried to negate the material ways of thinking. That does not mean that they have become liberated. Thus they fall down. In the *Bhagavad-gītā* it is stated that the impersonalist has to undergo great tribulation in realizing the ultimate goal. At the beginning of the *Śrīmad-Bhāgavatam,* it is also stated that without devotional service to the Supreme Personality of Godhead, one cannot achieve liberation from the bondage of fruitive activities. The statement of Lord Kṛṣṇa is there in the *Bhagavad-gītā,* and in the *Śrīmad-Bhāgavatam* the statement of the great sage Nārada is there, and here also the demigods confirm it. "Persons who have not taken to devotional service are understood to have come short of the ultimate purpose of knowledge and are not favored by Your grace." The impersonalists simply *think* that they are liberated, but actually they have no feeling for the Personality of Godhead. They think that when Kṛṣṇa comes into the material world, he accepts a material body. They therefore overlook the transcendental body of Kṛṣṇa. This is also confirmed in the *Bhagavad-gītā. Avajānanti māṁ mūḍhāḥ.* In spite of conquering material lust and rising up to the point of liberation, the impersonalists fall down. If they are engaged just in knowing things for the sake of knowledge and do not take to the devotional service of the Lord, they cannot achieve the desired result. Their achievement is the trouble they take, and that is all. It is clearly stated in the *Bhagavad-gītā* that to realize Brahman identification is not all. Brahman identification may help one become joyful without material attachment or detachment and to achieve the platform of equanimity, but after this stage, one has to take to devotional service. When one takes to devotional service after being elevated to the platform of Brahman realization, he is then admitted into the spiritual kingdom for permanent residence in association with the Supreme Personality of Godhead. That is the result of devotional service. Those who are devotees of the Supreme Personality of Godhead never fall down like the impersonalists. Even if the devotees fall down, they remain affectionately attached to their Lordship. They can meet all kinds of obstacles on the path of devotional service, and freely, without any fear, they can surmount such obstacles. Because of their surrender, they are certain that Kṛṣṇa will always protect them. As it is promised by Kṛṣṇa in the *Bhagavad-gītā:* "My devotees are never vanquished."

"Our dear Lord, You have appeared in Your original unalloyed form, the eternal form of goodness, for the welfare of all living entities within this material world. Taking advantage of Your appearance, all of them can now very easily understand the nature and form of the Supreme Personality of Godhead. Persons who belong to the four divisions of the social order (the *brahmacārīs,* the *gṛhasthas,* the *vānaprasthas* and the *sannyāsīs*) can all take advantage of Your appearance.

"Dear Lord, husband of the goddess of fortune, devotees who are dovetailed in Your service do not fall down from their high position like the impersonalists. Being protected by You, the devotees are able to traverse over the heads of many of *māyā's* commanders-in-chief, who can always put stumbling blocks on the path of liberation. My dear Lord, You appear in Your transcendental form for the benefit of the living entities so that they can see You face to face and offer their worshipful sacrifices by ritualistic performance of the *Vedas,* mystic meditation and devotional service as recommended in the scriptures. Dear Lord, if You did not appear in Your eternal transcendental form, full of bliss and knowledge—which can eradicate all kinds of speculative ignorance about Your position—then all people would simply speculate about You according to their respective modes of material nature."

The appearance of Kṛṣṇa is the answer to all imaginative iconography of the Supreme Personality of Godhead. Everyone imagines the form of the Supreme Personality of Godhead according to his mode of material nature. In the *Brahma-saṁhitā* it is said that the Lord is the oldest person. Therefore a section of religionists imagine that God must be very old, and therefore they depict a form of the Lord like a very old man. But in the same *Brahma-saṁhitā,* that is contradicted; although He is the oldest of all living entities, He has His eternal form as a fresh youth. The exact words used in this connection in the *Śrīmad-Bhāgavatam* are *vijñānam ajñānabhid āpamārjanam. Vijñānam* means transcendental knowledge of the Supreme Personality. *Vijñānam* is also experienced knowledge. Transcendental knowledge has to be accepted by the descending process of disciplic succession as Brahmā presents the knowledge of Kṛṣṇa in the *Brahma-saṁhitā. Brahma-saṁhitā* is *vijñānam* as realized by Brahmā's transcendental experience, and in that way he presented the form and the pastimes of Kṛṣṇa in the transcendental abode. *Ajñānabhid* means that which can match all kinds of speculation. In ignorance, people are imagining the form of the Lord; sometimes He has no form and sometimes He has form, according to their different imaginations. But the presentation of Kṛṣṇa in the *Brahma-saṁhitā* is *vijñānam*—scientific, experienced knowledge given by Lord Brahmā and accepted by Lord Caitanya. There is no doubt about it. Śrī Kṛṣṇa's form, Śrī Kṛṣṇa's flute, Kṛṣṇa's color—everything is reality. Here it is said that this *vijñānam* is always defeating all kinds of speculative knowledge. "Therefore, without Your appearing as Kṛṣṇa, as You are, neither *ajñānabhid* (nescience of speculative knowledge) nor *vijñānam* would be realized. *Ajñānabhid āpamārjanam*—by Your appearance the speculative knowledge of ignorance will be vanquished and the real experienced knowledge of authorities like Lord Brahmā will be established. Men influenced by the three modes of material nature imagine their own God according to the modes of material nature. In this way God is presented in various ways, but Your appearance will establish what the real form of God is."

The highest blunder committed by the impersonalist is to think that when the incarnation of God comes, He accepts the form of matter in the modes of goodness. Actually the form of Kṛṣṇa or Nārāyaṇa is transcendental to any material idea. Even the greatest impersonalist, Śaṅkarācārya, has admitted that *nārāyaṇaḥ paro'vyaktāt:* the material creation is caused by the *avyakta* impersonal manifestation of matter or the nonphenomenal total reservation of matter, and Kṛṣṇa is transcendental to that material conception. That is expressed in the *Śrīmad-Bhāgavatam* as *śuddha-sattva,* or transcendental. He does not belong to the material mode of goodness, and He is above the position of material goodness. He belongs to the transcendental eternal status of bliss and knowledge.

"Dear Lord, when You appear in Your different incarnations, You take different names and forms according to different situations. Lord Kṛṣṇa is Your name because You are all attractive; You are called Śyāmasundara because of Your transcendental beauty. *Śyāma* means blackish, yet they say that You are more beautiful than thousands of cupids. *Kandarpa-koṭi-kamanīya.* Although You appear in a color which is compared to the blackish cloud, because You are transcendental Absolute, Your beauty is many many times more attractive than the delicate body of Cupid. Sometimes You are called Giridhārī because You lifted the hill known as Govardhana. You are sometimes called Nandanandana or Vāsudeva or Devakīnandana because You appear as the son of Mahārāja Nanda or Devakī or Vasudeva. Impersonalists think that Your many names or forms are according to a particular type of work and quality because they accept You from the position of a material observer.

"Our dear Lord, the way of understanding is not to study Your absolute nature, form and activities by mental speculation. One must engage himself in devotional service; then one can understand Your absolute nature, transcendental form, name and quality. Actually only a person who has a little taste for the service of Your lotus feet can understand Your transcendental nature or form and quality. Others may go on speculating for millions of years, but it is not possible for them to understand even a single part of Your actual position." In other words, the Supreme Personality of Godhead, Kṛṣṇa, cannot be understood by the nondevotees because there is a curtain of *Yogamāyā* which covers Kṛṣṇa's actual features. As confirmed in the *Bhagavad-gītā, nāhaṁ prakāśaḥ sarvasya.* The Lord says, "I am not exposed to anyone and everyone." When Kṛṣṇa came, He was actually present on the battlefield of Kurukṣetra, and everyone saw Him. But not everyone could understand that He was the Supreme Personality of

Godhead. Still, everyone who died in His presence attained complete liberation from material bondage and was transferred to the spiritual world.

"O Lord, the impersonalists or nondevotees cannot understand that Your name is identical with Your form." Since the Lord is Absolute, there is no difference between His name and His actual form. In the material world there is a difference between form and name. The mango fruit is different from the name of the mango. One cannot taste the mango fruit simply by chanting, "Mango, mango, mango." But the devotee who knows that there is no difference between the name and the form of the Lord chants Hare Kṛṣṇa, Hare Kṛṣṇa, Kṛṣṇa Kṛṣṇa, Hare Hare, Hare Rāma, Hare Rāma, Rāma Rāma, Hare Hare, and realizes that he is always in Kṛṣṇa's company.

For persons who are not very advanced in absolute knowledge of the Supreme, Lord Kṛṣṇa exhibits His transcendental pastimes. They can simply think of the pastimes of the Lord and get the full benefit. Since there is no difference between the transcendental name and form of the Lord, there is no difference between the transcendental pastimes and the form of the Lord. For those who are less intelligent (like women, laborers or the mercantile class), the great sage Vyāsadeva wrote *Mahābhārata.* In the *Mahābhārata,* Kṛṣṇa is present in His different activities. *Mahābhārata* is history, and simply by studying, hearing and memorizing the transcendental activities of Kṛṣṇa, the less intelligent can also gradually rise to the standard of pure devotees.

The pure devotees, who are always absorbed in the thought of the transcendental lotus feet of Kṛṣṇa and who are always engaged in devotional service in full Kṛṣṇa consciousness, are never to be considered to be in the material world. Śrī Rūpa Gosvāmī has explained that those who are always engaged in Kṛṣṇa consciousness, by body, mind and activities, are to be considered liberated even within this body. This is also confirmed in the *Bhagavad-gītā:* those who are engaged in the devotional service of the Lord have already transcended the material position.

Kṛṣṇa appears to give a chance both to the devotees and nondevotees for realization of the ultimate goal of life. The devotees get the direct chance to see Him and worship Him. Those who are not on that platform get the chance to become acquainted with His activities and thus become elevated to the same position.

"O dear Lord," the demigods continued, "You are unborn; therefore we do not find any reason for Your appearance other than for Your pleasurable pastimes." Although the reason for the appearance of the Lord is stated in the *Bhagavad-gītā* (He descends just to give protection to the devotee and vanquish the nondevotee), actually He descends for His pleasure-meeting with the devotees, not really to vanquish the nondevotees. The nondevotees can be vanquished simply by material nature. "The action and reaction of the external energy of material nature (creation, maintenance and annihilation) are being carried on automatically. But simply by taking shelter of Your holy name—because Your holy name and Your personality are nondifferent—the devotees are sufficiently protected." The protection of the devotees and the annihilation of the nondevotees are actually not the business of the Supreme Personality of Godhead when He descends. They are just for His transcendental pleasure. There cannot be any other reason for His appearance.

"Our dear Lord, You are appearing as the best of the Yadu dynasty, and we are offering our respectful humble obeisance unto Your lotus feet. Before this appearance, You also appeared as the fish incarnation, the horse incarnation, the tortoise incarnation, the swan incarnation, as King Rāmacandra, as Paraśurāma, and as many other incarnations. You appeared just to protect the devotees, and we request You in Your present appearance as the Supreme Personality of Godhead Himself to give us similar protection all over the three worlds and remove all obstacles for the peaceful execution of our lives.

"Dear mother Devakī, within your womb is the Supreme Personality of Godhead, appearing along with all His plenary extensions. He is the original Personality of Godhead appearing for our welfare. Therefore you should not be afraid of your brother, the King of Bhoja. Your son Lord Kṛṣṇa, who is the original Personality of Godhead, will appear for the protection of the pious Yadu dynasty. The Lord is appearing not only alone but accompanied by His immediate plenary portion, Balarāma."

Devakī was very much afraid of her brother Kaṁsa because he had already killed so many of her children. She used to remain very anxious about Kṛṣṇa. In the *Viṣṇu Purāṇa* it is stated that in order to pacify Devakī, all the demigods, along with their wives, used to always visit her to encourage her not to be afraid that her son would be killed by Kaṁsa. Kṛṣṇa, who was within her womb, was to appear not only to diminish the burden of the world but specifically to protect the interest of the Yadu dynasty, and certainly to protect Devakī and Vasudeva.

Thus ends the Bhaktivedanta purport of the Second Chapter of Kṛṣṇa, *"Prayers by the Demigods for Lord Kṛṣṇa in the Womb."*

3 / Birth of Lord Kṛṣṇa

As stated in the *Bhagavad-gītā,* the Lord says that His appearance, birth, and activities are all transcendental, and one who understands them factually becomes immediately eligible to be transferred to the spiritual world. The Lord's appearance or birth is not like that of an ordinary man who is forced to accept a material body according to his past deeds. The Lord's appearance is explained in the Second Chapter: He appears out of His own sweet pleasure. When the time was mature for the appearance of the Lord, thc constellations became very auspicious. The astrological influence of the star known as Rohiṇī was also predominant because this star is considered to be very auspicious. Rohiṇī is under the direct supervision of Brahmā. According to the astrological conclusion, besides the proper situation of the stars, there are auspicious and inauspicious moments due to the different situations of the different planetary systems. At the time of Kṛṣṇa's birth, the planetary systems were automatically adjusted so that everything became auspicious.

At that time, in all directions, east, west, south, north, everywhere, there was an atmosphere of peace and prosperity. There were auspicious stars visible in the sky, and on the surface in all towns and villages or pasturing grounds and within the minds of everyone there were signs of good fortune. The rivers were flowing full of waters, and lakes were beautifully decorated with lotus flowers. The forests were full with beautiful birds and peacocks. All the birds within the forests began to sing with sweet voices, and the peacocks began to dance along with their consorts. The wind blew very pleasantly, carrying the aroma of different flowers, and the sensation of bodily touch was very pleasing. At home, the *brāhmaṇas,* who were accustomed to offer sacrifices in the fire, found their homes very pleasant for offerings. Due to disturbances created by the demoniac kings, the sacrificial fire altar had been almost stopped in the houses of *brāhmaṇas,* but now they could find the opportunity to start the fire peacefully. Being forbidden to offer sacrifices, the *brāhmaṇas* were very distressed in mind, intelligence and activities, but just on the point of Kṛṣṇa's appearance, automatically their minds became full of joy because they could hear loud vibrations in the sky of transcendental sounds proclaiming the appearance of the Supreme Personality of Godhead.

The denizens of the Gandharva and Kinnara planets began to sing, and the denizens of Siddhaloka and the planets of the Cāraṇas began to offer prayers in the service of the Personality of Godhead. In the heavenly planets, the angels along with their wives, accompanied by the Apsaras, began to dance.

The great sages and the demigods, being pleased, began to shower flowers. At the seashore, there was the sound of mild waves, and above the sea there were clouds in the sky which began to thunder very pleasingly.

When things were adjusted like this, Lord Viṣṇu, who is residing within the heart of every living entity, appeared in the darkness of night as the Supreme Personality of Godhead before Devakī, who also appeared as one of the demigoddesses. The appearance of Lord Viṣṇu at that time could be compared with the full moon in the sky as it rises on the eastern horizon. The objection may be raised that, since Lord Kṛṣṇa appeared on the eighth day of the waning moon, there could be no rising of the full moon. In answer to this it may be said that Lord Kṛṣṇa appeared in the dynasty which is in the hierarchy of the moon; therefore, although the moon was incomplete on that night, because of the Lord's appearance in the dynasty wherein the moon is himself the original person, the moon was in an overjoyous condition, so by the grace of Kṛṣṇa he could appear just as a full moon.

In an astronomical treatise by the name *Khamānikya,* the constellations at the time of the appearance of Lord Kṛṣṇa are very nicely described. It is confirmed that the child born at that auspicious moment was the Supreme Brahman or the Absolute Truth.

Vasudeva saw that wonderful child born as a baby with four hands, holding conchshell, club, disc, and lotus flower, decorated with the mark of Śrīvatsa, wearing the jeweled necklace of *kaustubha* stone, dressed in yellow silk, appearing dazzling like a bright blackish cloud, wearing a helmet bedecked with the *vaidūrya* stone, valuable bracelets, earrings and similar other ornaments all over His body and an abundance of hair on His head. Due to the extraordinary features of the child, Vasudeva was struck with wonder. How could a newly born child be so decorated? He could therefore understand that Lord Kṛṣṇa had now appeared, and he became overpowered by the occasion. Vasudeva very humbly wondered that although he was an ordinary living entity conditioned by material nature and was externally imprisoned by Kaṁsa, the all-pervading Personality of Godhead, Viṣṇu or Kṛṣṇa, was appearing as a child in his home, exactly in His original position. No earthly child is born with four hands decorated with ornaments and nice clothing, fully equipped with all the signs of the Supreme Personality of Godhead. Over and over again, Vasudeva glanced at his child, and he considered how to celebrate this auspicious moment: "Generally, when a male child is born," he thought, "people observe the occasion with jubilant celebrations, and in my home, although I am imprisoned, the Supreme Personality of Godhead has taken birth. How many millions of millions of times should I be prepared to observe this auspicious ceremony!"

When Vasudeva, who is also called Ānakadundubhi, was looking at his newborn baby, he was so happy that he wanted to give many thousands of cows in charity to the *brāhmaṇas.* According to the Vedic system, whenever there is an auspicious ceremony in the *kṣatriya* king's palace, the king gives many things in charity. Cows decorated with golden ornaments are delivered to the *brāhmaṇas* and sages. Vasudeva wanted to perform a charitable ceremony to celebrate Kṛṣṇa's appearance, but because he was shackled within the walls of Kaṁsa's prison, this was not possible. Instead, within his mind he gave thousands of cows to the *brāhmaṇas.*

When Vasudeva was convinced that the newborn child was the Supreme Personality of Godhead Himself, he bowed down with folded hands and began to offer Him prayers. At that time Vasudeva was in the transcendental position, and he became completely free from all fear of Kaṁsa. The newborn baby was also flashing His effulgence within the room in which He appeared.

Vasudeva then began to offer his prayers. "My dear Lord, I can understand who You are. You are the Supreme Personality of Godhead, the Supersoul of all living entities and the Absolute Truth. You have appeared in Your own eternal form which is directly perceived by us. I understand that because I am afraid of Kaṁsa, You have appeared just to deliver me from that fear. You do not belong to this material world; You are the same person who brings about the cosmic manifestation simply by glancing over material nature."

One may argue that the Supreme Personality of Godhead, who creates the whole cosmic manifestation simply by His glance, cannot come within the womb of Devakī, the wife of Vasudeva. To eradicate this argument, Vasudeva said, "My dear Lord, it is not a very wonderful thing that You appear within the womb of Devakī because the creation was also made in that way. You were lying in the Causal Ocean as Mahā-Viṣṇu, and by Your breathing process, innumerable universes came into existence. Then You entered into each of the universes as Garbhodakaśāyī Viṣṇu. Then again You expanded Yourself as Kṣīrodakaśāyī Viṣṇu and entered into the hearts of all living entities and entered even within the atoms. Therefore Your entrance in the womb of Devakī is understandable in the same way. You appear to have entered, but You are simultaneously all-pervading. We can understand Your entrance and nonentrance from material examples. The total material energy remains intact even after being divided into sixteen elements. The material body is nothing but the combination of the five gross elements—namely earth, water, fire, air and ether. Whenever there is a material body, it appears that such elements are newly created, but actually the elements are always existing outside of the body. Similarly, although You appear as a child in the womb of Devakī, You are also existing outside. You are always in Your abode, but still You can simultaneously expand Yourself into millions of forms.

"One has to understand Your appearance with great intelligence because the material energy is also emanating from You. You are the original source of the material energy, just as the sun is the source of the sunshine. The sunshine cannot cover the sun globe, nor can the material energy—being an emanation from You—cover You. You appear to be in the three modes of material energy, but actually the three modes of material energy cannot cover You. This is understood by the highly intellectual philosophers. In other words, although You appear to be within the material energy, You are never covered by it."

We hear from the Vedic version that the Supreme Brahman exhibits His effulgence, and therefore everything becomes illuminated. We can understand from *Brahma-saṁhitā* that the *brahmajyoti,* or the Brahman effulgence, emanates from the body of the Supreme Lord. And from the Brahman effulgence, all creation takes place. It is further stated in the *Bhagavad-gītā* that the Lord is also the support of the Brahman effulgence. Originally He is the root cause of everything. But persons who are less intelligent think that when the Supreme Personality of Godhead comes within this material world, He accepts the material qualities. Such conclusions are not very mature, but are made by the less intelligent.

The Supreme Personality of Godhead is directly and indirectly existing everywhere; He is outside this material creation, and He is also within it. He is within this material creation not only as Garbhodakaśāyī Viṣṇu; He is also within the atom. Existence is due to His presence. Nothing can be separated from His existence. In the Vedic injunction we find that the Supreme Soul or the root cause of everything has to be searched out because nothing exists independent of the Supreme Soul. Therefore the material manifestation is also a transformation of His potency. Both inert matter and the living force–soul–are emanations from Him. Only the foolish conclude that when the Supreme Lord appears He accepts the conditions of matter. Even if He appears to have accepted the material body, He is still not subjected to any material condition. Kṛṣṇa has therefore appeared and defeated all imperfect conclusions about the appearance and disappearance of the Supreme Personality of Godhead.

"My Lord, Your appearance, existence and disappearance are beyond the influence of the material qualities. Because Your Lordship is the controller of everything and the resting place of the Supreme Brahman, there is nothing inconceivable or contradictory in You. As You have said, material nature works under Your superintendence. It is just like government officers working under the orders of the chief executive. The influence of subordinate activities cannot affect You. The Supreme Brahman and all phenomena are existing within You, and all the activities of material nature are controlled by Your Lordship.

"You are called *śuklam*. *Śuklam* or 'whiteness' is the symbolic representation of the Absolute Truth because it is unaffected by the material qualities. Lord Brahmā is called *rakta,* or red, because Brahmā represents the qualities of passion for creation. Darkness is entrusted to Lord Śiva because he annihilates the cosmos. The creation, annihilation and maintenance of this cosmic manifestation is conducted by Your potencies, yet You are always unaffected by those qualities. As confirmed in the *Vedas, Harir hi nirguṇaḥ sākṣāt:* the Supreme Personality of Godhead is always free from all material qualities. It is also said that the qualities of passion and ignorance are nonexistent in the person of the Supreme Lord.

"My Lord, You are the supreme controller, the Personality of Godhead, the supreme great, maintaining the order of this cosmic manifestation. And in spite of Your being the supreme controller, You have so kindly appeared in my home. The purpose of Your appearance is to kill the followers of the demonic rulers of the world who are in the dress of royal princes but are actually demons. I am sure that You will kill all of them and their followers and soldiers.

"I understand that You have appeared to kill the uncivilized Kaṁsa and his followers. But knowing that You were to appear to kill him and his followers, he has already killed so many of Your predecessors, elder brothers. Now he is simply awaiting the news of Your birth. As soon as he hears about it, he will immediately appear with all kinds of weapons to kill You."

After this prayer of Vasudeva, Devakī, the mother of Kṛṣṇa, offered her prayers. She was very frightened because of her brother's atrocities. Devakī said "My dear Lord, Your eternal forms, like Nārāyaṇa, Lord Rāma, Śeṣa, Varāha, Nṛsiṁha, Vāmana, Baladeva, and millions of similar incarnations emanating from Viṣṇu, are described in the Vedic literature as original. You are original because all Your forms as incarnations are outside of this material creation. Your form was existing before this cosmic manifestation was created. Your forms are eternal and all-pervading. They are self-effulgent, changeless and uncontaminated by the material qualities. Such eternal forms are ever-cognizant and full of bliss; they are situated in transcendental goodness and are always engaged in different pastimes. You are not limited to a particular form only; all such transcendental eternal forms are self-sufficient. I can understand that You are the Supreme Lord Viṣṇu.

"After many millions of years, when Lord Brahmā comes to the end of his life, the annihilation of the cosmic manifestation takes place. At that time the five elements–namely earth, water, fire, air and ether–enter into the *mahat-tattva.* The *mahat-tattva* again enters, by the force of time, into the nonmanifested total material energy; the total material energy enters into the energetic *pradhāna,* and the *pradhāna* enters into You. Therefore after the annihilation of the whole cosmic manifestation, You alone remain with Your transcendental name, form, quality and paraphernalia.

"My Lord, I offer my respectful obeisances unto You because You are the director of the unmanifested total energy, and the ultimate reservoir of the material nature. My Lord, the whole cosmic manifestation is under the influence of time, beginning from the moment up to the duration of the year. All act under Your direction. You are the original director of everything and the reservoir of all potent energies.

"Therefore my Lord, I request You to save me from the cruel hands of the son of Ugrasena, Kaṁsa. I am praying to Your Lordship to please rescue me from this fearful condition because You are always ready to give protection to Your servitors." The Lord has confirmed this statement in the *Bhagavad-gītā* by assuring Arjuna, "You may declare to the world, My devotee shall never be vanquished."

While thus praying to the Lord for rescue, mother Devakī expressed her motherly affection: "I understand that this transcendental form is generally perceived in meditation by the great sages, but I am still afraid because as soon as Kaṁsa understands that You have appeared, he might harm You. So I request that for the time being You become invisible to our material eyes." In other words, she requested the Lord to assume the form of an ordinary child. "My only cause of fear from my brother Kaṁsa is due to Your appearance. My Lord Madhusūdana, Kaṁsa may know that You are already born. Therefore I request You to conceal this four-armed form of Your Lordship which holds the four symbols of Viṣṇu—namely the conchshell, the disc, the club and the lotus flower. My dear Lord, at the end of the annihilation of the cosmic manifestation, You put the whole universe within Your abdomen; still by Your unalloyed mercy You have appeared in my womb. I am surprised that You imitate the activities of ordinary human beings just to please Your devotee."

On hearing the prayers of Devakī, the Lord replied, "My dear mother, in the millennium of Svāyambhuva Manu, My father Vasudeva was living as one of the *Prajāpatis*, and his name at that time was Sutapā, and you were his wife named Pṛśni. At that time, when Lord Brahmā was desiring to increase the population, he requested you to generate offspring. You controlled your senses and performed severe austerities. By practicing the breathing exercise of the *yoga* system, both you and your husband could tolerate all the influences of the material laws: the rainy season, the onslaught of the wind, and the scorching heat of the sunshine. You also executed all religious principles. In this way you were able to cleanse your heart and control the influence of material law. In executing your austerity, you used to eat only the leaves of the trees which fell to the ground. Then with steady mind and controlled sex drive, you worshiped Me, desiring some wonderful benediction from Me. Both of you practiced severe austerities for 12,000 years, by the calculation of the demigods. During that time, your mind was always absorbed in Me. When you were executing devotional service and always thinking of Me within your heart, I was very much pleased with you. O sinless mother, your heart is therefore always pure. At that time also I appeared before you in this form just to fulfill your desire, and I asked you to ask whatever you desired. At that time you wished to have Me born as your son. Although you saw Me personally, instead of asking for your complete liberation from the material bondage, under the influence of My energy, you asked Me to become your son."

In other words, the Lord selected His mother and father—namely Pṛśni and Sutapā—specifically to appear in the material world. Whenever the Lord comes as a human being, He must have someone as a mother and father, so He selected Pṛśni and Sutapā perpetually as His mother and father. And on account of this, both Pṛśni and Sutapā could not ask the Lord for liberation. Liberation is not so important as the transcendental loving service of the Lord. The Lord could have awarded Pṛśni and Sutapā immediate liberation, but He preferred to keep them within this material world for His different appearances, as will be explained in the following verses. On receiving the benediction from the Lord to become His father and mother, both Pṛśni and Sutapā returned from the activities of austerity and lived as husband and wife in order to beget a child who was the Supreme Lord Himself.

In due course of time Pṛśni became pregnant and gave birth to the child. The Lord spoke to Devakī and Vasudeva: "At that time My name was Pṛśnigarbha. In the next millennium also you took birth as Aditi and Kaśyapa, and I became your child of the name Upendra. At that time My form was just like a dwarf, and for this reason I was known as Vāmanadeva. I gave you the benediction that I would take birth as your son three times. The first time I was known as Pṛśnigarbha, born of Pṛśni and Sutapā, the next birth I was Upendra born of Aditi and Kaśyapa, and now for the third time I am born as Kṛṣṇa from you, Devakī and Vasudeva. I appeared in this Viṣṇu form just to convince you that I am the same Supreme Personality of Godhead again taken birth. I could have appeared just like an ordinary child, but in that way you would not believe that I, the Supreme Personality of Godhead, have taken birth in your womb. My dear father and mother, you have therefore raised Me many times as your child, with great affection and love, and I am therefore very pleased and obliged to you. And I assure you that this time you shall go back to home, back to Godhead, on account of your perfection in your mission. I know you are very concerned about Me and afraid of Kaṁsa. Therefore I order you to take me immediately to Gokula and replace Me with the daughter who has just been born to Yaśodā."

Having spoken thus in the presence of His father and mother, the Lord turned Himself into an ordinary child and remained silent.

Being ordered by the Supreme Personality of Godhead, Vasudeva attempted to take his son from the delivery room, and exactly at that time, a daughter was born of Nanda and Yaśodā. She was *Yogamāyā,* the internal potency of the Lord. By the influence of this internal potency, *Yogamāyā,* all the residents of Kaṁsa's palace, especially the doorkeepers, were overwhelmed with deep sleep, and all the palace doors opened, although they were barred and shackled with iron chains. The night was very dark, but as soon as Vasudeva took Kṛṣṇa on his lap and went out, he could see everything just as in the sunlight.

In the *Caitanya-caritāmṛta* it is said that Kṛṣṇa is just like sunlight, and wherever there is Kṛṣṇa, the illusory energy, which is compared to darkness, cannot remain. When Vasudeva was carrying Kṛṣṇa, the darkness of the night disappeared. All the prison doors automatically opened. At the same time there was a thunder in the sky and severe rainfall. While Vasudeva was carrying his son Kṛṣṇa in the falling rain, Lord Śeṣa in the shape of a serpent spread his hood over the head of Vasudeva so that he would not be hampered by the rainfall. Vasudeva came onto the bank of the Yamunā and saw that the water of the Yamunā was roaring with waves and that the whole span was full of foam. Still, in that furious feature, the river gave passage to Vasudeva to cross, just as the great Indian Ocean gave a path to Lord Rāma when He was bridging over the gulf. In this way Vasudeva crossed the River Yamunā. On the other side, he went to the place of Nanda Mahārāja situated in Gokula, where he saw that all the cowherd men were fast asleep. He took the opportunity of silently entering into the house of Yaśodā, and without difficulty he replaced his son, taking away the baby girl newly born in the house of Yaśodā. Then, after entering the house very silently and exchanging the boy with the girl, he again returned to the prison of Kaṁsa and silently put the girl on the lap of Devakī. He again clamped the shackles on himself so that Kaṁsa could not recognize that so many things had happened.

Mother Yaśodā understood that a child was born of her, but because she was very tired from the labor of childbirth, she was fast asleep. When she awoke, she could not remember whether she had given birth to a male or female child.

Thus ends the Bhaktivedanta purport of the Third Chapter of Kṛṣṇa, *"Birth of Lord Kṛṣṇa."*

4 / Kaṁsa Begins His Persecutions

After Vasudeva adjusted all the doors and gates, the gatekeepers awoke and heard the newborn child crying. Kaṁsa was waiting to hear the news of the child's birth, and the gatekeepers immediately approached him and informed him that the child was born. At that time, Kaṁsa got up from his bed very quickly and exclaimed, "Now the cruel death of my life is born!" Kaṁsa became perplexed now that his death was approaching, and his hair stood on end. Immediately he proceeded toward the place where the child was born.

Devakī, on seeing her brother approaching, prayed in a very meek attitude to Kaṁsa: "My dear brother, please do not kill this female child. I promise that this child will be the wife of your son; therefore don't kill her. You are not to be killed by any female child. That was the omen. You are to be killed by a male child, so please do not kill her. My dear brother, you have killed so many of my children who were just born, shining as the sun. That is not your fault. You have been advised by demoniac friends to kill my children. But now I beg you to excuse this girl. Let her live as my daughter."

Kaṁsa was so cruel that he did not listen to the beautiful prayers of his sister Devakī. He forcibly grabbed the newborn child to rebuke his sister and attempted to dash her on the stone mercilessly. This is a graphic example of a cruel brother who could sacrifice all relationships for the sake of personal gratification. But immediately the child slipped out of his hands, went up in the sky and appeared with eight arms as the younger sister of Viṣṇu. She was decorated with a nice dress and flower garlands and ornaments; in her eight hands she held a bow, lancet, arrows, bell, conchshell, disc, club and shield.

Seeing the appearance of the child (who was actually the goddess Durgā), all the demigods from different planets like Siddhaloka, Cāraṇaloka, Gandharvaloka, Apsaraloka, Kinnaraloka, and Uragaloka presented her articles and began to offer their respective prayers. From above, the goddess addressed Kaṁsa: "You rascal, how can you kill me? The child who will kill you is already born before me somewhere within this world. Don't be so cruel to your poor sister." After this appearance, the goddess Durgā became known by various names in various parts of the world.

After hearing these words, Kaṁsa became very much overwhelmed with fear. Out of pity, he immediately released Vasudeva and Devakī from the bondage of their shackles and very politely began to address them. He said, "My dear sister and brother-in-law, I have acted just like a demon in killing my own nephews. I have given up all consideration of our intimate relationship. I do not know what will be the result of these acts of mine. Probably I shall be sent to the hell where killers of the *brāhmaṇas* go. I am surprised, however, that the celestial prophecy has not come true. False propaganda is not found only in the human society. Now it appears that even the celestial denizens speak lies. Because I believed in the words of the celestial denizens, I have committed so many sins by killing the children of my sister. My dear Vasudeva and Devakī, you are both very great souls. I have nothing to instruct you, but still I request that you not be sorry for the death of your children. Every one of us is under the control of superior power, and that superior power does not allow us to remain together. We are bound to be separated from our friends and relatives in due course of time. But we must know for certain that even after the disappearance of the different material bodies, the soul remains intact eternally. For example, there are many pots made of earthly clay, and they are prepared and also broken. But in spite of this, the earth remains as it is perpetually. Similarly, the bodies of the soul under different conditions are made and destroyed, but the spirit soul remains eternally. So there is nothing to lament over. Everyone should understand that this material body is different from the spirit soul, and so long as one does not come to that understanding, he is sure to accept the processes of transmigration from one body to another. My dear sister Devakī, you are so gentle and kind. Please excuse me—don't be aggrieved by the death of your children, which I have caused. Actually this was not done by me because all these are predestined activities. One has to act according to the predestined plan, even unwillingly. People misunderstand that with the end of the body, the self dies, or they think that one can kill another living entity. All these misconceptions oblige one to accept the conditions of material existence. In other words, as long as one is not firmly convinced of the eternality of the soul, one is subjected to the tribulation of being killer and killed. My dear sister Devakī and brother-in-law Vasudeva, kindly excuse the atrocities I have committed against you. I am very poor-hearted, and you are so great-hearted, so take compassion upon me and excuse me."

While Kaṁsa was speaking to his brother-in-law and sister, tears flowed from his eyes and he fell down at their feet. Believing the words of Durgādevī, whom he had tried to kill, Kaṁsa immediately released his brother-in-law and sister. He personally unlocked the iron shackles and very sympathetically showed his friendship, just like a family member.

When Devakī saw her brother so repentent, she also became pacified and forgot all his atrocious activities against her children. Vasudeva also, forgetting all past incidents, spoke smilingly with his brother-in-law. Vasudeva told Kaṁsa, "My dear fortunate brother-in-law, what you are saying about the material body and the soul is correct. Every living entity is born ignorant, understanding this material body to be his self. This conception of life is due to ignorance, and on the basis of this ignorance we create enmity or friendship. Lamentation, jubilation, fearfulness, envy, greed, illusion and madness are different features of our material concept of life. A person influenced like this engages in enmity due only to the material body. Being engaged in such activities, we forget our eternal relationship with the Supreme Personality of Godhead."

Vasudeva took the opportunity of Kaṁsa's benevolence and informed him that his atheistic activities were also due to this misconception of life —namely taking the material body to be the self. When Vasudeva talked with Kaṁsa in such an illuminating way, Kaṁsa became very pleased, and his guilt for killing his nephews subdued. With the permission of his sister Devakī and brother-in-law Vasudeva, he returned to his home with a relieved mind.

But the next day Kaṁsa called all his counsellors together and narrated to them all the incidents that had happened the night before. All the counsellors of Kaṁsa were demons and eternal enemies of the demigods, so they became depressed upon hearing their master speak of the night's events. And although they were not very much experienced or learned, they began to give instructions to Kaṁsa as follows: "Dear sir, let us now make arrangements to kill all children who were born within the last ten days in all towns, countries, villages and pasturing grounds. Let us execute this plan indiscriminately. We think that the demigods cannot do anything against us if we perform these atrocities. They are always afraid of fighting with us, and even if they wish to check our activities, they will not dare to do so. Because of the immeasurable strength of your bow, they fear you. Indeed, we have practical experience that whenever you stood to fight with them and began to shower your arrows on them, they immediately began to flee in all directions just to save their lives. Many of the demigods were unable to fight with you, and they immediately surrendered themselves unto you by opening their turbans and the flag on their heads. With folded hands they begged you to spare them and said, 'My lord, we are all afraid of your strength. Please release us from this dangerous fight.' We have also seen many times that you would never kill such surrendered fighters when they were all fearful, their bows, arrows and chariots broken, forgetful of their military activities and unable to fight with you. So actually we have nothing to fear from these demigods. They are very proud of being great fighters in peacetime outside of the warfield, but actually they cannot show any talent or military power on the warfield. Although Lord Viṣṇu, Lord Siva and Lord Brahmā are always ready to help the demigods headed by Indra, we have no reason to be afraid of them. As far as Lord Viṣṇu is concerned, He has already hidden Himself within the hearts of all living entities, and He cannot come out. As far as Lord Śiva is concerned, he has renounced all activities; he has already entered into the forest. And Lord Brahmā is always engaged in different types of austerities and meditation. And what to speak of Indra–he is a straw in comparison to your strength. Therefore we have nothing to fear from all these demigods. But we must not neglect them because the demigods are our determined enemies. We must be careful to protect ourselves. To root them out from their very existence, we should just engage ourselves in your service and be always ready for your command."

The demons continued to say: "If there is some disease in the body which is neglected, it becomes incurable. Similarly, when one is not careful about restraining the senses and lets them loose, it is very difficult to control them at all. Therefore, we must always be very careful of the demigods before they get too strong to be subdued. The foundation of strength of the demigods is Lord Viṣṇu, because the ultimate goal of all religious principles is to satisfy Him. The Vedic injunctions, the *brāhmaṇas,* the cows, austerities, sacrifices, performances of charity and distribution of wealth are all for the satisfaction of Lord Viṣṇu. So let us immediately begin by killing all the *brāhmaṇas* who are in charge of the Vedic knowledge and the great sages who are in charge of sacrificial ritualistic performances. Let us kill all the cows which are the source of butter which is so necessary for performing sacrifices. Please give us your permission to kill all these creatures."

Actually the limbs of the transcendental body of Lord Viṣṇu are the *brāhmaṇas,* the cows, Vedic knowledge, austerity, truthfulness, sense and mind control, faithfulness, charity, tolerance and performance of sacrifices. Lord Viṣṇu is situated in everyone's heart and is the leader of all demigods, including Lord Śiva and Lord Brahmā. "We think that to kill Lord Viṣṇu is to persecute the great sages and *brāhmaṇas,*" said the ministers.

Thus being advised by the demonic ministers, Kaṁsa, who was from the very beginning the greatest rascal, decided to persecute the *brāhmaṇas* and Vaiṣṇavas, being entrapped by the shackles of all-devouring, eternal time. He ordered the demons to harass all kinds of saintly persons, and then he entered his house. The adherents of Kaṁsa were all influenced by the modes of passion as well as illusioned by the modes of ignorance, and their only business was to create enmity with saintly persons. Such activities can only reduce the duration of life. The demons accelerated the process and invited their deaths as soon as possible. The result of persecuting saintly persons is not only untimely death. The act is so offensive that the actor also gradually loses his beauty, his fame and his religious principles, and his promotion to higher planets is also checked. Driven by various kinds of mental concoctions, the demons diminish all kinds of welfare. An offense at the lotus feet of the devotees and *brāhmaṇas* is a greater offense than that committed at the lotus feet of the Supreme Personality of Godhead. Thus a godless civilization becomes the source of all calamities.

Thus ends the Bhaktivedanta purport of the Fourth Chapter of Kṛṣṇa, *"Kaṁsa Begins His Persecutions."*

5 / Meeting of Nanda and Vasudeva

Although Kṛṣṇa was the real son of Vasudeva and Devakī, because of Kaṁsa's atrocious activities Vasudeva could not enjoy the birth ceremony of his son. But Nanda Mahārāja, the foster father, celebrated the birth ceremony of Kṛṣṇa very joyfully. The next day, it was declared that a male child was born of Yaśodā. According to Vedic custom, Nanda Mahārāja called for learned astrologers and *brāhmaṇas* to perform the birth ceremony. After the birth of a child, the astrologers calculate the moment of the birth and make a horoscope of the child's future life. Another ceremony takes place after the birth of the child: the family members take baths, cleanse themselves and decorate themselves with ornaments and garlands; then they come before the child and the astrologer to hear of the future life of the child. Nanda Mahārāja and other members of the family dressed and sat down in front of the birth place. All the *brāhmaṇas* who were assembled there on this occasion chanted auspicious *mantras*, according to the rituals, while the astrologers performed the birth ceremony. All the demigods are also worshiped on this occasion, as well as the forefathers of the family. Nanda Mahārāja distributed 200,000 well decorated, dressed and ornamented cows to the *brāhmaṇas*. He not only gave cows in charity, but hills of grains, decorated with golden-bordered garments and many ornaments.

In the material world we possess riches and wealth in many ways, but sometimes not in very honest and pious ways, because that is the nature of accumulating wealth. According to Vedic injunction, therefore, such wealth should be purified by giving cows and gold in charity to the *brāhmaṇas*. A newborn child is also purified by giving grains in charity to the *brāhmaṇas*. In this material world it is to be understood that we are always living in a contaminated state. We therefore have to purify the duration of our lives, our possession of wealth and ourselves. The duration of life is purified by taking daily bath and cleansing the body inside and outside and accepting the ten kinds of purificatory processes. By austerities, by worship of the Lord, and by distribution of charity, we can purify the possession of wealth. We can purify ourselves by studying the *Vedas,* by striving for self-realization and by understanding the Supreme Absolute Truth. It is therefore stated in the Vedic literature that by birth everyone is born a *śūdra,* and by accepting the purificatory process one becomes twice-born. By studies of the *Vedas* one can become *vipra,* which is the preliminary qualification for becoming a *brāhmaṇa.* When one understands the Absolute Truth in perfection, he is called a *brāhmaṇa.* And when the *brāhmaṇa* reaches further perfection, he becomes a Vaiṣṇava or a devotee.

In that ceremony, all the *brāhmaṇas* assembled began to chant different kinds of Vedic *mantras* to invoke all good fortune for the child. There are different kinds of chanting known as *sūta, māgadha, vandī,* and *virudāvalī.* Along with this chanting of *mantras* and songs, bugles and kettledrums sounded outside the house. On this occasion, the joyous vibrations could be heard in all the pasturing grounds and all the houses. Within and outside of the houses there were varieties of artistic paintings, done with rice pulp, and scented water was sprinkled everywhere, even on the roads and streets. Ceilings and roofs were decorated with different kinds of flags, festoons and green leaves. The gates were made of green leaves and flowers. All the cows, bulls and calves were smeared with a mixture of oil and turmeric and painted with minerals like red oxide, yellow clay and manganese. They wore garlands of peacock feathers, and were covered with nice colored dresses and gold necklaces.

When all the ecstatic cowherd men heard that Nanda Mahārāja, father of Kṛṣṇa, was celebrating the birth ceremony of his son, they became spontaneously joyful. They dressed themselves with very costly garments and ornamented their bodies with different kinds of earrings and necklaces and wore great turbans on their heads. After dressing themselves in this gorgeous way, they took various kinds of presentations and thus approached the house of Nanda Mahārāja.

As soon as they heard that mother Yaśodā had given birth to a child, all the cowherd women became overwhelmed with joy, and they also dressed themselves with various kinds of costly garments and ornaments and smeared scented cosmetics on their bodies.

As the dust on the lotus flower exhibits the exquisite beauty of the flower, all the *gopīs* (cowherd girls) applied the dust of *kuṅkuma* on their lotus-like faces. These beautiful *gopīs* took their different presentations and very soon reached the house of Mahārāja Nanda. Overburdened with their heavy hips and swollen breasts, the *gopīs* could not proceed very quickly towards the house of Nanda Mahārāja, but out of ecstatic love for Kṛṣṇa they began to proceed as quickly as possible. Their ears were decorated with pearl rings, their necks were decorated with jewel padlocks, their lips and eyes were decorated with different kinds of lipstick and ointment, and their hands were decorated with nice golden bangles. As they were very hastily passing over the stone road, the flower garlands which were decorating their bodies fell to the ground, and it appeared that a shower of flowers was falling from the sky. From the movement of the different kinds of ornaments on their bodies, they were looking still more beautiful. In this way, they all reached the house of Nanda-Yaśodā and blessed the child: "Dear child, You live long just to protect us." While they were blessing child Kṛṣṇa in this way, they offered a mixture of turmeric powder with oil, yogurt, milk and water. They not only sprinkled this mixture on the body of child Kṛṣṇa but on all other persons who were present there. Also on that auspicious occasion, there were different bands of expert musicians playing.

When the cowherd men saw the pastimes of the cowherd women, they became very joyful, and in response they also began to throw yogurt, milk, clarified butter and water upon the bodies of the *gopīs*. Then both parties began to throw butter on each other's bodies. Nanda Mahārāja was also very happy to see the pastimes of the cowherd men and women, and he became very liberal in giving charity to the different singers who were assembled there. Some singers were reciting great verses from the *Upaniṣads* and *Purāṇas*, some were glorifying the family ancestors, and some were singing very sweet songs. There were also many learned *brāhmaṇas* present, and Nanda Mahārāja, being very satisfied on this occasion, began to give them different kinds of garments, ornaments, and cows in charity.

It is very important to note in this connection how wealthy the inhabitants of Vṛndāvana were simply by raising cows. All the cowherd men belonged to the *vaiśya* community, and their business was to protect the cows and cultivate crops. By their dress and ornaments and by their behavior, it appears that although they were in a small village, they still were rich in material possessions. They possessed such an abundance of various kinds of milk products that they were throwing butter lavishly on each other's bodies without restriction. Their wealth was in milk, yogurt, clarified butter and many other milk products, and by trading their agricultural products, they were rich in various kinds of jewelry, ornaments and costly dresses. Not only did they possess all these things, but they could give them away in charity, as did Nanda Mahārāja.

Thus Nanda Mahārāja, the foster father of Lord Kṛṣṇa, began to satisfy the desires of all the men assembled there. He respectively received them and gave them in charity whatever they desired. The learned *brāhmaṇas,* who had no other source of income, were completely dependent of the *vaiśya* and *kṣatriya* communities for their maintenance, and they received gifts on such festive occasions as birthdays, marriages, etc. While Nanda Mahārāja was worshiping Lord Viṣṇu on this occasion and was trying to satisfy all the people there, his only desire was that the newborn child Kṛṣṇa would be happy. Nanda Mahārāja had no knowledge that this child was the origin of Viṣṇu, but he was praying to Lord Viṣṇu to protect Him.

Rohiṇīdevī, mother of Balarāma, was the most fortunate wife of Vasudeva. She was away from her husband, yet just to congratulate Mahārāja Nanda on the occasion of the birth ceremony of his son, Kṛṣṇa, she dressed herself very nicely. Wearing a garland, a necklace and other bodily ornaments, she appeared on the scene and moved hither and thither. According to the Vedic system, a woman whose husband is not at home does not dress herself very nicely. But although Rohiṇī's husband was away, she still dressed herself on this occasion.

From the opulence of the birth ceremony of Kṛṣṇa, it is very clear that at that time Vṛndāvana was rich in every respect. Because Lord Kṛṣṇa took birth in the house of King Nanda and mother Yaśodā, the goddess of fortune was obliged to manifest her opulences in Vṛndāvana. It appeared that Vṛndāvana had already become a site for the pastimes of the goddess of fortune.

After the birth ceremony, Nanda Mahārāja decided to go to Mathurā to pay the annual tax to the government of Kaṁsa. Before leaving, he called for the able cowherd men of the village and asked them to take care of Vṛndāvana in his absence. When Nanda Mahārāja arrived in Mathurā, Vasudeva got the news and was very eager to congratulate his friend. He immediately went to the place where Nanda Mahārāja was staying. When Vasudeva saw Nanda, he felt that he had regained his life. Nanda, overwhelmed with joy, immediately stood up and embraced Vasudeva. Vasudeva was received very warmly and offered a nice place to sit. At that time Vasudeva was anxious about his two sons who had been put under the protection of Nanda without Nanda's knowledge. With great anxiety, Vasudeva inquired about them. Both Balarāma and Kṛṣṇa were the sons of Vasudeva. Balarāma was transferred to the womb of Rohiṇī, Vasudeva's own wife, but Rohiṇī was kept under the protection of Nanda Mahārāja. Kṛṣṇa was personally delivered to Yaśodā and exchanged with her daughter. Nanda Mahārāja knew that Balarāma was the son of Vasudeva, although he did not know that Kṛṣṇa was also Vasudeva's son. But Vasudeva was aware of this fact and inquired very eagerly about Kṛṣṇa and Balarāma.

Vasudeva then addressed him, "My dear brother, you were old enough and very anxious to beget a son, and yet you had none. Now by the grace of the Lord you are fortunate to have a very nice son. I think that this incident is very auspicious for you. Dear friend, I was imprisoned by Kaṁsa, and now I am released; therefore this is another birth for me. I had no hope of seeing you again, but by God's grace I can see you." Vasudeva then expressed his anxiety about Kṛṣṇa. Kṛṣṇa was sent incognito to the bed of mother Yaśodā, and after very pompously celebrating His birth ceremony, Nanda went to Mathurā. So Vasudeva was very pleased and said, "This is a new birth for me." He never expected that Kṛṣṇa would live because all his other sons were killed by Kaṁsa.

Vasudeva continued, "My dear friend, it is very difficult for us to live together. Although we have our family and relatives, sons and daughters, by nature's way we are generally separated from one another. The reason for this is that every living entity appears on this earth under different pressures of fruitive activities; although they assemble together, there is no certainty of their remaining together for a long time. According to one's fruitive activities, one has to act differently and thereby be separated. For example, many plants and creepers are floating on the waves of the ocean. Sometimes they come together and sometimes they separate forever: one plant goes one way and another plant goes another. Similarly, our family assembly may be very nice while we are living together, but after some time, in the course of the waves of time, we are separated."

The purport of this expression by Vasudeva is this: although he had eight sons born in the womb of Devakī, unfortunately they were all gone. He could not even keep his one son Kṛṣṇa with him. Vasudeva was feeling His separation, but he could not express the real fact. "Please tell me about the welfare of Vṛndāvana," he said. "You have many animals—are they happy? Are they getting sufficient grass and water? Please also let me know whether the place where you are now living is undisturbed and peaceful." This inquiry was made by Vasudeva because he was very anxious about Kṛṣṇa's safety. He knew that Kaṁsa and his followers were trying to kill Kṛṣṇa by sending various kinds of demons. They had already resolved that all children born within ten days of the birthday of Kṛṣṇa should be killed. Because Vasudeva was so anxious about Kṛṣṇa, he inquired about the safety of His residence. He also inquired about Balarāma and His mother Rohiṇī, who were entrusted to the care of Nanda Mahārāja. Vasudeva also reminded Nanda Mahārāja that Balarāma did not know His real father. "He knows you as His father. And now you have another child, Kṛṣṇa, and I think you are taking very nice care for both of Them." It is also significant that Vasudeva inquired about the welfare of Nanda Mahārāja's animals. The animals, and especially the cows, were protected exactly in the manner of one's children. Vasudeva was a *kṣatriya,* and Nanda Mahārāja was a *vaiśya.* It is the duty of the *kṣatriya* to give protection to the citizens of mankind, and it is the duty of the *vaiśyas* to give protection to the cows. The cows are as important as the citizens. Just as the human citizens should be given all kinds of protection, so the cows also should be given full protection.

Vasudeva continued to say that the maintenance of religious principles, economic development and the satisfactory execution of meeting the demands of the senses depend on cooperation among relatives, nations and all humanity. Therefore, it is everyone's duty to see that his fellow citizens and the cows are not put into difficulty. One should see to the peace and comfort of his fellow man and the animals. The development of religious principles, economic development and sense gratification can then be achieved without difficulty. Vasudeva expressed his sorrow due to not being able to give protection to his own sons born of Devakī. He was thinking that religious principles, economic development and the satisfaction of his senses were therefore all lost.

On hearing this, Nanda Mahārāja replied, "My dear Vasudeva, I know that you are very much aggrieved because the cruel king Kaṁsa has killed all your sons born of Devakī. Although the last child was a daughter, Kaṁsa could not kill her, and she has entered into the celestial planets. My dear friend, do not be aggrieved; we are all being controlled by our past unseen activities. Everyone is subjected to his past deeds, and one who is conversant with the philosophy of *karma* and its reaction is a man in knowledge. Such a person will not be aggrieved at any incident, happy or miserable."

Vasudeva then replied, "My dear Nanda, if you have already paid the government taxes, then return soon to your place, because I think that there may be some disturbances in Gokula."

After the friendly conversation between Nanda Mahārāja and Vasudeva, Vasudeva returned to his home. The cowherd men headed by Nanda Mahārāja, who had come to Mathurā to pay their taxes, also returned.

Thus ends the Bhaktivedanta purport of the Fifth Chapter of Kṛṣṇa, *"Meeting of Nanda and Vasudeva."*

6 / Pūtanā Killed

While Nanda Mahārāja was returning home, he considered Vasudeva's warning that there might be some disturbance in Gokula. Certainly the advice was friendly and not false. So Nanda thought, "There is some truth in it." Therefore, out of fear, he began to take shelter of the Supreme Personality of Godhead. It is quite natural for a devotee in danger to think of Kṛṣṇa because he has no other shelter. When a child is in danger, he takes shelter of his mother or father. Similarly, a devotee is always under the shelter of the Supreme Personality of Godhead, but when he specifically sees some danger, he remembers the Lord very rapidly.

After consulting with his demonic ministers, Kaṁsa instructed a witch named Pūtanā, who knew the black art of killing small children by ghastly sinful methods, to kill all kinds of children in the cities, villages and pasturing grounds. Such witches can play their black art only where there is no chanting or hearing of the holy name of Kṛṣṇa. It is said that wherever the chanting of the holy name of Kṛṣṇa is done, even negligently, all bad elements–witches, ghosts, and dangerous calamaties–immediately disappear. And this is certainly true of the place where the chanting of the holy name of Kṛṣṇa is done seriously–especially in Vṛndāvana when the Supreme Lord was personally present. Therefore, the doubts of Nanda Mahārāja were certainly based on affection for Kṛṣṇa. Actually there was no danger from the activities of Pūtanā, despite her powers. Such witches are called *khecarī*, which means they can fly in the sky. This black art of witchcraft is still practiced by some women in the remote northwestern side of India. They can transfer themselves from one place to another on the branch of an uprooted tree. Pūtanā knew this witchcraft, and therefore she is described in the *Bhāgavatam* as *khecarī*.

Pūtanā entered the county of Gokula, the residential quarter of Nanda Mahārāja, without permission. Dressing herself just like a beautiful woman, she entered the house of mother Yaśodā. She appeared very beautiful with raised hips, nicely swollen breasts, earrings, and flowers in her hair. She looked especially beautiful on account of her thin waist. She was glancing at everyone with very attractive looks and smiling face, and all the residents of Vṛndāvana were captivated. The innocent cowherd women thought that she was a goddess of fortune appearing in Vṛndāvana with a lotus flower in her hand. It seemed to them that she had personally come to see Kṛṣṇa, who is her husband. Because of her exquisite beauty, no one checked her movement, and therefore she freely entered the house of Nanda Mahārāja. Pūtanā, the killer of many, many children, found baby Kṛṣṇa lying on a small bed, and she could at once perceive that the baby was hiding His unparalleled potencies. Pūtanā thought, "This child is so powerful that He can destroy the whole universe immediately."

Pūtanā's understanding is very significant. The Supreme Personality of Godhead, Kṛṣṇa, is situated in everyone's heart. It is stated in the *Bhagavad-gītā* that He gives one necessary intelligence, and He also causes one to forget. Pūtanā was immediately aware that the child whom she was observing in the house of Nanda Mahārāja was the Supreme Personality of Godhead Himself. He was lying there as a small baby, but that does not mean that He was less powerful. The materialistic theory that God-worship is anthropomorphic is not correct. No living being can become God by undergoing meditation or austerities. God is always God. Kṛṣṇa as the child-baby is as complete as He is as a full-fledged youth. The Māyāvādī theory holds that the living entity was formerly God but has now become overwhelmed by the influence of *māyā*. Therefore they say that presently he is not God, but when the influence of *māyā* is taken away, then he again becomes God. This theory cannot be applied to the minute living entities. The living entities are minute parts and parcels of the Supreme Personality of Godhead; they are minute particles or sparks of the supreme fire, but are not the original fire, or Kṛṣṇa. Kṛṣṇa is the Supreme Personality of Godhead, even from the beginning of His appearance in the house of Vasudeva and Devakī.

Kṛṣṇa showed the nature of a small baby and closed His eyes, as if to avoid the face of Pūtanā. This closing of the eyes is interpreted and studied in different ways by the devotees. Some say that Kṛṣṇa closed His eyes because He did not like to see the face of Pūtanā, who had killed so many children and who had now come to kill Him. Others say that something extraordinary was being dictated to her, and in order to give her assurance, Kṛṣṇa closed His eyes so that she would not be frightened. And yet others interpret in this way: Kṛṣṇa appeared to kill the demons and give protection to the devotees, as it is stated in the *Bhagavad-gītā: paritrāṇāya sādhūnāṁ vināśāya ca duṣkṛtām.* The first demon to be killed was a woman. According to Vedic rules, the killing of a woman, a *brāhmaṇa,* cows, or of a child, is forbidden. Kṛṣṇa was obliged to kill the demon Pūtanā, and because the killing of a woman is forbidden according to Vedic Śāstra, He could not help but close His eyes. Another interpretation is that Kṛṣṇa closed His eyes because He simply took Pūtanā to be His nurse. Pūtanā came to Kṛṣṇa just to offer her breast for the Lord to suck. Kṛṣṇa is so merciful that even though He knew Pūtanā was there to kill Him, He took her as His nurse or mother.

There are seven kinds of mothers according to Vedic injunction: the real mother, the wife of a teacher or spiritual master, the wife of a king, the wife of a *brāhmaṇa,* the cow, the nurse, and the mother earth. Because Pūtanā came to take Kṛṣṇa on her lap and offer her breast's milk to be sucked by Him, she was accepted by Kṛṣṇa as one of His mothers. That is considered to be another reason He closed His eyes: He had to kill a nurse or mother. But His killing of His mother or nurse was no different from His love for His real mother or foster mother Yaśodā. We further understand from Vedic information that Pūtanā was also treated as a mother and given the same facility as Yaśodā. As Yaśodā was given liberation from the material world, so Pūtanā was also given liberation. When the baby Kṛṣṇa closed His eyes, Pūtanā took Him on her lap. She did not know that she was holding death personified. If a person mistakes a snake for a rope, he dies. Similarly, Pūtanā killed so many babies before meeting Kṛṣṇa, but now she was accepting the snake that would kill her immediately.

When Pūtanā was taking baby Kṛṣṇa on her lap, both Yaśodā and Rohiṇī were present, but they did not forbid her because she was so beautifully dressed and because she showed motherly affection towards Kṛṣṇa. They could not understand that she was a sword within a decorated case. Pūtanā had smeared a very powerful poison on her breasts, and immediately after taking the baby on her lap, she pushed her breastly nipple within His mouth. She was hoping that as soon as He would suck her breast, He would die. But baby Kṛṣṇa very quickly took the nipple in anger. He sucked the milk-poison along with the life air of the demon. In other words, Kṛṣṇa simultaneously sucked the milk from her breast and killed her by sucking out her life. Kṛṣṇa is so merciful that because the demon Pūtanā came to offer her breast-milk to Him, He fulfilled her desire and accepted her activity as motherly. But to stop her from further nefarious activities, He immediately killed her. And because the demon was killed by Kṛṣṇa, she got liberation. When Kṛṣṇa sucked out her very breath, Pūtanā fell down on the ground, spread her arms and legs and began to cry, "Oh child, leave me, leave me!" She was crying loudly and perspiring, and her whole body became wet.

As she died, screaming, there was a tremendous vibration both on the earth and in the sky, in all directions, and people thought that thunderbolts were falling. Thus the nightmare of the Pūtanā witch was over, and she assumed her real feature as a great demon. She opened her fierce mouth and spread her arms and legs all over. She fell exactly as Vṛtrāsura when struck by the thunderbolt of Indra. The long hair on her head was scattered all over her body. Her fallen body extended up to twelve miles and smashed all the trees to pieces, and everyone was struck with wonder upon seeing this gigantic body. Her teeth appeared just like ploughed roads, and her nostrils appeared just like mountain caves. Her breasts appeared like small hills, and her hair was a vast reddish bush. Her eye sockets appeared like blind wells, and her two thighs appeared like two banks of a river; her two hands appeared like two strongly constructed bridges, and her abdomen seemed like a dried-up lake. All the cowherd men and women became struck with awe and wonder upon seeing this. And the tumultuous sound of her falling shocked their brains and ears and made their hearts beat strongly.

When the *gopīs* saw little Kṛṣṇa fearlessly playing on Pūtanā's lap, they very quickly came and picked Him up. Mother Yaśodā, Rohiṇī, and other elderly *gopīs* immediately performed the auspicious rituals by taking the tail of a cow and circumambulating His body. The child was completely washed with the urine of a cow, and the dust created by the hooves of the cows was thrown all over His body. This was all just to save little Kṛṣṇa from future inauspicious accidents. This incident gives us a clear indication of how important the cow is to the family, society and to living beings in general. The transcendental body of Kṛṣṇa did not require any protection, but to instruct us on the importance of the cow, the Lord was smeared over with cow dung, washed with the urine of a cow, and sprinkled with the dust upraised by the walking of the cows.

After this purificatory process, the *gopīs*, headed by mother Yaśodā and Rohiṇī, chanted twelve names of Viṣṇu to give Kṛṣṇa's body full protection from all evil influences. They washed their hands and feet and sipped water three times, as is the custom before chanting *mantra*. They chanted as follows: "My dear Kṛṣṇa, may the Lord who is known as Maṇimān protect Your thighs; may Lord Viṣṇu who is known as Yajña protect Your legs; may Lord Acyuta protect Your arms; may Lord Hayagrīva protect Your abdomen; may Lord Keśava protect Your heart; may Lord Viṣṇu protect

Your arms; may Lord Urukrama protect Your face; may Lord Īśvara protect Your head; may Lord Cakradhara protect Your front; may Lord Gadādhara protect Your back; may Lord Madhusūdana who carries a bow in His hand protect Your eyesight; may Lord Viṣṇu with His conchshell protect Your left side; may the Personality of Godhead Upendra protect You from above, and may Lord Tārkṣya protect You from below the earth; may Lord Haladhara protect You from all sides; may the Personality of Godhead known as Hṛṣīkeśa protect all Your senses; may Lord Nārāyaṇa protect Your breath; and may the Lord of Śvetadvīpa, Nārāyaṇa, protect Your heart; may Lord Yogeśvara protect Your mind; may Lord Pṛśnigarbha protect Your intelligence, and may the Supreme Personality of Godhead protect Your soul. While You are playing, may Lord Govinda protect You from all sides, and when You are sleeping, may Lord Mādhava protect You from all danger; when You are working may the Lord of Vaikuṇṭha protect You from falling down; when You are sitting, may the Lord of Vaikuṇṭha give You all protection; and while You are eating, may the Lord of all sacrifices give You all protection."

Thus mother Yaśodā began to chant different names of Viṣṇu to protect the child Kṛṣṇa's different bodily parts. Mother Yaśodā was firmly convinced that she should protect her child from different kinds of evil spirits and ghosts–namely Ḍākinīs, Yātudhānīs, Kūṣmāṇḍās, Yakṣas, Rākṣasas, Vināyakas, Koṭarā, Revatī, Jyeṣṭhā, Pūtanā, Mātṛkās, Unmādas and similar other evil spirits who cause persons to forget their own existence and give trouble to the life-air and the senses. Sometimes they appear in dreams and cause much perturbation; sometimes they appear as old women and suck the blood of small children. But all such ghosts and evil spirits cannot remain where there is chanting of the holy name of God. Mother Yaśodā was firmly convinced of the Vedic injunctions about the importance of cows and the holy name of Viṣṇu; therefore she took all shelter in the cows and the name of Viṣṇu just to protect her child Kṛṣṇa. She recited all the holy names of Viṣṇu so that He might save the child. Vedic culture has taken advantage of keeping cows and chanting the holy name of Viṣṇu since the beginning of history, and persons who are still following the Vedic ways, especially the householders, keep at least one dozen cows and worship the Deity of Lord Viṣṇu, who is installed in their house.

The elderly *gopīs* of Vṛndāvana were so absorbed in affection for Kṛṣṇa that they wanted to save Him, although there was no need to, for He had already protected Himself. They could not understand that Kṛṣṇa was the Supreme Personality of Godhead playing as a child. After performing the formalities to protect the child, mother Yaśodā took Kṛṣṇa and let Him suck her own breast. When the child was protected by Viṣṇu *mantra,* mother Yaśodā felt that He was safe. In the meantime, all the cowherd men who went to Mathurā to pay tax returned home and were struck with wonder at seeing the gigantic dead body of Pūtanā.

Nanda Mahārāja recalled the prophecy of Vasudeva and considered him a great sage and mystic *yogī;* otherwise, how could he have foretold an incident that happened during his absence from Vṛndāvana. After this, all the residents of Vraja cut the gigantic body of Pūtanā into pieces and piled it up with wood for burning. When all the limbs of Pūtanā's body were burning, the smoke emanating from the fire created a good aroma. This aroma was due to her being killed by Kṛṣṇa. This means that the demon Pūtanā was washed of all her sinful activities and attained a celestial body. Here is an example of how the Supreme Personality of Godhead is all good: Pūtanā came to kill Kṛṣṇa, but because He sucked her milk, she was immediately purified, and her dead body attained a transcendental quality. Her only business was to kill small children; she was only fond of blood. But in spite of being envious of Kṛṣṇa, she attained salvation because she gave her milk to Him to drink. So what can be said of others who are affectionate to Kṛṣṇa in the relationship of mother or father?

The pure devotees always serve Kṛṣṇa with great love and affection, for He is the Supreme Personality of Godhead, the Supersoul of every living entity. It is concluded therefore that even a little energy expended in the service of the Lord gives one immense transcendental profit. This is explained in the *Bhagavad-gītā: svalpam apy asya dharmasya.* Devotional service in Kṛṣṇa consciousness is so sublime that even a little service to Kṛṣṇa, knowingly or unknowingly, gives one the greatest benefit. The system of worshiping Kṛṣṇa by offering flowers from a tree is also beneficial for the living entity who is confined to the bodily existence of that tree. When flowers and fruits are offered to Kṛṣṇa, the tree that bore them also receives much benefit, indirectly. The *arcanā* process, or worshiping procedure, is therefore beneficial for everyone. Kṛṣṇa is worshipable by great demigods like Brahmā and Lord Śiva, and Pūtanā was so fortunate that the same Kṛṣṇa played in her lap as a little child. The lotus feet of Kṛṣṇa, which are worshiped by great sages and devotees, were placed on the body of Pūtanā. People worship Kṛṣṇa and offer food, but automatically He sucked the milk from the body of Pūtanā. Devotees therefore pray that if simply by offering something as an enemy, Pūtanā got so much benefit, then who can measure the benefit of worshiping Kṛṣṇa in love and affection?

One should only worship Kṛṣṇa if for no other reason than so much benefit awaits the worshiper. Although Pūtanā was an evil spirit, she gained elevation just like the mother of the Supreme Personality of Godhead. It is clear that the cows and the elderly *gopīs* who offered milk to Kṛṣṇa were also elevated to the transcendental position. Kṛṣṇa can offer anyone anything, from liberation to anything materially conceivable. Therefore, there cannot be any doubt of the salvation of Pūtanā, whose bodily milk was sucked by Kṛṣṇa for such a long time. And how can there be any doubt about the salvation of the *gopīs* who were so fond of Kṛṣṇa? Undoubtedly all the *gopīs* and cowherd boys and cows who served Kṛṣṇa in Vṛndāvana with love and affection were liberated from the miserable condition of material existence.

When all the inhabitants of Vṛndāvana smelled the good aroma from the smoke of the burning Pūtanā, they inquired from each other, "Where is this good flavor coming from?" And while conversing, they came to understand that it was the fumes of the burning Pūtanā. They were very fond of Kṛṣṇa, and as soon as they heard that the demon Pūtanā was killed by Kṛṣṇa, they offered blessings to the little child out of affection. After the burning of Pūtanā, Nanda Mahārāja came home and immediately took up the child on his lap and began to smell His head. In this way, he was quite satisfied that his little child was saved from this great calamity. Śrīla Śukadeva Gosvāmī has blessed all persons who hear the narration of the killing of Pūtanā by Kṛṣṇa. They will surely attain the favor of Govinda.

Thus ends the Bhaktivedanta purport of the Sixth Chapter of Kṛṣṇa, *"Pūtanā Killed."*

7 / Salvation of Tṛṇāvarta

The Supreme Personality of Godhead, Kṛṣṇa, is always full of six opulences—namely complete wealth, complete strength, complete fame, complete knowledge, complete beauty and complete renunciation. The Lord appears in different complete, eternal forms of incarnation. The conditioned soul has immense opportunity to hear about the transcendental activities of the Lord in these different incarnations. In the *Bhagavad-gītā* it is said, *janma karma ca me divyam.* The pastimes and activities of the Lord are not material; they are beyond the material conception. But the conditioned soul can benefit by hearing such uncommon activities. Hearing is an opportunity to associate with the Lord; to hear His activities is to evolve to the transcendental nature—simply by hearing. The conditioned soul has a natural aptitude to hear something about other conditioned souls in the form of fiction, drama and novel. That inclination to hear something about others may be utilized in hearing the pastimes of the Lord. Then one can immediately evolve to his transcendental nature. Kṛṣṇa's pastimes are not only beautiful; they are also very pleasing to the mind.

If someone takes advantage of hearing the pastimes of the Lord, the material contamination of dust, accumulated in the heart due to long association with material nature, can be immediately cleansed. Lord Caitanya also instructed that simply by hearing the transcendental name of Lord Kṛṣṇa, one can cleanse the heart of all material contamination. There are different processes for self-realization, but this process of devotional service—of which hearing is the most important function—when adopted by any conditioned soul, will automatically cleanse him of the material contamination and enable him to realize his real constitutional position. Conditional life is due to this contamination only, and as soon as it is cleared off, then naturally the dormant function of the living entity—rendering service to the Lord—awakens. By developing his eternal relationship with the Supreme Lord, one becomes eligible to create friendship with the devotees. Mahārāja Parīkṣit recommended, from practical experience, that everyone try to hear about the transcendental pastimes of the Lord. This *Kṛṣṇa* treatise is meant for that purpose, and the reader may take advantage in order to attain the ultimate goal of human life.

The Lord, out of His causeless mercy, descends on this material world and displays His activities just like an ordinary man. Unfortunately the impious entities or the atheistic class of men consider Kṛṣṇa to be an ordinary man like themselves, and so they deride Him. This is condemned in the *Bhagavad-gītā* by the Lord Himself when He says, "*Avajānanti māṁ mūḍhāḥ.*" The *mūḍhas,* or the rascals, take Kṛṣṇa to be an ordinary man or a slightly more powerful man; out of their great misfortune, they cannot accept Him as the Supreme Personality of Godhead. Sometimes such unfortunate persons misrepresent themselves as incarnations of Kṛṣṇa without referring to the authorized scriptures.

When Kṛṣṇa grew up a little more, He began to turn Himself backside up; He did not merely lie down on His back. And another function was observed by Yaśodā and Nanda Mahārāja: Kṛṣṇa's first birthday. They arranged for Kṛṣṇa's birthday ceremony, which is still observed by all followers of the Vedic principles. (Kṛṣṇa's birthday ceremony is observed in India by all Hindus, irrespective of different sectarian views.) All the cowherd men and women were invited to participate, and they arrived in jubilation. A nice band played, and the people assembled enjoyed it. All the learned *brāhmaṇas* were invited, and they chanted Vedic hymns for the good fortune of Kṛṣṇa. During the chanting of the Vedic hymns and playing of the bands, Kṛṣṇa was bathed by mother Yaśodā. This bathing ceremony is technically called *abhiṣeka,* and even today this is observed in all the temples of Vṛndāvana as Janmāṣṭamī Day or the birthday anniversary of Lord Kṛṣṇa.

On this occasion, mother Yaśodā arranged to distribute a large quantity of grains, and first-class cows decorated with golden ornaments were made ready to be given in charity to the learned, respectable *brāhmaṇas.* Yaśodā took her bath and dressed herself nicely, and taking child Kṛṣṇa, duly dressed and bathed, on her lap, she sat down to hear the Vedic hymns chanted by the *brāhmaṇas.* While listening to the chanting of the Vedic hymns, the child appeared to be falling asleep, and therefore mother Yaśodā very silently laid Him down on the bed. Being engaged in receiving all the friends, relatives and residents of Vṛndāvana on that holy occasion, she forgot to feed the child milk. He was crying, being hungry, but mother Yaśodā could not hear Him cry because of the various noises. The child, however, became angry because He was hungry and His mother was not paying attention to Him. So He lifted His legs and began to kick His lotus feet just like an ordinary child. Baby Kṛṣṇa had been placed underneath a hand-driven cart, and while He was kicking His legs, He accidently touched the wheel of the cart, and it collapsed. Various kinds of utensils and brass and metal dishes had been piled up in the hand cart, and they all fell down with a great noise. The wheel of the cart separated from the axle, and the spokes of the wheel were all broken and scattered hither and thither. Mother Yaśodā and all the *gopīs,* as well as Mahārāja Nanda and the cowherd men, were astonished as to how the cart could have collapsed by itself. All the men and women who were assembled for the holy function crowded around and began to suggest how the cart might have collapsed. No one could ascertain the cause, but some small children who were entrusted to play with baby Kṛṣṇa informed the crowd that it was due to Kṛṣṇa's striking His feet against the wheel. They assured the crowd that they had seen how it happened with their own eyes, and they strongly asserted the point. Some were listening to the statement of the small children, but others said, "How can you believe the statements of these children?" The cowherd men and women could not understand that the all-powerful Personality of Godhead was lying there as a baby, and He could do anything. Both the possible and impossible were in His power. While the discussion was going on, baby Kṛṣṇa cried. Without remonstration, mother Yaśodā picked the child up on her lap and called the learned *brāhmaṇas* to chant holy Vedic hymns to counteract the evil spirits. At the same time she allowed the baby to suck her breast. If a child sucks the mother's breast nicely, it is to be understood that he is out of all danger. After this, all the stronger cowherd men put the broken cart in order, and all the scattered things were set up nicely as before. The *brāhmaṇas* thereafter began to offer oblations to the sacrificial fire with yogurt, butter, *kuśa* grass, and water. They worshiped the Supreme Personality of Godhead for the good fortune of the child.

The *brāhmaṇas* who were present at that time were all qualified because they were not envious; they never indulged in untruthfulness, they were never proud, they were nonviolent, and they never claimed any false prestige. They were all bona fide *brāhmaṇas,* and there was no reason to think that their blessing would be useless. With firm faith in the qualified *brāhmaṇas,* Nanda Mahārāja took his child on his lap and bathed Him with water mixed with various herbs while the *brāhmaṇas* chanted hymns from the *Ṛk, Yajus* and *Sāma Vedas.*

It is said that without being a qualified *brāhmaṇa,* one should not read the *mantras* of the *Vedas.* Here is the proof that the *brāhmaṇas* were qualified with all the brahminical symptoms. Mahārāja Nanda also had full faith in them. Therefore they were allowed to perform the ritualistic ceremonies by chanting the Vedic *mantras.* There are many different varieties of sacrifices recommended for different purposes, but the *mantras* are all to be chanted by qualified *brāhmaṇas.* And because in this age of Kali such qualified *brāhmaṇas* are not available, all Vedic ritualistic sacrifices are forbidden. Śrī Caitanya Mahāprabhu has therefore recommended only one kind of sacrifice in this age—namely *saṅkīrtana yajña,* or simply chanting the *mahāmantra,* Hare Kṛṣṇa, Hare Kṛṣṇa, Kṛṣṇa Kṛṣṇa, Hare Hare, Hare Rāma, Hare Rāma, Rāma Rāma, Hare Hare.

As the *brāhmaṇas* chanted the Vedic hymns and performed the ritualistic ceremonies for the second time, Nanda Mahārāja again gave huge quantities of grains and many cows to them. All the cows which were given in charity were covered with nice gold-embroidered garments, and their horns were bedecked with golden rings; the hooves were covered with silver plate, and they wore garlands of flowers. He gave so many cows just for the welfare of his wonderful child, and the *brāhmaṇas* in return bestowed their heartfelt blessing. And the blessings offered by the able *brāhmaṇas* were never to be baffled.

One day, shortly after this ceremony, when mother Yaśodā was patting her baby on her lap, the baby felt too heavy, and being unable to carry Him, she unwillingly placed Him on the ground. After a while, she became engaged in household affairs. At that time, one of the servants of Kaṁsa, known as Tṛṇāvarta, as instructed by Kaṁsa, appeared there in the shape of a whirlwind. He picked the child up on his shoulders and raised a great dust storm all over Vṛndāvana. Because of this, everyone's eyes became covered within a few moments, and the whole area of Vṛndāvana became densely dark so that no one could see himself or anyone else. During this great catastrophe, mother Yaśodā could not see her baby, who was taken away by the whirlwind, and she began to cry very piteously. She fell down on the ground exactly like a cow who has just lost her calf. When mother Yaśodā was so piteously crying, all the cowherd women immediately came and began to look for the baby, but they were disappointed and could not find Him. The Tṛṇāvarta demon who took baby Kṛṣṇa on his shoulder went high in the sky, but the baby assumed such a weight that suddenly he could not go any further, and he had to stop his whirlwind activities. Baby Kṛṣṇa made Himself heavy and began to weigh down the demon. The Lord caught hold of his neck. Tṛṇāvarta felt the baby to be as heavy as a big mountain, and he tried to get out of His clutches, but he was unable to do so, and his eyes popped out from their sockets. Crying very fiercely, he fell down to the ground of Vṛndāvana and died. The demon fell exactly like Tripurāsura, who was pierced by the arrow of Lord Śiva. He hit the stone ground, and His limbs were smashed. His body became visible to all the inhabitants of Vṛndāvana.

When the *gopīs* saw the demon killed and child Kṛṣṇa very happily playing on his body, they immediately picked Kṛṣṇa up with great affection. The cowherd men and women became very happy to get back their beloved child Kṛṣṇa. At that time they began to talk about how wonderful it was that the demon took away the child to devour Him but could not do so; instead he fell down dead. Some of them supported the situation: "This is proper because those who are too sinful die from their sinful reactions, and child Kṛṣṇa is pious; therefore He is saved from all kinds of fearful situations. And we too must have performed great sacrifices in our previous lives, worshiping the Supreme Personality of Godhead, giving great wealth in charity and acting philanthropically for the general welfare of men. Because of such pious activities, the child is saved from all danger."

The *gopīs* assembled there spoke among themselves: "What sort of austerities and penances we must have undergone in our previous lives! We must have worshiped the Supreme Personality of Godhead, offered different kinds of sacrifices, made charities and performed many welfare activities for the public such as growing banyan trees and excavating wells. As a result of these pious activities, we have got back our child, even though He was supposed to be dead. Now He has come back to enliven His relatives." After observing such wonderful happenings, Nanda Mahārāja began to think of the words of Vasudeva again and again.

After this incident, when Yaśodā once was nursing her child and patting Him with great affection, there streamed a profuse supply of milk from her breast, and when she opened the mouth of the child with her fingers, she suddenly saw the universal manifestation within His mouth. She saw within the mouth of Kṛṣṇa the whole sky, including the luminaries, stars in all directions, the sun, moon, fire, air, seas, islands, mountains, rivers, forests, and all other movable and immovable entities. Upon seeing this, mother Yaśodā's heart began to throb, and she murmured within herself, "How wonderful this is!" She could not express anything, but simply closed her eyes. She was absorbed in wonderful thoughts. Kṛṣṇa's showing the universal form of the Supreme Personality of Godhead, even when lying down on the lap of His mother, proves that the Supreme Personality of Godhead is always the Supreme Personality of Godhead, whether He is manifested as a child on the lap of His mother or as a charioteer on the battlefield of Kurukṣetra. The concoction of the impersonalist, that one can become God by meditation or by some artificial material activities, is herewith declared false. God is always God in any condition or status, and the living entities are always the parts and parcels of the Supreme Lord. They can never be equal to the inconceivable supernatural power of the Supreme Personality of Godhead.

Thus ends the Bhaktivedanta purport of the Seventh Chapter of Kṛṣṇa, *"Salvation of Tṛṇāvarta."*

8 / Vision of the Universal Form

After this incident, Vasudeva asked his family priest Gargamuni to visit the place of Nanda Mahārāja in order to astrologically calculate the future life of Kṛṣṇa. Gargamuni was a great saintly sage who underwent many austerities and penances and was appointed priest of the Yadu dynasty. When Gargamuni arrived at the home of Nanda Mahārāja, Nanda Mahārāja was very pleased to see him and immediately stood up with folded hands and offered his respectful obeisances. He received Gargamuni with the feeling of one who is worshiping God or the Supreme Personality of Godhead. He offered him a nice sitting place, and when he sat down, Nanda Mahārāja offered him a warm reception. Addressing him very politely, he said: "My dear *brāhmaṇa,* your appearance in a householder's place is only to enlighten. We are always engaged in household duties and are forgetting our real duty of self-realization. Your coming to our house is to give us some enlightenment about spiritual life. You have no other purpose to visit householders." Actually a saintly person or a *brāhmaṇa* has no business visiting householders who are always busy in the matter of dollars and cents. If it is asked, "Why don't the householders go to a saintly person or a *brāhmaṇa* for enlightenment?" the answer is that householders are very poor-hearted. Generally householders think that their engagement in family affairs is their prime duty and that self-realization or enlightenment in spiritual knowledge is secondary. Out of compassion only, saintly persons and *brāhmaṇas* go to householders' homes.

Nanda Mahārāja addressed Gargamuni as one of the great authorities in astrological science. The foretellings of astrological science, such as the occurrence of solar or lunar eclipses, are wonderful calculations, and by this particular science, a person can understand the future very clearly. Gargamuni was proficient in this knowledge. By this knowledge one can understand what his previous activities were, and by the result of such activities one may enjoy or suffer in this life.

Nanda Mahārāja also addressed Gargamuni as the "best of the *brāhmaṇas.*" A *brāhmaṇa* is one who is expert in the knowledge of the Supreme. Without knowledge of the Supreme Absolute, one cannot be recognized as a *brāhmaṇa.* The exact word used in this connection is *brahmavidām,* which means those who know the Supreme very well. An expert *brāhmaṇa* is able to give reformatory facilities to the sub-castes—namely the *kṣatriyas* and *vaiśyas.* The *śūdras* observe no reformatory performances. The *brāhmaṇa* is considered to be the spiritual master or priest for the *kṣatriya* and *vaiśya.* Nanda Mahārāja happened to be a *vaiśya,* and he accepted Gargamuni as a first class *brāhmaṇa.* He therefore offered his two foster sons—namely Kṛṣṇa and Balarāma—to Him to purify. He agreed that not only these boys, but all human beings just after birth should accept a qualified *brāhmaṇa* as spiritual master.

Upon this request, Gargamuni replied, "Vasudeva has sent me to see to the reformatory performances of these boys, especially Kṛṣṇa's. I am their family priest, and incidentally, it appears to me that Kṛṣṇa is the son of Devakī." By his astrological calculation, Gargamuni could understand that Kṛṣṇa was the son of Devakī but that He was being kept under the care of Nanda Mahārāja, which Nanda did not know. Indirectly he said that Kṛṣṇa, as well as Balarāma, were both sons of Vasudeva. Balarāma was known as the son of Vasudeva because His mother Rohiṇī was present there, but Nanda Mahārāja did not know about Kṛṣṇa. Gargamuni indirectly disclosed the fact that Kṛṣṇa was the son of Devakī. Gargamuni also warned Nanda Mahārāja that if he would perform the reformatory ceremony, then Kaṁsa, who was naturally very sinful, would understand that Kṛṣṇa was the son of Devakī and Vasudeva. According to astrological calculation, Devakī could not have a female child, although everyone thought that the eighth child of Devakī was female. In this way Gargamuni intimated to Nanda Mahārāja that the female child was born of Yaśodā and that Kṛṣṇa was born of Devakī, and they were exchanged. The female child, or Durgā, also informed Kaṁsa that the child who would kill him was already born somewhere else. Gargamuni stated, "If I give your child a name and if He fulfills the prophecy of the female child to Kaṁsa, then it may be that the sinful demon will come and kill this child also after the name-giving ceremony. But I do not want to become responsible for all these future calamities."

On hearing the words of Gargamuni, Nanda Mahārāja said, "If there is such danger, then it is better not to plan any gorgeous name-giving ceremony. It would be better for you to simply chant the Vedic hymns and perform the purificatory process. We belong to the twice-born caste, and I am taking this opportunity of your presence. So please perform the name-giving ceremony without external pomp." Nanda Mahārāja wanted to keep the name-giving ceremony a secret and yet take advantage of Gargamuni's performing the ceremony.

When Gargamuni was so eagerly requested by Nanda Mahārāja, he performed the name-giving ceremony as secretly as possible in the cowshed of Nanda Mahārāja. He informed Nanda Mahārāja that Balarāma, the son of Rohiṇī, would be very pleasing to his family members and relatives and therefore would be called Rāma. In the future He would be extraordinarily strong and therefore would be called Balarāma. Gargamuni said further, "Because your family and the family of the Yadus are so intimately connected and attracted, therefore His name will also be Saṅkarṣaṇa." This means that Gargamuni awarded three names to the son of Rohiṇī—namely Balarāma, Saṅkarṣaṇa, and Baladeva. But he carefully did not disclose the fact that Balarāma also appeared in the womb of Devakī and was subsequently transferred to the womb of Rohiṇī. Kṛṣṇa and Balarāma are real brothers, being originally sons of Devakī.

Gargamuni then informed Nanda Mahārāja, "As far as the other boy is concerned, this child has taken different bodily complexions in different *yugas* (millennia). First of all He assumed the color white, then He assumed the color red, then the color yellow and now He has assumed the color black. Besides that, He was formerly the son of Vasudeva; therefore His name should be Vāsudeva as well as Kṛṣṇa. Some people will call Him Kṛṣṇa, and some will call Him Vāsudeva. But one thing you must know: This son has had many, many other names and activities due to His different pastimes."

Gargamuni gave Nanda Mahārāja a further hint that his son will also be called Giridhārī because of His uncommon pastimes of lifting Goverdhana Hill. Since he could understand everything past and future, he said, "I know everything about His activities and name, but others do not know. This child will be very pleasing to all the cowherd men and cows. Being very popular in Vṛndāvana, He will be the cause of all good fortune for you. Because of His presence, you will overcome all kinds of material calamities, despite opposing elements."

Gargamuni continued to say, "My dear King of Vraja, in His previous births, this child many times protected righteous persons from the hands of rogues and thieves whenever there was political disruption. Your child is so powerful that anyone who will become a devotee of your boy will never be troubled by enemies. Just as demigods are always protected by Lord

Viṣṇu, so the devotees of your child will always be protected by Nārāyaṇa, the Supreme Personality of Godhead. This child will grow in power, beauty, opulence—in everything—on the level of Nārāyaṇa, the Supreme Personality of Godhead. Therefore I would advise that you protect Him very carefully so that He may grow without disturbance."

Gargamuni further informed Nanda Mahārāja that because he was a great devotee of Nārāyaṇa, Lord Nārāyaṇa gave a son who is equal to Him. At the same time he indicated, "Your son will be disturbed by so many demons, so be careful and protect Him." In this way, Gargamuni convinced Nanda Mahārāja that Nārāyaṇa Himself had become his son. In various ways he described the transcendental qualities of his son. After giving this information, Gargamuni returned to his home. Nanda Mahārāja began to think of himself as the most fortunate person, and he was very satisfied to be benedicted in this way.

A short time after this incident, both Balarāma and Kṛṣṇa began to crawl on Their hands and knees. When They were crawling like that, They pleased Their mothers. The bells tied to Their waist and ankles sounded fascinating, and They would move around very pleasingly. Sometimes, just like ordinary children, They would be frightened by others and would immediately hurry to Their mothers for protection. Sometimes They would fall into the clay and mud of Vṛndāvana and would approach Their mothers smeared with clay and saffron. They were actually smeared with saffron and sandalwood pulp by Their mothers, but due to crawling over muddy clay, They would simultaneously smear Their bodies with clay. As soon as They would come crawling to their mothers, Yaśodā and Rohiṇī would take Them on their laps and, covering the lower portion of their saris, allow Them to suck their breasts. When the babies were sucking their breasts, the mothers would see small teeth coming in. Thus their joy would be intensified to see their children grow. Sometimes the naughty babies would crawl up to the cowshed, catch the tail of a calf and stand up. The calves, being disturbed, would immediately begin running here and there, and the children would be dragged over clay and cow dung. To see this fun, Yaśodā and Rohiṇī would call all their neighboring friends, the *gopīs.* Upon seeing these childhood pastimes of Lord Kṛṣṇa, the *gopīs* would be merged in transcendental bliss. In their enjoyment they would laugh very loudly.

Both Kṛṣṇa and Balarāma were so restless that Their mothers Yaśodā and Rohiṇī would try to protect Them from cows, bulls, monkeys, water, fire and birds while they were executing their household duties. Always being anxious to protect the children and to execute their duties, they were not very tranquil. In a very short time, both Kṛṣṇa and Balarāma began to stand up and slightly move on Their legs. When Kṛṣṇa and Balarāma began to walk, other friends of the same age joined Them, and together they began to give the highest transcendental pleasure to the *gopīs*, specifically to mother Yaśodā and Rohiṇī.

All the *gopī* friends of Yaśodā and Rohiṇī enjoyed the naughty childish activities of Kṛṣṇa and Balarāma in Vṛndāvana. In order to enjoy further transcendental bliss, they all assembled and went to mother Yaśodā to lodge complaints against the restless boys. When Kṛṣṇa was sitting before mother Yaśodā, all the elderly *gopīs* began to lodge complaints against Him so that Kṛṣṇa could hear. They said, "Dear Yaśodā, why don't you restrict your naughty Kṛṣṇa. He comes to our houses along with Balarāma every morning and evening, and before the milking of the cows They let loose the calves, and the calves drink all the milk of the cows. So when we go to milk the cows, we find no milk, and we have to return with empty pots. If we warn Kṛṣṇa and Balarāma about doing this, They simply smile charmingly. We cannot do anything. Also, your Kṛṣṇa and Balarāma find great pleasure in stealing our stock of yogurt and butter from wherever we keep it. When Kṛṣṇa and Balarāma are caught stealing the yogurt and butter, They say, 'Why do you charge us with stealing? Do you think that butter and yogurt are in scarcity in our house?' Sometimes They steal butter, yogurt and milk and distribute them to the monkeys. When the monkeys are well fed and do not take any more, then your boys chide, 'This milk and butter and yogurt are useless—even the monkeys won't take it.' And They break the pots and throw them hither and thither. If we keep our stock of yogurt, butter and milk in a solitary dark place, your Kṛṣṇa and Balarāma find it in the darkness by the glaring effulgence of the ornaments and jewels on Their bodies. If by chance they cannot find the hidden butter and yogurt, They go to our little babies and pinch their bodies so that they cry, and then They go away. If we keep our stock of butter and yogurt high on the ceiling, hanging on a swing, although it is beyond Their reach, They arrange to reach it by piling all kinds of wooden crates over the grinding machine. And if They cannot reach, They make a hole in the pot. We think therefore that you better take all the jeweled ornaments from the bodies of your children."

On hearing this, Yaśodā would say, "All right, I will take all the jewels from Kṛṣṇa so that He can not see the butter hidden in the darkness." Then the *gopīs* would say, "No, no, don't do this. What good will you do by taking away the jewels? We do not know what kind of boys these are, but even without ornaments They spread some kind of effulgence so that even in darkness They can see everything." Then mother Yaśodā would inform them, "All right, keep your butter and yogurt carefully so that They may not reach it." In reply to this, the *gopīs* said, "Yes, actually we do so, but because we are sometimes engaged in our household duties, these naughty boys enter our house somehow or other and spoil everything. Sometimes being unable to steal our butter and yogurt, out of anger They pass urine on the clean floor and sometimes spit on it. Just see your boy now–He is hearing this complaint. All day They simply make arrangements to steal our butter and yogurt, and now They are sitting just like very silent good boys. Just see His face." When mother Yaśodā thought to chastise her boy after hearing all the complaints, she saw His pitiable face, and smiling, she did not chastise Him.

Another day, when Kṛṣṇa and Balarāma were playing with Their friends, all the boys joined Balarāma and told mother Yaśodā that Kṛṣṇa had eaten clay. On hearing this, mother Yaśodā caught hold of Kṛṣṇa's hand and said, "My dear Kṛṣṇa, why have You eaten earth in a solitary place? Just see, all Your friends including Balarāma are complaining about You." Being afraid of His mother, Kṛṣṇa replied, "My dear mother, all these boys, including My elder brother Balarāma, are speaking lies against Me. I have never eaten clay. My elder brother Balarāma, while playing with Me today, became angry, and therefore He has joined with the other boys to complain against Me. They have all combined together to complain so you will be angry and chastise Me. If you think they are truthful, then you can look within My mouth to see whether I have taken clay or not." His mother replied, "All right, if You have actually not taken any clay, then just open Your mouth. I shall see."

When the Supreme Personality of Godhead Kṛṣṇa was so ordered by His mother, He immediately opened His mouth just like an ordinary boy. Then mother Yaśodā saw within that mouth the complete opulence of creation. She saw the entire outer space in all directions, mountains, islands, oceans, seas, planets, air, fire, moon and stars. Along with the moon and the stars she also saw the entire elements, water, sky, the extensive ethereal existence along with the total ego and the products of the senses and the controller of the senses, all the demigods, the objects of the senses like sound, smell, etc., and the three qualities of material nature. She also could perceive that within His mouth were all living entities, eternal time, material nature, spiritual nature, activity, consciousness and different forms of the whole creation. Yaśodā could find within the mouth of her child everything necessary for cosmic manifestation. She also saw, within His mouth, herself taking Kṛṣṇa on her lap and having Him sucking her breast. Upon seeing all this, she became struck with awe and began to wonder whether she were dreaming or actually seeing something extraordinary. She concluded that she was either dreaming or seeing the play of the illusory energy of the Supreme Personality of Godhead. She thought that she had become mad, mentally deranged, to see all those wonderful things. Then she thought, "It may be cosmic mystic power attained by my child, and therefore I am perplexed by such visions within His mouth. Let me offer my respectful obeisances unto the Supreme Personality of Godhead under whose energy bodily self and bodily possessions are conceived." She then said, "Let me offer my respectful obeisances unto Him, under whose illusory energy I am thinking that Nanda Mahārāja is my husband and Kṛṣṇa is my son, that all the properties of Nanda Mahārāja belong to me and that all the cowherd men and women are my subjects. All this misconception is due to the illusory energy of the Supreme Lord. So let me pray to Him that He may protect me always."

While mother Yaśodā was thinking in this high philosophical way, Lord Kṛṣṇa again expanded His internal energy just to bewilder her with maternal affection. Immediately mother Yaśodā forgot all philosophical speculation and accepted Kṛṣṇa as her own child. She took Him on her lap and became overwhelmed with maternal affection. She thus began to think, "Kṛṣṇa is not understandable to the masses through the gross process of knowledge, but He can be received through the *Upaniṣads* and the Vedānta or mystic Yoga system and Saṅkhya philosophy." Then she began to think of the Supreme Personality of Godhead as her own begotten child.

Certainly mother Yaśodā had executed many, many pious activities as a result of which she got the Absolute Truth, Supreme Personality of Godhead, as her son who sucked milk from her breast. Similarly, Nanda Mahārāja also must have performed many great sacrifices and pious activities for Lord Kṛṣṇa to become his son and address him as father. But it is surprising that Vasudeva and Devakī did not enjoy the transcendental bliss of Kṛṣṇa's childhood pastimes, although Kṛṣṇa was their real son. The childhood pastimes of Kṛṣṇa are glorified even today by many sages and saintly persons, but Vasudeva and Devakī could not enjoy such childhood pastimes personally. The reason for this was explained by Śukadeva Gosvāmī to Mahārāja Parīkṣit as follows.

When the best of the Vasus of the name Droṇa along with his wife Dharā were ordered to increase progeny by Lord Brahmā, they said unto him, "Dear father, we are seeking your benediction." Droṇa and Dharā then took benediction from Brahmā that in the future—when they would take birth again within the universe—the Supreme Lord Kṛṣṇa in His most attractive feature of childhood would absorb their whole attention. Their dealings with Kṛṣṇa would be so powerful that simply by hearing of Kṛṣṇa's childhood activities with them, anyone could very easily cross over the nescience of birth and death. Lord Brahmā agreed to give them the benediction, and as a result the same Droṇa appeared as Nanda Mahārāja in Vṛndāvana, and the same Dharā appeared as mother Yaśodā, the wife of Nanda Mahārāja.

In this way, Nanda Mahārāja and his wife, mother Yaśodā, developed their unalloyed devotion for the Supreme Personality of Godhead, having gotten Him as their son. And all the *gopīs* and cowherd men who were associates of Kṛṣṇa naturally developed their own different feelings of love for Kṛṣṇa.

Therefore, just to fulfill the benediction of Lord Brahmā, Lord Kṛṣṇa appeared along with His plenary expansion, Balarāma, and performed all kinds of childhood pastimes in order to increase the transcendental pleasure of all residents of Vṛndāvana.

Thus ends the Bhaktivedanta purport of the Eighth Chapter of Kṛṣṇa, *"Vision of the Universal Form."*

9 / Mother Yaśodā Binding Lord Kṛṣṇa

Once upon a time, seeing that her maidservant was engaged in different household duties, mother Yaśodā personally took charge of churning butter. And while she churned butter, she sang the childhood pastimes of Kṛṣṇa and enjoyed thinking of her son.

The end of her sari was tightly wrapped while she churned, and on account of her intense love for her son, milk automatically dripped from her breasts which moved as she labored very hard, churning with two hands. The bangles and bracelets on her hands tinkled as they touched each other, and her earrings and breasts shook. There were drops of perspiration on her face, and the flower garland which was on her head scattered here and there. Before this picturesque sight, Lord Kṛṣṇa appeared as a child. He felt hungry, and out of love for His mother, He wanted her to stop churning. He indicated that her first business was to let Him suck her breast and then churn butter later.

Mother Yaśodā took her son on her lap and pushed the nipples of her breasts into His mouth. And while Kṛṣṇa was sucking the milk, she was smiling, enjoying the beauty of her child's face. Suddenly, the milk which was on the oven began to boil over. Just to stop the milk from spilling, mother Yaśodā at once put Kṛṣṇa aside and went to the oven. Left in that state by His mother, Kṛṣṇa became very angry, and His lips and eyes became red in rage. He pressed His teeth and lips, and taking up a piece of stone, He immediately broke the butter pot. He took butter out of it, and with false tears in His eyes, He began to eat the butter in a secluded place.

In the meantime, mother Yaśodā returned to the churning place after setting the overflowing milk pan in order. She saw the broken pot in which the churning yogurt was kept. Since she could not find her boy, she concluded that the broken pot was His work. She began to smile as she thought, "The child is very clever. After breaking the pot He has left this place, fearing punishment." After she sought all over, she found a big wooden grinding mortar which was kept upside down, and she found her son sitting on it. He was taking butter which was hanging from the ceiling on a swing, and He was feeding it to the monkeys. She saw Kṛṣṇa looking this way and that way in fear of her because He was conscious of His naughty behavior. After seeing her son so engaged, she very silently approached Him from behind. Kṛṣṇa, however, quickly saw her coming at Him with a stick in her hand, and immediately He got down from the grinding mortar and began to flee in fear.

Mother Yaśodā chased Him to all corners, trying to capture the Supreme Personality of Godhead who is never approached even by the meditations of great *yogīs*. In other words, the Supreme Personality of Godhead, Kṛṣṇa, who is never caught by the *yogīs* and speculators, was playing just like a little child for a great devotee like mother Yaśodā. Mother Yaśodā, however, could not easily catch the fast-running child because of her thin waist and heavy body. Still she tried to follow Him as fast as possible. Her hair loosened, and the flower in her hair fell to the ground. Although she was tired, she somehow reached her naughty child and captured Him. When He was caught, Kṛṣṇa was almost on the point of crying. He smeared His hands over His eyes, which were anointed with black eye cosmetics. The child saw His mother's face while she stood over Him, and His eyes became restless from fear. Mother Yaśodā could understand that Kṛṣṇa was unnecessarily afraid, and for His benefit she wanted to allay His fears.

Being the topmost well-wisher of her child, mother Yaśodā began to think, "If the child is too fearful of me, I don't know what will happen to Him." Mother Yaśodā then threw away her stick. In order to punish Him, she thought to bind His hands with some ropes. She did not know it, but it was actually impossible for her to bind the Supreme Personality of Godhead. Mother Yaśodā was thinking that Kṛṣṇa was her tiny child; she did not know that the child had no limitation. There is no inside or outside of Him, nor beginning or end. He is unlimited and all-pervading. Indeed, He is Himself the whole cosmic manifestation. Still, mother Yaśodā was thinking of Kṛṣṇa as her child. Although He is beyond the reach of all senses, she endeavored to bind Him up to a wooden grinding mortar. But when she tried to bind Him, she found that the rope she was using was too short–by two inches. She gathered more ropes from the house and added to it, but at the end she found the same shortage. In this way, she connected all the ropes available at home, but when the final knot was added, she saw that it was still two inches too short. Mother Yaśodā was smiling, but she was astonished. How was it happening?

In attempting to bind her son, she became tired. She was perspiring, and the garland on her head fell down. Then Lord Kṛṣṇa appreciated the hard labor of His mother, and being compassionate upon her, He agreed to be bound up by the ropes. Kṛṣṇa, playing as a human child in the house of mother Yaśodā, was performing His own selected pastimes. Of course no one can control the Supreme Personality of Godhead. The pure devotee surrenders himself unto the lotus feet of the Lord, who may either protect or vanquish the devotee. But for his part, the devotee never forgets his own position of surrender. Similarly, the Lord also feels transcendental pleasure by submitting Himself to the protection of the devotee. This was exemplified by Kṛṣṇa's surrender unto His mother, Yaśodā.

Kṛṣṇa is the supreme bestower of all kinds of liberation to His devotees, but the benediction which was bestowed upon mother Yaśodā was never experienced even by Lord Brahmā or Lord Śiva or the goddess of fortune.

The Supreme Personality of Godhead, who is known as the son of Yaśodā and Nanda Mahārāja, is never so completely known to the *yogīs* and speculators. But He is easily available to His devotees. Nor is He appreciated as the supreme reservoir of all pleasure by the *yogīs* and speculators.

After binding her son, mother Yaśodā engaged herself in household affairs. At that time, bound up to the wooden mortar, Kṛṣṇa could see a pair of trees before Him which were known as *arjuna* trees. The great reservoir of pleasure, Lord Śrī Kṛṣṇa, thus thought to Himself, "Mother Yaśodā first of all left without feeding Me sufficient milk, and therefore I broke the pot of yogurt and distributed the stock butter in charity to the monkeys. Now she has bound Me up to a wooden mortar. So I shall do something more mischievous than before." And thus He thought of pulling down the two very tall *arjuna* trees.

There is a history behind the pair of *arjuna* trees. In their previous lives, the trees were born as the human sons of Kuvera, and their names were Nalakūvara and Maṇigrīva. Fortunately, they came within the vision of the Lord. In their previous lives they were cursed by the great sage Nārada in order to receive the highest benediction of seeing Lord Kṛṣṇa. This benediction-curse was bestowed upon them because of their forgetfulness due to intoxication. This story will be narrated in the next chapter.

Thus ends the Bhaktivedanta purport of the Ninth Chapter of Kṛṣṇa, *"Mother Yaśodā Binding Lord Kṛṣṇa."*

10 / Deliverance of Nalakūvara and Manigrīva

The story of the cursing of Nalakūvara and Maṇigrīva and their deliverance by Kṛṣṇa, under the all-blissful desire of the great sage Nārada, is here described.

The two great demigods, Nalakūvara and Maṇigrīva, were sons of the treasurer of the demigods, Kuvera, who was a great devotee of Lord Śiva. By the grace of Lord Śiva, Kuvera's material opulences had no limit. As a rich man's sons often become addicted to wine and women, so these two sons of Kuvera were also addicted to wine and sex. Once, these two demigods, desiring to enjoy, entered the garden of Lord Śiva in the province of Kailāsa on the bank of Mandākinī Ganges. There they drank much and engaged in hearing the sweet singing of beautiful women who accompanied them in that garden of fragrant flowers. In an intoxicated condition, they both entered the water of the Ganges, which was full with lotus flowers, and there they began to enjoy the company of the young girls exactly as the male elephant enjoys the female elephants within the water.

While they were thus enjoying themselves in the water, all of a sudden Nārada, the great sage, happened to pass that way. He could understand that the demigods Nalakūvara and Maṇigrīva were too intoxicated and could not even see that he was passing. The young girls, however, were not so intoxicated as the demigods, and they at once became ashamed at being naked before the great sage Nārada. They began to cover themselves with all haste. The two demigod-sons of Kuvera were so intoxicated that they could not appreciate the presence of the sage Nārada and therefore did not cover their bodies. On seeing the two demigods so degraded by intoxication, Nārada desired their welfare, and therefore he exhibited his causeless mercy upon them by cursing them.

Because the great sage was compassionate upon them, he wanted to finish their false enjoyment of intoxication and association with young girls and wanted them to see Lord Kṛṣṇa eye to eye. He conceived of cursing them as follows. He said that the attraction for material enjoyment is due to an increase of the mode of passion. A person in the material world, when favored by the material opulence of riches, generally becomes addicted to three things–intoxication, sex and gambling. Materially opulent men, being puffed up with the accumulation of wealth, also become so merciless that they indulge in killing animals by opening slaughterhouses. And they think that they themselves will never die. Such foolish persons, forgetting the laws of nature, become overly infatuated with the body. They forget that the material body, even though very much advanced in civilization, up to the position of the demigods, will finally be burned to ashes. And while one is living, whatever the external condition of the body may be, within there is only stool, urine and various kinds of worms. Thus being engaged in jealousy and violence to other bodies, materialists cannot understand the ultimate goal of life, and without knowing this goal of life, they generally glide down to a hellish condition. In their next birth, such foolish persons commit all kinds of sinful activities on account of this temporary body, and they are even unable to consider whether this body actually belongs to them. Generally it is said that the body belongs to the persons who feed the body. One might therefore consider whether this body belongs to one personally or to the master to whom one renders service. The master of slaves claims full right to the bodies of the slaves because the master feeds the slaves. It may be questioned then whether the body belongs to the father, who is the seed-giving master of this body, or to the mother, who develops the child's body in her womb.

Foolish persons are engaged in committing all sorts of sins due to the misconception of identifying the material body with the self. But one should be intelligent enough to understand to whom this body belongs. A foolish person indulges in killing other animals to maintain the body, but he does not consider whether this body belongs to him or to his father or mother or grandfather. Sometimes a grandfather or a father gives his daughter in charity to a person with a view of getting back the daughter's child as a son. The body may also belong to a stronger man who forces it to work for him. Sometimes the slave's body is sold to the master on the basis that the body will belong to the master. And at the end of life, the body belongs to the fire, because the body is given to the fire and burned to ashes. Or the body is thrown into the street to be eaten by the dogs and vultures.

Before committing all kinds of sins to maintain the body, one should understand to whom the body belongs. Ultimately it is concluded that the body is a product of material nature, and at the end it merges into material nature; therefore, the conclusion should be that the body belongs to material nature. One should not wrongly think that the body belongs to him. To maintain a false possession, why should one indulge in killing? Why should one kill innocent animals to maintain the body?

When a man is infatuated with the false prestige of opulence, he does not care for any moral instruction but indulges in wine, women and animal killing. In such circumstances, a poverty-stricken man is often better situated because a poor man thinks of himself in relation to other bodies. A poor man often does not wish to inflict injuries to other bodies because he can understand more readily that when he himself is injured he feels pain. As such, the great sage Nārada considered that because the demigods Nalakūvara and Maṇigrīva were so infatuated by false prestige, they should be put into a condition of life devoid of opulence.

A person who has a pinprick in his body does not wish others to be pricked by pins; a considerate man in the life of poverty does not wish others to be also put into that condition. Generally it is seen that one who has risen from a poverty-stricken life and becomes wealthy creates some charitable institution at the end of his life so that other poverty-stricken men might be benefitted. In short, a compassionate poor man may consider others' pains and pleasures with empathy. A poor man may be seldom puffed with false pride, and he may be freed from all kinds of infatuation. He may remain satisfied by whatever he gets for his maintenance by the grace of the Lord.

To remain in the poverty-stricken condition is a kind of austerity. According to Vedic culture, therefore, the *brāhmaṇas,* as a matter of routine, keep themselves in a poverty-stricken condition to save themselves from the false prestige of material opulence. False prestige due to advancement of material prosperity is a great impediment for spiritual emancipation. A poverty-stricken man cannot become unnaturally fat by eating more and more. And on account of not being able to eat more than he requires, his senses are not very turbulent. When the senses are not very turbulent, he cannot become violent.

Another advantage of poverty is that a saintly person can easily enter a poor man's house, and thus the poor man can take advantage of the saintly person's association. A very opulent man does not allow anyone to enter his house; therefore, the saintly person cannot enter. According to the Vedic system, a saintly person takes the position of a mendicant so that on the plea of begging something from the householder, he can enter any house. The householder, who has usually forgotten everything about spiritual advancement because he is busy maintaining family affairs, can be benefitted by the association of a saintly person. There is a great chance for the poor man to become liberated through association with a saint. Of what use are persons who are puffed up with material opulence and prestige if they are bereft of the association of saintly persons and devotees of the Supreme Personality of Godhead?

The great sage Nārada thereafter thought that it was his duty to put those demigods into a condition where they could not be falsely proud of their material opulence and prestige. Nārada was compassionate and wanted to save them from their fallen life. They were in the mode of darkness, and being therefore unable to control their senses, they were addicted to sex life. It was the duty of a saintly person like Nārada to save them from their abominable condition. In animal life, the animal has no sense to understand that he is naked. But Kuvera was the treasurer of the demigods, a very responsible man, and Nalakūvara and Maṇigrīva were two of his sons. And yet they became so animalistic and irresponsible that they could not understand, due to intoxication, that they were naked. To cover the lower part of the body is a principle of human civilization, and when a man or woman forgets this principle, they become degraded. Nārada therefore thought that the best punishment for them was to make them immovable living entities, or trees. Trees are, by nature's laws, immovable. Although trees are covered by the mode of ignorance, they cannot do harm. The great sage Nārada thought it fitting that, although the brothers, by his mercy, would be punished to become trees, they continue to keep their memory to be able to know why they were being punished. After changing the body, a living entity generally forgets his previous life, but in special cases, by the grace of the Lord, as with Nalakūvara and Maṇigrīva, one can remember.

Sage Nārada therefore contemplated that the two demigods should remain for one hundred years, in the time of the demigods, in the form of trees, and after that they would be fortunate enough to see the Supreme Personality of Godhead, face to face, by His causeless mercy. And thus they would be again promoted to the life of the demigods and great devotees of the Lord.

After this, the great sage Nārada returned to his abode known as Nārāyaṇa Āśrama, and the two demigods turned into trees, known as twin *arjuna* trees. The two demigods were favored by the causeless mercy of Nārada and given a chance to grow in Nanda's courtyard and see Lord Kṛṣṇa face to face.

Although the child Kṛṣṇa was bound up to the wooden mortar, He began to proceed towards the growing trees in order to fulfill the prophecy of His great devotee Nārada. Lord Kṛṣṇa knew that Nārada was His great devotee and that the trees standing before Him as twin *arjuna* trees were actually the sons of Kuvera. "I must now fulfill the words of My great devotee Nārada," He thought. Then He began to proceed through the passage between the two trees. Although He was able to pass through the passage, the large wooden mortar stuck horizontally between the trees. Taking advantage of this, Lord Kṛṣṇa began to pull the rope which was tied to the mortar. As soon as He pulled, with great strength, the two trees, with all branches and limbs, fell down immediately with a great sound. Out of the broken, fallen trees came two great personalities, shining like blazing fire. All sides became illuminated and beautiful by their presence. The two purified bodies immediately came before child Kṛṣṇa and bowed down to offer their respects and prayers in the following words.

"Dear Lord Kṛṣṇa, You are the original Personality of Godhead, master of all mystic powers. Learned *brāhmaṇas* know very well that this cosmic manifestation is an expansion of Your potencies which are sometimes manifest and sometimes unmanifest. You are the original provider of the life, body and senses of all living entities. You are the eternal God, Lord Viṣṇu, who is all-pervading, the principal controller of everything. You are the original source of the cosmic manifestation which is acting under the spell of the three modes of material nature—goodness, passion and ignorance. You are living as the Supersoul in all the multi-forms of living entities, and You know very well what is going on within their bodies and minds. Therefore You are the supreme director of all activities of all living entities. But although You are in the midst of everything which is under the spell of the material modes of nature, You are not affected by such contaminated qualities. No one under the jurisdiction of the material modes can understand Your transcendental qualities, which existed before the creation; therefore You are called the Supreme Brahman who is always glorified by His personal internal potencies. In this material world You can be known only by Your different incarnations. Although You assume different types of bodies, these bodies are not part of the material creation. They are always full of transcendental potencies of unlimited opulence, strength, beauty, fame, wisdom and renunciation. In the material existence, there is a difference between the body and the owner of the body, but because You appear in Your original spiritual body, there is no such difference for You. When You appear, Your uncommon activities indicate that You are the Supreme Personality of Godhead. Such uncommon activities are not possible for anyone in material existence. You are that Supreme Personality of Godhead, now appearing to cause the birth and death as well as liberation of the living entities, and You are full with all Your plenary expansions. You can bestow on everyone all kinds of benediction. O Lord! O source of all fortune and goodness, we offer our respectful obeisances unto You. You are the all-pervading Supreme Personality of Godhead, the source of peace and the supreme person in the dynasty of King Yadu. O Lord, our father known as Kuvera, the demigod, is Your servant. Similarly, the great sage Nārada is also Your servitor, and by their grace only we have been able to see You personally. We therefore pray that we may always be engaged in Your transcendental loving service by speaking only about Your glories and hearing about Your transcendental activities. May our hands and other limbs be engaged in Your service and our minds always be concentrated at Your lotus feet and our heads always bowed down before the all-pervading universal form of Your Lordship."

When the demigods Nalakūvara and Maṇigrīva finished their prayers, the child, Lord Kṛṣṇa, the master and proprietor of Gokula, bound to the wooden grinding mortar by the ropes of Yaśodā, began to smile and said, "It was already known to Me that My great devotee-sage Nārada had shown his causeless mercy by saving you from the abominable condition of pride due to possessing extraordinary beauty and opulence in the family of the demigods. He has saved you from gliding down into the lowest condition of hellish life. All these facts are already known to Me. You are very fortunate because you were not only cursed by him, but you had the great opportunity to see him. If someone is able, by chance, to see a great saintly person like Nārada face to face, who is always serene and merciful to everyone, then immediately that conditioned soul becomes liberated. This is exactly like being situated in the full light of the sun: there cannot be any visionary impediment. Therefore, O Nalakūvara and Maṇigrīva, your lives have now become successful because you have developed ecstatic love for Me. This is your last birth within material existence. Now you can go back to your father's residence in the heavenly planet, and by remaining in the attitude of devotional service, you will be liberated in this very life."

After this, the demigods circumambulated the Lord many times and bowed down before Him again and again, and thus they left. The Lord remained bound up with ropes to the grinding mortar.

Thus ends the Bhaktivedanta purport of the Tenth Chapter of Kṛṣṇa, *"Deliverance of Nalakūvara and Maṇigrīva."*

The great sage Nārada Muni. (p. 67)

Mother Yaśodā saw within the mouth of Kṛṣṇa the whole sky, including all the luminaries, stars and all directions. (p. 54)

The family priest, Gargamuni, performed the name-giving ceremony when Kṛṣṇa was one year old. (p. 56)

Yaśodā and Rohiṇī would call all their neighboring friends to see the fun.
(p. 59)

The darling of Vraja. (p. 61)

Kṛṣṇa had to plan how to stop the destruction of His intimate friends. (p. 83)

Seeing Kṛṣṇa enjoying with His cowherd friends, Lord Brahmā decided to play a trick. (p. 88)

Kṛṣṇa always demanded mother Yaśodā's complete attention. (p. 64)

Out of the broken, fallen trees came two personalities, shining like blazing fire. (p. 71)

“I am offering my humble obeisances and prayers just to please You.”
(p. 96)

11 / Killing the Demons Vatsāsura and Bakāsura

When the twin *arjuna* trees fell to the ground, making a sound like the falling of thunderbolts, all the inhabitants of Gokula, including Nanda Mahārāja, immediately came to the spot. They were very much astonished to see how the two great trees had suddenly fallen. Because they could find no reason for their falling down, they were puzzled. When they saw child Kṛṣṇa bound up to the wooden mortar by the ropes of Yaśodā, they began to think that it must have been caused by some demon. Otherwise, how was it possible? At the same time, they were very much perturbed because such uncommon incidences were always happening to the child Kṛṣṇa. While the elderly cowherd men were thus contemplating, the small children who were playing there informed the men that the trees fell due to Kṛṣṇa's pulling the wooden mortar with the ropes to which He was bound. "Kṛṣṇa came in between the two trees," they explained, "and the wooden mortar was topsy-turvied and stuck in between the trees. Kṛṣṇa began to pull the rope, and the trees fell down. When the trees fell down, two very dazzling men came out of the trees, and they began to talk to Kṛṣṇa."

Most of the cowherd men did not believe the statement of the children. They could not believe that such things were at all possible. Some of them, however, believed them and told Nanda Mahārāja, "Your child is different from all other children. He just might have done it." Nanda Mahārāja began to smile, hearing about the extraordinary abilities of his son. He came forward and untied the knot just to free his wonderful child. After being freed by Nanda Mahārāja, Kṛṣṇa was taken onto the laps of the elderly *gopīs*. They took Him away to the courtyard of the house and began to clap, praising His wonderful activities. Kṛṣṇa began to clap along with them, just like an ordinary child. The Supreme Lord Kṛṣṇa, being completely controlled by the *gopīs*, began to sing and dance, just like a puppet in their hands.

Sometimes mother Yaśodā used to ask Kṛṣṇa to bring her a wooden plank for sitting. Although the wooden plank was too heavy to be carried by a child, still somehow or other Kṛṣṇa would bring it to His mother. Sometimes while worshiping Nārāyaṇa, His father would ask Him to bring his wooden slippers, and Kṛṣṇa, with great difficulty, would put the slippers on His head and bring them to His father. When He was asked to lift some heavy article and was unable to lift it, He would simply move His arms. In this way, daily, at every moment, He was the reservoir of all pleasure to His parents. The Lord was exhibiting such childish activities before the inhabitants of Vṛndāvana because He wanted to show the great philosophers and sages searching after the Absolute Truth how the Supreme Absolute Truth Personality of Godhead is controlled by and subject to the desires of His pure devotees.

One day, a fruit vendor came before the house of Nanda Mahārāja. Upon hearing the vendor call, "If anyone wants fruits please come and take them from me!" child Kṛṣṇa immediately took some grains in His palm and went to get fruits in exchange. In those days exchange was by barter; therefore Kṛṣṇa might have seen His parents exchange fruits and other things by bartering grains, and so He imitated. But His palms were very small, and He was not very careful to hold them tight, so He was dropping the grains. The vendor who came to sell fruits saw this and was very much captivated by the beauty of the Lord, so he immediately accepted whatever few grains were left in His palm and filled His hands with fruits. In this meantime, the vendor saw that his whole basket of fruit had become filled with jewels. The Lord is the bestower of all benediction. If someone gives something to the Lord, he is not the loser; he is the gainer by a million times.

One day Lord Kṛṣṇa, the liberator of the twin *arjuna* trees, was playing with Balarāma and the other children on the bank of the Yamunā, and because it was already late in the morning, Rohiṇī, the mother of Balarāma, went to call them back home. But Balarāma and Kṛṣṇa were so engrossed in playing with Their friends that They did not wish to come back; They just engaged Themselves in playing more and more. When Rohiṇī was unable to take Them back home, she went home and sent mother Yaśodā to call Them again. Mother Yaśodā was so affectionate toward her son that as soon as she came out to call Him back home, her breast filled up with milk. She loudly cried, "My dear child, please come back home. Your time for lunch is already past." She then said, "My dear Kṛṣṇa, O my dear lotus-eyed child, please come and suck my breast. You have played enough. You must be very hungry, my dear little child.

You must be tired from playing for so long." She also addressed Balarāma thus: "My dear, the glory of Your family, please come back with Your younger brother Kṛṣṇa immediately. You have been engaged in playing since morning, and You must be very tired. Please come back and take Your lunch at home. Your father Nandarāja is waiting for You. He has to eat, so You must come back so that he can eat."

As soon as Kṛṣṇa and Balarāma heard that Nanda Mahārāja was waiting for Them and could not take his food in Their absence, They started to return. Their other playmates complained, "Kṛṣṇa is leaving us just at the point when our playing is at the summit. Next time we shall not allow Him to leave."

His playmates then threatened not to allow Him to play with them again. Kṛṣṇa became afraid, and instead of going back home, He went back again to play with the boys. At that time, mother Yaśodā scolded the children and told Kṛṣṇa, "My dear Kṛṣṇa, do You think that You are a street boy? You have no home? Please come back to Your home! I see that Your body has become very dirty from playing since early morning. Now come home and take Your bath. Besides, today is Your birthday ceremony; therefore You should come back home and give cows in charity to the *brāhmaṇas*. Don't You see how Your playmates are decorated with ornaments by their mothers? You should also be cleansed and decorated with nice dress and ornaments. Please, therefore, come back, take Your bath, dress Yourself nicely, and then again You may go on playing."

In this way mother Yaśodā called back Lord Kṛṣṇa and Balarāma who are worshipable by great demigods like Lord Brahmā and Lord Śiva. She was thinking of Them as her children.

When mother Yaśodā's children, Kṛṣṇa and Balarāma, came home, she bathed Them very nicely and dressed Them with ornaments. She then called for the *brāhmaṇas,* and through her children she gave many cows in charity for the occasion of Kṛṣṇa's birthday. In this way she performed the birthday ceremony of Kṛṣṇa at home.

After this incident, all the elderly members of the cowherd men assembled together, and Nanda Mahārāja presided. They began to consult amongst themselves how to stop great disturbances in the Mahāvana on account of the demons. In this meeting, Upananda, brother of Nanda Mahārāja, was present. He was considered to be learned and experienced, and he was a well-wisher of Kṛṣṇa and Balarāma. He was a leader, and he began to address the meeting as follows: "My dear friends! Now we should leave here for another place because we are continually finding that great demons are coming here to disturb the peaceful situation, and they are especially attempting to kill the small children. Just consider Pūtanā and Kṛṣṇa. It was simply by the grace of Lord Hari that Kṛṣṇa was saved from the hands of such a great demon. Next the whirlwind demon took Kṛṣṇa away in the sky, but by the grace of Lord Hari He was saved, and the demon fell down on a stone slab and died. Very recently, this child was playing between two trees, and the trees fell down violently, and yet there was no injury to the child. So Lord Hari saved Him again. Just imagine the calamity if this child or any other child playing with Him were crushed by the falling trees! Considering all these incidences, we must conclude that this place is no longer safe. Let us leave. We have all been saved from different calamities by the grace of Lord Hari. Now we should be cautious and leave this place and reside somewhere where we can live peacefully. I think that we should all go to the forest known as Vṛndāvana, where just now there are newly grown plants and herbs. It is very suitable for pasturing ground for our cows, and we and our families, the *gopīs* with their children, can very peacefully live there. Near Vṛndāvana there is Govardhana Hill, which is very beautiful, and there is newly grown grass and fodder for the animals, so there will be no difficulty in living there. I therefore suggest that we start immediately for that beautiful place, as there is no need to waste any more time. Let us prepare all our carts immediately, and, if you like, let us go, keeping all the cows in front."

On hearing the statement of Upananda, all the cowherd men immediately agreed. "Let us immediately go there." Everyone then loaded all their household furniture and utensils on the carts and prepared to go to Vṛndāvana. All the old men of the village, the children and women were arranged on seats, and the cowherd men equipped themselves with bows and arrows to follow the carts. All the cows and bulls along with their calves were placed in the front, and the men surrounded the flocks with their bows and arrows and began to blow on their horns and bugles. In this way, with tumultuous sound, they started for Vṛndāvana.

And who can describe the damsels of Vraja? They were all seated on the carts and were very beautifully dressed with ornaments and costly saris. They began to chant the pastimes of child Kṛṣṇa as usual. Mother Yaśodā and mother Rohiṇī were seated on a separate cart, and Kṛṣṇa and Balarāma were seated on their laps. While mother Rohiṇī and Yaśodā were riding on the cart, they talked to Kṛṣṇa and Balarāma, and feeling the pleasure of such talks, they looked very, very beautiful.

In this way, after reaching Vṛndāvana, where everyone lives eternally, very peacefully and happily, they encircled Vṛndāvana and kept the carts all together. After seeing the beautiful appearance of Govardhana on the bank of the River Yamunā, they began to construct their places of residence. While those of the same age were walking together and children were talking with their parents, the inhabitants of Vṛndāvana felt very happy.

At this time Kṛṣṇa and Balarāma were given charge of the calves. The first responsibility of the cowherd boys was to take care of the little calves. The boys are trained in this from the very beginning of their childhood. So along with other little cowherd boys, Kṛṣṇa and Balarāma went into the pasturing ground and took charge of the calves and played with Their playmates. While taking charge of the calves, sometimes the two brothers played on Their flutes. And sometimes They played with *āmalakī* fruits and *bael* fruits, just like small children play with balls. Sometimes They danced and made tinkling sounds with Their ankle bells. Sometimes They made Themselves into bulls and cows by covering Themselves with blankets. Thus Kṛṣṇa and Balarāma played. The two brothers also used to imitate the sounds of bulls and cows and play at bullfighting. Sometimes They used to imitate the sounds of various animals and birds. In this way, They enjoyed Their childhood pastimes apparently like ordinary, mundane children.

Once, when Kṛṣṇa and Balarāma were playing on the bank of the Yamunā, a demon of the name Vatsāsura assumed the shape of a calf and came there intending to kill the brothers. By taking the shape of a calf, the demon could mingle with other calves. Kṛṣṇa, however, specifically noticed this, and He immediately told Balarāma about the entrance of the demon. Both brothers then followed him and sneaked up upon him. Kṛṣṇa caught hold of the demon-calf by the two hind legs and tail, whipped him around very forcibly and threw him up into a tree. The demon lost his life and fell down from the top of the tree to the ground. When the demon lay dead on the ground, all the playmates of Kṛṣṇa congratulated Him, "Well done, well done," and the demigods in the sky began to shower flowers with great satisfaction. In this way, the maintainers of the complete creation, Kṛṣṇa and Balarāma, used to take care of the calves in the morning every day, and thus They enjoyed Their childhood pastimes as cowherd boys in Vṛndāvana.

All the cowherd boys would daily go to the bank of the River Yamunā to water their calves. Usually, when the calves drank water from the Yamunā, the boys also drank. One day, after drinking, when they were sitting on the bank of the river, they saw a huge animal which looked something like a duck and was as big as a hill. Its top was as strong as a thunderbolt. When they saw that unusual animal, they became afraid of it. The name of this beast was Bakāsura, and he was a friend of Kaṁsa's. He appeared on the scene suddenly and immediately attacked Kṛṣṇa with his pointed, sharp beaks and quickly swallowed Him up. When Kṛṣṇa was thus swallowed, all the boys, headed by Balarāma, became almost breathless, as if they had died. But when the Bakāsura demon was swallowing up Kṛṣṇa, he felt a burning fiery sensation in his throat. This was due to the glowing effulgence of Kṛṣṇa. The demon quickly threw Kṛṣṇa up and tried to kill Him by pinching Him in his beaks. Bakāsura did not know that although Kṛṣṇa was playing the part of a child of Nanda Mahārāja, He was still the original father of Lord Brahmā, the creator of the universe. The child of mother Yaśodā, who is the reservoir of pleasure for the demigods and who is the maintainer of saintly persons, caught hold of the beaks of the great gigantic duck and, before His cowherd boy friends, bifurcated his mouth, just as a child very easily splits a blade of grass. From the sky, the denizens of the heavenly planets showered flowers like the *cāmeli*, the most fragrant of all flowers, as a token of their congratulations. Accompanying the showers of flowers was a vibration of bugles, drums and conchshells.

When the boys saw the showering of flowers and heard the celestial sounds, they became struck with wonder. When they saw Kṛṣṇa, they all, including Balarāma, were so pleased that it seemed as if they had regained their very source of life. As soon as they saw Kṛṣṇa coming towards them, they one after another embraced the son of Nanda and held Him to their chests. After this, they assembled all the calves under their charge and began to return home.

When they arrived home, they began to speak of the wonderful activities of the son of Nanda. When the *gopīs* and cowherd men all heard the story from the boys, they felt great happiness because naturally they loved Kṛṣṇa, and hearing about His glories and victorious activities, they became still more affectionate toward Him. Thinking that the child Kṛṣṇa was saved from the mouth of death, they began to see His face with great love and affection. They were full of anxieties, but they could not turn their faces from the vision of Kṛṣṇa. The *gopīs* and the men began to converse amongst themselves about how the child Kṛṣṇa was attacked in so many ways and so many times by so many demons, and yet the demons were killed and Kṛṣṇa was uninjured. They continued to converse amongst themselves about how so many great demons in such fierce bodies attacked Kṛṣṇa to kill Him, but by the grace of Hari, they could not cause even a slight injury. Rather, they died like small flies in a fire. Thus they remembered the words of Gargamuni who foretold, by dint of his vast knowledge of the *Vedas* and astrology, that this boy would be attacked by many demons. Now they actually saw that this was coming true, word for word.

All the elderly cowherd men, including Nanda Mahārāja, used to talk of the wonderful activities of Lord Kṛṣṇa and Balarāma, and they were always so much absorbed in those talks that they forgot the threefold miseries of this material existence. This is the effect of Kṛṣṇa consciousness. What was enjoyed 5,000 years ago by Nanda Mahārāja can still be enjoyed by persons who are in Kṛṣṇa consciousness simply by talking about the transcendental pastimes of Kṛṣṇa and His associates.

Thus both Balarāma and Kṛṣṇa enjoyed Their childhood pastimes, imitating the monkeys of Lord Rāmacandra who constructed the bridge over the ocean and Hanumān, who jumped over the water to Ceylon. And They used to imitate such pastimes among Their friends and so happily passed Their childhood life.

Thus ends the Bhaktivedanta purport of the Eleventh Chapter of Kṛṣṇa, *"Killing the Demons Vatsāsura and Bakāsura."*

12 / The Killing of the Aghāsura Demon

Once the Lord desired to go early in the morning with all His cowherd boy friends to the forest, where they were to assemble together and take lunch. As soon as He got up from bed, He blew a buffalo horn and called all His friends together. Keeping the calves before them, they started for the forest. In this way, Lord Kṛṣṇa assembled thousands of His boy friends. They were each equipped with a stick, flute and horn as well as lunch bag, and each of them was taking care of thousands of calves. All the boys appeared very jolly and happy in that excursion. Each and every one of them was attentive for his personal calves. The boys were fully decorated with various kinds of golden ornaments, and out of sporting propensities they began to pick up flowers, leaves, twigs, peacock feathers and red clay from different places in the forest, and they began to dress themselves in different ways. While passing through the forest, one boy stole another boy's lunch package and passed it to a third. And when the boy whose lunch package was stolen came to know of it, he tried to take it back. But one threw it to another boy. This sportive playing went on amongst the boys as childhood pastimes.

When Lord Kṛṣṇa went ahead to a distant place in order to see some specific scenery, the boys behind Him tried to run to catch up and be the first to touch Him. So there was a great competition. One would say, "I will go there and touch Kṛṣṇa," and another would say, "Oh you cannot go. I'll touch Kṛṣṇa first." Some of them played on their flutes or vibrated bugles made of buffalo horn. Some of them gladly followed the peacocks and imitated the onomatopoetic sounds of the cuckoo. While the birds were flying in the sky, the boys ran after the birds' shadows along the ground and tried to follow their exact courses. Some of them went to the monkeys and silently sat down by them, and some of them imitated the dancing of the peacocks. Some of them caught the tails of the monkeys and played with them, and when the monkeys jumped in a tree, the boys also followed. When a monkey showed its face and teeth, a boy imitated and showed his teeth to the monkey. Some of the boys played with the frogs on the bank of the Yamunā, and when, out of fear, the frogs jumped in the water, the boys immediately dove in after them, and they would come out of the water when they saw their own shadows and stand imitating, making caricatures and laughing. They would also go to an empty well and make loud sounds, and when the echo came back, they would call it ill names and laugh.

As stated personally by the Supreme Personality of Godhead in the *Bhagavad-gītā,* He is realized proportionately by transcendentalists as Brahman, Paramātmā and the Supreme Personality of Godhead. Here, in confirmation of the same statement, Lord Kṛṣṇa, who awards the impersonalist Brahman realization by His bodily effulgence, also gives pleasure to the devotees as the Supreme Personality of Godhead. Those who are under the spell of external energy, *māyā,* take Him only as a beautiful child. Yet He gave full transcendental pleasure to the cowherd boys who played with Him. Only after accumulating heaps of pious activities, those boys were promoted to personally associate with the Supreme Personality of Godhead. Who can estimate the transcendental fortune of the residents of Vṛndāvana? They were personally visualizing the Supreme Personality of Godhead face to face, He whom many *yogīs* cannot find even after undergoing severe austerities, although He is sitting within the heart. This is also confirmed in the *Brahma-saṁhitā.* One may search for Kṛṣṇa the Supreme Personality of Godhead through the pages of the *Vedas* and *Upaniṣads,* but if one is fortunate enough to associate with a devotee, he can see the Supreme Personality of Godhead face to face. After accumulating pious activities in many, many previous lives, the cowherd boys were seeing Kṛṣṇa face to face and playing with Him as friends. They could not understand that Kṛṣṇa is the Supreme Personality of Godhead, but they were playing as intimate friends with intense love for Him.

When Lord Kṛṣṇa was enjoying His childhood pastimes with His boy friends, one Aghāsura demon became very impatient. He was unable to see Kṛṣṇa playing, so he appeared before the boys intending to kill them all. This Aghāsura was so dangerous that even the denizens of heaven were afraid of him. Although the denizens of heaven drank nectar daily to prolong their lives, they were afraid of this Aghāsura and were wondering, "When will the demon be killed?" The denizens used to drink nectar to become immortal, but actually they were not confident of their immortality. On the other hand, the boys who were playing with Kṛṣṇa had no fear of the demons. They were free of fear. Any material arrangement for protecting oneself from death is always unsure, but if one is in Kṛṣṇa consciousness, then immortality is confidently assured.

The demon Aghāsura appeared before Kṛṣṇa and His friends. Aghāsura happened to be the younger brother of Pūtanā and Bakāsura, and he thought, "Kṛṣṇa has killed my brother and sister. Now I shall kill Him along with all His friends and calves." Aghāsura was instigated by Kaṁsa, so he had come with determination. Aghāsura also began to think that when he would offer grains and water in memory of his brother and kill Kṛṣṇa and all the cowherd boys, then automatically all the inhabitants of Vṛndāvana would die. Generally, for the householders, the children are the life and breath force. When all the children die, then naturally the parents also die on account of strong affection for them.

Aghāsura, thus deciding to kill all the inhabitants of Vṛndāvana, expanded himself by the yogic *siddhi* called *mahimā.* The demons are generally expert in achieving almost all kinds of mystic powers. In the *yoga* system, by the perfection called *mahima-siddhi,* one can expand himself as he desires. The demon Aghāsura expanded himself up to eight miles and assumed the shape of a very fat serpent. Having attained this wonderful body, he stretched his mouth open just like a mountain cave. Desiring to swallow all the boys at once, including Kṛṣṇa and Balarāma, he sat on the path.

The demon in the shape of a big fat serpent expanded his lips from land to sky; his lower lip was touching the ground and his upper lip was touching the clouds. His jaws appeared like a big mountain cave, without limitation, and his teeth appeared just like mountain summits. His tongue appeared to be a broad traffic way, and he was breathing just like a hurricane. The fire of his eyes was blazing. At first the boys thought that the demon was a statue, but after examining it, they saw that it was more like a big serpent lying down in the road and widening his mouth. The boys began to talk among themselves: "This figure appears to be a great animal, and he is sitting in such a posture just to swallow us all. Just see—is it not a big snake that has widened his mouth to eat all of us?"

One of them said, "Yes, what you say is true. This animal's upper lip appears to be just like the sunshine, and its lower lip is just like the reflection of red sunshine on the ground. Dear friends, just look to the right and left hand side of the mouth of the animal. Its mouth appears to be like a big mountain cave, and its height cannot be estimated. The chin is also raised just like a mountain summit. That long highway appears to be its tongue, and inside the mouth it is as dark as in a mountain cave. The hot wind that is blowing like a hurricane is his breathing, and the fishy bad smell coming out from his mouth is the smell of his intestines."

Then they further consulted among themselves: "If we all at one time entered into the mouth of this great serpent, how could it possibly swallow all of us? And even if it were to swallow all of us at once, it could not swallow Kṛṣṇa. Kṛṣṇa will immediately kill him, as He did Bakāsura." Talking in this way, all the boys looked at the beautiful lotus-like face of Kṛṣṇa, and they began to clap and smile. And so they marched forward and entered the mouth of the gigantic serpent.

Meanwhile, Kṛṣṇa, who is the Supersoul within everyone's heart, could understand that the big statuesque figure was a demon. While He was planning how to stop the destruction of His intimate friends, all the boys along with their cows and calves entered the mouth of the serpent. But Kṛṣṇa did not enter. The demon was awaiting Kṛṣṇa's entrance, and he was thinking, "Everyone has entered except Kṛṣṇa, who has killed my brothers and sisters."

Kṛṣṇa is the assurance of safety to everyone. But when He saw that His friends were already out of His hands and were lying within the belly of a great serpent. He became, momentarily, aggrieved. He was also struck with wonder how the external energy works so wonderfully. He then began to consider how the demon should be killed and how he could save the boys and calves. Although there was no factual concern on Kṛṣṇa's part, He was thinking like that. Finally, after some deliberation, He also entered the mouth of the demon. When Kṛṣṇa entered, all the demigods, who had gathered to see the fun and who were hiding within the clouds, began to express their feelings with the words, "Alas! alas!" At the same time, all the friends of Aghāsura, especially Kaṁsa, who were all accustomed to eating flesh and blood, began to express their jubilation, understanding that Kṛṣṇa had also entered the mouth of the demon.

While the demon was trying to smash Kṛṣṇa and His companions, Kṛṣṇa heard the demigods crying, "Alas, alas," and He immediately began to expand Himself within the throat of the demon. Although he had a gigantic body, the demon choked by the expanding of Kṛṣṇa. His big eyes moved violently, and he quickly suffocated. His life-air could not come out from any source, and ultimately it burst out of a hole in the upper part of his skull. Thus his life-air passed off. After the demon dropped dead, Kṛṣṇa, with His transcendental glance alone, brought all the boys and calves back to consciousness and came with them out of the mouth of the demon. While Kṛṣṇa was within the mouth of Aghāsura, the demon's spirit soul came out like a dazzling light, illuminating all directions, and waited in the sky. As soon as Kṛṣṇa with His calves and friends came out of the mouth of the demon, that glittering effulgent light immediately merged into the body of Kṛṣṇa within the vision of all the demigods.

The demigods became overwhelmed with joy and began to shower flowers on the Supreme Personality of Godhead, Kṛṣṇa, and thus they worshiped Him. The denizens of heaven began to dance in jubilation, and the denizens in Gandharvaloka began to offer various kinds of prayers. Drummers began to beat drums in jubilation, the *brāhmaṇas* began to recite Vedic hymns, and all the devotees of the Lord began to chant the words, "*Jaya! Jaya!* All glories to the Supreme Personality of Godhead!"

When Lord Brahmā heard those auspicious vibrations which sounded throughout the higher planetary system, he immediately came down to see what had happened. He saw that the demon was killed, and he was struck with wonder at the uncommon glorious pastimes of the Personality of Godhead. The gigantic mouth of the demon remained in an open position for many days and gradually dried up; it remained a spot of pleasure pastimes for all the cowherd boys.

The killing of Aghāsura took place when Kṛṣṇa and all His boy friends were under five years old. Children under five years old are called *kaumāra*. After five years up to the tenth year they are called *paugaṇḍa*, and after the tenth year up to the fifteenth year they are called *kaiśora*. After the fifteenth year, boys are called youths. So for one year there was no discussion of the incident of the Aghāsura demon in the village of Vraja. But when they attained their sixth year, they informed their parents of the incident with great wonder. The reason for this will be clear in the next chapter.

For Śrī Kṛṣṇa, the Supreme Personality of Godhead, who is far greater than such demigods as Lord Brahmā, it is not at all difficult to award one the opportunity of merging with His eternal body. This He awarded to Aghāsura. Aghāsura was certainly the most sinful living entity, and it is not possible for the sinful to merge into the existence of the Absolute Truth. But in this particular case, because Kṛṣṇa entered into Aghāsura's body, the demon became fully cleansed of all sinful reaction. Persons constantly thinking of the eternal form of the Lord in the shape of the Deity or in the shape of a mental form are awarded the transcendental goal of entering into the kingdom of God and associating with the Supreme Personality of Godhead. So we can just imagine the elevated position of someone like Aghāsura into whose body the Supreme Personality of Godhead, Kṛṣṇa, personally entered. Great sages, meditators and devotees constantly keep the form of the Lord within the heart, or they see the Deity form of the Lord in the temples; in that way, they become liberated from all material contamination and at the end of the body enter into the kingdom of God. This perfection is possible simply by keeping the form of the Lord within the mind. But in the case of Aghāsura, the Supreme Personality of Godhead personally entered. Aghāsura's position was therefore greater than the ordinary devotee's or the greatest *yogī's*.

Mahārāja Parīkṣit, who was engaged in hearing the transcendental pastimes of Lord Kṛṣṇa (who saved the life of Mahārāja Parīkṣit while he was in the womb of his mother), became more and more interested to hear about Him. And thus he questioned the sage Śukadeva Gosvāmī, who was reciting *Śrīmad-Bhāgavatam* before the King.

King Parīkṣit was a bit astonished to understand that the killing of the Aghāsura demon was not discussed for one year, until after the boys attained the *pauganda* age. Mahārāja Parīkṣit was very inquisitive to learn this, for he was sure that such an incident was due to the working of Kṛṣṇa's different energies.

Generally, the *kṣatriyas* or the administrative class are always busy with their political affairs, and they have very little chance to hear about the transcendental pastimes of Lord Kṛṣṇa. But while Parīkṣit Mahārāja was hearing these transcendental pastimes, he considered himself to be very fortunate because he was hearing from Śukadeva Gosvāmī, the greatest authority on the *Śrīmad-Bhāgavatam.* Thus being requested by Mahārāja Parīkṣit, Śukadeva Gosvāmī continued to speak about the transcendental pastimes of Lord Kṛṣṇa in the matter of His form, quality, fame and paraphernalia.

Thus ends the Bhaktivedanta purport of the Twelfth Chapter of Kṛṣṇa, *"The Killing of the Aghāsura Demon."*

13 / The Stealing of the Boys and Calves by Brahmā

Śukadeva Gosvāmī was very much encouraged when Mahārāja Parīkṣit asked him why the cowherd boys did not discuss the death of Aghāsura until after one year had passed. He explained thus: "My dear King, you are making the subject matter of the transcendental pastimes of Kṛṣṇa fresher by your inquisitiveness."

It is said that it is the nature of a devotee to constantly apply his mind, energy, words, ears, etc., in hearing and chanting about Kṛṣṇa. This is called Kṛṣṇa consciousness, and for one who is rapt in hearing and chanting Kṛṣṇa, the subject matter never becomes hackneyed or old. That is the significance of transcendental subejct matter in contrast to material subject matter. Material subject matter becomes stale, and one cannot hear a certain subject for a long time; he wants change. But as far as transcendental subject matter is concerned, it is called *nityanavanavāyamāna.* This means that one can go on chanting and hearing about the Lord and never feel tired but will remain fresh and eager to hear more and more.

It is the duty of the spiritual master to disclose all confidential subject matter to the inquisitive and sincere disciple. Thus Śukadeva Gosvāmī began to explain why the killing of Aghāsura was not discussed until one year had passed. Śukadeva Gosvāmī told the King, "Now hear of this secret with attention. After saving His friends from the mouth of Aghāsura and after killing the demon, Lord Kṛṣṇa brought His friends to the bank of Yamunā and addressed them as follows: 'My dear friends, just see how this spot is very nice for taking lunch and playing on the soft sandy Yamunā bank. You can see how the lotus flowers in the water are beautifully blown and how they distribute their flavor all around. The chirping of the birds along with cooing of the peacocks, surrounded by the whispering of the leaves in the trees, combine and present sound-vibrations that echo one another. And this just enriches the beautiful scenery created by the trees here. Let us have our lunch in this spot because it is already late and we are feeling hungry. Let the calves remain near us, and let them drink water from the Yamunā. While we engage in our lunch-taking, the calves may engage in eating the soft grasses that are in this spot.'"

On hearing this proposal from Kṛṣṇa, all the boys became very glad and said, "Certainly, let us all sit down here to take our lunch." They then let loose the calves to eat the soft grass. Sitting down on the ground and keeping Kṛṣṇa in the center, they began to open their different boxes brought from home. Lord Śrī Kṛṣṇa was seated in the center of the circle, and all the boys kept their faces toward Him. They ate and constantly enjoyed seeing the Lord face to face. Kṛṣṇa appeared to be the whorl of a lotus flower, and the boys surrounding Him appeared to be its different petals. The boys collected flowers, leaves of flowers and the barks of trees and placed them under their different boxes, and thus they began to eat their lunch, keeping company with Kṛṣṇa. While taking lunch, each boy began to manifest different kinds of relations with Kṛṣṇa, and they enjoyed each other's company with joking words. While thus enjoying lunch with His friends, Lord Kṛṣṇa's flute was pushed within the belt of His cloth, and His bugle and cane were pushed in on the left-hand side of His cloth. He was holding a lump of foodstuff prepared with yogurt, butter, rice and pieces of fruit salad in His left palm, which could be seen through His petal-like finger joints. The Supreme Personality of Godhead, who accepts the results of all great sacrifices, was laughing and joking, enjoying lunch with His friends in Vṛndāvana. And thus the scene was being observed by the demigods from heaven. As for the boys, they were simply enjoying transcendental bliss in the company of the Supreme Personality of Godhead.

At that time, the calves that were pasturing nearby entered into the deep forest, allured by new grasses, and gradually went out of sight. When the boys saw that the calves were not nearby, they became afraid for their safety, and they immediately cried out, "Kṛṣṇa!" Kṛṣṇa is the killer of fear personified. Everyone is afraid of fear personified, but fear personified is afraid of Kṛṣṇa. By crying out the word "Kṛṣṇa," the boys at once transcended the fearful situation. Out of His great affection, Kṛṣṇa did not want His friends to give up their pleasing lunch engagement and go searching for the calves. He therefore said, "My dear friends, you need not interrupt your lunch. Go on enjoying. I am going personally where the calves are." Thus Lord Kṛṣṇa immediately started to search out the calves in the caves and bushes. He searched in the mountain holes and in the forests, but nowhere could He find them.

At the time when Aghāsura was killed and the demigods were looking on the incident with great surprise, Brahmā, who was born out of the lotus flower growing out of the navel of Viṣṇu, also came to see. He was surprised how a little boy like Kṛṣṇa could act so wonderfully. Although he was informed that the little cowherd boy was the Supreme Personality of Godhead, he wanted to see more glorified pastimes of the Lord, and thus he stole all the calves and cowherd boys and took them to a different place. Lord Kṛṣṇa, therefore, in spite of searching for the calves, could not find them, and He even lost His boy friends on the bank of the Yamunā where they had been taking their lunch. In the form of a cowherd boy, Lord Kṛṣṇa was very little in comparison to Brahmā, but because He is the Supreme Personality of Godhead, He could immediately understand that all the calves and boys had been stolen by Brahmā. Kṛṣṇa thought, "Brahmā has taken away all the boys and calves. How can I alone return to Vṛndāvana? The mothers will be aggrieved!"

Therefore in order to satisfy the mothers of His friends as well as to convince Brahmā of the supremacy of the Personality of Godhead, He immediately expanded Himself as the cowherd boys and calves. In the *Vedas* it is said that the Supreme Personality of Godhead expands Himself in so many living entities by His energy. Therefore it was not very difficult for Him to expand Himself again into so many boys and calves. He expanded Himself to become exactly like the boys, who were of all different features, facial and bodily construction, and who were different in their clothing and ornaments and in their behavior and personal activities. In other words, everyone has different tastes; being individual soul, each person has entirely different activities and behavior. Yet Kṛṣṇa exactly expanded Himself into all the different positions of the individual boys. He also became the calves, who were also of different sizes, colors, activities, etc. This was possible because everything is an expansion of Kṛṣṇa's energy. In the *Viṣṇu Purāṇa* it is said, *parasya brahmaṇaḥ śakti.* Whatever we actually see in the cosmic manifestation—be it matter or the activities of the living entities—is simply an expansion of the energies of the Lord, as heat and light are the different expansions of fire.

Thus expanding Himself as the boys and calves in their individual capacities, and surrounded by such expansions of Himself, Kṛṣṇa entered the village of Vṛndāvana. The residents had no knowledge of what had happened. After entering the village, Vṛndāvana, all the calves entered their respective cowsheds, and the boys also went to their respective mothers and homes.

The mothers of the boys heard the vibration of their flutes before their entrance, and to receive them, they came out of their homes and embraced them. And out of maternal affection, milk was flowing from their breasts, and they allowed the boys to drink it. However, their offering was not exactly to their boys but to the Supreme Personality of Godhead who had expanded Himself into such boys. This was another chance for all the mothers of Vṛndāvana to feed the Supreme Personality of Godhead with their own milk. Therefore Lord Kṛṣṇa gave not only Yaśodā the chance of feeding Him, but this time He gave the chance to all the elderly *gopīs.*

All the boys began to deal with their mothers as usual, and the mothers also, on the approach of evening, began to bathe their respective children, decorate them with *tilaka* and ornaments and give them necessary food after the day's labor. The cows also, who were away in the pasturing ground, returned in the evening and began to call their respective calves. The calves immediately came to their mothers, and the mothers began to lick the bodies of the calves. These relations between the cows and the *gopīs* with their calves and boys remained unchanged, although actually the original calves and boys were not there. Actually the cows' affection for their calves and the elderly *gopīs'* affection for the boys causelessly increased. Their affection increased naturally, even though the calves and boys were not their offspring. Although the cows and elderly *gopīs* of Vṛndāvana had greater affection for Kṛṣṇa than for their own offspring, after this incident, their affection for their offspring increased exactly as it did for Kṛṣṇa. For one year continually, Kṛṣṇa Himself expanded as the calves and cowherd boys and was present in the pasturing ground.

As it is stated in the *Bhagavad-gītā,* Kṛṣṇa's expansion is situated in everyone's heart as the Supersoul. Similarly, instead of expanding Himself as the Supersoul, He expanded Himself as a portion of calves and cowherd boys for one continuous year.

One day, when Kṛṣṇa, along with Balarāma, was maintaining the calves in the forest, They saw some cows grazing on the top of Govardhana Hill. The cows could see down into the valley where the calves were being taken care of by the boys. Suddenly, on sighting their calves, the cows began to run towards them. They leaped downhill with joined front and rear legs. The cows were so melted with affection for their calves that they did not care about the rough path from the top of Govardhana Hill down to the pasturing ground. They began to approach the calves with their milk bags full of milk, and they raised their tails upwards. When they were coming down the hill, their milk bags were pouring milk on the ground out of intense maternal affection for the calves, although they were not their own calves. These cows had their own calves, and the calves that were grazing beneath Govardhana Hill were larger; they were not expected to drink milk directly from the milk bag but were satisfied with the grass. Yet all the cows came immediately and began to lick their bodies, and the calves also began to suck milk from the milk bags. There appeared to be a great bondage of affection between the cows and calves.

When the cows were running down from the top of Govardhana Hill, the men who were taking care of them tried to stop them. Elderly cows are taken care of by the men, and the calves are taken care of by the boys; and as far as possible, the calves are kept separate from the cows, so that the calves do not drink all the available milk. Therefore the men who were taking care of the cows on the top of Govardhana Hill tried to stop them, but they failed. Baffled by their failure, they were feeling ashamed and angry. They were very unhappy, but when they came down and saw their children taking care of the calves, they all of a sudden became very affectionate toward the children. It was very astonishing. Although the men came down disappointed, baffled and angry, as soon as they saw their own children, their hearts melted with great affection. At once their anger, dissatisfaction and unhappiness disappeared. They began to show paternal love for the children, and with great affection they lifted them in their arms and embraced them. They began to smell their children's heads and enjoy their company with great happiness. After embracing their children, the men again took the cows back to the top of Govardhana Hill. Along the way they began to think of their children, and affectionate tears fell from their eyes.

When Balarāma saw this extraordinary exchange of affection between the cows and their calves and between the fathers and their children—when neither the calves nor the children needed so much care—He began to wonder why this extraordinary thing happened. He was astonished to see all the residents of Vṛndāvana so affectionate for their own children, exactly as they had been for Kṛṣṇa. Similarly, the cows had grown affectionate for their calves—as much as for Kṛṣṇa. Balarāma therefore concluded that the extraordinary show of affection was something mystical, either performed by the demigods or by some powerful man. Otherwise, how could this wonderful change take place? He concluded that this mystical change must have been caused by Kṛṣṇa, whom Balarāma considered His worshipable Personality of Godhead. He thought, "It was arranged by Kṛṣṇa, and even I could not check its mystic power." Thus Balarāma understood that all those boys and calves were only expansions of Kṛṣṇa.

Balarāma inquired from Kṛṣṇa about the actual situation. He said, "My dear Kṛṣṇa, in the beginning I thought that all these cows, calves and cowherd boys were either great sages and saintly persons or demigods, but at the present it appears that they are actually Your expansions. They are all You; You Yourself are playing as the calves and cows and boys. What is the mystery of this situation? Where have those other calves and cows and boys gone? And why are You expanding Yourself as the cows, calves, and boys? Will You kindly tell Me what is the cause?" At the request of Balarāma, Kṛṣṇa briefly explained the whole situation: how the calves and boys were stolen by Brahmā and how He was concealing the incident by expanding Himself so people would not know that the original cows, calves, and boys were missing.

While Kṛṣṇa and Balarāma were talking, Brahmā returned after a moment's interval (according to the duration of his life). We have information of Lord Brahmā's duration of life from the *Bhagavad-gītā:* 1,000 times the duration of the four ages, or 4,300,000 x 1,000, comprise Brahmā's twelve hours. Similarly, one moment of Brahmā is equal to one year of our solar calculation. After one moment of Brahmā's calculation, Brahmā came back to see the fun caused by his stealing the boys and calves. But he was also afraid that he was playing with fire. Kṛṣṇa was his master, and he had played mischief for fun by taking away His calves and boys. He was really anxious, so he did not stay away very long; he came back after a moment (of his calculation). He saw that all the boys, calves and cows were playing with Kṛṣṇa in the same way as when he had come upon them, although he was confident that he had taken them and made them lie down asleep under the spell of his mystic power. Brahmā began to think, "All the boys, calves and cows were taken away by me, and I know they are still sleeping. How is it that a similar batch of cows, boys and calves are playing with Kṛṣṇa? Is it that they are not influenced by my mystic power? Have they been playing continually for one year with Kṛṣṇa?" Brahmā tried to understand who they were and how they were uninfluenced by his mystic power, but he could not ascertain it. In other words, he himself came under the spell of his own mystic power. The influence of his mystic power appeared like snow in darkness or the glow worm in daytime. During the night's darkness, the glow worm can show some glittering power, and the snow piled up on the top of a hill or on the ground can shine during the daytime. But at night the snow has no silver glitter; nor does the glow worm have any illuminating power during the daytime. Similarly, when the small mystic power exhibited by Brahmā was before the mystic power of Kṛṣṇa, it was just like snow or the glow worm. When a man of small mystic power wants to show potency in the presence of greater mystic power, he diminishes his own influence; he does not increase it. Even a great personality like Brahmā, when he wanted to show his mystic power before Kṛṣṇa, became ludicrous. Brahmā was thus confused about his own mystic power.

In order to convince Brahmā that all those cows, calves and boys were not the original ones, the cows, calves, and boys who were playing with Kṛṣṇa transformed into Viṣṇu forms. Actually, the original ones were sleeping under the spell of Brahmā's mystic power, but the present ones, seen by Brahmā, were all immediate expansions of Kṛṣṇa, or Viṣṇu. Viṣṇu is the expansion of Kṛṣṇa, so the Viṣṇu forms appeared before Brahmā. All the Viṣṇu forms were of bluish color and dressed in yellow garments; all of Them had four hands decorated with club, disc, lotus flower and conchshell. On Their heads were glittering golden jeweled helmets; They were bedecked with pearls and earrings, and garlanded with beautiful flowers. On Their chests was the mark of *śrīvatsa;* Their arms were decorated with armlets and other jewelry. Their necks were smooth just like the conchshell, Their legs were decorated with bells, Their waists decorated with golden bells, and Their fingers decorated with jeweled rings. Brahmā also saw that upon the whole body of Lord Viṣṇu, fresh *tulasī* buds were thrown, beginning from His lotus feet up to the top of the head. Another significant feature of the Viṣṇu forms was that all of Them were looking transcendentally beautiful. Their smiling resembled the moonshine, and Their glancing resembled the early rising of the sun. Just by Their glancing They appeared as the creators and maintainers of the modes of ignorance and passion. Viṣṇu represents the mode of goodness, Brahmā represents the mode of passion, and Lord Śiva represents the mode of ignorance. Therefore as maintainer of everything in the cosmic manifestation, Viṣṇu is also creator and maintainer of Brahmā and Lord Śiva.

After this manifestation of Lord Viṣṇu, Brahmā saw that many other Brahmās and Śivas and demigods and even insignificant living entities down to the ants and very small straws—movable and immovable living entities—were dancing, surrounding Lord Viṣṇu. Their dancing was accompanied by various kinds of music, and all of Them were worshiping Lord Viṣṇu. Brahmā realized that all those Viṣṇu forms were complete, beginning from the *aṇimā* perfection of becoming small like an atom, up to becoming infinite like the cosmic manifestation. All the mystic powers of Brahmā, Śiva, all the demigods and the twenty-four elements of cosmic manifestation were fully represented in the person of Viṣṇu. By the influence of Lord Viṣṇu, all subordinate mystic powers were engaged in

His worship. He was being worshiped by time, space, cosmic manifestation, reformation, desire, activity and the three qualities of material nature. Lord Viṣṇu, Brahmā also realized, is the reservoir of all truth, knowledge and bliss. He is the combination of three transcendental features, namely eternity, knowledge, and bliss, and He is the object of worship by the followers of the *Upaniṣads.* Brahmā realized that all the different forms of cows, boys and calves transformed into Viṣṇu forms were not transformed by a mysticism of the type that a *yogī* or a demigod can display by specific powers invested in him. The cows, calves and boys transformed into Viṣṇu *mūrtis* or Viṣṇu forms were not displays of Viṣṇu *māyā* or Viṣṇu energy, but were Viṣṇu Himself. The respective qualifications of Viṣṇu and Viṣṇu *māyā* are just like fire and heat. In the heat there is the qualification of fire, namely warmth; and yet heat is not fire. The manifestation of the Viṣṇu forms of the boys, cows and calves was not like the heat, but rather the fire—they were all actually Viṣṇu. Factually, the qualification of Viṣṇu is full truth, full knowledge and full bliss. Another example can be given with material objects, which are reflected in many, many forms. For example, the sun is reflected in many water pots, but the reflections of the sun in many pots are not actually the sun. There is no actual heat and light from the sun in the pot, although it appears as the sun. But the forms which Kṛṣṇa assumed were each and every one full Viṣṇu. *Satyam* means truth, *jñānam,* full knowledge, and *ānanda,* full bliss.

Transcendental forms of the Supreme Personality of Godhead in His person are so great that the impersonal followers of the *Upaniṣads* cannot reach the platform of knowledge to understand them. Particularly, the transcendental forms of the Lord are beyond the reach of the impersonalists who can only understand, through the studies of *Upaniṣads,* that the Absolute Truth is not matter and that the Absolute Truth is not materially restricted by limited potency. Lord Brahmā understood Kṛṣṇa and His expansion into Viṣṇu forms and could understand that, due to the expansion of energy of the Supreme Lord, everything movable and immovable within the cosmic manifestation is existing.

When Brahmā was thus standing baffled in his limited power and conscious of his limited activities within the eleven senses, he could at least realize that he was also a creation of the material energy, just like a puppet. As a puppet has no independent power to dance but dances according to the direction of the puppet master, so the demigods and living entities are all subordinate to the Supreme Personality of Godhead. As it is stated in the *Caitanya-caritāmṛta,* the only master is Kṛṣṇa, and all others are servants. The whole world is under the waves of the material spell, and beings are floating like straws in water. So their struggle for existence is continuing. But as soon as one becomes conscious that he is the eternal servant of the Supreme Personality of Godhead, this *māyā* or illusory struggle for existence is immediately stopped.

Lord Brahmā, who has full control over the goddess of learning and who is considered to be the best authority in Vedic knowledge, was thus perplexed, being unable to understand the extraordinary power manifested in the Supreme Personality of Godhead. In the mundane world, even a personality like Brahmā is unable to understand the potential mystic power of the Supreme Lord. Not only did Brahmā fail to understand, but he was perplexed even to see the display which was being manifested by Kṛṣṇa before him.

Kṛṣṇa took compassion upon Brahmā's inability to see even how He was displaying the force of Viṣṇu in transferring Himself into cows and cowherd boys, and thus, while fully manifesting the Viṣṇu expansion, He suddenly pulled His curtain of *yogamāyā* over the scene. In the *Bhagavad-gītā* it is said that the Supreme Personality of Godhead is not visible due to the curtain spread by *yogamāyā.* That which covers the reality is *mahā-māyā,* or the external energy, which does not allow a conditioned soul to understand the Supreme Personality of Godhead beyond the cosmic manifestation. But the energy which partially manifests the Supreme Personality of Godhead and partially does not allow one to see, is called *yogamāyā.* Brahmā is not an ordinary conditioned soul. He is far, far superior to all the demigods, and yet he could not comprehend the display of the Supreme Personality of Godhead; therefore Kṛṣṇa willingly stopped manifesting any further potency. The conditioned soul not only becomes bewildered, but he is completely unable to understand. The curtain of *yogamāyā* was drawn so that Brahmā would not become more and more perplexed.

When Brahmā was relieved from his perplexity, he appeared to be awakened from an almost dead state, and he began to open his eyes with great difficulty. Thus he could see the eternal cosmic manifestation with common eyes. He saw all around him the super-excellent view of Vṛndāvana—full with trees—which is the source of life for all living entities. He could appreciate the transcendental land of Vṛndāvana where all the living entities are transcendental to ordinary nature. In the forest of Vṛndāvana, even ferocious animals like tigers and others live peacefully along with the deer and human being. He could understand that, because of the presence of the Supreme Personality of Godhead in Vṛndāvana, that place is transcendental to all other places and that there is no lust and greed there. Brahmā thus found Śrī Kṛṣṇa, the Supreme Personality of Godhead, playing the part of a small cowherd boy; he saw that little child with a lump of food in His left hand, searching out His friends, cows and calves, just as He was actually doing one year before, after their disappearance.

Immediately Brahmā descended from his great swan carrier and fell down before the Lord just like a golden stick. The word used among the Vaiṣṇavas for offering respect is *daṇḍavat.* This word means falling down like a stick; one should offer respect to the superior Vaiṣṇava by falling down straight, with his body just like a stick. So Brahmā fell down before the Lord just like a stick to offer respect; and because the complexion of Brahmā is golden, he appeared to be like a golden stick lying down before Lord Kṛṣṇa. All the four helmets on the heads of Brahmā touched the lotus feet of Kṛṣṇa. Brahmā, being very joyful, began to shed tears, and he washed the lotus feet of Kṛṣṇa with his tears. Repeatedly he fell and rose as he recalled the wonderful activities of the Lord. After repeating obeisances for a long time, Brahmā stood up and smeared his hands over his eyes. Seeing the Lord before him, he, trembling, began to offer prayers with great respect, humility and attention.

Thus ends the Bhaktivedanta purport of the Thirteenth Chapter of Kṛṣṇa, *"The Stealing of the Boys and Calves by Brahmā."*

14 / Prayers Offered by Lord Brahmā to Lord Kṛṣṇa

Brahmā said, "My dear Lord, You are the only worshipful Supreme Lord, Personality of Godhead; therefore I am offering my humble obeisances and prayers just to please You. Your bodily features are of the color of clouds filled with water. You are glittering with a silver electric aura emanating from Your yellow garments.

"Let me offer my respectful repeated obeisances unto the son of Mahārāja Nanda who is standing before me with conchshell, earrings and peacock feather on His head. His face is beautiful; He is wearing a helmet, garlanded by forest flowers, and He stands with a morsel of food in His hand. He is decorated with cane and bugle, and He carries a buffalo horn and flute. He stands before me with small lotus feet.

"My dear Lord, people may say that I am the master of all Vedic knowledge, and I am supposed to be the creator of this universe, but it has been proved now that I cannot understand Your personality, even though You are present before me just like a child. You are playing with Your boy friends, calves and cows, which might imply that You do not even have sufficient education. You are appearing just like a village boy, carrying Your food in Your hand and searching for Your calves. And yet there is so much difference between Your body and mine that I cannot estimate the potency of Your body. As I have already stated in the *Brahma-saṁhitā*, Your body is not material."

In the *Brahma-saṁhitā* it is stated that the body of the Lord is all spiritual; there is no difference between the Lord's body and His self. Each limb of His body can perform the actions of all the others. The Lord can see with His hands, He can hear with His eyes, He can accept offerings with His legs and He can create with His mouth.

Brahmā continued: "Your appearance as a cowherd child is for the benefit of the devotees, and although I have committed offenses at Your lotus feet by stealing away Your cows, boys and calves, I can understand that You have mercy upon me. That is Your transcendental quality; You are very affectionate toward Your devotees. In spite of Your affection for me, I cannot estimate the potency of Your bodily activities. It is to be understood that when I, Lord Brahmā, the supreme personality of this universe, cannot estimate the child-like body of the Supreme Personality of Godhead, then what to speak of others? And if I cannot estimate the spiritual potency of Your child-like body, then what can I understand about Your transcendental pastimes? Therefore, as it is said in the *Bhagavad-gītā,* anyone who can understand a little of the transcendental pastimes, appearance and disappearance of the Lord becomes immediately eligible to enter into the kingdom of God after quitting the material body. This statement is also confirmed in the *Vedas,* and it is stated simply: by understanding the Supreme Personality of Godhead, one can overcome the chain of repeated birth and death. I therefore recommend that people should not try to understand You by their speculative knowledge.

"The best process of understanding You is to submissively give up the speculative process and try to hear about You, either from Yourself as You have given statements in the *Bhagavad-gītā* and many similar Vedic literatures, or from a realized devotee who has taken shelter at Your lotus feet. One has to hear from a devotee without speculation. One does not even need to change his worldly position; he simply has to hear Your message. Although You are not understandable by the material senses, simply by hearing about You, one can gradually conquer the nescience of misunderstanding. By Your own grace only, You become revealed to a devotee. You are unconquerable by any other means. Speculative knowledge without any trace of devotional service is simply a useless waste of time in the search for You. Devotional service is so important that even a little attempt can raise one to the highest perfectional platform. One should not, therefore, neglect this auspicious process of devotional service and take to the speculative method. By the speculative method one may gain partial knowledge of Your cosmic manifestation, but it is not possible to understand You, the origin of everything. The attempt of persons who are interested only in speculative knowledge is simply wasted labor, like the labor of a person who attempts to gain something by beating the empty husk of a rice paddy. A little quantity of paddy can be husked by the grinding wheel, and one can gain some grains of rice, but if the skin of the paddy is already beaten by the grinding wheel, there is no further gain in beating the husk. It is simply useless labor.

"My dear Lord, there are many instances in the history of human society where a person, after failing to achieve the transcendental platform, engaged himself in devotional service with his body, mind and words and thus attained the highest perfectional state of entering into Your abode. The processes of understanding You by speculation or mystic meditation are all useless without devotional service. One should therefore engage himself in Your devotional service even in his worldly activities, and one should always keep himself near You by the process of hearing and chanting Your transcendental glories. Simply by being attached to hearing and chanting Your glories, one can attain the highest perfectional stage and enter into Your kingdom. If a person, therefore, always keeps in touch with You by hearing and chanting Your glories and offers the results of his work for Your satisfaction only, he very easily and happily attains entrance into Your supreme abode. You are realizable by persons who have cleansed their hearts of all contamination. This cleansing of the heart is made possible by chanting and hearing the glories of Your Lordship."

The Lord is all-pervading. As it is stated by Lord Kṛṣṇa in the *Bhagavad-gītā,* "Everything is sustained by Me, but at the same time I am not in everything." Since the Lord is all-pervading, there is nothing existing without His knowledge. The all-pervasive nature of the Supreme Personality of Godhead can never be within the limited knowledge of a living entity; therefore, a person who has attained steadiness of the mind by fixing the mind on the lotus feet of the Lord is able to understand the Supreme Lord to some extent. It is the business of the mind to wander over varied subject matter for sense gratification. Therefore only a person who engages the senses always in the service of the Lord can control the mind and be fixed at the lotus feet of the Lord. This concentration of the mind upon the lotus feet of the Lord is called *samādhi.* Until one reaches the stage of *samādhi,* or trance, he cannot understand the nature of the Supreme Personality of Godhead. There may be some philosophers or scientists who can study the cosmic nature from atom to atom; they may be so advanced that they can count the atomic composition of the cosmic atmosphere or all the planets and stars in the sky, or even the shining molecular parts of the sun or other stars and luminaries in the sky. But it is not possible to count the qualities of the Supreme Personality of Godhead.

As described in the beginning of *Vedānta-sūtra,* the Supreme Person is the origin of all qualities. He is generally called *nirguṇa. Nirguṇa* means without qualities. *Guṇa* means quality, and *nir* means without. But impersonalists interpret this word *nirguṇa* as "having no quality." Because they are unable to estimate the qualities of the Lord in transcendental realization, they conclude that the Supreme Lord has no qualities. But that is actually not the position. The real position is that He is the original source of all qualities. All qualities are emanating constantly from Him. How, therefore, can a limited person count the qualities of the Lord? One may estimate the qualities of the Lord for one moment, but the next moment the qualities are increased; so it is not possible to make an estimation of the transcendental qualities of the Lord. He is therefore called *nirguṇa*. His qualities cannot be estimated.

One should not uselessly labor in mental speculation to estimate the Lord's qualities. There is no need of adopting the speculative method or exercising the body to attain mystic *yoga* perfection. One should simply understand that the distress and happiness of this body are predestined; there is no need to try to avoid the distress of this bodily existence or to attempt to achieve happiness by different types of exercises. The best course is to surrender unto the Supreme Personality of Godhead with body, mind and words and always be engaged in His service. This transcendental labor is fruitful, but other attempts to understand the Absolute Truth are never successful. Therefore an intelligent man does not try to understand the Supreme Person, Absolute Truth, by speculative or mystic power. Rather, he engages in devotional service and depends on the Supreme Personality of Godhead. He knows that whatever may happen to the body is due to his past fruitive activities. If one lives such a simple life in devotional service, then automatically he can inherit the transcendental abode of the Lord. Actually, every living entity is part and parcel of the Supreme Lord and a son of the Godhead. Each has the natural right to inherit and share the transcendental pleasures of the Lord, but due to the contact of matter, conditioned living entities have been practically disinherited. If one adopts the simple method of engaging himself in devotional service, automatically he becomes eligible to become freed from the material contamination and elevated to the transcendental position of associating with the Supreme Lord.

Lord Brahmā presented himself to Lord Kṛṣṇa as the most presumptuous living creature because he wanted to examine the wonder of His personal power. He stole the boys and calves of the Lord in order to see how the Lord would recover them. After his maneuver, Lord Brahmā admitted that his attempt was most presumptuous, for he was attempting to test his energy before the person of original energy. Coming to his senses, Lord Brahmā saw that although he was a very powerful living creature in the estimation of all other living creatures within this material world, in comparison to the power and energy of the Supreme Personality of

Godhead, his power was nothing. The scientists of the material world have discovered wonders such as atomic weapons, and when tested in a city or insignificant place on this planet, such powerful weapons create so-called havoc, but if the atomic weapons are tested on the sun, what is their significance? They are insignificant there. Similarly, Brahmā's stealing the calves and boys from Śrī Kṛṣṇa may be a wonderful display of mystic power, but when Śrī Kṛṣṇa exhibited His expansive power in so many calves and boys and maintained them without effort, Brahmā could understand that his own power was insignificant.

Brahmā addressed Lord Kṛṣṇa as *Acyuta* because the Lord is never forgetful of a little service rendered by His devotee. He is so kind and affectionate towards His devotees that a little service by them is accepted by Him as a great deal. Brahmā has certainly rendered much service to the Lord. As the supreme personality in charge of this particular universe, he is, without a doubt, a faithful servant of Kṛṣṇa; therefore he could appease Kṛṣṇa. He asked that the Lord understand him as a subordinate servant whose little mistake and impudence might be excused. He admitted that he was puffed up by his powerful position as Lord Brahmā. Because he is the qualitative incarnation of the mode of passion within this material world, this was natural for him, and therefore he committed the mistake. But after all, Lord Kṛṣṇa would kindly take compassion upon His subordinate and excuse him for his gross mistake.

Lord Brahmā realized his actual position. He is certainly the supreme teacher of this universe, in charge of the production of material nature consisting of complete material elements, false ego, sky, air, fire, water and earth. Such a universe may be gigantic, but it can be measured, just as we measure our body as seven cubits. Generally everyone's personal bodily measurement is calculated to be seven cubits of his hand. This particular universe may appear as a very gigantic body, but it is nothing but the measurement of seven cubits for Lord Brahmā. Aside from this universe, there are unlimited other universes which are outside the jurisdiction of this particular Lord Brahmā. Just as innumerable atomic infinitesimal fragments pass through the holes of a screened window, so millions and trillions of universes in their seedling form are coming out from the bodily pores of Mahā-Viṣṇu, and that Mahā-Viṣṇu is but a part of the plenary expansion of Kṛṣṇa. Under these circumstances, although Lord Brahmā is the supreme creature within this universe, what is his importance in the presence of Lord Kṛṣṇa?

Lord Brahmā therefore compared himself to a little child within the womb of his mother. If the child within the womb plays with his hands and legs, and while playing touches the body of the mother, is the mother offended with the child? Of course she isn't. Similarly, Lord Brahmā may be a very great personality, and yet not only Brahmā but everything that be is existing within the womb of the Supreme Personality of Godhead. The Lord's energy is all-pervading; there is no place in the creation where it is not acting. Everything is existing within the energy of the Lord, so the Brahmā of this universe or the Brahmās of the many other millions and trillions of universes are existing within the energy of the Lord; therefore the Lord is considered to be the mother, and everything existing within the womb of the mother is considered to be the child. And the good mother is never offended with the child, even if he touches the body of the mother by kicking his legs.

Lord Brahmā then admitted that his birth was from the lotus flower which blossomed from the navel of Nārāyaṇa after the dissolution of the three worlds, or three planetary systems, known as *Bhurloka, Bhuvarloka* and *Svarloka.* The universe is divided into three divisions, namely Svarga, Martya and Pātāla. These three planetary systems are merged into water at the time of dissolution. At that time Nārāyaṇa, the plenary portion of Kṛṣṇa, lies down on the water and gradually a lotus stem grows from His navel, and from that lotus flower, Brahmā is born. It is naturally concluded that the mother of Brahmā is Nārāyaṇa. Because the Lord is the resting place of all the living entities after the dissolution of the universe, He is called Nārāyaṇa. The word *nāra* means the aggregate total of all living entities, and *ayana* means the resting place. The form of Garbhodakaśāyī Viṣṇu is called Nārāyaṇa because He rests Himself on that water. In addition, He is the resting place of all living creatures. Besides that, Nārāyaṇa is also present in everyone's heart, as it is confirmed in the *Bhagavad-gītā.* In that sense, also, He is Nārāyaṇa, as *ayana* means the source of knowledge as well as the resting place. It is also confirmed in the *Bhagavad-gītā* that remembrance of the living entity is due to the presence of the Supersoul within the heart. After changing the body, a living creature forgets everything of his past life, but because Nārāyaṇa the Supersoul is present within his heart, he is reminded by Him to act according to his past desire. Lord Brahmā wanted to prove that Kṛṣṇa is the original Nārāyaṇa, that He is the source of Nārāyaṇa, and that Nārāyaṇa is not an exhibition of the external energy, *māyā,* but is an expansion of spiritual energy. The activities of the external energy or *māyā* are exhibited after the creation of this cosmic world, and the original spiritual energy of Nārāyaṇa was acting before the creation. So the expansions of Nārāyaṇa, from Kṛṣṇa to Garbhodakaśāyī Viṣṇu, from

Garbhodakaśāyī Viṣṇu to Kṣīrodakaśāyī Viṣṇu, and from Kṣīrodakaśāyī Viṣṇu to everyone's heart, are manifestations of His spiritual energy. They are not conducted by the material energy; therefore they are not temporary. Anything conducted by the material energy is temporary, but everything executed by the spiritual energy is eternal.

Lord Brahmā reconfirmed his statement establishing Kṛṣṇa as the original Nārāyaṇa. He said that the gigantic universal body is still resting on the water known as Garbhodaka. He spoke as follows: "This gigantic body of the universe is another manifestation of Your energy. On account of His resting on the water, this universal form is also Nārāyaṇa, and we are all within the womb of this Nārāyaṇa form. I see Your different Nārāyaṇa forms everywhere. I can see You on the water, I can feel You within my heart, and I can also see You before me now. You are the original Nārāyaṇa.

"My dear Lord, in this incarnation You have proved that You are the supreme controller of *māyā*. You remain within the cosmic manifestation, and yet the whole creation is within You. This fact has already been proved by You when You exhibited the whole universal creation within Your mouth before Your mother Yaśodā. By Your inconceivable potency of *yogamāyā*, You can make such things effective without external help.

"My dear Lord Kṛṣṇa, the whole cosmic manifestation that we are visualizing at present is all within Your body. Yet I am seeing You outside, and You are also seeing me outside. How can such things happen without being influenced by Your inconceivable energy?"

Lord Brahmā stressed herein that without accepting the inconceivable energy of the Supreme Personality of Godhead, one cannot explain things as they are. He continued: "My dear Lord, leaving aside all other things and just considering today's happenings—what I have seen—are they not all due to Your inconceivable energies? First of all I saw You alone; thereafter You expanded Yourself as Your friends, the calves and all the existence of Vṛndāvana; then I saw You and all the boys as four-handed Viṣṇus, and They were being worshiped by all elements and all demigods, including myself. Again They all became cowherd boys, and You remained alone as You were before. Does this not mean that You are the Supreme Lord Nārāyaṇa, the origin of everything, and from You everything emanates, and again everything enters unto You, and You remain the same as before?"

"Persons who are unaware of Your inconceivable energy cannot understand that You alone expand Yourself as the creator Brahmā, maintainer Viṣṇu, and annihilator Śiva. Persons who are not in awareness of things as they are contemplate that I, Brahmā, am the creator, Viṣṇu is the maintainer, and Lord Śiva is the annihilator. Actually, You are alone everything—creator, maintainer, and annihilator. Similarly, You expand Yourself in different incarnations; among the demigods You incarnate as Vāmanadeva, among the great sages You incarnate as Paraśurāma, among the human beings You appear as Yourself, as Lord Kṛṣṇa, or Lord Rāma, among the animals You appear as the boar incarnation, and among the aquatics You appear as the incarnation of fish. And yet You have no appearance; You are always eternal. Your appearance and disappearance are made possible by Your inconceivable energy just to give protection to the faithful devotees and to annihilate the demons. O my Lord, O all-pervading Supreme Personality of Godhead, O Supersoul, controller of all mystic powers, no one can appreciate Your transcendental pastimes as they are exhibited within these three worlds. No one can estimate how You have expanded Your *yogamāyā* and Your incarnation and how You act by Your transcendental energy. My dear Lord, this whole cosmic manifestation is just like a flashing dream, and its temporary existence simply disturbs the mind. As a result, we are full of anxiety in this existence; to live within this material world means simply to suffer and to be full of all miseries. And yet this temporary existence of the material world appears to be pleasing and dear on account of its having evolved from Your body, which is eternal and full of bliss and knowledge.

"My conclusion is, therefore, that You are the Supreme Soul, Absolute Truth, and the supreme original person; and although You have expanded Yourself in so many Viṣṇu forms, or in living entities and energies, by Your inconceivable transcendental potencies, You are the supreme one without a second, You are the supreme Supersoul. The innumerable living entities are simply like sparks of the original fire. Your Lordship, the conception of the Supersoul as impersonal is wrongly accepted because I see that You are the original person. A person with a poor fund of knowledge may think that, because You are the son of Mahārāja Nanda, You are not the original person, that You are born just like a human being. They are mistaken. You are the actual original person; that is my conclusion. In spite of Your being the son of Nanda, You are the original person, and there is no doubt about it. You are the Absolute Truth, and You are not of this material darkness. You are the source of the original *brahmajyoti* as well as the material luminaries. Your transcendental effulgence is identical with *brahmajyoti*. As it is described in the *Brahma-saṁhitā*, the *brahmajyoti* is nothing but Your personal bodily effulgence. There are many Viṣṇu incarnations and incarnations of Your different qualities, but all those incarnations are not on the same level. You are the original lamp. Other incarnations may possess the same candle power as the original lamp, but the original lamp is the beginning of all light. And because You are not one of the creations of this material world, even after the annihilation of this world, Your existence as You are will continue.

"Because You are the original person, You are therefore described in the *Gopāla-tāpanī* (the Vedic *Upaniṣad*), as well as in the *Brahma-saṁhitā,* as *govindam ādi-puruṣam.* Govinda is the original person, the cause of all causes. In the *Bhagavad-gītā* also it is stated that You are the source of the Brahman effulgence. No one should conclude that Your body is like an ordinary material body. Your body is *akṣara,* indestructible. The material body is always full of threefold miseries, but Your body is *sac-cid-ānanda-vigraha:* full of being, bliss, knowledge and eternality. You are also *nirañjana* because Your pastimes, as the little son of mother Yaśodā or the Lord of the *gopīs,* are never contaminated by the material qualities. And although You exhibited Yourself in so many cowherd boys, calves and cows, Your transcendental potency is not reduced. You are always complete. As it is described in the Vedic literature, even if the complete is taken away from the complete–Supreme Absolute Truth–it yet remains the complete, Supreme Absolute Truth. And although many expansions from the complete are visible, the complete is one without a second. Since all Your pastimes are spiritual, there is no possibility of their being contaminated by the material modes of nature. When You place Yourself subordinate to Your father and mother, Nanda and Yaśodā, You are not reduced in Your potency; this is an expression of Your loving attitude for Your devotees. There is no other competitor of second identity than Yourself. A person with a poor fund of knowledge concludes that Your pastimes and appearance are simply material designations. You are transcendental to both nescience and knowledge, as it is confirmed in the *Gopāla-tāpanī.* You are the original *amṛta* (nectar of immortality), indestructible. As it is confirmed in the *Vedas, amṛtaṁ śāśvataṁ brahme.* Brahman is the eternal, the supreme origin of everything, who has no birth or death.

"In the *Upaniṣads* it is stated that the Supreme Brahman is as effulgent as the sun and is the origin of everything, and anyone who can understand that original person becomes liberated from the material conditional life. Anyone who can simply be attached to You by devotional service can know Your actual position, Your birth, appearance, disappearance and activities. As confirmed in the *Bhagavad-gītā,* simply by understanding Your constitutional position, appearance and disappearance, one can be immediately elevated to the spiritual kingdom after quitting this present body. Therefore to cross over the ocean of material nescience, an intelligent person takes shelter of Your lotus feet and is easily transferred to the spiritual world. There are many so-called meditators who do not know that You are the Supreme Soul. As stated in the *Bhagavad-gītā,* You are the Supreme Soul present in everyone's heart. Therefore there is no necessity of one's meditating on something beyond You. One who is always absorbed in meditation on Your original form of Kṛṣṇa easily crosses over the ocean of material nescience. But persons who do not know that You are the Supreme Soul remain within this material world in spite of their so-called meditation. If, by the association of Your devotees, a person comes to the knowledge that Lord Kṛṣṇa is the original Supersoul, then it is possible for him to cross over the ocean of material ignorance. For instance, a person becomes transcendental to the mistake of thinking a rope is a snake; as soon as one understands that the rope is not a snake, he is liberated from fear. For one who understands You, therefore, through Your personal teachings, as stated in the *Bhagavad-gītā,* or through Your pure devotees, as stated in the *Śrīmad-Bhāgavatam* and all Vedic literatures –that You are the ultimate goal of understanding–he need no more fear this material existence.

"So-called liberation and bondage has no meaning for a person who is already engaged in Your devotional service, just as a person who knows that the rope is not a snake is unafraid. A devotee knows that this material world belongs to You, and he therefore engages everything in Your transcendental loving service. Thus there is no bondage for him. For a person who is already situated in the sun planet, there is no question of the appearance or disappearance of the sun in the name of day or night. It is also said that You, Kṛṣṇa, are just like the sun, and *māyā* is like darkness. When the sun is present, there is no question of darkness; so, for those who are always in Your presence, there is no question of bondage or liberation. They are already liberated. On the other hand, persons who falsely think themselves to be liberated without taking shelter of Your lotus feet, fall down because their intelligence is not pure.

"If one therefore thinks that the Supersoul is something different from Your personality and thus searches out the Supersoul somewhere else, in the forest or in the caves of the Himālayas, his condition is very lamentable.

"Your teachings in the *Bhagavad-gītā* are that one should give up all other processes of self-realization and simply surrender unto You, for that is complete. Because You are supreme in everything, those who are searching after the Brahman effulgence are also searching after You. And those who are searching after Supersoul realization are also searching after You. You have stated in the *Bhagavad-gītā* that You Yourself, by Your partial representation as the Supersoul, have entered into this material cosmic manifestation. You are present in everyone's heart, and there is no need to search out the Supersoul anywhere else. If someone does so, he is simply in ignorance. One who is transcendental to such a position understands that You are unlimited; You are both within and without. Your presence is everywhere. Instead of searching for the Supersoul anywhere else, a devotee only concentrates his mind on You within. Actually one who is liberated from the material concept of life can search for You; others cannot. The simile of thinking the rope to be a snake is applicable only to those who are still in ignorance of You. Actually the existence of a snake besides the rope is only within the mind. The existence of *māyā*, similarly, is only within the mind. *Māyā* is nothing but ignorance of Your personality. When one forgets Your personality, that is the conditional state of *māyā*. Therefore one who is fixed upon You both internally and externally is not illusioned.

"One who has attained a little devotional service can understand Your glories. Even one striving for Brahman realization or Paramātmā realization cannot understand the different features of Your personality unless he treads the devotional path. One may be the spiritual master of many impersonalists, or he may go to the forest or to a cave or mountain and meditate as a hermit for many, many years, but he cannot understand Your glories without being favored by a slight degree of devotional service. Brahman realization or Paramātmā realization are also not possible even after one searches for many, many years unless one is touched by the wonderful effect of devotional service.

"My dear Lord, I pray that I may be so fortunate that, in this life or in another life, wherever I may take my birth, I may be counted as one of Your devotees. Wherever I may be, I pray that I may be engaged in Your devotional service. I do not even care what form of life I get in the future, because I can see that even in the form of cows and calves or cowherd boys, the devotees are so fortunate to be always engaged in Your transcendental loving service and association. Therefore I wish to be one of them instead of such an exalted person as I am now, for I am full of ignorance. The *gopīs* and cows of Vṛndāvana are so fortunate that they have been able to supply their breast milk to You. Persons who are engaged in performing great sacrifices and offering many valuable goats in the sacrifice cannot attain the perfection of understanding You, but simply by devotional service these innocent village women and cows are all able to satisfy You with their milk. You have drunk their milk to satisfaction, yet You are never satisfied by those engaged in performing sacrifices. I am simply surprised, therefore, with the fortunate position of Mahārāja Nanda, mother Yaśodā and the cowherd men and *gopīs,* because You, the Supreme Personality of Godhead, the Absolute Truth, are existing here as their most intimate lovable object. My dear Lord, no one can actually appreciate the good fortune of these residents of Vṛndāvana. We are all demigods, controlling deities of the various senses of the living entities, and we are proud of enjoying such privileges, but actually there is no comparison between our position and the position of these fortunate residents of Vṛndāvana because they are actually relishing Your presence and enjoying Your association by dint of their activities. We may be proud of being controllers of the senses, but here the residents of Vṛndāvana are so transcendental that they are not under our control. Actually they are enjoying the senses through service to You. I shall therefore consider myself fortunate to be given a chance to take birth in this land of Vṛndāvana in any of my future lives.

"My dear Lord, I am therefore not interested in either material opulences or liberation. I am most humbly praying at Your lotus feet for You to please give me any sort of birth within this Vṛndāvana forest so that I may be able to be favored by the dust of the feet of some of the devotees of Vṛndāvana. Even if I am given the chance to grow just as the humble grass in this land, that will be a glorious birth for me. But if I am not so fortunate to take birth within the forest of Vṛndāvana, I beg to be allowed to take birth outside the immediate area of Vṛndāvana so that when the devotees go out they will walk over me. Even that would be a great fortune for me. I am just aspiring for a birth in which I will be smeared by the dust of the devotees' feet.

"I can see that everyone here is simply full of Kṛṣṇa consciousness; they do not know anything but Mukunda. All the *Vedas* are indeed searching after the lotus feet of Kṛṣṇa."

It is confirmed in the *Bhagavad-gītā* that the purpose of Vedic knowledge is to find Kṛṣṇa. And it is said in the *Brahma-saṁhitā* that it is very difficult to find Kṛṣṇa, the Supreme Personality of Godhead, by systematic reading of the Vedic literature. But He is very easily available through the mercy of a pure devotee. The pure devotees of Vṛndāvana are fortunate because they can see Mukunda (Lord Kṛṣṇa) all the time. This word "*mukunda*" can be understood in two ways. *Muk* means liberation. Lord Kṛṣṇa can give liberation and therefore transcendental bliss. The word also refers to His smiling face, which is just like the *kunda* flower. *Mukha* also means face. The *kunda* flower is very beautiful, and it appears to be smiling. Thus the comparison is made.

The difference between the pure devotees of Vṛndāvana and other devotees is that the residents of Vṛndāvana have no other desire but to be associated with Kṛṣṇa. Kṛṣṇa, being very kind to His devotees, fulfills their desire; because they always want Kṛṣṇa's association, the Lord is always prepared to give it to them. The devotees of Vṛndāvana are also spontaneous lovers. They do not follow the regulative principles. They are not required to strictly follow regulative principles because they are already naturally developed in transcendental love for Kṛṣṇa. Regulative principles are required for persons who have not achieved the position of transcendental love. Brahmā is also a devotee of the Lord, but he is subject to follow the regulative principles. He prays to Kṛṣṇa to give him the chance to take birth in Vṛndāvana so that he might be elevated to the platform of spontaneous love.

Lord Brahmā continued: "My Lord, sometimes I am puzzled as to how Your Lordship will be able to repay, in gratitude, the devotional service of these residents of Vṛndāvana. Although I know that You are the supreme source of all benediction, I am puzzled to know how You will be able to repay all the service that You are receiving from these residents of Vṛndāvana. I think of how You are so kind, so magnanimous, that even Pūtanā, who came to cheat You by dressing herself as a very affectionate mother, was awarded liberation and the actual post of a mother. And other demons belonging to the same family, such as Aghāsura and Bakāsura, were also favored with liberation. Under the circumstances, I am puzzled. These residents of Vṛndāvana have given You everything—their bodies, their minds, their love, their homes. Everything is being utilized for Your purpose. So how will You be able to repay their debt? You have already given Yourself to Pūtanā! I surmise that You shall ever remain a debtor to the residents of Vṛndāvana, being unable to repay their loving service. My Lord, I can understand that the superexcellent service of the residents of Vṛndāvana is due to their spontaneously engaging all natural instincts in Your service. It is said that attachment for material objects and home is due to illusion, which makes a living entity conditioned in the material world. But this is only the case for persons who are not in Kṛṣṇa consciousness. In the case of the residents of Vṛndāvana, such obstructions, as attachment to hearth and home, are nonexistent. Because their attachment has been converted unto You, and their home has been converted into a temple because You are always there, and because they have forgotten everything for Your sake, there is no impediment. For a Kṛṣṇa conscious person, there is no such thing as impediments in hearth and home. Nor is there illusion.

"I can also understand that Your appearance as a small cowherd boy, a child of the cowherd men, is not at all a material activity. You are so much obliged by their affection that You are here to enthuse them with more loving service by Your transcendental presence. In Vṛndāvana there is no distinction between material and spiritual because everything is dedicated to Your loving service. My dear Lord, Your Vṛndāvana pastimes are simply to enthuse Your devotees. If someone takes Your Vṛndāvana pastimes to be material, he will be misled.

"My dear Lord Kṛṣṇa, those who deride You, claiming that You have a material body like an ordinary man, are described in the *Bhagavad-gītā* as demonic and less intelligent. You are always transcendental. The non-devotees are cheated because they consider You to be a material creation. Actually, You have assumed this body, which resembles that of an ordinary cowherd boy, simply to increase the devotion and transcendental bliss of Your devotees.

"My dear Lord, I have nothing to say about people who advertise that they have already realized God or that by their realization they have themselves become God. But as far as I am concerned, I admit frankly that for me it is not possible to realize You by my body, mind or speech. What can I say about You, or how can I realize You by my senses? I cannot even think of You perfectly with my mind, which is the master of the senses. Your qualities, Your activities and Your body cannot be conceived by any person within this material world. Only by Your mercy can one understand, to some extent, what You are. My dear Lord, You are the Supreme Lord of all creation, although I sometimes falsely think that I am the master of this universe. I may be master of this universe, but there are innumerable universes, and there are innumerable Brahmās also who preside over these universes. But actually You are the master of them all. As the Supersoul in everyone's heart, You know everything. Please, therefore accept me as Your surrendered servant. I hope that You will excuse me for disturbing You in Your pastimes with Your friends and calves. Now if You will kindly allow me, I will immediately leave so You can enjoy Your friends and calves without my presence.

"My dear Lord Kṛṣṇa, Your very name suggests that You are all-attractive. The attraction of the sun and the moon are all due to You. By the attraction of the sun, You are beautifying the very existence of the Yadu dynasty. With the attraction of the moon, You are enhancing the potency of the land, the demigods, the *brāhmaṇas,* the cows and the oceans. Because of Your supreme attraction, demons like Kaṁsa and others are annihilated. Therefore it is my deliberate conclusion that You are the only worshipable Deity within the creation. Accept my humble obeisances until the annihilation of this material world. As long as there is sunshine within this material world, kindly accept my humble obeisances."

In this way, Brahmā, the master of this universe, after offering humble and respectful obeisances unto the Supreme Personality of Godhead and circumambulating Him three times, was ready to return to his abode known as Brahmaloka. By His gesture, the Supreme Personality of Godhead gave him permission to return. As soon as Brahmā left, Lord Śrī Kṛṣṇa immediately appeared as He had on the very day the cows and cowherd boys had vanished.

Kṛṣṇa had left His friends on the bank of the Yamunā while they were engaged in lunch, and although He returned exactly one year later, the cowherd boys thought that He had returned within a second. That is the way of Kṛṣṇa's different energies and activities. It is stated in the *Bhagavad-gītā* that Kṛṣṇa Himself is residing in everyone's heart, and He causes both remembrance and forgetfulness. All living entities are controlled by the supreme energy of the Lord, and sometimes they remember and sometimes they forget their constitutional position. His friends, being controlled in such a way, could not understand that for one whole year they were absent from the Yamunā bank and were under the spell of Brahmā's illusion. When Kṛṣṇa appeared before the boys, they thought, "Kṛṣṇa has returned within a minute." They began to laugh, thinking that Kṛṣṇa was not willing to leave their lunchtime company. They were very jubilant and invited Him, "Dear friend Kṛṣṇa, You have come back so quickly! All right, we have not as yet begun our lunch, not even taken one morsel of food. So please come and join us and let us eat together." Kṛṣṇa smiled and accepted their invitation, and He began to enjoy the lunchtime company of His friends. While eating, Kṛṣṇa was thinking, "These boys believe that I have come back within a second, but they do not know that for the last year I have been involved with the mystic activities of Lord Brahmā."

After finishing their lunch, Kṛṣṇa and His friends and calves began to return to their Vrajabhūmi homes. While passing, they enjoyed seeing the dead carcass of Aghāsura in the shape of a gigantic serpent. When Kṛṣṇa returned home to Vrajabhūmi, He was seen by all the inhabitants of Vṛndāvana. He was wearing a peacock feather in His helmet, which was also decorated with forest flowers. Kṛṣṇa was also garlanded with flowers and painted with different colored minerals collected from the caves of Govardhana Hill. Govardhana Hill is always famous for supplying natural red dyes, and Kṛṣṇa and His friends painted their bodies with them. Each of them had a bugle made of buffalo horn and a stick and a flute, and each called his respective calves by their particular names. They were so proud of Kṛṣṇa's wonderful activities that, while entering the village, they all sang His glories. All the *gopīs* in Vṛndāvana saw beautiful Kṛṣṇa entering the village. The boys composed nice songs describing how they were saved from being swallowed by the great serpent and how the serpent was killed. Some described Kṛṣṇa as the son of Yaśodā, and others as the son of Nanda Mahārāja. "He is so wonderful that He saved us from the clutches of the great serpent and killed him," they said. But little did they know that one year had passed since the killing of Aghāsura.

In this regard, Mahārāja Parīkṣit asked Śukadeva Gosvāmī how the inhabitants of Vṛndāvana suddenly developed so much love for Kṛṣṇa, although Kṛṣṇa was not a member of any of their families. Mahārāja Parīkṣit enquired, "During the absence of the original cowherd boys, when Kṛṣṇa expanded Himself, why is it that the boys' parents became more loving toward Him than toward their own sons? Also, why did the cows become so loving toward the calves, more than toward their own calves?"

Śukadeva Gosvāmī told Mahārāja Parīkṣit that every living entity is actually most attached to his own self. Outward paraphernalia such as home, family, friends, country, society, wealth, opulence, reputation, etc., are all only secondary in pleasing the living entity. They please only because they bring pleasure to the self. For this reason, one is self-centered and is attached to his body and self more than he is to relatives like wife, children, and friends. If there is some immediate danger to one's own person, he first of all takes care of himself, then others. That is natural. That means, more than anything else, he loves his own self. The next important object of affection, after his own self, is his material body. A person who has no information of the spirit soul is very much attached to his material body, so much so that even in old age he wants to preserve the body in so many artificial ways, thinking that his old and broken body can be saved. Everyone is working hard day and night just to give pleasure to his own self, under either the bodily or spiritual concept of life. We are attached to material possessions because they give pleasure to the senses or to the body. The attachment to the body is there only because the "I," the spirit soul, is within the body. Similarly, when one is further advanced, he knows that the spirit soul is pleasing because it is part and parcel of Kṛṣṇa. Ultimately, it is Kṛṣṇa who is pleasing and all-attractive. He is the Supersoul of everything. And in order to give us this information, Kṛṣṇa descends and tells us that the all-attractive center is He Himself. Without being an expansion of Kṛṣṇa, nothing can be attractive.

Whatever is attractive within the cosmic manifestation is due to Kṛṣṇa. Kṛṣṇa is therefore the reservoir of all pleasure. The active principle of everything is Kṛṣṇa, and highly elevated transcendentalists see everything in connection with Him. In the *Caitanya-caritāmṛta* it is stated that a *mahābhāgavata,* or highly advanced devotee, sees Kṛṣṇa as the active principle in all movable and immovable living entities. Therefore he sees everything within this cosmic manifestation in relation to Kṛṣṇa. For the fortunate person who has taken shelter of Kṛṣṇa as everything, liberation is already there. He is no longer in the material world. This is also confirmed in the *Bhagavad-gītā.* Whoever is engaged in the devotional service of Kṛṣṇa is already on the *brahma-bhūta* or spiritual platform. The very name Kṛṣṇa suggests piety and liberation. Anyone who takes shelter of the lotus feet of Kṛṣṇa enters the boat for crossing over the ocean of nescience. For him, this vast expansion of the material manifestation becomes as insignificant as a hoofprint. Kṛṣṇa is the center of all great souls, and He is the shelter of the material worlds.

For one who is on the platform of Kṛṣṇa consciousness, Vaikuṇṭha, or the spiritual world, is not far away. He does not live within the material world where there is danger at every step. In this way, Kṛṣṇa consciousness was fully explained by Śukadeva Gosvāmī to Mahārāja Parīkṣit. Śukadeva Gosvāmī even recited to the king the statements and prayers of Lord Brahmā. These descriptions of Lord Kṛṣṇa's pastimes with His cowherd boys, His eating with them on the bank of the Yamunā and Lord Brahmā's prayers unto Him, are all transcendental subject matters. Anyone who hears, recites or chants them surely gets all his spiritual desires fulfilled. Thus Kṛṣṇa's childhood appearance, His sporting with Balarāma in Vṛndāvana, was described.

Thus ends the Bhaktivedanta purport of the Fourteenth Chapter of Kṛṣṇa, *"Prayers Offered by Lord Brahmā to Lord Kṛṣṇa."*

15 / Killing of Dhenukāsura

In this way, Śrī Kṛṣṇa, along with His elder brother Balarāma, passed the childhood age known as *kaumāra* and stepped into the age of *paugaṇḍa,* from the sixth year up to the tenth. At that time, all the cowherd men conferred and agreed to give those boys who had passed their fifth year charge of the cows in the pasturing ground. Given charge of the cows, Kṛṣṇa and Balarāma traversed Vṛndāvana, purifying the land with Their footprints.

Accompanied by the cowherd boys and Balarāma, Kṛṣṇa brought forward the cows and played on His flute through the forest of Vṛndāvana, which was full of flowers, vegetables, and pasturing grass. The Vṛndāvana forest was as sanctified as the clear mind of a devotee and was full of bees, flowers and fruits. There were chirping birds and clear water lakes with waters that could relieve one of all fatigues. Sweet flavored breezes blew always, refreshing the mind and body. Kṛṣṇa, with His friends and Balarāma, entered the forest and, seeing the favorable situation, enjoyed the atmosphere to the fullest extent. Kṛṣṇa saw all the trees, overloaded with fruits and fresh twigs, coming down to touch the ground as if welcoming Him by touching His lotus feet. He was very pleased by the behavior of the trees, fruits and flowers, and He began to smile realizing their desires.

Kṛṣṇa then spoke to His elder brother Balarāma as follows: "My dear brother, You are superior to all of us, and Your lotus feet are worshiped by the demigods. Just see how these trees, full with fruits, have bent down to worship Your lotus feet. It appears that they are trying to get out of the darkness of being obliged to accept the form of trees. Actually, the trees born in the land of Vṛndāvana are not ordinary living entities. Having held the impersonal point of view in their past lives, they are now put into this stationary condition of life, but now they have the opportunity of seeing You in Vṛndāvana, and they are praying for further advancement in spiritual life through Your personal association. Generally the trees are living entities in the modes of darkness. The impersonalist philosophers are in that darkness, but they eradicate it by taking full advantage of Your presence. I think the drones that are buzzing all around You must have been Your devotees in their past lives. They cannot leave Your company because no one can be a better, more affectionate master than You. You are the supreme and original Personality of Godhead, and the drones are just trying to spread Your glories by chanting every moment. I think some of them must be great sages, devotees of Your Lordship, and they are disguising themselves in the form of drones because they are unable to give up Your company even for a moment. My dear brother, You are the supreme worshipable Godhead. Just see how the peacocks in great ecstasy are dancing before You. The deer, whose behavior is just like the *gopīs,* are welcoming You with the same affection. And the cuckoos who are residing in this forest are receiving You with great joy because they consider that Your appearance is so auspicious in their home. Even though they are trees and animals, these residents of Vṛndāvana are glorifying You. They are prepared to welcome You to their best capacity, as is the practice of great souls in receiving another great soul at home. As for the land, it is so pious and fortunate that the footprints of Your lotus feet are marking its body.

"It is quite natural for these Vṛndāvana inhabitants to thus receive a great personality like You. The herbs, creepers and plants are also so fortunate to touch Your lotus feet. And by Your touching the twigs with Your hands, these small plants are also made glorious. As for the hills and the rivers, they too are now glorious because You are glancing at them. Above all, the damsels of Vraja, the *gopīs,* attracted by Your beauty, are the most glorious, because You embrace them with Your strong arms."

In this way, both Lord Kṛṣṇa and Balarāma began to enjoy the residents of Vṛndāvana to their full satisfaction, along with the calves and cows on the bank of the Yamunā. In some places both Kṛṣṇa and Balarāma were accompanied by Their friends. The boys were singing, imitating the humming sound of the drones and accompanying Kṛṣṇa and Balarāma, who were garlanded with forest flowers. While walking, the boys sometimes imitated the quacking sound of the swans in the lakes, or when they saw the peacocks dancing, they imitated them before Kṛṣṇa. Kṛṣṇa also moved His neck, imitating the dancing and making His friends laugh.

The cows taken care of by Kṛṣṇa had different names, and Kṛṣṇa would call them with love. After hearing Kṛṣṇa calling, the cows would immediately respond by mooing, and the boys would enjoy this exchange to their hearts' content. They would all imitate the sound vibrations made by the different kinds of birds, especially the *cakoras*, peacocks, cuckoo and *bhāradvājas*. Sometimes, when they would see the weaker animals fleeing out of fear of the sounds of tigers and lions, the boys, along with Kṛṣṇa and Balarāma, would imitate the animals and run away with them. When they felt some fatigue, they would sit down, and Balarāma would put His head on the lap of one of the boys just to take rest, and Kṛṣṇa would immediately come and begin massaging the legs of Balarāma. And sometimes He would take a palm fan and fan the body of Balarāma, causing a pleasing breeze to relieve Him of His fatigue. Other boys would sometimes dance or sing while Balarāma took rest, and sometimes they would wrestle amongst themselves or jump. When the boys were thus engaged, Kṛṣṇa would immediately join them, and catching their hands, He would enjoy their company and laugh and praise their activities. When Kṛṣṇa would feel tired and fatigued, He would sometimes take shelter of the root of a big tree, or the lap of a cowherd boy, and lie down. When He would lie down with a boy or a root as His pillow, some of the boys would come and massage His legs, and some would fan His body with a fan made from leaves. Some of the more talented boys would sing in very sweet voices to please Him. Thus very soon His fatigue would go away. The Supreme Personality of Godhead, Kṛṣṇa, whose legs are tended by the goddess of fortune, shared Himself with the cowherd boys as one of them, expanding His internal potency to appear exactly like a village boy. But despite His appearing just like a village boy, there were occasions when He proved Himself to be the Supreme Personality of Godhead. Sometimes men pose themselves as the Supreme Personality of Godhead and cheat innocent people, but they can only cheat; they cannot exhibit the potency of God.

While Kṛṣṇa was thus engaged in exhibiting His internal potency along with the supermost fortunate friends, there occurred another chance for Him to exhibit the superhuman powers of Godhead. His most intimate friends Śrīdāmā, Subala and Stokakṛṣṇa began to address Kṛṣṇa and Balarāma with great love and affection thus: "Dear Balarāma, You are very powerful; Your arms are very strong. Dear Kṛṣṇa, You are very expert in killing all kinds of disturbing demons. Will You kindly note that just near this place there is a big forest of the name Tālavana. This forest is full of palm trees, and all the trees are filled with fruits. Some are falling down, and some of them are very ripe even in the trees. It is a very nice place, but because of a great demon, Dhenukāsura, it is very difficult to go there. No one can reach the trees to collect the fruits. Dear Kṛṣṇa and Balarāma, this demon is present there in the form of an ass, and he is surrounded by similar demon friends who assume the same shape. All of them are very strong, so it is very difficult to approach this place. Dear brothers, You are the only persons who can kill such demons. Other than You, no one can go there for fear of being killed. Not even animals go there, and no birds are sleeping there; they have all left. One can only appreciate the sweet aroma that is coming from that place. It appears that up until now, no one has tasted the sweet fruits there, either on the tree or on the ground. Dear Kṛṣṇa, to tell You frankly, we are very attracted by this sweet aroma. Dear Balarāma, let us all go there and enjoy these fruits. The aroma of the fruits is now spread everywhere. Don't You smell it from here?"

When Balarāma and Kṛṣṇa were thus petitioned by Their smiling, intimate friends, They were inclined to please them, and They began to proceed towards the forest, surrounded by all Their friends. Immediately upon entering the Tālavana, Balarāma began to yank the trees with His arms, exhibiting the strength of an elephant. Because of this jerking, all the ripe fruits fell down on the ground. Upon hearing the sound of the falling fruits, the demon Dhenukāsura, who was living there in the form of an ass, began to approach with great force, shaking the whole field so that all the trees began to move as if there were an earthquake. The demon appeared first before Balarāma and began to kick His chest with his hind legs. At first, Balarāma did not say anything, but the demon with great anger began to kick Him again more vehemently. This time Balarāma immediately caught hold of the legs of the ass with one hand and, wheeling him around, threw him into the treetops. While he was being wheeled around by Balarāma, the demon lost his life. Balarāma threw the demon into the biggest palm tree about, and the demon's body was so heavy that the palm tree fell upon other trees, and several fell down. It appeared as if a great hurricane had passed through the forest, and all the trees were falling down, one after another. This exhibition of extraordinary strength is not astonishing because Balarāma is the Personality of Godhead known as Ananta Śeṣanāga, who is holding all the planets on the hoods of His millions of heads. The whole cosmic manifestation is maintained by Him exactly as two threads hold the weaving of a cloth.

After the demon was thrown into the trees, all the friends and associates of Dhenukāsura immediately assembled and attacked Balarāma and Kṛṣṇa with great force. They were determined to retaliate and avenge the death of their friend. But Kṛṣṇa and Balarāma began to catch each of the asses by the hind legs and, exactly in the same way, wheel them around. Thus They killed all of them by throwing them into the palm trees. Because of the dead bodies of the asses, there was a panoramic scene. It appeared as if clouds of various colors were assembled in the trees. Hearing of this great incident, the demigods from the higher planets began to shower flowers on Kṛṣṇa and Balarāma and began to beat their drums and offer devotional prayers.

A few days after the killing of Dhenukāsura, people began to come into the Tālavana forest to collect the fruits, and animals began to return without fear to feed on the nice grasses grown there. Just by chanting or hearing these transcendental activities and pastimes of the brothers Kṛṣṇa and Balarāma, one can amass pious activities.

When Kṛṣṇa, Balarāma and Their friends entered the village of Vṛndāvana, They played Their flutes, and the boys praised Their uncommon activities in the forest. Their faces were decorated with *tilaka* and smeared with the dust raised by the cows, and Kṛṣṇa's head was decorated with a peacook feather. Both He and Balarāma played Their flutes, and the young *gopīs* were joyous to see Kṛṣṇa returning home. All the *gopīs* in Vṛndāvana remained very morose on account of Kṛṣṇa's absence. All day they were thinking of Kṛṣṇa in the forest or of Him herding cows in the pasture. When they saw Kṛṣṇa returning, all their anxieties were immediately relieved, and they began to look at His face the way drones hover over the honey of the lotus flower. When Kṛṣṇa entered the village, the young *gopīs* smiled and laughed. Kṛṣṇa, while playing the flute, enjoyed the beautiful smiling faces of the *gopīs*.

Then Kṛṣṇa and Balarāma were immediately received by Their affectionate mothers, Yaśodā and Rohiṇī, and, according to the time's demands, they began to fulfill the desires of their affectionate sons. Simultaneously, the mothers rendered service and bestowed benediction upon their transcendental sons. They very nicely took care of their children by bathing and dressing Them. Kṛṣṇa was dressed in bluish garments, and Balarāma was dressed in yellowish garments, and They were given all sorts of ornaments and flower garlands. Being relieved of the fatigue of Their day's work in the pasturing ground, They looked refreshed and very beautiful.

They were given palatable dishes by Their mothers, and They pleasantly ate everything. After eating, They were seated nicely on clean bedding, and the mothers began to sing various songs of Their activities. As soon as They sat down on the bedding, They very quickly fell fast asleep. In this way, Kṛṣṇa and Balarāma used to enjoy Vṛndāvana life as cowherd boys.

Sometimes Kṛṣṇa used to go with His boy friends and with Balarāma, and sometimes He used to go alone with His friends to the bank of the Yamunā and tend the cows. Gradually, the summer season arrived, and one day, while in the field, the boys and cows became very thirsty and began to drink the water of the Yamunā. The river, however, was made poisonous by the venom of the great serpent known as Kāliya.

Because the water was so poisonous, the boys and cows became visibly affected immediately after drinking. They suddenly fell down on the ground, apparently dead. Then Kṛṣṇa, who is the life of all lives, simply cast His merciful glance over them, and all the boys and cows regained consciousness and began to look at one another with great astonishment. They could understand that by drinking the water of Yamunā they had died and that the merciful glance of Kṛṣṇa restored their life. Thus they appreciated the mystic power of Kṛṣṇa, who is known as Yogeśvara, the master of all mystic *yogīs*.

Thus ends the Bhaktivedanta purport of the Fifteenth Chapter of Kṛṣṇa, *"Killing of Dhenukāsura."*

16 / Subduing Kāliya

When He understood that the water of the Yamunā was being polluted by the black serpent Kāliya, Lord Kṛṣṇa took action against him and made him leave the Yamunā and go elsewhere, and thus the water became purified.

When this story was being narrated by Śukadeva Gosvāmī, Mahārāja Parīkṣit became eager to hear more about Kṛṣṇa's childhood pastimes. He inquired from Śukadeva Gosvāmī how Kṛṣṇa chastised Kāliya, who was living in the water for many years. Actually, Mahārāja Parīkṣit was becoming more and more enthusiastic to hear the transcendental pastimes of Kṛṣṇa, and his inquiry was made with great interest.

Śukadeva Gosvāmī narrated the story as follows. Within the River Yamunā there was a great lake, and in that lake the black serpent Kāliya used to live. Because of his poison, the whole area was so contaminated that it emanated a poisonous vapor twenty-four hours a day. If a bird happened to even pass over the spot, he would immediately fall down in the water and die.

Due to the poisonous effect of the Yamunā's vapors, the trees and grass near the bank of the Yamunā had all dried up. Lord Kṛṣṇa saw the effect of the great serpent's poison: the whole river that ran before Vṛndāvana was now deadly.

Kṛṣṇa, who advented Himself just to kill all undesirable elements in the world, immediately climbed up in a big *kadamba* tree on the bank of the Yamunā. The *kadamba* is a round yellow flower, generally seen only in the Vṛndāvana area. After climbing to the top of the tree, He tightened His belt cloth, and, flapping His arms just like a wrestler, jumped in the midst of the poisonous lake. The *kadamba* tree from which Kṛṣṇa had jumped was the only tree there which was not dead. Some commentators say that due to touching the lotus feet of Kṛṣṇa, the tree became immediately alive. In some other *Purāṇas* it is stated that Garuḍa, the eternal carrier of Viṣṇu, knew that Kṛṣṇa would take this action in the future, so he put some nectar on this tree to preserve it. When Lord Kṛṣṇa jumped into the water, the river overflooded its banks, as if something very large had fallen into it. This exhibition of Kṛṣṇa's strength is not at all uncommon because He is the reservoir of all strength.

When Kṛṣṇa was swimming about, just like a great strong elephant, He made a tumultuous sound which the great black serpent Kāliya could hear. The tumult was intolerable for him, and he could understand that this was an attempt to attack his home. Therefore he immediately came before Kṛṣṇa. Kāliya saw that Kṛṣṇa was indeed worth seeing because His body was so beautiful and delicate; its color resembled that of a cloud, and His legs resembled a lotus flower. He was decorated with Śrīvatsa, jewels and yellow garments. He was smiling with a beautiful face and was playing in the River Yamunā with great strength. But in spite of Kṛṣṇa's beautiful features, Kāliya felt great anger within his heart, and thus he grabbed Kṛṣṇa with his mighty coils. Seeing the incredible way in which Kṛṣṇa was enveloped in the coils of the serpent, the affectionate cowherd boys and inhabitants of Vṛndāvana immediately became stunned out of fear. They had dedicated everything to Kṛṣṇa, their lives, property, affection, activities—everything was for Kṛṣṇa—and when they saw Him in that condition, they became overwhelmed with fear and fell down on the ground. All the cows, bulls and small calves became overwhelmed with grief, and they began to look at Him with great anxiety. Out of fear they could only cry in agony and stand erect on the bank, unable to help their beloved Kṛṣṇa.

While this scene was taking place on the bank of the Yamunā, there were ill omens manifest. The earth trembled, meteors fell from the sky, and the bodies of men shivered. All these are indications of great immediate danger. Observing the inauspicious signs, the cowherd men, including Mahārāja Nanda, became very anxious out of fear. At the same time they were informed that Kṛṣṇa had gone to the pasturing ground without His elder brother, Balarāma. As soon as Nanda and Yaśodā and the cowherd men heard this news, they became even more anxious. Out of their great affection for Kṛṣṇa, unaware of the extent of Kṛṣṇa's potencies, they became overwhelmed with grief and anxiety because they had nothing dearer than Kṛṣṇa and because they dedicated their everything—life, property, affection, mind and activities—to Kṛṣṇa. Because of their great attachment for Kṛṣṇa, they thought, "Today Kṛṣṇa is surely going to be vanquished!"

All the inhabitants of Vṛndāvana came out of the village to see Kṛṣṇa.

The assembly consisted of children, young and old men, women, animals and all living entities; they knew that Kṛṣṇa was their only means of sustenance. While this was happening, Balarāma, who is the master of all knowledge, stood there simply smiling. He knew how powerful His younger brother Kṛṣṇa was and that there was no cause for anxiety when Kṛṣṇa was fighting with an ordinary serpent of the material world. He did not, therefore, personally take any part in their concern. On the other hand, all the inhabitants of Vṛndāvana, being disturbed, began to search out Kṛṣṇa by following the impression of His footprints on the ground, and thus they moved towards the bank of the Yamunā. Finally, by following the footprints marked with flag, bow and conchshell, the inhabitants of Vṛndāvana arrived at the river bank and saw that all the cows and boys were weeping to behold Kṛṣṇa enwrapped in the coils of the black serpent. Then they became still more overwhelmed with grief. While Balarāma was smiling to see their lamentation, all the inhabitants of Vrajabhūmi merged into the ocean of grief because they thought that Kṛṣṇa was finished. Although the residents of Vṛndāvana did not know much about Kṛṣṇa, their love for Him was beyond comparison. As soon as they saw that Kṛṣṇa was in the River Yamunā enveloped by the serpent Kāliya and that all the boys and cows were lamenting, they simply began to think of Kṛṣṇa's friendship, His smiling face, His sweet words and His dealings with them. Thinking of all these and believing that their Kṛṣṇa was now within the clutches of Kāliya, they at once felt that the three worlds had become vacant. Lord Caitanya also said that He was seeing the three worlds as vacant for want of Kṛṣṇa. This is the highest stage of Kṛṣṇa consciousness. Almost all of the inhabitants of Vṛndāvana had the highest ecstasy, love for Kṛṣṇa.

When mother Yaśodā arrived, she wanted to enter the River Yamunā, and being checked, she fainted. Other friends who were equally aggrieved were shedding tears like torrents of rain or waves of the river, but in order to bring mother Yaśodā to consciousness, they began to speak loudly about the transcendental pastimes of Kṛṣṇa. Mother Yaśodā remained still, as if dead, because her consciousness was concentrated on the face of Kṛṣṇa. Nanda and all others who dedicated everything, including their lives, to Kṛṣṇa were ready to enter the waters of the Yamunā, but Lord Balarāma checked them because He was in perfect knowledge that there was no danger.

For two hours Kṛṣṇa remained like an ordinary child gripped in the coils of Kāliya, but when He saw that all the inhabitants of Gokula—including His mother and father, the *gopīs,* the boys and the cows—were just on the point of death and that they had no shelter for salvation from imminent death, Kṛṣṇa immediately freed Himself. He began to expand His body, and when the serpent tried to hold Him, he felt a great strain. On account of the strain, his coils slackened, and he had no other alternative but to let loose the Personality of Godhead, Kṛṣṇa, from his grasp. Kāliya then became very angry, and his great hoods expanded. He exhaled poisonous fumes from his nostrils, his eyes blazed like fire, and flames issued from his mouth. The great serpent remained still for some time, looking at Kṛṣṇa. Licking his lips with bifurcated tongues, the serpent looked at Kṛṣṇa with double hoods, and his eyesight was full of poison. Kṛṣṇa immediately pounced upon him, just as Garuḍa swoops upon a snake. Thus attacked, Kāliya looked for an opportunity to bite Him, but Kṛṣṇa moved around him. As Kṛṣṇa and Kāliya moved in a circle, the serpent gradually became fatigued, and his strength seemed to diminish considerably. Kṛṣṇa immediately pressed down the serpent's hoods and jumped up on them. The Lord's lotus feet became tinged with red from the rays of the jewels on the snake's hoods. Then He who is the original artist of all fine arts, such as dancing, began to dance upon the hoods of the serpent, although they were moving to and fro. Upon seeing this, denizens from the upper planets began to shower flowers, beat drums, play different types of flutes and sing various prayers and songs. In this way, all the denizens of heaven, such as the Gandharvas, Siddhas and demigods, became very pleased.

While Kṛṣṇa was dancing on his hoods, Kāliya tried to push Him down with some of his other hoods. Kāliya had about a hundred hoods, but Kṛṣṇa took control of them. He began to dash Kāliya with His lotus feet, and this was more than the serpent could bear. Gradually, Kāliya was reduced to struggling for his very life. He vomited all kinds of refuse and exhaled fire. While throwing up poisonous material from within, Kāliya became reduced in his sinful situation. Out of great anger, he began to struggle for existence and tried to raise one of his hoods to kill the Lord. The Lord immediately captured that hood and subdued it by kicking it and dancing on it. It actually appeared as if the Supreme Personality of Godhead Viṣṇu was being worshiped; the poisons emanating from the mouth of the serpent appeared to be like flower offerings. Kāliya then began to vomit blood instead of poison; he was completely fatigued. His whole body appeared to be broken by the kicks of the Lord. Within his mind, however, he finally began to understand that Kṛṣṇa was the Supreme Personality of Godhead, and he began to surrender unto Him. He realized that Kṛṣṇa was the Supreme Lord, the master of everything.

The wives of the serpent, known as the Nāgapatnīs, saw that their husband was being subdued by the kicking of the Lord, within whose womb the whole universe remains. Kāliya's wives prepared to worship the Lord, although, in their haste, their dress, hair and ornaments became disarrayed. They also surrendered unto the Supreme Lord and began to pray. They appeared before Him, put forward their offspring and anxiously offered respectful obeisances, falling down on the bank of the Yamunā. The Nāgapatnīs knew that Kṛṣṇa is the shelter of all surrendered souls, and they desired to release their husband from the impending danger by pleasing the Lord with their prayers.

The Nāgapatnīs began to offer their prayers as follows: "O dear Lord, You are equal to everyone. For You there is no distinction between Your sons, friends or enemies. Therefore the punishment which You have so kindly offered to Kāliya is exactly befitting. O Lord, You have descended especially for the purpose of annihilating all kinds of disturbing elements within the world, and because You are the Absolute Truth, there is no difference between Your mercy and punishment. We think, therefore, that this apparent punishment to Kāliya is actually some benediction. We consider that Your punishment is Your great mercy upon us because when You punish someone it is to be understood that the reactions of his sinful activities are eradicated. It is already clear that this creature appearing in the body of a serpent must have been overburdened with all kinds of sin; otherwise, how could he have the body of a serpent? Your dancing on his hoods reduces all the sinful results of actions caused by his having this body of a serpent. It is, therefore, very auspicious that You have become angry and have punished him in this way. We are very astonished to see how You have become so pleased with this serpent who evidently performed various religious activities in his past lives. Everyone must have been pleased by his undergoing all kinds of penances and austerities, and he must have executed universal welfare activities for all living creatures."

The Nāgapatnīs confirm that one cannot come in contact with Kṛṣṇa without having executed pious activities in devotional service in his previous lives. As Lord Caitanya advised in His *Śikṣāṣṭaka,* one has to execute devotional service by humbly chanting the Hare Kṛṣṇa *mantra*, thinking oneself lower than the straw in the street and not expecting honor for himself but offering all kinds of honor to others. The Nāgapatnīs were astonished that, although Kāliya had the body of a serpent as the result of grievous sinful activities, at the same time he was in contact with the Lord to the extent that the Lord's lotus feet were touching his hoods. Certainly this was not the ordinary result of pious activities. These two contradictory facts astonished them. Thus they continued to pray: "O dear Lord, we are simply astonished to see that he is so fortunate as to have the the dust of Your lotus feet on his head. This is a fortune sought after by great saintly persons. Even the goddess of fortune underwent severe austerities just to have the blessing of the dust of Your lotus feet, so how is it that Kāliya is so easily getting this dust on his head? We have heard from authoritative sources that those who are blessed with the dust of Your lotus feet do not care even for the highest post within the universe, namely the post of Lord Brahmā, or the kingship of heavenly planets, or the sovereignty of this planet. Nor do such persons desire to rule the planets above this earth, such as Siddhaloka; nor do they aspire for the mystic powers achieved by the *yoga* process. Nor do the pure devotees aspire for liberation by becoming one with You. My Lord, although he is born in a species of life which is fostered by the most abominable modes of material nature, accompanied with the quality of anger, this King of the serpents has achieved something very, very rare. Living entities who are wandering within this universe and getting different species of life can very easily achieve the greatest benediction only by Your mercy."

It is also confirmed in the *Caitanya-caritāmṛta* that the living entities are wandering within the universe in various species of life, but by the mercy of Kṛṣṇa and the spiritual master, they can get the seed of devotional service, and thus their path of liberation can be cleared.

"We therefore offer our respectful obeisances unto You," the Nāgapatnīs continued, "our dear Lord, because You are the Supreme Person, You are living as the Supersoul within every living entity; although You are transcendental to the cosmic manifestation, everything is resting in You. You are the personified indefatigable eternal time. The entire time force is existing in You, and You are therefore the seer and the embodiment of total time in the shape of past, present and future, month, day, hour, moment—everything. In other words, O Lord, You can see perfectly all the activities happening in every moment, in every hour, in every day, every year, past, present and future. You are Yourself the universal form, and yet You are different from this universe. You are simultaneously one and different from the universe. We therefore offer our respectful obeisances unto You. You are Yourself the whole universe, and yet You are the creator of the whole universe. You are the superintendent and maintainer of this whole universe, and You are its original cause. Although You are present within this universe by Your three qualitative incarnations, Brahmā, Viṣṇu, and Maheśvara, You are transcendental to the material creation. Although You are the cause of the appearance of all kinds of living entities—their senses, their lives, their minds, their intelligence—You are to be realized by Your internal energy. Let us therefore offer our respectful obeisances unto You, who are unlimited, finer than the finest, the center of all creation and knower of everything. Different varieties of philosophical speculators try to reach You. You are the ultimate goal of all philosophical efforts, and You are actually described by all philosophies and by different kinds of doctrines. Let us offer our respectful obeisances unto You, because You are the origin of all scripture and the source of knowledge. You are the root of all evidences, and You are the Supreme Person who can bestow upon us the supreme knowledge. You are the cause of all kinds of desires, and You are the cause of all kinds of satisfaction. You are the *Vedas* personified. Therefore we offer You our respectful obeisances.

"Our dear Lord, You are the Supreme Personality of Godhead, Kṛṣṇa, and You are also the supreme enjoyer now appeared as the son of Vasudeva, who is a manifestation of the pure state of goodness. You are the predominating Deity of mind and intelligence, Pradyumna and Aniruddha, and You are the Lord of all Vaiṣṇavas. By Your expansion as *caturvyūha*—namely Vāsudeva, Saṅkarṣaṇa, Aniruddha and Pradyumna—You are the cause of the development of mind and intelligence. By Your activities only, the living entities become covered by forgetfulness or discover their real identity. This is also confirmed in the *Bhagavad-gītā* (Fifteenth Chapter): the Lord is sitting as the Supersoul in everyone's heart, and due to His presence the living entity either forgets himself or revives his original identity. We can partially understand that You are within our hearts as the witness of all our activities, but it is very difficult to appreciate Your presence, although every one of us can do so to some extent. You are the supreme controller of both the material and spiritual energies; therefore You are the supreme leader, although You are different from this cosmic manifestation. You are the witness and creator and the very ingredient of this cosmic manifestation. We therefore offer our respectful obeisances unto You. Our dear Lord, in the matter of creating this cosmic manifestation, personally You have nothing to exert; by expending Your different kinds of energy—namely the mode of goodness, the mode of passion and the mode of ignorance—You can create, maintain and annihilate this cosmic manifestation. As the controller of the entire time force, You can simply glance over the material energy, create this universe and energize the different forces of material nature which are acting differently in different creatures. No one can estimate, therefore, how Your activities are going on within this world. Our dear Lord, although You have expanded into the three principal Deities of this universe—namely Lord Brahmā, Lord Viṣṇu and Lord Śiva—for creation, maintenance and destruction, Your appearance as Lord Viṣṇu is actually for the benediction of living creatures. Therefore, for those who are actually peaceful and who are aspiring after the supreme peace, worship of Your peaceful appearance as Lord Viṣṇu is recommended. O Lord, we are submitting our prayers unto You. You can appreciate that this poor serpent is going to give up his life. You know that for us women our lives and everything are our husband's; therefore, we are praying unto You that You kindly excuse Kāliya, our husband, because if this serpent dies, then we shall be in great difficulty. Looking upon us only, please excuse this great offender. Our dear Lord, every living creature is Your offspring, and You maintain everyone. This serpent is also Your offspring, and You can excuse him although he has offended You, undoubtedly without knowing Your potency. We are praying that he may be excused for this time. Our dear Lord, we are offering our loving service unto You because we are all eternal servitors of Your Lordship. You can order us and ask us to do whatever You please. Every living being can be relieved from all kinds of despair if he agrees to abide by Your orders."

After the Nāgapatnīs submitted their prayers, Lord Kṛṣṇa released Kāliya from his punishment. Kāliya was already unconscious from being struck by the Lord. Upon regaining consciousness and being released from the punishment, Kāliya got back his life force and the working power of his senses. With folded hands, he humbly began to pray to the Supreme Lord Kṛṣṇa: "My dear Lord, I have been born in such a species that by nature I am angry and envious, being in the darkest region of the mode of ignorance. Your Lordship knows well that it is very difficult to give up one's natural instincts, although by such instincts the living creature transmigrates from one body to another." It is also confirmed in the *Bhagavad-gītā* that it is very difficult to get out of the clutches of material nature, but if anyone surrenders unto the Supreme Personality of Godhead, Kṛṣṇa, the modes of material nature can no longer act on him. "My dear Lord," Kāliya continued, "You are therefore the original creator of all kinds of modes of material nature by which the universe is created. You are the cause of the different kinds of mentality possessed by living creatures by which they have obtained different varieties of bodies. My dear Lord, I am born as a serpent; therefore, by natural instinct, I am very angry. How is it then possible to give up my acquired nature without Your mercy? It is very difficult to get out of the clutches of Your *māyā*. By Your *māyā* we remain enslaved. My dear Lord, kindly excuse me for my inevitable material tendencies. Now You can punish me or save me as You desire."

After hearing this, the Supreme Personality of Godhead, who was acting as a small human child, ordered the serpent thus: "You must immediately leave this place and go to the ocean. Leave without delay. You can take with you all your offspring, wives and everything that you possess. Don't pollute the waters of the Yamunā. Let it be drunk by My cows and cowherd boys without hindrance." The Lord then declared that the order given to the Kāliya snake be recited and heard by everyone so that no one need fear Kāliya any longer.

Anyone who hears the narration of the Kāliya serpent and his punishment will need fear no more the envious activities of snakes. The Lord also declared: "If one takes a bath in the Kāliya lake where My cowherd boy friends and I have bathed, or if one, fasting for a day, offers oblations to the forefathers from the water of this lake, he will be relieved from all kinds of sinful reaction." The Lord also assured Kāliya: "You came here out of fear of Garuḍa, who wanted to eat you in the beautiful land by the ocean. Now, after seeing the marks where I have touched your head with My lotus feet, Garuḍa will not disturb you."

The Lord was pleased with Kāliya and his wives. Immediately after hearing His order, the wives began to worship Him with great offerings of nice garments, flowers, garlands, jewels, ornaments, sandal pulp, lotus flowers, and nice eatable fruits. In this way they pleased the master of Garuḍa, of whom they were very much afraid. Then, obeying the orders of Lord Kṛṣṇa, all of them left the lake within the Yamunā.

Thus ends the Bhaktivedanta purport of the Sixteenth Chapter of Kṛṣṇa, *"Subduing Kāliya."*

17 / Extinguishing the Forest Fire

King Parīkṣit, after hearing of the chastisement of Kāliya, inquired from Śukadeva Gosvāmī as to why Kāliya left his beautiful land and why Garuḍa was so antagonistic to him. Śukadeva Gosvāmī informed the King that the island known as Nāgālaya was inhabited by serpents and that Kāliya was one of the chief serpents there. Being accustomed to eating snakes, Garuḍa used to come to this island and kill many serpents at his will. Some of them he actually ate, but some were unnecessarily killed. The reptile society became so disturbed that their leader, Vāsuki, appealed to Lord Brahmā for protection. Lord Brahmā made an arrangement by which Garuḍa would not create a disturbance: on each half-moon day, the reptile community would offer a serpent to Garuḍa. The serpent was to be kept underneath a tree as a sacrificial offering to Garuḍa. Garuḍa was satisfied with this offering, and therefore he did not disturb any other serpents.

But gradually, Kāliya took advantage of this situation. He was unnecessarily puffed up by the volume of his accumulated poison, as well as by his material power, and he thought, "Why should Garuḍa be offered this sacrifice?" He then ceased offering any sacrifice; instead, he himself ate the offering intended for Garuḍa. When Garuḍa, the great devotee-carrier of Viṣṇu, understood that Kāliya was eating the offered sacrifices, he became very angry and quickly rushed to the island to kill the offensive serpent. Kāliya tried to fight Garuḍa and faced him with his many hoods and poisonous sharp teeth. Kāliya attempted to bite him, and Garuḍa, the son of Tārkṣya, in great anger and with the great force deserving the carrier of Lord Viṣṇu, struck the body of Kāliya with his effulgent golden wings. Kāliya, who is also known as Kadrūsuta, son of Kadrū, immediately fled to the lake known as Kāliyadaha, underneath the Yamunā River, which Garuḍa could not approach.

Kāliya took shelter within the water of the Yamunā for the following reason. Just as Garuḍa went to the island of the Kāliya snake, so he also used to go to the Yamunā to catch fish to eat. There was, however, a great *yogī* known as Saubhari Muni, who used to meditate within the water there and who was sympathetic with the fish. He asked Garuḍa not to come there and disturb the fish. Although Garuḍa was not under anyone's order, being the carrier of Lord Viṣṇu, he did not disobey the order of the great *yogī*. Instead of staying and eating many fish, he carried off one big fish, who was their leader. Saubhari Muni was sorry that one of the leaders of the fish was taken away by Garuḍa, and thinking of their protection, he cursed Garuḍa in the following words: "Henceforward from this day, if Garuḍa comes here to catch fish, then–I say this with all my strength–he will be immediately killed."

This curse was known only to Kāliya. Kāliya was, therefore, confident that Garuḍa would not be able to come there, and so he thought it wise to take shelter of the lake within the Yamunā. But Kāliya's taking shelter of Saubhari Muni was not successful; he was driven away from the Yamunā by Kṛṣṇa, the master of Garuḍa. It may be noted that Garuḍa is directly related to the Supreme Personality of Godhead and is so powerful that he is never subjected to anyone's order or curse. Actually the cursing of Garuḍa–who is stated in the *Śrīmad-Bhāgavatam* to be of the stature of the Supreme Personality of Godhead, Bhagavān–was an offense on the part of Saubhari Muni. Although Garuḍa did not try to retaliate, the Muni was not saved from his offensive act against a great Vaiṣṇava personality. Due to this offence, Saubhari fell down from his yogic position and afterwards became a householder, a sense enjoyer in the material world. The falldown of Saubhari Muni, who was supposed to be absorbed in spiritual bliss by meditation, is an instruction to the offender of Vaiṣṇavas.

When Kṛṣṇa finally came out of Kāliya's lake, He was seen by all His friends and relatives on the bank of Yamunā. He appeared before them nicely decorated, smeared all over with *candana* pulp, bedecked with valuable jewels and stones, and almost completely covered with gold. The inhabitants of Vṛndāvana, cowherd boys and men, mother Yaśodā, Mahārāja Nanda and all the cows and calves, saw Kṛṣṇa coming from the Yamunā, and it was as though they had recovered their very life. When a person regains his life, naturally he becomes absorbed in pleasure and joyfulness. They each in turn pressed Kṛṣṇa to their chests, and thus they felt a great relief. Mother Yaśodā, Rohiṇī, Mahārāja Nanda and the cowherd men became so happy that they embraced Kṛṣṇa and thought they had achieved their ultimate goal of life.

Balarāma also embraced Kṛṣṇa, but He was laughing because He had known what would happen to Kṛṣṇa when everyone else was so overwhelmed with anxiety. All the trees on the bank of the Yamunā, all the cows, bulls and calves were full of pleasure because of Kṛṣṇa's appearance there. The *brāhmaṇa* inhabitants of Vṛndāvana, along with their wives, immediately came to congratulate Kṛṣṇa and His family members. *Brāhmaṇas* are considered to be the spiritual masters of society. They offered their blessings to Kṛṣṇa and the family on account of Kṛṣṇa's release. They also asked Mahārāja Nanda to give them some charity on that occasion. Being so pleased by Kṛṣṇa's return, Mahārāja Nanda began to give many cows and much gold in charity to the *brāhmaṇas*. While Nanda Mahārāja was thus engaged, mother Yaśodā simply embraced Kṛṣṇa and made Him sit on her lap while she shed tears continually.

Since it was almost night, and all the inhabitants of Vṛndāvana, including the cows and calves, were very tired, they decided to take their rest on the river bank. In the middle of the night, while they were taking rest, there was suddenly a great forest fire, and it quickly appeared that the fire would soon devour all the inhabitants of Vṛndāvana. As soon as they felt the warmth of the fire, they immediately took shelter of Kṛṣṇa, the Supreme Personality of Godhead, although He was playing just like their child. They began to say, "Our dear Kṛṣṇa! O Supreme Personality of Godhead! Our dear Balarāma, the reservoir of all strength! Please try to save us from this all devouring and devastating fire. We have no other shelter than You. This devastating fire will swallow us all!" Thus they prayed to Kṛṣṇa, saying that they could not take any shelter other than His lotus feet. Lord Kṛṣṇa, being compassionate upon His own townspeople, immediately swallowed up the whole forest fire and saved them. This was not impossible for Kṛṣṇa because He is unlimited. He has unlimited power to do anything He desires.

Thus ends the Bhaktivedanta purport of the Seventeenth Chapter of Kṛṣṇa, *"Extinguishing the Forest Fire."*

18 / Killing the Demon Pralambāsura

After extinguishing the devastating fire, Kṛṣṇa, surrounded by His relatives, friends, cows, calves and bulls and glorified by their singing, again entered Vṛndāvana, which is always full of cows. While Kṛṣṇa and Balarāma were enjoying life in Vṛndāvana, in the midst of the cowherd boys and girls, the season gradually changed to summer. The summer season in India is not very much welcomed because of the excessive heat, but in Vṛndāvana everyone was pleased because summer there appeared just like spring. This was possible only because Lord Kṛṣṇa and Balarāma, who are the controllers even of Lord Brahmā and Lord Śiva, were residing there. In Vṛndāvana there are many falls which are always pouring water, and the sound is so sweet that it covers the sound of the crickets. And because water flows all over, the forest always looks very green and beautiful.

The inhabitants of Vṛndāvana were never disturbed by the scorching heat of the sun or the high summer temperatures. The lakes of Vṛndāvana are surrounded by green grasses, and various kinds of lotus flowers bloom there, such as the *kalhāra-kañjotpala,* and the air blowing in Vṛndāvana carries the aromatic pollen of those lotus flowers. When the particles of water from the waves of the Yamunā, the lakes and the waterfalls, touched the bodies of the inhabitants of Vṛndāvana, they automatically felt a cooling effect. Therefore they were practically undisturbed by the summer season.

Vṛndāvana is such a nice place. Flowers are always blooming, and there are even various kinds of decorated deer. Birds are chirping, peacocks are crowing and dancing, and bees are humming. The cuckoos there sing nicely in five kinds of tunes.

Kṛṣṇa, the reservoir of pleasure, blowing His flute, accompanied by His elder brother Balarāma and other cowherd boys and cows, entered the beautiful forest of Vṛndāvana to enjoy the atmosphere. They walked into the midst of newly grown leaves of trees whose flowers resembled peacock feathers. They were garlanded by those flowers and decorated with saffron chalk. Sometimes they were dancing and singing and sometimes wrestling with one another. While Kṛṣṇa danced, some of the cowherd boys sang, and others played on flutes; some bugled on buffalo horns or clapped their hands, praising Kṛṣṇa, "Dear brother, You are dancing very nicely." Actually, all these boys were demigods descended from higher planets to assist Kṛṣṇa in His pastimes. The demigods garbed in the dress of the cowherd boys were encouraging Kṛṣṇa in His dancing, just as one artist encourages another with praise. Up to that time, neither Balarāma nor Kṛṣṇa had undergone the haircutting ceremony; therefore Their hair was clustered like crows' feathers. They were always playing hide-and-seek with Their boy friends or jumping or fighting with one another. Sometimes, while His friends were chanting and dancing, Kṛṣṇa would praise them, "My dear friends, you are dancing and singing very nicely." The boys played at catching ball with bell shaped fruits and round *āmalakī*. They played blindman's buff, challenging and touching one another. Sometimes they imitated the forest deer and various kinds of birds. They joked with one another by imitating croaking frogs, and they enjoyed swinging underneath the trees. Sometimes they would play like a king and his subjects amongst themselves. In this way, Balarāma and Kṛṣṇa, along with all Their friends, played all kinds of sports and enjoyed the soothing atmosphere of Vṛndāvana, full of rivers, lakes, rivulets, fine trees and excellent fruits and flowers.

Once while they were engaged in their transcendental pastimes, a great demon of the name Pralambāsura entered their company, desiring to kidnap both Balarāma and Kṛṣṇa. Although Kṛṣṇa was playing the part of a cowherd boy, as the Supreme Personality of Godhead He could understand everything—past, present and future. So when Pralambāsura entered their company, Kṛṣṇa began to think how to kill the demon, but externally He received him as a friend. "O My dear friend," He said. "It is very good that you have come to take part in our pastimes." Kṛṣṇa then called all His friends and ordered them: "Now we shall play in pairs. We shall challenge one another in pairs." With this proposal, all the boys assembled together. Some of them took the side of Kṛṣṇa, and some of them took the side of Balarāma, and they arranged to play in duel. The defeated members in duel fighting had to carry the victorious members on their backs. They began playing, and at the same time tended the cows as they proceeded through the Bhāṇḍīravana forest. The party of Balarāma, accompanied by Śrīdāmā and Vṛṣabha, came out victorious, and Kṛṣṇa's party had to carry them on their backs through the Bhāṇḍīravana forest. The Supreme Personality of Godhead, Kṛṣṇa, being defeated, had to carry Śrīdāmā on His back, and Bhadrasena carried Vṛṣabha. Imitating their play, Pralambāsura, who appeared there as a cowherd boy, carried Balarāma on his back. Pralambāsura was the greatest of the demons, and he had calculated that Kṛṣṇa was the most powerful of the cowherd boys.

In order to avoid the company of Kṛṣṇa, Pralambāsura carried Balarāma far away. The demon was undoubtedly very strong and powerful, but he was carrying Balarāma, who is compared with a mountain; therefore he began to feel the burden, and thus he assumed his real form. When he appeared in his real feature, he was decorated with a golden helmet and earrings and looked just like a cloud with lightning carrying the moon. Balarāma observed the demon's body expanding up to the limits of the clouds, his eyes dazzling like blazing fire and his mouth flashing with sharpened teeth. At first, Balarāma was surprised by the demon's appearance, and He began to wonder, "How is it that all of a sudden this carrier has changed in every way?" But with a clear mind He could quickly understand that He was being carried away from His friends by a demon who intended to kill Him. Immediately He struck the head of the demon with His strong fist, just as the king of the heavenly planets strikes a mountain with his thunderbolt. Being stricken by the fist of Balarāma, the demon fell down dead, just like a snake with a smashed head, and blood poured from his mouth. When the demon fell, he made a tremendous sound, and it sounded as if a great hill were falling upon being struck by the thunderbolt of King Indra. All the boys then rushed to the spot. Being astonished by the ghastly scene, they began to praise Balarāma with the words, "Well done, well done." All of them then began to embrace Balarāma with great affection, thinking that He had returned from death, and they offered their blessings and congratulations. All the demigods in the heavenly planets became very satisfied and showered flowers on the transcendental body of Balarāma, and they also offered their blessings and congratulations for His having killed the great demon Pralambāsura.

Thus ends the Bhaktivedanta purport of the Eighteenth Chapter of Kṛṣṇa, *"Killing the Demon Pralambāsura."*

19 / Devouring the Forest Fire

While Kṛṣṇa and Balarāma and Their friends were engaged in the pastimes described above, the cows, being unobserved, began to wander off on their own, entering farther and farther into the deepest part of the forest, allured by fresh grasses. The goats, cows and buffalo travelled from one forest to another and entered the forest known as Iṣikāṭavi. This forest was full of green grass, and therefore they were allured; but when they entered, they saw that there was a forest fire, and they began to cry. On the other side, Balarāma and Kṛṣṇa, along with Their friends, could not find their animals, and they became very aggrieved. They began to trace the cows by following their footprints, as well as the path of eaten grass. All of the boys were fearing that their very means of livelihood, the cows, were now lost. Soon, however, they heard the crying of their cows. Kṛṣṇa began to call the cows by their respective names, with great noise. Upon hearing Kṛṣṇa calling, the cows immediately replied with joy. But by this time the forest fire surrounded all of them, and the situation appeared to be very fearful. The flames increased as the wind blew very quickly, and it appeared that everything movable and immovable would be devoured. All the cows and the boys became very frightened, and they looked towards Balarāma the way a dying man looks at the picture of the Supreme Personality of Godhead. They said, "Dear Kṛṣṇa and Balarāma, we are now burning from the heat of this blazing fire. Let us take shelter of Your lotus feet. We know You can protect us from this great danger. Our dear friend Kṛṣṇa, we are Your intimate friends. It is not right that we should suffer in this way. We are all completely dependent on You, and You are the knower of all religious life. We do not know anyone except You."

The Personality of Godhead heard the appealing voices of His friends, and casting a pleasing glance over them, He began to answer. By speaking through His eyes, He impressed His friends that there was no cause for fear. Then Kṛṣṇa, the supreme mystic, the powerful Personality of Godhead, immediately swallowed up all the flames of the fire. The cows and boys were thus saved from imminent danger. Out of fear, the boys were almost unconscious, but when they regained their consciousness and opened their eyes, they saw that they were again in the forest with Kṛṣṇa, Balarāma and the cows. They were astonished to see that they were completely free from the attack of the blazing fire and that the cows were saved. They secretly thought that Kṛṣṇa must not be an ordinary boy, but some demigod.

In the evening, Kṛṣṇa and Balarāma, along with the boys and cows, returned to Vṛndāvana, playing Their flutes. As they approached the village, all the *gopīs* became very joyous. Throughout the day the *gopīs* used to think of Kṛṣṇa while He was in the forest, and in His absence they were considering one moment to be like twelve years.

Thus ends the Bhaktivedanta purport of the Nineteenth Chapter of Kṛṣṇa, *"Devouring the Forest Fire."*

20 / Description of Autumn

The killing of Pralambāsura and the devouring of the devastating forest fire by Kṛṣṇa and Balarāma became household topics in Vṛndāvana. The cowherd men described these wonderful activities to their wives and to everyone else, and all were struck with wonder. They concluded that Kṛṣṇa and Balarāma were demigods who had kindly come to Vṛndāvana to become their children. In this way, the rainy season ensued. In India, after the scorching heat of the summer, the rainy season is very welcome. The clouds accumulating in the sky, covering the sun and the moon, become very pleasing to the people, and they expect rainfall at every moment. After summer, the advent of the rainy season is considered to be a life-giving source for everyone. The thunder and occasional lightning are also pleasurable to the people.

The symptoms of the rainy season may be compared to the symptoms of the living entities who are covered by the three modes of material nature. The unlimited sky is like the Supreme Brahman, and the tiny living entities are like the covered sky, or Brahman covered by the three modes of material nature. Originally, everyone is part and parcel of Brahman. The Supreme Brahman, or the unlimited sky, can never be covered by a cloud, but a portion of it can be covered. As stated in the *Bhagavad-gītā*, the living entities are part and parcel of the Supreme Personality of Godhead. But they are only an insignificant portion of the Supreme Lord. This portion is covered by the modes of material nature, and therefore the living entities are residing within this material world. The *brahmajyoti*–spiritual effulgence–is just like the sunshine; as the sunshine is full of molecular shining particles, so the *brahmajyoti* is full of minute portions of the Supreme Personality of Godhead. Out of that unlimited expansion of minute portions of the Supreme Lord, some are covered by the influence of material nature, whereas others are free.

Kṛṣṇa brought forward the cows and played on His flute through the forest of Vṛndāvana. (p. 113)

With tumultuous sound they started for Vṛndāvana. (p. 76)

Sometimes the boys would imitate the sounds of various animals and birds. (p. 77)

Kṛṣṇa bifurcated Bakāsura's mouth as easily as a child splits a blade of grass. (p. 78)

Returning home, Kṛṣṇa and Balārama were received by Their affectionate mothers. (p. 117)

“We think that this apparent punishment to Kāliya is actually some benediction.” (p. 123)

Garuḍa struck the body of Kāliya with his effulgent golden wings. (p. 128)

Kṛṣṇa would praise them, “My dear friends, you are dancing and singing very nicely.” (p. 132)

Pralambāsura looked just like a cloud with lightning carrying the moon. (p. 133)

Kṛṣṇa, the supreme mystic, immediately swallowed up all the flames of the fire. (p. 135)

Due to remaining in the water for a long time, the gopīs felt cold and were shivering. (p. 154)

Clouds are accumulated water drawn from the land by the sunshine. Continually for eight months the sun evaporates all kinds of water from the surface of the globe, and this water is accumulated in the shape of clouds, which are distributed as water when there is need. Similarly, a government exacts various taxes from the citizens which the citizens are able to pay by their different material activities: agriculture, trade and industry; thus the government can also exact taxes in the form of income tax and sales tax. This is compared to the sun drawing water from the earth. When there is again need of water on the surface of the globe, the same sunshine converts the water into clouds and distributes it all over the globe. Similarly, the taxes collected by the government must be distributed to the people again, as educational work, public work, sanitary work, etc. This is very essential for a good government. The government should not simply exact tax for useless squandering; the tax collection should be utilized for the public welfare of the state.

During the rainy season, there are strong winds blustering all over the country and carrying clouds from one place to another to distribute water. When water is urgently needed after the summer season, the clouds are just like a rich man who, in times of need, distributes his money even by exhausting his whole treasury. So the clouds exhaust themselves by distributing water all over the surface of the globe.

When Mahārāja Daśaratha, the father of Lord Rāmacandra, used to fight with his enemies, it was said that he approached them just like a farmer uprooting unnecessary plants and trees. And when there was need of giving charity, he used to distribute money exactly as the cloud distributes rain. The distribution of rain by clouds is so sumptuous that it is compared to the distribution of wealth by a great, munificent person. The clouds' downpour is so sufficient that the rains even fall on rocks and hills and on the oceans and seas where there is no need for water. It is like a charitable person who opens his treasury for distribution and who does not discriminate whether the charity is needed or not. He gives in charity openhanded.

Before the rainfall, the whole surface of the globe becomes almost depleted of all kinds of energies and appears very lean. After the rainfall, the whole surface of the earth becomes green with vegetation and appears to be very healthy and strong. Here, a comparison is made with the person undergoing austerities for fulfillment of a material desire. The flourishing condition of the earth after a rainy season is compared with the fulfillment of material desires. Sometimes, when a country is subjected by an undesirable government, persons and parties undergo severe penances and austerities to get control of the government, and when they attain control, they flourish by giving themselves generous salaries. This also is like the flourishing of the earth in the rainy season. Actually, one should undergo severe austerities and penances only to achieve spiritual happiness. In the *Śrīmad-Bhāgavatam* it is recommended that *tapasa* or penance should be accepted for realizing the Supreme Lord. By accepting austerity in devotional service, one regains his spiritual life, and as soon as one regains his spiritual life, he enjoys unlimited spiritual bliss. But if someone undertakes austerities and penances for some material gain, it is stated in the *Bhagavad-gītā* that the results are temporary and that they are desired by persons of less intelligence.

During the rainy season, in the evening, there are many glowworms visible about the tops of trees, hither and thither, and they glitter just like lights. But the luminaries of the sky, the stars and the moons, are not visible. Similarly, in the age of Kali, persons who are atheists or miscreants become very prominently visible, whereas persons who are actually following the Vedic principles for spiritual emancipation are practically obscured. This age, Kaliyuga, is compared to the cloudy season of the living entities. In this age, real knowledge is covered by the influence of material advancement of civilization. The cheap mental speculators, atheists and manufacturers of so-called religious principles become prominent like the glowworms, whereas persons strictly following the Vedic principles or scriptural injunctions become covered by the clouds of this age. People should learn to take advantage of the actual luminaries of the sky, the sun, moon, and stars, instead of the glowworm's light. Actually, the glowworm cannot give any light in the darkness of night. As clouds sometimes clear, even in the rainy season, and sometimes the moon, stars and sun become visible, so even in this Kaliyuga there are sometimes advantages. The Vedic movement of Lord Caitanya's—the distribution of chanting the Hare Kṛṣṇa *mantra*—is heard in this way. People seriously anxious to find real life should take advantage of this movement instead of looking toward the light of mental speculators and atheists.

After the first rainfall, when there is a thundering sound in the clouds, all the frogs begin to croak, like students suddenly engaged in reading their studies. Students are generally supposed to rise early in the morning. They do not usually arise of their own accord, however, but only when there is a bell sounded in the temple or in the cultural institution. By the order of the spiritual master they immediately rise, and after finishing their morning duties, they sit down to study the *Vedas* or chant Vedic *mantras*. Everyone is sleeping in the darkness of Kaliyuga, but when there is a great *ācārya*, by his calling only, everyone takes to the study of the *Vedas* to acquire actual knowledge. During the rainy season, many small ponds, lakes and rivulets become filled with water; otherwise the rest of the year they remain dry. Similarly, materialistic persons are dry, but sometimes, when they are in a so-called opulent position, with a home or children or a little bank balance, they appear to be flourishing, but immediately afterwards they become dry again, like the small rivulets and ponds. The poet Vidyāpati said that in the society of friends, family, children, wife, etc., there is certainly some pleasure, but that pleasure is compared to a drop of water in the desert. Everyone is hankering after happiness, just as in the desert everyone is hankering after water. If, in the desert, there is a drop of water, the water is there of course, but the benefit from that drop of water is very insignificant. In our materialistic way of life, we are hankering after an ocean of happiness, but in the form of society, friends and mundane love, we are getting no more than a drop of water. Our satisfaction is never achieved, as the small rivulets, lakes and ponds are never filled with water in the dry season.

Due to rainfall, the grass, trees and vegetation look very green. Sometimes the grass is covered by a certain kind of red insect, and when the green and red combine with umbrella-like mushrooms, the entire scene changes, just like a person who has suddenly become rich. The farmer then becomes very happy to see his field full of grains, but the capitalists—who are always unaware of the activities of a supernatural power—become unhappy because they are afraid of a competitive price. In some places certain capitalists in government restrict the farmer from producing too much grains, not knowing the actual fact that all food grains are supplied by the Supreme Personality of Godhead. According to the Vedic injunction, *eko bahūnāṁ yo vidadhāti kāmān,* the Supreme Personality of Godhead maintains this creation; therefore, He arranges for a supply of whatever is required for all living entities. When there is population increase, it is the business of the Supreme Lord to feed them. But persons who are atheists or miscreants do not like abundant production of food grains, especially if their business might be hampered.

During the rainy season, all living entities, in the land, sky and water, become very refreshed, exactly like one who engages in the transcendental loving service of the Lord. We have practical experience of this with our students in the International Society for Krishna Consciousness. Before becoming students, they were dirty looking, although they had naturally beautiful personal features; but due to having no information of Kṛṣṇa consciousness they appeared very dirty and wretched. Since they have taken to Kṛṣṇa consciousness, their health has improved, and by following the rules and regulations, their bodily luster has increased. When they are dressed with saffron colored cloth, with *tilaka* on their foreheads and beads in their hands and on their necks, they look exactly as if they come directly from Vaikuṇṭha.

In the rainy season, when the rivers swell and rush to the oceans and seas, they appear to agitate the ocean. Similarly, if a person who is engaged in the *yoga*-mystic process is not very advanced in spiritual life, he can become agitated by the sex impulse. High mountains, however, although splashed by torrents of rain, do not change; so a person who is advanced in Kṛṣṇa consciousness, even if put into difficulties, is not embarrassed because a person who is spiritually advanced accepts any adverse condition of life as the mercy of the Lord, and thus he is completely eligible to enter into the spiritual kingdom.

In the rainy season some of the roads are not frequently used, and they become covered with long grasses. This is exactly like a *brāhmaṇa* who is not accustomed to studying and practicing the reformatory methods of Vedic injunctions—he becomes covered with the long grasses of *māyā*. In that condition, forgetful of his constitutional nature, he forgets his position of eternal servitorship to the Supreme Personality of Godhead. By being deviated by the seasonal overgrowth of long grasses created by *māyā,* a person identifies himself with mayic production and succumbs to illusion, forgetting his spiritual life.

During the rainy season, lightning appears in one group of clouds and then immediately in another group of clouds. This phenomena is compared to a lusty woman who does not fix her mind on one man. A cloud is compared to a qualified person because it pours rain and gives sustenance to many people; a man who is qualified similarly gives sustenance to many living creatures, such as family members or many workers in business. Unfortunately, his whole life can be disturbed by a wife who divorces him; when the husband is disturbed, the whole family is ruined, the children are dispersed or the business is closed, and everything is effected. It is therefore recommended that a woman desiring to advance in Kṛṣṇa consciousness peacefully live with a husband and that the couple not separate under any condition. The husband and wife should control sex indulgence and concentrate their minds on Kṛṣṇa consciousness so their life may be successful. After all, in the material world a man requires a woman, and a woman requires a man. When they are combined, they should live peacefully in Kṛṣṇa consciousness and should not be restless like the lightning, flashing from one group of clouds to another.

Sometimes, in addition to the roaring thunder of the clouds, there is an appearance of a rainbow, which stands as a bow without a string. Actually, a bow is in the curved position, being tied at its two ends by the bowstring; but in the rainbow there is no such string, and yet it rests in the sky so beautifully. Similarly, when the Supreme Personality of Godhead descends to this material world, He appears just like an ordinary human being, but He is not resting on any material condition. In the *Bhagavad-gītā,* the Lord says that He appears by His internal potency, which is free from the bondage of the external potency. What is bondage for the ordinary creature is freedom for the Personality of Godhead. In the rainy season, the moonlight is covered by clouds but is visible at intervals. It sometimes appears that the moon is moving with the movement of the clouds, but actually the moon is still; due to the clouds it also appears to move. Similarly, for one who has identified himself with the moving material world, his actual spiritual luster is covered by illusion, and with the movement of material activities, he thinks that he is moving through different spheres of life. This is due to false ego, which is the demarcation between spiritual and material existence, just as the moving cloud is the demarcation between moonlight and darkness. In the rainy season, when the clouds appear for the first time, after seeing their appearance, the peacocks begin to dance with joy. This can be compared to persons who are very harassed in the materialistic way of life. If they can find the association of a person engaged in the loving devotional service of the Lord, they become enlightened, just like the peacocks when they dance. We have practical experience of this, because many of our students were dry and morose previous to their coming to Kṛṣṇa consciousness, but having come into contact with devotees, they are now dancing like jubilant peacocks.

Plants and creepers grow by drinking water from the ground. Similarly, a person practicing austerities becomes dry; after the austere performances are completed and he gets the result, he begins to enjoy life in sense gratification, with family, society, love, home and other paraphernalia. Sometimes it is seen that cranes and ducks meander continually on the banks of the lakes and rivers, although the banks are filled with muddy garbage and thorny creepers. Similarly, persons who are householders without Kṛṣṇa consciousness are constantly tarrying in material life, in spite of all kinds of inconveniences. In family life, or any life, one cannot be perfectly happy without being Kṛṣṇa conscious. Śrīla Narottama dāsa Ṭhākur prays that he will have the association of a person—either a householder or a man in the renounced order of life—who is engaged in the transcendental loving service of the Lord and is always crying the holy name of Lord Caitanya.

For the materialistic person, worldly affairs become too aggressive, whereas to a person who is in Kṛṣṇa consciousness, everything appears to be happily situated.

The barriers around the agricultural field sometimes break due to heavy torrents of rain. Similarly, the unauthorized atheistic propaganda in the age of Kali breaks the boundary of the Vedic injunctions. Thus people gradually degenerate to godlessness. In the rainy season, the clouds, tossed by the wind, deliver water which is welcomed like nectar. When the Vedic followers, the *brāhmaṇas,* inspire rich men like kings and the wealthy mercantile community to give charity in the performance of great sacrifices, the distribution of such wealth is also nectarean. The four sections of human society, namely the *brāhmaṇas,* the *kṣatriyas,* the *vaiśyas* and the *śūdras,* are meant to live peacefully in a cooperative mood; this is possible when they are guided by the expert Vedic *brāhmaṇas* who perform sacrifices and distribute wealth equally.

Vṛndāvana forest improved from the rains and was replete with ripened dates, mangoes, blackberries and other fruits. Lord Kṛṣṇa, the Supreme Personality of Godhead, and His boy friends and Lord Balarāma, entered the forest to enjoy the new seasonal atmosphere. The cows, being fed by new grasses, became very healthy, and their milk bags were all very full. When Lord Kṛṣṇa called them by name, they immediately came to Him out of affection, and in their joyful condition the milk flowed from their bags. Lord Kṛṣṇa was very pleased when passing through the Vṛndāvana forest by the side of Govardhana Hill. On the bank of the Yamunā He saw all the trees decorated with bee hives pouring honey. There were many waterfalls on Govardhana Hill, and their flowing made a nice sound. Kṛṣṇa heard them as He looked into the caves of the hill. When the rainy season was not ended completely but was gradually turning to autumn, sometimes, especially when there was rainfall within the forest, Kṛṣṇa and His companions would sit under a tree or within the caves of Govardhana Hill and enjoy eating the ripened fruits and talking with great pleasure. When Kṛṣṇa and Balarāma were in the forest all day, mother Yaśodā used to send Them some rice mixed with yogurt, fruits and sweetmeat. Kṛṣṇa would take them and sit on a slab of stone on the bank of the Yamunā. While Kṛṣṇa and Balarāma and Their friends were eating, they watched the cows, calves and bulls. The cows appeared to be tired from standing with their heavy milk bags. By sitting and chewing grass, they became happy, and Kṛṣṇa was pleased to see them. He was proud to see the beauty of the forest, which was nothing but the manifestation of His own energy.

At such times Kṛṣṇa would praise nature's special activities during the rainy season. It is stated in the *Bhagavad-gītā* that the material energy, or nature, is not independent in its actions. Nature is acting under the superintendence of Kṛṣṇa. It is also stated in the *Brahma-saṁhitā* that material nature, known as Durgā, is acting as the shadow of Kṛṣṇa. Whatever order is sent from Kṛṣṇa, material nature obeys. Therefore the natural beauty created by the rainy season was acted out according to the indications of Kṛṣṇa. Soon all the water reservoirs became very clean and pleasing, and refreshing air was blowing everywhere because of the appearance of autumn. The sky was completely cleared of all clouds, and it recovered its natural blue color. The blooming lotus flower in the clear water in the forest appeared like a person who has fallen down from *yoga* practice but again has become beautiful by resuming his spiritual life.

Everything becomes naturally beautiful with the appearance of the autumn season. Similarly, when a materialistic person takes to Kṛṣṇa consciousness and spiritual life, he also becomes as clear as the sky and water in autumn. The autumn season takes away the rolling of dark clouds in the sky as well as the polluted water. Filthy conditions on the ground also become cleansed. Similarly, a person who takes to Kṛṣṇa consciousness immediately becomes cleansed of all dirty things within and without. Kṛṣṇa is therefore known as Hari. "*Hari*" means "he who takes away." Kṛṣṇa immediately takes away all unclean habits from anyone who takes to Kṛṣṇa consciousness. The clouds of autumn are white, for they do not carry any water. Similarly, a retired man, being freed from all responsibility of family affairs (namely, maintaining the home, wife and children) and taking completely to Kṛṣṇa consciousness, becomes freed from all anxieties and looks as white as clouds in autumn. Sometimes in autumn the falls come down from the top of the hill to supply clean water, and sometimes they stop. Similarly, sometimes great saintly persons distribute clear knowledge, and sometimes they are silent. The small ponds which were filled with water because of the rainy season, gradually dry up in autumn. As for the tiny aquatics living in the reservoirs, they cannot understand that their numbers are diminishing day by day, as the materially engrossed persons cannot understand that their duration of life is being reduced day by day. Such persons are engaged in maintaining cows, property, children, wife, society and friendship. Due to the reduced water and scorching heat from the sun in the autumn season, the small creatures living in small reservoirs of water are much disturbed; they are exactly like uncontrolled persons who are always unhappy from being unable to enjoy life or maintain their family members. The muddy earth gradually dries up, and newly grown fresh vegetables begin to wither. Similarly, for one who has taken to Kṛṣṇa consciousness, desire for family enjoyment gradually dries up.

Because of the appearance of the autumn season, the water of the ocean becomes calm and quiet, just as a person developed in self-realization is no longer disturbed by the three modes of material nature. In autumn, farmers save the water within the fields by building strong walls so that the water contained within the field cannot run out. There is hardly any hope for new rainfalls; therefore they want to save whatever is in the field. Similarly, a person who is actually advanced in self-realization protects his energy by controlling the senses. It is advised that after the age of fifty, one should retire from family life and should conserve the energy of the body for utilization in the advancement of Kṛṣṇa consciousness. Unless one is able to control the senses and engage them in the transcendental loving service of Mukunda, there is no possibility of salvation.

During the daytime in autumn, the sun is very scorching, but at night, due to the clear moonshine, people get relief from the day's fatigue. If a person takes shelter of Mukunda, or Kṛṣṇa, he can be saved from the fatigue of misidentifying the body with the self. Mukunda, or Kṛṣṇa, is also the source of solace to the damsels of Vṛndāvana. The damsels of Vrajabhūmi are always suffering because of separation from Kṛṣṇa. When they meet Kṛṣṇa during the moonlit autumn night, their fatigue of separation is also satiated. When the sky is clear of all clouds, the stars at night shine very beautifully; similarly, when a person is actually situated in Kṛṣṇa consciousness, he is cleared of all dirty things, and he becomes as beautiful as the stars in the autumn sky. Although the *Vedas* prescribe *karma* in the form of offering sacrifices, their ultimate purpose is stated in the *Bhagavad-gītā:* one has to accept Kṛṣṇa consciousness after thoroughly understanding the purpose of the *Vedas.* Therefore the clean heart exhibited by a devotee in Kṛṣṇa consciousness can be compared to the clean sky of the autumn season. During autumn, the moon looks very bright along with the stars in the clear sky. Lord Kṛṣṇa Himself appeared in the sky of the Yadu dynasty, and He was exactly like the moon surrounded by the stars, or the members of the Yadu dynasty. When there are ample blooming flowers in the gardens in the forest, the fresh, aromatic breeze gives a great relief to the person who has suffered during the summer and rainy seasons. Unfortunately, such breezes could not give any relief to the *gopīs* because of their hearts' dedication to Kṛṣṇa. People in general might have taken pleasure in that nice autumn breeze, but the *gopīs,* not being embraced by Kṛṣṇa, were not very satisfied.

On arrival of the autumn season, all the cows, deer, birds and females in general become pregnant, because in that season generally all the husbands become impelled by sex desire. This is exactly like the transcendentalists who, by the grace of the Supreme Lord, are bestowed with the benediction of their destinations in life. Śrīla Rūpa Gosvāmī has instructed in his *Upadeśāmṛta* that one should follow devotional service with great enthusiasm, patience and conviction and should follow the rules and regulations, keep oneself clean from material contamination and stay in the association of devotees. By following these principles, one is sure to achieve the desired result of devotional service. For he who patiently follows the regulative principles of devotional service, the time will come when he will achieve the result, as the wives who reap results by becoming pregnant.

During the autumn, the lotus flowers in the lakes grow in large numbers because of the absence of lilies; both the lilies and the lotus flowers grow by sunshine, but during the autumn season, the scorching sunshine helps only the lotus. This example is given in the case of a country where the king or the government is strong; the rise of unwanted elements like thieves and robbers cannot prosper. When the citizens become confident that they will not be attacked by robbers, they develop very satisfactorily. A strong government is compared to the scorching sunshine in the autumn season; the lilies are compared to unwanted persons like robbers, and the lotus flowers are compared to the satisfied citizens of the government. During autumn, the fields become filled with ripened grains. At that time, the people become happy over the harvest and observe various ceremonies, such as Navānna–the offering of new grains to the Supreme Personality of Godhead. The new grains are first offered to the Deities in various temples, and all are invited to take sweet rice made of these new grains. There are other religious ceremonies and methods of worship, particularly in Bengal, where the greatest of all such ceremonies is held, called *Durgā Pūjā.*

In Vṛndāvana the autumn season was very beautiful then because of the presence of the Supreme Personality of Godhead, Kṛṣṇa and Balarāma. The mercantile community, the royal order and great sages were free to move to achieve their desired benedictions. Similarly, the transcendentalists, when freed from the encagement of the material body, also achieved their desired goal. During the rainy season, the mercantile community cannot move from one place to another and so do not get their desired profit. Nor can the royal order go from one place to another to collect taxes from the people. As for saintly persons who must travel to preach transcendental knowledge, they also are restrained by the rainy season. But during the autumn, all of them leave their confines. In the case of the transcendentalist, be he a *jñānī*, a *yogī*, or a devotee, because of the material body he cannot actually enjoy spiritual achievement. But as soon as he gives up the body, or after death, the *jñānī* merges into the spiritual effulgence of the Supreme Lord; the *yogī* transfers himself to the various higher planets, and the devotee goes to the planet of the Supreme Lord, Goloka Vṛndāvana, or the Vaikuṇṭhas, and thus enjoys his eternal spiritual life.

Thus ends the Bhaktivedanta purport of the Twentieth Chapter of Kṛṣṇa, *"Description of Autumn."*

21 / The Gopīs Attracted by the Flute

Kṛṣṇa was very pleased with the atmosphere of the forest where flowers bloomed and bees and drones hummed very jubilantly. While the birds, trees and branches were all looking very happy, Kṛṣṇa, tending the cows, accompanied by Śrī Balarāma and the cowherd boys, began to vibrate His transcendental flute. After hearing the vibration of the flute of Kṛṣṇa, the *gopīs* in Vṛndāvana remembered Him and began to talk amongst themselves about how nicely Kṛṣṇa was playing His flute. When the *gopīs* were describing the sweet vibration of Kṛṣṇa's flute, they also remembered their pastimes with Him; thus their minds became disturbed, and they were unable to describe completely the beautiful vibrations. While discussing the transcendental vibration, they remembered also how Kṛṣṇa dressed, decorated with a peacock feather on His head, just like a dancing actor, and with blue flowers pushed over His ear. His garment glowed yellow-gold, and He was garlanded with a *vaijayantī* necklace. Dressed in such an attractive way, Kṛṣṇa filled up the holes of His flute with the nectar emanating from His lips. So they remembered Him, entering the forest of Vṛndāvana, which is always glorified by the footprints of Kṛṣṇa and His companions.

Kṛṣṇa was very expert in playing the flute, and the *gopīs* were captivated by the sound vibration, which was not only attractive to them, but to all living creatures who heard it. One of the *gopīs* told her friends, "The highest perfection of the eyes is to see Kṛṣṇa and Balarāma entering the forest and playing Their flutes and tending the cows with Their friends."

Persons who are constantly engaged in the transcendental meditation of seeing Kṛṣṇa, internally and externally, by thinking of Him playing the flute and entering the Vṛndāvana forest, have really attained the perfection of *samādhi. Samādhi* (trance) means absorption of all the activities of the senses on a particular object, and the *gopīs* indicate that the pastimes of

Kṛṣṇa are the perfection of all meditation and *samādhi.* It is also confirmed in the *Bhagavad-gītā* that anyone who is always absorbed in the thought of Kṛṣṇa is the topmost of all *yogīs.*

Another *gopī* expressed her opinion that Kṛṣṇa and Balarāma, while tending the cows, appeared just like actors going to play on a dramatic stage. Kṛṣṇa was dressed in glowing garments of yellow, Balarāma in blue, and They held new twigs of mango tree, peacock feathers, and bunches of flowers in Their hands. Dressed with garlands of lotus flowers, They were sometimes singing very sweetly among Their friends. One *gopī* told her friend, "How is it Kṛṣṇa and Balarāma are looking so beautiful?" Another *gopī* said, "My dear friend, we cannot even think of His bamboo flute—what sort of pious activities did it execute so that it is now enjoying the nectar of the lips of Kṛṣṇa?" Kṛṣṇa sometimes kisses the *gopīs;* therefore the transcendental nectar of His lips is available only to them, and His lips are considered their property. Therefore the *gopīs* asked: "How is it possible that the flute, which is nothing but a bamboo rod, is always engaged in enjoying the nectar from Kṛṣṇa's lips? Because the flute is engaged in the service of the Supreme Lord, the mother and the father of the flute must be happy."

The lakes and the rivers are considered to be the mothers of the trees because the trees live simply by drinking water. So the waters of the lakes and rivers of Vṛndāvana were full of happy lotus flowers because the waters were thinking, "How is it our son, the bamboo rod, is enjoying the nectar of Kṛṣṇa's lips?" The bamboo trees standing by the banks of the rivers and the lakes were also happy to see their descendant so engaged in the service of the Lord, just as persons who are advanced in knowledge take pleasure to see their descendants engage in the service of the Lord. The trees were overwhelmed with joy and were incessantly yielding honey, which flowed from the beehives hanging on the branches.

Sometimes the *gopīs* spoke thus to their friends about Kṛṣṇa: "Dear friends, our Vṛndāvana is proclaiming the glories of this entire earth because this planet is glorified by the lotus footprints of the son of Devakī. Besides that, when Govinda plays His flute, the peacocks immediately become mad. When all the animals and trees and plants, either on the top of Govardhana Hill or in the valley, see the dancing of the peacock, they all stand still and listen to the transcendental sound of the flute with great attention. We think that this boon is not possible or available on any other planet." Although the *gopīs* were village cowherd women and girls, they had knowledge of Kṛṣṇa. Similarly, one can learn the highest truths simply by hearing the *Vedas* from authoritative sources.

Another *gopī* said, "My dear friends, just see the deer! Although they are dumb animals, they have approached the son of Mahārāja Nanda, Kṛṣṇa. Not only are they attracted by the dress of Kṛṣṇa and Balarāma, but as soon as they hear the playing of the flute, the deer, along with their husbands, offer respectful obeisances unto the Lord by looking at Him with great affection." The *gopīs* were envious of the deer because the deer were able to offer their service to Kṛṣṇa along with their husbands. The *gopīs* thought themselves not so fortunate because whenever they wanted to go to Kṛṣṇa, their husbands were not very happy.

Another *gopī* said, "My dear friends, Kṛṣṇa is so nicely dressed that He appears to be the impetus to various kinds of ceremonies held by the womenfolk. Even the wives of the denizens of heaven become attracted after hearing the transcendental sound of His flute. Although they are travelling in the air in their airplanes, enjoying the company of their husbands, on hearing the sound of Kṛṣṇa's flute, they immediately become perturbed. Their hair is loosened and their tight dresses are slackened." This means that the transcendental sound of the flute of Kṛṣṇa extended to all corners of the universe. Also, it is significant that the *gopīs* knew about the different kinds of airplanes flying in the sky.

Another *gopī* said to her friends, "My dear friends, the cows are also charmed as soon as they hear the transcendental sound of the flute of Kṛṣṇa. It sounds to them like the pouring of nectar, and they immediately spread their long ears just to catch the liquid nectar of the flute. As for the calves, they are seen with the nipples of their mothers pressed in their mouths, but they cannot suck the milk. They remain struck with devotion, and tears glide down their eyes, illustrating vividly how they are embracing Kṛṣṇa heart to heart." These phenomena indicate that even the cows and calves in Vṛndāvana knew how to cry for Kṛṣṇa and embrace Him heart to heart. Actually, Kṛṣṇa conscious affection can be culminated in shedding tears from the eyes.

A younger *gopī* told her mother, "My dear mother, the birds, who are all looking at Kṛṣṇa playing on His flute, are sitting very attentively on the branches and twigs of different trees. From their features it appears that they have forgotten everything and are engaged only in hearing Kṛṣṇa's flute. This proves that they are not ordinary birds; they are great sages and devotees, and just to hear Kṛṣṇa's flute they have appeared in Vṛndāvana forest as birds." Great sages and scholars are interested in Vedic knowledge, but the essence of Vedic knowledge is stated in the *Bhagavad-gīta: vedaiś ca sarvair aham eva vedyaḥ.* Through the knowledge of the *Vedas*, Kṛṣṇa has to be understood. From the behavior of these birds, it appeared that they were great scholars in Vedic knowledge and that they took to Kṛṣṇa's transcendental vibration and rejected all branches of Vedic knowledge. Even the River Yamunā, being desirous to embrace the lotus feet of Kṛṣṇa after hearing the transcendental vibration of His flute, broke her fierce waves to flow very nicely with lotus flowers in her hands, just to present flowers to Mukunda with deep feeling.

The scorching heat of the autumn sunshine was sometimes intolerable, and therefore the clouds in the sky appeared in sympathy above Kṛṣṇa and Balarāma and Their boy friends while They engaged in blowing Their flutes. The clouds served as a soothing umbrella over Their heads just to make friendship with Kṛṣṇa. The wanton aborigine girls also became fully satisfied when they smeared their faces and breasts with the dust of Vṛndāvana, which was reddish from the touch of Kṛṣṇa's lotus feet. The aborigine girls had very full breasts, and they were also very lusty, but when their lovers felt their breasts, they were not very satisfied. When they came out into the midst of the forest, they saw that while Kṛṣṇa was walking, some of the leaves and creepers of Vṛndāvana turned reddish from the *kuṅkuma* powder which fell from His lotus feet. His lotus feet were held by the *gopīs* on their breasts, which were also smeared with *kuṅkuma* powder, but when Kṛṣṇa travelled in the Vṛndāvana forest with Balarāma and His boy friends, the reddish powder fell on the ground of the Vṛndāvana forest. So the lusty aborigine girls, while looking toward Kṛṣṇa playing His flute, saw the reddish *kuṅkuma* on the ground and immediately took it and smeared it over their faces and breasts. In this way they became fully satisfied, although they were not satisfied when their lovers touched their breasts. All material lusty desires can be immediately satisfied if one comes in contact with Kṛṣṇa consciousness.

Another *gopī* began to praise the unique position of Govardhana Hill in this way: "How fortunate is this Govardhana Hill, for it is enjoying the association of Lord Kṛṣṇa and Balarāma who are accustomed to walk on it. Thus Govardhana is always in touch with the lotus feet of the Lord. And because Govardhana Hill is so obliged to Lord Kṛṣṇa and Balarāma, it is supplying different kinds of fruits, roots and herbs, as well as very pleasing crystal water from its lakes, in presentation to the Lord." The best presentation offered by Govardhana Hill, however, was newly grown grass for the cows and calves. Govardhana Hill knew how to please the Lord by pleasing His most beloved associates, the cows and the cowherd boys.

Another *gopī* said that everything appeared wonderful when Kṛṣṇa and Balarāma travelled in the forest of Vṛndāvana playing Their flutes and making intimate friendship with all kinds of moving and nonmoving living creatures. When Kṛṣṇa and Balarāma played on Their transcendental flutes, the moving creatures became stunned and stopped their activities, and the nonmoving living creatures, like trees and plants, began to shiver with ecstasy.

Kṛṣṇa and Balarāma carried binding ropes on Their shoulders and in Their hands, just like ordinary cowherd boys. While milking the cows, the boys bound the hind legs with a small rope. This rope almost always hung from the shoulders of the boys, and it was not absent on the shoulders of Kṛṣṇa and Balarāma. In spite of Their being the Supreme Personality of Godhead, They played exactly like cowherd boys, and therefore everything became wonderful and attractive. While Kṛṣṇa was engaged in tending the cows in the forest of Vṛndāvana or on Govardhana Hill, the *gopīs* in the village were always absorbed in thinking of Him and discussing His different pastimes. This is the perfect example of Kṛṣṇa consciousness: to somehow or other remain always engrossed in thoughts of Kṛṣṇa. The vivid example is always present in the behavior of the *gopīs;* therefore Lord Caitanya declared that no one can worship the Supreme Lord by any method which is better than the method of the *gopīs.* The *gopīs* were not born in very high *brāhmaṇa* or *kṣatriya* families; they were born in the families of *vaiśyas,* and not in big mercantile communities but in the families of cowherd men. They were not very well educated, although they heard all sorts of knowledge from the *brāhmaṇas,* the authorities of Vedic knowledge. The *gopīs'* only purpose was to remain always absorbed in thoughts of Kṛṣṇa.

Thus ends the Bhaktivedanta purport of the Twenty-first Chapter of Kṛṣṇa, *"The Gopīs Attracted by the Flute."*

22 / Stealing the Garments of the Unmarried Gopī Girls

According to Vedic civilization, unmarried girls from ten to fourteen years of age are supposed to worship either Lord Śiva or the goddess Durgā in order to get a nice husband. But the unmarried girls of Vṛndāvana were already attracted by the beauty of Kṛṣṇa. They were, however, engaged in the worship of the goddess Durgā in the beginning of the *hemanta* season (just prior to the winter season). The first month of *hemanta* is called Agrahāyana (October-November), and at that time all the unmarried *gopīs* of Vṛndāvana began to worship goddess Durgā with a vow. They first ate *haviṣyānna,* a kind of foodstuff prepared by boiling together mung dahl and rice without any spices or turmeric. According to Vedic injunction, this kind of foodstuff is recommended to purify the body before one enacts á ritualistic ceremony. All the unmarried *gopīs* in Vṛndāvana used to daily worship goddess Kātyāyanī early in the morning after taking bath in the River Yamunā. Kātyāyanī is another name for goddess Durgā. The goddess is worshiped by preparing a doll made out of sand mixed with earth from the bank of the Yamunā. It is recommended in the Vedic scriptures that a deity may be made from different kinds of material elements; it can be painted, made of metal, made of jewels, made of wood, earth or stone or can be conceived within the heart of the worshiper. The Māyāvādī philosopher takes all these forms of the deity to be imaginary, but actually they are accepted in the Vedic literatures to be identical with either the Supreme Lord or a respective demigod.

The unmarried *gopīs* used to prepare the deity of goddess Durgā and worship it with *candana* pulp, garlands, incense lamps and all kinds of presentations—fruits, grains and twigs of plants. After worshiping, it is the custom to pray for some benediction. The unmarried girls used to pray with great devotion to goddess Kātyāyanī, addressing her as follows: "O supreme eternal energy of the Personality of Godhead, O supreme mystic power, O supreme controller of this material world, O goddess, please be kind to us and arrange for our marriage with the son of Nanda Mahārāja, Kṛṣṇa." The Vaiṣṇavas generally do not worship any demigods. Śrīla Narottama dāsa Ṭhākur has strictly forbidden all worship of the demigods for anyone who wants to advance in pure devotional service. Yet the *gopīs,* who are beyond compare in their affection for Kṛṣṇa, were seen to worship Durgā. The worshipers of demigods also sometimes mention that the *gopīs* also worshiped goddess Durgā, but we must understand the purpose of the *gopīs.* Generally, people worship goddess Durgā for some material benediction. Here, the *gopīs* prayed to the goddess to become wives of Lord Kṛṣṇa. The purport is that if Kṛṣṇa is the center of activity, a devotee can adopt any means to achieve that goal. The *gopīs* could adopt any means to satisfy or serve Kṛṣṇa. That was the superexcellent characteristic of the *gopīs.* They worshiped goddess Durgā completely for one month in order to have Kṛṣṇa as their husband. Every day they prayed for Kṛṣṇa, the son of Nanda Mahārāja, to become their husband.

Early in the morning, the *gopīs* used to go to the bank of the Yamunā to take bath. They would assemble together, capturing each other's hands, and loudly sing of the wonderful pastimes of Kṛṣṇa. It is an old system among Indian girls and women that when they take bath in the river they place their garments on the bank and dip into the water completely naked. The portion of the river where the girls and women take bath was strictly prohibited to any male member, and this is still the system. The Supreme Personality of Godhead, knowing the minds of the unmarried young *gopīs,* benedicted them with their desired objective. They had prayed for Kṛṣṇa to become their husband, and Kṛṣṇa wanted to fulfill their desires.

At the end of the month, Kṛṣṇa, along with His friends, appeared on the scene. Another name of Kṛṣṇa is Yogeśvara, or master of all mystic powers. By practicing meditation, the *yogī* can study the psychic movement of other men, and certainly Kṛṣṇa could understand the desire of the *gopīs.* Appearing on the scene, Kṛṣṇa immediately collected all the garments of the *gopīs,* climbed up in a nearby tree, and with smiling face began to speak to them.

"My dear girls," He said. "Please come here one after another and pray for your garments and then take them away. I'm not joking with you. I'm just telling the truth. I have no desire to play any joke with you, for you have observed the regulative principles for one month by worshiping goddess Kātyāyanī. Please do not come here all at once. Come alone; I want to see each of you in your complete beauty, for you all have thin waists. I have requested you to come alone. Now please comply."

When the girls in the water heard such joking words from Kṛṣṇa, they began to look at one another and smile. They were very joyous to hear such a request from Kṛṣṇa because they were already in love with Him. Out of shyness, they looked at one another, but they could not come out of the water because they were naked. Due to remaining in the water for a long time, they felt cold and were shivering, yet upon hearing the pleasing and joking words of Govinda, their minds were perturbed with great joy. They began to tell Kṛṣṇa, "Dear son of Nanda Mahārāja, please do not joke with us in that way. It is completely unjust to us. You are a very respectable boy because You are the son of Nanda Mahārāja, and You are very dear to us, but You should not play this joke on us because now we are all shivering from the cold water. Kindly deliver our garments immediately, otherwise we shall suffer." They then began to appeal to Kṛṣṇa with great submission. "Dear Śyāmasundara," they said, "we are all Your eternal servitors. Whatever You order us to do, we are obliged to perform without hesitation because we consider it our religious duty. But if You insist on putting this proposal to us, which is impossible to perform, then certainly we will have to go to Nanda Mahārāja and lodge a complaint against You. If Nanda Mahārāja does not take action, then we shall tell King Kaṁsa about Your misbehavior."

Upon hearing this appeal by the unmarried *gopīs,* Kṛṣṇa answered, "My dear girls, if you think that you are My eternal servitors and you are always ready to execute My order, then My request is that, with your smiling faces, you please come here alone, one after another, and take away your garments. If you do not come here, however, and if you lodge complaints to My father, I shall not care anyway, for I know My father is old and cannot take any action against Me."

When the *gopīs* saw that Kṛṣṇa was strong and determined, they had no alternative but to abide by His order. One after another they came out of the water, but because they were completely naked, they tried to cover their nakedness by placing their left hand over their pubic area. In that posture they were all shivering. Their simple presentation was so pure that Lord Kṛṣṇa immediately became pleased with them. All the unmarried *gopīs* who prayed to Kātyāyanī to have Kṛṣṇa as their husband were thus satisfied. A woman cannot be naked before any male except her husband. The unmarried *gopīs* desired Kṛṣṇa as their husband, and He fulfilled their desire in this way. Being pleased with them, He took their garments on His shoulder and began to speak as follows. "My dear girls, you have committed a great offense by going naked in the River Yamunā. Because of this, the predominating deity of the Yamunā, Varuṇadeva, has become displeased with you. Please, therefore, just touch your foreheads with folded palms and bow down before the demigod Varuṇa in order to be excused from this offensive act." The *gopīs* were all simple souls, and whatever Kṛṣṇa said they took to be true. In order to be freed from the wrath of Varuṇadeva, as well as to fulfill the desired end of their vows and ultimately to please their worshipable Lord, Kṛṣṇa, they immediately abided by His order. Thus they became the greatest lovers of Kṛṣṇa, and His most obedient servitors.

Nothing can compare to the Kṛṣṇa consciousness of the *gopīs.* Actually, the *gopīs* did not care for Varuṇa or any other demigod; they only wanted to satisfy Kṛṣṇa. Kṛṣṇa became very ingratiated and satisfied by the simple dealings of the *gopīs,* and He immediately delivered their respective garments, one after another. Although Kṛṣṇa cheated the young unmarried *gopīs* and made them stand naked before Him and enjoyed joking words with them, and although He treated them just like dolls and stole their garments, they were still pleased with Him and never lodged complaints against Him. This attitude of the *gopīs* is described by Lord Caitanya Mahāprabhu when He prays, "My dear Lord Kṛṣṇa, You may embrace me or trample me under Your feet, or You may make me brokenhearted by never being present before me. Whatever You like, You can do, because You have complete freedom to act. But in spite of all Your dealings, You are my Lord eternally, and I have no other worshipable object." This is the attitude of the *gopīs* toward Kṛṣṇa.

Lord Kṛṣṇa was pleased with them, and since they all desired to have Him as their husband, He told them, "My dear well-behaved girls, I know of your desire for Me and why you worship goddess Kātyāyanī, and I completely approve of your action. Anyone whose full consciousness is always absorbed in Me, even if in lust, is elevated. As a fried seed cannot fructify, so any desire in connection with My loving service cannot produce any fruitive result, as in ordinary *karma.*"

There is a statement in the *Brahma-saṁhitā: karmāṇi nirdahati kintu ca bhakti-bhājām.* Everyone is bound by his fruitive activities, but the devotees, because they work completely for the satisfaction of the Lord, suffer no reactions. Similarly, the *gopīs'* attitude toward Kṛṣṇa, although seemingly lusty, should not be considered to be like the lusty desires of ordinary women. The reason is explained by Kṛṣṇa Himself. Activities in devotional service to Kṛṣṇa are transcendental to any fruitive result.

"My dear *gopīs,*" Kṛṣṇa continued, "your desire to have Me as your husband will be fulfilled because with this desire you have worshiped goddess Kātyāyanī. I promise you that during the next autumn season you shall be able to meet with Me, and you shall enjoy Me as your husband."

Taking shelter of the shade of the trees, Kṛṣṇa became very happy. While walking He began to address the inhabitants of Vṛndāvana. "My dear Stokakṛṣṇa, My dear Varūthapa, My dear Bhadrasena, My dear Sudāmā, My dear Subala, My dear Arjuna, My dear Viśāla, My dear Ṛṣabha—just look at these most fortunate trees of Vṛndāvana. They have dedicated their lives to the welfare of others. Individually they are tolerating all kinds of natural disturbances, such as hurricanes, torrents of rain, scorching heat and piercing cold, but they are very careful to relieve our fatigues and give us shelter. My dear friends, I think they are glorified in this birth as trees. They are so careful to give shelter to others that they are like noble, highly elevated charitable men who never deny charity to one who approaches them. No one is denied shelter by these trees. They supply various kinds of facilities to human society, such as leaves, flowers, fruit, shade, roots, bark, flavor extracts and fuel. They are the perfect example of noble life. They are like a noble person who has sacrificed everything possible—his body, mind, activities, intelligence and words—in engaging in the welfare of all living entities."

Thus the Supreme Personality of Godhead walked on the bank of the Yamunā, touching the leaves of the trees and their fruits, flowers and twigs, and praising their glorious welfare activities. Different people may accept certain welfare activities to be beneficial for human society, according to their own views, but the welfare activity that can be rendered to people in general, for eternal benefit, is the spreading of the Kṛṣṇa consciousness movement. Everyone should be prepared to propagate this movement. As instructed by Lord Caitanya, one should be humbler than the grass on the ground and more tolerant than the tree. The toleration of the trees is explained by Lord Kṛṣṇa Himself, and those who are engaged in the preaching of Kṛṣṇa consciousness should learn lessons from the teachings of Lord Kṛṣṇa and Lord Caitanya through Their direct disciplic succession.

While passing through the forest of Vṛndāvana on the bank of the Yamunā, Kṛṣṇa sat down at a beautiful spot and allowed the cows to drink the cold and transparent water of the Yamunā. Being fatigued, the cowherd boys, Kṛṣṇa and Balarāma also drank. After seeing the young *gopīs* taking bath in the Yamunā, Kṛṣṇa passed the rest of the morning with the boys.

Thus ends the Bhaktivedanta purport of the Twenty-second Chapter of Kṛṣṇa, *"Stealing the Garments of the Unmarried Gopī Girls."*

23/ Delivering the Wives of the Brāhmaṇas Who Performed Sacrifices

The morning passed, and the cowherd boys were very hungry because they had not eaten breakfast. They immediately approached Kṛṣṇa and Balarāma and said, "Dear Kṛṣṇa and Balarāma, You are both all-powerful; You can kill many, many demons, but today we are much afflicted with hunger, and this is disturbing us. Please arrange for something that will mitigate our hunger."

Requested in this way by Their friends, Lord Kṛṣṇa and Balarāma immediately showed compassion on certain wives of *brāhmaṇas* who were performing sacrifices. These wives were great devotees of the Lord, and Kṛṣṇa took this opportunity to bless them. He said, "My dear friends, please go to the house of the *brāhmaṇas* nearby. They are now engaged in performing Vedic sacrifices known as *āṅgirasa,* for they desire elevation to heavenly planets. All of you please go to them." Then Lord Kṛṣṇa warned His friends, "These *brāhmaṇas* are not Vaiṣṇavas. They cannot even chant Our names, Kṛṣṇa and Balarāma. They are very busy in chanting the Vedic hymns, although the purpose of Vedic knowledge is to find Me. But because they are not attracted by the names of Kṛṣṇa and Balarāma, you had better not ask them for anything in My name. Better ask for some charity in the name of Balarāma."

Charity is generally given to high class *brāhmaṇas,* but Kṛṣṇa and Balarāma did not appear in a *brāhmaṇa* family. Balarāma was known as the son of Vasudeva, a *kṣatriya,* and Kṛṣṇa was known in Vṛndāvana as the son of Nanda Mahārāja, who was a *vaiśya.* Neither belonged to the *brāhmaṇa* community. Therefore, Kṛṣṇa considered that the *brāhmaṇas* engaged in performing sacrifices might not be induced to give charity to a *kṣatriya* and *vaiśya.* "But at least if you utter the name of Balarāma, they may prefer to give in charity to a *kṣatriya,* rather than to Me, because I am only a *vaiśya.*"

Being thus ordered by the Supreme Personality of Godhead, all the boys went to the *brāhmaṇas* and began to ask for some charity. They approached them with folded hands and fell down on the ground to offer respect. "O earthly gods, kindly hear us who are ordered by Lord Kṛṣṇa and Balarāma. We hope you know Them both very well, and we wish you all good fortune. Kṛṣṇa and Balarāma are tending cows nearby, and we have accompanied Them. We have come to ask for some food from you. You are all *brāhmaṇas* and knowers of religious principles, and if you think that you should give us charity, then give us some food and we shall all eat along with Kṛṣṇa and Balarāma. You are the most respectable *brāhmaṇas* within the human society, and you are expected to know all the principles of religious procedure."

Although the boys were village boys and were not expected to be learned in all the Vedic principles of religious ritual, they hinted that because of their association with Kṛṣṇa and Balarāma, they knew all those principles. When the Supreme Personality of Godhead Kṛṣṇa and Balarāma, asked for food, the boys would immediately deliver it without hesitation because it is stated in the *Bhagavad-gītā* that one should perform *yajña* (sacrifices) only for the satisfaction of Viṣṇu.

The boys continued, "Lord Viṣṇu as Kṛṣṇa and Balarāma is standing waiting, and you should immediately deliver whatever food you have in your stock." They also explained to the *brāhmaṇas* how foodstuffs are to be accepted. Generally, the Vaiṣṇavas, or pure devotees of the Lord, do not take part in ordinary sacrificial performances. But they know very well the ceremonials called *dīkṣā paśusamtha sautrāmnya.* One is permitted to take food after the procedure of *dīkṣā* and before the animal sacrificial ceremony and the *Sautrāmaṇi,* or ceremony in which liquors are also offered. The boys said, "We can take your food at the present stage of your ceremony, for now it will not be prohibitory. So you can deliver us the foodstuff."

Although the companions of Lord Kṛṣṇa and Balarāma were simple cowherd boys, they were in a position to dictate even to the high class *brāhmaṇas* engaged in the Vedic rituals of sacrifices. But the *smārta brāhmaṇas,* who were simply sacrificial-minded, could not understand the dictation of the transcendental devotees of the Lord. They could not even appreciate the begging of the Supreme Lord, Kṛṣṇa and Balarāma. Although they heard all the arguments on behalf of Kṛṣṇa and Balarāma, they did not care for them, and they refused to speak to the boys. Despite being highly elevated in the knowledge of Vedic sacrificial rites, all such nondevotee *brāhmaṇas*, although they think of themselves as very highly elevated, are ignorant, foolish persons. All their activities are useless because they do not know the purpose of the *Vedas,* as it is explained in the *Bhagavad-gītā*: to understand Kṛṣṇa. In spite of their advancement in Vedic knowledge and rituals, they do not understand Kṛṣṇa; therefore their knowledge of the *Vedas* is superficial. Lord Caitanya, therefore, gave His valuable opinion that a person does not have to be born in a *brāhmaṇa* family; if he knows Kṛṣṇa or the science of Kṛṣṇa consciousness, he is more than a *brāhmaṇa,* and he is quite fit to become spiritual master.

There are various details to be observed in the performance of sacrifices, and they are known collectively as *deśa.* They are as follows: *kāla* means the time, *pṛthak dravya,* the different detailed paraphernalia, *mantra,* hymns, *tantra,* scriptural evidences, *agni,* fire, *ṛtvij,* learned performers of sacrifices, *devatā,* the demigods, *vajamāna,* the performer of the sacrifices, *kratu,* the sacrifice itself, and *dharma,* the procedures. All these are for satisfying Kṛṣṇa. It is confirmed that He is the actual enjoyer of all sacrifices because He is directly the Supreme Personality of Godhead and the Supreme Absolute Truth, beyond the conception or speculation of material senses. He is present just like an ordinary human boy. But for persons who identify themselves with this body, it is very difficult to understand Him. The *brāhmaṇas* were very interested in the comforts of this material body and in elevation to the higher planetary residences called *svarga-vāsa.* They were therefore completely unable to understand the position of Kṛṣṇa.

When the boys saw that the *brāhmaṇas* would not speak to them, they became very disappointed. They then returned to Lord Kṛṣṇa and Balarāma and explained everything that had happened. After hearing their statements, the Supreme Personality began to smile. He told them that they should not be sorry for being refused by the *brāhmaṇas* because that is the way of begging. He convinced them that while one is engaged in collecting or begging, one should not think that he will be successful everywhere. He may be unsuccessful in some places, but that should not be cause for disappointment. Lord Kṛṣṇa then asked all the boys to go again, but this time to the wives of those *brāhmaṇas* engaged in sacrifices. He also informed them that these wives were great devotees. "They are always absorbed in thinking of Us. Go there and ask for some food in My name and the name of Balarāma, and I am sure that they will deliver you as much food as you desire."

Carrying out Kṛṣṇa's order, the boys immediately went to the wives of the *brāhmaṇas.* They found the wives sitting inside their house. They were very beautifully decorated with ornaments. After offering them all respectful obeisances, the boys said, "Dear mothers, please accept our humble obeisances and hear our statement. May we inform you that Lord Kṛṣṇa and Balarāma are nearby. They have come here with the cows, and you may know also that we have come here under Their instructions. All of us are very hungry; therefore, we have come to you for some food. Please give us something to eat for Kṛṣṇa, Balarāma and ourselves."

Immediately upon hearing this, the wives of the *brāhmaṇas* became anxious for Kṛṣṇa and Balarāma. These reactions were spontaneous. They did not have to be convinced of the importance of Kṛṣṇa and Balarāma; immediately upon hearing Their names, they became very anxious to see Them. Being advanced by thinking of Kṛṣṇa constantly, they were performing the greatest form of mystic meditation. All the wives then became very busily engaged in filling up different pots with nice foodstuff. Due to the performance of the sacrifice, the various food was all very palatable. After collecting a feast, they prepared to go to Kṛṣṇa, their most lovable object, exactly in the way rivers flow to the sea.

For a long time the wives had been anxious to see Kṛṣṇa. However, when they were preparing to leave home to go see Him, their husbands, fathers, sons and relatives asked them not to go. But the wives did not comply. When a devotee is called by the attraction of Kṛṣṇa, he does not care for bodily ties. The women entered the forest of Vṛndāvana on the bank of the Yamunā, which was verdant with vegetation and newly grown vines and flowers. Within that forest, they saw Kṛṣṇa and Balarāma engaged in tending the cows, along with Their very affectionate boy friends.

The *brāhmaṇas'* wives saw Kṛṣṇa putting on a garment glittering like gold. He wore a nice garland of forest flowers and a peacock feather on His head. He was also painted with the minerals found in Vṛndāvana, and He looked exactly like a dancing actor on a theatrical stage. They saw Him keeping one hand on the shoulder of His friend, and in His other hand, He was holding a lotus flower. His ears were decorated with lilies, He wore marks of *tilaka,* and He was smiling charmingly. With their very eyes, the wives of the *brāhmaṇas* saw the Supreme Personality of Godhead, of whom they had heard so much, who was so dear to them, and in whom their minds were always absorbed. Now they saw Him eye to eye and face to face, and Kṛṣṇa entered within their hearts through their eyes.

They began to embrace Kṛṣṇa to their hearts' content, and the distress of separation was mitigated immediately. They were just like great sages who, by their advancement of knowledge, merge into the existence of the Supreme. As the Supersoul living in everyone's heart, Lord Kṛṣṇa could understand their minds; they had come to Him despite all the protests of their relatives, fathers, husbands, brothers, and all the duties of household affairs. They came just to see Him who was their life and soul. They were actually following Kṛṣṇa's instruction in the *Bhagavad-gītā:* one should surrender to Him, giving up all varieties of occupational and religious duties. The wives of the *brāhmaṇas* actually carried out the instruction of the *Bhagavad-gītā* in total. He therefore began to speak to them, smiling very magnificently. It should be noted in this connection that when Kṛṣṇa entered into the wives' hearts and when they embraced Him and felt the transcendental bliss of being merged with Him, the Supreme Lord Kṛṣṇa did not lose His identity, nor did the individual wives lose theirs. The individuality of both the Lord and the wives remained, yet they felt oneness in existence. When a lover submits to his lover without any pinch of personal consideration, that is called oneness. Lord Caitanya has taught us this feeling of oneness in His *Śikṣāṣṭaka:* Kṛṣṇa may act freely, doing whatever He likes, but the devotee should always be in oneness or in agreement with His desires. That oneness was exhibited by the wives of the *brāhmaṇas* in their love for Kṛṣṇa.

Kṛṣṇa welcomed them with the following words: "My dear wives of the *brāhmaṇas*, you are all very fortunate and welcomed here. Please let Me know what I can do for you. Your coming here, neglecting all the restrictions and hindrances of relatives, fathers, brothers and husbands, in order to see Me, is completely befitting. One who does this actually knows his self interest, because rendering transcendental loving service unto Me, without motive or restriction, is actually auspicious for the living entities."

Lord Kṛṣṇa here confirms that the highest perfectional stage of the conditional soul is surrender to Him. One must give up all other responsibilities. This complete surrender unto the Supreme Personality of Godhead is the most auspicious path for the conditioned soul because the Supreme Lord is the supreme objective of love. Everyone is loving Kṛṣṇa ultimately, but realization is according to the advancement of his knowledge. One comes to understand that his self is the spirit soul, and the spirit soul is nothing but a part and parcel of the Supreme Lord; therefore the Supreme Lord is the ultimate goal of love, and thus one should surrender unto Him. This surrender is considered auspicious for the conditioned soul. Our life, property, home, wife, children, house, country, society and all paraphernalia which are very dear to us are expansions of the Supreme Personality of Godhead. He is the central object of love because He gives us all bliss, expanding Himself in so many ways according to our different situations, namely bodily, mental or spiritual.

"My dear wives of the *brāhmaṇas,*" Kṛṣṇa said. "You can now return to your homes. Engage yourselves in sacrificial activities and be engaged in the service of your husbands and household affairs so that your husbands will be pleased with you, and the sacrifice which they have begun will be properly executed. After all, your husbands are householders, and without your help how can they execute their prescribed duties?"

The wives of the *brāhmaṇas* replied, "Dear Lord, this sort of instruction does not befit You. Your eternal promise is that You will always protect Your devotees, and now You must fulfill this promise. Anyone who comes and surrenders unto You never goes back to the conditioned life of material existence. We expect that You will now fulfill Your promise. We have surrendered unto Your lotus feet, which are covered by the *tulasī* leaves, so we have no more desire to return to the company of our so-called relatives, friends, and society and give up the shelter of Your lotus feet. And what shall we do, returning home? Our husbands, brothers, fathers, sons, mothers and our friends do not expect to see us because we have already left them all. Therefore we have no shelter to return to. Please, therefore, do not ask us to return home, but arrange for our stay under Your lotus feet so that we can eternally live under Your protection."

The Supreme Personality of Godhead replied, "My dear wives, rest assured that your husbands will not neglect you on your return, nor will your brothers, sons, or fathers refuse to accept you. Because you are My pure devotees, not only your relatives but also people in general, as well as the demigods, will be satisfied with you." Kṛṣṇa is situated as the Supersoul in everyone's heart. So if someone becomes a pure devotee of Lord Kṛṣṇa, he immediately becomes pleasing to everyone. The pure devotee of Lord Kṛṣṇa is never inimical to anyone. A sane person cannot be an enemy of a pure devotee. "Transcendental love for Me does not depend upon bodily connection," Kṛṣṇa said further, "but anyone whose mind is always absorbed in Me will surely, very soon, come to Me for My eternal association."

After being instructed by the Supreme Personality of Godhead, all the wives again returned home to their respective husbands. Pleased to see their wives back home, the *brāhmaṇas* executed the performances of sacrifices by sitting together, as it is enjoined in the *śāstras*. According to Vedic principle, religious rituals must be executed by the husband and wife together. When the *brāhmaṇas'* wives returned, the sacrifice was duly and nicely executed. One of the *brāhmaṇas'* wives, however, who was forcibly checked from going to see Kṛṣṇa, began to remember Him as she heard of His bodily features. Being completely absorbed in His thought, she gave up her material body conditioned by the laws of nature.

Śrī Govinda, the ever-joyful Personality of Godhead, revealed His transcendental pastimes, appearing just like an ordinary human being, and enjoyed the food offered by the wives of the *brāhmaṇas*. In this way, He attracted common persons to Kṛṣṇa consciousness. He attracted to His words and beauty all the cows, cowherd boys and damsels in Vṛndāvana.

After the return of their wives from Kṛṣṇa, the *brāhmaṇas* engaged in the performance of sacrifices began to regret their sinful activities in refusing food to the Supreme Personality of Godhead. They could finally understand their mistake; engaged in the performance of Vedic rituals, they had neglected the Supreme Personality of Godhead who had appeared just like an ordinary human being and asked for some food. They began to condemn themselves after seeing the faith and devotion of their wives. They regretted very much that, although their wives were elevated to the platform of pure devotional service, they themselves could not understand even a little bit of how to love and offer transcendental loving service to the Supreme Soul. They began to talk among themselves. "To hell with our being born *brāhmaṇas!* To hell with our learning all Vedic literatures! To hell with our performing great sacrifices and observing all the rules and regulations! To hell with our family! To hell with our expert service in performing the rituals exactly to the description of scriptures! To hell with it all, for we have not developed transcendental loving service to the Supreme Personality of Godhead, who is beyond the speculation of the mind, body and senses."

The learned *brāhmaṇas*, expert in Vedic ritualistic performances, were properly regretful, because without developing Kṛṣṇa consciousness, all discharge of religious duties is simply a waste of time and energy. They continued to talk among themselves; "The external energy of Kṛṣṇa is so strong that it can create illusion to overcome even the greatest mystic *yogī*. Although we expert *brāhmaṇas* are considered to be the teachers of all other sections of human society, we also have been illusioned by the external energy. Just see how fortunate these women are who have so devotedly dedicated their lives to the Supreme Personality of Godhead, Kṛṣṇa. They could easily give up their family connection, which is so difficult to do. Family life is just like a dark well for the continuation of material miseries."

Women in general, being very simple in heart, can very easily take to Kṛṣṇa consciousness, and when they develop love of Kṛṣṇa they can easily get liberation from the clutches of *māyā*, which is very difficult for even so-called intelligent and learned men to surpass. According to Vedic injunction, women are not allowed to undergo the purificatory process of initiation by the sacred thread, nor are they allowed to live as *brahmacāriṇī* in the *āśrama* of the spiritual master; nor are they advised to undergo the strict disciplinary procedure; nor are they very much expert in discussing philosophy or self-realization. And by nature they are not very pure; nor are they very much attached to auspicious activities. "But how wonderful it is that they have developed transcendental love for Kṛṣṇa, the Lord of all mystic *yogīs!*" the *brāhmaṇas* exclaimed. "They have surpassed all of us in firm faith and devotion unto Kṛṣṇa. Being too attached to the materialistic way of life, although we are considered to be masters in all purificatory processes, we did not actually know what the goal is. Even though we were reminded of Kṛṣṇa and Balarāma by the cowherd boys, we disregarded Them. We think now that it was simply a trick of mercy upon us by the Supreme Personality of Godhead that He sent His friends to beg foodstuff from us. Otherwise, He had no need to send them. He could have satisfied their hunger then and there just by willing to do so."

If someone denies Kṛṣṇa's self-sufficiency on hearing that He was tending the cows for livelihood, or if someone doubts His not being in need of the foodstuff, thinking that He was actually hungry, then one should understand that the goddess of fortune is always engaged in His service. In this way the goddess can break her faulty habit of restlessness. In Vedic literatures like *Brahma-saṁhitā* it is stated that Kṛṣṇa is served in His abode with great respect by not only one goddess of fortune but many thousands. Therefore it is simply illusion for one to think that Kṛṣṇa begged food from the *brāhmaṇas*. It was actually a trick to show them the mercy of accepting Him in pure devotional service. The Vedic ceremonial paraphernalia, the suitable place, suitable time, different grades of articles for performing ritualistic ceremonies, the Vedic hymns, the priest who is able to perform such sacrifice, the fire and the demigods, the performer of the sacrifice and the religious principles are all meant for understanding Kṛṣṇa, for Kṛṣṇa is the Supreme Personality of Godhead. He is the Supreme Lord Viṣṇu, and the Lord of all mystic *yogīs.*

"Because He has appeared as a child in the dynasty of the Yadus, we were so foolish that we could not understand that He is the Supreme Personality of Godhead," the *brāhmaṇas* said. "But on the other hand, we are very proud because we have such exalted wives who have developed pure transcendental service of the Lord without being shackled by our rigid position. Let us therefore offer our respectful obeisances unto the lotus feet of Lord Kṛṣṇa, under whose illusory energy, called *māyā*, we are absorbed in fruitive activities. We therefore pray to the Lord to be kind enough to excuse us because we are simply captivated by His external energy. We transgressed His order without knowing His transcendental glories."

The *brāhmaṇas* repented for their sinful activities. They wanted to go personally to offer their obeisances unto Him, but being afraid of Kaṁsa, they could not go. In other words, it is very difficult for one to surrender fully unto the Personality of Godhead without being purified by devotional service. The example of the learned *brāhmaṇas* and their wives is vivid. The wives of the *brāhmaṇas*, because they were infused by pure devotional service, did not care for any kind of opposition. They immediately went to Kṛṣṇa. But although the *brāhmaṇas* had come to know the supremacy of the Lord and were repenting, they were still afraid of King Kaṁsa because they were too addicted to fruitive activities.

Thus ends the Bhaktivedanta purport of the Twenty-third Chapter of Kṛṣṇa, *"Delivering the Wives of the Brāhmaṇas Who Performed Sacrifices."*

24 / Worshiping Govardhana Hill

While engaged with the *brāhmaṇas* who were too involved in the performance of Vedic sacrifices, Kṛṣṇa and Balarāma also saw that the cowherd men were preparing a similar sacrifice in order to pacify Indra, the King of heaven, who is responsible for supplying water. As stated in the *Caitanya-caritāmṛta,* a devotee of Kṛṣṇa has strong and firm faith in the understanding that if he is simply engaged in Kṛṣṇa consciousness and Kṛṣṇa's transcendental loving service, then he is freed from all other obligations. A pure devotee of Lord Kṛṣṇa doesn't have to perform any of the ritualistic functions enjoined in the *Vedas*; nor is he required to worship any demigods. Being a devotee of Lord Kṛṣṇa, one is understood to have performed all kinds of Vedic rituals and all kinds of worship to the demigods. Just by performing the Vedic ritualistic ceremonies or worshiping the demigods, one does not develop devotional service for Kṛṣṇa. But one who is engaged fully in the service of the Lord has already finished all Vedic injunctions.

Kṛṣṇa ordered a stop to all such activities by His devotees, for He wanted to firmly establish exclusive devotional service during His presence in Vṛndāvana. Kṛṣṇa knew that the cowherd men were preparing for the Indra sacrifice because He is the omniscient Personality of Godhead, but as a matter of etiquette, he began to inquire with great honor and submission from elder personalities like Mahārāja Nanda and others.

Kṛṣṇa asked His father, "My dear father, what is this arrangement going on for a great sacrifice? What is the result of such sacrifice, and for whom is it meant? How is it performed? Will you kindly let Me know? I am very anxious to know this procedure, so please explain to Me the purpose of this sacrifice." Upon this inquiry, His father, Nanda Mahārāja, remained silent, thinking that his young boy would not be able to understand the intricacies of performing the *yajña*. Kṛṣṇa, however, persisted: "My dear father, for those who are liberal and saintly, there is no secrecy. They do not think anyone to be a friend or enemy because they are always open to everyone. And even for those who are not so liberal, nothing should be secret for the family members and friends, although secrecy may be maintained for persons who are inimical. Therefore you cannot keep any secrets from Me. All persons are engaged in fruitive activities. Some know what these activities are, and they know the result, and some execute activities without knowing the purpose or the result. A person who acts with full knowledge gets the full result; one who acts without knowledge does not get such a perfect result. Therefore, please let Me know the purpose of the sacrifice which you are going to perform. Is it according to Vedic injunction? Or is it simply a popular ceremony? Kindly let Me know in detail about the sacrifice."

On hearing this inquiry from Kṛṣṇa, Mahārāja Nanda replied, "My dear boy, this ceremonial performance is more or less traditional. Because rainfall is due to the mercy of King Indra and the clouds are his representatives, and because water is so important for our living, we must show some gratitude to the controller of this rainfall, Mahārāja Indra. We are arranging, therefore, to pacify King Indra, because he has very kindly sent us clouds to pour down sufficient quantity of rain for successful agricultural activities. Water is very important; without rainfall we cannot farm or produce grains. We cannot live if there is no rainfall. It is necessary for successful religious ceremonies, economic development, and, ultimately, liberation. Therefore we should not give up the traditional ceremonial function; if one gives it up, being influenced by lust, or greed or fear, then it does not look very good for him."

After hearing this, Kṛṣṇa, the Supreme Personality of Godhead, in the presence of His father and all the cowherd men of Vṛndāvana, spoke in such a way as to make heavenly King Indra very angry. He suggested that they forego the sacrifice. His reasons for discouraging the sacrifice performed to please Indra were twofold. First, as stated in the *Bhagavad-gītā,* there is no need to worship the demigods for any material advancement; all results derived from worshiping the demigods are simply temporary, and only those who are less intelligent are interested with temporary results. Secondly, whatever temporary result one derives from worshiping the demigods is actually granted by the permission of the Supreme Personality of Godhead. It is clearly stated in the *Bhagavad-gītā, mayaiva vihitān hi tān.* Whatever benefit is supposed to be derived from the demigods is actually bestowed by the Supreme Personality of Godhead. Without the permission of the Supreme Personality of Godhead, one cannot bestow any benefit upon others. But sometimes the demigods become puffed up by the influence of material nature; thinking themselves as all in all, they try to forget the supremacy of the Supreme Personality of Godhead. In the *Śrīmad-Bhāgavatam*, it is clearly stated that in this instance Kṛṣṇa wanted to make King Indra angry. Kṛṣṇa's advent was especially meant for the annihilation of the demons and protection of the devotees. King Indra was certainly a devotee, not a demon, but because he was puffed up, Kṛṣṇa wanted to teach him a lesson. He first tried to make Indra angry by stopping the Indra Pūjā which was arranged by the cowherd men in Vṛndāvana.

With this purpose in mind, Kṛṣṇa began to talk as if He were an atheist supporting the philosophy of *karma-mīmāṁsā*. Advocates of this type of philosophy do not accept the supreme authority of the Personality of Godhead. They put forward the argument that if anyone works nicely, the result is sure to come. Their opinion is that even if there is a God who gives man the result of his fruitive activities, there is no need to worship Him because unless man works He cannot bestow any good result. They say that instead of worshiping a demigod or God, people should give attention to their own duties, and thus the good result will surely come. Lord Kṛṣṇa began to speak to His father according to these principles of the *karma-mīmāṁsā* philosophy. "My dear father," He said, "I don't think you need to worship any demigod for the successful performance of your agricultural activities. Every living being is born according to his past *karma* and leaves this life simply taking the result of his present *karma*. Everyone is born in different types or species of life according to his past activities, and he gets his next birth according to the activities of this life. Different grades of material happiness and distress, comforts and disadvantages of life, are different results of different kinds of activities, either from the past or present life."

Mahārāja Nanda and other elderly members argued that without satisfying the predominating god, one cannot derive any good result simply by material activities. This is actually the fact. For example, it is sometimes found that, in spite of first-class medical help and treatment by a first-class physician, a diseased person dies. It is concluded, therefore, that first-class medical treatment or the attempts of a first-class physician are not in themselves the cause for curing a patient; there must be the hand of the Supreme Personality of Godhead. Similarly, a father's and mother's taking care of their children is not the cause of the children's comfort. Sometimes it is found that in spite of all care by the parents, the children go bad or succumb to death. Therefore material causes are not sufficient for results.

There must be the sanction of the Supreme Personality of Godhead. Nanda Mahārāja therefore advocated that, in order to get good results for agricultural activities, they must satisfy Indra, the superintending deity of the rain supply. Lord Kṛṣṇa nullified this argument, saying that the demigods give results only to persons who have executed their prescribed duties. The demigods cannot give any good results to the person who has not executed the prescribed duties; therefore demigods are dependent on the execution of duties and are not absolute in awarding good results to anyone.

"My dear father, there is no need to worship the demigod Indra," Lord Kṛṣṇa said. "Everyone has to achieve the result of his own work. We can actually see that one becomes busy according to the natural tendency of his work; and according to that natural tendency, all living entities—either human beings or demigods—achieve their respective results. All living entities achieve higher or lower bodies and create enemies, friends or neutral parties only because of their different kinds of work. One should be careful to discharge duties according to his natural instinct and not divert attention to the worship of various demigods. The demigods will be satisfied by proper execution of all duties, so there is no need to worship them. Let us, rather, perform our prescribed duties very nicely. Actually one cannot be happy without executing his proper prescribed duty. One who does not, therefore, properly discharge his prescribed duties, is compared with an unchaste woman. The proper prescribed duty of the *brāhmaṇas* is the study of the *Vedas;* the proper duty of the royal order, the *kṣatriyas,* is engagement in protecting the citizens; the proper duty of the *vaiśya* community is agriculture, trade and protection of the cows; and the proper duty of the *śūdras* is service to the higher classes, namely the *brāhmaṇas, kṣatriyas,* and *vaiśyas.* We belong to the *vaiśya* community, and our proper duty is to farm, or to trade with the agricultural produce, to protect cows, or take to banking."

Kṛṣṇa identified Himself with the *vaiśya* community because Nanda Mahārāja was protecting many cows, and Kṛṣṇa was taking care of them. He enumerated four kinds of business engagements for the *vaiśya* community, namely agriculture, trade, protection of cows and banking. Although the *vaiśyas* can take to any of these occupations, the men of Vṛndāvana were engaged primarily in the protection of cows.

Kṛṣṇa further explained to His father: "This cosmic manifestation is going on under the influence of three modes of material nature—goodness, passion, and ignorance. These three modes are the causes of creation, maintenance, and destruction. The cloud is caused by the action of the mode of passion; therefore it is the mode of passion which causes the rainfall. And after the rainfall, the living entities derive the result—success in agricultural work. What, then, has Indra to do in this affair? Even if you do not please Indra, what can he do? We do not derive any special benefit from Indra. Even if he is there, he pours water on the ocean also, where there is no need of water. So he is pouring water on the ocean or on the land; it does not depend on our worshiping him. As far as we are concerned, we do not need to go to another city or village or foreign country. There are palatial buildings in the cities, but we are satisfied living in this forest of Vṛndāvana. Our specific relationship is with Govardhana Hill and Vṛndāvana forest and nothing more. I therefore request you, My dear father, to begin a sacrifice which will satisfy the local *brāhmaṇas* and Govardhana Hill, and let us have nothing to do with Indra."

After hearing this statement by Kṛṣṇa, Nanda Mahārāja replied, "My dear boy, since You are asking, I shall arrange for a separate sacrifice for the local *brāhmaṇas* and Govardhana Hill. But for the present let me execute this sacrifice known as *Indra-yajña."*

But Kṛṣṇa replied, "My dear father, don't delay. The sacrifice you propose for Govardhana and the local *brāhmaṇas* will take much time. Better take the arrangement and paraphernalia you have already made for sacrificing Indra-yajña and immediately engage it to satisfy Govardhana Hill and the local *brāhmaṇas."*

Mahārāja Nanda finally relented. The cowherd men then inquired from Kṛṣṇa how He wanted the *yajña* performed, and Kṛṣṇa gave them the following directions. "Prepare very nice foodstuffs of all descriptions from the grains and ghee collected for the *yajña.* Prepare rice, dahl, then halavah, *pākorā, puri* and all kinds of milk preparations like sweet rice, sweetballs, *sandeśa, rasagullā* and *lāḍḍu* and invite the learned *brāhmaṇas* who can chant the Vedic hymns and offer oblations to the fire. The *brāhmaṇas* should be given all kinds of grains in charity. Then decorate all the cows and feed them well. After performing this, give money in charity to the *brāhmaṇas.* As far as the lower animals are concerned, such as the dogs, and the lower grades of people, such as the *cāṇḍālas,* or the fifth class of men who are considered untouchable, they also may be given sumptuous *prasādam.* After giving nice grasses to the cows, the sacrifice known as *Govardhana Pūjā* may immediately begin. This sacrifice will very much satisfy Me."

In this statement, Lord Kṛṣṇa practically described the whole economy of the *vaiśya* community. In all communities of human society, and in the animal kingdom, among the cows, dogs, goats, etc., everyone has his part to play. Each is to work in cooperation for the total benefit of all society, which includes not only animate objects but also inanimate objects like hills and land. The *vaiśya* community is specifically responsible for the economic improvement of the society by producing grains, by giving protection to the cows, by transporting food when needed, and by banking and finance.

From this statement we learn also that the cats and dogs, although not so important, are not to be neglected. Cow protection is actually more important than protection of cats and dogs. Another hint we get from this statement is that the *cāṇḍālas* or the untouchables are also not to be neglected by the higher classes. Everyone is important, but some are directly responsible for the advancement of human society, and some are only indirectly responsible. However, when Kṛṣṇa consciousness is there, then everyone's total benefit is taken care of.

The sacrifice known as Govardhana Pūjā is observed in the Kṛṣṇa consciousness movement. Lord Caitanya has recommended that since Kṛṣṇa is worshipable, so His land, Vṛndāvana and Govardhana Hill, are also worshipable. To confirm this statement, Lord Kṛṣṇa said that Govardhana Pūjā is as good as worship of Him. From that day, the Govardhana Pūjā has been still going on and is known as *Annakūṭa.* In all the temples of Vṛndāvana or outside of Vṛndāvana, huge quantities of food are prepared in this ceremony and are very sumptuously distributed to the general population. Sometimes the food is thrown to the crowds, and they enjoy collecting it off the ground. From these instances, we can understand that *prasādam* offered to Kṛṣṇa never becomes polluted or contaminated, even if it is thrown on the ground. The people, therefore, collect it and eat with great satisfaction.

The Supreme Personality of Godhead, Kṛṣṇa, therefore advised the cowherd men to stop the Indra-yajña and begin the Govardhana Pūjā in order to chastise Indra who was very much puffed up at being the supreme controller of the heavenly planets. The honest and simple cowherd men headed by Nanda Mahārāja accepted Kṛṣṇa's proposal and executed in detail everything He advised. They performed Govardhana worship and circumambulation of the hill. (Following the inauguration of Govardhana Pūjā, people in Vṛndāvana still dress nicely and assemble near Govardhana Hill to offer worship and circumambulate the hill, leading their cows all around.) According to the instruction of Lord Kṛṣṇa, Nanda Mahārāja and the cowherd men called in learned *brāhmaṇas* and began to worship Govardhana Hill by chanting Vedic hymns and offering *prasādam.* The inhabitants of Vṛndāvana assembled together, decorated their cows and gave them grass. Keeping the cows in front, they began to circumambulate Govardhana Hill. The *gopīs* also dressed themselves very luxuriantly and sat in bull-driven carts, chanting the glories of Kṛṣṇa's pastimes. Assembled there to act as priests for Govardhana Pūjā, the *brāhmaṇas* offered their blessings to the cowherd men and their wives, the *gopīs*. When everything was complete, Kṛṣṇa assumed a great transcendental form and declared to the inhabitants of Vṛndāvana that He was Himself Govardhana Hill in order to convince the devotees that Govardhana Hill and Kṛṣṇa Himself are identical. Then Kṛṣṇa began to eat all the food offered there. The identity of Kṛṣṇa and Govardhana Hill is still honored, and great devotees take rocks from Govardhana Hill and worship them exactly as they worship the Deity of Kṛṣṇa in the temples. Devotees therefore collect small rocks or pebbles from Govardhana Hill and worship them at home, because this worship is as good as Deity worship. The form of Kṛṣṇa who began to eat the offerings was separately constituted, and Kṛṣṇa Himself along with other inhabitants of Vṛndāvana began to offer obeisances to the Deity as well as Govardhana Hill. In offering obeisances to the huge form of Kṛṣṇa Himself and Govardhana Hill, Kṛṣṇa declared, "Just see how Govardhana Hill has assumed this huge form and is favoring us by accepting all the offerings." Kṛṣṇa also declared at that meeting, "One who neglects the worship of Govardhana Pūjā, as I am personally conducting it, will not be happy. There are many snakes on Govardhana Hill, and persons neglecting the prescribed duty of Govardhana Pūjā will be bitten by these snakes and killed. In order to assure the good fortune of the cows and themselves, all people of Vṛndāvana near Govardhana must worship the hill, as prescribed by Me."

Thus performing the Govardhana Pūjā sacrifice, all the inhabitants of Vṛndāvana followed the instructions of Kṛṣṇa, the son of Vasudeva, and afterwards they returned to their respective homes.

Thus ends the Bhaktivedanta purport of the Twenty-fourth Chapter of Kṛṣṇa, *"Worshiping Govardhana Hill."*

25 / Devastating Rainfall in Vṛndāvana

When Indra understood that the sacrifice offered by the cowherd men in Vṛndāvana was stopped by Kṛṣṇa, he became angry, and he vented his anger upon the inhabitants of Vṛndāvana, who were headed by Nanda Mahārāja, although Indra knew perfectly well that Kṛṣṇa was personally protecting them. As the director of different kinds of clouds, Indra called for the *sāṁvartaka.* This cloud is invited when there is a need to devastate the whole cosmic manifestation. The *sāṁvartaka* was ordered by Indra to go over Vṛndāvana and inundate the whole area with an extensive flood. Demonically, Indra thought himself to be the all-powerful supreme personality. When demons become very powerful, they defy the supreme controller, Personality of Godhead. Indra, though not a demon, was puffed up by his material position, and he wanted to challenge the supreme controller. He thought himself, at least for the time being, as powerful as Kṛṣṇa. Indra said, "Just see the impudence of the inhabitants of Vṛndāvana! They are simply inhabitants of the forest, but being infatuated with their friend Kṛṣṇa, who is nothing but an ordinary human being, they have dared to defy the demigods."

Kṛṣṇa has declared in the *Bhagavad-gītā* that the worshipers of the demigods are not very intelligent. He has also declared that one has to give up all kinds of worship and simply concentrate on Kṛṣṇa consciousness. Kṛṣṇa's invoking the anger of Indra and later on chastising him is a clear indication to His devotee that those who are engaged in Kṛṣṇa consciousness have no need to worship any demigod, even if it is found that the demigod has become angry. Kṛṣṇa gives His devotees all protection, and they should completely depend on His mercy.

Indra cursed the action of the inhabitants of Vṛndāvana and said, "By defying the authority of the demigods, the inhabitants of Vṛndāvana will suffer in material existence. Having neglected the sacrifice to the demigods, they cannot cross over the impediments of the ocean of material misery." Indra further declared, "These cowherd men in Vṛndāvana have neglected my authority on the advice of this talkative boy who is known as Kṛṣṇa. He is nothing but a child, and by believing this child, they have enraged me." Thus he ordered the *sāṁvartaka* cloud to go and destroy the prosperity of Vṛndāvana. "The men of Vṛndāvana," said Indra, "have become too puffed up over their material opulence and their confidence in the presence of their tiny friend, Kṛṣṇa. He is simply talkative, childish, and unaware of the complete cosmic situation, although He is thinking Himself very advanced in knowledge. Because they have taken Kṛṣṇa so seriously, they must be punished, and so I have ordered the *sāṁvartaka* cloud to go there and inundate the place. They should be destroyed with their cows."

It is indicated here that in the villages or outside the towns, the inhabitants must depend on the cows for their prosperity. When the cows are destroyed, the people are destitute of all kinds of opulences. When King Indra ordered the *sāṁvartaka* and companion clouds to go to Vṛndāvana, the clouds were afraid of the assignment. But King Indra assured them, "You go ahead, and I will also go, riding on my elephant, accompanied by great storms. And I shall apply all my strength to punish the inhabitants of Vṛndāvana."

Ordered by King Indra, all the dangerous clouds appeared above Vṛndavana and began to pour water incessantly, with all their strength and power. There was constant lightning and thunder, blowing of severe wind and incessant falling of rain. The rainfall seemed to fall like piercing sharp arrows. By pouring water as thick as pillars, without cessation, the clouds gradually filled all the lands in Vṛndāvana with water, and there was no visible distinction between higher and lower land. The situation was very dangerous, especially for the animals. The rainfall was accompanied by great winds, and every living creature in Vṛndāvana began to tremble from the severe cold. Unable to find any other source of deliverance, they all approached Govinda to take shelter at His lotus feet. The cows especially, being much aggrieved from the heavy rain, bowed down their heads, and taking their calves underneath their bodies, they approached the Supreme Personality of Godhead to take shelter of His lotus feet. At that time all the inhabitants of Vṛndāvana began to pray to Lord Kṛṣṇa. "Dear Kṛṣṇa," they prayed, "You are all-powerful, and You are very affectionate to Your devotees. Now please protect us who have been much harrassed by angry Indra."

Upon hearing their prayer, Kṛṣṇa could also understand that Indra, being bereft of his sacrificial honor, was pouring down rain that was accompanied by heavy pieces of ice and strong winds, although all this was out of season. Kṛṣṇa understood that this was a deliberate exhibition of anger by Indra. He therefore concluded, "This demigod who thinks himself supreme has shown his great power, but I shall answer him according to My position, and I shall teach him that he is not autonomous in managing universal affairs. I am the Supreme Lord over all, and I shall thus take away his false prestige which has risen from his power. The demigods are My devotees, and therefore it is not possible for them to forget My supremacy, but somehow or other he has become puffed up with material power and thus is now maddened. I shall act in such a way to relieve him of this false prestige. I shall give protection to My pure devotees in Vṛndāvana, who are at present completely at My mercy and whom I have taken completely under My protection. I will save them by My mystic power."

Thinking in this way, Lord Kṛṣṇa immediately picked up Govardhana Hill with one hand, exactly as a child picks up a mushroom from the ground. Thus He exhibited His transcendental pastime of lifting Govardhana Hill. Lord Kṛṣṇa then began to address His devotees, "My dear brothers, My dear father, My dear inhabitants of Vṛndāvana, you can now safely enter under the umbrella of Govardhana Hill, which I have just lifted. Do not be afraid of the hill and think that it will fall from My hand. You have been too much afflicted from the heavy rain and strong wind; therefore I have lifted this hill, which will protect you exactly like a huge umbrella. I think this is a proper arrangement to relieve you from your immediate distress. Be happy along with your animals underneath this great umbrella." Being assured by Lord Kṛṣṇa, all the inhabitants of Vṛndāvana entered beneath the great hill and appeared to be safe along with their property and animals.

The inhabitants of Vṛndāvana and their animals remained there for one week without being disturbed by hunger, thirst or any other discomforts. They were simply astonished to see how Kṛṣṇa was holding up the mountain with the little finger of His left hand. Seeing the extraordinary mystic power of Kṛṣṇa, Indra, the King of heaven, was thunderstruck and baffled in his determination. He immediately called for all the clouds and asked them to desist. When the sky became completely cleared of all clouds and there was sunrise again, the strong winds stopped. At that time Kṛṣṇa, the Supreme Personality of Godhead, known now as the lifter of Govardhana Hill, said, "My dear cowherd men, now you can leave and take your wives, children, cows and valuables, because everything is ended. The inundation has gone down, along with the swelling waters of the river."

All the men loaded their valuables on carts and slowly left with their cows and other paraphernalia. After they had cleared out everything, Lord Kṛṣṇa very slowly replaced Govardhana Hill exactly in the same position as it had been before. When everything was done, all the inhabitants of Vṛndāvana approached Kṛṣṇa and embraced Him with great ecstacy. The *gopīs*, being naturally very affectionate to Kṛṣṇa, began to offer Him curd mixed with their tears, and they poured incessant blessings upon Him. Mother Yaśodā, mother Rohiṇī, Nanda, and Balarāma, who is the strongest of the strong, embraced Kṛṣṇa one after another and, from spontaneous feelings of affection, blessed Him over and over again. In the heavens, different demigods from different planetary systems, such as Siddhaloka, Gandharvaloka and Cāraṇaloka, also began to show their complete satisfaction. They poured showers of flowers on the surface of the earth and sounded different conchshells. There was beating of drums, and being inspired by godly feelings, residents of Gandharvaloka began to play on their tampouras to please the Lord. After this incident, the Supreme Personality of Godhead, surrounded by His dear friends and animals, returned to His home. As usual, the *gopīs* began to chant the glorious pastimes of Lord Kṛṣṇa with great feeling, for they were chanting from the heart.

Thus ends the Bhaktivedanta purport of the Twenty-fifth Chapter of Kṛṣṇa, *"Devastating Rainfall in Vṛndāvana."*

26 / Wonderful Kṛṣṇa

Without understanding the intricacies of Kṛṣṇa, the Supreme Personality of Godhead, and without knowing His uncommon spiritual opulences, the innocent cowherd boys and men of Vṛndāvana began to discuss the wonderful activities of Kṛṣṇa which surpass the activities of all men.

One of them said, "My dear friends, considering His wonderful activities, how is it possible that such an uncommon boy would come and live with us in Vṛndāvana? It is really not possible. Just imagine! He is now only seven years old! How was it possible for Him to lift Govardhana Hill in one hand and hold it up just like the king of elephants holds a lotus flower? To lift a lotus flower is a most insignificant thing for an elephant, and similarly Kṛṣṇa lifted Govardhana Hill without exertion. When He was simply a small baby and could not even see properly, He killed a great demon, Pūtanā. While sucking her breast, He also sucked out her life-air. Kṛṣṇa killed the Pūtanā demon exactly as eternal time kills a living creature in due course. When He was only three months old, He was sleeping underneath a hand-driven cart. Being hungry for His mother's breast, He began to cry and throw His legs upwards. And from the kicking of his small feet the cart immediately broke apart and fell to pieces. When He was only one year old, He was carried away by the Tṛṇāvarta demon disguised as a whirlwind, and although He was taken very high in the sky, He simply hung on the neck of the demon and forced him to fall from the sky and immediately die. Once His mother, being disturbed by His stealing butter, tied Him to a wooden mortar, and the child pushed it towards a pair of trees known as *yamala arjuna* and caused them to fall. Once, when He was engaged in tending the calves in the forest along with His elder brother, Balarāma, a demon named Bakāsura appeared, and Kṛṣṇa at once bifurcated the demon's beaks. When the demon known as Vatsāsura entered among the calves tended by Kṛṣṇa with a desire to kill Him, He immediately detected the demon, killed him, and threw him into a tree. When Kṛṣṇa, along with His brother, Balarāma, entered the Tālavana forest, the demon known as Dhenukāsura, in the shape of an ass, attacked Them and was immediately killed by Balarāma, who caught his hind legs and threw him in a palm tree. Although the Dhenukāsura demon was assisted by his cohorts, also in the shape of asses, all were killed, and the Tālavana forest was then open for the use of the animals and inhabitants of Vṛndāvana. When Pralambāsura entered amongst His cowherd boy friends, He caused his death by Balarāma. Thereafter, Kṛṣṇa saved His friends and cows from the severe forest fire, and He chastised the Kāliya serpent in the lake of Yamunā and forced him to leave the vicinity of the Yamunā River; He thereby made the water of the Yamunā poisonless."

Another one of the friends of Nanda Mahārāja said, "My dear Nanda, we do not know why we are so attracted by your son Kṛṣṇa. We want to forget Him, but this is impossible. Why are we so naturally affectionate toward Him? Just imagine how wonderful it is! On one hand He is only a boy of seven years old, and on the other hand there is a huge hill like Govardhana Hill, and He lifted it so easily! O Nanda Mahārāja, we are now in great doubt—your son Kṛṣṇa must be one of the demigods. He is not at all an ordinary boy. Maybe He is the Supreme Personality of Godhead."

On hearing the praises of the cowherd men in Vṛndāvana, King Nanda said, "My dear friends, in reply to you I can simply present the statement of Gargamuni so that your doubts may be cleared. When he came to perform the name-giving ceremony, he said that this boy descends in different periods of time in different colors and that this time He has appeared in Vṛndāvana in a dark color and is known as Kṛṣṇa. Previously, He has white color, then red color, then yellow color. He also said that this boy was once the son of Vasudeva, and everyone who knows of His previous birth calls Him Vāsudeva. Actually he said that my son has many varieties of names, according to His different qualities and activities. Gargācārya assured me that this boy will be all-auspicious for my family and that He will be able to give transcendental blissful pleasure to all the cowherd men and cows in Vṛndāvana. Even though we will be put into various kinds of difficulties, by the grace of this boy we will be very easily freed from them. He also said that formerly this boy saved the world from an unregulated condition, and He saved all honest men from the hands of the dishonest. He also said that any fortunate man who becomes attached to this boy, Kṛṣṇa, is never vanquished or defeated by his enemy. On the whole, He is exactly like Lord Viṣṇu, who always takes the side of the demigods, who are consequently never defeated by the demons.

Gargācārya thus concluded that my child will grow to be exactly like Viṣṇu in transcendental beauty, qualification, activities, influence and opulence, and so we should not be very astonished by His wonderful activities. After telling me this, Gargācārya returned home, and since then we have been continually seeing the wonderful activities of this child. According to the version of Gargācārya, I consider that He must be Nārāyaṇa Himself, or maybe a plenary portion of Nārāyaṇa."

When all the cowherd men very attentively heard the statements of Gargācārya through Nanda Mahārāja, they better appreciated the wonderful activities of Kṛṣṇa and became very jubilant and satisfied. They began to praise Nanda Mahārāja, because by consulting him their doubts about Kṛṣṇa were cleared. They said, "Let Kṛṣṇa, who is so kind, beautiful and merciful, protect us. When angry Indra sent torrents of rain, accompanied by showers of ice blocks and high wind, He immediately took compassion upon us and saved us and our families, cows and valuable possessions by picking up the Govardhana Hill, just as a child picks up a mushroom. He saved us so wonderfully. May He continue to mercifully glance over us and our cows. May we live peacefully under the protection of wonderful Kṛṣṇa."

Thus ends the Bhaktivedanta purport of the Twenty-sixth Chapter of Kṛṣṇa, *"Wonderful Kṛṣṇa."*

27 / Prayers by Indra, the King of Heaven

When Kṛṣṇa saved the inhabitants of Vṛndāvana from the wrath of Indra by lifting Govardhana Hill, a *surabhi* cow from Goloka Vṛndāvana, as well as King Indra from the heavenly planet, appeared before Him. Indra, the King of heaven, was conscious of his offence before Kṛṣṇa; therefore he stealthily appeared before Him from a secluded place. He immediately fell down at the lotus feet of Kṛṣṇa, although his own crown was dazzling like sunshine. Indra knew about the exalted position of Kṛṣṇa because Kṛṣṇa is the master of Indra, but he could not believe that Kṛṣṇa could come down and live in Vṛndāvana among the cowherd men. When Kṛṣṇa defied the authority of Indra, Indra became angry because he thought that he was all in all within this universe and that no one was as powerful as he. But after this incident, his false puffed up prestige was destroyed. Being conscious of his subordinate position, he appeared before Kṛṣṇa with folded hands and began to offer the following prayers.

"My dear Lord," Indra said, "being puffed up by my false prestige, I thought that You had offended me by not allowing the cowherd men to perform the Indra-*yajña,* and I thought that You wanted to enjoy the offerings that were arranged for the sacrifice. I thought that in the name of a Govardhana sacrifice, You were taking my share of profit, and therefore I mistook Your position. Now by Your grace I can understand that You are the Supreme Lord, Personality of Godhead, and that You are transcendental to all the material qualities. Your transcendental position is *viśuddha-sattvam,* which is above the platform of the material mode of goodness, and Your transcendental abode is beyond the disturbance of the material qualities. Your name, fame, form, quality and pastimes are all beyond this material nature, and they are never disturbed by the three material modes. Your abode is accessible only for one who undergoes severe austerities and penances and who is completely freed from the onslaught of material qualities like passion and ignorance. If someone thinks that when You come within this material world You accept the modes of material nature, he is mistaken. The webs of the material qualities are never able to touch You, and You certainly do not accept them when You are present within this world. Your Lordship is never conditioned by the laws of material nature.

"My dear Lord, You are the original father of this cosmic manifestation. You are the supreme spiritual master of this cosmic world, and You are the original proprietor of everything. As eternal time, You are competent to chastise offenders. Within this material world there are many fools like myself who consider themselves to be the Supreme Lord or the all in all within the universe. You are so merciful that without punishing their offenses, You devise means so that their false prestige is subdued and they can know that You, and none else, are the Supreme Personality of Godhead.

"My dear Lord, You are the supreme father, the supreme spiritual master and supreme king. Therefore, You have the right to chastise all living entities whenever there is any discrepancy in their behavior. The father, the spiritual master, and the supreme executive officer of the state are always well-wishers of their sons, their students and their citizens respectively. As such, the well-wishers have the right to chastise their dependents. By Your own desire You appear auspiciously on the earth in Your eternal varieties of forms; You come to glorify the earthly planet and specifically to chastise persons who are falsely claiming to be God. In the material world there is regular competition between different types of living entities to become supreme leaders of society, and after being frustrated in achieving the supreme positions of leadership, foolish persons claim to be God, the Supreme Personality. There are many such foolish personalities in this world, like me, but in due course of time, when they come to their senses, they surrender unto You and again engage themselves properly by rendering service unto You. And that is the purpose of Your chastising persons envious of You.

"My dear Lord, I committed a great offense unto Your lotus feet, being falsely proud of my material opulences, not knowing Your unlimited power. Therefore, my Lord, kindly excuse me, because I am fool number one. Kindly give me Your blessings so that I may not act so foolishly again. If You think, my Lord, that the offence is very great and cannot be excused, then I appeal to You that I am Your eternal servant; Your appearance in this world is to give protection to Your eternal servants and to destroy the demons who maintain great military strength just to burden the very existence of the earth. As I am Your eternal servant, kindly excuse me.

"My dear Lord, You are the Supreme Personality of Godhead. I offer my respectful obeisances unto You because You are the Supreme Person and the Supreme Soul. You are the son of Vasudeva, and You are the Supreme Lord, Kṛṣṇa, the master of all pure devotees. Please accept my prostrated obeisances. You are the personification of supreme knowledge. You can appear anywhere according to Your desire in any one of Your eternal forms. You are the root of all creation and the Supreme Soul of all living entities. Due to my gross ignorance, I created great disturbance in Vṛndāvana by sending torrents of rain and heavy hailstorm. I acted out of severe anger caused by Your stopping the sacrifice which was to be held to satisfy me. But my dear Lord, You are so kind to me that You have bestowed Your mercy upon me by destroying all my false pride. I therefore take shelter unto Your lotus feet. My dear Lord, You are not only the supreme controller, but also the spiritual master of all living entities."

Thus praised by Indra, Lord Kṛṣṇa, the Supreme Personality of Godhead, smiling beautifully, said, "My dear Indra, I have stopped your sacrifice just to show My causeless mercy and to revive your memory that I am your eternal master. I am not only your master, but I am the master of all the other demigods as well. You should always remember that all your material opulences are due to My mercy. Everyone should always remember that I am the Supreme Lord. I can show anyone My favor, and I can chastise anyone, because no one is superior to Me. If I find someone overpowered by false pride, in order to show him My causeless mercy, I withdraw all his opulences."

It is noteworthy that Kṛṣṇa sometimes removes all opulences in order to facilitate a rich man's becoming a surrendered soul to Him. This is a special favor of the Lord's. Sometimes it is seen that a person is very opulent materially, but due to his devotional service to the Lord, he may be reduced to poverty. One should not think, however, that because he worshiped the Supreme Lord he became poverty-stricken. The real purport is that when a person is a pure devotee, but at the same time, by miscalculation, he wants to lord it over material nature, the Lord shows His special mercy by taking away all material opulences until at last he surrenders unto the Supreme Lord.

After instructing Indra, Lord Kṛṣṇa asked him to return to his kingdom in the heavenly planet and to remember always that he is never the supreme but is always subordinate to the Supreme Personality of Godhead. He also advised him to remain as King of heaven, but to be careful of false pride.

After this, the transcendental *surabhi* cow, who also came with Indra to see Kṛṣṇa, offered her respectful obeisances unto Him and worshiped Him.

The *surabhi* offered her prayer as follows. "My dear Lord Kṛṣṇa, You are the most powerful of all mystic *yogīs* because You are the soul of the complete universe, and from You only all this cosmic manifestation has taken place. Therefore, although Indra tried his best to kill my descendant cows in Vṛndāvana, they remained under Your shelter, and You have protected them all so well. We do not know anyone else as the Supreme, nor do we go to any other god or demigods for protection. Therefore, You are our Indra, You are the Supreme Father of the whole cosmic manifestation, and You are the protector and elevator of all the cows, *brāhmaṇas*, demigods and others who are pure devotees of Your Lordship. O Supersoul of the universe, let us bathe You with our milk because You are our Indra. O Lord, You appear just to diminish the burden of impure activities on the earth."

In this way, Kṛṣṇa was bathed by the milk of the *surabhi* cows, and Indra was bathed by the water of the celestial Ganges through the trunk of his carrier elephant. After this, the heavenly King Indra, along with *surabhi* cows and all other demigods and their mothers, worshiped Lord Kṛṣṇa by bathing Him with Ganges water and the milk of the *surabhis*. Thus Govinda, Lord Kṛṣṇa, was pleased with all of them. The residents of all higher planetary systems, such as Gandharvaloka, Pitṛloka, Siddhaloka, and Cāraṇaloka, all combined and began to glorify the Lord by chanting His holy name. Their wives and damsels began to dance with great joy. They very much satisfied the Lord by incessantly pouring flowers from the sky. When everything was very nicely and joyfully settled, the cows overflooded the surface of the earth with their milk. The water of the rivers began to flow and give nourishment to the trees, producing fruits and flowers of different colors and taste. The trees began to pour drops of honey. The hills and mountains began to produce potent medicinal plants and valuable stones. Because of Kṛṣṇa's presence, all these things happened very nicely, and the lower animals, who were generally envious, were envious no longer.

After satisfying Kṛṣṇa, who is the Lord of all the cows in Vṛndāvana, who is known as Govinda, King Indra took His permission to return to his heavenly kingdom. He was surrounded by all kinds of demigods who passed with him through cosmic space. This great incident is a powerful example of how Kṛṣṇa consciousness can benefit the world. Even the lower animals forget their envious nature and become elevated to the qualities of the demigods.

Thus ends the Bhaktivedanta purport of the Twenty-seventh Chapter of Kṛṣṇa, *"Prayers by Indra, the King of Heaven."*

28 / Releasing Nanda Mahārāja from the Clutches of Varuna

The Govardhana Ceremony took place on the new moon day. After this, there were torrents of rain and hailstorms imposed by King Indra for seven days. Nine days of the waxing moon having passed, on the tenth day King Indra worshiped Lord Kṛṣṇa, and thus the matter was satisfactorily settled. After this, on the eleventh day of the full moon, there was *Ekādaśī*. Mahārāja Nanda observed fasting for the whole day, and just early in the morning of the *Dvādaśī,* the day after *Ekādaśī,* he went to take bath in the River Yamunā. He entered deep into the water of the river, but he was arrested immediately by one of the servants of Varuṇadeva. These servants brought Nanda Mahārāja before the demigod Varuṇa and accused him of taking a bath in the river at the wrong time. According to astronomical calculations, the time in which he took bath was considered demoniac. The fact was, Nanda Mahārāja wanted to take a bath in the River Yamunā early in the morning before the sunrise, but somehow or other he was a little too early, and he bathed at an inauspicious time. Consequently he was arrested.

When Nanda Mahārāja was taken away by Varuṇa's servants, his companions began to call loudly for Kṛṣṇa and Balarāma. Immediately Kṛṣṇa and Balarāma could understand that Nanda Mahārāja was taken by Varuṇa, and thus They went to the abode of Varuṇa, for They were pledged to give protection. The inhabitants of Vrndāvana, the unalloyed devotees of the Lord, having no shelter other than the Supreme Personality of Godhead, naturally cried to Him for help, exactly like children who do not know anything but the protection of their parents. Demigod Varuṇa received Lord Kṛṣṇa and Balarāma with great respect and said, "My dear Lord, actually at this very moment, because of Your presence, I am materially defeated. Although I am the proprietor of all the treasures in the water, I know that such possessions do not make for a successful life.

But this moment, as I look at You, my life is made completely successful because by seeing You I no longer have to accept a material body. Therefore, O Lord, Supreme Personality of Godhead, Supreme Brahman and Supersoul of everything, let me offer my respectful obeisances unto You. You are the supreme transcendental personality; there is no possibility of imposing the influence of material nature upon You. I am very sorry that by being foolish, by not knowing what to do or what not to do, I have mistakenly arrested Your father, Nanda Mahārāja. So I beg Your pardon for the offence of my servants. I think that it was Your plan to show me Your mercy by Your personal presence here. My dear Lord Kṛṣṇa, Govinda, be merciful upon me—here is Your father. You can take him back immediately."

In this way Lord Kṛṣṇa, the Supreme Personality of Godhead, rescued His father and presented him before his friends with great jubilation. Nanda Mahārāja was surprised that, although the demigod was so opulent, he offered such respect to Kṛṣṇa. That was very astonishing to Nanda, and he began to describe the incident to his friends and relatives with great wonder.

Actually, although Kṛṣṇa was acting so wonderfully, Mahārāja Nanda and mother Yaśodā could not think of Him as the Supreme Personality of Godhead. Instead, they always accepted Him as their beloved child. Thus Nanda Mahārāja did not accept the fact that Varuṇa worshiped Kṛṣṇa because Kṛṣṇa was the Supreme Personality of Godhead; rather he took it that because Kṛṣṇa was such a wonderful child He was respected even by Varuṇa. The friends of Nanda Mahārāja, all the cowherd men, became eager to know if Kṛṣṇa were actually the Supreme Personality and if He were going to give them all salvation. When they were all thus consulting among themselves, Kṛṣṇa understood their minds, and in order to assure them of their destiny in the spiritual kingdom, He showed them the spiritual sky. Generally, ordinary persons are engaged simply in working hard in the material world, and they have no information that there is another kingdom or another sky, which is known as the spiritual sky, where life is eternal, blissful, and full of knowledge. As it is stated in the *Bhagavad-gītā,* a person returning to that spiritual sky never returns to this material world of death and suffering.

Kṛṣṇa, the Supreme Personality of Godhead, is always anxious to give information to the conditioned soul that there is a spiritual sky far, far beyond this material sky, transcendental to the innumerable universes created within the total material energy. Kṛṣṇa is, of course, always very kind to every conditioned soul, but, as stated in the *Bhagavad-gītā,* He is especially inclined to the devotees. Hearing their inquiries, Kṛṣṇa immediately thought that His devotees in Vṛndāvana should be informed of the spiritual sky and the Vaikuṇṭha planets therein. Within the material world, every conditioned soul is in the darkness of ignorance. This means that all conditioned souls are under the concept of this bodily existence.

Everyone is under the impression that he is of this material world, and with this concept of life, everyone is working in ignorance in different forms of life. The activities of the particular type of body are called *karma,* or fruitive action. All conditioned souls under the impression of the bodily concept are working according to their particular types of body. These activities are creating their future conditional life. Because they have very little information of the spiritual world, they do not generally take to spiritual activities, which are called *bhakti-yoga.* Those who successfully practice *bhakti-yoga,* after giving up this present body, go directly to the spiritual world and become situated in one of the Vaikuṇṭha planets. The inhabitants of Vṛndāvana are all pure devotees. Their destination after quitting the body is Kṛṣṇaloka. They even surpass the Vaikuṇṭhalokas. The fact is, those who are always engaged in Kṛṣṇa consciousness and mature, pure devotional service are given the chance, after death, to gain Kṛṣṇa's association in the universes within the material world. Kṛṣṇa's pastimes are continually going on, either in this universe or in another universe. Just as the sun globe is passing through many places across this earthly planet, so *Kṛṣṇa-līlā,* or the transcendental advent and pastimes of Kṛṣṇa, are also going on continually, either in this or another universe. The mature devotees, who have completely executed Kṛṣṇa consciousness, are immediately transferred to the universe where Kṛṣṇa is appearing. In that universe the devotees get their first opportunity to associate with Kṛṣṇa personally and directly. The training goes on, as we see in the Vṛndāvana *līlā* of Kṛṣṇa within this planet. Kṛṣṇa therefore revealed the actual feature of the Vaikuṇṭha planets so that the inhabitants of Vṛndāvana could know their destination.

Thus Kṛṣṇa showed them the eternal ever-existing spiritual sky which is unlimited and full of knowledge. Within this material world there are different gradations of forms, and according to the gradations, knowledge is proportionately manifested. For example, the knowledge in the body of a child is not as perfect as the knowledge in the body of an adult man. Everywhere there are different gradations of living entities, in aquatic animals, in the plants and trees, in the reptiles and insects, in birds and beasts and in the civilized and uncivilized human forms of life. Above the human form of life there are demigods, Cāraṇas and Siddhas on up to

Brahmaloka where Lord Brahmā lives, and among these demigods there are always different gradations of knowledge. But past this material world, in the Vaikuṇṭha sky, everyone is in full knowledge. All the living entities there are engaged in devotional service to the Lord, either in the Vaikuṇṭha planets or in Kṛṣṇaloka.

As it is confirmed in the *Bhagavad-gītā,* full knowledge means knowing Kṛṣṇa to be the Supreme Personality of Godhead. In the *Vedas* and *Bhagavad-gītā* it is also stated that in the *brahmajyoti* or spiritual sky there is no need of sunlight, moonlight, or electricity. All those planets are self-illuminating, and all of them are eternally situated. There is no question of creation and annihilation in the *brahmajyoti,* spiritual sky. *Bhagavad-gītā* also confirms that beyond the material sky there is another eternal spiritual sky where everything is eternally existing. Information of the spiritual sky can be had only from great sages and saintly persons who have already surpassed the influence of the three material modes of nature. Unless one is constantly situated on that transcendental platform, it is not possible to understand the spiritual nature.

Therefore it is recommended that one should take to *bhakti-yoga* and keep himself engaged twenty-four hours in Kṛṣṇa consciousness, which places one beyond the reach of the modes of material nature. One in Kṛṣṇa consciousness can easily understand the nature of the spiritual sky and Vaikuṇṭhaloka. The inhabitants of Vṛndāvana, being always engaged in Kṛṣṇa consciousness, could therefore very easily understand the transcendental nature of the Vaikuṇṭhalokas.

Thus Kṛṣṇa led all the cowherd men, headed by Nanda Mahārāja, to the lake where Akrūra was later shown the Vaikuṇṭha planetary system. They took their bath immediately and saw the real nature of the Vaikuṇṭhalokas. After seeing the spiritual sky and the Vaikuṇṭhalokas, all the men, headed by Nanda Mahārāja, felt wonderfully blissful, and coming out of the river, they saw Kṛṣṇa, who was being worshiped with excellent prayers.

Thus ends the Bhaktivedanta purport of the Twenty-eighth Chapter of Kṛṣṇa, *"Releasing Nanda Mahārāja from the Clutches of Varuṇa."*

29 / The Rāsa Dance: Introduction

In the *Śrīmad-Bhāgavatam* it is stated the *rāsa* dance took place on the full moon night of the *śarat* season. From the statement of previous chapters, it appears that the festival of Govardhana Pūjā was performed just after the dark moon night of the month of Kārttika, and thereafter the ceremony of *Bhrātṛdvitīya* was performed; then the wrath of Indra was exhibited in the shape of torrents of rain and hailstorm, and Lord Kṛṣṇa held up Govardhana Hill for seven days, up until the ninth day of the moon. Thereafter, on the tenth day, the inhabitants of Vṛndāvana were talking amongst themselves about the wonderful activities of Kṛṣṇa, and the next day, *Ekādaśī* was observed by Nanda Mahārāja. On the next day, *Dvādaśī,* Nanda Mahārāja went to take a bath in the Ganges and was arrested by the men of Varuṇa; then he was released by Lord Kṛṣṇa. Then Nanda Mahārāja, along with the cowherd men, was shown the spiritual sky.

In this way, the full moon night of *śarat* season came to an end. The full moon night of Āśvina is called *śārad-pūrṇimā.* It appears from the statement of *Śrīmad-Bhāgavatam* that Kṛṣṇa had to wait another year for such a moon before enjoying the *rāsa* dance with the *gopīs.* At the age of seven years, He lifted Govardhana Hill. Therefore, the *rāsa* dance took place during His eighth year.

From Vedic literature it appears that when a theatrical actor dances among many dancing girls, the group-dance is called a *rāsa* dance. When Kṛṣṇa saw the full moon night of the *śarat* season, He decorated Himself with various seasonal flowers, especially the *mallikā* flowers, which are very fragrant. He remembered the *gopīs'* prayers to goddess Kātyāyanī, wherein they prayed for Kṛṣṇa to be their husband. He thought that the full night of the *śarat* season was just suitable for a nice dance. So their desire to have Kṛṣṇa as their husband would then be fulfilled.

The words used in this connection in the *Śrīmad-Bhāgavatam* are *bhagavān api.* This means that although Kṛṣṇa is the Supreme Personality of Godhead, He has no desire that needs to be fulfilled because He is always full with six opulences. Yet He wanted to enjoy the company of the *gopīs. Bhagavān api* signifies that this is not like the ordinary dancing of young boys and young girls. The specific word used in the *Śrīmad-Bhāgavatam* is *yogamāyām upāśritaḥ,* which means that this dancing with the *gopīs* is on the platform of *yogamāyā,* not *mahāmāyā.* The dancing of young boys and girls within this material world is in the kingdom of *mahāmāyā,* or the external energy. The *rāsa* dance of Kṛṣṇa with the *gopīs* is on the platform of *yogamāyā.* The difference between the platform of *yogamāyā* and *mahāmāyā* is compared in the *Caitanya-caritāmṛta* to the difference between gold and iron. From the viewpoint of metallurgy, gold and iron are both metals, but the quality is completely different. Similarly, although the *rāsa* dance and Lord Kṛṣṇa's association with the *gopīs* appear like the ordinary mixing of young boys and girls, the quality is completely different. The difference is appreciated by great Vaiṣṇavas because they can understand the difference between love of Kṛṣṇa and lust.

On the *mahāmāyā* platform, dances take place on the basis of sense gratification. But when Kṛṣṇa called the *gopīs* by sounding His flute, the *gopīs* very hurriedly rushed towards the spot of *rāsa* dance with the transcendental desire of satisfying Kṛṣṇa. The author of *Caitanya-caritāmṛta,* Kṛṣṇadāsa Kavirāja Gosvāmī, has explained that lust means sense gratification, and love also means sense gratification–but for Kṛṣṇa. In other words, when activities are enacted on the platform of personal sense gratification, they are called material activities, but when they are enacted for the satisfaction of Kṛṣṇa, then they are spiritual activities. On any platform of activities, the principle of sense gratification is there. But on the spiritual platform, sense gratification is for the Supreme Personality of Godhead, Kṛṣṇa, whereas on the material platform it is for the performer. For example, on the material platform, when a servant serves a master, he is not trying to satisfy the senses of the master, but rather his own senses. The servant would not serve the master if the payment stopped. That means that the servant engages himself in the service of the master just to satisfy his senses. On the spiritual platform, the servitor of the Supreme Personality of Godhead serves Kṛṣṇa without payment, and he continues his service in all conditions. That is the difference between Kṛṣṇa consciousness and material consciousness.

It appears that Kṛṣṇa enjoyed the *rāsa* dance with the *gopīs* when He was eight years old. At that time, many of the *gopīs* were married, because in India, especially in those days, girls were married at a very early age. There are even many instances of a girl giving birth to a child at the age of twelve. Under the circumstances, all the *gopīs* who wanted to have Kṛṣṇa as their husband were already married. At the same time, they continued to hope that Kṛṣṇa would be their husband. Their attitude toward Kṛṣṇa was that of paramour love. Therefore, the loving affairs of Kṛṣṇa with the *gopīs* is called *parakīya-rasa.* A married man or a wife who desires another wife or husband is called *parakīya-rasa.*

Actually, Kṛṣṇa is the husband of everyone because He is the supreme enjoyer. The *gopīs* wanted Kṛṣṇa to be their husband, but factually there was no possibility of His marrying all the *gopīs.* But because they had that natural tendency to accept Kṛṣṇa as their supreme husband, the relationship between the *gopīs* and Kṛṣṇa is called *parakīya-rasa.* This *parakīya-rasa* is ever-existent in Goloka Vṛndāvana in the spiritual sky where there is no possibility of the inebriety which characterizes *parakīya-rasa* in the material world. In the material world, *parakīya-rasa* is abominable, whereas in the spiritual world it is present in the superexcellent relationship of Kṛṣṇa and the *gopīs.* There are many other relationships with Kṛṣṇa: master and servant, friends and friend, parent and son, and lover and beloved. Out of all these *rasas,* the *parakīya-rasa* is considered to be the topmost.

This material world is the perverted reflection of the spiritual world; it is just like the reflection of a tree on the bank of a reservoir of water: the topmost part of the tree is seen as the lowest part. Similarly, *parakīya-rasa,* when pervertedly reflected in this material world, is abominable. When people, therefore, imitate the *rāsa* dance of Kṛṣṇa with the *gopīs,* they simply enjoy the perverted, abominable reflection of the transcendental *parakīya-rasa.* There is no possibility of enjoying this transcendental *parakīya-rasa* within the material world. It is stated in the *Śrīmad-Bhāgavatam* that one should not imitate this *parakīya-rasa* even in dream or imagination. Those who do so drink the most deadly poison.

When Kṛṣṇa, the supreme enjoyer, desired to enjoy the company of the *gopīs* on that full moon night of the *śarat* season, exactly at that very moment, the moon, the lord of the stars, appeared in the sky, displaying its most beautiful features. The full moon night of the *śarat* season is the most beautiful night in the year. In India there is a great monument called Taj Mahal in Agra, a city in the Uttar Pradesh province, and the tomb is made of first-class marble stone. During the night of the full moon of the *śarat* season, many foreigners go to see the beautiful reflections of the moon on the tomb. Thus this full moon night is celebrated even today for its beauty.

When the full moon rose in the east, it tinged everything with a reddish color. With the rising of the moon, the whole sky appeared smeared by red *kuṅkuma*. When a husband long separated from his wife returns home, he decorates the face of his wife with red *kuṅkuma*. This long-expected moonrise of the *śarat* season was thus smearing the eastern sky.

The appearance of the moon increased Kṛṣṇa's desire to dance with the *gopīs*. The forests were filled with fragrant flowers. The atmosphere was cooling and festive. When Lord Kṛṣṇa began to blow His flute, the *gopīs* all over Vṛndāvana became enchanted. Their attraction to the vibration of the flute increased a thousand times due to the rising full moon, the red horizon, the calm and cool atmosphere, and the blossoming flowers. All these *gopīs* were by nature very much attracted to Kṛṣṇa's beauty, and when they heard the vibration of His flute, they became apparently lustful to satisfy the senses of Kṛṣṇa.

Immediately upon hearing the vibration of the flute, they all left their respective engagements and proceeded to the spot where Kṛṣṇa was standing. While they ran very swiftly, all their earrings swung back and forth. They all rushed toward the place known as Vaṁśīvaṭa. Some of them were engaged in milking cows, but they left their milking business half finished and immediately went to Kṛṣṇa. One of them had just collected milk and put it in a milk pan on the oven to boil, but she did not care whether the milk overboiled and spilled—she immediately left to go see Kṛṣṇa. Some of them were breast feeding their small babies, and some were engaged in distirbuting food to the members of their families, but they left all such engagements and immediately rushed towards the spot where Kṛṣṇa was playing His flute. Some were engaged in serving their husbands, and some were themselves engaged in eating, but neither caring to serve their husbands nor eat, they immediately left. Some of them wanted to decorate their faces with cosmetic ointments and to dress themselves very nicely before going to Kṛṣṇa, but unfortunately they could not finish their cosmetic decorations nor put on their dresses in the right way because of their anxiety to meet Kṛṣṇa immediately. Their faces were decorated hurriedly and were haphazardly finished; some even put the lower part of their dresses on the upper part of their bodies and the upper part on the lower part.

While all the *gopīs* were hurriedly leaving their respective places, their husbands, brothers and fathers were all struck with wonder to know where they were going. Being young girls, they were protected either by husbands, elderly brothers or fathers. All their guardians forbade them to go to Kṛṣṇa, but they disregarded them. When a person becomes attracted by

Kṛṣṇa and is in full Kṛṣṇa consciousness, he does not care for any worldly duties, even though very urgent. Kṛṣṇa consciousness is so powerful that it gives everyone relief from all material activities. Śrīla Rūpa Gosvāmī has written a very nice verse wherein one *gopī* advises another, "My dear friend, if you desire to enjoy the company of material society, friendship and love, then please do not go to see this smiling boy Govinda, who is standing on the bank of the Yamunā and playing His flute, His lips brightened by the beams of the full moonlight." Śrīla Rūpa Gosvāmī indirectly instructs that one who has been captivated by the beautiful smiling face of Kṛṣṇa has lost all attraction for material enjoyments. This is the test of advancement in Kṛṣṇa consciousness: a person advancing in Kṛṣṇa consciousness must lose interest in material activities and personal sense gratification.

Some of the *gopīs* were factually detained from going to Kṛṣṇa by their husbands and were locked up by force within their rooms. Being unable to go to Kṛṣṇa, they began to meditate upon His transcendental form by closing their eyes. They already had the form of Kṛṣṇa within their minds. They proved to be the greatest *yogīs;* as is stated in the *Bhagavad-gītā,* a person who is constantly thinking of Kṛṣṇa within his heart with faith and love is considered to be the topmost of all *yogīs.* Actually, a *yogī* concentrates his mind on the form of Lord Viṣṇu. That is real *yoga.* Kṛṣṇa is the original form of all Viṣṇu *tattvas.* The *gopīs* could not go to Kṛṣṇa personally, so they began to meditate on Him as perfect *yogīs.*

In the conditioned stage of the living entities, there are two kinds of results of fruitive activities: the conditioned living entity who is constantly engaged in sinful activities has suffering as his result, and he who is engaged in pious activities has material enjoyment as a result. In either case—material suffering or material enjoyment—the enjoyer or sufferer is conditioned by material nature.

The *gopī* associates of Kṛṣṇa, who assemble in the place where Kṛṣṇa is appearing, are from different groups. Most of the *gopīs* are eternal companions of Kṛṣṇa. As stated in the *Brahma-saṁhitā, ānanda-cin-maya-rasa-pratibhāvitābhiḥ:* in the spiritual world the associates of Kṛṣṇa, especially the *gopīs,* are the manifestation of the pleasure potency of Lord Kṛṣṇa. They are expansions of Śrīmatī Rādhārāṇī. But when Kṛṣṇa exhibits His transcendental pastimes within the material world in some of the universes, not only the eternal associates of Kṛṣṇa come, but also those who are being promoted to that status from this material world. The *gopīs* who joined Kṛṣṇa's pastimes within this material world were coming from the status of ordinary human beings. If they had been bound by fruitive action, they were fully freed from the reaction of *karma* by constant meditation on Kṛṣṇa. Their severe painful yearnings caused by their not being able to see Kṛṣṇa freed them from all sinful reactions, and their ecstacy of transcendental love for Kṛṣṇa in His absence was transcendental to all their reactions of material pious activities. The conditioned soul is subjected to birth and death, either by pious or sinful activities, but the *gopīs* who began to meditate on Kṛṣṇa transcended both positions and became purified and thus elevated to the status of the *gopīs* already expanded by His pleasure potency. All the *gopīs* who concentrated their minds on Kṛṣṇa in the spirit of paramour love became fully uncontaminated from all the fruitive reactions of material nature, and some of them immediately gave up their material bodies developed under the three modes of material nature.

Mahārāja Parīkṣit heard Śukadeva Gosvāmī explain the situation of the *gopīs* who assembled with Kṛṣṇa in the *rāsa* dance. When he heard that some of the *gopīs,* simply by concentrating on Kṛṣṇa as their paramour, became freed from all contamination of material birth and death, he said, "The *gopīs* did not know that Kṛṣṇa is the Supreme Personality of Godhead. They accepted Him as a beautiful boy and considered Him to be their paramour. So how was it possible for them to get freed from the material condition just by thinking of a paramour?" One should consider here that Kṛṣṇa and ordinary living beings are qualitatively one. The ordinary living beings, being part and parcel of Kṛṣṇa, are also Brahman, but Kṛṣṇa is the Supreme–Parabrahman. The question is, if it is possible for the devotee to get free from the material, contaminated stage simply by thinking of Kṛṣṇa, then why not others who are also thinking of someone? If one is thinking of a husband or son, or if anyone at all is thinking of another living entity, since all living entities are also Brahman, then why are they not all freed from the contaminated stage of material nature? This is a very intelligent question, because the atheists are always imitating Kṛṣṇa. In these days of Kaliyuga, there are many rascals who think themselves to be as great as Kṛṣṇa and who cheat people into believing that thinking of them is as good as thinking of Lord Kṛṣṇa. Parīkṣit Mahārāja, apprehending the dangerous condition of blind followers of demonic imitators, therefore asked this question, and fortunately it is recorded in the *Śrīmad-Bhāgavatam* to warn innocent people that thinking of an ordinary man and thinking of Kṛṣṇa are not the same.

Actually, even thinking of the demigods cannot compare with thinking of Kṛṣṇa. It is also warned in *Vaiṣṇava Tantra* that one who puts Viṣṇu, Nārāyaṇa, or Kṛṣṇa on the same level of the demigods is called *pāsaṇḍa,* or a rascal. On hearing this question of Mahārāja Parīkṣit, Śukadeva Gosvāmī replied, "My dear King, your question is already answered, even before this incident."

Because Parīkṣit Mahārāja wanted to clear up the situation, his spiritual master answered him very intelligently, "Why are you again asking the same subject matter which has already been explained to you? Why are you so forgetful?" A spiritual master is always in the superior position, so he has the right to chastise his disciple in this way. Śukadeva Gosvāmī knew that Mahārāja Parīkṣit asked the question not for his own understanding, but as a warning to the future innocent people who might think others to be equal to Kṛṣṇa.

Śukadeva Gosvāmī then reminded Parīkṣit Mahārāja about the salvation of Śiśupāla. Śiśupāla was always envious of Kṛṣṇa, and because of his envy Kṛṣṇa killed him. Since Kṛṣṇa is the Supreme Personality of Godhead, Śiśupāla gained salvation simply by seeing Him. If an envious person can get salvation simply by concentrating his mind on Kṛṣṇa, then what to speak of the *gopīs* who are so dear to Kṛṣṇa and always thinking of Him in love? There must be some difference between the enemies and the friends. If Kṛṣṇa's enemies could get freed from material contamination and become one with the Supreme, then certainly His dear friends like the *gopīs* are freed and with Him.

Besides that, in the *Bhagavad-gītā* Kṛṣṇa is called Hṛṣīkeśa. Śukadeva Gosvāmī also said that Kṛṣṇa is Hṛṣīkeśa, the Supersoul, whereas an ordinary man is a conditioned soul covered by the material body. Kṛṣṇa and Kṛṣṇa's body are the same because He is Hṛṣīkeśa. Any person making a distinction between Kṛṣṇa and Kṛṣṇa's body is fool number one. Kṛṣṇa is Hṛṣīkeśa and Adhokṣaja. These two particular words have been used by Parīkṣit Mahārāja in this instance. Hṛṣīkeśa is the Supersoul, and Adhokṣaja is the Supreme Personality of Godhead, transcendental to the material nature. Just to show favor to the ordinary living entities, out of His causeless mercy, He appears as He is. Unfortunately, foolish persons mistake Him to be another ordinary person, and so they become eligible to go to hell. Śukadeva Gosvāmī reconfirmed that Kṛṣṇa is the Supreme Personality of Godhead, imperishable, immeasurable, and free from all material contamination.

Śukadeva Gosvāmī continued to inform Mahārāja Parīkṣit that Kṛṣṇa is not an ordinary person. He is the Supreme Personality of Godhead, full of all spiritual qualities. He appears in this material world out of His causeless mercy, and whenever He appears, He appears as He is without change. This is also confirmed in the *Bhagavad-gītā*. There the Lord says that He appears in His spiritual potency. He does not appear under the control of this material potency. The material potency is under His control. In the *Bhagavad-gītā* it is stated that the material potency is working under His superintendence. It is also confirmed in the *Brahma-saṁhitā* that the material potency known as Durgā is acting just as a shadow which moves with the movement of the substance. The conclusion is that if one somehow or other becomes attached to Kṛṣṇa or attracted to Him, either because of His beauty, quality, opulence, fame, strength, renunciation or knowledge, or even through lust, anger or fear, or affection or friendship, then one's salvation and freedom from material contamination is assured.

In the *Bhagavad-gītā,* Eighteenth Chapter, the Lord also states that one who is engaged in preaching Kṛṣṇa consciousness is very dear to Him. A preacher has to face many difficulties in his struggle to preach pure Kṛṣṇa consciousness. Sometimes he has to suffer bodily injuries, and sometimes he has to meet death also. All this is taken as a great austerity on behalf of Kṛṣṇa. Kṛṣṇa therefore has said that such a preacher is very, very dear to Him. If Kṛṣṇa's enemies can expect salvation simply by concentrating their minds on Him, then what to speak of persons who are so dear to Kṛṣṇa? The conclusion should be that the salvation of those who are engaged in preaching Kṛṣṇa consciousness in the world is guaranteed in all circumstances. But such preachers never care for salvation, because factually one who is engaged in Kṛṣṇa consciousness, devotional service, has already achieved salvation. Śukadeva Gosvāmī therefore assured King Parīkṣit that he should always rest assured that one attracted by Kṛṣṇa attains liberation from material bondage because Kṛṣṇa is the transcendental master of all mystic power.

When all the *gopīs* assembled, as described, before Kṛṣṇa, He began to speak to them, welcoming them as well as discouraging them by word jugglery. Kṛṣṇa is the supreme speaker; He is the speaker of the *Bhagavad-gītā.* He can speak on the highest elevated subjects of philosophy, politics, economics—everything. And He also spoke before the *gopīs* who were so dear to Him. He wanted to enchant them by word jugglery, and thus He began to speak as follows.

"O ladies of Vṛndāvana," Kṛṣṇa said. "You are very fortunate, and you are very dear to Me. I am very pleased that you have come here, and I hope everything is well in Vṛndāvana. Now please order Me. What can I do for you? What is the purpose of coming here in this dead of night. Kindly take your seats and let Me know what I can do for you."

The *gopīs* had come to Kṛṣṇa to enjoy His company, to dance with Him, embrace Him and kiss Him, and when Kṛṣṇa began to receive them very officially, showing all kinds of etiquette, they were surprised. He was treating them as ordinary society women. Therefore they began to smile among themselves, and they very eagerly listened to Kṛṣṇa talk in that way. When He saw that they were smiling at Him, He said, "My dear friends, you must know now that it is the dead of night, and the forest is very dangerous. At this time all the ferocious jungle animals, the tigers, bears, jackals and wolves, are prowling in the forest. Therefore it is very dangerous for you. You cannot select a secure place now. Everywhere you go you will find that all these animals are loitering to find their prey. I think, therefore, that you are taking a great risk in coming here in the dead of night. Please turn back immediately, without delay."

When He saw that they continued to smile, He said, "I very much appreciate your bodily features. All of you have nice, very thin waists." All of the *gopīs* there were exquisitely beautiful. They are described by the word *sumadhyamā;* the standard of beauty of a woman is said to be *sumadhyamā* when the middle portion of the body is slender.

Kṛṣṇa wanted to impress on them that they were not old enough to take care of themselves. Actually, they required protection. It was not very wise for them to come in the dead of night to Kṛṣṇa. Kṛṣṇa also indicated that He was young and that they were young girls. "It does not look very well for young girls and boys to remain together in the dead of night." After hearing this advice, the *gopīs* did not seem very happy; therefore Kṛṣṇa began to stress the point in a different way.

"My dear friends, I can understand that you have left your homes without the permission of your guardians; therefore I think your mothers, your fathers, your elderly brothers or even your sons, and what to speak of your husbands, must be very anxious to find you. As long as you are here, they must be searching in different places, and their minds must be very agitated. So don't tarry. Please go back and make them peaceful."

When the *gopīs* appeared to be a little bit disturbed and angry from the free advice of Kṛṣṇa, they diverted their attention to looking at the beauty of the forest. At that time the whole forest was illuminated by the bright shining of the moon, and the air was blowing very silently over the blooming flowers, and the green leaves of the trees were moving in the breeze. Kṛṣṇa took the opportunity of their looking at the forest to advise them. "I think you have come out to see the beautiful Vṛndāvana forest on this night," He said, "but you must now be satisfied. So return to your homes without delay. I understand that you are all very chaste women, so now that you have seen the beautiful atmosphere of the Vṛndāvana forests, please return home and engage in the faithful service of your respective husbands. Some of you must have babies by this time, although you are very young. You must have left your small babies at home, and they must be crying. Please immediately go back home and just feed them with your breast milk. I can also understand that you have very great affection for Me, and out of that transcendental affection you have come here, hearing My playing on the flute. Your feelings of love and affection for Me are very appropriate because I am the Supreme Personality of Godhead. All living creatures are My parts and parcels, and naturally they are affectionate to Me. So this affection for Me is very much welcome, and I congratulate you for this. Now you can go back to your homes. Another thing I must explain to you is that for a chaste woman, service to the husband without duplicity is the best religious principle. A woman should be not only faithful and chaste to the husband, but affectionate to the friends of her husband, obedient to the father and mother of the husband, and affectionate to the younger brothers of the husband. And most importantly, the woman must take care of the children."

In this way, Kṛṣṇa explained the duty of a woman. He also stressed the point of serving the husband: "Even if he is not of very good character, or even if he is not very rich or fortunate, or even if he is old or invalid on account of continued diseases, whatever her husband's condition, a woman should not divorce her husband if she actually desires to be elevated to the higher planetary systems after leaving this body. Besides that, it is considered abominable in society if a woman is unfaithful and goes searching for another man. Such habits will deter a woman from being elevated to the heavenly planets, and the results of such habits are very degrading. A married woman should not search for a paramour, for this is not sanctioned by the Vedic principles of life. If you think that you are very much attached to Me and you want My association, I advise you not to personally try to enjoy Me. It is better for you to go home, simply talk about Me, think of Me, and by this process of constantly remembering Me and chanting My names, you will surely be elevated to the spiritual platform. There is no need to stand near Me. Please go back home."

The instruction given herein by the Supreme Personality of Godhead to the *gopīs* was not at all sarcastic. Such instructions should be taken very seriously by all honest women. The chastity of women is specifically stressed herein by the Supreme Personality of Godhead. Therefore this principle should be followed by any serious woman who wants to be elevated to a higher status of life. Kṛṣṇa is the center of all affection for all living creatures. When this affection is developed for Kṛṣṇa, then one surpasses and transcends all Vedic injunctions. This was possible for the *gopīs* because they saw Kṛṣṇa face to face. This is not possible for any women in the conditioned state. Unfortunately, by imitating the behavior of Kṛṣṇa with the *gopīs,* sometimes a rascal takes the position of Kṛṣṇa, following the philosophy of monism or oneness, and he very irresponsibly takes advantage of this *rāsa-līlā* to entice many innocent women and mislead them in the name of spiritual realization. As a warning, Lord Kṛṣṇa has herein hinted that what was possible for the *gopīs* is not possible for ordinary women. Although a woman can actually be elevated by advanced Kṛṣṇa consciousness, she should not be enticed by an imposter who says that he is Kṛṣṇa. She should concentrate her devotional activities in chanting and meditating upon Kṛṣṇa, as is advised herein. One should not follow the men called *sahajiyā,* the so-called devotees who take everything very lightly.

When Kṛṣṇa spoke in such a discouraging way to the *gopīs,* they became very sad, for they thought that their desire to enjoy *rāsa* dance with Kṛṣṇa would be frustrated. Thus they became full of anxiety. Out of great sadness, the *gopīs* began to breathe very heavily. Instead of looking at Kṛṣṇa face to face, they bowed their heads and looked to the ground, and they began to draw various types of curved lines on the ground with their toes. They were shedding heavy tears, and their cosmetic decorations were being washed from their faces. The water from their eyes mixed with the *kuṅkuma* of their breasts and fell to the ground. They could not say anything to Kṛṣṇa, but simply stood there silently. By their silence they expressed that their hearts were grieviously wounded.

The *gopīs* were not ordinary women. In essence they were on an equal level with Kṛṣṇa. They are His eternal associates. As it is confirmed in the *Brahma-saṁhitā,* they are expansions of the pleasure potency of Kṛṣṇa, and as His potency they are nondifferent from Him. Although they were depressed by the words of Kṛṣṇa, they did not like to use harsh words against Him. Yet they wanted to rebuke Kṛṣṇa for His unkind words, and therefore they began to speak in faltering voices. They did not like to use harsh words against Kṛṣṇa because He was their dearmost, their heart and soul. The *gopīs* had only Kṛṣṇa within their hearts. They were completely surrendered and dedicated souls. Naturally, when they heard such unkind words, they tried to reply, but in the attempt torrents of tears fell from their eyes. Finally they managed to speak.

"Kṛṣṇa," they said, "You are very cruel! You should not talk like that. We are full-fledged surrendered souls. Please accept us, and don't talk in that cruel way. Of course, You are the Supreme Personality of Godhead, and You can do whatever You like, but it is not worthy of Your position to treat us in such a cruel way. We have come to You, leaving everything behind, just to take shelter of Your lotus feet. We know that You are completely independent and can do whatever You like, but we request You, don't reject us. We are Your devotees. You should accept us as Lord Nārāyaṇa accepts His devotees. There are many devotees of Lord Nārāyaṇa who worship Him for salvation, and He awards them salvation. Similarly, how can You reject us when we have no other shelter than Your lotus feet?

"O dear Kṛṣṇa," they continued, "You are the supreme instructor. There is no doubt about it. Your instructions to the women to be faithful to their husbands and to be merciful to their children, to take care of homely affairs and to be obedient to the elderly members of the family, are surely just according to the tenets of *śāstras*. But we know also that all these instructions of the *śāstras* may be observed perfectly by keeping oneself under the protection of Your lotus feet. Our husbands, friends, family members and children are all dear and pleasing to us only because of Your presence, for You are the Supersoul of all living creatures. Without Your presence, one is worthless. When You leave the body, the body immediately dies, and according to the injunction of the *śāstra,* a dead body must immediately be thrown in a river or burned. Therefore, ultimately You are the dearmost personality in this world. By placing our faith and love in Your personality, there is no chance of our being bereft of husband, friends, sons or daughters. If a woman accepts You as the supreme husband, then she will never be bereft of her husband, as in the bodily concept of life. If we accept You as our ultimate husband, then there is no question of being separated, divorced or widowed. You are the eternal husband, eternal son, eternal friend, and eternal master, and one who enters into a relationship with You is eternally happy. Since You are the teacher of all religious principles, Your lotus feet first have to be worshiped. Accordingly, the *śāstras* state, *ācārya-upāsanā:* the worship of Your lotus feet is the first principle. Besides that, as stated in the *Bhagavad-gītā,* You are the only enjoyer, You are the only proprietor, and You are the only friend. As such, we have come to You, leaving aside all so-called friends, society and love, and now You have become our enjoyer. Let us be everlastingly enjoyed by You. Be our proprietor, for that is Your natural claim, and be our supreme friend, for You are naturally so. Let us thus embrace You as the supreme beloved."

Then the *gopīs* told the lotus-eyed Kṛṣṇa, "Please do not discourage our long-cherished desires to have You as our husband. Any intelligent man who cares for his own self-interest reposes all his loving spirit in You. Persons who are simply misled by the external energy, who want to be satisfied by false concepts, try to enjoy themselves apart from You. The so-called husband, friend, son, daughter, or father and mother are all simply sources of material misery. No one is made happy in this material world by having a so-called father, mother, husband, son, daughter and friend. Although the father and mother are expected to protect the children, there are many children who are suffering for want of food and shelter. There are many good physicians, but when a patient dies, no physician can revive him. There are many means of protection, but when one is doomed, none of the protective measures can help, and without Your protection the so-called sources of protection simply become sources of continued distress. We therefore appeal to You, dear Lord of all lords, please do not kill our long-cherished desires to have You as our supreme husband.

"Dear Kṛṣṇa, as women, we are certainly satisfied when our hearts are engaged in the activities of family affairs, but our hearts have already been stolen by You. We can no longer engage them in family affairs. Besides that, You are asking us repeatedly to return home, and that is a very appropriate instruction, but unfortunately we have been stunned here. Our legs have no power to move a step from Your lotus feet. Therefore, if even at Your request we return home, what shall we do there? We have lost all our capacity to act without You. Instead of engaging our hearts in family affairs as women, we have now developed a different type of lust which is continually blazing in our hearts. Now we request You, dear Kṛṣṇa, to extinguish that fire with Your beautiful smile and the transcendental vibration emanating from Your lips. If You do not agree to do us this favor, we shall certainly be burned in the fire of separation. In that condition, we shall simply think of You and Your beautiful features and give up our bodies immediately. In that way we think it will be possible for us to reside at Your lotus feet in the next life. Dear Kṛṣṇa, if You say that if we go home our respective husbands will satisfy the lusty flame of our desire, we can only say that that is no longer possible. You have given us a chance to be enjoyed by You in the forest and have touched our breasts once in the past, which we accepted as a blessing, as did the goddesses of fortune, who are enjoyed in the Vaikuṇṭhalokas by You. Since we have tasted this transcendental enjoyment, we are no longer interested in going to anyone but You for the satisfaction of our lust. Dear Kṛṣṇa, the lotus feet of the goddess of fortune are always worshiped by the demigods, although she is always resting on Your chest in the

“Do not be afraid of the hill and think that it will fall from my hand.”
(p. 175)

King Indra from the heavenly planet appeared before Kṛṣṇa from a secluded place. (p. 180)

The god of the waters was holding Nanda captive underneath the sea. (p. 184)

B. G. Sharma

The *gopīs* remembered their pastimes with Kṛṣṇa. (p. 208)

The wives of the *brāhmanas* saw the Supreme Personality of Godhead, and He entered within their hearts through their eyes. (p. 160)

Kṛṣṇa, the supreme enjoyer, desired to enjoy the company of the *gopīs*. (p. 190)

Out of many thousands of *gopīs*, Rādhārāṇī is the most prominent. (p. 211)

Kṛṣṇa appeared on the scene and touched the serpent with His lotus feet. (p. 226)

Mohan Mādhurī. (p. 215)

appeared that
golden necklace. (p

It appeared that Kṛṣṇa was a greenish sapphire locket in the midst of a golden necklace. (p. 214)

Being kicked by Kṛṣṇa, Ariṣṭāsura rolled over and began to move his legs violently. (p. 237)

Vaikuṇṭha planets. She underwent great austerity and penance to have some shelter at Your lotus feet, which are always covered by *tulasī* leaves. Your lotus feet are the proper shelter of Your servitors, and the goddess of fortune, instead of abiding on Your chest, comes down and worships Your lotus feet. We have now placed ourselves under the dust of Your feet. Please do not reject us, for we are fully surrendered souls.

"Dear Kṛṣṇa, You are known as Hari. You destroy all the miseries of all living entities, specifically of those who have left their homes and family attachment and have completely taken to You. We have left our homes with the hope that we shall completely devote and dedicate our lives to Your service. We are simply begging to be engaged as Your servants. We do not wish to ask You to accept us as Your wives. Simply accept us as Your maidservants. Since You are the Supreme Personality of Godhead and like to enjoy the *parakīya-rasa* and are famous as a transcendental woman hunter, we have come to satisfy Your transcendental desires. We are also after our own satisfaction, for simply by looking at Your smiling face we have become very lusty. We have come before You decorated with all ornaments and dress, but until You embrace us, all our dresses and beautiful features remain incomplete. You are the Supreme Person, and if You complete our dressing attempt as the *puruṣa-bhūṣaṇa,* or the male ornament, then all our desires and bodily decorations are complete.

"Dear Kṛṣṇa, we have simply been captivated by seeing You with *tilaka* and with earrings and by seeing Your beautiful face covered with scattered hair and Your extraordinary smile. Not only that, but we are also attracted by Your arms, which always give assurance to the surrendered souls. And although we are also attracted by Your chest, which is always embraced by the goddess of fortune, we do not wish to take her position. We shall simply be satisfied by being Your maidservants. If You, however, accuse us of encouraging prostitution, then we can only ask where is that woman within these three worlds who is not captivated by Your beauty and the rhythmic songs vibrated by Your transcendental flute? Within these three worlds there is no distinction between men and women in relation to You because both men and women belong to the marginal potency or *prakṛti.* No one is actually the enjoyer or the male; everyone is meant to be enjoyed by You. There is no woman within these three worlds who cannot but deviate from her path of chastity once she is attracted to You because Your beauty is so sublime that not only men and women, but cows, birds, beasts and even trees, fruits and flowers—everyone and everything—become enchanted, and what to speak of ourselves? It is, however, definitely decided that as Lord Viṣṇu is always protecting the demigods from the onslaught of demons, so You have also advented in Vṛndāvana just to give the residents protection from all kinds of distress. O dear friend of the distressed, kindly place Your hand on our burning breasts as well as on our heads, because we have surrendered unto You as Your eternal maidservants. If You think, however, that Your lotus-like palms might be burned to ashes if placed on our burning breasts, let us assure You that Your palms will feel pleasure instead of pain, as the lotus flower, although very delicate and soft, enjoys the scorching heat of the sun."

Upon hearing the anxious plea of the *gopīs,* the Supreme Personality of Godhead began to smile, and being very kind to the *gopīs,* the Lord, although self-sufficient, began to embrace them and kiss them as they desired. When Kṛṣṇa, smiling, looked at the faces of the *gopīs,* the beauty of their faces became a hundred times enhanced. When He was enjoying them in their midst, He appeared just like the full moon surrounded by millions of shining stars. Thus the Supreme Personality of Godhead, surrounded by hundreds of *gopīs* and decorated with a flower garland of many colors, began to wander within the Vṛndāvana forest, sometimes singing to Himself and sometimes singing with the *gopīs.* In this way, both the Lord and the *gopīs* reached the cool sandy bank of the Yamunā where there were lilies and lotus flowers. In such a transcendental atmosphere, both the *gopīs* and Kṛṣṇa began to enjoy one another. While they were walking on the bank of the Yamunā, Kṛṣṇa would sometimes put His arms around a *gopī's* head, breast or waist. Pinching one another and joking and looking at one another, they enjoyed. When Kṛṣṇa touched the bodies of the *gopīs,* their lust to embrace Him increased. They all enjoyed these pastimes. Thus the *gopīs* were blessed with all mercy by the Supreme Personality of Godhead, for they enjoyed His company without a tinge of mundane sex life.

The *gopīs,* however, soon began to feel very proud, thinking themselves to be the most fortunate women in the universe by being favored by the company of Kṛṣṇa. Lord Kṛṣṇa, who is known as Keśava, could immediately understand their pride caused by their great fortune of enjoying Him personally, and in order to show them His causeless mercy and to curb their false pride, He immediately disappeared from the scene, exhibiting His opulence of renunciation. The Supreme Personality of Godhead is always full with six kinds of opulences, and this is an instance of the opulence of renunciation. This renunciation confirms Kṛṣṇa's total nonattachment. He is always self-sufficient and is not dependent on anything. This is the platform on which the transcendental pastimes are enacted.

Thus ends the Bhaktivedanta purport of the Twenty-ninth Chapter of Kṛṣṇa, *"The Rāsa Dance: Introduction."*

30 / Kṛṣṇa's Hiding from the Gopīs

When Kṛṣṇa suddenly disappeared from the company of the *gopīs,* they began to search for Him in every place. After not finding Him anywhere, they became afraid and almost mad after Him. They were simply thinking of the pastimes of Kṛṣṇa in great love and affection. Being absorbed in thought, they experienced loss of memory, and with dampened eyes they began to see the very pastimes of Kṛṣṇa, His beautiful talks with them, His embracing, kissing, and other activities. Being so attracted to Kṛṣṇa, they began to imitate His dancing, His walking and smiling, as if they themselves were Kṛṣṇa. Due to Kṛṣṇa's absence, they all became crazy; each one of them began to tell the others that she was Kṛṣṇa Himself. Soon they all began to assemble together and chant Kṛṣṇa's name very loudly, and they moved from one part of the forest to another searching for Him. Actually, Kṛṣṇa is all-pervasive; He is in the sky, and He is in the forest; He is within the heart, and He is always everywhere.

The *gopīs* therefore began to question the trees and plants about Kṛṣṇa. There were various types of big trees and small plants in the forest, and the *gopīs* began to address them. "Dear banyan tree, have you seen the son of Mahārāja Nanda passing this way, laughing and playing on His flute? He has stolen our hearts and has gone away. If you have seen Him, kindly inform us which way He has gone. Dear *aśoka* tree, dear *nāga* flower tree and *campaka* flower tree, have you seen the younger brother of Balarāma pass this way? He has disappeared because of our pride." The *gopīs* were aware of the reason for Kṛṣṇa's sudden disappearance. They could understand that when they were enjoying Kṛṣṇa, they thought themselves to be the most fortunate women within the universe, and since they were feeling proud, Kṛṣṇa disappeared immediately just to curb their pride. Kṛṣṇa does not like His devotees to be proud of their service to Him. He accepts everyone's service, but He does not like one devotee to be prouder than others. If sometimes there are such feelings, Kṛṣṇa ends them by changing His attitude toward the devotee.

The *gopīs* then began to address the *tulasī* plants: "Dear *tulasī*, you are much beloved by Lord Kṛṣṇa because your leaves are always at His lotus feet. Dear *mālatī* flower, dear *mallikā* flower, dear jasmine flower, all of you must have been touched by Kṛṣṇa while He was passing this way after giving us transcendental enjoyment. Have you seen Mādhava passing this way? O mango trees, O trees of jack fruit, O pear trees and *asana* trees! O blackberries and *bael* trees and trees of *kadamba* flower—you are all very pious trees to be living on the bank of Yamunā. Kṛṣṇa must have passed through this way. Will you kindly let us know which way He has gone?

The *gopīs* then looked upon the ground they were traversing and began to address the earth, "Dear earthly planet, we do not know how many penances and austerities you have undergone to be now living with the footprints of Lord Kṛṣṇa upon you. You are very jolly; the hairs on your body are these jubilant trees and plants. Lord Kṛṣṇa must have been very much pleased with you, otherwise how could He have embraced you in the form of Varāha the boar? When you were submerged in water, He delivered you, taking the whole weight of your existence on His tusks."

After addressing the innumerable trees and plants, they turned their faces toward the beautiful deer who were looking on them very pleasingly. "It appears," they addressed the deer, "that Kṛṣṇa, who is the Supreme Nārāyaṇa Himself, must have passed through this way along with His companion, Lakṣmī, the goddess of fortune. Otherwise, how is it possible that the aroma of His garland, which is smeared with the red *kuṅkuma* from the breast of the goddess of fortune, can be perceived in the breeze blowing here? It appears that they must have passed through here and touched your bodies, and thus you are feeling so pleasant and are looking toward us with sympathy. Will you kindly, therefore, inform us which way Kṛṣṇa has gone? Kṛṣṇa is the well-wisher of Vṛndāvana. He is as kind to you as to us; therefore after leaving us, He must have been present in your company. O fortunate trees, we are thinking of Kṛṣṇa, the younger brother of Balarāma. While passing through here, with one hand resting on the shoulder of the goddess of fortune and the other hand whirling a lotus flower, He must have been very pleased to accept your obeisances, and He must have glanced at you with great pleasure.

Some of the *gopīs* then began to address their other *gopī* friends, "Dear friends, why don't you question these creepers who are so jubilantly embracing the big trees as if the trees were their husbands? It appears that the flowers of the creepers must have been touched by the nails of Kṛṣṇa. Otherwise, how could they feel so jubilant?"

After searching for Kṛṣṇa here and there, when the *gopīs* became fatigued, they began to talk like madwomen. They could only satisfy themselves by imitating the different pastimes of Kṛṣṇa. One of them imitated the demon, Pūtanā, and one of them imitated Kṛṣṇa and sucked her breast. One *gopī* imitated a hand-driven cart, and another *gopī* lay down beneath the cart and began to throw up her legs, touching the wheels of the cart, as Kṛṣṇa did to kill the demon Śakaṭāsura. They imitated child Kṛṣṇa, lying down on the ground, and one *gopī* became the demon Tṛṇāvarta and carried the small child Kṛṣṇa by force into the sky; and one of the *gopīs* began to imitate Kṛṣṇa while He was attempting to walk, ringing His ankle bells. Two *gopīs* imitated Kṛṣṇa and Balarāma, and many others imitated Their cowherd boy friends. One *gopī* assumed the form of Bakāsura, and another forced her to fall down as the demon Bakāsura did when he was killed; similarly, another *gopī* defeated Vatsāsura. Just as Kṛṣṇa used to call His cows by their different names, so the *gopīs* imitated Him, calling the cows by their respective names. One of the *gopīs* began to play on a flute, and another praised her the way Kṛṣṇa's boy friends praised Him while He played on His flute. One of the *gopīs* took another *gopī* on her shoulders, just as Kṛṣṇa used to take His boy friends. Absorbed in thoughts of Kṛṣṇa, the *gopī* who was carrying her friend began to boast that she was Kṛṣṇa herself: "All of you just see my movement!" One of the *gopīs* raised her hand with her covering garments and said, "Now don't be afraid of torrents of rain and severe hurricanes. I'll save you!" In this way she imitated the lifting of Govardhana Hill. One *gopī* forcibly put her feet on the head of another *gopī* and said, "You rascal Kāliya! I shall punish you severely. You must leave this place. I have descended on this earth to punish all kinds of miscreants!" Another *gopī* told her friends, "Just see! The flames of the forest fire are coming to devour us. Please close your eyes, and I shall immediately save you from this imminent danger."

In this way all the *gopīs* were madly feeling the absence of Kṛṣṇa. They enquired for Him from the trees and plants. In some places they found the imprints of the marks on the sole of His feet—namely the flag, the lotus flower, the trident, the thunderbolt, etc. After seeing those footprints, they exclaimed, "O here is the impression of the marks on the sole of Kṛṣṇa. All the marks, such as the flag, the lotus flower, the trident and the thunderbolt, are distinctly visible here." They began to follow the footprints, and shortly they saw another set of footprints beside them, and immediately they became very sorry. "Dear friends, just see! Whose are these other footprints? They are beside the footprints of the son of Mahārāja Nanda. It is certainly Kṛṣṇa passing through, resting His hand on some other *gopī*, exactly as an elephant goes side by side with his beloved mate. We must, therefore, understand that this particular *gopī* served Kṛṣṇa with greater affectionate love than ourselves. Because of this, although He has left us, He could not leave Her company. He has taken Her along with Him. Dear friends, just imagine how the dust of this place is transcendentally glorious. The dust of the lotus feet of Kṛṣṇa is worshiped even by Lord Brahmā and Lord Śiva, and the goddess of fortune, Lakṣmī. But at the same time, we are very sorry that this particular *gopī* has gone along with Kṛṣṇa, for She is sharing the nectar of Kṛṣṇa's kisses and leaving us aside to lament. O friends, just see! At this particular spot we do not see the footprints of that *gopī*. It appears that because there were some pin-pricks from the dried grass, Kṛṣṇa took Rādhārāṇī on His shoulder. O, She is so dear to Him! Kṛṣṇa must have picked some flowers in this spot to satisfy Rādhārāṇī, because here, where He stood erect to get the flowers from the high branches of the tree, we find only half the impression of His feet. Dear friends, just see how Kṛṣṇa must have sat down here with Rādhārāṇī and tried to set flowers in Her hair. You can be certain that both of Them sat together here. Kṛṣṇa is self-sufficient; He has nothing to enjoy from any other source, yet just to satisfy His devotee He has treated Rādhārāṇī exactly as a lusty boy treats his girl friend. Kṛṣṇa is so kind that He always tolerates the disturbances created by His girl friends."

In this way, all the *gopīs* began to point out the faults of the particular *gopī* who had been taken alone by Kṛṣṇa. They began to say that the chief *gopī*, Rādhārāṇī, who was taken alone by Kṛṣṇa, must be very proud of Her position, thinking Herself the greatest of the *gopīs*. "Yet how could Kṛṣṇa take Her away alone, leaving all of us aside, unless She be extraordinarily qualified and beautiful? She must have taken Kṛṣṇa in the deep forest and told Him, 'My dear Kṛṣṇa, I am now very tired. I cannot go any further. Please carry Me wherever You like.' When Kṛṣṇa was spoken to in this way, He might have told Rādhārāṇī, 'All right, better get on My shoulder.' But immediately Kṛṣṇa must have disappeared, and now Rādhārāṇī must be lamenting for Him, 'My dear lover, My dearest, You are so fine and so powerful. Where have You gone? I am nothing but Your most obedient maidservant. I am very much aggrieved. Please come and be with Me again.' Kṛṣṇa, however, is not coming to Her. He must be watching Her from a distant place and enjoying Her sorrow."

All the *gopīs* then went further and further into the forest, searching out Kṛṣṇa, but when they learned that actually Rādhārāṇī was left alone by Kṛṣṇa, they became very sorry. This is the test of Kṛṣṇa consciousness. In the beginning they were a little envious that Kṛṣṇa had taken Rādhārāṇī alone, leaving aside all other *gopīs,* but as soon as they knew that Kṛṣṇa had also left Rādhārāṇī and that She was alone lamenting for Him, they became more sympathetic to Her. The *gopīs* found Rādhārāṇī and heard everything from Her, about how She misbehaved with Kṛṣṇa and how She was proud and was insulted for Her pride. After hearing all this, they became actually very sympathetic. Then all the *gopīs,* including Rādhārāṇī, began to proceed further into the forest until they could no longer see the moonlight.

When they saw that it was getting gradually darker, they stopped. Their mind and intelligence became absorbed in the thoughts of Kṛṣṇa; they all imitated the activities of Kṛṣṇa and His speeches. Due to their heart and soul being completely given to Kṛṣṇa, they began to chant His glories, completely forgetting their family interests. In this way, all the *gopīs* assembled together on the bank of Yamunā, and expecting that Kṛṣṇa must return to them, they simply engaged in the chanting of the glories of Śrī Kṛṣṇa—Hare Kṛṣṇa, Hare Kṛṣṇa, Kṛṣṇa Kṛṣṇa, Hare Hare, Hare Rāma, Hare Rāma, Rāma Rāma, Hare Hare.

Thus ends the Bhaktivedanta purport of the Thirtieth Chapter of Kṛṣṇa, *"Kṛṣṇa's Hiding from the Gopīs."*

31 / Songs by the Gopīs

One *gopī* said, "My dear Kṛṣṇa, ever since You took Your birth in this land of Vrajabhūmi, everything appears to be glorious. The land of Vṛndāvana has become glorious, and it is as if the goddess of fortune is personally always existing here. But it is only we who are very unhappy, because we are searching for You, but cannot see You with our greatest effort. Our life is completely dependent upon You; therefore we request that You again come to us."

Another *gopī* said, "My dear Kṛṣṇa, You are the life and soul even of the lotus flower that grows on the water of lakes made transparent by the clear rains of autumn. Although the lotus flowers are so beautiful, without Your glance they fade away. Similarly, without You, we are also dying. Actually, we are neither Your wives nor slaves. You never spent any money for us, yet we are simply attracted by Your glance. Now, if we die without receiving Your glance, You'll be responsible for our deaths. Certainly the killing of women is a great sin, and if You do not come to see us and we die, You will suffer the reactions of sin. So please come see us. Do not think that one can be killed only by certain weapons. We are being killed by Your absence. You should consider how You are responsible for killing women. We are always grateful to You because You have protected us many times: from the poisonous water of Yamunā, from the serpent Kāliya, from Bakāsura, from the anger of Indra and his torrents of rain, from forest fire and so many other incidents. You are the greatest and most powerful of all. It is wonderful for You to protect us from so many dangers, but we are surprised that You are neglecting us at this moment. Dear Kṛṣṇa, dear friend, we know very well that You are not actually the son of mother Yaśodā or the cowherd man Nanda Mahārāja. You are the Supreme Personality of Godhead and the Supersoul of all living entities. You have, out of Your own causeless mercy, appeared in this world, requested by Lord Brahmā for the protection of the world. It is by Your kindness only that You have appeared in the dynasty of Yadu. O best in the dynasty of Yadu, if anyone afraid of this materialistic way of life takes shelter at Your lotus feet, You never deny him protection. Your movements are sweet, and You are independent, touching the goddess of fortune with one hand and in the other bearing a lotus flower. That is Your extraordinary feature. Please, therefore, come before us and bless us with the lotus flower in Your hand.

"Dear Kṛṣṇa, You are the killer of all the fears of the inhabitants of Vṛndāvana. You are the supremely powerful hero, and we know that You can kill the unnecessary pride of Your devotee as well as the pride of women like us simply by Your beautiful smile. We are simply Your maid-servants and slaves; please, therefore, accept us by showing us Your lotus-like beautiful face.

"Dear Kṛṣṇa, actually we have become very lusty, having been touched by Your lotus feet. Your lotus feet certainly kill all kinds of sinful activities of devotees who have taken shelter there. You are so kind that even the ordinary animals take shelter under Your lotus feet. Your lotus feet are also the residence of the goddess of fortune, yet You dance on the head of the Kāliya serpent with them. Now we are requesting You to kindly place Your lotus feet on our breasts and pacify our lusty desires to touch You.

"O Lord, Your attractive eyes, like the lotus, are so nice and pleasing. Your sweet words are so fascinating that they please even the greatest scholars, who also become attracted to You. We are also attracted by Your speaking and by the beauty of Your face and eyes. Please, therefore, satisfy us by Your nectarean kisses. Dear Lord, words spoken by You or words describing Your activities are full of nectar, and simply by speaking or hearing Your words one can be saved from the blazing fire of material existence. Great demigods like Lord Brahmā and Lord Śiva are always engaged in chanting the glories of Your words. They do so to eradicate the sinful activities of all living entities in the material world. If one simply tries to hear Your transcendental words, he can very quickly be elevated to the platform of pious activities. For the Vaiṣṇavas, Your words give transcendental pleasure, and saintly persons who are engaged in distributing Your transcendental message all over the world are first-class charitable persons." (This is confirmed by Rūpa Gosvāmī also when he addressed Lord Caitanya as the most munificent incarnation because Lord Caitanya distributed the words of Kṛṣṇa and love of Kṛṣṇa free of charge all over the world.)

"Dear Kṛṣṇa," the *gopīs* continued, "You are very cunning. You can imagine how much we are distressed simply by remembering Your cunning smile, Your pleasing glance, Your walking with us in the forest of Vṛndāvana, and Your auspicious meditations. Your talks with us in lonely places were heart-warming. Now we are all aggrieved to remember Your behavior. Please save us. Dear Kṛṣṇa, certainly You know how much we are saddened when You go out of Vṛndāvana village to tend the cows in the forest. How we are afflicted simply to think that Your soft lotus feet are being pricked by the dry grass and the tiny stones in the forest! We are so attached to You that we always think simply of Your lotus feet.

"O Kṛṣṇa, when You return from the pasturing ground with the animals, we see Your face covered by Your curly hair and dusted by the hoof-dust of the cows. We see Your mildly smiling face, and our desire to enjoy You increases. O dear Kṛṣṇa, You are the supreme lover, and You always give shelter to surrendered souls. You fulfill everyone's desire; Your lotus feet are even worshiped by Lord Brahmā, the creator of the universe. To whomever worships Your lotus feet, You without a doubt always bestow Your benedictions. So kindly be pleased with us and keep Your lotus feet on our breasts and thus relieve our present distresses. Dear Kṛṣṇa, we are seeking Your kisses which You offer even to Your flute. The vibration of Your flute enchants the whole world and our hearts also. Kindly, therefore, return and kiss us with Your mouth of nectar."

When Lord Kṛṣṇa finally reappeared and assembled with the *gopīs,* He looked very beautiful, just befitting a person with all kinds of opulences. In the *Brahma-saṁhitā,* it is stated, *ānanda-cin-maya-rasa-pratibhāvitābhiḥ:* Kṛṣṇa alone is not particularly beautiful, but when His energy—especially His pleasure energy, represented by Rādhārāṇī—expands, He looks very magnificent. The Māyāvāda conception of the perfection of the Absolute Truth without potency is due to insufficient knowledge. Actually, outside the exhibition of His different potencies, the Absolute Truth is not complete. *Ānanda-cin-maya-rasa* means that His body is a transcendental form of eternal bliss and knowledge. Kṛṣṇa is always surrounded by different potencies, and therefore He is perfect and beautiful. We understand from *Brahma-saṁhitā* and *Skanda Purāṇa* that Kṛṣṇa is always surrounded by many thousands of goddesses of fortune. The *gopīs* are all goddesses of fortune, and Kṛṣṇa took them hand in hand on the bank of the Yamunā.

It is said in the *Skanda Purāṇa* that out of many thousands of *gopīs,* 16,000 are predominant; out of those 16,000 *gopīs,* 108 *gopīs* are especially prominent; and out of 108 *gopīs,* eight *gopīs* are still more prominent; out of eight *gopīs,* Rādhārāṇī and Candrāvalī are prominent; and out of these two *gopīs,* Rādhārāṇī is the most prominent.

When Kṛṣṇa entered the forest on the bank of the Yamunā, the moonlight dissipated the surrounding darkness. Due to the season, flowers like the *kunda* and *kadamba* were blooming, and a gentle breeze was carrying their aroma. Due to the aroma, the bees were also flying in the breeze, thinking that the aroma was honey. The *gopīs* made a seat for Kṛṣṇa by leveling the soft sand and placing cloths over it.

The *gopīs* who were gathered there were mostly all followers of the *Vedas.* In their previous births, during Lord Rāmacandra's advent, they were Vedic scholars who desired the association of Lord Rāmacandra in conjugal love. Rāmacandra gave them the benediction that they would be present for the advent of Lord Kṛṣṇa, and He would fulfill their desires. During Kṛṣṇa's advent, the Vedic scholars took birth in the shape of the *gopīs* in Vṛndāvana; as young *gopīs,* they got the association of Kṛṣṇa in fulfillment of their previous births' desire. The ultimate goal of their perfect desire was attained, and they were so joyous that they had nothing further to desire. This is confirmed in the *Bhagavad-gītā:* if one attains the Supreme Personality of Godhead, then he has no desire for anything. When the *gopīs* had Kṛṣṇa in their company, not only all their grief, but their lamenting in the absence of Kṛṣṇa was relieved. They felt they had no desire to be fulfilled. Fully satisfied in the company of Kṛṣṇa, they spread their cloths on the ground. These garments were made of fine linen and smeared with the red *kuṅkuma* which decorated their breasts. With great care they spread a sitting place for Kṛṣṇa. Kṛṣṇa was their life and soul, and they created a very comfortable seat for Him.

Sitting on the seat amongst the *gopīs,* Kṛṣṇa became more beautiful. Great *yogīs* like Lord Śiva, Lord Brahmā or even Lord Śeṣa and others always try to fix their attention upon Kṛṣṇa in their heart, but here the *gopīs* actually saw Kṛṣṇa seated before them on their cloths. In the society of the *gopīs,* Kṛṣṇa looked very beautiful. They were the most beautiful damsels within the three worlds, and they assembled together around Kṛṣṇa.

It may be asked herein how Kṛṣṇa seated Himself beside so many *gopīs* and yet sat alone. There is a significant word in this verse: *īśvara.* As it is stated in the *Bhagavad-gītā, īśvaraḥ sarva-bhūtānām. Īśvara* refers to the Supreme Lord as the Supersoul seated in everyone's heart. Kṛṣṇa also manifested this potency of expansion as Paramātmā in this gathering with the *gopīs.* Kṛṣṇa was sitting by the side of each *gopī,* unseen by the others. Kṛṣṇa was so kind to the *gopīs* that instead of sitting in their hearts to be appreciated in yogic meditation, He seated Himself by their sides. By seating Himself outside, He showed special favor to the *gopīs,* who were the selected beauties of all creation. Having gotten their most beloved Lord, the *gopīs* began to please Him by moving their eyebrows and smiling and also by suppressing their anger. Some of them took His lotus feet in their laps and began to massage Him. And while smiling, they confidentially expressed their suppressed anger and said, "Dear Kṛṣṇa, we are ordinary women of Vṛndāvana, and we do not know much about Vedic knowledge—what is right and what is wrong. We therefore put a question to You, and, since You are very learned, You can answer it properly. In dealing between lovers, we find that there are three classes of men. One class simply receives, another class reciprocates favorably, even if the lover is very contrary, and the third class neither acts contrary nor answers favorably in dealings of love. So out of these three classes, which do You prefer, or which do You call honest?"

In answer, Kṛṣṇa said, "My dear friends, persons who simply reciprocate the loving dealings of the other party are just like merchants. They give in loving affairs as much as they get from the other party. Practically there is no question of love. It is simply business dealing, and it is self-interested or self-centered. Better the second class of men, who love in spite of the opposite party's contrariness; even those without a tinge of loving affairs are better than the merchants. Sincere love can be seen when the father and mother love their children in spite of their children's neglect. The third class neither reciprocates nor neglects. They can be further divided into two classes. One is the self-satisfied, who do not require anyone's love. They are called *ātmārāma,* which means they are absorbed in the thought of the Supreme Personality of Godhead and so do not care whether one loves them or not. But another class are ungrateful men. They are called callous. The men in this group revolt against superior persons. For instance, a son, in spite of receiving all kinds of things from loving parents, may be callous and not reciprocate. Those in this class are generally known as *gurudruha,* which means they receive favors from the parents or the spiritual master and yet neglect them."

Kṛṣṇa indirectly answered the questions of the *gopīs,* even those questions which implied that Kṛṣṇa did not properly receive their dealings. In answer, Kṛṣṇa said that He, as the Supreme Personality of Godhead, is self-satisfied. He does not require anyone's love, but at the same time He said that He is not ungrateful.

"My dear friends," Kṛṣṇa continued, "you might be aggrieved by My words and acts, but you must know that sometimes I do not reciprocate my devotees' dealings with Me. It appears that my devotees are very much attached to Me, but sometimes I do not reciprocate their feelings properly in order to increase their love for Me more and more. If I can very easily be approached by them, they might think, 'Kṛṣṇa is so easily available.' So sometimes I do not respond. If a person has no money but after some time accumulates some wealth and then loses it, he will think of the lost property twenty-four hours a day. Similarly, in order to increase the love of My devotees, sometimes I appear to be lost to them, and instead of forgetting Me, they feel their loving sentiments for Me increase. My dear friends, do not think for a moment that I have been dealing with You just like ordinary devotees. I know what you are. You have forsaken all kinds of social and religious obligations; you have given up all connection with your parents. Without caring for social convention and religious obligations, you have come to Me and loved Me, and I am so much obliged to you that I cannot treat you as ordinary devotees. Do not think that I was away from you. I was near to you. I was simply seeing how much you were anxious for Me in My absence. So please do not try to find fault in Me. Because you consider Me so dear to you, kindly excuse Me if I have done anything wrong. I cannot repay your continual love for Me, even throughout the lifetimes of the demigods in the heavenly planets. It is impossible to repay you or show gratitude for your love; therefore please be satisfied by your own pious activities. You have displayed exemplary attraction for Me, overcoming the greatest difficulties arising from family connections. Please be satisfied with your highly exemplary character, for it is not possible for Me to repay your debt."

The exemplary character of devotional service manifested by the devotees of Vṛndāvana is the purest type of devotion. It is enjoined in authoritative *śāstra* that devotional service must be *ahaituka* and *apratihata.* This means that devotional service to Kṛṣṇa cannot be checked by political or religious convention. The stage of devotional service is always transcendental. The *gopīs* particularly showed pure devotional service towards Kṛṣṇa, so much so that Kṛṣṇa Himself remained indebted to them. Lord Caitanya thus said that the devotional service manifested by the *gopīs* in Vṛndāvana excelled all other methods of approaching the Supreme Personality of Godhead.

Thus ends the Bhaktivedanta purport of the Thirty-first Chapter of Kṛṣṇa, *"Songs by the Gopīs."*

32 / Description of the Rāsa Dance

Thus hearing the Supreme Personality of Godhead, Kṛṣṇa, speaking to pacify them, the *gopīs* became very much pleased. And not only by hearing His words, but also by touching the hands and legs of the Supreme Personality of Godhead, they became completely relieved from the great suffering of separation. After this, the Supreme Personality of Godhead began His *rāsa* dance. When one dances in the midst of many girls, it is called a *rāsa* dance. So Kṛṣṇa began to dance among the most beautiful and fortunate girls within the three worlds. The *gopīs* of Vṛndāvana, who were so attracted to Him, danced with Kṛṣṇa, hand in hand.

Kṛṣṇa's *rāsa* dance should never be compared with any kind of material dance, such as a ball dance or a society dance. The *rāsa* dance is a completely spiritual performance. In order to establish this fact, Kṛṣṇa, the supreme mystic, expanded Himself in many forms and stood beside each *gopī*. Placing His hands on the shoulders of the *gopīs* on both sides of Him, He began to dance in their midst. The mystic expansions of Kṛṣṇa were not perceived by the *gopīs* because Kṛṣṇa appeared alone to each of them. Each *gopī* thought that Kṛṣṇa was dancing with her alone. Above that wonderful dance flew many airplanes carrying the denizens of the heavenly planets, who were very anxious to see the wonderful dance of Kṛṣṇa with the *gopīs*. The Gandharvas and Kinnaras began to sing, and, accompanied by their respective wives, all the Gandharvas began to shower flowers on the dancers.

As the *gopīs* and Kṛṣṇa danced together, a very blissful musical sound was produced from the tinkling of their bells, ornaments and bangles. It appeared that Kṛṣṇa was a greenish sapphire locket in the midst of a golden necklace decorated with valuable stones. While Kṛṣṇa and the *gopīs* danced they displayed extraordinary bodily features. The movements of their legs, their placing their hands on one another, the movements of their eyebrows, their smiling, the movements of the breasts of the *gopīs* and their clothes, their earrings, their cheeks, their hair with flowers—as they sang and danced these combined together to appear like clouds, thunder, snow and lightning. Kṛṣṇa's bodily features appeared just like a group of clouds, their songs were like thunder, the beauty of the *gopīs* appeared to be just like lightning in the sky, and the drops of perspiration visible on their faces appeared like falling snow. In this way, both the *gopīs* and Kṛṣṇa fully engaged in dancing.

The necks of the *gopīs* became tinted with red due to their desire to enjoy Kṛṣṇa more and more. To satisfy them, Kṛṣṇa began to clap His hands in time with their singing. Actually the whole world is full of Kṛṣṇa's singing, but it is appreciated in different ways by different kinds of living entities. This is confirmed in the *Bhagavad-gītā: ye yathā māṁ prapadyante.* Kṛṣṇa is dancing, and every living entity is also dancing, but there is a difference in the dancing in the spiritual world and in the material world. This is expressed by the author of *Caitanya-caritāmṛta,* who says that the master dancer is Kṛṣṇa and everyone is His servant. Everyone is trying to imitate Kṛṣṇa's dancing. Those who are actually in Kṛṣṇa consciousness respond rightly to the dancing of Kṛṣṇa: they do not try to dance independently. But those in the material world try to imitate Kṛṣṇa as the Supreme Personality of Godhead. The living entities are dancing under the direction of Kṛṣṇa's *māyā* and are thinking that they are equal to Kṛṣṇa. But this is not a fact. In Kṛṣṇa consciousness, this misconception is absent, for a person in Kṛṣṇa consciousness knows that Kṛṣṇa is the supreme master and everyone is His servant. One has to dance to please Kṛṣṇa, not to imitate or to become equal to the Supreme Personality of Godhead. The *gopīs* wanted to please Kṛṣṇa, and therefore as Kṛṣṇa sang, they responded and encouraged Him by saying, "Well done, well done." Sometimes they presented beautiful music for His pleasure, and He responded by praising their singing.

When some of the *gopīs* became very tired from dancing and moving their bodies, they placed their hands on the shoulders of Śrī Kṛṣṇa. Then their hair loosened and flowers fell to the ground. When they placed their hands on Kṛṣṇa's shoulder, they became overwhelmed by the fragrance of His body which emanated from the lotus, other aromatic flowers, and the pulp of sandalwood. They became filled with attraction for Him, and they began to kiss one another. Some *gopīs* touched Kṛṣṇa cheek to cheek, and Kṛṣṇa began to offer them chewed betel nuts from His mouth, which they exchanged with great pleasure by kissing. And by accepting those betel nuts, the *gopīs* spiritually advanced.

The *gopīs* became tired after long singing and dancing. Kṛṣṇa was dancing beside them, and to alleviate their fatigue they took Śrī Kṛṣṇa's hand and placed it on their raised breasts. Kṛṣṇa's hand, as well as the breasts of the *gopīs,* are eternally auspicious; therefore when they combined, both of them became spiritually enhanced. The *gopīs* so enjoyed the company of Kṛṣṇa, the husband of the goddess of fortune, that they forgot that they had any other husband in the world, and upon being embraced by the arms of Kṛṣṇa and dancing and singing with Him, they forgot everything. The *Śrīmad-Bhāgavatam* thus describes the beauty of the *gopīs* while they were *rāsa* dancing with Kṛṣṇa. There were lotus flowers over both their ears, and their faces were decorated with sandalwood pulp. They wore *tilaka,* and there were drops of sweat on their smiling mouths. From their feet came the tinkling sound of ankle bells as well as bangles. The flowers within their hair were falling to the lotus feet of Kṛṣṇa, and He was very satisfied.

As stated in the *Brahma-saṁhitā,* all these *gopīs* are expansions of Kṛṣṇa's pleasure potency. Touching their bodies with His hands and looking at their pleasing eyes, Kṛṣṇa enjoyed the *gopīs* exactly as a child enjoys playing with the reflection of his body in a mirror. When Kṛṣṇa touched the different parts of their bodies, the *gopīs* felt surcharged with spiritual energy. They could not adjust their loosened clothes, although they tried to keep them properly. Their hair and garments became scattered, and their ornaments loosened as they forgot themselves in company with Kṛṣṇa.

While Kṛṣṇa was enjoying the company of the *gopīs* in the *rāsa* dance, the astonished demigods and their wives gathered in the sky. The moon, being afflicted with a sort of lust, began to watch the dance and became stunned with wonder. The *gopīs* had prayed to the goddess Kātyāyanī to have Kṛṣṇa as their husband. Now Kṛṣṇa was fulfilling their desire by expanding Himself in as many forms as there were *gopīs* and enjoying them exactly as a husband.

Śrīla Śukadeva Gosvāmi has remarked that Kṛṣṇa is self-sufficient—He is *ātmārāma.* He doesn't need anyone else for His satisfaction. Because the *gopīs* wanted Kṛṣṇa as their husband, He fulfilled their desire. When Kṛṣṇa saw that the *gopīs* were tired from dancing with Him, He immediately began to smear His hands over their faces so that their fatigue would be satiated. In order to reciprocate the kind hospitality of Kṛṣṇa, the *gopīs* began to look at Him lovingly. They were overjoyed by the auspicious touch of the hand of Kṛṣṇa. Their smiling cheeks shone with beauty, and they began to sing the glories of Kṛṣṇa with transcendental pleasure. As pure devotees, the more the *gopīs* enjoyed Kṛṣṇa's company, the more thev became enlightened with His glories, and thus they reciprocated with Him. They wanted to satisfy Kṛṣṇa by glorifying His transcendental pastimes. Kṛṣṇa is the Supreme Personality of Godhead, the master of all masters, and the *gopīs* wanted to worship Him for His unusual exhibition of mercy upon them.

Both the *gopīs* and Kṛṣṇa entered the water of the Yamunā just to relieve their fatigue from the *rāsa* dance. The lily flower garlands around the necks of the *gopīs* were strewn to pieces due to their embracing the body of Kṛṣṇa, and the flowers were reddish from being smeared with the *kuṅkuma* on their breasts. The bumblebees were humming about in order to get honey from the flowers. Kṛṣṇa and the *gopīs* entered the water of Yamunā just as an elephant enters a water tank with his many female companions. Both the *gopīs* and Kṛṣṇa forgot their real identity, playing in the water, enjoying each others' company and relieving the fatigue of *rāsa* dancing. The *gopīs* began to splash water on the body of Kṛṣṇa, all the while smiling, and Kṛṣṇa enjoyed this. As Kṛṣṇa was taking pleasure in the joking words and splashing water, the demigods in the heavenly planets began to shower flowers. The demigods thus praised the super-excellent *rāsa* dance of Kṛṣṇa, the supreme enjoyer, and His pastimes with the *gopīs* in the water of Yamunā.

After this, Lord Kṛṣṇa and the *gopīs* came out of the water and began to stroll along the bank of the Yamunā, where a nice breeze was blowing, carrying the aroma of different kinds of flowers over the water and land. While strolling on the bank of the Yamunā, Kṛṣṇa recited various kinds of poetry. He thus enjoyed the company of the *gopīs* in the soothing moon-light of autumn.

Sex desire is especially excited in the autumn season, but the wonderful thing about Kṛṣṇa's association with the *gopīs* is that there was no question of sex desire. It was, as clearly stated in the *Bhāgavata* description by Śukadeva Gosvāmī, *avaruddha-sauratah,* namely the sex impulse was completely controlled. There is a distinction between Lord Kṛṣṇa's dancing with the *gopīs* and the ordinary dancing of living entities within the material world. In order to clear up further misconceptions about the *rāsa* dance and the affairs of Kṛṣṇa and the *gopīs,* Mahārāja Parīkṣit, the hearer of *Śrīmad-Bhāgavatam,* told Śukadeva Gosvāmī, "Kṛṣṇa appeared on the earth to establish the regulative principles of religion and to curb the predominance of irreligion. But the behavior of Kṛṣṇa and the *gopīs* might encourage irreligious principles in the material world. I am simply surprised that He would act in such a way, enjoying the company of others' wives in the dead of night." This statement of Mahārāja Parīkṣit's was very much appreciated by Śukadeva Gosvamī. The answer anticipates the abominable acts of the Māyāvādī impersonalists who place themselves in the position of Kṛṣṇa and enjoy the company of young girls and women.

The basic Vedic injunctions never allow a person to enjoy sex with any woman except one's own wife. Kṛṣṇa's appreciation of the *gopīs* appeared to be distinctly in violation of these rules. Mahārāja Parīkṣit understood the total situation from Śukadeva Gosvāmī, yet to further clear the transcendental nature of Kṛṣṇa and the *gopīs* in *rāsa* dance, he expressed his surprise. This is very important in order to check the unrestricted association with women by the *prakṛta-sahajiyā.*

In his statement, Mahārāja Parīkṣit has used several important words which require clarification. The first word, *jugupsitam,* means abominable. The first doubt of Mahārāja Parīkṣit was as follows: Lord Kṛṣṇa is the Supreme Personality of Godhead who has advented Himself to establish religious principles. Why then did He mix with others' wives in the dead of night and enjoy dancing, embracing and kissing? According to the Vedic injunctions, this is not allowed. Also, when the *gopīs* first came to Him, He gave instructions to them to return to their homes. To call the wives of other persons or young girls and enjoy dancing with them is certainly abominable according to the *Vedas.* Why should Kṛṣṇa have done this?

Another word used here is *āptakāma.* Some may take it for granted that Kṛṣṇa was very lusty among young girls, but Parīkṣit Mahārāja said that this was not possible. He could not be lusty. First of all, from the material calculation He was only eight years old. At that age a boy cannot be lusty. *Āptakāma* means that the Supreme Personality of Godhead is self-satisfied. Even if He were lusty, He doesn't need to take help from others to satisfy His lusty desires. The next point is that, although not lusty Himself, He might have been induced by the lusty desires of the *gopīs.* But Mahārāja Parīkṣit then used another word, *yadu-pati,* which indicates that Kṛṣṇa is the most exalted personality in the dynasty of the Yadus. The kings in the dynasty of Yadu were considered to be the most pious, and their descendants were also like that. Having taken birth in that family, how could Kṛṣṇa have been induced, even by the *gopīs?* It is concluded, therefore, that it was not possible for Kṛṣṇa to do anything abominable. But Mahārāja Parīkṣit was in doubt as to *why* Kṛṣṇa acted in that way. What was the real purpose? Another word Mahārāja Parīkṣit used when he addressed Śukadeva Gosvāmī is *suvrata,* which means to take a vow to enact pious activities. Śukadeva Gosvāmī was an educated *brahmacārī,* and under the circumstances, it was not possible for him to indulge in sex. This is strictly prohibited for *brahmacārīs,* and what to speak of a *brahmacārī* like Śukadeva Gosvāmī. But because the circumstances of the *rāsa* dance were very suspect, Mahārāja Parīkṣit inquired for clarification from Śukadeva Gosvāmī. Śukadeva Gosvāmī immediately replied that transgressions of religious principles by the supreme controller testify to His great power. For example, fire can consume any abominable thing; that is the manifestation of the supremacy of fire. Similarly, the sun can absorb water from a urinal or from stool, and the sun is not polluted; rather, due to the influence of sunshine, the polluted, contaminated place becomes disinfected and sterilized.

One may also argue that since Kṛṣṇa is the supreme authority, His activities should be followed. In answer to this question, Śukadeva Gosvāmī has very clearly said that *īśvarāṇām,* or the supreme controller, may sometimes violate His instructions, but this is only possible for the controller Himself, not for the followers. Unusual and uncommon activities by the controller can never by imitated. Śukadeva Gosvāmī warned that the conditioned followers, who are not actually in control, should never even imagine imitating the uncommon activities of the controller. A Māyāvādī philosopher may falsely claim to be God or Kṛṣṇa, but he cannot actually act like Kṛṣṇa. He can persuade his followers to falsely imitate *rāsa* dance, but he is unable to lift Govardhana Hill. We have many experiences in the past of Māyāvādī rascals deluding their followers by posing themselves as Kṛṣṇa in order to enjoy *rāsa-līlā.* In many instances they were checked by the government, arrested and punished. In Orissa, Ṭhākur Bhaktivinode also punished a so-called incarnation of Viṣṇu, who was imitating *rāsa-līlā* with young girls. There were many complaints against him. At that time, Bhaktivinode Ṭhākur was magistrate, and the government deputed him to deal with that rascal, and he punished him very severely. The *rāsa-līlā* dance cannot be imitated by anyone. Śukadeva Gosvāmī warns that one should not even think of imitating it. He specifically mentions that if, out of foolishness, one tries to imitate Kṛṣṇa's *rāsa* dance, he will be killed, just like a person who wants to imitate Lord Śiva's drinking of an ocean of poison. Lord Śiva drank an ocean of poison and kept it within his throat. The poison made his throat turn blue; and therefore Lord Śiva is called Nīlakaṇṭa. But if any ordinary person tries to imitate Lord Śiva by drinking poison or smoking *gañja,* he is sure to be vanquished and will die within a very short time. Lord Śrī Kṛṣṇa's dealing with the *gopīs* was under special circumstances.

Most of the *gopīs* in their previous lives were great sages, expert in the studies of the *Vedas,* and when Lord Kṛṣṇa appeared as Lord Rāmacandra, they wanted to enjoy with Him. Lord Rāmacandra gave them the benediction that their desires would be fulfilled when He would appear as Kṛṣṇa. Therefore the desire of the *gopīs* to enjoy the appearance of Lord Kṛṣṇa was long cherished. So they approached goddess Kātyāyanī to have Kṛṣṇa as their husband. There are many other circumstances also which testify to the supreme authority of Kṛṣṇa and show that He is not bound to the rules and regulations of the material world. In special cases, He acts as He likes to favor His devotees. This is only possible for Him, because He is the supreme controller. People in general should follow the instructions of Lord Kṛṣṇa as given in the *Bhagavad-gītā* and should not even imagine imitating Lord Kṛṣṇa in the *rāsa* dance.

Kṛṣṇa's lifting of Govardhana Hill, His killing great demons like Pūtanā and others are all obviously extraordinary activities. Similarly, the *rāsa* dance is also an uncommon activity and cannot be imitated by any ordinary man. An ordinary person engaged in his occupational duty, like Arjuna, should execute his duty for the satisfaction of Kṛṣṇa; that is within his power. Arjuna was a fighter, and Kṛṣṇa wanted him to fight for His satisfaction. Arjuna agreed, although at first he was not willing to fight. Duties are required for ordinary persons. They should not jump up and try to imitate Kṛṣṇa and indulge in *rāsa-līlā* and thus bring about their ruin. One should know with certainty that Kṛṣṇa had no personal interest in whatever He did for the benediction of the *gopīs*. As stated in the *Bhagavad-gītā, na māṁ karmāṇi limpanti:* Kṛṣṇa never enjoys or suffers the result of His activities. Therefore it is not possible for Him to act irreligiously. He is transcendental to all activities and religious principles. He is untouched by the modes of material nature. He is the supreme controller of all living entities, either in human society, in the demigod society in heavenly planets, or in lower forms of life. He is the supreme controller of all living entities and of material nature; therefore, He has nothing to do with religious or irreligious principles.

Śukadeva Gosvāmī further concludes that the great sages and devotees, who are washed clean of all conditional life, can move freely even within the contamination of material nature by keeping Kṛṣṇa the Supreme Personality of Godhead within their hearts. In this way also they do not become subject to the laws of pleasure and pain in the modes of material nature. How, then, is it possible for Kṛṣṇa, who appears in His own internal potency, to be subjected to the laws of *karma?*

In the *Bhagavad-gītā* the Lord clearly says that whenever He appears He does so by His internal potency; He is not forced to accept a body by the laws of *karma* like an ordinary living entity. Every other living entity is forced to accept a certain type of body by his previous actions. But when Kṛṣṇa appears, He always appears in a body; it is not forced upon Him by the action of His past deeds. His body is a vehicle for His transcendental pleasure which is enacted by His internal potency. He has no obligation to the laws of *karma.* The Māyāvādī monist must accept a certain type of body, being forced by the laws of nature; therefore, his claim to be one with Kṛṣṇa or God is only theoretical. Such persons who claim to be equal with Kṛṣṇa and indulge in *rāsa-līlā* create a dangerous situation for the people in general. Kṛṣṇa, the Supreme Personality of Godhead, is already present as Supersoul within the bodies of the *gopīs* and their husbands. He is the guide of all living entities, as is confirmed in the *Kaṭha Upaniṣad, nityo nityānāṁ cetanaś cetanānām.* The Supersoul directs the individual soul to act, and the Supersoul is the actor and witness of all action.

It is confirmed in the *Bhagavad-gītā* that Kṛṣṇa is present in everyone's heart, and from Him come all action, remembrance and forgetfulness. He is the original person to be known by Vedic knowledge. He is the author of *Vedānta* philosophy, and He knows the *Vedānta* philosophy perfectly well. The so-called Vedāntists and Māyāvādīs cannot understand Kṛṣṇa as He is; they simply mislead followers by imitating the actions of Kṛṣṇa in an unauthorized way. Kṛṣṇa, the Supersoul of everyone, is already within the body of everyone; therefore if He sees someone or embraces someone there is no question of propriety.

Some ask that if Kṛṣṇa is self-sufficient, why should He at all manifest pastimes with the *gopīs* which are disturbing to the so-called moralists of the world? The answer is that such activities show special mercy to the fallen, conditioned souls. The *gopīs* are also expansions of His internal energy, but because Kṛṣṇa wanted to exhibit the *rāsa-līlā,* they also appeared as ordinary human beings. In the material world, pleasure is ultimately manifested in the sex attraction between man and woman. The man lives simply to be attracted by women, and the woman lives simply to be attracted by men. That is the basic principle of material life. As soon as these attractions are combined, people become more and more implicated in material existence. In order to show them special favor, Kṛṣṇa exhibited this *rāsa-līlā* dance. It is just to captivate the conditioned soul. Since they are very much attracted by sexology, they can enjoy the same life with Kṛṣṇa and thus become liberated from the material condition. In the Second Canto of *Śrīmad-Bhāgavatam,* Mahārāja Parīkṣit also explains that the pastimes and activities of Lord Kṛṣṇa are medicine for the conditioned souls. If they simply hear about Kṛṣṇa they become relieved from the material disease. They are addicted to material enjoyment and are accustomed to reading sex literature, but by hearing these transcendental pastimes of Kṛṣṇa with the *gopīs,* they will be relieved from material contamination.

How they should hear and from whom is also explained by Śukadeva Gosvāmī. The difficulty is that the whole world is full of Māyāvādīs, and when they become professional reciters of *Śrīmad-Bhāgavatam,* and when people, without knowing the effect of the Māyāvāda philosophy, hear from such persons, they become confused. Discussion of *rāsa-līlā* among people in general is not recommended because they are affected by the Māyāvāda philosophy, but if one who is advanced explains, and people hear from him, certainly the hearers will be gradually elevated to the position of Kṛṣṇa consciousness and liberated from materially contaminated life.

Another important point is that all the *gopīs* who danced with Kṛṣṇa were not in their material bodies. They danced with Kṛṣṇa in their spiritual bodies. All their husbands thought that their wives were sleeping by their sides. The so-called husbands of the *gopīs* were already enamored by the influence of the external energy of Kṛṣṇa; so by dint of this very energy they could not understand that their wives had gone to dance with Kṛṣṇa. What then is the basis of accusing Kṛṣṇa of dancing with others' wives? The bodies of the *gopīs,* which were their husbands', were lying in bed, but the spiritual parts and parcels of Kṛṣṇa were dancing with Him. Kṛṣṇa is the supreme person, the whole spirit, and He danced with the spiritual bodies of the *gopīs.* There is therefore no reason to accuse Kṛṣṇa in any way.

After the *rāsa* dance was over, the night turned into the *brāhma-muhūrta* (the night of Brahmā, a very, very long period, as mentioned in the *Bhagavad-gītā).* The *brāhma-muhūrta* takes place about one and a half hours before sunrise. It is recommended that one should rise from bed at that time and, after finishing daily ablutions, take to spiritual activities by performing *Maṅgala-ārātrika* and chanting the Hare Kṛṣṇa *mantra.* This period is very convenient for the execution of spiritual activities. When that auspicious moment arrived, Kṛṣṇa asked the *gopīs* to leave. Although they were not willing to quit His company, they were very obedient and dear to Him. As soon as Kṛṣṇa asked them to go home, they immediately left and returned home. Śukadeva Gosvāmī concludes this episode of *rāsa-līlā* by pointing out that if a person hears from the right source of the pastimes of Kṛṣṇa, who is Viṣṇu Himself, and the *gopīs,* who are expansions of His energy, then he will be relieved from the most dangerous type of disease, namely lust. If one actually hears *rāsa-līlā,* he will become completely freed from the lusty desire of sex life and elevated to the highest level of spiritual understanding. Generally, because they hear from Māyāvādīs and they themselves are Māyāvādīs, people become more and more implicated in sex life. The conditioned soul should hear the *rāsa-līlā* dance from an authorized spiritual master and be trained by him so that he can understand the whole situation; thus one can be elevated to the highest standard of spiritual life, otherwise one will be implicated. Material lust is a kind of heart disease, and to cure the material heart disease of the conditioned soul, it is recommended that one should hear, but not from the impersonalist rascals. If one hears from the right sources with right understanding, then his situation will be different.

Śukadeva Gosvāmī has used the word *śraddhānvita* for one who is trained in the spiritual life. *Śraddhā,* or faith, is the beginning. One who has developed his faith in Kṛṣṇa as the Supreme Personality of Godhead, the Supreme Spirit Soul, can both describe and hear. Śukadeva also uses the word *anuśṛṇuyāt.* One must hear from disciplic succession. *Anu* means following, and *anu* means always. So one must always follow the disciplic succession and not hear from any stray professional reciter, Māyāvādī or ordinary man. *Anuśṛṇuyāt* means that one must hear from an authorized person who is in the disciplic succession and is always engaged in Kṛṣṇa consciousness. When a person wants to hear in this way, then the effect will be sure. By hearing *rāsa-līlā,* one will be elevated to the highest position of spiritual life.

Śukadeva Gosvāmī uses two specific words, *bhaktim* and *parām. Bhaktim parām* means execution of devotional service above the neophyte stage. Those who are simply attracted to temple worship but do not know the philosophy of *bhakti* are in the neophyte stage. That sort of *bhakti* is not the perfectional stage. The perfectional stage of *bhakti,* or devotional service, is completely free from material contamination. The most dangerous aspect of contamination is lust or sex life. *Bhaktim parām* devotional service is so potent that the more one advances in this line, the more he loses his attraction for material life. One who is actually deriving benefit from hearing *rāsa-līlā* dance surely achieves the transcendental position. He surely loses all traces of lust in his heart.

Śrīla Viśvanātha Cakravartī Ṭhākur points out that according to *Bhagavad-gītā,* the Brahmā day and Brahmā night are periods of solar years expanding to 4,300,000 multiplied by 1,000. According to Viśvanātha Cakravartī Ṭhākur, the *rāsa* dance was performed during the long period of Brahmā's night, but the *gopīs* could not understand that. In order to fulfill their desire, Kṛṣṇa extended the night to cover such a great period of time. One may ask how this was possible, and Viśvanātha Cakravartī Ṭhākur reminds us that Kṛṣṇa, although bound by a small rope, could show His mother the whole universe within His mouth. How was this possible? The answer is that He can do anything for the pleasure of His devotees. Similarly, because the *gopīs* wanted to enjoy Kṛṣṇa, they were given the opportunity to associate with Him for a long period. This was done according to His promise. When Kṛṣṇa stole the garments of the *gopīs* while they were taking bath at Cirghat on Yamunā, Kṛṣṇa promised to fulfill their desire in some future night. In one night, therefore, they enjoyed the company of Kṛṣṇa as their beloved husband, but that night was not an ordinary night. It was a night of Brahmā, and lasted millions and millions of years. Everything is possible for Kṛṣṇa, for He is the supreme controller.

Thus ends the Bhaktivedanta purport of the Thirty-second Chapter of Kṛṣṇa, *"Description of the Rāsa Dance."*

33 / Vidyādhara Liberated and the Demon Śaṅkhāsura Killed

Once upon a time, the cowherd men of Vṛndāvana, headed by Nanda Mahārāja, desired to go to Ambikāvana to perform the *Śivarātri* performance. The *rāsa-līlā* was performed during the autumn, and after that the next big ceremony is *Holi* or the *Dolayātrā* ceremony. Between the *Dolayātrā* ceremony and the *rāsa-līlā* ceremony there is one important ceremony which is called *Śivarātri,* which is especially observed by the Śaivites, or devotees of Lord Śiva. But sometimes the Vaiṣṇavas also observe this ceremony because they accept Lord Śiva as the foremost Vaiṣṇava. But the function of *Śivarātri* is not observed very regularly by the *bhaktas,* or devotees of Kṛṣṇa. Under the circumstances, it is stated in *Śrīmad-Bhāgavatam* that the cowherd men headed by Nanda Mahārāja "once upon a time desired." That means that they were not regularly observing the *Śivarātri* function, but that once upon a time they wanted to go to Ambikāvana out of curiosity. Ambikāvana is situated somewhere in the Gujarat province. Ambikāvana is said to be situated on the river Sarasvatī, yet we do not find any Sarasvatī River in the Gujarat province; the only river there is Savarmati. In India, all the big places of pilgrimage are situated on nice rivers like the Ganges, Yamunā, Sarasvatī, Narmadā, Godāvarī, Kāverī, etc. Ambikāvana was situated on the bank of Sarasvatī, and all the cowherd men and Nanda Mahārāja went there.

They very devotedly began to worship the deity of Lord Śiva and Ambikā. It is the general practice that wherever there is a temple of Lord Śiva, there must be another temple of Ambikā (or Durgā) because Ambikā is the wife of Lord Śiva and is the most exalted of chaste women. She doesn't live outside the association of her husband. After reaching Ambikāvana, the cowherd men of Vṛndāvana first bathed themselves in the River Sarasvatī. If one goes to any place of pilgrimage, his first duty is to take a bath and sometimes to shave his head. That is the first business. After taking bath, they worshiped the Deities and then distributed charity in the holy places.

According to the Vedic system, charity is given to the *brāhmaṇas.* It is stated in the Vedic *śāstras* that only the *brāhmaṇas* and the *sannyāsīs* can accept charity. The cowherd men from Vṛndāvana gave cows decorated with golden ornaments and beautiful garlands. The *brāhmaṇas* are given charity because they are not engaged in any business profession. They are supposed to be engaged in brahminical occupations, as described in the *Bhagavad-gītā*—namely, they must be very learned and must perform austerity and penances. They must not only themselves be learned, but they must also teach others. *Brāhmaṇas* are not meant to be *brāhmaṇas* alone; they should create other *brāhmaṇas* also. If a man is found who agrees to become a *brāhmaṇa's* disciple, he is also given the chance to become a *brāhmaṇa.* The *brāhmaṇa* is always engaged in the worship of Lord Viṣṇu. Therefore the *brāhmaṇas* are eligible to accept all kinds of charity. But if the *brāhmaṇas* receive excess charity, they are to distribute it for the service of Viṣṇu. In the Vedic scripture, therefore, one is recommended to give in charity to the *brāhmaṇas,* and by so doing one pleases Lord Viṣṇu and all the demigods.

The pilgrims take bath, worship the Deity, and give in charity; they are also recommended to fast one day. They should go to a place of pilgrimage and stay there at least for three days. The first day is spent fasting, and at night they can drink a little water because water does not break the fast.

The cowherd men, headed by Nanda Mahārāja, spent that night on the bank of the Sarasvatī. They fasted all day and drank a little water at night. But while they were taking their rest, a great serpent from the nearby forest appeared before them and hungrily began to swallow up Nanda Mahārāja. Nanda began to cry helplessly, "My dear son, Kṛṣṇa, please come and save me from this danger! This serpent is swallowing me!" When Nanda Mahārāja cried for help, all the cowherd men got up and saw what was happening. They immediately took up burning logs and began to beat the snake to kill it. But in spite of being beaten with burning logs, the serpent was not about to give up swallowing Nanda Mahārāja.

At that time Kṛṣṇa appeared on the scene and touched the serpent with His lotus feet. Immediately upon being touched by the lotus feet of Kṛṣṇa, the serpent shed its reptilian body and appeared as a very beautiful demigod named Vidyādhara. His bodily features were so beautiful that he appeared to be worshipable. There was a luster and effulgence emanating from his body, and he was garlanded with a gold necklace. He offered obeisances to Lord Kṛṣṇa and stood before Him with great humility. Kṛṣṇa then asked the demigod, "You appear to be a very nice demigod and to be favored by the goddess of fortune. How is it that you performed such abominable activities, and how did you get the body of a serpent?" The demigod then began to narrate the story of his previous life.

"My dear Lord," he said, "in my previous life I was named Vidyādhara and was known all over the world for my beauty. Because I was a celebrated personality, I used to travel all over in my airplane. While traveling, I saw a great sage named Āṅgirā. He was very ugly, and because I was very proud of my beauty, I laughed at him. Due to this sinful action, I was condemned by the great sage to assume the form of a serpent."

One should note here that before being favored by Kṛṣṇa, a person is always under the modes of material nature, however elevated he may be materially. Vidyādhara was a materially elevated demigod, and he was very beautiful. He also held a great material position and was able to travel all over by airplane. Yet he was condemned to become a serpent in his next life. Any materially elevated person can be condemned to an abominable species of life if he is not careful. It is a misconception that after reaching the human body one is never degraded. Vidyādhara himself states that even though he was a demigod, he was condemned to become a serpent. But because he was touched by the lotus feet of Kṛṣṇa, he immediately came to Kṛṣṇa consciousness. He admitted, however, that in his previous life he was actually sinful. A Kṛṣṇa conscious person knows that he is always the servant of the servant of Kṛṣṇa; he is most insignificant, and whatever good he does is by the grace of Kṛṣṇa and the spiritual master.

The demigod Vidyādhara continued to speak to Śrī Kṛṣṇa. "Because I was very proud of the exquisite beauty of my body," he said, "I derided the ugly features of the great sage Āṅgirā. He cursed me for my sin, and I became a snake. Now I consider that this curse by the sage was not at all a curse; it was a great benediction for me. Had he not cursed me, I would not have assumed the body of a serpent and would not have been kicked by Your lotus feet and thus freed from all material contamination."

In material existence, four things are very valuable: to be born in a decent family, to be very rich, to be very learned, and to be very beautiful. These are considered to be material assets. Unfortunately, without Kṛṣṇa consciousness, these material assets sometimes become sources of sin and degradation. Despite Vidyādhara's being a demigod and having a beautiful body, he was condemned to the body of a snake due to pride. A snake is considered to be the most cruel and envious living entity, but those who are human beings and are envious of others are considered to be even more vicious than snakes. The snake can be subdued or controlled by charming *mantras* and herbs, but a person who is envious cannot be controlled by anyone.

"My dear Lord," Vidyādhara continued, "Now since I think I have become freed from all kinds of sinful activities, I am asking Your permission to return to my abode, the heavenly planet." This request indicates that persons who are attached to fruitive activities, desiring promotion to the comforts of higher planetary systems, cannot achieve their ultimate goal of life without the sanction of the Supreme Personality of Godhead. It is also stated in the *Bhagavad-gītā* that the less intelligent want to achieve material benefits and therefore worship different kinds of demigods, but they actually get the benediction from the demigods through the permission of Lord Viṣṇu, or Kṛṣṇa. Demigods have no power to bestow material profit. Even if one is attached to material benediction, he can worship Kṛṣṇa the Supreme Personality of Godhead and ask Him. Kṛṣṇa is completely able to give even material benediction. There is a difference, however, in asking material benediction from the demigods and from Kṛṣṇa. Dhruva Mahārāja worshiped the Supreme Personality of Godhead for material benediction, but when he actually achieved the favor of the Supreme Lord and saw Him, he was so satisfied that he refused to accept any material benediction. The intelligent person does not ask favors from or worship the demigods; he directly becomes Kṛṣṇa conscious, and if he has any desire for material benefit, he asks Kṛṣṇa, not the demigods.

Vidyādhara, awaiting permission of Kṛṣṇa to return to the heavenly planets, said, "Now because I am touched by Your lotus feet, I am relieved from all kinds of material pangs. You are the most powerful of all mystics. You are the original Supreme Personality of Godhead. You are the master of all the devotees. You are the provider of the planetary systems, and therefore I am asking Your permission. You may accept me as fully surrendered unto You. I know very well that persons who are constantly engaged in chanting Your holy name attain release from all sinful reactions, and certainly persons who are fortunate enough to be personally touched by Your lotus feet are freed. Therefore I am sure that I am now relieved from the curse of the *brāhmaṇa* simply by being touched by Your lotus feet."

In this way, Vidyādhara got permission from Lord Kṛṣṇa to return to his home in the higher planetary system. After receiving this honor, he began to circumambulate the Lord. And after offering his respectful obeisances unto Him, he returned to his heavenly planet. Thus Nanda

Mahārāja also became relieved from the imminent danger of being devoured by the snake.

The cowherd men who had come to execute the ritualistic function of worshiping Lord Śiva and Ambikā finished their business and prepared to return to Vṛndāvana. While returning, they recalled the wonderful activities of Kṛṣṇa. By relating the incident of Vidyādhara's deliverance, they became more attached to Kṛṣṇa. They had come to worship Lord Śiva and Ambikā, but they became more and more attached to Kṛṣṇa. Similarly, the *gopīs* also worshiped goddess Kātyāyanī to become more and more attached to Kṛṣṇa. It is stated in the *Bhagavad-gītā* that persons who are attached to worshiping demigods like Lord Brahmā, Śiva, Indra and Candra, for some personal benefit, are less intelligent and have forgotten the real purpose of life. But the cowherd men, inhabitants of Vṛndāvana, were no ordinary men. Whatever they did, they did for Kṛṣṇa. If one worships demigods like Lord Śiva and Lord Brahmā to become more attached to Kṛṣṇa, that is approved. But if one goes to the demigods for some personal benefit, that is condemned.

After this incident, on a very pleasant night, both Kṛṣṇa and His elder brother Balarāma, who are inconceivably powerful, went into the forest of Vṛndāvana. They were accompanied by the damsels of Vrajabhūmi, and they began to enjoy each other's company. The young damsels of Vraja were very nicely dressed and anointed with pulp of sandalwood and decorated with flowers. The moon was shining in the sky, surrounded by glittering stars, and the breeze was blowing, bearing the aroma of *mallikā* flowers, and the bumblebees were mad after the aroma. Taking advantage of the pleasing atmosphere, both Kṛṣṇa and Balarāma began to sing very melodiously. The damsels became so absorbed in their rhythmical song that they almost forgot themselves; their hair loosened, their dresses slackened, and their garlands began to fall to the ground.

At that time, while they were so much absorbed, almost in madness, a demon associate of Kuvera (the treasurer of the heavenly planets) appeared on the scene. The demon's name was Śaṅkhāsura because on his head there was a valuable jewel resembling a conchshell. Just as the two sons of Kuvera were puffed up over their wealth and opulence and did not care for Nārada Muni's presence, this Śaṅkhāsura was also puffed up over material opulence. He thought that Kṛṣṇa and Balarāma were two ordinary cowherd boys enjoying the company of many beautiful girls. Generally, in the material world, a person with riches thinks that all beautiful women should be enjoyed by him. Śaṅkhāsura also thought that, since he belonged to the rich community of Kuvera, he, not Kṛṣṇa and Balarāma, should enjoy the company of so many beautiful girls. He therefore decided to take charge of them. He appeared before Kṛṣṇa and Balarāma and the damsels of Vraja and began to lead the girls away to the north. He commanded them as if he were their proprietor and husband, despite the presence of Kṛṣṇa and Balarāma. Being forcibly taken away by Śaṅkhāsura, the damsels of Vraja began to call the names of Kṛṣṇa and Balarāma for protection. The two brothers immediately began to follow them, taking up big logs in Their hands. "Don't be afraid, don't be afraid," They called to the *gopīs*. "We are coming at once to chastise this demon." Very quickly They reached Śaṅkhāsura. Thinking the brothers too powerful, Śaṅkhāsura left the company of the *gopīs* and ran for fear of his life. But Kṛṣṇa would not let him go. He entrusted the *gopīs* to the care of Balarāma and followed Śaṅkhāsura wherever he fled. Kṛṣṇa wanted to take the valuable jewel resembling a conchshell from the head of the demon. After following him a very short distance, Kṛṣṇa caught him, struck his head with His fist and killed him. He then took the valuable jewel and returned. In the presence of all the damsels of Vraja, He presented the valuable jewel to His elder brother Balarāma.

Thus ends the Bhaktivedanta purport of the Thirty-third Chapter of Kṛṣṇa, *"Vidyādhara Liberated and the Demon Śaṅkhāsura Killed."*

34 / The Gopīs' Feelings of Separation

The *gopīs* of Vṛndāvana were so attached to Kṛṣṇa that they were not satisfied simply with the *rāsa* dance at night. They wanted to associate with Him and enjoy His company during the daytime also. When Kṛṣṇa went to the forest with His cowherd boy friends and cows, the *gopīs* did not physically take part, but their hearts went with Him. And because their hearts went, they were able to enjoy His company through strong feelings of separation. To acquire this strong feeling of separation is the teaching of Lord Caitanya and His direct disciplic succession of Gosvāmīs. When we are not in physical contact with Kṛṣṇa, we can associate with Him like the *gopīs,* through feelings of separation. Kṛṣṇa's transcendental form, qualities, pastimes, and entourage are all identical with Him. There are nine different kinds of devotional service. Devotional service to Kṛṣṇa in feelings of separation elevates the devotee to the highest perfectional level, to the level of the *gopīs.*

It is stated in Śrīnivāsācārya's prayer to the six Gosvāmīs that they left the material opulences of government service and the princely status of life and went to Vṛndāvana, where they lived just like ordinary mendicants, begging from door to door. But they were so much enriched with the *gopīs'* feelings of separation that they enjoyed transcendental pleasure at every moment. Similarly, when Lord Caitanya was at Jagannātha Purī, He was in the role of Rādhārāṇī, feeling the separation of Kṛṣṇa. Those who are in the disciplic succession of the Mādhva-Gauḍīya-sampradāya should also feel the separation of Kṛṣṇa, worship His transcendental form, and discuss His transcendental teachings, His pastimes, His qualities, His entourage and His associations. The spiritual masters should enrich the devotees to the highest devotional perfection. Feeling constant separation while engaged in the service of the Lord is the perfection of Kṛṣṇa consciousness.

The *gopīs* used to discuss Kṛṣṇa amongst themselves, and their talks were as follows. "My dear friends," one *gopī* said, "do you know that when Kṛṣṇa lies on the ground He rests on His left elbow, and His head rests on His left hand. He moves His attractive eyebrows while playing His flute with His delicate fingers, and the sound He produces creates such a nice atmosphere that the denizens of the heavenly planets, who travel in space with their wives and beloved, stop their airplanes, for they are stunned by the vibration of the flute. The wives of the demigods who are seated in the planes then become very much ashamed of their singing and musical qualifications. Not only that, but they become afflicted with conjugal love, and their hair and tightened dresses immediately loosen."

Another *gopī* said, "My dear friends, Kṛṣṇa is so beautiful that the goddess of fortune always remains on His chest, and He is always adorned with a golden necklace. Beautiful Kṛṣṇa plays His flute in order to enliven the hearts of many devotees. He is the only friend of the suffering living entities. When He plays His flute, all the cows and other animals of Vṛndāvana, although engaged in eating, simply take a morsel of food in their mouths and stop chewing. Their ears raise up and they become stunned. They do not appear alive but like painted animals. Kṛṣṇa's flute playing is so attractive that even the animals become enchanted, and what to speak of ourselves."

Another *gopī* said, "My dear friends, not only living animals, but even inanimate objects like the rivers and lakes of Vṛndāvana also become stunned when Kṛṣṇa passes with peacock feathers on His head and His body smeared with the minerals of Vṛndāvana. With leaves and flowers decorating His body, He looks like some hero. When He plays on His flute and calls the cows with Balarāma, the River Yamunā stops flowing and waits for the air to carry dust from His lotus feet. The River Yamunā is unfortunate like us; it does not get Kṛṣṇa's mercy. The river simply remains stunned, stopping its waves just as we also stop crying out of frustration for Kṛṣṇa."

In the absence of Kṛṣṇa the *gopīs* were constantly shedding tears, but sometimes, when they expected that Kṛṣṇa was coming, they would stop crying. But when they saw that Kṛṣṇa was not coming, then again they would become frustrated and begin to cry. Kṛṣṇa is the original Personality of Godhead, the origin of all Viṣṇu forms, and the cowherd boys are all demigods. Lord Viṣṇu is always worshiped and surrounded by different demigods like Lord Śiva, Lord Brahmā, Indra, Candra, and others. When Kṛṣṇa traveled through the Vṛndāvana forest or walked on the Govardhana

Hill, He was accompanied by the cowherd boys. While walking, He played His flute, just to call His cows. Just by His association, the trees, plants and other vegetation in the forest immediately became Kṛṣṇa conscious. A Kṛṣṇa conscious person sacrifices everything for Kṛṣṇa. Although trees and plants are not very advanced in consciousness, by the association of Kṛṣṇa and His friends they also become Kṛṣṇa conscious. They then want to deliver everything—whatever they have—their fruits, flowers, and the honey incessantly falling from their branches.

When Kṛṣṇa walked on the bank of the Yamunā, He was seen nicely decorated with *tilaka* on His head. He was garlanded with different kinds of forest flowers, and His body was smeared by the pulp of sandalwood and *tulasī* leaves. The bumblebees became mad after the treasure and sweet nectar of the atmosphere. Being pleased by the humming sound of the bees, Kṛṣṇa would play His flute, and together the sounds became so sweet to hear that the aquatics, the cranes, swans and ducks and other birds were charmed. Instead of swimming or flying, they became stunned. They closed their eyes and entered a trance of meditation in worship of Kṛṣṇa.

One *gopī* said, "My dear friend, Kṛṣṇa and Balarāma are nicely dressed with earrings and pearl necklaces. They enjoy Themselves on the top of Govardhana Hill, and everything becomes absorbed in transcendental pleasure when Kṛṣṇa plays on His flute, charming the whole created manifestation. When He plays, the clouds stop their loud thundering, out of fear of Him. Rather than disturb the vibration of His flute, they respond with mild thunder and so congratulate Kṛṣṇa, their friend."

Kṛṣṇa is accepted as the friend of the cloud because both the cloud and Kṛṣṇa satisfy the people when they are disturbed. When the people are burning due to excessive heat, the cloud satisfies them with rain. Similarly, when people in materialistic life become disturbed by the blazing fire of material pangs, Kṛṣṇa gives them relief. The cloud and Kṛṣṇa, having the same bodily color also, are considered to be friends. Desiring to congratulate its superior friend, the cloud poured not water, but small flowers and covered the head of Kṛṣṇa to protect Him from the scorching sunshine.

One of the *gopīs* told mother Yaśodā, "My dear mother, your son is very expert among the cowherd boys. He knows all the different arts, how to tend the cows and how to play the flute. He composes His own songs, and to sing them He puts His flute to His mouth. When He plays, either in the morning or in the evening, all the demigods, like Lord Śiva, Brahmā, Indra and Candra, bow their heads and listen with great attention. Although they are very learned and expert, they cannot understand the musical arrangements of Kṛṣṇa's flute. They simply listen attentively and try to understand, but become bewildered and nothing more."

Another *gopī* said, "My dear friend, when Kṛṣṇa returns home with His cows, the footprint of the soles of His feet—with flag, thunderbolt, trident, and lotus flower—relieves the pain the earth feels when the cows traverse it. He walks in a stride which is so attractive, and He carries His flute. Just by looking at Him we become lusty to enjoy His company. At that time, our movements cease. We become just like trees and stand perfectly still. We even forget what we look like."

Kṛṣṇa had many thousands of cows, and they were divided into groups according to their colors. They were also differently named according to color. When He would return from the pasturing ground, He would find all the cows gathered. As Vaiṣṇavas count 108 beads, which represent the 108 individual *gopīs,* so Kṛṣṇa would also chant 108 different groups of cows.

"When Kṛṣṇa returns, He is garlanded with *tulasī* leaves," a *gopī* describes Him to a friend. "He puts His hand on the shoulder of a cowherd boy friend, and begins to blow His transcendental flute. The wives of the black deer become enchanted upon hearing the vibration of His flute, which resembles the vibration of the *vīṇā.* The deer come to Kṛṣṇa and become so charmed that they stand still, forgetting their homes and husbands. Like us, who are enchanted by the ocean of the transcendental qualities of Kṛṣṇa, the she-deer become enchanted by the vibration of His flute."

Another *gopī* told mother Yaśodā, "My dear mother, when your son returns home, He decorates Himself with the buds of the *kunda* flower, and just to enlighten and gladden His friends, He blows His flute. The breeze blowing from the south pleases the atmosphere because it is fragrant and very cool. Demigods like the Gandharvas and Siddhas take advantage of this atmosphere and offer prayers to Kṛṣṇa by sounding their bugles and drums. Kṛṣṇa is very kind to the inhabitants of Vrajabhūmi, Vṛndāvana, and when He returns with His cows and friends, He is remembered as the lifter of Govardhana Hill. Taking advantage of this opportunity, the most exalted demigods like Lord Brahmā and Lord Śiva come down to offer their evening prayers, and they accompany the cowherd boys in glorifying the qualities of Kṛṣṇa.

"Kṛṣṇa is compared with the moon, born in the ocean of the womb of Devakī. When He returns in the evening, it appears that He is fatigued, but He still tries to gladden the inhabitants of Vṛndāvana by His auspicious presence. When Kṛṣṇa returns, garlanded with flowers, His face looks beautiful. He walks into Vṛndāvana with a stride just like the elephant and slowly enters His home. Upon His return, the men, women, and cows of Vṛndāvana immediately forget the scorching heat of the day."

Such descriptions of Kṛṣṇa's transcendental pastimes and activities were remembered by the *gopīs* during His absence from Vṛndāvana. They give us some idea of Kṛṣṇa's attraction. Everyone and everything is attracted to Kṛṣṇa—that is the perfect description of Kṛṣṇa's attraction. The example of the *gopīs* is very instructive to persons who are trying to be absorbed in Kṛṣṇa consciousness. One can very easily associate with Kṛṣṇa simply by remembering His transcendental pastimes. Everyone has a tendency to love someone. That Kṛṣṇa should be the object of love is the central point of Kṛṣṇa consciousness. By constantly chanting the Hare Kṛṣṇa *mantra* and remembering the transcendental pastimes of Kṛṣṇa, one can be fully in Kṛṣṇa consciousness and thus make his life sublime and fruitful.

Thus ends the Bhaktivedanta purport of the Thirty-fourth Chapter of Kṛṣṇa, *"The Gopīs' Feelings of Separation."*

35 / Kaṁsa Sends Akrūra for Kṛṣṇa

Vṛndāvana was always absorbed in the thought of Kṛṣṇa. Everyone remembered His pastimes and was constantly merged in the ocean of transcendental bliss. But the material world is so contaminated that even in Vṛndāvana the *asuras* or demons tried to disturb the peaceful situation.

One demon named Ariṣṭāsura entered the village like a great bull with a gigantic body and horns, digging up the earth with his hoofs. When the demon entered Vṛndāvana, it appeared that the whole land trembled, as if there were an earthquake. He roared fiercely, and after digging up the earth on the riverside, he entered the village proper. The fearful roaring of the bull was so piercing that some of the pregnant cows and women had miscarriages. Its body was so big, stout and strong that a cloud hovered over its body just as clouds hover over mountains. Ariṣṭāsura entered Vṛndāvana with such a fearful appearance that just on seeing this great demon, all the men and women were afflicted with great fear, and the cows and other animals fled the village.

The situation became very terrible, and all the inhabitants of Vṛndāvana began to cry, "Kṛṣṇa! Kṛṣṇa, please save us!" Kṛṣṇa also saw that the cows were running away, and He immediately replied, "Don't be afraid. Don't be afraid." He then appeared before Ariṣṭāsura and said, "You are the lowest of living entities. Why are you frightening the inhabitants of Gokula? What will you gain by this action? If you have come to challenge My authority, then I am prepared to fight you." In this way, Kṛṣṇa challenged the demon, and the demon became very angry by the words of Kṛṣṇa. Kṛṣṇa stood before the bull, resting His hand on the shoulder of a friend. The bull began to proceed towards Kṛṣṇa in anger. Digging the earth with his hoofs, Ariṣṭāsura lifted his tail, and it appeared that clouds were hovering about the tail. His eyes were reddish and moving in anger. Pointing his horns at Kṛṣṇa, he began to charge Him, just like the thunderbolt of Indra. But Kṛṣṇa immediately caught his horns and tossed him away, just as a gigantic elephant repels a small inimical elephant. Although the demon appeared to be very tired and although he was perspiring, he took courage and got up. Again he charged Kṛṣṇa with great force and anger. While rushing towards Kṛṣṇa, he breathed very heavily. Kṛṣṇa again caught his horns and immediately threw him on the ground, breaking his horns. Kṛṣṇa then began to kick his body, just as one squeezes a wet cloth on the ground. Being thus kicked by Kṛṣṇa, Ariṣṭāsura rolled over and began to move his legs violently. Bleeding and passing stool and urine, his eyes starting from their sockets, he passed to the kingdom of death.

The demigods in the celestial planets began to shower flowers on Kṛṣṇa for His wonderful achievements. Kṛṣṇa was already the life and soul of the inhabitants of Vṛndāvana, and after killing this demon in the shape of a bull, He became the cynosure of all eyes. With Balarāma, He triumphantly entered Vṛndāvana village, and the inhabitants glorified Him and Balarāma with great jubilation. When a person performs some wonderful feat, his kinsmen and relatives and friends naturally become jubilant.

It was after this incident that the great sage Nārada disclosed the secret of Kṛṣṇa. Nārada Muni is generally known as *devadarśana,* which means that he can be seen only by demigods or persons on the same level with the demigods. But Nārada visited Kaṁsa, who was not at all on the level of the demigods, and yet Kaṁsa saw him. Of course Kaṁsa also saw Kṛṣṇa, what to speak of Nārada Muni, but generally one must have purified eyes to see the Lord and His devotees. Of course, by association with a pure devotee, one can derive an imperceptible benefit, which is called *ajñatasukṛti.* He cannot understand how he is making progress, yet he makes progress by seeing the devotee of the Lord. Nārada Muni's mission was to finish things quickly. Kṛṣṇa appeared to kill the demons, and Kaṁsa was the chief among them. Nārada wanted to expedite things; therefore, he immediately approached Kaṁsa with all the real information. "You are to be killed by the eighth son of Vasudeva," Nārada told Kaṁsa. "That eighth son is Kṛṣṇa. You were misled by Vasudeva into believing that the eighth issue of Vasudeva was a daughter. Actually, the daughter was born of Yaśodā, the wife of Nanda Mahārāja, and Vasudeva exchanged the daughter, so you were misled. Kṛṣṇa is the son of Vasudeva, as is Balarāma. Being afraid of your atrocious nature, Vasudeva has tactfully hidden Them in Vṛndāvana, out of your sight." Nārada further informed Kaṁsa, "Kṛṣṇa and Balarāma have been living incognito in the care of Nanda Mahārāja. All the *asuras,* your companions who were sent to Vṛndāvana to kill different children, were all killed by Kṛṣṇa and Balarāma."

As soon as Kaṁsa got this information from Nārada Muni, he took out his sharpened sword and prepared to kill Vasudeva for his duplicity. But Nārada pacified him. "You are not to be killed by Vasudeva," he said. "Why are you so anxious to kill him? Better try to kill Kṛṣṇa and Balarāma." But in order to satisfy his wrath, Kaṁsa arrested Vasudeva and his wife and shackled them in iron chains. Acting on the new information, Kaṁsa immediately called for the Keśī demon and asked him to go to Vṛndāvana immediately to fetch Balarāma and Kṛṣṇa. In actuality, Kaṁsa asked Keśī to go to Vṛndāvana to be killed by Kṛṣṇa and Balarāma and thus get salvation. Then Kaṁsa called for the expert elephant trainers, Cāṇūra, Muṣṭika, Śala, Tośala, etc., and he told them, "My dear friends, try to hear me attentively. At Nanda Mahārāja's place in Vṛndāvana there are two brothers, Kṛṣṇa and Balarāma. They are actually two sons of Vasudeva. As you know, I have been destined to be killed by Kṛṣṇa; there is a prophecy to this effect. Now I am requesting you to arrange for a wrestling match. People from different parts of the country will come to see the festival. I will arrange to get those two boys here, and you will try to kill Them in the wrestling arena."

Wrestling matches are still enjoyed by the indigenous people in the northern part of India, and it appears from the statements of *Śrīmad-Bhāgavatam* that 5,000 years ago wrestling was popular. Kaṁsa planned to arrange such a wrestling competition and to invite people to visit. He also told the trainers of the elephants, "Be sure to bring the elephant named Kuvalayāpīḍa and keep him at the gate of the wrestling camp. Try to capture Kṛṣṇa and Balarāma on Their arrival and kill Them."

Kaṁsa also advised his friends to arrange to worship Lord Śiva by offering animal sacrifices and performing the sacrifice called *Dhanur-yajña* and the sacrifice performed on the fourteenth day of the moon known as *Caturdaśī.* This date falls three days after *Ekādaśī,* and it is set aside for the worship of Lord Śiva. One of the plenary portions of Lord Śiva is called Kālabhairava. This form of Lord Śiva is worshiped by the demons who offer skinned animals before him. The process is still current in India in a place called Vaidyanātha-dhāma where the demons offer animal sacrifices to the deity of Kālabhairava. Kaṁsa belonged to this demonic group. He was also an expert diplomat, and so he quickly arranged for his demon friends to kill Kṛṣṇa and Balarāma.

He then called for Akrūra, one of the descendants in the family of Yadu in which Kṛṣṇa was born as the son of Vasudeva. When Akrūra came to see Kaṁsa, Kaṁsa very politely shook hands with him and said, "My dear Akrūra, actually I've no better friend than you in the Bhoja and Yadu dynasties. You are the most munificent person, so as a friend I am begging charity from you. Actually I have taken shelter of you exactly as King Indra takes shelter of Lord Viṣṇu. I request you to go immediately to Vṛndāvana and find the two boys named Kṛṣṇa and Balarāma. They are sons of Nanda Mahārāja. Take this nice chariot, especially prepared for the boys, and bring Them here immediately. That is my request to you. Now, my plan is to kill these two boys. As soon as They come in the gate, there will be a giant elephant named Kuvalayāpīḍa awaiting, and possibly he will be able to kill Them. But if somehow or other They escape, They will next meet the wrestlers and will be killed by them. That is my plan. And after killing these two boys, I shall kill Vasudeva and Nanda, who are supporters of the Vṛṣṇi and Bhoja dynasties. I shall also kill my father Ugrasena and his brother Devaka, because they are actually my enemies and are hindrances to my diplomacy and politics. Thus I shall get rid of all my enemies. Jarāsandha is my father-in-law, and I have a great monkey friend named Dvivida. With their help it will be easy to kill all the kings on the surface of the world who support the demigods. This is my plan. In this way I shall be free from all opposition, and it will be very pleasant to rule the world without obstruction. You may know also that Śambara, Narakāsura and Bāṇāsura are my intimate friends, and when I begin this war against the kings who support the demigods, they will help me considerably. Surely I shall be rid of all my enemies. Please go immediately to Vṛndāvana and encourage the boys to come here to see the beauty of Mathurā and take pleasure in the wrestling competition."

After hearing this plan of Kaṁsa's, Akrūra replied, "My dear King, your plan is very excellently made to counteract the hindrances to your diplomatic activities. But you should maintain some discretion, or your plans will not be fruitful. After all, man proposes, God disposes. We may make very great plans, but unless they are sanctioned by the supreme authority, they will fail. Everyone in this material world knows that the supernatural power is the ultimate disposer of everything. One may make a very great plan with his fertile brain, but he must know that he will become subjected to the fruits, misery and happiness. But I have nothing to say against your proposal. As a friend, I shall carry out your order and bring Kṛṣṇa and Balarāma here, as you desire."

After instructing his friends in various ways, Kaṁsa retired, and Akrūra went to Vṛndāvana.

Thus ends the Bhaktivedanta purport of the Thirty-fifth Chapter of Kṛṣṇa, *"Kaṁsa Sends Akrūra for Kṛṣṇa."*

36 / Killing the Keśī Demon and Vyomāsura

After being instructed by Kaṁsa, the demon Keśī assumed the form of a terrible horse. He entered the area of Vṛndāvana, his great mane flying and his hooves digging up the earth. He began to whinny and terrify the whole world. Kṛṣṇa saw that the demon was terrifying all the residents of Vṛndāvana with his whinnying and his tail wheeling in the sky like a big cloud. Kṛṣṇa could understand that the horse was challenging Him to fight. The Lord accepted his challenge and stood before the Keśī demon. As He called him to fight, the horse began to proceed towards Kṛṣṇa, making a horrible sound like a roaring lion. Keśī rushed toward the Lord with great speed and tried to trample Him with his legs, which were strong, forceful, and as hard as stone. Kṛṣṇa, however, immediately caught hold of his legs and thus baffled him. Being somewhat angry, Kṛṣṇa began to move around the horse dextrously. After a few rounds, He threw him a hundred yards away, just as Garuḍa throws a big snake. Thrown by Kṛṣṇa, the horse immediately passed out, but after a little while he regained consciousness and with great anger and force rushed toward Kṛṣṇa again, this time with his mouth open. As soon as Keśī reached Him, Kṛṣṇa pushed His left hand within the horse's mouth. The horse felt great pain because the hand of Kṛṣṇa felt to him like a hot iron rod. Immediately his teeth fell out. Kṛṣṇa's hand within the mouth of the horse at once began to inflate, and Keśī's throat choked up. As the great horse began to suffocate, perspiration appeared on his body, and he began to throw his legs hither and thither. As his last breath came, his eyeballs bulged in their sockets, and he passed stool and urine simultaneously. Thus the vital force of his life expired. When the horse was dead, his mouth became loose and Kṛṣṇa could extract His hand without difficulty. He did not feel any surprise that the Keśī demon was killed so easily, but the demigods were amazed, and out of their great appreciation they offered Kṛṣṇa greetings by showering flowers.

After this incident, Nārada Muni, the greatest of all devotees, came to see Kṛṣṇa in a solitary place and began to talk with Him. "My dear Lord Kṛṣṇa," he said, "You are the unlimited Supersoul, the supreme controller of all mystic powers, the Lord of the whole universe, the all-pervading Personality of Godhead. You are the resting place of the cosmic manifestation, the master of all the devotees and the Lord of everyone. My dear Lord, as the Supersoul of all living entities, You remain concealed within their hearts exactly as fire remains concealed in every piece of fuel. You are the witness of all the activities of the living entities, and You are the supreme controller within their hearts. You are self-sufficient; before the creation, you existed, and by Your energy You have created the whole material universe. According to Your perfect plan, this material world is created by the interaction of the modes of nature, and by You they are maintained and annihilated. Although You are unaffected by all these activities, You are the supreme controller eternally. My dear Lord, You have advented Yourself on the surface of this world just to kill all the so-called kings who are actually demons. These hobgoblins are cheating people in the dress of the princely order. You have advented Yourself to fulfill Your own statement that You come within this material world just to protect the principles of religion and annihilate unwanted miscreants. My dear Lord, I am therefore sure that the day after tomorrow I shall see demons like Cāṇūra, Muṣṭika and the other wrestlers and elephants, as well as Kaṁsa himself, killed by You. And I shall see this with my own eyes. After this, I hope I shall be able to see the killing of other demons like Śaṅkha, Yavana, Mura, and Narakāsura. I shall also see how You take away the *pārijāta* flower from the kingdom of heaven, and how You defeat the king of heaven himself.

"My dear Lord," Nārada Muni continued, "I shall then be able to see how You marry princesses, the daughters of chivalrous kings, by paying the price of *kṣatriya* strength." (Whenever a *kṣatriya* wants to marry a very beautiful and qualified princess of a great king, he must fight his competitors and emerge victorious. Then he is given the hand of the princess in charity.)

"I shall also see how You save King Nṛga from a hellish condition," said Nārada Muni. "This You shall enact in Dvārakā. I shall also be able to see how You get Your wife and the Syamantaka jewel and how You save the son of a *brāhmaṇa* from death after he has already been transferred to another planet. After this, I will be able to see You kill the Pauṇḍraka demon and burn to ashes the kingdom of Kāśī. I will see how You kill the King of Cedi and Dantavakra in great fights, on behalf of Mahārāja

Yudhiṣṭhira. Besides all this, it will be possible for me to see many other chivalrous activities while You remain in Dvārakā. And all these activities performed by Your grace will be sung by great poets for all time. And at the battle of Kurukṣetra You will take part as the chariot driver of Your friend Arjuna, and as the invincible death incarnation, eternal time, You will vanquish all belligerents assembled there. I shall see a large number of military forces killed in that battlefield. My Lord, let me offer my respectful obeisances unto Your lotus feet. You are situated completely in the transcendental position in perfect knowledge and bliss. You are complete in Yourself and are beyond all desires. By exhibiting Your internal potency, You have set up the influence of *māyā*. Your unlimited potency cannot even be measured by anyone. My dear Lord, You are the supreme controller. You are under Your own internal potency, and it is simply vain to think that You are dependent on any of Your creations.

"You have taken birth in the Yadu dynasty, or the Vṛṣṇi dynasty. Your advent on the surface of the earth in Your original form of eternal blissful knowledge is Your own pastime. You are not dependent on anything but Yourself; therefore I offer my respectful obeisances unto Your lotus feet."

Nārada Muni wanted to impress upon people in general that Kṛṣṇa is fully independent. His activities, such as His appearance in the family of Yadu or His friendship with Arjuna, do not necessarily oblige Him to act to enjoy their results. They are all pastimes, and for Him they are all play. But for us they are actual, tangible facts.

After offering his respectful obeisances to Lord Kṛṣṇa, Nārada Muni took permission and left. After He had killed the Keśī demon, Kṛṣṇa returned to tending the cows with His friends in the forest as though nothing had happened. Thus Kṛṣṇa is eternally engaged in His transcendental activities in Vṛndāvana with His friends, the cowherd boys and *gopīs*, but sometimes He exhibits the extraordinary prowess of the Supreme Personality of Godhead by killing different types of demons.

Later that morning Kṛṣṇa went to play with His cowherd boy friends on the top of the Govardhana Hill. They were imitating the play of thieves and police. Some of the boys became police constables, and some became thieves, and some took the role of lambs. While they were thus enjoying their childhood pastimes, a demon known by the name of Vyomāsura, "the demon who flies in the sky," appeared on the scene. He was the son of another great demon named Maya. These demons can perform wonderful magic. Vyomāsura took the part of a cowherd boy playing as thief and stole many boys who were playing the parts of lambs. One after another he took away almost all the boys and put them in the caves of the mountain and sealed the mouths of the caves with stones. Kṛṣṇa could understand the trick the demon was playing; therefore He caught hold of him exactly as a lion catches hold of a lamb. The demon tried to expand himself like a hill to escape arrest, but Kṛṣṇa did not allow him to get out of His clutches. He was immediately thrown on the ground with great force and killed, just as an animal is killed in the slaughterhouse. After killing the Vyoma demon, Lord Kṛṣṇa released all His friends from the caves of the mountain. He was then praised by His friends and by the demigods for these wonderful acts. He again returned to Vṛndāvana with His cows and friends.

Thus ends the Bhaktivedanta purport of the Thirty-sixth Chapter of Kṛṣṇa, *"Killing the Keśī Demon and Vyomāsura."*

37 / Akrūra's Arrival in Vṛndāvana

Nārada Muni did not mention Kṛṣṇa's killing Vyomāsura, which means that he was killed on the same day as the Keśī demon. The Keśī demon was killed in the early morning, and after that the boys went to tend the cows on Govardhana Hill, and it was there that Vyomāsura was killed. Both demons were killed in the morning. Akrūra was requested by Kaṁsa to arrive in Vṛndāvana by evening. After receiving instruction from Kaṁsa, Akrūra started the next morning via chariot for Vṛndāvana. Because Akrūra himself was a great devotee of the Lord, while going to Vṛndāvana he began to praise the Lord. Devotees are always absorbed in thoughts of Kṛṣṇa, and Akrūra was constantly thinking of Lord Kṛṣṇa's lotus eyes.

He did not know what sort of pious activities he must have done to gain an opportunity to go see Lord Kṛṣṇa. Akrūra thought that if Kṛṣṇa willed, he would be able to see Him. Akrūra considered himself most fortunate that he was going to see Kṛṣṇa, whom great mystic *yogīs* desire to see. He was confident that on that day all the sinful reactions of his past life would be finished and his fortunate human form of life would be successful. Akrūra also considered that he was very much favored by Kaṁsa, who was sending him to bring back Kṛṣṇa and Balarāma and thus enabling him to see the Lord. Akrūra continued to consider that formerly great sages and saintly persons were liberated from the material world simply by seeing the shining nails of the lotus feet of Kṛṣṇa.

"That Supreme Personality of Godhead has now come just like an ordinary human being, and it is my great fortune to be able to see Him face to face," Akrūra thought. He was thrilled with expectations of seeing the very lotus feet which are worshiped by great demigods like Brahmā, Nārada, and Lord Śiva, which traverse the ground of Vṛndāvana and which touch the breasts of the *gopīs* covered with tinges of *kuṅkuma.* He thought, "I am so fortunate that I will be able to see those very lotus feet on this day, and certainly I shall be able to see the beautiful face of Kṛṣṇa, which is marked on the forehead and the nose with *tilaka.* And I shall also see His smile and His curling black hair. I can be sure of this opportunity because I see that today the deer are passing on my right side. Today it will be possible for me to actually see the beauty of the spiritual kingdom of Viṣṇuloka because Kṛṣṇa is the Supreme Viṣṇu, and He has advented Himself out of His own good will. He is the reservoir of all beauty; therefore my eyes will be filled today."

Akrūra knew beyond doubt that Lord Kṛṣṇa is the Supreme Viṣṇu. Lord Viṣṇu glances over the material energy, and thus the cosmic manifestation comes into being. And although Lord Viṣṇu is the creator of this material world, He is free, by His own energy, from the influence of material energy. By His internal potency He can pierce the darkness of material energy. Similarly, Kṛṣṇa the original Viṣṇu, by expansion of His internal potency, created the inhabitants of Vṛndāvana. In the *Brahma-saṁhitā* it is also confirmed that the paraphernalia and the abode of Kṛṣṇa are expansions of His internal potency. The same internal potency is exhibited on earth as Vṛndāvana, where Kṛṣṇa enjoys Himself with His parents and in the company of His friends, the cowherd boys and *gopīs.* By the statement of Akrūra, it is clear that, since Kṛṣṇa is transcendental to the modes of material nature, the inhabitants of Vṛndāvana, who are engaged in loving service of the Lord, are also transcendental.

Akrūra also considered the necessity of the transcendental pastimes of the Lord. He thought that the transcendental activities, instructions, qualities and pastimes of Kṛṣṇa are all for the good fortune of people in general. The people can remain constantly in Kṛṣṇa consciousness by discussing the Lord's transcendental form, qualities, pastimes, and paraphernalia. By doing so, the whole universe can actually live auspiciously and advance peacefully. But without Kṛṣṇa consciousness, civilization is but a decoration for a dead body. A dead body may be decorated very nicely, but without consciousness such decorations are useless. Human society without Kṛṣṇa consciousness is useless and lifeless.

Akrūra thought, "That Supreme Personality of Godhead, Kṛṣṇa, has now appeared as one of the descendants of the Yadu dynasty. The principles of religion are His enacted laws. Those who are abiding by such laws are the demigods, and those who are not abiding are demons. He has advented Himself to give protection to the demigods, who are very obedient to the laws of the Supreme Lord. The demigods and the devotees of the Lord take pleasure in abiding by the laws of Kṛṣṇa, and Kṛṣṇa takes pleasure in giving them all sorts of protection. These activities of Kṛṣṇa,

His protection of the devotees and killing the demons, as confirmed in the *Bhagavad-gītā*, are always good for men to hear and narrate. The glorious activities of the Lord will ever increasingly be chanted by the devotees and demigods.

"Kṛṣṇa, the Supreme Personality of Godhead, is the spiritual master of all spiritual masters; He is the deliverer of all fallen souls and the proprietor of the three worlds. Anyone is able to see Him by eyes smeared with love of Godhead. Today I shall be able to see the Supreme Personality of Godhead, who by His transcendental beauty has attracted the goddess of fortune to live with Him perpetually. As soon as I arrive in Vṛndāvana, I will get down from this chariot and fall prostrate to offer my obeisances to the Supreme Lord, the master of material nature and all living entities. The lotus feet of Kṛṣṇa are always worshiped by great mystic *yogīs,* so I shall also worship His lotus feet and become one of His friends in Vṛndāvana like the cowherd boys. When I bow down before Lord Kṛṣṇa in that way, certainly He will place His fearless lotus hand on my head. His hand is offered to all conditioned souls who take shelter under His lotus feet. Kṛṣṇa is the ultimate goal of life for all people who fear material existence, and certainly when I see Him He will give me the shelter of His lotus feet. I am aspiring for the touch of His lotus-like hands on my head."

In this way Akrūra expected blessings from the hand of Kṛṣṇa. He knew that Indra, who is the king of heaven and the master of the three worlds—the upper, middle, and lower planetary systems—was blessed by the Lord simply for his offering a little water which Kṛṣṇa accepted. Similarly, Bali Mahārāja gave only three feet of land in charity to Vāmanadeva, and he also offered a little water which Lord Vāmanadeva accepted, and thereby Bali Mahārāja attained the position of Indra. When the *gopīs* were dancing with Kṛṣṇa in the *rāsa* dance, they became fatigued, and Kṛṣṇa smeared His hand, which is as fragrant as a lotus flower, over the pearl-like drops of perspiration on the faces of the *gopīs,* and immediately they became refreshed. Thus Akrūra was expecting benediction from that supreme hand of Kṛṣṇa. Kṛṣṇa's hand is capable of bestowing benediction to all kinds of men if they take to Kṛṣṇa consciousness. If one wants material happiness like the king of heaven, he can derive that benediction from the hand of Kṛṣṇa; if one wants liberation from the pangs of material existence, he can also get benediction from the hand of Kṛṣṇa; and if one in pure transcendental love for Kṛṣṇa wants personal association and the touch of His transcendental body, he can also gain benediction from His hand.

Akrūra was afraid, however, of being deputed by Kaṁsa, the enemy of Kṛṣṇa. He thought, "I am going to see Kṛṣṇa as a messenger of the enemy."

And at the same time, he thought, "Kṛṣṇa is in each and everyone's heart as the Supersoul, so He must know my heart." Although Akrūra was trusted by the enemy of Kṛṣṇa, his heart was clear. He was a pure devotee of Kṛṣṇa. He risked Kaṁsa's wrath just to meet Kṛṣṇa. He was certain that although he was going as a representative of Kaṁsa, Kṛṣṇa would not accept him as an enemy. "Even though I am on a sinful mission, being deputed by Kaṁsa, when I approach the Supreme Personality of Godhead, I shall stand before Him with all humility and folded hands. Surely, He will be pleased with my devotional attitude, and maybe He will smile lovingly and look upon me and thereby free me from all kinds of sinful reaction. I shall then be on the platform of transcendental bliss and knowledge. Since Kṛṣṇa knows my heart, certainly when I approach Him, He will embrace me. I am not only one of the members of the Yadu dynasty, but I am an unalloyed pure devotee. By His merciful embrace, my body, my heart and soul will be completely cleansed of the actions and reactions of my past life. When our bodies touch, I will immediately stand up with folded hands, with all humility. Certainly Kṛṣṇa and Balarāma will call me, 'Akrūra, uncle,' and at that time my whole life will be glorious. Unless one is recognized by the Supreme Personality of Godhead, his life cannot be successful."

It is clearly stated here that one should try to be recognized by the Supreme Personality of Godhead by one's service and devotion, without which the human form of life is condemned. As stated in the *Bhagavad-gītā,* the Supreme Lord, Personality of Godhead, is equal to everyone. He has no friends and no enemies. But He is inclined to a devotee who renders Him service with devotional love. The *Bhagavad-gītā* also declares that the Supreme Lord is responsive to the devotional service rendered by the devotee. Akrūra thought that Kṛṣṇa was like the desire tree in the heavenly planets which gives fruit according to the desire of the worshiper. The Supreme Personality of Godhead is also the source of everything. A devotee must know how to render service unto Him and thus be recognized by Him. In the *Caitanya-caritāmṛta* it is therefore explained that one should serve both the spiritual master and Kṛṣṇa simultaneously and in that way make progress in Kṛṣṇa consciousness. Service rendered to Kṛṣṇa under the direction of the spiritual master is bona fide service because the spiritual master is the manifested representative of Kṛṣṇa. Śrī Viśvanātha Cakravartī Ṭhākur says that when one satisfies the spiritual master, he satisfies the Supreme Lord. It is exactly like service in a government office. One has to work under the supervision of the departmental head. If the supervisor of the department is satisfied with the service of a particular person, a promotion and increase in pay will automatically come.

Akrūra then thought, "When Kṛṣṇa and Balarāma are pleased with my prayers, certainly They will take my hand, receive me within Their homes and offer me all kinds of respectable hospitalities, and They will surely ask me of the activities of Kaṁsa and his friends."

In this way, Akrūra, who was the son of Śvaphalka, meditated on Śrī Kṛṣṇa on his journey from Mathurā. He reached Vṛndāvana by the end of the day. Akrūra passed the whole journey without knowing how long it took. When he reached Vṛndāvana, the sun was setting. As soon as he entered the boundary of Vṛndāvana, he saw the footprints of the cows and Lord Kṛṣṇa's footprints, impressed with the signs of His sole, the flag, trident, thunderbolt and lotus flower. Upon seeing the footprints of Kṛṣṇa, Akrūra immediately jumped down from the chariot, out of respect. He became overwhelmed with all the symptoms of ecstasy; he wept, and his body trembled. Out of extreme jubilation upon seeing the dust touched by the lotus feet of Kṛṣṇa, Akrūra fell flat on his face and began to roll on the ground.

Akrūra's journey to Vṛndāvana is exemplary. One who intends to visit Vṛndāvana should follow the ideal footsteps of Akrūra and always think of the pastimes and activities of the Lord. As soon as one reaches the boundary of Vṛndāvana, he should immediately smear the dust of Vṛndāvana over his body without thinking of his material position and prestige. Narottamadāsa Ṭhākur has sung in his celebrated song, *Viṣaya-chāriyā kave śuddha have mana:* "When my mind will be purified after leaving the contamination of material sense enjoyment, I shall be able to visit Vṛndāvana." Actually, one cannot go to Vṛndāvana by purchasing a ticket. The process of going to Vṛndāvana is shown by Akrūra.

When Akrūra entered Vṛndāvana, he saw Kṛṣṇa and Balarāma engaged in supervising the milking of the cows. Kṛṣṇa was dressed in yellow garments and Balarāma in bluish. Akrūra also saw that Kṛṣṇa's eyes were exactly like the beautifully grown lotus flower of the autumn season. He saw both Kṛṣṇa and Balarāma in the spring of Their youth. Although both were similar in bodily features, Kṛṣṇa was blackish in complexion, whereas Balarāma was whitish. Both were the shelter of the goddess of fortune. They had well-constructed bodies, beautiful hands and pleasing faces, and They were as strong as elephants. Now, after seeing Their footprints, Akrūra actually saw Kṛṣṇa and Balarāma, face to face. Although They were the most influential personalities, They were glancing at him with smiling faces. Akrūra could understand that both Kṛṣṇa and Balarāma had returned from tending cows in the forest; They had taken Their baths and were dressed with fresh clothing and garlanded with flowers and necklaces made of valuable jewels. Their bodies were smeared with the pulp of sandalwood. Akrūra greatly appreciated the aroma of flowers and sandalwood and Their bodily presence. He considered himself very fortunate to see Kṛṣṇa, the Supreme Personality of Godhead, and His plenary expansion, Balarāma, face to face, for he knew that They were the original personalities of the creation.

As stated in the *Brahma-saṁhitā,* Kṛṣṇa is the original Personality of Godhead and the cause of all causes. Akrūra could understand that the Supreme Personality of Godhead appeared personally for the welfare of His creation, to reestablish the principles of religion and to annihilate the demons. With Their bodily effulgence, the brothers were dissipating all the darkness of the world, as if They were mountains of sapphire and silver. Without hesitating, Akrūra immediately got down from his chariot and fell flat, just like a rod, before Kṛṣṇa and Balarāma. Upon touching the lotus feet of the Supreme Personality of Godhead, he became overwhelmed with transcendental bliss; his voice choked up and he could not speak. Due to Kṛṣṇa's transcendental presence, incessant torrents of tears fell from his eyes. He remained stunned in ecstasy, as if devoid of all powers to see and speak. Lord Kṛṣṇa, who is very kind to His devotees, raised Akrūra with His hand and embraced him. It appeared that Lord Kṛṣṇa was very pleased with Akrūra. Balarāma also embraced Akrūra. Taking him by the hand, Kṛṣṇa and Balarāma brought him to Their sitting room where They offered him a very nice sitting place and water for washing his feet. They also worshiped him with suitable presentations of honey and other ingredients. When Akrūra was thus comfortably seated, both Kṛṣṇa and Balarāma offered Him a cow in charity and then brought very palatable dishes of eatables, and Akrūra accepted them. When Akrūra finished eating, Balarāma gave him betel nut and spices, as well as pulp of sandalwood, just to make him more pleased and comfortable. The Vedic system of receiving a guest was completely observed by Lord Kṛṣṇa Himself to teach all others how to receive a guest at home. It is a Vedic injunction that even if a guest is an enemy, he should be received so well that he does not apprehend any danger from the host. If the host is a poor man, he should at least offer a straw mat as a sitting place and a glass of water to drink. Kṛṣṇa and Balarāma welcomed Akrūra just befitting his exalted position.

After Akrūra was thus properly received and seated, Nanda Mahārāja, the foster father of Kṛṣṇa, said, "My dear Akrūra, what shall I inquire from you? I know that you are being protected by Kaṁsa, who is most cruel and demoniac. His protection is just like the slaughterhouse keeper's protection of animals he will kill in the future. Kaṁsa is so selfish that he has killed the sons of his own sister, so how can I honestly believe that he is protecting the citizens of Mathurā?" This statement is most significant. If the political or executive heads of the state are simply interested in themselves, they can never look after the welfare of the citizens.

As Nanda Mahārāja spoke to Akrūra with pleasing words, Akrūra forgot all the fatigue of his day's journey from Mathurā to Vṛndāvana.

Thus ends the Bhaktivedanta purport of the Thirty-seventh Chapter of Kṛṣṇa, *"Akrūra's Arrival in Vṛndāvana."*

38/Akrūra's Return Journey and His Visiting of Viṣṇuloka Within the Yamunā River

Akrūra was warmly received by Lord Kṛṣṇa and Nanda Mahārāja and offered a resting place for the night. In the meantime, the two brothers Balarāma and Kṛṣṇa went to take Their supper. Akrūra sat on his bed and began to reflect that all the desires which he had anticipated while coming from Mathurā to Vṛndāvana had been fulfilled. Lord Kṛṣṇa is the husband of the goddess of fortune; being pleased with His pure devotee, He can offer whatever the devotee desires. But the pure devotee does not ask anything from the Lord for his personal benefit.

After taking Their supper, Kṛṣṇa and Balarāma came to bid goodnight to Akrūra. Kṛṣṇa asked about His maternal uncle, Kaṁsa, "How is he dealing with his friends?" And He asked, "How are my relatives?" He also inquired into Kaṁsa's plans. The Supreme Personality of Godhead then informed Akrūra that his presence was very much welcome. He inquired from him whether all his relatives and friends were well and free from all kinds of ailments. Kṛṣṇa stated that He was very sorry that His maternal uncle Kaṁsa was the head of the kingdom; He said that Kaṁsa was the greatest anachronism in the whole system of government and that they could not expect any welfare for the citizens while he ruled. Then Kṛṣṇa said, "My father has undergone much tribulation simply from My being his son. For this reason also he has lost many other sons. I think Myself so fortunate that you have come as My friend and relative. My good friend Akrūra, please tell me the purpose of your coming to Vṛndāvana."

After this inquiry, Akrūra, who belonged to the dynasty of Yadu, explained the recent events in Mathurā, including Kaṁsa's attempt to kill Vasudeva, the father of Kṛṣṇa. He related the things which happened after the disclosure by Nārada that Kṛṣṇa was the son of Vasudeva. Sitting by Him in the house of Nanda Mahārāja, Akrūra narrated all the stories regarding Kaṁsa. He told how Nārada met Kaṁsa and how he himself was deputed by Kaṁsa to come to Vṛndāvana. Akrūra explained to Kṛṣṇa that

Nārada had told Kaṁsa all about Kṛṣṇa's being transferred from Mathurā to Vṛndāvana just after His birth and about His killing all the demons sent by Kaṁsa. Akrūra then explained to Kṛṣṇa the purpose of his coming to Vṛndāvana: to take him back to Mathurā. After hearing of these arrangements, Balarāma and Kṛṣṇa, who are very expert in killing opponents, mildly laughed at the plans of Kaṁsa.

They asked Nanda Mahārāja to invite all the cowherd boys to go to Mathurā to participate in the ceremony known as *Dhanur-yajña*. Kaṁsa wanted them all to go there to participate in the function. On Kṛṣṇa's word, Nanda Mahārāja at once called for the cowherd boys and asked them to collect all kinds of milk preparations and milk to present in the ceremony. He also sent instructions to the police chief of Vṛndāvana to tell all the inhabitants about Kaṁsa's great Dhanur-yajña function and invite them to join. Nanda Mahārāja informed the cowherd boys that they would start the next morning. They therefore arranged for the cows and bulls to carry them all to Mathurā.

When the *gopīs* saw that Akrūra had come to take Kṛṣṇa and Balarāma away to Mathurā, they became overwhelmed with anxiety. Some of them became so aggrieved that their faces turned black, and they began to breathe warmly and had palpitations of the heart. They discovered that their hair and dress immediately loosened. Hearing the news that Kṛṣṇa and Balarāma were leaving for Mathurā, others who were engaged in household duties stopped working as if they had forgotten everything, like a person who is called forth to die and leave this world at once. Others immediately fainted due to separation from Kṛṣṇa. Remembering His attractive smile and His talks with them, the *gopīs* became overwhelmed with grief. They all remembered the characteristics of the Personality of Godhead, how He moved within the area of Vṛndāvana and how, with joking words, He attracted all their hearts. Thinking of Kṛṣṇa and of their imminent separation from Him, the *gopīs* assembled together with heavy beating hearts. Completely absorbed in thought of Kṛṣṇa, tears fell from their eyes. They began to converse as follows.

"O Providence, you are so cruel! It appears that you do not know how to show mercy to others. By your arrangement, friends contact one another, but without fulfilling their desires you separate them. This is exactly like children's play that has no meaning. It is very abominable that you arrange to show us beautiful Kṛṣṇa, whose bluish curling hair beautifies His broad forehead and sharp nose, who is always smiling to minimize all contention in this material world, and then arrange to separate Him from us. O Providence, You are so cruel! But most astonishingly You appear now as 'Akrūra,' which means 'not cruel.' In the beginning we appreciated Your workmanship in giving us these eyes to see the beautiful face of Kṛṣṇa, but now, just like a foolish creature, You are trying to take out our eyes so we may not see Kṛṣṇa here again. Kṛṣṇa, the son of Nanda Mahārāja, is also very cruel! He must always have new friends; He does not like to keep friendship for a long time with anyone. We *gopīs* of Vṛndāvana, having left our homes, friends, and relatives, have become Kṛṣṇa's maidservants, but He is neglecting us and going away. He does not even look upon us, although we are completely surrendered unto Him. Now all the young girls in Mathurā will have the opportunity. They are expecting Kṛṣṇa's arrival, and they will enjoy His sweet smiling face and will drink its honey. Although we know that Kṛṣṇa is very steady and determined, we are threatened that as soon as He sees the beautiful faces of the young girls in Mathurā, He will forget Himself. We fear He will become controlled by them and will forget us, for we are simple village girls. He will no longer be kind to us. We therefore do not expect Kṛṣṇa to return to Vṛndāvana. He will not leave the company of the girls in Mathurā."

The *gopīs* began to imagine the great functions in the city of Mathurā. Kṛṣṇa would pass through the streets, and the ladies and young girls of the city would see Him from the balconies of their respective houses. Mathurā City contained different communities, known then as Daśārha, Bhoja, Andhaka and Sātvata. All these communities were different branches of the same family in which Kṛṣṇa appeared, namely the Yadu dynasty. They were also expecting the arrival of Kṛṣṇa. It had already been ascertained that Kṛṣṇa, who is the rest of the goddess of fortune and reservoir of all pleasure and transcendental qualities, was going to visit Mathurā City.

The *gopīs* then began to condemn the activities of Akrūra. They stated that he was taking Kṛṣṇa, who was more dear than the dearest to them and who was the pleasure of their eyes. He was being taken from their sight without their being informed or solaced by Akrūra. Akrūra should not have been so merciless but should have taken compassion on them. The *gopīs* went on to say: "The most astonishing feature is that Kṛṣṇa, the son of Nanda, without consideration, has already seated Himself on the chariot. From this it appears that Kṛṣṇa is not very intelligent. Yet He may be very intelligent—but He is not very civilized. Not only Kṛṣṇa, but all the cowherd men are so callous that they are already yoking the bulls and calves for the journey to Mathurā. The elderly persons in Vṛndāvana are also merciless; they do not take our plight into consideration and stop Kṛṣṇa's journey to Mathurā. Even the demigods are very unkind to us; they are not impeding His going to Mathurā."

The *gopīs* prayed to the demigods to create some natural disturbance, such as a hurricane, storm or heavy rainfall, so that Kṛṣṇa could not go to Mathurā. They then began to consider: "Despite our elderly parents and guardians, we shall personally stop Kṛṣṇa from going to Mathurā. We have no other alternative than to take this direct action. Everyone has gone against us to take away Kṛṣṇa from our sight. Without Him we cannot live for a moment." The *gopīs* thus decided to obstruct the passage through which the chariot of Kṛṣṇa was supposed to pass. They began to talk among themselves: "We have passed a very long night—which seemed only a moment—engaged in the *rāsa* dance with Kṛṣṇa. We were looking at His sweet smile and were embracing and talking. Now, how shall we live even for a moment if He goes away from us? At the end of the day, in the evening, along with His elder brother Balarāma, Kṛṣṇa would return home with His friends. His face would be smeared with the dust raised by the hooves of the cows, and He would smile and play on His flute and look upon us so kindly. How shall we be able to forget Him? How shall we be able to forget Kṛṣṇa, who is our life and soul? He has already taken away our hearts in so many ways throughout our days and nights, and if He goes away, there is no possibility of our continuing to live." Thinking like this, the *gopīs* became more and more griefstricken at Kṛṣṇa's leaving Vṛndāvana. They could not check their minds, and they began to cry loudly, calling the different names of Kṛṣṇa, "O dear Dāmodara! Dear Mādhava!"

The *gopīs* cried all night before the departure of Kṛṣṇa. As soon as the sun rose, Akrūra finished his morning bath, got on the chariot and began to start for Mathurā with Kṛṣṇa and Balarāma. Nanda Mahārāja and the cowherd men got up on bullock carts, after loading them with milk preparations, such as yogurt, milk, and ghee, filled in big earthen pots, and began to follow the chariot of Kṛṣṇa and Balarāma. In spite of Kṛṣṇa's asking them not to obstruct their way, all the *gopīs* surrounded the chariot and stood up to see Kṛṣṇa with pitiable eyes. Kṛṣṇa was very much affected upon seeing the plight of the *gopīs,* but His duty was to start for Mathurā, for this was foretold by Nārada. Kṛṣṇa, therefore, consoled the *gopīs*. He told them that they should not be aggrieved; He was coming back very soon after finishing His business. But they could not be persuaded to disperse. The chariot, however, began to head west, and as it proceeded, the minds of the *gopīs* followed it as far as possible. They watched the flag on the chariot as long as it was visible; finally they could only see the dust of the chariot in the distance. The *gopīs* did not move from their places but stood until the chariot could not be seen at all. They remained standing still, as if they were painted pictures. All the *gopīs* decided that Kṛṣṇa was not returning immediately, and with greatly disappointed hearts, they returned to their respective homes. Being greatly disturbed by the absence of Kṛṣṇa, they simply thought all day and night about His pastimes and thus derived some consolation.

The Lord, accompanied by Akrūra and Balarāma, drove the chariot with great speed towards the bank of the Yamunā. Simply by taking a bath in the Yamunā, anyone can diminish the reaction of his sinful activities. Both Kṛṣṇa and Balarāma took Their baths in the river and washed Their faces. After drinking the transparent crystal clear water of the Yamunā, They took Their seats again on the chariot. The chariot was standing underneath the shade of big trees, and both brothers sat down there. Akrūra then took Their permission to also take bath in the Yamunā. According to Vedic ritual, after taking bath in the river, one should stand at least half-submerged and murmur the *Gāyatrī mantra.* While he was standing in the river, Akrūra suddenly saw both Balarāma and Kṛṣṇa within the water. He was surprised to see Them there because he was confident that They were sitting on the chariot. Confused, he immediately came out of the water and went to see where the boys were, and he was very surprised to see that They were sitting on the chariot as before. When he saw Them on the chariot, he began to wonder whether he saw Them in the water. He therefore went back to the river. This time he saw not only Balarāma and Kṛṣṇa there, but many of the demigods and all the Siddhas, Cāraṇas, and Gandharvas. They were all standing before the Lord, who was lying down. He also saw the Śeṣa Nāga with thousands of hoods. Lord Śeṣa Nāga was covered with bluish garments, and His necks were all white. The white necks of Śeṣa Nāga appeared exactly like snowcapped mountains. On the curved lap of Śeṣa Nāga, Akrūra saw Kṛṣṇa sitting very soberly, with four hands. His eyes were like the reddish petals of the lotus flower.

In other words, after returning, Akrūra saw Balarāma turned into Śeṣa Nāga and Kṛṣṇa turned into Mahā-Viṣṇu. He saw the fourhanded Supreme Personality of Godhead, smiling very beautifully. He was very pleasing to all and was looking towards everyone. He appeared beautiful with His raised nose, broad forehead, spread-up ears and reddish lips. His arms, reaching to the knees, were very strongly built. His shoulders were high, His chest very broad and shaped like the conchshell. His navel was very deep, and His abdomen was marked with three lines. His waist was broad and big, resembling the hips of a woman, and His thighs resembled the trunks of elephants. The other parts of His legs, the joints and lower extremities, were all very beautiful, the nails of His feet were dazzling, and His toes were as beautiful as the petals of the lotus flower. His helmet was decorated with very valuable jewels. There was a nice belt around the waist, and He wore a sacred thread across His broad chest. Bangles were on His hands and armlets on the upper portion of His arms. He wore bells on His ankles. He possessed dazzling beauty, and His palms were like the lotus flower. He was still more beautiful with different emblems of the Viṣṇu-mūrti, the conchshell, club, disc and lotus flower, which He held in His four hands. His chest was marked with the particular signs of Viṣṇu, and He wore fresh flower garlands. All in all, He was very beautiful to look at. Akrūra also saw His Lordship surrounded by intimate associates like the four Kumāras, Sanaka, Sanātana, Sananda and Sanatkumāra, and other associates like Sunanda and Nanda, as well as demigods like Brahmā and Lord Śiva. The nine great learned sages were there, and devotees like Prahlāda and Nārada were engaged in offering prayers to the Lord with clean hearts and pure words. After seeing the transcendental Personality of Godhead, Akrūra immediately became overwhelmed with great devotion, and all over his body there was transcendental shivering. Although for the moment he was bewildered, he retained his clear consciousness and bowed down his head before the Lord. With folded hands and faltering voice, he began to offer prayers to the Lord.

Thus *ends the Bhaktivedanta purport of the Thirty-eighth Chapter of* Kṛṣṇa, *"Akrūra's Return Journey and His Visiting of Viṣṇuloka Within the Yamunā River."*

39/ Prayers by Akrūra

Akrūra offered his prayers as follows: "My dear Lord, I here pay my respectful obeisances unto You because You are the supreme cause of all causes and the original inexhaustible Personality, Nārāyaṇa. From Your navel a lotus flower grows, and from that lotus, Brahmā, the creator of this universe, is born. Since Brahmā is the cause of this universe, You are the cause of all causes. All the elements of this cosmic manifestation—earth, water, fire, air, ether, ego and the total material energy, as well as nature, the marginal energy, the living entities, mind, senses, the sense objects and the demigods who control the affairs of the cosmos—are all produced from Your body. You are the Supersoul of everything, but no one knows Your transcendental form. Everyone within this material world is influenced by the modes of material nature. Demigods like Lord Brahmā, being covered by the influence of material nature, do not exactly know Your transcendental existence beyond the cosmic manifestation of the three modes of material nature. Great sages and mystics worship You as the Supreme Personality of Godhead, the original cause of all living entities, all cosmic manifestation and all demigods. They worship You as all-inclusive. Some of the learned *brāhmaṇas* also worship You by observing the ritualistic ceremony of the *Ṛg-veda.* They offer different kinds of sacrifices in the names of different gods. And there are others also who are fond of worshiping transcendental knowledge. They are very peaceful and wish to give up all kinds of material activities. They engage themselves in the philosophical search for You, known as *jñāna-yoga.*

"There are devotees also known as *Bhāgavatas* who worship You as the Supreme Personality of Godhead. After being properly initiated in the method of *Pāñcarātra,* they decorate their bodies with *tilaka* and engage in worshiping Your different forms of Viṣṇu *mūrti.* There are others also, known as Śaivites, followers of the different *ācāryas,* who worship You in the form of Lord Śiva."

It is stated in the *Bhagavad-gītā* that worship of demigods is also indirectly worship of the Supreme Lord. But such worship is not orthodox, because the worshipable Lord is the Supreme Personality of Godhead, Nārāyaṇa. Demigods such as Brahmā and Śiva are incarnations of the material qualities, which are also emanations from the body of Nārāyaṇa. Actually, there was no one existing before the creation except Nārāyaṇa, the Supreme Personality of Godhead. The worship of a demigod is not on the level with worship of Nārāyaṇa.

Akrūra said, "Although the minds of those who are devotees of the demigods are fixed on a particular demigod, because You are the Supersoul of all living entities, including the demigods, worship of demigods indirectly goes to You. Sometimes, after flowing down from the mountains during the rainy season, small rivers fail to reach the sea; some reach the sea and some do not. Similarly, the worshipers of the demigods may or may not reach You. There is no guarantee. Their success depends on the strength of their worship."

According to Vedic principle, when a worshiper worships a particular demigod, he also conducts some ritual for Nārāyaṇa, *Yajñeśvara,* for it is mentioned in *Bhagavad-gītā* that demigods cannot fulfill the desires of their worshipers without the sanction of Nārāyaṇa, or Kṛṣṇa. The exact words used in the *Bhagavad-gītā* are *mayaiva vihitān hi tān,* which means that the demigods can award some benediction after being authorized by the Supreme Lord. When the demigod worshiper comes to his senses, he can reason as follows: "The demigod can offer benediction only after being empowered by the Supreme Lord, so why not worship the Supreme Lord directly?" Worshipers of the demigods may come to the Supreme Personality of Godhead, but others, who take the demigod as all in all, cannot reach the ultimate goal.

Akrūra continued to pray: "My dear Lord, the whole world is filled with the three material modes of nature, namely, goodness, passion and ignorance. Everyone within this material world is covered by these modes, from Lord Brahmā down to the immovable plants and trees. My dear Lord, I offer my respectful obeisances unto You, because You are beyond the influence of the three modes. Except for You, everyone is being carried away by the waves of these modes. My dear Lord, fire is Your mouth, the earth is Your feet, the sun is Your eye, the sky is Your navel, and the directions are Your ears. Space is Your head, the demigods are Your arms, the oceans and seas are Your abdomen, and the winds and air are Your strength and vitality. All the plants and herbs are the hair on Your body; the clouds are Your hair, the mountains are Your bones and nails, the days and nights are the twinkling of Your eyelids; Prajāpati (the progenitor) is

Your genitals, and the rains are Your semina.

"My dear Lord, all living entities, including different grades of demigods, different grades of overlords, kings and other living entities, are supposed to be resting in You. As part and parcel of the big unit, one cannot know You by experimental knowledge. One can simply understand Your transcendental existence as the great ocean in which different grades of living entities are included, or as the fruit *kadamba* out of which small mosquitoes come. My dear Lord, whatever eternal forms and incarnations You accept and which appear in this world are meant for relieving the living entities from their ignorance, illusion and lamentation. All people, therefore, can appreciate the incarnations and pastimes of Your Lordship and eternally glorify Your activities. No one can estimate how many forms and incarnations You have, nor can anyone estimate the number of universes that are existing within You.

"Let me therefore offer my respectful obeisances unto the incarnation of fish, who appeared in devastation, although Your Lordship is the cause of all causes. Let me offer my respectful obeisances unto the Hayagrīva incarnation who killed the two demons, Madhu and Kaiṭabha; let me offer my respectful obeisances unto You who appeared as the gigantic tortoise and held up the great mountain Mandara, and who appeared as the boar who rescued the earth planet which had fallen into the water of Garbhodaka. Let me offer my respectful obeisances unto Your Lordship, who appeared as Nṛsiṁhadeva, who delivered all kinds of devotees from the fearful condition of atheistic atrocities. Let me offer my respectful obeisances unto You who appeared as Vāmanadeva and covered the three worlds simply by expanding Your lotus feet. Let me offer my respectful obeisances unto You who appeared as the Lord of the Bhṛgus in order to kill all the infidel administrators of the world. And let me offer my respectful obeisances unto You who appeared as Lord Rāma to kill demons like Rāvaṇa. You are worshiped by all devotees as the chief of the Raghu dynasty, Lord Rāmacandra. Let me offer my respectful obeisances unto You who appeared as Lord Vāsudeva, Lord Saṅkarṣaṇa, Lord Pradyumna and Lord Aniruddha. Let me offer my respectful obeisances unto You, who appeared as Lord Buddha in order to bewilder the atheistic and demoniac. And let me offer my respectful obeisances unto You, who appeared as Kalki in order to chastise the so-called royal order degraded to the abominable condition of the *mlecchas*, who are below the jurisdiction of Vedic regulative principles.

"My dear Lord, everyone within this material world is conditioned by Your illusory energy. Under the impression of false identification and false possession, everyone is transmigrating from one body to another in the path of fruitive activities and their reactions. My dear Lord, I am also no exception to these conditioned souls. I am falsely thinking myself happy in possessing my home, wife, children, state, property and effects. In this way I am acting as if in a dreamland because none of these are permanent. I am a fool to be always absorbed in such thoughts, accepting them as permanent and true. My dear Lord, due to my false identification, I have accepted everything which is nonpermanent, such as this material body, which is not spiritual and is the source of all kinds of miserable conditions. Being bewildered by such concepts of life, I am always absorbed in thoughts of duality, and I have forgotten You who are the reservoir of all transcendental pleasure. I am bereft of Your transcendental association and am just like a foolish creature who goes in search of water in the desert, leaving the water spot which is covered by water-nourished vegetables. The conditioned souls want to quench their thirst, but they do not know where to find water. They give up the spot where there is actually a reservoir of water and run into the desert where there is no water. My dear Lord, I am completely incapable of controlling my mind, which is now driven by the unbridled senses and is attracted by fruitive activities and their results. My dear Lord, Your lotus feet cannot be appreciated by any person in the conditional stage of material existence, but somehow or other I have come near Your lotus feet, and I consider this to be Your causeless mercy upon me. You can act in any way because You are the supreme controller. I can thus understand that when a person becomes eligible to be delivered from the path of repeated birth and death, it is only by Your causeless mercy that he further progresses to become attached to Your causeless devotional service."

Akrūra fell down before the Lord and said, "My dear Lord, Your transcendental eternal form is full of knowledge. Simply by concentrating one's mind upon Your form, one can understand in full knowledge everything that be, because You are the original source of all knowledge. You are the supreme powerful, possessing all kinds of energies. You are the Supreme Brahman and the Supreme Person, supreme controller and master of the material energies. I offer my respectful obeisances unto You because You are Vāsudeva, the resting place of all creation. You are the all-pervading Supreme Personality of Godhead, and You are also the Supreme Soul residing in everyone's heart and giving direction to act. Now, my Lord, I am completely surrendered unto You. Please give me Your protection."

Thus ends the Bhaktivedanta purport of the Thirty-ninth Chapter of Kṛṣṇa, *"Prayers by Akrūra."*

40 / Kṛṣṇa Enters Mathurā

While Akrūra was offering his prayers to the Supreme Personality of Godhead, the Lord disappeared from the water, exactly as an expert dramatic actor changes his dress and assumes his original feature. After the Viṣṇu-mūrti disappeared, Akrūra got out of the water. Finishing the rest of his ritualistic performance, he went near the chariot of Balarāma and Kṛṣṇa and was struck with wonder. Kṛṣṇa asked whether he had seen something wonderful within the water or in space. Akrūra said, "My dear Lord, all wonderful things taht are happening within this world, either in the sky or in the water or on the land, are factually appearing in Your universal form. So when I have seen You, what wonderful things have I not seen?" This statement confirms the Vedic version that one who knows Kṛṣṇa knows everything, and one who has seen Kṛṣṇa has seen everything, regardless of how wonderful a thing may be. "My dear Lord," Akrūra continued, "there cannot be anything more wonderful than Your transcendental form. When I have seen Your transcendental form, what is there left to see?"

After saying this, Akrūra immediately started the chariot. By the end of the day, they had almost reached the precincts of Mathurā. When passing from Vṛndāvana to Mathurā, all passersby along the way who saw Kṛṣṇa and Balarāma could not help but look at Them again and again. In the meantime, the other inhabitants of Vṛndāvana, headed by Nanda and Upananda, had already reached Mathurā by going through forests and rivers, and they were awaiting the arrival of Kṛṣṇa and Balarāma. Upon reaching the entrance to Mathurā, Kṛṣṇa and Balarāma got down from the chariot and shook hands with Akrūra. Kṛṣṇa informed Akrūra, "You may go home now because We shall enter Mathurā along with Our associates." Akrūra replied, "My dear Lord, I cannot go to Mathurā alone, leaving You aside. I am Your surrendered servant. Please do not try to avoid me. Please, come along with me, with Your elder brother and cowherd boy friends, and sanctify my house. My dear Lord, if You come, my home will be sanctified by the dust of Your lotus feet. The water emanating from the perspiration of Your lotus feet, namely the Ganges, purifies everyone, including the forefathers, the fire-god and all other demigods. King Bali Mahārāja has become famous simply by washing Your lotus feet, and all his relatives have achieved the heavenly planet due to his contact with the Ganges water. Bali Mahārāja himself enjoyed all material opulences and later on was elevated to the highest exalted position of liberation. The Ganges water not only sanctifies the three worlds but is carried on the head of Lord Śiva. O Supreme Lord of all lords! O master of the universe! I offer my respectful obeisances unto You."

On hearing this, the Supreme Personality of Godhead, Kṛṣṇa, replied, "Akrūra, I shall surely come to your home with My elder brother Balarāma, but only after killing all the demons who are envious of the Yadu dynasty. In this way I shall please all My relatives." Akrūra became a little disappointed by these words of the Supreme Personality of Godhead, but he could not disregard the order. He therefore entered Mathurā and informed Kaṁsa about the arrival of Kṛṣṇa, and then he entered his own home.

After the departure of Akrūra, Lord Kṛṣṇa, Balarāma and the cowherd boys entered Mathurā to see the city. They observed that the gate of Mathurā was made of first-class marble, very well constructed, and the doors were made of pure gold. There were gorgeous gardens all around, and the whole city was encircled by cannons so that no enemy could enter very easily. They saw that all the crossings of the roads were decorated with gold. And there were many richmen's houses, all appearing symmetrical, as if constructed by one engineer. The houses were decorated with costly jewels, and each and every house had nice compounds of trees, fruits and flowers. The gardens, corridors and verandas of the houses were decorated with silk cloth and embroidery work in jewels and pearls. In front of the balcony windows were pigeons and peacocks walking and cooing. All the grain dealers' shops within the city were decorated with different kinds of flowers and garlands, newly grown grass and blossoming roses. The central doors of the houses were decorated with water pots filled with water, and a mixture of water and yogurt was sprinkled all around. There were flowers decorated with burning lamps of different sizes over the doors, and there were also decorations of fresh mango leaves and silk festoons on all the doors of the houses.

When the news spread that Kṛṣṇa, Balarāma and the cowherd boys were within Mathurā City, all the inhabitants gathered, and the ladies and girls immediately went up to the roofs of the houses to see Them. They had been awaiting the arrival of Kṛṣṇa and Balarāma with great anxiety, and in their extreme eagerness to see Kṛṣṇa and Balarāma, the ladies did not dress themselves very properly. Some of them placed their dress in the wrong place. Some annointed their eyes on one side only, and some wore ankle bells only on one leg or only one earring. Thus in great haste, not even decorated properly, they came to see Kṛṣṇa from the roofs. Some of them had been taking their lunch, but as soon as they heard that Kṛṣṇa and Balarāma were in the city, they left their eating and ran to the roof. Some of them were in the bathroom, taking their baths, but without properly finishing their baths, they came to see Kṛṣṇa and Balarāma. Passing by very slowly and smiling, Lord Kṛṣṇa immediately stole their hearts. He who is the husband of the goddess of fortune passed through the street like an elephant. For a very long time the women of Mathurā had heard about Kṛṣṇa and Balarāma and Their uncommon characteristics, and they were very much attracted and eager to see Them. Now when they actually saw Kṛṣṇa and Balarāma passing on the street and saw Them sweetly smiling, the ladies' joy reached the point of ecstasy. When they actually saw Them with their eyes, they took Kṛṣṇa and Balarāma within their hearts and began to embrace Them to their fullest desire. Their hairs stood up in ecstasy. They had heard of Kṛṣṇa, but they had never seen Him, and now their longing was relieved. After going up on the roofs of the palaces of Mathurā, the ladies began to shower flowers upon Kṛṣṇa and Balarāma. When the brothers were passing through the streets, all the *brāhmaṇas* in the neighborhood also went out with sandalwood and flowers and respectfully welcomed Them to the city. All the residents of Mathurā began to talk among themselves about the elevated and pious activities of the people of Vṛndāvana. The residents of Mathurā were surprised at the pious activities the cowherd men in Vṛndāvana must have performed in their previous lives to be able to see Kṛṣṇa and Balarāma daily as cowherd boys.

While Kṛṣṇa and Balarāma were passing in this way, They saw a washerman and dyer of clothing. Kṛṣṇa was pleased to ask him for some nice clothing. He also promised that if the washerman would deliver the nicest dyed cloth to Him, he would be very happy, and all good fortune would be his. Kṛṣṇa was neither beggar nor was He in need of clothing, but by this request He indicated that everyone should be ready to offer to Kṛṣṇa whatever He wants. That is the purpose of Kṛṣṇa consciousness.

Unfortunately, this washerman was a servant of Kaṁsa and therefore could not appreciate the demand of Lord Kṛṣṇa, the Supreme Personality of Godhead. This is the effect of bad association. He could have immediately delivered the clothing to the Supreme Personality of Godhead, who promised him all good fortune, but being a servant of Kaṁsa, the sinful demon could not accept the offer. Instead of being pleased, he was very angry and refused the Lord's request saying, "How is it that You are asking clothing which is meant for the king?" The washerman then began to instruct Kṛṣṇa and Balarāma: "My dear boys, in the future don't be so impudent as to ask for things which belong to the king. Otherwise, You will be punished by the government men. They will arrest You and punish You, and You will be in difficulty. I have practical experience of this fact. Anyone who unlawfully wants to use the king's property is very severely punished."

On hearing this, Lord Kṛṣṇa, the son of Devakī, became very angry at the washerman, and striking him with the upper portion of His hand, He separated the man's head from his body. The washerman fell down dead on the ground. In this way Lord Kṛṣṇa confirmed the statement that every limb of His body is capable of doing everything He likes. Without a sword, but simply with His hand, he cut off the head of the washerman. This is proof that the Supreme Lord is omnipotent. If He wants to do something, He can do it without extraneous help.

After this ghastly incident, the employees of the washerman immediately dispersed, leaving the clothing. Kṛṣṇa and Balarāma took possession of it and dressed according to Their choice; the rest of the clothes were offered to the cowherd boys, who also used them as they desired. What they did not use remained there. They then continued to proceed. In the meantime, a devotee-tailor took the opportunity of service and prepared some nice clothes from the cloth for Kṛṣṇa and Balarāma. Thus being very nicely attired, Kṛṣṇa and Balarāma looked like elephants dressed with colored clothings on the full moon day of the dark moon. Kṛṣṇa was very much pleased with the tailor and gave him the benediction of *sārūpya-mukti,* which means that after leaving his body, he would be liberated and would attain a body exactly like fourhanded Nārāyaṇa's in the Vaikuṇṭha planets. He also granted him that as long as he would live he would earn sufficient opulence to be able to enjoy sense gratification. By this incident Kṛṣṇa proved that those who are Kṛṣṇa conscious devotees will not be lacking material enjoyment or sense gratification. They will have sufficient opportunity for such things, but after leaving this life they will be allowed to enter the spiritual planets of Vaikuṇṭhaloka or Kṛṣṇaloka, Goloka Vṛndāvana.

After dressing nicely, Kṛṣṇa and Balarāma went to a florist of the name Sudāmā. As soon as they reached the precinct of his house, the florist

The hand of Kṛṣṇa felt to Keśī like a hot iron rod. (p. 240)

Akrūra became overwhelmed with all the symptoms of ecstasy; he wept, and his body trembled. (p. 248)

Akrūra saw Balarāma turned into Śeṣa Nāga and Kṛṣṇa turned into Mahā-Viṣṇu. (p. 255)

“O Dear Dāmodara! Dear Mādhava!” (p. 254)

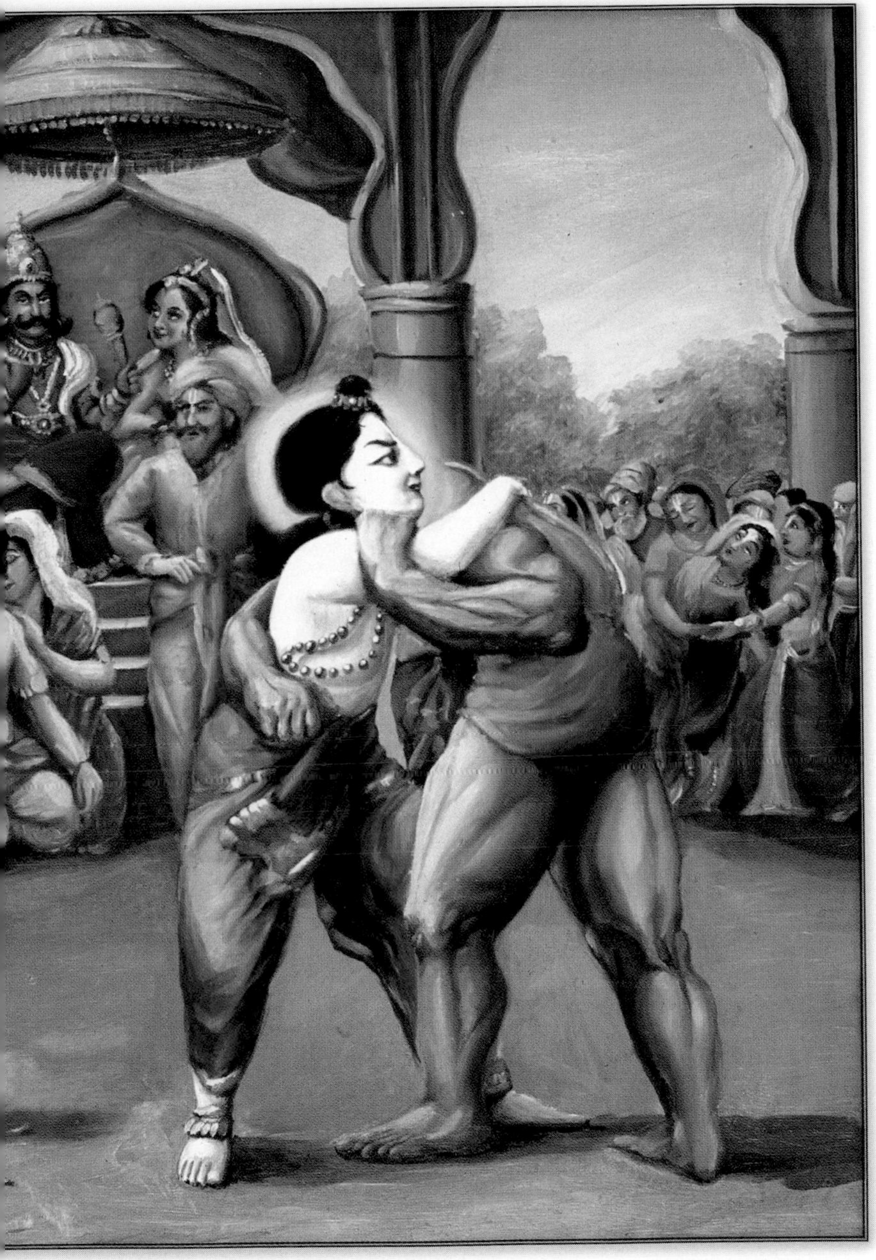

The audience was not very satisfied because the wrestlers did not appear to be equally matched. (p. 275)

Simply from the strokes of His fist, Kaṁsa lost his vital force. (p. 278)

The florist begged from the Lord that he might remain His eternal servant. (p. 265)

The elephant moved before Kṛṣṇa like inevitable death. (p. 271)

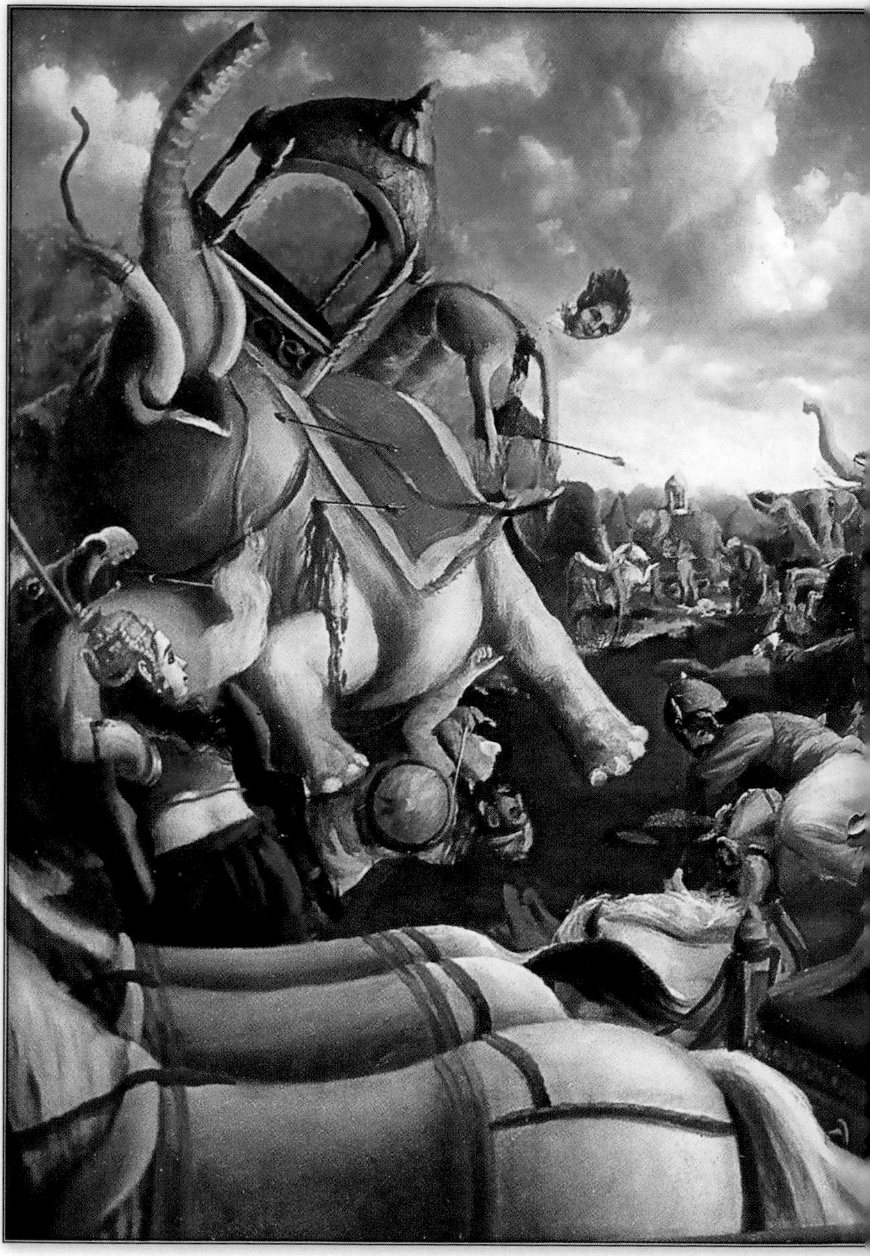

Their blood began to flow just like the waves of a river. (p. 330)

“Bumblebee, you are the unreliable servant of an unreliable master.” (p. 299)

"Some time back you caused the drowning of the son of Our teacher. I order you to return him." (p. 288)

immediately came out and with great devotion fell down on his face to offer his respectful obeisances. He offered a nice seat to Kṛṣṇa and Balarāma and asked his assistant to bring out flowers and betel nuts smeared with pulp of *candana.* The florist's welcome greatly satisfied the Lord.

The florist very humbly and submissively offered his prayers to the Lord, saying, "My dear Lord, because You have come to my place, I think all my forefathers and all my worshipable superiors are pleased and delivered. My dear Lord, You are the supreme cause of all causes of this cosmic manifestation, but for the benefit of the residents of this earthly planet, You have appeared with Your plenary portion to give protection to Your devotees and annihilate the demons. You are equally disposed as the friend of all living entities; You are the Supersoul, and You do not discriminate between friend and enemy. Yet You are pleased to give Your devotees the special result of their devotional activities. My Lord, I am praying that You please tell me whatever You wish me to do, because I am Your eternal servant. If You will allow me to do something, it will be a great favor to me." The florist, Sudāmā, was greatly pleased within his heart by seeing Kṛṣṇa and Balarāma in his place, and thus, as his choicest desire, he made two exquisite garlands of various flowers and presented them to the Lord. Both Kṛṣṇa and Balarāma were very pleased with his sincere service, and Kṛṣṇa offered the florist His salutation and benediction, which He is always prepared to bestow upon the surrendered souls. When the florist was offered benediction, he begged from the Lord that he might remain His eternal servant in devotional service and by such service do good to all living creatures. By this, it is clear that a devotee of the Lord in Kṛṣṇa consciousness should not be simply satisfied by his own advancement in devotional service; he must be willing to work for the welfare of all others. This example was followed by the six Gosvāmīs of Vṛndāvana. It is therefore stated in their prayer, *lokānāṁ hitakāriṇau:* Vaiṣṇavas, or devotees of the Lord, are not selfish. Whatever benefit they derive from the Supreme Personality of Godhead as benediction they want to distribute to all other persons. That is the greatest of all humanitarian activities. Being satisfied with the florist, Lord Kṛṣṇa not only gave him benediction for whatever he wanted, but over and above that, He offered him all material opulences, family prosperity, long duration of life, and whatever else his heart desired within the material world.

Thus ends the Bhaktivedanta purport of the Fortieth Chapter of Kṛṣṇa, *"Kṛṣṇa Enters Mathurā."*

41 / The Breaking of the Bow in the Sacrificial Arena

After leaving the florist's place, Kṛṣṇa and Balarāma saw a hunchbacked young woman carrying a dish of sandalwood pulp through the streets. Since Kṛṣṇa is the reservoir of all pleasure, He wanted to make all His companions joyous by cutting a joke with the hunchbacked woman. Kṛṣṇa addressed her, "O tall young woman, who are you? Tell Me, for whom are you carrying this sandalwood pulp in your hand? I think you should offer this sandalwood to Me, and if you do so I am sure you will be fortunate." Kṛṣṇa is the Supreme Personality of Godhead, and He knew everything about the hunchback. By His inquiry He indicated that there was no use in serving a demon; one had better serve Kṛṣṇa and Balarāma and get rid of the result of sins.

The woman replied to Kṛṣṇa, "My dear Śyāmasundara, dear beautiful dark boy, You may know that I am engaged as maidservant of Kaṁsa. I am supplying him pulp of sandalwood daily. The king is very pleased with me for supplying this nice thing, but now I see that there is no one who can better be served by this pulp of sandalwood than You two brothers." Being captivated by the beautiful features of Kṛṣṇa and Balarāma, Their talking, Their smiling, Their glancing and other activities, the hunchbacked woman began to smear the pulp of sandalwood over Their bodies with great satisfaction and devotion. The two transcendental beggars, Kṛṣṇa and Balarāma, were naturally beautiful and had beautiful complexions, and They were nicely dressed in colorful garments. The upper portions of Their bodies were already very attractive, and when the hunchbacked woman smeared Their bodies with sandalwood pulp, They looked even more beautiful. Kṛṣṇa was very pleased by this service, and He began to consider how to reward her. In other words, in order to draw the attention of the Lord, the Kṛṣṇa conscious devotee has to serve Him in great love and devotion. Kṛṣṇa cannot be pleased by any action other than transcendental loving service unto Him. Thinking like this, Lord Kṛṣṇa pressed the feet of the hunchbacked woman with His toes and, capturing her cheeks with His fingers, gave her a jerk in order to make her straight. At once the hunchbacked woman looked like a beautiful straight girl, with broad hips, thin waist and very nice, well shaped breasts. Since Kṛṣṇa was pleased with the service of the hunchbacked woman, and since she was touched by Kṛṣṇa's hands, she became the most beautiful girl among women. This incident shows that by serving Kṛṣṇa the devotee immediately becomes elevated to the most exalted position. In all respects, devotional service is so potent that anyone who takes to it becomes qualified with all godly qualities. Kṛṣṇa was attracted to the hunchbacked woman not for her beauty but for her service; as soon as she rendered service, she immediately became the most beautiful woman. A Kṛṣṇa conscious person does not have to be qualified or beautiful; after becoming Kṛṣṇa conscious and rendering service unto Kṛṣṇa, he becomes very qualified and beautiful.

When the woman was turned by Kṛṣṇa's favor into an exquisitely beautiful young girl, she naturally felt very much obliged to Kṛṣṇa, and she was also attracted by His beauty. Without hesitation, she caught the rear part of His cloth and began to snatch it. She smiled flirtatiously and admitted that she was agitated by lusty desires. She forgot that she was on the street and before the elder brother of Kṛṣṇa and His friends.

She frankly proposed to Kṛṣṇa: "My dear hero, I cannot leave You in this way. You must come to my place. I am already very much attracted to Your beauty, so I must receive You well, for You are the best among males. You must also be very kind upon me." In plain words she proposed that Kṛṣṇa come to her home and satisfy her lusty desires. Kṛṣṇa, of course, felt a little bit embarassed in front of His elder brother, Balarāma, but He knew that the girl was simple and attracted; therefore He simply smiled at her words. Looking towards His cowherd boy friends, he replied to the girl, "My dear beautiful girl, I am very much pleased by your invitation, and I must come to your home after finishing My other business here. Such a beautiful girl like you is the only means of solace for a person like Me, for I am away from home and not married. Certainly, as a suitable girl friend, you can give us relief from all kinds of mental agitation." Kṛṣṇa satisfied the girl in this way with sweet words. Leaving her there, He began to proceed down the street of the marketplace where the citizens were prepared to receive Him with various kinds of presentations, especially betel nuts, flowers and sandalwood.

The mercantile men in the market worshiped Kṛṣṇa and Balarāma with great respect. When Kṛṣṇa was passing through the street, all the women in the surrounding houses came to see Him, and some of the younger ones almost fainted, being captivated by His beauty. Their hair and tight dresses loosened, and they forgot where they were standing.

Kṛṣṇa next inquired from the citizens as to the location of the place of sacrifice. Kaṁsa had arranged for the sacrifice called *Dhanur-yajña,* and to designate this particular sacrifice he had placed a big bow near the sacrificial altar. The bow was very big and wonderful and resembled the rainbow in the sky. Within the sacrificial arena, this bow was protected by many constables and watchmen engaged by King Kaṁsa. As Kṛṣṇa and Balarāma approached the bow, they were warned not to go nearer, but Kṛṣṇa ignored this warning. He forcibly went up and immediately took the big bow in His left hand. After stringing the bow in the presence of the crowd, He drew it and broke it at the middle into two parts, exactly as an elephant breaks sugar cane in the field. Everyone present appreciated Kṛṣṇa's power. The sound of the bow cracking filled both sky and land and was heard by Kaṁsa. When Kaṁsa heard what had happened, he began to fear for his life. The caretaker of the bow, who was standing by watching, became very angry. He ordered his men to take up weapons, and he began to rush towards Kṛṣṇa, shouting, "Arrest Him! Kill Him! Kill Him!" Kṛṣṇa and Balarāma were surrounded. When They saw the threatening motions of the guards, they became angry, and taking up the two pieces of the broken bow, They began to beat off all the caretaker's men. While this turmoil was going on, Kaṁsa sent a small group of troops to assist the caretakers, but both Kṛṣṇa and Balarāma fought with them also and killed them.

After this, Kṛṣṇa did not proceed further into the sacrificial arena but went out the gate and proceeded towards Their resting camp. Along the way, He visited various places in Mathurā City with great delight. Seeing the activities and wonderful prowess of Kṛṣṇa, all the citizens of Mathurā began to consider the two brothers to be demigods who had come down to Mathurā, and they all looked upon Them with great astonishment. The two brothers strolled carefree in the street, not caring for the law and order of Kaṁsa.

When evening came, Kṛṣṇa and Balarāma, with Their cowherd boy friends, went to the outskirts of the city where all their cars were assembled. Thus Kṛṣṇa and Balarāma gave some preliminary hints of Their arrival to Kaṁsa, and he could understand what severe type of danger was awaiting him the next day in the sacrificial arena.

When Kṛṣṇa and Balarāma were going from Vṛndāvana to Mathurā, the inhabitants of Vṛndāvana had imagined the great fortune of the citizens of Mathurā in being able to see the wonderful beauty of Kṛṣṇa, who is worshiped by His pure devotees as well as the goddess of fortune. The fantasies of the residents of Vṛndāvana were actually realized, for the citizens of Mathurā became fully satisfied by seeing Kṛṣṇa.

When Kṛṣṇa returned to His camp, He was taken care of by servants who washed His lotus feet, gave Him a nice seat and offered Him milk and palatable dishes of foodstuffs. After taking supper and thinking of the next day's program, He very peacefully began to take rest. Thus He passed the night there.

On the other side, when Kaṁsa came to understand about the breaking of his wonderful bow and the killing of the caretaker and soldiers by Kṛṣṇa, he could partially realize the power of the Supreme Personality of Godhead. He could realize that the eighth son of Devakī had appeared and that now his death was imminent. Thinking of his imminent death, he could not rest the entire night. He began to have many inauspicious visions, and he could understand that both Kṛṣṇa and Balarāma, who had approached the precincts of the city, were his messengers of death. Kaṁsa began to see various kinds of inauspicious signs, both awake and dreaming. When he looked in the mirror he could not see his head, although the head was actually present. He could see the luminaries in the sky in double, although there was only one set factually. He began to see holes in his shadow, and he could hear high buzzing sound within his ears. All the trees before him appeared to be made of gold, and he could not see his own footprints in dust or muddy clay. In dream he saw various kinds of ghosts being carried in a carriage drawn by donkeys. He also dreamed that someone gave him poison, and he was drinking it. He dreamed also that he was going naked with a garland of flowers and was smearing oil all over his body. Thus, as Kaṁsa saw various signs of death both awake and sleeping, he could understand that death was certain, and thus in great anxiety he could not rest that night. Just after the night expired, he busily arranged for the wrestling match.

The wrestling arena was nicely cleansed and decorated with flags, festoons and flowers, and the match was announced by the beating of kettledrums. The platform appeared very beautiful due to streamers and flags. Different types of galleries were arranged for respectable persons—kings, *brāhmaṇas* and *kṣatriyas*. The various kings had reserved thrones, and others had arranged seats also. Kaṁsa finally arrived, accompanied by various ministers and secretaries, and he sat on the raised platform especially meant for him. Unfortunately, although he was sitting in the center of all governing executive heads, his heart was palpitating in fear of death. Cruel death evidentally does not care even for a person as powerful as Kaṁsa.

When death comes, it does not care for anyone's exalted position.

When everything was complete, the wrestlers, who were to exhibit their skills before the assembly, walked into the arena. They were decorated with bright ornaments and dress. Some of the famous wrestlers were Cāṇūra, Muṣṭika, Śala, Kūṭa and Tośala. Being enlivened by the musical concert, they passed through with great alacrity. All the respectable cowherd men who came from Vṛndāvana, headed by Nanda, were also welcomed by Kaṁsa. After presenting Kaṁsa with the milk products they had brought with them, the cowherd men also took their respective seats by the side of the king, on a platform especially meant for them.

Thus ends the Bhaktivedanta purport of the Forty-first Chapter of Kṛṣṇa, *"The Breaking of the Bow in the Sacrificial Arena."*

42/The Killing of the Elephant Kuvalayāpīḍa

After taking their baths and finishing all other morning duties, Kṛṣṇa and Balarāma could hear the beating of the kettledrums in the wrestling camp. They immediately prepared Themselves to proceed to the spot to see the fun. When Kṛṣṇa and Balarāma reached the gate of the wrestling camp, They saw a big elephant of the name Kuvalayāpīḍa being tended by a caretaker. The caretaker was deliberately blocking Their entrance by keeping the elephant in front of the gateway. Kṛṣṇa could understand the purpose of the caretaker, and He prepared Himself by tightening His dress before combatting the elephant. He began to address the caretaker in a very grave voice, as resounding as a cloud: "You miscreant caretaker, give way and let Me pass through the gate. If you block My way, I shall send you and your elephant to the house of death personified."

The caretaker, being thus insulted by Kṛṣṇa, became very angry, and in order to challenge Kṛṣṇa, as was previously planned, he provoked the elephant to attack. The elephant then moved before Kṛṣṇa like inevitable death. It rushed towards Him and tried to catch Him with its trunk, but Kṛṣṇa very dexterously moved behind the elephant. Being able to see only to the end of its nose, the elephant could not see Kṛṣṇa hiding behind its legs, but it tried to capture Him with its trunk. Kṛṣṇa again very quickly escaped capture, and He again ran behind the elephant and caught its tail. Holding the elephant by its tail, Kṛṣṇa began to pull it, and with very great strength He dragged it for at least twenty-five yards, just as Garuḍa drags an insignificant snake. Kṛṣṇa pulled the elephant from this side to that, from right to left, just as He used to pull the tail of a calf in His childhood. After this, Kṛṣṇa went in front of the elephant and gave it a strong slap. He then slipped away from the elephant's view and ran to its back. Then, falling down on the ground, Kṛṣṇa placed Himself in front of the elephant's two legs and caused it to trip and fall. Kṛṣṇa immediately got up, but the elephant, thinking that He was still lying down, tried to push an ivory tusk through the body of Kṛṣṇa by forcibly stabbing it into the ground. Although the elephant was harassed and angry, the caretaker riding on its head tried to provoke it further. The elephant then rushed madly towards Kṛṣṇa. As soon as it came within reach, Kṛṣṇa caught hold of the trunk and pulled the elephant down. When the elephant and caretaker fell, Kṛṣṇa jumped up on the elephant's back and broke it and killed the caretaker also. After killing the elephant, Kṛṣṇa took an ivory tusk on His shoulder. Decorated with drops of perspiration and sprinkled with the blood of the elephant, He felt very blissful, and thus He began to proceed towards the wrestling camp. Lord Balarāma took the other tusk of the elephant on His shoulder. Accompanied by Their cowherd boy friends, They entered the arena.

When Kṛṣṇa entered the wrestling arena with Balarāma and Their friends, He appeared differently to different people according to their different relationships *(rasas)* with Him. Kṛṣṇa is the reservoir of all pleasure and all kinds of *rasas,* both favorable and unfavorable. He appeared to the wrestlers exactly like a thunderbolt. To the people in general He appeared as the most beautiful personality. To the females He appeared to be the most attractive male, Cupid personified, and thus increased their lust. The cowherd men who were present there looked upon Kṛṣṇa as their own kinsman, coming from the same village of Vṛndāvana. The *kṣatriya* kings who were present saw Him as the strongest ruler. To the parents of Kṛṣṇa, Nanda and Yaśodā, He appeared to be the most loving child. To Kaṁsa, the king of the Bhoja dynasty, He appeared to be death personified. To the unintelligent, He appeared to be an incapable personality. To the *yogīs* present, He appeared to be the Supersoul. To the members of the Vṛṣṇi dynasty He appeared to be the most celebrated descendant. Thus appreciated differently by different kinds of men present, Kṛṣṇa entered the wrestling arena with Balarāma and His cowherd boy friends. Having heard that Kṛṣṇa had already killed the elephant, Kuvalayāpīḍa, Kaṁsa knew beyond doubt that Kṛṣṇa was formidable. He thus became very much afraid of Him. Kṛṣṇa and Balarāma had long hands. They were beautifully dressed, and They were attractive to all the people assembled there. They were dressed as if They were going to act on a dramatic stage, and They drew the attention of all people.

The citizens of Mathurā City who saw Kṛṣṇa, the Supreme Personality of Godhead, became very pleased and began to look on His face with insatiable glances, as if they were drinking the nectar of heaven. Seeing Kṛṣṇa gave them so much pleasure that it appeared that they were not only drinking the nectar of seeing His face, but were smelling the aroma and licking up the taste of His body and were embracing Him and Balarāma with their arms. They began to talk among themselves about the two transcendental brothers. For a long time they had heard of the beauty and activities of Kṛṣṇa and Balarāma, but now they were personally seeing Them face to face. They thought that Kṛṣṇa and Balarāma were two plenary incarnations of the Supreme Personality of Godhead, Nārāyaṇa, who had appeared in Vṛndāvana.

The citizens of Mathurā began to recite Kṛṣṇa's pastimes, His birth as the son of Vasudeva, His being taken into the care of Nanda Mahārāja and his wife in Gokula, and all those events leading to His coming to Mathurā. They spoke of the killing of the demon Pūtanā, as well as the killing of Tṛṇāvarta, who came as a whirlwind. They also recalled the deliverance of the twin brothers from within the *yamala arjuna* trees. The citizens of Mathurā spoke among themselves: Śaṅkhāsura, Keśī, Dhenukāsura and many other demons were killed by Kṛṣṇa and Balarāma in Vṛndāvana. Kṛṣṇa also saved all the cowherd men of Vṛndāvana from devastating fire. He chastised the Kāliya snake in the water of Yamunā, and He curbed the false pride of the heavenly king, Indra. Kṛṣṇa held up the great Govardhana Hill in one hand for seven continuous days and saved all the people of Gokula from incessant rain, hurricane and windstorm." They also began to remember other enlivening activities: "The damsels of Vṛndāvana were so pleased by seeing Kṛṣṇa's beauty and participating in His activities that they forgot the purpose of material existence. By seeing and thinking of Kṛṣṇa, they forgot all sorts of material fatigue." The Mathurā citizens discussed the dynasty of Yadu, saying that because of Kṛṣṇa's appearance in this dynasty, the Yadus would remain the most celebrated family in the whole universe. While they were thus talking about the activities of Kṛṣṇa and Balarāma, they heard the vibrations of different bands announcing the wrestling match.

The famous wrestler Cāṇūra then began to talk with Kṛṣṇa and Balarāma. "My dear Kṛṣṇa and Balarāma," he said, "we have heard about Your past activities. You are great heroes, and therefore the king has called you. We have heard that Your arms are very strong. The king and all the people present here desire to see a display of Your wrestling abilities. A citizen should be obedient and please the mind of the ruling king; acting in that way, the citizen attains all kinds of good fortune. One who does not care to act obediently is made unhappy because of the king's anger. You are cowherd boys, and we have heard that while tending Your cows in the forest, You enjoy wrestling with each other. We wish, therefore, for You to join with us in wrestling so that all the people present here, along with the king, will be pleased."

Kṛṣṇa immediately understood the purpose of Cāṇūra's statements, and He prepared to wrestle with him. But according to the time and circumstances, He spoke as follows: "You are the subject of the King of Bhoja, and you live in the jungle. We are also indirectly his subjects, and we try to please him as far as possible. This offer of wrestling is a great favor of his, but the fact is that We are simply boys. We sometimes play in the forest of Vṛndāvana with our friends who are our own age. We think that to combat persons of equal age and strength is good for us, but to fight great wrestlers like you would not be good for the audience. It would contradict their religious principles." Kṛṣṇa thus indicated that the celebrated, strong wrestlers should not challenge Kṛṣṇa and Balarāma to fight.

In reply to this, Cāṇūra said, "My dear Kṛṣṇa, we can understand that You are neither a child nor a young man. You are transcendental to everyone, as is Your big brother, Balarāma. You have already killed the elephant Kuvalayāpīḍa, who was capable of fighting and defeating other elephants. You have killed him in a wonderful way. Because of Your strength, it behooves You to compete with the stronger wrestlers amongst us. I therefore wish to wrestle with You, and Your elder brother, Balarāma, will wrestle with Muṣṭika."

Thus ends the Bhaktivedanta purport of the Forty-second Chapter of Kṛṣṇa, *"The Killing of the Elephant Kuvalayāpīḍa."*

43 / The Killing of Kaṁsa

After Kaṁsa's wrestlers expressed their determination, the Supreme Personality of Godhead, the killer of Madhu, confronted Cāṇūra, and Lord Balarāma, the son of Rohiṇī, confronted Muṣṭika. Kṛṣṇa and Cāṇūra and then Balarāma and Muṣṭika locked themselves hand to hand, leg to leg, and each began to press against the other with a view to come out victorious. They joined palm to palm, calf to calf, head to head, chest to chest and began to strike each other. The fighting increased as they pushed one another from one place to another. One captured another and threw him down on the ground, and another rushed from the back to the front of another and tried to overcome him with a hold. The fighting increased step by step. There was picking up, the dragging and pushing, and then the legs and hands were locked together. All the arts of wrestling were perfectly exhibited by the parties, as each tried his best to defeat his opponent.

But the audience in the wrestling arena was not very satisfied because the combatants did not appear to be equally matched. They considered Kṛṣṇa and Balarāma to be mere boys before the wrestlers Cāṇūra and Muṣṭika, who were huge men as solid as stone. Being compassionate and favoring Kṛṣṇa and Balarāma, many members of the audience began to talk as follows. "Dear friends, there is danger here." Another said, "Even in front of the king this wrestling is going on between incompatable sides." The audience had lost their sense of enjoyment. They could not encourage the fighting between the strong and the weak. "Muṣṭika and Cāṇūra are just like thunderbolts, as strong as great mountains, and Kṛṣṇa and Balarāma are two delicate boys of very tender age. The principle of justice has already left this assembly. Persons who are aware of the civilized principles of justice will not remain to watch this unfair match. Those taking part in this wrestling match are not very much enlightened; therefore whether they speak or remain silent, they are being subjected to the reactions of sinful activities." "But my dear friends," another in the assembly spoke out, "just look at the face of Kṛṣṇa. There are drops of perspiration on His face from chasing His enemy, and His face appears like the lotus flower with drops of water. And do you see how the face of Lord Balarāma has turned especially beautiful? There is a reddish hue on His white face because He is engaged in a strong wrestling match with Muṣṭika."

Ladies in the assembly also addressed one another. "Dear friends, just imagine how fortunate the land of Vṛndāvana is where the Supreme Personality of Godhead Himself is present, always decorated with flower garlands and engaged in tending cows along with His brother, Lord Balarāma. He is always accompanied by His cowherd boy friends, and He plays His transcendental flute. The residents of Vṛndāvana are fortunate to be able to constantly see the lotus feet of Kṛṣṇa and Balarāma, which are worshiped by great demigods like Lord Śiva and Brahmā and the goddess of fortune. We cannot estimate how many pious activities were executed by the damsels of Vrajabhūmi so that they were able to enjoy the Supreme Personality of Godhead and look on the unparalleled beauty of His transcendental body. The beauty of the Lord is beyond compare. No one is higher or equal to Him in beauty of complexion or bodily luster. Kṛṣṇa and Balarāma are the reservoir of all kinds of opulence—namely wealth, strength, beauty, fame, knowledge and renunciation. The *gopīs* are so fortunate that they can see and think of Kṛṣṇa twenty-four hours a day, beginning from their milking the cows or husking the paddy or churning the butter in the morning. While engaged in cleaning their houses and washing their floors, they are always absorbed in the thought of Kṛṣṇa."

The *gopīs* give a perfect example of how one can execute Kṛṣṇa consciousness even if he is in different types of material engagement. By constantly being absorbed in the thought of Kṛṣṇa, one cannot be affected by the contamination of material activities. The *gopīs* are, therefore, perfectly in trance, *samādhi,* the highest perfectional stage of mystic power. In the *Bhagavad-gītā,* it is confirmed that one who is constantly thinking of Kṛṣṇa is a first-class *yogī* among all kinds of *yogīs.* "My dear friends," one lady told another, "we must accept the *gopīs'* activities to be the highest form of piety; otherwise, how could they have achieved the opportunity of seeing Kṛṣṇa both morning and evening when He goes to the pasturing ground with His cows and cowherd boy friends and returns in the evening? They frequently see Him playing on His flute and smiling very brilliantly."

When Lord Kṛṣṇa, the Supersoul of every living being, understood that the ladies in the assembly were anxious for Him, He decided not to continue wrestling but to kill the wrestlers immediately. The parents of Kṛṣṇa and Balarāma, namely Nanda Mahārāja, Yaśodā, Vasudeva and Devakī, were also very anxious because they did not know the unlimited strength of their children. Lord Balarāma was fighting with the wrestler Muṣṭika in the same way that Kṛṣṇa, the Supreme Personality of Godhead, was fighting and wrestling with Cāṇūra. Lord Kṛṣṇa appeared to be cruel to Cāṇūra, and He immediately struck him thrice with His fist. The great wrestler was jolted, to the astonishment of the audience. Cāṇūra then took his last chance and attacked Kṛṣṇa, just as one hawk swoops upon another. Folding his two hands, he began to strike the chest of Kṛṣṇa, but Lord Kṛṣṇa was not even slightly disturbed, no more than an elephant that is hit by a flower garland. Kṛṣṇa quickly caught the two hands of Cāṇūra and began to wheel him around, and simply by this centrifugal action, Cāṇūra lost his life. Kṛṣṇa then threw him to the ground. Cāṇūra fell just like the flag of Indra, and all his nicely decorated ornaments were scattered hither and thither.

Muṣṭika also struck Balarāma, and Balarāma returned the stroke with great force. Muṣṭika began to tremble, and blood and vomit flowed from his mouth. Distressed, he gave up his vital force and fell down just as a tree falls down in a hurricane. After the two wrestlers were killed, a wrestler named Kūṭa came forward. Lord Balarāma immediately caught him in His left hand and killed him nonchalantly. Another wrestler of the name Śala came forward, and Kṛṣṇa immediately kicked him and cracked his head. Another wrestler named Tośala came forward and was killed in the same way. Thus all the great wrestlers were killed by Kṛṣṇa and Balarāma, and the remaining wrestlers began to flee from the assembly out of fear for their lives. All the cowherd boy friends of Kṛṣṇa and Balarāma approached Them and congratulated Them with great pleasure. While drums beat and they talked of the victory, the leg bells on the feet of Kṛṣṇa and Balarāma tinkled.

All people gathered there began to clap in great ecstasy, and no one could estimate the bounds of their pleasure. The *brāhmaṇas* present began to praise Kṛṣṇa and Balarāma ecstatically. Only Kaṁsa was morose; he neither clapped nor offered benediction to Kṛṣṇa. Kaṁsa resented the drums' being beaten for Kṛṣṇa's victory, and he was very sorry that the wrestlers had been killed and had fled the assembly. He therefore immediately ordered the drum playing to stop and began to address his friends as follows: "I order that these two sons of Vasudeva be immediately driven out of Mathurā. The cowherd boys who have come with Them should be plundered and all their riches taken away. Nanda Mahārāja should immediately be arrested and killed for his cunning behavior, and the rascal Vasudeva should also be killed without delay. Also my father, Ugrasena, who has always supported my enemies against my will, should be killed."

When Kaṁsa spoke in this way, Lord Kṛṣṇa became very angry with him, and within a second He jumped over the high guards of King Kaṁsa. Kaṁsa was prepared for Kṛṣṇa's attack, for he knew from the beginning that He was to be the cause of his death. He immediately unsheathed his sword and prepared to answer the challenge of Kṛṣṇa with sword and shield. As Kaṁsa wielded his sword up and down, hither and thither, Lord Kṛṣṇa, the supreme powerful Lord, caught hold of him with great force. The Supreme Personality of Godhead, who is the shelter of the complete creation and from whose lotus navel the whole creation is manifested, immediately knocked the crown from the head of Kaṁsa and grabbed his long hair in His hand. He then dragged Kaṁsa from his seat to the wrestling dias and threw him down. Then Kṛṣṇa at once straddled his chest and began to strike him over and over again. Simply from the strokes of His fist, Kaṁsa lost his vital force.

In order to assure His parents that Kaṁsa was dead, Lord Kṛṣṇa dragged him just as a lion drags an elephant after killing it. On sight of this, there was a great roaring sound from all sides, as some spectators expressed their jubilation and others cried in lamentation. From the day Kaṁsa heard that he would be killed by the eighth son of Devakī, he was always thinking of Kṛṣṇa twenty-four hours a day without any stoppage—even while he was eating, while he was walking, while he was breathing—and naturally he got the blessing of liberation. In the *Bhagavad-gītā* it is stated, *sadā tad-bhāva-bhāvitaḥ:* a person gets his next life according to the thoughts in which he is always absorbed. Kaṁsa was thinking of Kṛṣṇa with His wheel, which means Nārāyaṇa who holds a wheel, conchshell, lotus flower and club.

According to the opinion of authorities, Kaṁsa attained *sārūpya-mukti* after death, that is to say he attained the same form as Nārāyaṇa (Viṣṇu). On the Vaikuṇṭha planets all the inhabitants have the same bodily features as Nārāyaṇa. After his death, Kaṁsa attained liberation and was promoted to Vaikuṇṭhaloka. From this instance we can understand that even a person who thinks of the Supreme Personality of Godhead as an enemy gets liberation and a place in a Vaikuṇṭha planet, so what to speak of the pure devotees who are always absorbed in favorable thoughts of Kṛṣṇa? Even an enemy who is killed by Kṛṣṇa gets liberation and is placed in the impersonal *brahmajyoti.* Since the Supreme Personality of Godhead is all good, anyone thinking of Him, either as enemy or as friend, gets liberation. But the liberation of the devotee and the liberation of the enemy are not the same. The enemy generally gets the liberation of *sāyujya,* and sometimes he gets *sārūpya* liberation.

Kaṁsa had eight brothers, headed by Kaṅka. All of them were younger than he, and when they learned that their elder brother had been killed, they combined together and rushed towards Kṛṣṇa in great anger to kill Him. Kaṁsa and his brothers were all Kṛṣṇa's maternal uncles. They were all brothers of Kṛṣṇa's mother, Devakī. When Kṛṣṇa killed Kaṁsa He killed His maternal uncle, which is against the regulation of Vedic injunction. Although Kṛṣṇa is independent of all Vedic injunction, He violates the Vedic injunction only in inevitable cases. Kaṁsa could not be killed by anyone but Kṛṣṇa; therefore Kṛṣṇa was obliged to kill him. As far as Kaṁsa's eight brothers were concerned, Balarāma took charge of killing them. Balarāma's mother, Rohiṇī, although the wife of Vasudeva, was not the sister of Kaṁsa; therefore Balarāma took charge of killing all of Kaṁsa's eight brothers. He immediately took up an available weapon (most probably the elephant's tusk which He carried) and killed the eight brothers one after another, just as a lion kills a flock of deer. Kṛṣṇa and Balarāma thus verified the statement that the Supreme Personality of Godhead appears to give protection to the pious and to kill the impious demons who are always enemies of the demigods.

The demigods from the higher planetary systems began to shower flowers, congratulating Kṛṣṇa and Balarāma. Among the demigods were powerful personalities like Lord Brahmā and Śiva, and all joined together in showing their jubilation over Kaṁsa's death. There was beating of drums and showering of flowers from the heavenly planets, and the wives of the demigods began to dance in ecstasy.

The wives of Kaṁsa and his eight brothers became aggrieved on account of their husbands' sudden deaths, and all of them were striking their foreheads and shedding torrents of tears. They were crying very loudly and embracing the bodies of their husbands. The wives of Kaṁsa and his brothers began to lament, addressing the dead bodies: "Our dear husbands, you are so kind and are the protectors of your dependents. Now, after your death, we are also dead, along with your homes and children. We are no longer looking very auspicious. On account of your death, the auspicious functions which were to take place, such as the sacrifice of the bow, have all been spoiled. Our dear husbands, you treated persons ill who were faultless, and as a result you have been killed. This is inevitable because a person who torments an innocent person must be punished by the laws of nature. We know that Lord Kṛṣṇa is the Supreme Personality of Godhead. He is the supreme master of everything and the supreme enjoyer of everything, and therefore anyone who neglects His authority can never be happy, and ultimately, as you have, he meets death."

Since Kṛṣṇa was kind and affectionate to His aunts, He began to give them solace as far as was possible. The ritualistic ceremonies after death were then conducted under the personal supervision of Kṛṣṇa because He happened to be the nephew of all the dead princes. After finishing this business, Kṛṣṇa and Balarāma immediately released Their father and mother, Vasudeva and Devakī who had been imprisoned by Kaṁsa. Kṛṣṇa and Balarāma fell at Their parents' feet and offered them prayers. Vasudeva and Devakī had suffered so much trouble because Kṛṣṇa was their son; it was because of Kṛṣṇa that Kaṁsa was always giving them trouble. Devakī and Vasudeva were fully conscious of Kṛṣṇa's exalted position as the Supreme Personality of Godhead; therefore, although Kṛṣṇa touched their feet and offered obeisances and prayers to them, they did not embrace Him, but simply stood up to hear the Supreme Personality of Godhead. Although Kṛṣṇa was born as their son, Vasudeva and Devakī were always conscious of His position.

Thus ends the Bhaktivedānta purport of the Forty-third Chapter of Kṛṣṇa, *"The Killing of Kaṁsa."*

44 / Kṛṣṇa Recovers the Son of His Teacher

When Lord Kṛṣṇa saw that Vasudeva and Devakī were remaining standing in a reverential attitude, He immediately expanded His influence of *yogamāyā* so that they could treat Him and Balarāma as children. As in the material world the relationship existing between father and mother and children can be established amongst different living entities by the influence of the illusory energy, so, by the influence of *yogamāyā,* the devotee can establish a relationship in which the Supreme Personality of Godhead is his child. After creating this situation by His *yogamāyā,* Kṛṣṇa, appearing with His elder brother Balarāma as the most illustrious sons in the dynasty of the Sātvatas, very submissively and respectfully addressed Vasudeva and Devakī: "My dear father and mother, although you have always been very anxious for the protection of Our lives, you could not enjoy the pleasure of having Us as your babies, as your growing boys and as your adolescent youths." Kṛṣṇa indirectly praised the fatherhood of Nanda Mahārāja and motherhood of Yaśodā as most glorious because although He and Balarāma were not their born sons, Nanda and Yaśodā actually enjoyed Their childhood pastimes. By nature's own arrangement, the childhood of the embodied living being is enjoyed by the parents. Even in the animal kingdom the parents are found to be affectionate to the cubs. Being captivated by the activities of their children, they take much care for their well-being. As for Vasudeva and Devakī, they were always very anxious for the protection of their sons, Kṛṣṇa and Balarāma. That is why Kṛṣṇa, after His appearance, was immediately transferred to another's house. Balarāma was also transferred from Devakī's womb to Rohiṇī's womb.

Vasudeva and Devakī were full of anxieties for Kṛṣṇa's and Balarāma's protection, and they could not enjoy Their childhood pastimes. Kṛṣṇa said, "Unfortunately, being ordered by Our fate, We could not be raised by Our own parents to enjoy childhood pleasures at home. My dear father and mother, a man has a debt to pay to his parents, from whom he gets this body which can bestow upon him all the benefits of material existence. According to the Vedic injunction, this human form of life enables one to perform all kinds of religious activities, fulfill all kinds of desires and acquire all kinds of wealth. And only in this human form is there every possibility that one can get liberation from material existence. This body is produced by the combined efforts of the father and mother. Every human being should be obliged to his parents and understand that he cannot repay his debt to them. If, after growing up, a son does not try to satisfy his parents by his actions or by an endowment of riches, he is surely punished after death by the superintendent of death and made to eat his own flesh. If a person is able to care for or give protection to old parents, children, the spiritual master, *brāhmaṇas* and other dependents, but does not do so, he is considered to be already dead, although he is supposedly breathing. My dear father and mother, you have always been very anxious for Our protection, but unfortunately We could not render any service unto you. Up to date We have simply wasted Our time; We could not serve you for reasons beyond Our control. Mother and father, please excuse Us for Our sinful action."

When the Supreme Personality of Godhead was speaking as an innocent boy in very sweet words, both Vasudeva and Devakī became captivated by parental affection and embraced Them with great pleasure. They were amazed and could not speak or answer the words of Kṛṣṇa, but simply embraced Him and Balarāma in great affection and remained silent, shedding incessant tears.

Thus consoling His father and mother, the Supreme Personality of Godhead, appearing as the beloved son of Devakī, approached His grandfather Ugrasena and announced that Ugrasena would now be the King of the Yadu kingdom. Kaṁsa had been forcibly ruling over the kingdom of Yadu, in spite of the presence of his father, whom he had arrested. But after the death of Kaṁsa, Kaṁsa's father was released and announced to be the King of the Yadu kingdom. It appears that in those days, in the western part of India, there were many small kingdoms, and they were ruled by the Yadu dynasty, Andhaka dynasty, Vṛṣṇi dynasty and Bhoja dynasty. Mahārāja Ugrasena belonged to the Bhoja dynasty; therefore Kṛṣṇa indirectly declared that the king of the Bhoja dynasty would be emperor of the other small kingdoms. He willingly asked Mahārāja Ugrasena to rule over Them because They were his subjects. The word *prajā* is used both for the progeny and for the citizens, so Kṛṣṇa belonged to the *prajā*, both as a grandson to Mahārāja Ugrasena and as a member of the Yadu dynasty. He voluntarily accepted the rule of Mahārāja Ugrasena. He informed Ugrasena: "Being cursed by the Yayāti, the kings of the Yadu dynasty will not rise against the throne. It will be Our pleasure to serve you as your servants. Our full cooperation with you will make your position more exalted and secure so that the kings of other dynasties will not hesitate to pay their respective revenues. Protected by Us, you will be honored even by the demigods from the heavenly planets. My dear grandfather, out of fear of My late uncle Kaṁsa, all the kings belonging to the Yadu dynasty, Vṛṣṇi dynasty, Andhaka dynasty, Madhu dynasty, Daśārha dynasty and Kukura dynasty were very anxious and disturbed. Now you can pacify them all and give them assurance of security. The whole kingdom will be peaceful."

All the kings in the neighboring area had left their homes in fear of Kaṁsa and were living in distant parts of the country. Now, after the death of Kaṁsa and the reinstatement of Ugrasena as king, the neighboring kings were given all kinds of presentations and comforts. Then they returned to their respective homes. After this nice political arrangement, the citizens of Mathurā were pleased to live in Mathurā, being protected by the strong arms of Kṛṣṇa and Balarāma. On account of good government in the presence of Kṛṣṇa and Balarāma, the inhabitants of Mathurā felt complete satisfaction in the fulfillment of all their material desires and necessities, and because they saw Kṛṣṇa and Balarāma daily, eye to eye, they soon forgot all material miseries completely. As soon as they saw Kṛṣṇa and Balarāma coming out on the street, very nicely dressed and smiling and looking here and there, the citizens were immediately filled with loving ecstasies, simply by seeing the personal presence of Mukunda. *Mukunda* refers to one who can award liberation and transcendental bliss. Kṛṣṇa's presence acted as such a vitalizing tonic that not only the younger generation, but even the old men of Mathurā became fully invigorated with youthful energy and strength by regularly seeing Him.

Nanda Mahārāja and Yaśodā were also living in Mathurā because Kṛṣṇa and Balarāma were there, but after some time they wanted to go back to Vṛndāvana. Kṛṣṇa and Balarāma went before them and very feelingly and affectionately embraced Nanda and Yaśodā, and Kṛṣṇa began to speak as follows: "My dear father and mother, although I was born of Vasudeva and Devakī, you have been Our real father and mother, because from Our very birth and childhood, you raised Us with great affection and love. Your affectionate love for Us was more than anyone can offer one's own children. You are actually Our father and mother, because you raised Us as your own children at a time when We were just like orphans. For certain reasons We were rejected by Our father and mother, and you protected Us. My dear father and mother, I know you will be feeling separation by returning to Vṛndāvana and leaving Us here, but please rest assured that I shall be coming back to Vṛndāvana just after giving some satisfaction to My real father and mother, Vasudeva and Devakī, My grandfather, and other relatives and family members." Kṛṣṇa and Balarāma satisfied Nanda and Yaśodā by sweet words and by presentation of various clothing, ornaments and properly made utensils. They satisfied them, along with their friends and neighbors who had come with them from Vṛndāvana to Mathurā, as fully as possible. On account of his excessive parental affection for Balarāma and Kṛṣṇa, Nanda Mahārāja felt tears in his eyes, and he embraced Them and started with the cowherd men for Vṛndāvana.

After this, Vasudeva had his son initiated by sacred thread as the token of second birth, which is essential for the higher castes of human society. Vasudeva called for his family priest and learned *brāhmaṇas,* and the sacred thread ceremony of Kṛṣṇa and Balarāma was duly performed. During this ceremony, Vasudeva gave various ornaments in charity to the *brāhmaṇas* and endowed them with cows decorated with silken cloths and golden ornaments. Previously, during the birth of Kṛṣṇa and Balarāma, Vasudeva had wanted to give cows in charity to the *brāhmaṇas,* but being imprisoned by Kaṁsa, he was able to do so only within his mind. With the death of Kaṁsa the actual cows were given to the *brāhmaṇas.* Then Balarāma and Kṛṣṇa were duly initiated with the sacred thread ceremony, and They repeated the chanting of the *Gāyatrī mantra.* The *Gāyatrī mantra* is offered to the disciples after the sacred thread ceremony, and Balarāma and Kṛṣṇa properly discharged the duties of chanting this *mantra.* Anyone who executes the chanting of this *mantra* has to abide by certain principles and vows. Although Balarāma and Kṛṣṇa were both transcendental personalities, They strictly followed the regulative principles. Both were initiated by Their family priest Gargācārya, usually known as Gargamuni, the *ācārya* of the Yadu dynasty. According to Vedic culture, every respectable person has an *ācārya,* or spiritual master. One is not considered to be a perfectly cultured man without being initiated and trained by an *ācārya.* It is said, therefore, that one who has approached an *ācārya* is actually in perfect knowledge. Lord Kṛṣṇa and Balarāma were the Supreme Personality of Godhead, the master of all education and knowledge. There was no need for Them to accept a spiritual master or *ācārya,* yet for the instruction of ordinary men, They also accepted a spiritual master for advancement in spiritual knowledge.

It is customary, after being initiated in the *Gāyatrī mantra,* for one to live away from home for some time under the care of the *ācārya* in order to be trained in spiritual life. During this period one has to work under the spiritual master as an ordinary menial servant. There are many rules and regulations for a *brahmacārī* living under the care of an *ācārya,* and both Lord Kṛṣṇa and Balarāma strictly followed those regulative principles while living under the instruction of their spiritual master, Sāndīpani Muni, in his place in northern India. According to scriptural injunctions, a spiritual master should be respected and be regarded on an equal level with the Supreme Personality of Godhead. Both Kṛṣṇa and Balarāma exactly followed those principles with great devotion and underwent the regulations of *brahmacarya,* and thus They satisfied Their spiritual master, who instructed Them in Vedic knowledge. Being very satisfied, Sāndīpani Muni instructed Them in all the intricacies of Vedic wisdom as well as in supplementary literatures such as the *Upaniṣads.* Because Kṛṣṇa and Balarāma happened to be *kṣatriyas,* They were specifically trained in military science, politics and mathematics. In politics there are six departments of knowledge—how to make peace, how to fight, how to pacify, how to divide and rule, how to give shelter, etc. All these items were fully explained and instructed to Kṛṣṇa and Balarāma.

The ocean is the source of water in a river. The cloud is created by the evaporation of ocean water, and the same water is distributed as rain all over the surface of the earth and then returns toward the ocean in rivers. So Kṛṣṇa and Balarāma, the Supreme Personality of Godhead, are the source of all kinds of knowledge, but because They were playing like ordinary human boys, They set the example so that everyone would receive knowledge from the right source. Thus They agreed to take knowledge from a spiritual master.

After hearing only once from the teacher, Kṛṣṇa and Balarāma learned all the arts and sciences. In sixty-four days and sixty-four nights They learned all the necessary arts and sciences that are required in human society. During daytime They took lessons on a subject from the teacher, and by nightfall, after having heard from the teacher, They were expert in that department of knowledge.

First of all They learned how to sing, how to compose songs and how to recognize the different tunes; They learned the favorable and unfavorable accents and meters, how to sing different kinds of rhythms and melodies, and how to follow them by beating different kinds of drums. They learned how to dance with rhythm, melody and different songs.

They learned how to write dramas, and They learned the various types of paintings, beginning from different village arts up to the highest perfectional stage. They also learned how to paint *tilaka* on the face and make different kinds of dots on the forehead and cheeks. Then They learned the art of painting on the floor with liquid paste of rice and flour; such paintings are very popular at auspicious ceremonies performed at household affairs or in the temple. They learned how to make a resting place with flowers and how to decorate clothing and leaves with colorful paintings. They also learned how to set different valuable jewels in ornaments. They learned the art of ringing water pots. Water pots are filled with water to a certain measurement so that when one beats on the pots, different tunes are produced, and when the pots are beaten together they produce a melodious sound. They also learned how to throw water in the rivers or the lakes while taking a bath among friends. They also learned how to decorate with flowers. This art of decorating can still be seen in various temples of Vṛndāvana during the summer season. It is called *phulabāḍi*. The dais, the throne, the walls and the ceiling are all fully decorated, and a small, aromatic fountain of flowers is fixed in the center. Because of these floral decorations, the people, fatigued from the heat of the summer season, become refreshed.

Kṛṣṇa and Balarāma learned the art of dressing hair in various styles and fixing a helmet in different positions on the head. They also learned how to perform on the theatrical stage, how to decorate dramatic actors with flower ornaments over the ear, and how to sprinkle sandalwood pulp and water to produce a nice fragrance. They also learned the art of performing magical feats. Within the magical field there is an art called *bahurūpī* by which a person dresses himself in such a way that when he approaches a friend he cannot be recognized. They also learned how to make beverages which are required at various times, and They studied syrups and tastes and the effects of intoxication. They learned how to manipulate thin threads for dancing puppets, and They learned how to string wires on musical instruments, such as the *vīṇā,* sitar and tampura, to produce melodious sound. Then They learned puzzles and how to set and solve them. They learned the art of reading books from which even a foolish student can very quickly learn to read the alphabet and comprehend writing. Then They learned how to rehearse and act out a drama. They also studied the art of solving crossword puzzles, filling up the missing space and making complete words.

They also learned how to draw pictographic literature. In some countries in the world, pictographic literature is still current. A story is represented by pictures; for instance, a man and a house are pictured to represent a man going home. Kṛṣṇa and Balarāma also learned the art of architecture—how to construct residential buildings. They learned to recognize valuable jewels by studying the luster and the quality of their colors. Then They learned the art of setting jewels with gold and silver. They also learned how to study soil to find minerals. This study of soil is now a greatly specialized science, but formerly it was common knowledge even for the ordinary man. They learned to study herbs and plants and to extract medicine from the elements. By studying the different species of plants, They learned how to crossbreed plants and get different types of fruits. They learned how to train and engage lambs and cocks in fighting for sporting purposes. They then learned how to teach parrots to speak and answer the questions of human beings.

They learned practical psychology—how to influence another's mind and thus induce another to act according to one's own desire. Sometimes this is called hypnotism. They learned how to wash hair, dye it in different colors and curl it in different ways. They learned the art of telling what is written in someone's book without actually seeing it. They learned to tell what is contained in another's fist. Sometimes children imitate this art, although not very accurately. One child keeps something within his fist and asks his friend, "Can you tell what is within?" and the friend gives some suggestion, although He actually cannot tell. But there is an art by which one can understand and actually tell what is held within the fist.

Kṛṣṇa and Balarāma learned how to speak and understand the languages of various countries. They learned not only the languages of human beings. Kṛṣṇa could also speak even with animals and birds. Evidence of this is found in Vaiṣṇava literature compiled by the Gosvāmīs. Then They learned how to make carriages and airplanes from flowers. It is said in the *Rāmāyaṇa* that after defeating Rāvaṇa, Rāmacandra was carried from Laṅkā to Bhāratavarṣa on a plane of flowers called *puṣpa-ratha.* Kṛṣṇa then learned the art of foretelling events by seeing signs. In a book called *Khanār vacana,* the various types of signs and omens are described. If, when one is going out, one sees someone with a bucket full of water, that is a very good sign. But if one sees someone with an empty bucket, it is not a very good sign. Similarly, if one sees cow's milk along with her calf, it is a good sign. The result of understanding these signs is that one can foretell events, and Kṛṣṇa learned the science. Kṛṣṇa also learned the art of composing *mātṛkā.* A *mātṛkā* is a crossword section with three letters in a line; counting any three from any side, it will count nine. The *mātṛkās* are of different kinds and are for different purposes.

Kṛṣṇa learned the art of cutting valuable stones such as diamonds, and

He learned the art of questioning and answering by immediately composing poetry within His mind. He learned the science of the action and reaction of physical combinations and permutations. He learned the art of a psychiatrist, who can understand the psychic movements of another person. He learned how to satisfy one's desires. Desires are very difficult to fulfill; but if one desires something which is unreasonable and can never be fulfilled, the desire can be subdued and satisfied, and that is an art. By this art one can also subdue sex impulses when they are aroused, as they are even in *brahmacārī* life. By this art one can make even an enemy his friend or transfer the direct action of a physical element to other things.

Lord Kṛṣṇa and Balarāma, the reservoir of all knowledge of arts and sciences, exhibited Their perfect understanding when They offered to serve Their teacher by awarding him anything he desired. This offering by the student to the teacher or spiritual master is called *guru-dakṣiṇā*. It is essential that a student satisfy the teacher in return for any learning received, either material or spiritual. When Kṛṣṇa and Balarāma offered Their service in this way, the teacher, Sāndīpani Muni, thought it wise to ask Them for something extraordinary, something which no common student could offer. He therefore consulted with his wife about what to ask from Them. They had already seen the extraordinary potencies of Kṛṣṇa and Balarāma and could understand that the two boys were the Supreme Personality of Godhead. They decided to ask for the return of their son, who had drowned in the ocean on the bank of Prabhāsakṣetra.

When Kṛṣṇa and Balarāma heard from Their teacher about the death of his son on the bank of Prabhāsakṣetra, They immediately started for the ocean on Their chariot. Reaching the beach, They asked the controlling deity of the ocean to return the son of Their teacher. The ocean deity immediately appeared before the Lord and offered Him all respectful obeisances with great humility.

The Lord said, "Some time back you caused the drowning of the son of Our teacher. I order you to return him."

The ocean deity replied, "The boy was not actually taken by me, but was captured by a demon named Pañcajana. This great demon generally remains deep in the water in the shape of a conchshell. The son of Your teacher might be within the belly of the demon, having been devoured by him."

On hearing this, Kṛṣṇa dove deep into the water and caught hold of the demon Pañcajana. He killed him on the spot, but could not find the son of His teacher within his belly. Therefore He took the demon's dead body (in the shape of a conchshell) and returned to His chariot on the beach of

Prabhāsakṣetra. From there He started for Saṁyamanī, the residence of Yamarāja, the superintendent of death. Accompanied by His elder brother Balarāma, who is also known as Halāyudha, Kṛṣṇa arrived there and blew on His conchshell.

Hearing the vibration, Yamarāja appeared and received Śrī Kṛṣṇa with all respectful obeisances. Yamarāja could understand who Kṛṣṇa and Balarāma were, and therefore he immediately offered his humble service to the Lord. Kṛṣṇa had appeared on the surface of the earth as an ordinary human being, but actually Kṛṣṇa and Balarāma are the Supersoul living within the heart of every living entity. They are Viṣṇu Himself, but were playing just like ordinary human boys. As Yamarāja offered his services to the Lord, Śrī Kṛṣṇa asked him to return His teacher's son, who had come to him as a result of his work. "Considering My ruling as supreme," said Kṛṣṇa, "you should immediately return the son of My teacher."

Yamarāja returned the boy to the Supreme Personality of Godhead, and Kṛṣṇa and Balarāma brought him to his father. The brothers asked if Their teacher had anything more to ask from Them, but he replied, "My dear sons, You have done enough for me. I am now completely satisfied. What further want can there be for a man who has disciples like You? My dear boys, You can go home now. These glorious acts of Yours will always be renowned all over the world. You are above all blessing, yet it is my duty to bless You. I give You the benediction that whatever You speak will remain as eternally fresh as the instruction of the *Vedas.* Your teachings will not only be honored within this universe or in this millennium, but in all places and ages and will remain increasingly new and important." Due to this benediction from His teacher, Lord Kṛṣṇa's *Bhagavad-gītā* is ever increasingly fresh and is not only renowned within this universe, but in other planets and in other universes also.

Being ordered by Their teacher, Kṛṣṇa and Balarāma immediately returned home on Their chariots. They traveled at great speeds like the wind and made sounds like the crashing of clouds. All the residents of Mathurā, who had not seen Kṛṣṇa and Balarāma for a long time, were very pleased to see Them again. They felt joyful, like a person who has regained his lost property.

Thus ends the Bhaktivedanta purport of the Forty-fourth Chapter of Kṛṣṇa, *"Kṛṣṇa Recovers the Son of His Teacher."*

45 / Uddhava Visits Vṛndāvana

Nanda Mahārāja returned to Vṛndāvana without Kṛṣṇa and Balarāma. He was accompanied only by the cowherd boys and men. It was certainly a very pathetic scene for the *gopīs,* mother Yaśodā, Śrīmatī Rādhārāṇī and all the inhabitants and residents of Vṛndāvana. Many devotees have tried to make adjustments to Kṛṣṇa's being away from Vṛndāvana because according to expert opinion, Kṛṣṇa, the original Supreme Personality of Godhead, never goes even a step out of Vṛndāvana. He always remains there. The explanation of expert devotees is that Kṛṣṇa was actually not absent from Vṛndāvana; He came back with Nanda Mahārāja as promised.

When He was going to Mathurā on the chariot driven by Akrūra and the *gopīs* were practically blocking the way, Kṛṣṇa assured them that He was coming back just after finishing His business in Mathurā. He told them not to be overwhelmed, and in this way He pacified them. But when He did not come back with Nanda Mahārāja, it appeared that He either cheated them or could not keep His promise. Expert devotees, however, have decided that Kṛṣṇa was neither a cheater nor a breaker of promises. Kṛṣṇa, in His original identity, returned with Nanda Mahārāja and stayed with the *gopīs* and mother Yaśodā in His *bhava* expansion. Kṛṣṇa and Balarāma remained in Mathurā, not in Their original forms, but in Their expansions as Vāsudeva and Saṅkarṣaṇa. The real Kṛṣṇa and Balarāma were in Vṛndāvana in Their *bhava* manifestation, whereas in Mathurā They appeared in the *prabhava* and *vaibhava* expansions. This is the expert opinion of advanced devotees of Kṛṣṇa. But when Nanda Mahārāja was preparing to return to Vṛndāvana, there was discussion among him, Kṛṣṇa and Balarāma as to how the boys could live in separation from Nanda. The conclusion to separate was reached by mutual agreement.

Vasudeva and Devakī happened to be Kṛṣṇa and Balarāma's real parents. They wanted to keep Them now because of the death of Kaṁsa. While

Kaṁsa was alive, They were kept under the protection of Nanda Mahārāja in Vṛndāvana. Now, naturally, the father and mother of Kṛṣṇa and Balarāma wanted Them to remain with them, specifically for the reformatory function of purification, the sacred thread ceremony. They also wanted to give Them a proper education, for this is the duty of the father. Another consideration was that all the friends of Kaṁsa outside Mathurā were planning to attack Mathurā. For that reason also Kṛṣṇa's presence was required. Kṛṣṇa did not want Vṛndāvana to be disturbed by enemies like Dantavakra and Jarāsandha. If Kṛṣṇa were to go to Vṛndāvana, these enemies would not only attack Mathurā, but would go on to Vṛndāvana, and the peaceful inhabitants of Vṛndāvana would be disturbed. Kṛṣṇa therefore decided to remain in Mathurā, and Nanda Mahārāja went back to Vṛndāvana. Although the inhabitants of Vṛndāvana were feeling separation from Kṛṣṇa, Kṛṣṇa was always present with them by His *līlā,* or pastimes, and this made them ecstatic.

Since Kṛṣṇa had departed from Vṛndāvana to Mathurā, the inhabitants of Vṛndāvana, especially mother Yaśodā, Nanda Mahārāja, Śrīmatī Rādhārāṇī, the *gopīs* and the cowherd boys, were simply thinking of Kṛṣṇa at every step. They were thinking, "Kṛṣṇa was playing in this way. Kṛṣṇa was blowing His flute. Kṛṣṇa was joking with us, and Kṛṣṇa was embracing us." This is called *līlā-smaraṇa,* and it is the process of association with Kṛṣṇa most recommended by great devotees; even Lord Caitanya enjoyed *līlā-smaraṇa* association of Kṛṣṇa when He was at Purī. Those who are in the most exalted position of devotional service and ecstasy can live with Kṛṣṇa always by remembering His pastimes. Śrīla Viśvanātha Cakravartī Ṭhākur has given us a transcendental literature entitled ***Kṛṣṇa-bhāvanāmṛta,*** which is full with Kṛṣṇa's pastimes. Devotees can remain absorbed in Kṛṣṇa-thought by reading such books. Any book of Kṛṣṇa *līlā,* even this book, *Kṛṣṇa,* and our *Teachings of Lord Caitanya,* is actually solace for devotees who are feeling the separation of Kṛṣṇa.

That Kṛṣṇa and Balarāma did not come to Vṛndāvana can be adjusted as follows: They did not break Their promise to return to Vṛndāvana, nor were They absent, but Their presence was necessary in Mathurā.

In the meantime, Uddhava, a cousin-brother of Kṛṣṇa, came to see Kṛṣṇa from Dvārakā. He was the son of Vasudeva's brother and was almost the same age as Kṛṣṇa. His bodily features resembled Kṛṣṇa's almost exactly. After returning from His teacher's home, Kṛṣṇa was pleased to see Uddhava, who happened to be His dearmost friend. He wanted to send him to Vṛndāvana with a message to the residents to pacify their deep feeling of separation.

As stated in the *Bhagavad-gītā, ye yathā māṁ prapadyante:* Kṛṣṇa is very responsive. He responds in proportion to the devotee's advancement in devotional service. The *gopīs* were thinking of Kṛṣṇa in separation twenty-four hours a day. Kṛṣṇa was also always thinking of the *gopīs,* mother Yaśodā, Nanda Mahārāja and the residents of Vṛndāvana, although He appeared to be away from them. He could understand how they were transcendentally aggrieved, and so He immediately wanted to send Uddhava to give them a message of solace.

Uddhava is described as the most exalted personality in the Vṛṣṇi dynasty, almost equal to Kṛṣṇa. He was a great friend, and on account of being the direct student of Bṛhaspati, the teacher and priest of the heavenly planets, he was very intelligent and sharp in decision. From the intellectual standpoint, he was highly qualified. Kṛṣṇa, being a very loving friend of Uddhava, wanted to send him to Vṛndāvana just to study the highly elevated ecstatic devotional service practiced there. Even if one is highly elevated in material education and is even the disciple of Bṛhaspati, he still has to learn from the *gopīs* and the residents of Vṛndāvana how to love Kṛṣṇa to the highest degree. Sending Uddhava to Vṛndāvana with a message to the residents of Vṛndāvana to pacify them was Kṛṣṇa's special favor to Uddhava.

Lord Kṛṣṇa's name is Hari, which means one who takes away all the distress from the surrendered souls. Lord Caitanya states that there cannot be, at any time, a worship as exalted as that realized by the *gopīs.* Being very anxious about the *gopīs'* grief, Kṛṣṇa talked with Uddhava and politely requested him to go to Vrndāvana. Shaking Uddhava's hand with His own hands, He said, "My dear gentle friend Uddhava, please go immediately to Vṛndāvana and try to pacify My father and mother, Nanda Mahārāja and Yaśodādevī, and the *gopīs.* They are very much griefstricken, as if suffering from great ailments. Go and give them a message. I hope their ailments will be partially relieved. The *gopīs* are always absorbed in thoughts of Me. They have dedicated body, desire, life and soul to Me. I am anxious not only for the *gopīs,* but for anyone who sacrifices society, friendship, love and personal comforts for Me. It is My duty to protect such exalted devotees. The *gopīs* are the most dear. They are always thinking of Me in such a way that they remain overwhelmed and almost dead in anxiety due to separation from Me. They are keeping alive simply by thinking that I am returning to them very soon."

Requested by Lord Kṛṣṇa, Uddhava immediately left on His chariot and carried the message to Gokula. He approached Vṛndāvana at sunset, when the cows were returning home from the pasturing ground. Uddhava and his chariot were covered by the dust raised by the hooves of the cows. He saw bulls running after cows for mating; other cows, with overladened milkbags, were running after the calves to fill them with milk. Uddhava saw that the entire land of Vṛndāvana was filled with white cows and their calves. Cows were running here and there all over Gokula, and he could hear the sound of milking. Every residential house in Vṛndāvana was decorated for the worship of the sun-god and the fire-god and for the reception of guests, cows, *brāhmaṇas* and demigods. Every home was illuminated with light and incense arranged for sanctification. All over Vṛndāvana there were nice flower garlands, flying birds and the humming sound of the bees. The lakes were filled with lotus flowers and with ducks and swans.

Uddhava entered the house of Nanda Mahārāja and was received as a representative of Vāsudeva. Nanda Mahārāja offered him a place and sat down with him to ask about messages from Kṛṣṇa, Balarāma and other family members in Mathurā. He could understand that Uddhava was a very confidential friend of Kṛṣṇa and therefore must have come with good messages. "My dear Uddhava, how is my friend Vasudeva enjoying life? He is now released from the prison of Kaṁsa, and he is now with his friends and his children, Kṛṣṇa and Balarāma. So he must be very happy. Tell me about him and his welfare. We are also very happy that Kaṁsa, the most sinful demon, is now killed. He was always envious of the family of the Yadus, his friends and relatives. Now because of his sinful activities, he is dead and gone, along with all his brothers.

"Please let us now know whether Kṛṣṇa is remembering His father and mother and His friends and companions in Vṛndāvana. Does He like to remember His cows, His *gopīs,* His Govardhana Hill, His pasturing ground in Vṛndāvana? Or has He forgotten all these now? Is there any possibility of His coming back to His friends and relatives so that we can again see His beautiful face with its raised nose and lotus-like eyes? We remember how He saved us from the forest fire, how He saved us from the great snake Kāliya in the Yamunā, how He saved us from so many other demons, and we simply think how much we are obliged to Him for giving us protection in so many dangerous situations. My dear Uddhava, when we think of Kṛṣṇa's beautiful face and eyes and His different activities here in Vṛndāvana, we become so overwhelmed that all our activities cease. We simply think of Kṛṣṇa, how He used to smile and how He looked upon us. When we go to the banks of the Yamunā and other lakes of Vṛndāvana or near Govardhana Hill or the pasturing field, we see that the impressions of Kṛṣṇa's footprints are still on the surface of the earth. We remember Him playing in those places, because He was constantly visiting them. When His appearance within our minds becomes manifest, we immediately become absorbed in thought of Him.

"We think, therefore, that Kṛṣṇa and Balarāma may be chief demigods in heaven who have appeared before us like ordinary boys in order to execute particular duties on earth. This was also foretold by Gargamuni when making Kṛṣṇa's horoscope. If Kṛṣṇa were not a great personality, how could He have killed Kaṁsa, who possessed the strength of 10,000 elephants? Besides Kaṁsa, there were very strong wrestlers, as well as the giant elephant, Kuvalayāpīḍa. All these animals and demons were killed by Him just as a lion kills an ordinary animal. How wonderful it is that Kṛṣṇa took in one hand the big, heavy bow made of three joined palm trees and broke it very quickly. How wonderful it is that continually for seven days He held up Govardhana Hill in one hand. How wonderful it is that He has killed all the demons, like Pralambāsura, Dhenukāsura, Ariṣṭāsura, Tṛṇāvarta and Bakāsura. They were so strong that even the demigods in the heavenly planets were afraid of them, but Kṛṣṇa killed them as easily as anything."

While describing the uncommon activities of Kṛṣṇa before Uddhava, Nanda Mahārāja gradually became overwhelmed and could not speak anymore. As for mother Yaśodā, she sat by the side of her husband and heard the pastimes of Kṛṣṇa without speaking. She was simply crying incessantly, and milk was pouring from her breasts. When Uddhava saw Mahārāja Nanda and Yaśodā so extraordinarily overwhelmed with thoughts of Kṛṣṇa, the Supreme Personality of Godhead, and when he experienced their extraordinary affection for Him, he also became overwhelmed and began to speak as follows. "My dear mother Yaśodā and Nanda Mahārāja, you are most respectable among human beings because no one but you can meditate in such transcendental ecstasy."

Both Balarāma and Kṛṣṇa are the original Personalities of Godhead from whom the cosmic manifestation is emanating. They are chief among all personalities. Both of Them are the effective cause of this material creation. Material nature is conducted by the *puruṣa* incarnations, who are all acting under Kṛṣṇa and Balarāma. By Their partial representation They enter in the hearts of all living entities. They are the source of all knowledge and all forgetfulness also. This is confirmed in the *Bhagavad-gītā,* Fifteenth Chapter: "I am present in everyone's heart, and I cause one to remember and to forget. I am the original compiler of the *Vedānta,* and I am the actual knower of the *Vedas.*" If, at the time of death, a person can fix his pure mind upon Kṛṣṇa even for a moment, he becomes eligible to give up this material body and appear in his original spiritual body, just as the sun rises with all illumination. Passing from his life in this way, he immediately enters into the spiritual kingdom, Vaikuṇṭha. This is the result of Kṛṣṇa conscious practice.

If we practice Kṛṣṇa consciousness in this present body while we are in a healthy condition and in good mind, simply by chanting the holy *mahā-mantra,* Hare Kṛṣṇa, we will have every possibility of fixing our mind upon Kṛṣṇa at the time of death. If that is done, then our life becomes successful without any doubt. Similarly, if we keep our mind always absorbed in fruitive activities for material enjoyment, then naturally at the time of death we shall think of such activities and again be forced to enter into a material, conditioned body to suffer the threefold miseries of material existence. Therefore, to remain always absorbed in Kṛṣṇa consciousness was the standard of the inhabitants of Vṛndāvana, as exhibited by Mahārāja Nanda, Yaśodā and the *gopīs*. If we can simply follow their footsteps, even to a minute proportion, our lives will surely become successful, and we will enter into the spiritual kingdom, Vaikuṇṭha.

"My dear mother Yaśodā and Nanda Mahārāja," Uddhava continued, "you have thus fixed your minds wholly and solely upon that Supreme Personality of Godhead, Nārāyaṇa, in His transcendental form, the cause of impersonal Brahman. The Brahman effulgence is only the bodily ray of Nārāyaṇa, and because you are always absorbed in ecstatic thought of Kṛṣṇa and Balarāma, what activity remains to be performed by you? I have brought a message from Kṛṣṇa to the effect that He will soon come back to Vṛndāvana and satisfy you both by His personal presence. Kṛṣṇa promised that He would come back to Vṛndāvana after finishing His business in Mathurā. This promise He will surely fulfill. I therefore request you both, who are the best among all fortunates, to be not aggrieved on account of Kṛṣṇa's absence.

"You are already perceiving His presence twenty-four hours a day, and yet He will come and see you very soon. Actually He is present everywhere and in everyone's heart, just as fire is present in wood. Since Kṛṣṇa is the Supersoul, no one is His enemy, no one is His friend, no one is equal to Him, and no one is lower or higher than Him. Actually He has no father, mother, brother or relative, nor does He require society, friendship and love. He does not have a material body; He never appears or takes birth as an ordinary human being. He does not appear in higher or lower species of life like ordinary living entities, who are forced to take birth on account of their previous activities. He appears by His internal potency just to give protection to His devotee. He is never influenced by the modes of material nature, but when He appears within this material world, it seems that He acts like an ordinary living entity under the spell of the modes of material nature. In fact, He is the overseer of this material creation and is not affected by the material modes of nature. He creates, maintains and dissolves the whole cosmic manifestation. We wrongly think of Kṛṣṇa and Balarāma as ordinary human beings. We are like dizzy men who see the whole world wheeling around them. The Personality of Godhead is no one's son; He is actually everyone's father, mother and supreme controller. There is no doubt of this. Whatever is being experienced, whatever is already in existence, whatever is not in existence, whatever will be in existence in the future, whatever is the smallest and whatever is the biggest have no separate existence outside the Supreme Personality of Godhead. Everything is resting in Him, but He is out of touch with everything manifested."

Nanda and Uddhava thus passed the whole night in discussing Kṛṣṇa. In the morning, the *gopīs* prepared for morning *ārātrika* by lighting their lamps and sprinkling butter mixed with yogurt. After finishing their *maṅgala-ārātrika,* they engaged themselves in churning butter from yogurt. While the *gopīs* were thus engaged, the lamps reflected on their ornaments became still more illuminated. The churning rod, their arms, their earrings, their bangles, their breasts—everything moved, and the *kuṅkuma* powder gave their faces a saffron luster comparable to the rising sun. While churning, they also sang the glories of Kṛṣṇa. The two sound vibrations mixed together, ascended to the sky and sanctified the whole atmosphere. After sunrise the *gopīs* came as usual to offer their respects to Nanda Mahārāja and Yaśodā, but when they saw the golden chariot of Uddhava at the door, they began to inquire among themselves. What was that chariot, and to whom did it belong? Some of them inquired whether Akrūra, who had taken away Kṛṣṇa, had again returned. They were not very pleased with Akrūra because, being engaged in the service of Kaṁsa, he took Kṛṣṇa away to the city of Mathurā. All the *gopīs* conjectured that Akrūra might have come again to fulfill another cruel plan. But they thought, "We are now dead bodies without our supreme master, Kṛṣṇa. What further act can he perpetrate on these dead bodies?" While they were talking in this way, Uddhava finished his morning ablutions, prayers and chanting and came before them.

Thus ends the Bhaktivedanta purport of the Forty-fifth Chapter of Kṛṣṇa, *"Uddhava Visits Vṛndāvana."*

46 / Delivery of the Message of Kṛṣṇa to the Gopīs

When the *gopīs* saw Uddhava, they observed that his features almost exactly resembled the features of Kṛṣṇa, and they could understand that he was a great devotee of Kṛṣṇa's. His hands were very long, and his arms were just like the petals of the lotus flower. He was dressed in yellow colored garments and wore a garland of lotus flowers. His face was very beautiful. Having achieved the liberation of *sārūpya* and having the same bodily features as the Lord, Uddhava looked almost like Kṛṣṇa. In Kṛṣṇa's absence, the *gopīs* had been coming dutifully to visit mother Yaśodā's house early in the morning. They knew that Nanda Mahārāja and mother Yaśodā were always griefstricken, and they had made it their first duty to come and pay their respects to the most exalted elderly personalities of Vṛndāvana. Seeing the friends of Kṛṣṇa, Nanda and Yaśodā would remember Kṛṣṇa Himself and be satisfied, and the *gopīs* also would be pleased by seeing Nanda and Yaśodā.

When the *gopīs* saw that Uddhava was representing Kṛṣṇa even in his bodily features, they thought that he must be a soul completely surrendered unto the Supreme Personality of Godhead. They began to contemplate, "Who is this boy who looks just like Kṛṣṇa? He has the same eyes like lotus petals, the same raised nose and beautiful face, and he is smiling in the same way. In all respects he is resembling Kṛṣṇa, Śyāmasundara, the beautiful dark boy. He is even dressed exactly like Kṛṣṇa. Where has this boy come from? Who is the fortunate girl who has him for her husband?" Thus they talked among themselves. They were very anxious to know about him, and because they were simply unsophisticated village girls, they surrounded Uddhava.

When the *gopīs* understood that Uddhava had a message from Kṛṣṇa, they became very happy and called him to a secluded place to sit down. They wanted to talk with him very freely and did not want to be embarrassed before unknown persons. They began to welcome him with polite words, in great submissiveness. "We know that you are a most confidential associate of Kṛṣṇa and that He has therefore sent you to Vṛndāvana to give solace to His father and mother. We can understand that family affection is very strong. Even great sages who have taken to the renounced order of life cannot give up family members. Kṛṣṇa has therefore sent you to His father and mother; otherwise He has no further business in Vṛndāvana. He is now in town. What does He have to know about Vṛndāvana Village or the cows' pasturing grounds? These things are not at all useful for Kṛṣṇa because He is now a man in the city.

"Surely He has nothing to do with persons who do not happen to be His family members. Why should one bother about those who are outside the family, especially and specifically those who are attached as the wives of others. Kṛṣṇa is interested in them as long as there is a need of gratification, like the bumblebees who have interest in the flowers as long as they want to take the honey out of them. It is very natural and psychological that a prostitute does not care for her paramour as soon as he loses his money. Similarly, when the citizens find that a government is incapable of giving them full protection, they leave the country. A student, after finishing his education, gives up his relationship with the teacher and the school. A rich man, after taking his reward from his worshiper, gives him up. When the fruit season is over, the birds are no longer interested in the tree. Just after eating in the house of a lord, the guest gives up his relationship with the host. After a forest fire, when there is a scarcity of green grass, the deer and other animals give up the forest. And so a man, after enjoying his girl friend, gives up his connection with her." In this way, all the *gopīs* began to indirectly accuse Kṛṣṇa by citing so many similes.

Uddhava understood that the *gopīs* of Vṛndāvana were all simply absorbed in the thought of Kṛṣṇa and His childhood activities. While talking about Kṛṣṇa with Uddhava, they forgot all about their household business. They even forgot about themselves as their interest in Kṛṣṇa increased more and more.

One of the *gopīs,* namely Śrīmatī Rādhārāṇī, was so much absorbed in thoughts of Kṛṣṇa by dint of Her personal touch with Him that She actually began to talk with a bumblebee which was flying there and trying to touch Her lotus feet. While another *gopī* was talking with Kṛṣṇa's messenger Uddhava, Śrīmatī Rādhārāṇī took that bumblebee to be a messenger from Kṛṣṇa and began to talk with it as follows. "Bumblebee, you are accustomed to drinking honey from the flowers, and therefore you have preferred to be a messenger of Kṛṣṇa, who is of the same nature as you. I have seen on your moustaches the red powder of *kuṅkuma,* which was smeared on the flower garland of Kṛṣṇa while He was pressing the breast of some other girl who is My competitor. You are feeling very proud by touching that flower, and your moustaches have become reddish. You have come here carrying a message for Me. You are anxious to touch My feet. But my dear bumblebee, let me warn you—don't touch Me! I don't want any messages from your unreliable master. You are the unreliable servant of an unreliable master." It may be that Śrīmatī Rādhārāṇī purposely addressed that bumblebee sarcastically in order to criticize the messenger Uddhava. Indirectly, Śrīmatī Rādhārāṇī saw Uddhava as not only resembling Kṛṣṇa's bodily features but as being equal to Kṛṣṇa. In this way She indicated that Uddhava was as unreliable as Kṛṣṇa Himself. Śrīmatī Rādhārāṇī wanted to give specific reasons why She was dissatisfied with Kṛṣṇa and His messengers.

She addressed the bumblebee, "Your master Kṛṣṇa is exactly of your quality. You sit down on a flower, and after taking a little honey you immediately fly away and sit in another flower and taste. You're just like your master Kṛṣṇa. He gave us the chance of tasting the touch of His lips and then left altogether. I know also that the goddess of fortune, Lakṣmī, who is always in the midst of the lotus flower, is constantly engaged in Kṛṣṇa's service. But I do not know why she has become so captivated by Kṛṣṇa. She is attached to Him, although she knows His actual character. As far as we are concerned, we are more intelligent than that goddess of fortune. We are not going to be cheated anymore by Kṛṣṇa or His messengers."

According to expert opinion, Lakṣmī, the goddess of fortune is a subordinate expansion of Śrīmatī Rādhārāṇī. As Kṛṣṇa has numerous expansions of Viṣṇu-*mūrtis,* so His pleasure potency, Rādhārāṇī, also has innumerable expansions of goddesses of fortune. Therefore the goddess of fortune, Lakṣmījī, is always anxious to be elevated to the position of the *gopīs*.

Śrīmatī Rādhārāṇī continued: "You foolish bumblebee, you are trying to satisfy Me and get a reward by singing the glories of Kṛṣṇa, but it is a useless attempt. We are bereft of all our possessions. We are away from our homes and families. We know very well about Kṛṣṇa. We know even more than you. So whatever you make up about Him will be old stories to us. Kṛṣṇa is now in the city and is better known as the friend of Arjuna. He now has many new girl friends, and they are no doubt very happy in association with Him. Because the lusty burning sensation of their breasts has been satisfied by Kṛṣṇa, they are now happy. If you go there and glorify Kṛṣṇa, they may be pleased to reward you. You are just trying to pacify Me by your behavior as a flatterer, and therefore you have put your head under My feet. But I know the trick which you are trying to play. I know that you are a messenger coming from a great trickster, Kṛṣṇa. Therefore please leave me.

"I can understand that you are very expert in reuniting two opposing parties, but at the same time you must know that I cannot place My reliance upon you, nor upon your master Kṛṣṇa. We left our families, husbands, children and relatives only for Kṛṣṇa, and yet He did not feel any obligation in exchange. He has left us for lost. Do you think we can place our faith in Him again? We know that Kṛṣṇa cannot be long without the association of young women. That is His nature. He is finding difficulty in Mathurā because He is no longer in the village among innocent cowherd girls. He is in the aristocratic society and must be feeling difficulty in making friendships with the young girls. Perhaps you have come here to canvass again or to take us there. But why should Kṛṣṇa expect us to return there? He is greatly qualified to entice all other girls, not only in Vṛndāvana or Mathurā, but all over the universe. His wonderfully enchanting smile is so attractive and the movement of His eyebrows so beautiful that He can call for any woman from the heavenly, middle or plutonic planets. Mahā-Lakṣmī, the greatest of all goddesses of fortune, also hankers to render Him some service. In comparison to all these women of the universe, what are we? We are very insignificant.

"Kṛṣṇa advertises Himself as very magnanimous, and He is praised by great saints. His qualifications could be perfectly utilized if He would only show us mercy because we are downtrodden and neglected by Him. You poor messenger, you are only a less intelligent servant. You do not know much about Kṛṣṇa, how ungrateful and hardhearted He has been, not only in this life, but in His previous lives also. We have all heard this from our grandmother, Paurṇamāsī. She has informed us that Kṛṣṇa was born in a *kṣatriya* family previous to this birth and was known as Rāmacandra. In that birth, instead of killing Vāli, an enemy of His friend, in the manner of a *kṣatriya,* He killed him just like a hunter. A hunter takes a secure hiding place and then kills an animal without facing it. So Lord Rāmacandra, as a *kṣatriya,* should have fought with Vāli face to face, but instigated by His friend, He killed him from behind a tree. Thus He deviated from the religious principles of a *kṣatriya.* Also, He was so attracted by the beauty of Sītā that He converted Śūrpaṇakhā, the sister of Rāvaṇa, into an ugly woman by cutting off her nose and ears. Śūrpaṇakhā proposed an intimate relationship with Him, and as a *kṣatriya,*

He should have satisfied her. But He was so selfish that He could not forget Sītādevī and converted Śūrpaṇakhā into an ugly woman. Before that birth as a *kṣatriya*, He took His birth as a *brāhmaṇa* boy known as Vāmanadeva and asked charity from Bali Mahārāja. Bali Mahārāja was so magnanimous that he gave Him whatever he had, yet Kṛṣṇa as Vāmanadeva ungratefully arrested him just like a crow and pushed him down to the Pātāla kingdom. We know all about Kṛṣṇa and how ungrateful He is. But here is the difficulty: in spite of His being so cruel and hardhearted, it is very difficult for us to give up talking about Him. Not only are we unable to give up this talk, but great sages and saintly persons are also engaged in talking about Him. We *gopīs* of Vṛndāvana do not want to make anymore friendships with this blackish boy, but we do not know how we shall be able to give up remembering and talking about His activities."

Since Kṛṣṇa is absolute, His so-called unkind activities are as relishable as His kind activities. Saintly persons and great devotees like the *gopīs* cannot give up Kṛṣṇa in any circumstances. Lord Caitanya therefore prayed, "Kṛṣṇa, You are free and independent in all respects. You can either embrace me or crush me under Your feet–whatever You like. You may make me brokenhearted by not letting me see You throughout my whole life, but You are my only object of love."

"In my opinion," Śrīmatī Rādhārāṇī continued, "one should not hear about Kṛṣṇa, because as soon as a drop of the nectar of His transcendental activities is poured into the ear, one immediately rises above the platform of duality, attraction and rejection. Being completely freed from the attraction of material attachment, one gives up the attachment for this material world, family, home, wife, children and everything which is materially dear to every person. Being dispossessed of all material acquisition, one makes his relatives and himself unhappy. Then he wanders in search of Kṛṣṇa, either as a human being or in other species of life, even as a bird. It is very difficult to actually understand Kṛṣṇa, His name, His quality, His form, His pastimes, His paraphernalia and His entourage."

Śrīmatī Rādhārāṇī continued to speak to the black messenger of Kṛṣṇa. "Please do not talk anymore about Kṛṣṇa. It is better to talk about something else. We are already doomed, like the black-spotted she-deer in the forest who are enchanted by the sweet musical vibration of the hunter. In the same way, we have been enchanted by the sweet words of Kṛṣṇa, and again and again we are thinking of the rays of the nails of His toes. We are becoming more and more lustful for His association; therefore, I request you not to talk of Kṛṣṇa anymore."

This talk of Rādhārāṇī with the bumblebee messenger and Her accusing

Kṛṣṇa, and, at the same time, Her inability to give up talking about Him, are symptoms of the topmost transcendental ecstasy, called *mahābhāva.* The ecstatic *mahābhāva* manifestation is possible only in the persons of Rādhārāṇī and Her associates. Great *ācāryas* like Śrīla Rūpa Gosvāmī and Viśvanātha Cakravartī Ṭhākur have analyzed these *mahābhāva* speeches of Śrīmatī Rādhārāṇī, and they have described the different sentiments such as *udghūrṇā,* bewilderment, and *jalpapratijalpa,* talking in different ways. In Rādhārāṇī is found the science of *ujjala,* or the brightest jewel or love of God. While Rādhārāṇī was talking with the bee and the bee was flying hither and thither, it all of a sudden disappeared from Her sight. She was in full mourning due to separation from Kṛṣṇa and was feeling ecstasy by talking with the bee. But as soon as the bee disappeared, She became almost mad, thinking that the messenger-bee might have returned to Kṛṣṇa to inform Him all about Her talking against Him. "Kṛṣṇa must have been very sorry to hear it," She thought. In this way She was very much overwhelmed with another type of ecstasy.

In the meantime, the bee, flying hither and thither, appeared before Her again. She thought, "Kṛṣṇa is still kind to Me. In spite of the messenger carrying disruptive messages, He is so kind that He has again sent the bee to take Me to Him." Śrīmatī Rādhārāṇī was very careful this time not to say anything against Kṛṣṇa. "My dear friend, I welcome you," she said. "Kṛṣṇa is so kind that He has again sent you. Kṛṣṇa is so kind and affectionate to Me that He has sent you back, fortunately, in spite of your carrying My message against Him. My dear friend, you can ask from Me whatever you want. I shall give you anything because you are so kind upon Me. You have come to take Me to Kṛṣṇa because He is not able to come here. He is surrounded by new girl friends in Mathurā. But you are a tiny creature. How can you take Me there? How will you be able to help Me in meeting Kṛṣṇa while He is taking rest there along with the goddess of fortune and embracing her to His chest? Never mind. Let us forget all these things about My going there or sending you. Please let Me know how Kṛṣṇa is faring in Mathurā. Tell Me if He still remembers His foster father, Nanda Mahārāja, His affectionate mother, Yaśodā, His cowherd friends and His poor friends like us, the *gopīs.* I am sure that He must sometimes sing about us. We served Him just like maidservants, without any payment. Is there any possibility that Kṛṣṇa will again come back and place His arms around us? His limbs are always fragrant with the *aguru* scent. Please put all these inquiries to Kṛṣṇa."

Uddhava was standing near, and he heard Rādhārāṇī talking in this way, as if She had become almost mad after Kṛṣṇa. He was exceedingly surprised at how the *gopīs* were accustomed to think of Kṛṣṇa constantly in that topmost ecstasy of *mahābhāva* love. He had brought a message in writing from Kṛṣṇa, and now he wanted to present it before the *gopīs,* just to pacify them. He said, "My dear *gopīs,* your mission of human life is now successful. You are all wonderful devotees of the Supreme Personality of Godhead; therefore you are eligible to be worshiped by all kinds of people. You are worshipable throughout the three worlds because your minds are wonderfully absorbed in the thought of Vāsudeva, Kṛṣṇa. He is the goal of all kinds of pious activities and ritualistic performances, such as giving in charity, rigidly following the austerity of vows, undergoing severe penances and igniting the fire of sacrifice. He is the purpose behind the chanting of different *mantras,* the reading of the *Vedas,* controlling the senses and concentrating the mind in meditation. These are some of the many different processes for self-realization and attainment of perfection of life. But actually they are only meant for realizing Kṛṣṇa and dovetailing oneself in the transcendental loving service of the Supreme Personality of Godhead. This is the last instruction of *Bhagavad-gītā* also; although there are descriptions of different kinds of processes of self-realization, at the end Kṛṣṇa recommended one should give up everything and simply surrender unto Him. All other processes are meant for teaching one how to surrender ultimately unto the lotus feet of Kṛṣṇa. The *Bhagavad-gītā* also says that this surrendering process is completed by a sincere person executing the processes of self-realization in wisdom and austerity after many births."

Since the perfection of such austerity was completely manifested in the life of the *gopīs,* Uddhava was fully satisfied upon seeing their transcendental position. He continued to say: "My dear *gopīs,* the mentality which you have developed in relationship with Kṛṣṇa is very, very difficult to attain, even for great sages and saintly persons. You have attained the highest perfectional stage of life. It is a great boon for you that you have fixed your mind upon Kṛṣṇa and have decided to have Kṛṣṇa only, giving up your family, home, relatives, husbands and children for the sake of the Supreme Personality. Because your mind is now fully absorbed in Kṛṣṇa, the Supreme Soul, universal love has automatically developed in you. I think myself very fortunate that I have been favored, by your grace, to see you in this situation."

When Uddhava said that he had a message from Kṛṣṇa, the *gopīs* were more interested in hearing the message than in hearing about their exalted position. They did not very much like being praised for their high position. They showed their anxiety to hear the message which Uddhava had brought from Kṛṣṇa. Uddhava said, "My dear *gopīs,* I am especially deputed to carry this message to you, who are such great and gentle devotees. Kṛṣṇa has specifically sent me to you because I am His most confidential servitor."

The written message which Uddhava brought from Kṛṣṇa was not delivered to the *gopīs* by Uddhava, but he personally read it before them. The message was very gravely written, so that not only the *gopīs,* but all empiric philosophers might understand how pure love of God is intrinsically integrated with all the different energies of the Supreme Lord. From Vedic information it is understood that the Supreme Lord has multi-energies, *parāsya śaktir vividhaiva śrūyate.* Also, the *gopīs* were such intimate personal friends of Kṛṣṇa that while He was writing the message for them, He was much moved and could not write distinctly. Uddhava, as the student of Bṛhaspati, had very sharp intelligence, so instead of handing over the written message, he thought it wise to read it personally and explain it to them.

Uddhava continued: "These are the words from the Personality of Godhead. 'My dear *gopīs,* My dear friends, please know that separation between ourselves is impossible at any time, at any place or under any circumstances, because I am all-pervading.'"

This all-pervasiveness of Kṛṣṇa is explained in the *Bhagavad-gītā,* both in the Ninth and Seventh Chapters. Kṛṣṇa is all-pervasive in His impersonal feature; everything is resting in Him, but He is not personally present everywhere. In the Seventh Chapter also, it is stated that the five gross elements, earth, water, fire, air and sky, and the three subtle elements, mind, intelligence, and ego, are all His inferior energies. But there is another, superior energy, which is called the living entity. The living entities are also directly part and parcel of Kṛṣṇa. Therefore Kṛṣṇa is the source of both the material and spiritual energies. He is always intermingled with everything as cause and effect. Not only the *gopīs,* but all living entities are always inseparably connected with Kṛṣṇa in all circumstances. The *gopīs,* however, are perfectly and thoroughly in cooperation in their relationship with Kṛṣṇa, whereas the living entities under the spell of *māyā* are forgetful of Kṛṣṇa. They think themselves as separate identities having no connection with Kṛṣṇa.

Love of Kṛṣṇa, or Kṛṣṇa consciousness, is therefore the perfectional stage of real knowledge in understanding things as they are. Our minds can never be vacant. The mind is constantly occupied with some kind of thought, and the subject matter of such thought cannot be outside the eight elements of Kṛṣṇa's energy. One who knows this philosophical aspect of all thoughts is actually a wise man, and he surrenders unto Kṛṣṇa. The *gopīs* are the typical example of this perfectional stage of knowledge. They are not simple mental speculators. Their minds are always in Kṛṣṇa. The mind is nothing but the energy of Kṛṣṇa. Actually, any person who can think, feel, act and will cannot be separated from Kṛṣṇa. But the stage in which he can understand his eternal realtionship is called Kṛṣṇa consciousness. The diseased condition in which he cannot understand his eternal relationship with Kṛṣṇa is the contaminated stage, or *māyā.* Since the *gopīs* are on the platform of pure transcendental knowledge, their minds are always filled with Kṛṣṇa consciousness. For example, as there is no separation between fire and air, so there is no separation between Kṛṣṇa and the living entities. When the living entities forget Kṛṣṇa, they are not in their normal condition. As for the *gopīs,* because they are always thinking of Kṛṣṇa they are on the absolute stage of perfection in knowledge. The so-called empiric philosophers sometimes think that the path of *bhakti* is meant for the less intelligent, but unless the so-called man of knowledge comes to the platform of *bhakti,* his knowledge is certainly impure and imperfect. Actually, the stage of perfecting one's eternal relationship with Kṛṣṇa is love in separation. But that is also illusory because there is no separation. The *gopīs* were never separated from Kṛṣṇa. Even from the philosophical point of view, there was no separation.

The cosmic manifestation is also not separate from Kṛṣṇa. "Nothing is separate from Me; the whole cosmic manifestation is resting on Me and is not separate from Me. Before the creation, I was existing." This is confirmed in the Vedic literature: before creation, there was only Nārāyaṇa. There were no Brahmā and no Śiva as assistants. The whole cosmic manifestation is manipulated by the three modes of material nature. Brahmā is the incarnation of the quality of passion. It is said that Brahmā created this universe, but Brahmā is the secondary creator; the original creator is Narāyaṇa. This is also confirmed by Śaṅkarācārya: *nārāyaṇaḥ paro'vyaktāt.* Nārāyaṇa is transcendental, beyond this cosmic creation.

Kṛṣṇa creates, maintains, and annihilates the whole cosmic manifestation by expanding Himself in different incarnations. Everything is Kṛṣṇa, and everything is depending on Kṛṣṇa, but He is not perceived in the material energy. Material energy is called *māyā,* or illusion. In the spiritual energy, however, Kṛṣṇa is perceived at every step, in all circumstances. This perfectional stage of understanding is present in the *gopīs.* As Kṛṣṇa is always aloof from the cosmic manifestation, although it is completely dependent on Him, so a living entity is also completely aloof from his material conditional life. The material body has developed on the basis of spiritual existence. In the *Bhagavad-gītā* the whole cosmic manifestation is accepted as the mother of the living entities, and Kṛṣṇa is the father. As the father impregnates the mother by injecting the living entity within the womb, so all the living entities are injected by Kṛṣṇa in the womb of the material nature. They come out in different bodies according to their different fruitive activities. In all circumstances, the living entity is aloof from this material conditional life.

If we simply study our own bodies, we can understand how a living entity is always aloof from this bodily encagement. Every action of the body is taking place by the interaction of the three modes of material nature. We can see at every moment many changes taking place in bodies, but the spirit soul is aloof from all changes. One can neither create nor annihilate nor interfere with the actions of material nature. The living entity is therefore entrapped by the material body and is conditioned in three stages, namely while awake, asleep and unconscious. The mind is acting through all the three conditions of life; the living entity in his sleeping or dreaming condition sees something as real, and in his awake condition he sees the same thing as unreal. It is concluded, therefore, that under certain circumstances he accepts something as real, and under other circumstances he accepts the very same thing as unreal. These matters are the subject matter of study for the empiric philosopher or the *sāṅkhya-yogī.* In order to come to the right conclusion, *sāṅkhya-yogīs* undergo severe austerities and penances. They practice control of the senses and renunciation.

All these different ways of determining the ultimate goal of life are compared to rivers. Kṛṣṇa is the ocean. As the rivers flow down toward the ocean, all attempts for knowledge flow toward Kṛṣṇa. After many, many births of endeavor, when one actually comes to Kṛṣṇa, he attains the perfectional stage. Kṛṣṇa says in the *Bhagavad-gītā:* All are pursuing the path of realizing Me, but those who have adopted courses without any *bhakti* find their endeavor very troublesome." *Kleśo'dhikataras teṣām:* Kṛṣṇa cannot be understood unless one comes to the point of *bhakti.*

Three paths are enunciated in the *Gītā: karma-yoga, jñāna-yoga* and *bhakti-yoga.* Those who are too addicted to fruitive activities are advised to perform actions which will bring them to *bhakti.* Those who are addicted to the frustration of empiric philosophy are also advised to realize *bhakti. Karma-yoga* is different from ordinary *karma,* and *jñāna-yoga* is different from *jñāna.* Ultimately, as stated by the Lord in the *Bhagavad-gītā, bhaktyā māṁ abhijānāti:* only through execution of devotional service can one understand Kṛṣṇa. The perfectional stage of devotional service was achieved by the *gopīs* because they did not care to know anything but Kṛṣṇa. It is confirmed in the *Vedas, yasmin eva vijñāte sarvam eva vijñātam bhavanti.* This means that simply by knowing Kṛṣṇa all other knowledge is automatically acquired.

Kṛṣṇa continued: "Transcendental knowledge of the Absolute is no longer necessary for you. You were accustomed to love Me from the very beginning of your lives." Knowledge of the Absolute Truth is specifically required for persons who want liberation from material existence. But one who has attained love for Kṛṣṇa is already on the platform of liberation. As stated in the *Bhagavad-gītā,* anyone engaged in unalloyed devotional service is to be considered situated on the transcendental platform of liberation. The *gopīs* were not actually feeling any pangs of material existence, but they were feeling the separation of Kṛṣṇa. Kṛṣṇa therefore said, "My dear *gopīs,* in order to increase your superexcellent love for Me, I have purposely separated Myself from you. I have done this so that you may be in constant meditation on Me."

The *gopīs* are in the perfectional stage of meditation. The *yogīs* are generally more fond of meditation than the execution of devotional service to the Lord, but they do not know that the perfectional stage of devotion is the attainment of the perfection of the *yoga* system. This constant meditation on Kṛṣṇa by the *gopīs* is confirmed in the *Bhagavad-gītā* to be the topmost *yoga.* Kṛṣṇa knew very well the psychology of women. When a woman's beloved is away, she thinks of him meditatively, and he is present before her. Kṛṣṇa wanted to teach through the behavior of the *gopīs.* One who is constantly in trance like the *gopīs* surely attains the lotus feet of Kṛṣṇa.

Lord Caitanya taught people in general the method of *vipralambha,* which is the method of rendering service unto the Supreme Personality of Godhead in the feeling of separation. The six Gosvāmīs also taught worship of Kṛṣṇa in the feeling of the *gopīs* in separation. The prayers of Śrīnivāsa Ācārya about the Gosvāmīs explain these matters very clearly. Śrīnivāsa Ācārya said that the Gosvāmīs were always absorbed in the ocean of transcendental feelings in the mood of the *gopīs.* When they lived in Vṛndāvana they were searching for Kṛṣṇa, crying, "Where is Kṛṣṇa? Where are the *gopīs?* Where are You, Śrīmatī Rādhārāṇī?" They never said, "We have now seen Rādhā and Kṛṣṇa, and therefore our mission is fulfilled." Their mission remained always unfulfilled; they never met Rādhā and Kṛṣṇa. At the time of the *rāsa* dance, those *gopīs* who could not join the *rāsa-līlā* with Kṛṣṇa gave up their bodies simply by thinking of Him. Absorption in Kṛṣṇa consciousness by feeling separation is thus the quickest method for attainment of the lotus feet of Kṛṣṇa. By the personal statement of Kṛṣṇa, the *gopīs* were convinced about the strength of feelings of separation. They were actually experiencing the supernatural method of Kṛṣṇa worship and were much relieved and happy to understand it.

They began to speak as follows: "We have heard that King Kaṁsa, who was always a source of trouble for the Yadu dynasty, has now been killed. This is good news for us. We hope, therefore, that the members of the Yadu dynasty are very happy in the association of Kṛṣṇa, who can fulfill all the desires of His devotees. My dear Uddhava, kindly let us know whether Kṛṣṇa sometimes thinks of us while in the midst of highly enlightened society girls in Mathurā. We know that the women and girls in Mathurā are not village women. They are enlightened and beautiful. Their bashful smiling glances and other feminine features must be very pleasing to Kṛṣṇa. We know very well that Kṛṣṇa is always fond of the behavior of beautiful women. It seems, therefore, that He has been entrapped by the women of Mathurā. My dear Uddhava, will you kindly let us know if Kṛṣṇa sometimes remembers us while He is in the midst of other women?"

Another *gopī* inquired: "Does He remember that night in the midst of *kumadini* flowers and moonlight, when Vṛndāvana became exceedingly beautiful? Kṛṣṇa was dancing with us, and the atmosphere was surcharged with the sound of foot bells. We exchanged pleasing conversation then. Does He remember that particular night? We remember that night, and we feel separation. Separation from Kṛṣṇa makes us agitated, as if there were fire in our bodies. He proposed to come back to Vṛndāvana to extinguish the fire, just as a cloud appears in the sky to extinguish the forest fire by its downpour."

Another *gopī* said, "Kṛṣṇa has killed His enemy, and He has victoriously achieved the kingdom of Kaṁsa. Maybe He is married with a king's daughter by this time and living very happily among His kinsmen and friends. Therefore, why should He come to this village of Vṛndāvana?"

Another *gopī* said, "Kṛṣṇa is the Supreme Personality of Godhead, the husband of the goddess of fortune, and He is self-sufficient. He has no business either with us, the girls in the Vṛndāvana forest, or with the city girls in Mathurā. He is the great Supersoul; He has nothing to do with any of us, either here or there."

Another *gopī* said, "It is an unreasonable hope for us to expect Kṛṣṇa to come back to Vṛndāvana. We should try instead to be happy in disappointment. Even Piṅgalā, the great prostitute, said that disappointment is the greatest pleasure. We all know these things, but it is very difficult for us to give up the expectation of Kṛṣṇa's coming back again. Who can forget a solitary conversation with Kṛṣṇa, on whose breast the goddess of fortune always remains, in spite of Kṛṣṇa's not desiring her? My dear Uddhava, Vṛndāvana is the land of rivers, forests and cows. Here the vibration of the flute is heard, and Kṛṣṇa, along with His elder brother, Śrī Balarāma, enjoyed the atmosphere in our company. Thus the environment of Vṛndāvana is constantly reminding us of Kṛṣṇa and Balarāma. The impression of His footprints is on the land of Vṛndāvana, which is the residential place of the goddess of fortune, but such signs cannot help us to get Kṛṣṇa."

The *gopīs* further expressed that Vṛndāvana was still full of all opulence and good fortune; there was no scarcity or want in Vṛndāvana as far as material necessities were concerned, but in spite of such opulence they could not forget Kṛṣṇa and Balarāma.

"We are constantly remembering various attractive features of beautiful Kṛṣṇa, His walking, His smiling and His joking words. We have all become lost by the dealings of Kṛṣṇa, and it is impossible for us to forget Him. We are always praying for Him, exclaiming, 'Dear Lord, dear husband of the goddess of fortune, dear Lord of Vṛndāvana and deliverer of the distressed devotees! We are now fallen and merged into an ocean of distress. Please, therefore, come back again to Vṛndāvana and deliver us from this pitiable condition.'"

Uddhava minutely studied the transcendental abnormal condition of the *gopīs* in their separation from Kṛṣṇa, and he thought it wise to repeat all the pastimes of Śrī Kṛṣṇa over and over again. Materialistic persons are always in a burning condition on account of the blazing fire of material miseries. The *gopīs* also were burning in a transcendental blazing fire due to separation from Kṛṣṇa. The blazing fire which was exasperating the *gopīs,* however, is different from the fire of the material world. The *gopīs* constantly want the association of Kṛṣṇa, whereas the materialistic person wants the advantage of material comforts.

It is stated by Viśvanātha Cakravartī Ṭhākur that Kṛṣṇa saved the cowherd boys from the blazing forest fire within a second, while their eyes were closed. Similarly, Uddhava advised the *gopīs* that they could be saved from the fire of separation by closing their eyes and meditating on the activities of Kṛṣṇa from the very beginning of their association with Him. From the outside, the *gopīs* could visualize all the pastimes of Kṛṣṇa by hearing the descriptions of Uddhava, and from inside they could remember those pastimes. From the instruction of Uddhava, the *gopīs* could understand that Kṛṣṇa was not separate from them. As they were constantly thinking of Kṛṣṇa, Kṛṣṇa was also thinking of them constantly while at Mathurā.

Uddhava's messages and instructions saved the *gopīs* from immediate death, and the *gopīs* acknowledged the benediction from Uddhava. Uddhava practically acted as the preceptor spiritual master of the *gopīs*, and they in return worshiped him as they would worship Kṛṣṇa. It is recommended in authoritative scriptures that the spiritual master should be worshiped on the level of the Supreme Personality of Godhead, because of his being His very confidential servitor, and it is accepted by great authorities that the spiritual master is the external manifestation of Kṛṣṇa. The *gopīs* were relieved from their transcendental burning condition by realizing that Kṛṣṇa was with them. Internally, they remembered His association within their hearts, and externally Uddhava helped them to appreciate Kṛṣṇa by conclusive instructions.

The Supreme Personality of Godhead is described in the scriptures as *adhokṣaja*, which indicates that He is beyond the perception of all material senses. Although He is beyond the perception of material senses, He is present in everyone's heart. At the same time, He is present everywhere by His all-pervasive feature of Brahman. All three transcendental features of the Absolute Truth (*Bhagavān* the Personality of Godhead, *Paramātmā* the localized Supersoul, and the all-pervasive *Brahman*) can be realized simply by studying the condition of the *gopīs* in their meeting with Uddhava, as described by the *Śrīmad-Bhāgavatam*.

It is said by Śrīnivāsa Ācārya that the six Gosvāmīs were always merged in thoughts of the activities of the *gopīs*. Caitanya Mahāprabhu has also recommended the *gopīs'* method of worship of the Supreme Personality of Godhead as superexcellent. Śrīla Śukadeva Gosvāmī has also recommended that anyone who hears from the right source about the dealings of the *gopīs* with Kṛṣṇa and who follows the instructions will be elevated to the topmost position of devotional service and will be able to give up the lust of material enjoyment.

All the *gopīs* were solaced by the instruction of Uddhava, and they requested him to stay in Vṛndāvana for a few days more. Uddhava agreed to their proposal and stayed with them not only for a few days, but for a few months. He always kept them engaged in thinking of the transcendental message of Kṛṣṇa and His pastimes, and the *gopīs* were feeling as if they were experiencing direct association with Kṛṣṇa. While Uddhava remained in Vṛndāvana, the inhabitants enjoyed his association. As they discussed the activities of Kṛṣṇa, the days passed just like moments. Vṛndāvana's natural atmosphere, with the presence of the River Yamunā, its nice orchards of trees decorated with various fruits, Govardhana Hill, caves, blooming flowers—all combined to inspire Uddhava to narrate Kṛṣṇa's pastimes. The inhabitants enjoyed Uddhava's association in the same way as they enjoyed the association of Kṛṣṇa.

Uddhava was attracted by the attitude of the *gopīs* because they were completely attached to Kṛṣṇa, and Uddhava was inspired by the *gopīs'* anxiety for Kṛṣṇa. He began to offer them his respectful obeisances and composed songs in praise of their transcendental qualities as follows: "Among all the living entities who have accepted the human form of life, the *gopīs* are superexcellently successful in their mission. Their thought is thoroughly absorbed in the lotus feet of Kṛṣṇa. Great sages and saintly persons are also trying to be absorbed in meditation upon the lotus feet of Kṛṣṇa, who is Mukunda Himself, the giver of liberation, but the *gopīs,* having lovingly accepted the Lord, are automatically accustomed to this habit. They do not depend on any yogic practice. The conclusion is that one who has attained the *gopīs'* condition of life does not have to take birth as Lord Brahmā or be born in a *brāhmaṇa* family or be initiated as a *brāhmaṇa.*"

Śrī Uddhava confirmed the statement of *Bhagavad-gītā* spoken by Lord Kṛṣṇa; one who takes shelter of Him for the right purpose, be he a *śūdra* or lower, will attain the highest goal of life. The *gopīs* have set the standard of devotion for the whole world. By following in the footsteps of the *gopīs* by constantly thinking of Kṛṣṇa, one can attain the highest perfectional stage of spiritual life. The *gopīs* were not born of any highly cultured family; they were born of cowherd men, and yet they developed the highest love of Kṛṣṇa. For self-realization or God realization there is no need to take birth in a high family. The only thing needed is ecstatic development of love of God. In achieving perfection in Kṛṣṇa consciousness, no other qualification is required than to be constantly engaged in the loving service of Kṛṣṇa. Kṛṣṇa is the supreme nectar, the reservoir of all pleasure. The effect of taking up Kṛṣṇa consciousness is just like that of drinking nectar; with or without one's knowledge, it will act. The active principle of Kṛṣṇa consciousness will manifest itself everywhere; it does not matter how and where one has taken his birth. Kṛṣṇa will bestow His benediction upon anyone who takes to Kṛṣṇa consciousness, without any doubt. The supreme benediction attained by the *gopīs* in spite of their being born in the family of cowherd men was never attained even by the goddess of fortune herself, and certainly not by the denizens of heaven, though their bodily forms are like lotuses. The *gopīs* are so fortunate that during *rāsa-līlā* Kṛṣṇa personally embraced them with His arms. Kṛṣṇa kissed them face to face. Certainly it is not possible for any women in the three worlds to achieve this except the *gopīs.*

Uddhava appreciated the exalted position of the *gopīs* and wished to fall down and take the dust of their feet on his head. Yet he did not dare to ask the *gopīs* to offer the dust from their feet; perhaps they would not be agreeable. He therefore desired to have his head smeared with the dust of the *gopīs'* feet without their knowledge. He desired to become only an insignificant clump of grass or herbs in the land of Vṛndāvana.

The *gopīs* were so much attracted to Kṛṣṇa that when they heard the vibration of His flute, they instantly left their families, children, honor and feminine bashfulness and ran towards the place where Kṛṣṇa was standing. They did not consider whether they were passing over the road or through the jungles. Imperceptibly, the dust of their feet was bestowed on small grasses and herbs of Vṛndāvana. Not daring to place the dust of the *gopīs'* feet on his own head, Uddhava aspired to have a future birth in the position of a clump of grass and herbs. He would then be able to have the dust of the *gopīs'* feet.

Uddhava appreciated the extraordinary fortune of the *gopīs,* who relieved themselves of all kinds of material contamination by placing on their high, beautiful breasts the lotus feet of Kṛṣṇa, which are not only worshiped by the goddess of fortune, but by such exalted demigods as Brahmā and Lord Śiva, and which are meditated upon by great *yogīs* within their hearts. Thus Uddhava desired to be able to constantly pray to be honored by the dust of the *gopīs'* lotus feet. The *gopīs'* chanting of the transcendental pastimes of Lord Kṛṣṇa has become celebrated all over the three worlds.

After living in Vṛndāvana for some days, Uddhava desired to go back to Kṛṣṇa, and he begged permission to leave from Nanda Mahārāja and Yaśodā. He had a farewell meeting with the *gopīs,* and taking permission of them also, he mounted his chariot to start for Mathurā.

When Uddhava was about to leave, all the inhabitants of Vṛndāvana, headed by Mahārāja Nanda and Yaśodā, came to bid him good-bye and presented him with various kinds of valuable goods secured in Vṛndāvana. They expressed their feelings with tears in their eyes due to intense attachment for Kṛṣṇa. All of them desired benediction from Uddhava. They desired always to remember the glorious activities of Kṛṣṇa and wanted their minds to be always fixed upon His lotus feet, their words always engaged in glorifying Kṛṣṇa, and their bodies always engaged in bowing down and constantly remembering Him. This prayer of the inhabitants of Vṛndāvana is the superexcellent type of self-realization. The method is very simple: to fix the mind always on the lotus feet of Kṛṣṇa, to talk always of Kṛṣṇa without passing on to any other subject matter, and to engage the body in Kṛṣṇa's service constantly. Specifically in this human form of life, one should engage his life, his resources, words and intelligence for the service of the Lord. Such kinds of activities only can elevate a human being to the highest level of perfection. This is the verdict of all authorities.

The inhabitants of Vṛndāvana said: "By the will of the supreme authority and according to the results of our own work, we may take our birth anywhere. It doesn't matter where we are born, but our only prayer is that we may simply be engaged in Kṛṣṇa consciousness." A pure devotee of Lord Kṛṣṇa never desires to be promoted to the heavenly planets, or even to Vaikuṇṭha or Goloka Vṛndāvana, because he has no desire for his own personal satisfaction. A pure devotee regards both heaven and hell to be on an equal level. Without Kṛṣṇa, heaven is hell; and with Kṛṣṇa, hell is heaven. When Uddhava had sufficiently honored the worship of the pure devotees of Vṛndāvana, he returned to Mathurā and to his master, Kṛṣṇa. After offering respects by bowing down before Lord Kṛṣṇa and Balarāma, he began to describe the wonderful devotional life of the inhabitants of Vṛndāvana. He presented all of the gifts given by the inhabitants of Vṛndāvana to Vasudeva, the father of Kṛṣṇa, and Ugrasena, the grandfather of Kṛṣṇa.

Thus ends the Bhaktivedanta purport of the Forty-sixth Chapter of Kṛṣṇa, *"Delivery of the Message of Kṛṣṇa to the Gopīs."*

47 / Kṛṣṇa Pleases His Devotees

For days together, Kṛṣṇa heard from Uddhava all the details of his visit to Vṛndāvana, of the condition of His father and mother, and of the *gopīs* and the cowherd boys. Lord Kṛṣṇa was fully satisfied that Uddhava was able to solace them by his instruction and by the message delivered to them.

Lord Kṛṣṇa then decided to go to the house of Kubjā, the hunchback woman who had pleased Him by offering Him sandalwood when He was entering the city of Mathurā. As stated in the *Bhagavad-gītā,* Kṛṣṇa always tries to please His devotees, and the devotees try to please Kṛṣṇa. As the devotees always think of Kṛṣṇa within their hearts, so Kṛṣṇa also thinks of His devotees within Himself. When Kubjā was converted into a beautiful society girl, she wanted Kṛṣṇa to come to her place so that she could try to receive and worship Him in her own way. Society girls generally try to satisfy their clients by offering their bodies to the men to enjoy. But this society girl, Kubjā, was actually captivated by a lust to satisfy her senses with Kṛṣṇa. When Kṛṣṇa desired to go to the house of Kubjā, He certainly had no desire for sense gratification. By supplying the sandalwood pulp to Kṛṣṇa, Kubjā had already satisfied His senses. On the plea of her sense gratification, He decided to go to her house, not actually for sense gratification, but to turn her into a pure devotee. Kṛṣṇa is always served by many thousands of goddesses of fortune; therefore He has no need to satisfy His senses by going to a society girl. But as He is kind to everyone, He decided to go there. It is said that the moon does not withhold its shining from the courtyard of a crooked person. Similarly, Kṛṣṇa's transcendental mercy is never denied to anyone, whether one has rendered service unto Him through lust, anger, fear or pure love. In the *Caitanya-caritāmṛta* it is stated that if one wants to serve Kṛṣṇa and at the same time wants to satisfy his own lusty desires, Kṛṣṇa will handle it so that the devotee forgets his lusty desire and becomes fully purified and constantly engaged in the service of the Lord.

In order to fulfill His past promise, Kṛṣṇa, along with Uddhava, went to the house of Kubjā. When Kṛṣṇa reached her house, He saw that it was completely decorated in a way to excite the lusty desires of a man. This suggests that there were many nude pictures, on top of which were canopies and flags embroidered with pearl necklaces, along with comfortable beds and cushioned chairs. The rooms were provided with flower garlands and were nicely scented with incense and sprinkled with scented water. And the rooms were illuminated by nice lamps.

When Kubjā saw that Lord Kṛṣṇa had come to her house in order to fulfill His promised visit, she immediately got up from the chair to receive Him. Accompanied by her many girl friends, she began to talk with Him with great respect and honor. After offering Him a nice place to sit, she worshiped Lord Kṛṣṇa in a manner just suitable to her position. Uddhava was similarly received by Kubjā and her girl friends, but he was not on an equal level with Kṛṣṇa, and he simply sat down on the floor.

Without wasting time, as one does in such situations, Kṛṣṇa entered the bedroom of Kubjā. In the meantime, Kubjā took her bath and smeared her body with sandalwood pulp. She dressed herself with nice garments, valuable jewelry, ornaments and flower garlands. Chewing betel nut and other intoxicating eatables and spraying herself with scents, she appeared before Kṛṣṇa. Her smiling glance and moving eyes were full of feminine bashfulness as she stood gracefully before Lord Kṛṣṇa, who is known as Mādhava, the husband of the goddess of fortune. When Kṛṣṇa saw that Kubjā was hesitating to come before Him, He immediately caught hold of her hand, which was decorated with bangles. With great affection, He dragged her beside Him and made her sit by His side. Simply by having previously supplied pulp of sandalwood to the Supreme Lord, Kṛṣṇa, Kubjā became free from all sinful reactions and eligible to enjoy with Him. She then took Kṛṣṇa's lotus feet and placed them on her breasts, which were burning with the blazing fire of lust. By smelling the fragrance of Kṛṣṇa's lotus feet, she immediately became relieved of all lusty desires. She was thus allowed to embrace Kṛṣṇa with her two arms and thus mitigate her long-cherised desire to have Kṛṣṇa as a visitor in her house.

It is stated in the *Bhagavad-gītā* that without being freed of all material sinful reactions, one cannot be engaged in the transcendental loving service of the Lord. Simply by supplying sandalwood pulp to Kṛṣṇa, Kubjā was thus rewarded. She was not trained to worship Kṛṣṇa in any other way; therefore she wanted to satisfy Him by her profession. It is confirmed in the *Bhagavad-gītā* that the Lord can be worshiped even by one's profession, if it is sincerely offered for the pleasure of the Lord. Kubjā then told

Kṛṣṇa, "My dear friend, kindly remain with me at least for a few days. Enjoy with me, You and Your lotus-eyed friend. I cannot leave You immediately. Please grant my request."

As stated in the Vedic versions, the Supreme Personality of Godhead has multi-potencies. According to expert opinion, Kubjā represents the *puruṣa-śakti* potency of Kṛṣṇa, just as Śrīmatī Rādhārāṇī represents His *cit-śakti* potency. Although she requested Kṛṣṇa to remain with her for some days, Kṛṣṇa politely impressed upon her that it was not possible for Him to stay. Kṛṣṇa visits this material world occasionally, whereas His connection with the spiritual world is eternal. Kṛṣṇa is always present either in the Vaikuṇṭha planets or in the Goloka Vṛndāvana planet. The technical term for His presence in the spiritual world is *prakaṭa-līlā.*

After satisfying Kubjā with sweet words, Kṛṣṇa returned to His place along with Uddhava. There is a warning in the *Śrīmad-Bhāgavatam* that Kṛṣṇa is not very easily worshiped because He is the Supreme Personality of Godhead, the chief among the *Viṣṇu-tattvas.* To worship Kṛṣṇa or have association with Him is not a very easy job. Specifically, there is a warning for devotees who are attracted to Kṛṣṇa through conjugal love; it is not good for them to desire to have sense gratification by direct association with Kṛṣṇa. Actually, the activities of sense gratification are material. In the spiritual world there are symptoms like kissing and embracing, but there is no sense-gratificatory process as it exists in the material world. This warning is specifically for those known as *sahajiyā,* who take it for granted that Kṛṣṇa is an ordinary human being. They desire to enjoy sex life with Him in a perverted way. In a spiritual relationship, sense gratification is most insignificant. Anyone who desires a relationship of perverted sense gratification with Kṛṣṇa must be considered to be less intelligent. His mentality requires to be reformed.

After a while, Kṛṣṇa fulfilled His promise to visit Akrūra at his house. Akrūra was in relationship with Kṛṣṇa as His servitor, and Kṛṣṇa wanted to get some service from him. He went there accompanied by both Lord Balarāma and Uddhava. When Kṛṣṇa, Balarāma and Uddhava were approaching the house of Akrūra, Akrūra came forward, embraced Uddhava and offered respectful obeisances, bowing down before Lord Kṛṣṇa and Balarāma. Kṛṣṇa, Balarāma and Uddhava offered him obeisances in turn and were offered appropriate sitting places by Akrūra. When all were comfortably seated, Akrūra washed their feet and sprinkled the water on his head. Then he offered nice flowers and sandalwood pulp in regular worship. All three of them became very satisfied by the behavior of Akrūra. Akrūra then bowed down before Kṛṣṇa, putting his head on the ground.

Then, keeping Kṛṣṇa's lotus feet on his lap, Akrūra began to gently massage them. When Akrūra was fully satisfied in the presence of Kṛṣṇa and Balarāma, his eyes became filled with tears of love for Kṛṣṇa, and he began to offer his prayers as follows.

"My dear Lord Kṛṣṇa, it is very kind of You to have killed Kaṁsa and his associates. You have delivered the whole family of the Yadu dynasty from the greatest calamity. Your saving of the great Yadu dynasty will always be remembered by them. My dear Lord Kṛṣṇa and Balarāma, You are the original personality from whom everything has emanated. You are the original cause of all causes. You have inconceivable energy, and You are all-pervasive. But for Yourself, there is no other cause and effect, gross or subtle. You are the Supreme Brahman realized by the study of the *Vedas.* By Your inconceivable energy, You are actually visible before us. You create this cosmic manifestation by Your own potencies, and You enter into it Yourself. As the five material elements, earth, water, fire, air, and sky, are distributed in everything manifested by different kinds of bodies, so You alone enter into different varieties of bodies, created by Your own energy. You enter the body as the individual soul as well as independently as the Supersoul. The material body is created by Your inferior energy. The living entities, individual souls, are part and parcel of You, and the Supersoul is Your localized representation. This material body, the living entity and the Supersoul constitute an individual living being, but originally they are all different energies of the one Supreme Lord.

"In the material world, You are creating, maintaining and dissolving the whole manifestation by interaction of three qualities, namely goodness, passion and ignorance. You are not implicated by the activities of those material qualities because Your supreme knowledge is never overcome, as is the case with the individual living entity."

As the Supreme Lord enters into this material creation and thus the creation, maintenance and destruction are going on in their due course, so the part and parcel living entity enters the material elements and has his material body created for him. The difference between the living entity and the Lord is that the living entity is part and parcel of the Supreme Lord and has the tendency to be overcome by the interaction of material qualities. Kṛṣṇa, the *Parambrahman* or the Supreme Brahman, being always situated in full knowledge, is never overcome by such activities. Therefore Kṛṣṇa's name is *Acyuta,* meaning He who never falls down. Kṛṣṇa's knowledge of spiritual identity is never overcome by material action, whereas the identity of the minute part and parcel living entities is prone to be overcome by material action. The individual living entities are eternally part and parcel of God. As minute sparks of the original fire, Kṛṣṇa, they have the tendency to become extinguished.

Akrūra continued: "The less intelligent class of men misunderstand Your transcendental form to be also made of material energy. That concept is not at all applicable to You. Actually, You are all spiritual, and there is no difference between You and Your body. Because of this, there is no question of Your being conditioned or liberated. You are ever-liberated in any condition of life. As stated in the *Bhagavad-gītā,* 'Only the fools and rascals consider You to be an ordinary man.' To consider Your Lordship to be one of us, conditioned by the material nature, is a mistake due to our imperfect knowledge. When people deviate from the original knowledge of the *Vedas,* they try to identify the ordinary living entities with Your Lordship. Your Lordship has appeared on this earth in Your original form in order to reestablish the real knowledge that the living entities are neither one with nor equal to the Supreme God. My dear Lord, You are always situated in uncontaminated goodness *(śuddha-sattva).* Your appearance is necessary to reestablish actual Vedic knowledge, as opposed to the atheistic philosophy which tries to establish that God and living entities are one and the same. My dear Lord Kṛṣṇa, this time You have appeared in the home of Vasudeva as His son, along with Your plenary expansion, Śrī Balarāma. Your mission is to kill all the atheistic royal families, along with their huge military strength. You have advented Yourself to minimize the overburden of the world, and in order to fulfill this mission, You have glorified the dynasty of Yadu, appearing in the family as one of its members.

"My dear Lord, today my home has become purified by Your presence. I have become the most fortunate person in the world. The Supreme Personality of Godhead, who is worshipable by all different kinds of demigods, Pitṛs, living entities, kings and emperors, and who is the Supersoul of everything, has come into my home. The water of His lotus feet is purifying the three worlds, and now He has kindly come to my place. Who is there in the three worlds among factually learned men who will not take shelter of Your lotus feet and surrender unto You? Who, knowing well that no one can be as affectionate as You are to Your devotees, is so foolish that he will decline to become Your devotee? Throughout the Vedic literature it is declared that You are the dearmost friend of every living entity. This is confirmed in the *Bhagavad-gītā: suhṛdaṁ sarva-bhūtānām.* You are the Supreme Personality of Godhead, completely capable of fulfilling the desires of Your devotees. You are the real friend of everyone. In spite of giving Yourself to Your devotees, You are never depleted of Your original potency. Your potency neither decreases nor increases in volume.

"My dear Lord, it is very difficult for even the great mystic *yogīs* and demigods to ascertain Your movement. You cannot be approached by them, and yet out of Your causeless mercy You have kindly consented to come to my home. This is the most auspicious moment in the journey of my material existence. By Your grace only, I can just understand that my home, my wife, my children and my worldly possessions are all different bonds to material existence. Please cut the knot and save me from this entanglement of false society, friendship and love."

Lord Śrī Kṛṣṇa was very pleased by Akrūra's offering of prayers. His smile was captivating Akrūra more and more. The Lord replied him as follows: "My dear Akrūra, in spite of your submissiveness, I consider you to be My superior, on the level with My father and teacher and most well-wishing friend. You are, therefore, worshipable by Me, and since You are My uncle, I am always to be protected by you. I desire to be maintained by you because I am one of your own children. Apart from this filial relationship, you are always to be worshiped. Anyone who desires good fortune must offer his respectful obeisances unto personalities like you. You are more than the demigods. People go to worship the demigods when they are in need of some sense gratification; the demigods offer benediction to their devotees after being worshiped by them. But a devotee like Akrūra is always ready to offer the greatest benediction to the people. A saintly person or devotee is free to offer benediction to everyone, whereas the demigods can offer benediction only after being worshiped. One can take advantage of the place of pilgrimage only after going there. By worshiping the particular demigod, it takes a long time for fulfillment of the desire; but saintly persons like you, My dear Akrūra, can immediately fulfill all the desires of the devotees. My dear Akrūra, you are always our friend and well-wisher. You are always ready to act for our welfare. Kindly, therefore, go to Hastināpura and see what arrangement has been made for the Pāṇḍavas."

Kṛṣṇa was very anxious to know about the sons of Pāṇḍu, because at a very young age, they had lost their father. Being very friendly to His devotees, Kṛṣṇa was anxious to know about them, and therefore He deputed Akrūra to go to Hastināpura and get information of the real situation. Kṛṣṇa continued to say, "I have heard that after the death of King Pāṇḍu, his young sons, Yudhiṣṭhira, Bhīma, Arjuna, Nakula and Sahadeva, along with their widowed mother, have come under the charge of Dhṛtarāṣṭra, who is to look after them as their guardian. But I have also heard that Dhṛtarāṣṭra is not only blind from birth, but also blind in his affection for his cruel son, Duryodhana. The five Pāṇḍavas are the sons of King Pāṇḍu, but Dhṛtarāṣṭra, due to his plans and designs, is not favorably disposed towards the Pāṇḍavas. Kindly go there and study how Dhṛtarāṣṭra is dealing with the Pāṇḍavas. On receipt of your report, I shall consider how to favor the Pāṇḍavas." In this way the Supreme Personality of Godhead, Kṛṣṇa, ordered Akrūra to go to Hastināpura, and then He returned home, accompanied by Balarāma and Uddhava.

Thus ends the Bhaktivedanta purport of the Forty-seventh Chapter of Kṛṣṇa, "*Kṛṣṇa Pleases His Devotees.*"

48 / Ill-motivated Dhṛtarāṣṭra

Thus being ordered by the Supreme Personality of Godhead, Śrī Kṛṣṇa, Akrūra visited Hastināpura. Hastināpura is said to be the site of what is now New Delhi. The part of New Delhi, which is still known as Indraprastha, is accepted by people in general as the old capital of the Pāṇḍavas. The very name Hastināpura suggests that there were many *hastīs,* or elephants. Because the Pāṇḍavas kept many elephants in the capital, it was called Hastināpura. Keeping elephants is a very expensive job; to keep many elephants, therefore, the kingdom must be very rich, and Hastināpura was full of elephants, horses, chariots and other opulences. When Akrūra reached Hastināpura, he saw that the capital was full of all kinds of opulences. The kings of Hastināpura were taken to be the ruling kings of the whole world. Their fame was widely spread throughout the entire kingdom, and their administration was conducted under the good counsel of learned *brāhmaṇas.*

After seeing the very opulent capital city, Akrūra met King Dhṛtarāṣṭra. He also saw grandfather Bhīṣma sitting with him. After meeting them, he went to see Vidura and then Vidura's sister, Kuntī. One after another, he saw the son of Somadatta, and the King of Bāhlīka, Droṇācārya, Kṛpācārya, Karṇa and Suyodhana. (Suyodhana is another name of Duryodhana.) He saw the five Pāṇḍava brothers and other friends and relatives living in the city. Akrūra was known as the son of Gāndī, so whomever he met was very pleased to receive him. He was offered a good seat at his receptions, and he inquired all about his relatives' welfare and other activities.

Since he was deputed by Lord Kṛṣṇa to visit Hastināpura, it is understood that he was very intelligent in studying a diplomatic situation. Dhṛtarāṣṭra was unlawfully occupying the throne after the death of the King Pāṇḍu, despite the presence of Pāṇḍu's sons. Akrūra wanted to study the whole situation by remaining there. He could understand very well that ill-motivated Dhṛtarāṣṭra was much inclined in favor of his own sons. In fact, Dhṛtarāṣṭra had already usurped the kingdom and was now instigating and planning to dispose of the five Pāṇḍava brothers. Akrūra knew also that all the sons of Dhṛtarāṣṭra, headed by Duryodhana, were very crooked politicians. Dhṛtarāṣṭra did not act in accordance with the good instruction given by Bhīṣma and Vidura, but he was being conducted by the ill instruction of such persons as Karṇa, Śakuni and others. Akrūra decided to stay in Hastināpura for a few months to study the whole political situation.

Gradually Akrūra learned from Kuntī and Vidura that Dhṛtarāṣṭra was very intolerant and envious of the five Pāṇḍava brothers because of their extraordinary learning in military science and their greatly developed bodily strength. They acted as true chivalrous heroes, exhibited all the good qualities of *kṣatriyas,* and were very responsible princes, always thinking of the welfare of the citizens. Akrūra also learned that the envious Dhṛtarāṣṭra, in consultation with his ill-advised son, had tried to kill the Pāṇḍavas by poisoning them.

Akrūra happened to be one of the cousins of Kuntī; therefore, after meeting him, she began to inquire about her paternal relatives. Thinking of her birthplace, she began to cry. She asked Akrūra whether her father, mother, brothers, sisters and other friends at home were still remembering her. She especially inquired about Kṛṣṇa and Balarāma, her glorious nephews. She asked: "Does Kṛṣṇa, who is the Supreme Personality of Godhead, who is very affectionate to His devotees, remember my sons? Does Balarāma remember us?" Inside herself, Kuntī felt like a she-deer in the midst of tigers, and actually her position was like that. After the death of her husband, King Pāṇḍu, she was supposed to take care of the five Pāṇḍava children, but Dhṛtarāṣṭra was always planning to kill them. She was certainly living as a poor innocent animal in the midst of several tigers. Being a devotee of Lord Kṛṣṇa, she was always thinking of Him and expecting that one day Kṛṣṇa would come and save them from their dangerous position. She inquired from Akrūra whether Kṛṣṇa proposed to come to advise the fatherless Pāṇḍavas how to get free of the intriguing policy of Dhṛtarāṣṭra and his sons. By talking with Akrūra about all these affairs, she felt herself helpless and began to exclaim: "My dear Kṛṣṇa, my dear Kṛṣṇa, You are the supreme mystic, the Supersoul of the universe. You are the real well-wisher of the whole universe. My dear Govinda, at this time You are far away from me, yet I pray to surrender unto Your lotus feet. At the present moment I am very much griefstricken with my five fatherless sons. I can fully understand that but for Your lotus feet there is no shelter or protection. Your lotus feet can deliver all aggrieved souls because You are the Supreme Personality of Godhead. One can be safe from the clutches of repeated birth and death by Your mercy only. My dear Kṛṣṇa, You are the supreme pure one, the Supersoul and the master of all *yogīs.* What can I say? I can simply offer my respectful obeisances unto You. Accept me as Your fully surrendered devotee."

Although Kṛṣṇa was not present before her, Kuntī offered her prayers to Him as if she were in His presence face to face. This is possible for anyone following in the footsteps of Kuntī. Kṛṣṇa does not have to be physically present everywhere. He is actually present everywhere by spiritual potency, and one simply has to surrender unto Him sincerely. When Kuntī was offering her prayers very feelingly to Kṛṣṇa, she could not check herself and began to cry loudly before Akrūra. Vidura was also present, and both Akrūra and Vidura became very sympathetic to the mother of the Pāṇḍavas. They began to solace her by glorifying her sons, Yudhiṣṭhira, Arjuna and Bhīma. They pacified her, saying that her sons were extraordinarily powerful; she should not be perturbed about them, since they were born of great demigods, Yamarāja, Indra and Vāyu.

Akrūra decided to return and report on the extreme circumstances in which he found Kuntī and her five sons. He first wanted to give good advice to Dhṛtarāṣṭra, who was so favorably inclined toward his own son and unfavorably inclined toward the Pāṇḍavas. When Kuntī and Dhṛtarāṣṭra were sitting among friends and relatives, Akrūra began to address him, calling him "Vārcitravīrya." *Vārcitravīrya* means the son of Vicitravīrya. Vicitravīrya was the name of the father of Dhṛtarāṣṭra, but Dhṛtarāṣṭra was not actually the begotten son of Vicitravīrya. He was the begotten son of Vyāsadeva. Formerly it was the system that if a man were unable to beget a child, his brother could beget a child in the womb of his wife. That system is now forbidden in this age of Kali. Akrūra called Dhṛtarāṣṭra "Vārcitravīrya" sarcastically because he was not actually begotten by his father. He was the son of Vyāsadeva. When a child was begotten in the wife by the husband's brother, the child was claimed by the husband, but of course the child was not begotten by the husband. This sarcastic remark pointed out that Dhṛtarāṣṭra was falsely claiming the throne on heriditary grounds. Actually the son of Pāṇḍu was the rightful king, and in the presence of Pāṇḍu's sons, the Pāṇḍavas, Dhṛtarāṣṭra should not have occupied the throne.

Akrūra then said, "My dear son of Vicitravīrya, you have unlawfully usurped the throne of the Pāṇḍavas. Anyway, somehow or other you are now on the throne. Therefore I beg to advise you to please rule the kingdom on moral and ethical principles. If you do so and try to teach your subjects in that way, then your name and fame will be perpetual." Akrūra hinted that although Dhṛtarāṣṭra was ill-treating his nephews, the Pāṇḍavas, they happened to be his subjects. "Even if you treat them not as the owners of the throne, but as your subjects, you should impartially think of their welfare as though they were your own sons. But if you do not follow this principle and act in just the opposite way, then you will be unpopular among your subjects, and in the next life you will have to live in a hellish condition. I therefore hope you will treat your sons and the sons of Pāṇḍu equally. Akrūra hinted that if Dhṛtarāṣṭra did not treat the Pāṇḍavas and his sons as equals, then surely there would be a fight between the two camps of cousins. Since the Pāṇḍavas cause was just, they would come out victorious, and the sons of Dhṛtarāṣṭra would be killed. This was a prophecy told by Akrūra to Dhṛtarāṣṭra.

Akrūra further advised Dhṛtarāṣṭra, "In this material world, no one can remain as an eternal companion to another. By chance only we assemble together in the family, in the society, in the community or in the nation, but at the end, because every one of us has to give up the body, we must be separated. One should not, therefore, be unnecessarily affectionate toward family members." Dhṛtarāṣṭra's affection was also unlawful and did not show much intelligence. In plain words, Akrūra hinted to Dhṛtarāṣṭra that his staunch family affection was due to his gross ignorance of fact. Although we appear to be combined together in family, society or nation, each one of us has an individual destiny. Everyone takes birth according to individual past work; therefore everyone has to individually enjoy or suffer the result of his own *karma*. There is no possibility of improving one's destiny by cooperate living. Sometimes it happens that one's father accumulates wealth by illegal ways, and the son takes away the money, although it is hard-earned by the father. It is just like a small fish in the ocean who eats the material body of the large, old fish. One ultimately cannot accumulate wealth illegaly for the gratification of his family, society, community or nation. That many great empires which developed in the past are no longer existing because their wealth was squandered away by later descendants is an illustration of this principle. One who does not know this subtle law of fruitive activities and thus gives up the principles of moral and ethical principles only carries with him the reactions of his sinful activities. His ill-gotten wealth and possessions are taken by someone else, and he goes to the darkest region of hellish life. One should not, therefore, accumulate more wealth than is alloted to him by destiny; otherwise he will be factually blind to his own interest. Instead of fulfilling his self-interest, he will act in just the opposite way for his own downfall.

Akrūra continued: "My dear Dhṛtarāṣṭra, I beg to advise you not to be blind about the fact of this material existence. Material conditional life, either in distress or in happiness, is to be accepted as a dream. One should try to bring his mind and senses under control and live very peacefully for spiritual advancement in Kṛṣṇa consciousness." In the *Caitanya-caritāmṛta* it is said that except for persons who are in Kṛṣṇa consciousness, everyone is always in a disturbed condition of mind and is full of anxiety. Even those who are trying for liberation, or merging into the Brahman effulgence, or the *yogīs* who are trying to achieve perfection in mystic power, cannot have peace of mind. Pure devotees of Kṛṣṇa have no demands to make of Kṛṣṇa. They are simply satisfied with service to Him. Actual peace and mental tranquility can be attained only in perfect Kṛṣṇa consciousness.

After hearing moral instructions from Akrūra, Dhṛtarāṣṭra replied: "My dear Akrūra, you are very charitable in giving me good instructions, but unfortunately I cannot accept it. A person who is destined to die does not utilize the effect of nectar, although it may be administered to him. I can understand that your instructions are very valuable. Unfortunately, they do not stay in my flickering mind, just as the glittering lightning in the sky does not stay in a fixed cloud. I can understand only that no one can stop the onward progress of the supreme will. I understand that the Supreme Personality of Godhead, Kṛṣṇa, has appeared in the family of the Yadus in order to decrease the overburdened load of this earth."

Dhṛtarāṣṭra gave hints to Akrūra that he had complete faith in Kṛṣṇa, the Supreme Personality of Godhead. At the same time, he was very much partial to his family members. In the very near future, Kṛṣṇa would vanquish all the members of his family, and in a helpless condition, Dhṛtarāṣṭra would take shelter of Kṛṣṇa's feet. In order to show His special favor to a devotee, Kṛṣṇa usually takes away all the objects of his material affection. He thus forces the devotee to be materially helpless, with no alternative than to accept the lotus feet of Kṛṣṇa. This actually happened to Dhṛtarāṣṭra after the end of the Battle of Kurukṣetra.

Dhṛtarāṣṭra could realize two opposing factors acting before him. He could understand that Kṛṣṇa was there to remove all the unnecessary burdens of the world. His sons were an unnecessary burden, and so he expected that they would be killed. At the same time, he could not rid himself of his unlawful affection for his sons. Understanding these two contradictory factors, he began to offer his respectful obeisances to the Supreme Personality of Godhead. "The contradictory ways of material existence are very difficult to understand; they can only be taken as the inconceivable execution of the plan of the Supreme, who by His inconceivable energy creates this material world and enters into it and sets into action the three modes of nature. When everything is created, He enters into each and every living entity and into the smallest atom. No one can understand the incalculable plans of the Supreme Lord."

After hearing this statement, Akrūra could clearly understand that Dhṛtarāṣṭra was not going to change his policy of discriminating against the Pāṇḍavas in favor of his sons. He at once took leave of his friends in Hastināpura and returned to his home in the kingdom of the Yadus. After returning home, he vividly informed Lord Kṛṣṇa and Balarāma of the actual situation in Hastināpura and the intentions of Dhṛtarāṣṭra. Akrūra was sent to Hastināpura by Kṛṣṇa to study. By the grace of the Lord, he was successful and informed Kṛṣṇa about the actual situation.

Thus ends the Bhaktivedanta purport of the Forty-eighth Chapter of Kṛṣṇa, *"Ill-Motivated Dhṛtarāṣṭra."*

49 / Kṛṣṇa Erects the Dvārakā Fort

After his death, Kaṁsa's two wives became widows. According to Vedic civilization, a woman is never independent. She has three stages of life: In childhood a woman should live under the protection of her father, a youthful woman should live under the protection of her young husband, and in the event of the death of her husband she should live either under the protection of her grown-up children, or if she has no grown-up children, she must go back to her father and live as a widow under his protection. It appears that Kaṁsa had no grown-up sons. After becoming widows, his wives returned to the shelter of their father. Kaṁsa had two queens. One was Asti, and the other Prāpti, and both happened to be the daughters of King Jarāsandha, the lord of the Behar Province (known in those days as Magadharāja). After reaching home, both queens explained their awkward position following Kaṁsa's death. The King of Magadha, Jarāsandha, was mortified on hearing their pitiable condition due to the slaughter. When informed of the death of Kaṁsa, Jarāsandha decided on the spot that he would rid the world of all the members of the Yadu dynasty. He decided that since Kṛṣṇa had killed Kaṁsa, the whole dynasty of the Yadus should be killed.

He began to make extensive arrangements to attack the kingdom of Mathurā with his innumerable military phalanxes, consisting of many thousands of chariots, horses, elephants and infantry soldiers. Jarāsandha prepared thirteen such military phalanxes in order to retaliate the death of Kaṁsa. Taking with him all his military strength, he attacked the capital of the Yadu kings, Mathurā, surrounding it from all directions. Śrī Kṛṣṇa, who appeared as an ordinary human being, saw the immense strength of Jarāsandha, which appeared as an ocean about to cover a beach at any moment. He also perceived that the inhabitants of Mathurā were overwhelmed with fear. He began to think within Himself about the situation of His mission as an incarnation and how to tackle the present situation before Him. His mission was to diminish the overburdened population of the whole world; therefore He took the opportunity of facing so many men, chariots, elephants, and horses. The military strength of Jarāsandha had appeared before Him, and He decided to kill the entire force of Jarāsandha so that they would not be able to go back and again reorganize their military strength.

While Lord Kṛṣṇa was thinking in that way, two military chariots, fully equipped with drivers, weapons, flags and other implements, arrived for Him from outer space. Kṛṣṇa saw the two chariots present before Him, and immediately addressed His attendant brother, Balarāma, who is also known as Saṅkarṣaṇa: "My dear elder brother, You are the best among the Āryans, You are the Lord of the universe, and specifically, You are the protector of the Yadu dynasty. The members of the Yadu dynasty sense great danger before the soldiers of Jarāsandha, and they are very much aggrieved. Just to give them protection, Your chariot is also here, filled with military weapons. I request You to sit down on Your chariot and kill all these soldiers, the entire military strength of the enemy. Naturally, both of Us have descended on this earth just to annihilate such unnecessary bellicose forces and to give protection to the pious devotees. So we have the opportunity to fulfill Our mission. Please let Us execute it." Thus Kṛṣṇa and Balarāma, the descendants of the Gadaha King, Daśārha, decided to annihilate the thirteen military companies of Jarāsandha.

Kṛṣṇa went upon the chariot on which Dāruka was the driver and with a small army, and to the blowing of conchshells, He came out of the city of Mathurā. Curiously enough, although the other party was equipped with greater military strength, just after hearing the vibration of Kṛṣṇa's conchshell, their hearts were shakened. When Jarāsandha saw both Balarāma and Kṛṣṇa, he was a little bit compassionate, because both Kṛṣṇa and Balarāma happened to be related to him as grandsons. He specifically addressed Kṛṣṇa as Puruṣādhama, meaning the lowest among men. Actually Kṛṣṇa is known in all Vedic literatures as Puruṣottama, the highest among men. Jarāsandha had no intention of addressing Kṛṣṇa as Puruṣottama, but great scholars have determined the true meaning of the word *puruṣādhama* to be "one who makes all other personalities go downward." Actually no one can be equal to or greater than the Supreme Personality of Godhead.

Jarāsandha said, "It will be a great dishonor for me to fight with boys like Kṛṣṇa and Balarāma." Because Kṛṣṇa had killed Kaṁsa, Jarāsandha specifically addressed Him as the killer of His own relatives. Kaṁsa had killed so many of his own nephews, yet Jarāsandha did not take notice of it; but because Kṛṣṇa had killed His maternal uncle, Kaṁsa, Jarāsandha tried to criticize Him. That is the way of demoniac dealing. Demons do not try to find their own faults, but try to find the faults of their friends. Jarāsandha also criticized Kṛṣṇa for not even being a *kṣatriya.* Because He was raised by Mahārāja Nanda, Kṛṣṇa was not a *kṣatriya,* but a *vaiśya. Vaiśyas* are generally called *guptas,* and the word *gupta* can also be used to mean "hidden." So Kṛṣṇa was both hidden and raised by Nanda Mahārāja. Jarāsandha accused Kṛṣṇa of three faults: that He killed His own maternal uncle, that He was hidden in His childhood, and that He was not even a *kṣatriya.* And therefore Jarāsandha felt ashamed to fight with Him.

Next he turned toward Balarāma and addressed Him: "You, Balarāma! If You like You can fight along with Him, and if You have patience, then You can wait to be killed by my arrows. Thus You can be promoted to heaven." It is stated in the *Bhagavad-gītā* that a *kṣatriya* can become benefited in two ways while fighting. If a *kṣatriya* gains victory in the fight, he enjoys the results of victory, but even if he is killed in the fight, he is promoted to the heavenly kingdom.

After hearing Jarāsandha speak in that way, Kṛṣṇa answered: "My dear King Jarāsandha, those who are heroes do not talk much. Rather, they show their prowess. Because you are talking much, it appears that you are assured of your death in this battle. We do not care to hear you anymore, because it is useless to hear the words of a person who is going to die or one who is very distressed." In order to fight with Kṛṣṇa, Jarāsandha surrounded Him from all sides with great military strength, and the sun appeared covered by the cloudy air and dust. Similarly, Kṛṣṇa, the supreme sun, was covered by the military strength of Jarāsandha. Kṛṣṇa's and Balarāma's chariots were marked with pictures of Garuḍa and palm trees. The women of Mathurā were all standing on the tops of the houses and palaces and gates to see the wonderful fight, but when Kṛṣṇa's chariot was surrounded by Jarāsandha's military force, they became so frightened that some of them fainted. Kṛṣṇa saw Himself overwhelmed by the military strength of Jarāsandha. His small number of soldiers were being harassed by them, so He immediately took up His bow, named Śārṅga.

He began to take His arrows from their case, and one after another He set them on the bowstring and shot them toward the enemy. They were so accurate that the elephants, horses and infantry soldiers of Jarāsandha were quickly killed. The incessant arrows thrown by Kṛṣṇa appeared as a whirlwind of blazing fire killing all the military strength of Jarāsandha. As Kṛṣṇa released His arrows, gradually all the elephants began to fall down, their heads severed by the arrows. Similarly, all the horses fell, and the chariots also, along with their flags. The chariot fighters and the chariot drivers fell as well. Almost all the infantry soldiers fell on the field of battle, their heads, hands and legs cut off. In this way, many thousands of elephants and horses were killed, and their blood began to flow just like the waves of a river. In that river, the severed arms of the men appeared to be snakes, their heads appeared to be tortoises, and the dead bodies of the elephants appeared to be small islands. The dead horses appeared to be sharks. By the arrangement of the supreme will, there was a great river of blood filled with paraphernalia. The hands and legs of the infantry soldiers were floating like seaweed, and the floating bows of the soldiers appeared to be waves of the river. And all the jewelry from the bodies of the soldiers and commanders appeared to be so many pebbles flowing down the river of blood.

Lord Balarāma, who is also known as Saṅkarṣaṇa, began to fight with His club in such a heroic way that the river of blood created by Kṛṣṇa overflooded. Those who were cowards became very much afraid upon seeing the ghastly and horrible scene, and those who were heroes began to talk delightedly among themselves about the heroism of the two brothers. Although Jarāsandha was equipped with a vast ocean of military strength, the fighting of Lord Kṛṣṇa and Balarāma converted the whole situation into a ghastly scene which was far beyond ordinary fighting. Persons of ordinary mind cannot estimate how it could be possible, but when such activities are accepted as pastimes of the Supreme Personality of Godhead, under whose will everything is possible, then this can be understood. The Supreme Personality of Godhead is creating, maintaining and dissolving the cosmic manifestation by His will only. For Him to create such a vast scene of devastation while fighting with an enemy is not so wonderful. And yet, because Kṛṣṇa and Balarāma were fighting with Jarāsandha just like ordinary human beings, the affair appeared to be wonderful.

All the soldiers of Jarāsandha were killed, and he was the only one left alive. Certainly he became very depressed at this point. Śrī Balarāma immediately arrested him, just as, with great strength, one lion captures another lion. But while Lord Balarāma was binding Jarāsandha with the rope of Varuṇa and ordinary ropes also, Lord Kṛṣṇa, with a greater plan in mind for the future, asked Him not to arrest him. Jarāsandha was then released by Kṛṣṇa. As a great fighting hero, Jarāsandha became very much ashamed, and he decided that he would no longer live as a king, but would resign from his position in the royal order and go to the forest to practice meditation under severe austerities and penances.

As he was returning home with other royal friends, however, they advised him not to retire, but to regain strength to fight again with Kṛṣṇa in the near future. The princely friends of Jarāsandha began to instruct him that ordinarily it would not have been possible for him to have been defeated by the strength of the Yadu kings, but the defeat which he had experienced was simply due to his ill luck. The princely order encouraged King Jarāsandha. His fighting, they said, was certainly heroic; therefore, he should not take his defeat very seriously, as it was due only to his past mistakes. After all, there was no fault in his fighting.

In this way, Jarāsandha, the King of Magadha Province, having lost all his strength and having been insulted by his arrest and subsequent release, could do nothing but return to his kingdom. Thus Lord Kṛṣṇa conquered the soldiers of Jarāsandha. Although Kṛṣṇa's army was tiny in comparison to Jarāsandha's, not a pinch of His strength was lost, whereas all of Jarāsandha's men were killed.

At that time the denizens of heaven became very pleased and began to offer their respects by chanting in glorification of the Lord and by showering Him with flowers. They accepted the victory with great appreciation. Jarāsandha returned to his kingdom, and Mathurā City was made safe from the danger of an imminent attack. The citizens of Mathurā organized the combined services of a circus of professional singers, like *sūtas, māgadhas*, and poets who could compose nice songs, and they began to chant the victory glorification of Lord Kṛṣṇa. When Lord Kṛṣṇa entered the city after the victory, many bugles, conches and kettledrums were sounded, and the vibrations of various musical instruments, like *bherya, tūrya, vīṇā*, flute and *mṛdaṅga*—all joined together to make a beautiful reception. While Kṛṣṇa was entering, the whole city was very much cleansed, all the different streets and roads were sprinkled with water, and the inhabitants, being joyous, decorated their respective houses, roads and shops with flags and festoons. The *brāhmaṇas* chanted Vedic *mantras* at numerous places. The people constructed road crossings, entrances, lanes and streets. When Lord Kṛṣṇa was entering the nicely decorated city of Mathurā in a festive attitude, the ladies and girls of Mathurā prepared different kinds of flower garlands to make the ceremony more auspicious. In accordance with the Vedic custom, they took yogurt mixed with freshly grown green grass and began to strew it here and there to make the victory jubilation even more auspicious. As Kṛṣṇa passed through the street, all the ladies and women began to regard Him with great affection. Kṛṣṇa and Balarāma carried various kinds of booty, ornaments and jewels carefully collected from the battlefield and presented them to King Ugrasena. Kṛṣṇa thus offered His respect to His grandfather because he was at that time the crowned king of the Yadu dynasty.

Jarāsandha, the King of Magadha, not only besieged the city of Mathurā once, but he attacked it seventeen times in the same way, equipped with the same number of military phalanxes. Each and every time, he was defeated, and all his soldiers were killed by Kṛṣṇa, and each time he had to return disappointed in the same way. Each time, the princely order of the Yadu dynasty arrested Jarāsandha in the same way and again released him in an insulting manner, and each time Jarāsandha shamelessly returned home.

While Jarāsandha was attempting one such attack, a Yavana king somewhere to the south of Mathurā became attracted by the opulence of the Yadu dynasty and also attacked the city. It is said that the king of the Yavanas, known as Kālayavana, was induced to attack by Nārada. This story is narrated in the *Viṣṇu Purāṇa.* Once, Gargamuni, the priest of the Yadu dynasty, was taunted by his brother-in-law. When the kings of the Yadu dynasty heard the taunt they laughed at him, and Gargamuni became angry at the Yadu kings. He decided that he would produce someone who would be very fearful to the Yadu dynasty, so he pleased Lord Śiva and received from him the benediction of a son. He begot this son, Kālayavana, in the wife of a Yavana king. This Kālayavana inquired from Nārada, "Who are the most powerful kings in the world?" Nārada informed him that the Yadus were the most powerful. Being thus informed by Nārada, Kālayavana attacked the city of Mathurā at the same time that Jarāsandha attempted to attack it for the eighteenth time. Kālayavana was very anxious to declare war on a king of the world who would be a suitable combatant for him, but he had not found any. However, being informed about Mathurā by Nārada, he thought it wise to attack this city. When he attacked Mathurā he brought with him thirty million Yavana soldiers. When Mathurā was thus besieged, Lord Śrī Kṛṣṇa began to consider how much the Yadu dynasty was in distress, being threatened by the attacks of two formidable enemies, Jarāsandha and Kālayavana. Time was growing very short. Kālayavana was already besieging Mathurā from all sides, and it was expected that the next day Jarāsandha would also come, equipped with the same number of divisions of soldiers as in his previous seventeen attempts. Kṛṣṇa was certain that Jarāsandha would take advantage of the opportunity to capture Mathurā when it was also being besieged by Kālayavana. He therefore thought it wise to take precautionary measures to defend the strategic points of Mathurā. If both Kṛṣṇa and Balarāma were engaged in fighting with Kālayavana at one place, Jarāsandha might come at another place to attack the whole Yadu family and take his revenge. Jarāsandha was very powerful, and having been defeated seventeen times, he might vengefully kill the members of the Yadu family or arrest them and take them to his kingdom. Kṛṣṇa therefore decided to construct a formidable fort in a place where no two-legged animal, either man or demon, could enter. He decided to keep His relatives there so that He would then be free to fight with the enemy. It appears that formerly Dvārakā was also part of the kingdom of Mathurā, because in the *Śrīmad-Bhāgavatam* it is stated that Kṛṣṇa constructed a fort in the midst of the sea. Remnants of the fort which Kṛṣṇa constructed are still existing on the Bay of Dvārakā.

He first of all constructed a very strong wall covering ninety-six square miles, and the wall itself was within the sea. It was certainly wonderful and was planned and constructed by Viśvakarmā. No ordinary architect could construct such a fort within the sea, but an architect like Viśvakarmā, who is considered to be the engineer among the demigods, can execute such wonderful craftmanship anywhere in any part of the universe. If huge planets can be floated in weightlessness in the outer space by the arrangement of the Supreme Personality of Godhead, surely the architectural construction of a fort within the sea covering a space of ninety-six square miles was not a very wonderful act.

It is stated in the *Śrīmad-Bhāgavatam* that this new, well-constructed city, developed within the sea, had regular planned roads, streets and lanes. Not only were there well-planned roads, trees and lanes, but there were well-planned paths and gardens filled with plants known as *kalpavṛkṣas,* or desire trees. These desire trees are not like the ordinary trees of the material world; the desire trees are found in the spiritual world. By Kṛṣṇa's supreme will, everything is possible, so such desire trees were planted in this city of Dvārakā constructed by Kṛṣṇa. The city was also filled with many palaces and *gopuras,* or big gates. These *gopuras* are still found in some of the larger temples. They are very high and constructed with extreme artistic skill. Such palaces and gates held golden waterpots *(kalaśa).* These water pots on the gates or in the palaces are considered to be auspicious signs.

Almost all the palaces were skyscrapers. In each and every house there were big pots of gold and silver and grains stocked in underground rooms. And there were many golden waterpots within the rooms. The bedrooms were all bedecked with jewels, and the floors were mosiac pavements of *marakata* jewels. The Viṣṇu Deity, worshiped by the descendants of Yadu, was installed in each house in the city. The residential quarters were so arranged that the different castes, *brāhmaṇas, kṣatriyas, vaiśyas* and *śūdras,* had their respective quarters. It appears from this that the caste system was existing even at that time. In the center of the city there was another residential quarter made specifically for King Ugrasena. This place was the most dazzling of all the houses.

When the demigods saw that Kṛṣṇa was constructing a particular city of His own choice, they sent the celebrated *pārijāta* flower of the heavenly planet to be planted in the new city, and they also sent a parliamentary house, Sudharmā. The specific quality of this assembly house was that anyone participating in a meeting within it would overcome the influence of invalidity due to old age. The demigod Varuṇa also presented a horse, which was all white except for black ears and which could run at the speed of the mind. Kuvera, the treasurer of the demigods, presented the art of attaining the eight perfectional stages of material opulences. In this way, all the demigods began to present their respective gifts according to their different capacities. There are thirty-three million demigods, and each of them is entrusted with a particular department of universal management. All the demigods took the opportunity of the Supreme Personality of Godhead's constructing a city of His own choice to present their respective gifts, making the city of Mathurā unique within the universe. This proves that there are undoubtedly innumerable demigods, but none of them are independent of Kṛṣṇa. As stated in the *Caitanya-caritāmṛta,* Kṛṣṇa is the supreme master, and all others are servants. So all the servants took the opportunity of rendering service to Kṛṣṇa when He was personally present within this universe. This example should be followed by all, especially those who are Kṛṣṇa conscious, for they should serve Kṛṣṇa by their respective abilities.

When the new city was fully constructed according to plan, Kṛṣṇa transferred all the inhabitants of Mathurā and entrusted Śrī Balarāma as the city father. After this He consulted with Balarāma, and being garlanded with lotus flowers, He came out of the city to meet Kālayavana, who had already seized Mathurā without taking up any weapons.

When Kṛṣṇa came out of the city, Kālayavana, who had never seen Kṛṣṇa before, saw Him to be extraordinarily beautiful, dressed in yellow garments. Passing through His assembly of soldiers, Kṛṣṇa appeared like the moon in the sky passing through the assembled clouds. Kālayavana was fortunate enough to see the lines of *Śrīvatsa,* a particular impression on the chest of Śrī Kṛṣṇa, and the *Kaustubha* jewel which He was wearing.

Kālayavana saw Him, however, in His Viṣṇu form, with a well-built body, with four hands, and eyes like newly blooming lotus petals. Kṛṣṇa appeared blissful, with a handsome forehead and beauitful face, with smiling restless eyes and moving earrings. Before seeing Kṛṣṇa, Kālayvana had heard about Him from Nārada, and now the descriptions of Nārada were confirmed. He noticed Kṛṣṇa's specific marks and the jewels on His chest, His beautiful garland of lotus flowers, His lotus-like eyes and similarly beautiful bodily features. He concluded that this beautiful personality must be Vāsudeva, because every description of Nārada's which he had heard previously was substantiated by the presence of Kṛṣṇa. Kālayavana was very much astonished to see that He was passing through without any weapon in His hands and without any chariot. He was simply walking on foot. Kālayavana had come to fight with Kṛṣṇa, and yet he had sufficient principles not to take up any kind of weapon. He decided to fight with Him hand to hand. Thus he prepared to capture Kṛṣṇa and fight.

Kṛṣṇa, however, went ahead without looking at Kālayavana, and Kālayavana began to follow Him with a desire to capture Him. But in spite of all his swift running, he could not capture Kṛṣṇa. Kṛṣṇa cannot be captured even by the mental speed attained by great *yogīs.* He can be captured only by devotional service, and Kālayavana was not practiced in devotional service. He wanted to capture Kṛṣṇa, and as he could not do so he was following him from behind.

Kālayavana began running very fast, and he was thinking, "Now I am nearer; I will capture Him," but he could not. Kṛṣṇa led him far away, and He entered the cave of a hill. Kālayavana thought that Kṛṣṇa was trying to avoid fighting with him and was therefore taking shelter of the cave. He began to chastise Him with the following words: "Oh You, Kṛṣṇa! I heard that You are a great hero born in the dynasty of Yadu, but I see that You are verily running away from fighting, like a coward. It is not worthy of Your good name and family tradition." Kālayavana was following, running very fast, but still he could not catch Kṛṣṇa because he was not freed from all contaminations of sinful life.

According to Vedic culture, anyone who does not live following the regulative principles of life observed by the higher castes like the *brāhmaṇas, kṣatriyas, vaiśyas* and even the laborer class is called *mleccha.* The Vedic social situation is so planned that persons who are accepted as *śūdras* can gradually be elevated to the position of *brāhmaṇas* by the cultural advancement known as *saṁskāra,* or the purificatory process. The version of the Vedic scriptures is that no one becomes a *brāhmaṇa* or a *mleccha* simply by birth; by birth everyone is accepted as *śūdra.* One has to elevate himself by the purificatory process to the stage of brahminical life. If he doesn't, if he degrades himself further, then he is called *mleccha.* Kālayavana belonged to the class of *mleccha* and *yavanas.* He was contaminated by sinful activities and could not approach Kṛṣṇa. The principles from which higher class men are restricted, namely illicit sex indulgence, meat eating, gambling and intoxication, are part and parcel of the lives of the *mlecchas* and *yavanas.* Being bound by such sinful activities one cannot make any advancement in God realization. The *Bhagavad-gītā* confirms that only one who is completely freed from all sinful reactions can be engaged in devotional service or Kṛṣṇa consciousness.

When Kṛṣṇa entered the cave of the hill, Kālayavana followed, chastising Him with various harsh words. Kṛṣṇa suddenly disappeared from the demon's sight, but Kālayavana followed and also entered the cave. The first thing he saw was a man lying down asleep within the cave. Kālayavana was very anxious to fight with Kṛṣṇa, and when he could not see Kṛṣṇa, but saw instead only a man lying down, he thought that Kṛṣṇa was sleeping within this cave. Kālayavana was very puffed up and proud of his strength, and he thought Kṛṣṇa was avoiding the fight. Therefore, he very strongly kicked the sleeping man, thinking him to be Kṛṣṇa. The sleeping man had been lying down for a very long time. When he was awakened by the kicking of Kālayavana, he immediately opened his eyes and began to look around in all directions. At last he began to see Kālayavana, who was standing nearby. This man was untimely awakened and therefore very angry, and when he looked upon Kālayavana in his angry mood, rays of fire emanated from his eyes, and Kālayavana burned into ashes within a moment.

Thus ends the Bhaktivedanta purport of the Forty-ninth Chapter of Kṛṣṇa, *"Kṛṣṇa Erects the Dvārakā Fort."*

50 / Deliverance of Mucukunda

When Mahārāja Parīkṣit heard this incident of Kālayavana's being burned to ashes, he inquired about the sleeping man from Śukadeva Gosvāmī: "Who was he? Why was he sleeping there? How had he achieved so much power that instantly, by his glance, Kālayavana was burned to ashes? How did he happen to be lying down in the cave of the hill?" Many questions were put before Śukadeva Gosvāmī, and Śukadeva also answered, as follows.

"My dear King, this person was born in the very great family of King Ikṣvāku, in which Lord Rāmacandra was also born, and he happened to be the son of a great king known as Māndhātā. He himself was also a great soul and was known popularly as Mucukunda. King Mucukunda was a very strict follower of the Vedic principles of brahminical culture, and he was truthful to his promise. He was so powerful that even demigods like Indra and others used to ask him to please help in fighting with the demons, and as such, he often fought against the demons to protect the demigods."

The commander-in-chief of the demigods, known as Kārttikeya, was satisfied with the fighting of King Mucukunda, but once he asked that the King, having taken too much trouble in fighting with the demons, retire from fighting and take rest. The commander-in-chief, Kārttikeya, addressed King Mucukunda, "My dear King, you have sacrificed everything for the sake of the demigods. You had a very nice kingdom undisturbed by any kind of enemy. You left that kingdom, you neglected your opulence and possessions, and you never cared for fulfillment of your personal ambition. Due to your long absence from your kingdom while fighting with the demons on behalf of the demigods, your family, your children, your relatives and your ministers have all passed away in due course of time. Time and tide wait for no living man. Now even if you retire to your home, you will find that no one is living there. The influence of time is very strong; all your relatives have passed away in due course of time. Time is so strong and powerful because it is a representation of the Supreme Personality of Godhead; time is therefore stronger than the strongest. By the influence of time, changes in subtle things can be effected without any difficulty. No one can check the process of time. As an animal tamer tames the animals according to his own will, so time also enters things according to its own will. None can supersede the arrangement made by the supreme time."

Thus addressing Mucukunda, the demigods requested him to ask for any kind of benediction he might be pleased with, excepting the benediction of liberation. Liberation cannot be awarded by any living entity except the Supreme Personality of Godhead, Viṣṇu. Therefore another name of Lord Viṣṇu or Kṛṣṇa is Mukunda, He who can award liberation.

King Mucukunda had not slept for many, many years. He was engaged in the duty of fighting, and therefore he was very tired. So when the demigod offered benediction, Mucukunda simply thought of sleeping. He replied as follows: "My dear Kārttikeya, the best of the demigods, I want to sleep now, and I want from you the following benediction. Grant me the power to burn, by my mere glance, anyone to ashes who tries to disturb my sleeping and awakens me untimely. Please give me this benediction." The demigod agreed and also gave him the benediction that he would be able to take complete rest. Then King Mucukunda entered the cave of the mountain.

On the strength of the benediction of Kārttikeya, Kālayavana was burnt into ashes simply by Mucukunda's glancing at him. When the incident was over, Kṛṣṇa came before King Mucukunda. Kṛṣṇa had actually entered the cave to deliver King Mucukunda from his austerity, but He did not first appear before him. He arranged that first Kālayavana should come before him. That is the way of the activities of the Supreme Personality of Godhead; He does one thing in such a way that many other purposes are served. He wanted to deliver King Mucukunda, who was sleeping in the cave, and at the same time He wanted to kill Kālayavana, who had attacked Mathurā city. By this action He served all purposes.

When Lord Kṛṣṇa appeared before Mucukunda, the King saw Him dressed in a yellow garment, His chest marked with the symbol of *Śrīvatsa,* and the *Kaustubha-maṇi* hanging around His neck. Kṛṣṇa appeared before him with four hands, as Viṣṇu-mūrti, with a garland called *vaijayantī* hanging from His neck down to His knees. He was looking very lustrous, His face was very beautifully smiling, and He had nice jeweled earrings in both His ears. Kṛṣṇa appeared more beautiful than a human can conceive.

Not only did He appear in this feature, but He glanced over Mucukunda with great splendor, attracting the King's mind. Although He was the Supreme Personality of Godhead, the oldest of all, He looked like a fresh young boy, and His movement was just like that of a free deer. He appeared extremely powerful; His excellence in power is so great that every human being should be afraid of Him.

When King Mucukunda saw Kṛṣṇa's magnificent features, he wondered about His identity, and with great humility he began to inquire from the Lord: "My dear Lord, may I inquire how it is that You happened to be in the cave of this mountain? Who are You? I can see that Your feet are just like soft lotus flowers. How could You walk in this forest full of thorns and hedges? I am simply surprised to see this! Are You not, therefore, the Supreme Personality of Godhead, who is the most powerful amongst the powerful? Are You not the original source of all illumination and fire? Can I consider You one of the great demigods, like the sun, the moon, or Indra, King of heaven? Or are You the predominating deity of any other planet?"

Mucukunda knew well that every higher planetary system has a predominating deity. He was not ignorant like modern men who consider that this earthly planet is full of living entities and all others are vacant. The inquiry from Mucukunda about Kṛṣṇa's being the predominating deity of a planet unknown to him is quite appropriate. Because he was a pure devotee of the Lord, King Mucukunda could immediately understand that Lord Kṛṣṇa, who had appeared before him in such an opulent feature, could not be one of the predominating deities in the material planets. He must be the Supreme Personality of Godhead, Kṛṣṇa, who has His many Viṣṇu forms. He therefore took Him to be Puruṣottama, Lord Viṣṇu. He could see also that the dense darkness within the mountain cave had already been dissipated due to the Lord's presence; therefore He could not be other than the Supreme Personality of Godhead. He knew very well that wherever the Lord is personally present by His transcendental name, quality, form, etc., there cannot be any darkness of ignorance. He is like a lamp placed in the darkness; He immediately illuminates a dark place.

King Mucukunda became very much anxious to know about the identity of Lord Kṛṣṇa, and therefore he said, "O best of human beings, if You think that I am fit to know about Your identity, then kindly tell me who You are. What is Your parentage? What is Your occupational duty, and what is Your family tradition?" King Mucukunda thought it wise, however, to identify himself to the Lord; otherwise he had no right to ask the Lord's identity. Etiquette is such that a person of less importance cannot ask the identity of a person of higher importance without first disclosing his own identity. King Mucukunda therefore informed Lord Kṛṣṇa, "My dear Lord, I must inform You of my identification. I belong to the most celebrated dynasty of King Ikṣvāku, but personally I am not as great as my forefather. My name is Mucukunda. My father's name was Māndhātā, and my grandfather's name was Yuvanāśva, the great king. I was very much fatigued due to not resting for many thousands of years, and because of this all my bodily limbs were flattened and almost incapable of acting. In order to revive my energy, I was taking rest in this solitary cave, but I have been awakened by some unknown man who has forced me to wake up although I was not willing to do so. For such an offensive act, this person has been burnt into ashes simply by my glancing over him. Fortunately, now I can see You in Your grand and beautiful features. I think, therefore, that You are the cause of killing my enemy. My dear Lord, I must admit that due to the effulgence of Your body, unbearable to my eyes, I cannot see You properly. I can fully realize that by the influence of Your effulgence my powerful potency has been diminished. I can understand that You are quite fit for being worshiped by all living entities."

Seeing King Mucukunda so anxious to know about His identity, Lord Kṛṣṇa began to answer smilingly, as follows: "My dear King, it is practically impossible to tell about My birth, appearance, disappearance and activities. Perhaps you know that My incarnation Anantadeva has unlimited mouths, and for an unlimited time he has been trying to narrate fully about My name, fame, qualities, activities, appearance, disappearance and incarnation, but still he has not been able to finish. Therefore, it is not possible to know exactly how many names and forms I possess. It may be possible for a material scientist to estimate the number of atomic particles which make up this earthly planet, but the scientist cannot enumerate My unlimited names, forms and activities. There are many great sages and saintly persons who are trying to make a list of My different forms and activities, yet they have failed to make a complete list. But since you are so anxious to know about Me, I may inform you that presently I have appeared on this planet just to annihilate the demoniac principles of the people in general and to reestablish the religious principles enjoined in the *Vedas*. I have been invited for this purpose by Brahmā, the superintending deity of this universe, and thus I have now appeared in the dynasty of the Yadus as one of their family members. I have specifically taken My birth as the son of Vasudeva in the Yadu Dynasty, and people therefore know Me as Vāsudeva, the son of Vasudeva. You may also know that I have killed Kaṁsa, who was in a previous life known as Kālanemi, as well as Pralambāsura and many other demons. They have acted as My enemies and have been killed by Me. The demon who was present before you also acted as My enemy, and you have very kindly burned him into ashes by glancing over him. My dear King Mucukunda, you are My great devotee, and just to show you My causeless mercy, I have appeared in this form. I am very affectionately inclined toward My devotees, and in your previous life, before your present condition, you acted as My great devotee and prayed for My causeless mercy. I have, therefore, come to see you to fulfill your desire. Now you can see Me to your heart's content. My dear King, now you can ask from Me any benediction that you wish, and I am prepared to fulfill your desire. It is my eternal principle that anyone who comes under My shelter must have all his desires fulfilled by My grace."

When Lord Kṛṣṇa ordered King Mucukunda to ask a benediction from Him, the King became very joyful, and he immediately remembered the prediction of Gargamuni, who had foretold long before that in the twenty-eighth millennium of Vaivasvata Manu, Lord Kṛṣṇa would appear on this planet. As soon as he remembered this prediction, he began to understand that the Supreme Person, Nārāyaṇa, was present before Him as Lord Kṛṣṇa. He immediately fell down at His lotus feet and began to pray as follows.

"My dear Lord, O Supreme Personality of Godhead, I can understand that all living entities on this planet are illusioned by Your external energy and are enamored of the illusory satisfaction of sense gratification. Being fully engaged in illusory activities, they are reluctant to worship Your lotus feet, and because they are unaware of the benefits of surrendering unto Your lotus feet they are subjected to various miserable conditions of material existence. They are foolishly attached to so-called society, friendship and love, which simply produce different kinds of miserable conditions. Illusioned by Your external energy, everyone, both man and woman, is attached to this material existence, and all are engaged in cheating one another in a great society of the cheaters and the cheated. These foolish persons do not know how fortunate they are to have obtained this human form of life, and they are reluctant to worship Your lotus feet. By the influence of Your external energy, they are simply attached to the glare of material activities. They are attached to so-called society, friendship and love like dumb animals that have fallen into a dark well." The example of a dark well is given because in the fields there are many wells, unused for years and covered over by grass, and the poor animals, without knowing of them, fall into them, and unless they are rescued, they die. Being captivated by a few blades of grass, the animals fall into a dark well and meet death. Similarly, foolish persons, without knowing the importance of the human form of life, spoil it simply for sense gratification and die unnecessarily, without any useful purpose.

"My dear Lord, I am not an exception to this universal law of material nature. I am also one of those foolish persons who has wasted his time for nothing. And my position is especially difficult. On account of my being situated in the royal order, I was more puffed up than ordinary persons. An ordinary man thinks of becoming the proprietor of his body or of his family, but I began to think in that way on a larger scale. I wanted to be the master of the whole world, and as I became puffed up with ideas of sense gratification, my bodily concept of life became stronger and stronger. My attachment for home, wife and children, for money and for supremacy over the world, became more and more acute; in fact, it was limitless. So I remained always attached to thoughts of my material living conditions.

" Therefore , my dear Lord, I wasted so much of my valuable lifetime without any benefit. My misconception of life having been intensified, I began to think of this material body, which is just a bag of flesh and bones, as the all in all, and in my vanity I was like a dog who believes that he has become the king of human society. In this misconception of bodily life, I began to travel all over the world, accompanied by my military strength—soldiers, charioteers, elephants and horses. Assisted by many commanders and puffed up by power, I could not trace out Your Lordship, who is always sitting within my heart as the most intimate friend. I did not care for You, and this was the fault of my so-called exalted material condition. I think that, like me, all living creatures are careless about spiritual realization and are always full of anxieties, thinking, 'What is to be done?' 'What is next?' But because we are strongly bound by material desires, we continue to remain in craziness.

"Yet in spite of our being so absorbed in material thought, inevitable time, which is only a form of Yourself, is always careful about its duty, and as soon as the alloted time is over, Your Lordship immediately ends all the activities of our material dreams. As the time factor, You end all our activities, as the hungry blacksnake swiftly swallows up a small rat without any leniency. Due to the action of cruel time, the royal body which was always decorated with gold ornaments during life and which moved on a chariot drawn by beautiful horses or on the back of an elephant nicely decorated with golden ornaments, and which was advertised as the king of human society—that same royal body decomposes under the influence of inevitable time and becomes fit for being eaten by worms and insects or being turned into ashes or the stool of an animal.

This beautiful body may be nice while in the living condition, but after death even the body of a king is eaten by an animal and therefore turns into stool or is cremated in the crematorium and turned into ashes or is put into an earthly grave where different kinds of worms and insects are produced out of it.

"My dear Lord, not only do we become under the full control of this inevitable time after death, but also while living, in a different way. For example, I may be a powerful king, and yet when I come home after conquering over the world I become subjected to many material conditions. It may be that when I come back after being victorious all subordinate kings come and offer their respects, but as soon as I enter into the inner section of my palace, I myself become an instrument in the hands of the queens, and for sense gratification I have to fall down at the feet of women. The material way of life is so complicated that before taking the enjoyment of material life one has to work so hard that there is scarcely an opportunity for enjoying. And to attain the youthful condition with all material facilities one has to undergo severe austerities and penances and become elevated to the heavenly planets. If one gets the opportunity of taking birth in a very rich or royal family, even then in that condition he is always anxious to maintain the status quo and prepare for the next life by performing various kinds of sacrifices and by distributing charity. Even in the royal condition of life one is not only full of anxieties because of political administration, but he is also in anxiety over being elevated to heavenly planets.

"It is therefore very difficult to get out of the material entanglement, but somehow or other if one is favored by You, by Your mercy only he is given the opportunity to associate with a pure devotee. That is the beginning point of liberation from the entanglement of material conditional life. My dear Lord, only by the association of pure devotees is one entrapped by Your Lordship, who is the controller of both the material and spiritual existences. You are the supreme goal of all pure devotees, and by association with pure devotees one can develop his dormant love for You. Therefore, development of Kṛṣṇa consciousness in the association of pure devotees is the cause of liberation from this material entanglement.

"My dear Lord, You are so merciful that in spite of my being reluctant to associate with Your great devotees You have shown Your extreme mercy upon me as a result of my slight contact with a pure devotee like Gargamuni. By Your causeless mercy only have I lost all my material opulences, my kingdom and my family. I do not think that I could have gotten rid of all these entanglements without Your causeless mercy. Kings and emperors accept the life of austerity to forget the royal condition of life, but by Your special causeless mercy I have already been bereft of the royal condition. Other kings exert themselves to get out of the attachment of kingdom and family by acceptance of the hardships of renunciation, but by Your mercy I do not need to become a mendicant or to practice renunciation.

"My dear Lord, I therefore pray that I may simply be engaged in rendering transcendental loving service unto Your lotus feet, which is the ambition of the pure devotees who are freed from all kinds of material contamination. You are the Supreme Personality of Godhead, and You can offer me anything I want, including liberation. But who is such a foolish person that after pleasing You he would ask from You something which might be the cause of entanglement in this material world? I do not think any sane man would ask such a benediction from You. I therefore surrender unto You because You are the Supreme Personality of Godhead, You are the Supersoul living in everyone's heart, and You are the impersonal Brahman effulgence. Moreover, You are also this material world, because this material world is only the manifestation of Your external energy. Therefore, from any angle of vision, You are the supreme shelter for everyone. Everyone, either in the material plane or in the spiritual plane, must take shelter under Your lotus feet. I therefore submit unto You, my Lord. For many, many births I have been suffering from the threefold miseries of this material existence, and I am now tired of it. I have simply been impelled by my senses, and I was never satisfied. I therefore take shelter of Your lotus feet, which are the source of all peaceful conditions of life and which can eradicate all kinds of lamentation caused by material contamination. My dear Lord, You are the Supersoul of everyone, and You can understand everything. Now I am free from all contamination of material desire. I do not wish to enjoy this material world, nor do I wish to take advantage of merging into Your spiritual effulgence, nor do I wish to meditate upon Your localized aspect of Paramātmā, for I know that simply by taking shelter of You, I shall become completely peaceful and undisturbed."

On hearing this statement of King Mucukunda, Lord Kṛṣṇa replied, "My dear King, I am very much pleased with your statement. You have been the King of all the lands on this planet, but I am surprised to find that your mind is now freed from all material contamination. You are now fit to execute devotional service. I am most pleased to see that although I offered you the opportunity of asking from Me any kind of benediction, you did not take advantage of asking for material benefit. I can understand that your mind is now fixed in Me, and it is not disturbed by any material fault.

"The material qualities are three, namely goodness, passion and ignorance. When one is placed in the mixed material qualities of passion and ignorance, he is impelled by various kinds of dirtiness and lusty desires to try to find comfort in this material world. When he is situated in the material quality of goodness, he tries to purify himself by performing various kinds of penances and austerities. When one reaches the platform of a real *brāhmaṇa,* he aspires to merge into the existence of the Lord, but when one desires simply to render service unto the lotus feet of the Lord, that is transcendental to all these three qualities. The pure Kṛṣṇa conscious person is therefore always free from all material qualities. My dear King, I offered to give you any kind of benediction, just to test how much you have advanced in devotional service. Now I can see that you are on the platform of the pure devotees because your mind is not disturbed by any kind of greedy or lusty desires of this material world. The *yogīs* who are trying to elevate themselves by controlling the senses and who meditate upon Me by practicing the breathing exercise of *prāṇāyāma* are not so thoroughly freed from material desires. It has been seen in several cases that as soon as there is allurement, such *yogīs* again come down to the material platform."

The vivid example verifying this statement is Viśvāmitra Muni. Viśvāmitra Muni was a great *yogī* who practiced *prāṇāyāma,* a breathing exercise, but still when he was visited by Menakā, a society woman of the heavenly planet, he lost all control and begot in her a daughter named Śakuntalā. But the pure devotee Haridāsa Ṭhākur was never disturbed, even when all such allurements were offered by the prostitutes.

"My dear King," Lord Kṛṣṇa continued, "I therefore give you the special benediction that you will always think of Me. Thus you will be able to traverse this material world freely, without being contaminated by the qualities." This statement of the Lord confirms that a person in true Kṛṣṇa consciousness, engaged in the transcendental loving service of the Lord under the direction of the spiritual master, is never subjected to the contamination of material qualities.

"My dear King," the Lord said, "because you are a *kṣatriya,* you have committed the offense of slaughtering animals, both in hunting and in political engagements. To become purified, just engage yourself in *bhakti-yoga* practice and always keep your mind absorbed in Me. Very soon you will be freed from all reactions to such sordid activities." In this statement it appears that although the *kṣatriyas* are allowed to kill animals in the hunting process, they are not freed from the contamination of other sinful reactions. Therefore it does not matter whether one is *kṣatriya, vaiśya,* or *brāhmaṇa;* everyone is recommended to take *sannyāsa* at the end of life, to engage himself completely in the service of the Lord and thus become freed from all sinful reactions of his past life.

The Lord then assured King Mucukunda, "In your next life you will take your birth as a first-class Vaiṣṇava, the best of *brāhmaṇas,* and in that life your only business will be to engage yourself in My transcendental service." The Vaiṣṇava is the first-class *brāhmaṇa,* because one who has not acquired the qualification of a bona fide *brāhmaṇa* cannot come to the platform of a Vaiṣṇava. When one comes to the platform of a Vaiṣṇava, he is completely engaged in welfare activities for all living entities. The highest welfare activity for living entities is the preaching of Kṛṣṇa consciousness. It is stated herein that those who are specifically favored by the Lord can become absolutely Kṛṣṇa conscious and be engaged in the preaching work of the Vaiṣṇava philosophy.

Thus ends the Bhaktivedanta purport of the Fiftieth Chapter of Kṛṣṇa, *"Deliverance of Mucukunda."*

51 / Kṛṣṇa, the Ranchor

When Mucukunda, the celebrated descendant of the Ikṣvāku dynasty, was favored by Lord Kṛṣṇa, he circumambulated the Lord within the cave and then came out. On coming out of the cave, Mucukunda saw that the stature of the human species had surprisingly been reduced to pigmy size. Similarly, the trees had also far reduced in size, and Mucukunda could immediately understand that the current age was Kali-yuga. Therefore, without diverting his attention, he began to travel north. Eventually he reached the mountain known as Gandhamādana. It appeared there were many trees on this mountain, such as sandalwood and other flower trees, the flavor of which made anyone joyful who reached them. He decided to remain in that Gandhamādana Mountain region in order to execute austerities and penances for the rest of his life. It appears that this place is situated in the northernmost part of the Himalayan Mountains, where the abode of Nara-Nārāyaṇa is situated. This place is still existing and is called Badarikāśrama. In Badarikāśrama he engaged himself in the worship of Lord Kṛṣṇa, forgetting all pain and pleasure and the other dualities of this material world. Lord Kṛṣṇa also returned to the vicinity of the city of Mathurā and began to fight with the soldiers of Kālayavana and kill them one after another. After this, He collected all the booty from the dead bodies, and under His direction, it was loaded on bullock carts by big men and brought back to Dvārakā.

Meanwhile, Jarāsandha again attacked Mathurā, this time with bigger divisions of soldiers, numbering twenty-three *akṣauhiṇīs.*

Lord Śrī Kṛṣṇa wanted to save Mathurā from the eighteenth attack of the great military divisions of King Jarāsandha. In order to prevent further killing of soldiers and to attend to other important business, Lord Kṛṣṇa left the battlefield without fighting. Actually He was not at all afraid, but He pretended to be an ordinary human being frightened by the immense quantity of soldiers and resources of Jarāsandha. Without any weapons He left the battlefield. Although His lotus feet were as soft as the petals of the lotus flower, He proceeded for a very long distance on foot.

This time, Jarāsandha thought that Kṛṣṇa and Balarāma were very much afraid of His military strength and were fleeing from the battlefield. He began to follow Them with all his chariots, horses and infantry. He thought Kṛṣṇa and Balarāma to be ordinary human beings, and he was trying to measure the activities of the Lord. Kṛṣṇa is known as Ranchor, which means "one who has left the battlefield." In India, especially in Gujarat, there are many temples of Kṛṣṇa which are known as temples of Ranchorjī. Ordinarily, if a king leaves the battlefield without fighting he is called a coward, but when Kṛṣṇa enacts this pastime, leaving the battlefield without fighting, He is worshiped by the devotee. A demon always tries to measure the opulence of Kṛṣṇa, whereas the devotee never tries to measure His strength and opulence, but always surrenders unto Him and worships Him. By following the footsteps of pure devotees we can know that Kṛṣṇa, the Ranchorjī, did not leave the battlefield because He was afraid, but because He had some other purpose. The purpose, as it will be revealed, was to attend to a confidential letter sent by Rukmiṇī, His future first wife. The act of Kṛṣṇa's leaving the battlefield is a display of one of His six opulences. Kṛṣṇa is the supreme powerful, the supreme wealthy, the supreme famous, the supreme wise, the supreme beautiful; similarly He is the supreme renouncer. *Śrīmad-Bhāgavatam* clearly states that He left the battlefield in spite of having ample military strength. Even without His militia, however, He alone would have been sufficient to defeat the army of Jarāsandha, as He had done seventeen times before. Therefore, His leaving the battlefield is an example of His supermost opulence of renunciation.

After traversing a very long distance, the brothers pretended to become very tired. To mitigate Their weariness They climbed up a very high mountain several miles above sea level. This mountain was called Pravarṣaṇa due to constant rain. The peak was always covered with clouds sent by Indra. Jarāsandha took it for granted that the two brothers were afraid of his military power and had hidden Themselves at the top of the mountain. First he tried to find Them, searching for a long time, but when he failed he decided to trap and kill Them by setting fires around the peak. He therefore surrounded the peak with oil and set it on fire. As the blaze spread more and more, Kṛṣṇa and Balarāma jumped from the top of the mountain down to the ground—a distance of eighty-eight miles. Thus, while the peak was burning up, Kṛṣṇa and Balarāma escaped without being seen by Jarāsandha. Jarāsandha concluded that the two brothers had been burned to ashes and that there was no need of further fighting. Thinking himself successful in his efforts, he left the city of Mathurā and returned to his home in the kingdom of Magadha. Gradually Kṛṣṇa and Balarāma reached the city of Dvārakā, which was surrounded on all sides by the sea.

Following this, Śrī Balarāma married Revatī, daughter of King Raivata, ruler of the Ānarta province. This is explained in the Ninth Canto of *Śrīmad-Bhāgavatam.* After the marriage of Baladeva, Kṛṣṇa married Rukmiṇī. Rukmiṇī was the daughter of King Bhīṣmaka, ruler of the province known as Vidarbha. Just as Kṛṣṇa is the Supreme Personality of Godhead, Vāsudeva, Rukmiṇī is the supreme goddess of fortune, Mahā-Lakṣmī. According to the authority of *Caitanya-caritāmṛta,* the expansion of Kṛṣṇa and Śrī Rādhārāṇī is simultaneous; Kṛṣṇa expands Himself into various *Viṣṇu-tattva* forms, and Śrīmatī Rādhārāṇī expands Herself into various *śakti-tattva* forms by Her internal potency, as multi-forms of the goddess of fortune.

According to Vedic convention, there are eight kinds of marriages. In the first-class marriage system, the parents of the bride and bridegroom arrange the marriage date. Then, in royal style, the bridegroom goes to the house of the bride, and in the presence of *brāhmaṇas,* priests and relatives, the bride is given in charity to the bridegroom. Besides this, there are other systems, such as the *gandharva* and *rākṣasa* marriages. Rukmiṇī was married to Kṛṣṇa in the *rākṣasa* style because she was kidnapped by Him in the presence of His many rivals, like Śiśupāla, Jarāsandha, Śālva and others. While Rukmiṇī was being given in charity to Śiśupāla, she was snatched from the marriage arena by Kṛṣṇa, exactly as Garuḍa snatched the pot of nectar from the demons. Rukmiṇī, the only daughter of King Bhīṣmaka, was exquisitely beautiful. She was known as Rucirānanā, which means "one who has a beautiful face, expanding like a lotus flower."

Devotees of Kṛṣṇa are always anxious to hear about the transcendental activities of the Lord. His activities of fighting, kidnapping and running away from the battlefield are all transcendental, being on the absolute platform, and devotees take a transcendental interest in hearing of them. The pure devotee does not make the distinction that some activities of the Lord should be heard and others should be avoided. There is, however, a class of so-called devotees known as *prākṛta sahajiyā* who are very interested in hearing about Kṛṣṇa's *rāsa-līlā* with the *gopīs,* but not about His fighting activities with His enemies. They do not know that His bellicose activities and His friendly activities with the *gopīs* are equally transcendental, being on the absolute platform. The transcendental pastimes of

Kṛṣṇa described in the *Śrīmad-Bhāgavatam* are relished by pure devotees through submissive aural reception. They do not reject even a drop.

The story of Kṛṣṇa's marriage with Rukmiṇī is described as follows. The King of Vidarbha, Mahārāja Bhīṣmaka, was a very qualified and devoted prince. He had five sons and only one daughter. The first son was known as Rukmī; the second, Rukmaratha; the third, Rukmabāhu; the fourth and youngest, Rukmakeśa; and the fifth, Rukmamālī. The brothers had one young sister, Rukmiṇī. She was beautiful and chaste and was meant to be married to Lord Kṛṣṇa. Many saintly persons and sages like Nārada Muni and others used to visit the palace of King Bhīṣmaka. Naturally Rukmiṇī had a chance to talk with them, and in this way she obtained information about Kṛṣṇa. She was informed about the six opulences of Kṛṣṇa, and simply by hearing about Him, she desired to surrender herself to His lotus feet and become His wife. Kṛṣṇa had also heard of Rukmiṇī. She was the reservoir of all transcendental qualities: intelligence, liberal-mindedness, exquisite beauty and righteous behavior. Kṛṣṇa therefore decided that she was fit to be His wife. All of the family members and relatives of King Bhīṣmaka decided that Rukmiṇī should be given in marriage to Kṛṣṇa. However her elder brother, Rukmī, despite the desire of the others, arranged for her marriage with Śiśupāla, a determined enemy of Kṛṣṇa. When the black-eyed, beautiful Rukmiṇī heard the settlement, she immediately became very morose. However, being a king's daughter, she understood political diplomacy and decided that there was no use in simply becoming morose. Some steps should be taken immediately. After some deliberation, she decided to send a message to Kṛṣṇa, and so that she might not be deceived, she selected a qualified *brāhmaṇa* as her messenger. Such a qualified *brāhmaṇa* is always truthful and is a devotee of Viṣṇu. Without delay, the *brāhmaṇa* was sent to Dvārakā.

Reaching the gate of Dvārakā, the *brāhmaṇa* informed the doorkeeper of his arrival, and the doorkeeper led him to the place where Kṛṣṇa was sitting on a golden throne. Since the *brāhmaṇa* had the opportunity of being Rukmiṇī's messenger, he was fortunate enough to see the Supreme Personality of Godhead, Kṛṣṇa, who is the original cause of all causes. A *brāhmaṇa* is the spiritual teacher of all the social divisions. Lord Śrī Kṛṣṇa, in order to teach everyone the Vedic etiquette of how to respect a *brāhmaṇa*, immediately got up and offered him His throne. When the *brāhmaṇa* was seated on the golden throne, Lord Śrī Kṛṣṇa began to worship him exactly in the manner in which the demigods worship Kṛṣṇa. In this way, He taught everyone that worshiping His devotee is more valuable than worshiping Himself.

In due time, the *brāhmaṇa* took his bath, accepted his meals and took to rest on a bedstead completely bedecked with soft silk. As he was resting, Lord Śrī Kṛṣṇa silently approached and, with great respect, put the *brāhmaṇa's* legs on His lap and began to massage them. In this way, Kṛṣṇa appeared before the *brāhmaṇa* and said, "My dear *brāhmaṇa,* I hope that you are executing the religious principles without any difficulty and that your mind is always in a peaceful condition." Different classes of people in the social system are engaged in various professions, and when one inquires as to the well-being of a particular person, it must be done on the basis of that person's occupation. Therefore, when one inquires as to the welfare of a *brāhmaṇa,* the questions should be worded according to his condition of life so as not to disturb him. A peaceful mind is the basis for becoming truthful, clean, equipoised, self-controlled and tolerant. Thus by attaining knowledge and knowing its practical application in life, one becomes convinced about the Absolute Truth. The *brāhmaṇa* knew Kṛṣṇa to be the Supreme Personality of Godhead, and still he accepted the respectful service of the Lord on the grounds of Vedic social convention. Lord Śrī Kṛṣṇa was playing just like a human being. Belonging to the *kṣatriya* division of the social system, and being a young boy, it was His duty to show respect to such a *brāhmaṇa.*

Lord Kṛṣṇa continued: "O best of all the *brāhmaṇas,* you should always remain satisfied because if a *brāhmaṇa* is always self-satisfied he will not deviate from his prescribed duties; and simply by sticking to one's prescribed duties, everyone, especially the *brāhmaṇas,* can attain the highest perfection of all desires. Even if a person is as opulent as the King of heaven, Indra, if he is not satisfied he inevitably has to transmigrate from one planet to another. Such a person can never be happy under any circumstances; but if a person's mind is satisfied, even if he is bereft of his high position, he can be happy living anywhere and everywhere."

This instruction of Kṛṣṇa to the *brāhmaṇa* is very significant. The purport is that a true *brāhmaṇa* should not be disturbed in any situation. In this modern age of Kali-yuga, the so-called *brāhmaṇas* have accepted the abominable position of the *śūdras* or less than *śūdras* and still want to pass as qualified *brāhmaṇas.* Actually, a qualified *brāhmaṇa* always sticks to his own duties and never accepts those of a *śūdra* or of one less than a *śūdra.* It is advised in the authorized scriptures that a *brāhmaṇa* may, under awkward circumstances, accept the profession of a *kṣatriya* or even a *vaiśya,* but never is he to accept the profession of a *śūdra.* Lord Kṛṣṇa declared that a *brāhmaṇa* should never be disturbed by any adverse conditions of life if he scrupulously sticks to his religious principles. In conclusion, Lord Śrī Kṛṣṇa said: "I offer My respectful obeisances to the *brāhmaṇas* and Vaiṣṇavas, because the *brāhmaṇas* are always self-satisfied, and the Vaiṣṇavas are always engaged in actual welfare activities for the human society. They are the best friends of the people in general; both are free from false egoism and are always in a peaceful condition of mind."

Lord Kṛṣṇa then desired to know about the rulers (*kṣatriyas*) in the *brāhmaṇa's* kingdom, so He inquired whether the citizens of the kingdom were all happy. A king's qualification is judged by the temperament of the people in the kingdom. If they are very happy in all respects, it is to be understood that the king is honest and executing his duties rightly. Kṛṣṇa said that the king in whose kingdom the citizens are happy is very dear to Him. Of course Kṛṣṇa could understand that the *brāhmaṇa* had come with a confidential message; therefore he said, "If you have no objection, I am giving you permission to speak about your mission." Thus, being very satisfied by these transcendental pastimes with the Lord, the *brāhmaṇa* narrated the whole story of his mission to come and see Kṛṣṇa. He got out the letter which Rukmiṇī had written to Kṛṣṇa and said, "These are the words of Princess Rukmiṇī: 'My dear Kṛṣṇa, O infallible and most beautiful one, any human being who happens to hear about Your transcendental form and pastimes immediately absorbs through his ears Your name, fame and qualities; thus all his material pangs subside, and he fixes Your form in his heart. Through such transcendental love for You, he sees You always within himself; and by this process all his desires become fulfilled. Similarly, I have heard of Your transcendental qualities. I may be shameless in expressing myself so directly, but You have captivated me and taken my heart. You may suspect that I am an unmarried girl, young in age, and may doubt my steadiness of character, but my dear Mukunda, You are the supreme lion among the human beings, the supreme person among persons. Any girl, although not yet out of her home, or any woman who may be of the highest chastity, would desire to marry You, being captivated by Your unprecedented character, knowledge, opulence and position. I know that You are the husband of the goddess of fortune and that You are very kind toward Your devotees; therefore I have decided to become Your eternal maidservant. My dear Lord, I dedicate my life and soul unto Your lotus feet. I have accepted Your Lordship as my selected husband, and I therefore request You to accept me as Your wife. You are the supreme powerful, O lotus-eyed one. Now I belong to You. If that which is enjoyable for the lion to eat is taken away by the jackal, it will be a ludicrous affair; therefore I request You to immediately take care of me before I am taken away by Śiśupāla and other princes like him.

My dear Lord, in my previous life I may have done public welfare work like digging wells and growing trees, or pious activities such as performing ritualistic ceremonies and sacrifices and serving the superior spiritual master, the *brāhmaṇas* and Vaiṣṇavas. By these activities, perhaps I have pleased the Supreme Personality of Godhead, Nārāyaṇa. If this is so, then I wish that You, Lord Kṛṣṇa, the brother of Lord Balarāma, would please come here and catch hold of my hand so that I may not be touched by Śiśupāla and his company.'"

Rukmiṇī's marriage with Śiśupāla was already settled; therefore she suggested that Kṛṣṇa kidnap her so that this might be changed. This sort of marriage, in which the girl is kidnapped by force, is known as *rākṣasa* and is practiced among the *kṣatriyas,* or the administrative, martial spirited type of men. Because her marriage was already arranged to take place the next day, Rukmiṇī suggested that Kṛṣṇa come there incognito to kidnap her and then fight with Śiśupāla and his allies like the King of Magadha. Knowing that no one could conquer Kṛṣṇa and that He would certainly emerge victorious, she addressed Him as Ajita—the unconquerable. Rukmiṇī told Kṛṣṇa not to be concerned that many of her family members, including other women, might be wounded or even killed if the fighting took place within the palace. As the king of a country thinks of diplomatic ways to achieve his object, similarly Rukmiṇī, being the daughter of a king, was diplomatic in suggesting how this unnecessary and undesirable killing could be avoided.

She explained that it was the custom of her family to visit the temple of the goddess Durgā, their family deity, before a marriage. (The *kṣatriya* kings were mostly staunch Vaiṣṇavas, worshiping Lord Viṣṇu in either the Rādhā-Kṛṣṇa or Lakṣmī-Nārāyaṇa form; still, for their material welfare, they used to worship the goddess Durgā. They never made the mistake, however, of accepting the demigods as the Supreme Lord on the level of *Viṣṇu-tattva,* as did some of the less intelligent men.) In order to avoid the unnecessary killing of her relatives, Rukmiṇī suggested that it would be easiest for Him to kidnap her while she was either going from the palace to the temple or else while she was returning home.

She also explained to Kṛṣṇa why she was so anxious to be married to Him, even though her marriage was to take place with Śiśupāla, who was also qualified, being the son of a great king. Rukmiṇī said that she did not think anyone was greater than Kṛṣṇa, not even Lord Śiva, who is known as Mahādeva, the greatest of all demigods. Lord Śiva also seeks the pleasure of Lord Kṛṣṇa in order to be delivered from his entanglement in the quality of ignorance within the material world. In spite of the fact that Lord

Śiva is the greatest of all great souls, *mahātmās,* he keeps on his head the purifying water of the Ganges, which emanates from a hole in this material universe made by the toe of Lord Viṣṇu. Lord Śiva is in charge of the material quality of ignorance, and in order to keep himself in a transcendental position, he always meditates on Lord Viṣṇu. Therefore Rukmiṇī knew very well that obtaining the favor of Kṛṣṇa was not an easy job. If even Lord Śiva must purify himself for this purpose, surely it would be difficult for Rukmiṇī, who was only the daughter of a *kṣatriya* king. Thus she desired to dedicate her life to observing severe austerities and penances, such as fasting and going without bodily comforts. If it were not possible in this lifetime to gain Kṛṣṇa's favor by these activities, she was prepared to do the same lifetime after lifetime. In the *Bhagavad-gītā* it is said that pure devotees of the Lord execute devotional service with great determination. Such determination, as exhibited by Rukmiṇīdevī, is the only price for purchasing Kṛṣṇa's favor and is the way to ultimate success in Kṛṣṇa consciousness.

After explaining Rukmiṇīdevī's statement to Kṛṣṇa, the *brāhmaṇa* said: "My dear Kṛṣṇa, chief of the Yadu dynasty, I have brought this confidential message for You from Rukmiṇī; now it is placed before You for Your consideration. After due deliberation You can act as You please, but if You want to do something, You must do it immediately. There is not much time left for action."

Thus ends the Bhaktivedanta purport of the Fifty-first Chapter of Kṛṣṇa, *"Kṛṣṇa, the Ranchor."*

52 / Kṛṣṇa Kidnaps Rukmiṇī

After hearing Rukmiṇī's statement, Lord Kṛṣṇa was very pleased. He immediately shook hands with the *brāhmaṇa* and said: "My dear *brāhmaṇa*, I am very glad to hear that Rukmiṇī is anxious to marry Me, since I am also anxious to get her hand. My mind is always absorbed in the thought of the daughter of Bhīṣmaka, and sometimes I cannot sleep at night because I am thinking of her. I can understand that the marriage of Rukmiṇī with Śiśupāla has been arranged by her elder brother in a spirit of animosity toward Me; so I am determined to give a good lesson to all of these princes. Just as fire is extracted and utilized after manipulating ordinary wood, similarly, after dealing with these demoniac princes, I shall bring forth Rukmiṇī, like fire, from their midst."

Kṛṣṇa, upon being informed of the specific date of Rukmiṇī's marriage, became anxious to leave immediately. He asked His driver, Dāruka, to harness the horses for His chariot and prepare to go to the kingdom of Vidarbha. The driver, just after hearing this order, brought Kṛṣṇa's four special horses. The names and descriptions of these horses are mentioned in the *Padma Purāṇa.* The first one, Śaivya, was greenish; the second, Sugrīva, was grayish like ice; the third, Meghapuṣpa, was the color of a new cloud; and the last, Balāhaka, was of ashen color. When the horses were yoked and the chariot ready to go, Kṛṣṇa helped the *brāhmaṇa* up and gave him a seat by His side. Immediately they started from Dvārakā and within one night arrived at the province of Vidarbha. The kingdom of Dvārakā is situated in the western part of India, and Vidarbha is situated in the northern part. They are separated by a distance of not less than 1,000 miles, but the horses were so fast that they reached their destination, a town called Kuṇḍina, within one night, or at most, twelve hours.

King Bhīṣmaka was not very enthusiastic about handing his daughter over to Śiśupāla, but he was obliged to accept the marriage settlement due to his affectionate attachment for his eldest son, who had negotiated it. As a matter of duty, he was decorating the city for the marriage ceremony and was acting in great earnestness to make it very successful. Water was sprinkled all over the streets, and the city was cleansed very nicely. Since India is situated in the tropical zone, the atmosphere is always dry. Due to this, dust always accumulates on the streets and roads; so they must be sprinkled with water at least once a day, and in big cities like Calcutta, twice a day. The roads of Kuṇḍina were arranged with colored flags and festoons, and gates were constructed at particular crossings. The whole city was decorated very nicely. The beauty of the city was enhanced by the inhabitants, both men and women, who were dressed in washed cloth, decorated with sandalwood pulp, pearl necklaces and flower garlands. Incense was burning everywhere, and fragrances like *aguru* scented the air. Priests and *brāhmaṇas* were sumptuously fed and, according to ritualistic ceremony, were given sufficient wealth and cows in charity. In this way, they were engaged in chanting Vedic hymns. The King's daughter, Rukmiṇī, was exquisitely beautiful. She was very clean and had beautiful teeth. The auspicious sacred girdle was tied on her wrist. She was given various types of jewelry to put on and long silken cloth to cover the upper and lower parts of her body. Learned priests gave her protection by chanting *mantras* from the *Sāma Veda, Ṛg Veda* and *Yajur Veda.* After this they chanted *mantras* from the *Atharva Veda* and offered oblations in the fire to pacify the ominous conjunctions of different stars.

King Bhīṣmaka was very experienced in dealing with the *brāhmaṇas* and priests when such ceremonies were held. He specifically distinguished the *brāhmaṇas* by giving them large quantities of gold and silver, grains mixed with molasses, and cows decorated with golden ornaments. Damaghoṣa, Śiśupāla's father, executed all kinds of ritualistic performances to invoke good fortune for his own family. Śiśupāla's father was known as Damaghoṣa due to his superior ability to cut down unregulated citizens. *Dama* means curbing down, and *ghoṣa* means famous; so he was famous for controlling the citizens. Damaghoṣa thought that if Kṛṣṇa came to disturb the marriage ceremony, he would certainly cut Him down with his military power. Therefore, after performing the various auspicious ceremonies, Damaghoṣa gathered his military divisions, known as Madasravi. He took many elephants, garlanded with golden necklaces, and many chariots and horses which were similarly decorated. It appeared that Damaghoṣa, along with his son and other companions, was going to Kuṇḍina, not completely forgetting the marriage, but mainly intent on fighting.

When King Bhīṣmaka learned that Damaghoṣa and his party were arriving, he left the city to receive them. Outside the city gate there were many gardens where the guests were welcomed to stay. In the Vedic system of marriage, the bride's father receives the large party of the bridegroom and accomodates them in a suitable place for two or three days until the marriage ceremony is performed. The party led by Damaghoṣa contained thousands of men, among whom the prominent kings and personalities were Jarāsandha, Dantavakra, Vidūratha and Pauṇḍraka. It was an open secret that Rukmiṇī was meant to be married to Kṛṣṇa but that her elder brother, Rukmī, had arranged her marriage to Śiśupāla. There was also some whispering going on about a rumor that Rukmiṇī had sent a messenger to Kṛṣṇa; therefore the soldiers suspected that Kṛṣṇa might cause a disturbance by attempting to kidnap Rukmiṇī. Even though they were not without fear, they were all prepared to give Kṛṣṇa a nice fight in order to prevent the girl from being taken away. Śrī Balarāma received the news that Kṛṣṇa had left for Kuṇḍina accompanied only by a *brāhmaṇa;* He also heard that Śiśupāla was there with a large number of soldiers. Suspecting that they would attack Kṛṣṇa, Balarāma took strong military divisions of chariots, infantry, horses and elephants and arrived at the precinct of Kuṇḍina.

Meanwhile, inside the palace, Rukmiṇī was expecting Kṛṣṇa to arrive, but when neither He nor the *brāhmaṇa* who took her message appeared, she became full of anxiety and began to think how unfortunate she was. "There is only one night between today and my marriage day, and still neither the *brāhmaṇa* nor Śyāmasundara has returned. I cannot ascertain any reason for this." Having little hope, she thought perhaps Kṛṣṇa had found reason to become dissatisfied and had rejected her fair proposal. As a result, the *brāhmaṇa* might have become disappointed and not come back. Although she was thinking of various causes for the delay, she expected them both at every moment.

Rukmiṇī further began to think that demigods such as Lord Brahmā, Lord Śiva and the goddess Durgā might have been displeased. It is generally said that the demigods become angry when they are not properly worshiped. For instance, when Indra found that the inhabitants of Vṛndāvana were not worshiping him (Kṛṣṇa having stopped the Indra-yajña), he became very angry and wanted to chastise them. Thus Rukmiṇī was thinking that since she did not worship Lord Śiva or Lord Brahmā very much, they might have become angry and tried to frustrate her plan. Similarly she thought that the goddess Durgā, the wife of Lord Śiva, might have taken the side of her husband. Lord Śiva is known as Rudra, and his wife is known as Rudrāṇī. Rudrāṇī and Rudra refer to those who are very accustomed to putting others in a distressed condition so they might cry forever. Rukmiṇī was thinking of the goddess Durgā as Girijā, the daughter of the Himalayan Mountains. The Himalayan Mountains are very cold and hard, and she thought of the goddess Durgā as hardhearted and cold. In her anxiety to see Kṛṣṇa, Rukmiṇī, who was after all still a child, thought this way about the different demigods. The *gopīs* worship goddess Kātyāyanī to get Kṛṣṇa as their husband; similarly Rukmiṇī was thinking of the various types of demigods, not for material benefit, but in respect to Kṛṣṇa. Praying to the demigods to achieve the favor of Kṛṣṇa is not irregular, and Rukmiṇī was fully absorbed in thoughts of Kṛṣṇa.

Even though she pacified herself by thinking that the time for Govinda to arrive had not yet expired, Rukmiṇī felt that she was hoping against hope. She began to shed tears, and when they became more forceful, she closed her eyes in helplessness. While Rukmiṇī was in such deep thought, auspicious symptoms appeared in different parts of her body. Trembling began to occur in her left eyelid and in her arms and thighs. When trembling occurs in these parts of the body, it is an auspicious sign indicating that something lucrative can be expected.

Just then, Rukmiṇī, full of anxiety, saw the *brāhmaṇa* messenger. Kṛṣṇa, being the Supersoul of all living beings, could understand Rukmiṇī's anxiety; therefore he sent the *brāhmaṇa* inside the palace to let her know that He had arrived. When Rukmiṇī saw the *brāhmaṇa,* she could understand the auspicious trembling of her body and immediately became elated. She smiled and inquired from him whether or not Kṛṣṇa had already come. The *brāhmaṇa* replied that the son of the Yadu dynasty, Śrī Kṛṣṇa, had arrived; he further encouraged her by saying that Kṛṣṇa had promised to carry her away without fail. Rukmiṇī was so elated by the *brāhmaṇa's* message that she wanted to give him in charity everything she possessed. However, finding nothing suitable for presentation, she simply offered him her respectful obeisances. The significance of offering respectful obeisances to a superior is that the one offering obeisances is obliged to the respected person. In other words, Rukmiṇī implied that she would remain ever grateful to the *brāhmaṇa.* Anyone who gets the favor of the goddess of fortune, as did this *brāhmaṇa,* is without a doubt always happy in material opulence.

When King Bhīṣmaka heard that Kṛṣṇa and Balarāma had come, he invited Them to see the marriage ceremony of his daughter. Immediately he arranged to receive Them, along with Their soldiers, in a suitable garden house. As was the Vedic custom, the King offered Kṛṣṇa and

Balarāma honey and fresh washed cloth. He was hospitable not only to Kṛṣṇa, Balarāma and kings such as Jarāsandha, but he also received many other kings and princes according to their respective personal strength, age and material possessions. Out of curiosity and eagerness, the people of Kuṇḍina assembled before Kṛṣṇa and Balarāma and began to drink the nectar of Their beauty. With tearful eyes, they offered Them their silent respects. They were very pleased, considering Lord Kṛṣṇa the suitable match for Rukmiṇī. They were so eager to unite Kṛṣṇa and Rukmiṇī that they began to pray to the Personality of Godhead: "My dear Lord, if we have performed any pious activities that You are satisfied with, kindly be merciful upon us and accept the hand of Rukmiṇī." It appears that Rukmiṇī was a very popular princess, and all the citizens, out of intense love for her, prayed for her best fortune. In the meantime, Rukmiṇī, being very nicely dressed and protected by bodyguards, came out of the palace to visit the temple of Ambikā, the goddess Durgā.

Deity worship in the temple has been in existence since the beginning of Vedic culture. There is a class of men described in the *Bhagavad-gītā* as the *veda-vāda-rata;* they only believe in the Vedic ritualistic ceremonies, but not in the temple worship. Such foolish people may here take note that although this marriage of Kṛṣṇa and Rukmiṇī took place more than 5,000 years ago, there were arrangements for temple worship. In the *Bhagavad-gītā* the Lord says, *yānti deva-vratā devān:* "The worshipers of the demigods attain the abodes of the demigods." There were many people who worshiped the demigods and many who directly worshiped the Supreme Personality of Godhead. The system of demigod worship was directed mainly to Lord Brahmā, Lord Siva, Lord Gaṇeśa, the sun-god and the goddess Durgā. Lord Śiva and the goddess Durgā were worshiped even by the royal families; other minor demigods were worshiped by silly inferior people. As far as the *brāhmaṇas* and Vaiṣṇavas are concerned, they simply worship Lord Viṣṇu, the Supreme Personality of Godhead. In the *Bhagavad-gītā* the worship of demigods is condemned, but not forbidden; there it is clearly stated that the less intelligent class of men worship the different kinds of demigods for material benefit. On the other hand, even though Rukmiṇī was the goddess of fortune, she went to the temple of the goddess Durgā because the family deity was worshiped there. In the *Śrīmad-Bhāgavatam* it is stated that as Rukmiṇī was proceeding towards the temple of the goddess Durgā, within her heart she was always thinking of the lotus feet of Kṛṣṇa. Therefore when Rukmiṇī went to the temple it was not with the intention of an ordinary person, who goes to beg for material benefits; her only target was Kṛṣṇa. When people go to the temple of a demigod, the objective is actually Kṛṣṇa, since it is He who empowers the demigods to provide material benefits.

As Rukmiṇī proceeded toward the temple, she was very silent and grave. Her mother and her girl friend were by her side, and the wife of a *brāhmaṇa* was in the center; surrounding her were royal bodyguards. (This custom of a would-be bride going to the temple of a demigod is still practiced in India.) As the procession continued, various musical sounds were heard. Drums, conchshells, and bugles of different sizes such as *paṇavas, turyas* and *bheris* combined to make a sound which was not only auspicious but very sweet to hear. There were thousands of wives of respectable *brāhmaṇas* present. These women were all dressed very nicely with suitable ornaments. They presented Rukmiṇī with flower garlands, sandalwood pulp and a variety of colorful garments to assist her in worshiping Lord Śiva and the goddess Durgā. Some of these ladies were very old and knew perfectly well how to chant prayers to the goddess Durgā and Lord Siva; so, followed by Rukmiṇī and others, they led these prayers before the deity.

Rukmiṇī offered her prayers to the deity by saying, "My dear goddess Durgā, I offer my respectful obeisances unto you as well as to your children." The goddess Durgā has four famous children: two daughters–the goddess of fortune, Lakṣmī, and the goddess of learning, Sarasvatī–and two famous sons, Lord Gaṇeśa and Lord Kārttikeya. They are all considered to be demigods and goddesses. Since the goddess Durgā is always worshiped along with her famous children, Rukmiṇī specifically offered her respectful obeisances to the deity in that way; however her prayers were different. Ordinary people pray to the goddess Durgā for material wealth, fame, profit, strength and so on; Rukmiṇī, however, desired to have Kṛṣṇa for her husband and therefore prayed to the deity to be pleased upon her and bless her. Since she desired only Kṛṣṇa, her worship of the demigods is not condemned. While Rukmiṇī was praying, a variety of items were presented before the deity, chief of which were water, different kinds of flames, incense, garments, garlands and various foodstuffs prepared with ghee, such as *puris* and *kacuris.* There were also fruits, sugar cane, betel nuts and spices offered. With great devotion, Rukmiṇī offered them to the deity according to the regulative principles directed by the old *brāhmaṇa* ladies. After this ritualistic ceremony, the ladies offered the remnants of the foodstuffs to Rukmiṇī as *prasādam,* which she accepted with great respect. Then Rukmiṇī offered her obeisances to the ladies and to the goddess Durgā. After the business of deity worship was finished, Rukmiṇī caught hold of the hand of one of her girl friends and left the temple, accompanied by the others.

All the princes and visitors who came to Kuṇḍina for the marriage were assembled outside the temple to see Rukmiṇī. The princes were especially very eager to see her because they all actually thought that they would have Rukmiṇī as their wife. Struck with wonder upon seeing Rukmiṇī, they thought that she was specially manufactured by the Creator to bewilder all the great chivalrous princes. Her body was well-constructed, the middle portion being thin. She had green eyes, pink lips, and a beautiful face which was enhanced by her scattered hair and by different kinds of earrings. Around her feet she wore jeweled lockets. The bodily luster and beauty of Rukmiṇī appeared as if painted by an artist perfectly presenting beauty following the description of great poets. The breast of Rukmiṇī is described as being a little bit high, indicating that she was just a youth not more than thirteen or fourteen years old. Her beauty was specifically intended to attract the attention of Krsna. Although the princes gazed upon her beautiful features, she was not at all proud. Her eyes moved restlessly, and when she smiled very simply, like an innocent girl, her teeth appeared just like lotus flowers. Expecting Kṛṣṇa to take her away at any moment, she proceeded very slowly towards her home. Her legs moved just like a full-grown swan, and her ankle bells tinkled very mildly.

As already explained, the great chivalrous princes who assembled there were so overwhelmed by Rukmiṇī's beauty that they almost became unconscious. Full of lust, they hopelessly desired Rukminī's hand, comparing their own beauty with hers. Śrīmatī Rukminī, however, was not interested in any of them; in her heart she was simply expecting Kṛṣṇa to come and carry her away. As she was adjusting the ornaments on her left-hand finger, she happened to look upon the princes and suddenly saw that Kṛṣṇa was present amongst them. Although Rukmiṇī had never before seen Kṛṣṇa, she was always thinking of Him; thus she had no difficulty in recognizing Him amongst the princely order. Krsna, not being concerned with the other princes, immediately took the opportunity of placing Rukmiṇī on His chariot, marked by a flag bearing an image of Garuda. He then proceeded slowly, without fear, taking away Rukminī exactly as the lion takes the deer from the midst of the jackals. Meanwhile Balarāma appeared on the scene with the soldiers of the Yadu dynasty.

Jarāsandha, who had many times experienced defeat by Kṛṣṇa, began to roar: "How is this? Kṛṣṇa is taking Rukmiṇī away from us without any opposition! What is the use in our being chivalrous fighters with arrows? My dear princes, just look! We are losing our reputation by this action. It is just like the jackal taking away the booty from the lion."

Thus ends the Bhaktivedanta purport of the Fifty-second Chapter of Kṛṣṇa, *"Kṛṣṇa Kidnaps Rukminī."*

53 / Kṛṣṇa Defeats All the Princes and Takes Rukmiṇī Home to Dvārakā

All the princes led by Jarāsandha became very angry at Kṛṣṇa's kidnapping Rukmiṇī. Struck by the beauty of Rukmiṇī, they had fallen from the backs of their horses and elephants, but now they began to stand up and properly arm themselves. Picking up their bows and arrows, they began to chase Kṛṣṇa on their chariots, horses and elephants. To check their progress, the soldiers of the Yadu dynasty turned and faced them. Thus terrible fighting between the two belligerant groups began. The princes opposing Kṛṣṇa were led by Jarāsandha, and they were all very expert in fighting. They began to shoot their arrows at the soldiers of Yadu just as a cloud splashes the face of a mountain with torrents of rain. Gathered on the face of a mountain, a cloud does not move very much, and therefore the force of rain is much more severe on a mountain than it is anywhere else.

The opposing princes were determined to defeat Kṛṣṇa and recapture Rukmiṇī from His custody, and they fought with Him as severely as possible. Rukmiṇī, seated by the side of Kṛṣṇa, saw arrows raining from the opposing party onto the faces of the soldiers of Yadu. In a fearful attitude, she began to look on the face of Kṛṣṇa, expressing her gratefulness that He had taken such a great risk for her sake only. Her eyes moving, she appeared to be very sorry, and Kṛṣṇa could immediately understand her mind. He encouraged her with these words: "My dear Rukmiṇī, don't worry. Please rest assured that the soldiers of the Yadu dynasty will kill all the opposing soldiers without delay."

As Kṛṣṇa was speaking with Rukmiṇī, the commanders of the Yadu dynasty's soldiers, headed by Lord Balarāma, who is also known as Saṅkarṣaṇa, as well as by Gadadhara, not tolerating the defiant attitude of the opposing soldiers, began to strike their horses, elephants, and chariots with arrows. As the fighting progressed, the princes and soldiers of the enemy camp began to fall from their horses, elephants and chariots. Within a very short time, it was seen that millions of severed heads, decorated with helmets and earrings, had fallen on the battlefield. The soldiers' hands were cut up along with their bows and arrows and clubs; one head was piled upon another, and one horse was piled upon another. All the infantry soldiers, as well as their camels, elephants and asses, fell down with severed heads.

When the enemy, headed by Jarāsandha, found that they were gradually being defeated by the soldiers of Kṛṣṇa, they thought it unwise to risk losing in the battle for the sake of Śiśupāla. Śiśupāla himself should have fought to rescue Rukmiṇī from the hands of Kṛṣṇa, but when the soldiers saw that Śiśupāla was not competent enough to fight with Kṛṣṇa, they decided not to lose their strength unnecessarily; therefore they ceased fighting and dispersed.

Some of the princes, as a matter of etiquette, appeared before Śiśupāla. They saw that Śiśupāla was very much discouraged, like one who has lost his wife. His face appeared to be dried up, he had lost all his energy, and all the luster of his body had disappeared. They began to address Śiśupāla thus: "My dear Śiśupāla, don't be discouraged in this way. You belong to the royal order and are the chief amongst the fighters. There is no question of distress or happiness for a person like you because neither of these conditions is everlasting. Take courage. Don't be disappointed by this temporary reverse. After all, we are not the final actor; as puppets dance in the hands of a magician, we are all dancing by the will of the Supreme, and according to His grace only we suffer distress or enjoy happiness, which therefore balance equally in all circumstances."

The whole catastrophe of the defeat was due to the envious nature of Rukmiṇī's elder brother, Rukmī. Having seen his sister forcibly taken away by Kṛṣṇa after he had planned to marry her with Śiśupāla, Rukmī was frustrated. So he and Śiśupāla, his friend and intended brother-in-law, returned to their respective homes. Rukmī, very much agitated, was determined to personally teach Kṛṣṇa a lesson. He called for his own soldiers—a military phalanx consisting of several thousand elephants, horses, chariots and infantry—and, equipped with this military strength, he began to follow Kṛṣṇa to Dvārakā. In order to show his prestige, Rukmī began to promise before all the returning kings, "You could not help Śiśupāla marry my sister Rukmiṇī, but I cannot allow Rukmiṇī to be taken away by Kṛṣṇa. I shall teach Him a lesson. Now I am going there." He presented himself as a big commander and vowed before all the princes present, "Unless I kill Kṛṣṇa in the fight and bring back my sister from

His clutches, I shall no more return to my capital city, Kuṇḍina. I make this vow before you all, and you will see that I shall fulfill it." After thus vibrating all these boasting words, Rukmī immediately got on his chariot and told his chariot driver to pursue Kṛṣṇa. He said, "I want to fight with Him immediately. This cowherd boy has become very proud because of His tricky way of fighting with the *kṣatriyas*, but today I shall teach Him a good lesson. Because He has the impudency to kidnap my sister, I, with my sharpened arrows, shall teach Him very good lessons indeed." Thus this unintelligent man, Rukmī, ignorant of the extent of the strength and activities of the Supreme Personality of Godhead, began to voice impudent threats.

In great stupidity he soon stood before Kṛṣṇa, telling Him repeatedly, "Stop for a minute and fight with me!" After saying this he drew his bow and directly shot three forceful arrows against Kṛṣṇa's body. Then he condemned Kṛṣṇa as the most abominable descendant of the Yadu dynasty and asked Him to stand before him for a minute so that he could teach Him a good lesson. "You are carrying away my sister just like a crow stealing clarified butter meant for use in a sacrifice. You are simply proud of Your military strength, but You cannot fight according to regulative principles. You have stolen my sister; now I shall relieve You of Your false prestige. You can keep my sister under Your possession only as long as I do not pinion You to the ground for good with my arrows."

Lord Kṛṣṇa, after hearing all these crazy words from Rukmī, immediately shot an arrow and severed the string of Rukmī's bow, making him unable to use another arrow. Rukmī immediately took another bow and shot another five arrows at Kṛṣṇa. Being attacked for the second time by Rukmī, Kṛṣṇa again severed his bowstring. Rukmī took a third bow, and Kṛṣṇa again cut off its string. This time, in order to teach Rukmī a lesson, Kṛṣṇa personally shot six arrows at him, and then He shot another eight arrows. Thus four horses were killed by four arrows, the chariot driver was killed by another arrow, and the upper portion of Rukmī's chariot, including the flag, was chopped off with the remaining three arrows.

Having run out of arrows, Rukmī took the assistance of swords, shields, tridents, lances and similar other weapons used for fighting hand-to-hand, but Kṛṣṇa immediately severed them all in the same way. Being repeatedly baffled in his attempts, Rukmī simply took his sword and ran very swiftly toward Kṛṣṇa, just as a fly proceeds toward a fire. As soon as Rukmī reached Kṛṣṇa, Kṛṣṇa cut his weapon to pieces. This time Kṛṣṇa took out His sharp sword and was about to kill him immediately, but Rukmī's sister Rukmiṇī, understanding that this time Kṛṣṇa would not excuse her brother, fell down at the lotus feet of Kṛṣṇa and in a very grievous tone, trembling with great fear, began to plead with her husband.

Rukmiṇī first addressed Kṛṣṇa as "Yogeśvara." Yogeśvara means one who is possessed of inconceivable opulence and energy. Kṛṣṇa possesses inconceivable opulence and energy, whereas Rukmiṇī's brother had only limited military potency. Kṛṣṇa is immeasurable, whereas her brother was measured in every step of his life. Therefore, Rukmī was not even comparable to an insignificant insect before the unlimited power of Kṛṣṇa. She also addressed Kṛṣṇa as the God of the gods. There are many powerful demigods, such as Lord Brahmā, Lord Śiva, Indra, and Candra; Kṛṣṇa is the Lord of all these gods, whereas Rukmiṇī's brother was not only an ordinary human being, but was, in fact, the lowest of all because he had no understanding of Kṛṣṇa. In other words, a human being who has no conception of the actual position of Kṛṣṇa is the lowest in human society. Rukmiṇī also addressed Kṛṣṇa as "Jagatpati," the master of the whole cosmic manifestation. In comparison, her brother was only a ordinary prince.

In this way, Rukmiṇī compared the position of Rukmī to that of Kṛṣṇa and very feelingly pleaded with her husband not to kill her brother just before the auspicious time of her being united with Kṛṣṇa, but to excuse him. In other words, she displayed her real position as a woman. She was happy to get Kṛṣṇa as her husband just at the moment when her marriage to another was to be performed, but she did not want it to be at the loss of her elder brother, who, after all, loved his young sister and wanted to hand her over to one who was, according to his own calculations, a better man. While Rukmiṇī was praying to Kṛṣṇa for the life of her brother, her whole body trembled, and because of her anxiety, her face appeared to be dried up, her throat became choked, and, due to her trembling, the ornaments on her body loosened and fell scattered on the ground. Lord Kṛṣṇa immediately became compassionate and agreed not to kill the foolish Rukmī. But, at the same time, He wanted to give him some light punishment, so He tied him up with a piece of cloth and snipped at his moustache, beard and hair, keeping some spots here and there.

While Kṛṣṇa was dealing with Rukmī in this way, the soldiers of the Yadu dynasty, commanded by Balarāma Himself, broke the whole strength of Rukmī's army just as an elephant in a tank discards the feeble stem of a lotus flower. In other words, as an elephant breaks the whole construction of a lotus flower while bathing in the reservoir of water, so the military strength of the Yadus broke up Rukmī's forces. Yet when the commanders of the Yadu dynasty came back to see Kṛṣṇa, they were all surprised to see the condition of Rukmī. Lord Balarāma became especially compassionate for His sister-in-law, who was newly married to His brother. In order to please Rukmiṇī, Balarāma personally untied Rukmī, and in order to further please her, Balarāma, as the elder brother of Kṛṣṇa, spoke some words of chastisement. "Kṛṣṇa, Your action is not at all satisfactory," He said. "This is an abomination very much contrary to our family tradition! To cut someone's hair and shave his moustache and beard is almost comparable to killing him. Whatever Rukmī might have been, he is now our brother-in-law, a relative of our family, and You should not have put him in such a condition."

After this, in order to pacify her, Lord Balarāma said to Rukmiṇī, "You should not be sorry because your brother has been made very odd-looking. Everyone suffers or enjoys the results of his own actions." Lord Balarāma wanted to impress upon Rukmiṇī that she should not have been sorry for the consequences suffered by her brother due to his actions. There was no need of being too affectionate toward such a brother. Lord Balarāma again turned toward Kṛṣṇa and said, "My dear Kṛṣṇa, a relative, even though he commits such a blunder and deserves to be killed, should be excused. For when such a relative is conscious of his own fault, that consciousness itself is like death. Therefore, there is no need in killing him." He again turned toward Rukmiṇī and informed her that the current duty of the *kṣatriya* in the human society is so fixed that, according to the principles of fighting, one's own brother may become an enemy on the opposite side. A *kṣatriya* does not hesitate to kill his own brother. In other words, Lord Balarāma wanted to instruct Rukmiṇī that Rukmī and Kṛṣṇa were right in not showing mercy to each other in the fighting, despite the family consideration that they happened to be brothers-in-law. Śrī Balarāma continued to inform Rukmiṇī that *kṣatriyas* are typical emblems of the materialistic way of life; they become puffed-up whenever there is a question of material acquisition. Therefore, when there is a fight between two belligerent *kṣatriyas* on account of kingdom, land, wealth, women, prestige or power, they try to put one another into the most abominable condition. Balarāma instructed Rukmiṇī that her affection toward her brother Rukmī, who had created enmity with so many persons, was a perverse consideration befitting an ordinary materialistic person. Her brother's character was not at all adorable, considering his treatment toward other friends, and yet Rukmiṇī, as an ordinary woman, was so affectionate toward him. He was not fit to be her brother, and still Rukmiṇī was lenient toward him.

"Besides that," Balarāma continued, "the consideration that a person is neutral or is one's friend or enemy is generally made by persons who are in the bodily concept of life. Such foolish persons become bewildered by the illusory energy of the Supreme Lord. The spirit soul is of the same pure quality in any embodiment of matter, but those who are not sufficiently intelligent see only the bodily differentiations of animals and men, literates and illiterates, rich and poor, and so on, which cover the pure spirit soul. Such differentiation, observed purely on the basis of the body, is exactly like differentiation between fires in terms of the different types of fuel they consume. Whatever the size and shape of the fuel, there is no such variety of size and shape of the fire which comes out. Similarly, in the sky there are no differences in size or shape."

In this way Balarāma appeased them by His moral and ethical instruction. He stated further: "This body is part of the material manifestation. The living entity or spirit soul, being in contact with matter, is transmigrating, due to illusory enjoyment, from one body to another, and that is known as material existence. This contact of the living entity with the material manifestation has neither integration nor disintegration. My dear chaste sister-in-law, the spirit soul is, of course, the cause of this material body, as much as the sun is the cause of sunlight, eyesight and the forms of material manifestation. The example of the sunshine and the material manifestation is very appropriate in the matter of understanding the living entities' contact with this material world. In the morning, there is sunrise, and the heat and light expand gradually throughout the whole day. The sun is the cause of all material production and shapes and forms; it is due to the sun that integration and disintegration of material elements take place. But as soon as the sun is set, the whole manifestation is no longer connected to the sun, which has passed from one place to another. When the sun passes from the eastern to the western hemisphere, the result of interaction due to the sunshine in the eastern hemisphere remains, but the sunshine itself is visible again on the western hemisphere. Similarly, the living entity accepts or produces different bodies and different bodily relationships in a particular circumstance, but as soon as he gives up the present body and accepts another, he has nothing to do with the former body. Similarly, the living entity has nothing to do with the next body which he accepts. He is always free from the contact of this bodily contamination. Therefore, the conclusion is that the appearance and disappearance of the body have nothing to do with the living entity, as much as the waxing and waning of the moon have nothing to do with the moon. When there is waxing of the moon, we falsely think that the moon is developing, and when there is waning of the moon we think that the moon is decreasing. Factually the moon, as it is, is always the same; it has nothing to do with such visible waxing and waning activities.

"Consciousness of material existence can be compared to sleeping and dreaming. When a man sleeps, he dreams of many nonfactual happenings, and as a result of dreaming he becomes subjected to different kinds of distress and happiness. Similarly, when a person is in the dreaming condition of material consciousness, he suffers the effects of accepting a body and giving it up again in material existence. Opposite to this material consciousness is Kṛṣṇa consciousness. In other words, when a man is elevated to the platform of Kṛṣṇa consciousness he becomes free from this false conception of life."

In this way, Śrī Balarāma instructed them in spiritual knowledge. He addressed his sister-in-law thus: "Sweet, smiling Rukmiṇī, do not be aggrieved by false motives caused by ignorance. Due to false notions only one becomes unhappy, but this unhappiness is immediately removed by discussing the philosophy of actual life. Be happy on that platform only."

After hearing such enlightening instruction from Śrī Balarāma, Rukmiṇī immediately became pacified and happy and adjusted her mental condition, which was very much afflicted by seeing the degraded position of her brother, Rukmī. As far as Rukmī was concerned, neither was his promise fulfilled nor his mission successful. He had come from home with his soldiers and military phalanx to defeat Kṛṣṇa and release his sister, but on the contrary, he lost all his soldiers and military strength. He was personally much degraded, and in that condition he was very sorry; but by the grace of the Lord he could continue his life to the fixed destination. Because he was a *kṣatriya*, he could remember his promise that he would not return to his capital city, Kuṇḍina, without killing Kṛṣṇa and releasing his sister, which he had failed to do; therefore, he decided in anger not to return to his capital city, and he constructed a small cottage in the village known as Bhojakaṭa and began to reside there for the rest of his life.

After defeating all the opposing elements and forcibly carrying away Rukmiṇī, Kṛṣṇa brought her to His capital city, Dvārakā, and then married her according to the Vedic ritualistic principle. After this marriage, Kṛṣṇa became the King of the Yadus at Dvārakā. On the occasion of His marriage with Rukmiṇī, all the inhabitants were happy, and in every house there were great ceremonies. The inhabitants of Dvārakā City became so pleased that they dressed themselves with the nicest possible ornaments and garments, and they went to present gifts according to their means to the newly married couple, Kṛṣṇa and Rukmiṇī. All the houses of Yadupurī

(Dvārakā) were decorated with flags, festoons and flowers. Each and every house had an extra gate specifically prepared for this occasion, and on both sides of the gate there were big water jugs filled with water. The whole city was flavored by the burning of high quality incense, and at night there was illumination by thousands of lamps, decorating each and every building.

The entire city appeared jubilant on the occasion of Lord Kṛṣṇa's marriage with Rukmiṇī. Everywhere in the city there was profuse decoration of banana trees and betel nut trees. These two trees are considered very auspicious in happy ceremonies. At the same time there was an assembly of many elephants, who carried the respective kings of different friendly kingdoms. It is the habit of the elephant that whenever he sees some small plants and trees, out of his sportive frivolous nature, he uproots the trees and throws them hither and thither. The elephants assembled on this occasion also scattered the banana and betel nut trees, but in spite of such intoxicated action, the whole city, with the trees thrown here and there, looked very nice.

The friendly kings of the Kurus and the Pāṇḍavas were represented by Dhṛtarāṣṭra, the five Pāṇḍu brothers, King Drupada, King Santardana, as well as Rukmiṇī's father, Bhīṣmaka. Because of Kṛṣṇa's kidnapping Rukmiṇī, there was initially some misunderstanding between the two families, but Bhīṣmaka, King of Vidarbha, being approached by Śrī Balarāma and persuaded by many saintly persons, was induced to participate in the marriage ceremony of Kṛṣṇa and Rukmiṇī. Although the incidence of Kṛṣṇa's kidnapping was not a very happy occurrence in the kingdom of Vidarbha, kidnapping was not an unusual affair among the *kṣatriyas.* Kidnapping was, in fact, current in almost all marriages. Anyway, King Bhīṣmaka was from the very beginning inclined to hand over his beautiful daughter to Kṛṣṇa. In one way or another his purpose had been served, and so he was pleased to join the marriage ceremony, even though his eldest son was degraded in the fight. It is mentioned in the *Padma Purāṇa* that Mahārāja Nanda and the cowherd boys of Vṛndāvana joined the marriage ceremony. Kings from the kingdoms of Kuru, Sṛñjaya, Kekaya, Vidarbha and Kunti came to Dvārakā on this occasion with all their royal paraphernalia.

The story of Rukmiṇī's being kidnapped by Kṛṣṇa was poeticized, and the professional readers recited it everywhere. All the assembled kings and, especially, their daughters were struck with wonder and became very pleased upon hearing the chivalrous activities of Kṛṣṇa. In this way, all visitors as well as the inhabitants of Dvārakā City became joyful seeing Kṛṣṇa and Rukmiṇī together. In other words, the Supreme Lord, the maintainer of everyone, and the goddess of fortune were united, and all the people felt extremely jubilant.

Thus ends the Bhaktivedanta purport of the Fifty-third Chapter of Kṛṣṇa, *"Kṛṣṇa Defeats all the Princes and Takes Rukmiṇī Home to Dvārakā."*

54 / Pradyumna Born to Kṛṣṇa and Rukmiṇī

It is said that Cupid, who is directly part and parcel of Lord Vāsudeva and who was formerly burnt to ashes by the anger of Lord Śiva, took birth in the womb of Rukmiṇī begotten by Kṛṣṇa. This is Kāmadeva, a demigod of the heavenly planets especially capable of inducing lusty desires. The Supreme Personality of Godhead, Kṛṣṇa, has many grades of parts and parcels, but the quadruple expansions of Kṛṣṇa—Vāsudeva, Saṅkarṣaṇa, Pradyumna and Aniruddha—are directly in the Viṣṇu category. Kāma, or the Cupid demigod, who later on took his birth in the womb of Rukmiṇī, was also named Pradyumna, but he cannot be the Pradyumna of the Viṣṇu category. He belongs to the category of *jīva-tattva,* but for special power in the category of demigods, he was a part and parcel of the super prowess of Pradyumna. That is the verdict of the Gosvāmīs. Therefore, when Cupid was burnt into ashes by the anger of Lord Śiva he merged into the body of Vāsudeva, and in order to get his body again, he was begotten by Lord Kṛṣṇa Himself; he was directly released from his body in the womb of Rukmiṇī and was born as the son of Kṛṣṇa, celebrated by the name Pradyumna. Because he was begotten by Lord Kṛṣṇa directly, his qualities were most similar to those of Kṛṣṇa.

There was a demon of the name Śambara who was destined to be killed by this Pradyumna. The Śambara demon knew of his destiny, and as soon as he learned that Pradyumna was born, he took the shape of a woman and kidnapped the baby from the maternity home less than ten days after his birth. The demon took him and threw him directly into the sea. But, as it is said, "Whoever is protected by Kṛṣṇa, no one can kill; and whoever is destined to be killed by Kṛṣṇa, no one can protect." When Pradyumna was thrown in the sea, a big fish immediately swallowed him. Later on this fish was caught by the net of a fisherman, and the fish was later on sold to the Śambara demon. In the kitchen of the demon there was a maidservant whose name was Māyāvatī. This woman had formerly been the wife of Cupid, and had been called Rati. When the fish was presented to the demon Śambara, it was taken charge of by his cook, who was to make it into a palatable fish preparation. Demons and the *rākṣasas* are accustomed to eat meat, fish and similar non-vegetarian foods. Similarly, other demons, like Rāvaṇa, Kaṁsa and Hiraṇyakaśipu, although born of *brāhmaṇa* and *kṣatriya* fathers, used to take meat and flesh without discrimination. This practice is still prevalent in India, and those who are meat and fish eaters are generally called demons and *rākṣasas*.

When the cook was cutting the fish, he found a nice baby within the belly of the fish, and he immediately presented him to the charge of Māyāvatī, who was an assistant in the kitchen affairs. This woman was surprised to see how such a nice baby could remain within the belly of a fish, and the situation perplexed her. The great sage Nārada then appeared and explained to her about the birth of Pradyumna, how the baby had been taken away by Śambara and later on thrown into the sea, and so on. In this way the whole story was disclosed to Māyāvatī, who had formerly been Rati, the wife of Cupid. Māyāvatī knew that she had previously been the wife of Cupid; after her husband was burnt into ashes by the wrath of Lord Śiva, she was always expecting him to come back again in the material form. This woman was engaged for cooking rice and dahl in the kitchen, but when she got this nice baby and understood that he was Cupid, her own husband, she naturally took charge of him and with great affection began to bathe him. Miraculously, the baby very swiftly grew up, and within a very short period he became a very beautiful young man. His eyes were just like the petals of lotus flowers, his arms were very long, down to the knees, and any woman who happened to see him became captivated by his bodily beauty.

Māyāvatī could understand that her former husband, Cupid, born as Pradyumna, had grown into such a nice young man, and she also gradually became captivated and lusty. She was smiling before him with a feminine attractiveness, expressing her desire for sexual unity. He therefore inquired from her, "How is it possible that first of all you were affectionate like a mother, and now you are expressing the symptoms of a lusty woman? What is the reason for such a change?" On hearing this statement from Pradyumna, the woman, Rati, replied, "My dear sir, you are the son of Lord Kṛṣṇa. Before you were ten days old, you were stolen by the Śambara demon and later on thrown into the water and swallowed up by a fish. In this way you have come under my care, but actually, in your former life as Cupid, I was your wife; therefore, my manifestation of conjugal symptoms is not at all incompatible. Śambara wanted to kill you, and he is endowed with various kinds of mystic powers. Therefore, before he again attempts to kill you, please kill him as soon as possible with your divine power. Since you were stolen by Śambara, your mother, Rukmiṇīdevī, has been in a very grievous condition, like a cuckoo bird who has lost her babies. She is very affectionate toward you, and since you have been taken away from her, she has been living like a cow aggrieved over the loss of its calf."

Māyāvatī had mystic knowledge of supernatural power. Supernatural powers are generally known as *māyā*, and to supersede all such supernatural power there is another supernatural power, which is called *mahāmāyā*. Māyāvatī had the knowledge of the mystic power of *mahāmāyā*, and she delivered to Pradyumna this specific energetic power in order to defeat the mystic powers of the Śambara demon. Thus being empowered by his wife, Pradyumna immediately went before Śambara and challenged him to fight. Pradyumna began to address him in very strong language, so that his temper might be agitated and he would be moved to fight. At Pradyumna's words, the demon Śambara, being insulted, felt just like a snake feels after being struck by one's leg. A serpent cannot tolerate being kicked by another animal or by a man, and he immediately bites the opponent.

Śambara felt the words of Pradyumna as if they were a kick. He immediately took his club in his hand and appeared before Pradyumna to fight. In great anger, he began to beat Pradyumna with his club, just as a thunderbolt beats a mountain. The demon was also groaning and making a noise like a thundering cloud. Pradyumna protected himself with his own club, and eventually he struck the demon very severely. In this way, the fighting between Śambarāsura and Pradyumna began very seriously.

But Śambarāsura knew the art of mystic powers and could raise himself in the sky and fight from outer space. There is another demon of the name Maya, and Śambarāsura learned many mystic powers from him. He thus raised himself high in the sky and began to throw various types of nuclear weapons at the body of Pradyumna. In order to combat the mystic powers or Śambarāsura, Pradyumna remembered another mystic power, known as *mahāvidyā*, which was different from the black mystic power. The *mahāvidyā* mystic power is based on the quality of goodness. Understanding that his enemy was formidable, Śambara took assistance from various kinds of demonic mystic powers belonging to the *Guhyakas*, the *Gandharvas*, the *Piśācas*, the snakes and the *Rākṣasas*. But although the demon exhibited his mystic powers and took shelter of supernatural strength, Pradyumna was able to counteract his strength and powers by the superior power of *mahāvidyā*. When Śambarāsura was defeated in every respect, Pradyumna then took his sharpened sword and immediately cut off the demon's head, which was decorated with a helmet and with valuable jewels. When Pradyumna thus killed the demon, all the demigods in the higher planetary systems began to shower flowers on him.

Pradyumna's wife, Māyāvatī, could travel in outer space, and therefore they directly reached his father's capital, Dvārakā, by the airways. They passed above the palace of Lord Kṛṣṇa and began to come down as a cloud comes down with lightning. The inner section of a palace is known as *antaḥpura* (private apartments). Pradyumna and Māyāvatī could see that there were many women there, and they sat down among them. When the women saw Pradyumna, dressed in bluish garments, with very long arms, curling hair, beautiful eyes, a smiling reddish face, jewelry and ornaments, they first of all could not recognize him as Pradyumna, a personality different from Kṛṣṇa. They all felt themselves to be very much blessed by the sudden presence of Kṛṣṇa, and they wanted to hide in a different corner of the palace.

When the women saw, however, that all the characteristics of Kṛṣṇa were not present in the personality of Pradyumna, out of curiosity they came back again to see him and his wife, Māyāvatī. All of them were conjecturing as to who he was, for he was so beautiful. Among the women was Rukmiṇīdevī, who was equally beautiful, with her lotus-like eyes. Seeing Pradyumna, she naturally remembered her own son, and milk began to flow from her breast out of motherly affection. She then began to wonder, "Who is this beautiful young boy? He appears to be the most beautiful person. Who is the fortunate young woman able to give birth to this nice boy in her womb and become his mother? And who is that young woman who has accompanied him? How have they met? Remembering my own son, who was stolen even from the maternity home, I can only guess that if he is living somewhere, he might have grown by this time to be like this boy." Simply by intuition, Rukmiṇī could understand that Pradyumna was her own lost son. She could also observe that Pradyumna resembled Lord Kṛṣṇa in every respect. She was struck with wonder as to how he acquired all the symptoms of Kṛṣṇa. She therefore began to think more confidently that the boy must be her own grown-up son because she felt much affection for him, and, as an auspicious sign, her left arm was trembling.

At that very moment, Lord Kṛṣṇa, along with His father and mother, Devakī and Vasudeva, appeared on the scene. Kṛṣṇa, the Supreme Personality of Godhead, could understand everything, yet in that situation He remained silent. However, by the desire of Lord Śrī Kṛṣṇa, the great sage Nārada also appeared on the scene, and he began to disclose all the incidences—how Pradyumna had been stolen from the maternity home and how he had grown up and had come there with his wife Māyāvatī, who formerly had been Rati, the wife of Cupid. When everyone was informed of the mysterious disappearance of Pradyumna and how he had grown up, they all became struck with wonder because they had gotten back their dead son after they were almost hopeless of his return. When they understood that it was Pradyumna who was present, they began to receive him with great delight. One after another, all of the members of the family—Devakī, Vasudeva, Lord Śri Kṛṣṇa, Lord Balarāma, and Rukmiṇī and all the women of the family—began to embrace both Pradyumna and his wife Māyāvatī. When the news of Pradyumna's return was spread all over the city of Dvārakā, all the astonished citizens began to come with great anxiety to see the lost Pradyumna. They began to say, "The dead son has come back. What can be more pleasing than this?"

Śrīla Śukadeva Gosvāmī has explained that, in the beginning, all the residents of the palace, who were all mothers and stepmothers of Pradyumna, mistook him to be Kṛṣṇa and were all bashful, infected by the desire for conjugal love. The explanation is that Pradyumna's personal appearance is exactly like Kṛṣṇa's, and he was factually Cupid himself. There was no cause of astonishment, therefore, when the mothers of Pradyumna and other women mistook him in that way. It is clear from the statement that Pradyumna's bodily characteristics were so similar to Kṛṣṇa's that he was mistaken to be Kṛṣṇa even by his mother.

Thus ends the Bhaktivedanta purport of the Fifty-fourth Chapter of Kṛṣṇa, *"Pradyumna Born to Kṛṣṇa and Rukmiṇī."*

55 / The Story of the Syamantaka Jewel

There was a king of the name Satrājit within the jurisdiction of Dvārakādhāma. He was a great devotee of the sun-god, who awarded him the benediction of a jewel known as Syamantaka. Because of this Syamantaka jewel, there was a misunderstanding between King Satrājit and the Yadu dynasty. Later on the matter was settled when Satrājit voluntarily offered Kṛṣṇa his daughter, Satyabhāmā, along with the jewel Syamantaka. Not only was Satyabhāmā married to Kṛṣṇa on account of the Syamantaka jewel, but Jāmbavatī, the daughter of Jāmbavān, was also married to Kṛṣṇa. These two marriages took place before the appearance of Pradyumna, as described in the last chapter. How King Satrājit offended the Yadu dynasty and how he later on came to his senses and offered his daughter and the Syamantaka jewel to Kṛṣṇa is described as follows.

Since he was a great devotee of the sun-god, King Satrājit gradually entered into a very friendly relationship with him. The sun-god was much pleased with him and delivered to him an exceptional jewel known as Syamantaka. When this jewel was worn by Satrājit in a locket around his neck, he appeared exactly like an imitation sun-god. Putting on this jewel, he would enter the city of Dvārakā, and people would think that the sun-god had come into the city to see Kṛṣṇa. They knew that Kṛṣṇa, being the Supreme Personality of Godhead, was sometimes visited by the demigods, so while Satrājit was visiting the city of Dvārakā all the inhabitants except Kṛṣṇa took him to be the sun-god himself. Although King Satrājit was known to everyone, he could not be recognized because of the dazzling effulgence of the Syamantaka jewel.

Once, mistaking him to be the sun-god, some of the important citizens of Dvārakā immediately went to Kṛṣṇa to inform Him that the sun-god had arrived to see Him. At that time, Kṛṣṇa was playing chess. One of the important residents of Dvārakā spoke thus: "My dear Lord Nārāyaṇa, You are the Supreme Personality of Godhead. In Your plenary portion of Nārāyaṇa or Viṣṇu, You have four hands with different symbols—the conchshell, disc, club and lotus flower. You are actually the owner of everything, but in spite of Your being the Supreme Personality of Godhead, Nārāyaṇa, You have descended in Vṛndāvana to act as the child of Yaśodāmātā, who sometimes used to tie You up with her ropes, and You are celebrated, therefore, by the name Dāmodara."

That Kṛṣṇa is the Supreme Personality of Godhead, Nārāyaṇa, as accepted by the citizens of Dvārakā, was later on confirmed by the great Māyāvādī philosophical leader, Śaṅkarācārya. By accepting the Lord as impersonal, he did not reject the Lord's personal form. He meant that everything which has form in this material world is subjected to creation, maintenance and annihilation, but the Supreme Personality of Godhead, Nārāyaṇa, does not have a material form subjected to these limitations. In order to convince the less intelligent class of men who take Kṛṣṇa to be an ordinary human being, Śaṅkarācārya therefore said that God is impersonal. This impersonality means that He is not a person of this material condition. He is a transcendental personality without a material body.

The citizens of Dvārakā addressed Lord Kṛṣṇa not only as Dāmodara, but also as Govinda, which indicates that Kṛṣṇa is very affectionate to the cows and calves; and just to refer to their intimate connection with Kṛṣṇa, they addressed Him as Yadunandana. He is the son of Vasudeva, born in the Yadu dynasty. In this way, the citizens of Dvārakā concluded that they were addressing Kṛṣṇa as the supreme master of the whole universe. They addressed Kṛṣṇa in many different ways, proud of being citizens of Dvārakā who could see Kṛṣṇa daily.

When Satrājit was visiting the city of Dvārakā, the citizens felt great pride to think that although Kṛṣṇa was living in Dvārakā like an ordinary human being, the demigods were coming to see Him. Thus they informed Lord Kṛṣṇa that the sun-god, with his appealing bodily effulgence, was coming to see Him. The citizens of Dvārakā confirmed that the sun-god's coming into Dvārakā was not very wonderful, because people all over the universe who were searching after the Supreme Personality of Godhead knew that He had appeared in the family of the Yadu dynasty and was living in Dvārakā as one of the members of that family. Thus the citizens expressed their joy on this occasion. On hearing the statement of His citizens, the all-pervasive Personality of Godhead, Kṛṣṇa, simply smiled. Being pleased with the citizens of Dvārakā, Kṛṣṇa informed them that the person whom they described as the sun-god was actually King Satrājit, who had come to visit Dvārakā City to show his opulence in the form of the valuable jewel obtained from the sun-god.

Satrājit, however, did not come to see Kṛṣṇa; he was instead overwhelmed by the jewel of Syamantaka. He installed the jewel in a temple to be worshiped by *brāhmaṇas* he engaged for this purpose. This is an instance of a less intelligent person worshiping a material thing. In the *Bhagavad-gītā* it is stated that less intelligent persons, in order to get immediate results from their fruitive activities, worship the demigods who are created within this universe. The word "materialist" means one concerned with gratification of the senses within this material world. Although Kṛṣṇa later asked for this Syamantaka jewel, King Satrājit did not deliver it to Him, but he installed the jewel for his purposes of worship. And who would not worship that jewel? The Syamantaka jewel was so powerful that it was daily producing a large quantity of gold. A quantity of gold is counted by a measurement called a *bhāra.* According to Vedic formulas, one *bhāra* is equal to sixteen pounds of gold; one *mound* equals eighty-two pounds. The jewel was producing about 170 pounds of gold every day. Besides that, it is learned from Vedic literature that in whatever part of the world this jewel is worshiped there is no possibility of famine; not only that, but wherever the jewel is present, there is no possibility of anything inauspicious, such as pestilence or disease.

Lord Kṛṣṇa wanted to teach the world that the best of everything should be offered to the ruling chief of the country. King Ugrasena was the overlord of many dynasties and happened to be the grandfather of Kṛṣṇa, and Kṛṣṇa asked Satrājit to present the Syamantaka jewel to King Ugrasena. Kṛṣṇa pleaded that the best should be offered to the king. But Satrājit, being a worshiper of the demigods, had become too materialistic and, instead of accepting the request of Kṛṣṇa, thought it wiser to worship the jewel in order to get the 170 pounds of gold every day. Materialistic persons who can achieve such huge quantities of gold every day are not interested in Kṛṣṇa consciousness. Sometimes, therefore, in order to show special favor, Kṛṣṇa takes away great accumulations of materialistic wealth from a person and thus makes him a great devotee. But Satrājit refused to abide by the order of Kṛṣṇa and did not deliver the jewel to him.

After this incident, Satrājit's younger brother, in order to display the opulence of the family, took the jewel, put it on his neck and rode on horseback into the forest making a show of his material opulence. While the brother of Satrājit, who was known as Prasena, was moving here and there in the forest, a big lion attacked him, killing both him and the horse on which he was riding, and took away the jewel to his cave. The news was received by the gorilla king, Jāmbavān, who then killed that lion in the cave and took away the jewel. Jāmbavān had been a great devotee of the Lord since the time of Lord Rāmacandra, so he did not take the valuable jewel as something he very much needed. He gave it to his young son to play with as a toy.

In the city, when Satrājit's younger brother Prasena did not return from the forest with the jewel, Satrājit became very upset. He did not know that his brother had been killed by a lion and that the lion had been killed by Jāmbavān. He was thinking instead that because Kṛṣṇa wanted that jewel and it had not been delivered to Him, Kṛṣṇa might have therefore taken the jewel away from Prasena by force and killed him. This idea grew into a rumor which was being spread by Satrājit in every part of Dvārakā.

The false rumor that Kṛṣṇa had killed Prasena and had taken away the jewel was spread everywhere like wildfire. Kṛṣṇa did not like to be defamed in that way, and therefore He decided that He would go to the forest and find the Syamantaka jewel, taking with Him some of the inhabitants of Dvārakā. Along with important men of Dvārakā, Kṛṣṇa went to search out Prasena, the brother of Satrājit, and He found him dead, killed by the lion. At the same time, Kṛṣṇa also found the lion which had been killed by Jāmbavān, who is generally called by the name Ṛkṣa. It was found that the lion had been killed by the hand of Ṛkṣa without the assistance of any weapon. Kṛṣṇa and the citizens of Dvārakā then found in the forest a great tunnel, said to be the path to Ṛkṣa's house. Kṛṣṇa knew that the inhabitants of Dvārakā would be afraid to enter the tunnel; therefore He asked them to remain outside, and He Himself entered the dark tunnel alone to find Ṛkṣa, Jāmbavān. After entering the tunnel, Kṛṣṇa saw that the very valuable jewel known as Syamantaka had been given to the son of Ṛkṣa as a toy, and in order to take the jewel from the child, He went there and stood before him. When the nurse who was taking care of Ṛkṣa's child saw Kṛṣṇa standing before her, she was afraid, thinking the valuable Syamantaka jewel might be taken away by Him. She began to cry loudly out of fear.

Hearing the nurse crying, Jāmbavān appeared on the scene in a very angry mood. Jāmbavān was actually a great devotee of Lord Kṛṣṇa, but because he was in an angry mood he could not recognize his master; he thought Him to be an ordinary man. This brings to mind the statement of the *Bhagavad-gītā* in which the Lord advises Arjuna to get free from anger, greed and lust in order to rise up to the spiritual platform. Lust, anger and greed run parallel in the heart and check one's progress on the spiritual path.

Not recognizing his master, Jāmbavān first challenged Him to fight. There was then a great fight between Kṛṣṇa and Jāmbavān in which they fought like two opposing vultures. Whenever there is an eatable corpse the vultures fight heartily over the prey. Kṛṣṇa and Jāmbavān first of all began fighting with weapons, then with stones, then with big trees, then hand to hand, until at last they were hitting one another with their fists, and the blows were like the striking of thunderbolts. Each was expecting victory over the other, but the fighting continued for days, both in daytime and at night, without stopping. In this way the fighting continued for twenty-eight days.

Although Jāmbavān was the strongest living entity of that time, practically all the joints of his bodily limbs became slackened and his strength reduced to practically nil after being constantly struck by the fists of Śrī Kṛṣṇa. Feeling very tired, with perspiration all over his body, Jāmbavān was astonished. Who was this opponent who was weakening him? Jāmbavān was quite aware of his own superhuman bodily strength, but when he felt tired from being struck by Kṛṣṇa, he could understand that Kṛṣṇa was no one else but his worshipable Lord, the Supreme Personality of Godhead. This incident has a special significance for the devotees. In the beginning, Jāmbavān could not understand Kṛṣṇa because his vision was obscured by material attachment. He was attached to his boy and to the greatly valuable Syamantaka jewel, which he did not want to spare for Kṛṣṇa. In fact, when Kṛṣṇa came there he became angry, thinking that He had come to take away the jewel. This is the material position; although one is very strong in body, that cannot help him understand Kṛṣṇa.

In a sporting attitude, Kṛṣṇa wanted to engage in a mock fight with His devotee. As we have experienced from the pages of the *Śrīmad-Bhāgavatam,* the Supreme Personality of Godhead has all the propensities and instincts of a human being. Sometimes, in a sportive spirit, He wishes to fight to make a show of bodily strength, and when He so desires, He selects one of His suitable devotees to give Him that pleasure. Kṛṣṇa desired this pleasure of mock fighting with Jāmbavān. Although Jāmbavān was a devotee by nature, he was without knowledge of Kṛṣṇa while giving service to the Lord by his bodily strength. But as soon as Kṛṣṇa was pleased by the fighting, Jāmbavān immediately understood that his opponent was none other than the Supreme Lord Himself. The conclusion is that he could understand Kṛṣṇa by his service. Kṛṣṇa is sometimes satisfied by fighting also.

Jāmbavān therefore said to the Lord, "My dear Lord, I can now understand who You are. You are the Supreme Personality of Godhead, Lord Viṣṇu, the source of everyone's strength, wealth, reputation, beauty, wisdom and renunciation." This statement of Jāmbavān's is confirmed by the *Vedānta-sūtra,* wherein the Supreme Lord is declared to be the source of everything. Jāmbavān identified Lord Kṛṣṇa as the Supreme Personality, Lord Viṣṇu: "My dear Lord, You are the creator of the creators of the universal affairs." This statement is very instructive to the ordinary man, who is amazed by the activities of a person with an exceptional brain. The ordinary man is surprised to see the inventions of a great scientist, but the statement of Jāmbavān confirms that although a scientist may be a creator of many wonderful things, Kṛṣṇa is the creator of the scientist. He is not only the creator of one scientist, but of millions and trillions, all over the universe. Jāmbavān said further, "You are not only creator of the creator, but You are also creator of the material elements which are manipulated by the so-called creators." Scientists utilize the physical elements or laws of material nature and do something wonderful, but actually such laws and elements are also the creation of Kṛṣṇa. This is actual scientific understanding. Less intelligent men do not try to understand who created the brain of the scientist; they are simply satisfied by seeing the wonderful creation or invention of the scientist.

Jāmbavān continued: "My dear Lord, the time factor which combines all the physical elements is also Your representative. You are the supreme time factor in which all creation takes place, is maintained, and is finally annihilated. And not only the physical elements and the time factors but also the persons who manipulate the ingredients and advantages of creation are part and parcel of You. The living entity is not, therefore, an independent creator. By studying all factors in the right perspective, one can see that You are the supreme controller and Lord of everything. My dear Lord, I can therefore understand that You are the same Supreme Personality of Godhead whom I worship as Lord Rāmacandra. My Lord Rāmacandra wanted to construct a bridge over the ocean, and I saw personally how the ocean became agitated simply by my Lord's glancing over it. And when the whole ocean became agitated, the living entities like the whales, alligators and *timiṅgila* fish, all became perturbed. [The *timiṅgila* fish in the ocean can swallow big aquatics like whales in one gulp.] In this way the ocean was forced to give way and allow Rāmacandra to cross to the island known as Laṅkā [now supposed to be Ceylon]. This construction of a bridge over the ocean from Cape Comorin to Ceylon is still well-known to everyone. After the construction of the bridge, a fire was set all over the kingdom of Rāvaṇa. During the fighting with Rāvaṇa, each and every part of Rāvaṇa's limbs was slashed and cut into pieces by Your sharp arrows, and his head fell to the face of the earth. Now I can understand that You are none other than my Lord Rāmacandra. No one else has such immeasurable strength; no one else could defeat me in this way."

Lord Kṛṣṇa became satisfied by the prayers and statements of Jāmbavān, and to mitigate the pains of his body, He began to smear the lotus palm of His hand all over the body of Jāmbavān. Jāmbavān at once felt relieved from the fatigue of the great fight. Lord Kṛṣṇa then addressed him as King Jāmbavān, because he and not the lion was actually the king of the forest; with his naked hand, without a weapon, Jāmbavān had killed the lion. Kṛṣṇa informed Jāmbavān that He had come to him to ask for the Syamantaka jewel because since the Syamantaka jewel had been stolen His name had been defamed by the less intelligent. Kṛṣṇa plainly informed him that he had come there to ask him for the jewel in order to be free from this defamation. Jāmbavān understood the whole situation, and to satisfy the Lord he not only immediately delivered the Syamantaka jewel, but he also brought his daughter Jāmbavatī, who was of marriagable age, and presented her to Lord Kṛṣṇa.

The episode of Jāmbavatī's marriage with Kṛṣṇa and the delivery of the jewel known as Syamantaka was finished within the mountain cave. Although the fighting between Kṛṣṇa and Jāmbavān went on for twenty-eight days, the inhabitants of Dvārakā waited outside the tunnel for twelve days, and after that they decided that something undesirable must have happened. They could not understand what had actually happened for certain, and being very sorry and tired, they had returned to the city of Dvārakā.

All the members of the family, namely the mother of Kṛṣṇa, Devakī, His father Vasudeva, and His chief wife Rukmiṇī, along with all other friends, relatives and residents of the palace, became very sorry when the citizens returned home without Kṛṣṇa. Because of their natural affection for Kṛṣṇa, they began to call Satrājit ill names, for he was the cause of Kṛṣṇa's disappearance. They went to worship the goddess Candrabhāgā, praying for the return of Kṛṣṇa. The goddess was satisfied by the prayers of the citizens of Dvārakā, and she immediately offered them her benediction. Simultaneously, Kṛṣṇa appeared on the scene accompanied by His new wife Jāmbavatī, and all the inhabitants of Dvārakā and relatives of Kṛṣṇa became joyful. The inhabitants of Dvārakā became as joyful as someone receiving a dear relative back from the dead. The inhabitants of Dvārakā had concluded that Kṛṣṇa had been put into great difficulties due to the fighting; therefore, they had become almost hopeless of His return. But when they saw that Kṛṣṇa had actually returned, not alone but with a new wife, Jāmbavatī, they immediately performed another celebration ceremony.

King Ugrasena then called for a meeting of all important kings and chiefs. He also invited Satrājit, and Kṛṣṇa explained before the whole assembly the incident of the recovery of the jewel from Jāmbavān. Kṛṣṇa wanted to return the valuable jewel to King Satrājit. Satrājit, however, became ashamed because he had unnecessarily defamed Kṛṣṇa. He accepted the jewel in his hand, but he remained silent, bending his head downwards, and without speaking anything in the assembly of the kings and chiefs, he returned home with the jewel. Then he thought about how he could clear himself from the abominable action he had performed by defaming Kṛṣṇa. He was conscious that he had offended Kṛṣṇa very grievously and that he had to find a remedial measure so that Kṛṣṇa would again be pleased with him.

King Satrājit was eager to get relief from the anxiety he had foolishly created due to being attracted by a material thing, specifically the Syamantaka jewel. Satrājit was truly afflicted by the offense he had committed toward Kṛṣṇa, and he sincerely wanted to rectify it. From within, Kṛṣṇa gave him good intelligence, and Satrājit decided to hand over to Kṛṣṇa both the jewel and his beautiful daughter, Satyabhāmā. There was no alternative for mitigating the situation, and therefore he arranged the marriage ceremony of Kṛṣṇa and his beautiful daughter. He gave in charity both the jewel and his daughter to the Supreme Personality of Godhead. Satyabhāmā was so beautiful and qualified that Satrājit, in spite of being asked for the hand of Satyabhama by many princes, was waiting to find a suitable son-in-law. By the grace of Kṛṣṇa he decided to hand his daughter over to Him.

Lord Kṛṣṇa, being pleased upon Satrājit, informed him that He did not have any need of the Syamantaka jewel. "It is better to let it remain in the temple as you have kept it," He said, "and every one of us will derive benefit from the jewel. Because of the jewel's presence in the city of Dvārakā, there will be no more famine or disturbances created by pestilence or excessive heat and cold."

Thus ends the Bhaktivedanta purport of the Fifty-fifth Chapter of Kṛṣṇa, *"The Story of the Syamantaka Jewel."*

56/ The Killing of Satrājit and Śatadhanvā

After Akrūra visited Hastināpura and reported the condition of the Pāṇḍavas to Kṛṣṇa, there were further developments. The Pāṇḍavas were transferred to a house which was made of shellac and was later on set ablaze, and everyone understood that the Pāṇḍavas along with their mother, Kuntī, had been killed. This information was also sent to Lord Kṛṣṇa and Balarāma. After consulting together, They decided to go to Hastināpura to show sympathy to Their relatives. Kṛṣṇa and Balarāma certainly knew that the Pāṇḍavas could not have been killed in the devastating fire, but in spite of this knowledge They wanted to go to Hastināpura to take part in the bereavement. On arriving in Hastināpura, Kṛṣṇa and Balarāma first of all went to see Bhīṣmadeva, because he was the chief of the Kuru dynasty. They then saw Vidura, Gāndhārī and Droṇa. Other members of the Kuru dynasty were not sorry, because they wanted the Pāṇḍavas and their mother to be killed. But some family members, headed by Bhīṣma, were actually very sorry for the incident, and Kṛṣṇa and Balarāma expressed equal sorrow, without disclosing the actual situation.

When Kṛṣṇa and Balarāma were away from the city of Dvārakā, there was a conspiracy to take away the Syamantaka jewel from Satrājit. The chief conspirator was Śatadhanvā. Along with others, Śatadhanvā wanted to marry Satyabhāmā, the beautiful daughter of Satrājit. Satrājit had promised that he would give his beautiful daughter in charity to various candidates, but later on the decision was changed, and Satyabhāmā was given to Kṛṣṇa along with the Syamantaka jewel. Satrājit had no desire to give the jewel away along with his daughter, and Kṛṣṇa, knowing his mentality, accepted his daughter but returned the jewel. After getting back the jewel from Kṛṣṇa, he was satisfied and kept it with him always. But in the absence of Kṛṣṇa and Balarāma there was a conspiracy by many men, including even Akrūra and Kṛtavarmā, who were devotees of Lord Kṛṣṇa, to take the jewel from Satrājit. Akrūra and Kṛtavarmā joined the conspiracy because they wanted the jewel for Kṛṣṇa. They knew that Kṛṣṇa wanted the jewel and that Satrājit had not delivered it properly. Others joined the conspiracy because they were disappointed in not having the hand of Satyabhāmā. Some of them incited Śatadhanvā to kill Satrājit and take away the jewel.

The question is generally raised, Why did a great devotee like Akrūra join this conspiracy? And why did Kṛtavarmā, although a devotee of the Lord, join the conspiracy also? The answer is given by great authorities like Jīva Gosvāmī and others that although Akrūra was a great devotee, he was cursed by the inhabitants of Vṛndāvana because of his taking Kṛṣṇa away from their midst. Because of his wounding their feelings, Akrūra was forced to join the conspiracy declared by sinful men. Similarly, Kṛtavarmā was a devotee, but because of his intimate association with Kaṁsa, he was also contaminated by sinful reaction, and he also joined the conspiracy.

Being inspired by all the members of the conspiracy, Śatadhanvā one night entered the house of Satrājit and killed him while he was sleeping. Śatadhanvā was a sinful man of abominable character, and although due to his sinful activities he was not to live for many days, he decided to kill Satrājit while Satrājit was sleeping at home. When he entered the house to kill Satrājit, all the women there began to cry very loudly, but in spite of their great protests, Śatadhanvā mercilessly butchered Satrājit without hesitation, exactly as a butcher kills an animal in the slaughterhouse. Since Kṛṣṇa was absent from home, His wife Satyabhāmā was also present on the night Satrājit was murdered, and she began to cry, "My dear father! My dear father! How mercilessly you have been killed!" The dead body of Satrājit was not immediately removed for cremation because Satyabhāmā wanted to go to Kṛṣṇa in Hastināpura. Therefore the body was preserved in a tank of oil so that Kṛṣṇa could come back and see the dead body of Satrājit and take real action against Śatadhanvā. Satyabhāmā immediately started for Hastināpura to inform Kṛṣṇa about the ghastly death of her father.

When Kṛṣṇa was informed by Satyabhāmā of the murder of His father-in-law, He began to lament like an ordinary man. His great sorrow is, again, a strange thing. Lord Kṛṣṇa has nothing to do with action and reaction, but because He was playing the part of a human being He expressed His full sympathy for the bereavement of Satyabhāmā, and His eyes filled with tears upon hearing about the death of His father-in-law. He thus began to lament, "Oh, what unhappy incidents have taken place!" In this way both Kṛṣṇa and Balarāma, along with Satyabhāmā, the wife of Kṛṣṇa, immediately returned to Dvārakā and began to make plans to kill Śatadhanvā and take away the jewel. Although he was a great outlaw in the city, Śatadhanvā was still very much afraid of Kṛṣṇa's power, and thus he became most afraid on Kṛṣṇa's arrival.

Understanding Kṛṣṇa's plan to kill him, he immediately went to take shelter of Kṛtavarmā. But on being approached by him, Kṛtavarmā said, "I shall never be able to offend Lord Kṛṣṇa and Balarāma because They are not ordinary persons. They are the Supreme Personality of Godhead. Who can be saved from death if he has offended Balarāma and Kṛṣṇa? No one can be saved from Their wrath." Kṛtavarmā further said that Kaṁsa, although powerful and assisted by many demons, could not be saved from the wrath of Kṛṣṇa, and what to speak of Jarāsandha, who had been defeated by Kṛṣṇa eighteen times and each time had to return from the fighting in disappointment.

When Śatadhanvā was refused help by Kṛtavarmā he went to Akrūra and implored him to help. Akrūra also replied, "Both Balarāma and Kṛṣṇa are Themselves the Supreme Personality of Godhead, and anyone who knows Their unlimited strength would never dare to offend Them or fight with Them." He further informed Śatadhanvā, "Kṛṣṇa and Balarāma are so powerful that simply by willing They are creating the whole cosmic manifestation, maintaining it and dissolving it. Unfortunately, persons who are bewildered by the illusory energy cannot understand the strength of Kṛṣṇa, although the whole cosmic manifestation is fully under His control." He cited, as an example, that Kṛṣṇa, even at the age of seven years, had lifted Govardhana Hill and had continued to hold up the mountain for seven days, exactly as a child carries a small umbrella. Akrūra plainly informed Śatadhanvā that he would always offer his most respectful obeisances to Kṛṣṇa, the Supersoul of everything that is created and the original cause of all causes. When Akrūra also refused to give him shelter, Śatadhanvā decided to deliver to the hands of Akrūra the Syamantaka jewel. Then, riding on a horse which could run at great speed and up to four hundred miles at a stretch, he fled the city.

When Kṛṣṇa and Balarāma were informed of the flight of Śatadhanvā, They mounted Their chariot, its flag marked by the picture of Garuḍa, and followed immediately. Kṛṣṇa was particularly angry with Śatadhanvā and wanted to kill him because he had killed Satrājit, a superior personality. Satrājit happened to be the father-in-law of Kṛṣṇa, and it is the injunction of the *śāstras* that anyone who has rebelled against a superior person, or *gurudruha*, must be punished in proportion to the volume of offense. Because Śatadhanvā had killed His father-in-law, Kṛṣṇa was determined to kill him by any means.

Śatadhanvā's horse became exhausted and died near a garden house in Mithilā. Unable to take help of the horse, Śatadhanvā began to run with great speed. In order to be fair to Śatadhanvā, Kṛṣṇa and Balarāma also left Their chariot and began to follow Śatadhanvā on foot. While both Śatadhanvā and Kṛṣṇa were running on foot, Kṛṣṇa took His disk and cut off the head of Śatadhanvā. After Śatadhanvā was killed, Kṛṣṇa searched through his clothing for the Syamantaka jewel, but He could not find it. He then returned to Balarāma and said, "We have killed this person uselessly because the jewel is not to be found on his body." Śrī Balarāma suggested, "The jewel might have been kept in custody of another man in Dvārakā, so You'd better return and search it out." Śrī Balarāma expressed His desire to remain in Mithilā City for some days because He enjoyed an intimate friendship with the king. Therefore, Kṛṣṇa returned to Dvārakā, and Balarāma entered the city of Mithilā.

When the King of Mithilā saw the arrival of Śrī Balarāma in his city, he became most pleased and received the Lord with great honor and hospitality. He presented many valuable presents to Balarāmajī in order to seek His pleasure. At this time Śrī Balarāma lived in the city for several years as the honored guest of the King of Mithilā, Janaka Mahārāja. During this time, Duryodhana, the eldest son of Dhṛtarāṣṭra, took the opportunity of coming to Balarāma and learning from Him the art of fighting with a club.

After killing Śatadhanvā, Kṛṣṇa returned to Dvārakā, and in order to please His wife Satyabhāmā, He informed her of the death of Śatadhanvā, the killer of her father. But He also informed her that the jewel had not been found in his possession. Then, according to religious principles, Kṛṣṇa, along with Satyabhāmā, performed all kinds of ceremonies in honor of the death of His father-in-law. In that ceremony all the friends and relatives of the family joined together.

Akrūra and Kṛtavarmā, who were prominent members in the conspiracy to kill Satrājit, had incited Śatadhanvā to kill him, but when they heard of the death of Śatadhanvā at Kṛṣṇa's hand, and when they heard also that Kṛṣṇa had returned to Dvārakā, they both immediately left Dvārakā. The citizens of Dvārakā felt themselves threatened with pestilence and natural disturbances due to the absence of Akrūra from the city. This was a kind of superstition because while Lord Kṛṣṇa was present there could not be any pestilence, famine or natural disturbances. But in the absence of Akrūra there were some disturbances in Dvārakā. Once in the province of Kāśī within the barricade of Vārāṇasī there was severe drought and practically no rainfall. At that time the King of Kāśī arranged the marriage of his daughter, known as Gāndinī, with Śvaphalka, the father of Akrūra. This was done by the King of Kāśī on the advice of an astrologer, and actually it so happened that after the marriage of the King's daughter with Śvaphalka there was sufficient rainfall in the province. Due to this supernatural power of Śvaphalka, his son Akrūra was also considered equally powerful, and people were under the impression that wherever Akrūra or his father remained, there would be no natural disturbance, famine or drought. That kingdom is considered to be happy where there is no famine, pestilence, or excessive heat and cold and where people are happy mentally, spiritually and bodily. As soon as there is some disturbance, people consider the cause to be due to the absence of an auspicious personality in the city. Thus there was a rumor that because of the absence of Akrūra inauspicious things were happening. After the departure of Akrūra, some of the elderly members of the town began to perceive that there were also inauspicious signs due to the absence of the Syamantaka jewel. When Lord Śrī Kṛṣṇa heard these rumors spread by the people He decided to summon Akrūra from the kingdom of Kāśī. Akrūra was Kṛṣṇa's uncle; therefore, when he came back to Dvārakā Lord Kṛṣṇa first of all welcomed him as befitting a superior person. Kṛṣṇa is the Supersoul in everyone's heart; He knows everything going on in everyone's heart. He knew everything that had happened in connection with Akrūra's conspiracy with Śatadhanvā. Therefore, He smilingly began to address Akrūra.

Addressing him as the chief among magnificent men, Kṛṣṇa said, "My dear uncle, it is already known to Me that the Syamantaka jewel was left by Śatadhanvā with you. Presently there is no direct claimant of the Syamantaka jewel, for King Satrājit has no male issue. His daughter Satyabhāmā is not very anxious for this jewel, yet her expected son, as grandson of Satrājit, would, after performing the regulative principles of inheritance, be the legal claimant of the jewel." Lord Kṛṣṇa indicated by this statement that Satyabhāmā was already pregnant and that her son would be the real claimant for the jewel and would certainly take the jewel from him.

Kṛṣṇa continued, "This jewel is so powerful that no ordinary man is able to keep it. I know that you are very pious in activities, so there is no objection to the jewel being kept with you. There is one difficulty, and that is that My elder brother, Śrī Balarāma, does not believe My version that the jewel is with you. I therefore request you, O large-hearted one, to show Me the jewel before My other relatives so that they may be pacified. You cannot deny that the jewel is with you because from various kinds of rumors we can understand that you have enhanced your opulence and are performing sacrifices on an altar made of solid gold." The properties of the jewel were known: wherever the jewel remained, it would produce for the keeper almost nine *mounds* of pure gold daily. Akrūra was getting gold in that proportion and was distributing it very profusely at sacrificial performances. Lord Kṛṣṇa cited Akrūra's lavishly spending in gold as positive evidence of his possessing the Syamantaka jewel.

When Lord Kṛṣṇa, in friendly terms and in sweet language, impressed Akrūra about the real fact and Akrūra understood that nothing could be concealed from the knowledge of Śrī Kṛṣṇa, he brought the valuable jewel, shining like the sun and covered by cloth, and presented it before Kṛṣṇa. Lord Kṛṣṇa took the Syamantaka jewel in His hand and showed it to all His relatives and friends present there and then again returned the jewel to Akrūra in their presence so that they would know that the jewel was actually being kept by Akrūra in Dvārakā City.

This story of the Syamantaka jewel is very significant. In the *Śrīmad-Bhāgavatam* it is said that anyone who hears the story of the Syamantaka jewel or describes it or simply remembers it will be free from all kinds of defamation and the reactions of all impious activities and thus will attain the highest perfectional condition of peace.

Thus ends the Bhaktivedanta purport of the Fifty-sixth Chapter of Kṛṣṇa, *"The Killing of Satrājit and Śatadhanvā.*

57 / Five Queens Married by Kṛṣṇa

There was a great rumor that the five Pāṇḍava brothers, along with their mother Kuntī, had, under the plan of Dhṛtarāṣṭra, died in a fire accident in the house of shellac in which they were living. But then the five brothers were detected at the marriage ceremony of Draupadī; so again another rumor spread that the Pāṇḍavas and their mother were not dead. It was a rumor, but actually it was so; they returned to their capital city, Hastināpura, and people saw them face to face. When this news was carried to Kṛṣṇa and Balarāma, Kṛṣṇa wanted to see them personally, and therefore Kṛṣṇa decided to go to Hastināpura.

This time, Kṛṣṇa visited Hastināpura in state, as a royal prince, accompanied by His commander-in-chief, Yuyudhāna, and by many other soldiers. He had not actually been invited to visit the city, yet He went to see the Pāṇḍavas out of His affection for His great devotees. He visited the Pāṇḍavas without warning, and all of them got up from their respective seats as soon as they saw Him. Kṛṣṇa is called Mukunda because as soon as one comes in constant touch with Kṛṣṇa or sees Him in full Kṛṣṇa consciousness, one immediately becomes freed from all material anxieties. Not only that, but he immediately becomes blessed with all spiritual bliss.

On receiving Kṛṣṇa, the Pāṇḍavas became very enlivened, just as if awakened from unconsciousness or from loss of life. When a man is lying unconscious, his senses and the different parts of his body are not active, but when he regains his consciousness, the senses immediately become active. Similarly, the Pāṇḍavas received Kṛṣṇa as if they had just regained their consciousness, and so they became very much enlivened. Lord Kṛṣṇa embraced every one of them, and by the touch of the Supreme Personality of Godhead, the Pāṇḍavas immediately became freed from all reactions of material contamination, and therefore they were smiling in spiritual bliss. By seeing the face of Lord Kṛṣṇa, everyone was transcendentally satisfied.

Lord Kṛṣṇa, although the Supreme Personality of Godhead, was playing the part of an ordinary human being, and thus He immediately touched the feet of Yudhiṣṭhira and Bhīma because they were His two older cousins. Arjuna embraced Kṛṣṇa as a friend of the same age, whereas the two younger brothers, namely Nakula and Sahadeva, touched the lotus feet of Kṛṣṇa to show Him respect. After an exchange of greetings according to the social etiquette befitting the position of the Pāṇḍavas and Lord Kṛṣṇa, Kṛṣṇa was offered an exalted seat. When He was comfortably seated, the newly married Draupadī, young and very beautiful in her natural feminine gracefulness, came before Lord Kṛṣṇa to offer her respectful greetings. The Yādavas who accompanied Kṛṣṇa to Hastināpura were also very respectfully received; specifically, Sātyaki, or Yuyudhāna, was also offered a nice seat. In this way, when everyone else was properly seated, the five brothers took their seats nearby Lord Kṛṣṇa.

After meeting with the five brothers, Lord Kṛṣṇa personally went to visit Śrīmatī Kuntīdevī, the mother of the Pāṇḍavas, who was also the paternal aunt of Kṛṣṇa. In offering His respects to His aunt, Kṛṣṇa also touched her feet. Kuntīdevī's eyes became wet, and, in great love, she feelingly embraced Lord Kṛṣṇa. She then inquired from Him about the well-being of her paternal family members—her brother Vasudeva, his wife, and other members of the family. Similarly, Kṛṣṇa also inquired from His aunt about the welfare of the Pāṇḍava families. Although Kuntīdevī was related to Kṛṣṇa by family ties, she knew immediately after meeting Him that He was the Supreme Personality of Godhead. She remembered the past calamities of her life and how by the grace of Kṛṣṇa the Pāṇḍavas and their mother had been saved. She knew perfectly well that no one, without Kṛṣṇa's grace, could have saved them from the fire accident designed by Dhṛtarāṣṭra and his sons. In a choked up voice, she began to narrate before Kṛṣṇa the past history of their life.

Śrīmatī Kuntī said: "My dear Kṛṣṇa, I remember the day when You sent my brother Akrūra to gather information about us. This means that You always remember us automatically. When You sent Akrūra, I could understand that there was no possibility of our being put into danger. All good fortune in our life began when You sent Akrūra to us. Since then, I have been convinced that we are not without protection. We may be put into various types of dangerous conditions by our family members, the Kurus, but I am confident that You remember us and that You always keep us safe and sound. Devotees who simply think of You are always immune from all kinds of material dangers, and what to speak of ourselves, who are personally remembered by You. So, my dear Kṛṣṇa, there is no question of bad luck; we are always in an auspicious position because of Your grace. But because You have bestowed a special favor on us, people should not mistakenly think that You are partial to some and inattentive to others. You make no such distinction. No one is Your favorite and no one is Your enemy. As the Supreme Personality of Godhead, You are equal to everyone, and everyone can take advantage of Your special protection. The fact is that although You are equal to everyone, You are especially inclined to the devotees who always think of You. The devotees are related to You by ties of love. As such, they cannot forget You even for a moment. You are present in everyone's heart, but because the devotees always remember You, You also respond accordingly. Although the mother has affection for all the children, she takes special care of the one who is fully dependent. I know certainly, my dear Kṛṣṇa, that being seated in everyone's heart, You always create auspicious situations for Your unalloyed devotees."

Then King Yudhiṣṭhira also praised Kṛṣṇa as the Supreme Personality and universal friend of everyone, but because Kṛṣṇa was taking special care of the Pāṇḍavas, King Yudhiṣṭhira said: "My dear Kṛṣṇa, we do not know what sort of pious activities we have executed in our past lives that have made You so kind and graceful to us. We know very well that the great mystics who are always engaged in meditation to capture You do not find it easy to obtain such grace, nor can they draw any personal attention from You. I cannot understand why You are so kind upon us. We are not *yogīs*, but, on the contrary, we are attached to material contaminations. We are householders dealing in politics, worldly affairs. I do not know why You are so kind upon us."

Being requested by King Yudhiṣṭhira, Kṛṣṇa agreed to stay in Hastināpura for four months during the rainy season. The four months of the rainy season are called *Cāturmāsya.* During this period, the generally itinerant preachers and *brāhmaṇas* stop at a certain place and live under rigid regulative principles. Although Lord Kṛṣṇa is above all regulative principles, He agreed to stay at Hastināpura out of affection for the Pāṇḍavas. Taking this opportunity of Kṛṣṇa's residence in Hastināpura, all the citizens of the town got the privilege of seeing Him now and then, and thus they merged into transcendental bliss simply by seeing Lord Kṛṣṇa eye to eye.

One day while Kṛṣṇa was staying with the Pāṇḍavas, He and Arjuna prepared themselves to go to the forest to hunt. Both of them sat down on the chariot, which flew a flag with a picture of Hanumān. Arjuna's special chariot is always marked with the picture of Hanumān, and therefore his name is also Kapidhvaja. (*Kapi* means Hanumān, and *dhvaja* means "flag.")

Full of feminine bashfulness, Kubjā stood gracefully before Kṛṣṇa. (p. 315)

Kṛṣṇa and Balarāma jumped from the top of the mountain. (p. 348)

Rukmiṇi was praying to Kṛṣṇa for the life of her brother. (p. 365)

Kālyavana burnt to ashes within a moment. (p. 336)

The cook found a nice baby within the belly of the fish. (p. 372)

Kṛṣṇa and Jāmbavān fought like two opposing vultures. (p. 379)

While Kṛṣṇa and Arjuna were resting and drinking water, they saw a beautiful girl of marriageable age walking alone at the bank of the Yamunā. (p. 393)

Kṛṣṇa pulled them strongly, just as a child pulls a toy wooden bull. (p. 395)

Lord Kṛṣṇa saw that the trident of the Mura demon was gradually rushing toward His carrier, Garuḍa. (p. 401)

Rukmiṇī fell down straight, like a banana tree cut down by a whirlwind. (p. 414)

Balarāma took a club in His hand and, without further talk, struck Rukmī on the head. (p. 427)

When Bāṇāsura saw him, Aniruddha was engaged in playing with Usā.
(p. 432)

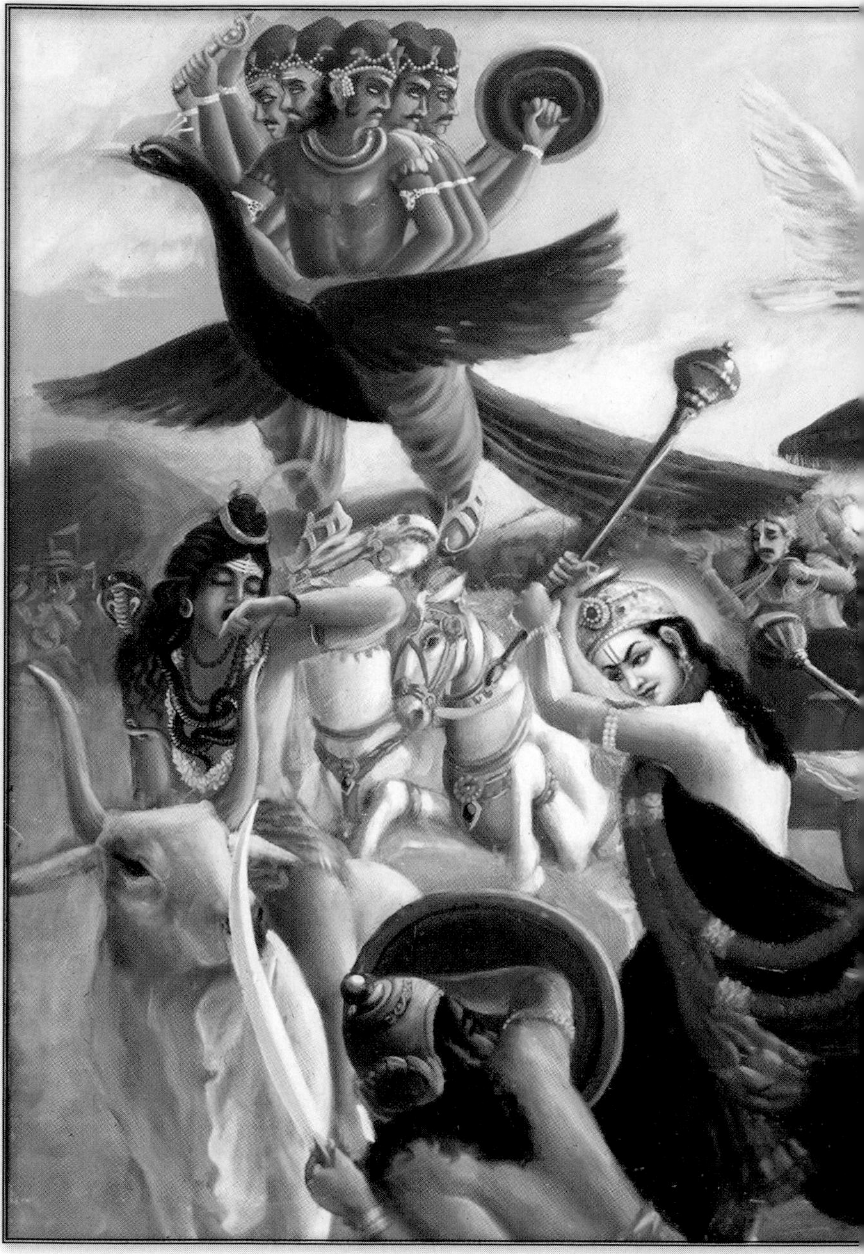

Bāṇāsura rushed towards Kṛṣṇa simultaneously working 500 bows and 2,000 arrows. (p. 436)

Balarāma passed every night with the *gopīs* in the forest of Vṛndāvana. (p. 453)

Thus Arjuna went to the forest with his bow and infallible arrows. He dressed himself with suitable protective garments, for he was to practice killing many enemies. He specifically entered that part of the forest where there were many tigers, deer and various other animals. Kṛṣṇa did not go with Arjuna to practice animal killing because He doesn't have to practice anything; He is self-sufficient. He accompanied Arjuna to see how he was practicing because in the future he would have to kill many enemies. After entering the forest, Arjuna killed many tigers, boars, bisons, *gavayas* (a kind of wild animal), rhinoceroses, deer, hares, porcupines and similar other animals, which he pierced with his arrows. Some of the dead animals, which were fit to be offered in the sacrifices, were carried by the servants and sent to King Yudhiṣṭhira. Other ferocious animals, such as tigers and rhinoceroses, were killed only to stop disturbances in the forest. Since there are many sages and saintly persons who are residents of the forests, it is the duty of the *kṣatriya* kings to keep even the forest in a peaceful condition for living.

Arjuna felt tired and thirsty from hunting, and therefore he went to the bank of the Yamunā along with Kṛṣṇa. When both the Kṛṣṇas, namely Kṛṣṇa and Arjuna (Arjuna is sometimes called Kṛṣṇa, as is Draupadī), reached the bank of the Yamunā, they washed their hands and feet and mouths and drank the clear water of the Yamunā. While they were resting and drinking water, they saw a beautiful girl of marriagable age walking alone on the bank of the Yamunā. Kṛṣṇa asked His friend Arjuna to go forward and ask the girl who she was. By the order of Kṛṣṇa, Arjuna immediately approached the girl, who was very beautiful. She had an attractive body and nice glittering teeth and smiling face. Arjuna inquired, "My dear girl, you are so beautiful with your raised breasts—may I ask you who you are? We are surprised to see you loitering here alone. What is your purpose in coming here? We can guess only that you are searching after a suitable husband. If you don't mind, you can disclose your purpose. I shall try to satisfy you."

The beautiful girl was the river Yamunā personified. She replied, "Sir, I am the daughter of the sun-god, and I am now performing penance and austerity to have Lord Viṣṇu as my husband. I think He is the Supreme Person and just suitable to become my husband. I disclose my desire thus because you wanted to know it."

The girl continued, "My dear sir, I know you are the hero Arjuna; so I may further say that I'll not accept anyone as my husband besides Lord Viṣṇu, because He is the only protector of all living entities and the bestower of liberation for all conditioned souls. I shall be thankful unto you if you pray to Lord Viṣṇu to become pleased with me." The girl Yamunā knew it well that Arjuna was a great devotee of Lord Kṛṣṇa and that if he would pray, Kṛṣṇa would never deny his request. To approach Kṛṣṇa directly may sometimes be futile, but to approach Kṛṣṇa through His devotee is sure to be successful. She further told Arjuna, "My name is Kālindī, and I live within the water of the Yamunā. My father was kind enough to construct a special house for me within the waters of the Yamunā, and I have vowed to remain in the water as long as I cannot find Lord Kṛṣṇa." The message of the girl Kālindī was duly carried to Kṛṣṇa by Arjuna although Kṛṣṇa, as the Supersoul of everyone's heart, knew everything. Without further discussion, Kṛṣṇa immediately accepted Kālindī and asked her to sit down on the chariot. Then all of them approached King Yudhiṣṭhira.

After this, Kṛṣṇa was asked by King Yudhiṣṭhira to help in constructing a suitable house to be planned by the great architect Viśvakarmā, the celestial engineer in the heavenly kingdom. Kṛṣṇa immediately called for Viśvakarmā, and He made him construct a wonderful city according to the desire of King Yudhiṣṭhira. When this city was constructed, Mahārāja Yudhiṣṭhira requested Kṛṣṇa to live with them a few days more in order to give them the pleasure of His association. Lord Kṛṣṇa accepted the request of Mahārāja Yudhiṣṭhira and remained there for many days more.

In the meantime, Kṛṣṇa engaged in the pastime of offering Khāṇḍava Forest, which belonged to King Indra. Kṛṣṇa wanted to give it to Agni, the fire-god. Khāṇḍava Forest contained many varieties of drugs, and Agni required to eat them for rejuvenation. Agni, however, did not touch Khāṇḍava Forest directly, but requested Kṛṣṇa to help him. Agni knew that Kṛṣṇa was very much pleased with him because he had formerly given Him the Sudarśana disc. So in order to satisfy Agni, Kṛṣṇa became the chariot driver of Arjuna, and both went to the Khāṇḍava Forest. After Agni had eaten up the Khāṇḍava Forest, he was very much pleased. This time, he offered a specific bow known as Gāṇḍīva, four white horses, one chariot, and an invincible quiver with two specific arrows considered to be talismans, which had so much power that no warrior could counteract them. When the Khāṇḍava Forest was being devoured by the fire-god, Agni, there was a demon of the name Maya who was saved by Arjuna from the devastating fire. For this reason, that former demon became a great friend of Arjuna, and in order to please Arjuna he constructed a nice assembly house within the city constructed by Viśvakarmā. This assembly house had some corners so puzzling that when Duryodhana came to visit this house he was misdirected, accepting water as land and land as water.

Duryodhana thus became insulted by the opulence of the Pāṇḍavas, and he became their determined enemy.

After a few days, Kṛṣṇa took permission from King Yudhiṣṭhira to return to Dvārakā. When he got permission, he went to his country, accompanied by Sātyaki, the leader of the Yadus who were living in Hastināpura with Him. Kālindī also returned with Kṛṣṇa to Dvārakā. After returning, Kṛṣṇa consulted many learned astrologers to find the suitable moment at which to marry Kālindī, and then He married her with great pomp. This marriage ceremony gave much pleasure to the relatives of both parties, and all of them enjoyed the great occasion.

The kings of Avantīpura (now known as Ujjain) were named Vinda and Anuvinda. Both kings were under the control of Duryodhana. They had one sister named Mitravindā, who was a very qualified, learned and elegant girl. She was the daughter of one of Kṛṣṇa's aunts. She was to select her husband in the assembly of princes, but she strongly desired to have Kṛṣṇa as her husband. During the assembly for selecting her husband, however, Kṛṣṇa was present, and He forcibly carried away Mitravindā in the presence of all other royal princes. Being unable to resist Kṛṣṇa, the princes were left simply looking at each other.

After this incident, Kṛṣṇa married the daughter of the King of Kośala. The King of Kośala Province was called Nagnajit. He was very pious and was a follower of the Vedic ritualistic ceremonies. His most beautiful daughter was named Satyā. Sometimes Satyā was called Nāgnajitī, for she was the daughter of King Nagnajit. King Nagnajit wanted to give the hand of his daughter to any prince who could defeat seven very strong, stalwart bulls maintained by him. No one in the princely order could defeat the seven bulls, and therefore no one could claim the hand of Satyā. The seven bulls were very strong, and they could hardly bear even the smell of any prince. Many princes approached this kingdom and tried to subdue these bulls, but instead of controlling them, they themselves were defeated. This news was spread all over the country, and when Kṛṣṇa heard that the girl Satyā could be achieved only by defeating the seven bulls, He prepared Himself to go to the kingdom of Kośala. With many soldiers, He approached that part of the country, known as Ayodhyā, making a regular state visit.

When it was known to the King of Kośala that Kṛṣṇa had come to ask the hand of his daughter, he became very pleased. With great respect and pomp, he welcomed Kṛṣṇa to the kingdom. When Kṛṣṇa approached him, he offered Him a suitable sitting place and articles for reception. Everything appeared to be very elegant. Kṛṣṇa also offered him respectful obeisances, thinking him to be His future father-in-law.

When Satyā, the daughter of King Nagnajit, understood that Kṛṣṇa Himself had come to marry her, she was very much pleased that the husband of the goddess of fortune had so kindly come there to accept her. She had cherished the idea of marrying Kṛṣṇa for a long time and was following the principles of austerities in order to obtain her desired husband. She then began to think, "If I have performed any pious activities to the best of my capacity and if I have sincerely thought all along to have Kṛṣṇa as my husband, then Kṛṣṇa may be pleased to fulfill my long-cherished desire." She began to offer prayers to Kṛṣṇa mentally, thinking, "I do not know how the Supreme Personality of Godhead can be pleased upon me. He is the master and Lord of everyone. Even the goddess of fortune, whose place is next to the Supreme Personality of Godhead, and Lord Śiva, Lord Brahmā and many other demigods of different planets always offer their respectful obeisances unto the Lord. The Lord also sometimes descends on this earth in different incarnations in order to fulfill the desire of His devotees. He is so exalted and great that I do not know how to satisfy Him." She thought that the Supreme Personality of Godhead could be pleased only out of His own causeless mercy upon the devotee; otherwise, there was no other means to please Him. Lord Caitanya, in the same way, prayed in His *Śikṣāṣṭaka* verses, "My Lord, I am Your eternal servant. Somehow or other I have fallen into this material existence. If You kindly pick me up and fix me as an atom of dust at Your lotus feet, it will be a great favor to Your eternal servant." The Lord can be pleased only by a humble attitude in the service spirit. The more we render service unto the Lord under the direction of the spiritual master, the more we make advancement on the path of approaching the Lord. We cannot demand any grace or mercy from the Lord because of our service rendered to Him. He may accept or not accept our service, but the only means to satisfy the Lord is through the service attitude, and nothing else.

King Nagnijit was already a pious king, and having Kṛṣṇa in his palace, he began to worship Him to the best of his knowledge and capacity. He presented himself before the Lord thus: "My dear Lord, You are the proprietor of the whole cosmic manifestation, and You are Nārāyaṇa, the rest of all living creatures. You are self-sufficient and pleased with Your personal opulences, so how can I offer You anything? And how could I please You by such offering? It is not possible, because I am an insignificant living being. Actually I have no capacity to render any service unto You."

Kṛṣṇa is the Supersoul of all living creatures, so He could understand the mind of Satyā, the daughter of King Nagnajit. He was also very much pleased with the respectful worship of the King in offering Him a sitting place, eatables, residence, etc. He was appreciative, therefore, that both the girl and the father of the girl were anxious to have Him as their intimate relative. He began to smile and in a great voice said, "My dear King Nagnajit, you know very well that anyone in the princely order who is regular in his position will never ask anything from anyone, however exalted he may be. Such requests by a *kṣatriya* king from another person have been deliberately forbidden by the learned Vedic followers. If a *kṣatriya* breaks this regulation, his action is condemned by learned scholars. But in spite of this rigid regulative principle, I am asking you for the hand of your beautiful daughter just to establish our relationship in return for your great reception of Me. You may also be pleased to be informed that in our family tradition there is no scope for our offering anything in exchange for accepting your daughter. We cannot pay any price which you may impose for delivering her." In other words, Kṛṣṇa wanted the hand of Satyā from the King without fulfilling the condition of defeating the seven bulls.

After hearing the statement of Lord Kṛṣṇa, King Nagnajit said, "My dear Lord, You are the reservoir of all pleasure, all opulences and all qualities. The goddess of fortune, Lakṣmījī, always lives on Your chest. Under these circumstances, who can be a better husband for my daughter? Both myself and my daughter have always prayed for this opportunity. You are the chief of the Yadu dynasty. You may kindly know that from the very beginning I have made a vow to marry my daughter to a suitable candidate, one who can come out victorious in the test I have devised. I have imposed this test just to understand the prowess and position of my intended son-in-law. You are Lord Kṛṣṇa, and You are the chief of all heroes. I am sure You shall be able to bring these seven bulls under control without any difficulty. Until now they have never been subdued by any prince; anyone who has attempted to bring them under control has simply had his limbs broken."

King Nagnajit continued his request: "Kṛṣṇa, if You'll kindly bridle the seven bulls and bring them under control, then undoubtedly You will be selected as the desired husband of my daughter, Satyā." After hearing this statement, Kṛṣṇa could understand that the King did not want to break his vow. Thus, in order to fulfill his desire, He tightened His belt and prepared to fight with the bulls. He immediately divided Himself into seven Kṛṣṇas, and each one of Them immediately caught hold of a bull and bridled its nose, thus bringing it under control as if it were a plaything.

Kṛṣṇa's dividing Himself into seven is very significant. It was known to Satyā, the daughter of King Nagnajit, that Kṛṣṇa had already married many other wives, and still she was attached to Kṛṣṇa. In order to encourage her, He immediately expanded Himself into seven. The purport is that Kṛṣṇa is one, but He has unlimited forms of expansions. He married many hundreds of thousands of wives, but this does not mean that while He was with one wife the others were bereft of His association. Kṛṣṇa could associate with each and every wife by His expansions.

When Kṛṣṇa brought the bulls under His control by bridling their noses, their strength and pride were immediately smashed. The name and fame which the bulls had attained was thus vanquished. When the bulls had been bridled by Kṛṣṇa, He pulled them strongly, just as a child pulls a toy wooden bull. Upon seeing this advantage of Kṛṣṇa, King Nagnajit became very much astonished and immediately, with great pleasure, brought his daughter Satyā before Kṛṣṇa and handed her over to Him. Kṛṣṇa also immediately accepted Satyā as His wife. Then there was a marriage ceremony with great pomp. The queens of King Nagnajit also were very much pleased because their daughter Satyā got Kṛṣṇa as her husband. Since the King and queens were very pleased on this auspicious occasion, there was a celebration all over the city in honor of the marriage. Everywhere was heard the sounds of the conchshell and kettledrum and various other vibrations of music and song. The learned *brāhmaṇas* began to shower their blessings upon the newly married couple. In jubilation, all the inhabitants of the city dressed themselves with colorful garments and ornaments. King Nagnajit was so pleased that he began to give a dowry to the daughter and son-in-law, as follows.

First of all he gave them ten thousand cows and three thousand well-dressed young maidservants, ornamented up to their necks. This system of dowry is still current in India especially for the *kṣatriya* princes. Also, when a *kṣatriya* prince is married, at least a dozen maidservants of similar age are given along with the bride. After giving the cows and maidservants, the King also enriched the dowry by giving 9,000 elephants and a hundred times more chariots than elephants. This means that he gave 900,000 chariots. And he gave a hundred times more horses than chariots, or 90,000,000 horses, and a hundred times more slaves than horses. Such slaves and maidservants were maintained by the royal princes with all provisions, as if they were their own children or family members. After giving this dowry as described, the King of the Kośala Province bade his daughter and great son-in-law be seated on a chariot. He allowed them to go to their home, guarded by a division of well-equipped soldiers. When they were travelling fast to their new home, his heart became enlivened with affection for them.

Before this marriage of Satyā with Kṛṣṇa, there had been many competitive engagements with the bulls of King Nagnajit, and many other princes of the Yadu dynasty and of other dynasties as well had tried to win the hand of Satyā. When the frustrated princes of the other dynasties heard that Kṛṣṇa was successful in getting the hand of Satyā by subduing the bulls, naturally they became envious. While Kṛṣṇa was travelling to Dvārakā, all the frustrated and defeated princes encircled Him and began to shower their arrows on the bridal party. When they attacked Kṛṣṇa's party and threw arrows like incessant torrents of rain, Arjuna, the best friend of Kṛṣṇa, took charge of the challenge, and he alone drove them off very easily to please his great friend Kṛṣṇa on the occasion of His marriage. He immediately took up his bow of the name Gāṇḍīva and chased away all the princes; exactly as a lion drives away all other small animals simply by chasing them, Arjuna drove away all the princes without killing even one of them. After this, the chief of the Yadu dynasty, Lord Kṛṣṇa, along with His newly married wife and a huge dowry, entered the city of Dvārakā with great pomp. Kṛṣṇa then lived there with His wife very peacefully.

Kṛṣṇa had another aunt, His father's sister, whose name was Śrutakīrti, and who was married and lived in the Kekaya province. She had a daughter whose name was Bhadrā. Bhadrā also wanted to marry Kṛṣṇa, and her brother handed her over to Him unconditionally. Kṛṣṇa also accepted her as His bona fide wife. Thereafter, Kṛṣṇa married a daughter of the king of the Madras Province, and her name was Lakṣmaṇā. Lakṣmaṇā had all good qualities. She was also forcibly married by Kṛṣṇa, who took her in the same way that Garuḍa snatched the jar of nectar from the hands of the demons. Kṛṣṇa kidnapped this girl in the presence of many other princes in the assembly of her *svayaṁvara. Svayaṁvara* is a ceremony in which the bride can select her own husband from an assembly of many princes.

The description of Kṛṣṇa's marriage with the five girls mentioned in this chapter is not sufficient. He had many other thousands of wives besides them. The other thousands of wives were accepted by Kṛṣṇa after killing one demon named Bhaumāsura. All these thousands of girls were held captive in the palace of Bhaumāsura, and Kṛṣṇa released them and married them.

Thus ends the Bhaktivedanta purport of the Fifty-seventh Chapter of Kṛṣṇa, *"Five Queens Married by Kṛṣṇa."*

58/ Deliverance of the Demon Bhaumāsura

The story of Bhaumāsura—how he kidnapped and made captive 16,000 princesses by collecting them from the palaces of various kings and how he was killed by Kṛṣṇa, the Supreme Lord of wonderful character—is all described by Śukadeva Gosvāmī to King Parīkṣit in the *Śrīmad-Bhāgavatam.* Generally, the demons are always against the demigods. This demon, Bhaumāsura, having become very powerful, took by force the umbrella from the throne of the demigod Varuṇa. He also took the earrings of Aditi, the mother of the demigods. He conquered a portion of heavenly Mount Meru and occupied the portion which was known as Maṇiparvata. The King of the heavenly planets, Indra, therefore came to Dvārakā to complain about Bhaumāsura before Lord Kṛṣṇa.

Hearing this complaint by Indra, the King of heaven, Lord Kṛṣṇa, accompanied by His wife Satyabhāmā, immediately started for the abode of Bhaumāsura. Both of them rode on the back of Garuḍa, who flew them to Prāgjyotiṣapura, the capital city of Bhaumāsura. It was not a very easy task to enter into the city of Prāgjyotiṣapura, because it was very well fortified. First of all, there were four formidable forts guarding the four directions of the city, and it was well-protected on all sides by formidable military strength. The next boundary was a water canal all around the city, and in addition the whole city was surrounded with electric wires. The next fortification was of *anila,* a gaseous substance. After this, there was a network of barbed wiring constructed by a demon of the name Mura. It appeared that the city was well-protected even in terms of today's scientific advancements.

When Kṛṣṇa arrived, He broke all the forts to pieces by the strokes of His club, and the military strength scattered here and there by the constant onslaught of the arrows of Kṛṣṇa. With His celebrated Sudarśana-cakra He counteracted the electrified boundary; the channels of water and the gaseous boundary were made null and void, and He cut to pieces the electrified network fabricated by the demon Mura. By the vibration of His conchshell, He not only broke the hearts of great fighters, but also the fighting machines which were there. Similarly, the walls around the city were broken by His invincible club.

The vibration of His conchshell sounded like the thunderbolt at the time of the dissolution of the whole cosmic situation. The demon Mura heard the vibration of the conchshell, awakened from his sleep, and personally came out to see what had happened. He had five heads and had long been living within the water. The Mura demon was as brilliant as the sun at the time of the dissolution of the cosmic manifestation, and his temper was like blazing fire. The effulgence of his body was so dazzling that it was difficult to see him with open eyes. When he came out, he first of all took out his trident and began to rush the Supreme Personality of Godhead. The onslaught of the demon Mura was like a big snake attacking Garuḍa. His angry mood was very severe, and he appeared ready to devour the three worlds. First of all he attacked the carrier of Kṛṣṇa, Garuḍa, by whirling his trident and he began to vibrate sounds through his five faces like the roaring of a lion. The roaring produced by the vibration of his mouths spread all over the atmosphere until it extended not only all over the world, but also into outer space, up and down and out to the ten directions. In this way, the sound was rumbling throughout the whole universe.

Lord Kṛṣṇa saw that the trident of the Mura demon was gradually rushing toward His carrier, Garuḍa. Immediately, by a trick of His hand, He took two arrows and threw them toward the trident, cutting it to pieces. Simultaneously, using many arrows, He pierced the mouths of the demon Mura. When he saw himself outmaneuvered by the Supreme Personality of Godhead, the Mura demon immediately began to strike Him in great anger with his club. But Lord Kṛṣṇa, with His own club, broke the club of Mura to pieces before it could reach Him. The demon, bereft of his weapon, decided to attack Kṛṣṇa with his strong arms, but by the aid of His Sudarśana-cakra, Kṛṣṇa immediately separated the demon's five heads from his body. The demon then fell into the water, just as the peak of a mountain falls into the ocean after being struck by the thunderbolt of Indra.

This demon Mura had seven sons, named Tāmra, Antarikṣa, Śravaṇa, Vibhāvasu, Vasu, Nabhasvān and Aruṇa. All of them became puffed up and vengeful because of the death of their father, and in order to retaliate, they prepared in great anger to fight with Kṛṣṇa. They equipped themselves with necessary weapons and situated Pīṭha, another demon, to act as commander in the battle. By the order of Bhaumāsura, all of them combinedly attacked Kṛṣṇa.

When they came before Lord Kṛṣṇa, they began to shower Him with many kinds of weapons, like swords, clubs, lances, arrows and tridents. But they did not know that the strength of the Supreme Personality of Godhead is unlimited and invincible. Kṛṣṇa, with His arrows, cut all the weapons of the men of Bhaumāsura into pieces, like grains. Kṛṣṇa then threw His weapons, and Bhaumāsura's commander-in-chief, Pīṭha, along with his assistants, fell down, their military dress cut off and their heads, legs, arms and thighs severed. All of them were sent to the superintendent of death, Yamarāja.

Bhaumāsura was also known as Narakāsura, for he happened to be the son of the earth personified. When he saw that all his soldiers, commanders and fighters were killed on the battlefield by the strokes of the weapons of the Personality of Godhead, he became exceedingly angry at the Lord. He then came out of the city with a great number of elephants who had all been born and brought up on the seashore. All of them were highly intoxicated. When they came out, they saw that Lord Kṛṣṇa and His wife were beautifully situated high in outer space just like a blackish cloud about the sun, glittering with the light of electricity. The demon Bhaumāsura immediately released a weapon called Śataghnī, by which he could kill hundreds of warriors with one stroke, and simultaneously all his assistants also threw their respective weapons at the Supreme Personality of Godhead. Lord Kṛṣṇa began to counteract all these weapons by releasing His feathered arrows. The result of this fight was that all the soldiers and commanders of Bhaumāsura fell to the ground, their arms, legs and heads separated from their trunks, and all their horses and elephants also fell with them. In this way, all the weapons released by Bhaumāsura were cut to pieces by the reaction of the Lord's arrows.

The Lord was fighting on the back of Garuḍa, and Garuḍa was also helping the Lord by striking the horses and the elephants with his wings and scratching their heads with his nails and sharpened beak. The elephants were feeling much pain by Garuḍa's attack on them, and they were all dispersing from the battlefield. Bhaumāsura alone remained on the battlefield, and he engaged himself in fighting with Kṛṣṇa. He saw that Kṛṣṇa's carrier, Garuḍa, was causing great disturbance to his soldiers and elephants, and in great anger he struck Garuḍa with all his strength, which defied the strength of the thunderbolt. Fortunately, Garuḍa was not an ordinary bird, and he felt the strokes given by Bhaumāsura just as a great elephant feels the impact of a garland of flowers.

Bhaumāsura thus came to see that none of his tricks would act upon Kṛṣṇa, and he became aware that all his attempts to kill Kṛṣṇa would be frustrated. Yet he attempted for the last time, taking a trident in his hand to strike Him. Kṛṣṇa was so dexterous that before Bhaumāsura could touch his trident, his head was cut off by the sharp Sudarśana-cakra. His head, illuminated by earrings and helmets, fell down on the battlefield. On the occasion of Bhaumāsura's being killed by Lord Kṛṣṇa, all the demon's relatives began to scream in disappointment, and the saintly persons began to glorify the chivalrous activities of the Lord. Taking this opportunity, the denizens of the heavenly planets began to shower flowers on the Lord.

At this time, the earth personified appeared before Lord Kṛṣṇa and greeted Him with a garland of *vaijayantī* jewels. She also returned the dazzling earrings of Aditi, bedecked with jewels and gold. She also returned the umbrella of Varuṇa, along with another valuable jewel, which she presented to Kṛṣṇa. After this, the earth personified began to offer her prayers to Kṛṣṇa, the Supreme Personality and master of the world, who is always worshiped by very exalted demigods. She fell down in obeisances and, in great devotional ecstasy, began to speak.

"Let me offer my respectful obeisances unto the Lord, who is always present with four kinds of symbols, namely His conchshell, disc, lotus and club, and who is the Lord of all demigods. Please accept my respectful obeisances unto You. My dear Lord, You are the Supersoul, and in order to satisfy the aspiration of Your devotees, You descend on the earth in Your various transcendental incarnations, which are just appropriate to the devotees' worshipful desire. Kindly accept my respectful obeisances.

"My dear Lord, the lotus flower is grown out of Your navel, and You are always decorated with a garland of lotus flowers. Your eyes are always spread like the petals of the lotus flower, and therefore they are all-pleasing to the eyes of others. Your lotus feet are so soft and delicate that they are always worshiped by Your unalloyed devotees, and they pacify their lotus-like hearts. I therefore repeatedly offer my respectful obeisances unto You.

"You possess all kinds of religions, fame, property, knowledge and renunciation; You are the shelter of all five opulences. Although You are all-pervading, You have nevertheless appeared as the son of Vasudeva. Please, therefore, accept my respectful obeisances. You are the original Supreme Personality of Godhead and the supreme cause of all causes. Only Your Lordship is the reservoir of all knowledge. Let me offer my respectful obeisances unto You. Personally You are unborn; still, You are the father of the whole cosmic manifestation. You are the reservoir and shelter of all kinds of energies. The manifestive appearance of this world is caused by You, and You are both the cause and effect of this cosmic manifestation. Please therefore accept my respectful obeisances.

"My dear Lord, as for the three gods—Brahmā, Viṣṇu and Śiva—they are also not independent of You. When there is necessity of creating this cosmic manifestation, You create Your passionate appearance of Brahmā, and when You want to maintain this cosmic manifestation, You expand Yourself as Lord Viṣṇu, the reservoir of all goodness. Similarly, You appear as Lord Śiva, master of the modes of ignorance, and thus dissolve the whole creation. Your transcendental position is always maintained, in spite of creating these three modes of material nature. You are never entangled like the ordinary living entities with these modes of material nature.

"Actually, my Lord, You are the material nature, You are the father of the universe, and You are the eternal time that has caused the combination of nature and the material creator. Still, You are always transcendental to all these material activities. My dear Lord, O Supreme Personality of Godhead, I know that earth, water, fire, air, sky, the five sense objects, mind, the senses and their deities, egotism, as well as the total material energy—everything animate and inanimate in this phenomenal world is resting upon You. Since everything is produced of You, nothing can be separated from You. Yet, since You are transcendentally situated, neither can anything material be identified with Your personality. Everything is, therefore, simultaneously one and different from You, and the philosophers who try to separate everything from you are certainly mistaken in their viewpoint.

"My dear Lord, may I inform You that this boy, whose name is Bhagadatta, is the son of my son, Bhaumāsura. He has been very much affected by the ghastly situation created by the death of his father and has become very much confused, being afraid of the present situation. I have therefore brought him to surrender unto Your lotus feet. I request Your Lordship to give shelter to this boy and bless him with Your lotus feet. I am bringing him to You so that he may become relieved from the reactions of all the sinful activities of his father."

When Lord Kṛṣṇa heard the prayers of mother Earth, He immediately assured her of immunity from all fearful situations. He said to Bhagadatta, "Don't be afraid." Then He entered the palace of Bhaumāsura, which was equipped with all kinds of opulences. In the palace of Bhaumāsura Lord Kṛṣṇa saw 16,100 young princesses, who had been kidnapped and held captive there. When the princesses saw the Supreme Personality of

Godhead, Kṛṣṇa, enter the palace, they immediately became captivated by the beauty of the Lord and prayed for His causeless mercy. Within their minds, they decided to accept Lord Kṛṣṇa as their husband without any hesitation. Each one of them began to pray to providence that Kṛṣṇa might become her husband. Sincerely and seriously, they offered their hearts to the lotus feet of Kṛṣṇa with an unalloyed devotional attitude. As the Supersoul in everyone's heart, Kṛṣṇa could understand their uncontaminated desire, and He agreed to accept them as His wives. Thus, He arranged for suitable dresses and ornaments for them, and each of them, seated on a palanquin, was dispatched to Dvārakā City. Kṛṣṇa also collected unlimited wealth from the palace, along with chariots, horses, jewels and treasure. He took from the palace fifty white elephants, each with four tusks, and all of them were dispatched to Dvārakā.

After this incident, Lord Kṛṣṇa and Satyabhāmā entered Amarāvatī, the capital city of the heavenly planet, and they immediately entered the palace of King Indra and his wife, Śacīdevī, who welcomed them. Kṛṣṇa then presented Indra with the earrings of Aditi.

When Kṛṣṇa and Satyabhāmā were returning from the capital city of Indra, Satyabhāmā remembered Kṛṣṇa's promise to give her the plant of the *pārijāta* flower. Taking the opportunity of having come to the heavenly kingdom, she plucked a *pārijāta* plant and kept it on the back of Garuḍa. Once Nārada took a *pārijāta* flower and presented it to Kṛṣṇa's senior wife, Śrī Rukmiṇīdevī. On account of this, Satyabhāmā developed an inferiority complex; she also wanted a flower from Kṛṣṇa. Kṛṣṇa could understand the competitive womanly nature of His co-wives, and He smiled. He immediately asked Satyabhāmā, "Why are you asking for only one flower? I would like to give you a whole tree of *pārijāta* flowers."

Actually, Kṛṣṇa had purposely taken His wife Satyabhāmā with Him so she could collect the *pārijāta* with her own hand. But the denizens of the heavenly planet, including Indra, became very irritated. Without their permission, Satyabhāmā had plucked a *pārijāta* plant, which is not to be found on the earth planet. Indra, along with other demigods, offered opposition to Kṛṣṇa and Satyabhāmā for taking away the plant, but in order to please His favorite wife Satyabhāmā, Kṛṣṇa became determined and adamant, so there was a fight between the demigods and Kṛṣṇa. As, usual, Kṛṣṇa came out victorious, and He triumphantly brought the *pārijāta* plant chosen by His wife to this earth planet, to Dvārakā. After this, the plant was installed in the palace garden of Satyabhāmā. On account of this extraordinary tree, the garden house of Satyabhāmā became extraordinarily beautiful. As the *pārijāta* plant came down to the earthly planet, the fragrance of the flower also came down, and the celestial swans also migrated to this earth in search of its fragrance and honey.

King Indra's behavior toward Kṛṣṇa was not very much appreciated by great sages like Śukadeva Gosvāmī. Out of His causeless mercy, Kṛṣṇa had gone to the heavenly kingdom, Amarāvatī, to present King Indra with his mother's earrings, which had been lost to Bhaumāsura, and Indra had been very glad to receive them. But when a flower plant from the heavenly kingdom was taken by Kṛṣṇa, Indra offered to fight with Him. This was self-interest on the part of Indra. He offered his prayer, tipping down his head to the lotus feet of Kṛṣṇa, but as soon as his purpose was served, he became a different creature. That is the way of the dealings of materialistic men. Materialistic men are always interested in their own profit. For this purpose they can offer any kind of respect to anyone, but when their personal interest is over, they are no longer friends. This selfish nature is not only found among the richer class of men on this planet, but is present even in personalities like Indra and other demigods. Too much wealth makes a man selfish. A selfish man is not prepared to take to Kṛṣṇa consciousness and is condemned by great devotees like Śukadeva Gosvāmī. In other words, possession of too many worldly riches is a disqualification for advancement in Kṛṣṇa consciousness.

After defeating Indra, Kṛṣṇa arranged to marry the 16,100 girls brought from the custody of Bhaumāsura. By expanding Himself in 16,100 forms, He simultaneously married them all in different palaces in one auspicious moment. He thus established the truth that Kṛṣṇa and no one else is the Supreme Personality of Godhead. There is nothing impossible, for Kṛṣṇa is the Supreme Personality of Godhead; He is all-powerful, omnipresent and imperishable, and as such there is nothing wonderful in this pastime. All the palaces of the more than 16,000 queens of Kṛṣṇa were full with suitable gardens, furniture and other paraphernalia, of which there is no parallel in this world. There is no exaggeration in this story from *Śrīmad-Bhāgavatam.* The queens of Kṛṣṇa were all expansions of the goddess of fortune, Lakṣmījī. Kṛṣṇa used to live with them in different palaces, and He treated them in exactly the same way as an ordinary man treats his wife.

We should always remember that the Supreme Personality of Godhead Kṛṣṇa was playing exactly like a human being; although He showed His extraordinary opulences by simultaneously marrying more than 16,000 wives in more than 16,000 palaces, He behaved with them just like an ordinary man, and He strictly followed the relationship between husband and wife required in ordinary homes. Therefore, it is very difficult to understand the characteristics of the Supreme Brahman, the Personality of Godhead. Even demigods like Brahmā and others are unable to probe into the transcendental pastimes of the Lord. The wives of Kṛṣṇa were so fortunate that they got the Supreme Personality of Godhead as their husband, although their husband's personality was unknown even to the demigods like Brahmā.

In their dealings as husband and wife, Kṛṣṇa and His queens would smile, talk, joke, embrace, and so on, and their conjugal relationship ever increasingly developed. In this way, both Kṛṣṇa and the queens enjoyed transcendental happiness in their household life. Although each and every queen had thousands of maidservants engaged for her service, the queens were all personally attentive in serving Kṛṣṇa. Each one of them used to receive Kṛṣṇa personally when He entered the palace. They engaged in getting Him seated on a nice couch, presenting Him with all kinds of worshipable paraphernalia, washing His lotus feet with Ganges water, offering Him betel nuts and massaging His legs. In this way, they were giving Him relief from the fatigue of being away from home. They saw to fanning Him nicely, offering Him fragrant essential floral oil, decorating Him with flower garlands, dressing His hair, asking Him to lie down to take rest, bathing Him personally and feeding Him nice palatable dishes. All these things were done by each queen herself. They did not wait for the maidservants. In other words, Kṛṣṇa and His different queens displayed on this earth an ideal household life.

Thus ends the Bhaktivedanta purport of the Fifty-eighth Chapter of Kṛṣṇa, *"Deliverance of the Demon Bhaumāsura."*

59 / Talks Between Kṛṣṇa and Rukmiṇī

Once upon a time, Lord Kṛṣṇa the Supreme Personality of Godhead, the bestower of all knowledge to all living entities from Brahmā to the insignificant ant, was sitting in the bedroom of Rukmiṇī, who was engaged in the service of the Lord along with her assistant maidservants. Kṛṣṇa was sitting on the bedstead of Rukmiṇī, and the maidservants were engaged in fanning Him with *cāmaras* (yak-tail fly-whisks).

Lord Kṛṣṇa's dealings with Rukmiṇī as a perfect husband is a perfect manifestation of the supreme perfection of the Personality of Godhead. There are many philosophers who propound a concept of the Absolute Truth in which God cannot do this or that. They deny the incarnation of God, or the Supreme Absolute Truth in human form. But actually, the fact is different: God cannot be subjected to our imperfect sensual activities. He is the all-powerful, omnipresent Personality of Godhead, and by His supreme will, He can not only create, maintain and annihilate the whole cosmic manifestation, but He can also descend as an ordinary human being in order to execute the highest mission. As stated in the *Bhagavad-gītā,* whenever there are discrepancies in the discharge of human occupational duties, He descends. He is not forced to appear by any external agency, but descends by His own internal potency in order to reestablish the standard functions of human activities as well as to simultaneously annihilate the disturbing elements in the progressive march of human civilization. In accordance with this principle of the transcendental pastimes of the Supreme Personality of Godhead, He descended in His eternal form of Śrī Kṛṣṇa in the dynasty of the Yadus.

The palace of Rukmiṇī was wonderfully finished. There were many canopies hanging on the ceiling with laces bedecked with pearl garlands, and the whole palace was illuminated by the effulgence of valuable jewels. There were many flower orchards of *baela* and *cāmeli,* which are con-

considered to be the most fragrant flowers in India. There were many clusters of these plants, with blooming flowers enhancing the beauty of the palace. And because of the exquisite fragrance of the flowers, little groups of humming bees were gathered around the trees, and at night the pleasing moonshine glittered through the network of holes in the windows. There were many heavily flowered trees of *pārijāta*, and the mild wind stirred the flavor of the flowers all around. Within the walls of the palace, there was incense burning, and the fragrant smoke was leaking out of the window shutters. Within the room there were mattresses covered with white bedsheets resembling the foam of milk; the bedding was as soft and white as milk foam. In this situation, Lord Śrī Kṛṣṇa was very comfortably sitting and enjoying the service of Rukmiṇījī assisted by her maidservants.

Rukmiṇī was also very eager to get the opportunity of serving the Supreme Personality of Godhead as her husband. She therefore wanted to serve the Lord personally and took the handle of the *cāmara* from the hand of the maidservant and began to move the fan. The handle of the *cāmara* was made of gold, decorated and bedecked with valuable jewels, and it became more beautiful when it was taken by Rukmiṇī, because all of her fingers were beautifully set with jeweled rings. Her legs were decorated with ankle bells and jewels, which rang very softly between the pleats of her sari. Rukmiṇī's raised breasts were smeared with *kuṅkuma* and saffron; thus her beauty was enhanced by the reflection of the reddish color emanating from her covered breasts. The highly raised lower part of her buttocks was decorated with a jeweled lace girdle, and a locket of great effulgence hung on her neck. Above all, because she was engaged in the service of Lord Kṛṣṇa—although at that time she was old enough to have grown-up sons—her beautiful body was beyond compare in the three worlds. When we take account of her beautiful face, it appears that the curling hair on her head, the beautiful earrings on her ears, her smiling mouth, and her necklace of gold, all combined to shower rains of nectar; and it was definitely proved that Rukmiṇī was none other than the original goddess of fortune who is always engaged in the service of the lotus feet of Nārāyaṇa.

The pastimes of Kṛṣṇa and Rukmiṇī in Dvārakā are accepted by great authorities as manifestations of those of Nārāyaṇa and Lakṣmī, which are of an exalted opulence. The pastimes of Rādhā and Kṛṣṇa in Vṛndāvana are simple and rural, distinguished from the polished urban characteristics of those of Dvārakā. The characteristics of Rukmiṇī were unusually bright, and Kṛṣṇa was very much satisfied with her behavior.

Kṛṣṇa had experienced that when Rukmiṇī was offered a *pārijāta* flower by Nārada Muni, Satyabhāmā had become envious of her co-wife and had immediately demanded a similar flower from Kṛṣṇa. In fact, she could not be pacified until she was promised the whole tree. That was actually done by Kṛṣṇa; the tree was brought down to the earth planet from the heavenly kingdom. After this episode, Kṛṣṇa expected that because Satyabhāmā had been rewarded by a full tree of *pārijāta,* Rukmiṇī would also demand something. Rukmiṇī did not mention anything of the incident, however, for she was grave and simply satisfied in her service. Kṛṣṇa wanted to see her a bit irritated, and therefore He schemed in order to see the beautiful face of Rukmiṇī in an irritated condition. Although Kṛṣṇa had more than 16,100 wives, He used to behave with each of them with familial affection; He would create a particular situation between Himself and His wife in which the wife would criticize Him in the irritation of love, and Kṛṣṇa would enjoy this. In this case, because Kṛṣṇa could not find any fault with Rukmiṇī, for she was very great and always engaged in His service, He smilingly, in great love, began to speak to her. Rukmiṇī was the daughter of King Bhīṣmaka, a powerful king. Thus Kṛṣṇa did not address her as Rukmiṇī; He addressed her this time as the princess. "My dear princess, it is very surprising. Many great personalities in the royal order wanted to marry you. Although not all of them were kings, all possessed the opulence and riches of the kingly order; they were well-behaved, learned, famous among kings, beautiful in their bodily features and personal qualifications, liberal, very powerful in strength, and advanced in every respect. They were not unfit in any way, and over and above that, your father and your brother had no objection to such marriages. On the contrary, they gave their word of honor that you would be married with Śiśupāla; the marriage was sanctioned by your parents. Śiśupāla was a great king and was so lusty and mad after your beauty that if he had married you, I think he would always have remained with you just like your faithful servant.

"In comparison to Śiśupāla, with his personal qualities, I am nothing. And you may personally realize it. I am surprised that you rejected the marriage with Śiśupāla and accepted Me, who am inferior in comparison to Śiśupāla. I think myself completely unfit to be your husband because you are so beautiful, sober, grave and exalted. May I inquire from you the reason that induced you to accept Me? Now, of course, I can address you as My beautiful wife, but still I may inform you of My actual position—that I am inferior to all those princes who wanted to marry you.

"First of all, you may know that I was so much afraid of Jarāsandha that I could not dare to live on the land, and thus I have constructed this house within the water of the sea. It is not my business to disclose this secret to others, but you must know that I am not very heroic; I am a coward and am afraid of them. Still I am not safe, because all the great kings of the land are inimical to Me. I have personally created this inimical feeling by fighting with them in many ways. Another fault is that although I am on the throne of Dvārakā, I have no immediate claim. Although I got a kingdom by killing My maternal uncle, Kaṁsa, the kingdom was to go to My grandfather; so actually I have no possession of a kingdom. Besides that, I have no fixed aim in life. People cannot understand Me very well. What is the ultimate goal of My life? They know very well that I was a cowherd boy in Vṛndāvana. People expected that I would follow the footsteps of My foster father, Nanda Mahārāja, and be faithful to Śrīmatī Rādhārāṇī and all Her friends in the village of Vṛndāvana. But all of a sudden I left them. I wanted to become a famous prince. Still I could not have any kingdom, nor could I rule as a prince. People are bewildered about My ultimate goal of life; they do not know whether I am a cowherd boy or a prince, whether I am the son of Nanda Mahārāja or the son of Vasudeva. Because I have no fixed aim in life, people may call Me a vagabond. Therefore, I am surprised that you could select such a vagabond husband.

"Besides this, I am not very much polished, even in social etiquette. A person should be satisfied with one wife, but you see I have married many times, and I have more than 16,000 wives. I cannot please all of them as a polished husband. My behavior with them is not very nice, and I know you are very much conscious of it. I sometimes create a situation with My wives which is not very happy. Because I was trained in a village in My childhood, I am not well acquainted with the etiquette of urban life. I do not know the way to please a wife with nice words and behavior. And from practical experience it is found that any woman who follows My way or who becomes attracted by Me is ultimately left to cry for the rest of her life. In Vṛndāvana, many *gopīs* were attracted to Me, and now I have left them, and they are living but are simply crying for Me in separation. I have heard from Akrūra and Uddhava that since I left Vṛndāvana, all my cowherd boy friends, the *gopīs* and Rādhārāṇī, and My foster father Nanda Mahārāja are simply crying constantly for Me. I have left Vṛndāvana for good and am now engaged with the queens in Dvārakā, but I am not well-behaved with any of you. So you can very easily understand that I have no steadiness of character; I am not a very reliable husband. The net result of being attracted to Me is to acquire a life of bereavement only.

"My dear beautiful princess, you may also know that I am always penniless. Just after My birth, I was carried penniless to the house of Nanda Mahārāja, and I was raised just like a cowherd boy. Although My foster father possessed many hundreds of thousands of cows, I was not proprietor of even one of them. I was simply entrusted to take care of them and tender them, but I was not the proprietor. Here also, I am not proprietor of anything, but am always penniless. There is no cause to lament for such a penniless condition; I possessed nothing in the past, so why should I lament that I do not possess anything at present? You may note also that My devotees are not very opulent persons; they also are very poor in worldly goods. Those who are very rich, possessing worldly wealth, are not interested in devotion to Me or Kṛṣṇa consciousness. On the contrary, when a person becomes penniless, whether by force or by circumstances, he may become interested in Me if he gets the proper opportunity. Persons who are proud of their riches, even if they are offered association with My devotees, do not take advantage of consciousness of Me. In other words, the poorer class of men may have some interest in Me, but the richer class of men have no interest. I think, therefore, that your selection of Me was not very intelligent. You appear to be very intelligent, trained by your father and brother, but ultimately you have made a great mistake in selecting your life's companion.

"But there is no harm; it is better late than never. You are at liberty to select a suitable husband who is actually an equal to you in opulence, family tradition, wealth, beauty, education—in all respects. Whatever mistakes you may have made may be forgotten. Now you may chalk out your own lucrative path of life. Usually a person does not establish a marital relationship with a person who is either higher or lower than his position. My dear daughter of the King of Vidarbha, I think you did not consider very sagaciously before your marriage. Thus you made a wrong selection by choosing Me as your husband. You mistakenly heard about My having very exalted character, although factually I was nothing more than a beggar. Without seeing Me and My actual position, simply by hearing about Me, you selected Me as your husband. That was not very rightly done. Therefore I advise you that it is better late than never; you can now select one of the great *kṣatriya* princes and accept him as your life's companion, and you can reject Me."

Kṛṣṇa was proposing that Rukmiṇī divorce Him at a time when Rukmiṇī already had many grown-up children. Therefore Kṛṣṇa's whole proposition to Rukmiṇī appeared to be something unexpected, because according to Vedic culture there was no such thing as separation of husband and wife by divorce. Nor was it possible for Rukmiṇī to do so in advanced age, when she had many married sons. Each and every one of Kṛṣṇa's proposals appeared to Rukmiṇī to be crazy, and she was surprised that Kṛṣṇa could say such things. Simple as she was, her anxiety was increasing more and more at the thought of separation from Kṛṣṇa.

Kṛṣṇa continued: "After all, you have to prepare yourself for your next life. I therefore advise that you select someone who can help you both in this life and the next life, for I am completely unable to help. My dear beautiful princess, you know that all the members of the princely order, including Śiśupāla, Śālva, Jarāsandha, Dantavakra and even your elder brother Rukmī, are all My enemies; they do not like Me at all. They hate Me from the core of their hearts. All these princes were very much puffed up with their worldly possessions, and they did not care a fig for anyone who came before them. In order to teach them some lessons, I agreed to kidnap you according to your desire; otherwise I actually have no love for you, although you loved Me even before the marriage.

"As I have already explained, I am not very much interested in family life or love between husband and wife. By nature, I am not very fond of family life, wife, children, home and opulences. As My devotees are always neglectful of all these worldly possessions, I am also like that. Actually, I am interested in self-realization; that gives Me pleasure, and not this family life." After submitting His statement, Lord Kṛṣṇa suddenly stopped.

The great authority Śukadeva Gosvāmī remarks that Kṛṣṇa almost always passed His time with Rukmiṇī, and Rukmiṇī was a bit proud to be so fortunate that Kṛṣṇa never left her even for a moment. Kṛṣṇa, however, does not like any of His devotees to be proud. As soon as a devotee becomes so, by some tactic He cuts down that pride. In this case also, Kṛṣṇa said many things which were hard for Rukmiṇī to hear. She could only conclude that although she was proud of her position, Kṛṣṇa could be separated from her at any moment.

Rukmiṇī was conscious that her husband was not an ordinary human being. He was the Supreme Personality of Godhead, the master of the three worlds. By the way He was speaking, she was afraid of being separated from the Lord, for she had never heard such harsh words from Kṛṣṇa before. Thus she became perplexed with fear of separation, and her heart began to palpitate. Without replying to a word of Kṛṣṇa's statement, she simply cried in great anxiety, as if being drowned in an ocean of grief. She silently scratched the ground with the nails of her toes, which were reflecting reddish light on the ground. The tears from her eyes were pink, mixed with the black cosmetic ointment from her eyelids, and the waters were dropping down, washing the *kuṅkuma* and saffron from her breasts. Choked up on account of great anxiety, unable to speak even a word, she kept her head downward and remained standing just like a stick. Due to extremely painful fearfulness and lamentation, she lost all her reasoning powers and became so weak that immediately her body lost so much weight that the bangles on her wrists became slackened. The *cāmara* rod with which she was serving Kṛṣṇa immediately fell from her hand. Her brain and memory became puzzled, and she lost consciousness. The nicely combed hair on her head scattered here and there, and she fell down straight, like a banana tree cut down by a whirlwind.

Lord Kṛṣṇa immediately realized that Rukmiṇī had not taken His words in a joking spirit. She had taken them very seriously, and in her extreme anxiety over immediate separation from Him, she had fallen into this condition. Lord Śrī Kṛṣṇa is naturally very affectionate toward His devotees, and seeing Rukmiṇī's condition, His heart immediately became softened. At once He became merciful to her. The relationship between Kṛṣṇa and Rukmiṇī was as Lakṣmī-Nārāyaṇa; therefore, He appeared before her in His four-handed manifestation of Nārāyaṇa. He got down from the bedstead, brought her up by her hands, and, placing His cooling hands on her face, smoothed the scattered hairs on her head. Lord Kṛṣṇa dried the wet breast of Rukmiṇījī with His hand. Understanding the seriousness of Rukmiṇī's love for Him, He embraced her to His chest.

The Supreme Personality is very expert in putting a thing reasonably for one's understanding, and thus He tried to retract all that He said before. He is the only resort for all the devotees, and so He knows very well how to satisfy His pure devotees. Kṛṣṇa understood that Rukmiṇī could not follow the statements which He had made in a joking way. To counteract her confusion, He again began to speak, as follows.

"My dear daughter of King Vidarbha, My dear Rukmiṇī, please do not misunderstand Me. Don't be unkind unto Me like this. I know you are sincerely and seriously attached to Me; you are My eternal companion. The words which have affected you so much are not factual. I wanted to irritate you a bit, and I was expecting you to make counter answers to those joking words. Unfortunately, you have taken them seriously; I am very sorry for it. I expected that your red lips would tremble in anger on hearing My statement and you would chastise Me in many words. O perfection of love, I never expected that your condition would be like this. I expected that you would put your blinking eyes upon Me in retaliation, and in that way, I would be able to see your beautiful face in that angry mood.

"My dear beautiful wife, you know that we are householders. We are always busy in many household affairs, so we long for a time that we can enjoy some joking words between us. That is our ultimate game in household life. Actually, the householders work very hard day and night, but all fatigue of the day's labor becomes minimized as soon as they meet, husband and wife together, and enjoy life in many ways." Lord Kṛṣṇa wanted to exhibit Himself just as an ordinary householder who delights himself by exchanging joking words with his wife. He therefore repeatedly requested Rukmiṇī not to take those words very seriously.

In this way, when Lord Kṛṣṇa pacified Rukmiṇī by His sweet words, she could understand that what was formerly spoken by Him was not actually meant, but was spoken to evoke some joking pleasure between themselves. She was therefore pacified by hearing the words of Kṛṣṇa. Gradually she was freed from all fearfulness of separation from Him, and she began to look on His face very cheerfully with her naturally smiling face. She said, "My dear lotus-eyed Lord, Your statement that we are not a fit combination is completely right. It is not possible for me to come to an equal level with You because You are the reservoir of all qualities, the unlimited Supreme Personality of Godhead. How can I be a fit match for You? There is no possibility of comparison with You, who are the master of all greatness, controller of the three qualities and the object of worship for great demigods like Brahmā and Lord Śiva. As far as I am concerned, I am a production of the three modes of material nature. The three modes of material nature are impediments towards the progressive advancement of devotional service. When and where can I be a fit match for You? My dear husband, You have rightly said also that being afraid of the kings, You have taken shelter in the water of the sea. But who is the king of this material world? I do not think that the so-called royal families are kings of the material world. The kings of the material world are the three modes of material nature. They are actually the controllers of this material world. You are situated in the core of everyone's heart, where You remain completely aloof from the touch of the three modes of material nature, and there is not doubt about it.

"You say You always maintain enmity with the worldly kings. But who are the worldly kings? I think the worldly kings are the senses. They are most formidable, and they control everyone. Certainly You maintain enmity with these material senses. You are never under the control of the senses; rather, You are the controller of the senses, Hṛṣīkeśa. My dear Lord, You have said that You are bereft of all royal power, and that is also correct. Not only are You bereft of material world supremacy, but even Your servants, those who have some attachment to Your lotus feet, also give up the material world supremacy because they consider the material position to be the darkest region, which checks the progress of spiritual enlightenment. Your servants do not like material supremacy, so what to speak of You? My dear Lord, Your statement that You do not act as an ordinary person with a particular aim in life is also perfectly correct. Even Your great devotees and servants, known as great sages and saintly persons, remain in such a state that no one can get any clue to the aim of their lives. They are considered by the human society to be crazy and cynical. Their aim of life remains a mystery to the common human being; the lowest of the mankind can know neither You nor Your servant. A contaminated human being cannot even imagine the pastimes of You and Your devotees. O unlimited one, when the activities and endeavors of Your devotees remain a mystery to the common human being, how can they understand Your motive and endeavor? All kinds of energies and opulences are engaged in Your service, but still they are resting at Your shelter.

"You have described Yourself as penniless, but this condition is not poverty. Since there is nothing in existence but Yourself, You do not require to possess anything—You Yourself are everything. Unlike others, You do not require to purchase anything extraneously. With You all contrary things can be adjusted because You are absolute. You do not possess anything, but no one is richer than You. In the material world no one can be rich without possessing. Since Your Lordship is absolute, You can adjust the contradiction of possessing nothing but at the same time being the richest. In the *Vedas* it is stated that although You have no material hands and legs, You accept everything which is offered in devotion by the devotees. You have no material eyes and ears, but still You can see everything everywhere, and You can hear everything everywhere. Although You do not possess anything, the great demigods who accept prayers and worship from others come and worship You to solicit Your mercy. How can You be categorized among the poor?

"My dear Lord, You have also stated that the richest section of human society does not worship You. This is also correct, because persons who are puffed up with material possessions think of utilizing their property for sense gratification. When a poverty-stricken man becomes rich, he makes a program for sense gratification. This is due to his ignorance of how to utilize his hard-earned money. Under the spell of the external energy, he thinks that his money is properly employed in sense gratification, and thus he neglects to render transcendental service. My dear Lord, You have stated that persons who possess nothing are very dear to You; renouncing everything, Your devotee wants to possess You only. I see, therefore, that a great sage like Nārada Muni who does not possess any material property is still very dear to You. And such persons do not care for anything but Your Lordship.

"My dear Lord, You have stated that a marriage between persons equal in status of social standing, beauty, riches, strength, influence and renunciation can be a suitable match. But this status of life can only be possible by Your grace. You are the supreme perfectional source of all opulences. Whatever opulent status of life one may have is all derived from You. As described in the *Vedānta-sūtra, janmādyasya yataḥ:* You are the supreme source from which everything emanates, the reservoir of all pleasures. Therefore, persons who are endowed with knowledge desire only to achieve You, and nothing else. To achieve Your favor, they give up everything—even the transcendental realization of Brahman. You are the supreme ultimate goal of life. You are the reservoir of all interests of the living entities. Those who are actually well-motivated desire only You, and for this reason they give up everything to attain success. They therefore deserve to be associated with You. In the society of the servitors and served in Kṛṣṇa consciousness, one is not subjected to the pains and pleasures of material society, which functions according to sex attraction. Therefore, everyone, man or woman, should seek to be an associate in Your society of servitors and served. You are the Supreme Personality of Godhead; no one can excel You, nor can anyone come up to an equal level with You. The perfect social system is that in which You remain in the center, being served as the Supreme, and all others engage as Your servitors. In such a perfectly constructed society, everyone can remain eternally happy and blissful.

"My Lord, You have stated that only the beggars praise Your glories, and that is also perfectly correct. But who are those beggars? Those beggars are all exalted devotees, liberated personalities and those in the renounced order of life. They are all great souls and devotees who have no other business than to glorify You. Such great souls forgive even the worst offender. These so-called beggars execute their spiritual advancement of life, tolerating all kinds of tribulations in the material world. My dear husband, do not think that out of my inexperience I accepted You as my husband; actually, I followed all these great souls. I followed the path of these great beggars and decided to surrender my life unto Your lotus feet.

"You have said that You are penniless, and that is correct. You distribute Yourself completely to these great souls and devotees. Knowing this fact perfectly well, I rejected even such great personalities like Lord Brahmā and King Indra. My Lord, the great time factor acts under Your direction only. The time factor is so great and powerful that within moments it can effect devastation anywhere within the creation. Considering all these factors, I thought Jarāsandha, Śiśupāla and similar other princes who wanted to marry Me to be no more important than ordinary insects.

"My dear all-powerful son of Vasudeva, Your statement that You have taken shelter within the water of the ocean, being afraid of all the great princes, is quite suitable, but my experience with You contradicts this. I have actually seen that You kidnapped me forcibly in the presence of all these princes. At the time of my marriage ceremony, simply by giving a jerk to the string of Your bow, You very easily drove the others away and kindly gave me shelter at Your lotus feet. I still remember vividly that You kidnapped me in the same way as a lion forcibly takes his share of hunted booty, driving away all other small animals within the twinkling of an eye.

"My dear lotus-eyed Lord, I cannot understand Your statement that women and other persons who have taken shelter under Your lotus feet pass their days only in bereavement. From the history of the world we can see that princes like Aṅga, Pṛthu, Bharata, Yayāti and Gaya were all great emperors of the world, and there were no competitors to their exalted positions. But in order to achieve the favor of Your lotus feet, they renounced their exalted positions and entered into the forest to practice penances and austerities. When they voluntarily accepted such a position, accepting Your lotus feet as all in all, does it mean that they were in lamentation and bereavement?

"My dear Lord, You have advised me that I can still select another from the princely order and divorce myself of Your companionship. But, my dear Lord, it is perfectly well-known to me that You are the reservoir of all good qualities. Great saintly persons like Nārada Muni are always engaged simply in glorifying Your transcendental characteristics. If someone simply takes shelter of such a saintly person, he immediately becomes freed from all material contamination. And by coming in direct contact with Your service the goddess of fortune agrees to bestow all her blessings. Under the circumstances, what woman who has once heard of Your glories from authoritative sources and somehow or other has tasted the nectarean flavor of Your lotus feet can be foolish enough to agree to marry someone of this material world who is always afraid of death, disease, old age and rebirth? I have therefore accepted Your lotus feet, not without consideration, but after mature and deliberate decision. My dear Lord, You are the master of the three worlds. You can fulfill all the desires of all Your devotees in this world and the next, because You are the Supreme Soul of everyone. I have therefore selected You as my husband, considering You to be the only fit personality. You may throw me in any species of life according to the reaction of my fruitive activities, and I haven't the least concern for this. My only ambition is that I may always remain fast to Your lotus feet, because You can deliver Your devotees from the illusory material existence and are always prepared to distribute Yourself to Your devotees.

"My dear Lord, You have advised me to select one of the princes such as Śiśupāla, Jarāsandha or Dantavakra, but what is their position in this world? They are always engaged in hard labor to maintain their household life, just like the bulls working hard day and night with the oil-pressing machine. They are compared to asses, beasts of burden. They are always dishonored like the dogs, and they are miserly like the cats. They have sold themselves like slaves to their wives. Any unfortunate woman who has never heard of Your glories may accept such a man as her husband, but a woman who has learned about You—that You are praised not only in this world, but in the halls of the great demigods like Lord Brahmā and Lord Śiva—will not accept anyone besides Yourself as her husband. A man within this material world is just a dead body. In fact, superficially, the living entity is covered by this body, which is nothing but a bag of skin decorated with beards and moustaches, hairs on the body, nails on the fingers and hairs on the head. Within this decorated bag there are bunches of muscles, bundles of bones, and pools of blood, always mixed up with stool, urine, mucus, bile and polluted air, and enjoyed by different kinds of insects and germs. A foolish woman accepts such a dead body as her husband and, in sheer misunderstanding, loves him as her dear companion. This is only possible because such a woman has never tasted the ever-blissful flavor of Your lotus feet.

"My dear lotus-eyed husband, You are self-satisfied. You do not care whether or not I am beautiful or qualified; You are not at all concerned about it. Therefore Your nonattachment for me is not at all astonishing; it is quite natural. You cannot be attached to any woman, however exalted her position and beauty. Whether You are attached to me or not, may my devotion and attention be always engaged at Your lotus feet. The material mode of passion is also Your creation, so when You passionately glance upon me, I accept it as the greatest boon of my life. I am ambitious only for such auspicious moments."

After hearing Rukmiṇī's statement and her clarification of each and every word which He had used to arouse her anger of love toward Him, Kṛṣṇa addressed Rukmiṇī as follows: "My dear chaste wife, My dear princess, I was expecting such an explanation from you, and for this purpose only I spoke all those joking words, so that you might be cheated of the real point of view. Now My purpose has been served. The wonderful explanation that you have given to each and every word of Mine is completely factual and approved by Me. O most beautiful Rukmiṇī, You are My dearmost wife. I am greatly pleased to understand how much love you have for Me. Please take it for granted that no matter what ambition and desire you might have and no matter what you might expect from Me, I am always at your service. And it is a fact also that My devotees, My dearmost friends and servitors, are always free from material contamination, even though they are not inclined to ask from Me such liberation. My devotees never desire anything from Me except to be engaged in My service. And yet because they are completely dependent upon Me, even if they are found to ask something from Me, that is not material. Such ambitions and desires, instead of becoming the cause of material bondage, become the source of liberation from this material world.

"My dear chaste and pious wife, I have tested, on the basis of strict chastity, your love for your husband, and you have passed the examination most successfully. I have purposely agitated you by speaking many words which were not applicable to your character, but I am surprised to see that not a pinch of your devotion to Me has been deviated from its fixed position. My dear wife, I am the bestower of all benedictions, even up to the standard of liberation from this material world, and it is I only who can stop the continuation of material existence and call one back to home, back to Godhead. One whose devotion for Me is adulterated worships Me for some material benefit, just to keep himself in the world of material happiness, culminating in the pleasure of sex life. One who engages himself in severe penance and austerities just to attain this material happiness is certainly under the illusion of My external energy. Persons who are engaged in My devotional service simply for the purpose of material gains and sense gratification certainly are very foolish. Material happiness based on sex life is available in the most abominable species of life, such as the hogs and dogs. No one should try to approach Me for such happiness, because it is available even if one is put into a hellish condition of life. It is better, therefore, for persons who are simply after material happiness and not after Me to remain in that hellish condition."

Material contamination is so strong that everyone is working very hard day and night for material happiness. The show of religiousness, austerity, penance, humanitarianism, philanthropy, politics, science—everything is aimed at realizing some material benefit. For the immediate success of material benefit, the materialistic persons generally worship different demigods, and under the spell of material propensities they sometimes take to the devotional service of the Lord. Sometimes it so happens that if a person sincerely serves the Lord and at the same time maintains material ambition, the Lord very kindly removes the sources of material happiness. Without finding any recourse in material happiness, the devotee then engages himself absolutely in pure devotional service.

Lord Kṛṣṇa continued, "My dear best of the queens, it is clearly understood by Me that you have no material ambition; your only purpose is to serve Me, and you have long been engaged in unalloyed service. Exemplary unalloyed devotional service not only can bestow upon the devotee liberation from this material world, but it also promotes him to the spiritual world for being eternally engaged in My service. Persons who are too addicted to material happiness cannot render such service. Women whose hearts are polluted and full of material desires devise various means of sense gratification while outwardly showing themselves to be great devotees.

"My dear honored wife, although I have thousands of wives, I do not think that any one of them can love Me more than you. The practical proof of your extraordinary position is that you had never seen Me before your marriage; you had simply heard about Me from a third person, and still your faith in Me was so fixed that even in the presence of many qualified, rich and beautiful men of the royal order, you did not select any one of them as your husband, but insisted on having Me. You neglected all the princes present, and very politely you sent Me a confidential letter inviting Me to kidnap you. While I was kidnapping you, your elder brother Rukmī violently protested and fought with Me. As a result of the fight, I defeated him mercilessly and disfigured his body. At the time of Aniruddha's marriage, when we were all engaged in playing chess, there was another fight with your brother Rukmī on a controversial verbal point, and My elder brother Balarāma finally killed him. I was surprised to see that you did not utter even a word of protest over this incidence. Because of your great anxiety that you might be separated from Me, you suffered all the consequences without speaking even a word. As the result of this great silence, My dear wife, you have purchased Me for all time; I have become eternally under your control. You sent your messenger to Me inviting Me to kidnap you, and when you found that there was a little delay in My arriving on the spot, you began to see the whole world as vacant. At that time you concluded that your beautiful body was not fit to be touched by anyone else; therefore, thinking that I was not coming, you decided to commit suicide and immediately end that body. My dear Rukmiṇī, such great and exalted love for Me will always remain within My soul. As far as

I am concerned, it is not within My power to repay you for your unalloyed devotion to Me."

The Supreme Personality of Godhead Kṛṣṇa certainly has no business being anyone's husband or son or father, because everything belongs to Him and everyone is under His control. He does not require anyone's help for His satisfaction. He is *ātmārāma*, self-satisfied; He can derive all pleasure by Himself, without anyone's help. When the Lord descends to play the part of a human being, He plays a role either as a husband, son, friend or enemy, in full perfection. As such, when He was playing as the perfect husband of the queens, especially of Rukmiṇījī, He enjoyed conjugal love in complete perfection.

According to Vedic culture, although polygamy is allowed, none of the wives should be ill-treated. In other words, one may take many wives only if he is able to satisfy all of them equally as an ideal householder; otherwise it is not allowed. Lord Kṛṣṇa is the world-teacher; therefore, even though He had no need for a wife, He expanded Himself into as many forms as He had wives, and He lived with them as an ideal householder, observing the regulative principles, rules and commitments in accordance with the Vedic injunctions and the social laws and customs of society. For each of His 16,108 wives, He simultaneously maintained different palaces, different establishments and different atmospheres. Thus the Lord, although one, exhibited Himself as 16,108 ideal householders.

Thus ends the Bhaktivedanta purport of the Fifty-ninth Chapter of Kṛṣṇa, "*Talks Between Kṛṣṇa and Rukmiṇī.*"

60 / The Genealogical Table of the Family of Kṛṣṇa

Kṛṣṇa had 16,108 wives, and in each of them He begot ten sons, all of them equal to their father in the opulences of strength, beauty, wisdom, fame, wealth and renunciation. "Like father like son." All the 16,108 wives of Kṛṣṇa were princesses, and when each saw that Kṛṣṇa was always present in her respective palace and did not leave home, they considered Kṛṣṇa to be a henpecked husband who was very much attached to them. Every one of them thought that Kṛṣṇa was her very obedient husband, but actually Kṛṣṇa had no attraction for any of them. Although each thought that she was the only wife of Kṛṣṇa and was very, very dear to Him, Lord Kṛṣṇa, since He is *ātmārāma,* self-sufficient, was neither dear nor inimical to any one of them; He was equal to all the wives and treated them as a perfect husband just to please them. For Him, there was no need for even a single wife. In fact, since they were women, the wives could not understand the exalted position of Kṛṣṇa nor the truths about Him.

All the princesses who were wives of Kṛṣṇa were exquisitely beautiful, and each one of them was attracted by Kṛṣṇa's eyes, which were just like lotus petals, and by His beautiful face, long arms, broad ears, pleasing smile, humorous talk and sweet words. Influenced by these features of Kṛṣṇa, they all used to dress themselves very attractively, desiring to attract Kṛṣṇa by their feminine bodily appeal. They used to exhibit their feminine characteristics by smiling and moving their eyebrows, thus throwing sharpened arrows of conjugal love just to awaken Kṛṣṇa's lusty desires for them. Still, they could not arouse the mind of Kṛṣṇa or His sex appetite. This means that Kṛṣṇa never had any sex relations with any of His many wives, save and except to beget children.

The queens of Dvārakā were so fortunate that they got Lord Śrī Kṛṣṇa as their husband and personal companion, although He is not approachable by exalted demigods like Brahmā. They remained together as husband and wife, and Kṛṣṇa, as an ideal husband, treated them in such a way that at every moment there was an increase of transcendental bliss in their smiling exchanges, talking and mixing together. Each and every wife had hundreds and thousands of maidservants, yet when Kṛṣṇa entered the palaces of His thousands of wives, each one of them used to receive Kṛṣṇa personally by seating Him in a nice chair, worshiping Him with all requisite paraphernalia, personally washing His lotus feet, offering Him betel nuts, massaging His legs to relieve them from fatigue, fanning Him to make Him comfortable, offering all kinds of scented sandalwood pulp, oils and aromatics, putting flower garlands on His neck, dressing His hair, getting Him to lie down on the bed and assisting Him in taking His bath. Thus they served always in every respect, especially when Kṛṣṇa was eating. They were always engaged in the service of the Lord.

Of the 16,108 queens of Kṛṣṇa, each of whom had ten sons, there is the following list of the sons of the first eight queens. By Rukmiṇī, Kṛṣṇa had ten sons: Pradyumna, Cārudeṣṇa, Sudeṣṇa, Cārudeha, Sucāru, Cārugupta, Bhadracāru, Cārucandra, Vicāru, and Cāru. None of them were inferior in their qualities to their divine father, Lord Kṛṣṇa. Similarly, Satyabhāmā had ten sons, and their names are as follows: Bhānu, Subhānu, Svarbhānu, Prabhānu, Bhānumān, Candrabhānu, Bṛhadbhānu, Atibhānu, Śrībhānu and Pratibhānu. The next queen, Jāmbavatī, had ten sons, headed by Sāmba. Their names are as follows: Sāmba, Sumitra, Purujit, Śatajit, Sahasrajit, Vijaya, Citraketu, Vasumān, Draviḍa and Kratu. Lord Kṛṣṇa was specifically very affectionate to the sons of Jāmbavatī. By His wife Satyā, the daughter of King Nagnajit, Lord Kṛṣṇa had ten sons. They are as follows: Vīra, Candra, Aśvasena, Citragu, Vegavān, Vṛṣa, Āma, Śaṅku, Vasu and Kunti. Amongst all of them, Kunti was very powerful. Kṛṣṇa had ten sons by Kālindī, and they are as follows: Śruta, Kavi, Vṛṣa, Vīra, Subāhu, Bhadra, Śānti, Darśa, Pūrṇamāsa and the youngest, Somaka. For His next wife, Lakṣmaṇā, the daughter of the King of Madras Province, He begot ten sons, of the names Praghoṣa, Gātravān, Siṁha, Bala, Prabala, Ūrdhvaga, Mahāśakti, Saha, Oja and Aparājita. Similarly, His next wife, Mitravindā, had ten sons. They are as follows: Vṛka, Harṣa, Anila, Gṛdhra, Vardhana, Annāda, Mahāṁsa, Pāvana, Vahni and Kṣudhi. His next wife, Bhadrā, had ten sons, of the names Saṅgrāmajit, Bṛhatsena, Śūra, Praharaṇa, Arijit, Jaya, Subhadra, Vāma, Āyu and Satyaka. Besides these eight chief queens, Kṛṣṇa had 16,100 other wives, and all of them had ten sons each.

The eldest son of Rukmiṇī, Pradyumna, was married with Māyāvatī from his very birth, and afterwards he was again married with Rukmavatī, the daughter of his maternal uncle, Rukmī. From this Rukmavatī, Pradyumna had a son named Aniruddha. In this way, Kṛṣṇa's family—Kṛṣṇa and His wives, along with their sons and grandsons and even great-grandsons—all combined together to include very nearly one billion family members.

Rukmī, the elder brother of Kṛṣṇa's first wife, Rukmiṇī, was greatly harrassed and insulted in his fight with Kṛṣṇa, but on the request of Rukmiṇī his life was saved. Since then Rukmī had held a great grudge against Kṛṣṇa and was always inimical toward Him. Nevertheless, his daughter was married with Kṛṣṇa's son, and his granddaughter was married with Kṛṣṇa's grandson, Aniruddha. This fact appeared to be a little astonishing to Mahārāja Parīkṣit when he heard it from Śukadeva Gosvāmī. "I am surprised that Rukmī and Kṛṣṇa, who were so greatly inimical to one another, could again be united by marital relationships between their descendants." Parīkṣit Mahārāja was curious about the mystery of this incident, and therefore he inquired further from Śukadeva Gosvāmī. Because Śukadeva Gosvāmī was a practical *yogī,* nothing was hidden from his power of insight. A perfect *yogī* like Śukadeva Gosvāmī can see past, present and future in all details. Therefore, from such *yogīs* or mystics there can be nothing concealed. When Parīkṣit Mahārāja inquired from Śukadeva Gosvāmī, Śukadeva Gosvāmī answered as follows.

Pradyumna, the eldest son of Kṛṣṇa, born of Rukmiṇī, was Cupid himself. He was so beautiful and attractive that the daughter of Rukmī, namely Rukmavatī, could not select any husband other than Pradyumna during her *svayaṁvara.* Therefore, in that selection meeting, she garlanded Pradyumna in the presence of all other princes. When there was a fight among the princes, Pradyumna came out victorious, and therefore Rukmī was obliged to offer his beautiful daughter to him. Although a far-off enmity was always blazing in the heart of Rukmī because of his being insulted by Kṛṣṇa's kidnapping of his sister Rukmiṇī, when his daughter selected Pradyumna as her husband Rukmī could not resist consenting to the marriage ceremony just to please his sister, Rukmiṇī. And so Pradyumna became the nephew of Rukmī. Besides the ten sons described above, Rukmiṇī had one beautiful daughter with big eyes, and she was married to the son of Kṛtavarmā, whose name was Balī.

Although Rukmī was a veritable enemy of Kṛṣṇa, he had great affection for his sister, Rukmiṇī, and he wanted to please her in all respects. On this account, when Rukmiṇī's grandson Aniruddha was to be married, Rukmī offered his granddaughter Rocanā to Aniruddha. Such marriage between immediate cousins is not very much sanctioned by the Vedic culture, but in order to please Rukmiṇī, Rukmī offered his daughter and granddaughter to the son and grandson of Kṛṣṇa. In this way, when the negotiation of the marriage of Aniruddha with Rocanā was complete, a big marriage party accompanied Aniruddha and started from Dvārakā. They travelled until they reached Bhojakaṭa, which Rukmī had colonized after his sister had been kidnapped by Kṛṣṇa. This marriage party was led by the grandfather, namely Lord Kṛṣṇa, accompanied by Lord Balarāma, as well as Kṛṣṇa's first wife, Rukmiṇī, His son Pradyumna, Jāmbavatī's son Sāmba and many other relatives and family members. They reached the town of Bhojakaṭa, and the marriage ceremony was peacefully performed.

The King of Kaliṅga was a friend of Rukmī's, and he gave him the ill advice to play with Balarāma and thus defeat Him in a bet. Amongst the *kṣatriya* kings, betting and gambling in chess was not uncommon. If someone challenged a friend to play on the chessboard, the friend could not deny the challenge. Śrī Balarāmajī was not a very expert chess player, and this was known to the King of Kaliṅga. So Rukmī was advised to retaliate against the family members of Kṛṣṇa by challenging Balarāma to play chess. Although not a very expert chess player, Śrī Balarāmajī was very enthusiastic in sporting activities. He accepted the challenge of Rukmī and sat down to play. Betting was with gold coins, and Balarāma first of all challenged with one hundred coins, then 1,000 coins, then 10,000 coins. Each time, Balarāma lost, and Rukmī became victorious.

Śrī Balarāma's losing the game was an opportunity for the King of Kaliṅga to criticize Kṛṣṇa and Balarāma. Thus the King of Kaliṅga was talking jokingly and purposefully showing his teeth to Balarāma. Because Balarāma was the loser in the game, He was a little intolerant of the sarcastic joking words. He became a little agitated, and when Rukmī again challenged Balarāma, he made a bet of 100,000 gold coins. Fortunately, this time Balarāma won. Although Balarāmajī had won, Rukmī, out of his cunningness, began to claim that Balarāma was the loser and that he himself had won. Because of this lie, Balarāmajī became most angry with Rukmī. His agitation was so sudden and great that it appeared like a tidal wave in the ocean on a full moon day. Balarāma's eyes are naturally reddish, and when He became agitated and angry His eyes became more reddish. This time He challenged and made a bet of a hundred million coins.

Again Balarāma was the winner according to the rules of chess, but Rukmī again cunningly began to claim that he had won. Rukmī appealed to the princes present, and He especially mentioned the name of the King of Kaliṅga. At that time there was a voice from the air during the dispute, and it announced that for all honest purposes Balarāma, the actual winner of this game, was being abused and that the statement of Rukmī that he had won was absolutely false.

In spite of this divine voice, Rukmī insisted that Balarāma had lost, and by his persistence it appeared that he had death upon his head. Falsely puffed up by the ill advice of his friend, he did not give much importance to the oracle, and he began to criticize Balarāmajī. He said, "My dear Balarāmajī, You two brothers, cowherd boys only, may be very expert in tending cows, but how can You be expert in playing chess or shooting arrows on the battlefield? These arts are well-known only to the princely order." Hearing this kind of pinching talk by Rukmī and hearing the loud laughter of all the other princes present there, Lord Balarāma became as agitated as burning cinders. He immediately took a club in His hand and, without any further talk, struck Rukmī on the head. From that one blow, Rukmī fell down immediately and was dead and gone. Thus Rukmī was killed by Balarāma on that auspicious occasion of Aniruddha's marriage.

These things are not very uncommon in *kṣatriya* society, and the King of Kaliṅga, being afraid that he would be the next to be attacked, fled from the scene. Before he could escape even a few steps, however, Balarāmajī immediately captured him and, because the King was always showing his teeth while criticizing Balarāma and Kṛṣṇa, broke all his teeth with His club. The other princes who were supporting the King of Kaliṅga and Rukmī were also captured, and Balarāma beat them with His club, breaking their legs and hands. They did not try to retaliate but thought it wise to run away from the bloody scene.

During this strife between Balarāma and Rukmī, Lord Kṛṣṇa did not utter a word, for He knew that if He supported Balarāma Rukmiṇī would be unhappy, and if He said that the killing of Rukmī was unjust, then Balarāma would be unhappy. Therefore, Lord Kṛṣṇa was silent on the death of His brother-in-law, Rukmī, on the occasion of His grandson's marriage. He did not disturb either His affectionate relationship with Balarāma or with Rukmiṇī. After this, the bride and the bridegroom were ceremoniously seated on the chariot, and they started for Dvārakā, accompanied by the bridegroom's party. The bridegroom's party was always protected by Lord Kṛṣṇa, the killer of the Madhu demon. Thus they left Rukmī's kingdom, Bhojakaṭa, and happily started for Dvārakā.

Thus ends the Bhaktivedanta purport of the Sixtieth Chapter of Kṛṣṇa, *"The Genealogical Table of the Family of Kṛṣṇa."*

61 / The Meeting of Uṣā and Aniruddha

The meeting of Aniruddha and Uṣā, which caused a great fight between Lord Kṛṣṇa and Lord Śiva, is very mysterious and interesting. Mahārāja Parīkṣit was anxious to hear the whole story from Śukadeva Gosvāmī, and thus Śukadeva narrated it. "My dear King, you must have heard the name of King Bali. He was a great devotee who gave away in charity all that he had–namely, the whole world–to Lord Vāmana, the incarnation of Viṣṇu as a dwarf *brāhmaṇa.* King Bali had one hundred sons, and the eldest of all of them was Bāṇāsura."

This great hero Bāṇāsura, born of Mahārāja Bali, was a great devotee of Lord Śiva and was always ready to render service unto him. Because of his devotion, he achieved a great position in society, and he was honored in every respect. Actually, he was very intelligent and liberal also, and his activities are all praiseworthy because he never deviated from his promise and word of honor; he was very truthful and fixed in his vow. In those days, he was ruling over the city of Śonitapura. By the grace of Lord Śiva, Bāṇāsura had one thousand hands, and he became so powerful that even demigods like King Indra were serving him as most obedient servants.

Long ago, when Lord Śiva was dancing in his celebrated fashion called *tāṇḍava-nṛtya,* for which he is known as Naṭarāja, Bāṇāsura helped Lord Śiva in his dancing by rythmically beating drums with his one thousand hands. Lord Śiva is well-known as Āśutoṣa, very easily pleased, and he is also very affectionate to his devotees. He is a great protector for persons who take shelter of him and is the master of all living entities in this material world. Being pleased with Bāṇāsura, he said, "Whatever you desire you can have from me because I am very much pleased with you." Bāṇāsura replied, "My dear lord, if you please, you can remain in my city just to protect me from the hands of my enemies."

Once upon a time, Bāṇāsura came to offer his respects to Lord Śiva. By touching the lotus feet of Lord Śiva with his helmet, which was shining like the sun globe, he offered his obeisances unto him. While offering his respectful obeisances, Bāṇāsura said, "My dear lord, anyone who has not fulfilled his ambition will be able to do so by taking shelter of your lotus feet, which are just like desire trees—one can take from them anything he desires. My dear lord, you have given me one thousand arms, but I do not know what to do with them. Please pardon me, but it appears that I cannot use them properly in fighting. I cannot find anyone competent to fight with me except your lordship, the original father of the material world. Sometimes I feel a great tendency to fight with my arms, and I go out to find a suitable warrior. Unfortunately, everyone flees, knowing my extraordinary power. Being baffled at not finding a match, I simply satisfy the itching of my arms by beating them against the mountains. In this way, I tear many great mountains to pieces."

Lord Śiva realized that his benediction had become troublesome for Bāṇāsura and addressed him, "You rascal! You are very eager to fight, but since you have no one to fight with, you are distressed. Although you think that there is no one in the world to oppose you except me, I say that you will eventually find such a competent person. At that time your days will come to an end, and your flag of victory will no longer fly. Then you will see your false prestige smashed to pieces!"

After hearing Lord Śiva's statement, Bāṇāsura became very puffed up with his power. He was elated that he would meet someone who would be able to smash him to pieces. Bāṇāsura then returned home with great pleasure, and he always waited for the day when the suitable fighter would come to cut down his strength. He was such a foolish demon. It appears that foolish, demonic human beings, when unnecessarily overpowered with material opulences, want to exhibit these opulences, and such foolish people feel satisfaction when these opulences are exhausted. The idea is that they do not know how to expend their energy for right causes, being unaware of the benefit of Kṛṣṇa consciousness. Actually, there are two classes of men—one is Kṛṣṇa conscious, the other is non-Kṛṣṇa conscious. The non-Kṛṣṇa conscious men are generally devoted to the demigods, whereas the Kṛṣṇa conscious men are devoted to the Supreme Personality of Godhead. Kṛṣṇa conscious persons utilize everything for the service of the Lord. The non-Kṛṣṇa conscious persons utilize everything for sense gratification, and Bāṇāsura is a perfect example of such a person. He was very anxious to utilize for his own satisfaction his extraordinary power to fight. Not finding any combatant, he struck his powerful hands against the mountains, breaking them into pieces. In contrast to this, Arjuna also possessed extraordinary powers for fighting, but he utilized them only for Kṛṣṇa.

Bāṇāsura had a very beautiful daughter, whose name was Uṣā. When she had attained the age of marriage and was sleeping amongst her many girl friends, she dreamt one night that Aniruddha was by her side and that she was enjoying a conjugal relationship with him, although she had never actually seen him nor heard of him before. She awoke from her dream exclaiming very loudly, "My dear beloved, where are you?" Being exposed to her other friends in this way, she became a little bit ashamed. One of Uṣā's girl friends was Citralekhā, who was the daughter of Bāṇāsura's prime minister. Citralekhā and Uṣā were intimate friends, and out of great curiosity Citralekhā asked, "My dear beautiful princess, as of yet you are not married to any young boy, nor have you seen any boys until now; so I am surprised that you are exclaiming like this. Who are you searching after? Who is your suitable match?"

On hearing Citralekhā's inquiries, Uṣā replied, "My dear friend, in my dream I saw a nice young man who is very, very beautiful. His complexion is swarthy, his eyes are just like lotus petals, and he is dressed in yellow garments. His arms are very long, and his general bodily features are so pleasing that any young girl would be attracted. I feel much pride in saying that this beautiful young man was kissing me, and I was very much enjoying the nectar of his kissing. I am sorry to inform you that just after this he disappeared, and I have been thrown into the whirlpool of disappointment. My dear friend, I am very anxious to find this wonderful young man, the desired lord of my heart."

After hearing Uṣā's words, Citralekhā immediately replied, "I can understand your bereavement, and I assure you that if this boy is within these three worlds—the upper, middle, and lower planetary systems—I must find him for your satisfaction. If you can identify him from your dream, I shall bring you peace of mind. Now, let me draw some pictures for you to inspect, and as soon as you find the picture of your desired husband, let me know. It doesn't matter where he is; I know the art of bringing him here. So, as soon as you identify him, I shall immediately arrange for it."

Citralekhā, while talking, began to draw many pictures of the demigods inhabiting the higher planetary systems, then pictures of the Gandharvas, Siddhas, Cāraṇas, Pannagas, Daityas, Vidyādharas and Yakṣas, as well as many human beings. (The statements of *Śrīmad-Bhāgavatam* and other Vedic literature prove definitely that on each and every planet there are living entities of different varieties. Therefore, it is foolish to assert that there are no living entities but those on this earth.) Citralekhā painted many pictures. Among those of the human beings was the Vṛṣṇi dynasty, including Vasudeva, the father of Kṛṣṇa, Śūrasena, the grandfather of Kṛṣṇa, Śrī Balarāmajī, Lord Kṛṣṇa and many others. When Uṣā saw the picture of Pradyumna, she became a little bashful, but when she saw the picture of Aniruddha, she became so bashful that she immediately lowered her head and smiled, having found the man she was seeking. She identified the picture to Citralekhā as that of the man who had stolen her heart.

Citralekhā was a great mystic *yoginī,* and as soon as Uṣā identified the picture, although neither of them had ever seen him nor knew his name, Citralekhā could immediately understand that the picture was of Aniruddha, a grandson of Kṛṣṇa. That very night she traveled in outer space and within a very short time reached the city of Dvārakā, which was well-protected by Kṛṣṇa. She entered the palace and found Aniruddha sleeping in his bedroom on a very opulent bed. Citralekhā, by her mystic power, immediately brought Aniruddha, in that sleeping condition, to the city of Śonitapura so that Uṣā might see her desired husband. Uṣā immediately bloomed in happiness and began to enjoy the company of Aniruddha with great satisfaction.

The palace in which Uṣā and Citralekhā lived was so well fortified that it was impossible for any male to either enter or see inside. Uṣā and Aniruddha lived together in the palace, and day after day the love of Uṣā for Aniruddha grew four times upon four times. Uṣā pleased Aniruddha with her valuable dresses, flowers, garlands, scents and incense. By his bedside sitting place were other paraphernalia for residential purposes—nice drinks such as milk and sherbet and nice eatables which could be chewed or swallowed. Above all, she pleased him with sweet words and very obliging service. Aniruddha was worshiped by Uṣā as if he were the Supreme Personality of Godhead. By her excellent service, Uṣā made Aniruddha forget all other things and was able to draw his attention and love upon her without deviation. In such an atmosphere of love and service, Aniruddha practically forgot himself and could not recall how many days he had been away from his real home.

In due course of time, Uṣā exhibited some bodily symptoms by which it could be understood that she was having intercourse with a male friend. The symptoms were so prominent that her actions could no longer be concealed from anyone. Uṣā was always cheerful in the association of Aniruddha, but she did not know the bounds of her satisfaction. The housekeeper and the watchmen of the palace could guess very easily that she was having relations with a male friend, and without waiting for further development, all of them informed their master, Bāṇāsura. In Vedic culture, an unmarried girl having association with a male is the greatest disgrace to the family, and so the caretaker cautiously informed his master that Uṣā was developing symptoms indicating a disgraceful association. The servants informed their master that they were not at all neglectful in guarding the house, being alert day and night against any young man who might enter. They were so careful that a male could not even see what was going on there, and so they were surprised that she had become contaminated. Since they could not trace out the reason for it, they submitted the whole situation before their master.

Bāṇāsura was shocked to understand that his daughter Uṣā was no longer a virgin maiden. This weighed heavily on his heart, and without delay he rushed towards the palace where Uṣā was living. There he saw that Uṣā and Aniruddha were sitting together and talking. Uṣā and Aniruddha looked very beautiful together, Aniruddha being the son of Pradyumna, who was Cupid himself. Bāṇāsura saw his daughter and Aniruddha as a suitable match, yet for family prestige, he did not like the combination at all. Bāṇāsura could not understand who the boy actually was. He appreciated the fact that Uṣā could not have selected anyone in the three worlds more beautiful. Aniruddha's complexion was brilliant and swarthy. He was dressed in yellow garments and had eyes just like lotus petals. His arms were very long, and he had nice, curling, bluish hair. The glaring rays of his glittering earrings and the beautiful smile on his lips were certainly captivating. Still, Bāṇāsura was very angry.

When Bāṇāsura saw him, Aniruddha was engaged in playing with Uṣā. Aniruddha was nicely dressed, and Uṣā had garlanded him with various beautiful flowers. The reddish *kuṅkuma* powder put on the breasts of women was spotted here and there on the garland, indicating that Uṣā had embraced him. Bāṇāsura was struck with wonder that, even in his presence, Aniruddha was peacefully sitting in front of Uṣā. Aniruddha knew, however, that his would-be father-in-law was not at all pleased and that he was gathering many soldiers in the palace to attack him.

Thus, not finding any other weapon, Aniruddha took hold of a big iron rod and stood up before Bāṇāsura and his soldiers. He firmly took a posture indicating that if he were attacked he would strike all of the soldiers down to the ground with the iron rod. Bāṇāsura and his company of soldiers saw that the boy was standing before them just like the superintendent of death with his invincible rod. Now, under the order of Bāṇāsura, the soldiers from all sides attempted to capture and arrest him. When they dared to come before him, Aniruddha struck them with the rod, breaking their heads, legs, arms and thighs, and one after another, they began to fall to the ground. He killed them just as the leader of a flock of hawks kills barking dogs, one after another. In this way, Aniruddha was able to escape the palace.

Bāṇāsura knew various arts of fighting, and by the grace of Lord Śiva, he knew how to arrest his opposing enemy by the use of a *nāgapāśa,* snake-noose, and so Aniruddha was seized as he came out of the palace. When Uṣā received the news that her father had arrested Aniruddha, she became overwhelmed with grief and confusion. Tears began to glide down her eyes, and being unable to check herself, she began to cry very loudly.

Thus ends the Bhaktivedanta purport of the Sixty-first Chapter of Kṛṣṇa, *"The Meeting of Uṣā and Aniruddha."*

62 / Lord Kṛṣṇa Fights with Bāṇāsura

When the four months of the rainy season passed and still Aniruddha had not returned home, all the members of the Yadu family became much perturbed. They could not understand how the boy was missing. Fortunately, one day the great sage Nārada came and informed the family about Aniruddha's disappearance from the palace. He explained how Aniruddha had been carried to the city of Śonitapura, the capital of Bāṇāsura's empire, and how Bāṇāsura had arrested him with the *nāgapāśa,* even though Aniruddha had defeated his soldiers. This news was given in detail, and the whole story was disclosed. Then the members of the Yadu dynasty, all of whom had great affection for Kṛṣṇa, prepared to attack the city of Śonitapura. Practically all the leaders of the family, including Pradyumna, Sātyaki, Gada, Sāmba, Sāraṇa, Nanda, Upananda and Bhadra, combined together and gathered eighteen *akṣauhiṇī* military divisions into phalanxes. Then they all went to Śonitapura and surrounded it with soldiers, elephants, horses and chariots.

Bāṇāsura heard that the soldiers of the Yadu dynasty were attacking the whole city, tearing down various walls, gates and nearby gardens. Becoming very angry, he immediately ordered his soldiers, who were of equal caliber, to go and face them. Lord Śiva was so kind to Bāṇāsura that he personally came as the commander-in-chief of the military force, assisted by his heroic sons Kārttikeya and Gaṇapati. Seated on his favorite bull, Nandīśvara, Lord Śiva, led the fighting against Lord Kṛṣṇa and Balarāma. We can simply imagine how fierce the fighting was—Lord Śiva with his valiant sons on one side and Lord Kṛṣṇa, the Supreme Personality of Godhead, and His elder brother, Śrī Balarāmajī, on the other. The fighting was so fierce that those who saw the battle were struck with wonder, and the hairs on their bodies stood up. Lord Śiva was engaged in fighting directly with Lord Kṛṣṇa, Pradyumna was engaged with Kārttikeya, and Lord Balarāma was engaged with Bāṇāsura's commander-in-chief, Kumbhāṇḍa, who was assisted by Kūpakarṇa. Sāmba, the son of Kṛṣṇa, was engaged in fighting with the son of Bāṇāsura, and Bāṇāsura was engaged in fighting with Sātyaki, commander-in-chief of the Yadu dynasty. In this way the fighting was waged.

News of the fighting spread all over the universe. Demigods such as Lord Brahmā, from higher planetary systems, along with great sages and saintly persons, Siddhas, Cāraṇas and Gandharvas—all being very curious to see the fight between Lord Śiva, Lord Kṛṣṇa and their assistants—were hovering over the battlefield in their airplanes. Lord Śiva is called the *bhūta-nātha,* being assisted by various types of powerful ghosts and denizens of the inferno—*bhūtas, pretas, pramathas, guhyakas, ḍākinīs, piśācas, kūṣmāṇḍas, vetālas, vināyakas,* and *brahma-rākṣasas.* (Of all kinds of ghosts, the *brahma-rākṣasas* are very powerful. *Brāhmaṇas* transferred to the role of ghosts become *brahma-rākṣasas.)*

The Supreme Personality of Godhead Śrī Kṛṣṇa simply drove all these ghosts away from the battlefield, beating them with His celebrated bow, Śārṅgadhanu. Lord Śiva then began to release all his selected weapons upon the Personality of Godhead. Lord Śrī Kṛṣṇa, without any difficulty, counteracted all these weapons with counter-weapons. He counteracted the *brahmāstra,* similar to the atomic bomb, by another *brahmāstra,* and an air weapon by a mountain weapon. When Lord Śiva released a particular weapon bringing about a violent hurricane on the battlefield, Lord Kṛṣṇa presented just the opposing element, a mountain weapon which checked the hurricane on the spot. Similarly when Lord Śiva released his weapon of devastating fire, Kṛṣṇa counteracted it with torrents of rain.

At last, when Lord Śiva released his personal weapon, called *pāśupata-śastra,* Kṛṣṇa immediately counteracted it by the *nārāyaṇa-śastra.* Lord Śiva then became exasperated in fighting with Lord Kṛṣṇa. Kṛṣṇa then took the opportunity to release His yawning weapon. When this weapon is released, the opposing party becomes tired, stops fighting, and begins to yawn. Consequently, Lord Śiva became so fatigued that he refused to fight anymore and began to yawn. Kṛṣṇa was now able to turn His attention from the attack of Lord Śiva to the efforts of Bāṇāsura, and He began to kill his personal soldiers with swords and clubs. Meanwhile, Lord Kṛṣṇa's son Pradyumna was fighting fiercely with Kārttikeya, the commander-in-chief of the demigods. Kārttikeya was wounded, and his body was bleeding profusely. In this condition, he left the battlefield and, without fighting anymore, rode away on the back of his peacock carrier. Similarly, Lord Balarāma was smashing Bāṇāsura's commander-in-chief, Kumbhāṇḍa, with the strokes of his club. Kūpakarṇa was also wounded in this way, and both he and Kumbhāṇḍa fell on the battlefield, the commander-in-chief being fatally wounded. Without guidance, all of Bāṇāsura's soldiers scattered here and there.

When Bāṇāsura saw that his soldiers and commanders had been defeated, his anger only increased. He thought it wise to stop fighting with Sātyaki, Kṛṣṇa's commander-in-chief, and instead directly attacked Lord Kṛṣṇa. Now having the opportunity to use his one thousand hands, he rushed towards Kṛṣṇa, simultaneously working 500 bows and 2,000 arrows. Such a foolish person could never measure Kṛṣṇa's strength. Immediately, without any difficulty, Kṛṣṇa cut each of Bāṇāsura's bows into two pieces and, to check him from going further, made his chariot horses lay on the ground. The chariot then broke to pieces. After doing this, Kṛṣṇa blew His conchshell, Pāñcajanya.

There was a demigoddess named Koṭarā who was worshiped by Bāṇāsura, and their relationship was as mother and son. Mother Koṭarā was upset that Bāṇāsura's life was in danger, so she appeared on the scene. With naked body and scattered hair, she stood before Lord Kṛṣṇa. Śrī Kṛṣṇa did not like the sight of this naked woman, and to avoid seeing her, He turned His face. Bāṇāsura, getting this chance to escape Kṛṣṇa's attack, left the battlefield. All the strings of his bows were broken, and there was no chariot or driver, so he had no alternative than to return to his city. He lost everything in the battle.

Being greatly harassed by the arrows of Kṛṣṇa, all the associates of Lord Śiva, the hobgoblins and ghostly *bhūtas, pretas* and *kṣatriyas,* left the battlefield. Lord Śiva then took to his last resort. He released his greatest death weapon, known as Śivajvara, which destroys by excessive temperature. It is said that at the end of this creation the sun becomes twelve times more scorching than usual. This twelve-times-hotter temperature is called Śivajvara. When the Śivajvara personified was released, he had three heads and three legs, and as he came toward Kṛṣṇa it appeared that he was burning everything into ashes. He was so powerful that he made blazing fire appear in all directions, and Kṛṣṇa observed that he was specifically coming toward Him.

As there is a Śivajvara weapon, there is also a Nārāyaṇajvara weapon. Nārāyaṇajvara is represented by excessive cold. When there is excessive heat, one can somehow or other tolerate it, but when there is excessive cold, everything collapses. This is actually experienced by a person at the time of death. At the time of death, the temperature of the body first of all increases to 107 degrees, and then the whole body collapses and immediately becomes as cold as ice. To counteract the scorching heat of the Śivajvara, there was no other weapon but Nārāyaṇajvara.

When Lord Kṛṣṇa saw that the Śivajvara had been released by Lord Śiva, He had no other recourse than to release Nārāyaṇajvara. Lord Śrī Kṛṣṇa is the original Nārāyaṇa and the controller of the Nārāyaṇajvara weapon. When the Nārāyaṇajvara was released, there was a great fight between the two *jvaras*. When excessive heat is counteracted by extreme cold, it is natural for the hot temperature to gradually reduce, and this is what occurred in the fight between Śivajvara and Nārāyaṇajvara. Gradually, Śivajvara's temperature diminished, and Śivajvara began to cry for help from Lord Śiva, but Lord Śiva was unable to help him in the presence of the Nārāyaṇajvara. Unable to get any help from Lord Śiva, the Śivajvara could understand that he had no means of escape outside surrendering unto Nārāyaṇa, Lord Kṛṣṇa Himself. Lord Śiva, the greatest of the demigods, could not help him, what to speak of the lesser demigods, and therefore Śivajvara ultimately surrendered unto Kṛṣṇa, bowing before Him and offering a prayer so that the Lord might be pleased and give him protection.

By this incidence of the fight between the ultimate weapons of Lord Śiva and Lord Kṛṣṇa it is proved that if Kṛṣṇa gives someone protection, no one can kill him. But if Kṛṣṇa does not give one any protection, then no one can save him. Lord Śiva is called Mahādeva, greatest of all demigods, although sometimes Lord Brahmā is considered the greatest of all demigods, because he can create, whereas Lord Śiva can annihilate the creations of Brahmā. But both Lord Brahmā and Lord Śiva act only in one capacity. Lord Brahmā can create, and Lord Śiva can annihilate, but neither of them can maintain. Lord Viṣṇu, however, not only maintains, but He creates, and annihilates also. Factually, the creation is not effected by Brahmā, because Brahmā himself is created by Lord Viṣṇu. Lord Śiva is created, or born, of Brahmā. The Śivajvara thus understood that without Kṛṣṇa or Nārāyaṇa, no one could help him. He therefore rightly took shelter of Lord Kṛṣṇa and, with folded hands, began to pray as follows.

"My dear Lord, I offer my respectful obeisances unto You because You have unlimited potencies. No one can surpass Your potencies, and thus You are the Lord of everyone. Generally people consider Lord Śiva to be the most powerful personality in the material world, but Lord Śiva is not all-powerful; You are all-powerful. This is factual. You are the original consciousness or knowledge. Without knowledge or consciousness, nothing can be powerful. A material thing might be very powerful, but without the touch of knowledge or consciousness it cannot act. A material machine may be very gigantic and wonderful, but without the touch of someone conscious and in knowledge, the material machine is useless for all purposes. My Lord, You are complete knowledge, and there is not a pinch of material contamination in Your personality. Lord Śiva may be a powerful demigod because of his specific power to annihilate the whole creation, and similarly, Lord Brahmā may be very powerful because he can create the entire universe, but actually neither Brahmā nor Lord Śiva is the original cause of this cosmic manifestation. You are the Absolute Truth, the Supreme Brahman, and You are the original cause. The original cause of the cosmic manifestation is not the impersonal Brahman effulgence. That impersonal Brahman effulgence is resting on Your personality. As is confirmed in the *Bhagavad-gītā,* the cause of the impersonal Brahman is Lord Kṛṣṇa. This Brahman effulgence is likened to the sunshine which emanates from the sun globe. Therefore, impersonal Brahman is not the ultimate cause. The ultimate cause of everything is the supreme eternal form of Kṛṣṇa. All material actions and reactions are taking place in the impersonal Brahman, but in the personal Brahman, the eternal form of Kṛṣṇa, there is no action and reaction. My Lord, Your body is therefore completely peaceful, completely blissful and is devoid of material contamination.

"In the material body there are actions and reactions of the three modes of material nature. The time factor is the most important element and is above all others, because the material manifestation is effected by time agitation. Thus natural phenomena come into existence, and as soon as there is the appearance of phenomena, fruitive activities are visible. As the result of these fruitive activities, a living entity takes his form. He acquires a particular type of nature which is packed up in a subtle body and gross body formed by the life air, the ego, the ten sense organs, the mind and the five gross elements. These then create the type of body which later becomes the root or cause of various other bodies, which are acquired one after another by the transmigration of the soul. All these phenomenal manifestations are the combined actions of Your material energy. Unaffected by the action and reaction of different elements, You are the cause of this external energy, and because You are transcendental to such compulsions of material energy, You are the supreme tranquility. You are the last word in freedom from material contamination. I am therefore taking shelter at Your lotus feet, giving up all other shelter.

"My dear Lord, Your appearance as the son of Vasudeva in Your role as a human being is one of the pastimes of Your complete freedom. To benefit Your devotees and to vanquish the nondevotees, You appear in multi-incarnations. All such incarnations descend in fulfillment of Your promise in the *Bhagavad-gītā* that You appear as soon as there are discrepancies in the system of progressive life. When there are disturbances by irregular principles, my dear Lord, You appear by Your internal potency. Your main business is to protect and maintain the demigods and spiritually inclined persons and maintain the standard of material law and order. Simultaneous to the maintenance of such law and order, Your violence to the miscreants and demons is quite befitting. This is not the first time You have incarnated; it is to be understood that You have done so many, many times before.

"My dear Lord, I beg to submit that I have been very greatly chastised by the release of Your Nārāyaṇajvara. It is certainly very cooling, yet at the same time very severely dangerous and unbearable for all of us. My dear Lord, as long as one is forgetful of Kṛṣṇa consciousness, driven by the spell of material desires and ignorant of the ultimate shelter at Your lotus feet, one who has accepted this material body becomes disturbed by the three miserable conditions of material nature. Because one does not surrender unto You, he therefore continues to suffer perpetually."

After hearing the Śivajvara, Lord Kṛṣṇa replied, "O three-headed one, I am pleased with your statement. Be assured there is no more suffering for you from the Nārāyaṇajvara. Not only are you now free from fear of Nārāyaṇajvara, but anyone in the future who simply recollects this fight between Śivajvara and Nārāyaṇajvara will also be freed from all kinds of fearfulness." After hearing the Supreme Personality of Godhead, the Śivajvara offered his respectful obeisances unto His lotus feet and left.

In the meantime Bāṇāsura somehow or other recovered from his setbacks and, with rejuvenated energy, returned to fight. This time Bāṇāsura appeared before Lord Kṛṣṇa, who was seated on His chariot, with different kinds of weapons in his one thousand hands. Bāṇāsura was very much agitated. He began to splash his different weapons, like torrents of rain, upon the body of Lord Kṛṣṇa. When Lord Kṛṣṇa saw the weapons of Bāṇāsura coming at Him, like water coming out of a strainer, He took His sharp-edged Sudarśana disc and began to cut off the demon's one thousand hands one after another, just as a gardener trims the twigs of a tree with sharp cutters. When Lord Śiva saw that his devotee Bāṇāsura could not be saved even in his presence, he came to his senses and personally came before Lord Kṛṣṇa and began to pacify Him by offering the following prayers.

Lord Śiva said, "My dear Lord, You are the worshipable object of the Vedic hymns. One who does not know You considers the impersonal *brahmajyoti* to be the ultimate Supreme Absolute Truth, without any knowledge that You are existing behind Your spiritual effulgence in Your eternal abode. My dear Lord, You are therefore called *Parambrahman.* This word, *Parambrahman,* has been used in the *Bhagavad-gītā* to identify You. Saintly persons who have completely cleansed their hearts of all material contamination can realize Your transcendental form, although You are all-pervading like the sky, unaffected by any material thing. Only the devotees can realize You, and no one else. In the impersonalists' conception of Your supreme existence, the sky is just like Your navel, the fire is Your mouth, and the water is Your semina. The heavenly planets are Your head, all the directions are Your ears, the Urvī planet is Your lotus feet, the moon is Your mind, and the sun is Your eye. As far as I am concerned, I act as Your ego. The ocean is Your abdomen, and the King of heaven, Indra, is Your arm. Trees and plants are the hairs of Your body, the cloud is the hair on Your head, and Lord Brahmā is Your intelligence. All the great progenitors, known as Prajāpatis, are Your symbolic representatives. And religion is Your heart. The impersonal feature of Your supreme body is conceived of in this way, but You are ultimately the Supreme Person. The impersonal feature of Your supreme body is only a small expansion of Your energy. You are likened to the original fire, and the expansions are Your light and heat."

Lord Śiva continued: "My dear Lord, although You are manifested universally, different parts of the universe are the different parts of Your body, and by Your inconceivable potency You can simultaneously be both localized and universal. In the *Brahma-saṁhitā* we also find it stated that although You always remain in Your abode, Goloka Vṛndāvana, You are nevertheless present everywhere. As stated in the *Bhagavad-gītā,* You appear to protect the devotees, which indicates good fortune for all the universe. All of the demigods are directing different affairs of the universe by Your grace only. Thus the seven upper planetary systems are being maintained by Your grace. At the end of this creation, all manifestations of Your energies, whether in the shape of demigods, human beings or lower animals, enter into You, and all immediate and remote causes of cosmic manifestation rest in You without distinctive features of existence. Ultimately, there is no possibility of distinction between Yourself and any other thing on an equal level with You or subordinate to You. You are simultaneously the cause of this cosmic manifestation and its ingredients as well. You are the Supreme Whole, one without a second. In the phenomenal manifestation there are three stages: the stage of consciousness, the stage of semiconsciousness in dreaming, and the stage of unconsciousness.

But Your Lordship is transcendental to all these different material stages of existence. You exist, therefore, in a fourth dimension, and Your appearance and disappearance do not depend on anything beyond Yourself. You are the supreme cause of everything, but for Yourself there is no cause. You Yourself cause Your own appearance and disappearance. Despite Your transcendental position, my Lord, in order to show Your six opulences and advertise Your transcendental qualities, You have appeared in Your different incarnations—fish, tortoise, boar, Nṛsiṁha, Keśava, etc.—by Your personal manifestation; and You have appeared as different living entities by Your separated manifestations. By Your internal potency, You appear as the different incarnations of Viṣṇu, and by Your external potency You appear as the phenomenal world.

"Because it is a cloudy day to the common man's eyes, the sun appears to be covered. But the fact is that because the sunshine creates the cloud, even though the whole sky is cloudy, the sun can never actually be covered. Similarly, the less intelligent class of men claims that there is no God, but when the manifestation of different living entities and their activities is visible, enlightened persons see You present in every atom and through the via media of Your external and marginal energies. Your unlimited potential activities are experienced by the most enlightened devotees, but those who arc bewildered by the spell of Your external energy identify themselves with this material world and become attached to society, friendship and love. Thus they embrace the threefold miseries of material existence and are subjected to the dualities of pain and pleasure. They are sometimes drowned in the ocean of attachment and sometimes taken out of it.

"My dear Lord, only by Your mercy and grace can the living entity get the human form of life, which is a chance to get out of the miserable condition of material existence. However, a person who possesses a human body but who cannot bring the senses under control is carried away by the waves of sensual enjoyment. As such, he cannot take shelter of Your lotus feet and thus engage in Your devotional service. The life of such a person is very unfortunate, and anyone living such a life of darkness is certainly cheating himself and thus cheating others also. Therefore, human society without Kṛṣṇa consciousness is a society of cheaters and the cheated.

"My Lord, You are actually the dearmost Supersoul of all living entities and the supreme controller of everything. The human being who is always illusioned is afraid of ultimate death. A man who is simply attached to sensual enjoyment voluntarily accepts the miserable material existence and thus wanders after the will-o'-the-wisp of sense pleasure. He is certainly the most foolsih man, for he drinks poison and puts aside the nectar. My dear

Lord, all the demigods, including myself and Lord Brahmā, as well as great saintly persons and sages who have cleansed their hearts of this material attachment, have, by Your grace, wholeheartedly taken shelter of Your lotus feet. We have all taken shelter of You, because we have accepted You as the Supreme Lord and the dearmost life and soul of all of us. You are the original cause of this cosmic manifestation, You are its supreme maintainer, and You are the cause of its dissolution also. You are equal to everyone, the most peaceful supreme friend of every living entity. You are the supreme worshipable object for every one of us. My dear Lord, let us always be engaged in Your transcendental loving service so that we may get free from this material entanglement.

"Lastly, my Lord, I may inform You that this Bāṇāsura is very dear to me. He has rendered very valuable service unto me; therefore I want to see him always happy. Being pleased with him, I have given him the assurance of safety. I pray to You, my Lord, that as You were pleased upon his forefathers King Prahlāda and Bali Mahārāja, You will also be pleased with him."

After hearing Lord Śiva's prayer, Lord Kṛṣṇa addressed him also as lord and said, "My dear Lord Śiva, I accept your statements, and your desire for Bāṇāsura is also accepted by Me. I know that this Bāṇāsura is the son of Bali Mahārāja, and as such I cannot kill him because that is My promise. I gave a benediction to King Prahlāda that all the demons who would appear in his family would never be killed by Me. Therefore, without killing this Bāṇāsura, I have simply cut off his arms to deprive him of his false prestige. The large number of soldiers which he was maintaining became a burden on this earth, and I have killed them all in order to minimize the burden. Now he has four remaining arms, and he will remain immortal, without being affected by the material pains and pleasures. I know that he is one of the chief devotees of your lordship, so you can now rest assured that henceforward he need have no fear from anything."

When Bāṇāsura was benedicted by Lord Kṛṣṇa in this way, he came before the Lord and bowed down before Him, touching his head to the earth. He immediately arranged to bring Aniruddha along with his daughter Uṣā, seated on a nice chariot, and presented them before Lord Kṛṣṇa. After this, Lord Kṛṣṇa took charge of Aniruddha and Uṣā, who had become very opulent materially because of the blessings of Lord Śiva. Thus, keeping forward a division of one *akṣauhiṇī* of soldiers, Kṛṣṇa began to proceed toward Dvārakā. In the meantime, all the people at Dvārakā, having received the news that Lord Kṛṣṇa was returning with Aniruddha and Uṣā in great opulence, decorated every corner of the city with flags, festoons and garlands. All the big roads and crossings were carefully cleansed and sprinkled with sandalwood pulp mixed with water. Everywhere there was the flavor of sandalwood. All the citizens, accompanied by their friends and relatives, welcomed Lord Kṛṣṇa with great pomp and jubilation. At that time, there was a tumultuous vibration of conchshells and drums and bugles to receive the Lord. In this way the Supreme Personality of Godhead Kṛṣṇa entered His capital, Dvārakā.

Śukadeva Gosvāmī assured King Parīkṣit that the narration of the fight between Lord Śiva and Lord Kṛṣṇa is not at all inauspicious like ordinary fights. On the contrary, if one remembers the narration of this fight between Lord Kṛṣṇa and Lord Śiva in the morning and takes pleasure in the victory of Lord Kṛṣṇa, he will never experience defeat anywhere in his struggle of life.

This episode of Bāṇāsura's fighting with Kṛṣṇa and later on being saved by the grace of Lord Śiva is confirmation of the statement in the *Bhagavad-gītā* that the worshipers of demigods cannot achieve any benediction without its being sanctioned by the Supreme Lord, Kṛṣṇa. Here, in this narration, we find that although Bāṇāsura was a great devotee of Lord Śiva, when he faced death by Kṛṣṇa, Lord Śiva was not able to save him. But Lord Śiva appealed to Kṛṣṇa to save his devotee, and it was thus sanctioned by the Lord. This is the position of Lord Kṛṣṇa. The exact words used in this connection in the *Bhagavad-gītā* are *mayaiva vihitān hi tān*. This means that without the sanction of the Supreme Lord, no demigod can award any benediction to the worshiper.

Thus ends the Bhaktivedanta purport of the Sixty-second Chapter of Kṛṣṇa, *"Lord Kṛṣṇa Fights with Bāṇāsura."*

63 / The Story of King Nṛga

Once the family members of Lord Kṛṣṇa, such as Sāmba, Pradyumna, Cārubhānu and Gada, all princes of the Yadu dynasty, went for a long picnic in the forest near Dvārakā. In the course of their excursion, all of them became thirsty, and so they began to try to find out where water was available in the forest. When they approached a well, they found that there was no water in it, but on the contrary, within the well was a wonderful living entity. It was a large lizard, and all of them became astonished to see such a wonderful animal. They could understand that the animal was trapped and could not escape by its own effort, so out of compassion they tried to take the large lizard out of the well. Unfortunately, they could not get the lizard out, even though they tried to do so in many ways.

When the princes returned home, their story was narrated before Lord Kṛṣṇa. Lord Kṛṣṇa is the friend of all living entities. Therefore, after hearing the appeal from His sons, He personally went to the well and easily got the great lizard out simply by extending His left hand. Immediately upon being touched by the hand of Lord Kṛṣṇa, that great lizard gave up its former shape and appeared as a beautiful demigod, an inhabitant of the heavenly planets. His bodily complexion glittered like molten gold. He was decorated with fine garments, and he wore costly ornaments around his neck.

How the demigod had been obliged to accept the body of a lizard was not a secret to Lord Kṛṣṇa, but still, for others' information, the Lord inquired, "My dear fortunate demigod, now I see that your body is so beautiful and lustrous. Who are you? We can guess that you are one of the best demigods in the heavenly planets. All good fortune to you. I think that you are not meant to be in this situation. It must be due to the results of your past activities that you have been put into the species of lizard life. Still, I want to hear from you how you were put in this position. If you think that you can disclose this secret, then please tell us your identity."

Actually this large lizard was King Nṛga, and when he was questioned by the Supreme Personality of Godhead he immediately bowed down before the Lord, touching to the ground the helmet on his head, which was as dazzling as the sunshine. In this way, he first of all offered his respectful obeisances unto the Supreme Lord. He then said, "My dear Lord, I am the son of King Ikṣvāku, and am King Nṛga. If you have ever taken account of all charitably disposed men, I am sure that You must have heard my name. My Lord, You are the witness. You are aware of every bit of work done by the living entities—past, present and future. Nothing can be hidden from Your eternal cognizance. Still, You have ordered me to explain my history, and I shall therefore narrate the full story."

King Nṛga proceeded to narrate the history of his degradation, caused by his *karma-kāṇḍa* activities. He was very charitably disposed and had given away so many cows that he said the number was equal to the amount of dust on the earth, the stars in the sky and the rainfall. According to the Vedic ritualistic ceremonies, a man who is charitably disposed is commanded to give cows to the *brāhmaṇas.* From King Nṛga's statement, it appears that he followed this principle earnestly; however, as a result of a slight discrepancy in his action, he was forced to take birth as a lizard. Therefore it is recommended by the Lord in the *Bhagavad-gītā* that one who is charitably disposed and desires to derive the benefit of his charity should offer his gifts to please Kṛṣṇa. To give in charity means to perform pious activities. As a result of pious activities one may be elevated to the higher planetary systems; but promotion to the heavenly planets is no guarantee that one will never fall down. Rather, from the example of King Nṛga, it is definitely proved that fruitive activities, even if they are very pious, cannot give us eternal blissful life. As stated in the *Bhagavad-gītā,* the result of work, either pious or impious, is sure to bind a man unless it is discharged as *yajña* on behalf of the Supreme Personality of Godhead.

King Nṛga continued to say that the cows given in charity were not ordinary cows. Each one was very young and had given birth to only one calf. They were full of milk, very peaceful and healthy. All the cows were purchased with money that had been earned legally. Furthermore, their horns were gold-plated, their hooves were bedecked with silver plates, and they were covered with silken wrappers which were embroidered with pearls and necklaces. He stated that these valuably decorated cows were not given to any worthless person, but were distributed to the first-class *brāhmaṇas,* whom he had also decorated with nice garments and gold ornaments. The *brāhmaṇas* were well qualified, none of them were rich, and their family members were always in want for the necessities of life. A real *brāhmaṇa* never hoards money for a luxurious life, like the *kṣatriyas* or the *vaiśyas,* but always keeps himself in a poverty-stricken condition, knowing that money diverts the mind to materialistic ways of life. To live in this way is the vow of a qualified *brāhmaṇa,* and all of these *brāhmaṇas* were well situated in that exalted vow. They were well learned in Vedic knowledge. They executed the required austerities and penances in their lives, and were liberal, meeting the standard of qualified *brāhmaṇas.* They were equally friendly to everyone; above all, they were young and quite fit to act as qualified *brāhmaṇas.* Besides the cows, they were also given land, gold, houses, horses and elephants. Those who were not married were given wives, maidservants, grains, silver, utensils, garments, jewels, household furniture, chariots, etc. This charity was nicely performed as a sacrifice according to the Vedic rituals. The King also stated that not only had he bestowed gifts on the *brāhmaṇas,* but he had performed other pious activities, such as digging a well, planting trees on the roadside and installing ponds on the highways.

The King continued, "In spite of all this, unfortunately one of the *brāhmaṇa's* cows chanced to enter amongst my other cows. Not knowing this, I again gave it in charity to another *brāhmaṇa.* As the cow was being taken away by the *brāhmaṇa,* its former master claimed it as his own, stating, 'This cow was formerly given to me, so how is it that you are taking it away?' Thus there was arguing and fighting between the two *brāhmaṇas,* and they came before me and charged that I had taken back a cow that I had previously given in charity." To give something to someone and then to take it away is considered a great sin, especially in dealing with a *brāhmaṇa.* When both the *brāhmaṇas* charged the King with the same complaint, he was simply puzzled as to how it had happened. Thereafter, with great humility, the King offered each of them one hundred thousand cows in exchange for the one cow that was causing the fight between them. He prayed to them that he was their servant and that there had been some mistake. Thus, in order to rectify it, he prayed that they would be very kind upon him and accept his offer in exchange for the cow. The King fervently appealed to the *brāhmaṇas* not to cause his downfall into hell because of this mistake. A *brāhmaṇa's* property is called *brahma-sva,* and according to Manu's law, it cannot be acquired even by the government. Both *brāhmaṇas* insisted that the cow was theirs and could not be taken back under any condition; neither of them agreed to exchange it for the one hundred thousand cows. Thus disagreeing with the King's proposal, both *brāhmaṇas* left the palace in anger, thinking that their lawful position had been usurped.

After this incident, when the time came for the King to give up his body, he was taken before Yamarāja, the superintendent of death. Yamarāja asked him whether he wanted to first enjoy the results of his pious activities or first suffer the results of his impious activities. Yamarāja also hinted that since the King had executed so many pious activities and charities, the limit of Nṛga's enjoyment would be unknown to him. There was practically no end to the King's material happiness, but in spite of this hint, he was bewildered. He decided to first suffer the results of his impious activities and then to accept the results of his pious activities; therefore Yamarāja immediately turned him into a lizard.

King Nṛga had remained in a well as a big lizard for a very long time. He told Lord Kṛṣṇa: "In spite of being put into that degraded condition of life, I simply thought of You, my dear Lord, and my memory was never vanquished." It appears from these statements of King Nṛga that persons who follow the principles of fruitive activities and derive some material benefits are not very intelligent. Being given the choice by the superintendent of death, Yamarāja, King Nṛga could have first accepted the results of his pious activities. Instead he thought it would be better to first receive the effects of his impious activities and then enjoy the effects of his pious activities without disturbance. On the whole, he had not developed Kṛṣṇa consciousness. The Kṛṣṇa conscious person develops love of God, Kṛṣṇa, not love for pious or impious activities; therefore he is not subjected to the results of such action. As stated in the *Brahma-saṁhitā,* a devotee, by the grace of the Lord, does not become subjected to the resultant reactions of fruitive activities.

Somehow or other, as a result of his pious activities, King Nṛga had aspired to see the Lord. He continued to say: "My dear Lord, I had a great desire that someday I might be able to see You personally. I think that my tendency to perform ritualistic and charitable activities, combined with this great desire to see You personally, has enabled me to retain the memory of who I was in my former life, even though I became a lizard." (Such a person, who remembers his past life, is called *jāti-smara.*) "My dear Lord, You are the Supersoul seated in everyone's heart. There are many great mystic *yogīs* who have eyes to see You through the *Vedas* and *Upaniṣads.* In order to achieve the elevated position of being equal in quality with You, they always meditate on You within their hearts. Although such exalted saintly persons may see You constantly within their hearts, they still cannot see You eye to eye; therefore I am very much surprised that I am able to see You personally. I know that I was engaged in so many activities, especially as a king. Although I was in the midst of luxury and opulence and was subjected to so much of the happiness and misery of material existence, I am so fortunate to be seeing You personally. As far as I know, when one becomes liberated from material existence, he can see You in this way."

When King Nṛga elected to receive the results of his impious activities, he was given the body of a lizard because of the mistake in his pious activities; thus he could not be directly converted to a higher status of life like a great demigod. However, along with his pious activities, he thought of Kṛṣṇa, so he was quickly released from the body of a lizard and given the body of a demigod. By worshiping the Supreme Lord, those who desire material opulences are given the bodies of powerful demigods. Sometimes these demigods can see the Supreme Personality of Godhead eye to eye, but they are still not yet eligible to enter into the spiritual kingdom, the Vaikuṇṭha planets. However, if the demigods continue to become devotees of the Lord, the next chance they get they will enter into the Vaikuṇṭha planets.

Having attained the body of a demigod, King Nṛga, continuing to remember everything, said, "My dear Lord, You are the Supreme Lord and are worshiped by all the demigods. You are not one of the living entities, but You are the Supreme Person, Puruṣottama. You are the source of all happiness to all living entities; therefore You are known as Govinda. You are the Lord of those living entities who have accepted a material body and those who have not yet accepted a material body." (Among the living entities who have not accepted a material body are those who are hovering in the material world as evil spirits or living in the ghostly atmosphere. However, those who live in the spiritual kingdom, the Vaikuṇṭhalokas, have bodies that are not made of material elements.) "You are, my Lord, infallible. You are the Supreme, the purest of all living entities. You are living in everyone's heart. You are the shelter of all living entities, Nārāyaṇa. Being seated in the heart of all living entities, You are the supreme director of everyone's sensual activities; therefore, You are called Hṛṣīkeśa.

"My dear Supreme Lord Kṛṣṇa, because You have given me this body of a demigod, I will have to go to some heavenly planet; so I am taking this opportunity to beg for Your mercy, that I may have the benediction of never forgetting Your lotus feet, no matter to which form of life or planet I may be transferred. You are all-pervading, present everywhere as cause and effect. You are the cause of all causes, and Your potency and power are unlimited. You are the Absolute Truth, the Supreme Personality of Godhead and the Supreme Brahman. I therefore offer my respectful obeisances unto You again and again. My dear Lord, Your body is full of transcendental bliss and knowledge, and You are eternal. You are the master of all mystic powers; therefore You are known as Yogeśvara. Kindly accept me as insignificant dust at Your lotus feet."

Before entering the heavenly planets, King Nṛga circumambulated the Lord. He touched his helmet to the lotus feet of the Lord and bowed before Him. Seeing the airplane from the heavenly planets present before him, he was given permission by the Lord to board it. After the departure of King Nṛga, Lord Kṛṣṇa expressed His appreciation for the King's devotion to the *brāhmaṇas* as well as his charitable disposition and his performance of Vedic rituals. Therefore, it is recommended that if one cannot directly become a devotee of the Lord, one should follow the Vedic principles of life. This will enable him, one day, to see the Lord by being promoted either directly to the spiritual kingdom or indirectly to the heavenly kingdom, where he has hope of being transferred to the spiritual planets.

At this time, Lord Kṛṣṇa was present among His relatives who were members of the *kṣatriya* class. To teach them through the exemplary character of King Nṛga, He said: "Even though a *kṣatriya* king may be as powerful as fire, it is not possible for him to usurp the property of a *brāhmaṇa* and utilize it for his own purpose. If this is so, how can ordinary kings, who falsely think of themselves as the most powerful beings within the material world, usurp a *brāhmaṇa's* property? I do not think that taking poison is as dangerous as taking a *brāhmaṇa's* property. For ordinary poison there is treatment—one can be relieved from its effects; but if one drinks the poison of taking a *brāhmaṇa's* property, there is no remedy for the mistake. The perfect example was King Nṛga. He was very powerful and very pious, but due to the small mistake of unknowingly usurping a *brāhmaṇa's* cow, he was condemned to the abominable life of a lizard. Ordinary poison affects only those who drink it, and ordinary fire can be extinguished simply by pouring water on it; but the *araṇi* fire ignited by the spiritual potency of a *brāhmaṇa* can burn to ashes the whole family of a person who provokes such a *brāhmaṇa*." (Formerly, the *brāhmaṇas* used to ignite the fire of sacrifice not with matches or any other external fire but with their powerful *mantras*, called *araṇi*.) "If someone even touches a *brāhmaṇa's* property, he is ruined for three generations. However, if a *brāhmaṇa's* property is forcibly taken away, the taker's family for ten generations before him and for ten generations after him will become subject to ruination. On the other hand, if someone becomes a Vaiṣṇava or devotee of the Lord, ten generations of his family before his birth and ten generations after will become liberated."

Lord Kṛṣṇa continued: "If some foolish king who is puffed up by his wealth, prestige and power wants to usurp a *brāhmaṇa's* property, it should be understood that such a king is clearing his path to hell; he does not know how much he has to suffer for such unwise action. If someone takes away the property of a very liberal *brāhmaṇa* who is encumbered by a large dependent family, then such a usurper is put into the hell known as Kumbhīpāka; not only is he put into this hell, but his family members also have to accept such a miserable condition of life. A person who takes away property which has either been awarded to a *brāhmaṇa* or given away by him is condemned to live for at least 60,000 years as miserably as an insect in stool. Therefore I instruct you, all My boys and relatives present here, do not, even by mistake, take the possession of a *brāhmaṇa* and thereby pollute Your whole family. If someone even wishes to possess such property, let alone attempts to take it away by force, the duration of his life will be reduced. He will be defeated by his enemies, and after being bereft of his royal position, when he gives up his body he will become a serpent. A serpent gives trouble to all other living entities. My dear boys and relatives, I therefore advise you that even if a *brāhmaṇa* becomes angry with you and calls you by ill names or cuts you, still you should not retaliate. On the contrary, you should smile, tolerate him and offer your respects to the *brāhmaṇa.* You know very well that even I Myself offer My obeisances to the *brāhmaṇas* with great respect three times daily. You should therefore follow My instruction and example. I shall not forgive anyone who does not follow them, and I shall punish him. You should learn from the example of King Nṛga that even if someone unknowingly usurps the property of a *brāhmaṇa,* he is put into a miserable condition of life."

Thus Lord Kṛṣṇa, who is always engaged in purifying the conditioned living entities, gave instruction not only to His family members and the inhabitants of Dvārakā, but to all the members of human society. After this the Lord entered His palace.

Thus ends the Bhaktivedanta purport of the Sixty-third Chapter of Kṛṣṇa, *"The Story of King Nṛga."*

64 / Lord Balarāma Visits Vṛndāvana

Lord Balarāma became very anxious to see His father and mother, Mahārāja Nanda and Yaśodā. Therefore He started for Vṛndāvana on a chariot with great enthusiasm. The inhabitants of Vṛndāvana had been anxious to see Kṛṣṇa and Balarāma for a very long time. When Lord Balarāma returned to Vṛndāvana, all the cowherd boys and the *gopīs* had grown up; but still, on His arrival, they all embraced Him, and Balarāma embraced them in reciprocation. After this He came before Mahārāja Nanda and Yaśodā and offered His respectful obeisances unto them. In response, mother Yaśodā and Nanda Mahārāja offered their blessings unto Him. They addressed Him as Jagadīśvara, or the Lord of the universe who maintains everyone. The reason for this was that both Kṛṣṇa and Balarāma maintain all living entities, and yet Nanda and Yaśodā were put into such difficulties on account of Their absence. Feeling like this, they embraced Balarāma and, seating Him on their laps, began their perpetual crying, wetting Balarāma with their tears. Lord Balarāma then offered His respectful obeisances to the elderly cowherd men and accepted the obeisances of the younger cowherd men. Thus, according to their different ages and relationships, Lord Balarāma exchanged feelings of friendship with them. He shook hands with those who were His equals in age and friendship, and with loud laughing embraced each one of them.

After being received by the cowherd men and boys, the *gopīs,* and King Nanda and Yaśodā, Lord Balarāma sat down, feeling satisfied, and they all surrounded Him. First Lord Balarāma inquired from them about their welfare, and then, not having seen Him for such a long time, they began to ask Him different questions. The inhabitants of Vṛndāvana had sacrificed everything for Kṛṣṇa, simply being captivated by the lotus eyes of the Lord. Because of their great desire to love Kṛṣṇa, they never desired anything like elevation to the heavenly planets or merging into the effulgence of Brahman to become one with the Absolute Truth. They were not even interested in enjoying a life of opulence, but were satisfied in living a simple life in the village as cowherd men. They were always absorbed in thoughts of Kṛṣṇa and did not desire any personal benefits, and they were all so much in love with Him that in His absence their voices faltered when they began to inquire from Balarāmajī.

First Nanda Mahārāja and Yaśodāmayī inquired, "My dear Balarāma, are our friends like Vasudeva and others in the family doing well? Now You and Kṛṣṇa are grown-up married men with children. In the happiness of family life, do You sometimes remember Your poor father and mother, Nanda Mahārāja and Yaśodādevī? It is very good news that the most sinful King Kaṁsa has been killed by You and that our friends like Vasudeva and the others, who had been harrassed by him, have now been relieved. It is also very good news that both You and Kṛṣṇa defeated Jarāsandha and Kālayavana, who now is dead, and that You are now living in a fortified residence in Dvārakā."

When the *gopīs* arrived, Lord Balarāma glanced over them with loving eyes. Being overjoyed, the *gopīs,* who had so long been mortified on account of Kṛṣṇa's and Balarāma's absence, began to ask about the welfare of the two brothers. They specifically asked Balarāma whether Kṛṣṇa was enjoying His life surrounded by the enlightened women of Dvārakā Purī. "Does He sometimes remember His father Nanda and His mother Yaśodā and the other friends with whom He so intimately behaved while He was in Vṛndāvana? Does Kṛṣṇa have any plans to come here to see His mother Yaśodā, and does He remember us *gopīs* who are now pitiably bereft of His company? Kṛṣṇa might have forgotten us in the midst of the cultured women of Dvārakā, but as far as we are concerned, we are still remembering Him by collecting flowers and sewing them into garlands. When He does not come, however, we simply pass our time by crying. If only He would come here and accept these garlands that we have made. Dear Lord Balarāma, descendant of Daśārha, You know that we would give up everything for Kṛṣṇa's friendship. Even in great distress one cannot give up the connection of family members, but although it might be impossible for others, we gave up our fathers, mothers, sisters and relatives without caring at all about our renunciation. Then, all of a sudden, Kṛṣṇa renounced us and went away. He broke off our intimate relationship without any serious consideration and left for a foreign country. But He was so clever and cunning that He manufactured very nice words. He said, 'My dear *gopīs,* please do not worry. The service that you have rendered Me is impossible for Me to repay.' After all, we are women, so how could we disbelieve Him? Now we can understand that His sweet words were simply for cheating us."

Another *gopī,* protesting Kṛṣṇa's absence from Vṛndāvana, began to say: "My dear Balarāmajī, we are of course village girls, so Kṛṣṇa could cheat us in that way, but what about the women of Dvārakā? Don't think they are as foolish as we are! We village women might be misled by Kṛṣṇa, but the women in the city of Dvārakā are very clever and intelligent. Therefore I would be surprised if such city women could be misled by Kṛṣṇa and could believe His words."

Then another *gopī* began to speak. "My dear friend," she said, "Kṛṣṇa is very clever in using words. No one can compete with Him in that art. He can manufacture such colorful words and talk so sweetly that the heart of any woman would be misled. Besides that, He has perfected the art of smiling very attractively, and by seeing His smile women become mad after Him and would give themselves to Him without any hesitation."

Another *gopī,* after hearing this, said, "My dear friends, what is the use in talking about Kṛṣṇa? If you are at all interested in passing away time by talking, let us talk on some subject other than Him. If cruel Kṛṣṇa can pass His time without us, why can't we pass our time without Kṛṣṇa? Of course, Kṛṣṇa is passing His days very happily without us, but the difference is that we cannot pass our days very happily without Him."

When the *gopīs* were talking in this way, their feelings for Kṛṣṇa became more and more intensified, and they were experiencing Kṛṣṇa's smiling, Kṛṣṇa's words of love, Kṛṣṇa's attractive features, Kṛṣṇa's characteristics and Kṛṣṇa's embraces. By the force of their ecstatic feelings, it appeared to them that Kṛṣṇa was personally present and dancing before them. Because of their sweet remembrance of Kṛṣṇa, they could not check their tears, and they began to cry without consideration.

Lord Balarāma could, of course, understand the ecstatic feelings of the *gopīs,* and therefore He wanted to pacify them. He was expert in presenting an appeal, and thus, treating the *gopīs* very respectfully, He began to narrate the stories of Kṛṣṇa so tactfully that the *gopīs* became satisfied. In order to keep the *gopīs* in Vṛndāvana satisfied, Lord Balarāma stayed there continually for two months, namely the months of Caitra (March-April) and Vaiśākha (April-May). For those two months He kept Himself among the *gopīs,* and He passed every night with them in the forest of Vṛndāvana in order to satisfy their desire for conjugal love. Thus Balarāma also enjoyed the *rāsa* dance with the *gopīs* during those two months. Since the season was springtime, the breeze on the bank of the Yamunā was blowing very mildly, carrying the aroma of different flowers, especially of the flower known as *kaumudī.* Moonlight filled the sky and spread everywhere, and thus the banks of the Yamunā appeared to be very bright and pleasing, and Lord Balarāma enjoyed the company of the *gopīs* there.

The demigod known as Varuṇa sent his daughter Vāruṇī in the form of liquid honey oozing from the hollows of the trees. Because of this honey the whole forest became aromatic, and the sweet aroma of the liquid honey, Vāruṇī, captivated Balarāmajī. Balarāmajī and all the *gopīs* became very much attracted by the taste of Vāruṇī, and all of them drank it together. While drinking this natural beverage, Vāruṇī, all the *gopīs* chanted the glories of Lord Balarāma, and Lord Balarāma felt very happy, as if He had become intoxicated by drinking that Vāruṇī beverage. His eyes rolled in a pleasing attitude. He was decorated with long garlands of forest flowers, and the whole situation appeared to be a great function of happiness because of this transcendental bliss. Lord Balarāma smiled beautifully, and the drops of perspiration decorating His face appeared to be soothing morning dew.

While Balarāma was in that happy mood, He desired to enjoy the company of the *gopīs* in the water of the Yamunā. Therefore He called Yamunā to come nearby. But Yamunā neglected the order of Balarāmajī, considering Him to be intoxicated. Lord Balarāma became very much displeased at Yamunā's neglecting His order. He immediately wanted to scratch the land near the river with His plowshare. Lord Balarāma has two weapons, a plow and a club, and He takes service from them when they are required. This time He wanted to bring the Yamunā by force, and He took the help of His plow. He wanted to punish Yamunā because she did not come in obedience to His order. He addressed Yamunā: "You wretched river! You did not care for My order. Now I shall teach you a lesson! You did not come to Me voluntarily. Now with the help of My plow I shall force you to come. I shall divide you into hundreds of scattered streams!"

When Yamunā was threatened like this, she became greatly afraid of the power of Balarāma and immediately came in person, falling at His lotus feet and praying thus: "My dear Balarāma, You are the most powerful personality, and You are pleasing to everyone. Unfortunately, I forgot Your glorious, exalted position, but now I have come to my senses, and I remember that You hold all the planetary systems on Your head merely by Your partial expansion as Śeṣa. You are the sustainer of the whole universe. My dear Supreme Personality of Godhead, You are full of six opulences. Because I forgot Your omnipotence, I have mistakenly disobeyed Your order, and thus I have become a great offender. But, my dear Lord, please know that I am a surrendered soul unto You. You are very much affectionate to Your devotees. Therefore please excuse my impudence and mistakes and, by Your causeless mercy, may You now release me."

Upon displaying this submissive attitude, Yamunā was forgiven, and when she came nearby, Lord Balarāma wanted to enjoy the pleasure of swimming within her water along with the *gopīs* in the same way an elephant enjoys himself along with his many she-elephants. After a long time, when Lord Balarāma had enjoyed to His full satisfaction, He came out of the water, and immediately a goddess of fortune offered Him a nice blue garment and a valuable necklace made of gold. After taking bath in the Yamunā, Lord Balarāma, dressed in blue garments and decorated with golden ornaments, looked very attractive to everyone. Lord Balarāma's complexion is white, and when He was properly dressed He looked exactly like the white elephant of King Indra in the heavenly planet. The River Yamunā still has many small branches due to being scratched by the plowshare of Lord Balarāma. And all these branches of the River Yamunā are still glorifying the omnipotency of Lord Balarāma.

Lord Balarāma and the *gopīs* enjoyed transcendental pastimes together every night for two months, and time passed away so quickly that all those nights appeared to be only one night. In the presence of Lord Balarāma, all the *gopīs* and inhabitants of Vṛndāvana became as cheerful as they had been before in the presence of both brothers, Lord Kṛṣṇa and Lord Balarāma.

Thus ends the Bhaktivedanta purport of the Sixty-fourth Chapter of Kṛṣṇa, *"Lord Balarāma Visits Vṛndāvana."*

65 / Deliverance of Pauṇḍraka and the King of Kāśī

The story of King Pauṇḍraka is very interesting because there have always been many rascals and fools who have considered themselves to be God. Even in the presence of the Supreme Personality of Godhead, Kṛṣṇa, there was such a foolish person. His name was Pauṇḍraka, and He wanted to declare himself to be God. While Lord Balarāma was absent in Vṛndāvana, this King Pauṇḍraka, the King of the Karūṣa province, being foolish and puffed up, sent a messenger to Lord Kṛṣṇa. Lord Kṛṣṇa is accepted as the Supreme Personality of Godhead, and King Pauṇḍraka directly challenged Kṛṣṇa through the messenger, who stated that Pauṇḍraka, and not Kṛṣṇa, was Vāsudeva. In the present day there are many foolish followers of such rascals. Similarly, in his day, many foolish men accepted Pauṇḍraka as the Supreme Personality of Godhead. Because he could not estimate his own position, Pauṇḍraka falsely thought himself to be Lord Vāsudeva. Thus the messenger declared to Kṛṣṇa that out of his causeless mercy, King Pauṇḍraka, the Supreme Personality of Godhead, had descended on the earth just to deliver all distressed persons.

Surrounded by many other foolish persons, this rascal Pauṇḍraka had actually concluded that he was Vāsudeva, the Supreme Personality of Godhead. This kind of conclusion is certainly childish. When children are playing, they sometimes create a king amongst themselves, and the child who is so selected thinks that he is the king. Similarly, many foolish persons, due to ignorance, select another fool as God, and then the rascal considers himself God, as if God could be created by childish play or by the votes of men. Under this false impression, thinking himself the Supreme Lord, Pauṇḍraka sent his messenger to Dvārakā to challenge the position of Kṛṣṇa. The messenger reached the royal assembly of Kṛṣṇa in Dvārakā and conveyed the message given by his master, Pauṇḍraka. The message contained the following statements.

"I am the only Supreme Personality of Godhead, Vāsudeva. There is no man who can compete with me. I have descended as King Pauṇḍraka, taking compassion on the distressed conditioned souls out of my unlimited causeless mercy. You have falsely taken the position of Vāsudeva without authority, but you should not propagate this false idea. You must give up Your position. O descendant of the Yadu dynasty, please give up all the symbols of Vāsudeva which You have falsely assumed. And after giving up this position, come and surrender unto me. If out of Your gross impudence You do not care for my words, then I challenge You to fight. I am inviting You to a battle in which the decision will be settled."

When all the members of the royal assembly, including King Ugrasena, heard this message sent by Pauṇḍraka, they laughed very loudly for a considerable time. After enjoying the loud laughter of all the members of the assembly, Kṛṣṇa replied to the messenger as follows. "O messenger of Pauṇḍraka, you may carry My message to your master: He is a foolish rascal. I directly call him a rascal, and I refuse to follow his instructions. I shall never give up the symbols of Vāsudeva, especially My disc. I shall use this disc to kill not only King Pauṇḍraka but all his followers also. I shall destroy this Pauṇḍraka and his foolish associates, who merely constitute a society ot cheaters and cheated. When this action is taken, foolish King, you will have to conceal your face in disgrace, and when your head is severed from your body by My disc, it will be surrounded by meat-eating birds like vultures, hawks and eagles. At that time, instead of becoming My shelter as you have demanded, you will be subjected to the mercy of these low-born birds. At that time your body will be thrown to the dogs, who will eat it with great pleasure."

The messenger carried the words of Lord Kṛṣṇa to his master, Pauṇḍraka, who patiently heard all these insults. Without waiting longer, Lord Śrī Kṛṣṇa immediately started out on His chariot to punish the rascal Pauṇḍraka. Because at that time the King of Karūṣa was living with his friend the King of Kāśī, Kṛṣṇa surrounded the whole city of Kāśī.

King Pauṇḍraka was a great warrior, and as soon as he heard of Kṛṣṇa's attack, he came out of the city along with two *akṣauhiṇī* divisions of soldiers. The King of Kāśī was also a friend to King Pauṇḍraka, and he came out with three *akṣauhiṇī* divisions. When the two kings came before Lord Kṛṣṇa to oppose Him, Kṛṣṇa saw Pauṇḍraka face to face for the first time. Kṛṣṇa saw that Pauṇḍraka had decorated himself with the symbols of the conchshell, disc, lotus and club. He carried the Śārṅga bow, and on his chest was the insignia of Śrīvatsa. His neck was decorated with a false Kaustubha jewel, and he wore a flower garland in exact imitation of Lord

Vāsudeva. He was dressed in yellow colored silken garments, and the flag on his chariot carried the symbol of Garuḍa, exactly imitating Kṛṣṇa's. He had a very valuable helmet on his head, and his earrings, like swordfish, glittered brilliantly. On the whole, however, his dress and makeup were clearly imitation. Anyone could understand that he was just like someone onstage playing the part of Vāsudeva in false dress. When Lord Śrī Kṛṣṇa saw Pauṇḍraka imitating His posture and dress, He could not check His laughter, and thus He laughed with great satisfaction.

The soldiers on the side of King Pauṇḍraka began to shower their weapons upon Kṛṣṇa. The weapons, including various kinds of tridents, clubs, poles, lances, swords, daggers and arrows, came flying in waves, and Kṛṣṇa counteracted them. He smashed not only the weapons but also the soldiers and assistants of Pauṇḍraka, just as during the dissolution of this universe the fire of devastation burns everything to ashes. The elephants, chariots, horses, and infantry belonging to the opposite party were scattered by the weapons of Kṛṣṇa. The whole battlefield became scattered with the bodies of animals and chariots. There were fallen horses, elephants, men, asses and camels. Although the devastated battlefield appeared like the dancing place of Lord Śiva at the time of the dissolution of the world, the warriors who were on the side of Kṛṣṇa were very much encouraged by seeing this, and they fought with greater strength.

At this time, Lord Kṛṣṇa told Pauṇḍraka, "Pauṇḍraka, you requested Me to give up the symbols of Lord Viṣṇu, specifically My disc. Now I will give it up to you. Be careful! You falsely declare yourself to be Vāsudeva, imitating Myself. Therefore no one is a greater fool than you." From this statement of Kṛṣṇa's it is clear that any rascal who advertises himself as God is the greatest fool in human society. Kṛṣṇa continued: "Now, Pauṇḍraka, I shall force you to give up this false representation. You wanted Me to surrender unto you. Now this is your opportunity. We shall now fight, and if I am defeated and you become victorious, I shall certainly surrender unto you." In this way, after chastising Pauṇḍraka very severely, He smashed his chariot to pieces by shooting an arrow. With the help of His disc He separated the head of Pauṇḍraka from his body, just as Indra shaves off the peaks of mountains by striking them with his thunderbolt. Similarly, He also killed the King of Kāśī with His arrows. Lord Kṛṣṇa specifically arranged to throw the head of the King of Kāśī into the city of Kāśī itself so that his relatives and family members could see it. This was done by Kṛṣṇa just as a hurricane carries a lotus petal here and there. Lord Kṛṣṇa killed Pauṇḍraka and his friend Kāśīrāja on the battlefield, and then He returned to His capital city, Dvārakā.

When Lord Kṛṣṇa returned to the city of Dvārakā, all the Siddhas from the heavenly planets were singing the glories of the Lord. As far as Pauṇḍraka was concerned, somehow or other he was always thinking of Lord Vāsudeva by falsely dressing himself in that way, and therefore Pauṇḍraka achieved *sārūpya,* one of the five kinds of liberation, and was thus promoted to the Vaikuṇṭha planets, where the devotees have the same bodily features as Viṣṇu, with four hands holding the four symbols. Factually, his meditation was concentrated on the Viṣṇu form, but because he thought himself to be Lord Viṣṇu, it was offensive. After being killed by Kṛṣṇa, however, that offense was also mitigated. Thus he was given *sārūpya* liberation, and he attained the same form as the Lord.

When the head of the King of Kāśī was thrown through the city gate, people gathered and were astonished to see that wonderful thing. When they found out that there were earrings on it, they could understand that it was someone's head. They conjectured as to whose head it might be. Some thought it was Kṛṣṇa's head because Kṛṣṇa was the enemy of Kāśīrāja, and they calculated that the King of Kāśī might have thrown Kṛṣṇa's head into the city so that the people might take pleasure that the enemy was killed. But it was finally detected that the head was not Kṛṣṇa's, but that of Kāśīrāja himself. When it was so ascertained, the queens of the King of Kāśī immediately approached and began to lament the death of their husband. "My dear lord," they cried, "upon your death, we have become just like dead bodies."

The King of Kāśī had one son whose name was Sudakṣiṇa. After observing the ritualistic funeral ceremonies, he took a vow that since Kṛṣṇa was the enemy of his father, he would kill Kṛṣṇa and in this way liquidate his debts to his father. Therefore, accompanied by a learned priest qualified to help him, he began to worship Mahādeva, Lord Śiva. The lord of the kingdom of Kāśī is Viśvanātha (Lord Śiva). The temple of Lord Viśvanātha is still existing in Vārāṇasī, and many thousands of pilgrims still gather daily in that temple. By the worship of Sudakṣiṇa, Lord Śiva was very much pleased, and he wanted to give a benediction to his devotee. Sudakṣiṇa's purpose was to kill Kṛṣṇa, and therefore he prayed for a specific power by which he could kill Him. Lord Śiva advised that Sudakṣiṇa, assisted by the *brāhmaṇas,* execute the ritualistic ceremony for killing one's enemy. This ceremony is also mentioned in some of the *Tantras.* Lord Śiva informed Sudakṣiṇa that if such a black ritualistic ceremony were performed properly then the evil spirit named Dakṣiṇāgni would appear to carry out any order given to him. He would have to be employed, however, to kill someone other than a qualified *brāhmaṇa.* In such a case he would be accompanied by Lord Śiva's ghostly companions, and the desire of Sudakṣiṇa to kill his enemy would be fulfilled.

When Sudakṣiṇa was encouraged by Lord Śiva in that way, he became assured that he would be able to kill Kṛṣṇa. With a determined vow of austerity, he began to execute the black art of chanting *mantras*, assisted by the priests. After this, out of the fire came a great demonic form, whose hair, beard and moustache were exactly the color of hot copper. This form was very big and fierce. As the demon arose from the fire, cinders of fire emanated from the sockets of his eyes. The giant fiery demon appeared still more fierce due to the movements of his eyebrows. He exhibited long sharp teeth and, sticking out his long tongue, licked both sides of his lips. He was naked, and he carried a big trident, which was blazing like fire. After appearing from the fire of sacrifice, he stood wielding the trident in his hand. Instigated by Sudakṣiṇa, the demon proceeded toward the capital city, Dvārakā, along with many hundreds of ghostly companions, and it appeared that he was going to burn all outer space to ashes. The surface of the earth trembled because of his striking steps. When he entered the city of Dvārakā, all the residents panicked, just like animals at the time of a forest fire.

At that time Kṛṣṇa was engaged in playing chess in the royal assembly council hall. All the residents of Dvārakā approached and addressed Him, "Dear Lord of the three worlds, there is a great fiery demon ready to burn the whole city of Dvārakā. Please save us." Thus, after approaching Lord Kṛṣṇa, all the inhabitants of Dvārakā began to appeal to Him for protection from the fiery demon who had just appeared in Dvārakā to devastate the whole city.

Lord Kṛṣṇa, who specifically protects His devotees, saw that the whole population of Dvārakā was most perturbed by the presence of the great fiery demon. He immediately began to smile and assured them, "Don't worry. I shall give you all protection." The Supreme Personality of Godhead, Kṛṣṇa, is all-pervading. He is within everyone's heart, and He is without also in the form of the cosmic manifestation. He could understand that the fiery demon was a creation of Lord Śiva, and in order to vanquish him He took His Sudarśana-cakra and ordered him to take the necessary steps. The Sudarśana-cakra appeared with the effulgence of millions of suns, his temperature being as powerful as that of the fire created at the end of the cosmic manifestation. By his own effulgence, the Sudarśana-cakra began to illuminate the entire universe, on the surface of the earth as well as in outer space. Then the Sudarśana-cakra began to freeze the fiery demon created by Lord Śiva. In this way, the fiery demon was checked by the Sudarśana-cakra of Lord Kṛṣṇa, and being defeated in his attempt to devastate the city of Dvārakā, he turned back.

Having failed to set fire to Dvārakā, he went back to Vārāṇasī, the kingdom of Kāśīrāja. As a result of his return, all the priests who had helped instruct the black art of *mantras,* along with their employer, Sudakṣiṇa were burned into ashes by the glaring effulgence of the fiery demon. According to the methods of black art *mantras* instructed in the *Tantra,* if the *mantra* fails to kill the enemy, then, because it must kill someone, it kills the original creator. Sudakṣiṇa was the originator, and the priests assisted him; therefore all of them were burned to ashes. This is the way of the demons: the demons create something to kill God, but by the same weapon the demons themselves are killed.

Following just behind the fiery demon, the Sudarśana-cakra also entered Vārāṇasī. This city of Vārāṇasī had been very opulent and great for a very long time. Even now, the city of Vārāṇasī is very opulent and famous, and it is one of the important cities of India. There were then many big palaces, assembly houses, marketplaces and gates, with very important large monuments by the palaces and gates. Lecturing platforms could be found at each and every crossing of the roads. There was a treasury house, and elephant heads, horse heads, chariots, granaries and places for distribution of foodstuff. The city of Vārāṇasī had been filled with all these material opulences for a very long time, but because the king of Kāśī and his son Sudakṣiṇa were against Lord Kṛṣṇa, the Viṣṇu-cakra Sudarśana (the disc weapon of Lord Kṛṣṇa) devastated the whole city by burning all these important places. This excursion was more ravaging than modern bombing. The Sudarśana-cakra, having thus finished his duty, came back to his Lord Śrī Kṛṣṇa at Dvārakā.

This narration of the devastation of Vārāṇasī by Kṛṣṇa's disc weapon, the Sudarśana-cakra, is transcendental and auspicious. Anyone who narrates this story or anyone who hears this story with faith and attention will be released from all reaction to sinful activities. This is the assurance of Śukadeva Gosvāmī who narrated this story to Parīkṣit Mahārāja.

Thus ends the Bhaktivedanta purport of the Sixty-fifth Chapter of Kṛṣṇa, *"Deliverance of Pauṇḍraka and the King of Kāśī."*

66 / Deliverance of Dvivida Gorilla

While Śukadeva Gosvāmī continued to speak on the transcendental pastimes and characteristics of Lord Kṛṣṇa, King Parīkṣit, upon hearing him, became more and more enthusiastic and wanted to hear further. Śukadeva Gosvāmī next narrated the story of Dvivida, the gorilla who was killed by Lord Balarāma.

This gorilla was a great friend of Baumāsura's or Narakāsura's, who was killed by Kṛṣṇa in connection with his kidnapping sixteen thousand princesses from all over the world. Dvivida was the minister of King Sugrīva. His brother, Mainda, was also a very powerful gorilla king. When Dvivida gorilla heard the story of his friend Baumāsura's being killed by Lord Kṛṣṇa, he planned to create mischief throughout the country in order to avenge the death of Baumāsura. His first business was to set fires in villages, towns, and industrial and mining places, as well as the residential quarters of the mercantile men who were busy dairy farming and protecting cows. Sometimes he would uproot a big mountain and tear it to pieces. In this way he created great disturbances all over the country, especially in the province of Kathwar. The city of Dvārakā was situated in this Kathwar province, and because Lord Kṛṣṇa used to live in this city, Dvivida specifically made it his target of disturbance.

Dvivida was as powerful as 10,000 elephants. Sometimes he would go to the seashore, and with his powerful hands he would create so much disturbance in the sea that he would overflood the neighboring cities and villages. Often he would go to the hermitages of great saintly persons and sages and cause a great disturbance by smashing their beautiful gardens and orchards. Not only did he create disturbances in that way, but sometimes he would pass urine and stool on their sacred sacrificial arena. He would thus pollute the whole atmosphere. He also kidnapped both men and women, taking them away from their residential places to the caves of the mountains. Putting them within the caves, he would close the entrances with large chunks of stone, like the *bhṛṅgī* insect, which arrests and carries away many flies and other insects and puts them within the holes of the trees where he lives. He thus regularly defied the law and order of the country. Not only that, but he would sometimes pollute the female members of many aristocratic families by forcibly raping them.

While creating such great disturbance all over the country, sometimes he heard very sweet musical sounds from the Raivataka mountain, and so he entered that mountainous region. There he saw that Lord Balarāma was present in the midst of many beautiful young girls, enjoying their company while engaged in singing and dancing. He became captivated by the beautiful features of Lord Balarāma's body, each and every part of which was very beautiful, decorated as He was with a garland of lotus flowers. Similarly, all the young girls present, dressed and garlanded with flowers, exhibited much beauty. Lord Balarāma seemed to be fully intoxicated from drinking the Vāruṇī beverage, and His eyes appeared to be rolling in a drunken state. Lord Balarāma appeared just like the king of the elephants in the midst of many she-elephants.

This gorilla by the name of Dvivida could climb up on the trees and jump from one branch to another. Sometimes he would jerk the branches, creating a particular type of sound, "Kila, kila," so that Lord Balarāma was greatly distracted from the pleasing atmosphere. Sometimes Dvivida would come before the women and exhibit different types of caricatures. By nature young women are apt to enjoy everything with laughter and joking, and when the gorilla came before them they did not take him seriously, but simply laughed at him. However, the gorilla was so rude that even in the presence of Balarāma he began to show the lower part of his body to the women, and sometimes he would come forward to show his teeth while moving his eyebrows. He disrespected the women, even in the presence of Balarāma. Lord Balarāma's name suggests that He is not only very powerful, but that He takes pleasure in exhibiting extraordinary strength. So He took a stone and threw it at Dvivida. The gorilla, however, artfully avoided being struck by the stone. In order to insult Balarāma, the gorilla took away the earthen pot in which the Vāruṇī was kept. Dvivida, being thus intoxicated, with his limited strength began to tear off all the valuable clothes worn by Balarāma and the accompanying young girls. He was so puffed up that he thought that Balarāma could not do anything to chastise him, and he continued to offend Balarāmajī and His companions.

When Lord Balarāma personally saw the disturbances created by the gorilla and heard that he had already performed many mischievous activities all over the country, He became very angry and decided to kill him. Immediately He took His club in His hands. The gorilla could understand that now Balarāma was going to attack him. In order to counteract Balarāma, he immediately uprooted a big oak tree, and with great force he came and struck at Lord Balarāma's head. Lord Balarāma, however, immediately caught hold of the big tree and remained undisturbed, just like a great mountain. To retaliate, He took His club by the name of Sunanda and began to hit the gorilla with it. The gorilla's head was severely injured. Currents of blood flowed from his head with great force, but the stream of blood enhanced his beauty like a stream of liquid manganese coming out of a great mountain. The striking of Balarāma's club did not even slightly disturb him. On the contrary, he immediately uprooted another big oak tree, and after clipping off all its leaves, he began to strike Balarāma's head with it. But Balarāma, with the help of His club, tore the tree to pieces. Since the gorilla was very angry, he took another tree in his hands and began to strike Lord Balarāma's body. Again Lord Balarāma tore the tree to pieces, and the fighting continued. Each time the gorilla would bring out a big tree to strike Balarāma, Lord Balarāma would tear the tree to pieces by the striking of His club. The gorilla Dvivida would clutch another tree from another direction and again attack Balarāma in the same way. As a result of this continuous fighting, the forest became treeless. When no more trees were available, Dvivida took help from the hills and threw large pieces of stone, like rainfall, upon the body of Balarāma. Lord Balarāma, also in a great sporting mood, began to smash those big pieces of stone into mere pebbles. The gorilla, being bereft of all trees and stone slabs, now stood before Him and waved his strong fists. Then, with great force, he began to beat the chest of Lord Balarāma with his fists. This time Lord Balarāma became most angry. Since the gorilla was striking Him with his hands, He would not strike him back with His own weapons, the club or the plow. Simply with His fist He began to strike the collarbone of the gorilla. This striking proved to be fatal to Dvivida, who immediately vomited blood and fell unconscious upon the ground. When the gorilla fell, it appeared that all the hills and forests tottered.

After this horrible incident, all the Siddhas, great sages and saintly persons from the upper planetary system began to shower flowers on the person of Lord Balarāma, and sounds glorifying the supremacy of Lord Balarāma were vibrated. All of them began to chant, "All glories to Lord Balarāma! Let us offer our respectful obeisances unto Your lotus feet. By

Your killing this great demon, Dvivida, You have initiated an auspicious era for the world." All such jubilant sounds of victory were heard from outer space. After killing the great demon Dvivida and being worshiped by showers of flowers and glorious sounds of victory, Balarāma returned to His capital city, Dvārakā.

Thus ends the Bhaktivedanta purport of the Sixty-sixth Chapter of Kṛṣṇa, *"Deliverance of Dvivida Gorilla."*

67 / The Marriage of Sāmba

Duryodhana, the son of Dhṛtarāṣṭra, had a marriageable daughter by the name of Lakṣmaṇā. She was a very highly qualified girl of the Kuru dynasty, and many princes wanted to marry her. In such cases, the *svayaṁvara* ceremony is held so that the girl may select her husband according to her own choice. In Lakṣmaṇā's *svayaṁvara* assembly, when the girl was to select her husband, Sāmba appeared. He was the son of Kṛṣṇa by Jāmbavatī, one of the chief wives of Lord Kṛṣṇa. This son Sāmba is so named because he was a very bad child, and he always lived close to his mother. The name Sāmba indicates a son who is very much his mother's pet. *Ambā* means mother, and *sa* means with. So this special name was given to him because he always remained with his mother. He was also known as Jāmbavatīsuta for the same reason. As previously explained, all the sons of Kṛṣṇa were as qualified as their great father, Lord Kṛṣṇa. Sāmba wanted the daughter of Duryodhana, Lakṣmaṇā, although she was not inclined to have him. Therefore Sāmba kidnapped Lakṣmaṇā by force from the *svayaṁvara* assembly.

Because Sāmba took Lakṣmaṇā away from the assembly by force, all the members of the Kuru dynasty, namely, Dhṛtarāṣṭra, Bhīṣma, Vidura, Ujahan and Arjuna, thought it an insult to their family tradition that the boy, Sāmba, could possibly have kidnapped their daughter. All of them knew that Lakṣmaṇā was not at all inclined to select him as a husband and that she was not given the chance to select her own husband; instead she was forcibly taken away by this boy. Therefore, they decided that he must be punished. They unanimously declared that he was most impudent and that he had degraded the Kurus' family tradition. Therefore, all of them, under the counsel of the elderly members of the Kuru family, decided to arrest the boy but not kill him. They concluded that the girl could not be married to any boy other than Sāmba since she had already been touched by him. (According to the Vedic system, once being used by some boy, a girl cannot be married or given to any other boy. Nor would anyone agree to marry a girl who had already thus associated with another boy.) The elderly members of the family, such as Bhīṣma, wanted to arrest him. All the members of the Kuru dynasty, especially the great fighters, joined together just to teach him a lesson, and Karṇa was made the commander-in-chief for this small battle.

While the plan was being made to arrest Sāmba, the Kurus counciled amongst themselves that upon his arrest, the members of the Yadu dynasty would be very angry with them. There was every possibility of the Yadus' accepting the challenge and fighting with them. But they also thought, "If they came here to fight with us, what could they do? The members of the Yadu dynasty cannot equal the members of the Kuru dynasty because the kings of the Kuru dynasty are the emperors, whereas the kings of the Yadu dynasty are able to enjoy their landed property." The Kurus thought, "If they come here to challenge us because their son was arrested, we will nevertheless accept the fight. All of us will teach them a lesson, so that automatically they will become subdued under pressure, as the senses are subdued by the mystic *yoga* process, *prāṇāyāma*." (In the mechanical system of mystic *yoga*, the airs within the body are controlled, and the senses are subdued and checked from being engaged in anything other than meditation upon Lord Viṣṇu.)

After consultation and after receiving permission from the elderly members of the Kuru dynasty, such as Bhīṣma and Dhṛtarāṣṭra, six great warriors—Karṇa, Śala, Bhuriśravā, Yajñaketu, and Duryodhana, the father of the girl—all *mahā-rathīs* and guided by the great fighter Bhīṣmadeva, attempted to arrest the boy Sāmba. There are different grades of fighters, including *mahā-rathī, eka-rathī,* and *rathī,* classified according to their fighting capacity. These *mahā-rathīs* could fight alone with many thousands of men. All of them combined together to arrest Sāmba. Sāmba was also a *mahā-rathī,* but he was alone and had to fight with the six other *mahā-rathīs.* Still he was not deterred when he saw all the great fighters of the Kuru dynasty coming up behind him to arrest him.

Alone, he turned towards them and took his nice bow, posing exactly as a lion stands adamant in the face of other animals. Karṇa was leading the party, and he challenged Sāmba, "Why are you fleeing? Just stand, and we shall teach you a lesson!" When challenged by another *kṣatriya* to stand and fight, a *kṣatriya* cannot go away; he must fight. Therefore, as soon as Sāmba accepted the challenge and stood alone before them, he was overpowered by showers of arrows thrown by all the great warriors. As a lion is never afraid of being chased by many wolves and jackals, similarly, Sāmba, the glorious son of the Yadu dynasty, endowed with inconceivable potencies as the son of Lord Kṛṣṇa, became very angry at the warriors of the Kuru dynasty for improperly using arrows against him. He fought them with great talent. First of all, he struck each of the six charioteers with six separate arrows. Another four arrows were used to kill the charioteers' horses, four on each chariot. One arrow was used to kill the driver, and one arrow was used for Karṇa as well as the other celebrated fighters. While Sāmba was so diligently fighting alone with the six great warriors, they all appreciated the inconceivable potency of the boy. Even in the midst of fighting, they admitted frankly that this boy Sāmba was wonderful. But the fighting was conducted in the *kṣatriya* spirit, so all together, although it was improper, they obliged Sāmba to get down from his chariot, now broken to pieces. Of the six warriors, four took care to kill Sāmba's four horses, and one of them managed to cut the string of Sāmba's bow so that he could no longer fight with them. In this way, with great difficulty and after a severe fight, Sāmba was left bereft of his chariot, and they were able to arrest him. Thus, the warriors of the Kuru dynasty accepted their great victory and took their daughter, Lakṣmaṇā, away from him. Thereafter, they entered the city of Hastināpura in great triumph.

The great sage Nārada immediately carried the news to the Yadu dynasty that Sāmba was arrested and told them the whole story. The members of the Yadu dynasty became very angry at Sāmba's being arrested, and improperly so by six warriors. Now, with the permission of the head of the Yadu dynasty's king, Ugrasena, they prepared to attack the capital city of the Kuru dynasty.

Although Lord Balarāma knew very well that by slight provocation people are prepared to fight with one another in the age of Kali, He did not like the idea that the two great dynasties, the Kuru dynasty and the Yadu dynasty, would fight amongst themselves, even though they were influenced by Kali-yuga. "Instead of fighting with them," He wisely thought, "let Me go there and see the situation, and let Me try to see if the fight can be settled by mutual understanding." Balarāma's idea was that if the Kuru dynasty could be induced to release Sāmba along with his wife, Lakṣmaṇā, then the fight could be avoided. He therefore immediately arranged for a nice chariot to go to Hastināpura, accompanied by learned priests and *brāhmaṇas,* as well as by some of the elderly members of the Yadu dynasty. He was confident that the members of the Kuru dynasty would agree to this marriage and avoid fighting amongst themselves. As

Lord Balarāma proceeded towards Hastināpura in this chariot, accompanied by the learned *brāhmaṇas* and the elderly members of the Yadu dynasty, He looked like the moon shining in the clear sky amongst the glittering stars. When Lord Balarāma reached the precincts of the city of Hastināpura, He did not enter, but stationed Himself in a camp outside the city in a small garden house. Then He asked Uddhava to see the leaders of the Kuru dynasty and inquire from them whether they wanted to fight with the Yadu dynasty or to make a settlement. Uddhava went to see the leaders of the Kuru dynasty, and he met all the important members, including Bhīṣmadeva, Dhṛtarāṣṭra, Droṇācārya, Bali, Duryodhana and Bāhlīka. After offering them due respects, he informed them that Lord Balarāma had already arrived at the garden, outside the city door.

The leaders of the Kuru dynasty, especially Dhṛtarāṣṭra and Duryodhana, were very joyful because they knew very well that Lord Balarāma was a great well-wisher of their family. There were no bounds to their joy on hearing the news, and so immediately they welcomed Uddhava. In order to properly receive Lord Balarāma, they all took auspicious paraphernalia for His reception in their hands and went to see Him outside the city door. According to their respective positions, they welcomed Lord Balarāma by giving Him in charity nice cows and *argha* (an assortment of articles such as *ārātrika* water, sweet preparations of honey, butter, etc., and flowers, and garlands scented with pulp). Because all of them knew the exalted position of Lord Balarāma as the Supreme Personality of Godhead, they bowed their heads before the Lord with great respect. They all exchanged words of reception by asking one another of their welfare, and when such formality was finished, Lord Balarāma, in a great voice and very patiently, submitted before them the following words for their consideration. "My dear friends, this time I have come to you as a messenger with the order of the all-powerful King Ugrasena. Please, therefore, hear the order with attention and great care. Without wasting a single moment, please try to carry out the order. King Ugrasena knows very well that you warriors of the Kuru dynasty improperly fought with the pious Sāmba, who was alone, and that with great difficulty and tactics you have arrested him. We have all heard this news, but we are not very agitated because we are most intimately related to each other. I do not think we should disturb our good relationship; we should continue our friendship without any unnecessary fighting. Please, therefore, immediately release Sāmba and bring him, along with his wife, Lakṣmaṇā, before Me."

When Lord Balarāma spoke in a commanding tone full of heroic assertion, supremacy and chivalry, His statements were not appreciated by the leaders of the Kuru dynasty. Rather, all of them became agitated, and with great anger they said: "Hello! These words are very astonishing but quite befitting the age of Kali; otherwise how could Balarāma speak so vituperatively? The language and tone used by Balarāma are simply abusive, and due to the influence of this age, it appears that the shoes befitting the feet want to rise to the top of the head where the helmet is worn. We are connected with the Yadu dynasty by marriage, and because of this they have been given the chance to come live with us, dine with us, and sleep with us; now they are taking advantage of these privileges. They had practically no position before we gave them a portion of our kingdom to rule, and now they are trying to command us. We have allowed the Yadu dynasty to use the royal insignias like the whisk, fan, conchshell, white umbrella, crown, royal throne, sitting place, bedstead, and everything befitting the royal order. They should not have used such royal paraphernalia in our presence, but we did not check them due to our family relationships. Now they have the audacity to order us to do things. Well, this is enough of their impudence! We cannot allow them to do any more of these things, nor shall we allow them to use these royal insignias. It would be best to take all these things away; it is improper to feed a snake with milk, since such merciful activities simply increase his venom. The Yadu dynasty is now trying to go against those who have fed them so nicely. Their flourishing condition is due to our gifts and merciful behavior, and still they are so shameless that they are trying to order us. How regrettable are all these activities! No one in the world can enjoy anything if the members of the Kuru dynasty like Bhīṣma, Droṇācārya and Arjuna do not allow them to. Exactly as a lamb cannot enjoy life in the presence of a lion, without our desire it is not even possible for the demigods in heaven, headed by King Indra, to find enjoyment in life, not to speak of ordinary human beings!" Actually the members of the Kuru dynasty were very puffed up due to their opulence, kingdom, aristocracy, family tradition, great warriors, family members and vast expansive empire. They did not even observe common formalities of civilized society, and in the presence of Lord Balarāma they uttered insulting words about the Yadu dynasty. Speaking in this unmannerly way, they returned to their city of Hastināpura.

Although Lord Balarāma patiently heard their insulting words and simply observed their uncivil behavior, from His appearance it was clear that He was burning with anger and was thinking of retaliating with great vengeance. His bodily features became so agitated that it was difficult for anyone to look at Him. He laughed very loudly and said: "It is true that if a man becomes too puffed up because of his family, opulence, beauty and material advancement, he no longer wants a peaceful life but becomes belligerent toward all others. It is useless to give such a person good instruction for gentle behavior and peaceful life, but on the contrary, one should search out the ways and means to punish him." Generally, due to material opulence a man becomes exactly like an animal. To give an animal peaceful instructions is useless, and the only means is *argumentum vaculum.* In other words, the only means to keep animals in order is a stick. "Just see how impudent the members of the Kuru dynasty are! I wanted to make a peaceful settlement despite the anger of all the other members of the Yadu dynasty, including Lord Kṛṣṇa Himself. They were preparing to attack the whole kingdom of the Kuru dynasty, but I pacified them and took the trouble to come here to settle the affair without any fighting. Still these rascals behave like this! It is clear that they do not want a peaceful settlement, but that they are factually warmongers. With great pride they have repeatedly insulted Me by calling the Yadus dynasty ill names.

"Even the King of heaven, Indra, abides by the order of the Yadu dynasty; and you consider King Ugrasena, who is the head of the Bhojas, Vṛṣṇis, Andhakas and Yādavas, to be the leader of a small phalanx! Your conclusion is wonderful! You do not care for King Ugrasena, whose order is obeyed even by King Indra. Consider the exalted position of the Yadu dynasty. They have forcibly used both the assembly house and the *pārijāta* tree of the heavenly planet, and still you think that they cannot order you. Don't you even think that Lord Kṛṣṇa, the Supreme Personality of Godhead, can sit on the exalted royal throne and command everyone? All right! If your thinking is like that, then you deserve to be taught a very good lesson. You have thought it wise that the royal insignias like the whisk, fan, white umbrella, royal throne and other princely paraphernalia not be used by the Yadu dynasty. Does this mean that even Lord Kṛṣṇa, the Lord of the whole creation and the husband of the goddess of fortune, cannot use this royal paraphernalia? The dust of Kṛṣṇa's lotus feet is worshiped by all the great demigods. The Ganges water is inundating the whole world, and since it is emanating from His lotus feet, its banks have turned into great places of pilgrimage. The principal deities of all planets are engaged in His service, and they consider themselves most fortunate to take the dust of the lotus feet of Kṛṣṇa on their helmets. Great demigods like Lord Brahmā, Lord Śiva, and even the goddess of fortune and I are simply plenary parts of His spiritual identity, and still you think that He is not fit to use the royal insignia or even sit on the royal throne? Alas, how regrettable it is that these fools consider us, the members of the Yadu dynasty, to be like shoes and themselves like helmets. It is clear now that these leaders of the Kuru dynasty have become mad over their worldly possessions and opulence. Every statement they made was full of crazy proposals. I should immediately take them to task and bring them to their senses. If I do not take steps against them, it will be improper on My part. Therefore, on this very day, I shall rid the whole world of any trace of the Kuru dynasty. I shall finish them off immediately!" While talking like this, Lord Balarāma seemed so furious that He looked as if He could burn the whole cosmic creation to ashes. He stood up steadily, and taking His plow in His hand, began striking the earth with it. In this way the whole city of Hastināpura was separated from the earth. Lord Balarāma then began to drag the city toward the flowing water of the river Ganges. Because of this, there was a great tremor throughout Hastināpura, as if there had been an earthquake, and it seemed that the whole city would be dismantled.

When all the members of the Kuru dynasty saw that their city was about to fall into the water of the Ganges and when they heard their citizens howling in great anxiety, they immediately came to their senses and understood what was happening. Thus without waiting another second they brought forward their daughter Lakṣmaṇā. They also brought Sāmba, who had forcibly tried to take her away, keeping him in the forefront with Lakṣmaṇā at his back. All the members of the Kuru dynasty appeared before Lord Balarāma with folded hands just to beg the pardon of the Supreme Personality of Godhead. Now using good sense, they said: "O Lord Balarāma, You are the reservoir of all pleasures. You are the maintainer and support of the entire cosmic situation. Unfortunately we were all unaware of Your inconceivable potencies. Dear Lord, please consider us most foolish. Our intelligence was bewildered and not in order. Therefore we have come before You to beg Your pardon. Please excuse us. You are the original creator, sustainer and annihilator of the whole cosmic manifestation, and still Your position is always transcendental. O all-powerful Lord, great sages speak about You. You are the original puppeteer, and everything in the world is just like Your toys. O unlimited one, You have a hold on everything, and like child's play You hold all the planetary systems on Your head. When the time for dissolution comes, You close up the whole cosmic manifestation within Yourself. At that time nothing remains but Yourself lying in the Causal Ocean as Mahā-Viṣṇu. Our dear Lord, You have appeared on this earth in Your transcendental body just for the maintenance of the cosmic situation. You are above all anger, envy and enmity. Whatever You do, even in the form of chastisement, is auspicious for the whole material existence. We are offering our respectful obeisances unto You because You are the imperishable Supreme Personality of Godhead, the reservoir of all opulences and potencies. O creator of innumerable universes, let us fall down and offer You our respectful obeisances, again and again. We are now completely surrendered unto You. Please, therefore, be merciful upon us and give us Your protection." When the prominent members of the Kuru dynasty, beginning with grandfather Bhīṣmadeva down to Arjuna and Duryodhana, had offered their respectful prayers in that way, the Supreme Personality of Godhead, Lord Balarāma, immediately became softened and assured them there was no cause for fear and that they need not worry.

For the most part it was the practice of the *kṣatriya* kings to inaugurate some kind of fighting between the parties of the bride and bridegroom before the marriage. When Sāmba forcibly took away Lakṣmaṇā, the elderly members of the Kuru dynasty were pleased to see that he was actually the suitable match for her. In order to see his personal strength, however, they fought with him, and without any respect for the regulations of fighting, they all arrested him. When the Yadu dynasty decided to release Sāmba from the confinement of the Kurus, Lord Balarāma came personally to settle the matter, and as a powerful *kṣatriya,* He ordered them to free Sāmba immediately. The Kauravas became superficially insulted by this order, so they challenged Lord Balarāma's power. They simply wanted to see Him exhibit His inconceivable strength. Thus with great pleasure they handed over their daughter to Sāmba, and the whole matter was settled. Duryodhana, being affectionate towards his daughter Lakṣmaṇā, had her married to Sāmba in great pomp. For her dowry, he first gave 1,200 elephants, each of which were at least sixty years old; then he gave 10,000 nice horses, 6,000 chariots, which were dazzling just like the sunshine, and 1,000 maidservants who were decorated with golden ornaments. Lord Balarāma, the most prominent member of the Yadu dynasty, acted as guardian of the bridegroom Sāmba and very pleasingly accepted the dowry. Balarāma was very satisfied after His great reception from the side of the Kurus, and accompanied by the newly married couple, He started towards His capital city of Dvārakā.

Lord Balarāma triumphantly reached Dvārakā, where He met with many citizens who were all His devotees and friends. When they all assembled, Lord Balarāma narrated the whole story of the marriage, and they were astonished to hear how Balarāma had made the city of Hastināpura tremble. It is confirmed by Śukadeva Gosvāmī that the site of Hastināpura is now known as New Delhi, and the river flowing through the city is called the Yamunā, although in those days it was known as the Ganges. From authorities like Jīva Gosvāmī it is also confirmed that the Ganges and Yamunā are the same river flowing in different courses. The part of the Ganges which flows through Hastināpura to the area of Vṛndāvana is called the Yamunā because it is sanctified by the transcendental pastimes of Lord Kṛṣṇa. The part of Hastināpura which slopes towards the Yamunā becomes inundated during the rainy season and reminds everyone of Lord Balarāma's threatening to cast the city into the Ganges.

Thus ends the Bhaktivedanta purport of the Sixty-seventh Chapter of Kṛṣṇa, *"The Marriage of Sāmba."*

68 / The Great Sage Nārada Visits the Different Homes of Lord Kṛṣṇa

The great sage Nārada heard that Lord Kṛṣṇa had married 16,000 wives after He had killed the demon Narakāsura, sometimes called Bhaumāsura. Nārada became astonished that Lord Kṛṣṇa had expanded Himself into 16,000 forms and married these wives simultaneously in different palaces. Being inquisitive as to how Kṛṣṇa was managing His household affairs with so many wives, Nārada desired to see these pastimes and so set out to visit Kṛṣṇa's different homes. When Nārada arrived in Dvārakā, he saw that the gardens and parks were full of various flowers of different colors and orchards that were overloaded with a variety of fruits. Beautiful birds were chirping, and peacocks were delightfully crowing. There were tanks and ponds full of blue and red lotus flowers, and some of these sites were filled with varieties of lilies. The lakes were full of nice swans and cranes whose voices resounded everywhere. In the city there were as many as 900,000 great palaces built of first-class marble with gates and doors made of silver. The posts of the houses and palaces were bedecked with jewels such as touchstone, sapphires and emeralds, and the floors gave off a beautiful luster. The highways, lanes, streets, crossings and marketplaces were all beautifully decorated. The whole city was full of residential homes, assembly houses, and temples, all of different architectural beauty. All of this made Dvārakā a glowing city. The big avenues, crossings, lanes, streets, and also the thresholds of every residential house, were very clean. On both sides of every path there were bushes, and at regular intervals there were large trees that shaded the avenues so that the sunshine would not bother the passersby.

In this greatly beautiful city of Dvārakā, Lord Kṛṣṇa, the Supreme Personality of Godhead, had many residential quarters. The great kings and princes of the world used to visit these palaces just to worship Him. The architectural plans were made personally by Viśvakarmā, the engineer of the demigods, and in the construction of the palaces he exhibited all of his talents and ingenuity. These residential quarters numbered more than 16,000, and a different queen of Lord Kṛṣṇa resided in each of them. The great sage Nārada entered one of these houses and saw that the pillars were made of coral and the ceilings were bedecked with jewels. The walls as well as the arches between the pillars glowed from the decorations of different kinds of sapphires. Throughout the palace there were many canopies made by Viśvakarmā that were decorated with strings of pearls. The chairs and other furniture were made of ivory, bedecked with gold and diamonds, and jeweled lamps dissipated the darkness within the palace. There was so much incense and flavored gum burning that the scented fumes were coming out of the windows. The peacocks sitting on the steps became illusioned by the fumes, mistaking them for clouds, and began dancing jubilantly. There were many maidservants, all of whom were decorated with gold necklaces, bangles and beautiful saris. There were also many male servants, who were nicely dressed in cloaks and turbans and jeweled earrings. Beautiful as they were, the servants were all engaged in different household duties.

Nārada saw that Lord Kṛṣṇa was sitting with Rukmiṇīdevī, the mistress of that particular palace, who was bearing the rod of a *cāmara* whisk. Even though there were many thousands of maidservants who were equally beautiful and qualified, and who were of the same age, Rukmiṇīdevī personally was engaged in fanning Lord Kṛṣṇa. Kṛṣṇa is the Supreme Personality of Godhead, worshiped even by Nārada, but still, as soon as He saw Nārada enter the palace, Kṛṣṇa got down immediately from Rukmiṇī's bedstead and stood up to honor him. Lord Kṛṣṇa is the teacher of the whole world, and in order to instruct everyone how to respect a saintly person like Nārada Muni, Kṛṣṇa bowed down, touching His helmet to the ground. Not only did Kṛṣṇa bow down, but He also touched the feet of Nārada and with folded hands requested him to sit on His chair. Lord Kṛṣṇa is the Supreme Personality worshiped by all devotees. He is the most worshiped spiritual master of everyone. The Ganges water which emanates from His feet sanctifies the three worlds. All qualified *brāhmaṇas* worship Him, and therefore He is called *brahmaṇya-deva.*

Brahmaṇya means one who fully possesses the brahminical qualifications, which are said to be as follows: truthfulness, self-control, purity, mastery of the senses, simplicity, full knowledge by practical application, and engagement in devotional service. Lord Kṛṣṇa personally possesses all these qualities, and He is worshiped by persons who themselves possess such qualities. There are thousands and millions of names of Lord Kṛṣṇa—

Viṣṇu-sahasra-nāma—and all of them are given to Him because of His transcendental qualities.

Lord Kṛṣṇa in Dvārakā enjoyed the pastimes of a perfect human being. When, therefore, He washed the feet of the sage Nārada and took the water on His head, Nārada did not object, knowing well that the Lord did so to teach everyone how to respect saintly persons. The Supreme Personality of Godhead, Kṛṣṇa, who is the original Nārāyaṇa and eternal friend of all living entities, thus worshiped the sage Nārada according to Vedic regulative principles. Welcoming him with sweet nectarean words, He addressed Nārada as *bhagavān,* or one who is self-sufficient, possessing all kinds of knowledge, renunciation, strength, fame, beauty, and similar other opulences. He particularly asked Nārada, "What can I do in your service?"

Nārada replied, "My dear Lord, this kind of behavior by Your Lordship is not at all astonishing because You are the Supreme Personality of Godhead and master of all species of living entities. You are the supreme friend of all living entities, but at the same time You are the supreme chastiser of the miscreants and the envious. I know that Your Lordship has descended on this earth for the proper maintenance of the whole universe. Your appearance, therefore, is not forced by any other agency. By Your sweet will only, You agree to appear and disappear. It is my great fortune that I have been able to see Your lotus feet today. Anyone who becomes attached to Your lotus feet is elevated to the supreme position of neutrality and is uncontaminated by the material modes of nature. My Lord, You are unlimited; there is no limit to Your opulences. Great demigods like Lord Brahmā and Lord Śiva are always busy placing You within their hearts and meditating upon You. The conditioned souls who have now been put into the blind well of material existence can get out of this eternal captivity only by accepting Your lotus feet. Thus, You are the only shelter of all conditioned souls. My dear Lord, You have very kindly asked what You can do for me. In answer to this I simply request that I may not forget Your lotus feet at any time. I do not care where I may be, but I pray that I may be allowed to constantly remember Your lotus feet."

The benediction which the sage Nārada asked from the Lord is the ideal prayer of all pure devotees. A pure devotee never asks for any kind of material or spiritual benediction from the Lord, but his only prayer is that he may not forget the lotus feet of the Lord in any condition of life. A pure devotee does not care whether he is put in heaven or hell; he is satisfied anywhere, provided he can constantly remember the lotus feet of the Lord. Lord Caitanya also taught this same process of prayer in His

Śikṣāṣṭaka, in which He clearly stated that all He wanted was devotional service, birth after birth. A pure devotee does not even want to stop the repetition of birth and death. To a pure devotee, it does not matter whether he has to take birth again in the various species of life. His only ambition is that he may not forget the lotus feet of the Lord in any condition of life.

After departing from the palace of Rukmiṇī, Nāradajī wanted to see the activities of Lord Kṛṣṇa's internal potency, *yogamāyā;* thus he entered the palace of another queen. There he saw Lord Kṛṣṇa engaged in playing chess, along with His dear wife and Uddhava. The Lord immediately got up from His seat and invited Nārada Muni to sit on His personal seat. The Lord again worshiped him with as much paraphernalia for reception as He had in the palace of Rukmiṇī. After worshiping him properly, Lord Kṛṣṇa acted as if He did not know what had happened in the palace of Rukmiṇī. He therefore told Nārada, "My dear sage, when your holiness comes here, you are full in yourself. Although we are householders and are always in need, you don't require anyone's help because you are self-satisfied. Under the circumstances, what reception can we offer you, and what can we possibly give you? Yet, since your holiness is a *brāhmaṇa,* it is our duty to offer you something as far as possible. Therefore, I beg your pleasure to order Me. What can I do for you?"

Nāradajī knew everything about the pastimes of the Lord, so without any further discussion, he simply left the palace silently, in great astonishment over the Lord's activities. He then entered another palace. This time Nāradajī saw that Lord Kṛṣṇa was engaged as an affectionate father petting His small children. From there he entered another palace and saw Lord Kṛṣṇa preparing to take His bath. In this way, Saint Nārada entered each and every one of the sixteen thousand residential palaces of the queens of Lord Kṛṣṇa, and in each of them he found Kṛṣṇa engaged in different ways.

In one place he found Kṛṣṇa engaged in offering oblations to the sacrificial fire and performing the ritualistic ceremonies of the *Vedas* as enjoined for householders. In another palace, Kṛṣṇa was found performing the *pañca-yajña* sacrifice, which is compulsory for a householder. This *yajña* is also known as *pañca-śūna*. Knowingly or unknowingly, everyone, specifically the householder, is committing five kinds of sinful activities. When we receive water from a water pitcher, we kill many germs that are in it. Similarly, when we use a grinding machine or take foodstuff, we kill many germs. When sweeping a floor or igniting a fire we kill many germs, and when we walk on the street we kill many ants and other insects.

Consciously or unconsciously, in all our different activities, we are killing. Therefore, it is incumbent upon every householder to perform the *pañca-śūna* sacrifice to rid himself of the reactions to such sinful activities.

In one palace Lord Kṛṣṇa was found engaged in feeding *brāhmaṇas* after performing ritualistic *yajñas.* In another palace, Nārada found Kṛṣṇa engaged in silently chanting the Gāyatrī *mantra,* and in a third he found Him practicing fighting with a sword and shield. In some palaces Lord Kṛṣṇa was found riding on horses or elephants or chariots and wandering hither and thither. Elsewhere He was found lying down on His bedstead taking rest, and somewhere else He was found sitting in His chair, being praised by the prayers of His different devotees. In some of the palaces He was found consulting with ministers like Uddhava and others on important matters of business. In one palace He was found surrounded by many young society girls, enjoying in a swimming pool. In another palace He was found engaged in giving well-decorated cows in charity to the *brāhmaṇas,* and in another palace He was found hearing the narrations of the *Purāṇas* or histories, such as the *Mahābhārata,* which are supplementary literatures for disseminating Vedic knowledge to common people by narrating important instances in the history of the universe. Somewhere Lord Kṛṣṇa was found enjoying the company of a particular wife by exchanging joking words with her. Somewhere else He was found engaged along with His wife in religious ritualistic functions. Since it is necessary for householders to increase their financial assets for various expenditures, Kṛṣṇa was found somewhere engaged in matters of economic development. Somewhere else He was found enjoying family life according to the regulative principles of the *śāstras.*

In one palace He was found sitting in meditation as if He were concentrating His mind on the Supreme Personality of Godhead, who is beyond these material universes. Meditation, as recommended in authorized scripture, is meant for concentrating one's mind on the Supreme Personality of Godhead, Viṣṇu. Lord Kṛṣṇa is Himself the original Viṣṇu, but because He played the part of a human being, He taught us definitely by His personal behavior what is meant by meditation. Somewhere Lord Kṛṣṇa was found satisfying elderly superiors by supplying them things which they needed. Somewhere else Nāradajī found that Lord Kṛṣṇa was engaged in discussing topics of fighting, and somewhere else in making peace with enemies. Somewhere Lord Kṛṣṇa was found discussing the ultimate auspicious activity for the entire human society with His elder brother Lord Balarāma. Nārada saw Lord Kṛṣṇa engaged in getting His sons and daughters married with suitable brides and bridegrooms in due course of time, and the marriage ceremonies were being performed with great pomp.

In one palace He was found bidding farewell to His daughters, and in another He was found receiving a daughter-in-law. People throughout the whole city were astonished to see such pomp and ceremonies.

Somewhere the Lord was seen engaged in performing different types of sacrifices to satisfy the demigods, who are only His qualitative expansions. Somewhere He was seen engaged in public welfare activities, establishing deep wells for water supply, rest houses and gardens for unknown guests, and great monastaries and temples for saintly persons. These are some of the duties enjoined in the *Vedas* for householders for fulfillment of their material desires. Somewhere Kṛṣṇa was found as a *kṣatriya* king engaged in hunting animals in the forest and riding on very beautiful *sindhi* horses. According to Vedic regulations, the *kṣatriyas* were allowed to kill prescribed animals on certain occasions, either to maintain peace in the forests or to offer the animals in the sacrificial fire. *Kṣatriyas* are allowed to practice this killing art because they have to kill their enemies mercilessly to maintain peace in society. In one situation the great sage Nārada saw Lord Kṛṣṇa, the Supreme Personality of Godhead and master of mystic powers, acting as a spy by changing His usual dress in order to understand the motives of different citizens in the city and within the palaces.

Saint Nārada saw all these activities of the Lord, who is the Supersoul of all living entities but who played the role of an ordinary human being in order to manifest the activities of His internal potency. He was smiling within himself and began to address the Lord as follows: "My dear Lord of all mystic powers, object of the meditation of great mystics, the extent of Your mystic power is certainly inconceivable, even to mystics like Lord Brahmā and Lord Śiva. But by Your mercy, because of my being always engaged in the transcendental loving service of Your lotus feet, Your Lordship has very kindly revealed to me the actions of Your internal potency. My dear Lord, You are worshipable by all, and demigods and predominating deities of all fourteen planetary systems are completely aware of Your transcendental fame. Now please give me Your blessings so that I may be able to travel all over the universes singing the glories of Your transcendental activities."

The Supreme Personality of Godhead, Lord Kṛṣṇa, replied to Nārada as follows: "My dear Nārada, O sage among the demigods, you know that I am the supreme instructor and perfect follower of all religious principles, as well as the supreme enforcer of such principles. I am therefore personally executing such religious principles in order to teach the whole world how to act. My dear son, it is My desire that you not be bewildered by such demonstrations of My internal energy."

The Supreme Personality of Godhead was engaged in His so-called household affairs in order to teach people how one can sanctify one's household life although he may be attached to the imprisonment of material existence. Actually, one is obliged to continue the term of material existence because of household life. But the Lord, being very kind upon householders, demonstrated the path of sanctifying ordinary household life. Because Kṛṣṇa is the center of all activities, a Kṛṣṇa conscious householder's life is transcendental to Vedic injunctions and is automatically sanctified.

Thus Nārada saw one single Kṛṣṇa living in sixteen thousand palaces by His plenary expansions. Due to His inconceivable energy, He was visible in each and every individual queen's palace. Lord Kṛṣṇa has unlimited power, and Nārada's astonishment was boundless upon observing again and again the demonstration of Lord Kṛṣṇa's internal energy. Lord Kṛṣṇa behaved by His personal example as if He were very much attached to the four principles of civilized life, namely religiousness, economic development, sense gratification and salvation. These four principles of material existence are necessary for the spiritual advancement of human society, and although Lord Kṛṣṇa had no need to do so, He exhibited His household activities so that people might follow in His footsteps for their own interest. Lord Kṛṣṇa satisfied the sage Nārada in every way. Nārada was very much pleased by seeing the Lord's activities in Dvārakā, and thus he departed.

In narrating the activities of Lord Kṛṣṇa in Dvārakā, Śukadeva Gosvāmī explained to King Parīkṣit how Lord Kṛṣṇa, the Supreme Personality of Godhead, descends on this material universe by the agency of His internal potency and personally exhibits the principles which, if followed, can lead one to achieve the ultimate goal of life. All the queens in Dvārakā, more than sixteen thousand in number, engaged their feminine attractive features in the transcendental service of the Lord by smiling and serving, and the Lord was pleased to behave with them exactly as a perfect husband enjoying household life. One should know definitely that such pastimes cannot be performed by anyone but Lord Śrī Kṛṣṇa. Lord Śrī Kṛṣṇa is the original cause of the creation, maintenance and dissolution of the whole cosmic manifestation. Anyone who attentively hears the narrations of the Lord's pastimes in Dvārakā or supports a preacher of the Kṛṣṇa consciousness movement will certainly find it very easy to traverse the path of liberation and taste the nectar of the lotus feet of Lord Kṛṣṇa. And thus he will be engaged in His devotional service.

Thus ends the Bhaktivedanta purport of the Sixty-eighth Chapter of Kṛṣṇa, *"The Great Sage Nārada Visits the Different Homes of Lord Kṛṣṇa."*

69 / Lord Kṛṣṇa's Daily Activities

From the Vedic *mantras* we learn that the Supreme Personality of Godhead has nothing to do: *na tasya karyaṁ kranaṁ ca vidyate.* If the Supreme Lord has nothing to do, then how can we speak of the activities of the Supreme Lord? From the previous chapter it is clear that no one can act in the way that Lord Kṛṣṇa does. We should clearly note this fact: the activities of the Lord should be followed, but they cannot be imitated. For example, Kṛṣṇa's ideal life as a householder can be followed, but if one wants to imitate Kṛṣṇa by expanding into many forms, that is not possible. We should always remember, therefore, that Lord Kṛṣṇa, although playing the part of a human being, nevertheless simultaneously maintains the position of the Supreme Personality of Godhead. We can follow Lord Kṛṣṇa's dealing with His wives as an ordinary human being, but His dealing with more than sixteen thousand wives at one time cannot be imitated. The conclusion is that to become ideal householders we should follow in the footsteps of Lord Kṛṣṇa as He displayed His daily activities, but we cannot imitate Him at any stage of our life.

Lord Kṛṣṇa used to lie down with His sixteen thousand wives, but also He would rise up from bed very early in the morning, three hours before sunrise. By nature's arrangement the crowing of the cocks warns of the *brāhma-muhūrta* hour. There is no need of alarm clocks; as soon as the cocks crow early in the morning, it is to be understood that it is time to rise from bed. Hearing that sound, Kṛṣṇa would get up from bed, but His rising early was not very much to the liking of His wives. The wives of Kṛṣṇa were so much attached to Him that they would lie in bed embracing Him, but as soon as the cocks crowed, Kṛṣṇa's wives would be very sorry and would immediately condemn the crowing.

In the garden within the compound of each palace there were *pārijāta* flowers. *Pārijāta* is not an artificial flower. We remember that Kṛṣṇa brought the *pārijāta* trees from heaven and implanted them in all His palaces. Early in the morning, a mild breeze would carry the aroma of the *pārijāta* flower, and Kṛṣṇa would smell it just after rising from bed. Due to this aroma, the honeybees would begin their humming vibration, and the birds also would begin their sweet chirping sounds. All together it would sound like the singing of professional chanters engaged in offering prayers to Kṛṣṇa. Although Śrīmatī Rukmiṇīdevī, the first queen of Lord Kṛṣṇa, knew that *brāhma-muhūrta* is the most auspicious time in the entire day, she would feel disgusted at the appearance of *brāhma-muhūrta* because she was not very happy to have Kṛṣṇa leave her side in bed. Despite Śrīmatī Rukmiṇīdevī's disgust, Lord Kṛṣṇa would immediately get up from bed exactly on the appearance of *brāhma-muhūrta.* An ideal householder should learn from the behavior of Lord Kṛṣṇa how to rise early in the morning, however comfortably he may be lying in bed embraced by his wife.

After rising from bed, Lord Kṛṣṇa would wash His mouth, hands and feet and would immediately sit down and meditate on Himself. This does not mean, however, that we should also sit down and meditate on ourselves. We have to meditate upon Kṛṣṇa, Rādhā-Kṛṣṇa. That is real meditation, Kṛṣṇa is Kṛṣṇa Himself; therefore He was teaching us that *brāhma-muhūrta* should be utilized for meditation on Rādhā-Kṛṣṇa. By doing so, Kṛṣṇa would feel very much satisfied, and similarly we will also feel transcendentally pleased and satisfied if we utilize the *brāhma-muhūrta* period to meditate on Rādhā and Kṛṣṇa and if we think of how Śrī Rukmiṇīdevī and Kṛṣṇa acted as ideal householders to teach the whole human society to rise early in the morning and immediately engage in Kṛṣṇa consciousness. There is no difference between meditating on the eternal forms of Rādhā-Kṛṣṇa and chanting the *mahāmantra,* Hare Kṛṣṇa. As for Kṛṣṇa's meditation, He had no alternative but to meditate on Himself. The object of meditation is Brahman, Paramātmā or the Supreme Personality of Godhead, but Kṛṣṇa Himself is all three: He is the Supreme Personality of Godhead, Bhagavān; the localized Paramātmā is His plenary parcel expansion; and the all-pervading Brahman effulgence is the personal rays of His transcendental body. Therefore Kṛṣṇa is always one, and for Him there is no differentiation. That is the difference between an ordinary living being and Kṛṣṇa. For an ordinary living being there are many distinctions. An ordinary living being is different from his body, and he is different from other species of living entities. A human being is different from other human beings and different from the animals. Even in his own body, there are different bodily limbs. We have our hands and legs, but our hands are different from our legs. The hand cannot act like the leg, nor can the leg act like the hand. The eyes cannot hear like the ears, nor can the ears see like the eyes. All these differences are technically called *svajtiya vijtiya.*

The bodily limitation whereby one part of the body cannot act as another part is totally absent in the Supreme Personality of Godhead. There is no difference between His body and Himself. He is completely spiritual, and therefore there is no material difference between His body and His soul. Similarly, He is not different from His millions of incarnations and plenary expansions. Baladeva is the first expansion of Kṛṣṇa, and from Baladeva expand Saṇkarṣaṇa, Vāsudeva, Pradyumna and Aniruddha. From Saṅkarṣaṇa there is again an expansion of Nārāyaṇa, and from Nārāyaṇa there is a second quadruple expansion of Saṇkarṣaṇa, Vāsudeva, Pradyumna and Aniruddha. Similarly there are innumerable expansions of Kṛṣṇa, but all of them are one. Kṛṣṇa has many incarnations, such as Lord Nṛsiṁha, Lord Boar, Lord Fish and Lord Tortoise, but there is no difference between Kṛṣṇa's original two-handed form, like that of a human being, and these incarnations of gigantic animal forms. Nor is there any difference between the action of one part of His body and that of another. His hands can act as His legs, His eyes can act as His ears, or His nose can act as another part of His body. Kṛṣṇa's smelling and eating and hearing are all the same. We limited living entities have to use a particular part of our body for a particular purpose, but there is no such distinction for Kṛṣṇa. In the *Brahma-saṁhitā* it is said, *aṅgāni yasya sakalendriya-vṛtti*: He can perform the activities of one limb with any other limb. So by analytical study of Kṛṣṇa and His person, it is concluded that He is the complete whole. When He meditates, therefore, He meditates on Himself. The self-meditation by ordinary men, designated in Sanskrit as *so'ham,* is simply imitation. Kṛṣṇa may meditate on Himself because He is the complete whole, but we cannot imitate Him and meditate on ourselves. Our body is a designation; Kṛṣṇa's body is not a designation. Kṛṣṇa's body is also Kṛṣṇa. There is no existence of anything foreign in Kṛṣṇa. Whatever there is in Kṛṣṇa is also Kṛṣṇa. He is therefore the supreme, indestructible complete existence, or the supreme truth.

Kṛṣṇa's existence is not relative existence. Everything else but Kṛṣṇa is a relative truth, but Kṛṣṇa is the Supreme Absolute Truth. Kṛṣṇa does not depend on anything but Himself for His existence. Our existence, however is relative. For example, only when there is the light of the sun, the moon or electricity are we able to see. Our seeing, therefore, is relative, and the light of the sun and moon and electricity is also relative; they are called illuminating only because we see them as such. Dependence and relativity do not exist in Kṛṣṇa. His activities are not dependent on anyone else's appreciation, nor does He depend on anyone else's help. He is beyond the existence of limited time and space, and because He is transcendental to time and space, He cannot be covered by the illusion of *māyā,* whose activities are limited. In the Vedic literature we find that the Supreme Personality of Godhead has multi-potencies. Since all such potencies are emanations from Him, there is no difference between Him and His potencies. Certain philosophers say, however, that when Kṛṣṇa comes He accepts a material body. But even if it is accepted that when He comes to the material world He accepts a material body, it should be concluded also that because the material energy is not different from Him, this body does not act materially. In the *Bhagavad-gītā* it is said, therefore, that He appears by His own internal potency, *ātma-māyā.*

Kṛṣṇa is called the Supreme Brahman because He is the cause of creation, the cause of maintenance and the cause of dissolution. Lord Brahmā, Lord Viṣṇu and Lord Śiva are different expansions of these material qualities. All these material qualities can act upon the conditioned souls, but there is no such action and reaction upon Kṛṣṇa because these qualities are all simultaneously one and different from Him. Kṛṣṇa Himself is simply *sac-cid-ānanda-vigraha,* the eternal form of bliss and knowledge, and because of His inconceivable greatness, He is called the Supreme Brahman. His meditation on Brahman or Paramātmā or Bhagavān is on Himself only and not on anything else beyond Himself. This meditation cannot be imitated by the ordinary living entity.

After His meditation, the Lord would regularly bathe early in the morning with clear sanctified water. Then He would change into fresh clothing, cover Himself with a wrapper and then engage Himself in His daily religious functions. Out of His many religious duties, the first was to offer oblations into the sacrificial fire and silently chant the Gāyatrī *mantra.* Lord Kṛṣṇa, as the ideal householder, executed all the religious functions of a householder without deviation. When the sunrise became visible, the Lord would offer specific prayers to the sun-god. The sun-god and other demigods mentioned in the Vedic scriptures are described as different limbs of the body of Lord Kṛṣṇa, and it is the duty of the householder to offer respects to the demigods and great sages, as well as the forefathers.

As it is said in the *Bhagavad-gītā,* The Lord has no specific duty to perform in this world, and yet He acts just like an ordinary man living an ideal life within this material world. In accordance with Vedic ritualistic principles, the Lord would offer respects to the demigods. The regulative principle by which the demigods and forefathers are worshiped is called *tarpaṇa,* which means pleasing. One's forefathers might have to take a body on another planet, but by performance of this *tarpaṇa* system, they become very happy wherever they may be. It is the duty of the householder to make his family members happy, and by following this *tarpaṇa* system he can make his forefathers happy also. As the perfect exemplary householder, Lord Śrī Kṛṣṇa followed this *tarpaṇa* system and offered respectful obeisances to the elderly superior members of His family.

His next duty was to give cows in charity to the *brāhmaṇas.* Lord Kṛṣṇa used to give as many as 13,084 cows. Each of them was decorated with a silken cover and pearl necklace, their horns were covered with gold plating, and their hooves were silver-plated. All of them were full of milk, due to having their first-born calves with them, and they were very tame and peaceful. When the cows were given in charity to the *brāhmaṇas*, the *brāhmaṇas* also were given nice silken garments, and each was given a deerskin and sufficient quantity of sesame grains. The Lord is generally known as *go-brāhmaṇa-hitāya ca,* which means that His first duty is to see to the welfare of the cows and the *brāhmaṇas.* Thus He used to give cows in charity to the *brāhmaṇas,* with opulent decorations and paraphernalia. Then, wishing for the welfare of all living entities, He would touch auspicious articles such as milk, fire, honey, ghee (clarified butter), gold, jewels and fire. Although the Lord is by nature very beautiful due to the perfect figure of His transcendental body, still He would dress Himself in yellow colored garments and put on His necklace of Kaustubha jewels. He would wear flower garlands, smear His body with the pulp of sandalwood and decorate Himself with other similar cosmetics and ornaments. It is said that the ornaments themselves became beautiful upon being placed on the transcendental body of the Lord. After decorating Himself in this way, the Lord would then look at marble statues of the cow and calf and visit temples of God or demigods like Lord Śiva. There were many *brāhmaṇas* who would come daily to see the Supreme Lord before taking their breakfast; they were anxious to see Him, and He welcomed them.

His next duty was to please all kinds of men belonging to the different castes, both in the city and within the palace compound. He made them happy by fulfilling their different desires, and when the Lord saw them happy He also became very much pleased. The flower garlands, betel nuts, sandalwood pulp and other fragrant cosmetic articles which were offered to the Lord would be distributed by Him, first to the *brāhmaṇas* and elderly members of the family, then to the queens, then to the ministers, and if there were still some balance He would utilize it for His own personal use. By the time the Lord finished all these daily duties and activities,

His charioteer Dāruka would come with His wonderful chariot to stand before the Lord with folded hands, intimating that the chariot was ready, and the Lord would come out of the palace to travel. Then the Lord, accompanied by Uddhava and Sātyaki, would ride on the chariot just as the sun-god rides on his chariot in the morning, appearing with his blazing rays on the surface of the world. When the Lord was about to leave His palaces, all the queens would look at Him with feminine gestures. The Lord would respond to their greetings with smiles, attracting their hearts so much so that they would feel intense separation from the Lord.

Then the Lord would go to the assembly house known as Sudharmā. It may be remembered that the Sudharmā assembly house was taken away from the heavenly planet and was reestablished in the city of Dvārakā. The specific significance of the assembly house was that anyone who entered it would be freed from the six kinds of material pangs, namely hunger, thirst, lamentation, illusion, old age and death. These are the webs of material existence, and as long as one remained in that assembly house of Sudharmā he would not be infected by these six material webs. The Lord would say good-bye in all the sixteen thousand palaces, and again He would become one and enter the Sudharmā assembly house in procession with other members of the Yadu dynasty. After entering the assembly house, He used to sit on the exalted royal throne and would be seen to emanate glaring rays of transcendental effulgence. In the midst of all the great heroes of the Yadu dynasty, Kṛṣṇa resembled the full moon in the sky, surrounded by multi-luminaries. In the assembly house there were professional jokers, dancers, musicians and ballet girls, and as soon as the Lord sat on His throne, they would begin their respective functions in order to please the Lord and put Him in a happy mood. First of all the jokers would talk in such a way that the Lord and His associates would enjoy their humor which would refresh the morning mood. The dramatic actors would then play their parts, and the dancing ballet girls would separately display their artistic movements. All these functions would be accompanied by the beating of *mṛdaṅga* drums and the sounds of the *vīṇā* and flutes and bells, followed by the sound of the *pākhvaj,* another type of drum. Along with these musical vibrations, the auspicious sound of the conchshell would also be added. The professional singers called *sūtas* and *māgadhas* would sing, and others would perform their dancing art. In this way, as devotees, they would offer respectful prayers to the Supreme Personality of Godhead. Sometimes the learned *brāhmaṇas* present in that assembly would chant Vedic hymns and explain them to the audience to their best knowledge, and sometimes some of them would recite old historical accounts of the activities of prominent kings. The Lord, accompanied by His associates, would be very much pleased to hear them.

Once upon a time, a person arrived at the gateway of the assembly house who was unknown to all the members of the assembly, and with the permission of Lord Kṛṣṇa he was admitted into the assembly by the doorkeeper. The doorkeeper was ordered to present him before the Lord, and the man appeared and offered his respectful obeisances unto the Lord with folded hands. It had happened that when King Jarāsandha conquered all other kingdoms many kings did not bow their heads before Jarāsandha, and as a result of this all of them, numbering twenty thousand, were arrested and made his prisoners. The man who was brought before Lord Kṛṣṇa by the doorkeeper was a representative messenger from all these imprisoned kings. Being duly presented before the Lord, the man began to explain the actual situation as follows:

"My dear Lord, You are the eternal form of transcendental bliss and knowledge. As such, You are beyond the reach of the mental speculation or vocal description of any materialistic man within this world. A slight portion of Your glories can be known by persons who are fully surrendered unto Your lotus feet, and by Your grace only such persons become freed from all material anxieties. My dear Lord, I am not one of these surrendered souls; I am still within the duality and illusion of this material existence. I have therefore come to take shelter of Your lotus feet, for I am afraid of the cycle of birth and death. My dear Lord, I think that there are many living entities like me who are eternally entangled in fruitive activities and their resultant reactions. They are never inclined to follow Your instructions by performance of devotional service, although it is pleasing to the heart and most auspicious for one's existence. On the contrary, they are against the path of Kṛṣṇa conscious life, and they are wandering within the three worlds impelled by the illusory energy of material existence.

"My dear Lord, who can estimate Your mercy and Your powerful activities? You are present always as the insurmountable force of eternal time, engaged in baffling the indefatigable desires of the materialists, who are thus repeatedly becoming confused and frustrated. I therefore offer my respectful obeisances unto You in Your form of eternal time. My dear Lord, You are the proprietor of all the worlds, and You have incarnated Yourself along with Your plenary expansion Lord Balarāma. It is said that Your appearance in this incarnation is for the purpose of protecting the faithful and destroying the miscreants. Under the circumstances, how is it possible that miscreants like Jarāsandha can put us into such deplorable conditions of life against Your authority? We are puzzled at the situation and cannot understand how it is possible. It may be that Jarāsandha has been deputed to give us such trouble because of our past misdeeds, but we have heard from revealed scriptures that anyone who surrenders unto Your lotus feet immediately becomes immuned to the reactions of sinful life. I have therefore been deputed by all the imprisoned kings to whole-heartedly offer ourselves unto Your shelter, and we hope that Your Lordship will now give us full protection. We have now come to the real conclusion of our lives. Our kingly positions are nothing but the reward of our past pious activities, just as our suffering imprisonment by Jarāsandha is the result of our past impious activities. We realize now that the resultant reactions of both pious and impious activities are temporary and that we can never be happy in this conditioned life. This material body is awarded to us by the modes of material nature, and on account of this we are full of anxieties. The material condition of life simply involves bearing the burden of this dead body. As a result of fruitive activities we have thus been subjected to being beasts of burden for these bodies, and being forced by conditional life, we have given up the pleasing life of Kṛṣṇa consciousness. Now we realize that we are the most foolish persons. We have been entangled in the network of material reaction due to our ignorance. We have therefore come to the shelter of Your lotus feet, which can immediately eradicate all the results of fruitive action and thus free us from the contamination of material pains and pleasures.

Dear Lord, because we are now surrendered souls at Your lotus feet, You can give us relief from the entrapment of fruitive action made possible by the form of Jarāsandha. Dear Lord, it is known to You that Jarāsandha possesses the power of ten thousand elephants, and with this power he has imprisoned us, just as a lion hypnotizes a flock of sheep. My dear Lord, You have already fought with Jarāsandha eighteen times consecutively, out of which You have defeated him seventeen times by surpassing his extraordinary powerful position. But in Your eighteenth fight, You exhibited Your human behavior, and thus it appeared that You were defeated. My dear Lord, we know very well that Jarāsandha cannot defeat You at any time because Your power, strength, resources and authority are all unlimited. No one can equal You or surpass You. The appearance of defeat by Jarāsandha in the eighteenth engagement is nothing but an exhibition of human behavior. Unfortunately, foolish Jarāsandha could not understand Your tricks, and he has since then become puffed up over his material power and prestige. Specifically, he has arrested us and imprisoned us, knowing fully that as Your devotees, we are subordinate to Your sovereignty.

"Now I have explained our awful position, and Your Lordship can consider and do whatever You like. As the messenger and representative of all those imprisoned kings, I have submitted my words before Your Lordship and presented our prayers to You. All the kings are very anxious to see You so that they can all personally surrender at Your lotus feet. My dear Lord, be merciful upon them and act for their good fortune."

At the very moment the messenger of the imprisoned kings was presenting his appeal before the Lord, the great sage Nārada also arrived. Because he was a great saint, his hair was dazzling like gold, and when he entered the assembly house it appeared that the sun-god was personally present in the midst of the assembly. Lord Kṛṣṇa is the worshipable master of even Lord Brahmā and Lord Śiva, yet as soon as He saw that the sage Nārada had arrived, He immediately stood up along with His ministers and secretaries to receive the great sage and offer His respectful obeisances by bowing His head. The great sage Nārada took a comfortable seat, and Lord Kṛṣṇa worshiped him with all paraphernalia, as required for the regular reception of a saintly person. While He was trying to satisfy Nāradajī, Lord Kṛṣṇa spoke the following words in His sweet and natural voice.

"My dear great sage among the demigods, I think that now everything is well within the three worlds. You are perfectly eligible to travel everywhere in space in the upper, middle and lower planetary systems of this universe. Fortunately, when we meet you we can very easily take information from your holiness of all the news of the three worlds; within this cosmic manifestation of the Supreme Lord, there is nothing concealed from your knowledge. You know everything, and so I wish to question you. Are the Pāṇḍavas doing well, and what is the present plan of King Yudhiṣṭhira? Will you kindly let Me know what they want to do at present?"

The great sage Nārada spoke as follows: "My dear Lord, You have spoken about the cosmic manifestation created by the Supreme Lord, but I know that You are the all-pervading creator. Your energies are so extensive and inconceivable that even powerful personalities like Brahmā, the lord of this particular universe, cannot measure Your inconceivable power. My dear Lord, You are present as the Supersoul in everyone's heart by Your inconceivable potency, exactly like the fire which is present in everyone but which no one can see directly. In conditioned life, every living entity is within the jurisdiction of the three modes of material nature. As such, they are unable to see Your presence everywhere with their material eyes. By Your grace, however, I have seen many times the action of Your inconceivable potency, and therefore when You ask me for news of the Pāṇḍavas, which is not at all unknown to You, I am not surprised at Your inquiry. My dear Lord, by Your inconceivable potencies You create this cosmic manifestation, maintain it and again dissolve it. It is by dint of Your inconceivable potency only that this material world, although a shadow representation of the spiritual world, appears to be factual. No one can understand what You plan to do in the future. Your transcendental position is always inconceivable to everyone. As far as I am concerned, I can simply offer my respectful obeisances unto You again and again. In the bodily concept of knowledge, everyone is driven by material desires, and thus everyone develops new material bodies one after another in the cycle of birth and death. Being absorbed in such a concept of existence, one does not know how to get out of this encagement of the material body. Out of Your causeless mercy, my Lord, You descend to exhibit Your different transcendental pastimes, which are illuminating and full of glory. Therefore I have no alternative but to offer my respectful obeisances unto You. My dear Lord, You are the supreme Parambrahman, and Your pastimes as an ordinary human are another tactical resource, exactly like a play on the stage in which the actor plays parts different from his own identity. You have inquired about Your cousins the Pāṇḍavas in the role of their well-wisher, and therefore I shall let You know about their intentions. Now please hear me. First of all may I inform You that King Yudhiṣṭhira has all material opulences which are possible to achieve in the highest planetary system, Brahmaloka. He has no material opulence for which to aspire, and yet he wants to perform Rājasūya sacrifices only to get Your association and please You.

Nārada informed Lord Kṛṣṇa, "King Yudhiṣṭhira is so opulent that he has attained all the opulences of Brahmaloka even on this earthly planet. He is fully satisfied, and he does not need anything more. He is full in everything, but now he wants to worship You in order to achieve Your causeless mercy, and I beg to request You to fulfill his desires. My dear Lord, in these great sacrificial performances by King Yudhiṣṭhira there will be an assembly of all the demigods and all the famous kings of the world.

"My dear Lord, You are the Supreme Brahman, Personality of Godhead. One who engages himself in Your devotional service by the prescribed methods of hearing, chanting and remembering certainly becomes purified from the contamination of the modes of material nature, and what to speak of those who have the opportunity to see You and touch You directly. My dear Lord, You are the symbol of everything auspicious. Your transcendental name and fame have spread all over the universe, including the higher, middle and lower planetary systems. The transcendental water which washes Your lotus feet is known in the higher planetary system as Mandākinī, in the lower planetary system as Bhogavatī, and in this earthly planetary system as the Ganges. This sacred, transcendental water flows throughout the entire universe, purifying wherever it flows."

Just before the great sage Nārada arrived in the Sudharmā assembly house of Dvārakā, Lord Kṛṣṇa and His ministers and secretaries had been considering how to attack the kingdom of Jarāsandha. Because they were seriously considering this subject, Nārada's proposal that Lord Kṛṣṇa go to Hastināpura for Mahārāja Yudhiṣṭhira's great Rājasūya sacrifice did not much appeal to them. Lord Kṛṣṇa could understand the intentions of his associates because He is the ruler of even Lord Brahmā. Therefore, in order to pacify them, He smilingly said to Uddhava, "My dear Uddhava, you are always my well-wishing confidential friend. I therefore wish to see everything through you because I believe that your counsel is always right. I believe that you understand the whole situation perfectly. Therefore I am asking your opinion. What should I do? I have faith in you, and therefore I shall do whatever you advise." It was known to Uddhava that although Lord Kṛṣṇa was acting like an ordinary man, He knew everything—past, present and future. However, because the Lord was trying to consult with him, Uddhava, in order to render service to the Lord, began to speak.

Thus ends the Bhaktivedanta purport of the Sixty-ninth Chapter of Kṛṣṇa, *"Lord Kṛṣṇa's Daily Activities."*

70 / Lord Kṛṣṇa in Indraprastha City

In the presence of the great sage Nārada and all the other associates of Lord Kṛṣṇa, Uddhava considered the situation and then spoke as follows: "My dear Lord, first of all let me say that the great sage Nārada Muni has requested You to go to Hastināpura to satisfy King Yudhiṣṭhira, your cousin, who is making arrangements to perform the great sacrifice known as Rājasūya. I think, therefore, that Your Lordship should immediately go there to help the King in this great adventure. However, although to accept the invitation offered by the sage Nārada Muni as primary is quite appropriate, at the same time, my Lord, it is Your duty to give protection to the surrendered souls. Both purposes can be served if we understand the whole situation. Unless we are victorious over all the kings, no one can perform this Rājasūya sacrifice. In other words, it is to be understood that King Yudhiṣṭhira cannot perform this great sacrifice without gaining victory over the belligerent King Jarāsandha. The Rājasūya sacrifice can only be performed by one who has gained victory over all directions. Therefore, to execute both purposes, we first of all have to kill Jarāsandha. I think that if we can somehow or other gain victory over Jarāsandha, then automatically all our purposes will be served. The imprisoned kings will be released, and with great pleasure we shall enjoy the spread of Your transcendental fame at having saved the innocent kings whom Jarāsandha has imprisoned.

"But King Jarāsandha is not an ordinary man. He has proved a stumbling block even to great warriors because his bodily strength is equal to the strength of 10,000 elephants. If there is anyone who can conquer this king, he is none other than Bhīmasena because he also possesses the strength of 10,000 elephants. The best thing would be for Bhīmasena to fight alone with him. Then there would be no unnecessary killing of many soldiers. In fact, it will be very difficult to conquer Jarāsandha when he stands with his *akṣauhiṇī* divisions of soldiers. We may therefore adopt a policy more favorable to the situation. We know that King Jarāsandha is very much devoted to the *brāhmaṇas*. He is very charitably disposed towards them; he never refuses any request from a *brāhmaṇa*. I think, therefore, that Bhīmasena should approach Jarāsandha in the dress of a *brāhmaṇa*, beg charity from Him, and then personally engage in fighting Him. And in order to assure Bhīmasena's victory, I think that Your Lordship should also accompany him. If the fighting takes place in Your presence, I am sure Bhīmasena will emerge victorious because simply by Your presence everything impossible is made possible, just as Lord Brahmā creates this universe and Lord Śiva destroys it simply through Your influence.

"Actually, You are creating and destroying the entire cosmic manifestation; Lord Brahmā and Lord Śiva are only the superficially visible causes. Creation and destruction are actually being performed by the invisible time factor, which is Your impersonal representation. Everything is under the control of this time factor. If Your invisible time factor can perform such wonderful acts through Lord Brahmā and Lord Śiva, will not Your personal presence help Bhīmasena to conquer Jarāsandha? My dear Lord, when Jarāsandha is killed, then the queens of all the imprisoned kings will be so joyful at their husbands' being released by Your mercy that they will all begin to sing Your glories. They will be as pleased as the *gopīs* were when they were relieved from the hands of Śaṅkhāsura. All the great sages, the King of the elephants, Gajendra, the goddess of fortune, Sītā, and even Your father and mother, were all delivered by Your causeless mercy. We also have been thus delivered, and we are always singing the transcendental glories of Your activities.

"Therefore, I think that if the killing of Jarāsandha is undertaken first, that will automatically solve many other problems. As for the Rājasūya sacrifice arranged in Hastināpura, it will be held, either because of the pious activities of the imprisoned kings or the impious activities of Jarāsandha.

"My Lord, it appears that You are also personally to go to Hastināpura to perform this great sacrifice so that demoniac kings like Jarāsandha and Śiśupāla may be conquered, the pious imprisoned kings released, and at the same time the great Rājasūya sacrifice performed. Considering all these points, I think that Your Lordship should immediately proceed to Hastināpura."

This advice of Uddhava's was appreciated by all who were present in the assembly, and everyone considered that Lord Kṛṣṇa's going to Hastināpura would be beneficial from all points of view. The great sage Nārada, the elderly personalities of the Yadu dynasty, and the Supreme Personality of Godhead Kṛṣṇa Himself all supported the statement of Uddhava. Lord Kṛṣṇa then took permission from His father Vasudeva and grandfather Ugrasena, and He immediately ordered His servants Dāruka and Jaitra to arrange for travel to Hastināpura. When everything was prepared, Lord Kṛṣṇa especially bid farewell to Lord Balarāma and the King of the Yadus, Ugrasena, and after dispatching His queens along with their children and sending their necessary luggage ahead, He mounted His chariot, which bore the flag marked with the symbol of Garuḍa.

Before starting the procession, Lord Kṛṣṇa satisfied the great sage Nārada by offering him different kinds of worshipable articles. Nāradajī wanted to fall at the lotus feet of Kṛṣṇa, but because the Lord was playing the part of a human being, he simply offered his respects within his mind, and fixing the transcendental form of the Lord within his heart, he left the assembly house by the airways. Usually the sage Narada never walks on the surface of the globe, but travels in outer space. After the departure of Nārada, Lord Kṛṣṇa addressed the messenger who had come from the imprisoned kings. He told him that they should not be worried. He would very soon arrange to kill the King of Magadha, Jarāsandha. Thus He wished good fortune to all the imprisoned kings and the messenger. After receiving this assurance from Lord Kṛṣṇa, the messenger returned to the imprisoned kings and informed them of the happy news of the Lord's forthcoming visit. All the kings became joyful at the news and began to wait very anxiously for the Lord's arrival.

The chariot of Lord Kṛṣṇa began to proceed, accompanied by many other chariots, along with elephants, cavalry, infantry and similar royal paraphernalia. Bugles, drums, trumpets, conchshells, horns and coronets all began to produce a loud auspicious sound which vibrated in all directions. The 16,000 queens, headed by the goddess of fortune Rukmiṇīdevī, the ideal wife of Lord Kṛṣṇa, and accompanied by their respective sons, all followed behind Lord Kṛṣṇa. They were dressed in costly garments decorated with ornaments, and their bodies were smeared with sandalwood pulp and garlanded with fragrant flowers. Riding on palanquins which were nicely decorated with silks, flags, and golden lace, they followed their exalted husband, Lord Kṛṣṇa. The infantry soldiers carried shields, swords and lances in their hands and acted as royal bodyguards to the queens. In the rear of the procession were the wives and children of all the other followers, and there were many society girls also following. Many beasts of burden like bulls, buffaloes, mules, and asses carried the camps, bedding and carpets, and the women who were following were seated in separate palanquins on the backs of camels. This panoramic procession was accompanied by the shouts of the people and was full with the display of different colored flags, umbrellas and whisks and different varieties of weapons, dress, ornaments, helmets and armaments. The procession, being reflected in the sunshine, appeared just like an ocean with high waves and sharks.

In this way the procession of Lord Kṛṣṇa's party advanced towards Hastināpura (New Delhi) and gradually passed through the kingdoms of Ānarta (Gujarat Province), Sauvīra (Sauret), the great desert of Rājasthān, and then Kurukṣetra. In between those kingdoms there were many mountains, rivers, towns, villages, pasturing grounds and mining fields. The procession passed through all of these places in its advance. On His way to Hastināpura, the Lord crossed two big rivers, the Dṛṣvatī and the Sarasvatī. Then He crossed the province of Pañchāla and the province of Matsya. In this way, ultimately He arrived at Indraprastha.

The audience of the Supreme Personality of Godhead, Kṛṣṇa, is not very commonplace. Therefore, when King Yudhiṣṭhira heard that Lord Kṛṣṇa had already arrived in his capital city, Hastināpura, he became so joyful that all his hairs stood on end in great ecstasy, and he immediately came out of the city to properly receive Him. He ordered the musical vibration of different instruments and songs, and the learned *brāhmaṇas* of the city began to chant the hymns of the *Vedas* very loudly. Lord Kṛṣṇa is known as Hṛṣīkeśa, the master of the senses, and King Yudhiṣṭhira went forward to receive Him exactly as the senses meet the consciousness of life. King Yudhiṣṭhira was the elderly cousin of Kṛṣṇa. Naturally he had great affection for the Lord, and as soon as he saw Him, his heart became filled with great love and affection. He had not seen the Lord for many days, and therefore he thought himself most fortunate to see Him present before him. The King therefore began to embrace Lord Kṛṣṇa again and again in great affection.

The eternal form of Lord Kṛṣṇa is the everlasting residence of the goddess of fortune. As soon as King Yudhiṣṭhira embraced Him, he became free from all the contamination of material existence. He immediately felt transcendental bliss, and he merged in an ocean of happiness. There were tears in his eyes, and his body shook due to ecstasy. He completely forgot that he was living in this material world. After this, Bhīmasena, the second brother of the Pāṇḍavas, smiled and embraced Lord Kṛṣṇa, thinking of Him as his own maternal cousin, and thus he was merged in great ecstasy. Bhīmasena also was so filled with ecstasy that for the time being he forgot his material existence. Then Lord Śrī Kṛṣṇa Himself embraced the other three Pāṇḍavas, Arjuna, Nakula and Sahadeva. The eyes of all three brothers were inundated with tears, and Arjuna began to embrace Kṛṣṇa again and again because they were intimate friends. The two younger Pāṇḍava brothers, after being embraced by Lord Kṛṣṇa, fell down at His lotus feet to offer their respects. Lord Kṛṣṇa thereafter offered His obeisances to the *brāhmaṇas* present there, as well as to the elderly members of the Kuru dynasty, like Bhīṣma, Droṇa and Dhṛtarāṣṭra. There were many kings of different provinces such as Kuru, Sṛñjaya and Kekaya, and Lord Kṛṣṇa duly reciprocated greetings and respects with them. The professional reciters like the *sūtas, māgadhas,* and *vandinas,* accompanied by the *brāhmaṇas,* began to offer their respectful prayers to the Lord. Artists and musicians like the Gandharvas, as well as the royal jokers, began to play their drums, conchshells, kettledrums, *vīṇās, mṛdaṅgas,* and bugles, and they exhibited their dancing art in order to please the Lord. Thus the all-famous Supreme Personality of Godhead, Lord Kṛṣṇa, entered the great city of Hastināpura, which was opulent in every respect. While Lord Kṛṣṇa was entering the city, everyone was talking amongst themselves about the glories of the Lord, praising His transcendental name, quality, form, etc.

The roads, streets and lanes of Hastināpura were all sprinkled with fragrant water through the trunks of intoxicated elephants. In different places of the city there were colorful festoons and flags decorating the houses and streets. At important road crossings there were gates with golden decorations, and at the two sides of the gates there were golden water jugs. These beautiful decorations glorified the opulence of the city. Participating in this great ceremony, all the citizens of the city gathered here and there, dressed in colorful new clothing, decorated with ornaments, flower garlands, and fragrant scents. Each and every house was illuminated by hundreds and thousands of lamps placed in different corners of the cornices, walls, columns, bases and architraves, and from far away the rays of the lamps resembled the festival of Dīpāvalī (a particular festival observed on the New Year's Day of the Hindu calendar). Within the walls of the houses, fragrant incense was burning, and smoke rose through the windows, making the entire atmosphere very pleasing. On the top of every house flags were flapping, and the gold water pots kept on the roofs shone very brilliantly.

Lord Kṛṣṇa thus entered the city of the Pāṇḍavas, enjoyed the beautiful atmosphere and slowly proceeded ahead. When the young girls in every house heard that Lord Kṛṣṇa, the only object worth seeing, was passing on the road, they became very anxious to see this all-famous personality. Their hair loosened, and their tightened saris became slack due to their hastily rushing to see Him. They gave up their household engagements, and those who were lying in bed with their husbands immediately left them and came directly down onto the street to see Lord Kṛṣṇa.

The procession of elephants, horses, chariots, and infantry was very crowded; some, being unable to see properly in the crowd, got up on the roofs of the houses. They were pleased to see Lord Śrī Kṛṣṇa passing with His thousands of queens. They began to shower flowers on the procession, and they embraced Lord Kṛṣṇa within their minds and gave Him a hearty reception. When they saw Him in the midst of His many queens, like the full moon situated amidst many luminaries, they began to talk amongst themselves.

One girl said to another, "My dear friend, it is very difficult to guess what kind of pious activities these queens might have performed, for they are always enjoying the smiling face and loving glances of Kṛṣṇa." While Lord Kṛṣṇa was thus passing on the road, at intervals some of the opulent citizens, who were all rich, respectable and freed from sinful activities presented auspicious articles to the Lord, just to offer Him a reception to the city. Thus they worshiped Him as humble servitors.

When Lord Kṛṣṇa entered the palace, all the ladies there became overwhelmed with affection just upon seeing Him. They immediately received Lord Kṛṣṇa with glittering eyes expressing their love and affection for Him, and Lord Kṛṣṇa smiled and accepted their feelings and gestures of reception. When Kuntī, the mother of the Pāṇḍavas, saw her nephew Lord Kṛṣṇa, the Supreme Personality of Godhead, she became overpowered with love and affection. She at once got up from her bedstead and appeared before Him with her daughter-in-law, Draupadī, and in maternal love and affection she embraced Him. As he brought Kṛṣṇa within the palace, King Yudhiṣṭhira became so confused in his jubilation that he practically forgot what he was to do at that time in order to receive Kṛṣṇa and worship Him properly. Lord Kṛṣṇa delightfully offered His respects and obeisances to Kuntī and other elderly ladies of the palace. His younger sister, Subhadrā, was also standing there with Draupadī, and both offered their respectful obeisances unto the lotus feet of the Lord. At the indication of her mother-in-law, Draupadī brought clothing, ornaments and garlands, and with this paraphernalia they received the queens Rukmiṇī, Satyabhāmā, Bhadrā, Jāmbavatī, Kālindī, Mitravindā, Lakṣmaṇā and the devoted Satyā. These principal queens of Lord Kṛṣṇa were first received, and then the remaining queens were also offered a proper reception. King Yudhiṣṭhira arranged for Kṛṣṇa's rest and saw that all who came along with Him—namely His queens, His soldiers, His ministers and His secretaries—were comfortably situated. He had arranged that they would experience a new feature of reception everyday while staying as guests of the Pāṇḍavas.

It was during this time that Lord Śrī Kṛṣṇa, with the help of Arjuna, for the satisfaction of the fire-god, Agni, allowed Agni to devour the Khāṇḍava Forest. During the forest fire, Kṛṣṇa saved the demon Mayāsura, who was hiding in the forest. Upon being saved, Mayāsura felt obliged to the Pāṇḍavas and Lord Kṛṣṇa, and he constructed a wonderful assembly house within the city of Hastināpura. In this way, Lord Kṛṣṇa, in order to please King Yudhiṣṭhira, remained in the city of Hastināpura for several months. During His stay, He enjoyed strolling here and there. He used to drive on chariots along with Arjuna, and many warriors and soldiers used to follow them.

Thus ends the Bhaktivedanta purport of the Seventieth Chapter of Kṛṣṇa, *"Lord Kṛṣṇa in Indraprastha City."*

71 / Liberation of King Jarāsandha

In the great assembly of respectable persons, citizens, friends, relatives, *brāhmaṇas, kṣatriyas* and *vaiśyas,* King Yudhiṣṭhira, in the presence of all, including his brothers, directly addressed Lord Kṛṣṇa as follows: "My dear Lord Kṛṣṇa, the sacrifice known as the Rājasūya *yajña* is to be performed by the emperor, and it is considered to be the king of all sacrifices. By performing this sacrifice, I wish to satisfy all the demigods, who are Your empowered representatives within this material world, and I wish that You will kindly help me in this great adventure so that it may be successfully executed. As far as the Pāṇḍavas are concerned, we have nothing to ask from the demigods. We are personally fully satisfied by being Your devotees. As You say in the *Bhagavad-gītā,* "Persons who are bewildered by material desires worship the demigods," but our purpose is different. I want to perform this Rājasūya sacrifice and invite the demigods to show them that they have no power independent of You. They are all Your servants, and You are the Supreme Personality of Godhead. Foolish persons with a poor fund of knowledge consider Your Lordship an ordinary human being. Sometimes they try to find fault in You, and sometimes they defame You. Therefore I wish to perform this Rājasūya *yajña.* I wish to invite all the demigods, beginning from Lord Brahmā, Lord Śiva and other exalted chiefs of the heavenly planets, and in that great assembly of demigods from all parts of the universe, I want to substantiate that You are the Supreme Personality of Godhead and that everyone is Your servant.

"My dear Lord, those who are constantly in Kṛṣṇa consciousness and who think of Your lotus feet or of Your shoes certainly become free from all contamination of material life. Persons who are engaged in Your service in full Kṛṣṇa consciousness, who meditate upon You only or who offer prayers unto You, are purified souls. Being constantly engaged in Kṛṣṇa conscious service, such persons become freed from the cycle of repeated birth and death. They do not even desire to become freed from this material existence or to enjoy material opulences; their desires are fulfilled by Kṛṣṇa conscious activities. As far as we are concerned, we are fully surrendered unto Your lotus feet, and by Your grace we are so fortunate to see You personally. Therefore, naturally we have no desire for material opulences. The verdict of the Vedic wisdom is that You are the Supreme Personality of Godhead. I want to establish this fact, and I also want to show the world the difference between accepting You as the Supreme Personality of Godhead and accepting You as an ordinary powerful historical person. I wish to show the world that one can attain the highest perfection of life simply by taking shelter at Your lotus feet, exactly as one can satisfy the branches, twigs, leaves and flowers of an entire tree simply by watering the root. Thus, if one takes to Kṛṣṇa consciousness, his life becomes fulfilled both materially and spiritually.

"This does not mean that You are partial to the Kṛṣṇa conscious person and are indifferent to the non-Kṛṣṇa conscious person. You are equal to everyone; that is Your declaration. You cannot be partial to one and not interested in others because You are sitting in everyone's heart as the Supersoul and giving everyone the respective results of his fruitive activities. You give every living entity the chance to enjoy this material world as he desires. As Supersoul, You are sitting in the body along with the living entity, giving him the results of his own actions as well as opportunities to turn toward Your devotional service by developing Kṛṣṇa consciousness. You openly declare that one should surrender unto You, giving up all other engagements, and that You will take charge of him, giving him relief from the reactions of all sins. You are like the desire tree in the heavenly planets, which awards benediction according to one's desires. Everyone is free to achieve the highest perfection, but if one does not so desire, then Your awarding of lesser benedictions is not due to partiality."

On hearing this statement of King Yudhiṣṭhira, Lord Kṛṣṇa replied as follows: "My dear King Yudhiṣṭhira, O killer of enemies, O ideal justice personified, I completely support your decision to perform the Rājasūya sacrifice. By performing this great sacrifice, your good name will remain well established forever in the history of human civilization. My dear King, may I inform you that it is the desire of all great sages, your forefathers, the demigods, and your relatives and friends, including Myself, that you perform this sacrifice, and I think that it will satisfy every living entity. But, because it is necessary, I request that you first of all conquer all the kings of the world and collect all requisite paraphernalia for executing this great sacrifice. My dear King Yudhiṣṭhira, your four brothers are direct representatives of important demigods like Varuṇa, Indra, etc. [It is said that Bhīma was born of the demigod Varuṇa, and Arjuna was born of the demigod Indra, whereas King Yudhiṣṭhira himself was born of the demigod Yamarāja.] Your brothers are great heroes, and you are the most pious and self-controlled king and are therefore known as Dharmarāja. All of you are so qualified in devotional service unto Me that automatically I have become rivalled by you."

Lord Kṛṣṇa told King Yudhiṣṭhira that He becomes conquered by the love of one who has conquered his senses. One who has not conquered his senses cannot conquer the Supreme Personality of Godhead. This is the secret of devotional service. To conquer the senses means to engage them constantly in the service of the Lord. The specific qualification of all the Pāṇḍava brothers was that they always engaged their senses in the service of the Lord. One who thus engages his senses becomes purified, and with purified senses one can actually render service to the Lord. The Lord can thus be conquered by the devotee by loving transcendental service.

Lord Kṛṣṇa continued: "There is no one in the three worlds of the universe, including the powerful demigods, who can surpass My devotees in any of the six opulences, namely, wealth, strength, reputation, beauty, knowledge and renunciation. Therefore, if you want to conquer the worldly kings, there is no possibility of their emerging victorious."

When Lord Kṛṣṇa thus encouraged King Yudhiṣṭhira, the King's face brightened like a blossoming flower because of transcendental happiness, and thus he ordered his younger brothers to conquer all the worldly kings in all directions. Lord Kṛṣṇa empowered the Pāṇḍavas to execute His great mission of chastising the infidel miscreants of the world and giving protection to His faithful devotees. In His Viṣṇu form, the Lord therefore carries four kinds of weapons in His four hands. He carries a lotus flower and a conchshell in two hands, and in the other two hands He carries a club and a disc. The club and disc are meant for the nondevotees, but because the Lord is the Supreme Absolute, the resultant action of all His weapons is one and the same. With the club and the disc He chastises the miscreants so that they may come to their senses and know that they are not all in all. Over them there is the Supreme Lord. And by bugling with the conchshell and by offering blessings with the lotus flower, He always assures the devotees that no one can vanquish them, even in the greatest calamity. King Yudhiṣṭhira, being thus assured by the indication of Lord Kṛṣṇa, ordered his youngest brother, Sahadeva, accompanied by soldiers of the Sṛñjaya tribe, to conquer the southern countries. Similarly, he ordered Nakula, accompanied by the soldiers of Matsyadeśa, to conquer the kings of the western side. He sent Arjuna, accompanied by the soldiers of Kekayadeśa, to conquer the kings of the northern side, and Bhīmasena, accompanied by the soldiers of Madradeśa (Madras), was ordered to conquer the kings on the eastern side.

It may be noted that by dispatching his younger brothers to conquer in different directions, King Yudhiṣṭhira did not actually intend that they declare war with the kings. Actually, the brothers started for different directions to inform the respective kings about King Yudhiṣṭhira's intention to perform the Rājasūya sacrifice. The kings were thus informed that they were required to pay taxes for the execution of the sacrifice. This payment of taxes to Emperor Yudhiṣṭhira meant that the king accepted his subjugation before him. In case of a king's refusal to act accordingly, there was certainly a fight. Thus by their influence and strength, the brothers conquered all the kings in different directions, and they were able to bring in sufficient taxes and presentations. These were brought before King Yudhiṣṭhira by his brothers.

King Yudhiṣṭhira was very anxious, however, when he heard that King Jarāsandha of Magadha did not accept his sovereignty. Seeing King Yudhiṣṭhira's anxiety, Lord Kṛṣṇa informed him of the plan explained by Uddhava for conquering King Jarāsandha. Bhīmasena, Arjuna and Lord Kṛṣṇa then started together for Girivraja, the capital city of Jarāsandha, dressing themselves in the garb of *brāhmaṇas.* This was the plan devised by Uddhava before Lord Kṛṣṇa started for Hastināpura, and now it was given practical application.

King Jarāsandha was a very dutiful householder, and he had great respect for the *brāhmaṇas.* He was a great fighter, a *kṣatriya* king, but he was never neglectful of the Vedic injunctions. According to Vedic injunctions, the *brāhmaṇas* are considered to be the spiritual masters of all other castes. Lord Kṛṣṇa, Arjuna and Bhīmasena were actually *kṣatriyas,* but they dressed themselves as *brāhmaṇas,* and at the time when King Jarāsandha was to give charity to the *brāhmaṇas* and receive them as guests, they approached him.

Lord Kṛṣṇa, in the dress of a *brāhmaṇa,* said to the King: "We wish all glories to your majesty. We are three guests at your royal palace, and we are coming from a great distance. We have come to ask you for charity, and we hope that you will kindly bestow upon us whatever we ask from you. We know about your good qualities. A person who is tolerant is always prepared to tolerate everything, even though distressful. Just as a criminal can perform the most abominable acts, so a greatly charitable person like you can give anything and everything he is asked for. For a great personality like you, there is no distinction between relatives and outsiders. A famous man lives forever, even after his death; therefore, any person who is completely fit and able to execute acts which will perpetuate his good name and fame and yet does not do so becomes abominable in the eyes of great persons. Such a person cannot be condemned enough, and his refusal to give charity is lamentable throughout his whole life. Your majesty must have heard the glorious names of charitable personalities such as Hariścandra, Rantideva and Mudgala, who used to live only on grains picked up from the paddy field, and the great Mahārāja Śibi, who saved the life of a pigeon by supplying flesh from his own body. These great personalities have attained immortal fame simply by sacrificing this temporary and perishable body." Lord Kṛṣṇa, in the garb of a *brāhmaṇa,* thus informed Jarāsandha that fame is imperishable, but the body is perishable. If one can attain imperishable name and fame by sacrificing his perishable body, he becomes a very respectable figure in the history of human civilization.

While Lord Kṛṣṇa was speaking in the garb of a *brāhmaṇa* along with Arjuna and Bhīma, Jarāsandha marked that the three of them did not appear to be actual *brāhmaṇas.* There were signs on their bodies by which Jarāsandha could understand that they were *kṣatriyas.* Their shoulders were marked with an impression due to carrying bows; they had beautiful bodily structure, and their voices were grave and commanding. Thus he definitely concluded that they were not *brāhmaṇas,* but *kṣatriyas.* He was also thinking that he had seen them somewhere before. Although these three persons were *kṣatriyas,* they had come to his door begging alms like *brāhmaṇas.* Therefore he decided that he would fulfill their desires, in spite of their being *kṣatriyas.* He thought in this way because their position had already been diminished by their appearing before him as beggars. "Under the circumstances," he thought, "I am prepared to give them anything. Even if they ask for my body, I shall not hesitate to offer it to them." In this regard, he began to think of Bali Mahārāja. Lord Viṣṇu in the dress of a *brāhmaṇa* appeared as a beggar before Bali, and in that way He snatched away all of his opulence and kingdom. He did this for the benefit of Indra, who, having been defeated by Bali Mahārāja, was bereft of his kingdom. Although Bali Mahārāja was cheated, his reputation as a great devotee who was able to give anything and everything in charity is still glorified throughout the three worlds. Bali Mahārāja could guess that the *brāhmaṇa* was Lord Viṣṇu Himself and that He had come to him just to take away his opulent kingdom on behalf of Indra. Bali's spiritual master and family priest, Śukrācārya, repeatedly warned him about this, and yet Bali did not hesitate to give in charity whatever the *brāhmaṇa* wanted, and at last he gave up everything to that *brāhmaṇa.* "It is my strong determination," thought Jarāsandha, "that if I can achieve immortal reputation by sacrificing this perishable body, I must act for that purpose; the life of a *kṣatriya* who does not live for the benefit of the *brāhmaṇa* is certainly condemned."

Actually King Jarāsandha was very liberal in giving charity to the *brāhmaṇas,* and thus he informed Lord Kṛṣṇa, Bhīma and Arjuna: "My dear *brāhmaṇas,* you can ask from me whatever you like. If you so desire, you can take my head also. I am prepared to give it."

After this, Lord Kṛṣṇa addressed Jarāsandha as follows: "My dear King, please note that we are not actually *brāhmaṇas,* nor have we come to ask for foodstuffs or grains. We are all *kṣatriyas,* and we have come to beg a duel with you. We hope that you will agree to this proposal. You may note that here is the second son of King Pāṇḍu, Bhīmasena, and the third son of Pāṇḍu, Arjuna. As for Myself, you may know that I am your old enemy, Kṛṣṇa, the cousin of the Pāṇḍavas."

When Lord Kṛṣṇa disclosed their disguise, King Jarāsandha began to laugh very loudly, and then in great anger and in a grave voice he exclaimed, "You fools! If you want to fight with me, I immediately grant your request. But, Kṛṣṇa, I know that You are a coward. I refuse to fight with You because You become very confused when You face me in fighting. Out of fear of me You left Your own city, Mathurā, and now You have taken shelter within the sea; therefore I must refuse to fight with You. As far as Arjuna is concerned, I know that he is younger than me and is not an equal fighter. I refuse to fight with him because he is not in any way an equal competitor. But as far as Bhīmasena is concerned, I think he is a suitable competitor to fight with me." After speaking in this way, King Jarāsandha immediately handed a very heavy club to Bhīmasena, and he himself took another, and thus all of them went outside the city walls to fight.

Bhīmasena and King Jarāsandha engaged themselves in fighting, and with their respective clubs, which were as strong as thunderbolts, they began to strike one another very severely, both of them being eager to fight. They were both expert fighters with clubs, and their techniques of striking one another were so beautiful that they appeared to be two dramatic artists dancing on a stage. When the clubs of Jarāsandha and Bhīmasena loudly collided, they sounded like the impact of the big tusks of two fighting elephants or like a thunderbolt in a flashing electrical storm. When two elephants fight together in a sugarcane field, each of them snatches a stick of sugarcane and, by catching it tightly in its trunk, strikes the other. Each elephant heavily strikes his enemy's shoulders, arms, collarbones, chest, thighs, waist, and legs, and in this way the sticks of sugarcane are smashed. Similarly, all the clubs used by Jarāsandha and Bhīmasena were broken, and so the two enemies prepared to fight with their strong-fisted hands. Both Jarāsandha and Bhīmasena were very angry, and they began to smash each other with their fists. The striking of their fists sounded like the striking of iron bars or like the sound of thunderbolts, and they appeared to be like two elephants fighting. Unfortunately, however, neither was able to defeat the other because both were very expert in fighting, both were of equal strength, and their fighting techniques were equal also. Neither Jarāsandha nor Bhīmasena became fatigued or defeated in the fighting, although they struck each other continually. At the end of a day's fighting, both lived at night as friends in Jarāsandha's palace, and the next day they fought again. In this way they passed twenty-seven days in fighting.

On the twenty-eighth day, Bhīmasena told Kṛṣṇa, "My dear Kṛṣṇa, I must frankly admit that I cannot conquer Jarāsandha." Lord Kṛṣṇa, however, knew the mystery of the birth of Jarāsandha. Jarāsandha was born in two different parts from two different mothers. When his father saw that the baby was useless, he threw the two parts in the forest, where they were later found by a black-hearted witch named Jarā. She managed to join the two parts of the baby from top to bottom. Knowing this, Lord Kṛṣṇa therefore also knew how to kill him. He gave hints to Bhīmasena that since Jarāsandha was brought to life by the joining of the two parts of his body, he could be killed by the separation of these two parts. Thus Lord Kṛṣṇa transferred His power into the body of Bhīmasena and informed him of the device by which Jarāsandha could be killed. Lord Kṛṣṇa immediately picked up a twig from a tree and, taking it in His hand, bifurcated it. In this way He hinted to Bhīmasena how Jarāsandha could be killed. Lord Kṛṣṇa, the Supreme Personality of Godhead, is omnipotent, and if He wants to kill someone, no one can save that person. Similarly, if He wants to save someone, no one can kill him.

Informed by the hints of Lord Kṛṣṇa, Bhīmasena immediately took hold of the legs of Jarāsandha and threw him to the ground. When Jarāsandha fell to the ground, Bhīmasena immediately pressed one of Jarāsandha's legs to the ground and took hold of the other leg with his two hands. Catching Jarāsandha in this way, he tore his body in two, beginning from the anus up to the head. As an elephant breaks the branches of a tree in two, so Bhīmasena separated the body of Jarāsandha. The audience standing nearby saw that the body of Jarāsandha was now divided into two halves, so that each half had one leg, one thigh, one testicle, one breast, half a backbone, half a chest, one collarbone, one arm, one eye, one ear, and half a face.

As soon as the news of Jarāsandha's death was announced, all the citizens of Magadha began to cry, "Alas, alas," while Lord Kṛṣṇa and Arjuna embraced Bhīmasena to congratulate him. Although Jarāsandha was killed, neither Kṛṣṇa nor the two Pāṇḍava brothers made a claim to the throne. Their purpose in killing Jarāsandha was to stop him from creating a disturbance against the proper discharge of world peace. A demon always creates disturbances, whereas a demigod always tries to keep peace in the world. The mission of Lord Kṛṣṇa is to give protection to the righteous persons and to kill the demons who disturb a peaceful situation. Therefore Lord Kṛṣṇa immediately called for the son of Jarāsandha, whose name was Sahadeva, and with due ritualistic ceremonies He asked him to occupy the seat of his father and reign over the kingdom peacefully. Lord Kṛṣṇa is the master of the whole cosmic creation, and He wants everyone to live peacefully and execute Kṛṣṇa consciousness. After installing Sahadeva on the throne, He released all the kings and princes who had been imprisoned unnecessarily by Jarāsandha.

Thus ends the Bhaktivedanta purport of the Seventy-first Chapter of Kṛṣṇa, *"The Liberation of King Jarāsandha."*

72 / Lord Kṛṣṇa Returns to the City of Hastināpura

The kings and the princes released by Lord Kṛṣṇa after the death of Jarāsandha were rulers of different parts of the world. Jarāsandha was so powerful in military strength that he had conquered all these princes and kings, numbering 20,800. They were all incarcerated within a mountain cave especially constructed as a fort, and for a long time they were kept in that situation. When they were released by the grace of Lord Kṛṣṇa, they all looked very unhappy, their garments were niggardly, and their faces were almost dried up for want of proper bodily care. They were very weak due to hunger, and their faces had lost all beauty and luster. Because of the kings' long imprisonment, every part of their bodies had become slackened and invalid. But although suffering in that miserable condition of life, they had the opportunity to think about the Supreme Personality of Godhead, Viṣṇu.

Now before them they saw the color of the transcendental body of Lord Kṛṣṇa, exactly like the hue of a newly arrived cloud in the sky. He appeared before them nicely covered by yellow colored silken garments, with four hands like Viṣṇu, and carrying the different symbols of the club, the conchshell, the disc and the lotus flower. There were marks of golden lines on His chest, and the nipples of His breast appeared to be like the whorl of a lotus flower. His eyes appeared to be spread like the petals of a lotus flower, and His smiling face exhibited the symbol of eternal peace and prosperity. His glittering earrings were set beautifully, and His helmet was bedecked with valuable jewels. The Lord's necklace of pearls and the bangles and bracelets nicely situated on His body all shone with a transcendental beauty. The Kaustubha jewel hanging on His chest glittered with great luster, and the Lord wore a beautiful flower garland. After so much distress, when the kings and princes saw Lord Kṛṣṇa, with His beautiful transcendental features, they looked upon Him to their hearts' content, as if they were drinking nectar through their eyes, licking His body with their tongues, smelling the aroma of His body with their noses, and embracing Him with their arms. Just by dint of their being in front of the Supreme Personality of Godhead, all reactions to their sinful activities were washed away. Therefore, without reservation, they surrendered themselves at the lotus feet of the Lord. It is stated in the *Bhagavad-gītā* that unless one is freed from all kinds of sinful reactions, one cannot fully surrender unto the lotus feet of the Lord. All the princes who saw Lord Kṛṣṇa forgot all their past tribulations. With folded hands and with great devotion, they began to offer prayers to Lord Kṛṣṇa, as follows.

"Dear Lord, O Supreme Personality of Godhead, master of all demigods, You can immediately remove all Your devotees' pangs because Your devotees are fully surrendered unto You. O dear Lord Kṛṣṇa, O eternal Deity of transcendental bliss and knowledge, You are imperishable, and we offer our respectful obeisances unto Your lotus feet. It is by Your causeless mercy that we have been released from the imprisonment of Jarāsandha, but now we pray unto You to release us from the imprisonment with the illusory energy of this material existence. Please, therefore, stop our continuous cycle of birth and death. We now have sufficient experience of the miserable material condition of life in which we are fully absorbed, and having tasted its bitterness, we have come to take shelter under Your lotus feet. Dear Lord, O killer of the demon Madhu, we can now clearly see that Jarāsandha was not at fault in the least; it is actually by Your causeless mercy that we were bereft of our kingdoms because we were very proud of calling ourselves rulers and kings. Any ruler or king who becomes too puffed up with false prestige and power does not get the opportunity to understand his real constitutional position and eternal life. Such foolish so-called rulers and kings become falsely proud of their position under the influence of Your illusory energy; they are just like a foolish person who considers a mirage in the desert to be a reservoir of water. Foolish persons think that their material possessions will give them protection, and those who are engaged in sense gratification falsely accept this material world as a place of eternal enjoyment. O Lord, O Supreme Personality of Godhead, we must admit that, before this, we were puffed up with our material opulences. Because we were all envious of each other and wanted to conquer one another, we all engaged in fighting for supremacy, even at the cost of sacrificing the lives of many citizens."

This is the disease of political power. As soon as a king or a nation becomes rich in material opulences, it wants to dominate other nations by military aggression. Similarly, mercantile men want to monopolize a certain type of business and control other mercantile groups. Degraded by false prestige and infatuated by material opulences, human society, instead of striving for Kṛṣṇa consciousness, creates havoc and disrupts peaceful living. Thus men naturally forget the real purpose of life: to attain the favor of Lord Viṣṇu, the Supreme Personality of Godhead.

The kings continued: "O Lord, we were simply engaged in the abominable task of killing citizens and alluring them to be unnecessarily killed, just to satisfy our political whims. We did not consider that Your Lordship is always present before us in the form of cruel death. We were so fooled that we became the cause of death for others, forgetting our own impending death. But, dear Lord, the retaliation of the time element, which is Your representative, is certainly insurmountable. The time element is so strong that no one can escape its influence; therefore we have received the reactions of our atrocious activities, and we are now bereft of all opulences and stand before You like street beggars. We consider our position to be Your causeless, unalloyed mercy upon us because now we can understand that we were falsely proud and that our material opulences could be withdrawn from us within a second by Your will. By Your causeless mercy only, we are now able to think of Your lotus feet. This is our greatest gain. Dear Lord, it is known to everyone that the body is a breeding ground of diseases. Now we are sufficiently aged, and instead of being proud of our bodily strength, we are getting weaker day by day. We are no longer interested in sense gratification or the false happiness derived through the material body. By Your grace, we have now come to the conclusion that hankering after such material happiness is just like searching for water in a desert mirage. We are no longer interested in the results of our pious activities, such as performing great sacrifices in order to be elevated to the heavenly planets. We now understand that such elevation to a higher material standard of life in the heavenly planets may sound very relishable, but actually there cannot be any happiness within this material world. We pray for Your Lordship to favor us by instructing us how to engage in the transcendental loving service of Your lotus feet so that we may never forget our eternal relationship with Your Lordship. We do not want liberation from the entanglement of material existence. By Your will we may take birth in any species of life; it does not matter. We simply pray that we may never forget Your lotus feet under any circumstances. Dear Lord, we now surrender unto Your lotus feet by offering our respectful obeisances unto You because You are the Supreme Lord, the Personality of Godhead, Kṛṣṇa, the son of Vasudeva. You are the Supersoul in everyone's heart, and You are Lord Hari, who can take away all miserable conditions of material existence. Dear Lord, Your name is Govinda, the reservoir of all pleasure. One who is engaged in satisfying Your senses automatically satisfies his own senses also, and therefore You are known as Govinda. Dear Lord, You are ever famous, for You can put an end to all the miseries of Your devotees. Please, therefore, accept us as Your surrendered servants."

After hearing the prayers of the kings released from the prison of Jarāsandha, Lord Kṛṣṇa, who is always the protector of surrendered souls and the ocean of mercy for the devotees, replied to them as follows in His sweetly transcendental voice, which was grave and full of meaning. "My dear kings," He said, "I bestow upon you My blessings. From this day forth you will be attached to My devotional service without fail. I give you this benediction, as you have desired. You may know from Me that I am always sitting within your hearts as Supersoul, and because you have now turned your faces towards Me, I, as master of everyone, shall always give you good counsel so that you may never forget Me and so that gradually you will come back home, back to Godhead. My dear kings, your decision to give up all conceptions of material enjoyment and turn instead toward My devotional service is factually the symptom of your good fortune. Henceforward you will always be blessed with blissful life. I confirm that all you have spoken about Me in your prayers is factual. It is a fact that the materially opulent position of one who is not fully Kṛṣṇa conscious is the cause of his downfall and of his becoming a victim of the illusory energy. In the past, there were many rebellious kings, such as Haihaya, Nahuṣa, Vena, Rāvaṇa and Narakāsura. Some of them were demigods, and some of them were demons, but because of their false perception of their positions, they fell from their exalted posts, and thus they no longer remained the kings of their respective kingdoms.

"While lost in the violence of conditional life, every one of you must understand that anything material has its starting point, growth, expansion, deterioration, and, finally, disappearance. All material bodies are subjected to these six conditions, and any relative acquisitions which are accumulated by this body are definitely subject to final destruction. Therefore, no one should be attached to perishable things. As long as one is within this material body, he should be very cautious in worldly dealings. The most perfect way of life in this material world is simply to be devoted to My transcendental loving service and to honestly execute the prescribed duties of one's particular position of life. As far as you are concerned, you all belong to *kṣatriya* families. Therefore, you should live honestly, according to the prescribed duties befitting the royal order, and you should make your citizens happy in all respects. Keep to the standard of *kṣatriya* life. Do not beget children out of sense gratification, but simply take charge of the welfare of the people in general. Everyone takes birth in this material world because of the contaminated desires of his previous life, and thus he is subjected to the stringent laws of nature, such as birth and death, distress and happiness, profit and loss. One should not be disturbed by duality, but should always be fixed in My service and thus remain balanced in mind and satisfied in all circumstances, considering all things to be given by Me, and one should remain undeviated from engagement in devotional service. Thus one can live a very happy and peaceful life, even within this material condition. In other words, one should actually be callous to this material body and its by-products and should remain unaffected by them. He should remain fully satisfied in the interests of the spirit soul and be engaged in the service of the Supersoul. One should engage his mind only on Me, one should simply become My devotee, one should simply worship Me, and one should offer his respectful obeisances unto Me alone. In this way, one can cross over this ocean of nescience very easily and at the end come back to Me. In conclusion, your lives should constantly be engaged in My service."

After delivering His instructions to the kings and princes, Lord Kṛṣṇa immediately arranged for their comfort and asked many servants and maidservants to take care of them. Lord Kṛṣṇa requested Sahadeva, the son of King Jarāsandha, to supply all necessities to the kings and also asked him to show them all respect and honor. In pursuance of the order of Lord Kṛṣṇa, Sahadeva offered them all honor, and presented them with ornaments, garments, garlands, and other paraphernalia. After taking their baths and dressing very nicely, the kings appeared happy and gentle. Then they were supplied nice foodstuffs. Lord Kṛṣṇa supplied everything for their comfort, as was befitting their royal positions. Since the kings were so mercifully treated by Lord Kṛṣṇa, they felt great happiness, and all their bright faces appeared just like the stars in the sky after the end of the rainy season. They were all nicely dressed and ornamented, and their earrings glittered. Each one was then seated on a chariot bedecked with gold and jewels and drawn by decorated horses. After seeing that each was taken care of, Lord Kṛṣṇa, in a sweet voice, asked them to return to their respective kingdoms. By His very liberal behavior, unparalleled in the history of the world, Lord Kṛṣṇa released all the kings who had been in the clutches of Jarāsandha, and being fully satisfied, the kings began to engage in chanting His holy name, thinking of His holy form, and glorifying His transcendental pastimes as the Supreme Personality of Godhead. So engaged, they returned to their respective kingdoms. The citizens of their kingdoms were very greatly pleased to see them return, and when they heard of the kind dealings of Lord Kṛṣṇa, they all became very happy. The kings began to manage the affairs of their kingdoms in accordance with the instructions of Lord Kṛṣṇa, and all those kings and their subjects passed their days very happily. This is the vivid example of the Kṛṣṇa conscious society. If the people of the world divide the whole society, in terms of their respective material qualities, into four orders for material and spiritual progress, centering around Kṛṣṇa and following the instructions of Kṛṣṇa as stated in *Bhagavad-gītā*, the entire human society will undoubtedly be happy. This is the lesson that we have to take from this incident.

After thus causing the annihilation of Jarāsandha by Bhīmasena and after being properly honored by Sahadeva, the son of Jarāsandha, Lord Kṛṣṇa, accompanied by Bhīmasena and Arjuna, returned to the city of Hastināpura. When they reached the precincts of Hastināpura, they blew their respective conchshells, and by hearing the sound vibrations and understanding who was arriving, everyone immediately became cheerful. But upon hearing the conchshells, the enemies of Kṛṣṇa became very sorry. The citizens of Indraprastha felt their hearts become joyful simply by hearing the vibration of Kṛṣṇa's conchshell because they could understand that Jarāsandha had been killed. Now the performance of the Rājasūya sacrifice by King Yudhiṣṭhira was almost certain. Bhīmasena, Arjuna, and Kṛṣṇa, the Supreme Personality of Godhead, arrived before King Yudhiṣṭhira and offered their respects to the King. King Yudhiṣṭhira attentively heard the narration of the killing of Jarāsandha and the setting free of the kings. He also heard of the tactics which were adopted by Kṛṣṇa to kill Jarāsandha. The king was naturally affectionate toward Kṛṣṇa, but after hearing the story, he became even more bound in love for Kṛṣṇa; tears of ecstasy glided from his eyes, and he became so stunned that he was almost unable to speak.

Thus ends the Bhaktivedanta purport of the Seventy-second Chapter of Kṛṣṇa, *"Lord Kṛṣṇa Returns to the City of Hastināpura."*

73 / The Deliverance of Śiśupāla

King Yudhiṣṭhira became very happy after hearing the details of the Jarāsandha episode, and he spoke as follows: "My dear Kṛṣṇa, O eternal form of bliss and knowledge, all the exalted directors of the affairs of this material world, including Lord Brahmā, Lord Śiva and King Indra, are always anxious to receive and carry out orders from You, and whenever they are fortunate enough to receive such orders, they immediately take them and keep them in their hearts. O Kṛṣṇa, You are unlimited, and although we sometimes think of ourselves as royal kings and rulers of the world and become puffed up over our paltry positions, we are very poor in heart. Actually, we are fit to be punished by You, but the wonder is that instead of punishing us, You so kindly and mercifully accept our orders and carry them out properly. Others are very surprised that Your Lordship can play the part of an ordinary human, but we can understand that You are performing these activities just like a dramatic artist. Your real position is always exalted, exactly like that of the sun, which always remains at the same temperature both during the time of its rising and the time of its setting. Although we feel the difference in temperature between the rising and the setting sun, the temperature of the sun never changes. You are always transcendentally equiposed, and thus You are neither pleased nor disturbed by any condition of material affairs. You are the Supreme Brahman, the Personality of Godhead, and for You there are no relativities. My dear Mādhava, You are never defeated by anyone. Material distinctions—'This is me.' 'This is you.' 'This is mine.' 'This is yours.'—are all conspicuous by dint of their absence in You. Such distinctions are visible in the lives of everyone, even the animals, but those who are pure devotees are freed from these false distinctions. Since these distinctions are absent in Your devotees, they cannot possibly be present in You."

After satisfying Kṛṣṇa in this way, King Yudhiṣṭhira arranged to perform the Rājasūya sacrifice. He invited all the qualified *brāhmaṇas* and sages to take part and appointed them to different positions as priests in charge of the sacrificial arena. He invited the most expert *brāhmaṇas* and sages, whose names are as follows: Kṛṣṇa-dvaipāyana Vyāsadeva, Bharadvāja, Sumantu, Gautama, Asita, Vasiṣṭha, Cyavana, Kaṇva, Maitreya, Kavaṣa, Trita, Viśvāmitra, Vāmadeva, Sumati, Jaimini, Kratu, Paila, Parāśara, Garga, Vaiśampāyana, Atharvā, Kaśyapa, Dhaumya, Paraśurāma, Śukrācārya, Āsuri, Vītihotra, Madhucchandā, Vīrasena, and Akṛtavraṇa. Besides all these *brāhmaṇas* and sages, he invited such respectful old men as Droṇācārya, Bhīṣma, the grandfather of the Kurus, Kṛpācārya, and Dhṛtarāṣṭra. He also invited all the sons of Dhṛtarāṣṭra, headed by Duryodhana, and the great devotee Vidura was also invited. Kings from different parts of the world, along with their ministers and secretaries, were also invited to see the great sacrifice performed by King Yudhiṣṭhira, and the citizens, comprising learned *brāhmaṇas,* chivalrous *kṣatriyas,* well-to-do *vaiśyas,* and faithful *śūdras,* all visited the ceremony.

The *brāhmaṇa* priests and sages in charge of the sacrificial ceremony constructed the sacrificial arena as usual with a plow of gold, and they initiated King Yudhiṣṭhira as the performer of the great sacrifice, in accordance with Vedic rituals. Long years ago, when Varuṇa performed a similar sacrifice, all the sacrificial utensils were made of gold. Similarly, in the Rājasūya sacrifice of King Yudhiṣṭhira, all the utensils required for the sacrifice were golden.

In order to participate in the great sacrifice performed by King Yudhiṣṭhira, all the exalted demigods like Lord Brahmā, Lord Śiva, and Indra the King of heaven, accompanied by their associates, as well as the predominating deities of higher planetary systems like Gandharvaloka, Siddhaloka, Janaloka, Tapoloka, Nāgaloka, Yakṣaloka, Rākṣasaloka, Pakṣiloka and Cāraṇaloka, as well as famous kings and their queens, were all present by the invitation of King Yudhiṣṭhira. All the respectable sages, kings and demigods who assembled there unanimously agreed that King Yudhiṣṭhira was quite competent to take the responsibility of performing the Rājasūya sacrifice; no one was in disagreement on this fact. All of them knew thoroughly the position of King Yudhiṣṭhira; because he was a great devotee of Lord Kṛṣṇa, no accomplishment was extraordinary for him. The learned *brāhmaṇas* and priests saw to it that the sacrifice by Mahārāja Yudhiṣṭhira was performed in exactly the same way as in bygone ages by the demigod Varuṇa. According to the Vedic system, whenever there is an arrangement for sacrifice, the members participating in the sacrifice are offered the juice of the *soma* plant. The juice of the *soma* plant is a kind of life-giving beverage. On the day of extracting the *soma* juice, King Yudhiṣṭhira very respectfully received the special priest who had been engaged to detect any mistake in the formalities of sacrificial procedures. The idea is that the Vedic *mantras* must be enuciated perfectly and chanted with the proper accent; if the priests who are engaged in this business commit any mistake, the checker or referee priest immediately corrects the procedure, and thus the ritualistic performances are perfectly executed. Unless it is perfectly executed, a sacrifice cannot yield the desired result. In this age of Kali there is no such learned *brāhmaṇa* or priest available; therefore, all such sacrifices are forbidden. The only sacrifice recommended in the *śāstras* is the chanting of the Hare Kṛṣṇa *mantra.*

Another important procedure is that the most exalted personality in the assembly of such a sacrificial ceremony is first offered worship. After all arrangements were made for Yudhiṣṭhira's sacrifice, the next consideration was who should be worshiped first in the ceremony. This particular ceremony is called Agrapūjā. *Agra* means first, and *pūjā* means worship. This Agrapūjā is similar to election of the president. In the sacrificial assembly, all the members were very exalted. Some proposed to elect one person as the perfect candidate for accepting Agrapūjā, and others proposed someone else.

When the matter remained undecided, Sahadeva began to speak in favor of Lord Kṛṣṇa. He said, "Lord Kṛṣṇa, the best amongst the members of the Yadu dynasty and the protector of His devotees, is the most exalted personality in this assembly. Therefore I think that He should without any objection be offered the honor of being worshiped first. Although demigods such as Lord Brahmā, Lord Śiva, Indra, the King of heavenly planets, and many other exalted personalities are present in this assembly, no one can be equal to or greater than Kṛṣṇa in terms of time, space, riches, strength, reputation, wisdom, renunciation or any other consideration. Anything which is considered opulent is present originally in Kṛṣṇa. As an individual soul is the basic principle of the growth of his material body, similarly Kṛṣṇa is the Supersoul of this cosmic manifestation. All kinds of Vedic ritualistic ceremonies, such as the performance of sacrifices, the offering of oblations in the fire, the chanting of the Vedic hymns and the practice of mystic *yoga*—all are meant for realizing Kṛṣṇa. Whether one follows the path of fruitive activities or the path of philosophical speculation, the ultimate destination is Kṛṣṇa; all bona fide methods of self-realization are meant for understanding Kṛṣṇa. Ladies and gentlemen, it is superfluous to speak about Kṛṣṇa, because every one of you exalted personalities know the Supreme Brahman, Lord Kṛṣṇa, for whom there are no material differences between body and soul, between energy and the energetic, or between one part of the body and another. Since everyone is a part and parcel of Kṛṣṇa, there is no qualitative difference between Kṛṣṇa and all living entities. Everything is an emanation of Kṛṣṇa's energies, the material and spiritual energies. Kṛṣṇa's energies are like the heat and light of the fire; there is no difference between the quality of heat and light and the fire itself.

"Also, Kṛṣṇa can do anything He likes with any part of His body. We can execute a particular action with the help of a particular part of our body, but He can do anything and everything with any part of His body. And because His transcendental body is full of knowledge and bliss in eternity, He doesn't undergo the six kinds of material changes–birth, existence, growth, fruitive action, dwindling and vanishing. Unforced by any external energy, He is the supreme cause of the creation, maintenance and dissolution of everything that be. By the grace of Kṛṣṇa only, everyone is engaged in the practice of religiousness, the development of economic conditions, the satisfaction of the senses and, ultimately, the achievement of liberation from material bondage. These four principles of progressive life can be executed by the mercy of Kṛṣṇa only. He should therefore be offered the first worship of this great sacrifice, and no one should disagree. As by watering the root, the watering of the branches, twigs, leaves and flowers is automatically accomplished, or as by supplying food to the stomach, the nutrition and metabolism of all parts of the body are automatically established, so by offering the first worship to Kṛṣṇa, everyone present in this meeting–including the great demigods–will be satisfied. If anyone is charitably disposed, it will be very good for him to give in charity only to Kṛṣṇa, who is the Supersoul of everyone, regardless of his particular body or individual personality. Kṛṣṇa is present as the Supersoul in every living being, and if we can satisfy Him, then automatically every living being becomes satisfied."

Sahadeva was fortunate to know of the glories of Kṛṣṇa, and after describing them in brief, he stopped speaking. After this speech was delivered, all the members present in that great sacrificial assembly applauded, confirming his words continuously by saying, "Everything that you have said is completely perfect. Everything that you have said is completely perfect." King Yudhiṣṭhira, after hearing the confirmation of all present, especially of the *brāhmaṇas* and learned sages, worshiped Lord Kṛṣṇa according to the regulative principles of the Vedic injunctions. First of all, King Yudhiṣṭhira–along with his brothers, wives, children, other relatives and ministers–washed the lotus feet of Lord Kṛṣṇa and sprinkled the water on their heads. After this, Lord Kṛṣṇa was offered various kinds of silken garments of yellow color, and heaps of jewelry and ornaments were presented before Him for His use.

King Yudhiṣṭhira felt such ecstasy by honoring Kṛṣṇa, who was his only lovable object, that tears glided down from his eyes, and although He wanted to, he could not see Lord Kṛṣṇa very well. Lord Kṛṣṇa was thus worshiped by King Yudhiṣṭhira. At that time all the members present in that assembly stood up with folded hands and began to chant, "*Jaya! Jaya! Namaḥ! Namaḥ!*" When all joined together to offer their respectful obeisances to Kṛṣṇa, there were showers of flowers from the sky.

In that meeting, King Śiśupāla was also present. He was an avowed enemy of Kṛṣṇa for many reasons, especially because of Kṛṣṇa's having stolen Rukmiṇī from the marriage ceremony; therefore, he could not tolerate such honor to Kṛṣṇa and glorification of His qualities. Instead of being happy to hear the glories of the Lord, he became very angry. When everyone offered respect to Kṛṣṇa by standing up, Śiśupāla remained in his seat, but when he became angry at Kṛṣṇa's being honored, Śiśupāla stood up suddenly, and, raising his hand, began to speak very strongly and fearlessly against Lord Kṛṣṇa. He spoke in such a way that Lord Kṛṣṇa could hear him very distinctly.

"Ladies and gentlemen, I can appreciate now the statement of the *Vedas* that, after all, time is the predominating factor. In spite of all endeavors to the contrary, the time element executes its own plan without opposition. For example, one may try his best to live, but when the time for death comes, no one can check it. I see here that although there are many stalwart personalities present in this assembly, the influence of time is so strong that they have been misled by the statement of a boy who has foolishly spoken about Kṛṣṇa. There are many learned sages and elderly persons present, but still they have accepted the statement of a foolish boy. This means that by the influence of time, even the intelligence of such honored persons as are present in this meeting can be misdirected. I fully agree with the respectable persons present here that they are competent enough to select the personality who can be first worshiped, but I cannot agree with the statement of a boy like Sahadeva, who has spoken so highly about Kṛṣṇa and has recommended that Kṛṣṇa is fit to accept the first worship in the sacrifice. I can see that in this meeting there are many personalities who have undergone great austerities, who are highly learned and who have performed many penances. By their knowledge and direction, they can deliver many persons who are suffering from the pangs of material existence. There are great *ṛṣis* here whose knowledge has no bounds, as well as many self-realized persons and *brāhmaṇas* also, and therefore I think that any one of them could have been selected for the first worship because they are worshipable even by the great demigods, kings and emperors. I cannot understand how you could have selected this cowherd boy, Kṛṣṇa, and have left aside all these other great personalities. I think Kṛṣṇa to be no better than a crow—how can He be fit to accept the first worship in this great sacrifice?

"We cannot even ascertain as yet to which caste this Kṛṣṇa belongs or what His actual occupational duty is." Actually, Kṛṣṇa does not belong to any caste, nor does He have to perform any occupational duty. It is stated in the *Vedas* that the Supreme Lord has nothing to do as His prescribed duty. Whatever has to be done on His behalf is executed by His different energies.

Śiśupāla continued: "Kṛṣṇa does not belong to a high family. He is so independent that no one knows His principles of religious life. It appears that He is outside the jurisdiction of all religious principles. He always acts independently, not caring for the Vedic injunctions and regulative principles. Therefore He is devoid of all good qualities." Śiśupāla indirectly praised Kṛṣṇa by saying that He is not within the jurisdiction of Vedic injunction. This is true because He is the Supreme Personality of Godhead. That He has no qualities means that Kṛṣṇa has no material qualities, and because He is the Supreme Personality of Godhead, He acts independently, not caring for conventions or social or religious principles.

Siśupāla continued: "Under these circumstances, how can He be fit to accept the first worship in the sacrifice? Kṛṣṇa is so foolish that He has left Mathurā, which is inhabited by highly elevated persons following the Vedic culture, and He has taken shelter in the ocean, where there is not even talk of the *Vedas*. Instead of living openly, He has constructed a fort within the water and is living in an atmosphere where there is no discussion of Vedic knowledge. And whenever He comes out of the fort, He simply harrasses the citizens like a dacoit, thief or rogue."

Śiśupāla went crazy because of Kṛṣṇa's being elected the supreme first-worshiped person in that meeting, and he spoke so irresponsibly that it appeared that he had lost all his good fortune. Being overcast with misfortune, Śiśupāla continued to insult Kṛṣṇa further, and Lord Kṛṣṇa patiently heard him without protest. Just as a lion does not care when a flock of jackals howl, Lord Kṛṣṇa remained silent and unprovoked. Kṛṣṇa did not reply to even a single accusation made by Śiśupāla, but all the members present in the meeting, except a few who agreed with Śiśupāla, became very agitated because it is the duty of any respectable person not to tolerate blasphemy against God or His devotee. Some of them, who thought that they could not properly take action against Śiśupāla, left the assembly in protest, covering their ears with their hands in order not to hear further accusations. Thus they left the meeting condemning the action of Śiśupāla. It is the Vedic injunction that whenever there is blasphemy of the Supreme Personality of Godhead, one must immediately leave. If he does not do so, he becomes bereft of his pious activities and is degraded to the lower condition of life.

All the kings present, belonging to the Kuru dynasty, Matsya dynasty, Kekaya dynasty and Sṛñjaya dynasty, became very angry and immediately took up their swords and shields to kill Śiśupāla. Śiśupāla was so foolish that he did not become even slightly agitated, although all the kings present were ready to kill him. He did not care to think of the pros and cons of his foolish talking, and when he saw that all the kings were ready to kill him, instead of stopping, he stood to fight with them and took up his sword and shield. When Lord Kṛṣṇa saw that they were going to engage in fighting in the arena of the auspicious Rājāsūya *yajña,* He personally pacified them. Out of His causeless mercy He Himself decided to kill Śiśupāla. When Śiśupāla was abusing the kings who were about to attack him, Lord Kṛṣṇa took up His disc, which was as sharp as the blade of a razor, and immediately separated the head of Śiśupāla from his body.

When Śiśupāla was thus killed, a great roar and howl went up from the crowd of that assembly. Taking advantage of that disturbance, the few kings who were supporters of Śiśupāla quickly left the assembly out of fear of their lives. But despite all this, the fortunate Śiśupāla's spirit soul immediately merged into the body of Lord Kṛṣṇa in the presence of all members, exactly as a burning meteor falls to the surface of the globe. Śiśupāla's soul's merging into the transcendental body of Kṛṣṇa reminds us of the story of Jaya and Vijaya, who fell to the material world from the Vaikuṇṭha planets upon being cursed by the four Kumāras. For their return to the Vaikuṇṭha world, it was arranged that both Jaya and Vijaya for three consecutive births would act as deadly enemies of the Lord, and at the end of these lives they would again return to the Vaikuṇṭha world and serve the Lord as His associates.

Although Śiśupāla acted as the enemy of Kṛṣṇa, he was not for a single moment out of Kṛṣṇa consciousness. He was always absorbed in thought of Kṛṣṇa, and thus he got first the salvation of *sāyujya-mukti,* merging into the existence of the Supreme, and finally became reinstated in his original position of personal service. The *Bhagavad-gītā* corroborates the fact that if one is absorbed in the thought of the Supreme Lord at the time of death, he immediately enters the kingdom of God after quitting his material body. After the salvation of Śiśupāla, King Yudhiṣṭhira rewarded all the members present in the sacrificial assembly. He sufficiently remunerated the priests and the learned sages for their engagement in the execution of the sacrifice, and after performing all this routine work, he took his bath. This bath at the end of the sacrifice is also technical. It is called the *avabhṛtha* bath.

Lord Kṛṣṇa thus enabled the performance of the Rājasūya *yajña* arranged by King Yudhiṣṭhira to be successfully completed, and, being requested by His cousins and relatives, He remained in Hastināpura for a few months more. Although King Yudhiṣṭhira and his brothers were not willing to have Lord Kṛṣṇa leave Hastināpura, Kṛṣṇa arranged to take permission from the King to return to Dvārakā, and thus He returned home along with His queens and ministers.

The story of the fall of Jaya and Vijaya from the Vaikuṇṭha planets to the material world is described in the Seventh Canto of *Śrīmad-Bhāgavatam*. The killing of Śiśupāla has a direct link with that narration of Jaya and Vijaya, but the most important instruction that we get from this incident is that the Supreme Personality of Godhead, being absolute, can give salvation to everyone, whether one acts as His enemy or as His friend. It is therefore a misconception that the Lord acts with someone in the relationship of a friend and with someone else in the relationship of an enemy. His being an enemy or friend is always on the absolute platform. There is no material distinction.

After King Yudhiṣṭhira took his bath after the sacrifice and stood in the midst of all the learned sages and *brāhmaṇas*, he seemed exactly like the King of heaven and thus looked very beautiful. King Yudhiṣṭhira sufficiently rewarded all the demigods who participated in the *yajña*, and being greatly satisfied, all of them left praising the King's activities and glorifying Lord Kṛṣṇa.

When Śukadeva Gosvāmī was narrating these incidents of Kṛṣṇa's killing Śiśupāla and describing the successful execution of the Rājasūya *yajña* by Mahārāja Yudhiṣṭhira, he pointed out also that after the successful termination of the *yajña* there was only one person who was not happy. He was Duryodhana. Duryodhana by nature was very envious because of his sinful life, and he appeared in the dynasty of the Kurus as a chronic disease personified in order to destroy the whole family.

Śukadeva Gosvāmī assured Mahārāja Parīkṣit that the pastimes of Lord Kṛṣṇa—the killing of Śiśupāla and Jarāsandha and the releasing of the imprisoned kings—are all transcendental vibrations, and anyone who hears these narrations from the authorized persons will be immediately freed from all the reactions of the sinful activities of his life.

Thus ends the Bhaktivedanta purport of the Seventy-third Chapter of Kṛṣṇa, *"The Deliverance of Śiśupāla."*

74 / Why Duryodhana Felt Insulted at the End of the Rājasūya Sacrifice

King Yudhiṣṭhira was known as *ajātaśatru,* or a person who has no enemy. Therefore, when all men, all demigods, all kings, sages and saints saw the successful termination of the Rājasūya *yajña* performed by King Yudhiṣṭhira, they became very happy. That Duryodhana alone was not happy was astonishing to Mahārāja Parīkṣit, and therefore he requested Śukadeva Gosvāmī to explain this.

Śukadeva Gosvāmī said, "My dear King Parīkṣit, your grandfather, King Yudhiṣṭhira, was a great soul. His congenial disposition attracted everyone as his friend, and therefore he was known as *ajātaśatru,* one who never created an enemy. He engaged all the members of the Kuru dynasty in taking charge of different departments for the management of the Rājasūya sacrifice. For example, Bhīmasena was put in charge of the kitchen department, Duryodhana in charge of the treasury department, Sahadeva in charge of the reception department, Nakula in charge of the store department, and Arjuna was engaged in looking after the comforts of the elderly persons. The most astonishing feature was that Kṛṣṇa, the Supreme Personality of Godhead, took charge of washing the feet of all the incoming guests. The Queen, the goddess of fortune Draupadī, was in charge of administering the distribution of food, and because Karṇa was famous for giving charity, he was put in charge of the charity department. In this way Sātyaki, Vikarṇa, Hārdikya, Vidura, Bhūriśravā, and Santardana, the son of Bāhlīka, were all engaged in different departments for managing the affairs of the Rājasūya sacrifice. They were all so bound in loving affection for King Yudhiṣṭhira that they simply wanted to please him.

After Śiśupāla had died by the mercy of Lord Kṛṣṇa and had become merged in the spiritual existence, and after the end of the Rājasūya *yajña,* when all friends, guests and well-wishers had been sufficiently honored and rewarded, King Yudhiṣṭhira went to bathe in the Ganges. The city of

Hastināpura is today standing on the bank of the Yamunā, and the statement of *Śrīmad-Bhāgavatam* that King Yudhiṣṭhira went to bathe in the Ganges indicates, therefore, that during the time of the Pāṇḍavas, the River Yamunā was also known as the Ganges. While the King was taking the *avabhṛtha* bath, different musical instruments, such as *mṛdaṅgas*, conchshells, drums, kettledrums and bugles, vibrated. In addition, the ankle bells of the dancing girls jingled. Many groups of professional singers played *vīṇās*, flutes, gongs and cymbals, and thus a tumultuous sound vibrated in the sky. The princely guests from many kingdoms, like Sṛñjaya, Kāmboja, Kuru, Kekaya and Kośala, were present with their different flags and gorgeously decorated elephants, chariots, horses and soldiers. All were passing in a procession, and King Yudhiṣṭhira was in the forefront. The executive members, such as the priests, religious ministers and *brāhmaṇas*, were performing a sacrifice, and all were loudly chanting the Vedic hymns. The demigods, the inhabitants of the Pitṛloka and Gandharvaloka, as well as many sages, showered flowers from the sky. The men and women of Hastināpura, Indraprastha, their bodies smeared with scents and floral oils, were nicely dressed in colorful garments and decorated with garlands, jewels and ornaments. They were all enjoying the ceremony, and they threw on each other liquid substances like water, oil, milk, butter and yogurt. Some even smeared these on each other's bodies. In this way, they were enjoying the occasion. The professional prostitutes were also engaged by jubilantly smearing these liquid substances on the bodies of the men, and the men reciprocated in the same way. All the liquid substances had been mixed with turmeric and saffron, and their color was a lustrous yellow.

In order to observe the great ceremony, many wives of the demigods had come in different airplanes, and they were visible in the sky. Similarly, the queens of the royal family arrived gorgeously decorated and surrounded by bodyguards on the surface on different palaquins. During this time, Lord Kṛṣṇa, the maternal cousin of the Pāṇḍavas, and His special friend Arjuna, were both throwing the liquid substances on the bodies of the queens. The queens became bashful, but at the same time their beautiful smiling brightened their faces. Because of the liquid substances thrown on their bodies, the saris covering them became completely wet. The different parts of their beautiful bodies, particularly their breasts and their waists, became partially visible because of the wet cloth. The queens also brought in buckets of liquid substances and sprinkled them on the bodies of their brothers-in-law. As they engaged in such jubilant activities, their hair fell loose, and the flowers decorating their bodies began to fall. When Lord

Kṛṣṇa, Arjuna and the queens were thus engaged in these jubilant activities, persons who were not clean in heart became agitated by lustful desires. In other words, such behavior between pure males and females is enjoyable, but persons who are materially contaminated become lustful.

King Yudhiṣṭhira, in a gorgeous chariot yoked by excellent horses, was present with his queens, including Draupadī and others. The festivities of the sacrifice were so beautiful that it appeared as if Rājasūya was standing there in person with the functions of the sacrifice.

Following the Rājasūya sacrifice, there was the Vedic ritualistic duty known as *patnīsaṁyāja.* This sacrifice was performed along with one's wife, and it was also duly performed by the priests of King Yudhiṣṭhira. When Queen Draupadī and King Yudhiṣṭhira were taking their *avabhṛtha* bath, the citizens of Hastināpura as well as the demigods began to beat on drums and blow trumpets out of feelings of happiness, and there was a shower of flowers from the sky. When the King and the Queen finished their bath in the Ganges, all the other citizens, consisting of all the *varṇas* or castes—the *brāhmaṇas,* the *kṣatriyas,* the *vaiśyas,* and the *śūdras*—took their baths in the Ganges. Bathing in the Ganges is recommended in the Vedic literatures because by such bathing one becomes freed from all sinful reactions. This is still current in India, especially at particularly auspicious moments. At such times, millions of people bathe in the Ganges.

After taking his bath, King Yudhiṣṭhira dressed in a new silken cloth and wrapper and decorated himself with valuable jewelry. The King not only dressed himself and decorated himself, but he also gave clothing and ornaments to all the priests and to the others who had participated in the *yajñas.* In this way, they were all worshiped by King Yudhiṣṭhira. He constantly worshiped his friends, his family members, his relatives, his well-wishers and everyone present, and because he was a great devotee of Lord Nārāyaṇa, or because he was a Vaiṣṇava, he therefore knew how to treat everyone well. The Māyāvadi philosophers' endeavor to see everyone as God is an artificial way towards oneness, but a Vaiṣṇava or a devotee of Lord Nārāyaṇa sees every living entity as part and parcel of the Supreme Lord. Therefore, a Vaiṣṇava's treatment of other living entities is on the absolute platform. Since one cannot treat one part of his body differently from another part because they all belong to the same body, so a Vaiṣṇava does not see a human being as distinct from an animal because in both of them he sees the soul and the Supersoul seated simultaneously.

When everyone was refreshed after bathing and was dressed in silken clothing with jeweled earrings, flower garlands, turbans, long wrappers and pearl necklaces, they looked, altogether, like the demigods from heaven.

This was especially true of the women, who were very nicely dressed. Each wore a golden belt around the waist. They were all smiling. Spots of *tilaka* and curling hair were scattered here and there. This combination was very attractive.

Persons who had participated in the Rājasūya sacrifice—including the most cultured priests, the *brāhmaṇas* who had assisted in the performance of the sacrifice, the citizens of all *varṇas,* kings, demigods, sages, saints and citizens of the Pitṛloka—were all very much satisfied by the dealings of King Yudhiṣṭhira, and at the end they happily departed for their residences. While returning to their homes, they talked of the dealings of King Yudhiṣṭhira, and even after continuous talk of his greatness they were not satiated, just as one may drink nectar over and over again and never be satisfied. After the departure of all others, Mahārāja Yudhiṣṭhira restrained the inner circle of his friends, including Lord Kṛṣṇa, by not allowing them to leave. Lord Kṛṣṇa could not refuse the request of the King. He therefore sent back all the heroes of the Yadu dynasty, like Sāmba and others. All of them returned to Dvārakā, and Lord Kṛṣṇa personally remained in order to give pleasure to the King.

In the material world, everyone has a particular type of desire to be fulfilled, but one is never able to fulfill his desires to his full satisfaction. But King Yudhiṣṭhira, because of his unflinching devotion to Kṛṣṇa, could fulfill all his desires successfully by the performance of the Rājasūya *yajña.* From the description of the execution of the Rājasūya *yajña,* it appears that such a function is a great ocean of opulent desires. It is not possible for an ordinary man to cross over such an ocean; nevertheless, by the grace of Lord Kṛṣṇa, King Yudhiṣṭhira was able to cross over it very easily, and thus he became freed from all anxieties.

When Duryodhana saw that Mahārāja Yudhiṣṭhira had become very famous after performance of the Rājasūya *yajña* and was fully satisfied in every respect, he began to burn with the fire of envy because his mind was always poisonous. For one thing, he envied the imperial palace which had been constructed by the demon Maya for the Pāṇḍavas. The palace was excellent in its puzzling artistic workmanship and was befitting the position of great princes, kings or leaders of the demons. In that great palace, the Pāṇḍavas were living with their family members, and Queen Draupadī was serving her husbands very peacefully. And because in those days Lord Kṛṣṇa was also there, the palace was also decorated by His thousands of queens. When the queens, with their heavy breasts and thin waists, moved within the palace, and their ankle bells rang very melodiously with their movement, the whole palace appeared to be more opulent than the heavenly kingdoms. Because a portion of their breasts was sprinkled with saffron powder, the pearl necklaces on their breast appeared to be reddish. With their full earrings and flowing hair, the queens appeared very beautiful. After looking at such beauties in the palace of King Yudhiṣṭhira, Duryodhana became envious. He became especially envious and lustful upon seeing the beauty of Draupadī because he had cherished a special attraction for her from the very beginning of her marriage with the Pāṇḍavas. In the marriage selection assembly of Draupadī, Duryodhana had also been present, and with other princes he had been very much captivated by the beauty of Draupadī, but had failed to achieve her.

Once upon a time, King Yudhiṣṭhira was sitting on the golden throne in the palace constructed by the demon Maya. His four brothers and other relatives, as well as his great well-wisher, the Supreme Personality of Godhead, Kṛṣṇa, were present and the material opulence of King Yudhiṣṭhira seemed no less than that of Lord Brahmā. When he was sitting on the throne surrounded by his friends, and the reciters were offering prayers to him in the form of nice songs, Duryodhana, with his younger brother, came to the palace. Duryodhana was decorated with a helmet, and he carried a sword in his hand. He was always in an envious and angry mood, and therefore, on a slight provocation, he spoke sharply with the doorkeepers and became angry. He was irritated because he failed to distinguish between water and land. By the craftmanship of the demon Maya, the palace was so decorated in different places that one who did not know the tricks would consider water to be land and land to be water. Duryodhana was also illusioned by this craftmanship, and when he was crossing water thinking it to be land, he fell down. When Duryodhana, out of his foolishness, had thus fallen, the queens enjoyed the incident by laughing. King Yudhiṣṭhira, could understand the feelings of Duryodhana, and he tried to restrain the queens from laughing, but Lord Kṛṣṇa indicated that King Yudhiṣṭhira should not restrain them from enjoying the incident. Kṛṣṇa desired that Duryodhana might be fooled in that way and that all of them might enjoy his foolish behavior. When everyone laughed, Duryodhana felt very insulted, and his hair stood up in anger. Being thus insulted, he immediately left the palace, bowing his head. He was silent and did not protest. When Duryodhana left in such an angry mood, everyone regretted the incident, and King Yudhiṣṭhira also became very sorry. But despite all occurrences, Kṛṣṇa was silent. He did not say anything against or in favor of the incident. It appeared that Duryodhana had been put into illusion by the supreme will of Lord Kṛṣṇa, and this was the beginning of the enmity between the two sects of the Kuru dynasty. It appeared that it was a part of Kṛṣṇa's plan in His mission to decrease the burden of the world.

King Parīkṣit had inquired from Śukadeva Gosvāmī as to why Duryodhana was not satisfied after the termination of the great Rājasūya sacrifice, and thus it was explained by Śukadeva Gosvāmī.

Thus ends the Bhaktivedanta purport of the Seventy-fourth Chapter of Kṛṣṇa, *"Why Duryodhana Felt Insulted at the End of the Rājasūya Sacrifice."*

75 / The Battle Between Śālva and the Members of the Yadu Dynasty

While Śukadeva Gosvāmī was narrating various activities of Lord Kṛṣṇa in playing the role of an ordinary human being, he also narrated the history of the battle between the dynasty of Yadu and a demon of the name Śālva, who had managed to possess a wonderful airship named Saubha. King Śālva was a great friend of Śiśupāla's. When Śiśupala went to marry Rukmiṇī, Śālva was one of the members of the bridegroom's party. When there was a fight between the soldiers of the Yadu dynasty and the kings of the opposite side, Śālva was defeated by the soldiers of the Yadu dynasty. But, despite his defeat, he made a promise before all the kings that he would in the future rid the whole world of all the members of the Yadu dynasty. Since his defeat in the fight during the marriage of Rukmiṇī, he had maintained within himself an unforgettable envy of Lord Kṛṣṇa, and he was, in fact, a fool, because he had promised to kill Kṛṣṇa.

Usually such foolish demons take shelter of a demigod like Lord Śiva to execute their ulterior plans, and so Śālva, in order to get strength, took shelter of the lotus feet of Lord Śiva. He underwent a severe type of austerity during which he would eat no more than a handful of ashes daily. Lord Śiva, the husband of Pārvatī, is generally very merciful, and he becomes very quickly satisfied if someone undertakes severe austerities in order to please him. So after continued austerities by Śālva for one year, Lord Śiva became pleased with him and asked him to beg for the fulfillment of his desire.

Śālva begged from Lord Śiva the gift of an airplane which would be so strong that it could not be destroyed by any demigod, demon, human being, Gandharva, Nāga, or even by any Rākṣasa. Moreover, he desired that the airplane be able to fly anywhere and everywhere he would like to pilot it, and be specifically very dangerous and fearful to the dynasty of the Yadus. Lord Śiva immediately agreed to give him the benediction, and

Śālva took the help of the demon Maya to manufacture this iron airplane, which was so strong and formidable that no one could crash it. It was a very big machine, almost like a big city, and it could fly so high and at such a great speed that it was almost impossible to see where it was, and so there was no question of attacking it. Although it might be dark outside, the pilot could fly it anywhere and everywhere. Having acquired such a wonderful airplane, Śālva flew it to the city of Dvārakā, because his main purpose in obtaining the airplane was to attack the city of the Yadus, toward whom he maintained a continual feeling of animosity.

Śālva thus not only attacked the city of Dvārakā from the sky, but he also surrounded the city by a large number of infantry. The soldiers on the surface began to attack the beautiful spots of the city.They began to destroy the baths, the city gates, the palaces and the skyscraper houses, the high walls around the city and the beautiful spots where people would gather for recreation. While the soldiers were attacking on the surface, the airplane began to drop big slabs of stone, tree trunks, thunderbolts, poisonous snakes and many other dangerous things. Śālva also managed to create such a strong whirlwind within the city that all of Dvārakā became dark because of the dust that covered the sky. The airplane occupied by Śālva put the entire city of Dvārakā into distress equal to that caused on the earth long, long ago by the disturbing activities of Tripurāsura. The inhabitants of Dvārakā Purī became so harrassed that they were not in a peaceful condition for even a moment.

The great heroes of Dvārakā City, headed by commanders such as Pradyumna, counterattacked the soldiers and the airplane of Śālva. When he saw the extreme distress of the citizens, Pradyumna immediately arranged his soldiers and personally got upon a chariot, encouraging the citizens by assuring safety. Following his command, many warriors like Sātyaki, Cārudeṣṇa and Sāmba, all young brothers of Pradyumna, as well as Akrūra, Kṛtavarmā, Bhānuvinda, Gada, Śuka and Sāraṇa—all came out of the city to fight with Śālva. All of them were great fighters; each one could fight with thousands of men. All were fully equipped with necessary weapons and assisted by hundreds and thousands of charioteers, elephants, horses and infantry soldiers. Fierce fighting began between the two parties, exactly as was formerly carried on between the demigods and the demons. The fighting was very severe, and whoever observed the fierce nature of the fight felt his hairs stand on end.

Pradyumna immediately counteracted the mystic demonstration occasioned by the airplane of Śālva, the King of Saubha. By the mystic power of the airplane, Śālva had created a darkness as dense as night, but Pradyumna all of a sudden appeared like the rising sun. As with the rising of the sun the darkness of night is immediately dissipated, so with the appearance of Pradyumna the power exhibited by Śālva became null and void. Each and every one of Pradyumna's arrows had a golden feather at the end, and the shaft was fitted with a sharp iron edge. By releasing twenty-five such arrows, Pradyumna severely injured Śālva's commander-in-chief. He then released another one hundred arrows toward the body of Śālva. After this, he pierced each and every soldier by releasing one arrow, and he killed the chariot drivers by firing ten arrows at each one of them. The carriers like the horses and elephants were killed by the release of three arrows directed toward each one of them. When everyone present on the battlefield saw this wonderful feat of Pradyumna, the great fighters on both the sides began to praise his acts of chivalry.

But still the airplane occupied by Śālva was very mysterious. It was so extraordinary that sometimes there would appear to be many airplanes in the sky, and sometimes it would be seen that there was none. Sometimes it was visible, and sometimes it was not visible, and the warriors of the Yadu dynasty became puzzled about the whereabouts of the peculiar airplane. Sometimes they would see the airplane on the ground, and sometimes they would see it flying in the sky. Sometimes they would see the airplane resting on the peak of a hill, and sometimes it was seen floating on the water. The wonderful airplane was flying in the sky like a firefly in the wind—it was not steady even for a moment. But despite the mysterious maneuvering of the airplane, the commanders and the soldiers of the Yadu dynasty would immediately rush toward Śālva wherever he was present with his airplane and soldiers. The arrows released by the dynasty of the Yadus were as brilliant as the sun and as dangerous as the tongues of serpents. All the soldiers fighting on behalf of Śālva became soon distressed by the incessant release of arrows upon them by the heroes of the Yadu dynasty, and Śālva himself became unconscious from the attack of these arrows.

The soldiers and the fighters fighting on behalf of Śālva were also very strong, and the release of their arrows also harassed the heroes of the Yadu dynasty. But still the Yadus were so strong and determined that they did not move from their strategic positions. The heroes of the Yadu dynasty were determined to either die in the battlefield or gain victory. They were confident of the fact that if they would die in the fighting they would attain a heavenly planet, and if they would come out victorious they would enjoy the world. The name of Śālva's commander-in-chief was Dyumān. He was very powerful, and although bitten by twenty-five of Pradyumna's arrows, he suddenly attacked Pradyumna with his fierce club and struck him so strongly that Pradyumna became unconscious. Immediately there was a roaring, "Now he is dead! Now he is dead!" The force of the club on the chest of Pradyumna was very severe, enough to tear asunder the chest of an ordinary man.

Pradyumna's chariot was being driven by the son of Dāruka. According to Vedic military principles, the chariot driver and the hero on the chariot have to cooperate during the fighting. As such, it was the duty of the chariot driver to take care of the hero on the chariot during the dangerous and precarious fighting on the battlefield. Thus Dāruka removed the body of Pradyumna from the battlefield. Two hours later, in a quiet place, Pradyumna regained his consciousness, and when he saw that he was in a place other than the battlefield he addressed the charioteer and condemned him:

"Oh, you have done the most abominable act! Why have you moved me from the battlefield? My dear charioteer, I have never heard that anyone in our family was ever removed from the battlefield. None of them left the battlefield while fighting. By this removal you have overburdened me with a great defamation. It will be said that I left the battlefield while fighting was going on. My dear charioteer, I must accuse you—you are a coward and emasculator! Tell me, how can I go before my uncle Balarāma and before my father Kṛṣṇa, and what shall I say before them? Everyone will talk about me and say that I fled from the fighting place, and if they inquire from me about this, what will be my reply? My sisters-in-law will play jokes upon me with sarcastic words: 'My dear hero, how have you become such a coward? How have you become a eunuch? How have you become so low in the eyes of the fighters who opposed you?' I think, my dear charioteer, that you have committed a great offense by removing me from the battlefield."

The charioteer of Pradyumna replied, "My dear sir, I wish a long life for you. I think I did not do anything wrong, as it is the duty of the charioteer to help the fighter in the chariot when he is in a precarious condition. My dear sir, you are completely competent in the battlefield activities. It is the mutual duty of the charioteer and the warrior to give protection to each other in a precarious condition. I was completely aware of the regulative principles of fighting, and I did my duty. The enemy all of a sudden struck you with his club so severely that you lost consciousness. You were in a dangerous position, surrounded by your enemies. Therefore I was obliged to act as I did."

Thus ends the Bhaktivedanta purport of the Seventy-fifth Chapter of Kṛṣṇa, *"The Battle Between Śālva and Members of the Yadu Dynasty."*

76 / The Deliverance of Śālva

After talking with his charioteer, the son of Dāruka, Pradyumna could understand the real circumstances, and therefore he refreshed himself by washing his mouth and hands. Arming himself properly with bows and arrows, he asked his charioteer to take him near the place where Śālva's commander-in-chief was standing. During the short absence of Pradyumna from the battlefield, Dyumān, Śālva's commander-in-chief, had been taking over the position of the soldiers of the Yadu dynasty. By appearing in the battlefield, Pradyumna immediately stopped him and struck him with eight arrows. With four arrows he killed his four horses, with one arrow he killed his chariot driver and with another arrow he cut his bow in two; with another arrow, he cut his flag into pieces, and with another he severed his head from his body.

On the other fronts, heroes like Gada, Sātyaki and Sāmba were engaged in killing the soldiers of Śālva. The soldiers who were staying with Śālva in the airplane were also killed in the fighting, and they fell into the ocean. Each party began to strike the opposite party very severely. The battle was fierce and dangerous and continued for twenty-seven days without stop. While the fight was going on in the city of Dvārakā, Kṛṣṇa was staying at Indraprastha along with the Pāṇḍavas and King Yudhiṣṭhira. This fighting with Śālva took place after the Rājasūya *yajña* had been performed by King Yudhiṣṭhira and after the killing of Śiśupāla. When Lord Kṛṣṇa understood that there was great danger in the city of Dvārakā, He took permission from the elderly members of the Pāṇḍava family, especially from his aunt Kuntīdevī, and started immediately for Dvārakā.

Lord Kṛṣṇa began to think that while He was arriving in Hastināpura with Balarāma after the killing of Śiśupāla, Śiśupāla's men must have attacked Dvārakā. On reaching Dvārakā, Lord Kṛṣṇa saw that the whole city was greatly endangered. He placed Balarāmajī in a strategic position for the protection of the city, and He Himself asked His charioteer Dāruka to prepare to start. He said, "Dāruka, please immediately take Me to where Śālva is staying. You may know that this Śālva is a very powerful, mysterious man. Don't fear him in the least." As soon as he got his orders from Lord Kṛṣṇa, Dāruka had Him seated on the chariot and drove very quickly toward Śālva.

The chariot of Lord Kṛṣṇa was marked with the flag bearing the insignia of Garuḍa, and as soon as the soldiers and warriors of the Yadu dynasty saw the flag, they could understand that Lord Kṛṣṇa was on the battlefield. By this time, almost all the soldiers of Śālva had been killed, but when Śālva saw that Kṛṣṇa had come to the battlefield, he released a great, powerful weapon which flew through the sky with a roaring sound like a great meteor. It was so bright that the whole sky lit up by its presence. But as soon as Lord Kṛṣṇa appeared, He tore the great weapon into hundreds and thousands of pieces by releasing His own arrow.

Lord Kṛṣṇa struck Śālva with sixteen arrows, and with showers of arrows He overpowered the airplane, just as the sun in a clear sky overpowers the whole sky by an unlimited number of molecules of sunshine. Śālva struck a severe blow to Kṛṣṇa's left side, where the Lord was carrying His bow, Śārṅga, and as a result the Śārṅga bow fell from Lord Kṛṣṇa's hand. This dropping of the bow was indeed wonderful. Great personalities and demigods who were observing the fighting between Śālva and Kṛṣṇa became most perturbed by this, and they began to exclaim, "Alas! Alas!"

Śālva thought that he had become victorious, and with a roaring sound began to address Lord Kṛṣṇa as follows: "You rascal, Kṛṣṇa! You kidnapped Rukmiṇī forcibly, even in our presence. You baffled my friend Śiśupāla and married Rukmiṇī Yourself. And in the great assembly at King Yudhiṣṭhira's Rājasūya *yajña,* while my friend Śiśupāla was a little absent-minded, You took an opportunity to kill him. Everyone thinks that You are a great fighter and that no one can conquer You. So now You'll have to prove Your strength. I think that if You stand before me any longer, with my sharpened arrows I shall send You to a place wherefrom You will never return."

To this Lord Kṛṣṇa replied, "Foolish Śālva, you are talking nonsensically. You do not know that the moment of death is already upon your head. Those who are actually heroes do not talk much. They prove their prowess by practical exhibition of chivalrous activities." After saying this, Lord Kṛṣṇa, in great anger, struck Śālva on the collarbone with His club so severely that he began to bleed internally and tremble as if he were going to collapse from severe cold. Before Kṛṣṇa was able to strike him again, however, Śālva became invisible by his mystic power.

Within a few moments, a mysterious unknown man came before Lord Kṛṣṇa. Crying loudly, he bowed down at the Lord's lotus feet and said to Him, "Since You are the most beloved son of Your father Vasudeva, Your mother Devakī has sent me to inform You of the unfortunate news that Your father has been arrested by Śālva and taken away by force. He took him just as a butcher mercilessly takes away an animal." When Lord Kṛṣṇa heard this unfortunate news from the unknown man, He at first became most perturbed, just like an ordinary human being. His face showed signs of grief, and He began to cry in a pitious tone, "How could that happen? My brother Lord Balarāma is there, and it is impossible for anyone to conquer Balarāmajī. He is in charge of Dvārakā City, and I know He is always alert. How could Śālva possibly enter the city and arrest My father in that way? Whatever he may be, Śālva's power is limited, so how could it be possible that he has conquered the strength of Balarāmajī and taken away My father, arresting him as described by this man? Alas! Destiny is, after all, very powerful."

While Śrī Kṛṣṇa was thinking like this, Śālva brought before Him in custody a man exactly resembling Vasudeva, His father. These were all creations of the mystic power of Śālva.

Śālva began to address Kṛṣṇa, "You rascal, Kṛṣṇa! Look. This is Your father who has begotten You and by whose mercy You are still living. Now just see how I kill Your father. If You have any strength, try to save him." The mystic juggler, Śālva, speaking in this way before Lord Kṛṣṇa, immediately cut off the head of the false Vasudeva. Without hesitation he took away the dead body and got into his airplane. Lord Kṛṣṇa is the self-sufficient Supreme Personality of Godhead, yet because He was playing the role of a human being, He became very depressed for a moment, as if He had actually lost His father. But at the next moment He could understand that the arrest and killing of His father were demonstrations of the mystic powers which Śālva had learned from the demon Maya. Coming to His right consciousness, He could see that there was no messenger and no head of His father, but that only Śālva had left in his airplane, which was flying in the sky. He then began to think of slaying Śālva.

Kṛṣṇa's reaction is a controversial point among great authorities and saintly persons. How could Kṛṣṇa, the Supreme Personality of Godhead, the reservoir of all power and knowledge, be bewildered in such a way? Lamentation, aggrievement and bewilderment are characteristics of persons who are conditioned souls, but how can such things affect the person of the Supreme, who is full of knowledge, power and all opulence? Actually, it is not at all possible that Lord Kṛṣṇa was misled by the mystic jugglery of Śālva. He was displaying His pastime in playing the role of a human being. Great saintly persons and sages who are engaged in the devotional service of the lotus feet of Lord Kṛṣṇa and who have thus achieved the greatest perfection of self-realization have transcended the bewilderments of the bodily concept of life. Lord Kṛṣṇa is the ultimate goal of life for such saintly persons. How then could Kṛṣṇa have been bewildered by the mystic jugglery of Śālva? The conclusion is that Lord Kṛṣṇa's bewilderment was another opulence of His supreme personality.

When Śālva thought that Kṛṣṇa had been bewildered by his mystic representations, he became encouraged and began to attack the Lord with greater strength and energy by showering volumes of arrows upon Him. But the enthusiasm of Śālva can be compared to the speedy march of flies into a fire. Lord Kṛṣṇa, by hurling His arrows with unfathomable strength, injured Śālva, whose armor, bow and jewelled helmet all scattered into pieces. With a crashing blow from Kṛṣṇa's club, Śālva's wonderful airplane burst into pieces and fell into the sea. Śālva was very careful, and instead of crashing with the airplane, he managed to jump onto the land. He again rushed towards Lord Kṛṣṇa. When Śālva ran swiftly to attack Kṛṣṇa with His club, Lord Kṛṣṇa cut off his hand, which fell to the ground with the club. Finally deciding to kill him, the Lord took up His wonderful disc, which was shining like the brilliant sun at the time of the dissolution of the material creation. When Lord Śrī Kṛṣṇa stood up with His disc to kill Śālva, He appeared just like the red sun rising over a mountain. Lord Kṛṣṇa then cut off his head, and the head, with its earrings and helmet, fell on the ground. Śālva was thus killed in the same way as Vṛtrāsura was killed by Indra, the King of heaven.

When Śālva was killed, all his soldiers and followers began to cry, "Alas! Alas!" While Śālva's men were thus crying, the demigods from the heavenly planets showered flowers on Kṛṣṇa and announced the victory by beating on drums and blowing bugles. At this very moment, other friends of Śiśupāla, such as Dantavakra, appeared on the scene to fight with Kṛṣṇa in order to avenge the death of Śiśupāla. When Dantavakra appeared before Lord Kṛṣṇa, he was extremely angry.

Thus ends the Bhaktivedanta purport of the Seventy-sixth Chapter of Kṛṣṇa, *"The Deliverance of Śālva."*

77 / The Killing of Dantavakra, Vidūratha and Romaharṣaṇa

After the demise of Śiśupāla, Śālva and Pauṇḍra, another foolish demoniac king of the name Dantavakra wanted to kill Kṛṣṇa in order to avenge the death of his friend Śālva. He became so agitated that he personally appeared on the battlefield without the proper arms and ammunition and without even a chariot. His only weapon was his great anger, which was red-hot. He carried only a club in his hand, but he was so powerful that when he moved, everyone felt the earth tremble. When Lord Kṛṣṇa saw him approaching in a very heroic mood, He immediately got down from His chariot, for it was a rule of military etiquette that fighting should take place only between equals. Knowing that Dantavakra was alone and armed with only a club, Lord Kṛṣṇa responded similarly and prepared Himself by taking His club in His hand. When Kṛṣṇa appeared before him, Dantavakra's heroic march was immediately stopped just as the great, furious waves of the ocean are stopped by the beach.

At that time, Dantavakra, who was the King of Karūṣa, stood up firmly with his club and spoke to Lord Kṛṣṇa as follows: "It is a great pleasure and fortunate opportunity, Kṛṣṇa, that we are facing each other eye to eye. My dear Kṛṣṇa, after all, You are my eternal cousin, and I should not kill You in this way, but unfortunately You have commited a great mistake by killing my friend Śālva. Moreover, You are not satisfied by killing my friend, but I know that You want to kill me also. Because of Your determination, I must kill You by tearing You into pieces with my club. Kṛṣṇa, although You are my relative, You are foolish. You are our greatest enemy, so I must kill You today just as a person removes a boil on his body by a surgical operation. I am always very much obliged to my friends, and I therefore consider myself indebted to my dear friend Śālva. I can only liquidate my indebtedness to him by killing You."

As the caretaker of an elephant tries to control the animal by striking it with his trident, so Dantavakra tried to control Kṛṣṇa simply by speaking strong words. After finishing his vituperation, he struck Kṛṣṇa on the head with his club and made a roaring sound like a lion. Although struck strongly by the club of Dantavakra, Kṛṣṇa did not move even an inch, nor did He feel any pain. Taking His Kaumodakī club and moving very skillfully, Kṛṣṇa struck the chest of Dantavakra so fiercely that the heart of Dantavakra split in twain. As a result, Dantavakra began to vomit blood, his hairs became scattered, and he fell to the ground, spreading his hands and legs. Within only a few minutes all that remained of Dantavakra was a dead body on the ground. After the death of Dantavakra, just as at the time of Śiśupāla's death, in the presence of all persons standing there, a small particle of spiritual effulgence came out of the demon's body and very wonderfully merged into the body of Lord Kṛṣṇa.

Dantavakra had a brother named Vidūratha who became overwhelmed with grief at the death of Dantavakra. Out of grief and anger, Vidūratha was breathing very heavily, and just to avenge the death of his brother he also appeared before Lord Kṛṣṇa with a sword and a shield in his hands. He wanted to kill Kṛṣṇa immediately. When Lord Kṛṣṇa understood that Vidūratha was looking for the opportunity to strike l im with his sword, He employed His Sudarśana cakra, His disc, which was as sharp as a razor, and without delay he cut off the head of Vidūratha, with its helmet and earrings.

In this way, after killing Śālva and destroying his wonderful airplane and then killing Dantavakra and Vidūratha, Lord Kṛṣṇa at last entered His city, Dvārakā. It would not have been possible for anyone but Kṛṣṇa to kill these great heroes, and therefore all the demigods from heaven and the human beings on the surface of the globe were glorifying Him. Great sages and ascetics, the denizens of the Siddha and Gandharva planets, the denizens known as Vidyādharas, Vāsuki and the Mahānāgas, the beautiful angels, the inhabitants of Pitṛloka, the Yakṣas, the Kinnaras and the Cāraṇas all began to shower flowers upon Him and sing the songs of His victory in great jubilation. Decorating the entire city very festively, the citizens of Dvārakā held a great celebration, and when Lord Kṛṣṇa passed through the city all the members of the Vṛṣṇi dynasty and the heroes of the Yadu dynasty followed Him with great respect. These are some of the transcendental pastimes of Lord Kṛṣṇa, who is the master of all mystic power and the Lord of all cosmic manifestations. Those who are fools, who are like animals, sometimes think that Kṛṣṇa is defeated, but factually He is the Supreme Personality of Godhead, and no one can defeat Him. He always remains victorious over everyone. He is the only one God, and all others are His subservient order carriers.

Once upon a time, Lord Balarāma heard that there was an arrangement being made for a fight between the two rival parties in the Kuru dynasty, one headed by Duryodhana and the other by the Pāṇḍavas. He did not like the idea that He was to be only a mediator to stop the fighting. Finding it unbearable not to take an active part on behalf of either of the parties, He left Dvārakā on the plea of visiting various holy places of pilgrimage. He first of all visited the place of pilgrimage known as Prabhāsakṣetra. He took His bath there, and He pacified the local *brāhmaṇas* and offered oblations to the demigods, *pitās,* great sages and people in general, in accordance with Vedic ritualistic ceremonies. That is the Vedic method of visiting holy places. After this, accompanied by some respectable *brāhmaṇas,* He decided to visit different places on the bank of the River Sarasvatī. He gradually visited such places as Pṛthūdaka, Bindusara, Tritakūpa, Sudarśanatīrtha, Viśālatīrtha, Brahmatīrtha and Cakratīrtha. Besides these, He also visited all the holy places on the bank of Sarasvatī River running toward the east. After this He visited all the principal holy places on the bank of the Yamunā and on the bank of the Ganges. Thus He gradually came to the holy place known as Naimiṣāraṇya.

This holy place, Naimiṣāraṇya, is still existing in India, and in ancient times it was especially used for the meetings of great sages and saintly persons with the aim of understanding spiritual life and self-realization. When Lord Balarāma visited that place there was a great sacrifice being performed by a great assembly of transcendentalists. Such meetings were planned to last thousands of years. When Lord Balarāma arrived, all the participants of the meeting–great sages, ascetics, *brāhmaṇas* and learned scholars–immediately arose from their seats and welcomed Him with great honor and respect. Some offered Him respectful obeisances, and those who were elderly great sages and *brāhmaṇas* offered Him blessings by standing up. After this formality, Lord Balarāma was offered a suitable seat, and everyone present worshiped Him. Everyone in the assembly stood up in the presence of Balarāma because they knew Him to be the Supreme Personality of Godhead. Education or learning means to understand the Supreme Personality of Godhead; therefore, although Lord Balarāma appeared on the earth as a *kṣatriya,* all the *brāhmaṇas* and sages stood up because they knew who Lord Balarāma was.

Unfortunately, after being worshiped and seated at His place, Lord Balarāma saw Romaharṣaṇa, the disciple of Vyāsadeva (the literary incarnation of Godhead), still sitting on the Vyāsāsana. He had neither gotten up from his seat nor offered Him respects. Because he was seated on the Vyāsāsana, he foolishly thought himself greater than the Lord; therefore he did not get down from his seat or bow down before the Lord. Lord

Balarāma then considered the history of Romaharṣaṇa: he was born in a *sūta* family or a mixed family, born of a *brāhmaṇa* woman and *kṣatriya* man. Therefore although Romaharṣaṇa considered Balarāma a *kṣatriya,* he should not have remained sitting on a higher seat. Lord Balarāma considered that Romaharṣaṇa, according to his position by birth, should not have accepted the higher sitting position, because there were many learned *brāhmaṇas* and sages present. He also observed that Romaharṣaṇa not only did not come down from his exalted seat, but he did not even stand up and offer his respects when Balarāmajī entered the assembly. Lord Balarāma did not like the audacity of Romaharṣaṇa, and he became very angry with him.

When a person is seated on the Vyāsāsana, he does not generally have to stand up to receive a particular person entering the assembly, but in this case the situation was different because Lord Baladeva is not an ordinary human being. Therefore, although Romaharṣaṇa Sūta was voted to the Vyāsāsana by all the *brāhmaṇas,* he should have followed the behavior of other learned sages and *brāhmaṇas* who were present and should have known that Lord Balarāma is the Supreme Personality of Godhead. Respects are always due to Him, even though such respects can be avoided in the case of an ordinary man. The appearances of Kṛṣṇa and Balarāma are especially meant for reestablishment of the religious principles. As stated in the *Bhagavad-gītā,* the highest religious principle is to surrender unto the Supreme Personality of Godhead. It is also confirmed in the *Śrīmad-Bhagavatam* that the topmost perfection of religiousness is to be engaged in the devotional service of the Lord.

When Lord Balarāma saw that Romaharṣaṇa Sūta did not understand the highest principle of religiousness in spite of having studied all the *Vedas,* He certainly could not support his position. Romaharṣaṇa Sūta had been given a chance to become a perfect *brāhmaṇa,* but because of his ill behavior in his relationship with the Supreme Personality of Godhead, his low birth was immediately remembered. Romaharṣaṇa Sūta had been given the position of a *brāhmaṇa,* but he had not been born in the family of a *brāhmaṇa;* he had been born in a *pratiloma* family. According to the Vedic concept, there are two kinds of mixed family heritage. They are called *anuloma* and *pratiloma.* When a male is united with a female of a lower caste, the offspring is called *anuloma;* but when a male unites with a woman of a higher caste, the offspring is called *pratiloma.* Romaharṣaṇa Sūta belonged to the *pratiloma* family because his father was a *kṣatriya* and his mother a *brāhmaṇa.* Because Romaharṣaṇa's transcendental realization was not perfect, Lord Balarāma remembered his *pratiloma* heritage. The idea is that any man can be given the chance to become a *brāhmaṇa,* but if he improperly uses the position of a *brāhmaṇa* without actual realization, then his elevation to the brahminical position is not valid.

After seeing the deficiency of realization in Romaharṣaṇa Sūta, Lord Balarāma decided to chastise him for being puffed up. Lord Balarāma therefore said, "This man is liable to be awarded the death punishment because, although he has the good qualification of being a disciple of Lord Vyāsadeva and although he has studied all the Vedic literature from this exalted personality, he was not submissive in the presence of the Supreme Personality of Godhead." As stated in the *Bhagavad-gītā,* a person who is actually a *brāhmaṇa* and is very learned must automatically become very gentle also. In the case of Romaharṣaṇa Sūta, although he was very learned and had been given the chance to become a *brāhmaṇa*, he had not become gentle. From this we can understand that when one is puffed up by material acquisition, he cannot acquire the gentle behavior befitting a *brāhmaṇa.* The learning of such a person is as good as a valuable jewel decorating the hood of a serpent. Despite the valuable jewel on the hood, a serpent is still a serpent and is as fearful as an ordinary serpent. If a person does not become meek and humble, all his studies of the *Vedas* and *Purāṇas* and his vast knowledge in the *śāstras* become simply outward dress, like the costume of a theatrical artist dancing on the stage. Lord Balarāma began to consider thus: "I have appeared in order to chastise false persons who are internally impure but externally pose themselves to be very learned and religious. My killing of such persons is proper to check them from further sinful activity."

Lord Balarāma had avoided taking part in the Battle of Kurukṣetra, and yet because of His position, the reestablishment of religious principles was his prime duty. Considering these points, He killed Romaharṣaṇa Sūta simply by striking him with a *kuśa* straw, which was nothing but a blade of grass. If someone questions how Lord Balarāma could kill Romaharṣaṇa Sūta simply by striking him with a blade of *kuśa* grass, the answer is given in the *Śrīmad-Bhāgavatam* by the use of the word *prabhu* (master). The Lord's position is always transcendental, and because He is omnipotent He can act as He likes without being obliged to the material laws and principles. Thus it was possible for Him to kill Romaharṣaṇa Sūta simply by striking him with a blade of *kuśa* grass.

At the death of Romaharṣaṇa Sūta, everyone present became much aggrieved, and there was roaring and crying. Although all the *brāhmaṇas* and sages present there knew Lord Balarāma to be the Supreme Personality of Godhead, they did not hesitate to protest the Lord's action, and they humbly submitted, "Our dear Lord, we think that Your action is not in line with the religious principles. Dear Lord Yadunandana, we may inform You that we *brāhmaṇas* posted Romaharṣaṇa Sūta on that exalted position for the duration of this great sacrifice. He was seated on the Vyāsāsana by our election, and when one is seated on the Vyāsāsana, it is improper for him to stand up to receive a person. Moreover, we awarded Romaharṣaṇa Sūta an undisturbed duration of life. Under the circumstances, since Your Lordship has killed him without knowing all these facts, we think that Your action has been equal to that of killing a *brāhmaṇa.* Dear Lord, deliverer of all fallen souls, we know certainly that You are the knower of all Vedic principles. You are the master of all mystic powers; therefore ordinarily the Vedic injunctions cannot be applied to Your personality. But we request that You show Your causeless mercy upon others by kindly atoning for this killing of Romaharṣaṇa Sūta. We do not, however, suggest what kind of act You should perform to atone for killing him; we simply suggest that some method of atonement be adopted by You so that others may follow Your action. What is done by a great personality is followed by the ordinary man."

The Lord replied, "Yes, I must atone for this action, which may have been proper for Me, but is improper for others; therefore, I think it is My duty to execute a suitable act of atonement enjoined in the authorized scriptures. Simultaneously I can also give this Romaharṣaṇa Sūta life again, with a span of long duration, sufficient strength, and full power of the senses. Not only this, if you desire, I shall be glad to award him anything else which you may ask. I shall be very glad to grant all these boons in order to fulfill your desires."

This statement of Lord Balarāma definitely confirms that the Supreme Personality of Godhead is free to act in any way. Although it may be considered that His killing of Romaharṣaṇa Sūta was improper, He could immediately counteract the action with greater profit to all. Therefore, one should not imitate the actions of the Supreme Personality of Godhead; one should simply follow the instructions of the Lord. All the great learned sages present realized that although they considered the action of Lord Balarāma to be improper, the Lord was able to immediately compensate with greater profits. Not wanting to detract from the mission of the Lord in killing Romaharṣaṇa Sūta, all of them prayed, "Our dear Lord, the uncommon use of Your *kuśa* weapon to kill Romaharṣaṇa Sūta may remain as it is; because of Your desire to kill him, he should not be brought to life again. At the same time Your Lordship may remember that we sages and *brāhmaṇas* voluntarily gave him long life; therefore, such a benediction should not be nullified." Thus the request of all the learned *brāhmaṇas* in the assembly was ambiguous because they wanted to keep intact the benediction given by them that Romaharṣaṇa Sūta would continue to live until the end of the great sacrifice, but at the same time they did not want to nullify Balarāma's killing him.

The Supreme Personality of Godhead therefore solved the problem in a manner befitting His exalted position, and said, "Because the son is produced from the body of the father, it is the injunction of the *Vedas* that the son is the father's representative. Therefore I say that Ugraśravā Sūta, the son of Romaharṣaṇa Sūta, should henceforth take his father's position and continue the discourses on the *Purāṇas,* and because you wanted Romaharṣaṇa to have a long duration of life, this benediction will be transferred to his son. The son, Ugraśravā, will therefore have all the facilities you offered–long duration of life in a good and healthy body, without any disturbances and full strength of all the senses.

Lord Balarāma then implored all the sages and *brāhmaṇas* that aside from the benediction offered to the son of Romaharṣaṇa, they should ask from Him any other benediction, and He would be prepared to fulfill it immediately. The Lord thus placed Himself in the position of an ordinary *kṣatriya* and informed the sages that He did not know in what way He could atone for His killing of Romaharṣaṇa, but whatever they would suggest He would be glad to accept.

The *brāhmaṇas* could understand the purpose of the Lord, and thus, they suggested that He atone for His action in a manner which would be beneficial for them. They said, "Our dear Lord, there is a demon of the name Balvala. He is the son of Ilvala, but he is a very powerful demon, and he visits this sacred place of sacrifice every fortnight on the full moon and moonless days and creates a great disturbance to the discharge of our duties in the sacrifice. O descendant of the Daśārha family, we all request You to kill this demon. We think that if You kindly kill him, that will be Your atonement on our behalf. The demon occasionally comes here and profusely throws upon us contaminated, impure things like puss, blood, stool, urine and wine, and he pollutes this sacred place by showering such filth upon us. After killing Balvala, You may continue touring all these sacred places of pilgrimage for twelve months, and in that way You will be completely freed from all contamination. That is our prescription."

Thus ends the Bhaktivedanta purport of the Seventy-seventh Chapter of Kṛṣṇa, *"The Killing of Dantavakra, Vidūratha and Romaharṣaṇa."*

78 / The Liberation of Balvala, and Lord Balarāma's Touring the Sacred Places

Lord Balarāma prepared Himself to meet the demon Balvala. At the time when the demon usually attacked the sacred place, there appeared a great hailstorm, the whole sky became covered with dust and the atmosphere became surcharged with a filthy smell. Just after this, the mischievous demon Balvala began to shower torrents of stool and urine and other impure substances on the arena of sacrifice. After this onslaught, the demon himself appeared with a great trident in his hand. He was a gigantic person, and his black body was like a huge mass of carbon. His hair, his beard and his moustache appeared reddish, like copper, and because of his great beard and moustache, his mouth appeared to be very dangerous and fierce. As soon as He saw the demon, Lord Balarāma prepared to attack him. He first began to consider how He could smash the great demon to pieces. Lord Balarāma called for His plow and club, and they immediately appeared before Him. The demon Balvala was flying in the sky, and at the first opportunity Lord Balarāma dragged him down with His plow and angrily smashed the demon's head with His club. By Balarāma's striking, the forehead of the demon became fractured. There was a profuse flow of blood from his forehead, and he began to scream loudly. In this way the demon, who had been such a great disturbance to the pious *brāhmaṇas,* fell to the ground. His falling was like a great mountain with a red oxide peak being struck by a thunderbolt and smashed to the ground.

The inhabitants of Naimiṣāraṇya, learned sages and *brāhmaṇas,* became most pleased by seeing this, and they offered their respectful prayers to Lord Balarāma. They offered their heartfelt blessings upon the Lord, and all agreed that Lord Balarāma's attempt to do anything would never be a failure. The sages and *brāhmaṇas* then performed a ceremonial bathing of Lord Balarāma, just as King Indra is bathed by the demigods when he is victorious over the demons. The *brāhmaṇas* and sages honored Lord

Balarāma by presenting Him first-class new clothing and ornaments and the lotus flower garland of victory, the reservoir of all beauty, which was never to be dried up, being in everlasting existence.

After this incidence, Lord Balarāma took permission from the *brāhmaṇas* assembled at Naimiṣāraṇya and, accompanied by other *brāhmaṇas,* went to the bank of the River Kauṣikī. After taking His bath in this holy place, He proceeded toward the River Sarayū and visited the source of the river. He began to travel on the bank of the Sarayū River, and He gradually reached Prayāga, where there is a confluence of three rivers, the Ganges, Yamunā and Sarasvatī. Here also He regularly took His bath, worshiped the local temples of God and, as it is enjoined in the Vedic literature, offered oblations to the forefathers and sages. He gradually reached the *āśrama* of the sage Pulaha and from there went to Gaṇḍakī on the River Gomatī. After this He took His bath in the River Vipāśā. Then gradually He came to the bank of the Śoṇa River. (The Śoṇa River is still running as one of the big rivers in the Behar Province.) He also took His bath there and performed the Vedic ritualistic ceremonies. He continued His travels and gradually came to the pilgrimage city of Gayā where there is a celebrated Viṣṇu temple. According to the advice of His father Vasudeva, He offered oblations to the forefathers in this Viṣṇu temple. From here He traveled to the delta of the Ganges, where the sacred River Ganges mixes with the Bay of Bengal. This sacred place is called Gaṅgāsāgara, and at the end of January every year there is still a great assembly of saintly persons and pious men, just as there is an assembly of saintly persons in Prayāga every year which is called the Magh Mela Fair.

After finishing His bathing and ritualistic ceremonies at Gaṅgāsāgara, Lord Balarāma proceeded toward the mountain known as Mahendra Parvata. At this place He met Paraśurāma, the incarnation of Lord Kṛṣṇa, and He offered him respect by bowing down before him. After this He gradually turned toward southern India and visited the banks of the River Godāvarī. After taking His bath in the River Godāvarī and performing the necessary ritualistic ceremonies, He gradually visited the other rivers—the Veṇā, Pampā and Bhīmarathī. On the bank of the River Bhīmarathī there is the deity called Svāmī Kārttikeya. After visiting Kārttikeya Lord Balarāma gradually proceeded to Śailapura, a pilgrimage city in the province of Mahārāṣṭra. Śailapura is one of the biggest districts in Mahārāṣṭra Province. He then gradually proceeded towards the Draviḍadeśa. Southern India is divided into five parts, called Pañcadraviḍa. Northern India is also divided into five parts, called Pañcagaura. All the important *ācāryas* of the modern age, namely Śaṅkarācārya, Rāmānujācārya,

Madhvācārya, Viṣṇusvāmī, and Nimbārka, advented themselves in these Draviḍa Provinces. Lord Caitanya appeared in Bengal, which is part of the five Gauradeśas.

The most important place of pilgrimage in southern India, or Draviḍa, is Veṅkaṭācala, commonly known as Bālajī. After visiting this place Lord Balarāma proceeded toward Viṣṇukāñcī, and from there He proceeded on the bank of the Kāverī. He took His bath in the River Kāverī; then He gradually reached Raṅgakṣetra. The biggest temple in the world is in Raṅgakṣetra, and the Viṣṇu deity there is celebrated as Raṅganātha. A similar temple of Raṅganātha is in Vṛndāvana, although it is not as big as the temple in Raṅgakṣetra.

While going to Viṣṇukāñcī, Lord Balarāma also visited Śivakāñcī. After visiting Raṅgakṣetra, He gradually proceeded toward Mathurā, commonly known as the Mathurā of southern India. After visiting this place, He gradually proceeded toward Setubandha. Setubandha is the place where Lord Rāmacandra constructed the stone bridge from India to Laṅkā (Ceylon). In this particularly holy place, Lord Balarāma distributed ten thousand cows to the local *brāhmaṇa* priests. It is the Vedic custom that when a rich visitor goes to any place of pilgrimage he gives in charity to the local priests gifts of horses, cows, ornaments and garments. This system of visiting places of pilgrimage and providing the local *brāhmaṇa* priests with all necessities of life has greatly deteriorated in this age of Kali. The richer section of the population, because of its degradation in Vedic culture, is no longer attracted by these places of pilgrimage, and the *brāhmaṇa* priests who depended on such visitors have also deteriorated in their professional duty of helping the visitors. These *brāhmaṇa* priests in the places of pilgrimage are called *paṇḍa* or *paṇḍit*. This means that they formerly were very learned *brāhmaṇas* and used to guide the visitors in all details of the purpose of coming there, and thus both the visitors and the priests were benefitted by mutual cooperation.

It is clear from the description of *Śrīmad-Bhāgavatam* that when Lord Balarāma was visiting the different places of pilgrimage, He properly followed the Vedic system. After distributing cows at Setubandha, Lord Balarāma proceeded toward the Kṛtamālā and Tāmraparṇī Rivers. These two rivers are celebrated as sacred, and Lord Balarāma bathed in both. He then proceeded toward Malaya Hill. This Malaya Hill is very great, and it is said that it is one of seven peaks called the Malaya Hills. The great sage Agastya used to live there, and Lord Balarāma visited him and offered His respects by bowing down before him. After taking the sage's blessings, Lord Balarāma, with the sage's permission, proceeded toward the Indian Ocean.

At the point of the cape there is a big temple of the goddess Durgā where she is known as Kanyākumārī. This temple of Kanyākumārī was also visited by Lord Rāmacandra, and therefore it is to be understood that the temple has been existing for millions of years. From there, Lord Balarāma went on to visit the pilgrimage city known as Phālgunatīrtha, which is on the shore of the Indian Ocean, or the Southern Ocean. Phālgunatīrtha is celebrated because Lord Viṣṇu in His incarnation of Ananta is lying there. From Phālgunatīrtha, Lord Balarāma went on to visit another pilgrimage spot known as Pañcāpsarasa. There also He bathed according to the regulative principles and observed the ritualistic ceremonies. This site is also celebrated as a shrine of Lord Viṣṇu; therefore Lord Balarāma distributed ten thousand cows to the local *brāhmaṇa* priests.

From Cape Comarin Lord Balarāma turned toward Kerala. The country of Kerala is still existing in southern India under the name of South Kerala. After visiting this place, He came to Gokarṇatīrtha, where Lord Śiva is constantly worshiped. Balarāma then visited the temple of Āryādevī, which is completely surrounded by water. From that island, He went on to a place known as Śūrpāraka. After this He bathed in the rivers known as Tāpī, Payoṣṇī, and Nirvindhyā, and He came to the forest known as Daṇḍakāraṇya. This is the same Daṇḍakāraṇya Forest where Lord Rāmacandra lived while He was in exile. Lord Balarāma next came to the bank of the River Narmadā, the biggest river in central India. On the bank of this sacred Narmadā there is a pilgrimage spot known as Māhiṣmati Purī. After bathing there, according to regulative principles, Lord Balarāma returned to Prabhāsatīrtha, wherefrom He had begun His journey.

When Lord Balarāma returned to Prabhāsatīrtha He heard from the *brāhmaṇas* that most of the *kṣatriyas* in the Battle of Kurukṣetra had been killed. Balarāma felt relieved to hear that the burden of the world had been reduced. Lord Kṛṣṇa and Balarāma appeared on this earth to lessen the burden of military strength created by the ambitious *kṣatriya* kings. This is the way of materialistic life: not being satisfied by the absolute necessities of life, people ambitiously create extra demands, and their illegal desires are checked by the laws of nature or by laws of God, appearing as famine, war, pestilence and similar catastrophes. Lord Balarāma heard that although most of the *kṣatriyas* had been killed, the Kurus were still engaged in fighting. Therefore He returned to the battlefield just on the day Bhīmasena and Duryodhana were engaged in a personal duel As well-wisher of both of them, Lord Balarāma wanted to stop them, but they would not stop.

When Lord Balarāma appeared on the scene, King Yudhiṣṭhira and his young brothers, Nakula, Sahadeva, Lord Kṛṣṇa and Arjuna, immediately offered Him their respectful obeisances, but they did not speak at all. The reason they were silent was that Lord Balarāma was somewhat affectionate toward Duryodhana, and Duryodhana had learned from Balarāmajī the art of fighting with a club. Thus, when the fighting was going on, King Yudhiṣṭhira and others thought that Balarāma might come there to say something in favor of Duryodhana, and they therefore remained silent. Both Duryodhana and Bhīmasena were very enthusiastic in fighting with clubs, and in the midst of large audiences, each was very skillfully trying to strike the other, and while attempting to do so they appeared to be dancing. But although they appeared to be dancing, it was clear that both of them were very angry.

Lord Balarāma, wanting to stop the fighting, said, "My dear King Duryodhana and Bhīmasena, I know that both of you are great fighters and are well known in the world as great heroes, but still I think that Bhīmasena is superior to Duryodhana in bodily strength. On the other hand, Duryodhana is superior in the art of fighting with a club. Taking this into consideration, My opinion is that neither of you is inferior to the other in fighting. Under the circumstances, there is very little chance of one of you being defeated by the other. Therefore I request you not to waste your time in fighting in this way. I wish you to stop this unnecessary fight."

The good instruction given by Lord Balarāma to both Bhīmasena and Duryodhana was intended for the equal benefit of both of them. But they were so enwrapped in anger against each other that they could only remember their long-lasting personal enmity. Each thought only of killing the other, and they did not give much importance to the instruction of Lord Balarāma. Both of them then became like madmen in remembering the strong accusations and ill behavior they had exchanged with one another. Lord Balarāma, being able to understand the destiny which was awaiting them, was not eager to go further in the matter. Therefore, instead of staying, He decided to return to the city of Dvārakā.

When He returned to Dvārakā, He was received with great jubilation by relatives and friends, headed by King Ugrasena and other elderly persons; all of them came forward to welcome Lord Balarāma. After this, He again went to the holy place of pilgrimage at Naimiṣāraṇya, and the sages, saintly persons and *brāhmaṇas* all received Him standing. They understood that Lord Balarāma, although a *kṣatriya,* was now retired from the fighting business. The *brāhmanas* and the sages, who were always for peace and tranquility, were very pleased at this. All of them embraced Balarāma with great affection and induced Him to perform various kinds of sacrifices in that sacred spot of Naimiṣāraṇya. Actually Lord Balarāma had no business performing the sacrifices recommended for ordinary human beings; He is the Supreme Personality of Godhead, and therefore He Himself is the enjoyer of all such sacrifices. As such, His exemplary action in performing sacrifices was only to give a lesson to the common man to show how one should abide by the injunction of the *Vedas*.

The Supreme Personality of Godhead Balarāma instructed the sages and saintly persons at Naimiṣāranya on the subject matter of the living entities' relationship with this cosmic manifestation, on how one should accept this whole universe and on how one should relate with the cosmos in order to achieve the highest goal of perfection, the understanding that the whole cosmic manifestation is resting on the Supreme Personality of Godhead and that the Supreme Personality of Godhead is also all-pervading, even within the minutest atom, by the function of His Paramātmā feature.

Lord Balarāma then took the *avabhṛtha* bath which is accepted after finishing sacrificial performances. After taking His bath, He dressed Himself in new silken garments and decorated Himself with beautiful jewelry amidst His relatives and friends. He appeared to be a shining full moon amidst the luminaries in the sky. Lord Balarāma is the Personality of Godhead Ananta Himself; therefore He is beyond the scope of understanding by mind, intelligence or body. He descended exactly like a human being and behaved in that way for His own purpose; we can only explain His activities as the Lord's pastimes. No one can even estimate the extent of the unlimited demonstrations of His pastimes because He is all-powerful. Lord Balarāma is the original Viṣṇu; therefore anyone remembering these pastimes of Lord Balarāma in the morning and evening, will certainly become a great devotee of the Supreme Personality of Godhead, and thus his life will become successful in all respects.

Thus ends the Bhaktivedanta purport of the Seventy-eighth Chapter of Kṛṣṇa, *"The Liberation of Balvala, and Lord Balarāma's Touring Sacred Places."*

79 / Meeting of Lord Kṛṣṇa with Sudāmā Brāhmaṇa

King Parīkṣit was hearing the narrations of the pastimes of Lord Kṛṣṇa and Lord Balarāma from Śukadeva Gosvāmī. These pastimes are all transcendentally pleasurable to hear, and Mahārāja Parīkṣit addressed Śukadeva Gosvāmī as follows: "My dear Lord, the Supreme Personality of Godhead Kṛṣṇa is the bestower of both liberation and love of God simultaneously. Anyone who becomes a devotee of the Lord automatically attains liberation without having to make a separate attempt. The Lord is unlimited, and as such, His pastimes and activities for creating, maintaining and destroying the whole cosmic manifestation are unlimited. I therefore wish to hear about His other pastimes of which you may not have spoken as yet. My dear master, the conditioned souls within this material world have been frustrated by searching out the pleasure of happiness derived from sense gratification. Such desires for material enjoyment are always piercing the heart of conditioned souls. But I am actually experiencing how the transcendental topics of Lord Kṛṣṇa's pastimes can relieve one from the state of being affected by such sense gratificatory material activities. I think that no intelligent person can reject this method of hearing the transcendental pastimes of the Lord again and again; simply by hearing, one can remain always steeped in transcendental pleasure. Thus one will not be attracted by material sense gratification."

In this statement, Mahārāja Parīkṣit has used two important words: *viṣaṇṇaḥ* and *viśeṣajñaḥ: viṣaṇṇaḥ* means "morose." The materialistic persons are inventing many ways and means to become fully satisfied, but actually they remain morose. The point may be raised that sometimes those who are transcendentalists also remain morose. Parīkṣit Mahārāja has used, however, the word *viśeṣajñaḥ*. There are two kinds of transcendentalists, namely the impersonalists and the personalists. *Viśeṣajñaḥ* refers to the personalists, who are interested in transcendental variegatedness. The devotees become jubilant by hearing the descriptions of the personal activities of the Supreme Lord, whereas the impersonalists, who are actually more attracted by the impersonal feature of the Lord, are only superficially attracted by the personal activities of the Lord. As such, in spite of coming in contact with the pastimes of the Lord, the impersonalists do not fully realize the benefit to be derived, and thus they remain in exactly the same morose position, due to fruitive activity, with the materialists.

King Parīkṣit continued: "The capacity for talking can be perfected only by describing the transcendental qualities of the Lord. The capacity for working with one's hands can be successful only when one engages himself in the service of the Lord with those hands. Similarly, one's mind can be pacified only when he simply thinks of Kṛṣṇa in full Kṛṣṇa consciousness. This does not mean that one has to be very thoughtful, but one simply has to understand that Kṛṣṇa, the Absolute Truth, is all-pervasive, by His localized aspect as Paramātmā. If only one can think that Kṛṣṇa, as Paramātmā, is everywhere, even within the atom, then one can perfect the thinking, feeling and willing function of his mind. The perfect devotee does not see the material world as it appears to material eyes, but he sees everywhere the presence of his worshipable Lord in His Paramātmā feature."

Mahārāja Parīkṣit continued to say that the function of the ear can be perfected simply by engagement in hearing the transcendental activities of the Lord. He said further that the function of the head can be fully utilized when the head is engaged in bowing down before the Lord and His representative. That the Lord is represented in everyone's heart is a fact, and therefore the highly advanced devotee offers his respects to every living entity, considering that the body is the temple of the Lord. But it is not possible for all men to come to that stage of life immediately, because that stage is for the first-class devotee. The second-class devotee can consider the Vaiṣṇavas, or the devotees of the Lord, to be representatives of Kṛṣṇa, and the devotee who is just beginning, the neophyte or third-class devotee, can bow his head before the Deity in the temple and before the spiritual master, who is the direct manifestation of the Supreme Personality of Godhead. In the neophyte stage, in the intermediate stage, or in the fully advanced perfected stage, one can make the function of the head perfect by bowing down before the Lord or His representative. Similarly, he can perfect the function of the eyes by seeing the Lord and His representative. In this way, everyone can elevate the functions of the different parts of his body to the highest perfectional stage simply by engaging them in the service of the Lord or His representative. If one is able to do nothing more, he can simply bow down before the Lord and His representative and drink the *caraṇāmṛta,* the water which has washed the lotus feet of the Lord or His devotee.

On hearing these statements of Mahārāja Parīkṣit, Śukadeva Gosvāmī became overwhelmed with devotional ecstasy because of King Parīkṣit's advanced understanding of the Vaiṣṇava philosophy. Śukadeva Gosvāmī was already engaged in describing the activities of the Lord, and when he was asked by Mahārāja Parīkṣit to describe them further, he continued with great pleasure to narrate *Śrīmad-Bhāgavatam.*

There was a very nice *brāhmaṇa* friend of Lord Kṛṣṇa. As a perfect *brāhmaṇa,* he was very elevated in transcendental knowledge, and because of his advanced knowledge, he was not at all attached to material enjoyment. Therefore he was very peaceful and had achieved supreme control over his senses. This means that the *brāhmaṇa* was a perfect devotee because unless one is a perfect devotee, he cannot achieve the highest standard of knowledge. It is stated in the *Bhagavad-gītā* that a person who has come to the point of perfection of knowledge surrenders unto the Supreme Personality of Godhead. In other words, any person who has surrendered his life for the service of the Supreme Personality of Godhead has come to the point of perfect knowledge. The result of perfect knowledge is that one becomes detached from the materialistic way of life. This detachment means complete control of the senses, which are always attracted by material enjoyment. The senses of the devotee become purified, and in that stage the senses are engaged in the service of the Lord. That is the complete field of devotional service.

Although the *brāhmaṇa* friend of Lord Kṛṣṇa was a householder, he was not busy accumulating wealth for very comfortable living; therefore he was satisfied by the income which automatically came to him according to his destiny. This is the sign of perfect knowledge. A man who is in perfect knowledge knows that one cannot be happier than he is destined to be. In this material world, everyone is destined to suffer a certain amount of distress and to enjoy a certain amount of happiness. The amount of happiness and distress is already predestined for every living entity. No one can increase or decrease the happiness of the materialistic way of life. The *brāhmaṇa,* therefore, did not exert himself for more material happiness, but he used his time for advancement of Kṛṣṇa consciousness. Externally he appeared to be very poor because he had no rich dress and could not provide a very rich dress for his wife, and because their material condition was not very opulent they were not even eating sufficiently, and thus both he and his wife appeared to be very thin. The wife was not very anxious for her personal comfort, but she felt very concerned for her husband, who was such a pious *brāhmaṇa.* She was trembling due to her weak health, and although she did not like to dictate to her husband, she spoke as follows:

"My dear lord, I know that Lord Kṛṣṇa, who is the husband of the goddess of fortune, is your personal friend. You are also a devotee of Lord Kṛṣṇa, and He is always ready to help His devotee. Even if you think that you are not rendering any devotional service to the Lord, still you are surrendered to Him, and the Lord is the protector of the surrendered soul. Moreover, I know that Lord Kṛṣṇa is the ideal personality of Vedic culture. He is always in favor of brahminical culture and is very kind to the qualified *brāhmaṇas.* You are the most fortunate person because you have as your friend the Supreme Personality of Godhead. Lord Kṛṣṇa is the only shelter for personalities like you because you are fully surrendered unto Him. You are saintly, learned and fully in control of your senses. Under the circumstances, Lord Kṛṣṇa is your only shelter. Please, therefore, go to Him. I am sure that He will immediately understand your impoverished position. You are also a householder; therefore without any money you are in a distressed condition. But as soon as He understands your position, He will certainly give you sufficient riches so that you can live very comfortably. Lord Kṛṣṇa is now the King of the Bhoja, Vṛṣṇi and Andhaka dynasties, and I have heard that He never leaves His capital city, Dvārakā. He is living there without outside engagements. He is so kind and liberal that He immediately gives everything, even His personal self, to any person who surrenders unto Him. When He is prepared to give Himself personally to His devotee, then there is nothing wonderful in giving some material riches. Of course, He does not give much material wealth to His devotee if the devotee is not very fixed, but I think in your case He knows perfectly well how much you are fixed in devotional service. Therefore He will not hesitate to award you some material benefit for the bare necessities of life."

In this way, the wife of the *brāhmaṇa* again and again requested, in great humility and submission, that he go to Lord Kṛṣṇa. The *brāhmaṇa* thought that there was no need to ask any material benefit from Lord Śrī Kṛṣṇa, but he was induced by the repeated requests of his wife. Moreover, he thought, "If I go there I shall be able to see the Lord personally. That will be a great opportunity, even if I don't ask any material benefit from Him." When he had decided to go to Kṛṣṇa, he asked his wife if she had anything in the home that he could offer to Kṛṣṇa, because he must take some presentation for his friend. The wife immediately collected four palmsful of chipped rice from her neighboring friends and tied it in a small cloth, like a handkerchief, and gave it to her husband to present to Kṛṣṇa. Without waiting any longer, the *brāhmaṇa* took the presentation and began to proceed toward Dvārakā to see his Lord. While he was proceeding toward Dvārakā he was absorbed in the thought of how he could be able to see Lord Kṛṣṇa. He had no thought within his heart other than Kṛṣṇa.

It was of course very difficult to reach the palaces of the kings of the Yadu dynasty, but *brāhmaṇas* were allowed to visit, and when the *brāhmaṇa* friend of Lord Kṛṣṇa went there, he, along with other *brāhmaṇas,* had to pass through three military encampments. In each camp there were very big gates, and he also had to pass through them. After the gates and the camps, there were sixteen thousand big palaces, the residential quarters of the sixteen thousand queens of Lord Kṛṣṇa. The *brāhmaṇa* entered one palace which was very gorgeously decorated. When he entered this beautiful palace, he felt that he was swimming in the ocean of transcendental pleasure. Ḥe felt himself constantly diving and surfacing in that transcendental ocean.

At that time, Lord Kṛṣṇa was sitting on the bedstead of Queen Rukmiṇī. Even from a considerable distance He could see the *brāhmaṇa* coming to His home, and He could recognize him as His friend. Lord Kṛṣṇa immediately left His seat and came forward to receive His *brāhmaṇa* friend and, upon reaching him, embraced the *brāhmaṇa* with His two arms. Lord Kṛṣṇa is the reservoir of all transcendental pleasure, and yet He Himself felt great pleasure upon embracing the poor *brāhmaṇa* because He was meeting His very dear friend. Lord Kṛṣṇa had him seated on His own bedstead and personally brought him all kinds of fruits and drinks to offer him, as is proper in receiving a worshipable guest. Lord Śrī Kṛṣṇa is the supreme pure, but because He was playing the role of an ordinary human being, He immediately washed the *brāhmaṇa's* feet and, for His own purification, sprinkled the water onto His head. After this the Lord smeared the body of the *brāhmaṇa* with different kinds of scented pulp, such as sandalwood, *aguru* and saffron. He immediately burned several kinds of scented incense, and, as is usual, He offered him *ārātrika* with burning lamps. After thus offering him an adequate welcome and after the *brāhmaṇa* had taken food and drink, Lord Kṛṣṇa said, "My dear friend, it is a great fortune that you have come here."

The *brāhmaṇa,* being very poor, was not dressed nicely; his clothing was torn and dirty, and his body was also very lean and thin. He appeared not to be very clean, and because of his weak body, his bones were distinctly visible. The goddess of fortune Rukmiṇīdevī personally began to fan him with the *cāmara* fan, but the other women in the palace became astonished at Lord Kṛṣṇa's behavior in receiving the *brāhmaṇa* in that way. They were surprised to see how eager Lord Kṛṣṇa was to welcome this particular *brāhmaṇa.* They began to wonder how Lord Kṛṣṇa could personally receive a *brāhmaṇa* who was poor, not very neat or clean, and poorly dressed; but at the same time they could realize that the *brāhmaṇa* was not an ordinary living being. They knew that he must have performed great pious activities; otherwise why was Lord Kṛṣṇa, the husband of the goddess of fortune, taking so much care for him? They were still more surprised to see that the *brāhmaṇa* was seated on the bedstead of Lord Kṛṣṇa. They were especially surprised to see that Lord Kṛṣṇa had embraced him exactly as He embraced His elder brother, Balarāmaji, because Lord Kṛṣṇa used to embrace only Rukmiṇī or Balarāma, and no one else.

After receiving the *brāhmaṇa* nicely, and seating him on His own cushioned bed, Lord Kṛṣṇa said, "My dear *brāhmaṇa* friend, you are a most intelligent personality, and you know very well the principles of religious life. I believe that after you finished your education at the house of our teacher and after you sufficiently remunerated him, you must have gone back to your home and accepted a suitable wife. I know very well that from the beginning you were not at all attached to the materialistic way of life, nor did you desire to be very opulent materially, and therefore you are in need of money. In this material world, persons who are not attached to material opulence are very rarely found. Such unattached persons haven't the least desire to accumulate wealth and prosperity for sense gratification, but sometimes they are found to collect money just to exhibit the exemplary life of a householder. They show how by proper distribution of wealth one can become an ideal householder and at the same time become a great devotee. Such ideal householders are to be considered followers of My footsteps. I hope, My dear *brāhmaṇa* friend, you remember all those days of our school life when both you and I were living together at the boarding house. Actually, whatever knowledge both you and I received in our life was accumulated in our student life.

"If a man is sufficiently educated in student life under the guidance of a proper teacher, then his life becomes successful in the future. He can very easily cross over the ocean of nescience, and he is not subjected to the influence of illusory energy. My dear friend, everyone should consider his father to be his first teacher because by the mercy of one's father one gets this body. The father is therefore the natural spiritual master. Our next spiritual master is he who initiates us into transcendental knowledge, and he is to be worshiped as much as I am. The spiritual master may be more than one. The spiritual master who instructs the disciples about spiritual matters is called *śikṣa-guru*, and the spiritual master who initiates the disciple is called *dīksā-guru*. Both of them are My representatives. There may be many spiritual masters who instruct, but the initiator spiritual master is one. A human being who takes advantage of these spiritual masters and, receiving proper knowledge from them, crosses the ocean of material existence, is to be understood as having properly utilized his human form of life. He has practical knowledge that the ultimate interest of life, which is to be gained only in this human form, is to achieve spiritual perfection and thus be transferred back home, back to Godhead.

"My dear friend, I am Paramātmā, the Supersoul present in everyone's heart, and it is My direct order that human society must follow the principles of *varṇa* and *āśrama.* As I have stated in the *Bhagavad-gītā,* the human society should be divided, according to quality and action, into four *varṇas*. Similarly, everyone should divide his life into four parts. One should utilize the first part of life in becoming a bona fide student, receiving adequate knowledge and keeping oneself in the vow of *brahmacarya,* so that one may completely devote his life for the service of the spiritual master without indulging in sense gratification. A *brahmacārī* is meant to lead a life of austerities and penance. The householder is meant to live a regulated life of sense gratification, but no one should remain a householder for the third stage of life. In that stage, one has to return to the austerities and penances formerly practiced in *brahmacārī* life and thus relieve himself of the attachment to household life. After being relieved of his attachments to the materialistic way of life, one may accept the order of *sannyāsa.*

"As the Supersoul of the living entities, sitting in everyone's heart, I observe everyone's activity in every stage and order of life. Regardless of which stage one is in, when I see that one is engaged seriously and sincerely in discharging the duties ordered by the spiritual master, and is thus dedicating his life to the service of the spiritual master, that person becomes most dear to Me. As far as the life of *brahmacarya* is concerned, if one can continue the life of a *brahmacārī* under the direction of a spiritual master, that is extremely good; but if in *brahmacārī* life one feels sex impulses, then he should take leave of his spiritual master, satisfying him according to the *guru's* desire. According to the Vedic system, a gift is offered to the spiritual master, which is called *guru-dakṣiṇā.* Then the disciple should take to householder life and accept a wife according to religious rites."

These instructions given by Lord Kṛṣṇa while talking with His friend the learned *brāhmaṇa* are very good for the guidance of human society. A system of human civilization that does not promote *varṇa* and *āśrama* is nothing but polished animal society. Indulgence in sex life by a man or woman living single is never acceptable in human society. A man should either strictly follow the principles of *brahmacārī* life or, with the permission of the spiritual master, should get married. Single life with illicit sex is animal life. For the animals there is no marriage institution.

Modern society does not aim at fulfilling the mission of human life. The mission of human life is to go back home, back to Godhead. To fulfill this mission, the system of *varṇa* and *āśrama* must be followed. When the system is followed rigidly and consciously, it fulfills this mission of life. When it is followed indirectly, without guidance of superior order, then it simply creates a disturbing condition in human society, and there is no peace and prosperity.

Kṛṣṇa continued to talk with His *brāhmaṇa* friend: "My dear friend, I think you remember our activities during the days when we were living as students. You may remember that once we went to collect fuel from the forest on the order of the *guru's* wife. While we were collecting the dried wood, we by chance entered the dense forest and became lost. There was an unexpected dust storm and then clouds and lightning in the sky and the explosive sound of thunder. Then sunset came, and we were lost in the dark jungle. After this, there was severe rainfall; the whole ground was overflooded with water, and we could not trace out the way to return to our *guru's āśrama*. You may remember that heavy rainfall–it was not actually rainfall but a sort of devastation. On account of the dust storm and the heavy rain, we began to feel greatly pained, and in whichever direction we turned we were bewildered. In that distressed condition, we took each other's hand and tried to find our way out. We passed the whole night in that way, and early in the morning when our absence became known to our *gurudeva*, he sent his other disciples to search us out. He also came with them, and when they reached us in the jungle they found us to be very distressed.

"With great compassion our *gurudeva* said, 'My dear boys, it is very wonderful that you have suffered so much trouble for me. Everyone likes to take care of his body as the first consideration, but you are so good and faithful to your *guru* that without caring for bodily comforts you have taken so much trouble for me. I am also glad to see that bona fide students like you will undergo any kind of trouble for the satisfaction of the spiritual master. That is the way for a bona fide disciple to become free from his debt to the spiritual master. It is the duty of the disciple to dedicate his life to the service of the spiritual master. My dear best of the twice-born, I am greatly pleased by your action, and I bless you: May all your desires and ambitions be fulfilled. May the understanding of the *Vedas* which you have learned from me always continue to remain within your memory, so that at every moment you can remember the teachings of the *Vedas* and quote their instructions without difficulty. Thus you will never be disappointed in this life or in the next.'"

Kṛṣṇa continued: "My dear friend, you may remember that many such incidents occurred while we were in the *āśrama* of our spiritual master. Both of us can realize that without the blessings of the spiritual master no one can be happy. By the mercy of the spiritual master and by his blessings, one can achieve peace and prosperity and be able to fulfill the mission of human life."

On hearing this, the learned *brāhmaṇa* replied, "My dear Kṛṣṇa, You are the Supreme Lord and the supreme spiritual master of everyone, and since I was fortunate enough to live with You in the house of our *guru*, I think I have nothing more to do in the matter of prescribed Vedic duties. My dear Lord, the Vedic hymns, ritualistic ceremonies, religious activities, and all other necessities for the perfection of human life, including economic development, sense gratification and liberation, are all derived from one source: Your supreme personality. All the different processes of life are ultimately meant for the understanding of Your personality. In other words, they are the different parts of Your transcendental form. And yet You played the role of a student and lived with us in the house of the *guru*. This means that You adopted all these pastimes for Your pleasure only; otherwise there was no need for Your playing the role of a human being."

Thus ends the Bhaktivedanta purport of the Seventy-ninth Chapter of Kṛṣṇa, *"The Meeting of Lord Kṛṣṇa with Sudāmā Brāhmaṇa."*

80 / The Brāhmaṇa Sudāmā Benedicted by Lord Kṛṣṇa

Lord Kṛṣṇa, the Supreme Personality of Godhead, the Supersoul of all living entities, knows very well everyone's heart. He is especially inclined to the *brāhmaṇa* devotees. Lord Kṛṣṇa is also called *brahmaṇyadeva,* which means that He is worshiped by the *brāhmaṇas.* Therefore it is understood that a devotee who is fully surrendered unto the Supreme Personality of Godhead has already acquired the position of a *brāhmaṇa.* Without becoming a *brāhmaṇa,* one cannot approach the Supreme Brahman, Lord Kṛṣṇa. Kṛṣṇa is especially concerned with vanquishing the distress of His devotees, and He is the only shelter of pure devotees.

Lord Kṛṣṇa was engaged for a long time in talking with Sudāmā Vipra about their past association. Then, just to enjoy the company of an old friend, Lord Kṛṣṇa began to smile, and asked, "My dear friend, what have you brought for Me? Has your wife given you some nice eatable for Me?" While He was addressing His friend, Lord Kṛṣṇa was looking upon him and smiling with great love. He continued: "My dear friend, you must have brought some presentation for Me from your home."

Lord Kṛṣṇa knew that Sudāmā was hesitating to present Him the paltry chipped rice which was actually unfit for His eating, and understanding the mind of Sudāmā Vipra the Lord said, "My dear friend, certainly I am not in need of anything, but if My devotee gives Me something as an offering of love, even though it may be very insignificant, I accept it with great pleasure. On the other hand, if a person is not a devotee, even though he may offer Me very valuable things, I do not like to accept them. I actually accept only things which are offered to Me in devotion and love; otherwise, however valuable the thing may be, I do not accept it. If My pure devotee offers Me even the most insignificant things—a little flower, a little piece of leaf, a little water—but saturates the offering in devotional love, then I not only gladly accept such an offering, but I eat it with great pleasure."

Lord Kṛṣṇa assured Sudāmā Vipra that He would be very glad to accept the chipped rice which he had brought from home, yet out of great shyness, Sudāmā Vipra hesitated to present it to the Lord. He was thinking, "How can I offer such insignificant things to Kṛṣṇa?" and he simply bowed his head.

Lord Kṛṣṇa, the Supersoul, knows everything in everyone's heart. He knows everyone's determination and everyone's want. He knew, therefore, the reason for Sudāmā Vipra's coming to Him. He knew that, driven by extreme poverty, he had come there at the request of his wife. Thinking of Sudāmā as His very dear class friend, He knew that Sudāmā's love for Him as a friend was never tainted by any desire for material benefit. Kṛṣṇa thought, "Sudāmā has not come asking anything from Me, but being obliged by the request of his wife, he has come to see Me just to please her." Lord Kṛṣṇa therefore decided that He would give more material opulence to Sudāmā Vipra than could be imagined even by the King of heaven.

He then snatched the bundel of chipped rice which was hanging on the shoulder of the poor *brāhmaṇa,* packed in one corner of his wrapper, and said, "What is this? My dear friend, you have brought Me nice, palatable chipped rice!" He encouraged Sudāmā Vipra, saying, "I consider that this quantity of chipped rice will not only satisfy Me, but will satisfy the whole creation." It is understood from this statement that Kṛṣṇa, being the original source of everything, is the root of the entire creation. As watering the root of a tree immediately distributes water to every part of the tree, so an offering made to Kṛṣṇa, or any action done for Kṛṣṇa, is to be considered the highest welfare work for everyone, because the benefit of such an offering is distributed throughout the creation. Love for Kṛṣṇa becomes distributed to all living entities.

While Lord Kṛṣṇa was speaking to Sudāmā Vipra, He ate one morsel of chipped rice from his bundle, and when He attempted to eat a second morsel, Rukmiṇīdevī, who is the goddess of fortune herself, checked the Lord by catching hold of His hand. After touching the hand of Kṛṣṇa, Rukmiṇī said, "My dear Lord, this one morsel of chipped rice is sufficient to cause him who offered it to become very opulent in this life and to continue his opulence in the next life. My Lord, You are so kind to Your devotee that even this one morsel of chipped rice pleases You very greatly, and Your pleasure assures the devotee opulence both in this life and in the next." This indicates that when food is offered to Lord Kṛṣṇa with love and devotion and He is pleased and accepts it from the devotee, Rukmiṇīdevī, the goddess of fortune, becomes so greatly obliged to the devotee that she has to personally go to the devotee's home to turn it into the most opulent home in the world. If one feeds Nārāyaṇa sumptuously, the goddess of fortune, Lakṣmī, automatically becomes a guest in one's house, which means that one's home becomes opulent. The learned *brāhmaṇa* Sudāmā passed that night at the house of Lord Kṛṣṇa, and while he was there he felt as if he were living in the Vaikuṇṭha planet. Actually he was living in Vaikuṇṭha, because wherever Lord Kṛṣṇa, the original Nārāyaṇa, and Rukmiṇīdevī, the goddess of fortune, live is not different from the spiritual planet, Vaikuṇṭhaloka.

The learned *brāhmaṇa* Sudāmā did not appear to have received anything substantial from Lord Kṛṣṇa while he was at His place, and yet he did not ask anything from the Lord. The next morning he started for his home, thinking always about his reception by Kṛṣṇa, and thus he became merged in transcendental bliss. All the way home he was simply remembering the dealings of Lord Kṛṣṇa, and he was feeling very happy to have seen the Lord.

The *brāhmaṇa* began to think as follows: "It is most pleasurable to see Lord Kṛṣṇa, who is most devoted to the *brāhmaṇas*. How great a lover He is of the brahminical culture! He is the Supreme *Brahman* Himself, yet He reciprocates with the *brāhmaṇas*. He also respects the *brāhmaṇas* so much that He embraced to His chest a poor *brāhmaṇa* like me, although He never embraces anyone to His chest except the goddess of fortune. How can there be any comparison between me, a poor, sinful *brāhmaṇa,* and the Supreme Lord Kṛṣṇa, who is the only shelter of the goddess of fortune? And yet, considering me as a *brāhmaṇa,* He embraced me with heartfelt pleasure in His two transcendental arms. Lord Kṛṣṇa was so kind to me that He allowed me to sit down on the same bedstead where the goddess of fortune lies down. He considered me to be His real brother. How can I appreciate my obligation to Him? When I was tired, Śrīmatī Rukmiṇīdevī, the goddess of fortune, began to fan me, holding the *cāmara* whisk in her own hand. She never considered her exalted position as the first queen of Lord Kṛṣṇa. I was rendered service by the Supreme Personality of Godhead because of His high regard for the *brāhmaṇas,* and by massaging my legs and feeding me with His own hand, He practically worshiped me! Aspiring for elevation to the heavenly planets, or liberation or all kinds of material opulences, or perfection in the mystic *yoga* powers, everyone throughout the universe worships the lotus feet of Lord Kṛṣṇa. Yet the Lord was so kind to me that He did not give me even a farthing, knowing very well that I am a poverty-stricken man who, if I got some money, might become puffed up and mad after material opulence and so forget Him."

The statement of the *brāhmaṇa* Sudāmā is correct. An ordinary man who is very poor and prays to the Lord for benediction in material opulence, and who somehow or other becomes richer in material opulence, immediately forgets his obligation to the Lord. Therefore, the Lord does not offer opulences to His devotee unless the devotee is thoroughly destitute. Rather, if a neophyte devotee serves the Lord very sincerely and at the same time wants material opulence, the Lord keeps him from obtaining it.

Thinking in this way, the learned *brāhmaṇa* gradually reached his own home. But on reaching there he saw that everything was wonderfully changed. He saw that in place of his cottage there were big palaces made of valuable stones and jewels, glittering like the sun, moon and rays of fire. Not only were there big palaces, but at intervals there were beautifully decorated parks, in which many beautiful men and women were strolling. In those parks there were nice lakes full of lotus flowers and beautiful lilies, and there were flocks of multicolored birds. Seeing the wonderful conversion of his native place, the *brāhmaṇa* began to think to himself, "How am I seeing all these changes? Does this place belong to me, or to someone else? If it is the same place where I used to live, then how has it so wonderfully changed?"

While the learned *brāhmaṇa* was considering this, a group of beautiful men and women with features resembling those of the demigods, accompanied by musical chanters, approached to welcome him. All were singing auspicious songs. The wife of the *brāhmaṇa* became very glad on hearing the tidings of her husband's arrival, and with great haste she also came out of the palace. The *brāhmaṇa's* wife appeared so beautiful that it seemed as if the goddess of fortune herself had come to receive him. As soon as she saw her husband present before her, tears of joy began to fall from her eyes, and her voice became so choked up that she could not even address her husband. She simply closed her eyes in ecstasy. But with great love and affection she bowed down before her husband, and within herself she thought of embracing him. She was fully decorated with a gold necklace and ornaments, and while standing among the maidservants she appeared like the wife of a demigod just alighting from an airplane. The *brāhmaṇa* was surprised to see his wife so beautiful, and in great affection and without saying a word he entered the palace with his wife.

When the *brāhmaṇa* entered his personal apartment in the palace, he saw that it was not an apartment, but the residence of the King of heaven. The palace was surrounded by many columns of jewels. The couches and the bedsteads were made of ivory, bedecked with gold and jewels, and the bedding was as white as the foam of milk and as soft as a lotus flower. There were many whisks hanging from golden rods, and many golden thrones with sitting cushions as soft as the lotus flower. In various places there were velvet and silken canopies with laces of pearls hanging all around. The structure of the building was standing on first-class transparent marble, with engravings made of emerald stones. All the women in the palace were carrying lamps made of valuable jewels. The flames and the jewels combined to produce a wonderfully brilliant light. When the *brāhmaṇa* saw his position suddenly changed to one of opulence, and when he could not determine the cause for such a sudden change, he began to consider very gravely how it had happened.

He thus began to think, "From the beginning of my life I have been extremely poverty-stricken, so what could be the cause of such great and sudden opulence? I do not find any cause other than the all-merciful glance of my friend Lord Kṛṣṇa, the chief of the Yadu dynasty. Certainly these are gifts of Lord Kṛṣṇa's causeless mercy. The Lord is self-sufficient, the husband of the goddess of fortune, and thus He is always full with six opulences. He can understand the mind of His devotee, and He sumptuously fulfills the devotee's desires. All these are acts of my friend, Lord Kṛṣṇa. My beautiful dark friend Kṛṣṇa is far more liberal than the cloud which can fill up the great ocean with water. Without disturbing the cultivator with rain during the day, the cloud brings liberal rain at night just to satisfy him. And yet when the cultivator wakes up in the morning, he considers that it has not rained enough. Similarly, the Lord fulfills the desire of everyone according to his position, and yet one who is not in Kṛṣṇa consciousness considers all the gifts of the Lord to be less than his desire. On the other hand, when the Lord receives a little thing in love and affection from His devotee, He considers it a great and valuable gift. The vivid example is myself. I simply offered Him a morsel of chipped rice, and in exchange He has given me opulences greater than the opulence of the King of heaven."

What the devotee actually offers to the Lord is not needed by the Lord. He is self-sufficient. If the devotee offers something to the Lord, it acts for his own interest because whatever a devotee offers to the Lord comes back in a quantity a million times greater than what was offered. One does not become a loser by giving to the Lord, but he becomes a gainer by millions of times.

The *brāhmaṇa*, feeling great obligation to Kṛṣṇa, thought, "I pray to have the friendship of Lord Kṛṣṇa and to engage in His service, and to surrender fully unto Him in love and affection, life after life. I do not want any opulence. I only desire not to forget His service. I simply wish to be associated with His pure devotees. May my mind and activities be always engaged in His service. The unborn Supreme Personality of Godhead Kṛṣṇa knows that many great personalities have fallen from their positions because of extravagant opulence. Therefore, even when His devotee asks for some opulence from Him, the Lord sometimes does not give it. He is very cautious about His devotees. Because a devotee in an immature position of devotional service may, if offered great opulence, fall from his position due to being in the material world, the Lord does not offer opulence to him. This is another manifestation of the causeless mercy of the Lord upon His devotee. His first interest is that the devotee may not fall. He is exactly like a well-wishing father who does not give much wealth into the hand of his immature son, but who, when the son is grown up and knows how to spend money, gives him the whole treasury house."

The learned *brāhmaṇa* thus concluded that whatever opulences he had received from the Lord should not be used for his extravagant sense gratification, but for the service of the Lord. The *brāhmaṇa* accepted his newly-acquired opulence, but he did so in a spirit of renunciation, unattached to sense gratification, and thus he lived very peacefully with his wife, enjoying all the facilities of opulence as *prasādam* of the Lord. He enjoyed varieties of foodstuff by offering it to the Lord and then taking it as *prasādam.* Similarly, if by the grace of the Lord we get such opulences as material wealth, fame, power, education and beauty, it is our duty to consider that they are all gifts of the Lord and must be used for His service, not for our sense enjoyment. The learned *brāhmaṇa* remained in that position, and instead of deteriorating due to great opulence, his love and affection for Lord Kṛṣṇa increased day after day. Material opulence can be the cause of degradation and also the cause of elevation, according to the purposes for which it is used. If opulence is used for sense gratification, it is the cause of degradation, and if it is used for the service of the Lord, it is the cause of elevation.

It is evident from Lord Kṛṣṇa's dealings with Sudāmā Vipra that the Supreme Personality of Godhead is very, very pleased with a person who is possessed of brahminical qualities. A qualified *brāhmaṇa* like Sudāmā Vipra is naturally a devotee of Lord Kṛṣṇa. Therefore it is said, *brāhmaṇo vaiṣṇavaḥ:* a *brāhmaṇa* is a *Vaiṣṇava.* Or sometimes it is said, *brāhmaṇaḥ paṇḍitaḥ. Paṇḍita* means a highly learned person. A *brāhmaṇa* cannot be foolish or uneducated. Therefore there are two divisions of *brāhmaṇas,* namely *Vaiṣṇavas* and *paṇḍitas.* Those who are simply learned are *paṇḍits,* but not yet devotees of the Lord, or *Vaiṣṇavas.* Lord Kṛṣṇa is not especially pleased with them. Simply the qualification of being a learned *brāhmaṇa* is not sufficient to attract the Supreme Personality of Godhead. A *brāhmaṇa* must not only be well qualified according to the requirements stated in scriptures such as *Śrīmad Bhagavad-gītā* and *Śrīmad-Bhāgavatam,* but at the same time he must be a devotee of Lord Kṛṣṇa. The vivid example is Sudāmā Vipra. He was a qualified *brāhmaṇa,* unattached to all sorts of material sense enjoyment, and at the same time a great devotee of Lord Kṛṣṇa. Lord Kṛṣṇa, the enjoyer of all sacrifices and penances, is very fond of a *brāhmaṇa* like Sudāmā Vipra, and we have seen by the actual behavior of Lord Kṛṣṇa how much He adores such a *brāhmaṇa.* Therefore, the ideal stage of human perfection is to become a *brāhmaṇa-vaiṣṇava* like Sudāmā Vipra.

Sudāmā Vipra realized that although Lord Kṛṣṇa is unconquerable, He nevertheless agrees to be conquered by His devotees. He realized how kind Lord Kṛṣṇa was to him, and he was always in trance, constantly thinking of Kṛṣṇa. By such constant association with Lord Kṛṣṇa, whatever darkness of material contamination was remaining within his heart was completely cleared away, and very shortly he was transferred to the spiritual kingdom, which is the goal of all saintly persons in the perfectional stage of life. Śukadeva Gosvāmī has stated that all persons who hear this history of Sudāmā Vipra and Lord Kṛṣṇa will know how affectionate Lord Kṛṣṇa is to the *brāhmaṇa* devotees like Sudāmā. Therefore anyone who hears this history gradually becomes as qualified as Sudāmā Vipra, and he is thus transferred to the spiritual kingdom of Lord Kṛṣṇa.

Thus ends the Bhaktivedanta purport of the Eightieth Chapter of Kṛṣṇa, "The Brāhmaṇa Sudāmā Benedicted by Lord Kṛṣṇa."

81 / Lord Kṛṣṇa and Balarāma Meet the Inhabitants of Vṛndāvana

Once upon a time while Lord Kṛṣṇa and Balarāma were living peacefully in Their great city of Dvārakā, there was the rare occasion of a full solar eclipse, such as takes place at the end of every *kalpa,* or day of Brahmā. At the end of every *kalpa* the sun is covered by a great cloud, and incessant rain covers the lower planetary systems up to Svargaloka. By astronomical calculation, people were informed about this great eclipse prior to its taking place, and therefore everyone, both men and women, decided to assemble at the holy place in Kurukṣetra known as Samanta-pañcaka.

The Samanta-pañcaka pilgrimage site is celebrated because Lord Paraśurāma performed great sacrifices there after having killed all the *kṣatriyas* in the world twenty-one times. Lord Paraśurāma killed all the *kṣatriyas,* and their accumulated blood flowed like a stream. Lord Paraśurāma dug five big lakes at Samanta-pañcaka, and filled them with this blood. Lord Paraśurāma is *Viṣṇu-tattva.* As stated in the *Īśopaniṣad, Viṣṇu-tattva* cannot be contaminated by any sinful activity. Yet although Lord Paraśurāma is fully powerful and uncontaminated, in order to exhibit ideal character, He performed great sacrifices at Samanta-pañcaka to atone for His so-called sinful killing of the *kṣatriyas.* By His example, Lord Paraśurāma established that the killing art, although sometimes necessary, is not good. Lord Paraśurāma considered Himself culpable for the sinful killing of the *kṣatriyas;* therefore, how much more are we culpable for such abominable unsanctioned acts. Thus, killing of living entities is prohibited from time immemorial all over the world.

Taking advantage of the occasion of the solar eclipse, all important persons visited the holy place of pilgrimage. Some of the important personalities are mentioned as follows. Among the elderly persons there were Akrūra, Vasudeva and Ugrasena; among the younger generation there were Gada, Pradyumna, Sāmba, and many other members of the Yadu dynasty who had come there with a view to atone for sinful activities accrued in the course of discharging their respective duties. Because almost all the members of the Yadu dynasty went to Kurukṣetra, some important personalities, like Aniruddha, the son of Pradyumna, and Kṛtavarmā, the commander-in-chief of the Yadu dynasty, along with Sucandra, Śuka and Sāraṇa remained in Dvārakā to protect the city.

All the members of the Yadu dynasty were naturally very beautiful, and yet on this occasion, when they appeared duly decorated with gold necklaces and flower garlands, dressed in valuable clothing and properly armed with their respective weapons, their natural beauty and personalities were a hundred times enhanced. The members of the Yadu dynasty came to Kurukṣetra in their gorgeously decorated chariots resembling the airplanes of the demigods, pulled by big horses that moved like the waves of the ocean, and some of them rode on sturdy, stalwart elephants that moved like the clouds in the sky. Their wives were carried on beautiful palanquins by beautiful men whose features resembled those of the Vidyādharas. The entire assembly looked as beautiful as an assembly of the demigods of heaven.

After arriving in Kurukṣetra, the members of the Yadu dynasty took their baths ceremoniously, with self-control, as enjoined in the *śāstras,* and they observed fasting for the whole period of the eclipse in order to nullify the reactions of their sinful activities. Since it is a Vedic custom to give in charity as much as possible during the hours of the eclipse, the members of the Yadu dynasty distributed many hundreds of cows in charity to the *brāhmaṇas.* All those cows were fully decorated with nice dress and ornaments. The special feature of these cows was that they had golden ankle bells and flower garlands on their necks.

All the members of the Yadu dynasty again took their baths in the lakes created by Lord Paraśurāma. After this they sumptuously fed the *brāhmaṇas* with first-class cooked food, all prepared in butter. According to the Vedic system, there are two classes of food. One is called raw food, and the other is called cooked food. Raw food does not include raw vegetables and raw grains, but food boiled in water; whereas cooked food is made in ghee. *Capatis, dahl,* rice and ordinary vegetables are called raw foods, as are fruits and salads. But *purīs, kacuri, saṅgosas,* sweet balls, etc., are called cooked foods. All the *brāhmaṇas* invited on that occasion by the members of the Yadu dynasty were fed sumptuously with cooked food.

The ceremonial functions performed by the members of the Yadu dynasty externally resembled the ritualistic performances performed by the *karmīs*. When a *karmī* performs some ritualistic ceremony, his ambition is sense gratification–good position, good wife, good house, good children or good wealth; but the ambition of the members of the Yadu dynasty was different. Their ambition was to offer perpetual faith and devotion to Kṛṣṇa. All the members of the Yadu dynasty were great devotees. As such, after many births of accumulated pious activities, they were given the chance to associate with Lord Kṛṣṇa. In going to take their baths in the place of pilgrimage at Kurukṣetra or observing the regulative principles during the solar eclipse or feeding the *brāhmaṇas*–in all their activities–they simply thought of devotion to Kṛṣṇa. Their ideal worshipable Lord was Kṛṣṇa, and no one else.

After feeding the *brāhmaṇas,* it is the custom for the host, with their permission, to accept *prasādam*. Thus, with the permission of the *brāhmaṇas,* all the members of the Yadu dynasty took lunch. Then they selected resting places underneath big, shadowy trees, and when they had taken sufficient rest, they prepared to receive visitors, among whom there were relatives and friends, as well as many subordinate kings and rulers. There were the rulers of the Matsya Province, Uśīnara Province, Kośala Province, Vidarbha Province, Kuru Province, Sṛñjaya Province, Kāmboja Province, Kekaya Province and many other countries and provinces. Some of the rulers belonged to opposing parties, and some were friends. But above all, the visitors from Vṛndāvana were most prominent. The residents of Vṛndāvana, headed by Nanda Mahārāja, had been living in great anxiety because of separation from Kṛṣṇa and Balarāma. Taking advantage of the solar eclipse, they all came to see their life and soul, Kṛṣṇa and Balarāma.

The inhabitants of Vṛndāvana were well-wishers and intimate friends of the Yadu dynasty. This meeting of the two parties after long separation was a very touching incident. Both the Yadus and the residents of Vṛndāvana felt such great pleasure in meeting and talking together that it was a unique scene. Meeting after long separation, they were all jubilant; their hearts were throbbing, and their faces appeared like freshly bloomed lotus flowers. There were drops of tears falling from their eyes, the hair on their bodies stood on end, and because of their extreme ecstasy, they were temporarily speechless. In other words, they began to dive in the ocean of happiness.

While the men were meeting in that way, the women were also meeting one another in the same manner. They were embracing each other in great friendship, smiling very mildly, and looking at one another with much affection. When they were embracing each other in their arms, the saffron and *kuṅkuma* spread on their breasts was exchanged from one person to another, and they all felt heavenly ecstasy. Due to such heart-to-heart embracing, torrents of tears glided down their cheeks. The juniors were offering obeisances to the elders, and the elders were offering their blessings to the juniors. They were thus welcoming one another and asking after each other's welfare. Ultimately, however, all their talk was only of Kṛṣṇa. All the neighbors and relatives were connected with Lord Kṛṣṇa's pastimes in this world, and as such Kṛṣṇa was the center of all their activities. Whatever activities they performed—social, political, religious, or conventional—were transcendental.

The real elevation of human life rests on knowledge and renunciation. As stated in the *Śrīmad-Bhāgavatam,* in the First Canto, devotional service rendered to Kṛṣṇa automatically produces perfect knowledge and renunciation. The family members of the Yadu dynasty and the cowherd men of Vṛndāvana had their minds fixed on Kṛṣṇa. That is the symptom of all knowledge, and because their minds were always engaged in Kṛṣṇa, they were automatically freed from all material activities. This stage of life is called *yukta-vairāgya* as enunciated by Śrīla Rūpa Gosvāmī. Knowledge and renunciation, therefore, do not mean dry speculation and renunciation of activities. Rather, one must start speaking and acting only in relationship with Kṛṣṇa.

In this meeting at Kurukṣetra, Kuntīdevī and Vasudeva, who were sister and brother, met after a long period of separation, along with their respective sons and daughters-in-law, wives, children and other family members. By talking among themselves, they soon forgot all their past miseries. Kuntīdevī especially addressed her brother Vasudeva as follows: "My dear brother, I am very unfortunate, because not one of my desires has ever been fulfilled; otherwise how could it happen that although I have such a saintly brother as you, perfect in all respects, you did not inquire from me as to how I was passing my days in a distressed condition of life." It appears that Kuntīdevī was remembering the miserable days when she had been banished along with her sons through the mischevious plans of Dhṛtarāṣṭra and Duryodhana. She continued; "My dear brother, I can understand that when providence goes against someone, even one's nearest relatives also forget him. In such a condition, even one's father, one's mother or one's own children will forget him. Therefore, my dear brother, I do not accuse you."

Vasudeva replied to his sister: "My dear sister, do not be sorry, and do not blame me in that way. We should always remember that we all are only toys in the hands of providence. Everyone is under the control of the Supreme Personality of Godhead. It is under His control only that all kinds of fruitive actions and the resultant reactions take place. My dear sister, you know that we were very much harrassed by King Kaṁsa, and by his persecutions we were scattered here and there. We were always full of anxieties. Only in the last few days have we returned to our own places, by the grace of God."

After this conversation, Vasudeva and Ugrasena received the kings who came to see them, and they sufficiently welcomed them all. Seeing Lord Kṛṣṇa present on the spot, all the visitors felt transcendental pleasure and became very peaceful. Some of the prominent visitors were as follows: Bhīṣmadeva, Droṇācārya, Dhṛtarāṣṭra, Duryodhana, and Gāndhārī along with her sons; King Yudhiṣṭhira along with his wife, and the Pāṇḍavas along with Kuntī; Sṛñjaya, Vidura, Kṛpācārya, Kuntibhoja, Virāṭa, King Nagnajit, Purujit, Drupada, Śalya, Dhṛṣṭaketu, the King of Kāśī, Damaghoṣa, Viśālākṣa, the King of Mithilā, the King of Madras (formerly known as Madra), the King of Kekaya, Yudhāmanyu, Suśarmā, Bāhlīka along with his sons, and many other rulers who were subordinate to King Yudhiṣṭhira.

When they saw Lord Kṛṣṇa with His thousands of queens, they became fully satisfied at the sight of such beauty and transcendental opulence. All who were there personally visited Lord Balarāma and Kṛṣṇa, and being properly welcomed by the Lord they began to glorify the members of the Yadu dynasty, especially Kṛṣṇa and Balarāma. Because he was the King of the Bhojas, Ugrasena was considered the chief Yadu, and therefore the visitors specifically addressed him: "Your majesty Ugrasena, King of the Bhojas, factually the Yadus are the only persons within this world who are perfect in all respects. All glories unto you! All glories unto you! The specific condition of your perfection is that you are always seeing Lord Kṛṣṇa, who is sought after by many mystic *yogīs* undergoing severe austerities and penances for great numbers of years. All of you are in direct touch with Lord Kṛṣṇa at every moment.

"All the Vedic hymns are glorifying the Supreme Personality of Godhead, Kṛṣṇa. The Ganges water is considered sanctified because of its being the water used to wash the lotus feet of Lord Kṛṣṇa. The Vedic literatures are nothing but the injunctions of Lord Kṛṣṇa. The purpose of the study of all the *Vedas* is to know Kṛṣṇa; therefore, the words of Kṛṣṇa and the message of His pastimes are always purifying. By the influence of time and circumstances, all the opulences of this world had become almost completely wiped out, but since Kṛṣṇa has appeared on this planet, all auspicious features have again appeared due to the touch of His lotus feet. Because of His presence, all our ambitions and desires are gradually being fulfilled. Your majesty, King of the Bhojas, you are related with the Yadu dynasty by matrimonial relationship, and by blood relationship also. As a result, you are constantly in touch with Lord Kṛṣṇa, and you have no difficulty in seeing Him at any time. Lord Kṛṣṇa moves with you, talks with you, sits with you, rests with you, and dines with you. The Yadus appear to be always engaged in worldly affairs which are considered to lead to the royal road to hell, but due to the presence of Lord Kṛṣṇa, the original Personality of Godhead in the Viṣṇu category, who is omniscient, omnipresent and omnipotent, all of you are factually relieved from all material contamination, and are situated in the transcendental position of liberation and Brahman existence."

When they had heard that Kṛṣṇa would be present in Kurukṣetra because of the solar eclipse, the residents of Vṛndāvana, headed by Mahārāja Nanda, had also decided to go there, and therefore all the members of the Yadu dynasty were attending. King Nanda, accompanied by his cowherd men, had loaded all their necessary paraphernalia on bullock carts, and all of the Vṛndāvana residents had come to Kurukṣetra to see their beloved sons Lord Balarāma and Lord Kṛṣṇa. When the cowherd men of Vṛndāvana arrived in Kurukṣetra, all the members of the Yadu dynasty became most pleased. As soon as they saw the residents of Vṛndāvana, they stood up to welcome them, and it appeared that they had again regained their life. Both had been very eager to meet, and when they actually came forward and met, they embraced one another to their heart's satisfaction and remained in embrace for a considerable time.

As soon as Vasudeva saw Nanda Mahārāja, he jumped and ran over to him and embraced him very affectionately. Vasudeva began to narrate his past history—how he had been imprisoned by King Kaṁsa, how his babies had been killed, and how immediately after Kṛṣṇa's birth he had carried Him to the place of Nanda Mahārāja, and how Kṛṣṇa and Balarāma had been raised by Nanda Mahārāja and his queen, Yaśodā, as their own children. Similarly, Lord Balarāma and Kṛṣṇa also embraced King Nanda and mother Yaśodā and then offered Their respect unto their lotus feet by bowing down. Because of Their filial affection for Nanda and Yaśodā, both Lord Kṛṣṇa and Balarāma became choked up, and for a few seconds They could not speak. The most fortunate King Nanda and mother Yaśodā placed their sons on their laps and began to embrace Them to their full satisfaction. Because of separation from Kṛṣṇa and Balarāma, both King Nanda and Yaśodā had been merged in great distress for a very long time. Now, after meeting Them and embracing Them, all their sufferings were mitigated.

After this, Kṛṣṇa's mother, Devakī, and Balarāma's mother, Rohiṇī, both embraced mother Yaśodā. They said, "Dear Queen Yaśodādevī, both you and Nanda Mahārāja have been great friends to us, and when we remember you we are immediately overwhelmed by the thought of your friendly activities. We are so indebted to you that even if we were to return your benediction by giving you the opulence of the King of heaven, it would not be enough to repay you for your friendly behavior. We shall never forget your kindly behavior toward us. When both Kṛṣṇa and Balarāma were born, before they even saw Their real father and mother, They were entrusted to your care, and you raised Them as your own children, fostering Them as birds take care of their offspring in the nest. You have nicely fed, nourished and loved Them and have performed many auspicious religious ceremonies for Their benefit.

"Actually They are not our sons; They belong to you. Nanda Mahārāja and yourself are the real father and mother of Kṛṣṇa and Balarāma. As long as They were under your care They had not even a pinch of difficulty. Under your protection, They were completely out of the way of all kinds of fear. This most affectionate care which you have taken for Them is completely befitting your elevated position. The most noble personalities do not discriminate between their own sons and the sons of others, and there cannot be any personalities more noble than Nanda Mahārāja and yourself."

As far as the *gopīs* of Vṛndāvana were concerned, from the very beginning of their lives, they did not know anything beyond Kṛṣṇa. Kṛṣṇa and Balarāma were their life and soul. The *gopīs* were so attached to Kṛṣṇa that they could not even tolerate not seeing Him momentarily when their eyelids blinked and impeded their vision. They condemned Brahmā, the creator of the body, because he foolishly made eyelids which blinked and checked their seeing Kṛṣṇa. Because they had been separated from Kṛṣṇa for so many years, the *gopīs,* having come along with Nanda Mahārāja and mother Yaśodā, felt intense ecstasy in seeing Kṛṣṇa. No one can even imagine how anxious the *gopīs* were to see Kṛṣṇa again. As soon as Kṛṣṇa became visible to them, they took Him inside their hearts through their eyes and embraced Him to their full satisfaction. Even though they were embracing Kṛṣṇa only mentally, they became so ecstatic and overwhelmed with joy that for the time being they completely forgot themselves. The ecstatic trance which they achieved simply by mentally embracing Kṛṣṇa is impossible to achieve even for great *yogīs* constantly engaged in meditation on the Supreme Personality of Godhead. Kṛṣṇa could understand that the *gopīs* were rapt in ecstasy by embracing Him in their minds, and therefore, since He is present in everyone's heart, He also reciprocated the embracing from within.

Kṛṣṇa was sitting with mother Yaśodā and His other mothers, Devakī and Rohiṇī, but when the mothers engaged in talking, He took the opportunity and went to a secluded place to meet the *gopīs.* As soon as He approached the *gopīs,* the Lord began to smile, and after embracing them and inquiring about their welfare, He began to encourage them, saying, "My dear friends, you know that both Lord Balarāma and Myself left Vṛndāvana just to please Our relatives and family members. Thus We were long engaged in fighting with Our enemies and were obliged to forget you, who were so much attached to Me in love and affection. I can understand that by this action I have been ungrateful to you, but still I know you are faithful to Me. May I inquire if you have been thinking of Us although We had to leave you behind? My dear *gopīs,* do you now dislike remembering Me, considering Me to have been ungrateful to you? Do you take My misbehavior with you very seriously?

"After all, you should know it was not My intention to leave you; our separation was ordained by providence, who after all is the supreme controller and does as he desires. He causes the intermingling of different persons, and again disperses them as he desires. Sometimes we see that due to the presence of clouds and strong wind, atomic particles of dust and broken pieces of cotton are intermingled together, and after the strong wind subsides, all the particles of dust and cotton are again separated, scattered in different places. Similarly, the Supreme Lord is the creator of everything. The objects which we see are different manifestations of His energy. By His supreme will we are sometimes united and sometimes separated. We can therefore conclude that ultimately we are absolutely dependent on His will.

"Fortunately, you have developed loving affection for Me, which is the only way to achieve the transcendental position of association with Me. Any living entity who develops such unalloyed devotional affection for Me certainly at the end goes back to home, back to Godhead. In other words, unalloyed devotional service and affection for Me are the cause of supreme liberation.

"My dear *gopī* friends, you may know from Me that it is My energies only which are acting everywhere. Take, for example, an earthen pot. It is nothing but a combination of earth, water, air, fire and sky. It is always of the same physical composites, whether in its beginning, during its existence or after its annihilation. When it is created, the earthen pot is made of earth, water, fire, air and sky; while it remains, it is the same in composition; and when it is broken and annihilated, its different ingredients are conserved in different parts of the material energy. Similarly, at the creation of this cosmic manifestation, during its maintenance, and after its dissolution, everything is but a different manifestation of My energy. And because the energy is not separate from Me, it is to be concluded that I am existing in everything.

"In the same way, the body of a living being is nothing but a composition of the five elements, and the living entity embodied in the material condition is also part and parcel of Me. The living entity is imprisoned in the material condition on account of his false conception of himself as the supreme enjoyer. This false ego of the living entity is the cause of his imprisonment in material existence. As the Supreme Absolute Truth, I am transcendental to the living entity, as well as to his material embodiment. The two energies, material and spiritual, are both acting under My supreme control. My dear *gopīs,* I request that instead of being so afflicted, you try to accept everything with a philosophical attitude. Then you will understand that you are always with Me and that there is no cause of lamentation in our being separated from one another."

This important instruction of Lord Kṛṣṇa's to the *gopīs* can be utilized by all devotees engaged in Kṛṣṇa consciousness. The whole philosophy is considered on the basis of inconceivable, simultaneous oneness and difference. In *Bhagavad-gītā* the Lord says that He is present everywhere in His impersonal feature. Everything is existing in Him, but still He is not personally present everywhere. The cosmic manifestation is nothing but a display of Kṛṣṇa's energy, and because the energy is not different from the energetic, nothing is different from Kṛṣṇa. When this absolute consciousness, Kṛṣṇa consciousness, is absent, we are separated from Kṛṣṇa; but fortunately, if this Kṛṣṇa consciousness is present, then we are not separated from Kṛṣṇa. The process of devotional service is the revival of Kṛṣṇa consciousness, and if the devotee is fortunate enough to understand that the material energy is not separated from Kṛṣṇa, then he can utilize the material energy and its products in the service of the Lord. But in the absence of Kṛṣṇa consciousness, the forgetful living entity, although part and parcel of Kṛṣṇa, falsely puts himself in the position of enjoyer of the material world and, being thus implicated in material entanglement, is forced by the material energy to continue his material existence. This is also confirmed in the *Bhagavad-gītā.* Although a living entity is forced to act by the material energy, he falsely thinks that he is the all-in-all and the supreme enjoyer.

If the devotee knows perfectly that the *arcā-vigraha,* or Deity form of Lord Kṛṣṇa in the temple, is exactly the same *sac-cid-ānanda-vigraha* as Kṛṣṇa Himself, then his service to the temple Deity becomes direct service to the Supreme Personality of Godhead. Similarly, the temple itself, the temple paraphernalia and the food offered to the Deity are also not separate from Kṛṣṇa. One has to follow the rules and regulations prescribed by the *ācāryas,* and thus, under superior guidance, Kṛṣṇa-realization is fully possible, even in this material existence.

The *gopīs,* having been instructed by Kṛṣṇa in this philosophy of simultaneous oneness and difference, remained always in Kṛṣṇa consciousness and thus became liberated from all material contamination. The consciousness of the living entity who falsely presents himself as the enjoyer of the material world is called *jīva-kośa,* which means imprisonment by the false ego. Not only the *gopīs* but anyone who follows these instructions of Kṛṣṇa becomes immediately freed from the *jīva-kośa* imprisonment. A person in full Kṛṣṇa consciousness is always liberated from false egoism; he utilizes everything for Kṛṣṇa's service and is not at any time separated from Kṛṣṇa.

The *gopīs* therefore prayed to Kṛṣṇa, "Dear Kṛṣṇa, from Your navel emanated the original lotus flower which is the birthsite of Brahmā, the creator. No one can estimate Your glories or Your opulence, which therefore remain always a mystery even to the highest thoughtful men, the masters of all yogic power. The conditioned soul fallen in the dark well of this material existence can very easily, however, take shelter of the lotus feet of Lord Kṛṣṇa. Thus his deliverance is guaranteed." The *gopīs* continued: "Dear Kṛṣṇa, we are always busy in our family affairs. We therefore request that You remain within our hearts as the rising sun, and that will be Your greatest benediction."

The *gopīs* are always liberated souls, because they are fully in Kṛṣṇa consciousness. They only pretended to be entangled in household affairs in Vṛndāvana. In spite of their long separation, the inhabitants of Vṛndāvana, the *gopīs,* were not interested in the idea of going with Kṛṣṇa to His capital city, Dvārakā. They wanted to remain busy in Vṛndāvana and thus feel the presence of Kṛṣṇa in every step of their lives. They immediately invited Kṛṣṇa to come back to Vṛndāvana. This transcendental emotional existence of the *gopīs* is the basic principle of Lord Caitanya's teaching. The *Ratha-yātrā* Festival observed by Lord Caitanya is the emotional process of taking Kṛṣṇa back to Vṛndāvana. Śrīmatī Rādhārāṇī refused to go with Kṛṣṇa to Dvārakā to enjoy His company in the atmosphere of royal opulence, but wanted to enjoy His company in the original Vṛndāvana atmosphere. Lord Kṛṣṇa, being profoundly attached to the *gopīs,* never goes away from Vṛndāvana, and the *gopīs* and other residents of Vṛndāvana remain fully satisfied in Kṛṣṇa consciousness.

Thus ends the Bhaktivedanta purport of the Eighty-first Chapter of Kṛṣṇa, *"Lord Kṛṣṇa and Balarāma Meet the Inhabitants of Vṛndāvana."*

82 / Draupadī Meets the Queens of Kṛṣṇa

There were many visitors who came to see Kṛṣṇa, and among them were the Pāṇḍavas, headed by King Yudhiṣṭhira. After talking with the *gopīs* and bestowing upon them the greatest benediction, Lord Kṛṣṇa came to welcome King Yudhiṣṭhira and other relatives who had come to see Him. He first of all inquired from them whether their situation was auspicious. Actually, there is no question of ill fortune for anyone who sees the lotus feet of Lord Kṛṣṇa, yet when Lord Kṛṣṇa, as a matter of etiquette, inquired from King Yudhiṣṭhira about his welfare, the King became very happy by such a reception and began to address the Lord thus: "My dear Lord Kṛṣṇa, great personalities and devotees in full Kṛṣṇa consciousness always think of Your lotus feet and remain fully satisfied by drinking the nectar of transcendental bliss. The nectar which they constantly drink sometimes comes out of their mouths and is sprinkled on others as the narration of Your transcendental activities. This nectar coming from the mouth of a devotee is so powerful that if one is fortunate enough to have the opportunity to drink it, he immediately becomes freed from the continuous journey of birth and death. Our material existence is caused by our forgetfulness of Your personality, but fortunately, the darkness of forgetfulness is immediately dissipated if one is privileged to hear about Your glories. Therefore, my dear Lord, where is the possibility of ill fortune for one who is constantly engaged in hearing Your glorious activities?

"Since we are fully surrendered unto You and have no other shelter than Your lotus feet, we are always confident of our good fortune. My dear Lord, You are the ocean of unlimited knowledge and transcendental bliss. The result of the action of mental concoction is to exist in the three temporary phases of material life—wakefulness, sleep and deep sleep. But these conditions cannot exist in Kṛṣṇa consciousness. All such reactions are invalidated by practice of Kṛṣṇa consciousness. You are the ultimate destination of all liberated persons. Out of Your independent will only, You have descended on this earth by the use of Your own internal potency, *yogamāyā,* and in order to reestablish the Vedic principles of life, You have appeared just like an ordinary human being. Since You are the Supreme Person, there cannot, therefore, be any ill luck for one who has fully surrendered unto You."

When Lord Kṛṣṇa was busy meeting various kinds of visitors and while they were engaged in offering prayers to the Lord, the female members of the Kuru dynasty and the Yadu dynasty took the opportunity of meeting with one another and engaging in talk of Lord Kṛṣṇa's transcendental pastimes. The first inquiry was made by Draupadī to the wives of Lord Kṛṣṇa. She addressed them: "My dear Rukmiṇī, Bhadrā, Jāmbavatī, Satyā, Satyabhāmā, Kālindī, Śaibyā, Lakṣmaṇā, Rohiṇī and all other wives of Lord Kṛṣṇa, will you please let us know how Lord Kṛṣṇa, the Supreme Personality of Godhead, accepted you as His wives and married you in pursuance of the marriage ceremonies of ordinary human beings?

To this question, the chief of the queens, Rukmiṇīdevī, replied, "My dear Draupadī, it was practically a settled fact that princes like Jarāsandha and others wanted me to marry King Śiśupāla, and, as is usual, all the princes present during the marriage ceremony were prepared with their armor and weapons to fight with any rival who dared to stop the marriage. But the Supreme Personality of Godhead kidnapped me the way a lion takes away a lamb from the flock. This was not, however, a very wondrous act for Lord Kṛṣṇa, because anyone who claims to be a very great hero or king within this world is subordinate to the lotus feet of the Lord. All the kings touch their helmets to the lotus feet of Lord Kṛṣṇa. My dear Draupadī, it is my eternal desire that life after life I may be engaged in the service of Lord Kṛṣṇa, who is the reservoir of all pleasure and beauty. This is my only desire and ambition in life."

After this, Satyabhāmā began to speak. She said, "My dear Draupadī, my father was very much afflicted on the death of his brother, Prasena, and he falsely accused Lord Kṛṣṇa of killing his brother and stealing the Syamantaka jewel, which had actually been taken by Jāmbavān. Lord Kṛṣṇa, in order to establish His pure character, fought with Jāmbavān and rescued the Syamantaka jewel, which was later delivered to my father. My father was very much ashamed and sorry for accusing Lord Kṛṣṇa of his brother's death. After getting back the Syamantaka jewel, he thought it wise to rectify his mistake, so although he had promised others my hand in marriage, he submitted the jewel and myself at the lotus feet of Kṛṣṇa, and thus I was accepted as His maidservant and wife."

After this, Jāmbavatī replied to Draupadī's question. She said, "My dear Draupadī, when Lord Kṛṣṇa attacked my father Jāmbavān, the King of the *ṛkṣas,* my father did not know that Lord Kṛṣṇa was his former master, Lord Rāmacandra, the husband of Sītā. Not knowing the identity of Lord Kṛṣṇa, my father remained continually engaged in fighting with Him for twenty-seven days. After this period, when he became very tired and fatigued, he could understand that since no one but Lord Rāmacandra could defeat him, his opponent, Lord Kṛṣṇa, must be the same Lord Rāmacandra. He thus came to his senses and not only immediately returned the Syamantaka jewel, but in order to satisfy the Lord, he presented me to Him to become His wife. In this way I was married to the Lord, and thus my desire to remain life after life as a servitor of Kṛṣṇa was fulfilled."

After this, Kālindī said, "My dear Draupadī, I was engaged in great austerities and penances in order to get Lord Kṛṣṇa as my husband. When Lord Kṛṣṇa became aware of this fact, He very kindly came to me along with His friend Arjuna and accepted me as His wife. Lord Kṛṣṇa then took me away from the bank of Yamunā, and since then I have been engaged in the house of Lord Kṛṣṇa as a sweeper. And the Lord is treating me as His wife."

After this, Mitravindā said, "My dear Draupadī, there was a great assembly of princes at my *svayaṁvara* ceremony. Lord Kṛṣṇa was also present in that meeting, and He accepted me as His maidservant by defeating all the princes present there. He immediately took me away to Dvārakā, exactly as a lion takes a deer from a pack of dogs. When I was thus taken away by Lord Kṛṣṇa, my brothers wanted to fight with Him, and later on they were defeated. Thus my desire to become the maidservant of Kṛṣṇa life after life was fulfilled."

After this, Satyā addressed Draupadī in this way: "My dear Draupadī, my father arranged for an assembly for my *svayaṁvara* [the personal selection of a husband], and in order to test the strength and heroism of the prospective bridegrooms, my father stipulated that they each fight with his seven ferocious bulls, which had long, serpentine horns. Many heroic prospective bridegrooms tried to defeat the bulls, but unfortunately they were all severely struck, and they returned to their homes as defeated invalids. When Lord Śrī Kṛṣṇa came and fought with the bulls, they were just like playthings for Him. He captured the bulls and roped each one of them by their nostrils. Thus they came under His control, just like a goat's small kids come very easily under the control of children.

My father became very pleased and married me with Lord Kṛṣṇa in great pomp, giving as my dowry many divisions of soldiers, horses, chariots and elephants, along with hundreds of maidservants. Thus Lord Kṛṣṇa brought me to His capital city, Dvārakā. On the way back, He was also assaulted by many princes, but Lord Kṛṣṇa defeated all of them, and thus I have the privilege of serving His lotus feet as a maidservant."

After this, Bhadrā began to speak. She said, "My dear Draupadī, Lord Kṛṣṇa is the son of my maternal uncle. Fortunately, I became attracted to His lotus feet. When my father understood these feelings of mine, he personally arranged for my marriage, inviting Lord Kṛṣṇa to marry me and giving Him in dowry one *akṣauhiṇī,* or division of armed forces, along with many maidservants and other royal paraphernalia. I do not know whether I shall be able to have the shelter of Lord Kṛṣṇa life after life, but still I pray to the Lord that wherever I may take my birth I may not forget my relationship with His lotus feet."

Then Lakṣmaṇā said, "My dear Queen, many times I have heard the great sage Nārada glorifying the pastimes of Lord Kṛṣṇa. I became attracted to the lotus feet of Kṛṣṇa when I heard Nārada say that the goddess of fortune, Lakṣmī, was also attracted to His lotus feet. Since then I have always been thinking of Him, and thus my attraction for Him has increased. My dear Queen, my father was very affectionate toward me. When he understood that I was attracted to Kṛṣṇa, he devised a plan. His plan was like that devised by your father; during the *svayaṁvara,* the prospective bridegrooms had to pierce the eyes of a fish with their arrows. The difference between the competition in your *svayaṁvara* and mine was that in your case the fish was hanging openly on the ceiling, in clear view, but in my case the fish was covered with a cloth and could only be seen by the reflection of the cloth in a pot of water. That was the special feature of my *svayaṁvara.*

"The news of this device was spread all over the world, and when the princes heard of it, they arrived at my father's capital city from all directions, fully equipped with armor and guided by their military instructors. Each one of them desired to win me as his wife, and one after another they raised the bow and arrow which was left there for piercing the fish. Many could not even join the bowstring to the two ends of the bow, and without attempting to pierce the fish, they simply left the bow as it was and went away. Some with great difficulty drew the string from one end to the other, and being unable to tie the other end, they were suddenly knocked down by the spring-like bow. My dear Queen, you will be surprised to know that at my *svayaṁvara* meeting there were many famous kings and heroes present. Heroes like Jarāsandha, Ambaṣṭha, Śiśupāla, Bhīmasena, Duryodhana and Karṇa were, of course, able to string the bow, but they could not pierce the fish, because it was covered, and they could not trace it out from the reflection. The celebrated hero of the Pāṇḍavas, Arjuna, was able to see the reflection of the fish on the water, but although with great caution he traced out the location of the fish and shot an arrow, he did not pierce the fish in the right spot. His arrow at least touched the fish, and so he proved himself better than all other princes.

"All the princes who had tried to pierce the target were disappointed, being baffled in their attempts, and some candidates had even left the place without making an attempt, but when at last Lord Kṛṣṇa took up the bow, He was able to tie the bowstring very easily, just as a child plays with a toy. He placed the arrow, and looking only once at the reflection of the fish in the water, He shot the arrow, and the pierced fish immediately fell down. This victory of Lord Kṛṣṇa was accomplished at noon, during the moment called *abhijit,* which is astronomically calculated as auspicious. At that time the vibration of *'Jaya! Jaya!'* was heard all over the world, and from the sky came sounds of drums beat by the denizens of heaven. Great demigods were overwhelmed with joy and began to shower flowers on the earth.

"At that time, I entered the arena of competition, and the ankle bells on my legs were sounding very melodiously as I walked. I was nicely dressed with new silken garments, flowers were decorating my hair, and because of Lord Kṛṣṇa's victory, I was in ecstatic joy and smiling very pleasingly. I was carrying in my hands a golden necklace bedecked with jewels, which was glittered at intervals. My curling hair encircled my face, which was shining with a bright luster due to the reflection of my various rings. My eyes blinking, I first of all observed all the princes present, and when I reached my Lord I very slowly placed the golden necklace on His neck. As I have already informed you, from the very beginning my mind had been attracted by Lord Kṛṣṇa, and thus I considered the garlanding of the Lord to be my great victory. As soon as I placed my garland on the neck of the Lord, there sounded immediately the combined vibration of *mṛdaṅgas, paṭahas,* conchshells, drums, kettledrums and other instruments, causing a tumultuous sound, and while the music played, expert male and female dancers began to dance, and singers began to sing sweetly.

"My dear Draupadī, when I accepted Lord Kṛṣṇa as my worshipable husband, and He also accepted me as His maidservant, there was a tumultuous roaring among the disappointed princes. All of them became very agitated because of their lusty desires, but without caring for them, my husband, in His form as the four-handed Nārāyaṇa, immediately took me on His chariot, which was drawn by four excellent horses. Expecting opposition from the princes, He armored Himself and took up His bow named Śārṅga, but our celebrated driver, Dāruka, drove the beautiful chariot without a moment's delay toward the city of Dvārakā. Thus, in the presence of all the princes, I was carried away very quickly, exactly as a deer is carried away from the flock by a lion. Some of the princes, however, wanted to check our progress, and thus, equipped with proper weapons, they opposed us, just as dogs try to oppose the progressive march of a lion. At that time, due to the arrows released by the Śārṅga bow of Lord Kṛṣṇa, some of the princes were cut on their left hands, some of them lost their legs, and some lost their heads and their lives, and others fled from the battlefield.

"The Supreme Personality of Godhead then entered the most celebrated city of the universe, Dvārakā, and as He entered the city, He appeared like the shining sun. The whole city of Dvārakā was profusely decorated on that occasion. There were so many flags and festoons and gates all over Dvārakā that the sunshine could not even enter the city. I have already told you that my father was very much affectionate to me, so when he saw that my desire was fulfilled by getting Lord Kṛṣṇa as my husband, in great happiness he began to distribute to friends and relatives various kinds of gifts, such as valuable dresses, ornaments, bedsteads and sitting carpets. Lord Kṛṣṇa is always self-sufficient, yet my father, out of his own accord, offered my husband a dowry consisting of riches, soldiers, elephants, chariots, horses and many rare and valuable weapons. He presented all these to the Lord with great enthusiasm. My dear Queen, at that time I could guess that in my previous life I must have performed some wonderfully pious activity, and as a result I can in this life be one of the maidservants in the house of the Supreme Personality of Godhead."

When all the principal queens of Lord Kṛṣṇa had finished their statements, Rohiṇī, as the representative of the other sixteen thousand queens, began to narrate the incident of their becoming wives of Kṛṣṇa.

"My dear Queen, when Bhaumāsura was conquering all the world, he collected wherever possible all the beautiful daughters of the kings and kept us arrested within his palace. When news of our imprisonment reached Lord Kṛṣṇa, He fought with Bhaumāsura and released us. Lord Kṛṣṇa killed Bhaumāsura and all his soldiers, and although He had no need to accept even one wife, He nevertheless, by our request, married all sixteen thousand of us. My dear Queen, our only qualification was that we were always thinking of the lotus feet of Lord Kṛṣṇa, which is the way to release oneself from the bondage of repeated birth and death. My dear Queen Draupadī, please take it from us that we are not after any opulence such as kingdom, empire, or a position of heavenly enjoyment. We do not want to enjoy such material opulences, nor do we desire to achieve the yogic perfections, nor the exhalted post of Lord Brahmā. Nor do we want any of the different kinds of liberation—*sālokya, sārṣṭi, sāmīpya* or *sāyujya.* We are not at all attracted by any of these opulences. Our only ambition is to bear on our heads life after life the dust particles attached to the lotus feet of Lord Kṛṣṇa. The goddess of fortune also desired to keep that dust on her breast along with the fragrant saffron. We simply desire this dust, which accumulates underneath the lotus feet of Kṛṣṇa as He travels on the land of Vṛndāvana as a cowherd boy. The *gopīs* especially, and also the cowherd men and the aborigine tribeswomen, always desire to become the grass and straw on the street of Vṛndāvana, to be trampled on by the lotus feet of Kṛṣṇa. My dear Queen, we wish to remain as such life after life, without any other desire."

Thus ends the Bhaktivedanta purport of the Eighty-second Chapter of Kṛṣṇa, *"Draupadī Meets the Queens of Kṛṣṇa."*

83 / Sacrificial Ceremonies Performed by Vasudeva

Among the women present at Kurukṣetra during the solar eclipse were Kuntī, Gāndhārī, Draupadī, Subhadrā and the queens of many other kings, as well as the *gopīs* from Vṛndāvana. When the different queens of Lord Kṛṣṇa were submitting their statements as to how they were married and accepted by Lord Kṛṣṇa as His wives, all the female members of the Kuru dynasty were struck with wonder. They were filled with admiration at how all the queens of Kṛṣṇa were attached to Him with love and affection. When they heard about the queens' intensity of love and affection for Kṛṣṇa, they could not check their eyes from filling up with tears.

While the women were engaged in conversations among themselves and the men were similarly engaged in conversation, there arrived almost all the important sages and ascetics from all directions, who had come for the purpose of seeing Lord Kṛṣṇa and Balarāma. Chief among the sages were Kṛṣṇa-dvaipāyana Vyāsa, the great sage Nārada, Cyavana, Devala, Asita, Viśvāmitra, Śatānanda, Bharadvāja, Gautama, and Lord Paraśurāma along with his disciples; Vasiṣṭha, Gālava, Bhṛgu, Pulastya, Kaśyapa, Atri, Mārkaṇḍeya, Bṛhaspati, Dvita, Trita, Ekata; the four Kumāra sons of Brahmā, Sanaka, Sanandana, Sanātana and Sanatkumāra; Aṅgira and Agastya, Yājñavalkya and Vāmadeva.

As soon as the sages and ascetics arrived, all the kings, including Mahārāja Yudhiṣṭhira and the Pāṇḍavas and Lord Kṛṣṇa and Balarāma, immediately got up from their seats and offered their respects by bowing down to the universally respected sages. After this, the sages were properly welcomed by being offered seats and water for washing their feet. Palatable fruits, garlands of flowers, incense, and sandalwood pulp were presented, and all the kings, led by Kṛṣṇa and Balarāma, worshiped the sages according to the Vedic rules and regulations. When all the sages were comfortably seated, Lord Kṛṣṇa, who descended for the protection of religion, began to address them on behalf of all the kings. When Kṛṣṇa began to speak, all became silent, being eager to hear and understand His welcoming words to the sages.

Lord Kṛṣṇa spoke thus: "All glories to the assembled sages and ascetics! Today we are all feeling that our lives have become successful. Today we have achieved the desired goal of life, because we are now seeing face to face all the exalted liberated sages and ascetics whom even the great demigods in the heavens desire to see. Persons who are neophytes in devotional service and who simply offer their respectful obeisances to the Deity in the temple but cannot realize that the Lord is situated in everyone's heart, and those who simply worship different demigods for fulfillment of their own lusty desires, are unable to understand the importance of these sages. They cannot take advantage of receiving these sages by seeing them with their eyes, by touching their lotus feet, by inquiring about their welfare or by diligently worshiping them."

Neophyte devotees or religionists cannot understand the importance of great *mahātmās.* They go to the temple as a matter of formality and pay their respectful obeisances unto the Deity. When one is promoted to the next platform of trance consciousness, one can understand the importance of *mahātmās* and devotees, and in that stage the devotee tries to please them. Therefore, Lord Kṛṣṇa said that the neophyte cannot understand the importance of great sages, devotees or ascetics.

Kṛṣṇa continued, "One cannot purify himself by traveling to holy places of pilgrimage and taking bath there or by seeing the Deities in the temples. But if one happens to meet a great devotee, a *mahātmā* who is representative of the Personality of Godhead, one becomes immediately purified. In order to become purified, there is the injunction to worship the fire, the sun, the moon, the earth, the water, the air, the sky and the mind. By worshiping all the elements and their predominating deities, one can become free from the influence of envy, but all the sins of an envious person can be nullified immediately simply by serving a great soul. My dear revered sages and respectable kings, you can take it from Me that a person who accepts this material body made of three elements—mucus, bile and air—as his own self, who considers his family and relatives as his own, and who accepts material things as worshipable, or who visits holy places of pilgrimage just to take a bath there, but never associates with great personalities, sages and *mahātmās*—such a person, even in the form of a human being, is nothing but an animal, like an ass."

When the supreme authority, Lord Kṛṣṇa, was thus speaking with great gravity, all the sages and ascetics remained in dead silence. They became amazed upon hearing Him speaking the absolute philosophy of life in such a concise way. Unless one is very much advanced in knowledge, one thinks his body to be his self, his family members to be his kith and kin, and the land of his birth to be worshipable. From this concept of life, the modern ideology of nationalism has sprung up. Lord Kṛṣṇa condemned such ideas, and He also condemned persons who take the trouble to go to holy places of pilgrimage just to take a bath and come back without taking the opportunity to associate with the great devotees and *mahātmās* living there. Such persons are compared to the most foolish animal, the ass. All those who heard considered the speech of Lord Kṛṣṇa for some time, and they concluded that Lord Kṛṣṇa was actually the Supreme Personality of Godhead, playing the role of an ordinary human being who is forced to take a certain type of body as a result of the reactions of his past deeds. He was assuming this pastime as an ordinary human simply to teach the people in general how they should live for perfection of the human mission.

Having concluded that Kṛṣṇa was the Supreme Personality of Godhead, the sages began to address Him thus: "Dear Lord, we, the leaders of human society, are supposed to possess the proper philosophy of life, and yet we are becoming bewildered by the spell of Your external energy. We are surprised to see Your behavior, which is just like that of an ordinary human being and which conceals Your real identity as the Supreme Personality of Godhead, and we therefore consider Your pastimes to be all-wonderful.

"Our dear Lord, by Your own energy You are creating, maintaining and annhilating the whole cosmic manifestation of different names and forms, in the same way as the earth creates many forms of stone, trees and other varieties of names and forms and yet remains the same. Although You are creating varieties of manifestation through Your energy, You are unaffected by all those actions. Our dear Lord, we remain simply stunned by seeing Your wonderful actions. Although You are transcendental to this entire material creation and are the Supreme Lord and the Supersoul of all living entities, You nevertheless appear on this earth by Your internal potency to protect Your devotees and destroy the miscreants. By such appearance You reestablish the principles of eternal religion, which the human society forgets by long association with the material energy. Our dear Lord, You are the creator of the social orders and spiritual statuses of the human society according to quality and work, and when these orders are misguided by unscrupulous persons, You appear and set them right.

"Dear Lord, the Vedic knowledge is the representation of Your pure heart. Austerities, study of the *Vedas,* and meditative trances lead to

Seeing Pauṇḍraka imitating His posture and dress, He could not check His laughter. (p. 453)

The demigod was obliged to accept the body of a lizard. (p. 444)

This time, Nārada Muni saw that Lord Kṛṣṇa was engaged as an affectionate father petting His small children. (p. 478)

Śiśupāla continued to insult Kṛṣṇa, and Kṛṣṇa patiently heard him without a protest. (p. 519)

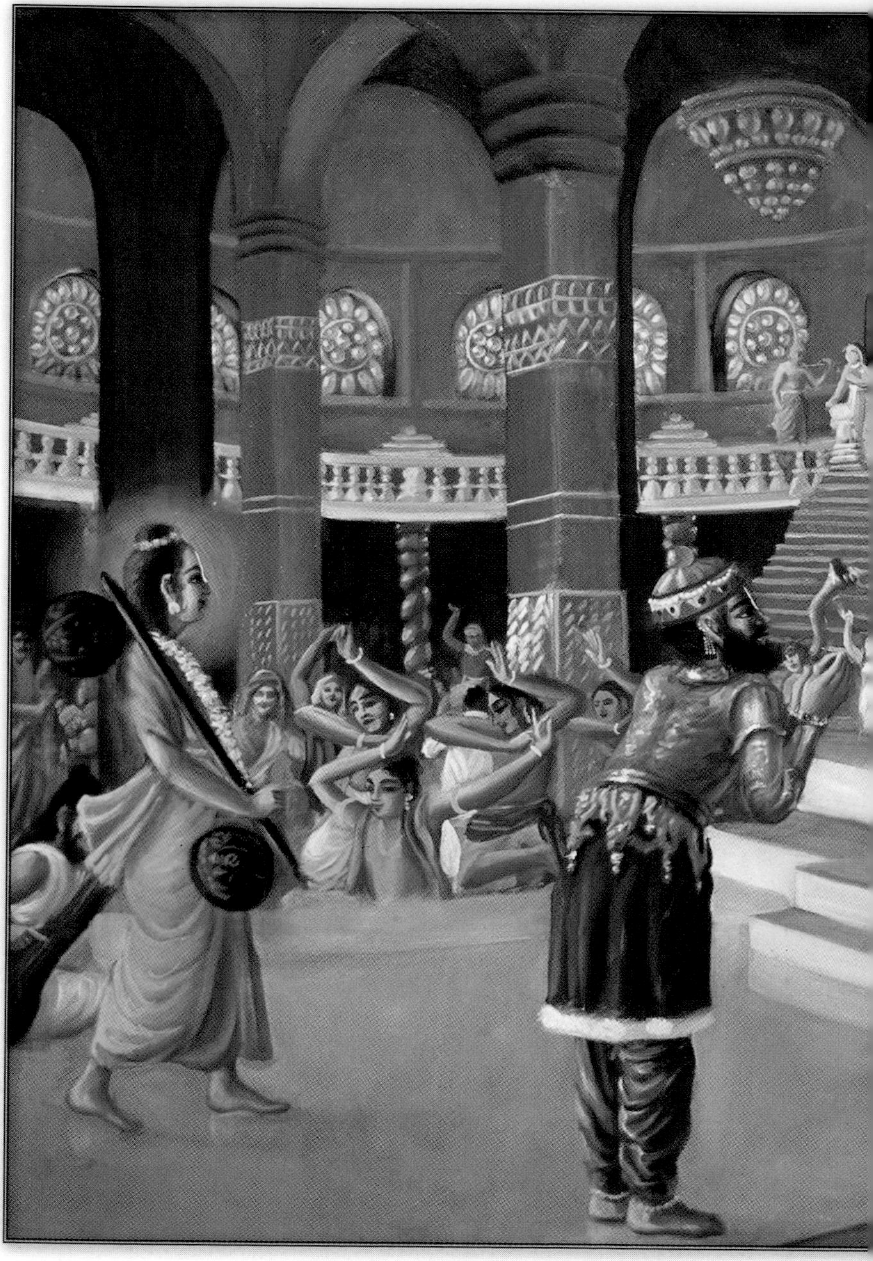

Lord Kṛṣṇa immediately stood up along with His ministers and secretaries to receive the great sage Nārada Muni. (p. 493)

They were all enjoying the occasion by throwing liquid substances on each other. (p. 523)

Kṛṣṇa cut off Śālva's head, and the head, with earrings and helmets, fell on the ground. (p. 535)

Balarāma killed Romaharṣaṇa simply by striking him with a blade of grass. (p. 540)

At the first opportunity Balarāma dragged the demon down with His plow. (p. 543)

The women in the palace were surprised to see that the poor *brāhmaṇa* was seated on the bedstead of Lord Kṛṣṇa. (p. 554)

Arjuna was simply looking over beautiful Subhadrā who was very enchanting even to the great heroes and kings. (p. 603)

The personified *Vedas* assembled around the Lord and began to glorify Him. (p. 618)

The Lord would sprinkle water on the bodies of the queens with a syringe-like instrument. (p. 717)

All the members of the Yadu dynasty again took their baths in the lakes created by Lord Paraśurāma. (p. 566)

different realizations of Your Self in Your manifested and nonmanifested aspects. The entire phenomenal world is a manifestation of Your impersonal energy, but You Yourself, as the original Personality of Godhead, are nonmanifested there. You are the Supreme Soul, the Supreme Brahman. Persons who are situated in brahminical culture, therefore, can understand the truth about Your transcendental form. Thus You always hold the *brāhmaṇas* in respect, and thus You are considered to be the topmost of all followers of brahminical culture. You are therefore known as *brahmaṇya-deva.* Our dear Lord, You are the last word in good fortune and the last resort of all saintly persons; therefore we all consider that we have achieved the perfection of our life, education, austerity and acquisition of transcendental knowledge by meeting You. Factually, You are the ultimate goal of all transcendental achievements.

"Our dear Lord, there is no end to Your unlimited knowledge. Your form is transcendental, eternally existing in full bliss and knowledge. You are the Supreme Personality of Godhead, the Supreme Brahman, the Supreme Soul. Being covered by the spell of Your internal potency, *yogamāyā,* You are now temporarily concealing Your unlimited potencies, but still we can understand Your exalted position, and therefore all of us offer You our respectful obeisances. Dear Lord, You are enjoying Your pastimes in the role of a human being, concealing Your real character of transcendental opulence; therefore, all the kings who are present here, even the members of the Yadu dynasty who are constantly mingling with You, eating with You, and sitting with You, cannot understand that You are the original cause of all causes, the soul of everyone, the original cause of all creation.

"When a person dreams at night, hallucinatory figures created by the dream are accepted as real, and the imaginary dream body is accepted as one's real body. For the time being one forgets that besides the body created in hallucination, there is another, real body in his awakened state. Similarly, in the awakened state also, the bewildered conditioned soul considers sense enjoyment to be real happiness.

"By the process of enjoyment of the senses of the material body, the spirit soul is covered, and his consciousness becomes materially contaminated. It is due to material consciousness that one cannot understand the Supreme Personality of Godhead, Kṛṣṇa. All great mystic *yogīs* endeavor to revive their Kṛṣṇa consciousness by mature practice of the *yoga* system and thus understand Your lotus feet and meditate upon Your transcendental form. In this way the accumulated result of sinful activities is counteracted. It is said that the water of the Ganges can vanquish volumes of a person's sinful actions, but the Ganges water is glorious only due to

Your lotus feet. The Ganges water is flowing as perspiration from the lotus feet of Your Lordship. And we are all so fortunate that today we have been able to directly see Your lotus feet. Dear Lord, we are all surrendered souls, devotees of Your Lordship; therefore, please be kind and bestow Your causeless mercy upon us. We know well that persons who have become liberated by constant engagement in Your devotional service are no longer contaminated by the material modes of nature; thus they have become eligible to be promoted to the kingdom of God in the spiritual world."

After first offering prayers to Lord Kṛṣṇa, the assembled sages wanted to take permission from King Dhṛtarāṣṭra and King Yudhiṣṭhira and then depart for their respective *āśramas.* At that time, however, Vasudeva, the father of Lord Kṛṣṇa and the most celebrated of all pious men, approached the sages and with great humility offered his respects by falling down at their feet. Vasudeva said, "My dear great sages, you are more respected than the demigods. I therefore offer my respectful obeisances unto you. I wish that you will accept my one request, if you so desire. I shall consider it a great blessing if you kindly explain the supreme fruitive activity by which one can counteract the reactions of all other activities."

The great sage Nārada was the leader of all the sages present there. Therefore he began to speak. "My dear sages," he said, "it is not very difficult to understand that because of his great goodness and simplicity, Vasudeva, who has become the father of the Personality of Godhead by accepting Kṛṣṇa as his son, is inclined to ask us about his welfare. It is said that familiarity breeds contempt. As such, Vasudeva, having Kṛṣṇa as his son, does not regard Kṛṣṇa with awe and veneration. Sometimes it is seen that persons who are living on the bank of the Ganges do not consider the Ganges to be very important, and they go far away in order to take their baths at a place of pilgrimage. Being that Lord Kṛṣṇa, whose knowledge is never second in any circumstances, is personally present, there is no need of Vasudeva's asking us for instruction.

"Lord Kṛṣṇa is not affected by the process of creation, maintenance and annihilation; His knowledge is never influenced by any agency beyond Himself. He is not agitated by the interaction of the material qualities, which changes things in the modes of time. His transcendental form is full of knowledge which never becomes agitated by ignorance, pride, attachment, envy or sense enjoyment. His knowledge is never subjected to the laws of *karma* regarding pious or impious activities; nor is it influenced by the three modes of material energy. No one is greater than or equal to Him, because He is the supreme authority, the Personality of Godhead.

"The ordinary conditioned human being may think the conditioned soul, who is covered by his materialistic senses, mind and intelligence, to be equal to Kṛṣṇa, but Lord Kṛṣṇa is just like the sun, which, although it sometimes may appear to be so, is never covered by the cloud, snow or fog or by other planets. When the eyes of less intelligent men are covered by such influences, they think the sun to be invisible. Similarly, persons influenced by the senses and addicted to material enjoyment cannot have a clear vision of the Supreme Personality of Godhead."

The sages present then began to address Vasudeva in the presence of Lord Kṛṣṇa, Balarāma and many other kings, and, as requested by him, they gave their instructions: "To counteract the reaction of *karma,* or desires impelling one to fruitive activities, one must execute the prescribed sacrifices which are meant for worshiping Lord Viṣṇu with faith and devotion. Lord Viṣṇu is the beneficiary of the results of all sacrificial performances. Great personalities and sages who are sufficiently experienced to possess vision of the three phases of the time element, namely past, present and future, and those who are able to see everything clearly through the eyes of revealed scriptures, have unanimously recommended that to purify the dust of material contamination accumulated in the heart and to clear the path of liberation and thereby achieve transcendental bliss, one must please Lord Viṣṇu. For everyone in the different social orders *(brāhmaṇa, kṣatriya* and *vaiśya)* who are living as householders, this worship of the Supreme Personality of Godhead Lord Viṣṇu, who is known as Puruṣottama, the original person, is recommended as the only auspicious path.

"All conditioned souls within this material world have deep-rooted desires to lord it over the resources of material nature. Everyone wants to accumulate riches, everyone wants to enjoy life to the greatest extent, everyone wants a wife, home and children, and everyone wants to become happy in this world and be elevated to the heavenly planets in the next life. But these desires are the causes of one's material bondage. Therefore, to get liberation from this bondage, one has to sacrifice his honestly earned riches for the satisfaction of Lord Viṣṇu.

"The only process to counteract all sorts of material desire is to engage oneself in the devotional service of Lord Viṣṇu. In this way a self-controlled person, even while remaining in householder life, should give up the three kinds of material desires, namely desire for the acquisition of material opulences, the enjoyment of wife and children, and elevation to higher planets. Eventually he may give up householder life and accept the renounced order of life, engaging himself completely in the devotional service of the Lord. Everyone, even if born in a higher status of life as *brāhmaṇa, kṣatriya,* or *vaiśya,* is certainly indebted to the demigods, to the sages, to the forefathers, to living entities and so on, and in order to liquidate all these debts, one has to perform sacrifices, study the Vedic literature, and generate children in religious householder life. If somehow one accepts the renounced order of life without fulfilling this debt, certainly he falls down from his position. Today you have already liquidated your debts to your forefathers and the sages. Now, by performing sacrifices, you can free yourself from indebtedness to the demigods and thus take complete shelter of the Supreme Personality of Godhead. My dear Vasudeva, certainly you have already performed many pious activities in your previous lives. Otherwise, how could you be the father of Kṛṣṇa and Balarāma, the Supreme Personality of Godhead?"

Saintly Vasudeva, after hearing all the sages, offered his respectful obeisances unto their lotus feet. In this way he pleased the sages, and then he elected for them to perform the *yajñas.* When the sages were elected as priests of the sacrifices, they also in their turn induced Vasudeva to collect the required paraphernalia for executing the *yajñas* in that place of pilgrimage. Thus Vasudeva was persuaded to start to perform the *yajñas,* and all the members of the Yadu dynasty took their baths, dressed themselves very nicely, and decorated themselves beautifully and garlanded themselves with lotus flowers. Vasudeva's wives, dressed with nice garments and ornaments and golden necklaces, approached the arena of sacrifice carrying in their hands the required articles to offer in the sacrifice.

When everything was complete, there was heard the vibration of *mṛdaṅgas,* conchshells, kettledrums and other musical instruments. Professional dancers, both male and female, began to dance. The *sūtas* and *māgadhas,* who were professional singers, began to offer prayers by singing. The Gandharvas and their wives, whose voices were very sweet, began to sing many auspicious songs. Vasudeva anointed his eyes with collyrium, smeared butter over his body, and then, along with his eighteen wives, headed by Devakī, sat before the priests to be purified by the *abhiṣeka* ceremony. All such ceremonies were observed strictly according to the principles of scriptures, as was done formerly in the case of the moon with the stars. Vasudeva, because he was being initiated for the sacrifice, was dressed in deerskin, but all his wives were dressed with very nice saris, bangles, necklaces, ankle bells, earrings and many other ornaments. Vasudeva looked very beautiful surrounded by his wives, exactly like the King of heaven when he performs such sacrifices.

At that time, when Lord Kṛṣṇa and Lord Balarāma, along with Their wives, children and relatives, sat down in that great sacrificial arena, it appeared that the Supreme Personality of Godhead was present along with all His part and parcel living entities and multi-energies. We have heard from the *śāstras* that Lord Kṛṣṇa has multi-energies and parts and parcels, but now in that sacrificial arena all could actually experience how the Supreme Personality of Godhead eternally exists along with His different energies. At that time, Lord Kṛṣṇa appeared as Lord Nārāyaṇa, and Lord Balarāma appeared as Saṅkarṣaṇa, the reservoir of all living entities.

Vasudeva satisfied Lord Viṣṇu by performing different kinds of sacrifices, such as *jyotiṣṭoma, darṣa* and *pūrṇamāsa.* Some of these *yajñas* are called *prākṛta,* and some of them are known as *sauryasatra* or *vaikṛta.* Thereafter, the other sacrifices, known as *agnihotra,* were also performed, and the prescribed articles were offered in the proper way. In this way Lord Viṣṇu became pleased. The ultimate purpose of offering oblations in sacrifice is to please Lord Viṣṇu. But in this age of Kali it is very difficult to collect the different articles required for offering sacrifices. People have neither the means to collect the required paraphernalia nor the necessary knowledge or tendency to offer such sacrifices. Therefore, in this age of Kali, when people are mostly unfortunate, full of anxieties and disturbed by various kinds of calamities, the only sacrifice recommended is the performance of *saṅkīrtana-yajña.* Worshiping Lord Caitanya by this *saṅkīrtana-yajña* is the only recommended process in this age.

After the performance of the different sacrifices, Vasudeva offered ample riches, clothing, ornaments, cows, land and maidservants to the priests. Thereafter, all the wives of Vasudeva took their *avabhṛtha* baths and performed the part of the sacrificial duties known as *patnīsaṁyāja.* After finishing the offering with all the required paraphernalia, they all took their baths together in the lakes constructed by Paraśurāma, which are known as the Rāma-hrada. After Vasudeva and his wives took their baths, all the garments and ornaments which they wore were distributed to the subordinate persons who were engaged in singing, dancing and similar activities. We may note that the performance of sacrifice necessitates the profuse distribution of riches. Charity is offered to the priests and the *brāhmaṇas* in the beginning, and used garments and ornaments are offered in charity to the subordinate assistants after the performance of the sacrifice.

After offering the used articles to the singers and reciters, Vasudeva and his wives, dressed with new ornaments and dresses, fed everyone very sumptuously, beginning from the *brāhmaṇas* down to the dogs. After this, all the friends, family members, wives and children of Vasudeva, along with all the kings and members of the Vidarbha, Kośala, Kuru, Kāśī, Kekaya and Sṛñjaya dynasties, assembled together. The priests, the demigods, the people in general, the forefathers, the ghosts and the *Cāraṇas* were all sufficiently remunerated by being offered ample gifts and respectful honor. Then all the persons assembled there took permission from Lord Kṛṣṇa, the husband of the goddess of fortune, and while glorifying the perfection of the sacrifice made by Vasudeva, they departed to their respective homes.

At that time, when King Dhṛtarāṣṭra, Vidura, Yudhiṣṭhira, Bhīma, Arjuna, Bhīṣmadeva, Droṇācārya, Kuntī, Nakula, Sahadeva, Nārada, Lord Vyāsadeva and many other relatives and kinsmen were about to part, they felt separation and therefore embraced each and every member of the Yadu dynasty with great feeling. Many others who were assembled in that sacrificial arena also departed. After this, Lord Kṛṣṇa and Lord Balarāma, along with King Ugrasena, satisfied the inhabitants of Vṛndāvana, headed by Mahārāja Nanda and the cowherd men, by profusely offering all kinds of gifts in order to worship them and please them. Out of their great feelings of friendship, the inhabitants of Vṛndāvana remained there for a considerable time along with the members of the Yadu dynasty.

After performing this sacrifice, Vasudeva felt so satisfied that there was no limit to his happiness. All the members of his family were with him, and in their presence he caught hold of the hands of Nanda Mahārāja and addressed him thus: "My dear brother, the Supreme Personality of Godhead has created a great tie of bondage which is known as the bondage of love and affection. I think it is a very difficult job for even the great sages and saintly persons to cut such a tie of love. My dear brother, you have exhibited feelings of love for me, which I was not able to return. I think, therefore, that I am ungrateful. You have behaved exactly as is characteristic of saintly persons, but I shall never be able to repay you. I have no means to repay you for your friendly dealings. Nevertheless I am confident that our tie of love will never break. Our relationship of friendship must ever continue, in spite of my inability to repay you. I hope you will excuse me for this inability.

"My dear brother, in the beginning, due to my being imprisoned, I could never serve you as a friend, and although at the present moment I am very opulent, because of my material prosperity I have become blind. I therefore cannot satisfy you properly even at this time. My dear brother, you are so nice and gentle that you offer all respect to others, but you don't care for any respect for yourself. A person seeking for auspicious progress in life must not possess too much material opulence with which to become blind and puffed up, but he should take care of his friends and relatives."

When Vasudeva was speaking to Nanda Mahārāja in this way, he was influenced by a great feeling for the friendship of Nanda Mahārāja and the beneficial activities executed by King Nanda on his behalf. As such, his eyes filled with tears, and he began to cry. Desiring to please his friend Vasudeva and being affectionately bound with love for Lord Kṛṣṇa and Balarāma, Nanda Mahārāja passed three months in their association. At the end of this time, all the members of the Yadu dynasty tried to please the inhabitants of Vṛndāvana to their hearts' content. The members of the Yadu dynasty tried to satisfy Nanda Mahārāja and his associates by offering them clothing, ornaments, and many other valuable articles, and they all became fully satisfied. Vasudeva, Ugrasena, Lord Kṛṣṇa, Lord Balarāma, Uddhava and all other members of the Yadu dynasty presented their individual gifts to Nanda Mahārāja and his associates. After Nanda Mahārāja received these farewell presentations, he, along with his associates, started for Vrajabhūmi, Vṛndāvana. The minds of the inhabitants of Vṛndāvana remained, however, with Kṛṣṇa and Balarāma, and therefore all of them started for Vṛndāvana without their minds.

When the members of the Vṛṣṇi family saw all their friends and visitors departing, they observed that the rainy season was approaching, and thus they decided to return to Dvārakā. They were fully satisfied, for they regarded Kṛṣṇa as everything. When they returned to Dvārakā, they began with great satisfaction to describe the sacrifice performed by Vasudeva, their meeting with various friends and well-wishers, and various other incidences which occurred during their travels in the places of pilgrimage.

Thus ends the Bhaktivedanta purport of the Eighty-third Chapter of Kṛṣṇa, *"Sacrificial Ceremonies Performed by Vasudeva."*

84 / Spiritual Instruction for Vasudeva and Return of the Six Dead Sons of Devakī by Lord Kṛṣṇa

It is a Vedic custom that the junior members of the family should offer respects to the elderly persons every morning. The children or the disciples especially should offer their respects to the parents or the spiritual master in the morning. In pursuance of this Vedic principle, Lord Kṛṣṇa and Balarāma used to offer Their obeisances to Their father, Vasudeva, along with his wives. One day, after having returned from the sacrificial performances at Kurukṣetra, when Lord Kṛṣṇa and Balarāma went to offer Their respect to Vasudeva, Vasudeva took the opportunity of appreciating the exalted position of his two sons. Vasudeva had the opportunity to understand the position of Kṛṣṇa and Balarāma from the great sages who had assembled in the arena of the sacrifice. He not only heard from the sages, but on many occasions he actually experienced that Kṛṣṇa and Balarāma were not ordinary human beings, but were very extraordinary. Thus he believed the words of the sages that his sons Kṛṣṇa and Balarāma were the Supreme Personality of Godhead.

With firm faith in his sons, he addressed them thus: "My dear Kṛṣṇa, You are the *sac-cid-ānanda-vigraha* Supreme Personality of Godhead, and my dear Balarāma, You are Saṅkarṣaṇa, the master of all mystic powers. I have now understood that You are eternal. Both of You are transcendental to this material manifestation and to its cause, the Supreme Person Mahā-Viṣṇu. You are the original controller of all. You are the rest of this cosmic manifestation. You are its creator, and You are also its creative ingredients. You are the master of this cosmic manifestation, and actually this manifestation is created for Your pastimes only.

"The different material phases from the beginning to the end of the cosmos manifest under different time formulas are also Yourself, because You are both the cause and effect of this manifestation. The two features of this material world, the predominator and the predominated, are also

You, and You are the supreme transcendental controller who stands above them. Therefore, You are beyond the perception of our senses. You are the supreme soul, unborn and unchanging. You are not affected by the six kinds of transformations which occur in the material body. The wonderful varieties of this material world are also created by You, and You have entered as the Supersoul into each living entity and even into the atom. You are the maintainer of everything.

"The vital force which is acting as the life principle in everything and the creative force derived from it are not acting independently, but are dependent upon You, the Supreme Person behind these forces. Without Your will, they cannot work. Material energy has no cognizance. It cannot act independently without being agitated by You. Because the material nature is dependent upon You, the living entities can only attempt to act. But without Your sanction and will they cannot perform anything or achieve the result they desire.

"The original energy is only an emanation from You. My dear Lord, the shining of the moon, the heat of the fire, the rays of the sun, the glittering of the stars, and the electric lightning which is manifested as very powerful, as well as the gravity of the mountains, the energy of the earth and the quality of its flavor—all are different manifestations of You. The pure taste of water and the vital force which maintains all life are also features of Your Lordship. The water and its taste are also Yourself.

"My dear Lord, although the forces of the senses, the mental power of thinking, willing and feeling, and the strength, movement and growth of the body appear to be performed by different movements of the airs within the body, they are all ultimately manifestations of Your energy. The vast expanse of outer space rests in Yourself. The vibration of the sky, its thunder, the supreme sound *omkāra* and the arrangement of different words to distinguish one thing from the other are symbolic representations of Yourself. Everything is Yourself. The senses, the controllers of the senses, the demigods, and the acquisition of knowledge which is the purpose of the senses, as well as the subject matter of knowledge—all are Yourself. The resolution of intelligence and the sharp memory of the living entity are also Yourself. You are the egotistic principle in ignorance which is the cause of this material world, the egotistic principle of passion which is the cause of the senses, and the egotistic principle of goodness which is the origin of the different controlling deities of this material world. The illusory energy, or *māyā,* which is the cause of the conditioned soul's perpetual transmigration from one form to another, is Yourself.

"My dear Supreme Personality of Godhead, You are the original cause of all causes, exactly as the earth is the original cause of different kinds of trees, plants and similar varieties of manifestation. As the earth is represented in everything, so You are present throughout this material manifestation as Supersoul. You are the supreme cause of all causes, the eternal principle. Everything is, in fact, a manifestation of Your one energy. The three qualities of material nature—*sattva, rajas* and *tamas*—and the result of their interaction, are linked up with You by Your agency of *yogamāyā*. They are supposed to be independent, but actually the total material energy is resting upon You, the Supersoul. Since You are the supreme cause of everything, the interactions of material manifestation—birth, existence, growth, transformation, deterioration and annihilation—are all absent in Yourself. Your supreme energy, *yogamāyā,* is acting in variegated manifestations, but because *yogamāyā* is Your energy, You are therefore present in everything."

In the *Bhagavad-gītā,* this fact is very nicely explained in the Ninth Chapter, wherein the Lord says, "In My impersonal form I am spread all over the material energy; everything is resting in Me, but I am not there." This very statement is also given by Vasudeva. To say He is not present everywhere means that He is aloof from everything, although His energy is acting everywhere. This can be understood by a crude example: In a big establishment, the energy, or the organization of the supreme boss, is working in every nook and corner of the business, but that does not mean that the original proprietor is present there, although in every department and every atmosphere the presence of the proprietor is felt by the worker. The physical presence of the proprietor in every department is formality only. Actually his energy is working everywhere. Similarly, the omnipresence of the Supreme Personality of Godhead is felt in the action of His energies. Therefore the philosophy of inconceivable simultaneous oneness with and difference from the Supreme Lord is confirmed everywhere. The Lord is one, but His energies are diverse.

Vasudeva said, "This material world is like a great flowing river, and its waves are the three material modes of nature—goodness, passion and ignorance. This material body, as well as the senses, the faculties of thinking, feeling and willing and the stages of distress, happiness, attachment and lust—all are different products of these three qualities of nature. The foolish person who cannot realize Your transcendental identity above all this material reaction continues to remain in the entanglement of fruitive activity and is subjected to the continuous process of birth and death without a chance of being freed.

This is also confirmed in a different way by the Lord in the Fourth

Chapter of *Bhagavad-gītā*. There it is said that anyone who knows the appearance and activities of the Supreme Lord Kṛṣṇa becomes freed from the clutches of material nature and goes back home, back to Godhead. Therefore Kṛṣṇa's transcendental name, form, activities and qualities are not products of this material nature.

"My dear Lord," Vasudeva continued, "despite all these defects of the conditioned soul, if someone somehow or other comes in contact with devotional service, he achieves this civilized human form of body with developed consciousness and thereby becomes capable of executing further progress in devotional service. And yet, illusioned by the external energy, people generally do not utilize this advantage of the human form of life. Thus they miss the chance of eternal freedom and unnecessarily spoil the progress they have made after thousands of births.

"In the bodily concept of life, one is attached to the offspring of the body, due to false egotism, and everyone in conditioned life is entrapped by false relationships and false affection. The whole world is moving under this false impression of material bondage. I know that neither of You are my sons; You are the original chief and progenitor, the Personalities of Godhead, known as Pradhāna and Puruṣa. But You have appeared on the surface of this globe in order to minimize the burden of the world by killing the *kṣatriya* kings who are unnecessarily increasing their military strength. You have already informed me about this in the past. My dear Lord, You are the shelter of the surrendered soul, the supreme well-wisher of the meek and humble. I am therefore taking shelter of Your lotus feet, which alone can give one liberation from the entanglement of material existence.

"For a long time I have simply considered this body to be myself, and although You are the Supreme Personality of Godhead, I consider You to be my son. My dear Lord, at the very moment when You first appeared in Kaṁsa's prison house, I was informed that You were the Supreme Personality of Godhead and that You had descended for the protection of the principles of religion as well as the destruction of the unfaithful. Although unborn, You descend in every millennium to execute Your mission. My dear Lord, as in the sky there are many forms appearing and disappearing, so You also appear and disappear in many eternal forms. Who, therefore, can understand Your pastimes or the mystery of Your appearance and disappearance? Our only business should be to glorify Your supreme greatness."

When Vasudeva was addressing his divine sons in that way, Lord Kṛṣṇa and Balarāma were smiling. Because They are very affectionate to Their devotees, They accepted all the appreciation of Vasudeva with a kindly smiling attitude. Kṛṣṇa then began to confirm all Vasudeva's statements as follows: "My dear father, whatever you may say, We are, after all, your sons. What you have said about us is certainly a highly philosophical understanding of spiritual knowledge. I accept it in total without exception."

Vasudeva was in the complete perfection of life in considering Lord Kṛṣṇa and Balarāma to be his sons, but because the sages assembled in the place of pilgrimage at Kurukṣetra had spoken about the Lord as the supreme cause of everything, Vasudeva simply repeated it out of his love for Kṛṣṇa and Balarāma. Lord Kṛṣṇa did not wish to detract from His relationship with Vasudeva as father and son; therefore in the very beginning of His reply He accepted the fact that He is the eternal son of Vasudeva and that Vasudeva is the eternal father of Kṛṣṇa. After this, Lord Kṛṣṇa informed His father of the spiritual identity of all living entities. He continued, "My dear father, everyone, including Myself and My brother Balarāma, as well as all the inhabitants of the city of Dvārakā and the whole cosmic manifestation, is exactly as you have already explained, but all of us are also qualitatively one."

Lord Kṛṣṇa intended for Vasudeva to see everything in the vision of a *mahābhāgavata,* a first-class devotee. A first-class devotee sees that all living entities are part and parcel of the Supreme Lord and that the Supreme Lord is situated in everyone's heart. In fact, every living entity has spiritual identity, but in contact with material existence he becomes influenced by the material modes of nature. He becomes covered by the concept of bodily life, forgetting that his spirit soul is of the same quality as the Supreme Personality of Godhead. One mistakenly considers one individual to be different from another simply because of their material bodily coverings. Because of differences between bodies, the spirit soul appears before us differently.

Lord Kṛṣṇa then gave a nice example in terms of the five material elements. The total material elements, namely, the sky, the air, the fire, the water and the earth, are present in everything in the material world, whether in an earthen pot or in a mountain or in the trees or in an earring. These five elements are present in everything, in different proportions and quantities. A mountain is a gigantic form of the combination of these five elements, and a small earthen pot is of the same elements, but in a smaller quantity. Therefore all material items, although in different shapes or different quantities, are of the same ingredients. Similarly, the living entities—beginning from Lord Kṛṣṇa and including the *Viṣṇu-tattva* and millions of Viṣṇu forms, and then the living entities in different forms, beginning from Lord Brahmā down to the small ant—are all of the same quality in spirit. Some are great in quantity, and some are small, but qualitatively they are of the same nature. It is therefore confirmed in the *Upaniṣads* that Kṛṣṇa, or the Supreme Lord, is the chief among all living entities, and He maintains them and supplies them with all necessities of life. Anyone who knows this philosophy is in perfect knowledge. The Vedic version *tat tvam asi,* "Thou art the same," does not mean that everyone is God, but everyone is qualitatively of the same nature as that of God.

After hearing Kṛṣṇa speak the entire philosophy of spiritual life in an abbreviated summation, Vasudeva was exceedingly pleased with his son. Being thus elated, he could not speak, but remained silent. In the meantime, Devakī, the mother of Lord Kṛṣṇa, sat by the side of her husband. Previously she had heard that both Kṛṣṇa and Balarāma were so kind upon Their teacher that They had brought back the teacher's dead sons from the clutches of the superintendent of death, Yamarāja. Since she had heard this incident, she had been also thinking of her own sons who were killed by Kaṁsa, and while remembering them she became overwhelmed with grief.

In compassion for her dead sons, Devakī began to appeal to Lord Kṛṣṇa and Balarāma thus: "My dear Balarāma, Your very name suggests that You give all pleasure and all strength to everyone. Your unlimited potency is beyond the reach of our minds and words, and my dear Kṛṣṇa, You are the master of all mystic *yogīs.* I also know that You are the master of the Prajāpatis like Brahmā and his assistants, and You are the original Personality of Godhead, Nārāyaṇa. I also know for certain that You have descended to annihilate all kinds of miscreants who have been misled in the course of time. They have lost control of their minds and senses, fallen from the quality of goodness, and have deliberately neglected the direction of the revealed scriptures by living a life of extravagancy and impudency. You have descended on the earth to minimize the burden of the world by killing such miscreant rulers. My dear Kṛṣṇa, I know that Mahā-Viṣṇu, who is lying in the causal ocean of the cosmic manifestation and who is the source of this whole creation, is simply an expansion of Your plenary portion. Creation, maintenance and annihilation of this cosmic manifestation are being effected only by Your plenary portion. I am, therefore, taking shelter of You without any reservation. I have heard that when You wanted to reward Your teacher, Sāndīpani Muni, and he asked You to bring back his dead son, You and Balarāma immediately brought him from the custody of Yamarāja, although he had been dead for a very long time. By this act I understand You to be the supreme master of all mystic *yogīs.* I am, therefore, asking You to fulfill my desire in the same way. In other words, I am asking You to bring back all my sons who were killed by Kaṁsa; upon Your bringing them back, my heart will be content, and it will be a great pleasure for me just to see them once."

After hearing Their mother speak in this way, Lord Balarāma and Kṛṣṇa immediately called for the assistance of *yogamāyā* and started for the lower planetary system known as Sutala. Formerly, in His incarnation of Vāmana, the Supreme Personality of Godhead was satisfied by the king of the demons, Bali Mahārāja, who donated to Him everything he had. Bali Mahārāja was then given the whole of Sutala for his residence and kingdom. Now when this great devotee, Bali Mahārāja, saw that Lord Balarāma and Kṛṣṇa had come to his planet, he immediately merged in the ocean of happiness. As soon as he saw Lord Kṛṣṇa and Balarāma in his presence, he and all his family members stood up from their seats and bowed down at the lotus feet of the Lord. Bali Mahārāja offered Lord Kṛṣṇa and Balarāma the best seat he had in his possession, and when both Lords were seated comfortably, he began to wash Their lotus feet. He then sprinkled the water on his head and on the heads of his family members. The water used to wash the lotus feet of Kṛṣṇa and Balarāma can purify even the greatest demigods, such as Lord Brahmā.

After this, Bali Mahārāja brought valuable garments, ornaments, sandalwood pulp, betel nuts, lamps and various nectarean foodstuffs, and along with his family members he worshiped the Lord according to the regulative principles and offered his riches and body unto the lotus feet of the Lord. King Bali was feeling such transcendental pleasure that he repeatedly grabbed the lotus feet of the Lord and kept them on his chest; and sometimes he put them on the top of his head, and in this way he was feeling transcendental bliss. Tears of love and affection began to flow down from his eyes, and all his hairs stood on end. He began to offer prayers to the Lords in a voice which choked up intermittently.

"My Lord Balarāma, You are the original Anantadeva. You are so great that Anantadeva Śeṣa and other transcendental forms have originally emanated from You and Lord Kṛṣṇa. You are the original Personality of Godhead, and Your eternal form is all-blissful and full of complete knowledge. You are the creator of the whole world. You are the original initiator and propounder of the systems of *jñāna-yoga* and *bhakti-yoga.* You are the Supreme Brahman, the original Personality of Godhead. I therefore with all respect offer my obeisances unto both of You. My dear Lords, it is very difficult for the living entities to get to see You, yet when You are merciful upon Your devotees it becomes easy for them to see You. As such, only out of Your causeless mercy have You agreed to come here and be visible to us, who are generally influenced by the qualities of ignorance and passion.

"My dear Lord, we belong to the *daitya* or demon category. The demons or demonic persons—the Gandharvas, the Siddhas, the Vidyādharas, the Cāraṇas, the Yakṣas, the Rākṣasas, the Piśācas, the ghosts and the hobgoblins—are incapable, by nature, of worshiping You or becoming Your devotees. Instead of becoming Your devotees, they simply become impediments on the path of devotion. But, opposed to them, You are the Supreme Personality of Godhead, representing all the *Vedas* and situated in the mode of uncontaminated goodness. Your position is always transcendental. For this reason, some of us, although born of the modes of passion and ignorance, have taken shelter of Your lotus feet and become devotees. Some of us are actually pure devotees, and some of us have taken shelter of Your lotus feet, desiring to gain something from devotion.

"By Your causeless mercy only we demons are in direct contact with Your personality. This contact is not possible even for the great demigods. No one knows how You act through Your *yogamāyā* potency. Even demigods cannot calculate the expanse of the activities of Your internal potency, so how is it possible for us to know it? I therefore place my humble prayers before You: please be kind to me, who am fully surrendered unto You, and favor me with Your causeless mercy so that I may simply remember Your lotus feet birth after birth. My only ambition is that I may live alone just like the *paramahaṁsas* who, traveling alone here and there in great peace of mind, depend simply upon Your lotus feet. I also desire that if I have to associate with anyone, they may be only Your pure devotees and no one else, because Your pure devotees are always well-wishers of all living entities.

"My dear Lord, You are the supreme master and director of the whole world. Please, therefore, engage me in Your service and let me thus become freed from all material contaminations. You can purify me in that way because if someone engages himself in the loving service of Your Lordship, he immediately becomes free from all kinds of regulative principles enjoined in the *Vedas*."

The word *paramahaṁsa* mentioned here means the supreme swan. It is said that the swan can draw milk out from a reservoir of water; it can take only the milk portion and reject the watery portion. Similarly, a person who can draw out the spiritual portion from this material world and who can live alone, depending only on the Supreme Spirit, not on the material world, is called *paramahaṁsa.* When one achieves the *paramahaṁsa* platform, he is no longer under the regulative principles of the Vedic injunctions. A *paramahaṁsa* accepts only the association of pure devotees and rejects others who are too materially addicted. In other words, those who are materially addicted cannot understand the value of the *paramahaṁsa,* but those who are fortunately advanced in spiritual sense take shelter of the *paramahaṁsa* and thus successfully complete the mission of human life.

After Lord Kṛṣṇa heard the prayers of Bali Mahārāja, He spoke as follows: "My dear King of the demons, in the millennium of the Svāyambhuva Manu, the Prajāpati known as Marīci begot six sons, all demigods, in the womb of his wife, Ūrṇā. Once upon a time, Lord Brahmā became captivated by the beauty of his daughter and was following her, impelled by sex desire. At that time, these six demigods looked at the action of Lord Brahmā with abhorrence. This criticism of Brahmā's action by the demigods constituted a great offense on their part, and for this reason they were condemned to take birth as the sons of the demon Hiraṇyakaśipu. These sons of Hiraṇyakaśipu were thereafter put in the womb of mother Devakī, and as soon as they took their birth, Kaṁsa killed them one after another. My dear King of the demons, again, mother Devakī is very anxious to see these six dead sons again, and she is very much aggrieved on account of their early death at the hand of Kaṁsa. I know that all of them are living with you. I have decided to take them with Me in order to pacify My mother Devakī. After seeing My mother, all these six conditioned souls will be liberated, and thus in great pleasure they will be transferred to their original planet. The names of these six conditioned souls are as follows: Smara, Udgītha, Pariṣvaṅga, Pataṅga, Kṣudrabhṛt and Ghṛṇī. They will be again reinstated in their former position as demigods."

After thus informing the King of the demons, Kṛṣṇa stopped speaking, and Bali Mahārāja understood the Lord's purpose. He worshiped Him sufficiently, and thereafter Lord Kṛṣṇa and Lord Balarāma took away the six conditioned souls and returned to the city of Dvārakā, where He presented them as little babies before His mother, Devakī. Mother Devakī became overwhelmed with joy and was so ecstatic in motherly feeling that immediately milk began to flow from her breasts, and she fed the babies with great satisfaction. She began to take them on her lap again and again, smelling their heads and thinking, "He has gotten my lost children back!" For the time being she became overpowered by the energy of Viṣṇu, and in great motherly affection she began to enjoy the company of her lost children.

The milk from the breast of Devakī was transcendental nectar because the same milk had been sucked by Lord Kṛṣṇa. As such, the babies who sucked the breast of Devakījī, which had touched the body of Lord Kṛṣṇa, immediately became self-realized persons. The babies therefore began to offer their obeisances unto Lord Kṛṣṇa, Balarāma, their father Vasudeva, and mother Devakī. After this, they were immediately transferred to their respective heavenly planets.

After they departed, Devakī became stunned with wonder that her dead children had come back and had again been transferred to their respective planets. She could adjust the events only by thinking of Lord Kṛṣṇa's pastimes, in which, because Lord Kṛṣṇa's potencies are all inconceivable, anything wonderful can be performed. Without accepting the inconceivable, unlimited potencies of the Lord, one cannot understand that Lord Kṛṣṇa is the Supreme Soul. By His unlimited potencies, He performs unlimited pastimes also, and no one can describe them in full nor can anyone know them all. Sūta Gosvāmī, speaking *Śrīmad-Bhāgavatam* before the sages of Naimiṣāraṇya, headed by Śaunaka Ṛṣi, gave his verdict in this connection as follows.

"Great sages, please understand that the transcendental pastimes of Lord Kṛṣṇa are all eternal. They are not ordinary narrations of historical incidences. Such narrations are identical with the Supreme Personality of Godhead Himself. Anyone, therefore, who hears such narrations of the Lord's pastimes becomes immediately freed from the contamination of material existence. And those who are pure devotees enjoy these narrations as nectar entering into their ears." Such narrations were described by Śukadeva Gosvāmī, the exalted son of Vyāsadeva, and anyone who hears them, as well as anyone who describes them for the hearing of others, becomes Kṛṣṇa conscious. And it is only the Kṛṣṇa conscious persons who become eligible for going back home, back to Godhead.

Thus ends the Bhaktivedanta purport of the Eighty-fourth Chapter of Kṛṣṇa, *"Spiritual Instruction for Vasudeva and Return of the Six Dead Sons of Devakī by Lord Kṛṣṇa."*

85 / The Kidnapping of Subhadrā and Lord Kṛṣṇa's Visiting Śrutadeva and Bahulāśva

After hearing this incident, King Parīkṣit became more inquisitive to hear about Kṛṣṇa and His pastimes, and thus he inquired from Śukadeva Gosvāmī how his grandmother Subhadrā was kidnapped by his grandfather Arjuna at the instigation of Lord Kṛṣṇa. King Parīkṣit was very much eager to learn about his grandfather's kidnapping and marriage of his grandmother.

Thus Śukadeva Gosvāmī began to narrate the story as follows: "Once upon a time, your grandfather Arjuna, the great hero, was visiting several holy places of pilgrimage, and while he was thus traveling all over he happened to come to the Prabhāsakṣetra. In the Prabhāsakṣetra he heard the news that Lord Balarāma was negotiating the marriage of Subhadrā, the daughter of Arjuna's maternal uncle, Vasudeva. Although her father, Vasudeva, and her brother, Kṛṣṇa, were not in agreement with Him, Balarāma was in favor of marrying Subhadrā to Duryodhana. Arjuna, however, desired to gain the hand of Subhadrā."

As he thought of Subhadrā and her beauty, Arjuna became more and more captivated with the idea of marrying her, and with a plan in mind he dressed himself like a Vaiṣṇava *sannyāsī,* carrying a *tridaṇḍa* in his hand. The Māyāvādī *sannyāsīs* take one *daṇḍa,* or one rod, whereas the Vaiṣṇava *sannyāsīs* take three *daṇḍa,* or three rods. The three rods, or *tridaṇḍa,* indicate that a Vaiṣṇava *sannyāsī* vows to render service to the Supreme Personality of Godhead by his body, mind and words. The system of *tridaṇḍa-sannyāsa* has been in existence for a long time, and the Vaiṣṇava *sannyāsīs* are called *tridaṇḍīs,* or sometimes *tridaṇḍi-svāmīs* or *tridaṇḍi-gosvāmīs.*

Sannyāsīs are generally meant to travel all over the country for preaching work, but during the four months of the rainy season in India, from September through December, they do not travel, but take shelter in one place and remain there without moving. This non-movement of the *sannyāsī* is called *Cāturmāsya-vrata.* When a *sannyāsī* stays in a place for four months, the local inhabitants of that place take advantage of his presence to become spiritually advanced. Arjuna, in the dress of a *tridaṇḍi-sannyāsī,* remained in the city of Dvārakā for four months, devising a plan whereby he could get Subhadrā as his wife. The inhabitants of Dvārakā as well as Lord Balarāma could not recognize the *sannyāsī* to be Arjuna; therefore all of them offered their respect and obeisances to the *sannyāsī* without knowing the actual situation.

One day Lord Balarāma invited this particular *sannyāsī* to lunch at His home. Balarāmajī very respectfully offered him all kinds of palatable dishes, and the so-called *sannyāsī* was eating sumptuously. While eating at the home of Balarāmajī, Arjuna was simply looking over beautiful Subhadrā, who was very enchanting even to the great heroes and kings. Out of love for her, Arjuna's eyes brightened, and he began to see her with glittering eyes. Arjuna decided that somehow or other he would achieve Subhadrā as his wife, and his mind became agitated on account of this strong desire.

Arjuna, the grandfather of Mahārāja Parīkṣit, was himself extraordinarily beautiful, and his bodily structure was very much attractive to Subhadrā. Subhadrā also decided within her mind that she would accept only Arjuna as her husband. As a simple girl, she was smiling with great pleasure, looking at Arjuna. Thus Arjuna also became more and more attracted by her. In this way, Subhadrā dedicated herself to Arjuna, and he resolved to marry her by any means. He then became absorbed twenty-four hours a day in the thought of how he could get Subhadrā as his wife. He was afflicted with the thought of getting Subhadrā, and had not a moment's peace of mind.

Once upon a time, Subhadrā, seated on a chariot, came out of the palace fort to see the gods in the temple. Arjuna took this opportunity, and with the permission of Vasudeva and Devakī, he kidnapped her. After getting on Subhadrā's chariot, he prepared himself for a fight. Taking up his bow and holding off with his arrows the soldiers ordered to check him, Arjuna took Subhadrā away. While Subhadrā was being thus kidnapped by Arjuna, her relatives and family members began to cry, but still he took her, just as a lion takes his share and departs. When it was disclosed to Lord Balarāma that the so-called *sannyāsī* was Arjuna and that he had planned such a device simply to take away Subhadrā and that he had actually taken her, He became very angry. Just as the waves of the ocean become agitated on a full moon day, Lord Balarāma became greatly disturbed.

Lord Kṛṣṇa was in favor of Arjuna; therefore, along with other members of the family, He tried to pacify Balarāma by falling at His feet and begging Him to pardon Arjuna. Lord Balarāma was then convinced that Subhadrā was attached to Arjuna, and He became pleased to know that she wanted Arjuna as her husband. The matter was settled, and in order to please the newly married couple, Lord Balarāma arranged to send a dowry, consisting of an abundance of riches, elephants, chariots, horses, servants and maidservants.

Mahārāja Parīkṣit was very anxious to hear more about Kṛṣṇa, and so, after finishing the narration of Arjuna's kidnapping Subhadrā, Śukadeva Gosvāmī began to narrate another story, as follows.

There was a householder *brāhmaṇa* in the city of Mithilā, the capital of the kingdom of Videha. This *brāhmaṇa,* whose name was Śrutadeva, was a great devotee of Lord Kṛṣṇa. Due to his being fully Kṛṣṇa conscious and always engaged in the service of the Lord, he was completely peaceful in mind and detached from all material attraction. He was very learned and had no other desire than to be fully situated in Kṛṣṇa consciousness. Although in the order of householder life, he never took great pains to earn anything for his livelihood; he was satisfied with whatever he could achieve without much endeavor, and somehow or other he lived in that way. Every day he would get necessities for life in just the quantity required, and not more. That was his destiny. The *brāhmaṇa* had no desire to get more than what he needed, and thus he was peacefully executing the regulative principles of a *brāhmaṇa's* life, as enjoined in the revealed scriptures.

Fortunately, the King of Mithilā was as good a devotee as the *brāhmaṇa.* The name of this famous King was Bahulāśva. He was very well established in his reputation as a good king, and he was not at all ambitious to extend his kingdom for the sake of sense gratification. As such, both the *brāhmaṇa* and King Bahulāśva remained pure devotees of Lord Kṛṣṇa in Mithilā.

Since Lord Kṛṣṇa was very merciful upon these two devotees, King Bahulāśva and the *brāhmaṇa,* Śrutadeva, He one day asked His driver, Dāruka, to take His chariot into the capital city of Mithilā. Lord Kṛṣṇa was accompanied by the great sages Nārada, Vāmadeva, Atri, Vyāsadeva, Paraśurāma, Asita, Aruṇi, Bṛhaspati, Kaṇva, Maitreya, Cyavana and others. Lord Kṛṣṇa and the sages were passing through many villages and towns, and everywhere the citizens would receive them with great respect and offer them articles in worship. When the citizens came to see the Lord and all of them assembled together in one place, it seemed that the sun was present along with his various satellite planets. In that journey, Lord Kṛṣṇa and the sages passed through the kingdoms of Ānarta, Dhanva,

Kurujāṅgala, Kaṅka, Matsya, Pāñcāla, Kunti, Madhu, Kekaya, Kośala and Arṇa, and thus all the citizens of these places, both men and women, could see Lord Kṛṣṇa eye to eye. In this way they enjoyed celestial happiness, with open hearts full of love and affection for the Lord, and when they saw the face of the Lord, it seemed to them that they were drinking nectar through their eyes. When they saw Kṛṣṇa, all the ignorant misconceptions of their lives dissipated. When the Lord passed through the various countries and the people came to visit Him, simply by glancing over them the Lord would bestow all good fortune upon them and liberate them from all kinds of ignorance. In some places, the demigods also would join with the human beings, and their glorification of the Lord would cleanse all directions of all inauspicious things. In this way, Lord Kṛṣṇa slowly and gradually reached the kingdom of Videha.

When the news of the Lord's arrival was received by the citizens, they all felt unlimited happiness and came to welcome Him, taking gifts in their hands to offer. As soon as they saw Lord Kṛṣṇa, their hearts immediately blossomed in transcendental bliss, just as a lotus flower blooms on the rising of the sun. Previously they had simply heard the names of the great sages, but had never seen them. Now, by the mercy of Lord Kṛṣṇa, they had the opportunity of seeing both the great sages and the Lord Himself.

King Bahulāśva, as well as the *brāhmaṇa,* Śrutadeva, knowing well that the Lord had come there just to grace them with favor, immediately fell at the Lord's lotus feet and offered their respects. With folded hands, the King and the *brāhmaṇa* each simultaneously invited Lord Kṛṣṇa and all the sages to his home. In order to please both of them, Lord Kṛṣṇa expanded Himself into two and went to the houses of each one of them; yet neither the King nor the *brāhmaṇa* could understand that the Lord had gone to the house of the other. Both thought that the Lord had gone only to his own house. That He and His companions were present in both houses, although both the *brāhmaṇa* and the King thought He was present in his house only, is another opulence of the Supreme Personality of Godhead. This opulence is described in the revealed scriptures as *vaibhava-prakāśa.* Similarly, when Lord Kṛṣṇa married sixteen thousand wives, He also expanded Himself into sixteen thousand forms, each one of them as powerful as He Himself. Similarly, in Vṛndāvana, when Brahmā stole away Kṛṣṇa's cows, calves and cowherd boys, Kṛṣṇa expanded Himself into many new cows, calves and cowherd boys.

Bahulāśva, the King of Videha, was very intelligent and was a perfect gentleman. He was astonished that so many great sages, along with the

Supreme Personality of Godhead, were personally present in his home. He knew perfectly well that the conditioned soul, especially when engaged in worldly affairs, cannot be a hundred percent pure, whereas the Supreme Personality of Godhead and His pure devotees are always transcendental to worldly contamination. Therefore, when he found that the Supreme Personality of Godhead Kṛṣṇa and all the great sages were at his home, he was astonished, and he began to thank Lord Kṛṣṇa for His causeless mercy.

Feeling very much obliged and wanting to receive his guests to the best of his capacity, he called for nice chairs and cushions, and Lord Kṛṣṇa, along with all the sages, sat down very comfortably. At that time, King Bahulāśva's mind was very restless, not because of any problems, but because of great ecstasy of love and devotion. His heart was filled with love and affection for the Lord and His associates, and his eyes were filled with tears of ecstasy. He arranged to wash the feet of his divine guests, and after washing them he and his family members sprinkled the water on their own heads. After this, he offered to the guests nice flower garlands, sandalwood pulp, incense, new garments, ornaments, lamps, cows and bulls. In a manner just befitting his royal position, he worshiped each one of them in this way. When all had been fed sumptuously and were sitting very comfortably, Bahulāśva came before Lord Kṛṣṇa and caught His lotus feet. He placed them on his lap and, while massaging the feet with his hands, began to speak about the glories of the Lord in a sweet voice.

"My dear Lord, You are the Supersoul of all living entities and as witness within the heart are cognizant of everyone's activities. As such, being duty-bound, we always think of Your lotus feet so that we can remain in a secure position without deviating from Your eternal service. As a result of our continuous remembrance of Your lotus feet, You have kindly visited my place personally to favor me with Your causeless mercy. We have heard, my dear Lord, that by Your various statements You confirm Your pure devotees to be more dear to You than Lord Balarāma or Your constant servitor the goddess of fortune. Your devotees are dearer to You than Your first son, Lord Brahmā, and I am sure that You have so kindly visited my place in order to prove Your divine statement. I cannot imagine how people can be godless and demoniac even after knowing of Your causeless mercy and affection for Your devotees who are constantly engaged in Kṛṣṇa consciousness. How can they forget Your lotus feet?

"My dear Lord, it is known to us that You are so kind and liberal that when a person leaves everything just to engage in Kṛṣṇa consciousness, You sometimes give Yourself in exchange for that unalloyed service. You have appeared in the Yadu dynasty to fulfill Your mission of reclaiming all conditioned souls rotting in the sinful activities of material existence, and this appearance is already famous all over the world. My dear Lord, You are the ocean of unlimited mercy, love and affection. Your transcendental form is full of bliss, knowledge and eternity. You can attract everyone's heart by Your beautiful form as Śyāmasundara, Kṛṣṇa. Your knowledge is unlimited, and to teach all people how to execute devotional service You have sent Your incarnation Nara-Nārāyaṇa, who is engaged in severe austerities and penances at Badarīnārāyaṇa. Kindly, therefore, accept my humble obeisances at Your lotus feet. My dear Lord, I beg to request You and Your companions, the great sages and *brāhmaṇas,* to remain at my place so that this family of the famous King Nimi may be sanctified by the dust of Your lotus feet at least for a few days." Lord Kṛṣṇa could not refuse the request of His devotee, and thus He remained there for a few days along with the sages in order to sanctify the city of Mithilā and all its citizens.

Meanwhile, the *brāhmaṇa,* simultaneously receiving Lord Kṛṣṇa and His associates at his home, became transcendentally overwhelmed with joy. After offering his guests nice sitting places, the *brāhmaṇa* began to dance, throwing his wrap around his body. Śrutadeva, being not at all rich, offered only mattresses, wooden planks, straw carpets, etc., to his distinguished guests, Lord Kṛṣṇa and the sages, but he welcomed them to his best capacity. He began to speak very highly of the Lord and the sages, and he and his wife washed the feet of each one of them. After this, he took the water and sprinkled it over all the members of his family, and although it appeared that the *brāhmaṇa* was very poor, he was at that time most fortunate. While Śrutadeva was welcoming Lord Kṛṣṇa and His associates, he simply forgot himself in transcendental joy. After welcoming the Lord and His companions, according to his capacity he brought fruits, incense, scented water, scented clay, *tulasī* leaves, *kuśa* straw and lotus flowers. They were not very costly items and could be secured very easily, but because they were offered with devotional love, Lord Kṛṣṇa and His associates accepted them very gladly. The *brāhmaṇa's* wife cooked very simple foods like rice and dahl, and Lord Kṛṣṇa and His followers were very pleased to accept them because they were offered in devotional love. When Lord Kṛṣṇa and His associates were fed in this way, the *brāhmaṇa* Śrutadeva was thinking thus: "I am fallen into the deep, dark well of householder life and am the most unfortunate person. How has it become possible that Lord Kṛṣṇa, who is the Supreme Personality of Godhead, and His associates, the great sages, whose very presence makes a place as sanctified as a pilgrimage site, have agreed to come to my place?" While the *brāhmaṇa* was thinking in this way, the guests finished their lunch and sat back very comfortably. At that time, the *brāhmaṇa*, Śrutadeva, and his wife, children and other relatives, appeared there to render service to the distinguished guests. While touching the lotus feet of Lord Kṛṣṇa, the *brāhmaṇa* began to speak.

"My dear Lord," he said, "You are the Supreme Person, Puruṣottama, situated transcendentally to the manifested and unmanifested material creation. The activities of this material world and of the conditioned souls have nothing to do with Your position. We can appreciate that it is not that only today You have given me Your audience. You are associating with all the living entities as Paramātmā since the beginning of creation."

This statement of the *brāhmaṇa* is very instructive. It is a fact that the Supreme Lord Personality of Godhead in His Paramātmā feature entered the creation of this material world as Mahā-Viṣṇu, Garbhodakaśāyī Viṣṇu and Kṣīrodakaśāyī Viṣṇu, and in a very friendly attitude the Lord is sitting along with the conditioned soul in the body. Therefore, every living entity has the Lord with him from the very beginning, but due to his mistaken consciousness of life, the living entity cannot understand this. When his consciousness is, however, changed into Kṛṣṇa consciousness, he can immediately understand how Kṛṣṇa is trying to assist the conditioned souls to get out of the material entanglement.

Śrutadeva continued, "My dear Lord, You have entered this material world as if in a sleeping condition. A conditioned soul, while sleeping, creates false or temporary worlds; he becomes busy in many illusory activities—sometimes becoming a king, sometimes being murdered or sometimes going to an unknown city—and all these are simply temporary affairs. Similarly, Your Lordship, apparently also in a sleeping condition, enters this material world to create a temporary manifestation, not for Your personal necessities, but for the conditioned soul who wants to imitate Your Lordship as enjoyer. The conditioned soul's enjoyment in the material world is temporary and illusory. And yet the conditioned soul is by himself unable to create such a temporary situation for his illusory enjoyment. In order to fulfill his desires, although they are temporary and illusory, You enter in this temporary manifestation to help him. Thus, from the beginning of the conditioned soul's entering into the material world, You are his constant companion. When, therefore, the conditioned soul comes in contact with a pure devotee and takes to devotional service, beginning from the process of hearing Your transcendental pastimes, glorifying Your transcendental activities, worshiping Your eternal form in the temple, offering prayers to You and engaging in discussion to understand Your transcendental position, he then gradually becomes freed from the contamination of material existence. His heart becomes cleansed of all material dust, and thus gradually You become visible in the heart of the devotee. Although You are constantly with the conditioned soul, only when he becomes purified by devotional service do You become revealed to him. Others, who are bewildered by fruitive activities, either by Vedic injunction or customary dealings, and who do not take to devotional service, become captivated by the external happiness of the bodily concept of life. You are not revealed to such persons. Rather, You remain far, far away from them. But for one who, being engaged in Your devotional service, has purified his heart by constant chanting of Your holy name, You become very easily understood as his eternal constant companion.

"It is said that Your Lordship, sitting in the heart of a devotee, gives him direction by which he can very quickly come back to home, back to You. This direct dictation by You reveals Your existence within the heart of the devotee. Only a devotee can immediately appreciate Your existence within his heart, whereas for a person who has only a bodily concept of life and is engaged in sense gratification You always remain covered by the curtain of *yogamāyā*. Such a person cannot realize that You are very near, sitting within his heart. For a nondevotee, You are appreciated only as ultimate death. The difference is like the difference between a cat's carrying its kittens in its mouth and a cat's carrying a rat in its mouth. In the mouth of the cat, the rat feels its death, whereas the kittens in the mouth of the cat feel motherly affection. Similarly, You are present to everyone, but the nondevotee feels You as ultimate cruel death, whereas for a devotee You are the supreme instructor and philosopher. The atheist, therefore, understands the presence of God as death, but the devotee understands the presence of God always within his heart, takes dictation from You, and lives transcendentally, not being affected by the contamination of the material world.

"You are the supreme controller and superintendent of the material nature's activities. The atheistic class of men simply observe the activities of material nature, but cannot find You as the original background. A devotee, however, can immediately see Your hand in every movement of material nature. The curtain of *yogamāyā* cannot cover the eyes of the devotee of Your Lordship, but it can cover the eyes of the nondevotee. The nondevotee is unable to see You eye to eye, just as a person whose eyes are interrupted by the covering of a cloud cannot see the sun, although persons who are flying above the cloud can see the sunshine brilliantly, as it is. My dear Lord, I offer my respectful obeisances unto You. My dear self-effulgent Lord, I am Your eternal servitor. Therefore, kindly order me —what can I do for You? The conditioned soul feels the pangs of material contamination as threefold miseries as long as You are not visible to him. And as soon as You are visible by development of Kṛṣṇa consciousness, all miseries of material existence simultaneously become vanquished."

The Supreme Personality of Godhead Kṛṣṇa is naturally very much affectionately inclined to His devotees. When He heard Śrutadeva's prayers of pure devotion, He was very much pleased and immediately caught his hands and began to address Him thus: "My dear Śrutadeva, all these great sages and saintly persons have been very kind to you by personally coming here to see you. You should consider this opportunity to be a great fortune for you. They are so kind that they are traveling with Me, and wherever they go they immediately make the whole atmosphere as pure as transcendence simply by the touch of the dust of their feet. People are accustomed to go to the temples of God. They also visit holy places of pilgrimage, and after prolonged association with such activities, for many days by touch and by worship, gradually they become purified. But the influence of great sages and saintly persons is so great that by seeing them one immediately becomes completely purified.

"Moreover, the very purifying potency of pilgrimages or worship of different demigods is also achieved by the grace of saintly persons. A pilgrimage site becomes a holy place because of the presence of the saintly persons there. My dear Śrutadeva, when a person is born as a *brāhmaṇa,* he immediately becomes the best of all human beings. And if such a brāhmaṇa, remaining self-satisfied, practices austerities, studies the *Vedas* and engages in My devotional service, as is the duty of the *brāhmaṇa* —or in other words, if a *brāhmaṇa* becomes a Vaiṣṇava—how wonderful is his greatness! My feature of four-handed Nārāyaṇa is not so pleasing or dear to Me as is a *brāhmaṇa* Vaiṣṇava. *Brāhmaṇa* means 'one well conversant with Vedic knowledge'; a *brāhmaṇa* is the insignia of perfect knowledge, and I am the full-fledged manifestation of all gods. The less intelligent class of men do not understand Me as the highest knowledge, nor do they understand the influence of the *brāhmaṇa* Vaiṣṇava. They are influenced by the three modes of material nature and thus dare to criticize Me and My pure devotees. A *brāhmaṇa* Vaiṣṇava, or a devotee already on the brahminical platform, can realize Me within his heart, and therefore he definitely concludes that the whole cosmic manifestation and its different features are effects of different energies of the Lord. Thus he has a clear conception of the whole material nature and the total material energy, and in every action such a devotee sees Me only, and nothing else.

"My dear Śrutadeva, you may therefore accept all these great saintly persons, *brāhmaṇas* and sages as My bona fide representatives. By worshiping them faithfully, you will be worshiping Me more diligently. I consider worship of My devotees to be better than direct worship of Me. If someone attempts to worship Me directly without worshiping My devotees, I do not accept such worship, even though it may be presented with great opulence."

In this way both the *brāhmaṇa,* Śrutadeva, and the King of Mithilā, under the direction of the Lord, worshiped both Kṛṣṇa and His followers, the great sages and saintly *brāhmaṇas,* on an equal level of spiritual importance. Both *brāhmaṇa* and King ultimately achieved the supreme goal of being transferred to the spiritual world. The devotee does not know anyone except Lord Kṛṣṇa, and Kṛṣṇa is most affectionate to His devotee. Lord Kṛṣṇa remained in Mithilā both at the house of the *brāhmaṇa* Śrutadeva and at the palace of King Bahulāśva. And after favoring them lavishly by His transcendental instructions, He went back to His capital city, Dvārakā.

The instruction we receive from this incident is that King Bahulāśva and Śrutadeva the *brāhmaṇa* were accepted by the Lord on the same level because both were pure devotees. This is the real qualification for being recognized by the Supreme Personality of Godhead. Because it has become the fashion of this age to become falsely proud of having taken birth in the family of a *kṣatriya* or of a *brāhmaṇa,* we see persons without any qualification other than birth claiming to be *brāhmaṇa* or *kṣatriya* or *vaiśya.* But as it is stated in the scriptures, *kalau śūdra-sambhava:* "In this age of Kali, everyone is a *śūdra.*" This is because there is no performance of the purificatory processes known as *saṁskāras,* which begin from the time of the mother's pregnancy and continue up to the point of the individual's death. No one can be classified as a member of a particular caste, especially of a higher caste—*brāhmaṇa, kṣatriya* or *vaiśya*—simply by birthright. If one is not purified by the process of the seed-giving ceremony, or *Garbhādhāna-saṁskāra*, he is immediately classified amongst the *śūdras,* because only the *śūdras* do not undergo this purificatory process. Sex life without the purificatory process of Kṛṣṇa consciousness is merely the seed-giving process of the *śūdras* or the animals. But Kṛṣṇa consciousness is the highest perfection, by which everyone can come to the platform of a Vaiṣṇava. This includes having all the qualifications of a *brāhmaṇa.* The Vaiṣṇavas are trained to become freed from the four kinds of sinful activities—illicit sex, indulgence in intoxicants, gambling, and eating animal foodstuffs. No one can be on the brahminical platform without having these preliminary qualifications, and without becoming a qualified *brāhmaṇa,* one cannot become a pure devotee.

Thus ends the Bhaktivedanta purport of the Eighty-fifth Chapter of Kṛṣṇa, *"The Kidnapping of Subhadrā and Lord Kṛṣṇa's Visiting Śrutadeva and Bahulāśva.*

86 / Prayers by the Personified Vedas

King Parīkṣit inquired from Śukadeva Gosvāmī about a very important topic in understanding transcendental subject matter. His question was, "Since Vedic knowledge generally deals with the subject matter of the three qualities of the material world, how then can it approach the subject matter of transcendence, which is beyond the approach of the three material modes? Since the mind is material and the vibration of words is a material sound, how can the Vedic knowledge, expressing by material sound the thoughts of the mind, approach transcendence? Description of a subject matter necessitates describing its source of emanation, its qualities and its activities. Such description can be possible only by thinking with the material mind and by vibrating material words. Although Brahman, or the Absolute Truth, has no material qualities, our power of speaking does not go beyond the material qualities. How then can Brahman, the Absolute Truth, be described by your words? I do not see how it is possible to understand transcendence from such expressions of material sound."

The purpose of King Parīkṣit's inquiring was to ascertain from Śukadeva Gosvāmī whether the *Vedas* ultimately describe the Absolute Truth as impersonal or as personal. Understanding of the Absolute Truth progresses in three features—impersonal Brahman, Paramātmā localized in everyone's heart and, at last, the Supreme Personality of Godhead Kṛṣṇa.

The *Vedas* deal with three departments of activities. One is called *karma-kāṇḍa,* or activities under Vedic injunction which gradually purify one to understand his real position; the next is *jñāna-kāṇḍa,* the process of understanding the Absolute Truth by speculative methods; and the third is *upāsanā-kāṇḍa,* or worship of the Supreme Personality of Godhead and sometimes of the demigods also. The worship of the demigods recommended in the *Vedas* is ordered with the understanding of the demigods' relationship to the Personality of Godhead. The Supreme Personality of Godhead has many parts and parcels; some are called *svāṁśas,* or His personal expansions, and some are called *vibhinnāṁśas,* the living entities. All such expansions, both *svāṁśas* and *vibhinnāṁśas,* are emanations from the original Personality of Godhead. *Śvāṁśa* expansions are called *Viṣṇu-tattva,* whereas the *vibhinnāṁśa* expansions are called *jīva-tattva.* The different demigods are *jīva-tattva.* The conditioned souls are generally put into the activities of the material world for sense gratification; therefore, as stated in the *Bhagavad-gītā,* to regulate those who are very much addicted to different kinds of sense gratification the worship of demigods is sometimes recommended. For example, for persons who are very much addicted to meat-eating, the Vedic injunction recommends that after worshiping the form of the goddess Kālī and sacrificing a goat (not any other animal) under *karma-kāṇḍa* regulation, the worshipers may be allowed to eat meat. The idea is not to encourage one to eat meat, but to allow one who is persistent to eat meat under certain restricted conditions. Therefore, worship of the demigods is not worship of the Absolute Truth, but by worshiping the demigods one gradually comes to accept the Supreme Personality of Godhead in an indirect way. This indirect acceptance is described in the *Bhagavad-gītā* as *avidhi. Avidhi* means not bona fide. Since demigod worship is not bona fide, the impersonalists stress concentration on the impersonal feature of the Absolute Truth. King Parīkṣit's question was, which is the ultimate target of Vedic knowledge—this concentration on the impersonal feature of the Absolute Truth or concentration on the personal feature? After all, both the impersonal and personal features of the Supreme Lord are beyond our material conception. The impersonal feature of the Absolute, the Brahman effulgence, is but the rays of the personal body of Kṛṣṇa. These rays of the personal body of Kṛṣṇa are cast all over the creation of the Lord, and the portion of the effulgence which is covered by the material cloud is called the created cosmos of the three material qualities—*sattva, rajas* and *tamas.* How can persons who are within this clouded portion called the material world conceive of the Absolute Truth by the speculative method?

In answering King Parīkṣit's question, Śukadeva Gosvāmī replied that the Supreme Personality of Godhead has created the mind, senses and living force for the purpose of sense gratification in transmigration from one kind of body to another, as well as for the purpose of allowing liberation from the material conditions. In other words, the senses, mind and living force can be utilized for sense gratification and transmigration from one body to another or for the matter of liberation. The Vedic injunctions are there just to give the conditioned souls the chance for sense gratification under regulative principles, and thereby also give them the chance for promotion to the higher conditions of life; ultimately, if the consciousness is purified, one comes to his original position and goes back home, back to Godhead.

The living force is intelligent. One therefore has to utilize his intelligence over the mind and the senses. When the mind and senses are purified by the proper use of intelligence, then the conditioned soul is liberated; otherwise, if the intelligence is not properly utilized in controlling the senses and mind, the conditioned soul continues to transmigrate from one kind of body to another simply for sense gratification. Another point clearly stated in the answer of Śukadeva Gosvāmī is that the Lord created the mind, senses and intelligence of the individual living force. It is not stated that the living entities themselves were ever created. Just as the shining particles of the sun's rays are always existing along with the sun, the living entities exist eternally as parts and parcels of the Supreme Personality of Godhead. The conditioned souls, although eternally existing as part of the Supreme Lord, are sometimes put within the cloud of the material concept of life, in the darkness of ignorance. The whole Vedic process is to alleviate that darkened condition. Ultimately, when the senses and mind of the conditioned being become fully purified, he then comes to the original position, called Kṛṣṇa consciousness, and that is liberation.

In the *Vedānta-sūtra,* the first *sūtra,* or code, questions about the Absolute Truth. *Athāto brahma-jijñāsā:* What is the nature of the Absolute Truth? The next *sūtra* answers that the nature of the Absolute Truth is that He is the origin of everything. Whatever we experience, even in this material condition of life, is but an emanation from Him. The Absolute Truth created the mind and senses and intelligence. This means that the Absolute Truth is not without mind, intelligence and senses. In other words, He is not impersonal. The very word "created" means that He has transcendental intelligence. For example, when the father begets a child, the child has senses because the father also has senses. The child is born with hands and legs because the father also has hands and legs. Sometimes it is said, therefore, that man is made after the image of God. The Absolute Truth is therefore the Supreme Personality, with transcendental mind, senses and intelligence. When one's mind, intelligence and senses are purified of material contamination, one can understand the original feature of the Absolute Truth as a person.

The Vedic process is to gradually promote the conditioned soul from the mode of ignorance to the mode of passion and from the mode of passion to the mode of goodness. In the mode of goodness there is sufficient light for understanding things as they are. For example, from earth a tree grows, and from the wood of the tree, fire is ignited. In that igniting process we first of all find the smoke, and the next stage is heat, and then fire. When there is actually fire, we can utilize it for various purposes; therefore, fire is the ultimate goal. Similarly, in the gross material stage of life the quality of ignorance is very much prominent. Dissipation of this ignorance takes place in the gradual progress of civilization from the barbarian stage to civilized life, and when one comes to the form of civilized life, he is said to be in the mode of passion. In the barbarian stage, or in the mode of ignorance, the senses are gratified in a very crude way, whereas in the mode of passion or in the civilized stage of life, the senses are gratified in a polished manner. But when one is promoted to the mode of goodness, one can understand that the senses and the mind are only engaged in material activities due to being covered by perverted consciousness. When this perverted consciousness is gradually transformed into Kṛṣṇa consciousness, then the path of liberation is opened. So it is not that one is unable to approach the Absolute Truth by the senses and the mind. The conclusion is, rather, that the senses, mind and intelligence in the gross stage of contamination cannot appreciate the nature of the Absolute Truth, but, when purified, the senses, mind and intelligence can understand what the Absolute Truth is. This purifying process is called devotional service, or Kṛṣṇa consciousness.

In the *Bhagavad-gītā* it is clearly stated that the purpose of Vedic knowledge is to understand Kṛṣṇa, and Kṛṣṇa is understood by devotional service, beginning with the process of surrender. As stated in the *Bhagavad-gītā,* one has to think of Kṛṣṇa always. One has to render loving service to Kṛṣṇa always, and one has to always worship and bow down before Kṛṣṇa. By this process only can one enter into the kingdom of God without any doubt.

When one is enlightened in the mode of goodness by the process of devotional service, he is freed from the modes of ignorance and passion. The word *ātmane* indicates the stage of brahminical qualification in which one is allowed to study the Vedic literatures known as the *Upaniṣads.* The *Upaniṣads* describe in different ways the transcendental qualities of the Supreme Lord. The Absolute Truth, the Supreme Lord, is called *nirguṇa.* That does not mean that He has no qualities. It is only because He has qualities that the conditioned living entities can have qualities. The purpose of studying the *Upaniṣads* is to understand the transcendental quality of the Absolute Truth, as opposed to the material qualities of ignorance, passion and goodness. That is the way of Vedic understanding. Great sages like the four Kumāras, headed by Sanaka, followed these principles of Vedic knowledge and came gradually from impersonal understanding to the platform of personal worship of the Supreme Lord. It is therefore recommended that we must follow the great personalities. Śukadeva Gosvāmī is also one of the great personalities, and his answer to the inquiry of Mahārāja Parikṣit is authorized. One who follows in the footsteps of such great personalities surely walks very easily on the path of liberation and ultimately goes back to home, back to Godhead. That is the way of perfecting this human form of life.

Śukadeva Gosvāmī continued to speak to Parīkṣit Mahārāja. "My dear King," he said, "I will narrate in this regard a nice story. This story is important because it is in connection with Nārāyaṇa, the Supreme Personality of Godhead. This narration is a conversation between Nārāyaṇa Ṛṣi and the great sage Nārada. Nārāyaṇa Ṛṣi still resides in Badarīkāśrama in the Himalayan hills and is accepted as an incarnation of Nārāyaṇa. Once when Nārada, the great devotee and ascetic amongst the demigods, was traveling in different planets, he desired to personally meet the ascetic Nārāyaṇa in Badarīkāśrama and offer him his respects. This great sage incarnation of Godhead, Nārāyaṇa Ṛṣi, has been undergoing great penances and austerities from the very beginning of the creation in order to teach the inhabitants of Bhāratavarṣa how to attain the highest perfectional stage of going back to Godhead. His austerities and penances are exemplary practices for the human being."

Badarīkāśrama is situated in the northernmost part of the Himalayan Mountains and is always covered with snow. Religious Indians still go to visit this place during the summer season, when the snowfall is not very severe. Once, the incarnation of God Nārāyaṇa Ṛṣi was sitting amongst many devotees in the village known as Kalāpagrāma. Of course, these were not ordinary sages who were sitting with him, and the great sage Nārada also appeared there. After offering his respects to Nārāyaṇa Ṛṣi, Nārada asked him exactly the same question asked by King Parīkṣit of Śukadeva Gosvāmī. When Nārada asked his question of Nārāyaṇa Ṛṣi, the Ṛṣi also answered by following in the footsteps of his predecessors. He narrated a story of how the same question had been discussed on the planet known as Janaloka. Janaloka is above the Svargaloka planets, such as the moon, Venus, etc. In this planet, great sages and saintly persons live, and they were also discussing the same point regarding the understanding of Brahman and His real identity.

The great sage Nārāyaṇa began to speak. "My dear Nārada," he said, "I will tell you a story which took place long, long ago. There was a great meeting of the denizens of the heavenly planets, and almost all the important *brahmacārīs,* such as the four Kumāras–Sanat, Sanandana, Sanaka and Sanātana Kumāra–attended. Their discussion was on the subject matter of understanding the Absolute Truth, Brahman. You were not present at that meeting because you went to see My expansion Aniruddha, who lives on the island of Śvetadvīpa. In this meeting, all the great sages and *brahmacārīs* very elaborately discussed the point about which you have asked me, and it was very interesting. The discussion was so delicate that even the *Vedas* were unable to answer the intricate questions raised.

Nārāyana Ṛṣi told Nāradajī that the same question which Nāradajī had raised had been discussed in that meeting in Janaloka. This is the way of understanding through the *paramparā,* or disciplic succession. Mahārāja Parikṣit was sent to Śukadeva Gosvāmī; Śukadeva Gosvāmī referred the matter to Nārada, who had in the same way questioned Nārāyana Ṛṣi, who had put the matter to still higher authorities in the planet of Janaloka, where it was discussed among the great Kumāras–Sanat, Sanātana, Sanaka Kumāra and Sanandana. These four *brahmacārīs* are recognized scholars in the *Vedas* and *śāstras.* Their unlimited volumes of knowledge, backed by austerities and penances, are exhibited by their sublime, ideal character. They are very amiable and gentle in behavior, and for them there is no distinction between friends, well-wishers and enemies. Being transcendentally situated, such personalities as the Kumāras are above all material considerations and are always neutral in respect to material dualities. In the discussions held among the four brothers, one of them, namely Sanandana, was selected to speak, and the other brothers became the audience to hear him.

Sanandana said, "After the dissolution of the whole cosmic manifestation, the entire energy and the whole creation in its nucleus form enters into the body of Garbhodakaśāyī Viṣṇu. The Lord at that time remains asleep for a long, long time, and where there is again necessity of creation, the *Vedas* personified assemble around the Lord and begin to glorify Him, describing His wonderful transcendental pastimes. It is exactly like a king: when he is asleep in the morning, the appointed reciters come around his bedroom and begin to sing of his chivalrous activities, and while hearing of his glorious activities, the king gradually awakens.

"The Vedic reciters or the personified *Vedas* sing thus: 'O unconquerable, You are the Supreme Personality. No one is equal to You or greater than You. No one can be more glorious in His activities. All glories unto

You! All glories unto You! By Your own transcendental nature You fully possess all six opulences. As such, You are able to deliver all conditioned souls from the clutches of *māyā.* O Lord, we fervently pray that You kindly do so. All the living entities, being Your parts and parcels, are naturally joyful, eternal and full of knowledge, but due to their own faults they try to imitate You by trying to become the supreme enjoyer; thus they disobey Your supremacy and become offenders. And because of their offenses, Your material energy has taken charge of them; thus, their transcendental qualities of joyfulness, bliss and wisdom have been covered by the clouds of the three material qualities. This cosmic manifestation, made of the three material qualities, is just like a prison house for the conditioned souls. The conditioned souls are struggling very hard to escape from the material bondage, and according to their different conditions of life they have been given different types of engagement. But all engagements are based on Your knowledge. Pious activities can be executed only when inspired by Your mercy. Therefore, without taking shelter at Your lotus feet one cannot surpass the influence of material energy. Actually, we, as personified Vedic knowledge, are always engaged in Your service to help the conditioned soul understand You.'"

This prayer of the *Vedas* personified illustrates that the *Vedas* are meant for helping the conditioned souls to understand Kṛṣṇa. All the *śrutis* or personified *Vedas* offered glories to the Lord again and again, singing, *"Jaya! Jaya!"* This indicates that the Lord is praised for His glories. Of all His glories the most important is His causeless mercy upon the conditioned souls in reclaiming them from the clutches of *māyā.*

There are unlimited numbers of living entities in different varieties of bodies, some moving and some standing in one place, and the conditioned life of these living entities is due only to their forgetfulness of their eternal relationship with the Supreme Personality of Godhead. When the living entity wants to lord it over the material energy by imitating the position of Kṛṣṇa, he is immediately captured by the material energy and, according to his desire, is offered a variety of 8,400,000 different kinds of bodies. Although undergoing the threefold miseries of material existence, the illusioned living entity falsely thinks himself the master of all he surveys. Under the spell of the material energy, which represents the threefold material qualities, the living entity is so entangled that it is not at all possible for him to become free unless he is graced by the Supreme Lord. The living entity cannot conquer the influence of the material modes of nature by his own endeavor, but because material nature is working under the control of the Supreme Lord, the Lord is beyond its jurisdiction.

Except for Him, all living entities, beginning from Brahmā down to an ant, are conquered by the contact of material nature.

Because He possesses in full the six opulences of wealth, strength, fame, beauty, knowledge and renunciation, the Lord alone is beyond the spell of material nature. Unless the living entity is situated in Kṛṣṇa consciousness, he cannot approach the Supreme Personality of Godhead, yet the Lord, by His omnipotency, can dictate from within as the Supersoul. In the *Bhagavad-gītā,* the Lord advises, "Whatever you do, do for Me; whatever you eat, first of all offer to Me; whatever charity you want to give, first give to Me; and whatever austerities and penances you want to perform, perform for Me." In this way the *karmīs* are directed to gradually develop Kṛṣṇa consciousness. Similarly, Kṛṣṇa directs the philosophers to approach Him gradually by discriminating between Brahman and *māyā.* At last when one is mature in knowledge, he surrenders unto Kṛṣṇa. As Kṛṣṇa says in *Bhagavad-gītā*, "After many, many births, the wise philosopher surrenders unto Me." The *yogīs* are also directed to concentrate their meditation upon Kṛṣṇa within the heart, and by such continued process of Kṛṣṇa consciousness the *yogī* can become free from the clutches of material energy. But, as is stated in *Bhagavad-gītā,* because the devotees are engaged in devotional service with love and affection from the very beginning, the Lord directs them so that they can approach Him without difficulty or deviation. Only by the grace of the Lord can the living entity understand the exact position of Brahman, Paramātmā and Bhagavān.

The statements of the personified *Vedas* give clear evidence that the Vedic literature is presented only for understanding Kṛṣṇa. It is confirmed in the *Bhagavad-gītā* that through all the *Vedas* it is Kṛṣṇa alone who has to be understood. Kṛṣṇa is always enjoying, either in the material world or in the spiritual world; because He is the supreme enjoyer, for Him there is no distinction between the material world and spiritual worlds. The material world is an impediment for the ordinary living entities because they are under its control, but Kṛṣṇa, being the controller of the material world, has nothing to do with the impediments it offers. Therefore, in different parts of the *Upaniṣads,* the *Vedas* declare: "Brahman is eternal, full of all knowledge and all bliss, but the one Supreme Personality of Godhead is existing in the heart of every living entity." Because of His all-pervasiveness, He is able to enter not only into the hearts of the living entities, but even into the atoms also. As the Supersoul, He is the controller of all activities of the living entities. He is living within all of them and witnessing their actions, allowing them to act according to their desires, and also giving them the results of their different activities. He is the living force of all things, but still He is transcendental to the material qualities. He is omnipotent; He is expert in manufacturing everything, and on account of His superior, natural knowledge, He can bring everyone under His control. As such, He is everyone's master. He is sometimes manifest on the surface of the globe, but He is simultaneously within all matter. Desiring to expand Himself in multi-forms, He glanced over the material energy, and thus innumerable living entities became manifest. Everything is created by His superior energy, and everything in His creation appears to be perfectly done without deficiency.

Those who aspire for liberation from this material world must therefore worship the Supreme Personality of Godhead, the ultimate cause of all causes. He is just like the total mass of earth, from which varieties of earthly pots are manufactured: the pots are made of earthly clay, they rest on the earth, and after being destroyed, their elements ultimately merge back into earth. Although the Personality of Godhead is the original cause of all varieties of manifestation, the impersonalists especially stress the Vedic statement, *sarvaṁ khalv idam brahma:* "Everything is Brahman." The impersonalists do not take into account the varieties of manifestation emanating from the supreme cause of Brahman. They simply take into consideration that everything emanates from Brahman and after destruction merges into Brahman and that the intermediate stage of manifestation is also Brahman. Although the Māyāvādīs believe that prior to its manifestation the cosmos was in Brahman, after creation it remains in Brahman and after destruction it merges into Brahman, they do not know what Brahman is. This fact is clearly described in the *Brahma-saṁhitā:* The living entities, space, time, and the material elements like fire, earth, sky, water and mind, constitute the total cosmic manifestation, known as *bhūr bhuvaḥ svaḥ,* which is manifested by Govinda. It flourishes on the strength of Govinda and after annihilation enters into and is conserved in Govinda. Lord Brahmā therefore says, "I worship Lord Govinda, the original personality, the cause of all causes."

The word Brahman indicates the greatest of all and the maintainer of everything. The impersonalists are attracted by the greatness of the sky, but because of their poor fund of knowledge they are not attracted by the greatness of Kṛṣṇa. In our practical life, however, we are attracted by the greatness of a person and not by the greatness of a big mountain. Actually the term *Brahman* can be applied to Kṛṣṇa only; therefore in the *Bhagavad-gītā* Arjuna admitted that Lord Kṛṣṇa is the *Parambrahman,* or the supreme rest of everything.

Kṛṣṇa is the Supreme Brahman because of His unlimited knowledge, unlimited potencies, unlimited strength, unlimited influence, unlimited beauty and unlimited renunciation. Therefore the word *Brahman* can be applied to Kṛṣṇa only. Arjuna affirms that because the impersonal Brahman is the effulgence emanating as rays of Kṛṣṇa's transcendental body, Kṛṣṇa is the Parambrahman. Everything is resting on Brahman, but Brahman itself is resting on Kṛṣṇa. Therefore Kṛṣṇa is the ultimate Brahman or Parambrahman. The material elements are accepted as inferior energies of Kṛṣṇa because by their interaction the cosmic manifestation takes place, rests on Kṛṣṇa, and after dissolution again enters into the body of Kṛṣṇa as His subtle energy. Kṛṣṇa is therefore the cause of both manifestation and dissolution.

Sarvaṁ khalv idaṁ brahma means everything is Kṛṣṇa, and that is the vision of the *mahābhāgavatas.* They see everything in relation to Kṛṣṇa. The impersonalists argue that Kṛṣṇa has transformed Himself into many and that therefore everything is Kṛṣṇa and worship of everything is worship of Him. This false argument is answered by Kṛṣṇa in the *Bhagavad-gītā:* although everything is a transformation of the energy of Kṛṣṇa, He is not present everywhere. He is simultaneously present and not present. By His energy He is present everywhere, but as the energetic He is not present everywhere. This simultaneous presence and non-presence is inconceivable to our present senses. But a clear explanation is given in the beginning of the *Īśopaniṣad,* in which it is stated that the Supreme Lord is so complete that although unlimited energies and their transformations are emanating from Kṛṣṇa, Kṛṣṇa's personality is not in the least bit transformed. Therefore, since Kṛṣṇa is the cause of all causes, intelligent persons should take shelter of His lotus feet.

Kṛṣṇa advises everyone just to surrender unto Him alone, and that is the way of Vedic instruction. Since Kṛṣṇa is the cause of all causes, He is worshiped by all kinds of sages and saints by observance of the regulative principles. When there is a necessity for meditation, great personalities meditate on the transcendental form of Kṛṣṇa within the heart. In this way the minds of great personalities are always engaged in Kṛṣṇa. With minds engaged in Kṛṣṇa, naturally the captivated devotees simply talk of Kṛṣṇa.

Talking of Kṛṣṇa or singing of Kṛṣṇa is called *kīrtana.* Lord Caitanya also recommends *kīrtanīyaḥ sadā hariḥ,* which means always thinking and talking of Kṛṣṇa and nothing else. That is called Kṛṣṇa consciousness. Kṛṣṇa consciousness is so sublime that anyone who takes to this process is elevated to the highest perfection of life—far, far beyond the concept of liberation. In the *Bhagavad-gītā,* therefore, Kṛṣṇa advises everyone to always think of Him, render devotional service to Him, worship Him and offer obeisances to Him. In this way a devotee becomes fully Kṛṣṇa-ized and, being always situated in Kṛṣṇa consciousness, ultimately goes back to Kṛṣṇa.

Although the *Vedas* have recommended worship of different demigods as different parts and parcels of Kṛṣṇa, it is to be understood that such instructions are meant for the less intelligent class of men, who are still attracted by material sense enjoyment. But the person who actually wants perfect fulfillment of the mission of human life should simply worship Lord Kṛṣṇa, and that will simplify the matter and completely guarantee the success of his human life. Although the sky, the water and the land are all part and parcel of the material world, when one stands on the solid land his position is more secure than when he stands in the sky or the water. An intelligent person, therefore, does not stand under the protection of different demigods, although they are part and parcel of Kṛṣṇa. Rather, he stands on the solid ground of Kṛṣṇa consciousness. That makes his position sound and secure.

Impersonalists sometimes give the example that if one stands on a stone or a piece of wood, one certainly stands on the surface of the land, because the stone and wood are both resting on the surface of the earth. But it may be replied that if one stands directly on the surface of the earth, he is more secure than on the wood or stone which are resting on the earth. In other words, taking shelter of Paramātmā or taking shelter of impersonal Brahman is not as secure a course as taking direct shelter of Kṛṣṇa in Kṛṣṇa consciousness. The position of the *jñānīs* and *yogīs* is therefore not as secure as the position of the devotees of Kṛṣṇa. Lord Kṛṣṇa has therefore advised in the *Bhagavad-gītā* that only a person who has lost his senses takes to the worship of demigods. And regarding persons who are attached to the impersonal Brahman, the *Śrīmad-Bhāgavatam* says, "My dear Lord, those who are thinking of themselves as liberated by mental speculation are not yet purified of the contamination of material nature because of their inability to find the shelter of Your lotus feet. Although they rise to the transcendental situation of existence in impersonal Brahman, they certainly fall from that exalted position because they have neglected to desire Your lotus feet." Lord Kṛṣṇa therefore advises that the worshipers of the demigods are not very intelligent persons because they derive only temporary, exhaustible results. Their endeavors are those of less intelligent men. But the Lord assures that His devotee has no fear of falling.

The personified *Vedas* continued to pray: "Dear Lord, considering all points of view, if one has to worship someone superior to him, then just out of good behavior one should stick to the worship of Your lotus feet because You are the ultimate controller of creation, maintenance and dissolution. You are the controller of the three worlds, Bhūr, Bhuvar and Svar, You are the controller of the fourteen upper and lower worlds, and You are the controller of the three material qualities. Demigods and persons advanced in spiritual knowledge are always engaged in hearing and chanting about Your transcendental pastimes because this has the specific potency of nullifying the accumulated results of sinful life. Intelligent persons factually take a dip in the ocean of Your nectarean activities and very patiently hear of them. Thus they immediately become freed from the contamination of the material qualities; they do not have to undergo severe penances and austerities for advancement of spiritual life. This chanting and hearing of Your transcendental pastimes is the easiest process for self-realization. Simply by submissive aural reception of the transcendental message, one's heart becomes cleansed of all dirty things. Thus Kṛṣṇa consciousness becomes fixed in the heart of a devotee.

"The great authority Bhīṣmadeva has also given the opinion that this process of chanting and hearing about the Supreme Personality of Godhead is the essence of all Vedic ritualistic performances. Dear Lord, the devotee who wants to elevate himself simply by this process of devotional activities, especially by hearing and chanting, very soon comes out of the clutches of the dualities of material existence. By this simple process of penance and austerity the Supersoul within the devotee's heart becomes very pleased and gives the devotee directions so that he may go back to home, back to Godhead. It is stated in the *Bhagavad-gītā* that one who engages all his activities and senses in the devotional service of the Lord becomes completely pacified because the Supersoul is satisfied with him; thus the devotee becomes transcendental to all kinds of dualities, such as heat and cold, honor and dishonor. Being freed from all dualities, he feels transcendental bliss, and he no longer suffers cares and anxieties due to material existence. *Bhagavad-gītā* confirms that the devotee who is always absorbed in Kṛṣṇa consciousness has no anxieties for his maintenance or protection. Being constantly absorbed in Kṛṣṇa consciousness, he ultimately achieves the highest perfection. While in the material existence, he lives very peacefully and blissfully without any cares and anxieties, and after quitting this body he goes back to home, back to Godhead. The Lord confirms in the *Bhagavad-gītā,* 'My supreme abode is a transcendental place where going no one returns to this material world. Anyone who attains the supreme perfection, being engaged in My personal devotional service in the eternal abode, reaches the highest perfection of human life and doesn't have to come back again to the miserable material world.'

"My dear Lord, it is imperative that the living entities be engaged in Kṛṣṇa consciousness, always rendering devotional service by prescribed methods such as hearing and chanting and executing Your orders. If a person is not engaged in Kṛṣṇa consciousness and devotional service, it is useless for him to exhibit the symptoms of life. Generally it is accepted that if a person is breathing he is alive. But a person without Kṛṣṇa consciousness may be compared to a bellows in a blacksmith's shop. The big bellows is a bag of skin which exhales and inhales air, and a human being who is simply living within the bag of skin and bones without taking to Kṛṣṇa consciousness and loving devotional service is no better than the bellows. Similarly, a nondevotee's long duration of life is compared to the long existence of a tree, his voracious eating capacity is compared to the eating of dogs and hogs, and his enjoyment in sex life is compared to that of hogs and goats.

"The cosmic manifestation has been possible because of the entrance of the Supreme Personality of Godhead as Mahā-Viṣṇu within this material world. The total material energy becomes agitated by the glance of Mahā-Viṣṇu, and only then does the interaction of the three material qualities begin. Therefore it should be concluded that whatever material facilities we are trying to enjoy are available only due to the mercy of the Supreme Personality of Godhead.

"Within the body there are five different departments of existence, known as *annamaya, prāṇamaya, manomaya, vijñānamaya,* and at last *ānandamaya.* In the beginning of life, every living entity is food conscious. A child or an animal is satisfied only by getting nice food. This stage of consciousness, in which the goal is to eat sumptuously, is called *annamaya. Anna* means food. After this one lives in the consciousness of being alive. If one can continue his life without being attacked or destroyed, one thinks himself happy. This stage is called *prāṇamaya,* or consciousness of one's existence. After this stage, when one is situated on the mental platform, that consciousness is called *manomaya.* The material civilization is primarily situated in these three stages, *annamaya, prāṇamaya* and *manomaya.* The first concern of civilized persons is economic development, the next concern is defense against being annihilated, and the next consciousness is mental speculation, the philosophical approach to the values of life.

"If by the evolutionary process of philosophical life one happens to reach to the platform of intellectual life and understands that he is not this material body, but is a spirit soul, then by evolution of spiritual life he comes to the understanding of the Supreme Lord or the Supreme Soul. When one develops his relationship with Him and executes devotional service, that stage of life is called Kṛṣṇa consciousness, the *ānandamaya* stage. *Ānandamaya* is the blissful life of knowledge and eternity. As it is said in the *Vedānta-sūtra, ānandamayo 'bhyāsāt.* The Supreme Brahman and the subordinate Brahman, or the Supreme Personality of Godhead and the living entities, are both joyful by nature. As long as the living entities are situated in the lower four stages of life, *annamaya, prāṇamaya, manomaya* and *vijñānamaya,* they are considered to be in the material condition of life, but as soon as one reaches the stage of *ānandamaya* he becomes a liberated soul. This *ānandamaya* stage is explained in the *Bhagavad-gītā* as the *brahma-bhūta* stage. There it is said that in the *brahma-bhūta* stage of life there is no anxiety and no hankering. This stage begins when one becomes equally disposed toward all living entities, and it then expands to the stage of Kṛṣṇa consciousness in which one always hankers to render service unto the Supreme Personality of Godhead. This hankering for advancement in devotional service is not the same as hankering for sense gratification in material existence. In other words, hankering remains in spiritual life, but it becomes purified. When our senses are purified, they become freed from all material stages, namely *annamaya, prāṇamaya, manomaya* and *vijñānamaya,* and they become situated in the highest stage—*ānandamaya,* or blissful life in Kṛṣṇa consciousness. The Māyāvādī philosophers consider *ānandamaya* to be the state of being merged in the Supreme. To them, *ānandamaya* means that the Supersoul and the individual soul become one. But the real fact is that oneness does not mean merging into the Supreme and losing one's own individual existence. Merging in the spiritual existence is the living entity's realization of qualitative oneness with the Supreme Lord in His eternity and knowledge aspects. But the actual *ānandamaya* (blissful) stage is obtained when one is engaged in devotional service. That is confirmed in the *Bhagavad-gītā. Mad-bhaktiṁ labhate parām:* the *brahma-bhūta ānandamaya* stage is complete only when there is the exchange of love between the Supreme and the subordinate living entities. Unless one comes to this *ānandamaya* stage of life, his breathing is like the breathing of a bellows in a blacksmith's shop, his duration of life is like that of a tree, and he is no better than the lower animals like the camels, hogs and dogs.

Undoubtedly the eternal living entity cannot be annihilated at any point. But the lower species of life exist in a miserable condition, whereas one who is engaged in devotional service of the Supreme Lord is situated in the pleasurable or *ānandamaya* status of life. The different stages described above are all in relationship with the Supreme Personality of Godhead. Although in all circumstances there exist both the Supreme Personality of Godhead and the living entities, the difference is that the Supreme Personality of Godhead always exists in the *ānandamaya* stage, whereas the subordinate living entities, because of their minute position as fragmental portions of the Supreme Lord, are prone to fall to the other stages of life. Although in all the stages both the Supreme Lord and the living entities exist, the Supreme Personality of Godhead is always transcendental to our concept of life, whether we are in bondage or in liberation. The whole cosmic manifestation becomes possible by the grace of the Supreme Lord, it exists by the grace of the Supreme Lord, and when it is annihilated, it merges into the existence of the Supreme Lord. As such, the Supreme Lord is the supreme existence, the cause of all causes. Therefore the conclusion is that without development of Kṛṣṇa consciousness, one's life is simply a waste of time.

Those who are very materialistic and cannot understand the situation of the spiritual world cannot understand the abode of Kṛṣṇa. For such persons, great sages have recommended the yogic process whereby one gradually rises from meditation on the adbomen, which is called *mūlādhāra* or *maṇipūraka* meditation. *Mūlādhāra* and *maṇipūraka* are technical terms which refer to the intestines within the abdomen. Grossly materialistic persons think that economic development is of foremost importance because they are under the impression that a living entity exists only by eating. Such grossly materialistic persons forget that although we may eat as much as we like, if the food is not digested it produces the troubles of indigestion and acidity. Therefore, in itself, eating is not the cause of the vital energy of life. For digestion of eatables we have to take shelter of another, superior energy, which is mentioned in the *Bhagavad-gītā* as *vaiśvānara.* Lord Kṛṣṇa says in the *Bhagavad-gītā* that He helps the digestion in the form of *vaiśvānara.* The Supreme Personality of Godhead is all-pervasive; therefore, His presence as *vaiśvānara* is not extraordinary.

Kṛṣṇa is actually present everywhere. The Vaiṣṇava, therefore, marks his body with temples of Viṣṇu: he first marks a *tilaka* temple on the abdomen, then on the chest, then between the collarbones, then on the forehead, and gradually he marks the top of the head, the *brahma-randhra.* The thirteen temples of *tilaka* marked on the body of a Vaiṣṇava are known as follows: On the forehead is the temple of Lord Keśava, on the belly is the temple of Lord Nārāyaṇa, on the chest is the temple of Lord Mādhava, and on the throat, between the two collarbones, is the temple of Lord Govinda. On the right side of the waist is the temple of Lord Viṣṇu, on the right arm is the temple of Lord Madhusūdana, and on the right side of the collarbone is the temple of Lord Trivikrama. Similarly, on the left side of the waist is the temple of Lord Vāmanadeva, on the left arm is the temple of Śrīdhara, on the left side of the collarbone is the temple of Hṛṣīkeśa, on the upper back the temple is called Padmanābha, and on the lower back the temple is called Dāmodara. On the top of the head the temple is called Vāsudeva. This is the process of meditation on the Lord's situation in the different parts of the body, but for those who are not Vaiṣṇavas, great sages recommend meditation on the bodily concept of life—meditation on the intestines, on the heart, on the throat, on the eyebrows, on the forehead and then on the top of the head. Some of the sages in the disciplic succession from the great saint Aruṇa meditate on the heart because the Supersoul is also staying within the heart along with the living entity. This is confirmed in *Bhagavad-gītā,* Fifteenth Chapter, wherein the Lord states, "I am situated in everyone's heart."

For the Vaiṣṇava, the protection of the body for the service of the Lord is a part of devotional service, but those who are gross materialists accept the body as the self. They worship the body by the yogic process of meditation on the different bodily parts, such as *maṇipūraka, dahara* and *hṛdaya,* gradually rising to the *brahma-randhra* on the top of the head. The first-class *yogī* who has attained perfection in the practice of the *yoga* system ultimately passes through the *brahma-randhra* to any one of the planets in either the material or spiritual worlds. How a *yogī* can transfer himself to another planet is very vividly described in the Second Canto of *Śrīmad-Bhāgavatam.*

In this regard, Śukadeva Gosvāmī has recommended that the beginners worship the *virāṭa puruṣa,* the gigantic universal form of the Lord. One who cannot believe that the Lord can be worshiped with equal success in the Deity or *arcā* form, or who cannot concentrate on this form, is advised to worship the universal form of the Lord. The lower part of the universe is considered the feet and legs of the Lord's universal form, the middle part of the universe is considered the navel or abdomen of the Lord, the upper planetary systems such as Janaloka and Maharloka are the heart of the Lord, and the topmost planetary system, Brahmaloka, is considered the top of the Lord's head. There are different processes recommended by great sages, according to the position of the worshiper, but the ultimate aim of all meditational and yogic processes is to go back home, back to Godhead. As stated in *Bhagavad-gītā,* anyone who reaches the highest planet, the abode of Kṛṣṇa, or even the Vaikuṇṭha planets, never has to come down again to this miserable material condition of life.

The Vedic recommendation, therefore, is that one make the lotus feet of Viṣṇu the target of all one's efforts. *Tad viṣṇoḥ paramaṁ padaṁ,* Viṣṇu-loka or the Viṣṇu planets, are situated above all the material planets. These Vaikuṇṭha planets are known as *sanātana-dhāma,* and they are eternal. They are never annihilated, not even by the annihilation of this material world. The conclusion is that if a human being does not fulfill the mission of his life by worshiping the Supreme Lord and does not go back to Godhead, then it is to be understood that he has been frustrated in fulfilling the main purpose of human life.

The next prayer of the personified *Vedas* to the Lord concerns His entering into different species of life. It is stated in *Bhagavad-gītā,* Fourteenth Chapter, that in every species and form of life the spiritual part and parcel of the Supreme Lord is present. The Lord Himself claims in the *Gītā* that He is the seed-giving father of all forms and species, and therefore they must all be considered sons of the Lord. The entrance of the Supreme Lord into everyone's heart as Paramātmā sometimes bewilders the impersonalists, who think in terms of the equality of the living entities with the Supreme Lord. They think that because the Supreme Lord enters into different bodies along with the individual soul, there is no distinction between the Lord and the individual entities. Their challenge is, "Why should individual souls worship the Paramātmā or Supersoul?" According to them, both the Supersoul and the individual soul are on the same level; they are one, without any difference between them. There is a difference, however, between the Supersoul and in the individual soul, and this is explained in *Bhagavad-gītā,* Fifteenth Chapter, wherein the Lord says that although He is situated with the living entity in the same body, He is superior. He is dictating to or giving intelligence to the individual soul from within. It is clearly stated in the *Gītā* that the Lord gives intelligence to the individual soul and that both memory and forgetfulness are due to the influence of the Supersoul. No one can act independently of the sanction of the Supersoul. Therefore, the individual soul acts according to his past *karma,* reminded by the Lord. The nature of the individual soul is forgetfulness, but the presence of the Lord within the heart reminds him of what he wanted to do in his past life. The intelligence of the individual soul is exhibited like fire in wood. Although fire is always fire, it is exhibited in a size proportionate to the size of the wood. Similarly, although the individual soul is qualitatively one with the Supreme Lord, he exhibits himself according to the limitations of his present body.

The Supreme Lord or the Supersoul is said to be *eka-rasa. Eka* means one, and *rasa* means mellow. The transcendental position of the Supreme Lord is that of eternity, bliss and full knowledge. His position of *eka-rasa* does not change in the slightest when He becomes a witness and advisor to the individual soul in each individual body.

The individual soul, beginning from Lord Brahmā down to the ant, exhibits his spiritual potency according to his present body. The demigods are in the same category with the individual souls in the bodies of the human beings or in the bodies of lower animals. Intelligent persons, therefore, do not worship different demigods, who are simply infinitesimal representatives of Kṛṣṇa manifesting in conditioned bodies. The individual soul can exhibit his power and potencies only in proportion to the shape and constitution of the body. The Supreme Personality of Godhead, however, can exhibit His full potencies in any shape or form without any change. The Māyāvādī philosophers' thesis that God and the individual soul are one and the same cannot be accepted because the individual soul has to develop his power and potencies according to the development of different types of bodies. The individual soul in the body of a baby cannot show the full power and potency of a grown man, but the Supreme Personality of Godhead Kṛṣṇa, even when lying on the lap of His mother as a baby, could exhibit His full potency and power by killing Pūtanā and other demons who tried to attack Him. Therefore the spiritual potency of the Supreme Personality of Godhead is said to be *eka-rasa,* or without change. Therefore the Supreme Personality of Godhead is the only worshipable object, and this is perfectly known to persons who are uncontaminated by the force of material nature. In other words, only the liberated souls can worship the Supreme Personality of Godhead. Less intelligent Māyāvādīs take to the worship of demigods, thinking that the demigods and the Supreme Personality of Godhead are on the same level.

The personified *Vedas* continued to offer their obeisances. "Dear Lord," they prayed, "after many, many births, those who have actually become wise take to the worship of Your lotus feet in complete knowledge." This is also confirmed in the *Bhagavad-gītā*, wherein the Lord says that after many, many births, a great soul or *mahātmā* surrenders unto the Lord, knowing well that Vāsudeva, Kṛṣṇa, is the cause of all causes. The *Vedas* continued: "As has already been explained, since our mind, intelligence and senses have been given to us by God, when these instruments are actually purified there is no alternative than to engage them all in the devotional service of the Lord. A living entity's entrapment in different species of life is due to the misapplication of his mind, intelligence and senses in material activities. Various kinds of bodies are awarded as the result of a living entity's actions, and they are created by the material nature according to the living entity's desire. Because a living entity desires and deserves a particular kind of body, it is given to him by the material nature under the order of the Supreme Lord.

In the *Śrīmad-Bhāgavatam,* Third Canto, it is explained that under the control of superior authority a living entity is put within the semina of a male and injected into the womb of a particular female in order to develop a particular type of body. A living entity utilizes his senses, intelligence, mind, etc., in a specific way of his own choosing and thus develops a particular type of body within which he becomes encaged. In this way the living entity becomes situated in different species of life, either in a demigod, human or animal body, according to different situations and circumstances.

It is explained in the Vedic literatures that the living entities entrapped in different species of life are part and parcel of the Supreme Lord. The Māyāvādī philosophers mistake the living entity for the Paramātmā, who is actually sitting with the living entity as a friend. Because the Paramātmā, the localized aspect of the Supreme Personality of Godhead, and the individual living entity are both within the body, a misunderstanding sometimes takes place that there is no difference between the two. But there is a definite difference between the individual soul and the Supersoul, and it is explained in the *Varāha Purāṇa* as follows. The Supreme Lord has two kinds of parts and parcels: the living entity is called *vibhinnāṁśa,* and the Paramātmā or the plenary expansion of the Supreme Lord is called *svāṁśa.* The *svāṁśa* plenary expansion of the Supreme Personality is as powerful as the Supreme Personality of Godhead Himself. There is not even the slightest difference between the potency of the Supreme Person and that of His plenary expansion as Paramātmā, but the *vibhinnāṁśa* parts and parcels possess only a minute portion of the potencies of the Lord. The *Nārāyaṇa-Pañcarātra* states that the living entities who are the marginal potency of the Supreme Lord are undoubtedly of the same quality of spiritual existence as the Lord Himself, but they are prone to be tinged with the material qualities. Because he is prone to be subjected to the influence of material qualities, the minute living entity is called *jīva.* Sometimes the Supreme Personality of Godhead is also known as Śiva, the all-auspicious. So the difference between Śiva and *jīva* is that the all-auspicious Personality of Godhead is never affected by the material qualities, whereas the minute portions of the Supreme Personality of Godhead are prone to be affected by the qualities of material nature.

The Supersoul within the body of a particular living entity, although a plenary portion of the Lord, is worshipable by the individual living entity. Great sages have therefore concluded that the process of meditation is designed so that the individual living entity may concentrate his attention on the lotus feet of the Supersoul form (Viṣṇu). That is the real form of *samādhi.* The living entity cannot become liberated from material entanglement by his own effort. He must therefore take to the devotional service of the lotus feet of the Supreme Lord, or the Supersoul within himself. Śrīdhara Svāmī, the great commentator on *Śrīmad-Bhāgavatam,* has composed a nice verse in this regard, the purport of which is as follows: "My dear Lord, I am eternally Your part and parcel, but I have been entrapped by the material potencies, which are also an emanation from You. As the cause of all causes, You have entered my body as the Supersoul, and I have the prerogative to enjoy the supreme blissful life of knowledge along with You. Therefore, my dear Lord, please order me to render You loving service so that I can again be brought to my original position of transcendental bliss."

Great personalities understand that a living entity entangled in this material world cannot become freed by his own efforts. With firm faith and devotion, such great personalities engage themselves in rendering transcendental loving service to the Lord. That is the verdict of the personified *Vedas.*

The personified *Vedas* continued: "Dear Lord, it is very difficult to achieve perfect knowledge of the Absolute Truth. Your Lordship is so kind to the fallen souls that You appear in different incarnations and execute different activities. You appear even as a historical personality of this material world, and Your pastimes are very nicely described in the Vedic literatures. Such pastimes are as attractive as the ocean of transcendental bliss. People in general have a natural inclination to read narrations in which ordinary *jīvas* are glorified, but when they become attracted by the Vedic literatures which delineate Your eternal pastimes, they actually dip into the ocean of transcendental bliss. As a fatigued man feels refreshed by dipping into a reservoir of water, so the conditioned soul who is very much disgusted with material activities becomes refreshed and forgets all the fatigue of material activities simply by dipping into the transcendental ocean of Your pastimes. And eventually he merges in the ocean of transcendental bliss. The most intelligent devotees, therefore, do not take to any means of self-realization except devotional service and constant engagement in the nine different processes of devotional life, especially hearing and chanting. When hearing and chanting about Your transcendental pastimes, Your devotees do not care even for the transcendental bliss derived from liberation or from merging into the existence of the Supreme. Such devotees are not interested even in so-called liberation, and certainly they have no interest in material activities for elevation to the heavenly planets for sense gratification. Pure devotees seek only the association of *paramahaṁsas,* or great liberated devotees, so that they can continually hear and chant about Your glories. For this purpose the pure devotees are prepared to sacrifice all comforts of life, even giving up the material comforts of family life and so-called society, friendship and love. Those who have tasted the nectar of devotion by relishing the transcendental vibration of chanting Your glories, Hare Kṛṣṇa, Hare Kṛṣṇa, Kṛṣṇa Kṛṣṇa, Hare Hare/ Hare Rāma, Hare Rāma, Rāma Rāma, Hare Hare, do not care for any other spiritual bliss or for material comforts, which appear to the pure devotee to be less important than the straw in the street."

The personified *Vedas* continued: "Dear Lord, when a person is able to purify his mind, senses and intelligence by engaging himself in devotional service in full Kṛṣṇa consciousness, his mind becomes his friend. Otherwise, his mind is always his enemy. When the mind is engaged in devotional service of the Lord, it becomes the intimate friend of the living entity because the mind can then think of the Supreme Lord always. Your Lordship is eternally dear to the living entity, so when the mind is engaged in thought of You, one immediately feels the great satisfaction for which he has been hankering life after life. When one's mind is thus fixed on the lotus feet of the Supreme Personality of Godhead, one does not take to any kind of inferior worship or inferior process of self-realization. By attempting to worship a demigod or by taking to any other process of self-realization, the living entity becomes a victim of the cycle of birth and death, and no one can estimate how much the living entity becomes degraded by entering the abominable species of life such as the cats and dogs."

Śrī Narottama dāsa Ṭhākur has sung that persons who do not take to devotional service of the Lord but are attracted to the process of philosophical speculation and fruitive activities drink the poisonous results of such actions. Such persons are forced to take birth in different species of life and are forced to adopt obnoxious practices like meat-eating and intoxication. Materialistic persons generally worship the transient material body and forget the welfare of the spirit soul within the body. Some take shelter of materialistic science to improve bodily comforts, and some take to the worship of demigods in order to be promoted to the heavenly planets. Their goal in life is to make the material body comfortable while forgetting the interest of the spirit soul. Such persons are described in the Vedic literature as suicidal because attachment for the material body and its comforts forces the living entity to wander through the process of birth and death perpetually and suffer the material pangs as a matter of course. The human form of life is a chance for one to understand his position, and the most intelligent person takes to devotional service just to engage his mind, senses and body in the service of the Lord without deviation.

The personified *Vedas* continued: "Dear Lord, there are many mystic *yogīs* who are very learned and deliberate in achieving the highest perfection of life. They engage themselves in the yogic process of controlling the life-air within the body. Concentrating the mind upon the form of Viṣṇu and controlling the senses very rigidly, they practice the *yoga* system, but even after much laborious austerity, penance, and regulation, they achieve the same destination as persons who are inimical toward You. In other words, both the *yogīs* and great, wise philosophical speculators ultimately attain the impersonal Brahman effulgence, which is also automatically attained by the demons who are regular enemies of the Lord. Demons like Kaṁsa, Śiśupāla and Dantavakra also attain the Brahman effulgence because they constantly meditate upon the Supreme Personality of Godhead. Women such as the *gopīs* were attached to Kṛṣṇa and captivated by His beauty, and their mental concentration on Kṛṣṇa was provoked by lust. They wanted to be embraced by the arms of Kṛṣṇa, which resemble the beautiful round shape of a snake. Similarly, there are the Vedic hymns, and we also simply concentrate our minds on the lotus feet of Your Lordship. Women like the *gopīs* concentrate upon You dictated by lust, and we concentrate upon Your lotus feet to go back home, back to Godhead. Your enemies also concentrate upon You, thinking always how to kill You, and the *yogīs* undertake great penances and austerities just to attain Your impersonal effulgence. All these different persons, although concentrating their minds in different ways, achieve spiritual perfection according to their different perspectives because You are equal to all Your devotees."

Śrīdhara Svāmī has composed a nice verse in this regard: "My dear Lord, to be engaged always in thinking of Your lotus feet is very difficult. It is possible by great devotees who have already achieved love for You and who are engaged in transcendental loving service. My dear Lord, I wish that my mind also may be engaged somehow or other on Your lotus feet, at least for some time."

The attainment of spiritual perfection by different spiritualists is explained in the *Bhagavad-gītā,* wherein the Lord says that He grants the perfection the devotee desires in proportion to the devotee's surrender unto Him. The impersonalists, *yogīs* and the enemies of the Lord enter into the Lord's transcendental effulgence, but the personalists who are following in the footsteps of the inhabitants of Vṛndāvana or strictly following the path of devotional service are elevated to the personal abode of Kṛṣṇa, Goloka Vṛndāvana, or to the Vaikuṇṭha planets. Both the impersonalists and the personalists enter into the spiritual realm or the spiritual sky, but the impersonalists are given their place in the impersonal Brahman effulgence, whereas the personalists are given a position in the Vaikuṇṭha planets or in the Vṛndāvana planet, according to their desire to serve the Lord in different mellows.

The personified *Vedas* stated that persons who are born after the creation of this material world cannot understand the existence of the Supreme Personality of Godhead by manipulating their material knowledge. Just as a person born in a particular family cannot understand the position of his great-grandfather who lived before the birth of the recent generation, we are unable to understand the Supreme Personality of Godhead, Nārāyaṇa or Kṛṣṇa, who exists eternally in the spiritual world. In the Eighth Chapter of the *Bhagavad-gītā* it is clearly said that the Supreme Person, who lives eternally in the spiritual kingdom of God *(sanātana-dhāma),* can be approached only by devotional service.

As for the material creation, Brahmā is the first created person. Before Brahmā there was no living creature within this material world; it was void and dark until Brahmā was born on the lotus flower sprouted from the abdomen of Garbhodakaśāyī Viṣṇu. Garbhodakaśāyī Viṣṇu is an expansion of Kāraṇodakaśāyī Viṣṇu, Kāraṇodakaśāyī Viṣṇu is an expansion of Saṅkarṣaṇa, and Saṅkarṣaṇa is an expansion of Balarāma. Balarāma is an immediate expansion of Lord Kṛṣṇa. After the creation of Brahmā, the two kinds of demigods were born: demigods like the four brothers Sanaka, Sanātana, Sananda and Sanat-kumāra, who are representatives of renunciation of the world, and demigods like Marīci and their descendants who are meant to enjoy this material world. From these two kinds of demigods were gradually manifested all other living entities, including the human beings. Thus any living creature within this material world, including Brahmā, all the demigods and all the *rākṣasas,* are to be considered modern. This means that they were all recently born. Therefore, just as a person recently born in a family cannot understand the situation of his distant forefather, so anyone within this material world cannot understand the position of the Supreme Lord in the spiritual world because the material world has only recently been created. Although they have a long duration of existence, all the manifestations of the material world, namely, the time elements, the living entities, the *Vedas,* and the gross and subtle elements, are all created at some point. Anything manufactured within this created situation or accepted as a means to understanding the original source of creation is to be considered modern.

Therefore by the process of self-realization or God realization through fruitive activities, philosophical speculation or mystic *yoga,* one cannot actually approach the supreme source of everything. When the creation is completely terminated, when there is no existence of the *Vedas,* no existence of material time, no existence of the gross and subtle material elements, and when all the living entities are in the nonmanifested stage resting within Nārāyaṇa, then all these manufactured processes become null and void and cannot act. Devotional service, however, is eternally going on in the eternal spiritual world. Therefore the only factual process of self-realization or God realization is devotional service, and if one takes to this process he takes to the real process of God realization. Śrīla Śrīdhara Svāmī has therefore composed a verse in this regard which conveys the idea that the supreme source of everything, the Supreme Personality of Godhead, is so great and unlimited that it is not possible for the living entity to understand Him by any material acquisition. Everyone should therefore pray to the Lord to be engaged in His devotional service eternally, so that by the grace of the Lord one can understand the supreme source of creation. The supreme source of creation, the Supreme Lord, reveals Himself only to the devotees. In the Fourth Chapter of *Bhagavad-gītā* the Lord says to Arjuna, "My dear Arjuna, because you are My devotee and because you are My intimate friend I shall therefore reveal to you the process of understanding Me." In other words, the supreme source of creation, the Supreme Personality of Godhead, cannot be understood by our own endeavor. We have to please Him with devotional service, and then He will reveal Himself to us. Then we can understand Him to some extent.

There are different kinds of philosophers who have tried to understand the supreme source by their mental speculation. There are generally six kinds of mental speculators, and they are called *ṣaḍ-darśana.* All these philosophers are impersonalists and are known as Māyāvādīs. Every one of them has tried to establish his own opinion, although they all have later compromised and stated that all opinions lead to the same goal and that every opinion is therefore valid. According to the prayers of the personified *Vedas,* however, none of them are valid because their process of knowledge is created within the temporary material world. They have all missed the real point: the Supreme Personality of Godhead or the Absolute Truth can be understood only by devotional service.

One class of philosophers, known as Mīmāṁsakas, represented by sages such as Jaimini, have concluded that everyone should be engaged in pious activities or prescribed duties and that such activities will lead one to the highest perfection. But this is contradicted in the Ninth Chapter of *Bhagavad-gītā,* where Lord Kṛṣṇa says that by pious activities one may be elevated to the heavenly planets, but as soon as one's accumulation of pious activities is used up, one has to leave the enjoyment of a higher standard of material prosperity in the heavenly planets and immediately come down again to these lower planets, where the duration of life is very short and where the standard of material happiness is of a lower grade. The exact words used in the *Gītā* are *kṣīṇe puṇye martya-lokaṁ viśanti.* Therefore the conclusion of the Mīmāṁsaka philosophers, that pious activities will lead one to the Absolute Truth, is not valid. Although a pure devotee is by nature inclined to pious activities, no one can attain the favor of the Supreme Personality of Godhead by pious activities alone. Pious activities may purify one of the contamination caused by ignorance and passion, but this is automatically attained by a devotee who is constantly engaged in hearing the transcendental message of Godhead in the form of the *Bhagavad-gītā, Śrīmad-Bhāgavatam* or similar scriptures. From the *Bhagavad-gītā* we understand that even a person who is not up to the standard of pious activities but who is absolutely engaged in devotional service is to be considered well situated on the path of spiritual perfection. It is also said in the *Bhagavad-gītā* that a person who is engaged in devotional service with love and faith is guided from within by the Supreme Personality of Godhead. The Lord Himself as Paramātmā, or the spiritual master sitting within one's heart, gives the devotee exact direction by which he can gradually go back to Godhead. The conclusion of the Mīmāṁsaka philosophers is not actually the truth which can lead one to real understanding.

Similarly, there are Sāṅkhya philosophers, metaphysicians or material scientists who study this cosmic manifestation by their invented scientific method and who do not recognize the supreme authority of God as the creator of the cosmic manifestation. Rather, they wrongly conclude that the reaction of material elements is the original cause of creation. The *Bhagavad-gītā,* however, does not accept this theory. It is clearly said therein that behind the cosmic activities is the direction of the Supreme Personality of Godhead. This fact is corroborated by the Vedic injunction *asad vā idam agra āsīt,* which means that the origin of the creation existed before the cosmic manifestation. Therefore, the material elements cannot be the cause of material creation. Although the material elements are accepted as material causes, the ultimate cause is the Supreme Personality of Godhead Himself. The *Bhagavad-gītā* says, therefore, that material nature works under the direction of Kṛṣṇa.

The conclusion of the atheistic Sāṅkhya philosophy is that because the effects of the material worlds are temporary or illusory, the cause is therefore also illusory. The Sāṅkhya philosophers are in favor of voidism, but the actual fact is that the original cause is the Supreme Personality of Godhead and this cosmic manifestation is the temporary manifestation of His material energy. When this temporary manifestation is annihilated, its cause, the eternal existence of the spiritual world, continues as it is, and therefore the spiritual world is called *sanātana-dhāma,* the eternal abode. The conclusion of the Sāṅkhya philosopher is therefore not valid.

Then there are the philosophers headed by Gautama and Kaṇāda. They have very minutely studied the cause and effect of the material elements and have ultimately come to the conclusion that atomic combination is the original cause of creation. Present material scientists also follow in the footsteps of Gautama and Kaṇāda, who propounded this theory of *paramāṇuvāda.* This theory, however, cannot be supported because the original cause of everything is not inert atoms. This is confirmed in *Bhagavad-gītā* and *Śrīmad-Bhāgavatam* as well as in the *Vedas,* wherein it is stated *eko nārāyaṇa āsīt,* only Nārāyaṇa existed before the creation. The *Śrīmad-Bhāgavatam* and *Vedānta-sūtra* also say that the original cause is sentient and both indirectly and directly cognizant of everything within this creation. In the *Bhagavad-gītā* Kṛṣṇa says, *ahaṁ sarvasya prabhavaḥ:* "I am the original cause of everything," and *mattaḥ sarvaṁ pravartate:* "From Me everything comes into existence." Therefore, atoms may form the basic combinations of material existence, but these atoms are generated from the Supreme Personality of Godhead. Thus the philosophy of Gautama and Kaṇāda cannot be supported.

Similarly, impersonalists headed by Aṣṭāvakra and later on by Śaṅkarācārya accept the impersonal Brahman effulgence as the cause of everything. According to their theory, the material manifestation is temporary and unreal, whereas the impersonal Brahman effulgence is reality. But this theory cannot be supported either, because the Lord Himself says in the *Bhagavad-gītā* that this Brahman effulgence is resting on His personality. It is also confirmed in the *Brahma-saṁhitā* that the Brahman effulgence is the personal bodily rays of Kṛṣṇa. As such, impersonal Brahman cannot be the original cause of the cosmic manifestation. The original cause is the all-perfect sentient Personality of Godhead, Govinda.

The most dangerous theory of the impersonalists is that when God comes as an incarnation He accepts a material body created by the three modes of material nature. This Māyāvādī theory has been condemned by Lord Caitanya as most offensive. He has said that anyone who accepts the transcendental body of the Personality of Godhead to be made of this material nature commits the greatest offense at the lotus feet of Viṣṇu. Similarly, the *Bhagavad-gītā* also states that only the fools and rascals deride the Personality of Godhead when He descends in a human form. Lord Kṛṣṇa, Lord Rāma and Lord Caitanya actually move within human society as human beings.

The personified *Vedas* condemn the impersonal conception as a gross misrepresentation. In the *Brahma-saṁhitā,* the body of the Supreme Personality of Godhead is described as *ānanda-cin-maya-rasa.* The Supreme Personality of Godhead possesses a spiritual body, not a material body. He can enjoy anything through any part of His body, and therefore He is omnipotent. The limbs of a material body can perform only a particular function, just as hands can hold, but they cannot see or hear. Because the body of the Supreme Personality of Godhead is made of *ānanda-cin-maya-rasa* or *sac-cid-ānanda-vigraha,* He can enjoy anything and do everything with any of His limbs. Acceptance of the spiritual body of the Lord as material is dictated by the tendency to make the Supreme Personality of Godhead equal to the conditioned soul. The conditioned soul has a material body. Therefore, if God also has a material body, then the impersonalistic theory that the Supreme Personality of Godhead and the living entities are one and the same can be very easily propagandized.

Factually, when the Supreme Personality of Godhead comes He exhibits different pastimes, and yet there is no difference between His childish body when He is lying on the lap of His mother Yaśodā and His so-called grown up body fighting with the demons. In His childhood body also, He fought with demons such as Pūtanā, Tṛṇāvarta, Aghāsura, etc., with strength equal to that with which He fought in His youth against demons like Dantavakra, Śiśupāla and others. In material life, as soon as a conditioned soul changes his body, he forgets everything of his past body, but from the *Bhagavad-gītā* we understand that Kṛṣṇa, because He has a *sac-cid-ānanda* body, did not forget instructing the sun-god about the *Bhagavad-gītā* millions of years ago. The Lord is therefore known as Puruṣottama because He is transcendental to both material and spiritual existence. That He is the cause of all causes means that He is the cause of the spiritual world and of the material world as well. The Supreme Personality of Godhead is omnipotent and omniscient. Therefore, because a material body can be neither omnipotent nor omniscient, the Lord's body surely is not material. The Māyāvādī theory that the Personality of Godhead comes within this material world with a material body cannot be supported by any means.

It can be concluded that all the theories of the material philosophers are generated from the temporary illusory existence, like the conclusions in a dream. Such conclusions certainly cannot lead us to the Absolute Truth. The Absolute Truth can only be realized through devotional service. As the Lord says in the *Bhagavad-gītā, bhaktyā mām abhijānāti,* "Only by devotional service can one understand Me." Śrīla Śrīdhara Svāmī has composed a nice verse in this regard, which states: "My dear Lord, let others be engaged in false argument and dry speculation, theorizing upon their great philosophical theses. Let them loiter in the darkness of ignorance and illusion, falsely enjoying as if very learned scholars, although they are without knowledge of the Supreme Personality of Godhead. As far as I am concerned, I wish to be liberated simply by chanting the holy names of the all-beautiful Supreme Personality of Godhead—Mādhava, Vāmana, Trinayana, Saṅkarṣaṇa, Śrīpati and Govinda. Simply by chanting His transcendental names, let me become free from the contamination of this material existence."

In this way the personified *Vedas* said, "My dear Lord, when a living entity, by Your grace only, comes to the right conclusion about Your exalted transcendental position, at that time he no longer bothers with the different theories manufactured by the mental speculators or so-called philosophers. This is a reference to the speculative theories of Gautama, Kaṇāda, Patañjali and Kapila (Nirīśvara). There are actually two Kapilas: one Kapila, the son of Kardama Muni, is an incarnation of God, and the other is an atheist of the modern age. The atheistic Kapila is often misrepresented to be the Supreme Personality of Godhead who appeared as the son of Kardama Muni during the time of Svāyambhuva Manu. Lord Kapila, the incarnation of Godhead, appeared long long ago; the modern age is the age of Vaivasvata Manu, whereas He appeared during the time of Svāyambhuva Manu.

According to Māyāvādī philosophy, this manifested world or the material world is *mithyā* or *māyā,* false. Their preaching principle is *brahma-satya jagat-mithyā.* According to them, only the Brahman effulgence is true, and the cosmic manifestation is illusory or false. But according to Vaiṣṇava philosophy, this cosmic manifestation is caused by the Supreme Personality of Godhead. In the *Bhagavad-gītā* the Lord says that He enters within this material world by one of His plenary portions, and thus the creation takes place. From the *Vedas* also, we can understand that this *asat* or temporary cosmic manifestation is also an emanation from the Supreme *sat* or fact. From the *Vedānta-sūtra* also it is understood that everything has emanated from the Supreme Brahman. As such the Vaiṣṇavas do not take this cosmic manifestation to be false. The Vaiṣṇava philosopher sees everything in this material world in relationship with the Supreme Lord.

This conception of the material world is very nicely explained by Śrīla Rūpa Gosvāmī, who said that renunciation of this material world as illusory or false without knowledge that the material world is also the manifestation of the Supreme Lord is of no practical value. The Vaiṣṇavas, however, are free of attachment to this world because generally the material world is accepted as an object of sense gratification. The Vaiṣṇavas are not in favor of sense gratification; therefore, they are not attached to material activities. The Vaiṣṇava accepts this material world according to the regulative principles of the Vedic injunctions. Since the Supreme Personality of Godhead is the original cause of everything, the Vaiṣṇava sees everything in relationship with Kṛṣṇa, even in this material world. By such advanced knowledge, everything becomes spiritualized. In other words, everything in the material world is already spiritual, but due to our lack of knowledge we see things as material.

The personified *Vedas* presented the example that those who are seeking after gold do not reject gold earrings, gold bangles or anything else made of gold simply because they are shaped differently from the original gold. All living entities are part and parcel of the Supreme Lord and are qualitatively one, but they are now differently shaped in 8,400,000 species of life, just like many different ornaments which have been manufactured from the same source of gold. As one who is interested in gold accepts all the differently shaped gold ornaments, so a Vaiṣṇava, knowing well that all living entities are of the same quality as the Supreme Personality of Godhead, accepts all living entities as eternal servants of God. As a Vaiṣṇava, then, one has ample opportunity to serve the Supreme Personality of Godhead simply by reclaiming these conditioned, misled living entities, training them in Kṛṣṇa consciousness and leading them back to home, back to Godhead. The fact is that the minds of the living entities are now agitated by the three material qualities, and the living entities are therefore transmigrating, as if in dreams, from one body to another. When their consciousness is changed into Kṛṣṇa consciousness, however, they immediately fix Kṛṣṇa within their hearts, and thus their path for liberation becomes clear.

In all the *Vedas* the Supreme Personality of Godhead and the living entities are stated to be of the same quality—*caitanya,* or spiritual. This is also confirmed in the *Padma Purāṇa,* wherein it is said that there are two kinds of spiritual entities; one is called the *jīva,* and the other is called the Supreme Lord. Beginning from Lord Brahmā down to the ant, all living entities are *jīvas,* whereas the Lord is the Supreme four-handed Viṣṇu or Janāradana. The word *ātmā* can be applied only to the Supreme Personality of Godhead, but because the living entities are His parts and parcels, sometimes the word *ātmā* is applied to them also. The living entities are therefore called *jivātmā,* and the Supreme Lord is called *Paramātmā.* Both the *Paramātmā* and *jivātmā* are within this material world, and therefore this material world has a purpose other than sense gratification. The conception of a life of sense gratification is illusion but the conception of service by the *jivātmā* to the *Paramātmā,* even in this material world, is not at all illusory. A Kṛṣṇa conscious person is fully aware of this fact, and thus he does not take this material world to be false, but acts in the reality of transcendental service. The devotee therefore sees everything in this material world as an opportunity to serve the Lord. He does not reject anything as material, but dovetails everything in the service of the Lord. Thus a devotee is always in the transcendental position, and everything that he uses becomes spiritually purified by being used in the service of the Lord.

Śrīdhara Svāmi has composed a nice verse in this regard: "I worship the Supreme Personality of Godhead who is always manifested as reality even within this material world, which is considered by some to be false." The conception of the falsity of this material world is due to lack of knowledge, but a person advanced in Kṛṣṇa consciousness sees the Supreme Personality of Godhead in everything. This is actually realization of the Vedic aphorism, *sarvaṁ khalv idaṁ brahma:* "Everything is Brahman."

The personified *Vedas* continued: "Dear Lord, less intelligent men take to other ways of self-realization, but actually there is no chance to become purified from material contamination or to stop the repeated cycle of birth and death unless one is a thoroughly pure devotee. Our dear Lord, everything is resting on Your different potencies; and everyone is supported by You, as is stated in the *Vedas (eko bahūnāṁ yo vidadhāti kāmān).* Therefore Your Lordship is the supporter and maintainer of all living entities—demigods, human beings and animals. Everyone is supported by You, and You are also situated in everyone's heart. In other words, You are the root of the whole creation. Therefore those who are engaged in Your devotional service without deviation always worship You. Such devotees actually pour water on the root of the universal tree. By devotional service, therefore, one satisfies not only the Personality of Godhead but also all others, because everyone is maintained and supported by Him. Because he understands the all-pervasive feature of the Supreme Personality of Godhead, a devotee is the most practical philanthropist and altruist. Such pure devotees, thoroughly engaged in Kṛṣṇa consciousness, very easily overcome the cycle of birth and death, and they as much as jump over the head of death."

A devotee is never afraid of death or of changing his body; his consciousness is transformed into Kṛṣṇa consciousness, and even if he does not go back to Godhead, even if he transmigrates to another material body, he has nothing to fear. A vivid example is Bharata Mahārāja. Although in his next life he became a deer, in the life after that he became completely free from all material contamination and was elevated to the kingdom of God. The *Bhagavad-gītā* affirms, therefore, that a devotee is never vanquished. A devotee's path to the spiritual kingdom, back home, back to Godhead, is guaranteed. Even though a devotee slips in one birth, the continuation of his Kṛṣṇa consciousness elevates him further and further until he goes back to Godhead. Not only does a pure devotee purify his own personal existence, but whoever becomes his disciple also ultimately becomes purified and able to enter the kingdom of God without difficulty. Not only can a pure devotee easily surpass death, but by his grace his followers also can do so without difficulty. The power of devotional service is so great that a pure devotee can electrify another person by his transcendental instruction on crossing over the ocean of nescience.

The instructions of a pure devotee to his disciple are also very simple. No one feels any difficulty in following in the footsteps of a pure devotee. Anyone who follows in disciplic succession from recognized devotees of the Lord, such as Lord Brahmā, Lord Śiva, the Kumāras, Manu, Kapila, King Prahlāda, King Janaka, Śukadeva Gosvāmī, Yamarāja, etc., very easily finds the door of liberation open. On the other hand, those who are not devotees but are engaged in uncertain processes of self-realization, such as *jñāna, yoga* and *karma,* are understood to be still contaminated. Such contaminated persons, although apparently advanced in self-realization, cannot even liberate themselves, not to speak of others who follow them. Such nondevotees are compared to chained animals, for they are not able to go beyond the jurisdiction of the formalities of a certain type of faith. In the *Bhagavad-gītā* they are condemned as *veda-vādah.* They cannot understand that the *Vedas* deal with activities of the material modes of nature—goodness, passion and ignorance.

Lord Kṛṣṇa advised Arjuna that one has to go beyond the jurisdiction of the duties prescribed in the *Vedas* and take to Kṛṣṇa consciousness, devotional service. It is said in the *Bhagavad-gītā, nistraiguṇyo bhavārjuna,* "My dear Arjuna, just try to become transcendental to the Vedic rituals." This transcendental position beyond the Vedic ritualistic performances is devotional service. In the *Bhagavad-gītā* the Lord clearly says that persons who are engaged in His devotional service without adulteration are situated in Brahman. Actual Brahman realization means Kṛṣṇa consciousness and engagement in devotional service. The devotees are therefore real *brahmacārīs* because their activities are always in Kṛṣṇa consciousness, devotional service.

The Kṛṣṇa consciousness movement is therefore a supreme call to all kinds of religionists asking them with great authority to join this movement by which one can learn how to love God and thus surpass all formulas and formalities of scriptural injunction. A person who cannot overcome the jurisdiction of stereotyped religious principles is compared to an animal chained up by his master. The purpose of all religion is to understand God and develop one's dormant love of Godhead. If one simply sticks to the religious formulas and formalities and does not become elevated to the position of love of God, he is considered to be a chained animal. In other words, if one is not in Kṛṣṇa consciousness, he is not eligible for liberation from the contamination of material existence.

Śrila Śrīdhara Svāmī has composed a nice verse which says, "Let others engage in severe austerities, let others fall to the land from the tops of hills and give up their lives, let others travel to many holy places of pilgrimage for salvation, or let them be engaged in deep study of philosophy and Vedic literatures; let the mystic *yogīs* engage in their meditational service, and let the different sects engage in unnecessary arguing as to which is the best. But it is a fact that unless one is Kṛṣṇa conscious, unless one is engaged in devotional service, and unless one has the mercy of the Supreme Personality of Godhead, he cannot cross over this material ocean." An intelligent person, therefore, gives up all stereotyped ideas and joins the Kṛṣṇa consciousness movement for factual liberation.

The personified *Vedas* continued their prayers. "Our dear Lord, Your impersonal feature is explained in the *Vedas:* You have no hands, but You can accept all sacrifices which are offered to You; You have no legs, but You can walk more swiftly than anyone. Although You have no eyes, You can see whatever happens in the past, present and future. Although You have no ears, You can hear everything that is said. Although You have no mind, You know everyone and everyone's activities, past, present and future, and yet no one knows who You are. You know everyone, but no one knows You; therefore, You are the oldest and supreme personality."

Similarly, in another part of the *Vedas* it is said, "You have nothing to do. You are so perfect in Your knowledge and potency that everything becomes manifest simply by Your will. There is no one equal to or greater than You, and everyone is acting as Your eternal servant." Thus the Vedic statements describe that the Absolute has no legs, no hands, no eyes, no ears and no mind, and yet He can act through His potencies and fulfill the needs of all living entities. As stated in the *Bhagavad-gītā,* His hands and legs are everywhere; He is all-pervasive. The hands, legs, ears and eyes of all living entities are acting and moving by the direction of the Supersoul sitting within the living entity's heart. Unless the Supersoul is present, it is not possible for the hands and legs to be active. The Supreme Personality of Godhead is so great, independent and perfect, however, that even without having any eyes, legs and ears, He is not dependent on others for His activities. On the contrary, others are dependent on Him for the activities of their different sense organs. Unless the living entity is inspired and directed by the Supersoul, he cannot act.

The fact is that ultimately the Absolute Truth is the Supreme Person. But because He is acting through His different potencies which are impossible for the gross materialists to see, the materialists accept Him as impersonal. For example, one can observe the personal artistic work in a painting of a flower, and one can understand that the color adjustment, the shape, etc., have demanded the minute attention of the artist. The artist's work is clearly exhibited in a painting of different blooming flowers. But the gross materialist, without seeing the hand of God in such artistic manifestations as the actual flowers blooming in nature, concludes that the Absolute Truth is impersonal. Actually, the Absolute is personal, but He is independent. He does not require to personally take a brush and colors to paint the flowers, but His potencies are acting so wonderfully that it appears as if flowers have come into being without the aid of an artist. The impersonal view of the Absolute Truth is accepted by less intelligent men because unless one is engaged in the service of the Lord, he cannot understand how the Supreme is acting—he cannot even know His name. Everything about His activities and personal features is revealed to the devotee only through his loving service attitude.

In the *Bhagavad-gītā* it is clearly said, *bhoktāraṁ yajña tapasām:* the Lord is the enjoyer of all kinds of sacrifices and of the results of all austerities. Then again the Lord says, *sarva-loka-maheśvaram:* "I am the proprietor of all planets." So that is the position of the Supreme Personality of Godhead. Although He is present in Vṛndāvana and enjoys transcendental pleasure in the company of His eternal associates, the *gopīs* and the cowherd boys, His potencies are acting under His direction all over the creation. They do not disturb His eternal pastimes.

Through devotional service only can one understand how the Supreme Personality of Godhead, by His inconceivable potencies, simultaneously acts impersonally and as a person. He is acting just like the supreme emperor, and many thousands of kings and chiefs are working under Him. The Supreme Personality of Godhead is the supreme independent controlling person, and all the demigods—including Lord Brahmā, Lord Śiva, Indra the king of heaven, the king of the moon planet, and the king of the sun planet—are working under His direction. It is confirmed in the *Vedas* that the sun is shining, the air is blowing, and fire is distributing heat out of fear of the Supreme Personality of Godhead. The material nature is producing all kinds of movable and immovable objects within the material world, but none of them can independently act or create without the direction of the Supreme Lord. All of them are acting as tributaries, just like subordinate kings who offer their annual taxes to the emperor.

The Vedic injunction states that every living entity lives by eating the remnants of foodstuffs offered to the Personality of Godhead. In great sacrifices the injunction is that Nārāyaṇa should be present as the supreme predominating Deity of the sacrifice, and after the sacrifice is performed, the remnants of foodstuffs are distributed amongst the demigods. This is called *yajña-bhāga.* Every demigod has an allotment of *yajña-bhāga* which he accepts as *prasādam.* The conclusion is that the demigods are not independently powerful; they are posted as different executives under the order of the Supreme Personality of Godhead, and they are eating *prasādam* or the remnants of sacrifices. They are executing the order of the Supreme Lord exactly according to His plan. The Supreme Personality of Godhead is in the background, and His orders are carried out by others. It only appears that He is impersonal. In our grossly materialistic way, we cannot conceive how the Supreme Person is above the impersonal activities of material nature. Therefore the Lord explains in the *Bhagavad-gītā* that there is nothing superior to Himself and that the impersonal Brahman is subordinately situated as a manifestation of His personal rays. Śrīpāda Śrīla Śrīdhara Svāmī has therefore composed a nice verse in this regard: "Let me offer my respectful obeisances unto the Supreme Personality of Godhead, who has no material senses but through whose direction and will all the material senses are working. He is the supreme potency of all material senses or sense organs. He is omnipotent, and He is the supreme performer of everything. Therefore He is worshipable by everyone. Unto that Supreme Person do I offer my respectful obeisances."

Kṛṣṇa Himself declares in the *Bhagavad-gītā* that He is Puruṣottama, which means the Supreme Personality. *Puruṣa* means person, and *uttama* means supreme or transcendental. Also in *Bhagavad-gītā* the Lord declares that because He is transcendental to all sentient and insentient beings, He is therefore known as the *puruṣottama.* In another place the Lord says that as the air is situated in the all-pervading sky, so everyone is situated in Him, and everyone is acting under His direction.

The *Vedas* personified continued. "Our dear Lord," they prayed, "You are equal to all, with no partiality toward a particular type of living entity. As Your parts and parcels, all living entities enjoy or suffer in different conditions of life. They are just like the sparks of a fire. Just as sparks dance on a blazing fire, so all living entities are dancing on Your support. You are providing them with everything they desire, and yet You are not responsible for their position of enjoyment or suffering. There are different types of living entities–demigods, human beings, animals, trees, birds, beasts, germs, worms, insects and aquatics–and all are enjoying or suffering in life by resting on You. The living entities are of two kinds: one class is called ever-liberated, *nitya-mukta,* and the other class is called *nitya-baddha.* The *nitya-mukta* living entities are in the spiritual kingdom, and the *nitya-baddha* are in the material world.

"In the spiritual world both the Lord and the living entities are manifest in their original status, like live sparks in a blazing fire. But in the material world, although the Lord is all-pervasive in His impersonal feature, the living entities have forgotten their Kṛṣṇa consciousness, just as sparks sometimes fall from a blazing fire and lose their original brilliant condition. Some sparks fall onto dry grass and thus ignite another big fire. This is a reference to the pure devotees who take compassion on the poor and innocent living entities. The pure devotee enlightens Kṛṣṇa consciousness in the hearts of the conditioned souls, and thus the blazing fire of the spiritual world becomes manifest even within this material world. Some sparks fall onto water; they immediately lose their original brilliance and become almost extinct. This is comparable to the living entities who take their birth in the midst of gross materialists, in which case their original Kṛṣṇa consciousness becomes almost extinct. Some sparks fall to the ground and remain midway between the blazing and extinct conditions. Thus some living entities are without Kṛṣṇa consciousness, some are between having and not having Kṛṣṇa consciousness, and some are actually situated in Kṛṣṇa consciousness. The demigods in the higher planets, beginning from Lord Brahmā, Indra, Candra, the sun-god, the moon-god, and various other demigods, are all Kṛṣṇa conscious. Human society is between the demigods and the animals, and thus some are more or less Kṛṣṇa conscious, and some are completely forgetful of Kṛṣṇa consciousness. The third-grade living entities, namely the animals, beasts, plants, trees and aquatics, have completely forgotten Kṛṣṇa consciousness. This example stated in the *Vedas* of the sparks of a blazing fire is very appropriate for understanding the condition of different types of living entities. But above all other living entities is the Supreme Personality of Godhead, Kṛṣṇa or Puruṣottama, who is always liberated from all material conditions.

"The question may be raised as to why the living entities have fallen by chance into different conditions of life. To answer this question, we first have to understand that there cannot be any influence of chance for the living entities; chance is for nonliving entities. According to the Vedic literatures, living entities have knowledge, and thus they are called *caitanya,* which means in knowledge. Their situation in different conditions of life, therefore, is not accidental. It is by their choice because they have knowledge. In the *Bhagavad-gītā* the Lord says, 'Give up everything and just surrender unto Me.' This process of realizing the Supreme Personality of Godhead is open for everyone, but still it is the choice of the particular living entity whether to accept or reject this proposal. In the last portion of the *Bhagavad-gītā,* Lord Kṛṣṇa very plainly said to Arjuna, 'My dear Arjuna, now I have spoken everything to You. Everything now depends on whether you choose to accept it.' Similarly, the living entities who have come down to this material world have made their own choice to enjoy this material world. It is not that Kṛṣṇa sent them into this material world. The material world is created for the enjoyment of living entities who wanted to give up the eternal service of the Lord to become the supreme enjoyer themselves. According to Vaiṣṇava philosophy, when a living entity desires to gratify his senses and forgets the service of the Lord, he is given a place in the material world to act freely according to his desire, and therefore he creates a condition of life in which he either enjoys or suffers. We should know definitely that both the Lord and the living entities are eternally cognizant. There is no birth and death for either the Lord or the living entities. When creation takes place, it does not mean that the living entities are created. The Lord creates this material world to give the conditioned souls a chance to elevate themselves to the higher platform of Kṛṣṇa consciousness. If the conditioned soul does not take advantage of this opportunity, then after the dissolution of this material world, he enters into the body of Nārāyaṇa and remains there in deep sleep until the time of another creation.

"In this connection the example of the rainy season is very appropriate. Seasonal rainfall may be taken as the agent for creation because after the rainfall the wet fields are favorable for growing different types of vegetation. Similarly, as soon as there is creation by the Lord's glancing over the material nature, immediately the living entities spring up in their different living conditions, just as different types of vegetation grow after a rainfall. The rainfall is one, but the creation of the different vegetables is varied. The rain falls equally on the whole field, but the different vegetables sprout up in different shapes and different forms according to the seeds planted. Similarly, the seeds of our desires are varied. Every living entity has a different type of desire, and that desire is the seed which causes his growth in a certain type of body. This is explained by Rūpa Gosvāmī by the word *pāpa-bīja. Pāpa* means sinful. All our material desires are to be taken as *pāpa-bīja,* or the seeds of sinful desires. *Bhagavad-gītā* explains that our sinful desire is that we do not surrender unto the Supreme Lord. The Lord therefore says in *Bhagavad-gītā,* 'I shall give you protection from the resultant actions of sinful desires.' These sinful desires are manifested in different types of bodies; therefore, no one can accuse the Supreme Lord of partiality in His giving one type of body to a certain type of living entity and another type of body to another living entity. All the bodies of the 8,400,000 species come according to the mental condition of the individual living entities. The Supreme Personality of Godhead, Puruṣottama, only gives them a chance to act according to their desires. Therefore, the living entities are acting, taking advantage of the facility given by the Lord.

"At the same time, they are born from the transcendental body of the Lord. This relationship between the Lord and the living entities is explained in the Vedic literatures, wherein it is said that the Supreme Lord maintains all His children, giving them whatever they want. Similarly, in the *Bhagavad-gītā,* the Lord says, 'I am the seed-giving father of all living entities.' It is very simple to understand that the father gives birth to the children, but the children act according to their own desires. Therefore the father is never responsible for the different futures of his children. Each child can take advantage of the father's property and instruction, but even though the inheritance and instruction may be the same for all the children, out of their different desires, each child creates a different life and thereby suffers or enjoys.

"Similarly, the *Bhagavad-gītā's* instructions are equal for everyone; everyone should surrender unto the Supreme Lord, and He will take charge of them and protect them from sinful reactions. The facilities of living in the creation of the Lord are equally offered to all living entities. Whatever there is, either on the land, on water or in the sky, is equally given to all living entities. Since they are all sons of the Supreme Lord, everyone can enjoy the material facilities given by the Lord, but unfortunate living entities create unfavorable conditions of life by fighting among themselves. The responsibility for this fighting and creating favorable and unfavorable situations of life lies with the living entities, not with the Supreme Personality of Godhead. Therefore, if the living entities take advantage of the Lord's instructions as given in the *Bhagavad-gītā* and develop Kṛṣṇa consciousness, then their lives become sublime, and they can go back to Godhead.

"One may argue that because this material world is created by the Lord, He is therefore responsible for its condition. Certainly He is indirectly responsible for the creation and maintenance of this material world, but He is never responsible for the different conditions of the living entities. The Lord's creation of this material world is compared to the cloud's creation of vegetation. In the rainy season the cloud creates different varieties of vegetables. The cloud pours water on the surface of the earth, but it never touches the earth directly. Similarly, the Lord creates this material world simply by glancing over the material energy. This is confirmed in the *Vedas:* He threw His glance over the material nature, and thus there was creation. In the *Bhagavad-gītā* it is also confirmed that simply by His transcendental glance over the material nature, He creates different varieties of entities, both movable and immovable, living and dead.

"The creation of the material world can therefore be taken as one of the pastimes of the Lord; it is called one of the pastimes of the Lord because He creates this material world whenever He desires. This desire of the Supreme Personality of Godhead is also extreme mercy on His part because it gives another chance to the conditioned souls to develop their original consciousness and thus go back to Godhead. Therefore no one can blame the Supreme Lord for creating this material world.

"From the subject matter under discussion, we can gain a clear understanding of the difference between the impersonalists and the personalists. The impersonal conception recommends merging in the existence of the Supreme, and the voidist philosophy recommends making all material varieties void. Both these philosophies are known as Māyāvāda. Certainly the cosmic manifestation comes to a close and becomes void when the living entities merge into the body of Nārāyaṇa to rest until another creation, and this may be called an impersonal condition, but these conditions are never eternal. The cessation of the variegatedness of the material world and the merging of the living entities into the body of the Supreme are not permanent because the creation will take place again, and the living entities who merge into the body of the Supreme without having developed their Kṛṣṇa consciousness will again appear in this material world when there is another creation. The *Bhagavad-gītā* confirms the fact that this material world is created and annihilated. This is going on perpetually, and conditioned souls who are without Kṛṣṇa consciousness come back again and again whenever the material creation is manifest. If such conditioned souls take advantage of this opportunity and develop Kṛṣṇa consciousness under the direct instruction of the Lord, then they are transferred to the spiritual world and do not have to come back again to the material creation. It is said, therefore, that the voidists and the impersonalists are not very intelligent because they do not take shelter under the lotus feet of the Lord. Because they are less intelligent, these voidists and impersonalists take to different types of austerities, either to attain the stage of *nirvāṇa,* which means finishing the material conditions of life, or to attain oneness by merging into the body of the Lord. All of them again fall down because they neglect the lotus feet of the Lord."

In the *Caitanya-caritāmṛta,* the author, Kṛṣṇadāsa Kavirāja Gosvāmī, after studying all the Vedic literature and hearing from all authorities, has given his opinion that Kṛṣṇa is the only supreme master and that all living entities are His eternal servants. His statement is confirmed in the prayers by the personified *Vedas.* The conclusion is, therefore, that everyone is under the control of the Supreme Personality of Godhead, everyone is serving under the supreme direction of the Lord, and everyone is afraid of the Supreme Personality of Godhead. It is out of fear of Him that activities are being rightly executed. Everyone's position is to be subordinate to the Supreme Lord, yet the Lord has no partiality in His view of the living entities. He is just like the unlimited sky; as the sparks of a fire dance in the fire, similarly, all living entities are like birds flying in the unlimited sky. Some of them are flying very high, some are flying at a lesser altitude, and some are flying at a still lesser altitude. The different birds are flying in different positions according to their respective abilities to fly, but the sky has nothing to do with this ability. In the *Bhagavad-gītā* also, the Lord confirms that He awards different positions to different living entities according to their proportionate surrender. This proportionate reward by the Personality of Godhead to the living entities is not partiality. Therefore, in spite of the living entities' being situated in different positions, in different spheres, and in different species of life, all of them are always under the control of the Supreme Personality of Godhead, and yet He is never responsible for their different living conditions. It is foolish and artificial, therefore, to think oneself equal to the Supreme Lord, and it is still more foolish to think that one has not seen God. Everyone is seeing

God in His different aspects; the only difference is that the theist sees God as the Supreme Personality, the most beloved, Kṛṣṇa, and the atheist sees the Absolute Truth as ultimate death.

The personified *Vedas* continued to pray. "Our dear Lord, from all Vedic information it is understood that You are the supreme controller, and all living entities are controlled. Both the Lord and the living entities are called *nitya,* eternal, and so are qualitatively one, yet the singular *nitya,* or the Supreme Lord, is the controller, whereas the plural *nityas* are controlled. The individual controlled living entity resides within the body, and the supreme controller, as Supersoul, is also present there, but the Supersoul is controlling the individual soul. That is the verdict of the *Vedas.* If the individual soul were not controlled by the Supersoul, then how could one explain the Vedic version that a living entity transmigrates from one body to another, enjoying and suffering the effects of his past deeds? Sometimes he is promoted to a higher standard of life, and sometimes he is degraded to a lower standard of life. Thus the conditioned souls are not only under the control of the Supreme Lord, but they are also conditioned by the control of the material nature. This relationship of the living entities to the Supreme Lord as the controlled and the controller definitely proves that although the Supersoul is all-pervasive, the individual living entities are never all-pervasive. If the individual souls were all-pervasive, there would be no question of their being controlled. The theory that the Supersoul and the individual soul are equal is therefore a polluted conclusion, and no sensible person accepts it; rather, one should try to understand the distinctions between the supreme eternal and the subordinate eternals."

The personified *Vedas* therefore concluded, "O Lord, both You and the limited *dhruvas,* the living entities, are eternal. The form of the unlimited eternal is sometimes calculated as the universal form, and in the Vedic literatures like the *Upaniṣads,* the form of the limited eternal is vividly described. It is said therein that the original spiritual form of the living entity is one ten-thousandth the size of the tip of a hair. It is stated that the spirit is greater than the greatest and smaller than the smallest. The individual living entities, who are eternally part and parcel of God, are smaller than the smallest. With our material senses, we can perceive neither the Supreme, who is greater than the greatest, nor the individual soul, who is smaller than the smallest. We have to understand both the greatest and the smallest from the authoritative sources of Vedic literature. Vedic literature states that the Supersoul is sitting within the body of a living entity and is as big as a thumb. Therefore the argument may be put forward, how can something the size of a thumb be accommodated within the heart of an ant? The answer is that this thumb measurement of the Supersoul is imagined in proportion to the body of the living entity. In all circumstances, therefore, the Supersoul and the individual living entity cannot be taken as one, although both of them enter within the material body of a living entity. The Supersoul living within the heart is for directing or controlling the individual living entity. Although both are *dhruva,* or eternal, the living entity is always under the direction of the Supreme.

"It may be argued that because the living entities are born of the material nature, they are all equal and independent. In the Vedic literature, however, it is said that the Supreme Personality of Godhead impregnates the material nature with the living entities, and then they come out. Therefore, the appearance of the individual living entities is not factually due to material nature alone, just as a child produced by a woman is not her independent production. A woman is first impregnated by a man, and then a child is produced. As such, the child produced by the woman is part and parcel of the man. Similarly, the living entities are apparently produced by the material nature, but not independently. It is due to the impregnation of material nature by the supreme father that the living entities are present. Therefore the argument that the individual living entities are not part and parcel of the Supreme cannot stand. For example, the different parts and parcels of the body cannot be taken as equal to the whole; rather, the whole body is the controller of the different limbs. Similarly, the parts and parcels of the supreme whole are always dependent and are always controlled by the source of the parts and parcels. It is confirmed in the *Bhagavad-gītā* that the living entities are part and parcel of Kṛṣṇa: *mamaivāṁśo.* No sane man, therefore, will accept the theory that the Supersoul and the individual soul are of the same category. They are equal in quality, but quantitatively the Supersoul is always the Supreme, and the individual soul is always subordinate to the Supersoul. That is the conclusion of the *Vedas.*"

Two significant words used in this connection are *yanmaya* and *cinmaya.* In Sanskrit grammar, the word *mayat* is used in the sense of transformation, and also in the sense of sufficiency. The Māyāvādī philosophers interpret that *yanmaya* or *cinmaya* indicates that the living entity is always equal to the Supreme. But one has to consider whether this affix, *mayat,* is used for sufficiency or for transformation. The living entity never possesses anything exactly in the same proportion as the Supreme Personality of Godhead. Therefore, this *mayat* affix cannot be used to mean that the individual living entity is self-sufficient. The individual living entity never has sufficient knowledge; otherwise, how could he have come under the control of *maya,* or the material energy? The word sufficient can be accepted, therefore, only in proportion to the magnitude of the living entity. The spiritual oneness of the Supreme Lord and the living entities is never to be accepted as homogeneity. Each and every living entity is individual. If homogeneous oneness is accepted, then by the liberation of one individual soul, all other individual souls would have been liberated immediately. But the fact is that every individual soul is differently enjoying and suffering in the material world.

The word *mayat* is also used in the sense of transformation, or sometimes it is used to mean by-product. The impersonalist theory is that Brahman Himself has accepted different types of bodies and that this is His *līlā* or pastime. There are, however, many hundreds and thousands of species of life in different standards of living conditions, such as human beings, demigods, animals, birds and beasts, and if all of them were expansions of the Supreme Absolute Truth, then there would be no question of liberation because Brahman is already liberated. Another interpretation put forward by the Māyāvādīs is that in every millennium different types of bodies are manifested, and when the millennium is closed, all the different bodies or expansions of Brahman automatically become one, ending all different manifestations. Then in the next millennium, according to this theory, Brahman again expands in different bodily forms. If we accept this theory, then Brahman becomes subject to change. But this cannot be accepted. From *Vedānta-sūtra* we understand that Brahman is by nature joyful. He cannot, therefore, change Himself into a body which is subject to painful conditions. Actually, the living entities who are part and parcel of Brahman are infinitesimal particles prone to be covered by the illusory energy. As explained before, the particles of Brahman are like sparks blissfully dancing within a fire, but there is a chance of their falling from the fire to smoke, although smoke is another condition of fire. This material world is just like smoke, and the spiritual world is just like a blazing fire. The innumerable living entities are prone to fall down to the material world from the spiritual world when influenced by illusory energy, and it is also possible for the living entity to become liberated again when by cultivation of real knowledge he becomes completely freed from the contamination of the material world.

The theory of the *asuras* is that the living entities are born of material nature, or *prakṛti,* in touch with the *puruṣa.* This theory also cannot be accepted because both the material nature and the Supreme Personality of Godhead are eternally existing. Neither the material nature nor the Supreme Personality of Godhead can be born. The Supreme Lord is known as *aja,* or unborn. Similarly, the material nature is also called *ajā.* Both these terms, *aja* and *ajā,* mean unborn. Because both the material nature and the Supreme Lord are unborn, it is not possible that they can beget the living entities. As water in contact with air sometimes presents innumerable bubbles, so a combination of material nature and the Supreme Person causes the appearence of the living entities within this material world. As bubbles in the water appear in different shapes, similarly the living entities also appear in the material world in different shapes and conditions, influenced by the modes of material nature. As such, it is not improper to conclude that the living entities appearing within this material world in different shapes, such as human beings, demigods, animals, birds, beasts, etc., all get their respective bodies due to different desires. No one can say when such desires were awakened in them, and therefore it is said, *anādi-karma:* the cause of such material existence is untraceable. No one knows when material life began, but it is a fact that it does have a point of beginning because originally every living entity is a spiritual spark. As sparks falling onto the ground from a fire have a beginning, similarly the living entities coming to this material world have a beginning, but no one can say when. Even during the time of dissolution, these living entities remain merged in the spiritual existence of the Lord, as if in deep sleep, but their original desires to lord it over the material nature do not subside. Again, when there is cosmic manifestation, they come out to fulfill the same desires, and therefore they appear in different species of life.

This merging into the Supreme at the time of dissolution is compared to honey. In the honeycomb, the taste of different flowers and fruits are conserved. When one drinks honey, one cannot distinguish what sort of honey has been collected from what sort of flower, but the palatable taste of the honey presupposes that the honey is not homogeneous, but is a combination of different tastes. Another example is that although different rivers ultimately mix with the water of the sea, that does not mean that the individual identities of the rivers are thereby lost. Although the water of the Ganges and the Yamunā mixes with the water of the sea, the River Ganges and River Yamunā still continue to exist independently. The merging of different living entities into Brahman at the time of dissolution involves the dissolution of different types of bodies, but the living entities, along with their different tastes, remain individually submerged in Brahman until another manifestation of the material world. As the salty taste of sea water and the sweet taste of Ganges water are different, and this difference continually exists, so the difference between the Supreme Lord and the living entities continually exists, even though it appears that at the time of dissolution they merge. The conclusion is, therefore, that even when the living entities become free from all contamination of material conditions, they merge into the spiritual kingdom, but still their individual tastes in relationship with the Supreme Lord continue to exist.

The personified *Vedas* continued: "Our dear Lord, it is our conclusion that all living entities are attracted by Your material energy, and only due to their mistakenly identifying themselves as products of the material nature are they transmigrating from one kind of body to another in forgetfulness of their eternal relationship with You. Because of ignorance, these living entities are misidentifying themselves in different species of life, and especially when they are elevated to the human form of life, they identify with a particular class of men, or a particular nation or race or so-called religion, forgetting their real identity as eternal servants of Your Lordship. Due to this faulty conception of life, they are undergoing repeated birth and death. Out of many millions of them, if one becomes intelligent enough, by association with pure devotees, he comes to the understanding of Kṛṣṇa consciousness and comes out of the jurisdiction of the material misconception."

In the *Caitanya-caritāmṛta* it is confirmed by Lord Caitanya that the living entities are wandering within this universe in different species of life, but if one of them becomes intelligent enough, by the mercy of the spiritual master and the Supreme Personality of Godhead, Kṛṣṇa, then he begins his devotional life in Kṛṣṇa consciousness. It is said, ***hariṁ vinā na mṛtim taranti:*** without the help of the Supreme Personality of Godhead, one cannot get out of the clutches of repeated birth and death. In other words, only the Supreme Lord, the Personality of Godhead, can relieve the conditioned souls from the cycle of repeated birth and death.

The personified *Vedas* continued: "The influence of time—past, present and future—and the material miseries, such as excessive heat, excessive cold, birth, death, old age, disease, are all simply the movement of Your eyebrows. Everything is working under Your direction. It is said in the *Bhagavad-gītā* that all material activity is going on under the direction of the Supreme Personality of Godhead, Kṛṣṇa. All the conditions of material existence are opposing elements for persons who are not surrendered unto You. But for those who are surrendered souls and are in full Kṛṣṇa consciousness, these things cannot be a source of fearfulness. When Lord Nṛsiṁhadeva appeared, Prahlāda Mahārāja was never afraid of Him, whereas his atheist father was immediately faced with death personified and was killed. Therefore, although Lord Nṛsiṁhadeva appears as death for an atheist like Hiraṇyakaśipu, He is always kind and is the reservoir of all pleasure to the devotees like Prahlāda. A pure devotee is not, therefore, afraid of birth, death, old age and disease.

Śrīpāda Śrīdhara Svāmī has composed a nice verse, the purport of which is as follows: "My dear Lord, I am a living entity perpetually disturbed by the conditions of material existence. I have been cracked into different pieces by the smashing wheel of material existence, and because of my various sinful activities while existing in this material world, I am burning in the blazing fire of material reaction. Somehow or other, my dear Lord, I have come to take shelter under Your lotus feet. Please accept me and give me protection." Śrīla Narottama dāsa Ṭhākur also prays like this: "My dear Lord, O son of Nanda Mahārāja, associated with the daughter of Vṛṣabhānu, I have come to take shelter under Your lotus feet after suffering greatly in the material condition of life, and I am praying that You please be merciful upon me. Please do not kick me away; I have no other shelter but You."

The conclusion is that any process of self-realization or God realization other than *bhakti-yoga,* or devotional service, is extremely difficult. Taking shelter of devotional service to the Lord in full Kṛṣṇa consciousness is therefore the only way to become free from the contamination of material conditional life, especially in this age. Those who are not in Kṛṣṇa consciousness are simply wasting their time, and they have no tangible proof of spiritual life.

It is said by Lord Rāmacandra, "I always give confidence and security to anyone who surrenders unto Me and decides definitely that He is My eternal servant because that is My natural inclination." Similarly, Lord Kṛṣṇa says in the *Bhagavad-gītā,* "The influence of the material nature is insurmountable, but anyone who surrenders unto Me can verily overcome the influence of material nature." The devotees are not at all interested in arguing with the nondevotees to nullify their theories. Rather than wasting their time, they always engage themselves in the transcendental loving service of the Lord in full Kṛṣṇa consciousness.

The personified *Vedas* continued: "Our dear Lord, although great mystic *yogīs* may have full control over the elephant of the mind and the hurricane of the senses, unless they take shelter of a bona fide spiritual master, they fall victims to the material influence and never become successful in their attempts at self-realization. Such unguided persons are compared to merchants going to sea on a ship without a captain. By his personal attempts, therefore, no one can get free from the clutches of material nature. One has to accept a bona fide spiritual master and work according to his direction. Then it is possible to cross over the nescience of material conditions. Śrīpāda Śrīdhara Svāmī has composed a nice verse in this connection, in which he says, "O all-merciful spiritual master, representative of the Supreme Personality of Godhead, when will my mind be completely surrendered unto your lotus feet? At that time, only by your mercy, I shall be able to get relief from all obstacles to spiritual life, and I shall be situated in blissful life."

Actually, ecstatic *samādhi* or absorption in the Supreme Personality of Godhead can be achieved by constant engagement in His service, and this constant engagement in devotional service can be performed only when one is working under the direction of a bona fide spiritual master. The *Vedas* therefore instruct that in order to know the science of devotional service, one has to submit himself unto the bona fide spiritual master. The bona fide spiritual master is he who knows the science of devotional service in disciplic succession. This disciplic succession is called *śrotriyam.* The prime symptom of one who has become a spiritual master in disciplic succession is that he is one hundred percent fixed in *bhakti-yoga.* Sometimes people neglect to accept a spiritual master, and instead they endeavor for self-realization by mystic *yoga* practice, but there are many instances of failure, even by great *yogīs* like Viśvāmitra. Arjuna said in the *Bhagavad-gītā* that controlling the mind is as impractical as stopping the blowing of a hurricane. Sometimes the mind is compared to a maddened elephant. Without following the direction of a spiritual master one cannot control the mind and the senses. In other words, if one practices *yoga* mysticism and does not accept a bona fide spiritual master, he will surely fail. He will simply waste his valuable time. The Vedic injunction is that no one can have full knowledge without being under the guidance of an *ācārya. Ācāryavān puruṣo veda:* one who has accepted an *ācārya* knows what is what. The Absolute Truth cannot be understood by arguments. One who has attained the perfect brahminical stage naturally becomes renounced; he does not strive for material gain because by spiritual knowledge he has come to the conclusion that in this world there is no insufficiency. Everything is sufficiently provided by the Supreme Personality of Godhead. A real *brāhmana,* therefore, does not endeavor for material perfection; rather, he approaches a bona fide spiritual master to accept orders from him. A spiritual master's qualification is that he is *brahmaniṣṭham,* which means that he has given up all other activities and has dedicated his life to working only for the Supreme Personality of Godhead, Kṛṣṇa. When a bona fide student approaches a bona fide spiritual master, he submissively prays to the spiritual master, "My dear Lord, kindly accept me as your student and train me in such a way that I will be able to give up all other kinds of processes for self-realization and simply engage in Kṛṣṇa consciousness, devotional service."

The devotee engaged by the direction of the spiritual master in the transcendental loving service of the Lord contemplates as follows: "My dear Lord, You are the reservoir of pleasure. Since You are present, what is the use of the transient pleasure derived from society, friendship and love? Persons who are unaware of the supreme reservoir of pleasure falsely engage in deriving pleasure from sense gratification, but this is transient and illusory." In this connection, Vidyāpati, a great Vaiṣṇava devotee and poet, says, "My dear Lord, undoubtedly there is some pleasure in the midst of society, friendship and love, although it is materially conceived, but such pleasure cannot satisfy my heart, which is like a desert." In a desert there is need of an ocean of water. But if only a drop of water is poured on the desert, what is the value of such water? Similarly, our material hearts are full of multi-desires, which cannot be fulfilled within the material society of friendship and love. When our hearts begin to derive pleasure from the supreme reservoir of pleasure, then we can be satisfied. That transcendental satisfaction is only possible in devotional service, in full Kṛṣṇa consciousness.

The personified *Vedas* continued: "Our dear Lord, You are *sac-cid-ānanda-vigraha,* the ever-blissful form of knowledge, and because the living entities are parts and parcels of Your personality, their natural state of existence is to be fully conscious of You. In this material world, anyone who has developed such Kṛṣṇa consciousness is no longer interested in the materialistic way of life. A Kṛṣṇa conscious being becomes disinterested in family life or opulent living conditions, and he requires only a little concession for his bodily needs. In other words, he is no longer interested in sense gratification. The perfection of human life is based on knowledge and renunciation, but it is very difficult to attempt to reach the stage of knowledge and renunciation while in family life. Kṛṣṇa conscious persons therefore take shelter of the association of devotees or sanctified places of pilgrimage. Such persons are aware of the relationship between the Supersoul and the individual living entities, and they are never in the bodily concept of life. Because they always carry You in full consciousness within their hearts, they are so purified that any place they go becomes a holy place of pilgrimage, and the water which washes their feet is able to deliver many sinful persons hovering within this material world."

When Prahlāda Mahārāja was asked by his atheistic father to describe something very good which he had learned, he replied to his father that for a materialistic person who is always full of anxieties due to being engaged in temporary and relative truths, the best course is to give up the blind well of family life and go to the forest to take shelter of the Supreme Lord. Those who are actually pure devotees are celebrated as *mahātmās,* or great sages, personalities perfect in knowledge. They always think of the Supreme Lord and His lotus feet, and thus they become automatically liberated. Devotees who are always situated in that position become electrified by the inconceivable potencies of the Lord, and thus they themselves become the source of liberation for their followers and devotees. A Kṛṣṇa conscious person is fully electrified spiritually, and therefore anyone who touches or takes shelter of such a pure devotee becomes similarly electrified with spiritual potencies. Such devotees are never puffed up with material opulences. Generally, the material opulences are good parentage, education, beauty and riches, but although a devotee of the Lord may possess all four of these material opulences, he is never carried away by the pride of possessing such distinctions. Great devotees of the Lord travel all over the world from one place of pilgrimage to another, and on their way they meet many conditioned souls and deliver them by their association and distribution of transcendental knowledge. They reside in places like Vṛndāvana, Mathurā, Dvārakā, Jagannātha Purī and Navadvīpa because only devotees assemble in such places. In this way they take advantage of saintly association, and by such association the devotees advance more and more in Kṛṣṇa consciousness. Such advancement is not possible in ordinary household life which is devoid of Kṛṣṇa consciousness.

The personified *Vedas* continue: "Our dear Lord, there are two classes of transcendentalists, the impersonalists and the personalists. The opinion of the impersonalists is that this material manifestation is false and that only the Absolute Truth is factual. The view of the personalist, however, is that the material world, although very temporary, is nevertheless not false, but is factual. Such transcendentalists have different arguments to establish the validity of their philosophies. Factually, the material world is simultaneously both truth and untruth. It is truth because everything is an expansion of the Supreme Absolute Truth, and it is untruth because the existence of the material world is temporary; it is created, and it is annihilated. Because of its different conditions of existence, the cosmic manifestation has no fixed position. Those who advocate acceptance of this material world as false are generally known by the maxim *brahma satya jagan mithyā.* They put forward the argument that everything in the material world is prepared from matter. For example, there are many things made of clay, such as earthen pots, dishes and balls. After their annihilation, these things may become transformed into many other material objects, but in all cases, their existence as clay continues. An earthen water jug, after being broken, may be transformed into a bowl or dish, but either as a dish, bowl or water jug, the earth itself continues to exist. Therefore, the forms of a water jug, bowl or dish are false, but their existence as earth is real. This is the impersonalists' version. This cosmic manifestation is certainly produced from the Absolute Truth, but because its existence is temporary, it is therefore false; the impersonalists' understanding is that the Absolute Truth, which is always present, is the only truth. In the opinion of other transcendentalists, however, this material world, being produced of the Absolute Truth, is also truth. The impersonalists' counter-argument is that the material world is not factual because sometimes it is found that matter is produced from spirit soul, and sometimes spirit soul is produced from matter. Such philosophers push forward the argument that although cow dung is dead matter, sometimes it is found that scorpions come out of cow dung. Similarly, dead matter like nails and hair comes out of the living body. Therefore, things produced of of a certain thing are not always the same. On the strength of this argument, Māyāvādī philosophers establish that although this cosmic manifestation is certainly an emanation from the Absolute Truth, the cosmic manifestation does not necessarily have truth in it. According to this view, the Absolute Truth, Brahman, should therefore be accepted as truth, whereas the cosmic manifestation, although a product of the Absolute Truth, cannot be taken as truth.

The view of the Māyāvādī philosopher, however, is stated in the *Bhagavad-gītā* to be the view of the *asuras,* or demons. The Lord says in *Bhagavad-gītā, asatyam apratiṣṭham te jagad āhur anīśvaram.* The *asuras'* view of this cosmic manifestation is that the whole creation is false. The *asuras* think that the mere interaction of matter is the source of the creation, and there is no controller or God. But actually that is not the fact. From the Seventh Chapter of the *Bhagavad-gītā,* we understand that the five gross elements–earth, water, air, fire and sky–plus the subtle elements–mind, intelligence and false ego–are the eight separated energies of the Supreme Lord. Beyond this inferior material energy, there is a spiritual energy, which is known as the living entities. The living entities are also accepted as the superior energy of the Lord. The whole cosmic manifestation is a combination of the inferior and superior energies, and the source of the energies is the Supreme Personality of Godhead. The Supreme Personality of Godhead has many different types of energies.

That is confirmed in the *Vedas: parāsya śaktir vividhaiva śrūyate* the transcendental energies of the Lord are variegated, and because such varieties have emanated from the Supreme Lord, they cannot be false. The Lord is ever-existing, and the energies are ever-existing. Some of the energy is temporary—sometimes manifested and sometimes unmanifested—but that does not mean that it is false. The example may be given that when a person is angry he does things which are different from his normal condition of life, but that the mood of anger only appears and disappears does not mean that the energy of anger is false. As such, the argument of the Māyāvādī philosophers that this world is false is not accepted by the Vaiṣṇava philosophers. It is confirmed by the Lord Himself that the view that there is no supreme cause of this material manifestation, that there is no God, and that everything is only the creation of the interaction of matter is a view of the *asuras*.

The Māyāvādī philosopher sometimes puts forward the argument of the snake and the rope. In the dark of evening, a curled up rope is sometimes, due to ignorance, taken for a snake. But mistaking the rope as a snake does not mean that the rope or the snake is false, and therefore this example, used by the Māyāvādīs to illustrate the falsity of this material world, is not valid. When a thing is taken as fact but actually has no existence at all, it is called false. But if something is mistaken for something else, that does not mean that it is false. The Vaiṣṇava philosophers use a very appropriate example comparing this material world to an earthen pot. When we see an earthen pot, it does not at once disappear and turn into something else. It may be temporary, but the earthen pot is taken into use for bringing water, and we continue to see it as an earthen pot. Therefore, although the earthen pot is temporary and is different from the original earth, still we cannot say that it is false. We should therefore conclude that the entire earth and the earthen pot are both truths because one is the product of the other. We understand from *Bhagavad-gītā* that after the dissolution of this cosmic manifestation, the energy enters into the Supreme Personality of Godhead. The Supreme Personality of Godhead is ever-existing with His varied energies. Because the material creation is an emanation from Him, we cannot say that this cosmic manifestation is a product of something void. Kṛṣṇa is not void. Whenever we speak of Kṛṣṇa, He is present with His form, quality, name, entourage and paraphernalia. Therefore, Kṛṣṇa is not impersonal. The original cause of everything is neither void nor impersonal, but is the Supreme Person. Demons may say that this material creation is *anīśvara*, without a controller or God, but such arguments ultimately cannot stand.

The example given by the Māyāvādī philosophers that inanimate matter like nails and hair comes out from the living body is not a very sound argument. Nails and hair are undoubtedly inanimate, but they come not from the animate living being, but from the inanimate material body. Similarly, the argument that the scorpion comes from cow dung, meaning that a living entity comes from matter, is also not sound. The scorpion which comes out of the cow dung is certainly a living entity, but the living entity does not come out of the cow dung. Only the living entity's material body, or the body of the scorpion, comes out of the cow dung. The sparks of the living entity, as we understand from *Bhagavad-gītā*, are impregnated within material nature, and then they come out. The body of the living entity in different forms is supplied by material nature, but the living entity himself is begotten by the Supreme Lord. The father and the mother give the body which is necessary for the living entity under certain conditions. The living entity transmigrates from one body to another according to his different desires. The desires in the subtle form of intelligence, mind and false ego accompany the living entity from body to body, and by superior arrangement a living entity is put into the womb of a certain type of material body, and then he develops a similar body. Therefore, the spirit soul is not produced from matter, but it takes on a particular type of body under superior arrangement. To our present experience, this material world is a combination of matter and spirit. The spirit is moving the matter. The spirit soul (the living entity) and matter are different energies of the Supreme Lord. Since both the energies are products of the supreme eternal or the supreme truth, they are therefore factual; they are not false. Because the living entity is part and parcel of the Supreme, he is existing eternally. Therefore, there cannot be any question of birth or death. So-called birth and death occur because of the material body. The Vedic version *sarvaṁ khalv idaṁ brahma* means that since both the energies have emanated from the Supreme Brahman, everything that we experience is not different from Brahman.

There are many arguments about the existence of this material world, but the Vaiṣṇava philosophical conclusion is the best. The example of the earthen pot is very suitable: the form of the earthen pot may be temporary, but it has a specific purpose. The purpose of the earthen pot is to carry water from one place to another. Similarly, this material body, although temporary, has a special use. The living entity is given a chance from the beginning of the creation to evolve different kinds of material bodies according to the reserve desires he has accumulated from time immemorial. The human form of body is a special chance in which the developed form of consciousness can be utilized.

Sometimes the Māyāvadī philosophers push forward the argument that if this material world is truth, then why are householders advised to give up their connection with this material world and take *sannyāsa*? But the Vaiṣṇava philosopher's view of *sannyāsa* is not that because the world is false, one must therefore give up material activities. The purpose of Vaiṣṇava *sannyāsa* is to utilize things as they are intended. Śrīla Rūpa Gosvāmī has given two formulas for our dealing with this material world. When a Vaiṣṇava renounces this materialistic way of life and takes to *sannyāsa*, it is not on the conception of the falsity of the material world, but to devote himself fully to engaging everything in the service of the Lord. Śrīla Rūpa Gosvāmī therefore gives this formula: one should be unattached to the material world because material attachment is meaningless. The entire material world, the entire cosmic manifestation, belongs to God, Kṛṣṇa. Therefore, everything should be utilized for Kṛṣṇa, and the devotee should remain unattached to material things. This is the purpose of Vaiṣṇava *sannyāsa.* A materialist sticks to the world for sense gratification, but a Vaiṣṇava *sannyāsī,* although not accepting anything for his personal sense gratification, knows the art of utilizing everything for the service of the Lord. Śrīla Rūpa Gosvāmī has therefore criticized the Māyāvādī *sannyāsīs* because they do not know that everything has a utilization for the service of the Lord. On the contrary, they take the world to be false and thus falsely think of being liberated from the contamination of the material world. Since everything is an expansion of the energy of the Supreme Lord, the expansions are as real as the Supreme Lord is.

That the cosmic world is only temporarily manifested does not mean that it is false or that the source of its manifestation is false. Since the source of its manifestation is truth, the manifestation is also truth, but one must know how to utilize it. The same example can be cited: the temporary earthen pot is produced from the whole earth, but when it is utilized for a proper purpose, the earthen pot is not false. The Vaiṣṇava philosophers know how to utilize the temporary construction of this material world, just as a sane man knows how to utilize the temporary construction of the earthen pot. When the earthen pot is utilized for a wrong purpose, that is false. Similarly, this human form of body, or this material world, when utilized for false sense gratification, is false. But if this human form of body and the material creation are utilized for the service of the Supreme Lord, their activities are never false. It is therefore confirmed in the *Bhagavad-gītā* that a little service attitude in utilizing this body and the material world for the service of the Lord can deliver a person from the gravest danger of life. When they are properly utilized, neither the superior nor inferior energies emanating from the Supreme Personality of Godhead are false. As far as fruitive activities are concerned, they are mainly based on the platform of sense gratification. Therefore an advanced Kṛṣṇa conscious person does not take to them. The result of fruitive activities can elevate one to the higher planetary system, but as it is said in the *Bhagavad-gītā,* foolish persons, after exhausting the results of their pious activities in the heavenly kingdom, come back again to this lower planetary system and then again try to go to the higher planetary system. Their only profit is to take the trouble of going and coming back, just as at present many material scientists are spoiling their time by trying to go to the moon planet and again come back. Those who are engaged in such activities are described by the *Vedas* personified as *andha-paramparā,* or blind followers of the Vedic ritualistic ceremonies. Although such ceremonies are certainly mentioned in the *Vedas,* they are not meant for the intelligent class of men. Men who are too much attached to material enjoyment are captivated by the prospect of being elevated to the higher planetary systems, and so they take to such ritualistic activities. But a person who is intelligent, or who has taken shelter of a bona fide spiritual master to see things as they are, does not take to fruitive activities, but engages himself in the transcendental loving service of the Lord.

Persons who are not devotees take to the Vedic ritualistic ceremonies for materialistic reasons, and then they are bewildered. A vivid example can be given: an intelligent person possessing millions of dollars in currency notes does not hold the money without using it, even though he knows perfectly well that the currency notes in themselves are nothing but paper. When one has one million dollars in currency notes, he is actually holding only a huge bunch of papers, but if he utilizes it for a purpose, then he benefits. Similarly, although this material world may be false, just like the paper, it has its proper beneficial utilization. Because the currency notes, although paper, are issued by the government, they therefore have full value. Similarly, this material world may be false or temporary, but because it is an emanation from the Supreme Lord, it has its full value. The Vaiṣṇava philosopher acknowledges the full value of this material world and knows how to properly utilize it, whereas the Māyāvādī philosopher, mistaking the currency note for false paper, gives it up and cannot utilize the money. Śrīla Rūpa Gosvāmī therefore declares that if one rejects this material world as false, not considering the importance of this material world as a means to serve the Supreme Personality of Godhead, such renunciation has very little value. A person who knows the intrinsic value of this material world for the service of the Lord, who is not attached to the material world, and who renounces the material world by not accepting it for sense gratification is situated in real renunciation. This material world is an expansion of the material energy of the Lord. Therefore it is real. It is not false, as it is sometimes concluded from the example of the snake and the rope.

The personified *Vedas* continued: "The cosmic manifestation, because of the flickering nature of its impermanent existence, appears to less intelligent men to be false." The Māyāvādī philosophers take advantage of the flickering nature of this cosmic manifestation to prove their thesis that this world is false. According to the Vedic version, before the creation this world had no existence, and after dissolution the world will no longer by manifested. Voidists also take advantage of this Vedic version and conclude that the cause of this material world is void. But Vedic injunction does not say that it is void. The Vedic injunction defines the source of creation and dissolution as *yato vā imāni bhūtāni jāyante,* "He from whom this cosmic manifestation has emanated and in whom, after annihilation, everything will merge." The same is explained in the *Vedānta-sūtra* and in the first verse of the First Chapter of *Śrīmad-Bhāgavatam* by the word *janmādyasya,* He from whom all things emanate. All these Vedic injunctions indicate that the cosmic manifestation is due to the Supreme Absolute Personality of Godhead, and when it is dissolved it merges into Him. The same is confirmed in the *Bhagavad-gītā:* this cosmic manifestation is coming into existence and again dissolving, and after dissolution it merges into the existence of the Supreme Lord. This statement definitely confirms that the particular energy known as *bahiraṅgā-māyā,* or the external energy, although of flickering nature, is the energy of the Supreme Lord, and as such it cannot be false. It simply appears to be false. The Māyāvādī philosophers conclude that because the material nature has no existence in the beginning and is nonexistent after dissolution, it is therefore false. But by the example of the earthen pots and dishes the Vedic version is presented: although the existence of the particular by-products of the Absolute Truth are temporary, the energy of the Supreme Lord is permanent. The earthen pot or water jug may be broken or transformed into another shape, such as that of a dish or bowl, but the ingredient, or the material basis, namely the earth, continues to be the same. The basic principle of this cosmic manifestation is always the same, Brahman, or the Absolute Truth; therefore, the Māyāvādī philosophers' theory that it is false is certainly only mental concoction. That the cosmic manifestation is flickering and temporary dose not mean that it is false. The definition of falsity is that which never had any existence but is existing only in name. For instance, the eggs of a horse or the flower of the sky or the horn of a rabbit are phenomena which exist only in name. There is no horse's eggs, there is no rabbit's horn, nor are there flowers growing in the sky. There are many things which exist in name or imagination but actually have no factual manifestation. Such things can be called false. But the Vaiṣṇava cannot take this material world to be false simply because its temporary nature is manifesting and again dissolving.

The personified *Vedas* continued to say that the Supersoul and the individual soul, or Paramātmā and *jīvātmā,* cannot be equal in any circumstance, although both of them are sitting within the same body, like two birds sitting in the same tree. As declared in the *Vedas,* these two birds, although sitting as friends, are not equal. One is simply a witness. This bird is Paramātmā, or the Supersoul. And the other bird is eating the fruit of the tree. That is *jīvātmā.* When there is cosmic manifestation, the *jīvātmā,* or the individual soul, appears in the creation in different forms, according to his previous fruitive activities, and due to his long forgetfulness of real existence, he identifies himself with a particular form awarded to him by the laws of material nature. After assuming a material form, he becomes subjected to the three material modes of nature and acts accordingly to continue his existence in the material world. While enwrapped in such ignorance, his natural opulences, although existing in minute quantity, are almost extinct. The opulences of the Supersoul, or the Supreme Personality of Godhead, however, are not diminished, although He appears within this material world. He maintains all opulences and perfections in full and yet keeps Himself apart from all the tribulations of this material world. The conditioned soul becomes entrapped in the material world, whereas the Supersoul, or the Supreme Personality of Godhead, leaves it without affection, just as a snake sheds his skin. The distinction between the Supersoul and the conditioned individual soul is that the Supersoul, or the Supreme Personality of Godhead, maintains His natural opulences, known as *ṣaḍ-aiśvarya, aṣṭa-siddhi and aṣṭa-guṇa.*

Because of their poor fund of knowledge, the Māyāvādī philosophers forget the fact that Kṛṣṇa is always full of six opulences, eight transcendental qualities and eight kinds of perfection. The six opulences are that no one is greater than Kṛṣṇa in wealth, in strength, in beauty, in fame, in knowledge and in renunciation. The first of Kṛṣṇa's six transcendental qualities is that He is always untouched by the contamination of material existence. This is also mentioned in the *Īśopaniṣad: apāpa-viddham:* just as the sun is never polluted by any contamination, the Supreme Lord is never polluted by any sinful activities. Similarly, although Kṛṣṇa's actions might sometimes seem to be impious, He is never polluted by such actions. The second transcendental quality is that Kṛṣṇa never dies. In the *Bhagavad-gītā,* Fourth Chapter, He informs Arjuna that both He and Arjuna had many appearances in this material world, but He alone remembers all such activities—past, present and future. This means that He never dies. Forgetfulness is due to death. As we die, we change our bodies. That is forgetfulness. Kṛṣṇa, however, is never forgetful. He can remember everything that has happened in the past. Otherwise, how could He remember that He first taught the *Bhagavad-gītā yoga* system to the sun-god, Vivasvān? Therefore, He never dies. Nor does He ever become an old man. Although Kṛṣṇa was a great-grandfather when He appeared on the Battlefield of Kurukṣetra, He did not appear as an old man. Kṛṣṇa cannot be polluted by any sinful activities, Kṛṣṇa never dies, Kṛṣṇa never becomes old, Kṛṣṇa never becomes subjected to any lamentation, Kṛṣṇa is never hungry, and He is never thirsty. Whatever He desires is perfectly lawful, and whatever He decides cannot be changed by anyone. These are the transcendental qualities of Kṛṣṇa. Besides that, Kṛṣṇa is known as Yogeśvara. He has all the opulences or facilities of mystic powers, such as *aṇima-siddhi,* the power to become smaller than the smallest. It is stated in the *Brahma-saṁhitā* that Kṛṣṇa has entered even within the atom, *aṇḍāntarastha-paramāṇu-cayāntarastham.* Similarly, Kṛṣṇa, as Garbhodakaśāyī Viṣṇu, is within the gigantic universe, and He is lying in the Causal Ocean as Mahā-Viṣṇu in a body so gigantic that when He exhales, millions and trillions of universes emanate from His body. This is called *mahima-siddhi.* Kṛṣṇa also has the perfection of *laghimā:* He can become the lightest. It is stated in the *Bhagavad-gītā* that it is because Kṛṣṇa enters within this universe and within the atoms that all the planets are floating in the air. That is the explanation of weightlessness. Kṛṣṇa also has the perfection of *prāpti:* He can get whatever He likes. Similarly, He has the facility of *īśitā,* controlling power. He is called the supreme controller, Parameśvara. In addition, Kṛṣṇa can bring anyone under His influence. This is called *vaśitā.*

Kṛṣṇa is endowed with all opulences, transcendental qualities and mystic powers. No ordinary living being can be compared to Him. Therefore, the Māyāvādīs' theory that the Supersoul and the individual soul are equal is only a misconception. The conclusion is, therefore, that Kṛṣṇa is worshipable and that all other living entities are simply His servants. This understanding is called self-realization. Any other realization of one's self beyond this relationship of eternal servitorship of Kṛṣṇa is impelled by *māyā.* It is said that the last snare of *māyā* is to dictate to the living entity to try to become equal to the Supreme Personality of Godhead. The Māyāvādī philosopher claims to be equal to God, but he cannot reply to the question of why he has fallen into material entanglement. If He is the Supreme God, then how is it that he has been overtaken by impious activities and thereby subjected to the tribulations of the law of *karma?* When the Māyāvādīs are asked about this, they cannot properly answer. The speculation that one is equal to the Supreme Personality of Godhead is another symptom of sinful life. One cannot take to Kṛṣṇa consciousness unless he is completely freed from all sinful activities. The very fact that the Māyāvādī claims to become one with the Supreme Lord means that he is not yet freed from the reactions of sinful activities. *Śrīmad-Bhāgavatam* says that such persons are *aviśuddha-buddhayā,* which means that they falsely think themselves liberated, although at the same time they think themselves equal with the Absolute Truth. Their intelligence is not purified.

The personified *Vedas* said that if the *yogīs* and the *jñānīs* do not free themselves from sinful desires, then their particular process of self-realization will never be successful. "My dear Lord," the personified *Vedas* continued, "if saintly persons do not take care to eradicate completely the roots of sinful desires, they cannot experience the Supersoul, although He is sitting side by side with the individual soul. *Samādhi,* or meditation, means that one has to find the Supersoul within himself. One who is not free from sinful reactions cannot see the Supersoul. If a person has a jeweled locket in his necklace but forgets the jewel, it is almost as though he does not possess it. Similarly, if an individual soul meditates but does not actually perceive the presence of the Supersoul within himself, he has not realized the Supersoul. Persons who have taken to the path of self-realization must therefore be very careful to be uncontaminated by the influence of *māyā.* Śrīla Rūpa Gosvāmī says that a devotee should be completely free from all sorts of material desires. A devotee should not be affected by the resultant actions of *karma* and *jñāna.* One simply has to understand Kṛṣṇa and carry out His desires. That is the pure devotional stage. Mystic *yogīs* who still have contaminated desires for sense gratification never become successful in their attempt, nor can they realize the Supersoul within the individual self. As such, the so-called *yogīs* and *jñānīs* who are simply wasting their time in different types of sense gratification, either by mental speculation or by exhibition of limited mystic powers, will never become liberated from conditional life and will continue to go through repeated births and deaths. For such persons, both this life and the next life become sources of tribulation. Such sinful persons are already suffering tribulation in this life, and because they are not perfect in self-realization, they will be plagued with further tribulation in the next life. Despite all endeavors to attain perfection, such *yogīs*, contaminated by desires for sense gratification, will continue to suffer in this life and in the next.

Śrīla Viśvanātha Cakravartī Ṭhākur remarks in this connection that if *sannyāsīs* and persons in the renounced order of life who have left their homes for self-realization do not engage themselves in the devotional service of the Lord but become attracted by philanthropic work, such as opening educational institutions, hospitals, or even monastaries, churches or temples of demigods, they find only trouble from such engagements, not only in this life but in the next. *Sannyāsīs* who do not take advantage of this life to realize Kṛṣṇa simply waste their time and energy in activities outside the jurisdiction of the renounced order of life. A devotee's attempt to engage his energies in such activities as constructing a Viṣṇu temple is, however, never wasted. Such engagements are called *Kṛṣṇārthe akhila-ceṣṭā,* variegated activities performed to please Kṛṣṇa. A philanthropist's opening a school building and a devotee's constructing a temple are not on the same level. Although a philanthropist's opening an educational institution may be pious activity, it comes under the laws of *karma,* whereas constructing a temple for Viṣṇu is devotional service.

Devotional service is never within the jurisdiction of the law of *karma.* It is stated in the *Bhagavad-gītā* that devotees transcend the reaction of the three modes of material nature and stand on the platform of Brahman realization: *brahma-bhūyāya kalpate.* The *Bhagavad-gītā* says, *sa guṇān samatityaitān brahma-bhūyāya: kalpate:* devotees of the Personality of Godhead transcend all the reactions of the three modes of material nature and are situated on the transcendental Brahman platform. The devotees are liberated both in this life and in the next life. Any work done in this material world for Yajña or Viṣṇu or Kṛṣṇa is considered to be liberated work, but without connection with Acyuta, the infallible Supreme Personality of Godhead, there is no possibility of stopping the resultant actions of the law of *karma.* The life of Kṛṣṇa consciousness is the life of liberation. The conclusion is that a devotee, by the grace of the Lord, is liberated, both in this life and the next, whereas *karmīs, jñānīs* and *yogīs* are never liberated, either in this life or in the next.

The personified *Vedas* continued: "Dear Lord, anyone who, by Your grace, has understood the glories of Your lotus feet is callous to material happiness and distress. The material pangs are inevitable as long as we are existing within the material world, but a devotee does not divert his attention to such actions and reactions, which are the result of pious and impious activities. Nor is a devotee very much disturbed or pleased by praise or condemnation by the people in general. A devotee is sometimes greatly praised by the people in general because of his transcendental activities, and sometimes he is criticized, even though there is no reason for adverse criticism. The pure devotee is always callous to praise or condemnation by the ordinary people. Actually, the devotee's activities are on the transcendental plane. He is not interested in the praise or condemnation of people engaged in material activities. If the devotee can thus maintain his transcendental position, then his liberation in this life and in the next life is guaranteed by the Supreme Personality of Godhead. A devotee's transcendental position within this material world is maintained in the association of pure devotees, simply by hearing the glorious activities enacted by the Lord in different ages and in different incarnations."

The Kṛṣṇa consciousness movement is based on this principle. Śrīla Narottama dāsa Ṭhākur has sung, "My dear Lord, let me be engaged in Your transcendental loving service, as indicated by the previous *ācāryas,* and let me live in the association of pure devotees. That is my desire, life after life." In other words, a devotee does not much care whether or not he is liberated, but he is anxious only for devotional service. Devotional service means that one does not do anything independently of the sanction of the *ācāryas.* The actions of the Kṛṣṇa consciousness movement are directed by the previous *ācāryas,* headed by Śrīla Rūpa Gosvāmī; in the association of devotees following these principles, a devotee is able to perfectly maintain his transcendental position.

In the *Bhagavad-gītā,* the Lord says that a devotee who knows Him perfectly is very dear to Him. Four kinds of pious men take to devotional service. If a man is pious, then in his distressed condition he approaches the Lord for mitigation of his distress. If a pious man is in need of material help, he also prays to the Lord for such help. If a pious man is actually inquisitive about the science of God, he also approaches the Supreme Personality of Godhead, Kṛṣṇa. Similarly, a pious man who is simply anxious to know the science of Kṛṣṇa also approaches the Supreme Lord. Out of these four classes of men, the last is praised by Kṛṣṇa Himself in the *Bhagavad-gītā.* A person who tries to understand Kṛṣṇa with full knowledge and devotion by following in the footsteps of previous *ācāryas* conversant with the scientific knowledge of the Supreme Lord is praiseworthy. Such a devotee can understand that all conditions of life, favorable and unfavorable, are created by the supreme will of the Lord. And when he has fully surrendered unto the lotus feet of the Supreme Lord, he does not care whether his condition of life is favorable or unfavorable. A devotee takes even an unfavorable condition to be the special favor of the Personality of Godhead. Actually, there are no unfavorable conditions for a devotee. He sees everything coming by the will of the Lord as favorable, and in any condition of life he is simply enthusiastic to discharge his devotional service. This devotional attitude is explained in the *Bhagavad-gītā:* a devotee is never distressed in reverse conditions of life, nor is he overjoyed in favorable conditions. In the higher stages of devotional service, a devotee is not even concerned with the list of do's and do not's. Such a position can be maintained only by following in the footsteps of the *ācāryas.* Because a pure devotee follows in the footsteps of the *ācāryas,* any action he performs to discharge devotional service is to be understood to be on the transcendental platform. Lord Kṛṣṇa therefore instructs us that an *ācārya* is above criticism. A neophyte devotee should not consider himself to be on the same plane as the *ācārya.* It should be accepted that the *ācāryas* are on the same platform as the Supreme Personality of Godhead, and as such, neither Kṛṣṇa nor His representative *ācārya* should be subject to any adverse criticism by the neophyte devotees.

The personified *Vedas* thus worshiped the Supreme Personality of Godhead in different ways. Offering worship to the Supreme Lord by praying means remembering His transcendental qualities, pastimes and activities. But the Lord's pastimes and qualities are unlimited. It is not possible for us to remember all the qualities of the Lord. Therefore, the personified *Vedas* worshiped to the best of their ability, and at the end they spoke as follows.

"Our dear Lord, although Lord Brahmā, the predominating deity of the highest planet, Brahmaloka, and King Indra, the predominating demigod of the heavenly planet, as well as the predominating deities of the sun planet, the moon planet, etc., are all very confidential directors of this material world, they have very little knowledge about You. And what to speak of ordinary human beings and mental speculators? It is not possible for anyone to enumerate the unlimited transcendental qualities of Your Lordship. No one, including the mental speculators and the demigods in higher planetary systems, is actually able to estimate the length and breadth of Your form and characteristics. We think that even Your Lordship does not have complete knowledge of Your transcendental qualities. The reason is that You are unlimited. Although it is not befitting in Your case to say that You do not know Yourself, it is nevertheless practical to understand that because You have unlimited qualities and energies and because Your knowledge is also unlimited, there is unlimited competition between Your knowledge and Your expansion of energies."

The idea is that because God and His knowledge are both unlimited, as soon as God is cognizant of some of His energies, He perceives that He has still more energies. In this way, both His energies and His knowledge increase. Because both of them are unlimited, there is no end to the energies and no end to the knowledge with which to understand the energies. God is undoubtedly omniscient, but the personified *Vedas* say that even God Himself does not know the full extent of His energies. This does not mean that God is not omniscient. When an actual fact is unknown to a certain person, this is called ignorance or lack of knowledge. This is not applicable to God, however, because He knows Himself perfectly, but still His energies and activities increase. Therefore He also increases His knowledge to understand it. Both are increasing unlimitedly, and there is no end to it. In that sense it can be said that even God Himself does not know the limit of His energies and qualities.

How God is unlimited in His expansion of energies and activities can be roughly calculated by any sane and sober living entity. It is said in the Vedic literature that innumerable universes issue forth when Mahā-Viṣṇu exhales in His *yoga-nidrā,* and innumerable universes enter His body when He again inhales. We have to imagine that these universes, which, according to our limited knowledge, are expanded unlimitedly, are so great that the gross ingredients, the five elements of the cosmic manifestation, namely earth, water, fire, air and sky, are not only within the universe, but are covering the universe in seven layers, each layer ten times bigger than the previous one. In this way, each and every universe is very securely packed, and there are numberless universes. All these universes are floating within the innumerable pores of the transcendental body of Mahā-Viṣṇu. It is stated that just as the atoms and particles of dust are floating within the air along with the birds and their number cannot be calculated, so innumerable universes are floating within the pores of the transcendental body of the Lord. For this reason, the *Vedas* say that God is beyond the capacity of our knowledge. *Abāṅmanasagocara:* to understand the length and breadth of God is beyond the jurisdiction of our mental speculation. Therefore, a person who is actually learned and sane does not claim to be God, but tries to understand God, making distinctions between spirit and matter. By such careful discrimination, one can clearly understand that the Supreme Soul is transcendental to both the superior and inferior energies, although He has a direct connection with both. In the *Bhagavad-gītā,* Lord Kṛṣṇa explains that although everything is resting on His energy, He is different or separate from the energy.

Nature and the living entities are sometimes designated as *prakṛti* and *puruṣa* respectively. The whole cosmic manifestation is an amalgamation of the *prakṛti* and *puruṣa.* Nature is the ingredient cause, and the living entities are the effective cause. These two causes combine together, and the effect is this cosmic manifestation. When one is fortunate enough to come to the right conclusion about this cosmic manifestation and everything which is going on within it, he knows it to be caused directly and indirectly by the Supreme Personality of Godhead Himself. It is concluded in the *Brahma-saṁhitā,* therefore, *īśvaraḥ paramaḥ kṛṣṇaḥ sac-cid-ānanda-vigrahaḥ anādir ādir govindaḥ sarva-kāraṇa-kāraṇam.*

After much deliberation and consideration, when one has attained the perfection of knowledge, he comes to the conclusion that Kṛṣṇa, or God, is the original cause of all causes. Instead of speculating about the measurement of God—whether He is so long or so wide—or philosophizing, one should come to the conclusion of *Brahma-saṁhitā: sarva-kāraṇa-kāraṇam:* "Kṛṣṇa, or God, is the cause of all causes." That is the perfection of knowledge.

Thus the *Veda-stuti,* or the prayers offered by the personified *Vedas* to the Garbhodakaśāyī Viṣṇu, were first narrated in disciplic succession by Sanandana to his brothers, all of whom were born of Brahmā. In the beginning the four Kumāras were the first-born of Brahmā; therefore they are known as *pūrva-jāta.* It is stated in the *Bhagavad-gītā* that the *paramparā* system, or the disciplic succession, begins with Kṛṣṇa Himself. Similarly, here, in the prayers of the personified *Vedas,* it is to be understood that the *paramparā* system begins with the Personality of Godhead Nārāyaṇa Ṛṣi. We should remember that this *Veda-stuti* is being narrated by Kumāra Sanandana, and the narration is being repeated by Nārāyaṇa Ṛṣi in Bodi Āśrama. Nārāyaṇa Ṛṣi is the incarnation of Kṛṣṇa for showing us the path of self-realization by undergoing severe austerities. In this age Lord Caitanya demonstrated the path of pure devotional service by putting Himself in the role of a pure devotee. Similarly, in the past Lord Nārāyaṇa Ṛṣi was an incarnation of Kṛṣṇa who performed severe austerities in the Himalayan ranges. Śrī Nārada Muni was hearing from Him. So in the statement given by Nārāyaṇa Ṛṣi to Nārada Muni, as it was narrated by Kumāra Sanandana in the form of *Veda-stuti,* it is understood that God is the one supreme and that all others are His servants.

In the *Caitanya-caritāmṛta* it is stated, *ekalā īśvara kṛṣṇa:* "Kṛṣṇa is the only Supreme God." *Āra sava bhṛtya:* "All others are His servants." *Yāre yaiche nācāya, se taiche kare nṛtya:* "The Supreme Lord, as He desires, is engaging all the living entities in different activities, and thus they are exhibiting their different talents and tendencies." This *Veda-stuti* is thus the original instruction regarding the relationship existing between the living entity their different talents and tendencies." This *Veda-stuti* is thus the original instruction regarding the relationship existing between the living entity and the Supreme Personality of Godhead. The highest platform of realization for the living entity is the attainment of this devotional life. One cannot be engaged in devotional life or Kṛṣṇa consciousness unless he is fully free from material contamination. Nārāyaṇa Ṛṣi informed Nārada Muni that the essence of all *Vedas* and Vedic literatures (namely, the four *Vedas,* the *Upaniṣads,* the *Purāṇas*) teaches the rendering of transcendental loving service to the Lord. In this connection Nārāyaṇa Ṛṣi has used one particular word–*rasa.* In devotional service this *rasa* is the via media or the basic principle for exchanging a relationship between the Lord and the living entity. A *rasa* is also described in the *Vedas* as *īśāvāsya:* "The Supreme Lord is the reservoir of all pleasure." All the Vedic literatures, the *Purāṇas,* the *Vedas,* the *Upaniṣads,* the *Vedānta-sūtras,* etc., are teaching the living entities how to attain the stage of *rasa.* The *Bhāgavatam* also says that the statements in the *Mahāpurāṇa (Śrīmad-Bhāgavatam)* contain the essence of *rasas* in all Vedic literatures. *Nigama-kalpa-taror galitaṁ phalaṁ.* The *Bhāgavatam* is the essence of the ripened fruit in the tree of the Vedic literature.

We understand that with the breathing of the Supreme Personality of Godhead there issued forth the four *Vedas,* namely the *Ṛg-veda,* the *Sāma-veda, Yajur-veda,* and the *Atharva-veda,* and the histories like the *Mahābhārata* and all the *Purāṇas,* which are also considered to be the history of the world. The Vedic histories like the *Purāṇas* and *Mahābhārata* are called the fifth *Veda.*

The verses of *Veda-stuti* are to be considered the essence of all Vedic knowledge. The four Kumāras and all other authorized sages know perfectly that devotional service in Kṛṣṇa consciousness is the essence of all Vedic literatures, and they are preaching this in different planets, traveling in outer space. It is stated herein that such sages, including Nārada Muni, hardly ever travel on land; they are perpetually traveling in space.

Sages like Nārada and the Kumāras travel throughout the universe in order to educate the conditioned souls and show them that their business in the world is not that of sense gratification, but of reinstating themselves again in their original position of devotional service to the Supreme Personality of Godhead. It is stated in several places that the living entities are like sparks of the fire, and the Supreme Personality of Godhead is like the fire itself. Somehow or other when the sparks fall out of the fire they lose their natural illumination; thus it is ascertained that the living entities come into this material world exactly as sparks fall from a great fire. The living entity wants to imitate Kṛṣṇa and tries to lord it over material nature; thus he forgets his original position, and his illuminating power, his spiritual identity, is extinguished. However, if a living entity takes to Kṛṣṇa consciousness, he is reinstated in his original position. Sages and saints like Nārada and the Kumāras are traveling all over the universe educating people and encouraging their disciples to preach this process of devotional service so that all the conditioned souls may be able to revive their original consciousness, or Kṛṣṇa consciousness, and thus gain relief from the miserable conditions of material life.

Śrī Nārada Muni is *naiṣṭika-brahmacārī.* There are four types of *brahmacārī,* and the first is called *sāvitra,* which refers to a *brahmacārī* who, after initiation and the sacred thread ceremony, must observe at least three days celibacy. The next is called *prājāpatya,* which refers to a *brahmacārī* who strictly observes celibacy for at least one year after initiation. The next is called *brāhma-brahmacārī,* which refers to a *brahmacārī* who observes celibacy from the time of initiation up to the time of the completion of his study of Vedic literature. The next stage is called *naiṣṭika,* which refers to a *brahmacārī* who is celibate throughout his whole life. Out of these, the first three are *upqrvma,* which means that the *brahmacārī* can marry later on after the *brahmacārī* period is over. The *naiṣṭika-brahmacārī* is completely reluctant to have any sex life; therefore the Kumāras and Nārada are known as *naiṣṭika-brahmacārīs.* The *brahmacārī* system of life is especially advantageous in that it increases the power of memory and determination. It is specifically mentioned in this connection that because Nārada was *naiṣṭika-brahmacārī* he could remember whatever he heard from his spiritual master and would never forget it. One who can remember everything perpetually is called *śruta-dhara.* A *śruta-dhara brahmacārī* can repeat all that he has heard verbatim without notes and without reference to books. The great sage Nārada has this qualification, and therefore, taking instruction from Nārāyaṇa Ṛṣi, he is engaged in propagating the philosophy of devotional service all over the world. Because such great sages can remember everything, they are very much thoughtful, self-realized and completely fixed in the service of the Lord. Thus the great sage Nārada, after hearing from his spiritual master Nārāyaṇa Ṛṣi, became completely realized. He became established in the truth, and he became so happy that he offered the following prayers to Nārāyaṇa Ṛṣi.

A *naiṣṭhika-brahmacārī* is also called *vīra-vrata.* Nārada Muni addressed Nārāyaṇa Ṛṣi as an incarnation of Kṛṣṇa, and he specifically addressed him as the supreme well-wisher of the conditioned souls. It is stated in the *Bhagavad-gītā* that Lord Kṛṣṇa descends in every millennium just to give protection to His devotees and to annihilate the nondevotees. Nārāyaṇa Ṛṣi, also being an incarnation of Kṛṣṇa, is also addressed as the well-wisher of the conditioned souls. As is stated in the *Bhagavad-gītā,* everyone should know that there is no well-wisher like Kṛṣṇa. Everyone should understand that Lord Kṛṣṇa is the well-wisher of everyone and should take shelter unto Kṛṣṇa. In this way one can become completely confident and satisfied knowing that he has someone who is able to give him all protection. Kṛṣṇa Himself, His incarnations and His plenary expansions are all supreme well-wishers of the conditioned souls, but Kṛṣṇa is the well-wisher even for the demons, for He gave salvation to all demons who came to kill Him at Vṛndāvana; therefore Kṛṣṇa's welfare activities are absolute, for even though He annihilates a demon or gives protection to a devotee, His activities are one and the same. It is said that the demon Pūtanā was elevated to the same position as Kṛṣṇa's mother. When Kṛṣṇa kills a demon it should be known that the demon is supremely benefitted by this; however, a pure devotee is always protected by the Lord.

Nārada Muni, after offering respects to his spiritual master, went to the *āśrama* of Vyāsadeva and narrated the entire story to his disciple. Thus Nārada Muni, being properly received by Vyāsadeva in his *āśrama* and seated very comfortably, began to narrate what he had heard from Nārāyaṇa Ṛṣi. In this way Śukadeva Gosvāmī informed Mahārāja Parīkṣit of the answers to his questions regarding the essence of Vedic knowledge and regarding what is considered to be the ultimate goal in the *Vedas.* The supreme goal in life is to seek the transcendental blessings of the Supreme Personality of Godhead and thus become engaged in the loving service of the Lord. One should follow in the footsteps of Śukadeva Gosvāmī and all the Vaiṣṇavas in the disciplic succession and should pay respectful obeisances unto Lord Kṛṣṇa the Supreme Personality of Godhead Hari. The four sects of Vaiṣṇava disciplic succession, namely the Madhva-sampradāya, the Rāmānuja-sampradāya, the Viṣṇusvāmī-sampradāya, and the Nimbārka-sampradāya, in pursuance of all Vedic conclusions, agree that one should surrender unto the Supreme Personality of Godhead.

The Vedic literatures are divided into two parts: the *śrutis* and the *smṛtis.* The *śrutis* are the four *Vedas: Ṛk, Sāma, Atharva* and *Yajus,* and the *Upaniṣads,* and the *smṛtis* are the *Purāṇas* like *Mahābhārata,* which includes *Bhagavad-gītā.* The conclusion of all these is that one should know Śrī Kṛṣṇa as the Supreme Personality of Godhead. He is the

Parampuruṣa, or the Supreme Personality of Godhead under whose superintendence material nature works, being created, maintained and destroyed. After the creation, the Supreme Lord incarnates into three, Brahmā, Viṣṇu and Lord Śiva. All of these take charge of the three qualities of material nature, but the ultimate direction is in the hand of Lord Viṣṇu. The complete activities of material nature under the three modes are being conducted under the direction of the Supreme Personality of Godhead, Kṛṣṇa. This is confirmed in the *Bhagavad-gītā, nyadarśana,* and in the *Vedas: sa aikṣata.*

The atheistic Sāṅkhyaite philosophers offer their arguments that this material cosmic manifestation is due to *prakṛti* and *puruṣa.* They argue that nature and material energy constitute the material cause and the effective cause. But Kṛṣṇa is the cause of all causes. He is the cause of all material and effective causes. *Prakṛti* and *puruṣa* are not the ultimate cause. Superficially it appears that a child is born due to the combination of the father and mother, but the ultimate cause of both the father and the mother is Kṛṣṇa. He is therefore the original cause, or the cause of all causes, as is confirmed in the *Brahma-saṁhitā.*

In the material nature, both the Supreme Lord and the living entities enter. The Supreme Lord Kṛṣṇa, by one of His plenary expansions, manifests as the Kṣīrodakaśāyī Viṣṇu and the Mahā-Viṣṇu, the gigantic Viṣṇu form lying in the Causal Ocean. Then from that gigantic form of the Mahā-Viṣṇu, the Garbhodakaśāyī Viṣṇu expands in every universe. From Him, Brahmā, Viṣṇu and Śiva expand. Viṣṇu enters into the hearts of all living entities, as well as into all material elements, including the atom. The *Brahma-saṁhitā* says: *aṇḍāntarastha-paramāṇu-cayāntarastham.* He is within this universe and also within every atom.

The living entity has a small material body taken from various species and forms, and similarly the whole universe is but the material body of the Supreme Personality of Godhead. This body is described in the *śāstras* as *virāṭa rūpa.* As the individual living entity maintains his particular body, the Supreme Personality of Godhead maintains the whole cosmic creation and everything within it. As soon as the individual living entity leaves the material body, the body is immediately annihilated, and similarly as soon as Lord Viṣṇu leaves the cosmic manifestation, everything is annihilated. Only when the individual living entity surrenders unto the Supreme Personality of Godhead is his liberation from material existence assured. This is confirmed in the *Bhagavad-gītā: mām eva ye prapadyante māyām etāṁ taranti te.* Surrendering unto the Supreme Personality of Godhead is therefore the cause of liberation and nothing else. How the living entity becomes liberated from the modes of material nature after surrendering unto the Supreme Personality of Godhead is illustrated by a sleeping man within a room. When a man is sleeping, everyone sees that he is present within the room, but actually the man himself is not within that body, for while sleeping a man forgets his bodily existence, although others may see that his body is present. Similarly, a liberated person engaged in devotional service of the Lord may be seen by others to be engaged in the household duties of the material world, but since his consciousness is fixed in Kṛṣṇa he does not live within this world. His engagements are different, exactly as the sleeping man's engagements are different from his bodily engagements. It is confirmed in the *Bhagavad-gītā* that a devotee engaged full time in the transcendental loving service of the Lord has already surpassed the influence of the three modes of material nature. He is already situated on the Brahman platform of spiritual realization, although he appears to be living with the body or within the material world.

Śrīla Rūpa Gosvāmī stated in this connection in his *Bhakti-rasāmṛta-sindhu* that the person whose only desire is to serve the Supreme Personality of Godhead may be situated in any condition in the material world, but he is to be understood as *jīvanmukta,* that is to say he is to be considered liberated while living within the body or the material world. The conclusion, therefore, is that a person fully engaged in Kṛṣṇa consciousness is a liberated person. Such a person has actually nothing to do with the material world. Those who are not in Kṛṣṇa consciousness are called *karmīs* and *jñānīs,* and they hover on the bodily and mental platform and thus are not liberated. This situation is called *kaivalya-nirasta-yoni.* A person situated on the transcendental platform becomes freed from the repetition of birth and death. This is also confirmed in *Bhagavad-gītā,* Fourth Chapter. Simply by knowing the transcendental nature of the Supreme Personality of Godhead Kṛṣṇa, one becomes free from the chains of the repetition of birth and death, and after quitting his present body he goes back home, back to Godhead. This is the conclusion of all the *Vedas.* Thus one should surrender unto the lotus feet of Lord Kṛṣṇa after understanding the prayers offered by the personified *Vedas.*

Thus end the Bhaktivedanta purports of the Eighty-sixth Chapter of Kṛṣṇa, *"Prayers by the Personified Vedas."*

87 / Deliverance of Lord Śiva

As a great devotee of Kṛṣṇa, King Parīkṣit was already liberated, but for clarification he was asking various questions of Śukadeva Gosvāmī. In the previous chapter, King Parīkṣit's question was, "What is the ultimate goal of the *Vedas?*" And Śukadeva Gosvāmī explained the matter, giving authoritative descriptions from the disciplic succession, beginning with Sanandana down to Nārāyaṇa Ṛṣi, Nārada, Vyāsadeva, and then he himself. The conclusion was that devotional service, or *bhakti,* is the ultimate goal of the *Vedas.* A neophyte devotee may question, "If the ultimate goal of life, or the conclusion of the *Vedas,* is to elevate oneself to the platform of devotional service, then why is it observed that a devotee of Lord Viṣṇu is generally not very prosperous materially, whereas a devotee of Lord Śiva is found to be very opulent?" In order to clarify this matter, Parīkṣit Mahārāja asked Śukadeva Gosvāmī: "My dear Śukadeva Gosvāmī, it is generally found that those who engage in the worship of Lord Śiva, whether in human, demoniac, or demigod society, become very opulent materially, although Lord Śiva himself lives just like a poverty-stricken person. On the other hand, the devotees of Lord Viṣṇu, who is the controller of the goddess of fortune, do not appear to be very prosperous, and sometimes they are even found to be living without any material opulence at all. Lord Śiva lives underneath a tree or in the snow of the Himalayan Mountains. He does not even construct a house for himself, but still the worshipers of Lord Śiva are very rich. Kṛṣṇa, or Lord Viṣṇu, however, lives very opulently, whether in Vaikuṇṭha or in this material world, but His devotees appear to be poverty-stricken. Why is this so?"

Mahārāja Parīkṣit's question is very intelligent. The two classes of devotees, namely the devotees of Lord Śiva and the devotees of Lord Viṣṇu, are always in disagreement. Even today in India these two classes of devotees still criticize each other, and especially in South India, the followers of Rāmānujācārya and the followers of Śaṅkarācārya hold occasional meetings for understanding the Vedic conclusion. Generally, the followers of Rāmānujācārya come out victorious in such meetings. So Parīkṣit Mahārāja wanted to clarify the situation by asking this question of Śukadeva Gosvāmī. That Lord Śiva lives as a poor man although his devotees appear to be very opulent, whereas Lord Kṛṣṇa or Lord Viṣṇu is always opulent, and yet His devotees appear to be poverty-stricken, is a situation which appears contradictory and puzzling to a discriminating person.

Śukadeva Gosvāmī began to reply to King Parīkṣit's inquiry about the apparent contradictions regarding the worship of Lord Śiva and that of Lord Viṣṇu. Lord Śiva is the master of the material energy. The material energy is represented by goddess Durgā, and Lord Śiva happens to be her husband. Since goddess Durgā is completely under the subjugation of Lord Śiva, it is to be understood that Lord Śiva is the master of this material energy. The material energy is manifested in three qualities, namely goodness, passion and ignorance, and therefore Lord Śiva is the master of these three qualities. Although he is in association with these qualities for the benefit of the conditioned soul, Lord Śiva is the director and is not affected. Although the conditioned soul is affected by the three qualities, Lord Śiva, because he is the master of these qualities, is not affected by them.

From the statements of Śukadeva Gosvāmī we can understand that the effects of worshiping different demigods are not, as some less intelligent persons suppose, the same as the effects of worshiping Lord Viṣṇu. He clearly states that by worshiping Lord Śiva one achieves one reward, whereas by worshiping Lord Viṣṇu one achieves a different reward. This is also confirmed in the *Bhagavad-gītā:* those who worship the different demigods achieve the desired results which the respective demigods can reward. Similarly, those who worship the material energy receive the suitable reward for such activities, and those who worship the *pitās* receive similar results. But those who are engaged in devotional service or worship of the Supreme Lord, Viṣṇu or Kṛṣṇa, go to the Vaikuṇṭha planets or Kṛṣṇaloka. One cannot approach the transcendental region or *paravyoma,* the spiritual sky, by worshiping Lord Śiva or Brahmā or any other demigod.

Since this material world is a product of the three qualities of material nature, all varieties of manifestations come from those three qualities. With the aid of materialistic science, modern civilization has created many machines and comforts of life, and yet they are only varieties of the interactions of the three material qualities. Although the devotees of Lord

Śiva are able to obtain many material acquisitions, we should know that they are simply collecting products manufactured by the three qualities. The three qualities are again subdivided into sixteen, namely the ten senses (five working senses and the five knowledge-acquiring senses), the mind, and the five elements (earth, water, air, fire and sky). These sixteen items are further extensions of the three qualities. Material happiness or opulence means gratification of the senses, specifically the genitals, the tongue and the mind. By exercising our minds we create many pleasurable things just for enjoyment by the genitals and the tongue. The opulence of a person within this material world is estimated in terms of his exercise of the genitals and the tongue, or in other words, how well he is able to utilize his sexual capacities and how well he is able to satisfy his fastidious taste by eating palatable dishes. Material advancement of civilization necessitates creating objects of enjoyment by mental concoction just to become happy on the basis of these two principles: pleasures for the genitals and pleasures for the tongue. Herein lies the answer to King Parīkṣit's question to Sukadeva Gosvāmī as to why the worshipers of Lord Śiva are so opulent.

The devotees of Lord Śiva are only opulent in terms of the material qualities. Factually, such so-called advancement of civilization is the cause of entanglement in material existence. It is actually not advancement, but degradation. The conclusion is that because Lord Śiva is the master of the three qualities, his devotees are given things manufactured by the interaction of these qualities for satisfaction of the senses. In the *Bhagavad-gītā*, however, we get instruction from Lord Kṛṣṇa that one has to transcend the qualitative existence. *Nistraiguṇyo bhavārjuna:* the mission of human life is to become transcendental to the three qualities. Unless one is *nistraiguṇya,* he cannot get free from material entanglement. In other words, favors received from Lord Śiva are not actually beneficial to the conditioned souls, although apparently such facilities seem to be opulent.

Śukadeva Gosvāmī continued: "The Supreme Personality of Godhead Hari is transcendental to the three qualities of material nature." It is stated in the *Bhagavad-gītā* that anyone who surrenders unto Him surpasses the control of the three qualities of material nature. Therefore, since Hari's devotees are transcendental to the control of the three material qualities, certainly He Himself is transcendental. It is stated, therefore, in the *Śrīmad-Bhāgavatam* that Hari, or Kṛṣṇa, is the original Supreme Personality. There are two kinds of *prakṛtis,* or potencies, namely the internal potency and the external potency, and Kṛṣṇa is the overlord of both these *prakṛtis* or potencies. He is *sarva-dṛk,* or the overseer of all the actions of the internal and external potencies, and He is also described as *upadraṣṭa,* the supreme advisor. Because He is the supreme advisor, He is above all the demigods, who merely follow the directions of the supreme advisor. As such, if one directly follows the instructions of the Supreme Lord, as inculcated in the *Bhagavad-gītā* and the *Śrīmad-Bhāgavatam,* then gradually one becomes *nirguṇa,* or above the interaction of the material qualities. To be *nirguṇa* means to be bereft of material opulences because, as we have explained, material opulence means an increase of the actions and reactions of the three material qualities. By worshiping the Supreme Personality of Godhead, instead of being puffed up with material opulences one becomes enriched with spiritual advancement of knowledge in Kṛṣṇa consciousness. To become *nirguṇa* means to achieve eternal peace, fearlessness, religiousness, knowledge and renunciation. All these are symptoms of becoming free from the contamination of the material qualities.

Śukadeva Gosvāmī, in answering Parīkṣit Mahārāja's question, went on to cite an historical instance regarding Parīkṣit Mahārāja's grandfather, King Yudhiṣṭhira. He said that after finishing the *aśvamedha* sacrifice in the great sacrificial arena, King Yudhiṣṭhira, in the presence of great authorities, enquired on that very same point: how is it that the devotees of Lord Śiva become materially opulent, whereas the devotees of Lord Viṣṇu do not? Śukadeva Gosvāmī specifically referred to King Yudhiṣṭhira as "your grandfather" so that Mahārāja Parīkṣit would be encouraged to think that he was related to Kṛṣṇa and that his grandfathers were intimately connected with the Supreme Personality of Godhead.

Although Kṛṣṇa is always very satisfied by nature, when this question was asked by Mahārāja Yudhiṣṭhira He became even more satisfied because these questions and their answers would bear a great meaning for the entire Kṛṣṇa conscious society. Whenever Lord Kṛṣṇa speaks about something to a specific devotee, it is not only meant for that devotee, but for the entire human society. Instructions by the Supreme Personality of Godhead are important even to the demigods, headed by Lord Brahmā, Lord Śiva and others, and anyone who does not take advantage of the instructions of the Supreme Personality of Godhead, who descends within this world for the benefit of all living entities, is certainly very unfortunate.

Lord Kṛṣṇa answered the question of Mahārāja Yudhiṣṭhira as follows: "If I especially favor a devotee and especially wish to care for him, the first thing I do is take away his riches." When the devotee becomes a penniless pauper or is put into a comparatively poverty-stricken position, his relatives and family members no longer take interest in him, and in most cases they give up their connection with him. The devotee then becomes doubly unhappy. First of all he becomes unhappy because his riches have been taken away by Kṛṣṇa, and he is made even more unhappy when his relatives desert him because of his poverty-stricken position. We should note, however, that when a devotee falls into a miserable condition in this way, it is not due to past impious activities, known as *karma-phala;* the poverty-stricken position of the devotee is a creation of the Personality of Godhead. Similarly, when a devotee becomes materially opulent, that is also not due to his pious activities. In either case, whether the devotee becomes poorer or richer, the arrangement is made by the Supreme Personality of Godhead. This arrangement is especially made by Kṛṣṇa for His devotee just to make him completely dependent upon Him and to free him from all material obligations. He can then concentrate his energies, mind and body—everything—for the service of the Lord, and that is pure devotional service. In the *Nārada-pañcarātra* it is therefore explained, *sarvopādhi-vinirmuktam,* which means "being freed from all designations." Works performed for family, society, community, nation, or humanity are all designated: "I belong to this society," "I belong to this community," "I belong to this nation," "I belong to this species of life." Such identities are all merely designations. When, by the grace of the Lord, a devotee becomes freed from all designation, his devotional service is actually *naiṣkarma. Jñānīs* are very much attracted by the position of *naiṣkarma,* in which one's actions no longer have material effect. When the devotee's actions are freed from effects, they are no longer in the category of *karma-phalam,* or fruitive activities. As explained before by the personified *Vedas,* the unhappiness and distress of a devotee are produced by the Personality of Godhead for the devotee, and the devotee therefore does not care whether he is in happiness or in distress. He goes on with his duties in executing devotional service. Although his behavior seems to be subject to the action and reaction of fruitive activities, he is actually freed from the results of action.

It may be questioned why a devotee is put into such tribulation by the Personality of Godhead. The answer is that this kind of arrangement by the Lord is just like the father's sometimes becoming unkind to his sons. Because the devotee is a surrendered soul and is taken charge of by the Supreme Lord, whenever the Lord puts him into any condition of life—either in distress or happiness—it is to be understood that behind this arrangement there is a large plan designed by the Personality of Godhead. For example, Lord Kṛṣṇa put the Pāṇḍavas into a distressed condition so acute that even Grandfather Bhīṣma could not comprehend how such distress could occur. He lamented that although the whole Pāṇḍava family was headed by King Yudhiṣṭhira, the most pious king, and protected by the two great warriors Bhīma and Arjuna, and although, above all, the Pāṇḍavas were all intimate friends and relatives of Lord Kṛṣṇa, they still had to undergo such tribulations. Later on, however, it was proved that this was planned by the Supreme Personality of Godhead Kṛṣṇa as part of His great mission to annihilate the miscreants and protect the devotees.

Another question may be raised: Since a devotee is put into different kinds of happy and distressful conditions by the arrangement of the Personality of Godhead, and a common man is put into such conditions as a result of his past deeds, then what is the difference? How is the devotee any better than the ordinary *karmī?* The answer is that the *karmīs* and the devotees are not on the same level. In whatever condition of life the *karmī* may be, he continues in the cycle of birth and death because the seed of *karma,* or fruitive activity, is there, and it fructifies whenever there is opportunity. By the law of *karma* a common man is perpetually entangled in repeated birth and death, whereas a devotee's distress and happiness, not being under the laws of *karma,* are part of a temporary arrangement by the Supreme Lord which does not entangle the devotee. Such an arrangement is made by the Lord only to serve a temporary purpose. If a *karmī* performs auspicious acts, he is elevated to the heavenly planets, and if he acts impiously, he is put into a hellish condition of life. But whether a devotee acts in a so-called pious or in an impious manner, he is neither elevated nor degraded, but is transferred to the spiritual kingdom. Therefore a devotee's happiness and distress and a *karmī's* happiness and distress are not on the same level. This fact is corroborated by a speech by Yamarāja to his servants in connection with the liberation of Ajāmila. Yamarāja advised his followers that persons who have never uttered the holy name of the Lord nor remembered the form, quality and pastimes of the Lord should be approached by his watchguards. Yamarāja also advised his servants never to approach the devotees. On the contrary, he instructed his messengers that if they meet a devotee they should offer their respectful obeisances. So there is no question of a devotee's being promoted or degraded within this material world. As there is a gulf of difference between the punishment awarded by the mother and the punishment awarded by an enemy, so a devotee's distressed condition is not the same as the distressed condition of a common *karmī.*

Here another question may be raised. If God is all-powerful, why should He try to reform His devotee by putting him into distress? The answer is that when the Supreme Personality of Godhead puts His devotee into a condition of distress, it is not without purpose. Sometimes the purpose is that in distress a devotee's feelings of attachment to Kṛṣṇa are magnified.

For example, when Kṛṣṇa, before leaving the capital of the Pāṇḍavas for His home, was asking for permission to leave, Kuntīdevī said, "My dear Kṛṣṇa, in our distressed condition You are always present with us. Now, because we have been elevated to a royal position, You are leaving us. I would therefore prefer to live in distress than to lose You." When a devotee is put into a situation of distress, his devotional activities are accelerated. Therefore, to show special favor to a devotee, the Lord sometimes puts him into distress. Besides that, it is stated that the sweetness of happiness is sweeter to those who have tasted bitterness. The Supreme Lord descends to this material world just to protect His devotees from distress. In other words, if devotees were not in a distressed condition, the Lord would not have come down. As for His killing the demons or the miscreants, this can be easily done by His various energies, just as many *asuras* are killed by His external energy, goddess Durgā. Therefore the Lord does not need to come down personally to kill such demons, but when His devotee is in distress He must come. Lord Nṛsiṁhadeva appeared not to kill Hiraṇyakaśipu but to see Prahlāda and to give him blessings. In other words, because Prahlāda Mahārāja was put into very great distress, the Lord appeared.

When, after the dense, dark night, there is finally sunrise in the morning, it is very pleasant. When there is scorching heat, cold water is very pleasant. And when there is freezing winter, hot water is very pleasant. Similarly, when a devotee, after experiencing the condition of the material world, relishes the spiritual happiness awarded by the Lord, his position becomes still more pleasant and enjoyable.

The Lord continued: "When My devotee is bereft of all material riches and is deserted by his relatives, friends and family members, because he has no one to look after him, he completely takes shelter of the lotus feet of the Lord." Śrīla Narottamadāsa Ṭhākur has sung in this connection, "My dear Lord Kṛṣṇa, O son of Nanda Mahārāja, You are now standing before me along with Śrīmatī Rādhārāṇī, the daughter of King Vṛṣabhānu. I am now surrendering unto You. Please accept me. Please do not kick me away. I have no shelter other than You."

When a devotee is thus put into so-called miserable conditions and is bereft of riches and family, he tries to revive his original position of material opulence. But although he tries again and again, Kṛṣṇa again and again takes away all his resources. Thus he finally becomes disappointed in material activities, and in that stage of frustration in all endeavors, he can fully surrender unto the Supreme Personality of Godhead. Such persons are advised by the Lord from within to associate with devotees. By associating with devotees they naturally become inclined to render service to the Personality of Godhead, and they immediately get all facilities from the Lord to advance in Kṛṣṇa consciousness. The non-devotees, however, are very careful about preserving their material condition of life. Generally, therefore, such nondevotees do not come to worship the Supreme Personality of Godhead, but worship Lord Śiva or other demigods for immediate material profit. In the *Bhagavad-gītā* it is said, therefore, *kāṅkṣantaḥ karmaṇāṁ siddhiṁ yajanta iha devatāḥ:* the *karmīs,* in order to achieve success within this material world, worship the various demigods. It is also stated by Lord Kṛṣṇa that those who worship the demigods are not mature in their intelligence. The devotees of the Supreme Personality of Godhead, therefore, because of their strong attachment for Him, do not foolishly go to the demigods.

Lord Kṛṣṇa said to King Yudhiṣṭhira: "My devotee is not deterred by any adverse conditions of life; he always remains firm and steady. Therefore I give Myself to him, and I favor him so he can achieve the highest success in life." The mercy bestowed upon the tried devotee by the Supreme Personality is described as *Brahman,* which indicates that the greatness of that mercy can be compared only to the all-pervasive greatness. *Brahman* means unlimitedly great and unlimitedly expanding. That mercy is also described as *parama,* for it has no comparison within this material world, and it is also called *sūkṣmam,* very fine. The Lord's mercy upon the tried devotee is not only great and unlimitedly expansive, but it is of the finest quality of transcendental love between the devotee and the Lord. Such mercy is further described as *cinmātram,* completely spiritual. The use of the word *mātram* indicates absolute spirituality, with no tinge of material qualities. That mercy is also called *sat,* eternal, and *anantakam,* unlimited. Since the devotee of the Lord is awarded such unlimited spiritual benefit, why should he worship the demigods? A devotee of Kṛṣṇa does not worship Lord Śiva or Brahmā or any other subordinate demigod. He completely devotes himself to the transcendental loving service of the Supreme Personality of Godhead.

Śukadeva Gosvāmī continued: "The demigods, headed by Lord Brahmā and Lord Śiva and including Lord Indra, Candra, Varuṇa and others, are apt to become very quickly satisfied and very quickly angered by the good and ill behavior of their devotees. But this is not so with the Supreme Personality of Godhead, Viṣṇu," This means that any living entity within this material world, including the demigods, is conducted by the three modes of material nature, and therefore the qualities of ignorance and passion are very prominent within the material world. Those devotees who take blessings from the demigods are also infected with the material qualities, especially passion and ignorance. Lord Śrī Kṛṣṇa has therefore stated in the *Bhagavad-gītā* that to take blessings from the demigods is less intelligent because when one takes benedictions from the demigods, the results of such benedictions are temporary. It is easy to get material opulence by worshiping the demigods, but the result is sometimes disastrous. As such, the benedictions derived from demigods are appreciated by the less intelligent class of men. Persons who derive benedictions from the demigods gradually become puffed up with material opulence and neglectful of their benefactors.

Śukadeva Gosvāmī addressed King Parīkṣit thus: "My dear King, Lord Brahmā, Lord Viṣṇu, and Lord Śiva, the principal trio of the material creation, are able to bless or to curse anyone. Of this trio, Lord Brahmā and Lord Śiva become very easily satisfied, and at the same time they become very easily angered. When they are satisfied they give benedictions without any consideration, and when they are angry, they curse the devotee without any consideration. But Lord Viṣṇu is not like that. Lord Viṣṇu is very considerate. Whenever a devotee wants something from Lord Viṣṇu, Lord Viṣṇu first of all considers whether such a benediction will ultimately be good for the devotee. Lord Viṣṇu never bestows any benediction which will ultimately prove disastrous to the devotee, He is, by His transcendental nature, always merciful; therefore, before giving any benediction, He considers whether it will prove beneficial for the devotee. Since the Supreme Personality of Godhead is always merciful, even when it appears that He has killed a demon, or even when He apparently becomes angry toward a devotee, His actions are always auspicious. The Supreme Personality of Godhead is therefore known as all-good. Whatever He does is good.

As for the benedictions given by demigods like Lord Śiva, there is the following historical incident cited by great sages. Once, Lord Śiva, after giving benediction to a demon named Vṛkāsura, the son of Śakuni, was himself entrapped in a very dangerous position. Vṛkāsura was searching after a benediction and was trying to decide which of the three presiding deities to worship in order to get it. In the meantime he happened to meet the great sage Nārada and consulted with him as to whom he should approach to achieve quick results from his austerity. He inquired, "Of the three deities, namely Lord Brahmā, Lord Viṣṇu and Lord Śiva, who is most quickly satisfied?" Nārada could understand the plan of the demon, and he advised him, "You had better worship Lord Śiva; then you will quickly get the desired result. Lord Śiva is very quickly satisfied and very quickly dissatisfied also. So you try to satisfy Lord Śiva." Nārada also cited instances wherein demons like Rāvaṇa and Bāṇāsura were enriched with great opulences simply by satisfying Lord Śiva with prayers. Because the great sage Nārada was aware of the nature of the demon Vṛkāsura, he did not advise him to approach Viṣṇu or Lord Brahmā. Persons such as Vṛkāsura who are situated in the material mode of ignorance, cannot stick to the worship of Viṣṇu.

After receiving instruction from Nārada, the demon Vṛkāsura went to Kedāranātha. The pilgrimage site of Kedāranātha still exists near Kashmere. It is almost always covered by snow, but for part of the year, during the month of July, it is possible to see the deity, and devotees go there to offer their respects. Kedāranātha is for the devotees of Lord Śiva. According to the Vedic principle, when something is offered to the deities to eat, it is offered in a fire. Therefore a fire sacrifice is necessary in all sorts of ceremonies. It is specifically stated in the *śāstras* that gods are to be offered something to eat through the fire. The demon Vṛkāsura therefore went to Kedāranātha and ignited a sacrificial fire to please Lord Śiva.

After igniting the fire in the name of Śiva, he began to offer his own flesh, by cutting it from his body so as to please Lord Śiva. Here is an instance of worship in the mode of ignorance. In the *Bhagavad-gītā*, different types of sacrifice are mentioned. Some sacrifices are in the mode of goodness, some are in the mode of passion, and some are in the mode of ignorance. There are different kinds of *tapasya* and worship because there are different kinds of people within this world. But the ultimate *tapasya*, Kṛṣṇa consciousness, is the topmost *yoga* and the topmost sacrifice. As confirmed in the *Bhagavad-gītā*, the topmost *yoga* is to think always of Lord Kṛṣṇa within the heart, and the topmost sacrifice is to perform the *saṅkīrtana-yajña*.

In the *Bhagavad-gītā* it is stated that the worshipers of the demigods have lost their intelligence. As will be revealed later in this chapter, Vṛkāsura wanted to satisfy Lord Śiva for a third-class materialistic objective, which was temporary and without real benefit. The *asuras* or persons within the mode of ignorance will accept such benedictions from the demigods. In complete contrast to this sacrifice in the modes of ignorance, the *arcanā-viddhi* process for worshiping Lord Viṣṇu or Kṛṣṇa is very simple. Lord Kṛṣṇa says in the *Bhagavad-gītā* that He accepts from His devotee even a little fruit, a flower or some water, which can be gathered by any person, poor or rich. Of course, those who are rich are not expected to offer only a little water, a little piece of fruit or a little leaf to the Lord. A rich man should offer according to his position, but if the devotee happens to be a very poor man the Lord will accept even the most meager offering. The worship of Lord Viṣṇu or Kṛṣṇa is very simple, and it can be executed by anyone in this world. But worship in the mode of ignorance, as exhibited by Vṛkāsura, is not only very difficult and painful, but it is also a useless waste of time. Therefore *Bhagavad-gītā* says that the worshipers of the demigods are bereft of intelligence; their process of worship is very difficult, and at the same time the result obtained is flickering and temporary.

Although Vṛkāsura continued his sacrifice for six days, he was nevertheless unable to personally see Lord Śiva, which was his objective; he wanted to see him face to face and ask him for a benediction. Here is another contrast between a demon and a devotee. A devotee is confident that whatever he offers to the Deity in full devotional service is accepted by the Lord, but a demon wants to see his worshipable deity face to face so that he can directly take the benediction. A devotee, however, does not worship Viṣṇu or Lord Kṛṣṇa for any benediction. Therefore a devotee is called *akāma,* free of desire, and a nondevotee is called *sarva-kāma,* or desirous of everything. On the seventh day, the demon Vṛkāsura decided that he should cut off his head and offer it to satisfy Lord Śiva. Thus he took bath in the nearby lake, and without drying his body and hair, he prepared to cut off his head. According to the Vedic system, an animal which is to be offered as a sacrifice has to be bathed first, and while the animal is wet he is sacrificed. When the demon was thus preparing to cut off his head, Lord Śiva became very compassionate. This compassion, however, is a symptom of the quality of goodness. Lord Śiva is called *triliṅga.* Therefore his manifestation of the nature of compassion is a sign of the quality of goodness. This compassion, however, is present in every living entity. The compassion of Lord Śiva was aroused because the demon was offering his flesh to the sacrificial fire. This is natural compassion. Even if a common man sees someone preparing to commit suicide, it is his duty to try to save him. He does so automatically. There is no need to appeal to him. Therefore when Lord Śiva appeared from the fire to check the demon from suicide, it was not as a very great favor to him.

The demon was saved from committing suicide by the touch of Lord Śiva; his bodily injuries immediately healed, and his body became as it was before. Then Lord Śiva told the demon, "My dear Vṛkāsura, you do not need to cut off your head. You can ask from me any benediction you like, and I shall fulfill your desire. I do not know why you wanted to cut off your head to satisfy me. I become satisfied even by an offering of a little water." Actually, according to the Vedic process, the Śiva *liṅga* in the temple or the form of Lord Śiva in the temple is worshiped simply by offering Ganges water because it is said that Lord Śiva is greatly satisfied when Ganges water is poured upon his head. Generally, devotees offer Ganges water and the leaves of the *bilva* tree, which are especially meant for offering to Lord Śiva and the goddess Durgā. The fruit of this tree also is offered to Lord Śiva. Lord Śiva assured Vṛkāsura that he becomes satisfied by a very simple process of worship. Why then was he so anxious to cut off his head, and why was he taking so much pain by cutting his body to pieces and offering it in the fire? There was no need of such severe penances. Anyway, out of compassion and sympathy, Lord Śiva prepared to give him any benediction he liked.

When the demon was offered this facility by Lord Śiva, he asked for a very fearful and abominable benediction. The demon was very sinful, and sinful persons do not know what sort of benediction should be asked from the deity. Therefore he asked Lord Śiva to be benedicted with such power that as soon as he would touch anyone's head, immediately it would crack, and the man would die. The demons are described in the *Bhagavad-gītā* as *duṣkṛtinas,* or miscreants. *Kṛtī* means very meritorious, but when *duṣ,* is added, it means abominable. Instead of surrendering unto the Supreme Personality of Godhead, the *duṣkṛtinas* worship different demigods in order to derive abominable material benefits. Sometimes such demons as material scientists discover lethal weapons. They cannot show their meritorious power by discovering something which can save man from death, but instead they discover weapons which accelerate the process of death. Because Lord Śiva is powerful enough to give any benediction, the demon could have asked of him something beneficial for human society, but for his personal interest he asked that anyone whose head would be touched by his hand would at once die.

Lord Śiva could understand the motive of the demon, and he was very sorry that he had assured him whatever benediction he liked. He would not withdraw his promise, but he was very sorry in his heart that he was to offer him a benediction so dangerous to human society. The demons are described as *duṣkṛtinas,* miscreants, because although they have brain power and merit, the merit and brain power are used for abominable activities. Sometimes, for example, the materialistic demons discover a lethal weapon. The scientific research for such a discovery certainly requires a very good brain, but instead of discovering something beneficial to human society, they discover something to accelerate the death which is already assured to every man. Similarly, Vṛkāsura, instead of asking Lord Śiva for something beneficial to human society, asked for something very dangerous to human society. Therefore Lord Śiva felt sorry within himself. Devotees of the Personality of Godhead, however, never ask any benediction from Lord Viṣṇu or Kṛṣṇa, and even if they ask something from the Lord, it is not at all dangerous for human society. That is the difference between the demons and the devotees, or the worshipers of Lord Śiva and the worshipers of Lord Viṣṇu.

While Śukadeva Gosvāmī was narrating the history of Vṛkāsura, he addressed Mahārāja Parīkṣit as *Bhārata,* referring to King Parīkṣit's birth in a family of devotees. Mahārāja Parīkṣit was saved by Lord Kṛṣṇa while he was in his mother's womb. Similarly, he could have asked Lord Kṛṣṇa to save him from the curse of the *brāhmaṇa,* but he did not do so. The demon, however, wanted to become immortal by killing everyone with the touch of his hand. Lord Śiva could understand this, but because he had promised, he gave him the benediction.

The demon, however, being very sinful, immediately decided that he would use the benediction to kill Lord Śiva and take away Gaurī (Pārvatī) for his personal enjoyment. He immediately decided to place his hand on the head of Lord Śiva. Thus Lord Śiva was put into an awkward position because he was endangered by his own benediction to a demon. This is also another instance of a materialistic devotee's misusing the power derived from the demigods.

Without further deliberation, the demon Vṛkāsura immediately approached Lord Śiva to place his hand on Lord Śiva's head. Lord Śiva was so afraid of him that his body trembled, and he began to flee from the land to the sky and from the sky to other planets until he reached the limits of the universe, above the higher planetary systems. Lord Śiva fled from one place to another, but the demon Vṛkāsura continued to chase him. The predominating deities of other planets, such as Brahmā, Indra and Candra, could not find any way to save Lord Śiva from the impending danger. Wherever Lord Śiva went, they remained silent.

At last Lord Śiva approached Lord Viṣṇu, who is situated within this universe in the planet known as Śvetadvīpa. Śvetadvīpa is the local Vaikuṇṭha planet beyond the jurisdiction of the influence of external energy. Lord Viṣṇu in His all-pervasive feature remains everywhere, but wherever He remains personally is the Vaikuṇṭha atmosphere. In the *Bhagavad-gītā* it is stated that the Lord remains within the heart of all living entities. As such, the Lord remains within the heart of many low-born living entities, but that does not mean that He is low-born. Wherever He remains is transformed into Vaikuṇṭha. So the planet within this universe known as Śvetadvīpa is also Vaikuṇṭhaloka. It is said in the *śāstras* that residential quarters within the forest are in the mode of goodness, residential quarters in big cities, towns and villages are in the mode of passion, and residential quarters in an atmosphere wherein indulgence in the four sinful activities of illicit sex, intoxication, meat-eating and gambling predominate are in the mode of ignorance. But residential quarters in a temple of Viṣṇu, the Supreme Lord, are in Vaikuṇṭha. It doesn't matter where the temple is situated, but the temple itself, wherever it may be, is Vaikuṇṭha. Similarly, the Śvetadvīpa planet, although within the material jurisdiction, is Vaikuṇṭha.

Lord Śiva finally entered Śvetadvīpa Vaikuṇṭha. In Śvetadvīpa there are great saintly persons who are completely freed from the envious nature of the material world and are beyond the jurisdiction of the four principles of material activities, namely, religiousness, economic development, sense gratification and liberation. Anyone who enters into that Vaikuṇṭha planet never comes back again to this material world. Lord Nārāyaṇa is celebrated as a lover of His devotees, and as soon as He understood that Lord Śiva was in great danger, He appeared as a *brahmacārī* and personally approached Lord Śiva to receive him from a distant place. The Lord appeared as a perfect *brahmacārī,* with a belt around His waist, sacred thread, deerskin, a *brahmacārī* stick and *raudra* beads. *(Raudra* beads are different from *tulasī* beads. *Raudra* beads are used by the devotees of Lord Śiva.) Dressed as a *brahmacārī,* Lord Nārāyaṇa stood before Lord Śiva. The shining effulgence emanating from His body attracted not only Lord Śiva but also the demon Vṛkāsura.

Lord Nārāyaṇa offered his respects and obeisances unto Vṛkāsura, just to attract his sympathy and attention. Thus checking the demon, the Lord addressed him as follows: "My dear son of Śakuni, you appear to be very tired, as if coming from a very distant place. What is your purpose? Why have you come so far? I see that you are very tired and fatigued, so I request you to take a little rest. You should not unnecessarily tire your body. Everyone greatly values his body because with this body only can one fulfill all the desires of one's mind. We should not, therefore, unnecessarily give trouble to this body."

The *brahmacārī* addressed Vṛkāsura as the son of Śakuni just to convince him that He was known to his father, Śakuni. Vṛkāsura then took the *brahmacārī* to be someone known to his family, and therefore the *brahmacārī's* sympathetic words appealed to him. Before the demon could argue that he had no time to take rest, the Lord began to inform him about the importance of the body, and the demon was convinced. Any man, especially a demon, takes his body to be very important. Thus Vṛkāsura became convinced about the importance of his body.

Then, just to pacify the demon, the *brahmacārī* told him, "My dear lord, if you think that you can disclose the mission for which you have taken the trouble to come here, maybe I shall be able to help you so that your purpose will be easily served." Indirectly, the Lord informed him that because the Lord is the Supreme Brahman, certainly He would be able to adjust the awkward situation created by Lord Śiva.

The demon was greatly pacified by the sweet words of Lord Nārāyaṇa in the form of a *brahmacārī,* and at last he disclosed all that had happened in regard to the benediction offered by Lord Śiva. The Lord replied to the demon as follows: "I myself cannot believe that Lord Śiva has in truth given you such a benediction. As far as I know, Lord Śiva is not in a sane mental condition. He had a quarrel with his father-in-law Dakṣa, and he has been cursed to become a *piśāca* (ghost). Thus he has become the leader of the ghosts and hobgoblins. Therefore I cannot put any faith in his words. But if you have faith still in the words of Lord Śiva, my dear king of the demons, then why don't you make an experiment by putting your hand on your head? If the benediction proves false, then you can immediately kill this liar, Lord Śiva, so that in the future he will not dare to give out false benedictions."

In this way, by Lord Nārāyaṇa's sweet words and by the expansion of His superior illusion, the demon became bewildered, and he actually forgot the power of Lord Śiva and his benediction. He was thus very easily persuaded to put his hand on his own head. As soon as the demon did that, his head cracked, as if struck by thunder, and he immediately died. The demigods from heaven began to shower flowers on Lord Nārāyaṇa, praising Him with all glories and all thanksgiving, and they offered their obeisances to the Lord. On the death of Vṛkāsura, all the denizens in the higher planetary systems, namely, the demigods, the *pitās,* the Gandharvas and the inhabitants of Janaloka, began to shower flowers on the Personality of Godhead.

Thus Lord Viṣṇu in the form of a *brahmacārī* released Lord Śiva from the impending danger and saved the whole situation. Lord Nārāyaṇa then informed Lord Śiva that this demon, Vṛkāsura, was killed as the result of his sinful activities. He was especially sinful and offensive because he wanted to experiment on his own master, Lord Śiva. Lord Nārāyaṇa then told Lord Śiva, "My dear lord, a person who commits an offense to great souls cannot continue to exist. He becomes vanquished by his own sinful activities, and this is certainly true of this demon, who has committed such an offensive act against you."

Thus, by the grace of the Supreme Personality of Godhead Nārāyaṇa, who is transcendental to all material qualities, Lord Śiva was saved from

being killed by a demon. Anyone who hears this history with faith and devotion certainly becomes liberated from material entanglement as well as from the clutches of his enemies.

Thus ends the Bhaktivedanta purport of the Eighty-seventh Chapter of Kṛṣṇa, *"Deliverance of Lord Śiva."*

88 / The Superexcellent Power of Kṛṣṇa

Long, long ago, there was an assembly of great sages on the bank of the River Sarasvatī, and they performed a great sacrifice of the name *Satrayajña.* In such assemblies, the great sages present usually discuss Vedic subject matters and philosophical topics, and in this particular meeting the following question was raised: The three predominating deities of this material world, namely, Lord Brahmā, Lord Viṣṇu and Lord Śiva, are directing all the affairs of the this cosmos, but who among them is the Supreme? After much discussion on this question, the great sage named Bhṛgu, who is the son of Lord Brahmā, was deputed to test all three predominating deities and report to the assembly as to who is the greatest.

Being thus deputed, the great sage Bhṛgumuni first of all went to his father's residence in Brahmaloka. The three deities are the controllers of the three material qualities, namely the qualities of goodness, passion and ignorance. The plan decided upon by the sages was for Bhṛgu to test which of the predominating deities possesses the quality of goodness in full. Therefore, when Bhṛgumuni reached his father, Lord Brahmā, because he wanted to test whether he had the quality of goodness, he purposely did not offer his respects to his father either by offering obeisances or by offering prayers. It is the duty of a son or a disciple to offer respects and recite suitable prayers when he approaches his father or spiritual master. But Bhṛgumuni purposefully failed to offer respects, just to see Lord Brahmā's reaction to this negligence. Lord Brahmā was very angry at his son's impudency, and he showed signs which definitely proved this to be so. He was even prepared to condemn Bhṛgu by cursing him, but because Bhṛgu was his son, Lord Brahmā controlled his anger with his great intelligence. This means that although the quality of passion was prominent in Lord Brahmā, he had the power to control it. Lord Brahmā's anger and his controlling his anger are likened to fire and water. Water is produced from fire, but at the same time, fire can be extinguished with water. Similarly, although Lord Brahmā was very angry due to his quality of passion, he could still control his passion because Bhṛgumuni was his son.

After testing Lord Brahmā, Bhṛgumuni went directly to the planet Kailāsa, where Lord Śiva resides. Bhṛgumuni happened to be Lord Śiva's brother. Therefore, as soon as Bhṛgumuni approached, Lord Śiva became very glad and personally rose to embrace him. But when Lord Śiva approached, Bhṛgumuni refused to embrace him. "My dear brother," he said, "you are always very impure. Because you smear your body with ashes, you are therefore not very clean. Please do not touch me." When Bhṛgumuni refused to embrace his brother, saying that Lord Śiva was very impure, the latter became very angry with him. It is said that an offense can be committed either with the body, with the mind or by speech. Bhṛgumuni's first offense, committed towards Lord Brahmā, was an offense with the mind. His second offense, committed towards Lord Śiva by insulting him, criticizing him for unclean habits, was an offense by speech. Because the quality of ignorance is prominent in Lord Śiva, when he heard Bhṛgu's insult, his eyes immediately became red with anger. With uncontrollable rage, he took up his trident and prepared to kill Bhṛgumuni. At that time, Lord Śiva's wife, Pārvatī, was present. Her personality is a mixture of the three qualities, and therefore she is called Triguṇamayī. In this case, she saved the situation by evoking Lord Śiva's quality of goodness. She fell down at the feet of her husband, and with her sweet words she talked him out of killing Bhṛgumuni.

After being saved from the anger of Lord Śiva, Bhṛgumuni went directly to the planet Śvetadvīpa, where Lord Viṣṇu was lying on a bed of flowers, accompanied by His wife, the goddess of fortune, who was engaged in massaging His lotus feet. There Bhṛgumuni purposely committed the greatest sin by offending Lord Viṣṇu by his bodily activities. The first offense committed by Bhṛgumuni was mental, the second offense was vocal, and the third offense was corporal. These different offenses are progressively greater in degree. An offense committed within the mind is a positive offense, the same offense, committed verbally is comparatively more grave, and when committed by bodily action it is superlative in offensiveness. So Bhṛgumuni committed the greatest offense by touching the chest of the Lord with his foot in the presence of the goddess of fortune. Of course, Lord Viṣṇu is all-merciful. He did not become angry at the activities of Bhṛgumuni because Bhṛgumuni was a great *brāhmaṇa.* A *brāhmaṇa* is to be excused even if he sometimes commits an offense, and Lord Viṣṇu set the example. Yet it is said that from the time of this incident, the goddess of fortune, Lakṣmī, has not been very favorably disposed towards the *brāhmaṇas,* and therefore because the goddess of fortune witholds her benedictions from them, the *brāhmaṇas* are generally very poor. Bhṛgumuni's touching the chest of Lord Viṣṇu with his foot was certainly a great offense, but Lord Viṣṇu is so great that He did not care. The so-called *brāhmaṇas* of the Kali-yuga are sometimes very proud that they can touch the chest of Lord Viṣṇu with their feet. But when Bhṛgumuni touched the chest of Lord Viṣṇu with his feet, it was different because although it was the greatest offense, Lord Viṣṇu, being greatly magnanimous, did not take it very seriously.

Instead of being angry or cursing Bhṛgumuni, Lord Viṣṇu immediately got up from His bed along with His wife, the goddess of fortune, and offered respectful obeisances to the *brāhmaṇa.* He addressed Bhṛgumuni as follows: "My dear *brāhmaṇa,* it is a great blessing for Me that you have come here. Please, therefore, sit down on this cushion for a few minutes. My dear *brāhmaṇa,* I am very sorry that when you first entered I could not receive you properly. It was a great offense on My part, and I beg you to pardon Me. You are so pure and great that the water which washes your feet can purify even the places of pilgrimage. Therefore, I request you to purify the Vaikuṇṭha planet where I live with My associates. My dear father, O great sage, I know that your feet are very soft, like a lotus flower, and that My chest is as hard as a thunderbolt. I am therefore afraid that you may have felt some pain by touching My chest with your feet. Let Me therefore touch your feet to relieve the pain you have suffered." Lord Viṣṇu then began to massage the feet of Bhṛgumuni.

The Lord continued to address Bhṛgumuni. "My dear lord," He said, "My chest has now become sanctified because of the touch of your feet, and I am now assured that the goddess of fortune, Lakṣmī, will be very glad to live there perpetually." Another name for Lakṣmī is Cañcalā. She does not stay in one place for a long time. Therefore, we see that a rich man's family sometimes becomes poor after a few generations, and sometimes we see that a poor man's family becomes very rich. Lakṣmī, the goddess of fortune, is Cañcalā in this material world, whereas in the Vaikuṇṭha planets she eternally lives at the lotus feet of the Lord. Because Lakṣmī is famous as Cañcalā, Lord Nārāyaṇa indicated that she might not have been living perpetually by His chest, but because His chest had been touched by the feet of Bhṛgumuni, it was now sanctified, and there was no chance that the goddess of fortune would leave. Bhṛgumuni, however, could understand his position and that of the Lord, and he was struck with wonder at the behavior of the Supreme Personality of Godhead. Because of his gratitude, his voice choked up, and he was not able to reply to the words of the Lord. Tears glided from his eyes, and he could not say anything. He simply stood silently before the Lord.

After testing Lord Brahmā, Lord Śiva and Lord Viṣṇu, Bhṛgumuni returned to the assembly of great sages on the bank of the River Sarasvatī and described his experience. After hearing him with great attention, the sages concluded that of all the predominating deities, certainly Viṣṇu is situated in the mode of goodness in the highest degree. In the *Śrīmad-Bhāgavatam,* these great sages are described as *brahma-vādinām. Brahma-vādinām* means those who talk about the Absolute Truth but have not yet come to a conclusion. Generally *brahma-vādi* refers to the impersonalists or to those who are students of the *Vedas.* It is to be understood, therefore, that all the gathered sages were serious students of Vedic literature, but had not come to definite conclusions as to who is the Supreme Absolute Personality of Godhead.

After hearing of Bhṛgumuni's experience in meeting all three predominating deities, Lord Śiva, Lord Brahmā, and Lord Viṣṇu, the sages concluded that Lord Viṣṇu is the Supreme Truth, the Personality of Godhead. It is said in the *Śrīmad-Bhāgavatam* that after hearing the details from Bhṛgumuni, the sages were astonished because although Lord Brahmā and Lord Śiva were immediately agitated, Lord Viṣṇu, in spite of being kicked by Bhṛgumuni, was not agitated in the least. The example is given that small lamps may become agitated by a little breeze, but the greatest lamp or the greatest illuminating source, the sun, is never moved, even by the greatest hurricane. One's greatness has to be estimated by one's ability to tolerate provoking situations. The sages gathered on the bank of the River Sarasvatī concluded that if anyone wants actual peace and freedom from all fearfulness, he should take shelter of the lotus feet of Viṣṇu. If Lord Brahmā and Lord Śiva lost their peaceful attitude upon a slight provocation, how could they maintain the peace and tranquility of their devotees? As for Lord Viṣṇu, however, it is stated in the *Bhagavad-gītā* that anyone who accepts Lord Viṣṇu or Kṛṣṇa as the supreme friend attains the highest perfection of peaceful life.

The sages thus concluded that by following the principles of *vaiṣṇava-dharma,* one becomes actually perfect. But if one follows all the religious principles of a particular sect and does not become advanced in understanding the Supreme Personality of Godhead, Viṣṇu, all such labor of love is fruitless. To execute religious principles means to come to the platform of perfect knowledge. If one comes to the platform of perfect knowledge, then he will be disinterested in material affairs. Perfect knowledge means to know one's own self and to know the Supreme Self. The Supreme Self and the individual self, although one in quality, are different in quantity. This analytical understanding of knowledge is perfect. Simply to understand, "I am not matter; I am spirit," is not perfect knowledge. The real religious principle is devotional service, or *bhakti.* This is confirmed in the *Bhagavad-gītā.* Lord Kṛṣṇa says, "Give up all other religious principles and simply surrender unto Me." Therefore, the term *dharma* applies only to the *vaiṣṇava-dharma* or *bhagavad-dharma,* following which all other good qualities and advancements in life are automatically achieved.

The highest perfectional knowledge is to know the Supreme Lord. He cannot be understood by any process of religion other than devotional service; therefore, the immediate result of perfect knowledge is achieved by executing devotional service. After attainment of knowledge, one becomes disinterested in the material world. This is not because of dry philosophical speculation. The devotees become disinterested in the material world, not simply because of theoretical understanding, but practical experience. When a devotee realizes the effect of association with the Supreme Lord, he naturally hates the association of so-called society, friendship and love. This detachment is not dry, but is due to achieving a higher status of life by relishing transcendental mellows. It is further stated in the *Śrīmad-Bhāgavatam* that after attainment of such knowledge and detachment from material sense gratification, one's advancement in the eight opulences attained by mystic *yoga* practice, namely the *aṇimā, laghimā* and *prāpti siddhis,* etc., are also achieved without separate effort. The perfect example is Mahārāja Ambarīṣa. He was not a mystic *yogī* but was a great devotee, yet in a disagreement with Mahārāja Ambarīṣa, the great mystic Durvāsā was defeated in the presence of his devotional attitude. In other words, a devotee does not need to practice the mystic *yoga* system to achieve power. The power is behind him by the grace of the Lord, just as when a small child is surrendered to a powerful father, all the powers of the father are behind him.

When a person becomes famous as a devotee of the Lord, his reputation is never to be extinguished. Lord Caitanya, when discoursing with Rāmānanda Rāya, questioned, "What is the greatest fame?" Rāmānanda Rāya replied that to be known as a pure devotee of Lord Kṛṣṇa is the perfect fame. The conclusion, therefore, is that Viṣṇu-*dharma,* or the religion of devotional service unto the Supreme Personality of Godhead, is meant for persons who are thoughtful. By proper utilization of thoughtfulness, one comes to the stage of thinking of the Supreme Personality of Godhead. By thinking of the Supreme Personality of Godhead, one becomes free from the contamination of the faulty association of the material world, and thus one becomes peaceful. The world is in a disturbed condition because of a scarcity of such peaceful devotees in human society. Unless one is a devotee, one cannot be equal to all living entities. A devotee is equally disposed towards the animals, the human beings and all living entities because he sees every living entity as a part and parcel of the Supreme Lord. In the *Īśopaniṣad* it is clearly stated that one who has come to the stage of seeing all living beings equally does not hate anyone or favor anyone. The devotee does not hanker to possess more than he requires. Devotees are therefore *akiñcana;* in any condition of life a devotee is satisfied. It is said that a devotee is evenminded whether he is in hell or in heaven. A devotee is callous to all subjects other than his engagement in devotional service. This mode of life is the highest perfectional stage, from which one can be elevated to the spiritual world, back home, back to Godhead. The devotees of the Supreme Personality of Godhead are especially attracted by the highest material quality, goodness, and the qualified *brāhmaṇa* is the symbolic representation of this goodness. Therefore, a devotee is attached to the brahminical stage of life. He is not very much interested in passion or ignorance, although these qualities also emanate from the Supreme Lord, Viṣṇu. In the *Śrīmad-Bhāgavatam* the devotees are described as *nipuṇa-buddhayaḥ,* which means that they are the most intelligent class of men. Uninfluenced by attachment or hatred, the devotee lives very peacefully and is not agitated by the influence of passion and ignorance.

It may be questioned here why a devotee should be attached to the quality of goodness in the material world if he is transcendental to all material qualities. The answer is that there are different kinds of people existing in the modes of material nature. Those who are in the mode of ignorance are called *rākṣasas,* those in the mode of passion are called *asuras,* and those in the mode of goodness are called *suras,* or demigods. Under the direction of the Supreme Lord, these three classes of men are created by material nature, but those who are in the mode of goodness have a greater chance to be elevated to the spiritual world, back home, back to Godhead.

Thus all the sages who assembled on the bank of the River Sarasvatī to try to determine who is the supreme predominating Deity became freed from all doubts about Viṣṇu worship. All of them thereafter engaged in devotional service, and thus they achieved the desired result and went back to Godhead.

Those who are actually anxious to become liberated from material entanglement would do better to accept at once the conclusion given by

Śrī Śukadeva Gosvāmī in the beginning of the *Śrīmad-Bhāgavatam.* It is said there that hearing the *Śrīmad-Bhāgavatam* is extremely conducive to liberation because it is spoken by Śukadeva Gosvāmī. The same fact is again confirmed by Sūta Gosvāmī: if anyone who is travelling aimlessly within this material world cares to hear the nectarean words spoken by Śukadeva Gosvāmī, certainly he will come to the right conclusion; simply by discharging devotional service to the Supreme Personality of Godhead he will be able to stop the fatigue of migrating from one material body to another perpetually. In other words, by proper hearing one will become fixed in loving devotional service to Viṣṇu. He will certainly be able to get relief from this material journey of life, and the process is very simple. One has to give aural reception to the sweet words spoken by Śukadeva Gosvāmī in the form of *Śrīmad-Bhāgavatam.*

Another conclusion is that we should never consider the demigods, even Lord Śiva and Lord Brahmā, to be on an equal level with Lord Viṣṇu. If we do this, then according to *Padma Purāṇa,* we immediately become atheists. In the Vedic literature known as *Harivaṁśa* it is also stated that only the Supreme Personality of Godhead, Viṣṇu, is to be worshiped. The Hare Kṛṣṇa *mahāmantra,* or any such Viṣṇu *mantra,* is always to be chanted. In the Second Canto of *Śrīmad-Bhāgavatam,* Lord Brahmā says, "Both Lord Śiva and myself are engaged by the Supreme Personality of Godhead to act in different capacities under His direction." In the *Caitanya-caritāmṛta* it is also stated that the only master is Kṛṣṇa, and everyone in all categories of life are servants of Kṛṣṇa only.

In the *Bhagavad-gītā* it is confirmed by the Lord that there is no truth superior to Kṛṣṇa. Śukadeva Gosvāmī also, in order to draw attention to the fact that among all *Viṣṇu-tattva* forms, Lord Kṛṣṇa is one hundred percent the Supreme Personality of Godhead, narrated the story of an incident which took place when Lord Kṛṣṇa was present.

Once upon a time, a *brāhmaṇa's* wife gave birth to a child. Unfortunately, however, just after being born and touching the ground, the child immediately died. The *brāhmaṇa* father took the dead child and went directly to Dvārakā to the palace of the king. The *brāhmaṇa* was very upset because of the untimely death of the child in the presence of his young father and mother. Thus his mind became very disturbed. Formerly, when there were responsible kings, up to the time of Dvāpara-yuga, when Lord Kṛṣṇa was present, the king was liable to be blamed for the untimely death of a child in the presence of his parents. Similarly, such responsibility was there during the time of Lord Rāmacandra. As we have explained in the First Canto of *Śrīmad-Bhāgavatam,* the king was so responsible for the comforts of the citizens that he was to see that there was not even excessive heat or cold. Although there was no fault on the part of the king, the *brāhmaṇa* whose child had died immediately went to the palace door and began to accuse the king as follows.

"The present king, Ugrasena, is envious of the *brāhmaṇas!*" The exact word used in this connection is *brāhma-dviṣaḥ*. One who is envious of the *Vedas* or one who is envious of a qualified *brāhmaṇa* or the *brāhmana* caste is called *brahma-dvit.* So the King was accused of being *brahma-dvit.* He was also accused of being *śaṭha-dhī,* falsely intelligent. The executive head of a state must be very intelligent to see to the comforts of the citizens, but, according to the *brāhmaṇa* the king was not at all intelligent, although he was occupying the royal throne. Therefore he also called him *lubdha,* which means greedy. In other words, a king or an executive head of state should not occupy the exalted post of presidency or kingship if he is greedy and self-interested. But it is natural that an executive head becomes self-interested when he is attached to material enjoyment. Therefore, another word used here is *viṣayātmanaḥ.*

The *brāhmaṇa* also accused the king of being *kṣatra-bandhu,* which refers to a person born in the family of *kṣatriyas* or the royal order who is without the qualifications of a royal personality. A king should protect brahminical culture and should be very alert to the welfare of his citizens; he should not be greedy due to attachment to material enjoyment. If a person with no qualifications represents himself as a *kṣatriya* of the royal order, he is not called a *kṣatriya,* but a *kṣatra-bandhu.* Similarly, if a person is born of a *brāhmaṇa* father but has no brahminical qualification, he is called *brahma-bandhu,* or *dvija-bandhu.* This means that a *brāhmaṇa* or a *kṣatriya* is not accepted simply by birth. One has to qualify himself for the particular position; only then is he accepted as a *brāhmaṇa* or a *kṣatriya.*

Thus the *brāhmaṇa* accused the king that his newly born baby was dead due to the disqualifications of the king. The *brāhmaṇa* took it most unnaturally, and therefore he held the king to be responsible. We also find in Vedic history that if a *kṣatriya* king were irresponsible, sometimes a consulting board of *brāhmaṇas* maintained by the monarchy would dethrone him. Considering all these points, it appears that the post of monarch in the Vedic civilization is a very responsible one.

The *brāhmaṇa* therefore said, "No one should offer respects or worship to a king whose only business is envy. Such a king spends his time either hunting and killing animals in the forest or killing citizens for criminal acts. He has no self-control and possesses bad character. If such a king is worshiped or honored by the citizens, the citizens will never be happy. They will always remain poor, full of anxieties and aggrievement, and always unhappy." Although in modern politics the post of monarch is abolished, the president is not held responsible for the comforts of the citizens. In this age of Kali, the executive head of a state somehow or other gets votes and is elected to an exalted post, but the condition of the citizens continues to be full of anxiety, distress, unhappiness, and dissatisfaction.

The *brāhmaṇa's* second child was also born dead, and the third also. He had nine children, and each of them was born dead, and each time he came to the gate of the palace to accuse the King. When the *brāhmaṇa* came to accuse the King of Dvārakā for the ninth time, Arjuna happened to be present with Kṛṣṇa. On hearing that a *brāhmaṇa* was accusing the King of not properly protecting him, Arjuna became inquisitive and approached the *brāhmaṇa.* He said, "My dear *brāhmaṇa,* why do you say that there are no proper *kṣatriyas* to protect the citizens of your country? Is there not even someone who can pretend to be a *kṣatriya,* who can carry a bow and arrow at least to make a show of protection? Do you think that all the royal personalities in this country simply engage in performing sacrifices with the *brāhmaṇas* but have no chivalrous power?" Thus Arjuna indicated that *kṣatriyas* should not sit back comfortably and engage only in performing Vedic rituals. Rather, they must be very chivalrous in protecting the citizens. *Brāhmaṇas,* being engaged in spiritual activities, are not expected to do anything which requires physical endeavor. Therefore, they need to be protected by the *kṣatriyas* so that they will not be disturbed in the execution of their higher occupational duties.

"If the *brāhmaṇas* feel unwanted separation from their wives and children," Arjuna continued, "and the *kṣatriya* kings do not take care of them, then such *kṣatriyas* are to be considered no more than stage players. In dramatical performances in the theater, an actor may play the part of a king, but no one expects any benefits from such a make-believe king. Similarly, if the king or the executive head of a state cannot give protection to the head of the social structure, he is considered merely a bluffer. Such executive heads simply live for their own livelihood while occupying exalted posts as chiefs of state. My lord, I promise that I shall give protection to your children, and if I am unable to do so, then I shall enter into blazing fire so that the sinful contamination which has infected me will be counteracted."

Upon hearing Arjuna speak in this way, the *brāhmaṇa* replied, "My dear Arjuna, Lord Balarāma is present, but He could not give protection to my children. Lord Kṛṣṇa is also present, but He also could not give them protection. There are also many other heroes, such as Pradyumna and Aniruddha, carrying bows and arrows, but they could not protect my children." The *brāhmaṇa* directly hinted that Arjuna could not do that which was impossible for the Supreme Personality of Godhead. He felt that Arjuna was promising something beyond his power. The *brāhmaṇa* said, "I consider your promise to be like that of an inexperienced child. I cannot put my faith in your promise."

Arjuna then understood that the *brāhmaṇa* had lost all faith in the *kṣatriya* kings. Therefore, to encourage him, Arjuna spoke as if criticizing even his friend, Lord Kṛṣṇa. While Lord Kṛṣṇa and others were listening, he specifically attacked Kṛṣṇa by saying, "My dear *brāhmaṇa,* I am neither Saṅkarṣaṇa nor Kṛṣṇa nor one of Kṛṣṇa's sons like Pradyumna or Aniruddha. My name is Arjuna, and I carry the bow known as Gāṇḍīva. You cannot insult me because I have satisfied even Lord Śiva by my prowess when we were both hunting in the forest. I had a fight with Lord Śiva, who appeared before me as a hunter, and when I satisfied him by my prowess, he gave me the weapon known as *paśupatāstra.* Do not doubt my chivalry. I shall bring back your sons even if I have to fight with death personified." When the *brāhmaṇa* was assured by Arjuna in such exalted words, he somehow or other was convinced, and thus he returned home.

When the *brāhmaṇa's* wife was to give birth to another child, the *brāhmaṇa* began to chant, "My dear Arjuna, please come now and save my child." After hearing him, Arjuna immediately prepared himself by touching sanctified water and uttering holy *mantras* to protect his bows and arrows from danger. He specifically took the arrow which was presented to him by Lord Śiva, and while going out, he began to remember Lord Śiva and his great favor. In this way, he appeared in front of the maternity home, equipped with his bow, known as Gāṇḍīva, and with various other weapons.

It appears that Arjuna did not leave Dvārakā because he had to fulfill his promise to the *brāhmaṇa.* He was called at night when the *brāhmaṇa's* wife was to give birth to the child. While going to the maternity home to attend to the delivery case of the *brāhmaṇa's* wife, Arjuna remembered Lord Śiva, and not his friend Kṛṣṇa; he thought that since Kṛṣṇa could not give protection to the *brāhmaṇa,* it was better to take shelter of Lord Śiva. This is another instance of how a person takes shelter of the demigods. This is explained in the *Bhagavad-gītā: kāmais tais tair hṛta-jñānāḥ:* a person who loses his intelligence because of greediness and lust forgets the Supreme Personality of Godhead and takes shelter of the demigods. Of course, Arjuna was not an ordinary living entity, but because of his friendly dealings with Kṛṣṇa, he thought that Kṛṣṇa was unable to give protection to the *brāhmaṇa* and that he would do better to remember Lord Śiva. Later on it was proved that Arjuna's taking shelter of Lord Śiva instead of Kṛṣṇa was not at all successful. Arjuna, however, did his best by chanting different *mantras,* and he took up his bow to guard the maternity home from all directions.

The *brāhmaṇa's* wife delivered a male child, and as usual the child began to cry. But suddenly, within a few minutes, both the child and Arjuna's arrows disappeared in the sky. It appeared that the *brāhmaṇa's* house was near Kṛṣṇa's residence and that Lord Kṛṣṇa was enjoying everything that was taking place apparently in defiance of His authority. It was He who played the trick of taking away the *brāhmana's* baby as well as the arrows, including the one given by Lord Śiva, of which Arjuna was so proud. *Tad bhavati alpamedhasām:* less intelligent men take shelter of the demigods due to bewilderment and are satisfied with the benefits they award.

In the presence of Lord Kṛṣṇa and others, the *brāhmaṇa* began to accuse Arjuna: "Everyone see my foolishness! I put my faith in the words of Arjuna, who is impotent and who is expert only in false promises. How foolish I was to believe Arjuna. He promised to protect my child when even Pradyumna, Aniruddha, Lord Balarāma and Lord Kṛṣṇa failed. If such great personalities could not protect my child, then who can do so? I therefore condemn Arjuna for his false promise, and I also condemn his celebrated bow Gāṇḍīva and his impudency in declaring himself greater than Lord Balarāma, Lord Kṛṣṇa, Pradyumna and Aniruddha. No one can save my child, for he has already been transferred to another planet. Due to sheer foolishness only, Arjuna thought that he could bring back my child from another planet."

Thus condemned by the *brāhmaṇa,* Arjuna empowered himself with a mystic *yoga* perfection so that he could travel to any planet to find the *brāhmaṇa's* baby. It seems that Arjuna had mastered the mystic yogic power by which *yogīs* can travel to any planet they desire. He first of all went to the planet known as Yamaloka, where the superintendent of death, Yamarāja, lives. There he searched for the *brāhmaṇa's* baby, but he was unable to find him. He then immediately went to the planet where the King of heaven, Indra, lives. When he was unable to find the baby there, he went to the planets of the fire demigods, Nairṛti, and then to the moon planet. Then he went to Vāyu and to Varuṇaloka. When he was unable to find the baby in those planets, he went down to the Rasātala planet, the lowest of the planetary systems. After traveling to all these different planets, he finally went to Brahmaloka, where even the mystic *yogīs* cannot go. By the grace of Lord Kṛṣṇa, Arjuna had that power, and he went above the heavenly planets to Brahmaloka. When he was unable to find the baby even after searching all possible planets, he then attempted to throw himself into a fire, as he had promised the *brāhmaṇa* if unable to bring back his baby. Lord Kṛṣṇa, however, was very kind toward Arjuna because Arjuna happened to be the most intimate friend of the Lord. Lord Kṛṣṇa persuaded Arjuna not to enter the fire in disgrace. Kṛṣṇa indicated that since Arjuna was His friend, if he were to enter the fire in hopelessness, indirectly it would be a blemish on Him. Lord Kṛṣṇa therefore checked Arjuna, assuring him that He would find the baby. He told Arjuna, "Do not foolishly commit suicide."

After addressing Arjuna in this way, Lord Kṛṣṇa called for His transcendental chariot. He mounted it along with Arjuna and began to proceed north. Lord Kṛṣṇa, the all-powerful Personality of Godhead, could have brought the child back without effort, but we should always remember that He was playing the part of a human being. As a human being has to endeavor to achieve certain results, so Lord Kṛṣṇa, like an ordinary human being, or like His friend Arjuna, left Dvārakā to bring back the *brāhmaṇa's* baby. By appearing in human society and exhibiting His pastimes as a human being, Kṛṣṇa definitely showed that there was not a single personality greater than He. "God is great." That is the definition of the Supreme Personality of Godhead. So at least within this material world, while He was present, Kṛṣṇa proved that there was no greater personality within the universe.

Seated on His chariot with Arjuna, Kṛṣṇa began to proceed north, crossing over many planetary systems. These are described in the *Śrīmad-Bhāgavatam* as *sapta-dvīpa. Dvīpa* means island. All these planets are sometimes described in the Vedic literature as *dvīpas.* The planet on which we are living is called Jambūdvīpa. Outer space is taken as a great ocean of air, and within that great ocean of air there are many islands, which are the different planets. In each and every planet there are oceans also. In some of the planets, the oceans are of salt water, and in some of them there are oceans of milk. In others there are oceans of liquor, and in others there are oceans of ghee or oil. There are different kinds of mountains also. Each and every planet has a different type of atmosphere.

Kṛṣṇa passed over all these planets and reached the covering of the universe. This covering is described in the *Śrīmad-Bhāgavatam* as great darkness. This material world as a whole is described as dark. In the open space there is sunlight, and therefore it is illuminated, but in the covering, because of the absence of sunlight, it is naturally dark. When Kṛṣṇa approached the covering layer of this universe, the four horses which were drawing His chariot—Śaibya, Sugrīva, Meghapuṣpa and Balāhaka—all appeared to hesitate to enter the darkness. This hesitation is also a part of the pastimes of Lord Kṛṣṇa because the horses of Kṛṣṇa are not ordinary. It is not possible for ordinary horses to go all over the universe and then enter into its outer covering layers. As Kṛṣṇa is transcendental, similarly His chariot and His horses and everything about Him are also transcendental, beyond the qualities of this material world. We should always remember that Kṛṣṇa was playing the part of an ordinary human being, and His horses also, by the will of Kṛṣṇa, played the parts of ordinary horses in hesitating to enter the darkness.

Kṛṣṇa is known as Yogeśvara, as is stated in the last portion of *Bhagavad-gītā*. *Yogeśvara Hari:* all mystic powers are under His control. In our experience, we can see many human beings who have yogic mystic power. Sometimes they perform very wonderful acts, but Kṛṣṇa is understood to be the master of all mystic power. Therefore, when He saw that His horses were hesitant to proceed into the darkness, He immediately released His disc, known as the Sudarśana cakra, which illuminated the sky a thousand times brighter than sunlight. The darkness of the covering of the universe is also a creation of Kṛṣṇa's, and the Sudarśana cakra is Kṛṣṇa's constant companion. Thus the darkness was penetrated by His keeping the Sudarśana cakra in front. *Śrīmad-Bhāgavatam* states that the Sudarśana cakra penetrated the darkness just as an arrow released from the Śārṅga bow of Lord Rāmacandra penetrated the army of Rāvaṇa. *Su* means very nice, and *darśana* means observation; by the grace of Lord Kṛṣṇa's disc, Sudarśana, everything can be seen very nicely, and nothing can remain in darkness. Thus Lord Kṛṣṇa and Arjuna crossed over the great region of darkness covering the material universes.

Arjuna then saw the effulgence of light known as the *brahmajyoti*. The *brahmajyoti* is situated outside the covering of the material universes, and because it cannot be seen with our present eyes, this *brahmajyoti* is sometimes called *avyakta*. This spiritual effulgence is the ultimate destination of the impersonalists known as Vedāntists. The *brahmajyoti* is also described as *anantapāram*, unlimited and unfathomed. When Lord Kṛṣṇa and Arjuna reached this region of the *brahmajyoti*, Arjuna could not tolerate the glaring effulgence, and he closed his eyes. Lord Kṛṣṇa's and Arjuna's reaching the *brahmajyoti* region is described in *Harivaṁśa*. In that portion of the Vedic literature, Kṛṣṇa informed Arjuna, "My dear Arjuna, the glaring effulgence, the transcendental light which you are seeing, is My bodily rays. O chief of the descendants of Bharata, this *brahmajyoti* is Myself." As the sun disc and the sunshine cannot be separated, similarly Kṛṣṇa and His bodily rays, the *brahmajyoti*, cannot be separated. Thus Kṛṣṇa claimed that the *brahmajyoti* is He Himself. This is clearly stated in the *Harivaṁśa* when Kṛṣṇa says, "*ahaṁ saḥ.*" The *brahmajyoti* is a combination of the minute particles known as spiritual sparks, or the living entities known as *citkana.* The Vedic word *so'ham,* or "I am the *brahmajyoti,*" can also be applied to the living entities, who can also claim to belong to the *brahmajyoti.* In the *Harivaṁśa,* Kṛṣṇa further explains, "This *brahmajyoti* is an expansion of My spiritual energy."

Kṛṣṇa told Arjuna, "The *brahmajyoti* is beyond the region of My external energy, known as *māyā-śakti.*" When one is situated within this material world, it is not possible for him to experience this Brahman effulgence. Therefore, in the material world this effulgence is not manifested, whereas in the spiritual world, it is manifested. That is the purport of the words *vyakta-avyakta.* In the *Bhagavad-gītā* it is said *avyakto-'vyaktāt sanātanaḥ:* both these energies are eternally manifested.

After this, Lord Kṛṣṇa and Arjuna entered a vast extensive spiritual water. This spiritual water is called the Kāraṇārṇava Ocean or Virajā which means that this ocean is the origin of the creation of the material world. In the *Mṛtyuñjaya Tantra,* a Vedic literature, there is a vivid description of this Kāraṇa Ocean, or Virajā. It is stated there that the highest planetary system within the material world is Satyaloka, or Brahmaloka. Beyond that there are Rudraloka and Mahā-Viṣṇuloka. Regarding this Mahā-Viṣṇuloka, it is stated in the *Brahma-saṁhitā, yaḥ kāraṇārṇava-jale bhajati sma yoga:* "Lord Mahā-Viṣṇu is lying in the Kāraṇa Ocean. When He exhales, innumerable universes come into existence, and when He inhales, innumerable universes enter within Him." In this way, the material creation is generated and again withdrawn. When Lord Kṛṣṇa and Arjuna entered the water, it appeared that there was a strong hurricane of transcendental effulgence brewing, and the water of the Kāraṇa Ocean was greatly agitated. By the grace of Lord Kṛṣṇa, Arjuna had the unique experience of being able to see the very beautiful Kāraṇa Ocean.

Accompanied by Kṛṣṇa, Arjuna saw a large palace within the water. There were many thousands of pillars and columns made of valuable jewels, and the glaring effulgence of those columns was so beautiful that Arjuna became charmed by it. Within that palace, Arjuna and Kṛṣṇa saw the gigantic form of Anantadeva, who is also known as Śeṣa. Lord Anantadeva or Śeṣanāga was in the form of a great serpent with thousands of hoods, and each one of them was decorated with valuable, effulgent jewels, which were beautifully dazzling. Each of Anantadeva's hoods had two eyes which appeared to be very fearful. His body was as white as the mountaintop of Kailāsa, which is always covered by snow. His neck was bluish, as were His tongues. Thus Arjuna saw the Śeṣanāga form, and he also saw that on the very soft, white body of Śeṣanāga, Lord Mahā-Viṣṇu was lying very comfortably. He appeared to be all-pervading and very powerful, and Arjuna could understand that the Supreme Personality of Godhead in that form is known as Puroṣottama. He is known as Puruṣottama, the best, or the Supreme Personality of Godhead, because from this form emanates another form of Viṣṇu, which is known as Garbhodakaśāyī Viṣṇu within the material world. The Mahā-Viṣṇu form of the Lord, *Puruṣottama,* is beyond the material world. He is also known as *Uttama. Tama* means darkness, and *ut* means above, transcendental; therefore, *Uttama* means above the darkest region of the material world. Arjuna saw that the bodily color of Puruṣottama, Mahā-Viṣṇu, was as dark as a new cloud in the rainy season; He was dressed in very nice yellow clothing. His face was always beautifully smiling, and His eyes, which were like lotus petals, were very attractive. Lord Mahā-Viṣṇu's helmet was bedecked with valuable jewels, and His beautiful earrings enhanced the beauty of the curling hair on His head. Lord Mahā-Viṣṇu had eight arms, all very long, reaching to His knees. His neck was decorated with the Kaustubha jewel, and His chest was marked with the symbol of *śrīvatsa,* which means the resting place of the goddess of fortune. The Lord wore a garland of lotus flowers down to His knees. This long garland is known as a *vaijayantī* garland.

The Lord was surrounded by His personal associates Nanda and Sunanda, and the personified Sudarśana disc was also standing by Him. As is stated in the *Vedas,* the Lord has innumerable energies, and they were also standing there personified. The most important among them were as follows: *puṣṭi,* the energy for nourishment, *śrī,* the energy of beauty, *kīrti,* the energy of reputation, and *ajā,* the energy of material creation. All these energies are invested in the administrators of the material world, namely Lord Brahmā, Lord Śiva and Lord Viṣṇu, and in the kings of the heavenly planets, Indra, Candra, Varuṇa and the sun-god. In other words, all these demigods, being empowered by the Lord with certain energies, engage in the transcendental loving service of the Supreme Personality of Godhead. The Mahā-Viṣṇu feature is an expansion of Kṛṣṇa's body. It is also confirmed in the *Brahma-saṁhitā* that Mahā-Viṣṇu is a portion of a plenary expansion of Kṛṣṇa. All such expansions are nondifferent from the Personality of Godhead, but since Kṛṣṇa appeared within this material world to manifest His pastimes as a human being, He and Arjuna immediately offered their respects to Lord Mahā-Viṣṇu by bowing down before Him. It is stated in the *Śrīmad-Bhāgavatam* that Lord Kṛṣṇa offered respect to Mahā-Viṣṇu; this means that He offered obeisances unto Him only because Lord Mahā-Viṣṇu is nondifferent from He Himself. This offering of obeisances by Kṛṣṇa to Mahā-Viṣṇu is not, however, the form of worship known as *ahaṅgraha-upāsanā,* which is sometimes recommended for persons who are trying to elevate themselves to the spiritual world by performing the sacrifice of knowledge. This is also stated in the *Bhagavad-gītā: jñāna-yajñena cāpy ante yajanto mām upāsate.*

Although there was no necessity for Kṛṣṇa to offer obeisances, because He is the master teacher, He taught Arjuna just how respect should be offered to Lord Mahā-Viṣṇu. Arjuna, however, became very much afraid upon seeing the gigantic form of everything, distinct from the material experience. Seeing Kṛṣṇa offering obeisances to Lord Mahā-Viṣṇu, he immediately followed Him and stood before the Lord with folded hands. After this, the gigantic form of Mahā-Viṣṇu, greatly pleased, smiled pleasingly and spoke as follows.

"My dear Kṛṣṇa and Arjuna, I was very anxious to see you both, and therefore I arranged to take away the babies of the *brāhmaṇa* and keep them here. I have been expecting to see you both at this palace. You have appeared in the material world as My incarnations in order to minimize the force of the demoniac persons who burden the world. Now after killing all these unwanted demons, you will please again come back to Me. Both of you are incarnations of the great sage Nara-Nārāyaṇa. Although you are both complete in yourselves, to protect the devotees and to annihilate the demons and especially to establish religious principles in the world so that peace and tranquility may continue, you are teaching the basic principles of factual religion so that the people of the world may follow you and thereby be peaceful and prosperous."

Both Lord Kṛṣṇa and Arjuna then offered their obeisances to Lord Mahā-Viṣṇu, and taking back the *brāhmaṇa's* children, they returned to Dvārakā via the same route by which they had entered the spiritual world. All the children of the *brāhmaṇa* had duly grown up. After returning to Dvārakā, Lord Kṛṣṇa and Arjuna delivered to the *brāhmaṇa* all of his sons.

Arjuna, however, was struck with great wonder after visiting the transcendental world by the grace of Lord Kṛṣṇa. And by the grace of Kṛṣṇa he could understand that whatever opulence there may be within this material world is an emanation from Him. Any opulent position a person may have within this material world is due to Kṛṣṇa's mercy. One should therefore always be in Kṛṣṇa consciousness, in complete gratefulness to Lord Kṛṣṇa, because whatever one may possess is all His mercy.

Arjuna's wonderful experience due to the mercy of Kṛṣṇa is one of the many thousands of pastimes performed by Lord Kṛṣṇa during His stay in this material world. They were all unique and have no parallel in the history of the world. All these pastimes prove fully that Kṛṣṇa is the Supreme Personality of Godhead, yet while He was present within this material world, He played just like an ordinary man possessing many worldly duties. He played the part of an ideal householder, and although He possessed 16,000 wives, 16,000 palaces and 160,000 children, He also performed many sacrifices, just to teach the royal order how to live in the material world for the welfare of humanity. As the ideal Supreme Personality, He fulfilled the desires of everyone, from the *brāhmaṇas,* the highest persons in human society, down to the ordinary living entities, including the lowest of men. Just as King Indra is in charge of distributing rain all over the world to satisfy everyone in due course, so Lord Kṛṣṇa satisfies everyone by pouring down His causeless mercy. His mission was to give protection to the devotees and to kill the demoniac kings; therefore, He killed many hundreds and thousands of demons. Some of them He killed personally, and some of them were killed by Arjuna, who was deputed by Kṛṣṇa. In this way He established many pious kings such as Yudhiṣṭhira at the helm of world affairs. Thus, by His divine arrangement He created the good government of King Yudhiṣṭhira, and there ensued peace and tranquility.

Thus ends the Bhaktivedanta purport of the Eighty-eighth Chapter of Kṛṣṇa, *"The Superexcellent Power of Kṛṣṇa."*

89 / Summary Description of Lord Kṛṣṇa's Pastimes

After returning from the spiritual kingdom, which he was able to visit personally along with Kṛṣṇa, Arjuna was very much astonished. He thought to himself that although he was only an ordinary living entity, by the grace of Kṛṣṇa it had been possible for him to see personally the spiritual world. Not only had he seen the spiritual world, but he had also personally seen the original Mahā-Viṣṇu, the cause of the material creation. It is said that Kṛṣṇa never goes out of Vṛndāvana. *Vṛndāvanaṁ parityajya na pādam ekaṁ gacchati.* Kṛṣṇa is supreme in Mathurā, He is more supreme in Dvārakā, and He is most supreme in Vṛndāvana. Kṛṣṇa's pastimes in Dvārakā are displayed by His Vāsudeva portion, yet there is no difference between the Vāsudeva portion manifested in Mathurā and Dvārakā and the original manifestation of Kṛṣṇa at Vṛndāvana. In the beginning of this book we have discussed that when Kṛṣṇa appears, all His incarnations, plenary portions and portions of the plenary portions come with Him. Thus some of His different pastimes are manifested not by the original Kṛṣṇa Himself but by His different portions and plenary portions of incarnation. Arjuna was therefore puzzled about how Kṛṣṇa went to see the Kāraṇārṇavaśāyī Viṣṇu in the spiritual world. This is fully discussed in the commentaries of Śrīla Viśvanātha Cakravartī Ṭhākur.

It is understood from the speech of Mahā-Viṣṇu that He was very anxious to see Kṛṣṇa. It may be said, however, that since Mahā-Viṣṇu took away the *brāhmaṇa's* sons, He certainly must have gone to Dvārakā to do so. Therefore, why did He not see Kṛṣṇa there? A possible answer is that Kṛṣṇa cannot be seen even by the Mahā-Viṣṇu who is lying in the Causal Ocean of the spiritual world, unless Kṛṣṇa gives His permission. Thus Mahā-Viṣṇu took away the *brāhmaṇa's* sons one after another just after their births so that Kṛṣṇa would come personally to retrieve them and then Mahā-Viṣṇu would be able to see Him there. If that is so, the next question is this: Why would Mahā-Viṣṇu come to Dvārakā personally if He were not able to see Kṛṣṇa? Why did He not send some of His associates to take away the sons of the *brāhmaṇa?* A possible answer is that it is very difficult to put any of the citizens of Dvārakā into trouble in the presence of Kṛṣṇa. Therefore, it was not possible for any of Mahā-Viṣṇu's associates to take away the *brāhmaṇa's* sons, and thus He personally came to take them.

Another question may also be raised: The Lord is known as *brahmaṇya-deva,* the worshipable Deity of the *brāhmaṇas,* so why was He inclined to put a *brāhmaṇa* into such a terrible condition of lamentation over one son after another until the ninth son was taken away? The answer is that Lord Mahā-Viṣṇu was so anxious to see Kṛṣṇa that He did not hesitate even to give trouble to a *brāhmaṇa.* Although giving trouble to a *brāhmaṇa* is a forbidden act, Lord Viṣṇu was prepared to do anything in order to see Kṛṣṇa—He was so anxious to see Him. After losing each of his sons, the *brāhmaṇa* would come to the gate of the palace and accuse the King of not being able to give the *brāhmaṇas* protection and of thus being unfit to sit on the royal throne. It was Mahā-Viṣṇu's plan that the *brāhmaṇa* would accuse the *kṣatriyas* and Kṛṣṇa, and Kṛṣṇa would be obliged to come see Him to take back the *brāhmaṇa's* sons.

Still another question may be raised: If Mahā-Viṣṇu cannot see Kṛṣṇa, then how was Kṛṣṇa obliged to come before Him after all to take back the sons of the *brāhmaṇa?* The answer is that Lord Kṛṣṇa went to see Lord Mahā-Viṣṇu not exactly to take away the sons of the *brāhmaṇa* but only for Arjuna's sake. His friendship with Arjuna was so intimate that when Arjuna prepared himself to die by entering the fire, Kṛṣṇa wanted to give him complete protection. Arjuna, however, would not desist from entering the fire unless the sons of the *brāhmaṇa* were brought back. Therefore Kṛṣṇa promised him, "I will bring back the *brāhmaṇa's* sons. Do not try to commit suicide."

If Lord Kṛṣṇa were going to see Lord Viṣṇu only to reclaim the sons of the *brāhmaṇa,* then He would not have waited until the ninth son was taken. But when the ninth son was taken away by Lord Mahā-Viṣṇu and Arjuna was therefore ready to enter the fire because his promise was going to prove false, that serious situation made Lord Kṛṣṇa decide to go with Arjuna to see Mahā-Viṣṇu. It is said that Arjuna is an empowered incarnation of Nara-Nārāyaṇa. He is even sometimes called Nara-Nārāyaṇa. The Nara-Nārāyaṇa incarnation is also one of Lord Viṣṇu's plenary expansions. Therefore, when Kṛṣṇa and Arjuna went to see Lord Viṣṇu, it is to be understood that Arjuna visited in His Nara-Nārāyaṇa capacity, just as

Kṛṣṇa, when He displayed His pastimes in Dvārakā, acted in His Vāsudeva capacity.

After visiting the spiritual world, Arjuna concluded that whatever opulence anyone can show within the material or spiritual worlds is all a gift of Lord Kṛṣṇa. Lord Kṛṣṇa is manifested in various forms, as *Viṣṇu-tattva* and *jīva-tattva,* or, in other words, as *sāṁśa* and *vibhinnāṁśa. Viṣṇu-tattva* is known as *sāṁśa,* and *jīva-tattva* is known as *vibhinnāṁśa.* He can, therefore, display Himself by His different transcendental pastimes, either in the portion of *sāṁśa* or *vibhinnāṁśa,* as He likes, but still He remains the original Supreme Personality of Godhead.

The concluding portion of Kṛṣṇa's pastimes is found in the Ninetieth Chapter of the Tenth Canto of *Śrīmad-Bhāgavatam,* and in this chapter Śukadeva Gosvāmī wanted to explain how Kṛṣṇa lived happily at Dvārakā with all opulences. Kṛṣṇa's opulence of strength has already been displayed in His different pastimes, and now it will be shown how His residence at Dvārakā displayed His opulences of wealth and beauty. In this material world, which is only a perverted reflection of the spiritual world, the opulences of wealth and beauty are considered to be the highest of all opulences. Therefore, while Kṛṣṇa stayed on this planet as the Supreme Personality of Godhead, His opulences of wealth and beauty had no comparison within the three worlds. Kṛṣṇa enjoyed sixteen thousand beautiful wives, and it is most significant that He lived at Dvārakā as the only husband of these hundreds and thousands of beautiful women. It is specifically stated in this connection that He was the only husband of sixteen thousand wives. It is, of course, not unheard of in the history of the world that a powerful king would keep many hundreds of queens, but although such a king might be the only husband of so many wives, he could not enjoy all of them at one time. Kṛṣṇa, however, enjoyed all of His sixteen thousand wives simultaneously.

Although it may be said that *yogīs* also can expand their bodies into many forms, the *yogīs'* expansion and Lord Kṛṣṇa's expansion are not one and the same. Kṛṣṇa is therefore sometimes called *yogeśvara,* the master of all *yogīs.* In the Vedic literature we find that the *yogī* Saubhari Muni expanded himself into eight. But that expansion was like a television expansion. The television image is manifested in millions of expansions, but those expansions cannot act differently; they are simply reflections of the original and can only act exactly as the original does. Kṛṣṇa's expansion is not material like the expansion of the television or the *yogī.* When Nārada visited the different palaces of Kṛṣṇa, he saw that Kṛṣṇa, in His different expansions, was variously engaged in each and every palace of the queens.

It is also said that Kṛṣṇa lived at Dvārakā as the husband of the goddess of fortune. Queen Rukmiṇī is the goddess of fortune, and all the other queens are her expansions. So Kṛṣṇa, the chief of the Vṛṣṇi dynasty, enjoyed with the goddess of fortune in full opulence. The queens of Kṛṣṇa are described as permanently youthful and beautiful. Although Kṛṣṇa had grandchildren and great-grandchildren, neither Kṛṣṇa nor His queens looked older than sixteen or twenty years of age. The young queens were so beautiful that when they moved they appeared like lightning moving in the sky. They were always dressed with exalted ornaments and garments and were always engaged in sportive activities like dancing, singing or playing ball on the roofs of the palaces. The dancing and tennis playing of girls in the material world appear to be perverted reflections of the original pastimes of the original Personality of Godhead, Kṛṣṇa, and His wives.

The roads and streets of the city of Dvārakā were always crowded with elephants, horses, chariots and infantry soldiers. When elephants are engaged in service, they are given liquor to drink, and it is said that the elephants in Dvārakā were given so much liquor that they would sprinkle a great quantity of it on the road and still would walk on the streets intoxicated. The infantry soldiers passing on the streets were profusely decorated with golden ornaments, and horses and golden chariots plied along the streets. In all directions of Dvārakā City, wherever one would turn his eyes he would find green parks and gardens, and each of them was filled with trees and plants laden with fruits and flowers. Because there were so many nice trees of fruits and flowers, all the sweetly chirping birds and the buzzing bumblebees joined together to make sweet vibrations. The city of Dvārakā thus fully displayed all opulences. The heroes in the dynasty of Yadu used to think themselves the most fortunate residents of the city, and actually they enjoyed all transcendental facilities.

All the sixteen thousand palaces of Kṛṣṇa's queens were situated in this beautiful city of Dvārakā, and Lord Kṛṣṇa, the supreme eternal enjoyer of all these facilities, expanded Himself into sixteen thousand forms and simultaneously engaged in different family affairs in those sixteen thousand palaces. In each and every one of the palaces there were nicely decorated gardens and lakes. The crystal clear water of the lakes contained many blooming lotus flowers of different colors like blue, yellow, white and red, and the saffron powder from the lotus flowers was blown all around by the breeze. All the lakes were full of beautiful swans, ducks and cranes, crying occasionally with melodious sounds. Lord Śrī Kṛṣṇa sometimes entered those lakes, or sometimes the rivers, with His wives and enjoyed swimming pastimes with them in full jubilation. Sometimes the wives of Lord Kṛṣṇa, who were all goddesses of fortune, would embrace the Lord in the midst of the water while swimming or taking bath, and the red vermilion of *kuṅkuma* decorating the beauty of their breasts would adorn the chest of the Lord with a reddish color.

The impersonalists would not dare to believe that in the spiritual world there are such varieties of enjoyment, but in order to demonstrate the factual, ever-blissful enjoyment in the spiritual world, Lord Kṛṣṇa descended on this planet and showed that the spiritual world is not devoid of such pleasurable facilities of life. The only difference is that in the spiritual world such facilities are eternal, never-ending occurrences, whereas in the material world they are simply impermanent perverted reflections. When Lord Kṛṣṇa was engaged in such enjoyment, the Gandharvas and professional musicians would glorify Him with melodious musical concerts, accompanied by *mṛdaṅgas,* drums, kettledrums, stringed instruments and brass bugles, and the whole atmosphere would change into a greatly festive celebration. In a festive mood, the wives of the Lord would sometimes sprinkle water on the Lord's body with a syringe-like instrument, and the Lord would similarly wet the bodies of the queens. When Kṛṣṇa and the queens engaged themselves in these pastimes, it seemed as if the heavenly King, Yakṣarāja, were engaged in such pastimes with his many wives. (Yakṣarāja is also known as Kuvera and is considered to be the treasurer of the heavenly kingdom.) When the wives of Lord Kṛṣṇa thus became wet, their breasts and thighs would increase in beauty a thousand times, and their long hair would fall down to decorate those parts of their bodies. The beautiful flowers which were placed in their hair would fall, and the queens, being seemingly harassed by the Lord's throwing water at them, would approach Him on the plea of snatching the syringe-like instrument, and this attempt would create a situation wherein the Lord could embrace them as they willingly approached Him. Upon being embraced, the wives of the Lord would feel on their mouths a clear indication of conjugal love, and this would create an atmosphere of spiritual bliss. When the garland on the neck of the Lord then touched the breasts of the queens, their whole bodies became covered with saffron yellow. Being engaged in their celestial pastimes, the queens forgot themselves, and their loosened hair appeared like the beautiful waves of a river. When the queens sprinkled water on the body of Kṛṣṇa or He sprinkled water on the bodies of the queens, the whole situation appeared just like an elephant enjoying in a lake along with many she-elephants.

After enjoying fully amongst themselves, the queens and Lord Kṛṣṇa would come out of the water, and their wet garments, which were very valuable, would be given up by them to be taken away by the professional singers and dancers. These singers and dancers had no other means of subsistence than the rewards of valuable garments and ornaments left by the queens and kings on such occasions. The whole system of society was so well planned that all the members of society in their different positions as *brāhmaṇas, kṣatriyas, vaiśyas,* and *śūdras* had no difficulty in earning their livelihood. There was no competition among the divisions of society. The original conception of the caste system was so planned that one group of men engaged in a particular type of occupation would not compete with another group of men engaged in a different occupation.

In this way, Lord Kṛṣṇa used to enjoy the company of His sixteen thousand wives. Devotees of the Lord who want to love the Supreme Personality of Godhead in the mellow of conjugal love are elevated to the position of becoming wives of Kṛṣṇa, and Kṛṣṇa also keeps them always attached to Him by His kind behavior. Kṛṣṇa's behavior with His wives, His movements, His talking with them, His smiling, His embracing, and similar other activities just like a loving husband kept them always very much attached to Him. That is the highest perfection of life. If someone remains always attached to Kṛṣṇa, it is to be understood that he is liberated, and his life is successful. With any devotee who loves Kṛṣṇa with his heart and soul, Kṛṣṇa reciprocates in such a way that the devotee cannot remain unattached to Him. The reciprocal dealings of Kṛṣṇa and His devotees are so attractive that a devotee cannot think of any subject matter other than Kṛṣṇa.

For all the queens, Kṛṣṇa only was their worshipable objective. They were always absorbed in thought of Kṛṣṇa, the lotus-eyed and beautifully blackish Personality of Godhead. Sometimes, in thought of Kṛṣṇa, they remained silent, and in great ecstasy of *bhāva* and *anubhāva* they sometimes spoke as if in delirium. Sometimes, even in the presence of Lord Kṛṣṇa, they vividly described the pastimes they had enjoyed in the lake or in the river with Him. Some of such talk may be described here.

One of the queens said to the bird *kurarī,* "My dear *kurarī,* now it is very late at night. Everyone is sleeping. The whole world is now calm and peaceful. At this time, the Supreme Personality of Godhead is sleeping, although His knowledge is undisturbed by any circumstance. Then why are you not sleeping? Why are you lamenting like this throughout the whole night? My dear friend, is it that you are also attracted by the lotus eyes of the Supreme Personality of Godhead and by His sweet smiling and attractive words, exactly as I am? Do those dealings of the Supreme Personality of Godhead pinch your heart as they do mine?

"Hello *cakravākī.* Why have you closed your eyes? Are you searching after your husband, who might have gone to foreign countries? Why are you lamenting so pitiably? Alas, it appears that you are very much aggrieved. Or is it a fact that you also are willing to become an eternal servitor of the Supreme Personality of Godhead? I think that you are anxious to put a garland on the lotus feet of the Lord and then place it on your hair.

"O my dear ocean, why are you roaring all day and night? Don't you like to sleep? I think that you have been attacked by insomnia, or, if I am not wrong, my dear Śyāmasundara has tactfully taken away your gravity and power of forbearence, which are your natural qualifications. Is it a fact that for this reason you are suffering from insomnia like me? Yes, I admit that there is no remedy for this disease.

"My dear moon-god, I think that you have been attacked by a severe type of tuberculosis. For this reason, you are becoming thinner and thinner day by day. O my lord, you are now so weak that your thin rays cannot dissipate the darkness of night. Or is it a fact that, just as I have, you also have been stunned by the mysteriously sweet words of my Lord Śyāmasundara. Is it a fact that it is because of this severe anxiety that you are so grave?

"O breeze from the Himalayas, what have I done to you that you are so intent on teasing me by awakening my lust to meet Kṛṣṇa? Do you not know that I have already been injured by the crooked policy of the Personality of Godhead? My dear Himalayan breeze, please know that I have already been stricken. There is no need to injure me more and more.

"My dear beautiful cloud, the color of your beautiful body exactly resembles my dearmost Śyāmasundara's bodily hue. I think, therefore, that you are very much dear to my Lord, the chief of the dynasty of the Yadus, and because you are so dear to Him, you are, exactly as I am, absorbed in meditation. I can appreciate that your heart is full of anxiety for Śyāmasundara. You appear to be excessively eager to see Him, and I see that for this reason only, there are drops of tears gliding down from your eyes, just as there are from mine. My dear black cloud, we must admit frankly that to establish an intimate relationship with Śyāmasundara means to purchase unnecessary anxieties while we are otherwise comfortable at home."

Generally the cuckoo sounds its cooing vibration at the end of night or early in the morning. When the queens heard the cooing of the cuckoo at the end of night, they said, "Dear cuckoo, your voice is very sweet. As soon as you vibrate your sweet voice, we immediately remember Śyāmasundara because your voice exactly resembles His. We must frankly admit that your voice is imbued with nectar, and it is so invigorating that it is competent to bring back life to those who are almost dead in separation from their dearmost friend. So we are very much obliged to you. Please let us know how we can welcome you or how we can do something for you."

The queens continued talking like that, and they addressed the mountain as follows: "Dear mountain, you are very generous. By your gravitation only, the whole crust of this earth is properly maintained, and because you are discharging your duties very faithfully, you do not know how to move. Because you are so grave, you do not move hither and thither, nor do you say anything. Rather, you always appear to be in a thoughtful mood. It may be that you are always thinking of a very grave and important subject matter, but we can guess very clearly what you are thinking of. We are sure that you are thinking of placing the lotus feet of Śyāmasundara on your raised peaks, as we want to place His lotus feet on our raised breasts.

"Dear dry rivers, we know that because this is the summer season, all your beds are dry and you have no water. Because all your water has now been dried up, you are no longer beautified by blooming lotus flowers. At the present moment, you appear to be very lean and thin, so we can understand that your position is exactly like ours. We have lost everything due to being separated from Śyāmasundara, and we no longer hear His pleasing words. Our hearts no longer work properly, and therefore we also have become very lean and thin. We think, therefore, that you are just like us. You have turned lean and thin because you are not getting any water from your husband, the ocean, through the clouds." The example given herewith by the queens is very appropriate. The river beds become dry when the ocean no longer supplies water through the clouds. The ocean is supposed to be the husband of the river and therefore is supposed to support her. Unless a woman is supported by the husband with the necessities of life, she also becomes as dry as a dry river.

One queen addressed a swan as follows. "My dear swan, please come here, come here. You are welcome. Please sit down and take some milk. My dear swan, can you tell me if you have any message from Śyāmasundara? I take you to be a messenger from Him. If you have any such news, please tell me. Our Śyāmasundara is always very independent. He never comes under the control of anyone. We have all failed to control Him, and therefore we ask you, is He keeping Himself well? I may inform you that Śyāmasundara is very fickle. His friendship is always temporary; it breaks even by slight agitation. But would you kindly explain why He is so unkind to me? Formerly He said that I alone am His dearmost wife. Does He remember this assurance? Anyway, you are welcome. Please sit down. But I cannot accept your entreaty to go to Śyāmasundara. When He does not care for me, why should I be mad after Him? I am very sorry to let you know that you have become the messenger of a poor-hearted soul. You are asking me to go to Him, but I am not going. What is that? You talk of His coming to me? Does He desire to come here to fulfill my long expectation for Him? All right. You can bring Him here. But don't bring with Him His most beloved goddess of fortune. Do you think that He cannot be separated from the goddess of fortune even for a moment? Could He not come here alone, without Lakṣmī? His behavior is very displeasing. Does it mean that without Lakṣmī, Śyāmasundara cannot be happy? Can't He be happy with any other wife? Does it mean that the goddess of fortune has the ocean of love for Him, and none of us can compare to her?"

All the wives of Lord Kṛṣṇa were completely absorbed in thought of Him. Kṛṣṇa is known as the *yogeśvara,* the master of all *yogīs,* and all the wives of Kṛṣṇa at Dvārakā used to keep this *yogeśvara* within their hearts. Instead of trying to be master of all yogic mystic powers, it is better if one simply keeps the supreme *yogeśvara,* Kṛṣṇa, within his heart. Thus one's life can become perfect, and one can very easily be transferred to the kingdom of God. It is to be understood that all the queens of Kṛṣṇa who lived with Him at Dvārakā were in their previous lives very greatly exalted devotees who wanted to establish a relationship with Kṛṣṇa in conjugal love. Thus they were given the chance to become His wives and enjoy a constant loving relationship with Him. Ultimately, they were all transferred to the Vaikuṇṭha planets.

The Supreme Absolute Truth Personality of Godhead is never impersonal. All the Vedic literatures glorify the transcendental performance of His various personal activities and pastimes. It is said that in the Vedas and in the *Rāmāyaṇa,* only the activities of the Lord are described. Everywhere in the Vedic literature, His glories are sung. As soon as soft-hearted people such as women hear those transcendental pastimes of Lord Kṛṣṇa, they immediately become attracted to Him. Soft-hearted women and girls are therefore very easily drawn to the Kṛṣṇa consciousness movement. One who is thus drawn to the Kṛṣṇa consciousness movement and tries to keep himself in constant touch with such consciousness certainly gets the supreme salvation, going back to Kṛṣṇa at Goloka Vṛndāvana. If simply by developing Kṛṣṇa consciousness one can be transferred to the spiritual world, one can simply imagine how blissful and blessed were the queens of Lord Kṛṣṇa, who talked with Him personally and who saw Lord Kṛṣṇa eye to eye. No one can properly describe the fortune of the wives of Lord Kṛṣṇa. They took care of Him personally by rendering various transcendental services like bathing Him, feeding Him, pleasing Him and serving Him. Thus no one's austerities can compare to the service of the queens at Dvārakā.

Śukadeva Gosvāmī informed Mahārāja Parīkṣit that for self-realization the austerities and penances performed by the queens at Dvārakā have no comparison. The objective of self-realization is one: Kṛṣṇa. Therefore, although the dealings of the queens with Kṛṣṇa appear just like ordinary dealings between husband and wife, the principal point to be observed is the queens' attachment for Kṛṣṇa. The entire process of austerity and penance is meant to detach one from the material world and to enhance one's attachment to Kṛṣṇa, the Supreme Personality of Godhead. Kṛṣṇa is the shelter of all persons advancing in self-realization. As an ideal householder, He lived with His wives and performed the Vedic rituals just to show less intelligent persons that the Supreme Lord is never impersonal. Kṛṣṇa lived with wife and children in all opulence, exactly like an ordinary conditioned soul, just to exemplify to those souls who are actually conditioned that one may enter into the circle of family life as long as Kṛṣṇa is the center. For example, the members of the Yadu dynasty lived in the family of Kṛṣṇa, and Kṛṣṇa was the center of all their activities.

Renunciation is not as important as enhancing one's attachment to Kṛṣṇa. The Kṛṣṇa consciousness movement is especially meant for this purpose. We are preaching on the principle that it does not matter whether a man is a *sannyāsī* or *gṛhastha.* One simply has to increase his attachment for Kṛṣṇa, and then his life is successful. Following in the footsteps of Lord Śrī Kṛṣṇa, one can live with his family members or within the society or nation, not for the purpose of indulging in sense gratification but to realize Kṛṣṇa by advancing in attachment for Him. There are four principles of elevation from conditional life to the life of liberation, which are technically known as *dharma, artha, kāma* and *mokṣa* (religion, economic development, sense gratification and liberation). If one lives a family life following in the footsteps of Lord Kṛṣṇa's family members, one can achieve all four of these principles of success simultaneously by making Kṛṣṇa the center of all activities.

It is already known to us that Kṛṣṇa had 16,108 wives. All these wives were exalted liberated souls, and among them Queen Rukmiṇī was the chief. After Rukmiṇī there were seven other principal wives, and the names of the sons of these eight principal queens have already been mentioned. Besides these eight queens, Lord Kṛṣṇa had ten sons by each of the other queens. Thus all together Kṛṣṇa's children numbered 16,108 times ten. One should not be astonished to hear that Kṛṣṇa had so many sons. One should always remember that Kṛṣṇa is the Supreme Personality of Godhead and that He has unlimited potencies. He claims all living entities as His sons, so even if He had sixteen million sons attached to Him personally, there would be no cause for astonishment.

Among Kṛṣṇa's greatly powerful sons, eighteen sons were *mahā-rathas.* The *mahā-rathas* could fight alone against many thousands of soldiers, charioteers, cavalry and elephants. The reputations of these eighteen sons are very widespread and are described in almost all the Vedic literatures. The eighteen *mahā-ratha* sons are listed as Pradyumna, Aniruddha, Dīptimān, Bhānu, Sāmba, Madhu, Bṛhadbhānu, Citrabhānu, Vṛka, Aruṇa, Puṣkara, Vedabāhu, Śrutadeva, Sunandana, Citrabāhu, Virūpa, Kavi and Nyagrodha. Of these eighteen *mahā-ratha* sons of Kṛṣṇa, Pradyumna is considered to be the foremost. Pradyumna happened to be the eldest son of Queen Rukmiṇī, and he inherited all the qualities of his great father, Lord Kṛṣṇa. He married the daughter of his maternal uncle, Rukmī, and Aniruddha, the son of Pradyumna, was born from that marriage. Aniruddha was so powerful that he could fight against ten thousand elephants. He married the granddaughter of Rukmī, the brother of his grandmother, Rukmiṇī. Because the relationship between these cousins was distant, such a marriage was not uncommon. Aniruddha's son was Vajra. When the whole Yadu dynasty was destroyed by the curse of a *brāhmaṇa,* only Vajra survived. Vajra had one son whose name was Pratibāhu. The son of Pratibāhu was named Subāhu, the son of Subāhu was named Śāntasena, and the son of Śāntasena was Śatasena.

It is stated by Śukadeva Gosvāmī that all the members of the Yadu dynasty had many children. Just as Kṛṣṇa had many sons, grandsons and great-grandsons, so each one of the kings named herewith also had similar family extensions. Not only did all of them have many children, but all were extraordinarily rich and opulent. None of them were weak or short-lived, and above all, all the members of the Yadu dynasty were staunch devotees of the brahminical culture. It is the duty of the *kṣatriya* kings to maintain the brahminical culture and to protect the qualified *brāhmaṇas,* and all these kings discharged their duties very rightly. The members of the Yadu dynasty were so numerous that it would be very difficult to describe them all even if one had a duration of life of many thousands of years. Śrīla Śukadeva Gosvāmī informed Mahārāja Parīkṣit that he had heard from reliable sources that simply to teach the children of the Yadu dynasty, there were as many as 38,800,000 tutors or *ācāryas.* If so many teachers were needed to educate their children, one can simply imagine how vast was the number of family members. As for their military strength, it is said that King Ugrasena alone had ten quadrillion soldiers as personal bodyguards.

Before the advent of Lord Kṛṣṇa within this universe, there were many battles between the demons and the demigods. Many demons died in the fighting, and they all were given the chance to take birth in high royal families on this earth. Because of their royal exalted posts, all these demons became very much puffed up, and their only business was to harass their subjects. Lord Kṛṣṇa appeared on this planet just at the end of Dvāpara-yuga in order to annihilate all these demonic kings. As it is said in the *Bhagavad-gītā, paritrāṇāya sādhūnāṁ vināśāya ca duṣkṛtām:* The Lord comes to protect the devotees and to annihilate the miscreants. Some of the demigods were also asked to appear on this earth to assist in the transcendental pastimes of Lord Kṛṣṇa. When Kṛṣṇa appeared, He came in the association of His eternal servitors, but the demigods also were requested to come down to assist Him, and thus all of them took their births in the Yadu dynasty. The Yadu dynasty had 101 clans in different parts of the country. All the members of these different clans respected Lord Kṛṣṇa in a manner befitting His divine position, and all of them were His devotees heart and soul. Thus all the members of the Yadu dynasty were very opulent, happy and prosperous, and they had no anxieties. Because of their implicit faith in and devotion to Lord Kṛṣṇa, they were never defeated by any other kings. Their love of Krsna was so intense that in their regular activities—in sitting, sleeping, traveling, talking, sporting, cleansing and bathing—they were simply absorbed in thoughts of Kṛṣṇa and paid no attention to bodily necessities. That is the symptom of a pure devotee of Lord Kṛṣṇa. Just as when a man is fully absorbed in some particular thought, he sometimes forgets his other bodily activities, so the members of the Yadu dynasty acted automatically for their bodily necessities, but their actual attention was always fixed on Kṛṣṇa. Their bodily activities were performed mechanically, but their minds were always absorbed in Kṛṣṇa consciousness.

Śrīla Śukadeva Gosvāmī has concluded the Ninetieth Chapter of the Tenth Canto of *Śrīmad-Bhāgavatam* by pointing out five particular excellences of Lord Kṛṣṇa. The first excellence is that before Lord Kṛṣṇa's appearance in the Yadu family, the River Ganges was known as the purest of all things; even impure things could be purified simply by touching the water of the Ganges. This superexcellent power of the Ganges water was due to its having emanated from the toe of Lord Viṣṇu. But when Lord Kṛṣṇa, the Supreme Viṣṇu, appeared in the family of the Yadu dynasty, He traveled personally throughout the kingdom of the Yadus, and by His intimate association with the Yadu dynasty, the whole family not only became very famous but also became more effective in purifying others than the water of the Ganges.

The next excellence of Lord Kṛṣṇa's appearance was that although apparently He gave protection to the devotees and annihilated the demons, both the devotees and the demons achieved the same result. Lord Kṛṣṇa is the bestower of five kinds of liberation, of which *sāyujya-mukti,* or the liberation of becoming one with the Supreme, was given to the demons like Kaṁsa, whereas the *gopīs* were given the chance to associate with Him personally. The *gopīs* kept their individuality to enjoy the company of Lord Kṛṣṇa, but Kaṁsa was accepted into His impersonal *brahmajyoti.* In other words, both the demons and the *gopīs* were spiritually liberated, but because the demons were enemies and the *gopīs* were friends, the demons were killed and the *gopīs* were protected.

The third excellence of Lord Kṛṣṇa's appearance was that the goddess of fortune, who is worshiped by demigods like Lord Brahmā, Indra and Candra, remained always engaged in the service of the Lord, even though the Lord gave more preference to the *gopīs.* Lakṣmījī, the goddess of fortune, tried her best to be on an equal level with the *gopīs,* but she was not successful. Nevertheless, she remained faithful to Kṛṣṇa, although generally she does not remain at one place even if worshiped by demigods like Lord Brahmā.

The fourth excellence of Lord Kṛṣṇa's appearance concerns the glories of His name. It is stated in the Vedic literature that by chanting the different names of Lord Viṣṇu a thousand times, one may be bestowed with the same benefits as by thrice chanting the holy name of Lord Rāma. And by chanting the holy name of Lord Kṛṣṇa only once, one receives the same benefit. In other words, of all the holy names of the Supreme Personality of Godhead, including Viṣṇu and Rāma, the holy name of Kṛṣṇa is the most powerful. The Vedic literature therefore specifically stresses the chanting of the holy name of Kṛṣṇa: Hare Kṛṣṇa, Hare Kṛṣṇa, Kṛṣṇa Kṛṣṇa, Hare Hare/ Hare Rāma, Hare Rāma, Rāma Rāma, Hare Hare. Lord Caitanya introduced this chanting of the holy name of Kṛṣṇa in this age, thus making liberation more easily obtainable than in other ages. In other words, Lord Kṛṣṇa is more excellent than His other incarnations, although all of them are equally the Supreme Personality of Godhead.

The fifth excellence of Lord Kṛṣṇa's appearance is that He established the most excellent of all religious principles by His one statement in the *Bhagavad-gītā* that simply by surrendering unto Him, one can discharge all the principles of religious rites. In the Vedic literature there are twenty kinds of religious principles mentioned, and each of them is described in different *śāstras.* But Lord Kṛṣṇa is so kind to the fallen conditioned souls of this age that He personally appeared and asked everyone to give up all kinds of religious rites and simply surrender unto Him. It is said that this age of Kali is three-fourths devoid of religious principles. Hardly one fourth of the principles of religion are still observed in this age. But by the mercy of Lord Kṛṣṇa, this vacancy of Kali-yuga has not only been completely filled, but the religious process has been made so easy that simply by rendering transcendental loving service unto Lord Kṛṣṇa by chanting His holy names, Hare Kṛṣṇa, Hare Kṛṣṇa, Kṛṣṇa Kṛṣṇa, Hare Hare/ Hare Rāma, Hare Rāma, Rāma Rāma, Hare Hare, one can achieve the highest result of religion, namely, being transferred to the highest planet within the spiritual world, Goloka Vṛndāvana. One can thus immediately estimate the benefit of Lord Kṛṣṇa's appearance and can understand that His giving relief to the people of the world by His appearance was not at all extraordinary.

Śrīla Śukadeva Gosvāmi thus concludes his description of the super-exalted position of Lord Kṛṣṇa by glorifying Him in the following way: "O Lord Kṛṣṇa, all glories unto You. You are present in everyone's heart as Paramātmā. Therefore You are known as Jananivāsa, one who lives in everyone's heart." As confirmed in the *Bhagavad-gītā, īśvaraḥ sarva-bhūtānāṁ hṛd-deśe 'rjuna tiṣṭhati:* The Supreme Lord in His Paramātma feature lives within everyone's heart. This does not mean, however, that Kṛṣṇa has no separate existence as the Supreme Personality of Godhead. The Māyāvādī philosophers accept the all-pervading feature of Parabrahman, but when Parabrahman, or the Supreme Lord, appears, they think that He appears under the control of material nature. Because Lord Kṛṣṇa appeared as the son of Devakī, the Māyāvādī philosophers accept Kṛṣṇa to be an ordinary living entity who takes birth within this material world. Therefore Śukadeva Gosvāmī warns them that *devakī-janma-vāda,* which means that although Kṛṣṇa is famous as the son of Devakī, actually He is the Supersoul or the all-pervading Supreme Personality of Godhead. The devotees, however, take this word *devakī-janma-vāda* in a different way. The devotees understand that actually Kṛṣṇa was the son of mother Yaśodā. Although Kṛṣṇa first of all appeared as the son of Devakī, He immediately transferred Himself to the lap of mother Yaśodā, and His childhood pastimes were blissfully enjoyed by mother Yaśodā and Nanda Mahārāja. This fact was also admitted by Vasudeva himself when he met Nanda Mahārāja and Yaśodā at Kurukṣetra. He admitted that Kṛṣṇa and Balarāma were actually the sons of mother Yaśodā and Nanda Mahārāja. Vasudeva and Devakī were only Their official father and mother. Their actual father and mother were Nanda and Yaśodā. Therefore Śukadeva Gosvāmī addressed Lord Kṛṣṇa as *devakī-janma-vāda.*

Śukadeva Gosvāmī then glorifies the Lord as one who is honored by the *yadu-vara-pariṣat*, the assembly house of the Yadu dynasty, and as the killer of different kinds of demons. Kṛṣṇa, the Supreme Personality of Godhead, could have killed all the demons by employing His different material energies, but He wanted to kill them personally in order to give them salvation. There was no need of Kṛṣṇa's coming to this material world to kill the demons. Simply by His willing, many hundreds and thousands of demons could have been killed without His personal endeavor. But actually He descended for His pure devotees, to play as a child with mother Yaśodā and Nanda Mahārāja and to give pleasure to the inhabitants of Dvārakā. By killing the demons and by giving protection to the devotees, Lord Kṛṣṇa established the real religious principle, which is simply love of God. By following the factual religious principles of love of God, even the living entities known as *sthira-cara* were also delivered of all material contamination and were transferred to the spiritual kingdom. *Sthira* means the trees and plants, which cannot move, and *cara* means the moving animals, specifically the cows. When Kṛṣṇa was present, He delivered all the trees, monkeys and other plants and animals who happened to see Him and serve Him both in Vṛndāvana and in Dvārakā.

Lord Kṛṣṇa is especially glorified for His giving pleasure to the *gopīs* and the queens of Dvārakā. Śukadeva Gosvāmī glorifies Lord Kṛṣṇa for His enchanting smile, by which He enchanted not only the *gopīs* at Vṛndāvana but also the queens at Dvārakā. The exact word used in this connection is *vardhayan kāmadevam.* In Vṛndāvana as the boy friend of many *gopīs* and in Dvārakā as the husband of many queens, Kṛṣṇa increased their lusty desires to enjoy with Him. For God realization or self-realization, one generally has to undergo severe austerities and penances for many, many thousands of years, and then it may be possible to realize God. But the *gopīs* and the queens of Dvārakā, simply by enhancing their lusty desires to enjoy Kṛṣṇa as their boy friend or husband, received the highest type of salvation.

This behavior of Lord Kṛṣṇa with the *gopīs* and queens is unique in the history of self-realization. Usually people understand that for self-realization one has to go to the forest or to the mountains and undergo severe austerities and penances. But the *gopīs* and the queens, simply by being attached to Kṛṣṇa in conjugal love and enjoying His company in a so-called sensuous life full of luxury and opulence, achieved the highest salvation, which is impossible to be achieved even by great sages and saintly persons. Similarly, the demons such as Kaṁsa, Dantavakra, Śiśupāla, etc., also got the highest benefit of being transferred to the spiritual world.

In the beginning of *Śrīmad-Bhāgavatam,* Śrīla Vyāsadeva offered his respectful obeisances to the Supreme Truth, Vāsudeva, Kṛṣṇa. After that he taught his son, Śukadeva Gosvāmī, to preach *Śrīmad-Bhāgavatam.* It is in this connection that Śukadeva Gosvāmī glorifies the Lord as *jayati.* Following in the footsteps of Śrīla Vyāsadeva, Śukadeva Gosvāmī and all the *ācāryas* in disciplic succession, the whole population of the world should glorify Lord Kṛṣṇa, and for their best interest they should take to this Kṛṣṇa consciousness movement. The process is easy and helpful. It is simply to chant the *mahāmantra,* Hare Kṛṣṇa, Hare Kṛṣṇa, Kṛṣṇa Kṛṣṇa, Hare Hare/Hare Rāma, Hare Rāma, Rāma Rāma, Hare Hare. Lord Caitanya has therefore recommended that one should be callous to the material ups and downs. Material life is temporary, and so the ups and downs of life may come and go. When they come, one should be as tolerant as a tree and as humble and meek as the straw in the street, but certainly he must engage himself in Kṛṣṇa consciousness by chanting Hare Kṛṣṇa, Hare Kṛṣṇa, Kṛṣṇa Kṛṣṇa, Hare Hare.

The Supreme Personality of Godhead, Kṛṣṇa, the Supersoul of all living entities, out of His causeless mercy comes down and manifests His different transcendental pastimes in different incarnations. Hearing the attractive pastimes of Lord Kṛṣṇa's different incarnations is a chance for liberation for the conditioned soul, and the most fascinating and pleasing activities of Lord Kṛṣṇa Himself are still more attractive because Lord Kṛṣṇa personally is all-attractive.

Following in the holy footsteps of Śrīla Śukadeva Gosvāmī, we have tried to present this book *Kṛṣṇa* for being read and heard by the conditioned souls of this age. By hearing the pastimes of Lord Kṛṣṇa, one is sure and certain to get salvation and be transferred back home, back to Godhead. It is recommended by Śukadeva Gosvāmī that as we hear the transcendental pastimes and activities of the Lord, we gradually cut the knots of material contamination. Therefore, regardless of what one is, if one wants the association of Lord Kṛṣṇa in the transcendental kingdom of God for eternity in blissful existence, one must hear about the pastimes of Lord Kṛṣṇa and chant the *mahāmantra,* Hare Kṛṣṇa,

Hare Kṛṣṇa, Kṛṣṇa Kṛṣṇa, Hare Hare/Hare Rāma, Hare Rāma, Rāma Rāma, Hare Hare.

The transcendental pastimes of the Supreme Personality of Godhead Kṛṣṇa are so powerful that simply by hearing, reading and memorizing this book *Kṛṣṇa,* one is sure to be transferred to the spiritual world, which is ordinarily very difficult to achieve. The description of the pastimes of Lord Kṛṣṇa is so attractive that automatically it gives us an impetus to study repeatedly, and the more we study the pastimes of the Lord, the more we become attached to Him. This very attachment to Kṛṣṇa makes one eligible to be transferred to His abode, Goloka Vṛndāvana. As we have learned from the previous chapter, to cross over the material world is to cross over the stringent laws of material nature. The stringent laws of material nature cannot check the progress of one who is attracted by the spiritual nature. This is confirmed in the *Bhagavad-gītā* by the Lord Himself: although the stringent laws of material nature are very difficult to overcome, if anyone surrenders unto the Lord, he can very easily cross over nescience. There is, however, no influence of material nature in the spiritual world. As we have learned from the Second Canto of *Śrīmad-Bhāgavatam,* the ruling power of the demigods and the influence of material nature are conspicuous by their absence in the spiritual world.

Śrīla Śukadeva Gosvāmī has therefore advised Mahārāja Parīkṣit in the beginning of the Second Canto that every conditioned soul should engage himself in hearing and chanting the transcendental pastimes of the Lord. Śrīla Śukadeva Gosvāmī also informed King Parīkṣit that previously many other kings and emperors went to the jungle to prosecute severe austerities and penances in order to go back home, back to Godhead. In India, it is still a practice that many advanced transcendentalists give up their family lives and go to Vṛndāvana to live there alone and completely engage in hearing and chanting of the holy pastimes of the Lord. This system is recommended in the *Śrīmad-Bhāgavatam,* and the six Gosvāmīs of Vṛndāvana followed it, but at the present moment many *karmīs* and pseudo-devotees have overcrowded the holy place of Vṛndāvana just to imitate this process recommended by Śukadeva Gosvāmī. It is said that many kings and emperors formerly went to the forest for this purpose, but Śrīla Bhaktisiddhānta Sarasvatī Ṭhākur Gosvāmī Mahārāja does not recommend that one take up this solitary life in Vṛndāvana prematurely.

One who goes prematurely to Vṛndāvana to live in pursuance of the instructions of Śukadeva Gosvāmī again falls a victim of *māyā,* even while residing in Vṛndāvana. To check such unauthorized residence in Vṛndāvana, Śrīla Bhaktisiddhānta Sarasvatī Ṭhākur has sung a nice song in this connection, the purport of which is as follows: "My dear mind, why are you so proud of being a Vaiṣṇava? Your solitary worship and chanting of the holy name of the Lord are based on a desire for cheap popularity, and therefore your chanting of the holy name is only a pretension. Such an ambition for a cheap reputation can be compared to the stool of a hog because such popularity is another extension of the influence of *māyā.*" One may go to Vṛndāvana for cheap popularity, and instead of being absorbed in Kṛṣṇa consciousness, one may always think of money and women, which are simply temporary sources of happiness. It is better that one engage whatever money and women he may have in his possession in the service of the Lord because sense enjoyment is not for the conditioned soul.

The master of the senses is Hṛṣīkeśa, Lord Kṛṣṇa. Therefore, the senses should always be engaged in His service. As for material reputation, there were many demons like Rāvaṇa who wanted to go against the laws of material nature, but they all failed. One should therefore not take to the demoniac activity of claiming to be a Vaiṣṇava just for false prestige, without performing service to the Lord. But when one engages oneself in the devotional service of the Lord, automatically the Vaiṣṇava reputation comes to him. There is no need to be envious of the devotees who are engaged in preaching the glories of the Lord. We have practical experience of being advised by the so-called *bābājīs* in Vṛndāvana that there is no need to preach and that it is better to live in Vṛndāvana in a solitary place and chant the holy name. Such *bābājīs* do not know that if one is engaged in preaching work or in glorifying the Supreme Personality of Godhead, the good reputation of a preacher automatically follows one. One should not, therefore, prematurely give up the honest life of a householder to lead a life of debauchery in Vṛndāvana. Śrīla Śukadeva Gosvāmī's recommendation to leave home and go to the forest in search of Kṛṣṇa is not for immature persons. Mahārāja Parīkṣit was mature. Even in his householder life, or from the very beginning of his life, he worshiped Lord Kṛṣṇa's *mūrti.* In his childhood he worshiped the Deity of Lord Kṛṣṇa, and later, although he was a householder, he was always detached, and therefore when he got the notice of his death, he immediately gave up all connection with household life and sat down on the bank of the Ganges to hear *Śrīmad-Bhāgavatam* in the association of devotees.

Thus ends the Bhaktivedanta purport of the Eighty-ninth Chapter of Kṛṣṇa, *"Summary Description of Lord Kṛṣṇa's Pastimes."*

Glossary

Aghāsura—demon who appeared in Vṛndāvana in the shape of a serpent

Ajita—the unconquerable one, a name of Kṛṣṇa

Akṣauhiṇī—a military division consisting of 21,870 chariots, 21,870 elephants, 206,950 infantry soldiers and 65,600 cavalry

Ātmārāma—self-satisfied sage

Bahulāśva—King of Videha who personally received the Supreme Lord as a guest in his home

Bali Mahārāja—king of the lower planetary system, Sutalaloka; he gave everything to Kṛṣṇa in His incarnation as Vāmana

Balvala—giant demon killed by Balarāma

Bāṇāsura—thousand-armed demon who arrested Aniruddha

Bhaumāsura—demon killed by Lord Kṛṣṇa after complaints by Lord Indra

Brahma-rākṣasas—*brāhmaṇas* who have become ghosts

Brāhmaṇas—the spiritual order of society whose occupation is the cultivation of Vedic knowledge

Cāmara—whisk or fan used by Kṛṣṇa's queens in Dvārakā to fan the Lord

Dantavakra—demon friend of Śālva, killed by a blow of Kṛṣṇa's club

Dhenukāsura—demon in the shape of an ass who was killed by Kṛṣṇa

Dvārakā—Lord Kṛṣṇa's opulent, fortified city built within the water

Dvivida—gorilla demon killed by Balarāma

Garuḍa—the giant bird carrier of Viṣṇu

Hastināpura—capital city of the Pāṇḍavas, entered by Kṛṣṇa at the time of the *Rājasūya* sacrifice

Jāmbavān—a devotee of Lord Rāmacandra who fought with Kṛṣṇa over the Syamantaka jewel

Jāmbavatī—one of Kṛṣṇa's wives, the daughter of Jāmbavān

Janmāṣṭamī—birthday anniversary of Lord Kṛṣṇa

Jarāsandha—demon who attacked Mathurā eighteen times and was finally killed by Bhīma

Kadamba—tree bearing a round yellow flower, seen generally only in the Vṛndāvana area

Kālayavana—demonic enemy of Kṛṣṇa who attacked Mathurā and was killed by Mucukunda

Kālindī—the Yamunā River personified, a wife of Kṛṣṇa

Kaumāra—childhood age of Kṛṣṇa

Kaumudī—an especially fragrant flower found on the bank of the Yamunā River

Kaustubha—transcendental jewel worn around the neck of the Supreme Personality of Godhead

Kṛṣṇa-kathā—narrations spoken by or about Kṛṣṇa

Kuṅkuma—a sweetly flavored reddish powder which is thrown upon the bodies of worshipable persons

Kuntīdevī—the mother of the Pāṇḍavas, a paternal aunt and pure devotee of Kṛṣṇa

Lakṣmaṇā—wife of Kṛṣṇa who heard of Him from Nārada and was taken by Kṛṣṇa during her *svayaṁvara*. Lakṣmaṇā is also the name of a wife of Sāmba.

Māgadhas—professional singers present at sacrifices

Mahā-ratha—a warrior who can fight against ten thousand others

Mahābhāgavata—highly advanced devotee

Mahāmāyā—external energy of the Supreme Lord, which covers the conditioned soul and does not allow him to understand the Supreme Personality of Godhead

Māyāvāda—the system of philosophy propounded by the impersonalists

Mitravindā—a wife whom Kṛṣṇa won in her *svayaṁvara* competition

Mukunda—Lord Kṛṣṇa, who awards liberation and whose smiling face is like a *kunda* flower

Nirguṇa—literally, without qualities (used to describe the Supreme Lord, whose qualities cannot be estimated)

Nāgapāśa—snake-noose, used by Bāṇāsura to subdue Aniruddha

Nāgapatnīs—wives of the Kāliya serpent

Nārāyaṇaśastra—weapon of Nārāyaṇa (Kṛṣṇa) used by Him to counteract Lord Śiva's *Pāśupataśastra* weapon

Nṛga—king who had to become a lizard due to his discrepancies in giving charity

Paramahaṁsa—(literally, the supreme swan) a person who can draw out the spiritual essence, just as a swan can extract milk from water

Pārijāta—a. type of flower found only in the heavenly planets
Pauṇḍraka—an imposter who, claiming to be the Supreme Personality of Godhead, challenged Kṛṣṇa and was killed by His Sudarśana-cakra
Pradyumna—son of Kṛṣṇa and Queen Rukmiṇī
Prakṛta sahajiyā—pseudo-devotees of Kṛṣṇa who fail to understand His absolute, transcendental position.
Prāṇāyāma—yogic breathing exercise
Paśughna—one who kills animals or is killing himself
Rājasūya-yajṣa—great sacrifice performed by Mahārāja Yudhiṣṭhira and attended by Lord Kṛṣṇa
Ranchor—literally, "one who has left the battlefield"—(describes Kṛṣṇa in His pastimes with Jarāsandha when He left the battle with the motive of renunciation)
Rasa—transcendental mellow relationship between the individual soul and the Supreme Lord
Rohinī—a wife of Kṛṣṇa
Romaharṣaṇa—disciple of Vyāsadeva who failed to offer Lord Balarāma respects and was killed by Balarāma with a blade of grass
Rukmiṇī—Lord Kṛṣṇa's principal queen at Dvārakā
Śālva—demon who attacked Dvārakā with a mystic airplane and was killed by Lord Kṛṣṇa
Samādhi—trance, absorption in meditation upon the Supreme Personality of Godhead
Saṅkarṣaṇa—Balarāma, the brother of Kṛṣṇa
Saṅkīrtana-yajṣa—the recommended sacrifice for the age of Kali, chanting of the holy names of God
Śāradia-pūrṇimā—full-moon night of the *śarat* season, during which Kṛṣṇa enjoyed the *rāsa* dance with the *gopīs*
Śāstras—revealed scriptures
Śatadhanvā—a demon who killed Satrājit for the Syamantaka jewel and was later killed by Kṛṣṇa's disc
Satyā—wife of Kṛṣṇa whom He won by subduing seven bulls
Satyabhāmā—one of Kṛṣṇa's principal queens
Sāyujya-mukti—merging into the existence of the Supreme. This type of impersonal liberation was awarded to demons, such as Śiśupāla, personally killed by Kṛṣṇa
Śiśupāla—demon who insulted Kṛṣṇa at the *Rājasūya-yajṣa* and was killed by Him

Śonitāpura—capital city of the demon Bhaumāsura

Śrutadeva—poor *brāhmaṇa* who received Kṛṣṇa in his home and pleased the Lord

Subhadrā—sister of Kṛṣṇa who was kidnapped and married by Arjuna

Sudāmā—*brāhmaṇa* devotee of Lord Kṛṣṇa who was an intimate boyhood friend of the Lord

Sudarśana-cakra—personal weapon of Śrī Kṛṣṇa

Śukadeva Gosvāmī—the exalted son of Vyāsadeva, the first narrator of the pastimes of Kṛṣṇa in *Śrīmad-Bhāgavatam*

Sūta Gosvāmī—the speaker of the *Śrīmad-Bhāgavatam* before the sages at Naimiṣāraṇya

Sūtas—professional singers present at sacrifices

Svayaṁvara—ceremony of open competition in which the conquering prince wins a princess in marriage

Tridaṇḍa—three rods carried by Vaiṣṇava *sannyāsīs,* indicating service to God in mind, body and words

Uṣā—girl who married Kṛṣṇa's grandson Aniruddha after a battle with Bhaumāsura's army

Vaiṣṇava—devotee of Lord Nārāyaṇa (Kṛṣṇa) who sees every living entity as part and parcel of the Lord

Vaiśya—the agricultural community in Vedic culture, who protect cows and cultivate crops

Vāruṇī—daughter of the demigod Varuṇa who came in the form of liquid honey which was drunk by Lord Balarāma

Viṣṇu—all-pervasive, fully empowered expansion of Lord Kṛṣṇa, qualified by full truth, full knowledge and full bliss.

Viṣṇu-tattva—expansions of Kṛṣṇa as the Supreme Personality of Godhead

Yadu dynasty—the family in which Kṛṣṇa appears; descending from Soma, the god of the moon planet

Yogamāyā—the principal, internal potency of the Supreme Lord *Yogeśvara*—a name of Kṛṣṇa, the master of all mystic powers

Yudhiṣṭhira Mahārāja—eldest Pāṇḍava brother, a cousin to Kṛṣṇa, and a pure devotee of the Lord

Index

Bibliography

Bhagavad-gītā, *xiii-xv, xv, xvi, xviii, xix, xxi, xxiii*, 13, 14, 17, 18, 20, 21, 23, 28, 44, 45, 48, 50, 51, 81, 89, 91, 94, 97, 98, 101, 104, 105, 106, 107, 109, 110, 112, 125, 126,136, 141, 143, 144, 148, 149,158, 159, 161, 167, 173, 185,187, 192, 194, 195,211,215,220, 221, 222, 223, 226, 228, 229, 246, 247, 258, 276, 278, 289, 292, 294, 303, 304, 306, 307, 311, 314, 315, 318,329,336, 354, 359, 378, 379, 438, 440, 443, 445, 485, 500, 509, 513, 520,539, 540, 551, 555, 573, 594, 595, 614, 616, 620, 621, 622, 623, 624, 626, 627, 628, 629, 630, 634, 636, 637, 638, 639,640, 643, 644, 645, 648, 648,649, 650, 651, 653, 656, 657, 658, 661, 662, 663, 664, 665, 668, 670, 671, 673, 674, 677, 678, 679, 681, 682, 683, 687, 688, 689, 690, 691, 692, 699, 700, 702, 705, 708, 709, 711, 724, 726, 729

Brahma-saṁhitā, *xix*, 16, 19, 26, 81, 96, 103, 104, 107, 143, 155, 164, 192, 198, 210, 216, 245, 249, 440, 447, 484, 638, 639, 668, 674, 678, 709

Caitanya-caritāmṛta, *xvii*,11, 30, 93, 112, 124, 166, 189, 215, 247, 314, 325, 334, 349, 652, 656, 674, 702

Īśopaniṣad, 565, 667, 701

Kaṭha Upaniṣad, 15, 480, 678

Kṛṣṇa-bhāvanāmṛta, 291

Mahābhārata, *xii*, 21

Mṛtyuñjaya-tantra, 709

Nārada-pañcarātra, 684

Nārāyaṇa-pañcarātra, 631

Padma Purāṇa, 355, 369, 641, 702

Śikṣāṣṭaka, 397,477-478

Skanda Purāṇa, 210

Śrīmad-Bhāgavatam, *xii, xix, xx, xxi, xxii, xxiii, xxiv*, 2, 17, 18, 19, 20, 85, 105, 129, 138, 168, 188, 190, 193, 216, 217, 221, 222, 225, 310, 316, 333, 348, 349, 350, 359, 389, 400, 430, 521, 523, 539, 542, 545, 551, 564, 568, 601, 623, 628,

631, 632, 637, 638, 666, 669, 675, 682, 683, 699, 700, 701, 702, 707, 715, 724, 728, 729
Teachings of Lord Caitanya, 291
Upadeśāmṛta, 145
Varāha Purāna, 632
Viṣṇu Purāṇa, 22, 88, 332
Vedānta-sūtra, 98, 104, 380, 417, 615, 626, 638, 640, 654, 666, 675
Vedas, 38, 53, 81, 97, 107, 138, 139, 144, 148, 159, 166, 218 219, 289, 307, 340, 447, 480, 519, 550, 557, 584, 613-679, 680, 699

Note on Transliterated Sanskrit Words

The vowels are pronounced almost as in Italian. The sound of the short ***a*** is like the *u* in b***u***t, the long **ā** is like the *a* in f***a***r and held twice as long as the short *a*, and ***e*** is like the *a* in ev***a***de. Long ***ī*** is like the *i* in p***i***que. The vowel ***ṛ*** is pronounced like the *re* in the English word fib***re***. The ***c*** is pronounced as in the English word ***ch***air, and the aspirated consonants ***(ch, jh, dh***, etc.) are pronounced as in staun***ch-h***eart, he***dge-h***og, re***d-h***ot, etc. The two spirants ***ś*** and ***ṣ*** are pronounced like the English ***sh; s*** is pronounced as in ***s***un.